Microsoft SQL Server 2012 Internals

Kalen Delaney
Bob Beauchemin
Conor Cunningham
Jonathan Kehayias
Benjamin Nevarez
Paul S. Randal

Published with the authorization of Microsoft Corporation by:
O'Reilly Media, Inc.
1005 Gravenstein Highway North
Sebastopol, California 95472

ISBN: 978-0-7356-5856-1

1 2 3 4 5 6 7 8 9 LSI 8 7 6 5 4 3

Printed and bound in the United States of America.

Microsoft Press books are available through booksellers and distributors worldwide. If you need support related to this book, email Microsoft Press Book Support at *mspinput@microsoft.com*. Please tell us what you think of this book at *http://www.microsoft.com/learning/booksurvey*.

Microsoft and the trademarks listed at *http://www.microsoft.com/about/legal/en/us/IntellectualProperty/ Trademarks/EN-US.aspx* are trademarks of the Microsoft group of companies. All other marks are property of their respective owners.

The example companies, organizations, products, domain names, email addresses, logos, people, places, and events depicted herein are fictitious. No association with any real company, organization, product, domain name, email address, logo, person, place, or event is intended or should be inferred.

This book expresses the author's views and opinions. The information contained in this book is provided without any express, statutory, or implied warranties. Neither the authors, O'Reilly Media, Inc., Microsoft Corporation, nor its resellers, or distributors will be held liable for any damages caused or alleged to be caused either directly or indirectly by this book.

Acquisitions and Developmental Editor: Michael Bolinger

Production Editor: Kara Ebrahim

Editorial Production: Box 12 Communications

Technical Reviewers: Benjamin Nevarez and Jonathan Kehayias

Copyeditor: Box 12 Communications

Indexer: Box 12 Communications

Cover Design: Twist Creative • Seattle

Cover Composition: Karen Montgomery

Illustrator: Rebecca Demarest

Contents at a glance

	Introduction	*xix*
CHAPTER 1	SQL Server 2012 architecture and configuration	1
CHAPTER 2	The SQLOS	35
CHAPTER 3	Databases and database files	99
CHAPTER 4	Special databases	139
CHAPTER 5	Logging and recovery	171
CHAPTER 6	Table storage	203
CHAPTER 7	Indexes: internals and management	297
CHAPTER 8	Special storage	381
CHAPTER 9	Special indexes	457
CHAPTER 10	Query execution	513
CHAPTER 11	The Query Optimizer	611
CHAPTER 12	Plan caching and recompilation	703
CHAPTER 13	Transactions and concurrency	765
CHAPTER 14	DBCC internals	837
	Index	*903*

Contents

Introduction . . . . *xix*

Chapter 1   SQL Server 2012 architecture and configuration   1

SQL Server editions 1

SQL Server installation and tools 2

SQL Server metadata 3

  Compatibility views 3

  Catalog views 4

  Dynamic Management Objects. 6

  Other metadata 7

Components of the SQL Server engine. 10

  Protocols 11

  Query processor. 12

  The storage engine 14

SQL Server 2012 configuration. 17

  Using SQL Server Configuration Manager. 18

  Managing services. 19

SQL Server system configuration. 21

  Operating system configuration 21

  Trace flags 23

  SQL Server configuration settings. 24

Conclusion 33

What do you think of this book? We want to hear from you!

Microsoft is interested in hearing your feedback so we can continually improve our books and learning resources for you. To participate in a brief online survey, please visit:

microsoft.com/learning/booksurvey

Chapter 2 The SQLOS   35

NUMA architecture 36

The scheduler 37

    Understanding SQL Server schedulers 38

    Binding schedulers to CPUs 41

    Observing scheduler internals 42

    Understanding the Dedicated Administrator Connection (DAC) . .45

Memory 47

    The buffer pool and the data cache 47

    Column store object pool 48

    Access to in-memory data pages 48

    Page management in the data cache 48

    The free buffer list and the lazywriter 49

    Checkpoints 50

    Memory management in other caches 52

    The Memory Broker 54

    Memory sizing 54

    Buffer pool sizing 55

SQL Server Resource Governor 61

    Resource Governor overview 61

    Resource Governor controls 70

    Resource Governor metadata 71

Extended Events 73

    Extended Events architecture 73

    Event execution life cycle 73

    Core concepts 75

    Extended Events DDL and querying 83

    Extended Events UI 86

Conclusion 97

Chapter 3 Databases and database files   99

Working with sample databases 100

    AdventureWorks 100

    pubs 101

Northwind 101

Understanding database files 101

    Creating a database 104

    Using CREATE DATABASE: an example 106

Expanding or shrinking a database 106

    Automatic file expansion 106

    Manual file expansion 107

    Fast file initialization 107

    Automatic shrinkage 108

    Manual shrinkage 108

Using database filegroups 109

    The default filegroup 110

    A FILEGROUP CREATION example 112

    Filestream filegroups 113

Altering a database 114

    ALTER DATABASE examples 115

    Databases under the hood 116

    Space allocation 116

Setting database options 119

    State options 122

    Cursor options 125

    Auto options 125

    SQL options 126

    Database recovery options 128

    Other database options 129

Understanding database security 129

    Database access 130

    Database security 132

    Databases vs. schemas 133

    Principals and schemas 133

    Default schemas 134

Moving or copying a database 134

    Detaching and reattaching a database 135

    Backing up and restoring a database 136

Understanding compatibility levels. 137

Conclusion 138

Chapter 4   Special databases   139

System databases 139

    Understanding the master database 139

    Understanding the model database. 140

    Introducing the tempdb database 140

    Understanding the resource database. 140

    Understanding the msdb database 141

    Moving system databases 142

    Moving the master database. 143

The tempdb database 144

    Objects in tempdb. 144

    Optimizations in tempdb 146

    Best practices 147

    tempdb contention 148

    tempdb space monitoring 153

Database snapshots 155

    Creating a database snapshot 156

    Understanding space used by database snapshots. 159

    Managing your snapshots 161

Partially contained databases. 162

    Configuring a contained database 162

    Creating contained users 163

    Understanding database collation changes 166

    Detecting uncontained features 168

Conclusion 169

Chapter 5   Logging and recovery   171

Transaction log internals 171

    Phases of recovery. 174

    Page LSNs and recovery. 175

    Log reading. 176

The log cache 177

Changes in log size. 178

Understanding virtual log files 178

Maintaining a recoverable log. 185

Automatically shrinking the log 187

Viewing the log file size 188

Database backup and restore. 188

Understanding the types of backups 189

Understanding recovery models. 190

Choosing a backup type. 194

Restoring a database. 195

Conclusion 201

Chapter 6   Table storage   203

Table creation 203

Naming tables and columns 204

Avoiding reserved keywords 205

Using delimited identifiers 206

Understanding naming conventions 207

Choosing a data type 208

The NULL problem. 233

User-defined data types. 235

IDENTITY property 237

Sequence object 240

Internal storage 243

The sys.indexes catalog view 244

Data storage metadata. 245

Catalog view queries. 246

Data pages 248

The structure of data rows 257

How to find a physical page. 259

Storage of fixed-length rows 262

Storage of variable-length rows 265

NULLS and variable-length columns 267

Storage of date and time data. 270

Storage of sql_variant data. 273

Constraints. 276

Constraint names and catalog view information 277

Constraint failures in transactions and multiple-row data
modifications 278

Altering a table 279

Changing a data type 280

Adding a new column. 281

Adding, dropping, disabling, or enabling a constraint 281

Dropping a column 283

Internals of altering tables 283

Heap modification internals 286

Allocation structures 286

Inserting rows. 288

Deleting rows 288

Updating rows 292

Conclusion 295

Chapter 7   Indexes: internals and management   297

Overview. 298

SQL Server B-tree indexes 299

Example 1: An index with a large key column 300

Example 2: An index with a very narrow key column 301

Tools for analyzing indexes. 302

Using the dm_db_index_physical_stats DMV 302

Using sys.dm_db_database_page_allocations 306

Understanding B-tree index structures. 308

Clustering key dependency 308

Nonclustered B-tree indexes 311

Constraints and indexes 312

Index creation options. 313

IGNORE_DUP_KEY 313

STATISTICS_NORECOMPUTE 314

MAXDOP 314

Index placement. 314

Physical index structures for B-trees 315

Index row formats 315

Clustered index structures 316

Non-leaf level(s) of a clustered index. 317

Analyzing a clustered index structure 317

Nonclustered index structures. 322

Indexes on computed columns and indexed views 333

SET options 333

Permissible functions. 334

Schema binding 335

Indexes on computed columns 335

Implementation of a computed column 336

Persisted columns 337

Indexed views 338

Additional requirements. 338

Creating an indexed view 339

Using an indexed view 340

Data modification internals. 341

Inserting rows. 342

Splitting pages 342

Deleting rows 346

Updating rows 354

Table-level vs. index-level data modification 357

Logging 358

Locking. 358

Fragmentation 359

Managing B-tree index structures. 360

Dropping indexes. 360

Using the ALTER INDEX command 361

Detecting fragmentation 363

Removing fragmentation 364

Rebuilding an index. 366

Online index building 367

Columnstore indexes 370

    Creation of columnstore indexes. 370

    Storage of columnstore indexes 371

    Columnstore index metadata 376

Conclusion 380

Chapter 8 Special storage   381

Large object storage 381

    Restricted-length large object data (row-overflow data) 382

    Unrestricted-length large object data 386

FILESTREAM and FileTable data 394

    Enabling FILESTREAM data for SQL Server .395

    Creating a FILESTREAM-enabled database .397

    Creating a table to hold FILESTREAM data .397

    Manipulating FILESTREAM data 399

    Exploring metadata with FILESTREAM data 404

    Creating a FileTable 406

    Considering performance for FILESTREAM data 409

    Summarizing FILESTREAM and FileTable 410

Sparse columns 411

    Management of sparse columns 411

    Column sets and sparse column manipulation. 414

    Physical storage 416

    Metadata 419

    Storage savings with sparse columns 420

Data compression 423

    Vardecimal. 423

    Row compression 424

    Page compression 433

Table and index partitioning 444

    Partition functions and partition schemes. 444

    Metadata for partitioning. 446

    The sliding window benefits of partitioning 450

Partitioning a columnstore index 452

Conclusion 455

Chapter 9   Special indexes   457

Special indexes vs. ordinary indexes 457

XML indexes. 458

Creating and maintaining XML indexes. .459

Using XQuery in SQL Server: internals 463

Understanding how a query plan uses an XML index. 465

Using secondary XML indexes. 468

Working with XML indexes and schema-validated columns 469

Using XML-specific information in query plans 470

Spatial indexes. 471

Purpose of spatial indexes 472

Composition of the spatial index. 475

How a spatial query uses a spatial index .477

How to ensure that your spatial index is being used. 478

Spatial query plans and spatial indexes 479

Nearest neighbor optimization in SQL Server 2012 481

Spatial index diagnostic stored procedures 484

Diagnostics with the SQL Server 2012 spatial functions. 491

Full-text indexes 492

Internal tables created by the full-text index 494

Full-text index metadata views 497

Full-text index creation. 498

Maintenance of a full-text index 499

Full-text status metadata, configuration, and diagnostic
information 500

How a full-text index is used in a query. .501

A full-text query plan 502

Extended event information for full-text queries. 503

Semantic indexes. 505

Conclusion 511

Chapter 10 Query execution   513

Introducing query processing and execution 513

    Iterators 513

    Properties of iterators 515

Reading query plans. 517

    Graphical plans. 517

    Text plans. 518

    XML plans 518

    Estimated vs. actual query plans. 518

    Query plan display options 520

Analyzing plans. 525

    Scans and seeks 526

    Seekable predicates and covered columns .528

    Bookmark lookup. 531

    Joins 533

    Aggregations 545

    Unions 555

    Advanced index operations 560

    Subqueries. 566

    Parallelism 580

    Inserts, updates, and deletes 598

Understanding data warehouses. 599

Using columnstore indexes and batch processing 603

    Adding new data 607

    Hints 609

Conclusion 610

Chapter 11 The Query Optimizer   611

Overview. 611

    Understanding the tree format 612

    Understanding optimization 613

Search space and heuristics. 614

    Rules. 614

    Properties 614

Storage of alternatives: the Memo 617
Operators. 617
Optimizer architecture. 624
Before optimization. 625
Simplification 625
Trivial plan/auto-parameterization. 625
Limitations. 627
The Memo: exploring multiple plans efficiently. 627
Statistics, cardinality estimation, and costing 630
Statistics design 631
Density/frequency information. 634
Filtered statistics. 636
String statistics 637
Cardinality estimation details. 638
Limitations. 642
Costing. 643
Index selection. 645
Filtered indexes. 648
Indexed views 649
Partitioned tables 654
Partition-aligned index views. 658
Windowing functions. 658
Data warehousing 659
Columnstore indexes. 660
Batch mode processing. 662
Plan shape. 667
Columnstore limitations and workarounds. 670
Updates. 670
Halloween Protection 674
Split/Sort/Collapse. 674
Merge. 676
Wide update plans. 679
Non-updating updates 681
Sparse column updates. 681

Partitioned updates 682

Locking. 685

Partition-level lock escalation 686

Distributed query 687

Extended indexes 689

Plan hinting 689

Debugging plan issues 691

{HASH | ORDER} GROUP 692

{MERGE | HASH | CONCAT} UNION 693

FORCE ORDER, {LOOP | MERGE | HASH} JOIN 693

INDEX=<indexname> | <indexid> 694

FORCESEEK 695

FAST <number_rows> 695

MAXDOP <N> 696

OPTIMIZE FOR 696

PARAMETERIZATION {SIMPLE | FORCED} 698

NOEXPAND. 699

USE PLAN. 699

Hotfixes. 700

Conclusion 701

Chapter 12 Plan caching and recompilation   703

The plan cache. 703

Plan cache metadata 704

Clearing plan cache 704

Caching mechanisms 705

Ad hoc query caching 706

Optimizing for ad hoc workloads 708

Simple parameterization. 711

Prepared queries 717

Compiled objects 719

Causes of recompilation 722

Plan cache internals 732

Cache stores 732

Compiled plans. 734

Execution contexts. 734

Plan cache metadata 735

Cache size management. 740

Costing of cache entries 743

Objects in plan cache: the big picture. 744

Multiple plans in cache 746

When to use stored procedures and other caching
mechanisms. 747

Troubleshooting plan cache issues 748

Optimization hints and plan guides 752

Optimization hints 752

Purpose of plan guides 754

Types of plan guides 755

Managing plan guides. 758

Plan guide considerations. 759

Conclusion 764

Chapter 13 Transactions and concurrency 765

Concurrency models. 765

Pessimistic concurrency 766

Optimistic concurrency. 766

Transaction processing. 766

ACID properties 767

Transaction dependencies 768

Isolation levels 770

Locking 774

Locking basics. 774

Spinlocks 775

Lock types for user data 775

Viewing locks 786

Locking examples. 789

Lock compatibility 794

Internal locking architecture 796

Row-level locking vs. page-level locking. 803

Lock escalation 804

Deadlocks 806

Row versioning 811

Row versioning details 811

Snapshot-based isolation levels. 813

Choosing a concurrency model. 830

Controlling locking. 832

Lock hints. 832

Conclusion 836

Chapter 14 DBCC internals   837

Shrinking files and databases. 837

Data file shrinking 838

Log file shrinking 840

DBCC SHRINKFILE 840

AUTO_SHRINK 841

Consistency checking. 841

Getting a consistent view of the database .842

Processing the database efficiently. 845

Performing primitive system catalog consistency checks. 855

Performing allocation consistency checks. .856

Performing per-table logical consistency checks. 860

Processing columns. 866

Performing cross-table consistency checks. 881

Understanding DBCC CHECKDB output 885

Reviewing DBCC CHECKDB options 890

Performing database repairs 893

Using consistency-checking commands other than
DBCC CHECKDB 898

Conclusion 901

Index   903

Introduction

The book you are now holding is the evolutionary successor to the *Inside SQL Server* series, which included *Inside SQL Server 6.5*, *Inside SQL Server 7*, *Inside SQL Server 2000*, and *Inside SQL Server 2005* (in four volumes) and the *SQL Server 2008 Internals* book. The name was changed for SQL Server 2008 because the *Inside* series was becoming too unfocused, and the name "Inside" had been usurped by other authors and even other publishers. I needed a title that was much more indicative of what this book is really about.

SQL Server 2012 Internals tells you how SQL Server, Microsoft's flagship relational database product, works. Along with that, I explain how you can use the knowledge of how it works to help you get better performance from the product, but that is a side effect, not the goal. There are dozens of other books on the market that describe tuning and best practices for SQL Server. This one helps you understand why certain tuning practices work the way they do, and it helps you determine your own best practices as you continue to work with SQL Server as a developer, data architect, or DBA.

Who should read this book

This book is intended to be read by anyone who wants a deeper understanding of what SQL Server does behind the scenes. The focus of this book is on the core SQL Server engine—in particular, the query processor and the storage engine. I expect that you have some experience with both the SQL Server engine and with the T-SQL language. You don't have to be an expert in either, but it helps if you aspire to become an expert and would like to find out all you can about what SQL Server is actually doing when you submit a query for execution.

This series doesn't discuss client programming interfaces, heterogeneous queries, business intelligence, or replication. In fact, most of the high-availability features are not covered, but a few, such as mirroring, are mentioned at a high level when we discuss database property settings. I don't drill into the details of some internal operations, such as security, because that's such a big topic it deserves a whole volume of its own.

My hope is that you'll look at the cup as half full instead of half empty and appreciate this book for what it does include. As for the topics that aren't included, I hope you'll find the information you need in other sources.

Organization of this book

SQL Server 2012 Internals provides detailed information on the way that SQL Server processes your queries and manages your data. It starts with an overview of the architecture of the SQL Server relational database system and then continues looking at aspects of query processing and data storage in 13 additional chapters. The content from the *SQL Server 2008 Internals* book has been enhanced to cover changes and relevant new features of SQL Server 2012. In addition, it contains an entire chapter on the SQLOS, drawn from and enhanced from sections in the previous book, and a whole chapter on system databases, also drawn from and enhanced from content in the *SQL Server 2008* book. There is also a brand new chapter on special indexes, including spatial indexes, XML indexes, fulltext indexes, and semantic indexes. Finally, the chapter on query execution from my *Inside SQL Server 2005: Query Tuning and Optimization* book has been include and updated for SQL Server 2012.

Companion content

This book features a companion website that makes available to you all the code used in the book, organized by chapter. The companion content also includes an extra chapter from my previous book, as well as the "History of SQL Server" chapter from my book *Inside Microsoft SQL Server 2000* (Microsoft Press, 2000). The site also provides extra scripts and tools to enhance your experience and understanding of SQL Server internals. As errors are found and reported, they will also be posted online. You can access this content from the companion site at this address: *http://www.SQLServerInternals. com/companion.*

System requirements

To use the code samples, you'll need Internet access and a system capable of running SQL Server 2012 Enterprise or Developer edition. To get system requirements for SQL Server 2012 and to obtain a trial version, go to *http://www.microsoft.com/en-us/download/details.aspx?id=29066.*

Acknowledgments

As always, a work like this is not an individual effort, and for this current volume, it is truer than ever. I was honored to have five other SQL Server experts join me in writing *SQL Server 2012 Internals*, and I truly could not have written this book alone. I am grateful to Benjamin Nevarez, Paul Randal, Conor Cunningham, Jonathan Kehayias, and Bob Beauchemin for helping to make this book a reality. In addition to my brilliant co-authors, this book could never have seen the light of day without help and encouragement from many other people.

First on my list is you, the reader. Thank you to all of you for reading what I have written. Thank you to those who have taken the time to write to me about what you thought of the book and what else you want to learn about SQL Server. I wish I could answer every question in detail. I appreciate all your input, even when I'm unable to send you a complete reply. One particular reader of one of my previous books, *Inside Microsoft SQL Server 2005: The Storage Engine* (Microsoft Press, 2006), deserves particular thanks. I came to know Ben Nevarez as a very astute reader who found some uncaught errors and subtle inconsistencies and politely and succinctly reported them to me through my website. Ben is now my most valued technical reviewer, and for this new edition, he is also an author!

As usual, the SQL Server team at Microsoft has been awesome. Although Lubor Kollar and Sunil Agarwal were not directly involved in much of the research for this book, I always knew they were there in spirit, and both of them always had an encouraging word whenever I saw them. Kevin Liu volunteered for the daunting task of coordinating my contracts with the SQL team, and always found me the right engineer to talk to when I had specific questions that needed to be answered.

Ryan Stonecipher, Kevin Farlee, Peter Byrne, Srini Acharya, and Susan Price met with me and responded to my (sometimes seemingly endless) emails. Fabricio Voznika, Peter Gvozdjak, Jeff East, Umachandar Jayachandran, Arkadi Brjazovski, Madhan Ramakrishnan, Cipri Clinciu, and Srikumar Rangarajan also offered valuable technical insights and information when responding to my emails. I hope they all know how much I appreciated every piece of information I received.

I am also indebted to Bob Ward, Bob Dorr, and Keith Elmore of the SQL Server Product Support team, not just for answering occasional questions but for making so much information about SQL Server available through white papers, conference presentations, and Knowledge Base articles. I am grateful to Alan Brewer and Gail Erickson for the great job they and their User Education team did putting together the SQL Server documentation in *SQL Server Books Online*.

I would like to extend my heartfelt thanks to all of the SQL Server MVPs, but most especially Erland Sommarskog. Erland wrote the section in Chapter 6 on collations just because he thought it was needed, and that someone who has to deal with only the 26 letters of the English alphabet could never do it justice. Also deserving of special mention are Ben Miller, Tibor Karaszi, and John Paul Cook, for all the personal support and encouragement they gave me. Other MVPs who inspired me during the writing of this volume are Hugo Kornelis, Rob Farley, and Allen White. Being a part of the SQL Server MVP team continues to be one of the greatest honors and privileges of my professional life.

I am deeply indebted to my students in my "SQL Server Internals" classes, not only for their enthusiasm for the SQL Server product and for what I have to teach and share with them, but for all they have to share with me. Much of what I have learned has been inspired by questions from my curious students. Some of my students, such as Cindy Gross and Lara Rubbelke, have become friends (in addition to becoming Microsoft employees) and continue to provide ongoing inspiration.

Most important of all, my family continues to provide the rock-solid foundation I need to do the work that I do. I am truly blessed to have my husband, Dan, my daughter, Melissa, and my three sons, Brendan, Kyle (aka Rickey), and Connor.

—*Kalen Delaney*

Thanks to Kalen for persisting even when it didn't look like this book would ever be published. I'd also like to thank the chapter reviewers: Joe Sack and Kalen Delaney (yes, she personally reviewed all of it). Thanks to product designers who reviewed the parts in their area of expertise: Ed Katibah, Shankar Pal (who reviewed my original XML index material), and the entire full-text and semantic search team: Mahadevan Venkatraman, Elnata Degefa, Shantanu Kurhekar, Chuan Liu, Ivan Mitic, Todd Porter, and Artak Sukhudyan, who reviewed the final prose, as well as Naveen Garg, Kunal Mukerjee, and others from the original full-text/semantic team. Thank you, one and all.

Special thanks to Mary, without whose encouragement, help, and the ability to provide me the space I needed to work in solitude, I'd never have written anything at all. Finally, special thanks to Ed Katibah, who taught me almost everything I know about spatial concepts and representing spatial data in databases.

—*Bob Beauchemin*

I'd like to thank my wife Shannon and daughter Savannah for allowing me the late nights and weekend days to complete the work for this book. I could not do it without you both.

—*Conor Cunningham*

When Kalen asked me to contribute to this book it was a great honor, and I owe a debt of gratitude to her for the opportunity to work on this project. While working on the SQLOS and Extended Events updates for this book, I spent a lot of time discussing changes to the internals of SQLOS with Jerome Halmans at Microsoft. Jerome was also one the primary developers for Extended Events in SQL Server 2008, and has been incredibly gracious in answering my questions for the last four years.

I'd also like to acknowledge my wife, Sarah, and kids, Charlotte and Michael, and their ability and willingness to put up with the late hours at night, spent locked in our home office, as well as the weekends spent sitting on my laptop when there were so many other things we could have been doing. Sarah has spent many nights wondering if I was actually going to make it to bed or not while writing and editing portions of this book. Additional recognition goes out to all of the mentors I've had over the years, the list of which is incredibly long. Without the commitment of SQL Server MVPs like Arnie Rowland, Paul Randal, Aaron Bertrand, Louis Davidson, and countless others, I would have never made it as far as I have with SQL Server.

—*Jonathan Kehayias*

First of all I would like to thank Kalen for first offering me the opportunity to work as technical reviewer of this and her previous three books and later as co-author of two of the chapters of this book, "Special databases" and "Query execution." It is truly an honor to work on her books as it was her *Inside SQL Server* books, which helped me to learn SQL Server in the first place. It is an honor to be updating Craig Freedman's work as well; his chapter and blog have always been one of my all-time favorites. I also would like to thank Jonathan Kehayias for doing the technical review of my two chapters as he provided invaluable feedback to improve their quality.

Finally, on the personal side, I would like to thank my family: my wife, Rocio, my three boy-scout sons, Diego, Benjamin, and David, and my parents, Guadalupe and Humberto; thanks all for your unconditional support and patience.

—*Benjamin Nevarez*

By the time we wrote *SQL Server 2008 Internals*, I'd been itching to write a complete description of what DBCC CHECKDB does for many years. When Kalen asked me to write the consistency checking chapter for that book, I jumped at the chance, and for that my sincere thanks go to Kalen. I'm very pleased to have been able to update that chapter for SQL Server 2012 in this book and to add a section on the internals of the shrink functionality as well. I'd like to reaffirm my special gratitude to two people from Microsoft, among the many great folks I worked with there. The first is Ryan Stoneci-pher, who I hired away from being an Escalation Engineer in SQL Product Support in late 2003 to work with me on DBCC, and who was suddenly thrust into complete ownership of 100K+ lines of DBCC code when I become the team manager two months later. I couldn't have asked for more capable hands to take over my precious DBCC, and I sincerely appreciate the time he took to explore the 2012 changes with me. The second is Bob Ward, who heads up the SQL Product Support team and has been a great friend since my early days at Microsoft. We must have collaborated on many hundreds of cases of corruption over the years and I've yet to meet someone with more drive for solving customer problems and improving SQL Server. Thanks must also go to Steve Lindell, the author of the original online consistency checking code for SQL Server 2000, who spent many hours patiently explaining how it worked in 1999. Finally, I'd like to thank my wife, Kimberly, and our daughters, Katelyn and Kiera, who are the other passions in my life apart from SQL Server.

—*Paul Randal*

Errata & book support

We've made every effort to ensure the accuracy of this book and its companion content. Any errors that have been reported since this book was published are listed at:

http://aka.ms/SQL2012Internals/errata

If you find an error that is not already listed, you can report it to us through the same page.

If you need additional support, email Microsoft Press Book Support at mspinput@ microsoft.com.

Please note that product support for Microsoft software is not offered through the addresses above.

We want to hear from you

At Microsoft Press, your satisfaction is our top priority, and your feedback our most valuable asset. Please tell us what you think of this book at:

http://aka.ms/tellpress

The survey is short, and we read every one of your comments and ideas. Thanks in advance for your input!

Stay in touch

Let's keep the conversation going! We're on Twitter: *http://twitter.com/MicrosoftPress*

CHAPTER 1

SQL Server 2012 architecture and configuration

Kalen Delaney

Microsoft SQL Server is Microsoft's premier database management system, and SQL Server 2012 is the most powerful and feature-rich version yet. In addition to the core database engine, which allows you to store and retrieve large volumes of relational data, and the world-class Query Optimizer, which determines the fastest way to process your queries and access your data, dozens of other components increase the usability of your data and make your data and applications more available and more scalable. As you can imagine, no single book could cover all these features in depth. This book, *SQL Server 2012 Internals*, covers only the main features of the core database engine.

This book delves into the details of specific features of the SQL Server Database Engine. This first chapter provides a high-level view of the components of that engine and how they work together. The goal is to help you understand how the topics covered in subsequent chapters fit into the overall operations of the engine.

SQL Server editions

Each version of SQL Server comes in various editions, which you can think of as a subset of the product features, with its own specific pricing and licensing requirements. Although this book doesn't discuss pricing and licensing, some of the information about editions is important because of the features available with each edition. *SQL Server Books Online* describes in detail the editions available and the feature list that each supports, but this section lists the main editions. You can verify what edition you are running with the following query:

```
SELECT SERVERPROPERTY('Edition');
```

You can also inspect a server property known as *EngineEdition*:

```
SELECT SERVERPROPERTY('EngineEdition');
```

The *EngineEdition* property returns a value of 2 through 5 (1 isn't a valid value in versions after SQL Server 2000), which determines what features are available. A value of 3 indicates that your SQL Server edition is either Enterprise, Enterprise Evaluation, or Developer. These three editions have exactly the same features and functionality. If your *EngineEdition* value is 2, your edition is either Standard, Web, or Business Intelligence, and fewer features are available. The features and behaviors discussed in this book are available in one of these two engine editions. The features in Enterprise edition (as well as in Developer and Enterprise Evaluation editions) that aren't in Standard edition generally relate to scalability and high-availability features, but other Enterprise-only features are available, as will be explained. For full details on what is in each edition, see the *SQL Server Books Online* topic, "Features Supported by the Editions of SQL Server 2012."

A value of 4 for *EngineEdition* indicates that your SQL Server edition is Express, which includes SQL Server Express, SQL Server Express with Advanced Services, and SQL Server Express with Tools. None of these versions are discussed specifically.

Finally, a value of 5 for *EngineEdition* indicates that you are running SQL Azure, a version of SQL Server that runs as a cloud-based service. Although many SQL Server applications can access SQL Azure with only minimum modifications because the language features are very similar between SQL Azure and a locally installed SQL Server (called an on-premises SQL Server), almost all the internal details are different. For this reason, much of this book's content is irrelevant for SQL Azure.

A *SERVERPROPERTY* property called *EditionID* allows you to differentiate between the specific editions within each of the different *EngineEdition* values—that is, it allows you to differentiate among Enterprise, Enterprise Evaluation, and Developer editions.

SQL Server installation and tools

Although installation of SQL Server 2012 is usually relatively straightforward, you need to make many decisions during installation, but this chapter doesn't cover all the details of every decision. You need to read the installation details, which are fully documented. Presumably, you already have SQL Server installed and available for use.

Your installation doesn't need to include every single feature because the focus in this book is on the basic SQL Server engine, although you should at least have installed a client tool such as SQL Server Management Studio that you can use for submitting queries. This chapter also refers to options available in the Object Explorer pane of the SQL Server Management Studio.

As of SQL Server 2012, you can install SQL Server on Windows Server 2008 R2 Server Core SP1 (referred to simply as Server Core). The Server Core installation provides a minimal environment for running specific server roles. It reduces the maintenance and management requirements and reduces the attack surface area. However, because Server Core provides no graphical interface capabilities, SQL Server must be installed using the command line and configuration file. Refer to the *Books Online* topic, "Install SQL Server 2012 from the Command Prompt," for details.

Also, because graphical tools aren't available when using Server Core, you can't run SQL Server Management Studio on a Server Core box. Your communications with SQL Server can be through a command line using the SQLCMD tool or by using SQL PowerShell. Alternatively, you can access your SQL Server running on Server Core from another machine on the network that does have the graphical tools available.

SQL Server metadata

SQL Server maintains a set of tables that store information about all objects, data types, constraints, configuration options, and resources available to SQL Server. In SQL Server 2012, these tables are called the *system base tables*. Some of the system base tables exist only in the *master* database and contain system-wide information; others exist in every database (including *master*) and contain information about the objects and resources belonging to that particular database. Beginning with SQL Server 2005, the system base tables aren't always visible by default, in *master* or any other database. You won't see them when you expand the *tables* node in the Object Explorer in SQL Server Management Studio, and unless you are a system administrator, you won't see them when you execute the *sp_help* system procedure. If you log on as a system administrator and select from the catalog view called *sys.objects* (discussed shortly), you can see the names of all the system tables. For example, the following query returns 74 rows of output on my SQL Server 2012 instance:

```
USE master;
SELECT name FROM sys.objects
WHERE type_desc = 'SYSTEM_TABLE';
```

But even as a system administrator, if you try to select data from one of the tables returned by the preceding query, you get a 208 error, indicating that the object name is invalid. The only way to see the data in the system base tables is to make a connection using the dedicated administrator connection (DAC), which Chapter 2, "The SQLOS," explains in the section titled "The scheduler." Keep in mind that the system base tables are used for internal purposes only within the Database Engine and aren't intended for general use. They are subject to change, and compatibility isn't guaranteed. In SQL Server 2012, three types of system metadata objects are intended for general use: Compatibility Views, Catalog Views, and Dynamic Management Objects.

Compatibility views

Although you could see data in the system tables in versions of SQL Server before 2005, you weren't encouraged to do so. Nevertheless, many people used system tables for developing their own troubleshooting and reporting tools and techniques, providing result sets that aren't available using the supplied system procedures. You might assume that due to the inaccessibility of the system base tables, you would have to use the DAC to utilize your homegrown tools when using SQL Server 2005 or later. However, you still might be disappointed. Many names and much of the content of the SQL Server 2000 system tables have changed, so any code that used them is completely unusable even with the DAC. The DAC is intended only for emergency access, and no support is provided for any other use of it. To save you from this problem, SQL Server 2005 and later versions offer a set of compatibility views that allow you to continue to access a subset of the SQL Server 2000 system tables. These views are accessible from any database, although they are created in a hidden resource database that Chapter 4, "Special databases," covers.

Some compatibility views have names that might be quite familiar to you, such as *sysobjects*, *sysindexes*, *sysusers*, and *sysdatabases*. Others, such as *sysmembers* and *sysmessages*, might be less familiar. For compatibility reasons, SQL Server 2012 provides views that have the same names as many of the system tables in SQL Server 2000, as well as the same column names, which means that any code that uses the SQL Server 2000 system tables won't break. However, when you select from these views, you're not guaranteed to get exactly the same results that you get from the corresponding tables in SQL Server 2000. The compatibility views also don't contain any metadata related to features added after SQL Server 2000, such as partitioning or the Resource Governor. You should consider the compatibility views to be for backward compatibility only; going forward, you should consider using other metadata mechanisms, such as the catalog views discussed in the next section. All these compatibility views will be removed in a future version of SQL Server.

> **More info** You can find a complete list of names and the columns in these views in *SQL Server Books Online*.

SQL Server also provides compatibility views for the SQL Server 2000 pseudotables, such as *sysprocesses* and *syscacheobjects*. Pseudotables aren't based on data stored on disk but are built as needed from internal structures and can be queried exactly as though they are tables. SQL Server 2005 replaced these pseudotables with Dynamic Management Objects, which are discussed shortly.

Catalog views

SQL Server 2005 introduced a set of catalog views as a general interface to the persisted system metadata. All catalog views (as well as the Dynamic Management Objects and compatibility views) are in the *sys* schema, which you must reference by name when you access the objects. Some of the names are easy to remember because they are similar to the SQL Server 2000 system table names. For example, in the *sys* schema is a catalog view called *objects*, so to reference the view, the following can be executed:

```
SELECT * FROM sys.objects;
```

Similarly, catalog views are named *sys.indexes* and *sys.databases*, but the columns displayed for these catalog views are very different from the columns in the compatibility views. Because the output from these types of queries is too wide to reproduce, try running these two queries on your own and observe the difference:

```
SELECT * FROM sys.databases;
SELECT * FROM sysdatabases;
```

The *sysdatabases* compatibility view is in the *sys* schema, so you can reference it as *sys.sysdatabases*. You can also reference it using *dbo.sysdatabases*. But again, for compatibility reasons, the schema name isn't required as it is for the catalog views. (That is, you can't simply select from a view called *databases*; you must use the schema *sys* as a prefix.)

When you compare the output from the two preceding queries, you might notice that many more columns are in the *sys.databases* catalog view. Instead of a bitmap *status* field that needs to be decoded, each possible database property has its own column in *sys.databases*. With SQL Server 2000, running the system procedure *sp_helpdb* decodes all these database options, but because *sp_helpdb* is a procedure, it is difficult to filter the results. As a view, *sys.databases* can be queried and filtered. For example, if you want to know which databases are in *simple* recovery model, you can run the following:

```
SELECT name FROM sys.databases
WHERE recovery_model_desc = 'SIMPLE';
```

The catalog views are built on an inheritance model, so you don't have to redefine internally sets of attributes common to many objects. For example, *sys.objects* contains all the columns for attributes common to all types of objects, and the views *sys.tables* and *sys.views* contain all the same columns as *sys.objects*, as well as some additional columns that are relevant only to the particular type of objects. If you select from *sys.objects*, you get 12 columns, and if you then select from *sys.tables*, you get exactly the same 12 columns in the same order, plus 16 additional columns that aren't applicable to all types of objects but are meaningful for tables. Also, although the base view *sys.objects* contains a subset of columns compared to the derived views such as *sys.tables*, it contains a superset of rows compared to a derived view. For example, the *sys.objects* view shows metadata for procedures and views in addition to that for tables, whereas the *sys.tables* view shows only rows for tables. So the relationship between the base view and the derived views can be summarized as follows: The base views contain a subset of columns and a superset of rows, and the derived views contain a superset of columns and a subset of rows.

Just as in SQL Server 2000, some metadata appears only in the *master* database and keeps track of system-wide data, such as databases and logins. Other metadata is available in every database, such as objects and permissions. The *SQL Server Books Online* topic, "Mapping System Tables to System Views," categorizes its objects into two lists: those appearing only in *master* and those appearing in all databases. Note that metadata appearing only in the *msdb* database isn't available through catalog views but is still available in system tables, in the schema *dbo*. This includes metadata for backup and restore, replication, Database Maintenance Plans, Integration Services, log shipping, and SQL Server Agent.

As views, these metadata objects are based on an underlying Transact-SQL (T-SQL) definition. The most straightforward way to see the definition of these views is by using the *object_definition* function. (You can also see the definition of these system views by using *sp_helptext* or by selecting from the catalog view *sys.system_sql_modules*.) So to see the definition of *sys.tables*, you can execute the following:

```
SELECT object_definition (object_id('sys.tables'));
```

If you execute this *SELECT* statement, notice that the definition of *sys.tables* references several completely undocumented system objects. On the other hand, some system object definitions refer only to documented objects. For example, the definition of the compatibility view *syscacheobjects* refers only to three fully documented Dynamic Management Objects (one view, *sys.dm_exec_cached_plans*, and two functions, *sys.dm_exec_sql_text* and *sys.dm_exec_plan_attributes*).

Dynamic Management Objects

Metadata with names starting with *sys.dm_*, such as the just-mentioned *sys.dm_exec_cached_plans*, are considered Dynamic Management Objects. Although Dynamic Management Objects include both views and functions, they are usually referred to by the abbreviation DMV.

DMVs allow developers and database administrators to observe much of the internal behavior of SQL Server. You can access them as though they reside in the *sys* schema, which exists in every SQL Server database, but they aren't real objects. They are similar to the pseudotables used in SQL Server 2000 for observing the active processes (*sysprocesses*) or the contents of the plan cache (*syscacheobjects*).

> **Note** A one-to-one correspondence doesn't always occur between SQL Server 2000 pseudotables and Dynamic Management Objects. For example, for SQL Server 2012 to retrieve most of the information available in *sysprocesses*, you must access three Dynamic Management Objects: *sys.dm_exec_connections*, *sys.dm_exec_sessions*, and *sys.dm_exec_requests*. Even with these three objects, information is still available in the old *sysprocesses* pseudotable that's not available in any of the new metadata.

The pseudotables in SQL Server 2000 don't provide any tracking of detailed resource usage and can't always be used to detect resource problems or state changes. Some DMVs allow tracking of detailed resource history, and you can directly query and join more than 175 such objects with T-SQL *SELECT* statements. The DMVs expose changing server state information that might span multiple sessions, multiple transactions, and multiple user requests. These objects can be used for diagnostics, memory and process tuning, and monitoring across all sessions in the server.

The DMVs aren't based on real tables stored in database files but are based on internal server structures, some of which are discussed in Chapter 2. More details about DMVs are discussed throughout this book, where the contents of one or more of the objects can illuminate the topics being discussed. The objects are separated into several categories based on the functional area of the information they expose. They are all in the *sys* schema and have a name that starts with *dm_*, followed by a code indicating the area of the server with which the object deals. The main categories are:

- **dm_exec_*** This category contains information directly or indirectly related to the execution of user code and associated connections. For example, *sys.dm_exec_sessions* returns one row per authenticated session on SQL Server. This object contains much of the same information that sysprocesses contains in SQL Server 2000 but has even more information about the operating environment of each sessions

- **dm_os_*** This category contains low-level system information such as memory and scheduling. For example, *sys.dm_os_schedulers* is a DMV that returns one row per scheduler. It's used primarily to monitor the condition of a scheduler or to identify runaway tasks.

- **dm_tran_*** This category contains details about current transactions. For example, *sys.dm_tran_locks* returns information about currently active lock resources. Each row represents a currently active request to the lock management component for a lock that has been granted or is waiting to be granted. This object replaces the pseudotable *syslockinfo* in SQL Server 2000.

- **dm_logpool*** This category contains details about log pools used to manage SQL Server 2012's log cache, a new feature added to make log records more easily retrievable when needed by features such as AlwaysOn. (The new log-caching behavior is used whether or not you're using the AlwaysOn features. Logging and log management are discussed in Chapter 5, "Logging and recovery.")

- **dm_io_*** This category keeps track of input/output activity on network and disks. For example, the function *sys.dm_io_virtual_file_stats* returns I/O statistics for data and log files. This object replaces the table-valued function *fn_virtualfilestats* in SQL Server 2000.

- **dm_db_*** This category contains details about databases and database objects such as indexes. For example, the *sys.dm_db_index_physical_stats* function returns size and fragmentation information for the data and indexes of the specified table or view. This function replaces *DBCC SHOWCONTIG* in SQL Server 2000.

SQL Server 2012 also has dynamic management objects for many of its functional components, including objects for monitoring full-text search catalogs, service broker, replication, availability groups, transparent data encryption, Extended Events, and the Common Language Runtime (CLR).

Other metadata

Although catalog views are the recommended interface for accessing the SQL Server 2012 catalog, other tools are also available.

Information schema views

Information schema views, introduced in SQL Server 7.0, were the original system table-independent view of the SQL Server metadata. The information schema views included in SQL Server 2012 comply with the SQL-92 standard, and all these views are in a schema called *INFORMATION_SCHEMA*. Some information available through the catalog views is available through the information schema views, and if you need to write a portable application that accesses the metadata, you should consider using these objects. However, the information schema views show only objects compatible with the SQL-92 standard. This means no information schema view exists for certain features, such as indexes, which aren't defined in the standard. (Indexes are an implementation detail.) If your code doesn't need to be strictly portable, or if you need metadata about nonstandard features such as indexes, filegroups, the CLR, and SQL Server Service Broker, using the Microsoft-supplied catalog views is suggested. Most examples in the documentation, as well as in this and other reference books, are based on the catalog view interface.

System functions

Most SQL Server system functions are property functions, which were introduced in SQL Server 7.0 and greatly enhanced in subsequent versions. Property functions provide individual values for many SQL Server objects as well as for SQL Server databases and the SQL Server instance itself. The values returned by the property functions are scalar as opposed to tabular, so they can be used as values returned by *SELECT* statements and as values to populate columns in tables. The following property functions are available in SQL Server 2012:

- *SERVERPROPERTY*
- *COLUMNPROPERTY*
- *DATABASEPROPERTYEX*
- *INDEXPROPERTY*
- *INDEXKEY_PROPERTY*
- *OBJECTPROPERTY*
- *OBJECTPROPERTYEX*
- *SQL_VARIANT_PROPERTY*
- *FILEPROPERTY*
- *FILEGROUPPROPERTY*
- *FULLTEXTCATALOGPROPERTY*
- *FULLTEXTSERVICEPROPERTY*
- *TYPEPROPERTY*
- *CONNECTIONPROPERTY*
- *ASSEMBLYPROPERTY*

The only way to find out what the possible property values are for the various functions is to check *SQL Server Books Online*.

You also can see some information returned by the property functions by using the catalog views. For example, the *DATABASEPROPERTYEX* function has a *Recovery* property that returns the recovery model of a database. To view the recovery model of a single database, you can use the following property function:

```
SELECT DATABASEPROPERTYEX('msdb', 'Recovery');
```

To view the recovery models of all your databases, you can use the *sys.databases* view:

```
SELECT name, recovery_model, recovery_model_desc
FROM sys.databases;
```

> **Note** Columns with names ending in *_desc* are known as the "friendly name" columns, and they are always paired with another column that is much more compact, but cryptic. In this case, the *recovery_model* column is a *tinyint* with a value of 1, 2, or 3. Both columns are available in the view because different consumers have different needs. For example, internally at Microsoft, the teams building the internal interfaces wanted to bind to more compact columns, whereas DBAs running ad hoc queries might prefer the friendly names.

In addition to the property functions, the system functions include functions that are merely shortcuts for catalog view access. For example, to find out the database ID for the *AdventureWorks2012* database, you can either query the *sys.databases* catalog view or use the *DB_ID()* function. Both of the following *SELECT* statements should return the same result:

```
SELECT database_id
FROM sys.databases
WHERE name = 'AdventureWorks2012';

SELECT DB_ID('AdventureWorks2012');
```

System stored procedures

System stored procedures are the original metadata access tool, in addition to the system tables themselves. Most of the system stored procedures introduced in the very first version of SQL Server are still available. However, catalog views are a big improvement over these procedures: You have control over how much of the metadata you see because you can query the views as though they were tables. With the system stored procedures, you have to accept the data that it returns. Some procedures allow parameters, but they are very limited. For the *sp_helpdb* procedure, for example, you can pass a parameter to see just one database's information or not pass a parameter and see information for all databases. However, if you want to see only databases that the login *sue* owns, or just see databases that are in a lower compatibility level, you can't do so using the supplied stored procedure. Through the catalog views, these queries are straightforward:

```
SELECT name FROM sys.databases
WHERE suser_sname(owner_sid) ='sue';

SELECT name FROM sys.databases
WHERE compatibility_level < 110;
```

Metadata wrap-up

Figure 1-1 shows the multiple layers of metadata available in SQL Server 2012, with the lowest layer being the system base tables (the actual catalog). Any interface that accesses the information contained in the system base tables is subject to the metadata security policies. For SQL Server 2012, that means that no users can see any metadata that they don't need to see or to which they haven't specifically been granted permissions. (The few exceptions are very minor.) "Other Metadata" refers to system information not contained in system tables, such as the internal information provided by the Dynamic Management Objects. Remember that the preferred interfaces to the system metadata are the catalog views and system functions. Although not all the compatibility views, *INFORMATION_ SCHEMA* views, and system procedures are actually defined in terms of the catalog views; thinking conceptually of them as another layer on top of the catalog view interface is useful.

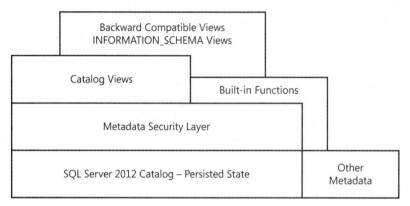

FIGURE 1-1 Layers of metadata in SQL Server 2012.

Components of the SQL Server engine

Figure 1-2 shows the general architecture of SQL Server and its four major components: the protocol layer, the query processor (also called the relational engine), the storage engine, and the SQLOS. Every batch submitted to SQL Server for execution, from any client application, must interact with these four components. (For simplicity, some minor omissions and simplifications have been made and certain "helper" modules have been ignored among the subcomponents.)

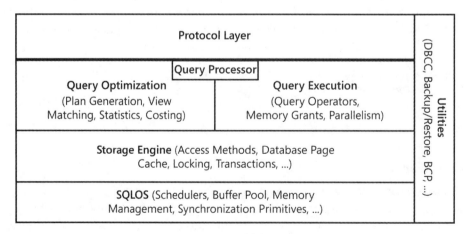

FIGURE 1-2 The major components of the SQL Server Database Engine.

The protocol layer receives the request and translates it into a form that the relational engine can work with. It also takes the final results of any queries, status messages, or error messages and translates them into a form the client can understand before sending them back to the client. The query processor accepts T-SQL batches and determines what to do with them. For T-SQL queries and programming constructs, it parses, compiles, and optimizes the request and oversees the process of executing the batch. As the batch is executed, if data is needed, a request for that data is passed to the storage engine. The storage engine manages all data access, both through transaction-based commands and bulk operations such as backup, bulk insert, and certain Database Console Commands (DBCCs). The SQLOS layer handles activities normally considered to be operating system responsibilities, such as thread management (scheduling), synchronization primitives, deadlock detection, and memory management, including the buffer pool.

The next section looks at the major components of the SQL Server Database Engine in more detail.

Protocols

When an application communicates with the Database Engine, the application programming interfaces (APIs) exposed by the protocol layer formats the communication using a Microsoft-defined format called a *tabular data stream (TDS) packet*. The SQL Server Network Interface (SNI) protocol layer on both the server and client computers encapsulates the TDS packet inside a standard communication protocol, such as TCP/IP or Named Pipes. On the server side of the communication, the network libraries are part of the Database Engine. On the client side, the network libraries are part of the SQL Native Client. The configuration of the client and the instance of SQL Server determine which protocol is used.

You can configure SQL Server to support multiple protocols simultaneously, coming from different clients. Each client connects to SQL Server with a single protocol. If the client program doesn't know which protocols SQL Server is listening on, you can configure the client to attempt multiple protocols sequentially. The following protocols are available:

- **Shared Memory**   The simplest protocol to use, with no configurable settings. Clients using the Shared Memory protocol can connect to only a SQL Server instance running on the same computer, so this protocol isn't useful for most database activity. Use this protocol for troubleshooting when you suspect that the other protocols are configured incorrectly. Clients using MDAC 2.8 or earlier can't use the Shared Memory protocol. If such a connection is attempted, the client is switched to the Named Pipes protocol.

- **Named Pipes**   A protocol developed for local area networks (LANs). A portion of memory is used by one process to pass information to another process, so that the output of one is the input of the other. The second process can be local (on the same computer as the first) or remote (on a network computer).

- **TCP/IP**   The most widely used protocol over the Internet. TCP/IP can communicate across interconnected computer networks with diverse hardware architectures and operating systems. It includes standards for routing network traffic and offers advanced security features. Enabling SQL Server to use TCP/IP requires the most configuration effort, but most networked computers are already properly configured.

> ## Tabular Data Stream endpoints
>
> SQL Server 2012 also allows you to create a TDS endpoint, so that SQL Server listens on an additional TCP port. During setup, SQL Server automatically creates an endpoint for each of the three protocols supported by SQL Server, and if the protocol is enabled, all users have access to it. For disabled protocols, the endpoint still exists but can't be used. An additional endpoint is created for the DAC, which only members of the *sysadmin* fixed server role can use. (Chapter 2 discusses the DAC in more detail.)

Query processor

As mentioned earlier, the query processor is also called the relational engine. It includes the SQL Server components that determine exactly what your query needs to do and the best way to do it. In Figure 1-2, the query processor is shown as two primary components: Query Optimization and query execution. This layer also includes components for parsing and binding (not shown in the figure). By far the most complex component of the query processor—and maybe even of the entire SQL Server product—is the Query Optimizer, which determines the best execution plan for the queries in the batch. Chapter 11, "The Query Optimizer," discusses the Query Optimizer in great detail; this section gives you just a high-level overview of the Query Optimizer as well as of the other components of the query processor.

The query processor also manages query execution as it requests data from the storage engine and processes the results returned. Communication between the query processor and the storage engine is generally in terms of Object Linking and Embedding (OLE) DB rowsets. (Rowset is the OLE DB term for a result set.)

Parsing and binding components

The parser processes T-SQL language events sent to SQL Server. It checks for proper syntax and spelling of keywords. After a query is parsed, a binding component performs name resolution to convert the object names into their unique object ID values. After the parsing and binding is done, the command is converted into an internal format that can be operated on. This internal format is known as a *query tree*. If the syntax is incorrect or an object name can't be resolved, an error is immediately raised that identifies where the error occurred. However, other types of error messages can't be explicit about the exact source line that caused the error. Because only parsing and binding components can access the source of the statement, the statement is no longer available in source format when the command is actually executed.

The Query Optimizer

The Query Optimizer takes the query tree and prepares it for optimization. Statements that can't be optimized, such as flow-of-control and Data Definition Language (DDL) commands, are compiled into an internal form. Optimizable statements are marked as such and then passed to the Query

Optimizer. The Query Optimizer is concerned mainly with the Data Manipulation Language (DML) statements *SELECT*, *INSERT*, *UPDATE*, *DELETE*, and *MERGE*, which can be processed in more than one way; the Query Optimizer determines which of the many possible ways is best. It compiles an entire command batch and optimizes queries that are optimizable. The query optimization and compilation result in an execution plan.

The first step in producing such a plan is to *normalize* each query, which potentially breaks down a single query into multiple, fine-grained queries. After the Query Optimizer normalizes a query, it *optimizes* it, which means that it determines a plan for executing that query. Query optimization is cost-based; the Query Optimizer chooses the plan that it determines would cost the least based on internal metrics that include estimated memory requirements, CPU utilization, and number of required I/Os. The Query Optimizer considers the type of statement requested, checks the amount of data in the various tables affected, looks at the indexes available for each table, and then looks at a sampling of the data values kept for each index or column referenced in the query. The sampling of the data values is called *distribution statistics*. (Chapter 11 discusses statistics in detail.) Based on the available information, the Query Optimizer considers the various access methods and processing strategies that it could use to resolve a query and chooses the most cost-effective plan.

The Query Optimizer also uses pruning heuristics to ensure that optimizing a query doesn't take longer than required to simply choose a plan and execute it. The Query Optimizer doesn't necessarily perform exhaustive optimization; some products consider every possible plan and then choose the most cost-effective one. The advantage of this exhaustive optimization is that the syntax chosen for a query theoretically never causes a performance difference, no matter what syntax the user employed. But with a complex query, it could take much longer to estimate the cost of every conceivable plan than it would to accept a good plan, even if it's not the best one, and execute it.

After normalization and optimization are completed, the normalized tree produced by those processes is compiled into the execution plan, which is actually a data structure. Each command included in it specifies exactly which table is affected, which indexes are used (if any), and which criteria (such as equality to a specified value) must evaluate to TRUE for selection. This execution plan might be considerably more complex than is immediately apparent. In addition to the actual commands, the execution plan includes all the steps necessary to ensure that constraints are checked. Steps for calling a trigger are slightly different from those for verifying constraints. If a trigger is included for the action being taken, a call to the procedure that comprises the trigger is appended. If the trigger is an *instead-of* trigger, the call to the trigger's plan replaces the actual data modification command. For *after* triggers, the trigger's plan is branched to right after the plan for the modification statement that fired the trigger, before that modification is committed. The specific steps for the trigger aren't compiled into the execution plan, unlike those for constraint verification.

A simple request to insert one row into a table with multiple constraints can result in an execution plan that requires many other tables to be accessed or expressions to be evaluated. Also, the existence of a trigger can cause many more steps to be executed. The step that carries out the actual *INSERT* statement might be just a small part of the total execution plan necessary to ensure that all actions and constraints associated with adding a row are carried out.

The query executor

The query executor runs the execution plan that the Query Optimizer produced, acting as a dispatcher for all commands in the execution plan. This module goes through each command of the execution plan until the batch is complete. Most commands require interaction with the storage engine to modify or retrieve data and to manage transactions and locking. You can find more information on query execution and execution plans in Chapter 10, "Query execution."

The storage engine

The SQL Server storage engine includes all components involved with the accessing and managing of data in your database. In SQL Server 2012, the storage engine is composed of three main areas: access methods, locking and transaction services, and utility commands.

Access methods

When SQL Server needs to locate data, it calls the access methods code, which sets up and requests scans of data pages and index pages and prepares the OLE DB rowsets to return to the relational engine. Similarly, when data is to be inserted, the access methods code can receive an OLE DB rowset from the client. The access methods code contains components to open a table, retrieve qualified data, and update data. It doesn't actually retrieve the pages; instead, it makes the request to the buffer manager, which ultimately serves up the page in its cache or reads it to cache from disk. When the scan starts, a look-ahead mechanism qualifies the rows or index entries on a page. The retrieving of rows that meet specified criteria is known as a *qualified retrieval*. The access methods code is used not only for *SELECT* statements but also for qualified *UPDATE* and *DELETE* statements (for example, *UPDATE* with a *WHERE* clause) and for any data modification operations that need to modify index entries. The following sections discuss some types of access methods.

Row and index operations   You can consider row and index operations to be components of the access methods code because they carry out the actual method of access. Each component is responsible for manipulating and maintaining its respective on-disk data structures—namely, rows of data or B-tree indexes, respectively. They understand and manipulate information on data and index pages.

The row operations code retrieves, modifies, and performs operations on individual rows. It performs an operation within a row, such as "retrieve column 2" or "write this value to column 3." As a result of the work performed by the access methods code, as well as by the lock and transaction management components (discussed shortly), the row is found and appropriately locked as part of a transaction. After formatting or modifying a row in memory, the row operations code inserts or deletes a row. The row operations code needs to handle special operations if the data is a large object (LOB) data type—*text*, *image*, or *ntext*—or if the row is too large to fit on a single page and needs to be stored as overflow data. Chapter 6, "Table storage"; Chapter 7, "Indexes: internals and management"; and Chapter 8, "Special storage," look at the different types of data-storage structures.

The index operations code maintains and supports searches on B-trees, which are used for SQL Server indexes. An index is structured as a tree, with a root page and intermediate-level and lower-level pages. (A very small tree might not have intermediate-level pages.) A B-tree groups records with similar index keys, thereby allowing fast access to data by searching on a key value. The B-tree's core feature is its ability to balance the index tree (B stands for *balanced*). Branches of the index tree are spliced together or split apart as necessary so that the search for any particular record always traverses the same number of levels and therefore requires the same number of page accesses.

Page allocation operations   The allocation operations code manages a collection of pages for each database and monitors which pages in a database have already been used, for what purpose they have been used, and how much space is available on each page. Each database is a collection of 8 KB disk pages spread across one or more physical files. (Chapter 3, "Databases and database files," goes into more detail about the physical organization of databases.)

SQL Server uses 13 types of disk pages. The ones this book discusses are data pages, two types of Large Object (LOB) pages, row-overflow pages, index pages, Page Free Space (PFS) pages, Global Allocation Map and Shared Global Allocation Map (GAM and SGAM) pages, Index Allocation Map (IAM) pages, Minimally Logged (ML) pages, and Differential Changed Map (DIFF) pages. Another type, File Header pages, won't be discussed in this book.

All user data is stored on data, LOB, or row-overflow pages. Index rows are stored on index pages, but indexes can also store information on LOB and row-overflow pages. PFS pages keep track of which pages in a database are available to hold new data. Allocation pages (GAMs, SGAMs, and IAMs) keep track of the other pages; they contain no database rows and are used only internally. BCM and DCM pages are used to make backup and recovery more efficient. Chapter 5 explains these page types in more detail.

Versioning operations   Another type of data access, which was added to the product in SQL Server 2005, is access through the version store. Row versioning allows SQL Server to maintain older versions of changed rows. The row-versioning technology in SQL Server supports snapshot isolation as well as other features of SQL Server 2012, including online index builds and triggers, and the versioning operations code maintains row versions for whatever purpose they are needed.

Chapters 3, 4, 6, 7, and 8 deal extensively with the internal details of the structures that the access methods code works with databases, tables, and indexes.

Transaction services

A core feature of SQL Server is its ability to ensure that transactions are *atomic*—that is, all or nothing. Also, transactions must be durable, which means that if a transaction has been committed, it must be recoverable by SQL Server no matter what—even if a total system failure occurs one millisecond after the commit was acknowledged. Transactions must adhere to four properties, called the ACID properties: *atomicity*, *consistency*, *isolation*, and *durability*. Chapter 13, "Transactions and concurrency," covers all four properties in a section on transaction management and concurrency issues.

In SQL Server, if work is in progress and a system failure occurs before the transaction is committed, all the work is rolled back to the state that existed before the transaction began. Write-ahead logging makes possible the ability to always roll back work in progress or roll forward committed work that hasn't yet been applied to the data pages. Write-ahead logging ensures that the record of each transaction's changes is captured on disk in the transaction log before a transaction is acknowledged as committed, and that the log records are always written to disk before the data pages where the changes were actually made are written. Writes to the transaction log are always synchronous—that is, SQL Server must wait for them to complete. Writes to the data pages can be asynchronous because all the effects can be reconstructed from the log if necessary. The transaction management component coordinates logging, recovery, and buffer management, topics discussed later in this book; this section looks just briefly at transactions themselves.

The transaction management component delineates the boundaries of statements that must be grouped to form an operation. It handles transactions that cross databases within the same SQL Server instance and allows nested transaction sequences. (However, nested transactions simply execute in the context of the first-level transaction; no special action occurs when they are committed. Also, a rollback specified in a lower level of a nested transaction undoes the entire transaction.) For a distributed transaction to another SQL Server instance (or to any other resource manager), the transaction management component coordinates with the Microsoft Distributed Transaction Coordinator (MS DTC) service, using operating system remote procedure calls. The transaction management component marks *save points* that you designate within a transaction at which work can be partially rolled back or undone.

The transaction management component also coordinates with the locking code regarding when locks can be released, based on the isolation level in effect. It also coordinates with the versioning code to determine when old versions are no longer needed and can be removed from the version store. The isolation level in which your transaction runs determines how sensitive your application is to changes made by others and consequently how long your transaction must hold locks or maintain versioned data to protect against those changes.

Concurrency models   SQL Server 2012 supports two concurrency models for guaranteeing the ACID properties of transactions:

- **Pessimistic concurrency**   This model guarantees correctness and consistency by locking data so that it can't be changed. Every version of SQL Server prior to SQL Server 2005 used this currency model exclusively; it's the default in both SQL Server 2005 and later versions.

- **Optimistic currency**   SQL Server 2005 introduced optimistic concurrency, which provides consistent data by keeping older versions of rows with committed values in an area of *tempdb* called the *version store*. With optimistic concurrency, readers don't block writers and writers don't block readers, but writers still block writers. The cost of these non-blocking operations must be considered. To support optimistic concurrency, SQL Server needs to spend more time managing the version store. Administrators also have to pay close attention to the *tempdb* database and plan for the extra maintenance it requires.

Five isolation-level semantics are available in SQL Server 2012. Three of them support only pessimistic concurrency: Read Uncommitted, Repeatable Read, and Serializable. Snapshot isolation level supports optimistic concurrency. The default isolation level, Read Committed, can support either optimistic or pessimistic concurrency, depending on a database setting.

The behavior of your transactions depends on the isolation level and the concurrency model you are working with. A complete understanding of isolation levels also requires an understanding of locking because the topics are so closely related. The next section gives an overview of locking; you'll find more detailed information on isolation, transactions, and concurrency management in Chapter 10.

Locking operations   Locking is a crucial function of a multiuser database system such as SQL Server, even if you are operating primarily in the snapshot isolation level with optimistic concurrency. SQL Server lets you manage multiple users simultaneously and ensures that the transactions observe the properties of the chosen isolation level. Even though readers don't block writers and writers don't block readers in snapshot isolation, writers do acquire locks and can still block other writers, and if two writers try to change the same data concurrently, a conflict occurs that must be resolved. The locking code acquires and releases various types of locks, such as share locks for reading, exclusive locks for writing, intent locks taken at a higher granularity to signal a potential "plan" to perform some operation, and extent locks for space allocation. It manages compatibility between the lock types, resolves deadlocks, and escalates locks if needed. The locking code controls table, page, and row locks as well as system data locks.

> **Note** Concurrency management, whether with locks or row versions, is an important aspect of SQL Server. Many developers are keenly interested in it because of its potential effect on application performance. Chapter 13 is devoted to the subject, so this chapter won't go into further detail here.

Other operations

Also included in the storage engine are components for controlling utilities such as bulk-load, DBCC commands, full-text index population and management, and backup and restore operations. Chapter 14, "DBCC internals," covers DBCC in detail. The log manager makes sure that log records are written in a manner to guarantee transaction durability and recoverability. Chapter 5 goes into detail about the transaction log and its role in backup-and-restore operations.

SQL Server 2012 configuration

This half of the chapter looks at the options for controlling how SQL Server 2012 behaves. Some options might not mean much until you've read about the relevant components later in the book, but you can always come back and reread this section. One main method of controlling the behavior of the Database Engine is to adjust configuration option settings, but you can configure behavior in a few other ways as well. First, look at using SQL Server Configuration Manager to control network protocols and SQL Server–related services. Then, look at other machine settings that can affect the behavior of SQL Server. Finally, you can examine some specific configuration options for controlling server-wide settings in SQL Server.

Using SQL Server Configuration Manager

Configuration Manager is a tool for managing the services associated with SQL Server, configuring the network protocols used, and managing the network connectivity configuration from client computers connecting to SQL Server. Configuration Manager is accessed by selecting All Programs on the Windows Start menu, and then selecting Microsoft SQL Server 2012 | Configuration Tools | SQL Server Configuration Manager.

Configuring network protocols

A specific protocol must be enabled on both the client and the server for the client to connect and communicate with the server. SQL Server can listen for requests on all enabled protocols at once. The underlying operating system network protocols (such as TCP/IP) should already be installed on the client and the server. Network protocols are typically installed during Windows setup; they aren't part of SQL Server setup. A SQL Server network library doesn't work unless its corresponding network protocol is installed on both the client and the server.

On the client computer, the SQL Native Client must be installed and configured to use a network protocol enabled on the server; this is usually done during Client Tools Connectivity setup. The SQL Native Client is a standalone data-access application programming interface (API) used for both OLE DB and Open Database Connectivity (ODBC). If the SQL Native Client is available, you can configure any network protocol for use with a particular client connecting to SQL Server. You can use SQL Server Configuration Manager to enable a single protocol or to enable multiple protocols and specify an order in which they should be attempted. If the Shared Memory protocol setting is enabled, that protocol is always tried first, but, as mentioned earlier in this chapter, it's available for communication only when the client and the server are on the same machine.

The following query returns the protocol used for the current connection, using the DMV *sys.dm_exec_connections*:

```
SELECT net_transport
FROM sys.dm_exec_connections
WHERE session_id = @@SPID;
```

Implementing a default network configuration

The network protocols used to communicate with SQL Server 2012 from another computer aren't all enabled for SQL Server during installation. To connect from a particular client computer, you might need to enable the desired protocol. The Shared Memory protocol is enabled by default on all installations, but because it can be used to connect to the Database Engine only from a client application on the same computer, its usefulness is limited.

TCP/IP connectivity to SQL Server 2012 is disabled for new installations of the Developer, Evaluation, and SQL Express editions. OLE DB applications connecting with MDAC 2.8 can't connect to the default instance on a local server using "." (period), "(local)", or (<blank>) as the server name. To resolve this, supply the server name or enable TCP/IP on the server. Connections to local named instances aren't affected, nor are connections using the SQL Native Client. Installations in which a previous installation of SQL Server is present might not be affected.

Table 1-1 describes the default network configuration settings.

TABLE 1-1 SQL Server 2012 default network configuration settings

SQL Server edition	Type of installation	Shared memory	TCP/IP	Named pipes
Enterprise	New	Enabled	Enabled	Disabled (available only locally)
Enterprise (clustered)	New	Enabled	Enabled	Enabled
Developer	New	Enabled	Disabled	Disabled (available only locally)
Standard	New	Enabled	Enabled	Disabled (available only locally)
Workgroup	New	Enabled	Enabled	Disabled (available only locally)
Evaluation	New	Enabled	Disabled	Disabled (available only locally)
Web	New	Enabled	Enabled	Disabled (available only locally)
SQL Server Express	New	Enabled	Disabled	Disabled (available only locally)
All editions	Upgrade or side-by-side installation	Enabled	Settings preserved from the previous installation	Settings preserved from the previous installation

Managing services

You can use Configuration Manager to start, pause, resume, or stop SQL Server–related services. The services available depend on the specific components of SQL Server you have installed, but you should always have the SQL Server service itself and the SQL Server Agent service. Other services might include the SQL Server Full-Text Search service and SQL Server Integration Services (SSIS). You can also use Configuration Manager to view the current properties of the services, such as whether the service is set to start automatically.

Configuration Manager, rather than the Windows service management tools, is the preferred tool for changing service properties. When you use a SQL Server tool such as Configuration Manager to change the account used by either the SQL Server or SQL Server Agent service, the tool automatically makes additional configurations, such as setting permissions in the Windows Registry so that the new account can read the SQL Server settings. Password changes using Configuration Manager take effect immediately without requiring you to restart the service.

SQL Server Browser

One related service that deserves special attention is the SQL Server Browser service, particularly important if you have named instances of SQL Server running on a machine. SQL Server Browser listens for requests to access SQL Server resources and provides information about the various SQL Server instances installed on the computer where the Browser service is running.

Prior to SQL Server 2000, only one installation of SQL Server could be on a machine at one time, and the concept of an "instance" really didn't exist. SQL Server always listened for incoming requests on port 1433, but any port can be used by only one connection at a time. When SQL Server 2000 introduced support for multiple instances of SQL Server, a new protocol called *SQL Server Resolution Protocol (SSRP)* was developed to listen on UDP port 1434. This listener could reply to clients with the names of installed SQL Server instances, along with the port numbers or named pipes used by the instance. SQL Server 2005 replaced SSRP with the SQL Server Browser service, which is still used in SQL Server 2012.

If the SQL Server Browser service isn't running on a computer, you can't connect to SQL Server on that machine unless you provide the correct port number. Specifically, if the SQL Server Browser service isn't running, the following connections won't work:

- Connecting to a named instance without providing the port number or pipe

- Using the DAC to connect to a named instance or the default instance if it isn't using TCP/IP port 1433

- Enumerating servers in SQL Server Management Studio

You are recommended to have the Browser service set to start automatically on any machine on which SQL Server will be accessed using a network connection.

SQL Server system configuration

You can configure the machine that SQL Server runs on, as well as the Database Engine itself, in several ways and through various interfaces. First, look at some operating system–level settings that can affect the behavior of SQL Server. Next, you can see some SQL Server options that can affect behavior that aren't especially considered to be configuration options. Finally, you can examine the configuration options for controlling the behavior of SQL Server 2012, which are set primarily using a stored procedure interface called *sp_configure*.

Operating system configuration

For your SQL Server to run well, it must be running on a tuned operating system on a machine that has been properly configured to run SQL Server. Although discussing operating system and hardware configuration and tuning is beyond the scope of this book, a few issues are very straightforward but can have a major effect on the performance of SQL Server.

Task management

The Windows operating system schedules all threads in the system for execution. Each thread of every process has a priority, and the operating system executes the next available thread with the highest priority. By default, it gives active applications a higher priority, but this priority setting might not be appropriate for a server application running in the background, such as SQL Server 2012. To remedy this situation, the SQL Server installation program modifies the priority setting to eliminate the favoring of foreground applications.

Periodically double-checking this priority setting is a good idea, in case someone has set it back. You'll need to use the Advanced tab in the Performance Options dialog box. If you're using Windows Server 2008 or Windows 7, click the Start menu, right-click Computer, and choose Properties. In the System information screen, select Advanced System Settings from the list on the left to open the System Properties sheet. Click the Settings button in the Performance section and then select the Advanced tab. Figure 1-3 shows the Performance Options dialog box.

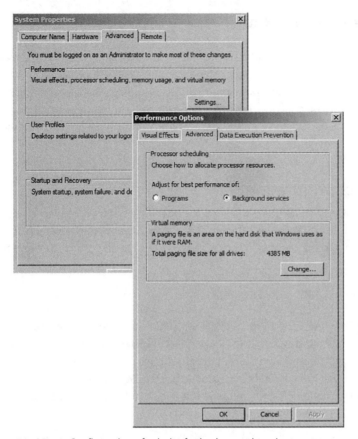

FIGURE 1-3 Configuration of priority for background services.

The first set of options specifies how to allocate processor resources, and you can adjust for the best performance of programs or background services. Select Background Services so that all programs (background and foreground) receive equal processor resources. If you plan to connect to SQL Server 2012 from a local client—that is, a client running on the same computer as the server—you can use this setting to improve processing time.

System paging file location

If possible, you should place the operating system paging file on a different drive than the files used by SQL Server. This is vital if your system will be paging. However, a better approach is to add memory or change the SQL Server memory configuration to effectively eliminate paging. In general, SQL Server is designed to minimize paging, so if your memory configuration values are appropriate for the amount of physical memory on the system, such a small amount of page-file activity will occur that the file's location is irrelevant.

Nonessential services

You should disable any services that you don't need. In Windows Server 2008, you can click the Start menu, right-click Computer, and choose Manage. Expand the Services and Applications node in the Computer Management tool, and click Services. In the right-hand pane is a list of all services available on the operating system. You can change a service's startup property by right-clicking its name and choosing Properties. Unnecessary services add overhead to the system and use resources that could otherwise go to SQL Server. No unnecessary services should be marked for automatic startup. Avoid using a server that runs SQL Server as a domain controller, the group's file or print server, the Web server, or the Dynamic Host Configuration Protocol (DHCP) server.

Connectivity

You should run only the network protocols that you actually need for connectivity. You can use the SQL Server Configuration Manager to disable unneeded protocols, as described earlier in this chapter.

Firewall setting

Improper firewall settings are another system configuration issue that can inhibit SQL Server connectivity across your network. Firewall systems help prevent unauthorized access to computer resources and are usually desirable, but to access an instance of SQL Server through a firewall, you'll need to configure the firewall on the computer running SQL Server to allow access. Many firewall systems are available, and you'll need to check the documentation for your system for the exact details of how to configure it. In general, you need to follow these steps:

1. Configure the SQL Server instance to use a specific TCP/IP port. Your default SQL Server uses port 1433 by default, but you can change that. Named instances use dynamic ports by default, but you can also change that through the SQL Server Configuration Manager.

2. Configure your firewall to allow access to the specific port for authorized users or computers.

3. As an alternative to configuring SQL Server to listen on a specific port and then opening that port, you can list the SQL Server executable (Sqlservr.exe) and the SQL Browser executable (Sqlbrowser.exe) when requiring a connection to named instances as exceptions to the blocked programs. You can use this method when you want to continue to use dynamic ports.

Trace flags

SQL Server Books Online lists only 17 trace flags that are fully supported. You can think of trace flags as special switches that you can turn on or off to change the behavior of SQL Server. Many dozens, if not hundreds, of trace flags exist, but most were created for the SQL Server development team's internal testing of the product and were never intended for use by anybody outside Microsoft.

You can toggle trace flags on or off by using the *DBCC TRACEON* and *DBCC TRACEOFF* commands or by specifying them on the command line when you start SQL Server using Sqlservr.exe. You can also use the SQL Server Configuration Manager to enable one or more trace flags every time the SQL Server service is started. (You can read about how to do that in *SQL Server Books Online*.) Trace flags enabled with *DBCC TRACEON* are valid only for a single connection unless you specified an additional parameter of *–1*, in which case they are active for all connections, even ones opened before you ran *DBCC TRACEON*. Trace flags enabled as part of starting the SQL Server service are enabled for all sessions.

A few of the trace flags are particularly relevant to topics covered in this book, and specific ones are discussed with topics they are related to.

Caution Because trace flags change the way SQL Server behaves, they can actually cause trouble if used inappropriately. Trace flags aren't harmless features that you can experiment with just to see what happens, especially on a production system. Using them effectively requires a thorough understanding of SQL Server default behavior (so that you know exactly what you'll be changing) and extensive testing to determine whether your system really will benefit from the use of the trace flag.

SQL Server configuration settings

If you choose to have SQL Server automatically configure your system, it dynamically adjusts the most important configuration options for you. It's best to accept the default configuration values unless you have a good reason to change them. A poorly configured system can destroy performance. For example, a system with an incorrectly configured memory setting can break an application.

In certain cases, tweaking the settings rather than letting SQL Server dynamically adjust them might lead to a tiny performance improvement, but your time is probably better spent on application and database designing, indexing, query tuning, and other such activities, which is covered later in this book. You might see only a 5 percent improvement in performance by moving from a reasonable configuration to an ideal configuration, but a badly configured system can kill your application's performance.

SQL Server 2012 has 69 server configuration options that you can query, using the catalog view *sys.configurations*.

You should change configuration options only when you have a clear reason for doing so and closely monitor the effects of each change to determine whether the change improved or degraded performance. Always make and monitor changes one at a time. The server-wide options discussed here can be changed in several ways. All of them can be set via the *sp_configure* system stored procedure. However, of the 69 options, all but 17 are considered advanced options and aren't manageable by default using *sp_configure*. You first need to change the *show advanced options* setting to be *1*:

```
EXEC sp_configure 'show advanced options', 1; RECONFIGURE;
GO
```

To see which options are advanced, you can query the *sys.configurations* view and examine a column called *is_advanced*, which lets you see which options are considered advanced:

```
SELECT * FROM sys.configurations
WHERE is_advanced = 1;
GO
```

You also can set many configuration options from the Server Properties sheet in the Object
Explorer pane of SQL Server Management Studio, but you can't see or change all configuration set-
tings from just one dialog box or window. Most of the options that you can change from the Server
Properties sheet are controlled from one of the property pages that you reach by right-clicking the
name of your SQL Server instance in Management Studio. You can see the list of property pages in
Figure 1-4.

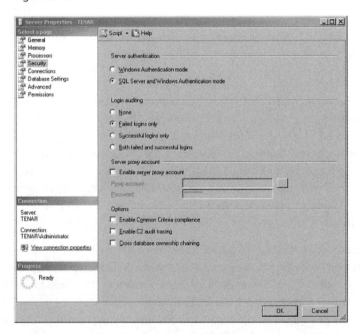

FIGURE 1-4 List of server property pages in SQL Server Management Studio.

If you use the *sp_configure* stored procedure, no changes take effect until the *RECONFIGURE*
command runs. In some cases, you might have to specify *RECONFIGURE WITH OVERRIDE* if you are
changing an option to a value outside the recommended range. Dynamic changes take effect immediately on reconfiguration, but others don't take effect until the server is restarted. If after running
RECONFIGURE an option's *run_value* and *config_value* as displayed by *sp_configure* are different, or if
the *value* and *value_in_use* in *sys.configurations* are different, you must restart the SQL Server service
for the new value to take effect. You can use the *sys.configurations* view to determine which options
are dynamic:

```
SELECT * FROM sys.configurations
WHERE is_dynamic = 1;
GO
```

This chapter doesn't look at every configuration option here—only the most interesting ones or ones related to SQL Server performance. In most cases, options that you shouldn't change are discussed. Some of these are resource settings that relate to performance only in that they consume memory, but if they are configured too high, they can rob a system of memory and degrade performance. Configuration settings are grouped by functionality. Keep in mind that SQL Server sets almost all these options automatically, and your applications can work well without you ever looking at them.

Memory options

Memory management involves a lot more than can be described in a few short paragraphs, and for the most part, you can do little to control how SQL Server uses the available memory. Chapter 2 goes into a lot more detail on how SQL Server manages memory, so this section will mention just the configuration options that deal directly with memory usage.

Min Server Memory and Max Server Memory   By default, SQL Server adjusts the total amount of the memory resources it will use. However, you can use the Min Server Memory and Max Server Memory configuration options to take manual control. The default setting for Min Server Memory is 0 MB, and the default setting for Max Server Memory is 2147483647. If you use the *sp_configure* stored procedure to change both of these options to the same value, you basically take full control and tell SQL Server to use a fixed memory size. The absolute maximum of 2147483647 MB is actually the largest value that can be stored in the integer field of the underlying system table. It's not related to the actual resources of your system.

The Min Server Memory option doesn't force SQL Server to acquire a minimum amount of memory at startup. Memory is allocated on demand based on the database workload. However, when the Min Server Memory threshold is reached, SQL Server does not release memory if it would be left with less than that amount. To ensure that each instance has allocated memory at least equal to the Min Server Memory value, therefore, you might consider executing a database server load shortly after startup. During normal server activity, the memory available per instance varies, but each instance never has less than the Min Server Memory value.

Set working set size   This configuration option is from earlier versions and has been deprecated. It's ignored in SQL Server 2012, even though you don't receive an error message when you try to use this value.

User connections   SQL Server 2012 dynamically adjusts the number of simultaneous connections to the server if this configuration setting is left at its default of 0. Even if you set this value to a different number, SQL Server doesn't actually allocate the full amount of memory needed for each user connection until a user actually connects. When SQL Server starts, it allocates an array of pointers with as many entries as the configured value for User Connections.

If you must use this option, don't set the value too high because each connection takes approximately 28 KB of overhead whether or not the connection is being used. However, you also don't want to set it too low because if you exceed the maximum number of user connections, you receive an error message and can't connect until another connection becomes available. (The exception is the

DAC connection, which can always be used.) Keep in mind that the User Connections value isn't the same as the number of users; one user, through one application, can open multiple connections to SQL Server. Ideally, you should let SQL Server dynamically adjust the value of the User Connections option.

Locks   This configuration option is a setting from earlier versions and has been deprecated. SQL Server 2012 ignores this setting, even though you don't receive an error message when you try to use this value.

Scheduling options

As you will see in detail in Chapter 2, SQL Server 2012 has a special algorithm for scheduling user processes using the SQLOS, which manages one scheduler per logical processor and ensures that only one process can run on a scheduler at any specific time. The SQLOS manages the assignment of user connections to workers to keep the number of users per CPU as balanced as possible. Five configuration options affect the behavior of the scheduler: Lightweight Pooling, Affinity Mask, Affinity64 Mask, Priority Boost, and Max Worker Threads.

Lightweight Pooling   By default, SQL Server operates in thread mode, which means that the workers processing SQL Server requests are threads. As described earlier, SQL Server also lets user connections run in fiber mode. Fibers are less expensive to manage than threads. The Lightweight Pooling option can have a value of 0 or 1; 1 means that SQL Server should run in fiber mode.

Using fibers can yield a minor performance advantage, particularly when you have eight or more CPUs and all available CPUs are operating at or near 100 percent. However, the tradeoff is that certain operations, such as running queries on linked servers or executing extended stored procedures, must run in thread mode and therefore need to switch from fiber to thread. The cost of switching from fiber to thread mode for those connections can be noticeable and in some cases offsets any benefit of operating in fiber mode.

If you're running in an environment that uses a high percentage of total CPU resources, and if System Monitor shows a lot of context switching, setting Lightweight Pooling to 1 might yield some performance benefit.

Max Worker Threads   SQL Server uses the operating system's thread services by keeping a pool of workers (threads or fibers) that take requests from the queue. It attempts to divide the worker threads evenly among the SQLOS schedulers so that the number of threads available to each scheduler is the Max Worker Threads setting divided by the number of CPUs. Having 100 or fewer users means having usually as many worker threads as active users (not just connected users who are idle). With more users, having fewer worker threads than active users often makes sense. Although some user requests have to wait for a worker thread to become available, total throughput increases because less context switching occurs.

The Max Worker Threads default value of 0 means that the number of workers is configured by SQL Server, based on the number of processors and machine architecture. For example, for a four-way 32-bit machine running SQL Server, the default is 256 workers. This doesn't mean that 256 workers are created on startup. It means that if a connection is waiting to be serviced and no worker is available, a new worker is created if the total is now below 256. If, for example, this setting is configured to 256 and the highest number of simultaneously executing commands is 125, the actual number of workers won't exceed 125. It might be even smaller than that because SQL Server destroys and trims away workers that are no longer being used.

You should probably leave this setting alone if your system is handling 100 or fewer simultaneous connections. In that case, the worker thread pool won't be greater than 100.

Table 1-2 lists the default number of workers, considering your machine architecture and number of processors. (Note that Microsoft recommends 1,024 as the maximum for 32-bit operating systems.)

TABLE 1-2 Default settings for Max Worker Threads

CPU	32-bit computer	64-bit computer
Up to 4 processors	256	512
8 processors	288	576
16 processors	352	704
32 processors	480	960

Even systems that handle 5,000 or more connected users run fine with the default setting. When thousands of users are simultaneously connected, the actual worker pool is usually well below the Max Worker Threads value set by SQL Server because from the perspective of the database, most connections are idle even if the user is doing plenty of work on the client.

Disk I/O options

No options are available for controlling the disk read behavior of SQL Server. All tuning options to control read-ahead in previous versions of SQL Server are now handled completely internally. One option is available to control disk write behavior; it controls how frequently the checkpoint process writes to disk.

Recovery interval This option can be configured automatically. SQL Server setup sets it to 0, which means autoconfiguration. In SQL Server 2012, this means that the recovery time should be less than one minute.

This option lets database administrators control the checkpoint frequency by specifying the maximum number of minutes that recovery should take, per database. SQL Server estimates how many data modifications it can roll forward in that recovery time interval. SQL Server then inspects the log of each database (every minute, if the recovery interval is set to the default of 0) and issues a checkpoint for each database that has made at least that many data modification operations since the last checkpoint. For databases with relatively small transaction logs, SQL Server issues a checkpoint when the log becomes 70 percent full, if that is less than the estimated number.

The Recovery Interval option doesn't affect the time it takes to undo long-running transactions. For example, if a long-running transaction takes two hours to perform updates before the server becomes disabled, the actual recovery takes considerably longer than the Recovery Interval value.

The frequency of checkpoints in each database depends on the amount of data modifications made, not on a time-based measure. So a database used primarily for read operations won't have many checkpoints issued. To avoid excessive checkpoints, SQL Server tries to ensure that the value set for the recovery interval is the minimum amount of time between successive checkpoints.

SQL Server provides a new feature called *indirect checkpoints* that allow the configuration of checkpoint frequency at the database level using a database option called *TARGET_RECOVERY_TIME*. Chapter 3 discusses this option, and Chapter 5 discusses both the server-wide option and the database setting in the sections about checkpoints and recovery. As you'll see, most writing to disk doesn't actually happen during checkpoint operations. Checkpoints are just a way to guarantee that all dirty pages not written by other mechanisms are still written to the disk in a timely manner. For this reason, you should keep the checkpoint options at their default values.

Affinity I/O Mask and Affinity64 I/O Mask   These two options control the affinity of a processor for I/O operations and work in much the same way as the two options for controlling processing affinity for workers. Setting a bit for a processor in either of these bitmasks means that the corresponding processor is used only for I/O operations.

You'll probably never need to set these options. However, if you do decide to use them, perhaps just for testing purposes, you should do so with the Affinity Mask or Affinity64 Mask option and make sure that the bit sets don't overlap. You should thus have one of the following combinations of settings: 0 for both Affinity I/O Mask and Affinity Mask for a CPU, 1 for the Affinity I/O Mask option and 0 for Affinity Mask, or 0 for Affinity I/O Mask and 1 for Affinity Mask.

Backup Compression DEFAULT   SQL Server 2008 added Backup Compression as a new feature, and for backward compatibility the default value is 0, meaning that backups aren't compressed. Although only Enterprise edition instances can create a compressed backup, any edition of SQL Server 2012 can restore a compressed backup. When Backup Compression is enabled, the compression is performed on the server before writing, so it can greatly reduce the size of the backups and the I/O required to write the backups to the external device. The amount of space reduction depends on many factors, including the following.

- **The type of data in the backup**   For example, character data compresses more than other types of data.

- **Whether the data is encrypted**   Encrypted data compresses significantly less than equivalent unencrypted data. If transparent data encryption is used to encrypt an entire database, compressing backups might not reduce their size by much, if at all.

After the backup is performed, you can inspect the *backupset* table in the *msdb* database to determine the compression ratio, using a statement like the following:

```
SELECT backup_size/compressed_backup_size FROM msdb..backupset;
```

Although compressed backups can use significantly fewer I/O resources, it also can significantly increase CPU usage when performing the compression. This additional load can affect other operations occurring concurrently. To minimize this effect, you can consider using the Resource Governor to create a workload group for sessions performing backups and assign the group to a resource pool with a limit on its maximum CPU utilization.

The configured value is the instance-wide default for Backup Compression, but it can be overridden for a particular backup operation by specifying *WITH COMPRESSION* or *WITH NO_COMPRESSION*. You can use compression for any type of backup: full, log, differential, or partial (file or filegroup).

> **Note** The algorithm used for compressing backups varies greatly from the database compression algorithms. Backup Compression uses an algorithm very similar to zip, where it's just looking for patterns in the data. Chapter 8 discusses data compression.

Filestream access level This option integrates the Database Engine with your NTFS file system by storing binary large object (BLOB) data as files on the file system and allowing you to access this data either using T-SQL or Win32 file system interfaces to provide streaming access to the data. Filestream uses the Windows system cache for caching file data to help reduce any effect that filestream data might have on SQL Server performance. The SQL Server buffer pool isn't used so that filestream doesn't reduce the memory available for query processing.

Before setting this configuration option to indicate the access level for filestream data, you must enable Filestream externally using the SQL Server Configuration Manager (if you haven't enabled Filestream during SQL Server setup). In the SQL Server Configuration Manager, right-click the name of the SQL Server service and choose Properties. The properties sheet has a separate tab for Filestream options. You must check the top box to enable Filestream for T-SQL access, and then you can choose to enable Filestream for file I/O streaming if you want.

After enabling Filestream for your SQL Server instance, you then set the configuration value. The following values are allowed:

- *0 Disables FILESTREAM* support for this instance

- *1 Enables FILESTREAM* for T-SQL access

- *2 Enables FILESTREAM* for T-SQL and Win32 streaming access

Databases that store filestream data must have a special filestream filegroup. Chapter 3 discusses filegroups; Chapter 8 provides more details about filestream storage.

Query processing options

SQL Server has several options for controlling the resources available for processing queries. As with all the other tuning options, your best bet is to leave the default values unless thorough testing indicates that a change might help.

Min Memory Per Query   When a query requires additional memory resources, the number of pages that it gets is determined partly by the this option. This option is relevant for sort operations that you specifically request using an *ORDER BY* clause; it also applies to internal memory needed by merge-join operations and by hash-join and hash-grouping operations.

This configuration option allows you to specify a minimum amount of memory (in kilobytes) that any of these operations should be granted before they are executed. Sort, merge, and hash operations receive memory very dynamically, so you rarely need to adjust this value. In fact, on larger machines, your sort and hash queries typically get much more than the Min Memory Per Query setting, so you shouldn't restrict yourself unnecessarily. If you need to do a lot of hashing or sorting, however, and have few users or a lot of available memory, you might improve performance by adjusting this value. On smaller machines, setting this value too high can cause virtual memory to page, which hurts server performance.

Query wait   This option controls how long a query that needs additional memory waits if that memory isn't available. A setting of –1 means that the query waits 25 times the estimated execution time of the query, but it always waits at least 25 seconds with this setting. A value of 0 or more specifies the number of seconds that a query waits. If the wait time is exceeded, SQL Server generates error 8645:

```
Server: Msg 8645, Level 17, State 1, Line 1
A time out occurred while waiting for memory resources to execute the query. Re-run the query.
```

Even though memory is allocated dynamically, SQL Server can still run out of memory if the memory resources on the machine are exhausted. If your queries time out with error 8645, you can try increasing the paging file size or even adding more physical memory. You can also try tuning the query by creating more useful indexes so that hash or merge operations aren't needed. Keep in mind that this option affects only queries that have to wait for memory needed by hash and merge operations. Queries that have to wait for other reasons aren't affected.

Blocked Process Threshold   This option allows administrators to request a notification when a user task has been blocked for more than the configured number of seconds. When Blocked Process Threshold is set to 0, no notification is given. You can set any value up to 86,400 seconds.

When the deadlock monitor detects a task that has been waiting longer than the configured value, an internal event is generated. You can choose to be notified of this event in one of two ways. You can create an Extended Events session to capture events of type *blocked_process_report*. As long as a resource stays blocked on a deadlock-detectable resource, the event is raised every time the deadlock monitor checks for a deadlock. (Chapter 2 discusses Extended Events.)

Alternatively, you can use event notifications to send information about events to a service broker service. You also can use event notifications, which execute asynchronously, to perform an action inside a SQL Server 2012 instance in response to events, with very little consumption of memory resources. Because event notifications execute asynchronously, these actions don't consume any resources defined by the immediate transaction.

Index Create Memory   The Min Memory Per Query option applies only to sorting and hashing used during query execution; it doesn't apply to the sorting that takes place during index creation. Another option, Index Create Memory, lets you allocate a specific amount of memory (in kilobytes) for index creation.

Query Governor Cost Limit   You can use this option to specify the maximum number of seconds that a query can run. If you specify a non-zero, non-negative value, SQL Server disallows execution of any query that has an estimated cost exceeding that value. Specifying 0 (the default) for this option turns off the query governor, and all queries are allowed to run without any time limit.

Note that the value set for seconds isn't clock-based. It corresponds to seconds on a specific hardware configuration used during product development, and the actual limit might be higher or lower on your machine.

Max Degree Of Parallelism and Cost Threshold For Parallelism   SQL Server 2012 lets you run certain kinds of complex queries simultaneously on two or more processors. The queries must lend themselves to being executed in sections; the following is an example:

```
SELECT AVG(charge_amt), category
FROM charge
GROUP BY category
```

If the charge table has 1 million rows and 10 different values for *category*, SQL Server can split the rows into groups and have only a subset of them processed on each processor. For example, with a four-CPU machine, categories 1 through 3 can be averaged on the first processor, categories 4 through 6 can be averaged on the second processor, categories 7 and 8 can be averaged on the third, and categories 9 and 10 can be averaged on the fourth. Each processor can come up with averages for only its groups, and the separate averages are brought together for the final result.

During optimization, the Query Optimizer always finds the cheapest possible serial plan before considering parallelism. If this serial plan costs less than the configured value for the Cost Threshold For Parallelism option, no parallel plan is generated. Cost Threshold For Parallelism refers to the cost of the query in seconds; the default value is 5. (As in the preceding section, this isn't an exact clock-based number of seconds.) If the cheapest serial plan costs more than this configured threshold, a parallel plan is produced based on assumptions about how many processors and how much memory will actually be available at runtime. This parallel plan cost is compared with the serial plan cost, and the cheaper one is chosen. The other plan is discarded.

A parallel query execution plan can use more than one thread; a serial execution plan, used by a nonparallel query, uses only a single thread. The actual number of threads used by a parallel query is determined at query plan execution initialization and is the Degree of Parallelism (DOP). The decision is based on many factors, including the Affinity Mask setting, the Max Degree Of Parallelism setting, and the available threads when the query starts executing.

You can observe when SQL Server is executing a query in parallel by querying the DMV *sys.dm_os_tasks*. A query running on multiple CPUs has one row for each thread, as follows:

```
SELECT
    task_address,
    task_state,
    context_switches_count,
    pending_io_count,
    pending_io_byte_count,
    pending_io_byte_average,
    scheduler_id,
    session_id,
    exec_context_id,
    request_id,
    worker_address,
    host_address
FROM sys.dm_os_tasks
ORDER BY session_id, request_id;
```

Be careful when you use the Max Degree Of Parallelism and Cost Threshold For Parallelism options. They affect the whole server.

Miscellaneous options   Most of the other configuration options that haven't been mentioned deal with aspects of SQL Server that are beyond the scope of this book. These include options for configuring remote queries, replication, SQL Agent, C2 auditing, and full-text search. A Boolean option allows use of the Common Language Runtime (CLR) in programming SQL Server objects; it is off (0) by default.

A few configuration options deal with programming issues, which this book doesn't cover. These options include ones for dealing with recursive and nested triggers, cursors, and accessing objects across databases.

Conclusion

This chapter looked at the general workings of the SQL Server engine, including the key components and functional areas that make up the engine. By necessity, the chapter has been simplified somewhat, but the information should provide some insight into the roles and responsibilities of the major components in SQL Server and the interrelationships among components.

This chapter also covered the primary tools for changing the behavior of SQL Server. The primary means of changing the behavior is by using configuration options, so you saw the options that can have the biggest impact on SQL Server behavior, especially its performance. To really know when changing the behavior is a good idea, you must understand how and why SQL Server works the way it does. This chapter has laid the groundwork for you to make informed decisions about configuration changes.

CHAPTER 2

The SQLOS

Jonathan Kehayias

The SQL Server Operating System (SQLOS) is a separate application layer at the lowest level of the SQL Server Database Engine that both SQL Server and SQL Reporting Services run atop. Earlier versions of SQL Server have a thin layer of interfaces between the storage engine and the actual operating system through which SQL Server makes calls to the operating system for memory allocation, scheduler resources, thread and worker management, and synchronization objects. However, the services in SQL Server that need to access these interfaces can be in any part of the engine. SQL Server requirements for managing memory, schedulers, synchronization objects, and so forth have become more complex. Rather than each part of the engine growing to support the increased functionality, a single application layer has been designed to manage all operating system resources specific to SQL Server.

The two main functions of SQLOS are scheduling and memory management, both of which are discussed in detail in this chapter. Other functions of SQLOS include the following.

- **Synchronization** This object type includes spinlocks, mutexes (mutual exclusions), and special reader/writer locks on system resources.

- **Memory brokers** Memory brokers distribute memory allocation between various components within SQL Server but don't perform any allocations, which are handled by the Memory Manager.

- **SQL Server exception handling** Exception handling involves dealing with user errors as well as system-generated errors.

- **Deadlock detection** The deadlock detection mechanism doesn't just involve locks but checks for any tasks holding onto resources that are mutually blocking each other. Chapter 13, "Transactions and concurrency," covers deadlocks involving locks (by far the most common kind).

- **Extended Events** Tracking extended events is similar to the SQL Trace capability but is much more efficient because the tracking runs at a much lower level than SQL Trace. Also, because the Extended Event layer is so low and deep, many more types of events can be tracked. The SQL Server 2012 Resource Governor manages resource usage via Extended Events. (In a future version, all tracing will be handled at this level by Extended Events.)

- **Asynchronous I/O** The difference between asynchronous and synchronous is what part of the system is actually waiting for an unavailable resource. When SQL Server requests a synchronous I/O, if the resource isn't available, the Windows kernel puts the thread on a wait queue until the resource becomes available. For asynchronous I/O, SQL Server requests that Windows initiate an I/O. Windows starts the I/O operation and doesn't stop the thread from running. SQL Server then places the server session in an I/O wait queue until it gets the signal from Windows that the resource is available.

- **CLR hosting** Hosting Common Language Runtime (CLR) inside the SQLOS allows managed .NET code to be used natively inside SQL Server. In SQL Server 2012, CLR hosting changed to .NET 4.0, which includes changes to memory reporting and garbage collection for AppDomains loaded by SQLOS. Memory allocations for SQLCLR can include any-page allocations inside SQLOS as well as virtual committed allocations from the Windows operating system.

NUMA architecture

Non-Uniform Memory Access (NUMA) architectures have become common in most datacenters today, and SQL Server has supported NUMA since it was first introduced in SQL Server 2000 with Service Pack 4 installed. However, since SQL Server 2005 the SQLOS has automatically recognized the existence of hardware NUMA support and optimizes scheduling and memory management by default. You can use some special configurations when you work with NUMA, so this section provides some general background before discussing scheduling and memory.

Only a few years ago, hardware NUMA required specialized hardware configurations using multiple server nodes that functioned as a single server through the use of a specialized interconnect between each node. Modern server processor architectures from AMD and Intel now offer hardware NUMA in most standard server configurations through the inclusion of an onboard memory controller for each processor die and interconnected paths between the physical sockets on the server motherboard. Regardless of the specific hardware implementation of NUMA, SQLOS performs the same internal configuration of SOS Memory Nodes and uses the same optimizations for memory management and scheduling.

The main benefit of NUMA is scalability, which has definite limits when you use symmetric multiprocessing (SMP) architecture. With SMP, all memory access is posted to the same shared memory bus. This works fine for a relatively small number of CPUs, but problems appear when you have many CPUs competing for access to the shared memory bus. The trend in hardware has been to have more than one system bus, each serving a small set of processors. NUMA limits the number of CPUs on any one memory bus. Each processor group has its own memory and possibly its own I/O channels. However, each CPU can access memory associated with other groups coherently, as discussed later in the chapter. Each group is called a *NUMA node*, which are linked to each other by a high-speed interconnection. The number of CPUs within a NUMA node depends on the hardware vendor. Accessing local memory is faster than accessing the memory associated with other NUMA nodes—the reason for the name *Non-Uniform Memory Access*. Figure 2-1 shows a NUMA node with four CPUs.

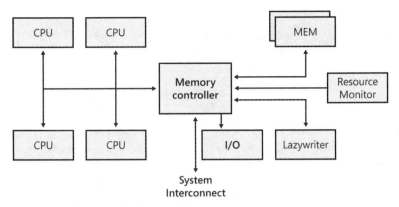

FIGURE 2-1 A NUMA node with four CPUs.

SQL Server 2012 allows you to subdivide one or more physical NUMA nodes into smaller NUMA nodes, referred to as *software NUMA* or *soft-NUMA*. You typically use soft-NUMA when you have many CPUs but no hardware NUMA, because soft-NUMA allows for the subdividing of CPUs but not memory. You can also use soft-NUMA to subdivide hardware NUMA nodes into groups of fewer CPUs than is provided by the hardware NUMA. Your soft-NUMA nodes can also be configured to listen on their own ports.

Only the SQL Server scheduler and Server Name Indication (SNI) are soft-NUMA–aware. Memory nodes are created based on hardware NUMA and therefore aren't affected by soft-NUMA.

TCP/IP, Virtual Interface Adapters (VIAs), Named Pipes, and shared memory can take advantage of NUMA round-robin scheduling, but only TCP and VIA can set the processor affinity to a specific set of NUMA nodes. See *SQL Server Books Online* for how to use the SQL Server Configuration Manager to set a TCP/IP address and port to single or multiple nodes.

The scheduler

Prior to SQL Server 7.0, scheduling depended entirely on the underlying Windows operating system. Although this meant that SQL Server could take advantage of the hard work done by Windows engineers to enhance scalability and efficient processor use, definite limits existed. Because the Windows scheduler knew nothing about the needs of a relational database system, it treated SQL Server worker threads the same as any other process running on the operating system. However, a high-performance system such as SQL Server functions best when the scheduler can meet its special needs. SQL Server 7.0 and all subsequent versions are designed to handle their own scheduling to gain a number of advantages, including the following.

- A private scheduler can support SQL Server tasks by using fibers as easily as it supports using threads.

- Context switching and switching into kernel mode can be avoided as much as possible.

Note The scheduler in SQL Server 7.0 and SQL Server 2000 was called the *User Mode Scheduler* (UMS) to reflect that it ran primarily in user mode, as opposed to kernel mode. SQL Server 2005 and later versions call the scheduler the SOS Scheduler and improve on UMS even more.

One major difference between the SOS Scheduler and the Windows scheduler is that the SQL Server scheduler runs as a cooperative rather than as a preemptive scheduler. It relies on the workers, threads, or fibers to yield voluntarily often enough so that one process or thread doesn't have exclusive control of the system. The SQL Server product team must make sure that its code runs efficiently and voluntarily yields the scheduler in appropriate places; the reward for this is much greater control and scalability than is possible with the Windows scheduler. Each task that executes inside SQL Server has a quantum of 4 milliseconds on the scheduler.

Even though the scheduler isn't preemptive, the SQL Server scheduler still adheres to a concept of a quantum. Rather than SQL Server tasks be forced to give up the CPU by the operating system, they can request to be put on a wait queue periodically, and if they have exceeded the internally defined 4 millisecond quantum and aren't in the middle of an operation that can't be stopped, they voluntarily relinquish the CPU.

Understanding SQL Server schedulers

In SQL Server 2012, each actual CPU (whether hyperthreaded or physical) has a scheduler created for it when SQL Server starts. This is true even if the Affinity Mask server configuration options are configured so that SQL Server is set to not use all available physical CPUs. In SQL Server 2012, each scheduler is set to either *ONLINE* or *OFFLINE* based on the process affinity settings; the default is that all schedulers are *ONLINE*.

Note The core-based licensing changes in SQL Server 2012 include upgrade licensing for Enterprise Edition using Server+CAL licensing under Software Assurance. This upgrade option provides a 20 core limitation that can result in schedulers being created but *OFFLINE* by default, which can result in an *ONLINE* scheduler imbalance for NUMA-based systems and potential performance problems because connections are assigned round-robin to NUMA nodes. If you are planning to upgrade to SQL Server 2012 under Software Assurance upgrades using the Enterprise Edition Server+CAL licensing, you might need to reconfigure the process affinity settings to balance the *ONLINE* schedulers across NUMA nodes to prevent performance problems.

Introduced for the first time in SQL Server 2008 R2, process affinity replaced the *'affinity mask'* sp_configure option and is accomplished through the use of ALTER SERVER CONFIGURATION for setting processor affinity in SQL Server. Changing the process affinity value can change the status of one or more schedulers to *OFFLINE*, which you can do without having to restart your SQL Server. Note that when a scheduler is switched from *ONLINE* to *OFFLINE* due to a configuration change, any work already assigned to the scheduler is first completed and no new work is assigned.

SQL Server workers

You can think of the SQL Server scheduler as a logical CPU used by SQL Server workers. A worker can be either a thread or a fiber bound to a logical scheduler. If the Affinity Mask configuration option is set (as discussed in Chapter 1, "SQL Server 2012 architecture and configuration"), or process affinity has been configured using *ALTER SERVER CONFIGURATION*, each scheduler is mapped to a particular CPU. (Later, this chapter covers additional configuration.) Thus, each worker is also associated with a single CPU. Each scheduler is assigned a worker limit based on the configured Max Worker Threads and the number of schedulers, and each scheduler is responsible for creating or destroying workers as needed. A worker can't move from one scheduler to another, but as workers are destroyed and created, it can appear as though workers are moving between schedulers.

Workers are created when the scheduler receives a request (a task to execute) and no workers are idle. A worker can be destroyed if it has been idle for at least 15 minutes or if SQL Server is under memory pressure. Each worker can use at least half a megabyte of memory on a 32-bit system and at least 2 MB on a 64-bit system, so destroying multiple workers and freeing their memory can yield an immediate performance improvement on memory-starved systems. SQL Server actually handles the worker pool very efficiently, and you might be surprised to know that even on very large systems with hundreds or even thousands of users, the actual number of SQL Server workers might be much lower than the configured value for Max Worker Threads. Later, this chapter explains some of the Dynamic Management Objects that let you see how many workers you actually have, as well as scheduler and task information.

SQL Server tasks

The unit of work for a SQL Server worker is a *request*, which you can think of as being equivalent to a single batch sent from the client to the server. When a request is received by SQL Server, it's bound to a task that's assigned to a worker, and that worker processes the entire request before handling any other request. If a request executes using parallelism, then multiple child tasks, and therefore workers, can be created based on the degree of parallelism being used to execute the request and the specific operation being performed. This holds true even if the request is blocked for some reason, such as waiting for a lock or for I/O to complete. The particular worker or workers don't handle any new requests but wait until the blocking condition is resolved and the request can be completed.

Keep in mind that a session ID (SPID) isn't the same as a task. A SPID is a connection or channel over which requests can be sent, but an active request isn't always available on any particular SPID. In SQL Server 2012, a SPID isn't bound to a particular scheduler. Each SPID has a preferred scheduler, which is one that most recently processed a request from the SPID. The SPID is initially assigned to the scheduler with the lowest load. (You can get some insight into the load on each scheduler by looking at the *load_factor* column in the DMV *sys.dm_os_schedulers*.) However, when subsequent requests are sent from the same SPID, if another scheduler has a load factor that is less than a certain percentage of the average of the scheduler's entire load factor, the new task is given to the scheduler with the smallest load factor. One restriction is that all tasks for one SPID must be processed by schedulers on the same NUMA node. The exception to this restriction is when a query is being executed as a parallel query across multiple CPUs. The optimizer can decide to use more available CPUs on the NUMA node processing the query so that other CPUs (and other schedulers) can be used.

Threads vs. fibers

As mentioned earlier, the UMS was designed to work with workers running on either threads or fibers. Windows fibers have less overhead associated with them than threads do, and multiple fibers can run on a single thread. You can configure SQL Server to run in fiber mode by setting the Lightweight Pooling option to 1. Although using less overhead and a "lightweight" mechanism sounds like a good idea, you should evaluate the use of fibers carefully.

Certain SQL Server components don't work—or don't work well—when SQL Server runs in fiber mode. These components include SQLMail and SQLXML. Other components, such as heterogeneous and CLR queries, aren't supported at all in fiber mode because they need certain thread-specific facilities provided by Windows. Although SQL Server can switch to thread mode to process requests that need it, the overhead might be greater than the overhead of using threads exclusively. Fiber mode was actually intended just for special niche situations in which SQL Server reaches a limit in scalability due to spending too much time switching between thread contexts or switching between user mode and kernel mode. In most environments, the performance benefit gained by fibers is quite small compared to the benefits you can get by tuning in other areas. If you're certain you have a situation that could benefit from fibers, be sure to test thoroughly before you set the option on a production server. Also, you might even want to contact Microsoft Customer Support Services (*http://support.microsoft.com/ph/2855*) just to be certain.

NUMA and schedulers

With a NUMA configuration, every node has some subset of the machine's processors and the same number of schedulers. If the machine is configured for hardware NUMA, the number of processors on each node is preset, but for soft-NUMA that you configure yourself, you can decide how many processors are assigned to each node. You still have the same number of schedulers as processors, however. When SPIDs are first created, they are assigned round-robin to nodes. The Scheduler Monitor then assigns the SPID to the least loaded scheduler on that node. As mentioned earlier, if the SPID is moved to another scheduler, it stays on the same node. A single processor or SMP machine is treated as a machine with a single NUMA node. Just like on an SMP machine, no hard mapping occurs between schedulers and a CPU with NUMA, so any scheduler on an individual node can run on any CPU on that node. However, if you have set the Affinity Mask configuration option, each scheduler on each node is fixed to run on a particular CPU.

Every hardware NUMA memory node has its own lazywriter (which the section "Memory" explains later in this chapter) as well as its own I/O Completion Port (IOCP), which is the network listener. Every node also has its own Resource Monitor, which a hidden scheduler manages (you can see the hidden schedulers in *sys.dm_os_schedulers*). Each Resource Monitor has its own SPID, which you can see by querying the *sys.dm_exec_requests* and *sys.dm_os_workers* DMVs:

```
SELECT session_id,
    CONVERT (varchar(10), t1.status) AS status,
    CONVERT (varchar(20), t1.command) AS command,
    CONVERT (varchar(15), t2.state) AS worker_state
FROM sys.dm_exec_requests AS t1
JOIN sys.dm_os_workers AS t2
ON t2.task_address = t1.task_address
WHERE command = 'RESOURCE MONITOR';
```

Every node has its own Scheduler Monitor, which runs on any SPID and in a preemptive mode. The Scheduler Monitor thread wakes up periodically and checks each scheduler to see whether it has yielded since the last time the Scheduler Monitor woke up (unless the scheduler is idle). The Scheduler Monitor raises an error (17883) if a non-idle thread hasn't yielded. This error can occur when an application other than SQL Server is monopolizing the CPU. The Scheduler Monitor knows only that the CPU isn't yielding; it can't ascertain what kind of task is using it. The Scheduler Monitor is also responsible for sending messages to the schedulers to help them balance their workload.

Dynamic affinity

In SQL Server 2012 (in all editions except SQL Server Express), processor affinity can be controlled dynamically. When SQL Server starts up, all scheduler tasks are started, so each CPU has one scheduler. If process affinity has been set, some schedulers are then marked as offline and no tasks are assigned to them.

When process affinity is changed to include additional CPUs, the new CPU is brought online. The Scheduler Monitor then notices an imbalance in the workload and starts picking workers to move to the new CPU. When a CPU is brought offline by changing process affinity, the scheduler for that CPU continues to run active workers, but the scheduler itself is moved to one of the other CPUs that are still online. No new workers are given to this scheduler, which is now offline, and when all active workers have finished their tasks, the scheduler stops.

Binding schedulers to CPUs

Remember that, normally, schedulers aren't bound to CPUs in a strict one-to-one relationship, even though you have the same number of schedulers as CPUs. A scheduler is bound to a CPU only when process affinity is set, even if you specify that process affinity use all the CPUs, which is the default setting. For example, the default process affinity is set to *AUTO*, which means to use all CPUs, with no hard binding of scheduler to CPU. In fact, in some cases when the machine is experiencing a heavy load, Windows can run two schedulers on one CPU.

The configuration of process affinity in SQL Server 2012 is designed to simplify configuration over the previous configuration using affinity masks in SQL Server 2008 and prior. Configuring process affinity using ALTER SERVER CONFIGURATION SET PROCESS AFFINITY CPU requires only that you specify the specific CPUIDs for the affinity or a range of CPUs using the starting *CPUID TO* the ending *CPUID*. For an eight-processor machine, a process affinity set with ALTER SERVER CONFIGURATION SET PROCESS AFFINITY CPU=0 TO 1 means that only CPUs 0 and 1 are used and two schedulers are bound to the two CPUs. If you set the process affinity set with ALTER SERVER CONFIGURATION SET PROCESS AFFINITY CPU 0 TO 7, all the CPUs are used, just as with the default. However, with the affinity mask set, the eight CPUs are bound to the eight schedulers.

In addition to being able to set process affinity based on specific CPUIDs, SQL Server 2012 can set process affinity based on NUMA nodes using ALTER SERVER CONFIGURATION SET PROCESS AFFINITY NUMANODE=<NUMA node range spec>. The NUMA node range specification is identical to the CPU range specification, except that it uses the NUMA NodeIDs instead of CPUIDs. If you want an instance to use only the CPUs within a specific NUMA node, you simply specify that NUMA NodeID for the process affinity.

In some situations, you might want to limit the number of CPUs available but not bind a particular scheduler to a single CPU—for example, if you are using a multiple-CPU machine for server consolidation. Suppose that you have a 64- processor machine on which you are running eight SQL Server instances, and you want each instance to use eight processors. Each instance has a different process affinity that specifies a different subset of the 64 processors. Because the process affinity is set, each instance has hard binding of scheduler to CPU. If you want to limit the number of CPUs but still not constrain a particular scheduler to running on a specific CPU, you can start SQL Server with trace flag 8002. This lets you have CPUs mapped to an instance, but within the instance, schedulers aren't bound to CPUs.

Observing scheduler internals

SQL Server 2012 has several Dynamic Management Objects (DMVs) that provide information about schedulers, workers, and tasks. These are primarily intended for use by Microsoft Customer Support Services, but you can use them to gain a greater appreciation for the information that SQL Server monitors.

The following sections discuss these Dynamic Management Objects.

> **Note** Selecting from these objects (as well as most of the other DMVs) requires a permission called *View Server State*. By default, only SQL Server administrators have that permission, but it can be granted to others. For each object, some of the more useful or interesting columns are listed, and a description is provided from *SQL Server 2012 Books Online* for each column. For the full list of columns (most of which are useful only to support personnel), refer to *SQL Server Books Online*, but even then, you'll find that some of the columns are listed as "for internal use only."

sys.dm_os_schedulers

This view returns one row per scheduler in SQL Server. Each scheduler is mapped to an individual processor in SQL Server. You can use this view to monitor the condition of a scheduler or to identify runaway tasks. Interesting columns include the following.

- **parent_node_id** The ID of the node that the scheduler belongs to, also known as the *parent node*. This represents a NUMA node.

- **scheduler_id** The ID of the scheduler. All schedulers that run regular queries have IDs of less than 1048576. Those with IDs greater than or equal to 1048576, such as the Dedicated Administrator Connection (DAC) scheduler, are used internally by SQL Server.

- **cpu_id** The CPUID assigned to the scheduler. A *cpu_id* of 255 no longer indicates no affinity as it did in SQL Server 2005. Please note that these tasks are accumulating signal wait time.

- **is_online** If SQL Server is configured to use only some of the available processors on the server, this can mean that some schedulers are mapped to processors not in the affinity mask. If that's the case, this column returns 0, meaning that the scheduler isn't being used to process queries or batches.

- **current_tasks_count** The number of current tasks associated with this scheduler, including the following. (When a task is completed, this count is decremented.)

  - Tasks waiting on a resource to be acquired before proceeding

  - Tasks that are currently running or that can run but are waiting to be executed

- **runnable_tasks_count** The number of tasks waiting to run on the scheduler.

- **current_workers_count** The number of workers associated with this scheduler, including workers not assigned any task.

- **active_workers_count** The number of workers assigned a task.

- **work_queue_count** The number of tasks waiting for a worker. If *current_workers_count* is greater than *active_workers_count*, this work queue count should be 0 and shouldn't grow.

- **pending_disk_io_count** The number of pending I/Os. Each scheduler has a list of pending I/Os that are checked on every context switch to determine whether the I/Os are completed. The count is incremented when the request is inserted and decremented when the request is completed. This number doesn't indicate the state of the I/Os.

- **load_factor** The internal value that indicates the perceived load on this scheduler. This value determines whether a new task should be put on this scheduler or another scheduler. It's useful for debugging purposes when schedulers appear to be unevenly loaded. In SQL Server 2000, a task was routed to a particular scheduler; in SQL Server 2012, the routing decision is based on the scheduler's load. SQL Server 2012 also uses a load factor of nodes and schedulers to help determine the best location to acquire resources. When a task is added to the queue, the load factor increases; when a task is completed, the load factor decreases. Using load factors helps the SQLOS better balance the workload.

sys.dm_os_workers

This view returns a row for every worker in the system. Interesting columns include the following.

- **is_preemptive**   A value of 1 means that the worker is running with preemptive scheduling. Any worker running external code is run under preemptive scheduling.

- **is_fiber**   A value of 1 means that the worker is running with lightweight pooling.

sys.dm_os_threads

This view returns a list of all SQLOS threads running under the SQL Server process. Interesting columns include the following.

- **started_by_sqlserver**   The thread initiator. A 1 means that SQL Server started the thread; 0 means that another component, such as an extended procedure from within SQL Server, started the thread.

- **creation_time**   The time when this thread was created.

- **stack_bytes_used**   The number of bytes actively being used on the thread.

- **affinity**   The CPU mask on which this thread is running. This depends on the value configured by the *ALTER SERVER CONFIGURATION SET PROCESS AFFINITY* statement, which might be different from the scheduler in the case of soft-affinity.

- **locale**   The cached locale LCID for the thread.

sys.dm_os_tasks

This view returns one row for each task that is active in the instance of SQL Server. Interesting columns include the following.

- **task_state**   The state of the task. The value can be one of the following.

  - **PENDING**   Waiting for a worker thread

  - **RUNNABLE**   Capable of being executed, but is waiting to receive a quantum

  - **RUNNING**   Currently running on the scheduler

  - **SUSPENDED**   Has a worker but is waiting for an event

  - **DONE**   Completed

  - **SPINLOOP**   Processing a spinlock, as when waiting for a signal

- **context_switches_count**   The number of scheduler context switches that this task has completed.

- **pending_io_count**   The number of physical I/Os performed by this task.

- **pending_io_byte_count**   The total byte count of I/Os performed by this task.

- **pending_io_byte_average**   The average byte count of I/Os performed by this task.

- **scheduler_id**   The ID of the parent scheduler. This is a handle to the scheduler information for this task.

- **session_id**   The ID of the session associated with the task.

sys.dm_os_waiting_tasks

This view returns information about the queue of tasks waiting on some resource. Interesting columns include the following.

- **session_id**   The ID of the session associated with the task.

- **exec_context_id**   The ID of the execution context associated with the task.

- **wait_duration_ms**   The total wait time (in milliseconds) for this wait type. This time is inclusive of *signal_wait_time*.

- **wait_type**   The name of the wait type.

- **resource_address**   The address of the resource for which the task is waiting.

- **blocking_task_address**   The task currently holding this resource.

- **blocking_session_id**   The ID of the session of the blocking task.

- **blocking_exec_context_id**   The ID of the execution context of the blocking task.

- **resource_description**   The description of the resource being consumed.

Understanding the Dedicated Administrator Connection (DAC)

Under extreme conditions, such as a complete lack of available resources, SQL Server can enter an abnormal state in which no further connections can be made to the SQL Server instance. Prior to SQL Server 2005, this situation meant that administrators couldn't get in to kill any troublesome connections or even begin to diagnose the possible cause of the problem. SQL Server 2005 introduced a special connection called the Dedicated Administrator Connection (DAC) that was designed to be accessible even when no other access can be made.

Access via the DAC must be specially requested. You can connect to the DAC using the command-line tool *SQLCMD* and specifying the *-A* (or */A*) flag. This method of connection is recommended because it uses fewer resources than the graphical user interface (GUI). Through Management Studio, you can specify that you want to connect using DAC by preceding the name of your SQL Server with *ADMIN*: in the Connection dialog box. For example, to connect to a default SQL Server instance on a machine named TENAR, you enter **ADMIN:TENAR**. To connect to a named instance called SQL2008 on the same machine, you enter **ADMIN:TENAR\SQL2008**.

The DAC is a special-purpose connection designed for diagnosing problems in SQL Server and possibly resolving them. It's not meant to be used as a regular user connection. Any attempt to connect using the DAC when a DAC connection is already active results in an error. The message returned to the client says only that the connection was rejected; it doesn't state explicitly that it was because of an active DAC. However, a message is written to the error log indicating the attempt (and failure) to get a second DAC connection. Under normal circumstances, you can check whether a DAC is in use by running the following query in SQL Server Management Studio when not connected to the DAC. If a DAC is active, the query returns the SPID for the DAC; otherwise, it returns no rows:

```
SELECT s.session_id
FROM sys.tcp_endpoints as e
INNER JOIN sys.dm_exec_sessions as s
    ON e.endpoint_id = s.endpoint_id
WHERE e.name=N'Dedicated Admin Connection';
```

Keep the following points in mind about using the DAC.

- By default, the DAC is available only locally. However, administrators can configure SQL Server to allow remote connection by using the *Remote Admin Connections* configuration option.

- The user login to connect via the DAC must be a member of the sysadmin server role.

- There are only a few restrictions on the SQL statements that can be executed on the DAC. (For example, you can't run parallel queries or commands—for example, *BACKUP* or *RESTORE*—using the DAC.) However, you are recommended not to run any resource-intensive queries that might exacerbate the problem that led you to use the DAC. The DAC connection is created primarily for troubleshooting and diagnostic purposes. In general, you use the DAC for running queries against the Dynamic Management Objects, some of which you've seen already and many more of which are discussed later in this book.

- A special thread is assigned to the DAC that allows it to execute the diagnostic functions or queries on a separate scheduler. This thread can't be terminated; you can kill only the DAC session, if needed. Prior to SQL Server 2008 R2, the DAC scheduler always used the *scheduler_id* value of 255, and this thread had the highest priority. In SQL Server 2008 R2 and SQL Server 2012, the DAC scheduler always uses the *scheduler_id* value of 1048576. The DAC has no lazywriter thread, but it does have its own I/O Completion Port (IOCP), a worker thread, and an idle thread.

You might not always be able to accomplish your intended tasks using the DAC. Suppose that you have an idle connection holding onto a lock. If the connection has no active task, no thread is associated with it, only a connection ID. Also, many other processes are trying to get access to the locked resource and are blocked. Those connections still have an incomplete task, so they don't release their worker. If enough processes try to get the same lock, all available workers might get used up and no more connections can be made to SQL Server. Because the DAC has its own scheduler, you can start it, and the expected solution would be to kill the connection that is holding the lock but not do any further processing to release the lock. But if you try to use the DAC to kill the process holding the lock, the attempt fails. SQL Server would need to give a worker to the task to kill it, and no workers are available. The only solution is to kill several of the (blameless) blocked processes that still have workers associated with them.

Note To conserve resources, SQL Server 2012 Express Edition doesn't support a DAC connection unless it's started with trace flag 7806.

The DAC isn't guaranteed to always be usable, but because it reserves memory and a private scheduler and is implemented as a separate node, a connection probably is possible when you can't connect in any other way.

Memory

Because memory management is a huge topic, covering every detail of it would require a whole book in itself. SQL Server 2012 introduces a significant rewrite of the SQLOS Memory Manager and has the first significant changes in memory management since SQLOS was introduced in SQL Server 2005. The goal of this section is twofold.

- To provide enough information about how SQL Server uses its memory resources so that you can determine whether memory is being managed well on your system

- To describe the aspects of memory management that you have control over so that you can understand when to exert that control

By default, SQL Server 2012 manages its memory resources almost completely dynamically. When allocating memory, SQL Server must communicate constantly with the operating system, which is one of the reasons the SQLOS layer of the engine is so important.

The buffer pool and the data cache

The main memory component in SQL Server is the buffer pool. All memory not used by another memory component remains in the buffer pool to be used as a data cache for pages read in from the database files on disk. The buffer manager manages disk I/O functions for bringing data and index pages into the data cache so that data can be shared among users. Other components requiring memory can request a buffer from the buffer pool.

A *buffer* is a page in memory that's the same size as a data or index page. You can think of it as a page frame that can hold one page from a database. Most buffers taken from the buffer pool for other memory components go to other kinds of memory caches, the largest of which is typically the cache for procedure and query plans, which is usually called the *plan cache*.

Prior to SQL Server 2012, memory requests that were larger than a single 8 KB page were obtained from memory outside the buffer pool and used a separate allocator in SQLOS. The buffer pool in SQL Server was allocated through the single-page allocator, and allocations for larger memory blocks occurred through the multi-page allocator. In SQL Server 2012, the Memory Manager has been rewritten to eliminate the separate page allocators in SQLOS; now memory allocations are made through a new any-page allocator in SQLOS. Having a simplified page allocation mechanism in SQLOS comes with numerous benefits, which the rest of this section covers.

Column store object pool

In addition to the buffer pool, SQL Server 2012 includes a new cache store specifically optimized for usage by the new column store indexing feature. The column store object pool allocates memory from the any-page allocator just like the buffer pool, but rather than cache data pages, the memory allocations are used for column store index objects. The memory for the column store object pool is tracked by a separate memory clerk, CACHESTORE_COLUMNSTOREOBJECTPOOL, in SQLOS. Because this memory is separate from the buffer pool, the allocations can pressure the buffer pool and result in page flushing from the data cache. To help prevent this, SQLOS tracks when buffer pages are removed from the data cache and are subsequently read back into cache, to monitor the effect that page flushing has on performance of the instance. These buffer simulations are used to adjust the sizing of the column store object pool and the buffer pool to optimize buffer reuse in the server dynamically based on the workload.

Access to in-memory data pages

Access to pages in the data cache must be fast. Even with real memory, scanning the whole data cache for a page would be ridiculously inefficient when you have gigabytes of data. Pages in the data cache are therefore hashed for fast access. *Hashing* is a technique that uniformly maps a key via a hash function across a set of hash buckets. A *hash table* is a structure in memory that contains an array of pointers (implemented as a linked list) to the buffer pages. If all pointers to buffer pages don't fit on a single hash page, a *linked list* chains to additional hash pages.

Given a *dbid-fileno-pageno* identifier (a combination of the database ID, file number, and page number), the hash function converts that key to the hash bucket that should be checked; in essence, the hash bucket serves as an index to the specific page needed. By using hashing, even when large amounts of memory are present, SQL Server can find a specific data page in cache with only a few memory reads. Similarly, it takes only a few memory reads for SQL Server to determine that a desired page isn't in cache and must be read in from disk.

> **Note** Finding a data page might require that multiple buffers be accessed via the hash buckets chain (linked list). The hash function attempts to uniformly distribute the *dbid-fileno-pageno* values throughout the available hash buckets. SQL Server sets the number of hash buckets internally, depending on the total size of the buffer pool.

Page management in the data cache

You can use a data page or an index page only if it exists in memory. Therefore, a buffer in the data cache must be available for the page to be read into. Keeping a supply of buffers available for immediate use is an important performance optimization. If a buffer isn't readily available, many memory pages might have to be searched simply to locate a buffer to free up for use as a workspace.

In SQL Server 2012, a single mechanism is responsible both for writing changed pages to disk and for marking as free those pages that haven't been referenced for some time. SQL Server maintains a linked list of the addresses of free pages, and any worker needing a buffer page uses the first page of this list.

Every buffer in the data cache has a header that contains information about the last two times the page was referenced and some status information, including whether the page is dirty (that is, it has been changed since it was read into memory or from disk). The reference information is used to implement the page replacement policy for the data cache pages, which uses an algorithm called *LRU-K* (introduced by Elizabeth O'Neil, Patrick O'Neil, and Gerhard Weikum in the Proceedings of the ACM SIGMOD Conference, May 1993). This algorithm is a great improvement over a strict Least Recently Used (LRU) replacement policy, which has no knowledge of how recently a page was used. It's also an improvement over a Least Frequently Used (LFU) policy involving reference counters because it requires far fewer adjustments by the engine and much less bookkeeping overhead. An LRU-K algorithm keeps track of the last *K* times a page was referenced and can differentiate between types of pages, such as index and data pages, with different frequency levels. It can actually simulate the effect of assigning pages to different buffer pools of specifically tuned sizes. SQL Server 2012 uses a *K* value of 2, so it keeps track of the two most recent accesses of each buffer page.

The data cache is periodically scanned from start to end by the lazywriter process, which functions similar to a ticking clock hand, processing 16 pages in the data cache for each tick. Because the buffer cache is all in memory, these scans are quick and require no I/O. During the scan, a value is associated with each buffer based on the time the buffer was last accessed. When the value gets low enough, the dirty page indicator is checked. If the page is dirty, a write is scheduled to commit the modifications to disk. Instances of SQL Server use write-ahead logging so that the write of the dirty data page is blocked while the log page recording the modification is first written to disk. (Chapter 5, "Logging and recovery," discusses logging in much more detail.) After the modified page is flushed to disk or if the page wasn't dirty to start with, it is freed. The association between the buffer page and the data page that it contains is removed by deleting information about the buffer from the hash table, and the buffer is put on the free list.

Using this algorithm, buffers holding pages considered more valuable remain in the active buffer pool, whereas buffers holding pages not referenced often enough eventually return to the free buffer list. The instance of SQL Server determines internally the size of the free buffer list, based on the size of the buffer cache. The size can't be configured.

The free buffer list and the lazywriter

The work of scanning the buffer pool, writing dirty pages, and populating the free buffer list is primarily performed by the lazywriter. Each instance of SQL Server has one lazywriter thread for each SOS Memory node created in SQLOS, with every instance having at least one lazywriter thread. As explained earlier, the lazywriter works like a clock hand and ticks, with each tick processing 16 buffers in the data cache. The location of the previous tick is tracked internally, and the buffers in the data cache are scanned sequentially from start to finish as the lazywriter ticks during execution. When the end of the data cache is reached, the process repeats from the beginning of the data cache on the next tick.

If the instance experiences memory pressure in the data cache, individual workers can assist the lazywriter as they allocate memory, and the number of pages available on the free list is too low. When this condition occurs, the individual workers execute an internal routine, *HelpLazyWriter*, which performs an additional lazywriter tick on the worker thread, processing the next 16 buffers in the data cache and returning buffers that exceed the current time of last access value to the free list. After the workers schedule an asynchronous read and before the read is completed, the worker gets the address of a section of the buffer pool containing 64 buffers from a central data structure in the SQL Server Database Engine. After the read is initiated, the worker checks to see whether the free list is too small. (Note that this process consumes one or more pages of the list for its own read.) If so, the worker searches for buffers to free up, examining all 64 buffers, regardless of how many it actually finds to free up in that group of 64. If a write must be performed for a dirty buffer in the scanned section, the write is also scheduled.

When SQL Server uses memory dynamically, it must constantly be aware of the amount of free memory available in Windows. One SQLOS component is the Resource Monitor, which, among other tasks, monitors the Windows operating system for low memory notifications by using the *QueryMemoryResourceNotification* Windows Server application programming interface (API) to get status. If the available memory in Windows drops below 32 MB for servers with 4 GB of RAM or 64 MB for servers with 8 GB or higher, a *LowMemoryResourceNotification* flag is set. This notification is returned by the *QueryMemoryResourceNotification* call, and Resource Monitor forces the external clock hands on the internal caches in SQLOS to sweep the caches to clean up and reduce memory usage, allowing SQL Server to return memory to Windows. As memory is released by SQLOS to Windows, it can be committed by other applications or, if a stable state occurs, the Windows operating system sets a *HighMemoryResourceNotification* when the available memory on the server is three times the low memory notification size. When this occurs, the Resource Monitor detects the change in notification, and the SQLOS can then commit additional memory from Windows, if required.

Checkpoints

The checkpoint process also scans the buffer cache periodically and writes all the dirty data pages for a particular database to disk. Checkpoint batches pages together to optimize the I/O being performed and to minimize page flushes through lazywrites. The difference between the checkpoint process and the lazywriter (or the worker threads' management of pages) is that the checkpoint process never puts buffers on the free list. The only purpose of the checkpoint process is to ensure that pages modified before a certain time are written to disk, so that the number of dirty pages in memory is always kept to a minimum, which in turn ensures that the length of time SQL Server requires for recovery of a database after a failure is kept to a minimum. In some cases, checkpoints might find few dirty pages to write to disk if most of the dirty pages have been written to disk by the workers or the lazywriters in the period between two checkpoints.

When a checkpoint occurs, SQL Server writes a checkpoint record to the transaction log, which lists all active transactions. This allows the recovery process to build a table containing a list of all the potentially dirty pages. Checkpoints occur automatically at regular intervals but can also be requested manually. Checkpoints are triggered when any of the following occurs.

- A database owner (or backup operator) explicitly issues a *CHECKPOINT* command to perform a checkpoint in that database. In SQL Server 2012, you can run multiple checkpoints (in different databases) concurrently by using the *CHECKPOINT* command.

- A backup or database snapshot is created of a database. An internal CHECKPOINT operation occurs to ensure that changes in the transaction log are also reflected on disk at the start of the operation.

- The log is filling up (more than 70 percent of capacity) and the database is in autotruncate mode. (Chapter 5 covers autotruncate.) A checkpoint is triggered to truncate the transaction log and free up space. However, if no space can be freed up—perhaps because of a long-running transaction—no checkpoint occurs.

- The recovery time exceeds the Recovery Interval server configuration option. In SQL Server 2012, the default configuration uses the same mechanism as previous versions of SQL Server to control automatic checkpoints. When recovery time is predicted to be longer than the Recovery Interval configuration option, a checkpoint is triggered. SQL Server 2012 uses a simple metric to predict recovery time because it can recover, or redo, in less time than the original operations needed to run. Thus, if checkpoints are taken about as often as the Recovery Interval frequency, recovery completes within the interval.

  A Recovery Interval setting of 1 means that checkpoints occur about every minute as long as transactions are being processed in the database. A minimum amount of work must be done for the automatic checkpoint to fire; this is currently 10 MB of logs per minute. In this way, SQL Server doesn't waste time taking checkpoints on idle databases. A default recovery interval of 0 means that SQL Server chooses an appropriate value; for the current version, this is one minute.

- The recovery time exceeds the Target Recovery Time database configuration option. In SQL Server 2012, each database can be configured with a specific Target Recovery Time that allows indirect checkpoints to occur using *ALTER DATABASE*. The indirect checkpoints improve on automatic checkpoints by setting a dirty page threshold for the database. As operations occur in the database, anytime the dirty page threshold is exceeded a background process, the Recovery Writer flushes dirty pages from memory to disk and updates the minimum recovery log sequence number (MinLSN) for the database. This feature can provide a more predictable recovery time for the database, but it can also affect performance of data manipulation language (DML) operations due to indirect checkpoint operations occurring too frequently.

- An orderly shutdown of SQL Server is requested, without the *NOWAIT* option. A checkpoint operation is then run in each database on the instance. An orderly shutdown occurs when you explicitly shut down SQL Server, unless you do so by using the *SHUTDOWN WITH NOWAIT* command. An orderly shutdown also occurs when the SQL Server service is stopped through Service Control Manager or the *net stop* command from an operating system prompt.

You can also use the *sp_configure* Recovery Interval option to influence checkpointing frequency, balancing the time to recover against any effect on runtime performance. If you're interested in tracing when checkpoints actually occur, you can use the SQL Server Extended Events *sqlserver.checkpoint_begin* and *sqlserver.checkpoint_end* to monitor checkpoint activity. (Details on Extended Events appear later in this chapter.)

The checkpoint process goes through the buffer pool, scanning the pages nonsequentially. When it finds a dirty page, it looks to see whether any physically contiguous (on the disk) pages are also dirty so that it can do a large block write. But this means that it might, for example, write buffers 12, 13, 14, 15, 16, and 17 when it sees that buffer 14 is dirty. (These pages have contiguous disk locations even though they can be in different memory regions in the buffer pool. In this case, the noncontiguous pages in the buffer pool can be written as a single operation called a *gather-write*.) The process continues to scan the buffer pool until it gets to page 17. In some cases, an already written page could potentially be dirty again and might need to be written out to disk a second time.

The larger the buffer pool, the greater the chance that an already written buffer will be dirty again before the checkpoint is done. To avoid this problem, SQL Server uses a bit associated with each buffer called a *generation number*. At the beginning of a checkpoint, all the bits are toggled to the same value—either all 0's or all 1's. As a checkpoint checks a page, it toggles the generation bit to the opposite value. When the checkpoint comes across a page whose bit has already been toggled, it doesn't write that page. Also, any new pages brought into cache during the checkpoint process get the new generation number, so they won't be written during that checkpoint cycle. Any pages already written because they're in proximity to other pages (and are written together in a gather write) aren't written a second time.

In some cases, checkpoints might issue a substantial amount of I/O, causing the I/O subsystem to get inundated with write requests, which can severely affect read performance. On the other hand, relatively low I/O activity can be utilized during some periods. SQL Server 2012 includes a command-line option that allows throttling of checkpoint I/Os. Use the SQL Server Configuration Manager and add the –*k* parameter, followed by a decimal number, to the list of startup parameters for the SQL Server service. The value specified indicates the number of megabytes per second that the checkpoint process can write. By using this –*k* option, the I/O overhead of checkpoints can be spread out and have a more measured effect. Remember that by default, the checkpoint process makes sure that SQL Server can recover databases within the recovery interval that you specify. If you enable this option, the default behavior changes, resulting in a long recovery time if you specify a very low value for the parameter. Backups might require slightly more time to finish because a checkpoint process that a backup initiates is also delayed. Before enabling this option on a production system, make sure that you have enough hardware to sustain the I/O requests posted by SQL Server and that you have thoroughly tested your applications on the system. The –k option doesn't apply to indirect checkpoints.

Memory management in other caches

Buffer pool memory not used for the data cache is used for other types of caches, primarily the plan cache. The page replacement policy for other caches, as well as the mechanism by which pages that can be freed are searched for, are quite a bit different than for the data cache.

SQL Server 2012 uses a common caching framework that all caches except the data cache use. The framework consists of the Resource Monitor and a set of three stores: cache stores, user stores (which don't actually have anything to do with users), and object stores. The plan cache is the main example of a cache store, and the metadata cache is the prime example of a user store. Both cache stores and user stores use the same LRU mechanism and the same costing algorithm to determine which pages can stay and which can be freed. Object stores, on the other hand, are just pools of memory blocks and don't require LRU or costing. One example of the use of an object store is the SNI, which uses the object store for pooling network buffers. For the rest of this section, the discussion of stores refers only to cache stores and user stores.

The LRU mechanism used by the stores is a straightforward variation of the clock algorithm. Imagine a clock hand sweeping through the store, looking at every entry; as it touches each entry, it decreases the cost. When the cost of an entry reaches 0, it can be removed from the cache. The cost is reset whenever an entry is reused.

Memory management in the stores takes into account both global and local memory management policies. Global policies consider the total memory on the system and enable the running of the clock algorithm across all the caches. Local policies involve looking at one store or cache in isolation and making sure it's not using a disproportionate amount of memory.

To satisfy global and local policies, the SQL Server stores implement two clock hands: external and internal. Each store has two clock hands, and you can observe them by examining the DMV *sys.dm_os_memory_cache_clock_hands*. This view contains one internal and one external clock hand for each cache store or user store. The external clock hands implement the global policy; the internal clock hands implement the local policy. The Resource Monitor is in charge of moving the external hands whenever it notices memory pressure. When the Resource Monitor detects memory pressure, it writes an entry into one of many in-memory ring buffers maintained by SQLOS for storing diagnostics information about SQL Server. A *ring buffer* is a memory structure that functions as a first-in-first-out queue with a fixed or variable number of entries that can be maintained within the memory structure. The ring buffer entries from the Resource Monitor can be monitored as follows:

```
SELECT *
FROM sys.dm_os_ring_buffers
WHERE ring_buffer_type=N'RING_BUFFER_RESOURCE_MONITOR';
```

If the memory pressure is external to SQL Server, the value of the IndicatorsSystem node is 2. If the memory pressure is internal to SQL Server, the value of the IndicatorsProcess node is 2. Also, if you look at the DMV *sys.dm_os_memory_cache_clock_hands*—specifically at the *removed_last_round_count* column—you can look for a value that is very large compared to other values. A dramatic increase in that value strongly indicates memory pressure. The companion website for this book contains a comprehensive white paper titled "Troubleshooting Performance Problems in SQL Server 2008," which includes many details on tracking down and dealing with memory problems.

The internal clock moves whenever an individual cache needs to be trimmed. SQL Server attempts to keep each cache reasonably sized compared to other caches. The internal clock hands move only in response to activity. If a worker running a task that accesses a cache notices a high number of entries in the cache or that the size of the cache is greater than a certain percentage of memory, the internal clock hand for that cache starts to free up memory for that cache.

The Memory Broker

Because so many SQL Server components need memory, and to make sure that each component uses memory efficiently, SQL Server uses a Memory Broker, whose job is to analyze the behavior of SQL Server with respect to memory consumption and to improve dynamic memory distribution. The Memory Broker is a centralized mechanism that dynamically distributes memory between the buffer pool, the query executor, the Query Optimizer, and all the various caches, and it attempts to adapt its distribution algorithm for different types of workloads. You can think of the Memory Broker as a control mechanism with a feedback loop. It monitors memory demand and consumption by component, and it uses the information that it gathers to calculate the optimal memory distribution across all components. It can broadcast this information to the component, which then uses the information to adapt its memory usage. You can monitor Memory Broker behavior by querying the Memory Broker ring buffer as follows:

```
SELECT *
FROM sys.dm_os_ring_buffers
WHERE ring_buffer_type=N'RING_BUFFER_MEMORY_BROKER';
```

The ring buffer for the Memory Broker is updated only when the Memory Broker wants the behavior of a specific component to change—that is, to grow, shrink, or remain stable (if it has previously been growing or shrinking). These updates can also correspond to Resource Monitor ring buffer entries that can assist in understanding the cause of the memory change notification by the Memory Broker.

Memory sizing

SQL Server memory involves more than just the buffer pool. As mentioned earlier in this discussion, SQL Server 2012 included a rewrite of the Memory Manager in SQLOS and no longer allocates or manages memory in the same manner as previous versions of SQL Server. Prior to SQL Server 2012, memory was managed separately for single-page allocations by the buffer pool, and non-buffer pool allocations were made using a separate multi-page allocator. Prior to SQL Server 2012, the sys.dm_os_memory_clerks DMV had a column called multi_pages_kb that shows how much space is used by a memory component outside the buffer pool:

```
SELECT type, sum(multi_pages_kb) AS multi_pages_kb
FROM sys.dm_os_memory_clerks
WHERE multi_pages_kb != 0
GROUP BY type;
```

In SQL Server 2012, the sys.dm_os_memory_clerks DMV has been reworked to reflect the changes to the Memory Manager and, therefore, no longer has separate single_page_kb and multi_pages_kb columns. Instead, a new pages_kb column reflects the total memory allocated by a component from the any-page allocator in SQLOS:

```
SELECT type, sum(pages_kb) AS pages_kb
FROM sys.dm_os_memory_clerks
WHERE pages_kb != 0
GROUP BY type;
```

Prior to SQL Server 2012, Address Windowing Extensions (AWE) could be used to access memory beyond the 32-bit address limit. This was considered to be a third memory area. Memory accessed using AWE was available only to the buffer pool and was tracked separately because it could be used only for the data cache pages. However, understand that support for AWE has been removed from SQL Server beginning with SQL Server 2012 and can no longer be used for memory allocations for the data cache.

> **Note** If AWE is enabled in previous SQL Server versions, the only way to get information about the actual memory consumption of SQL Server is by using SQL Server–specific counters or DMVs inside the server. You won't get this information from operating system–level performance counters.

Buffer pool sizing

When SQL Server starts, it computes the size of the virtual address space (VAS) of the SQL Server process. Each process running on Windows has its own VAS. The set of all virtual addresses available for process use constitutes the size of the VAS, which also depends on the architecture (32-bit or 64-bit) and the operating system. The VAS is just the set of all possible addresses; it might be much greater than the physical memory on the machine.

A 32-bit machine can directly address only 4 GB of memory and, by default, Windows itself reserves the top 2 GB of address space for its own use, which leaves only 2 GB as the maximum size of the VAS for any application, such as SQL Server. You can increase this by enabling a /3GB flag in the system's Boot.ini file, which allows applications to have a VAS of up to 3 GB. If your system has more than 3 GB of RAM, the only way a 32-bit process can access the memory above the 32-bit address limits is by enabling AWE, which (as just mentioned in the preceding section) is no longer available in SQL Server 2012. If you need to access more than 3 GB of RAM with SQL Server 2012, you have to use a 64-bit platform.

Memory management is much more straightforward on a 64-bit machine, both for SQL Server, which has so much more VAS to work with, and for administrators, who don't have to worry about special operating system flags or configuration options in SQL Server to be able to access the memory. On a 64-bit platform, the Windows policy option Lock Pages in Memory is available, although it's disabled by default. This policy determines which accounts can make use of a Windows feature to keep data in physical memory, preventing the system from paging the data to virtual memory on disk. If your SQL Server has problems with forced working set trims by the Windows operating system, enabling the use of Lock Pages in Memory can generally prevent forced working set trims from occurring.

Table 2-1 shows the possible memory configurations for various editions of SQL Server 2012.

TABLE 2-1 SQL Server 2012 Memory configurations

Configuration	VAS	Maximum physical memory	AWE/locked pages support
Native 32-bit on 32-bit operating system with /3GB boot parameter	2 GB 3 GB	2 GB 3 GB	None
32-bit on x64 operating system (Windows on Windows— WOW64)	4 GB	4 GB	None
Native 64-bit on x64 operating system	8 TB	1 TB	Locked pages

In addition to the VAS size, SQL Server also calculates a value called *Target Memory*, which is the number of 8 KB pages that it expects to be able to allocate. If the *Max Server Memory* configuration option is set, *Target Memory* is the lesser of these two values. Target Memory is recomputed periodically, particularly when it gets a memory notification from Windows. A decrease in the number of target pages on a normally loaded server might indicate a response to external physical memory pressure. You can see the number of target pages by using the Performance Monitor; examine the *Target Server Pages* counter in the *SQL Server: Memory Manager* object. Also, a DMV called *sys.dm_os_sys_info* contains one row of general-purpose SQL Server configuration information, including the following columns.

- **physical_memory_kb**   The amount of physical memory available

- **virtual_memory_kb**   The amount of virtual memory available to the process in user mode

- **commited_kb**   The committed memory in kilobytes in the Memory Manager; doesn't include reserved memory in the Memory Manager

- **commit_target_kb**   The amount of memory, in kilobytes, that SQL Server Memory Manager can consume

Also, a DMV called *sys.dm_os_process_memory* contains one row of information about the SQL Server process memory usage, including the following columns.

- **physical_memory_in_use_kb**   The size of the process working set in KB, as reported by Windows, as well as tracked allocations by using large page APIs

- **large_page_allocations_kb**   The amount of physical memory allocated by using large page APIs

- **locked_page_allocations_kb**   The amount of memory pages locked in memory

- **total_virtual_address_space_kb**   The total size of the user mode part of the virtual address space

- **virtual_address_space_reserved_kb**   The total amount of virtual address space reserved by the process

- **virtual_address_space_committed_kb** The amount of reserved virtual address space that has been committed or mapped to physical pages

- **virtual_address_space_available_kb** The amount of virtual address space that's currently free

Although the VAS is reserved, the physical memory up to the target amount is committed only when that memory is required for the current workload that the SQL Server instance is handling. The instance continues to acquire physical memory as needed to support the workload, based on the users connecting and the requests being processed. The SQL Server instance can continue to commit physical memory until it reaches its target or the operating system indicates that no more free memory is available. If Windows notifies SQL Server that free memory is running short, it frees up memory if it has more memory than the configured value for Min Server Memory. Note that SQL Server doesn't commit memory equal to Min Server Memory initially. It commits only what it needs and what the operating system can afford. The value for Min Server Memory comes into play only after the buffer pool size goes above that amount, and then SQL Server doesn't let memory go below that setting.

As other applications are started on a computer running an instance of SQL Server, they consume memory, and SQL Server might need to adjust its target memory. Normally, this should be the only situation in which target memory is less than commit memory, and it should stay that way only until memory can be released. The instance of SQL Server adjusts its memory consumption, if possible. If another application is stopped and more memory becomes available, the instance of SQL Server increases the value of its target memory, allowing the memory allocation to grow when needed. SQL Server adjusts its target and releases physical memory only when it's pressured to do so. Thus, a server that is busy for a while can commit large amounts of memory that won't necessarily be released if the system becomes quiescent.

> **Note** Multiple SQL Server instances aren't handled in any special way on the same machine, and balancing memory across all instances isn't attempted. Instances all compete for the same physical memory, so to make sure that none of the instances becomes starved for physical memory, you should use the Min and Max Server Memory option on all SQL Server instances on a multiple-instance machine.

DMVs for memory internals

SQL Server 2012 includes several Dynamic Management Objects that provide information about memory and the various caches. Like the DMVs containing information about the schedulers, these objects are intended primarily for use by customer support services to see what SQL Server is doing, but you can use them for the same purpose. To select from these objects, you must have the *View Server State* permission. Again, some of the more useful or interesting columns are listed for each object; most of these descriptions are taken from *SQL Server Books Online*.

- **sys.dm_os_memory_clerks** This view returns one row per memory clerk that's currently active in the instance of SQL Server. You can think of a clerk as an accounting unit. Each store described earlier is a clerk, but some clerks aren't stores, such as those for the CLR and for full-text search. The following query returns a list of all the types of clerks.

```
SELECT DISTINCT type
FROM sys.dm_os_memory_clerks;
```

Interesting columns include the following.

- **pages_kb**   The amount of page memory allocated in kilobytes for this memory clerk.

- **virtual_memory_reserved_kb**   The amount of virtual memory reserved by a memory clerk.

- **virtual_memory_committed_kb**   The amount of memory committed by the clerk. The amount of committed memory should always be less than the amount of Reserved Memory.

- **awe_allocated_kb**   The amount of memory in kilobytes locked in the physical memory and not paged out by Windows.

- **sys.dm_os_memory_cache_counters**   This view returns a snapshot of the health of each cache of type userstore and cachestore. It provides runtime information about the cache entries allocated, their use, and the source of memory for the cache entries. Interesting columns include the following.

  - **pages_kb**   The amount of memory in kilobytes allocated in the cache.

  - **pages_in_use_kb**   The amount of memory in kilobytes (KB) that is allocated and used in the cache.

  - **entries_count**   The number of entries in the cache.

  - **entries_in_use_count**   The number of entries in use in the cache.

- **sys.dm_os_memory_cache_hash_tables**   This view returns a row for each active cache in the SQL Server instance. This view can be joined to *sys.dm_os_memory_cache_counters* on the *cache_address* column. Interesting columns include the following.

  - **buckets_count**   The number of buckets in the hash table.

  - **buckets_in_use_count**   The number of buckets currently being used.

  - **buckets_min_length**   The minimum number of cache entries in a bucket.

  - **buckets_max_length**   The maximum number of cache entries in a bucket.

  - **buckets_avg_length**   The average number of cache entries in each bucket. If this number gets very large, it might indicate that the hashing algorithm isn't ideal.

  - **buckets_avg_scan_hit_length**   The average number of examined entries in a bucket before the searched-for item was found. As above, a big number might indicate a less-than-optimal cache. You might consider running *DBCC FREESYSTEMCACHE* to remove all unused entries in the cache stores. You can get more details on this command in *SQL Server Books Online*.

- **sys.dm_os_memory_cache_clock_hands**   This DMV, discussed earlier, can be joined to the other cache DMVs using the *cache_address* column. Interesting columns include the following.

  - **clock_hand**   The type of clock hand, either external or internal. Remember that every store has two clock hands.

  - **clock_status**   The status of the clock hand: suspended or running. A clock hand runs when a corresponding policy kicks in.

  - **rounds_count**   The number of rounds the clock hand has made. All the external clock hands should have the same (or close to the same) value in this column.

  - **removed_all_rounds_count**   The number of entries removed by the clock hand in all rounds.

NUMA and memory

As mentioned earlier, one major reason for implementing Non-Uniform Memory Access (NUMA) is to handle large amounts of memory efficiently. As clock speed and the number of processors increase, reducing the memory latency required to use this additional processing power becomes increasingly difficult. Large L3 caches can help alleviate part of the problem, but this is only a limited solution. NUMA is the scalable solution of choice. SQL Server 2012 has been designed to take advantage of NUMA-based computers without requiring any application changes.

Keep in mind that NUMA memory nodes depend completely on the hardware NUMA configuration. Defining your own soft-NUMA, as discussed earlier, doesn't affect the number of NUMA memory nodes. For example, if you have an SMP computer with eight CPUs and create four soft-NUMA nodes with two CPUs each, you have only one memory node serving all four NUMA nodes. Soft-NUMA doesn't provide memory to CPU affinity. However, each NUMA node has a network I/O thread, either hard or soft.

The principal reason for using soft-NUMA is to segregate workloads to specific CPUs through the use of the separate I/O completion port assigned to each logical thread, for connectivity. This can benefit computers with many CPUs and no hardware NUMA, but it can also benefit hardware NUMA systems. For instance, on a computer with eight CPUs and no hardware NUMA, you have one I/O completion port for connections and the connections are assigned round-robin, based on the load factor to the SOS Schedulers in SQLOS. Configuring four soft-NUMA nodes provides four I/O completion ports and managing threads, which allows separation of workloads by connecting to the port of a specific soft-NUMA node.

Configuring soft-NUMA doesn't provide additional lazywriter threads in SQL Server. Separate lazywriter threads are created only for physical hardware NUMA memory nodes.

If you have multiple physical NUMA memory nodes, SQL Server divides the total target memory evenly among all the nodes. So if you have 10 GB of physical memory and four NUMA memory nodes and SQL Server determines a 10 GB target memory value, all nodes eventually allocate and use 2.5 GB of memory as though it were their own. In fact, if one node physically has less memory than another, it must use memory from another one to reach its 2.5 GB allocation. This memory is called *foreign memory* and is considered local. If SQL Server readjusts its target memory and each node needs to release some memory, no attempt will be made to free up foreign pages first. Also, if SQL Server has been configured to run on a subset of the available NUMA nodes, the target memory is *not* limited automatically to the memory on those nodes. You must set the Max Server Memory value to limit the amount of memory.

Although the NUMA nodes function largely independently of each other, that's not always the case. For example, if a worker running on node *N1* needs to access a database page already in node *N2*'s memory, it does so by accessing *N2*'s memory, which is called *nonlocal memory*. (Note that nonlocal isn't the same as foreign memory.)

Read-ahead

SQL Server supports a mechanism called *read-ahead*, whereby the need for data and index pages can be anticipated and pages can be brought into the buffer pool before they're actually needed. This performance optimization allows large amounts of data to be processed effectively and typically keeps the necessary pages in the buffer pool before they are needed by the execution engine. Read-ahead is managed completely internally, and no configuration adjustments are necessary.

Read-ahead comes in two types: one for table scans on heaps and one for index ranges. For table scans, the table's allocation structures are consulted to read the table in disk order. Up to 32 extents (32 * 8 pages/extent * 8,192 bytes/page = 2 MB) of read-ahead might be outstanding at a time. Up to eight contiguous extents (64 contiguous pages) can be read at a time are read with a single 512 KB scatter read from one file. If the table is spread across multiple files in a file group, SQL Server attempts to distribute the read-ahead activity across the files evenly.

For index ranges, the scan uses level 1 of the index structure (the level immediately above the leaf) to determine which pages to read ahead. When the index scan starts, read-ahead is invoked on the initial descent of the index to minimize the number of reads performed. For instance, for a scan of *WHERE state = 'WA'*, read-ahead searches the index for *key = 'WA'*, and it can tell from the level-1 nodes how many pages must be examined to satisfy the scan. If the anticipated number of pages is small, all the pages are requested by the initial read-ahead; if the pages are noncontiguous, they're fetched in scatter reads. If the range contains a large number of pages, the initial read-ahead is performed and thereafter, every time another 16 pages are consumed by the scan, the index is consulted to read in another 16 pages. This has several interesting effects.

- Small ranges can be processed in a single read at the data page level whenever the index is contiguous.

- The scan range (for example, *state = 'WA'*) can be used to prevent reading ahead of pages that won't be used because this information is available in the index.

- Read-ahead isn't slowed by having to follow page linkages at the data page level. (Read-ahead can be done on both clustered indexes and nonclustered indexes.)

As you can see, memory management in SQL Server is a huge topic, and this discussion provided you with only a basic understanding of how SQL Server uses memory. This information should give you a start in interpreting the wealth of information available through the DMVs and troubleshooting. The companion website includes a white paper that offers many more troubleshooting ideas and scenarios.

SQL Server Resource Governor

Having sufficient memory and scheduler resources available is of paramount importance in having a system that runs well. Although SQL Server and the SQLOS have many built-in algorithms to distribute these resources equitably, you often understand your resource needs better than the SQL Server Database Engine does. This is where the Resource Governor comes in handy.

Resource Governor overview

SQL Server 2008 Enterprise Edition introduced an interface for assigning scheduler and memory resources to groups of processes based on your determination of their needs. This interface—still available only in Enterprise Edition in SQL Server 2012—is called the Resource Governor *and* has the following goals.

- It allows monitoring of resource consumption per workload. (A workload can be defined as a group of requests.)

- It enables workloads to be prioritized.

- It provides a means to specify resource boundaries between workloads to allow predictable execution of those workloads where they otherwise experience resource contention.

- It prevents or reduces the probability of runaway queries.

The Resource Governor's functionality is based on the concepts of workloads and resource pools, which the DBA sets up. By using just a few basic Data Definition Language (DDL) commands, you can define a set of workload groups, create a classifier function to determine which user sessions are members of which groups, and set up pools of resources to allow each workload group to have minimum and maximum settings for the amount of memory and the percentage of CPU resources that they can use.

Figure 2-2 illustrates a sample relationship between the classifier function applied to each session, workload groups, and resource pools. More details about groups and pools are provided throughout this section, but you can see in the figure that each new session is placed in a workload group based on the result of the classifier function. Also notice that groups and pools have a many-to-one relationship. Many workload groups can be assigned to the same pool, but each workload group only belongs on one pool.

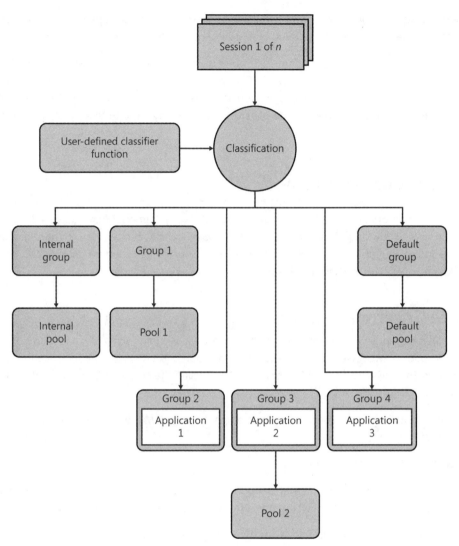

FIGURE 2-2 Resource Governor components.

To enable the Resource Governor, use the DDL statement *ALTER RESOURCE GOVERNOR*. With this statement, you can specify a classifier function to be used to assign sessions to a workload, enable or disable the Resource Governor, or reset the statistics being kept on the Resource Governor.

Classifier function

After a classifier function is defined and the Resource Governor is enabled, the function is applied to each new session to determine the name of the workload group to which the session will be assigned. The session stays in the same group until its termination, unless it's assigned explicitly to a differ-ent group. A maximum of only one classifier function can be active at any particular time, and if no classifier function is defined, all new sessions are assigned to a default group. The classifier function is typically based on properties of a connection and determines the workload group based on system functions such as *SUSER_NAME()*, *SUSER_SNAME()*, *IS_SRVROLEMEMBER()*, and *IS_MEMBER()*, and on property functions such as *LOGINPROPERTY* and *CONNECTIONPROPERTY*.

Resource pools

A *resource pool* is a subset of the server's physical resources. Each pool has two parts.

- One part doesn't overlap with other pools, which enables you to set a minimum value for the resource.

- The other part of the pool is shared with other pools, and this allows you to define the maximum possible resource consumption.

Pool resources are set by specifying one of the following for each resource.

- *MIN* or *MAX* for CPU

- *MIN* or *MAX* for memory percentage

MIN represents the minimum guaranteed resource availability and *MAX* represents the maximum size of the pool.

The shared part of the pool is used to indicate where available resources can go if resources are available. However, when resources are consumed, they go to the specified pool and aren't shared. This can improve resource utilization in cases in which no requests are in a specific pool and the resources configured to the pool can be freed up for other pools.

Here are more details about the six values that can be specified for each resource pool.

- **MIN_CPU_PERCENT** This value is a guaranteed average CPU bandwidth for all requests in the pool when CPU contention occurs. SQL Server attempts to distribute CPU bandwidth between individual requests as fairly as possible and takes the *IMPORTANCE* property for each workload group into account. The default value is 0, which means no minimum value.

- **MAX_CPU_PERCENT** This value is the maximum CPU bandwidth that all requests in the pool receive when CPU contention occurs. The default value is 100, which means no maximum value. If no contention is occurring for CPU resources, a pool can consume up to 100 percent of CPU bandwidth.

- **CAP_CPU_PERCENT** This value is a hard limit on the maximum CPU bandwidth that all requests in the pool receive. Although requests in the pool can exceed the *MAX_CPU_PERCENT* value if resources are available, they can't exceed the value set for *CAP_CPU_PERCENT*.

- **AFFINITY** This value attaches the resource pool to specific schedulers. The default value is *AUTO*, which allows the pool to use all schedulers in the server. Pool affinity can be configured using *SCHEDULER* to specify a specific scheduler range, or using *NUMANODE* to specify a specific NUMA node or range of nodes.

- ***MIN_MEMORY_PERCENT*** This value specifies the amount of memory reserved for this pool that can't be shared with other pools. If the pool has no requests but has a minimum memory value set, this memory can't be used for requests in other pools and is wasted. Within a pool, memory distribution between requests is first come, first served. Memory for a request can also be affected by properties of the workload group, such as *REQUEST_MAX_MEMORY_GRANT_PERCENT*. The default value of 0 means that no minimum memory is reserved.

- ***MAX_MEMORY_PERCENT*** This value specifies the percent of total server memory that all requests in the specified pool can use. This amount can go up to 100 percent, but the actual amount is reduced by memory already reserved by the *MIN_MEMORY_PERCENT* value specified by other pools. *MAX_MEMORY_PERCENT* is always greater than or equal to *MIN_MEMORY_PERCENT*. Workload group policy affects the amount of memory for an individual request—for example, *REQUEST_MAX_MEMORY_GRANT_PERCENT*. The default setting of 100 means that all server memory can be used for one pool. This setting can't be exceeded, even if it means that the server will be underused.

Some extreme cases of pool configuration are as follows.

- All pools define minimums that add up to 100 percent of the server resources. This is equivalent to dividing the server resources into non-overlapping pieces regardless of the resources consumed inside any particular pool.

- All pools have no minimums. They all compete for available resources, and their final sizes are based on each pool's resource consumption.

Resource Governor has two predefined resource pools for each SQL Server instance.

- **Internal pool** This pool represents the resources consumed by SQL Server itself. This pool always contains only the internal workload group and can't be altered in any way. Resources used by the internal pool have no restrictions. You can't affect the resource usage of the internal pool or add workload groups to it; however, you can monitor the resources used by the internal group.

- **Default pool** Initially, the default pool contains only the default workload group. This pool can't be dropped, but it can be altered and other workload groups can be added to it. Note that the default group can't be moved out of the default pool.

Pool sizing

Table 2-2, taken from *SQL Server 2012 Books Online*, illustrates the relationships between the *MIN* and *MAX* values in several pools and how the effective *MAX* values are computed. The table shows the settings for the internal pool, the default pool, and two user-defined pools. The following formulas are used for calculating the effective *MAX %* and the shared percentage.

- Min(X,Y) means the smaller value of *X* and *Y*.

- Sum(X) means the sum of value *X* across all pools.

- Total shared % = 100 – sum(MIN %).

- Effective MAX % = min(X,Y).

- Shared % = Effective MAX % – MIN %.

TABLE 2-2 MIN and MAX values for resource pools

Pool name	MIN % setting	MAX % setting	Calculated effective MAX %	Calculated shared %	Comment
internal	0	100	100	0	Effective MAX % and shared % aren't applicable to the internal pool.
default	0	100	30	30	The effective MAX value is calculated as min(100,100–(20+50)) = 30. The calculated shared % is effectively MAX – MIN = 30.
Pool 1	20	100	50	30	The effective MAX value is calculated as min(100,100–50) = 50. The calculated shared % is effectively MAX – MIN = 30.
Pool 2	50	70	70	20	The effective MAX value is calculated as min(70,100–20) = 70. The calculated shared % is effectively MAX – MIN = 20.

Table 2-3, also taken from *SQL Server Books Online*, shows how the values in Table 2-2 can change when a new pool is created. This new pool is Pool 3 and has a MIN % setting of 5.

TABLE 2-3 MIN and MAX values for resource pools

Pool name	MIN % setting	MAX % setting	Calculated effective MAX %	Calculated shared %	Comment
internal	0	100	100	0	Effective MAX % and shared % aren't applicable to the internal pool.
default	0	100	25	30	The effective MAX value is calculated as min(100,100−(20+50+5)) = 25. The calculated shared % is effectively MAX − MIN = 25.
Pool 1	20	100	45	25	The effective MAX value is calculated as min(100,100−55) = 45. The calculated shared % is effectively MAX − MIN = 30.
Pool 2	50	70	70	20	The effective MAX value is calculated as min(70,100−25) = 70. The calculated shared % is effectively MAX − MIN = 20.
Pool 3	5	100	30	25	The effective MAX value is calculated as min(100,100−70) = 30. The calculated shared % is effectively MAX − MIN = 25.

The number of resource pools that can be created in SQL Server is limited. For SQL Server 2012, 64-bit servers can have a maximum of 64 resource pools, including the internal and default pool. Previous versions of SQL Server are limited to a maximum of 20 resource pools.

Workload groups

A *workload group* is just a name defined by a DBA to allow multiple connections to share the same resources. Every SQL Server instance has two predefined workload groups.

- **Internal group**   This group is used for the internal activities of SQL Server. Users can't add sessions to the internal group or affect its resource usage. However, you can monitor the internal group.

- **Default group**   All sessions are classified into this group when no other classifier rules can be applied. This includes situations where the classifier function resulted in a nonexistent group or when the classifier function failed.

The same workload group can have many sessions assigned, and each session can start multiple sequential tasks (or batches). Each batch can be composed of multiple statements, and some of those statements, such as stored procedure calls, can be broken down further. Figure 2-3 illustrates this relationship between workload groups, sessions, batches, and statements.

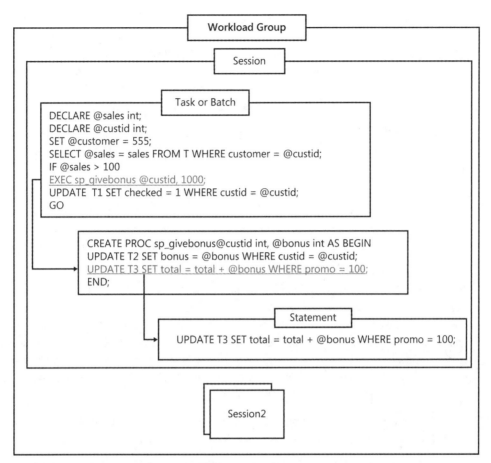

FIGURE 2-3 Workload groups, sessions, batches, and statements.

When you create a wor kload group, you give it a name and then supply values for up to six specific group properties. Any properties that aren't specified receive a default value. In addition to the group properties, the group is assigned to a resource pool; and if no pool is specified, the default pool is assumed. The following properties can be specified.

- **IMPORTANCE** Each workload group can have an importance of low, medium, or high within their resource pool. Medium is the default. This value determines the relative ratio of CPU bandwidth available to the group in a preset proportion (which is subject to change in future versions or services packs). Currently, the weighting is low = 1, medium =3, and high = 9, meaning that a scheduler tries to execute runnable sessions from high-priority workload groups three times more often than sessions from groups with medium importance, and nine times more often than sessions from groups with low importance. The DBA needs to be sure not to have too many sessions in the groups with high importance, or not to assign a high importance to too many groups. If you have nine times as many sessions from groups with high importance than from groups with low importance, the end result is that all sessions get equal time on the scheduler.

- **REQUEST_MAX_MEMORY_GRANT_PERCENT**   This value specifies the maximum amount of memory that a single task from this group can take from the resource pool. This percentage is relative to the pool size specified by the pool's *MAX_MEMORY_PERCENT* value, not the actual amount of memory in use. This amount refers only to memory granted for query execution and not for data buffers or cached plans, which many requests can share. The default value is 25 percent, which means a single request can consume one-fourth of the pool's memory.

- **REQUEST_MAX_CPU_TIME_SEC**   This value is the maximum amount of CPU time in seconds that any one request can consume in the workload group. The default setting is 0, which means the CPU time has no limit.

- **REQUEST_MEMORY_GRANT_TIMEOUT_SEC**   This value is the maximum time in seconds that a query waits for a resource to become available. If the resource doesn't become available, it might fail with a timeout error. (In some cases, the query might not fail, but it might run with substantially reduced resources.) The default value is 0, which means the server calculates the timeout based on query cost.

- **MAX_DOP**   This value specifies the maximum degree of parallelism (DOP) for a parallel query and takes precedence over the *Max Degree of Parallelism* configuration option and any query hints. The actual runtime DOP is also bound by the number of schedulers and availability of parallel threads. The *MAX_DOP* setting is a maximum limit only, meaning that the server is allowed to run the query using fewer processors than specified. The default setting is 0, meaning that the server handles the value globally. You should be aware of the following details about working with the *MAX_DOP* value.

  - *MAXDOP* as query hint is honored so long as it doesn't exceed the workload group *MAX_DOP* value.

  - *MAXDOP* as query hint always overrides the *Max Degree of Parallelism* configuration option.

  - If the query is marked as serial at compile time, it can't be changed back to parallel at runtime regardless of workload group or configuration setting.

  - After the degree of parallelism is decided, it can be lowered only when memory pressure occurs. Workload group reconfiguration won't be seen for tasks waiting in the grant memory queue.

- **GROUP_MAX_REQUESTS**   This value is the maximum number of requests allowed to be simultaneously executing in the workload group. The default is 0, which means unlimited requests.

Any of the properties of a workload group can be changed by using *ALTER WORKLOAD GROUP*.

Code example

This following code includes a few syntax examples of the Resource Governor DDL commands, to give you a further idea of how all these concepts work together. This isn't a complete list of all possible DDL command options; for that, you need to refer to *SQL Server Books Online*.

```sql
--- Create a resource pool for production processing
--- and set limits.
USE master;
GO
CREATE RESOURCE POOL pProductionProcessing
WITH
(
    MAX_CPU_PERCENT = 100,
    MIN_CPU_PERCENT = 50
);
GO
--- Create a workload group for production processing
--- and configure the relative importance.
CREATE WORKLOAD GROUP gProductionProcessing
WITH
(
    IMPORTANCE = MEDIUM
)
--- Assign the workload group to the production processing
--- resource pool.
USING pProductionProcessing;
GO
--- Create a resource pool for off-hours processing
--- and set limits.
CREATE RESOURCE POOL pOffHoursProcessing
WITH
(
    MAX_CPU_PERCENT = 50,
    MIN_CPU_PERCENT = 0
);
GO
--- Create a workload group for off-hours processing
--- and configure the relative importance.
CREATE WORKLOAD GROUP gOffHoursProcessing
WITH
(
    IMPORTANCE = LOW
)
--- Assign the workload group to the off-hours processing
--- resource pool.
USING pOffHoursProcessing;
GO
--- Any changes to workload groups or resource pools require that the
--- resource governor be reconfigured.
ALTER RESOURCE GOVERNOR RECONFIGURE;
GO
USE master;
GO
CREATE TABLE tblClassifierTimeTable (
    strGroupName    sysname         not null,
    tStartTime      time            not null,
    tEndTime        time            not null
);
GO
```

```
--- Add time values that the classifier will use to
--- determine the workload group for a session.
INSERT into tblClassifierTimeTable
     VALUES('gProductionProcessing', '6:35 AM', '6:15 PM');
GO
--- Create the classifier function
CREATE FUNCTION fnTimeClassifier()
RETURNS sysname
WITH SCHEMABINDING
AS
BEGIN
     DECLARE @strGroup sysname
     DECLARE @loginTime time
     SET @loginTime = CONVERT(time,GETDATE())
     SELECT TOP 1 @strGroup = strGroupName
     FROM dbo.tblClassifierTimeTable
     WHERE tStartTime <= @loginTime and tEndTime >= @loginTime
     IF(@strGroup is not null)
     BEGIN
          RETURN @strGroup
     END
--- Use the default workload group if there is no match
--- on the lookup.
     RETURN N'gOffHoursProcessing'
END;
GO
--- Reconfigure the Resource Governor to use the new function
ALTER RESOURCE GOVERNOR with (CLASSIFIER_FUNCTION = dbo.fnTimeClassifier);
ALTER RESOURCE GOVERNOR RECONFIGURE;
GO
```

Resource Governor controls

Your pool settings control the actual limitations of resources. In SQL Server 2012, you can control memory and CPU resources, but not I/O. In a future version, more resource controls might possibly become available.

The way that memory and CPU resource limits are applied is different. You can think of the memory specifications for a pool as hard limits, and no pool will ever use more than its maximum memory setting. Also, SQL Server always reserves the minimum memory for each pool, so that if no sessions in workload groups are assigned to a pool, its minimum memory reservation is unusable by other sessions.

However, CPU limits are soft limits under MAX_CPU_PERCENT, and other sessions can use unused scheduler bandwidth. The maximum values also aren't always fixed upper limits unless a value has been specified for CAP_CPU_PERCENT. Suppose that you have two pools: one with a MAX_CPU_PERCENT value of 25 percent and the other with a MAX_CPU_PERCENT value of 50 percent. As soon as the first pool has used its 25 percent of the scheduler, sessions from groups in the other pool can use all remaining CPU resources. As a soft limit, MAX_CPU_PERCENT can make CPU usage not quite as predictable as memory usage.

Each session is assigned to a scheduler, as described earlier, with no regard to the workload group that the session is in. Assume a minimal situation with only two sessions running on a dual CPU instance. Each will most likely be assigned to a different scheduler, and the two sessions can be in two different workload groups in two different resource pools.

Assume further that the session on CPU1 is from a workload group in the first pool with a MAX_CPU_PERCENT setting of 80 percent, and that the second session, on CPU2, is from a group in the second pool with a MAX_CPU_PERCENT setting of 20 percent. Because these are only two sessions, they each use 100 percent of their scheduler or 50 percent of the total CPU resources on the instance. If CPU1 is then assigned another task from a workload group from the 20 percent pool, the situation changes. Tasks using the 20 percent pool have 20 percent of CPU1 but still have 100 percent of CPU2, and tasks using the 80 percent pool still have only 80 percent of CPU1. This means tasks running from the 20 percent pool have 60 percent of the total CPU resources, and the one task from the 80 percent pool has only 40 percent of the total CPU resources. Of course, as more and more tasks are assigned to the schedulers, this anomaly can work itself out, but much less explicit control is available because of the way that scheduler resources are managed across multiple CPUs.

To configure hard limits to make CPU usage more predictable, you should use CAP_CPU_PERCENT to set fixed upper limits to each pool. In the previous configuration, if the session on CPU1 is from a workload group in the first pool that has a CAP_CPU_PERCENT setting of 80 percent, and the second session on CPU2 is from a group in a second pool with a CAP_CPU_PERCENT setting of 20 percent, the session on CPU1 would consume only 80 percent of the CPU and the session on CPU2 would consume only 20 percent of the CPU.

For testing and troubleshooting purposes, sometimes you want to be able to turn off all Resource Governor functionality easily. You can disable the Resource Governor with the command *ALTER RESOURCE GOVERNOR DISABLE*. You can then re-enable the Resource Governor with the command *ALTER RESOURCE GOVERNOR RECONFIGURE*. If you want to ensure that the Resource Governor stays disabled, you can start your SQL Server instance with trace flag 8040. When this trace flag is used, Resource Governor stays in the OFF state at all times, and all attempts to reconfigure it fails. The same behavior results if you start your SQL Server instance in single-user mode using the *–m* and *–f* flags. If the Resource Governor is disabled, you should notice the following behaviors.

- Only the *internal* workload group and resource pool exist.

- Resource Governor configuration metadata isn't loaded into memory.

- Your classifier function is never executed automatically.

- The Resource Governor metadata is visible and can be manipulated.

Resource Governor metadata

You want to consider three specific catalog views when working with the Resource Governor.

- **sys.resource_governor_configuration**   This view returns the stored Resource Governor state.

- **sys.resource_governor_resource_pools** This view returns the stored resource pool configuration. Each row of the view determines the configuration of an individual pool.

- **sys.resource_governor_workload_groups** This view returns the stored workload group configuration.

Also, three DMVs are devoted to the Resource Governor.

- **sys.dm_resource_governor_workload_groups** This view returns workload group statistics and the current in-memory configuration of the workload group.

- **sys.dm_resource_governor_resource_pools** This view returns information about the current resource pool state, the current configuration of resource pools, and resource pool statistics.

- **sys.dm_resource_governor_configuration** This view returns a row that contains the current in-memory configuration state for the Resource Governor.

Finally, six other DMVs contain information related to the Resource Governor.

- **sys.dm_exec_query_memory_grants** This view returns information about the queries that have acquired a memory grant or that still require a memory grant to execute. Queries that don't have to wait for a memory grant don't appear in this view. The following columns are added for the Resource Governor: *group_id*, *pool_id*, *is_small*, and *ideal_memory_kb*.

- **sys.dm_exec_query_resource_semaphores** This view returns the information about the current query-resource semaphore status. It provides general query-execution memory status information and allows you to determine whether the system can access enough memory. The *pool_id* column has been added for the Resource Governor.

- **sys.dm_exec_sessions** This view returns one row per authenticated session on SQL Server. The *group_id* column has been added for the Resource Governor.

- **sys.dm_exec_requests** This view returns information about each request executing within SQL Server. The *group_id* column is added for the Resource Governor.

- **sys.dm_exec_cached_plans** This view returns a row for each query plan cached by SQL Server for faster query execution. The *pool_id* column is added for the Resource Governor.

- **sys.dm_os_memory_brokers** This view returns information about allocations internal to SQL Server that use the SQL Server Memory Manager. The following columns are added for the Resource Governor: *pool_id*, *allocations_kb_per_sec*, *predicated_allocations_kb*, and *overall_limit_kb*.

Although at first glance the setup of the Resource Governor might seem unnecessarily complex, you should find that being able to specify properties for both workload groups and resource pools provides you with the maximum control and flexibility. You can think of the workload groups as tools that give control to your developers, and the resource pools as administrator tools for limiting what the developers can do.

Extended Events

Extended Events were first introduced in SQL Server 2008 as a general event infrastructure to provide debugging and diagnostics capabilities for various purposes. The lack of UI support for Extended Events in SQL Server 2008 made for a steep learning curve of all the new concepts introduced by Extended Events for even simple tracing. Although Extended Events exposed a number of new events that were never available in SQL Trace, it was missing a large number of the trace events required for normal day-to-day usage.

In SQL Server 2012, Extended Events has been expanded significantly and now contains all the events formerly available in SQL Trace as well as a new UI implementation in SQL Server Management Studio. SQL Trace also has been added to the deprecated feature list, marking it for removal in a future version of SQL Server and making Extended Events the future of all diagnostic troubleshooting in SQL Server. Also, Analysis Services was integrated into Extended Events, allowing data collected from the Database Engine to be correlated with data collected from Analysis Services in an easy-to-manage implementation.

Extended Events architecture

As a new implementation in SQL Server 2008, Extended Events reworked diagnostic data collection from the ground up to solve many limitations and problems that existed with SQL Trace. The Extended Events engine starts up inside SQL Server when the process loads and provides all the management functionality for Extended Events in SQL Server. The Extended Events engine is only an operating environment that provides management of the available package metadata, the event sessions running inside the instance, and a pool of dispatcher threads that send collected events to destination targets for consumption.

The individual modules inside SQL Server load packages into the Extended Events engine that contain all the metadata about the Extended Events objects exposed by the module. Packages are metadata containers that provide information about events, actions, targets, types, maps, and predicates available for use in defining event sessions. "The core concepts" section covers each object in further depth.

Event execution life cycle

When an event point in code is encountered during the execution of a task, the engine performs a very fast Boolean check to determine whether the event is enabled in an event session that is started on the server. If the event isn't enabled for an event session, it won't fire, and the code execution for the task continues with virtually no overhead to the SQL Server process. If the event is enabled, it begins the process of firing by collecting all the data columns associated with its default column schema.

At this point, the Extended Events engine looks up the active sessions that have the event enabled for collection and performs predicate evaluation to determine whether the event is supposed to continue executing. At the first point in the predicate definition that the Boolean expression being checked for evaluates to false, the event terminates executing and the engine returns to executing the original task with minimal overhead associated with evaluating the event predicates. If all predicate expressions for a session evaluate to true, the events data columns are copied into that session's context and the event execution continues.

Any actions added to the event are now executed in the engine, and any additional data is appended to the events output data synchronously on the executing thread. When the actions finish executing, the final event data is immediately dispatched to any synchronous targets defined for the event session, and then the event data is added to the event session's memory buffers to allow for future dispatching to the asynchronous targets by the dispatcher pool.

Figure 2-4 shows the full life cycle of an extended event.

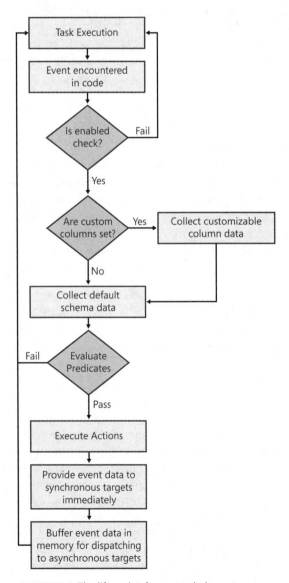

FIGURE 2-4 The life cycle of an extended event.

Core concepts

So that you can understand Extended Events better, wherever possible, corresponding concepts from SQL Trace are used to explain the concepts being covered. Unlike SQL Trace, Extended Events uses two-part naming for all objects that can be used in defining an event session. Objects are referenced by package name and the object name. (A package is a container of metadata information loaded by a module.) Understanding how to use the objects in Extended Events involves first understanding the packages being loaded for use, because these define the functional areas within SQL Server where events can originate.

In SQL Server 2012 there are seven packages for use by event sessions. An additional private package exists for the auditing feature (secaudit) that event sessions can't use, even though audits take advantage of Extended Events as the underlying mechanism for data collection. Also, SQL Server 2012 ships with an empty package, named XeDkPkg, that contains no useable objects or maps (explained later in this chapter) for Extended Events. The packages and objects in Extended Events available for use in user-defined event sessions can be determined using the capabilities column within the DMV, which will either be NULL or will return a value of 0 for a bitwise AND operation for a value of 1:

```
SELECT *
FROM sys.dm_xe_packages AS p
WHERE (p.capabilities IS NULL
    OR p.capabilities & 1 = 0);
```

The sys.dm_xe_packages DMV lists eight packages, including the seven mentioned earlier, plus the special *package0* package that is loaded by the Extended Events engine and contains generic objects. *Package0* loads all targets, as well as many of the types, predicate comparison functions, and a couple of generic actions that provide side effects when events execute. Because individual modules load packages, the *sys.dm_xe_packages* DMV lists two *sqlserver* packages that are the result of product changes that split parts of the engine into a new module in SQL Server 2012. The *package0* package loaded by the Extended Events engine contains generic objects. The *sys.dm_xe_packages* DMV also shows you packages for SQLOS (*sqlos*), SQLCLR (*sqlclr*), Filestream (*filestream*), and the Unified Communications Stack (*ucs*).

Events

Events correspond to well-known points in SQL Server code. Common examples would be *sp_statement_starting*, *sp_statement_completed*, *rpc_starting*, and *rpc_completed*. These have corresponding events in SQL Trace that most database administrators are already familiar with. However, other events are available, such as the *wait_info* and *latch_suspend_end* events provided by SQLOS any time a session waits on a resource or finishes waiting on a latch respectively. The following query lists of all events available in SQL Server 2012 from the *sys.dm_xe_objects* metadata view:

```
SELECT p.name AS package_name,
       o.name AS event_name,
       o.description
FROM sys.dm_xe_packages AS p
INNER JOIN sys.dm_xe_objects AS o
    ON p.guid = o.package_guid
WHERE (p.capabilities IS NULL
   OR p.capabilities & 1 = 0)
  AND (o.capabilities IS NULL
   OR o.capabilities & 1 = 0)
  AND o.object_type = N'event';
```

Events in Extended Events are categorized using the Event Tracing for Windows (ETW) method of categorizing events—using channels and keywords. The channel specifies the type of event and can be Admin, Analytic, Debug, or Operational. The following describes each event channel.

- **Admin** events are expected to be of most use to systems administrators. This channel includes events such as error reports and deprecation announcements.

- **Analytic** events fire regularly—potentially thousands of times per second on a busy system—and are designed to be aggregated to support analysis about system performance and health. This channel includes events around topics such as lock acquisition and SQL statements starting and completing.

- **Debug** events are expected to be used by DBAs and support engineers to help diagnose and solve engine-related problems. This channel includes events that fire when threads and processes start and stop, various times throughout a scheduler's life cycle, and for other similar themes.

- **Operational** events are expected to be of most use to operational DBAs for managing the SQL Server service and databases. This channel's events relate to databases being attached, detached, started, and stopped, as well as issues such as the detection of database page corruption.

Keywords provide the specific part of the engine that actually generated the event—for example, *io*, *memory*, *scheduling*, or *alwayson*.

Events have three different types of columns associated with them. Every event has a set of readonly columns that identify information about it, such as the specific channel and associated keyword, as well as a globally unique identifier (GUID), all of which are used for ETW integration. Events also return data columns when the event fires in the engine. For some events, some data columns are customizable, which allow the event session to specify whether to actually collect the column. A good example of this is the statement column of the *sql_statement_completed* event. This column is turned on by default but might not be necessary to collect in every case. Because providing the statement text has a higher overhead in the event payload, it can be turned off to save this overhead where it doesn't provide a significant benefit—for example, under ad hoc workloads in which the query_hash action is being collected for data aggregation instead. The column schema can be seen in the *sys.dm_xe_object_columns* metadata view as shown in the following query:

```
SELECT *
FROM sys.dm_xe_object_columns
WHERE object_name = N'sql_statement_completed';
```

Actions

Actions in Extended Events provide the capability to execute additional operations when an event fires inside the engine. Actions perform two types of tasks in Extended Events: adding data to an event's output and performing side-effecting tasks such as capturing a memory dump or inserting a debugger break in the SQL Server process where the event is executed. Typically, the only scenario in which you will use the side-effecting task actions is when you are working with product support services to capture additional diagnostic data about a problem occurring in SQL Server.

The most common usage of actions is to add global state data to a firing event—for example, *session_id, nt_username, client_app_name, query_hash, query_plan_hash*, and many others. Keep in mind that actions execute synchronously on the executing thread and add overhead to the event firing inside the engine. A best practice is to add actions only where the additional data will actually be used for diagnosing a problem. Collecting excessive actions increases the amount of data to be buffered and can cause events to be lost, depending on the configuration of the event session options (discussed later in this section).

To see a list of the available actions, you should query *sys.dm_xe_objects*:

```
SELECT p.name AS package_name,
       o.name AS action_name,
       o.description
FROM sys.dm_xe_packages AS p
INNER JOIN sys.dm_xe_objects AS o
    ON p.guid = o.package_guid
WHERE (p.capabilities IS NULL
  OR p.capabilities & 1 = 0)
  AND (o.capabilities IS NULL
  OR o.capabilities & 1 = 0)
  AND o.object_type = N'action';
```

SQL Server 2012 ships with 50 actions, two of which are private and can't be added directly to an event unless *TRACK_CAUSALITY* is enabled for the session. *TRACK CAUSALITY* maps to virtually every predicate source, if you want to filter on a specific source as well as include the actual value in your event's output.

Predicates

Predicates provide the ability to filter the events during event execution, as explained earlier in the "Event execution life cycle" section. Predicate evaluation allows for short-circuiting the event execution by carefully selecting the order of the predicate expression so that the expressions most likely to fail are evaluated first. Extended Events predicates are assigned based on event rather than to the entire session. This is quite a departure from SQL Trace, where filters were defined at the granularity of the entire trace, and so every event used within the trace must abide by the overarching filter set. In Extended Events, if filtering only some events and leaving other events totally unfiltered (or filtered using a different set of criteria) makes sense, that's a perfectly acceptable option.

Predicates can be defined by using *events data columns* or against global state data exposed as *pred_source* objects in the Extended Events metadata. When a predicate is defined using a *pred_source* object, the predicate evaluation during the Event Execution Life Cycle must execute to code to collect the *pred_source* data for use in evaluation. This occurs synchronously on the executing thread and, although very fast, adds a slight overhead to predicate evaluation. Whenever possible, as a best practice, consider defining predicates on *event data* columns first and then on *pred_source* objects to allow short-circuiting to prevent collection of the *pred_source* data if it's not necessary.

The available *pred_source* objects can be found in sys.dm_xe_objects using the following query:

```
SELECT p.name AS package_name,
       o.name AS source_name,
       o.description
FROM sys.dm_xe_objects AS o
INNER JOIN sys.dm_xe_packages AS p
    ON o.package_guid = p.guid
WHERE (p.capabilities IS NULL
   OR p.capabilities & 1 = 0)
  AND (o.capabilities IS NULL
   OR o.capabilities & 1 = 0)
  AND o.object_type = N'pred_source';
```

Predicates in Extended Events also can be defined using common Boolean expressions similar to the standard syntax used in Transact-SQL *WHERE* clause criteria. However, Extended Events also contains 77 comparison functions in SQL Server 2012 that you can use for defining the filtering criteria for events in text. These comparison functions are exposed as *pred_compare* objects in the metadata and can be found in *sys.dm_xe_objects* using the following query:

```
SELECT p.name AS package_name,
       o.name AS source_name,
       o.description
FROM sys.dm_xe_objects AS o
INNER JOIN sys.dm_xe_packages AS p
    ON o.package_guid = p.guid
WHERE (p.capabilities IS NULL
   OR p.capabilities & 1 = 0)
  AND (o.capabilities IS NULL
   OR o.capabilities & 1 = 0)
  AND o.object_type = N'pred_compare';
```

Most comparison functions are overloaded with standard syntax and therefore aren't generally used when defining events because each predicate is limited to just 3,000 characters. A couple of special predicate comparison functions maintain state information and provide advanced filtering capabilities in Extended Events. The *greater_than_max_<type>* and *less_than_min_<type>* comparison functions accept a starting value for comparison and then allow the event to execute only if the current value of the column being filtered is greater than the maximum value, or less than the minimum value respectively, that's stored in the state information for the predicate. The *divides_by_uint64* comparison function tests whether the current value of the column being filtered is evenly divisible by the value for comparison and can be used for defining sampling based filters—for example, to collect only events in which the *session_id* is evenly divisible by four.

Types and maps

In Extended Events, two kinds of data types can be defined: scalar *types* and *maps*. A scalar *type* is a single value—something like an integer, a single Unicode character, or a binary large object. A map, on the other hand, is very similar to an enumeration in most object-oriented systems. The idea for a *map* is that many events have greater value if they can convey to the consumer some human-readable text about what occurred, rather than just a set of machine-readable values. Much of this text can be predefined—for example, the list of wait types supported by SQL Server—and can be stored in a table indexed by an integer. When an event fires, rather than collect the actual text, the event can simply store the integer, thereby saving large amounts of memory and processing resources.

Types and *maps*, like the other objects, are visible in the *sys.dm_xe_objects* DMV. To see a list of both types and maps supported by the system, use the following query:

```
SELECT *
FROM sys.dm_xe_objects
WHERE object_type IN (N'type', N'map');
```

Although *types* are more or less self-describing, *maps* must expose their associated values so that consumers can display the human-readable text when appropriate. This information is available in a DMV called *sys.dm_xe_map_values*. The following query returns all the wait types exposed by the SQL Server engine, along with the *map* keys (the integer representation of the type) used within Extended Events that describe waits:

```
SELECT *
FROM sys.dm_xe_map_values
WHERE name = N'wait_types';
```

In SQL Server 2012, virtually all the *types* are exposed via the *package0* package, whereas each package contains many of its own map values. This makes sense, considering that a scalar *type* such as an integer doesn't need to be redefined repeatedly, whereas *maps* are more aligned to specific purposes.

If you look at this from an architectural point of view, some thought has been put into optimizing the type system by including pass-by-value and pass-by-reference semantics, depending on the object's size. Any object of 8 bytes or smaller is passed by value as the data flows through the system, whereas larger objects are passed by reference using a special Extended Events–specific 8-byte pointer type.

Targets

So far, we have seen events that fire when an instrumented code path is encountered, predicates that filter events so that only interesting data is collected, and actions that can add data to an event's payload. After all this takes place, the final package of event data needs to go somewhere to be collected. This destination for event data is one or more *targets*, which are the means by which Extended Events are consumed.

Targets make up the final object type that has metadata exposed within *sys.dm_xe_objects*. The list of available *targets* can be seen by running the following query:

```
SELECT p.name AS package_name,
       o.name AS target_name,
       o.description
FROM sys.dm_xe_packages AS p
INNER JOIN sys.dm_xe_objects AS o ON p.guid = o.package_guid
WHERE (p.capabilities IS NULL
   OR p.capabilities & 1 = 0)
  AND (o.capabilities IS NULL
   OR o.capabilities & 1 = 0)
  AND o.object_type = N'target';
```

SQL Server 2012 ships with nine *targets* for Extended Events. However, three of these are private *targets* used by the streaming API in .NET for buffering event data to a live reader connected to a session and can't be used in an event session definition. When the API opens a connection for streaming access to an active session, the Extended Events engine modifies the event session to use the required private *targets*. Of the remaining six *targets* available in Extended Events, two are marked *synchronous* in the *capabilities_desc* column. These *targets* collect event data synchronously—much like actions—before control is returned to the code that caused the event to fire. The other four *targets*, in comparison, are asynchronous, meaning that the data is buffered before being collected by the *target* at some point after the event fires. Buffering results in better performance for the code that caused the event to fire, but it also introduces latency into the process because the *target* might not collect the event for some time.

Extended Events *targets* can be classified into two different types of operations: data collecting and data aggregating. Four *targets*—three public and one *private* (the streaming API *target*)—collect the raw event data for further analysis.

- **event_file**   This target is similar to the SQL Trace file I/O provider, which buffers data before writing it out to a proprietary binary file format.

- **etw_classic_sync_target**   This file-based target synchronously writes data to a file format suitable for consumption by any number of ETW-enabled readers.

- **ring_buffer**   This target stores data in an in-memory ring buffer with a user-configurable size. A ring buffer loops back to the start of the buffer when it fills and begins overwriting data collected earlier. This means that the buffer can consume an endless quantity of data without using all available system memory, but only the newest data is available at any particular time.

■ **event_stream**   This private target provides streaming access to the event data through internal mechanisms that copy the buffers into an additional set of memory buffers whenever the streaming .NET API is connected to an active event session. It's used by the Live Data Viewer inside SQL Server Management Studio to read the event data from the server, but can also be used by third-party applications for accessing the data in near real time.

The data-aggregating *targets* store the event data in memory in SQL Server but don't store all event data in its original form.

■ **event_counter**   This target synchronously counts the number of times events have fired. Along these same lines the histogram target creates buckets based on a user-specified column or action, and counts the number of times that a specific event occurs within each bucket.

■ **pair_matching**   This target is designed to help find instances where a pair of events is expected to occur, but one or the other isn't firing due to a bug or some other problem. This target works by asynchronously collecting events defined by the user as begin events, and then matching them to events user-defined as end events. The actual matching can be performed using one or more of the event columns and actions defined for the event. When a pair of successfully matched events is found, both events are dropped, leaving only those events that didn't have a match.

This target shouldn't be used for certain event pairs in which SQL Server functionality can result in false unmatched pairs occurring in the target data. For example, you might consider using this target with the l*ock_acquired* and *lock_released* events. However, if lock escalation occurs, only a single *lock_released* event executes for escalated lock, resulting in unpaired events for all the lower granularity *lock_acquired* events that executed.

Because targets can be used with one another, you can bind multiple targets to a single session, rather than create many sessions to collect the same data. For example, you can create an event session using the *pair_matching* target with the *event_file* and/or *ring_buffer* target to record all data for troubleshooting the cause of unpaired events in the *pair_matching* target. You can apply the same method when using the *histogram* target to allow for further aggregation of the raw data for analysis of minimum, maximum, or average values later in another column.

As with the SQL Trace providers, some action must occur when more data enters the system than can be processed in a reasonable amount of time. With synchronous *targets*, things are simple; the calling code waits until the *target* returns control, and the target waits until its event data is fully consumed. With asynchronous *targets*, however, a number of configuration options dictate how to handle the situation.

When event data buffers begin to fill up, the engine can take one of three possible actions depending on how you configured the session.

■ **Block, waiting for buffer space to become available (no event loss)**   This is the same behavior characterized by the SQL Trace file provider and can cause performance degradation.

- **Drop the waiting event (allow single event loss)**   In this case, the system drops only a single event at a time while waiting for more buffer space to free up. This is the default mode.

- **Drop a full buffer (allow multiple event loss)**   Each buffer can contain many events, and the number of events lost depends on event size as well as buffer size (described shortly).

The various options are listed here in decreasing order of their impact on overall system performance should buffers begin filling up, and in increasing order of the number of events that can be lost while waiting for buffers to become free. Choosing an option that reflects the amount of acceptable data loss while keeping in mind that blocking occurs if too restrictive of an option is used is important. Liberal use of predicates, careful attention to the number of actions bound to each event, and attention to other configuration options, all help you avoid having to worry about buffers filling up and whether the choice of these options is a major issue.

Along with specifying what should happen when buffers fill up, you can specify how much memory is allocated, how the memory is allocated across CPU or NUMA node boundaries, and how often buffers are cleared.

By default, one central set of buffers, consuming a maximum of 4 MB of memory, is created for each Extended Events session (as described in the next section). The central set of buffers by default contains three buffers, each consuming one-third of the maximum amount of memory specified. You can override these defaults, creating one set of buffers per CPU or one set per NUMA node, and increasing or decreasing the amount of memory that each set of buffers consumes. Also, you can specify that events larger than the maximum allocated buffer memory should be allowed to fire. In that case, those events are stored in special large memory buffers.

Another default option is that buffers are cleared every 30 seconds or when they fill up. You can override this option, changing the value of the MAX_DISPATCH_LATENCY session option for the event session. Doing so causes the buffers to be checked and cleared both at a specific time interval (specified as a number of seconds) and when they fill up.

Note that each of these settings is applied not based on individual targets, but rather to any number of targets bound to a session. The next section explores how this works.

Event sessions

You've now gone through each element that makes up the core Extended Events infrastructure. Bringing each of these together into a cohesive unit at runtime are *sessions*, the Extended Events equivalent of a *trace* in SQL Trace parlance. A session describes the events that you are interested in collecting, predicates against which events should be filtered, actions that should fire with the events, the targets that should be used for data collection at the end of the cycle, and the event session options that control how the events fire and are buffered to the targets for the event session(s).

You can create any number of sessions if you have adequate server-level permission, and sessions, for the most part, are independent of one another, just as with SQL Trace. The main thread that links any number of sessions is a central bitmap that indicates whether a specific event is enabled. An event can be enabled simultaneously in any number of sessions, but the global bitmap is used to avoid having to check each of those sessions at runtime. Beyond this level, sessions are completely separate from one another, and each uses its own memory and has its own set of defined objects.

Extended Events DDL and querying

To complete the overview of Extended Events, we'll take a quick tour of the session-creation DDL and see how all the objects apply to what you can control when creating actual sessions. You will also see an example of how to query some of the data collected by an Extended Events session.

Creating an event session

The primary DDL hook for Extended Events is the *CREATE EVENT SESSION* statement, which allows you to create sessions and map all the various Extended Events objects. An *ALTER EVENT SESSION* statement also exists, allowing you to modify a session that has already been created. To modify the session level options for an existing session, it must not be active. Modifying the events or targets for an active event session can occur while the session is active.

The following T-SQL statement creates a session and shows how to configure all the Extended Events features and options reviewed in this chapter:

```
CREATE EVENT SESSION [statement_completed]
ON SERVER
ADD EVENT
    sqlserver.sp_statement_completed
    (   ACTION (sqlserver.session_id)
        WHERE (sqlserver.is_system = 0)),
ADD EVENT
    sqlserver.sql_statement_completed
    (   ACTION (sqlserver.session_id)
        WHERE (sqlserver.is_system = 0))
ADD TARGET
    package0.ring_buffer
    (   SET max_memory=4096)
WITH
(   MAX_MEMORY = 4096KB,
    EVENT_RETENTION_MODE = ALLOW_SINGLE_EVENT_LOSS,
    MAX_DISPATCH_LATENCY = 1 SECONDS,
    MEMORY_PARTITION_MODE = NONE,
    TRACK_CAUSALITY = OFF,
    STARTUP_STATE = OFF);
```

The session is called *statement_completed,* and two events are bound: *sp_statement_completed* and *sql_statement_completed,* both exposed by the *sqlserver* package. These events fire inside the engine whenever a stored procedure, function, or trigger statement completes execution or when a SQL statement completes inside a SQL batch, respectively. Both events collect the *session_id* action when they fire, and they have been filtered on the *is_system pred_source* object to exclude system sessions from generating events. One item to note, even though it isn't shown in this example, is that the *WHERE* clause supports *AND, OR,* and parentheses; you can create complex predicates that combine many different conditions, if needed.

When the *sql_statement_completed* event fires for session ID 53, the event session invokes the *session_id* action. This action collects the *session_id* of the session that executed the statement that caused the event to fire and adds it to the event's data. After the event data is collected, it's pushed to the *ring_buffer* target, which is configured to use a maximum of 4,096 KB of memory.

Some session-level options have also been configured. The session's asynchronous buffers can't consume more than 4,096 KB of memory, and if they fill up, events are allowed to be dropped. That's probably not likely to happen, though, because the dispatcher has been configured to clear the buffers every second. Because memory isn't partitioned across CPUs, three buffers are the result. Also, causality tracking isn't in use. Finally, after the session is created, it exists only as metadata; it doesn't start until the following statement is issued:

```
ALTER EVENT SESSION [statement_completed]
ON SERVER
STATE=START;
```

Querying event data

When the session is started, the ring buffer target is updated every second with new events (assuming that any exist). Each in-memory target exposes its data in XML format in the *target_data* column of the *sys.dm_xe_session_targets* DMV. Because the data is in XML format, using XQuery is necessary to query the data directly with Transact-SQL. However, if you don't know XQuery, you can use the new Extended Events UI (covered in detail in the next section) in Management Studio to read the target data of every target except for the *ring_buffer* target, even though it can read a live stream of events from a session that's using the *ring_buffer* target.

Consuming the XML in a tabular format requires knowledge of which nodes are present. In the case of the *ring buffer* target, a root node called *RingBufferTarget* includes one event node for each event that fires. The event node contains one data node for each attribute contained within the event data and one "action" node for actions bound to the event. These data and action nodes contain three nodes each: one node called *type,* which indicates the data type; one called *value*, which includes the value in most cases; and one called *text,* which is for longer text values.

Explaining how to query every possible event and target is beyond the scope of this book, but a quick sample query based on the *statement_completed* session follows. You can use this query as a base from which to work up queries against other events and actions when working with the *ring buffer* target:

```
SELECT
    ed.value('(@name)[1]', 'varchar(50)') AS event_name,
    ed.value('(data[@name="source_database_id"]/value)[1]', 'bigint') AS source_database_id,
    ed.value('(data[@name="object_id"]/value)[1]', 'bigint') AS object_id,
    ed.value('(data[@name="object_type"]/value)[1]', 'bigint') AS object_type,
    COALESCE(ed.value('(data[@name="cpu"]/value)[1]', 'bigint'),
            ed.value('(data[@name="cpu_time"]/value)[1]', 'bigint')) AS cpu,
    ed.value('(data[@name="duration"]/value)[1]', 'bigint') AS duration,
    COALESCE(ed.value('(data[@name="reads"]/value)[1]', 'bigint'),
            ed.value('(data[@name="logical_reads"]/value)[1]', 'bigint')) AS reads,
    ed.value('(data[@name="writes"]/value)[1]', 'bigint') AS writes,
    ed.value('(action[@name="session_id"]/value)[1]', 'int') AS session_id,
    ed.value('(data[@name="statement"]/value)[1]', 'varchar(50)') AS statement
FROM
(
    SELECT
        CONVERT(XML, st.target_data) AS target_data
    FROM sys.dm_xe_sessions s
    INNER JOIN sys.dm_xe_session_targets st ON
        s.address = st.event_session_address
    WHERE s.name = N'statement_completed'
        AND st.target_name = N'ring_buffer'
) AS tab
CROSS APPLY target_data.nodes('//RingBufferTarget/event') t(ed);
```

This query converts the *ring buffer* data to an XML instance and then uses the *nodes* XML function to create one row per event node found. It then uses the ordinal positions of the various data elements within the event nodes to map the data to output columns. Of course, more advanced sessions require more advanced XQuery to determine the type of each event and do some case logic if the events involved in the session have different schemas—which the two in this example don't. When you reach this point, the data is just that—standard tabular data, which can be aggregated, joined, inserted into a table, or whatever else you want to do with it.

You can also read from the *event_file* target via T-SQL, using the *sys.fn_xe_file_target_read_file* table-valued function. This function returns one row per event, but you still have to get comfortable with XML; the event's data, exposed in a column called *event_data,* is in an XML format similar to data in the *ring buffer* target. The new UI can also process files generated by the *event_file* target and is much more efficient at shredding the event data into an actionable form than native XQuery is.

Stopping and removing the event session

After you finish reading data from the event session, it can be stopped using the following code:

```
ALTER EVENT SESSION [statement_completed]
ON SERVER
STATE=STOP;
```

Stopping the event session doesn't remove the metadata. To eliminate the session from the server completely, you must drop it using the following statement:

```
DROP EVENT SESSION [statement_completed]
ON SERVER;
```

Extended Events UI

The new user interface in SQL Server 2012 for Extended Events simplifies using Extended Events similarly to the way Profiler simplifies using SQL Trace Trace, specifically for reading data. Although a number of the UI features have been targeted toward making Extended Events easier to use without understanding all the information that precedes this section, the UI also provides access to all the features and functionality of Extended Events to someone that understands everything that's possible. This section introduces the UI and the most important features for managing and consuming event data.

Creating and managing event sessions

The Extended Events UI provides two methods of creating new event sessions in SQL Server 2012; the *New Session Wizard* and the *New Session window*. The *New Session Wizard* is simply a trimmed-down version of the *New Session window* and provides a limited set of functionality to allow an event session to be created faster. Both features are available through the right-click context menu on the *Sessions* folder under the *Extended Events* node in *Object Explorer*.

Using the wizard restricts an event session to being able to filter only on columns that exist in every event in the session or to the predicate source data globally available to all events. Any actions selected in the wizard are also applied globally to every event in the session, and only *ring_buffer* or *event_file* targets can be added to the session. However, after the wizard creates an event session, it can be opened and manually edited to change the event predicates, add targets, or change the session options.

The *New Session window* provides more options over the wizard for creating an event session. The window's *General* page (see Figure 2-5) provides the session name and allows you to choose a template to use for the event session. Templates store the entire definition for an event session and can be used to rapidly re-create the session on a server. SQL Server 2012 ships with nine event session templates with default configurations and also enables you to create customized templates by exporting an existing event session to XML. The *General page* includes the most common event session options to help with streamlining session creation. You can toggle the option for the session to start automatically when SQL Server starts, which sets the *STARTUP_STATE* option to *ON*, and enable the *TRACK_CAUSALITY* option by selecting the option to Track How Events Are Related To One Another. Two additional options not related to the event session definition, but are instead additional features of creating the event session with the UI, are Start The Event Session Immediately After Session Creation and Watch Live Data On Screen As It Is Captured, which is covered later in this section.

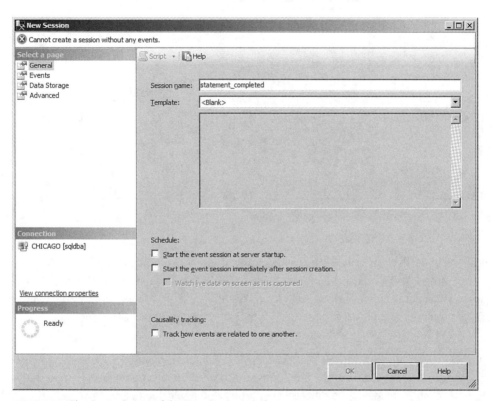

FIGURE 2-5 The General page of the New Session window.

The Events page in the window allows events to added or removed from the event session. You can search the event list by typing the search into the text box and selecting the appropriate search field in the drop-down list. For example, you can find any *statement_completed* events by searching the event names, as shown in Figure 2-6. More information about a specific event, including its description and column list, are displayed below the event list when an event is selected.

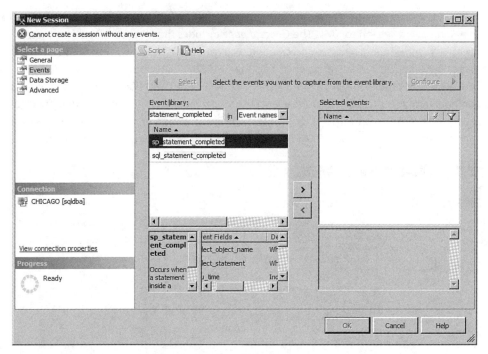

FIGURE 2-6 The Events page of the New Session window.

Note As you can probably already tell from the screenshots in this section, space in this UI is very limited. The screenshots were taken at 1024x768, the minimum resolution required for the UI to fit onscreen. If you have a lower resolution, you can't use the UI effectively; you generally have a better experience the higher your resolution is.

After the events are added to the event session, you can further configure the events to include actions and predicates by clicking the Configure button. You can select multiple events at the same time so that changes made on the different tabs affect all the selected events. However, just as in the wizard, only those columns that are common across all the events or the global predicate sources can be used to add filters to the events. You can add individual actions to the selected events by toggling the check box for the action in the Global Fields (Actions) tab. The Filtering (Predicate) tab, shown in Figure 2-7, provides a predicate editor grid that allows you to add new expressions to an event and group or ungroup expressions into complex predicates, which are expressed in the DDL using parenthesis around each grouping. The grid also allows the use of comparison functions or standard operators. The Event Fields tab allows the customizable columns for an event to be toggled on or off.

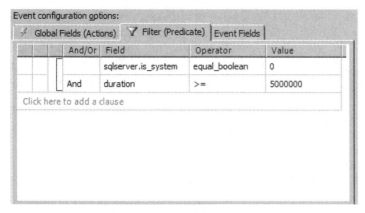

FIGURE 2-7 New Session Event Filter (Predicate) tab.

The Data Storage page allows targets to be added to the event session. When a specific target is selected in the grid, its specific configuration options are displayed below the grid. For example, selecting the *ring_buffer* target in the Type column changes the UI, as shown in Figure 2-8.

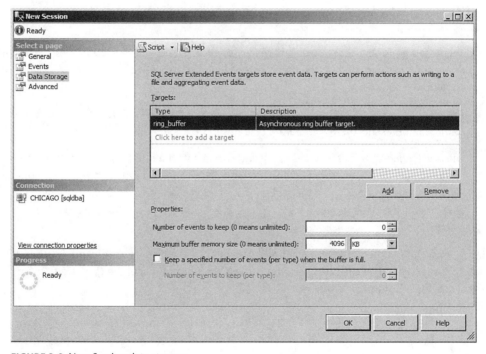

FIGURE 2-8 New Session data storage.

The *Advanced page* contains all remaining session options that haven't been shown in one of the previous pages. These include the event retention mode, dispatch latency, and memory configuration options for the session. Like every other window in Management Studio, the *New Session window* allows you to automatically perform the operation configured in the UI by clicking OK, or you can script the operation by using the *Script button* at the top of the window, which provides the same scripting options as other windows.

Viewing Target Data

The Extended Events UI provides the ability to read the current contents of many of the targets, removing the need to build XQuery statements to process the data. Two exceptions exist for this.

- The *etw_classic_sync_target* can't be read using the UI because the data is intended for use with other ETW data from Windows. Also, other steps and tools exist for performing ETW analysis, such as *xperf* and *xperfview* from the Windows Software Development Kit (SDK).

- The *ring_buffer* target returns the raw XML to the UI whenever the *View Target Data* menu option is selected from its context menu.

For the remaining in-memory targets, the UI handles the target data based on the target being viewed.

- The *histogram* target contains only the value of each bucket and the count of how many times that bucket has occurred, so the data viewer shows only a two-column table containing value and count columns.

- The event_counter target tracks only three columns of data—*package_name*, *event_name*, and *count*—and presents them as separate columns in the data table.

- The *pair_matching* target is based on having two events that are supposed to correlate to one another, so in theory the events should have similar column outputs and would be configured with a similar set of actions, if the matching is action based. When the *pair_matching* target data is read, the UI generates a table with all event columns and actions laid out in separate columns.

Each view for the in-memory targets has a refresh interval that you can configure through the right-click context menu on the grid. Also, you can export the contents of the grid to a CSV file or copy it to the clipboard for use elsewhere.

The most common use of the UI for viewing data is for watching live event streams in the live data view or reading files that have previously been saved from a live stream by the UI or created by the event_file target in the servers file system. These two features provide a very similar set of functionality, with the only difference being that you can't perform grouping and aggregation of data in the live data view.

When an event log file is opened in Management Studio or the live data view is opened initially, the UI presents a grid with two columns available: the event name and the timestamp for when the event was generated (see Figure 2-9). This default view is created because 1,174 distinct column names are available across the events in SQL Server 2012, and 50 possible actions can be added to the events in a session. This makes creating a common meaningful layout impossible for every event session, and because the only two columns guaranteed to exist for every event are the event name and timestamp, they are the only default columns in the grid.

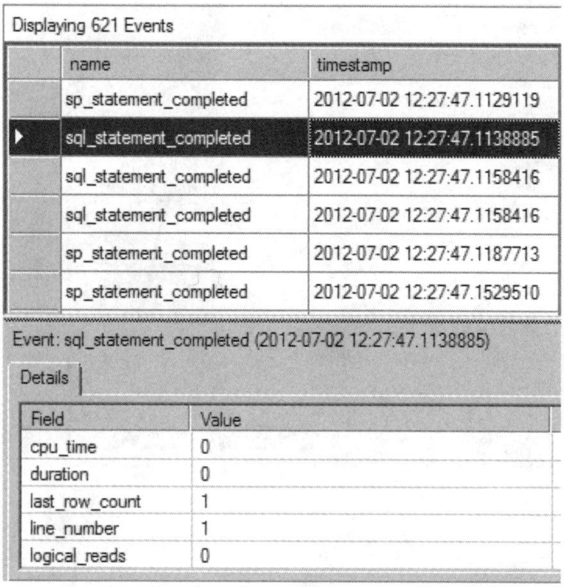

Displaying 621 Events

name	timestamp
sp_statement_completed	2012-07-02 12:27:47.1129119
sql_statement_completed	2012-07-02 12:27:47.1138885
sql_statement_completed	2012-07-02 12:27:47.1158416
sql_statement_completed	2012-07-02 12:27:47.1158416
sp_statement_completed	2012-07-02 12:27:47.1187713
sp_statement_completed	2012-07-02 12:27:47.1529510

Event: sql_statement_completed (2012-07-02 12:27:47.1138885)

Details

Field	Value
cpu_time	0
duration	0
last_row_count	1
line_number	1
logical_reads	0

FIGURE 2-9 Event log file and live data view.

Two methods exist to add columns to the grid layout. In the lower *Details pane* in Figure 2-9, the right-click context menu for a row contains the *Show Column In Table option*, which adds the selected column to the end of the columns now displayed. The UI also contains a *Choose Columns* dialog box that you can open from the right-click context menu on the grid column names, through the Extended Events menu, or by using the *Choose Columns* toolbar button. The *Choose Columns* dialog box, shown in Figure 2-10, helps you add multiple columns to the grid, change the column order in the grid, or create a merged column (see Figure 2-11) that presents the data from multiple columns in a single customized column in the grid.

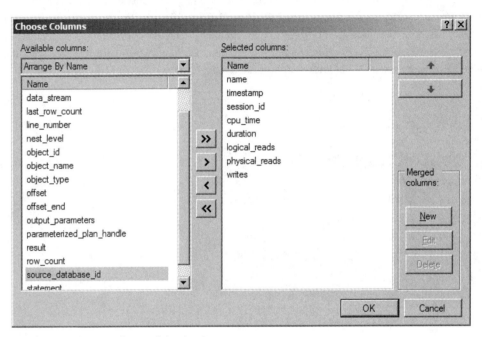

FIGURE 2-10 Choose Columns dialog box.

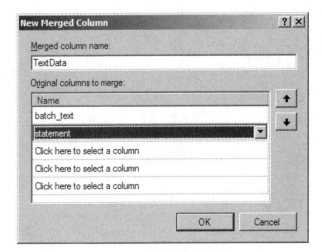

FIGURE 2-11 New Merged Column dialog box.

After you configure the display options for the grid, you can save them by using the *Display Settings menu* under the Extended Events menu, or by using the toolbar drop-down list of the same name. By saving the display options, you can reuse them in the future when viewing similar sets of events and actions in the data grid. The data in the grid can be searched, filtered, sorted, and—when the grid isn't connected to a live stream—grouped and aggregated to simplify analysis of the collected data. To search the grid, you can use the *Find menu* option in the Extended Events menu, use the binocular button on the toolbar, or right-click the context menu on the grid column names. Filtering events in the grid is a local operation only and affects what events the grid will display; it doesn't affect the data actually being collected by a live stream if the grid is still connected to the event session.

Grouping and aggregating the data in the grid is much more robust than the grouping capabilities of Profiler and can be used to simplify data analysis over long periods of time. Event grouping can be performed using one or more columns. Grouping by an individual column can be accomplished using the right-click context menu on the column name for the grid and selecting the *Group By This Column* option. To open the *Grouping dialog box* (see Figure 2-12), use the *Grouping option* on the Extended Events menu or the toolbar button with the same name. The dialog box enables you to group by multiple columns and to specify the column order to use.

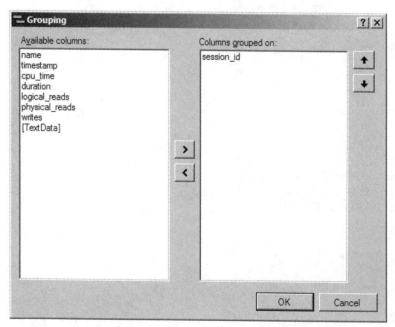

FIGURE 2-12 Grouping dialog box.

After the events are grouped (see Figure 2-13), you can calculate aggregations for the individual columns through the *Calculate Aggregation option* on the right-click context menu for the column names. You also can create aggregations for multiple columns via the Aggregation dialog box, which you can open with the *Aggregation option* on the Extended Events menu or the toolbar button with the same name. The aggregations can be made using *SUM, MIN, MAX, AVG,* or *COUNT* for each column. To remove an aggregation from a column, set *Aggregation to None* for the column. You can sort the aggregated values in the *Aggregation dialog box*, as shown in Figure 2-14, or through the right-click context menu on the column names in the grid. To sort the column data within an aggregated group, click the column name in the grid header. Figure 2-15 shows the data sorted by the duration column aggregation in the grid.

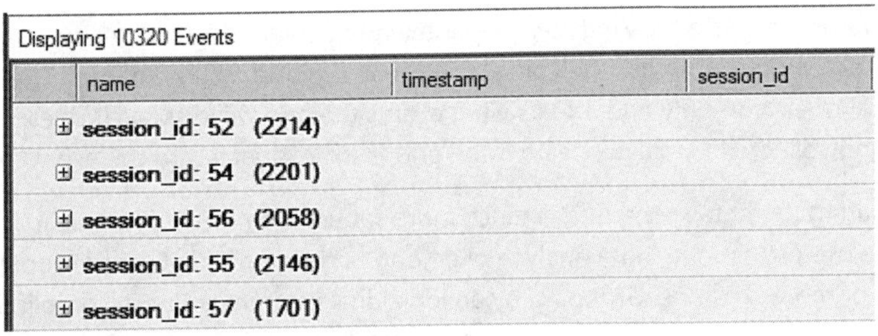

Displaying 10320 Events

name	timestamp	session_id
⊞ **session_id**: 52 (2214)		
⊞ **session_id**: 54 (2201)		
⊞ **session_id**: 56 (2058)		
⊞ **session_id**: 55 (2146)		
⊞ **session_id**: 57 (1701)		

FIGURE 2-13 Grid with events grouped.

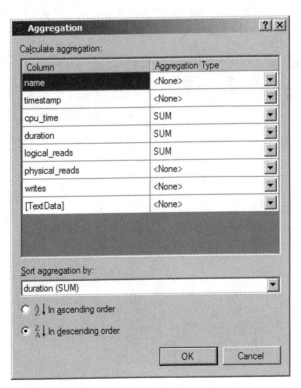

FIGURE 2-14 Aggregation dialog box.

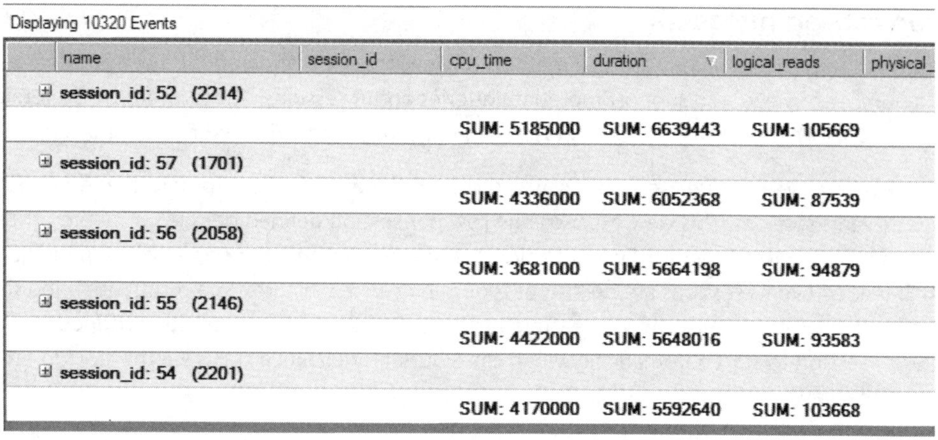

name	session_id	cpu_time	duration	logical_reads	physical_
⊞ **session_id: 52 (2214)**					
		SUM: 5185000	SUM: 6639443	SUM: 105669	
⊞ **session_id: 57 (1701)**					
		SUM: 4336000	SUM: 6052368	SUM: 87539	
⊞ **session_id: 56 (2058)**					
		SUM: 3681000	SUM: 5664198	SUM: 94879	
⊞ **session_id: 55 (2146)**					
		SUM: 4422000	SUM: 5648016	SUM: 93583	
⊞ **session_id: 54 (2201)**					
		SUM: 4170000	SUM: 5592640	SUM: 103668	

Displaying 10320 Events

FIGURE 2-15 Data grouped and aggregated in the UI.

One great benefit of the data grid in the UI is the improved performance over using the *sys.fn_xe_file_target_read_file* table-valued function and XQuery used through Transact-SQL. However, when connected to a live stream, an event session can generate events faster than the UI can actually consume the server-side buffers. When this occurs, the live stream is disconnected by the Extended Events engine to prevent a negative effect to server performance. If this occurs and you are relying on the live data stream for near real-time analysis, the session definition might need to be changed to reduce the number of events being generated or possibly to filter the existing events to reduce the number of events being generated. This is a good case for using the event_counter target to test how many events the session will generate before actually collecting the data. If the number of events can't be reduced, consider using the *event_file* target with rollover and then reading the files using the UI for analysis.

Any data captured by the live data stream, or read into the data grid from an event file, can be exported from the grid after it is filtered. You can export data to an event file in the file system, a table in a database, or to a CSV file using the *Export To option* on the *Extended Events menu*. The UI also enables you to merge event files using the *Merge Extended Event Files option* on the *File and Open menu*. This capability can be very useful when diagnosing problems for the new Availability Group feature in SQL Server 2012, where each replica in the topology has an *AlwaysOn_health* session running on it to monitor the health of the Availability Group, or for merging files for the *system_health* session running on every instance of SQL Server 2008 onward to monitor performance conditions that could negatively affect the SQL Server instance.

Session catalog metadata

Although the UI provides an easy-to-use method of viewing information about a server's event sessions, a number of views also support metadata queries about sessions. These might be preferable to use in situations where tasks need to be performed uniformly across many servers using scripting.

The *sys.server_event_sessions* catalog view is the central metadata store for information about Extended Events sessions. This view exposes one row per session defined on the SQL Server instance. Like traces in SQL Trace, Extended Events sessions can be started and stopped at will. But unlike traces, Extended Events sessions are persistent regarding service restarts; as a result, querying the view before and after a restart shows the same results unless a session is explicitly dropped. You can configure a session to start automatically when the SQL Server instance starts via the *startup_state* column of the view.

Along with the central *sys.server_event_sessions* views are a number of other views describing details of how the session was configured. The *sys.server_event_session_events* view exposes one row per event bound to each session and includes a predicate column that contains the definition of the predicate used to filter the event, if one has been set. Actions and targets have similar views, namely *sys.server_event_session_actions* and *sys.server_event_session_targets*. A final view, *sys.server_event_session_fields*, contains information about settings that you can customize for a particular event or target. For example, you can set the ring buffer target's memory consumption to a specific amount; if the target is used, the memory setting appears in this view.

Session-scoped configuration options

As mentioned earlier in this chapter, a number of settings are set globally for a session and, in turn, influence the runtime behavior of the objects that make up the session.

The first set of session-scoped options includes those already discussed: options that determine how asynchronous target buffers are configured, both from a memory and latency standpoint. These settings influence a process called the *dispatcher,* which is responsible for periodically collecting data from the buffers and sending it to each asynchronous target bound to the session. The frequency with which the dispatcher is activated depends on how you've configured the memory and latency settings. If a latency value of *infinite* is specified, the dispatcher doesn't dispatch data except when the buffers are full. Otherwise, the dispatcher dispatches data at the interval determined by the setting—as often as once a second.

You can use the *sys.dm_xe_sessions* DMV to monitor whether any problems are occurring dispatching asynchronous buffers. This DMV exposes one row per Extended Events session that has been started and exposes a number of columns that can provide insight into how buffers are being handled. The most important columns are the following.

- **regular_buffer_size and total_regular_buffers**   These columns expose the number of buffers created (based on the maximum memory and memory partitioning settings) as well as the size of each buffer. Knowing these numbers and estimating the approximate size for each event tells you how many events you might lose in case of a full buffer situation should you use the allow multiple event loss option.

- **dropped_event_count and dropped_buffer_count**   These columns expose the number of events and/or buffers dropped because not enough free buffer space is available to accommodate incoming event data.

- **blocked_event_fire_time**   This column exposes the amount of time that blocking occurred, if the no event loss option was used.

Another session-scoped option that you can enable is *CAUSALITY_TRACKING*. This option enables you to use a SQL Server engine feature to help correlate events either when parent-child relationships exist between tasks on the same thread or when one thread causes activity to occur on another thread. In the engine code, these relationships are tracked by each task defining a GUID, known as an *activity ID*. When a child task is called, the ID is passed along and continues down the stack as subsequent tasks are called. If activity needs to pass to another thread, the ID is passed in a structure called a *transfer block*, and the same logic continues.

These identifiers are exposed via two Extended Events actions: *package0.attach_activity_id* and *package0.attach_activity_id_xfer*. However, these actions can't be attached to an event by a user creating a session. Instead, you must enable the causality tracking option at the session level, which automatically binds the actions to every event defined for the session. When the actions are enabled, both the activity ID and activity transfer ID are added to each event's payload.

Conclusion

The SQLOS inside SQL Server provides the interfaces between the internal components in SQL Server and the actual operating system for thread scheduling, memory allocation, and synchronization objects. This centralized implementation makes SQL Server much more scalable and simplifies the design over previous versions of SQL Server, in which the individual components had to independently implement the interfaces with the operating system. In addition to providing centralization of the interfaces, SQLOS also provides implementations for tracking the memory usage by the individual components through the memory brokers, cache stores, and object pools internally. SQLOS also provides the capability to control session resource usage through the Resource Governor feature inside SQL Server, allowing you to control execution memory and CPU usage limits for different workload groups and pools defined in the engine, along with providing the framework for collecting diagnostics data from SQL Server with the Extended Events implementation.

CHAPTER 3

Databases and database files

Kalen Delaney

Simply put, a Microsoft SQL Server database is a collection of objects that hold and manipulate data. A typical SQL Server instance has only a handful of databases, but it's not unusual for a single instance to contain several dozen databases. The technical limit for one SQL Server instance is 32,767 databases. Practically speaking, however, this limit would never be reached.

To elaborate a bit, you can think of a SQL Server database as having the following properties and features.

- It's a collection of many objects, such as tables, views, stored procedures, functions, and constraints. The technical limit is 231–1 (more than 2 billion) objects. The number of objects typically ranges from hundreds to tens of thousands

- It's owned by a single SQL Server login account.

- It maintains its own set of user accounts, roles, schemas, and security.

- It has its own set of system tables to hold the database catalog.

- It's the primary unit of recovery and maintains logical consistency among objects within it. For example, primary and foreign key relationships always refer to other tables within the same database, not in other databases.

- It has its own transaction log and manages its own transactions.

- It can span multiple disk drives and operating system files.

- It can range in size from 2 MB to a technical limit of 1524,272 TB.

- It can grow and shrink automatically or manually.

- It can have objects joined in queries with objects from other databases in the same SQL Server instance or on linked servers.

- It can have specific properties enabled or disabled. For example, you can set a database to be read-only or to be a source of published data in replication.

Here is what a SQL Server database is *not*.

- It's not synonymous with an entire SQL Server instance.

- It's not a single SQL Server table.

- It's not a specific operating system file.

While a database isn't the same thing as an operating system file, it always exists in two or more such files. These files, known as SQL Server *database files*, are specified either at the time the database is created using the CREATE DATABASE command, or afterward using the ALTER DATABASE command.

Working with sample databases

Prior to SQL Server 2005, the installation program automatically installed sample databases so you would have some actual data for exploring SQL Server functionality. As part of Microsoft's efforts to tighten security, SQL Server 2012 doesn't automatically install any sample databases. However, several sample databases are widely available.

AdventureWorks

AdventureWorks actually comprises a family of sample databases created by the Microsoft User Education group as an example of what a "real" database might look like. The family includes Adventure-Works, AdventureWorksDW, and AdventureWorksLT. Each new version has updated these databases (the originals were created for SQL Server 2005). So you might see databases called Adventure-Works2008, AdventureWorks2008R2 and AdventureWorks2012. You can download these databases from the Microsoft codeplex site at *http://www.codeplex.com/SqlServerSamples*.

The *AdventureWorks* database was designed to showcase SQL Server features, including the organization of objects into different schemas. These databases are based on data needed by the fictitious Adventure Works Cycles company. The database is designed to support Online Transaction Processing (OLTP) applications; AdventureWorksDW, designed to support the business intelligence features of SQL Server, is based on a completely different database architecture. Both designs are highly normalized. Although normalized data and many separate schemas might map closely to a real production database's design, they can make it quite difficult to write and test simple queries and to learn basic SQL.

Database design isn't a major focus of this book, so most of the examples use simple tables created by the authors. If more than a few rows of data are needed, the authors sometimes copy data from one or more *AdventureWorks* tables into their own tables. Becoming familiar with the design of the *AdventureWorks* database is a good idea because many of the examples in SQL Server Books Online and in white papers published on the Microsoft website (*http://www.microsoft.com/sqlserver/2008/en/us/white-papers.aspx*) use data from this database.

Note If you want, you can install the AdventureWorksLT database, which is a highly simpli-fied and somewhat denormalized version of the AdventureWorks OLTP database that fo-cuses on a simple sales scenario with a single schema.

pubs

The *pubs* database is a sample database used extensively in earlier versions of SQL Server. Many older publications with SQL Server examples assume that you have this database because it was installed automatically on versions of SQL Server prior to SQL Server 2005. You can download a script for building this database from Microsoft's website; this script is also included with this book's companion content.

The *pubs* database is admittedly simple, but that simplicity is a feature, not a drawback. It provides good examples without a lot of peripheral issues to obscure the central points. Don't worry about modifying the *pubs* database as you experiment with SQL Server features. You can rebuild it from scratch by running the supplied script. In a query window, open the file named *instpubs.sql* and ex-ecute it. Make sure that no current connections to *pubs* are active because the current *pubs* database is dropped before the new one is created.

Northwind

The sample *Northwind* database was originally developed for use with Microsoft Office Access. Much of the pre–SQL Server 2005 documentation dealing with application programming interfaces (APIs) uses *Northwind*. *Northwind* is a bit more complex than *pubs* and, at almost 4 MB, is slightly larger. As with *pubs*, you can download a script (instnwnd.sql) from the Microsoft website to build it, or you can use the script provided with the companion content. Also, some sample scripts for this book use a modified copy of Northwind called Northwind2.

Understanding database files

A database file is nothing more than an operating system file. (In addition to database files, SQL Serv-er also has *backup devices,* which are logical devices that map to operating system files or to physical devices such as tape drives. This chapter won't discuss files used to store backups.) A database spans at least two, and possibly several, database files, which are specified when a database is created or altered. Every database must span at least two files: one for the data (as well as indexes and allocation pages) and one for the transaction log.

SQL Server 2012 allows the following three types of database files.

- **Primary data files**   Every database has one primary data file that keeps track of all the rest of the files in the database, in addition to storing data. By convention, a primary data file has the extension .mdf.

- **Secondary data files** A database can have zero or more secondary data files. By convention, a secondary data file has the extension .ndf.

- **Log files** Every database has at least one log file that contains the information necessary to recover all transactions in a database. By convention, a log file has the extension .ldf.

SQL Server 2012 databases also can have filestream and FileTable data files, as well as full-text data files. Filestream and FileTable data files are discussed later in the section "Filestream filegroups." Full-text data files are created and managed completely separately from other database files and are discussed in Chapter 9, "Special indexes."

Each database file has five properties that you can specify when you create the file: a logical filename, a physical filename, an initial size, a maximum size, and a growth increment. (Filestream data files have only the logical and physical name properties.) The values of these properties, along with other information about each file, can be seen through the metadata view *sys.database_files*, which contains one row for each file used by a database. Table 3-1 lists most columns shown in *sys.database_files*. The columns not mentioned here contain information dealing with transaction log backups relevant to the particular file. (Chapter 5, "Logging and recovery," discusses transaction logs.)

TABLE 3-1 The sys.database_files catalog view

Column	Description
Fileid	The file identification number (unique for each database).
file_guid	Globally unique identifier (GUID) for the file. *NULL* = Database was upgraded from an earlier version of SQL Server.
Type	File type: 0 = Rows (includes full-text catalogs upgraded to or created in SQL Server 2012) 1 = Log 2 = FILESTREAM 3 = Reserved for future use 4 = Full-text (full-text catalogs from versions earlier than SQL Server 2012; full-text catalogs upgraded to or created in SQL Server 2012 show a file type of 0)
type_desc	Description of the file type: *ROWS, LOG, FILESTREAM, FULLTEXT*
data_space_id	ID of the data space to which this file belongs. Data space is a filegroup. 0 = Log file
name	The logical filename.
physical_name	Operating system filename.
State	File state: 0 = ONLINE 1 = RESTORING 2 = RECOVERING 3 = RECOVERY_PENDING 4 = SUSPECT 5 = Reserved for future use 6 = OFFLINE 7 = DEFUNCT

Column	Description
state_desc	Description of the file state: ONLINE RESTORING RECOVERING RECOVERY_PENDING SUSPECT OFFLINE DEFUNCT
size	Current size of the file, in 8 KB pages. 0 = Not applicable For a database snapshot, size reflects the maximum space that the snapshot can ever use for the file.
max_size	Maximum file size, in 8 KB pages: 0 = No growth is allowed. −1 = File grows until the disk is full. 268435456 = Log file grows to a maximum size of 2 TB.
growth	0 = File is a fixed size and won't grow. >0 = File grows automatically. If *is_percent_growth* = 0, growth increment is in units of 8 KB pages, rounded to the nearest 64 KB. If *is_percent_growth* = 1, growth increment is expressed as a whole number percentage.
is_media_read_only	1 = File is on read-only media. 0 = File is on read/write media.
is_read_only	1 = File is marked read-only. 0 = File is marked read/write.
is_sparse	Sparse files are used with database snapshots, as discussed later in this chapter. 1 = File is a sparse file. 0 = File isn't a sparse file.
is_percent_growth	See description for *growth* column.
is_name_reserved	1 = Dropped filename (*name* or *physical_name*) is reusable only after the next log backup. When files are dropped from a database, the logical names stay in a reserved state until the next log backup. This column is relevant only under the full recovery model and the bulk-logged recovery model.

Creating a database

The easiest way to create a database is to use Object Explorer in Management Studio, which provides a graphical front end to the Transact-SQL (T-SQL) commands that actually create the database and set its properties. Figure 3-1 shows the New Database window, which you can use in place of the T-SQL CREATE DATABASE command for creating a new user database. Only a user with the appropriate permissions can create a database, either through Object Explorer or by using the CREATE DATABASE command. This includes anyone in the sysadmin role, anyone who has been granted CONTROL or ALTER permission on the server, and anyone who has been granted CREATE DATABASE permission by someone with the sysadmin or dbcreator role.

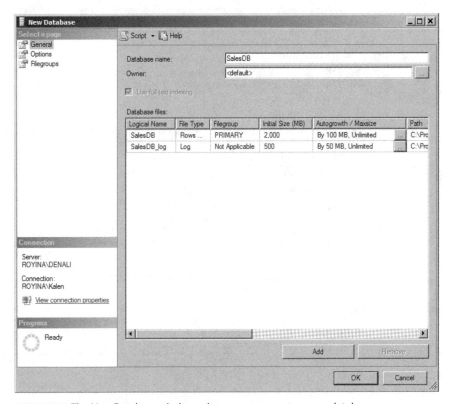

FIGURE 3-1 The New Database window, where you can create a new database.

When you create a new database, SQL Server copies the *model* database. If you have an object that you want created in every subsequent user database, you should create that object in *model* first. You can also use *model* to set default database options in all subsequently created databases. The *model* database includes 79 objects: 67 system tables, six objects used for SQL Server Query Notifications and Service Broker, one table used to help manage filestream data, one table used to help manage FileTable data, and one table used to help manage change tracking. You can see these objects by selecting from the system table called *sys.objects*. However, if you run the procedure *sp_help* in the *model* database, it lists two objects. It turns out that most of these objects aren't really stored in the *model* database but are accessible through it. Chapter 6, "Table storage," explains what the other kinds of objects are and how you can tell whether an object is really stored in a particular database. Most objects that you see in *model* show up when you run *sp_help* in any database, but your user databases will probably add more objects to this list. The contents of *model* are just the starting point.

A new user database must be 3 MB or larger (including the transaction log), and the primary data file size must be at least as large as the primary data file of the *model* database. (Because the *model* database has only one file and can't be altered to add more, the size of the primary data file and the size of the database are basically the same for *model*.) Almost all possible arguments to the CREATE DATABASE command have default values, so it's possible to create a database using a simple form of CREATE DATABASE, such as this:

```
CREATE DATABASE newdb;
```

This command creates a database *called newdb*, with a default size, on two files whose logical names—*newdb* and *newdb_log*—are derived from the name of the database. The corresponding physical files, *newdb.mdf* and *newdb_log.ldf*, are created in the default data directory, which is usually determined at the time SQL Server is installed.

The SQL Server login account that created the database is known as the *database owner*, and that information is stored with the information about the database properties in the *master* database. A database can have only one actual owner, which always corresponds to a login name. Any login that uses any database has a user name in that database, which might be the same name as the login name but doesn't have to be. The login that owns a database always has the special user name *dbo* when using the database it owns. (Later in this chapter, a section on the basics of database security covers database users.)

The default size of the data file is the size of the primary data file of the *model* database (which is 3 MB by default), and the default size of the log file is 0.75 MB. Whether the database name, *newdb*, is case-sensitive depends on the collation that you chose during setup. If you accepted the default, the name is case-insensitive. (Note that the actual command CREATE DATABASE is case-insensitive, regardless of the case sensitivity chosen for data.)

Other default property values apply to the new database and its files. For example, if the *LOG ON* clause isn't specified but data files are specified, SQL Server creates a log file with a size that is 25 percent of the sum of the sizes of all data files. If the *MAXSIZE* clause isn't specified for the files, the file grows until the disk is full. (In other words, the file size is considered unlimited.) You can specify the values for SIZE, MAXSIZE, and FILEGROWTH in units of terabytes (TB), gigabytes (GB), the default megabytes (MB), or kilobytes (KB). You can also specify the *FILEGROWTH* property as a percentage. A value of 0 for *FILEGROWTH* indicates no growth. If no *FILEGROWTH* value is specified, the default growth increment for data files is 1 MB. The log file *FILEGROWTH* default is specified as 10 percent

Using CREATE DATABASE: an example

The following is a complete example of the *CREATE DATABASE* command, specifying three files and all the properties of each file:

```
CREATE DATABASE Archive
ON
PRIMARY
( NAME = Arch1,
FILENAME =
    'C:\Program Files\Microsoft SQL Server\MSSQL11.MSSQLSERVER\MSSQL\DATA \archdat1.mdf',
SIZE = 100MB,
MAXSIZE = 200MB,
FILEGROWTH = 20MB),
( NAME = Arch2,
FILENAME =
    'C:\Program Files\Microsoft SQL Server\MSSQL11.MSSQLSERVER\MSSQL\DATA \archdat2.ndf',
SIZE = 10GB,
MAXSIZE = 50GB,
FILEGROWTH = 250MB)
LOG ON
( NAME = Archlog1,
FILENAME =
    'C:\Program Files\Microsoft SQL Server\MSSQL11.MSSQLSERVER\MSSQL\DATA \archlog1.ldf',
SIZE = 2GB,
MAXSIZE = 10GB,
FILEGROWTH = 100MB);
```

Expanding or shrinking a database

You can expand and shrink databases automatically or manually. The mechanism for automatic expansion is completely different from the mechanism for automatic shrinkage. Manual expansion is also handled differently from manual shrinkage. Log files have their own rules for growing and shrinking, as covered in Chapter 5.

Warning Shrinking a database or any data file is an extremely resource-intensive operation, so don't do it unless you absolutely must reclaim disk space. Shrinking a data file can also lead to excessive logical fragmentation within your database, as discussed in Chapter 7, "Indexes: internals and management."

Automatic file expansion

Expansion can happen automatically to any one of the database's files when that particular file becomes full. The file property FILEGROWTH determines how that automatic expansion happens. The FILEGROWTH property specified when the file is first defined can be qualified using the suffix *TB*, *GB*, *MB*, *KB*, or *%*, and it is always rounded up to the nearest 64 KB. If the value is specified as a percentage, the growth increment is the specified percentage of the size of the file when the expansion occurs. The file property MAXSIZE sets an upper limit on the size. Because Chapter 5 covers other considerations for the exact amount that a log file can grow, the remainder of this section discusses only data files.

Allowing SQL Server to grow your data files automatically is no substitute for good capacity planning before you build or populate any tables. Enabling autogrow might prevent some failures due to unexpected increases in data volume, but it can also cause problems. Suppose that a data file is full and your autogrow percentage is set to grow by 10 percent. If an application attempts to insert a single row and no space is available, the database might start to grow by a large amount (10 percent of 10,000 MB is 1,000 MB). This in itself can take a lot of time if fast file initialization (discussed in the next section) isn't being used. The growth might take so long that the client application's timeout value is exceeded, which means the insert query fails. The query would have failed anyway if autogrow weren't set, but with autogrow enabled, SQL Server spends a lot of time trying to grow the file, and you won't be informed of the problem immediately. File growth also can result in physical fragmentation on the disk. Again, the way to get maximum benefit from the database autogrow capabilities is to combine it with good capacity planning.

With autogrow enabled, your database files still can't grow the database size beyond the limits of the available disk space on the drives on which files are defined, or beyond the size specified in the MAXSIZE file property. So if you rely on the autogrow functionality to size your databases, you must still independently check your available hard disk space or the total file size. (The undocumented extended procedure *xp_fixeddrives* returns a list of the amount of free disk space on each of your local volumes, with the exception of mount points.) To reduce the possibility of running out of space, you can watch the Performance Monitor counter SQL Server: Databases Object: Data File Size and set up a performance alert to signal when the database file reaches a certain size.

Manual file expansion

You can expand a database file manually by using the ALTER DATABASE command with the *MODIFY FILE* option to change the SIZE property of one or more files. When you alter a database, the new file size must be larger than the current size. To decrease the file size, use the DBCC SHRINKFILE command, which is explained shortly.

Fast file initialization

You can initialize SQL Server 2012 data files (but not log files) instantly, allowing for fast execution of the file creation and growth. Instant file initialization adds space to the data file without filling the newly added space with zeros. Instead, the actual disk content is overwritten only as new data is written to the files. Until the data is overwritten, a hacker using an external file reader tool could possibly see the data previously on the disk.

Although the SQL Server 2012 documentation describes the instant file initialization feature as an "option," it's not really an option within SQL Server. It's actually controlled through a Windows security setting called *SE_MANAGE_VOLUME_NAME*, which is granted to Windows administrators by default. (This right can be granted to other Windows users by adding them to the Perform Volume

Maintenance Tasks security policy.) If your SQL Server service account is in the Windows Administrator role, instant file initialization is used. If you want to make sure that your database files are zeroed out as they are created and expanded, you can use *traceflag 1806* or deny *SE_MANAGE_VOLUME_NAME* rights to the account under which your SQL Server service is running.

Automatic shrinkage

The database property *autoshrink* allows a database to shrink automatically. The effect is the same as running *DBCC SHRINKDATABASE (dbname, 25)*. This option leaves 25 percent free space in a database after the shrink, and any free space beyond that is returned to the operating system. The thread that performs autoshrink shrinks databases at very frequent intervals, in some cases as often as every 30 minutes. Shrinking data files is so resource-intensive that it should be done only when you have no other way to reclaim needed disk space.

> **Important** Automatic shrinking is never recommended. In fact, Microsoft has announced that the autoshrink option will be removed in a future version of SQL Server and that you should avoid using it.

Manual shrinkage

You can shrink a database manually using one of the following Database Console Commands (DBCCs):

```
DBCC SHRINKFILE ( {file_name | file_id }
[, target_size][, {EMPTYFILE | NOTRUNCATE | TRUNCATEONLY} ]  )

DBCC SHRINKDATABASE (database_name [, target_percent]
[, {NOTRUNCATE | TRUNCATEONLY} ]  )
```

DBCC SHRINKFILE

DBCC SHRINKFILE allows you to shrink files in the current database. When you specify a *target_size*, DBCC SHRINKFILE attempts to shrink the specified file to the specified size in megabytes. Used pages in the part of the file to be freed are relocated to available free space in the retained part of the file. For example, for a 15 MB data file, a DBCC SHRINKFILE with a *target_size* of 12 causes all used pages in the last 3 MB of the file to be reallocated into any free slots in the first 12 MB of the file.

DBCC SHRINKFILE doesn't shrink a file past the size needed to store the data. For example, if 70 percent of the pages in a 10 MB data file are used, a DBCC SHRINKFILE statement with a *target_size* of 5 shrinks the file to only 7 MB, not 5 MB.

DBCC SHRINKDATABASE

DBCC SHRINKDATABASE shrinks all files in a database but doesn't allow any file to be shrunk smaller than its minimum size. The minimum size of a database file is the initial size of the file (specified when the database was created) or the size to which the file has been explicitly extended or reduced, using either the ALTER DATABASE or DBCC SHRINKFILE command. If you need to shrink a database smaller than its minimum size, use the DBCC SHRINKFILE command to shrink individual database files to a specific size. The size to which a file is shrunk becomes the new minimum size.

The numeric *target_percent* argument passed to the DBCC SHRINKDATABASE command is a percentage of free space to leave in each file of the database. For example, if you've used 60 MB of a 100 MB database file, you can specify a shrink percentage of 25 percent. SQL Server then shrinks the file to a size of 80 MB, and you have 20 MB of free space in addition to the original 60 MB of data. In other words, the 80 MB file has 25 percent of its space free. If, on the other hand, you've used 80 MB or more of a 100 MB database file, SQL Server can't shrink this file to leave 25 percent free space. In that case, the file size remains unchanged.

Because DBCC SHRINKDATABASE shrinks the database file by file, the mechanism used to perform the actual shrinking of data files is the same as that used with DBCC SHRINKFILE (when a data file is specified). SQL Server first moves pages to the front of files to free up space at the end, and then it releases the appropriate number of freed pages to the operating system. The actual internals details of how data files are shrunk are discussed in Chapter 14, "DBCC internals."

> **Note** Shrinking a log file is very different from shrinking a data file, and understanding how much you can shrink a log file and what exactly happens when you shrink it requires an understanding of how the log is used. For this reason, the discussion of shrinking log files is postponed until Chapter 5.

As the warning at the beginning of this section indicated, shrinking a database or any data files is a resource-intensive operation. If you absolutely need to recover disk space from the database, you should plan the shrink operation carefully and perform it when it has the least impact on the rest of the system. You should never enable the AUTOSHRINK option, which shrinks *all* the data files at regular intervals and wreaks havoc on system performance. Because shrinking data files can move data all around a file, it can also introduce fragmentation, which you then might want to remove. Defragmenting your data files can then have its own impact on productivity because it uses system resources. Chapter 6 discusses fragmentation and defragmentation in more detail.

A transaction enabled for a snapshot isolation level can block shrink operations. When this happens, DBCC SHRINKFILE and DBCC SHRINKDATABASE print out an informational message to the error log every 5 minutes in the first hour and then every hour after that. SQL Server also provides progress reporting for the SHRINK commands, available through the *sys.dm_exec_requests* view. Chapter 14 covers progress reporting.

Using database filegroups

You can group data files for a database into filegroups for allocation and administration purposes. In some cases, you can improve performance by controlling the placement of data and indexes into specific filegroups on specific drives or volumes. The filegroup containing the primary data file is called the *primary filegroup*. Only one primary filegroup exists, and if you don't ask specifically to place files in other filegroups when you create your database, *all* your data files end up in the primary filegroup.

In addition to the primary filegroup, a database can have one or more user-defined filegroups, which you can create by using the FILEGROUP keyword in the CREATE DATABASE or ALTER DATABASE statement.

Don't confuse the primary filegroup and the primary file. Here are the differences:

- The primary file is always the first file listed when you create a database, and it typically has the file extension .mdf. One special feature of the primary file is that it has pointers into a table in the master database that contains information about all the files belonging to the database. (You can access this table through the catalog view *sys.database_files*).

- The primary filegroup always contains the primary file. This filegroup contains the primary data file and any files not put into another specific filegroup. All pages from system tables are always allocated from files in the primary filegroup.

The default filegroup

One filegroup always has the property of DEFAULT. (Note that DEFAULT is a property of a filegroup, not a name.) Only one filegroup in each database can be the default filegroup. By default, the primary filegroup is also the default filegroup. A database owner can change which filegroup is the default by using the ALTER DATABASE statement. When a table or index is created, it's created in the default filegroup if no specific filegroup is specified.

Most SQL Server databases have a single data file in one (default) filegroup. In fact, most users probably never know enough about how SQL Server works to know what a filegroup is. As a user acquires greater database sophistication, she might decide to use multiple drives to spread out the input/output (I/O) for a database. The easiest way to do this is to create a database file on a redundant array of independent disks (RAID) device. Still, she has no need to use filegroups. At the next level of sophistication and complexity, the user might decide that she really wants multiple files—perhaps to create a database that uses more space than is available on a single drive. In this case, she still doesn't need filegroups; she can accomplish her goals using CREATE DATABASE with a list of files on separate drives.

More sophisticated database administrators might decide to have different tables assigned to different drives or to use the table and index partitioning feature. Only then do they need to use filegroups. They can use Object Explorer in SQL Server Management Studio to create the database on multiple filegroups. Then they can right-click the database name in Object Explorer and create a script of the CREATE DATABASE command that includes all the files in their appropriate filegroups. They can save and reuse this script when they need to re-create the database or build a similar database.

Why use multiple files?

You might wonder why you would want to create a database on multiple files located on one physical drive. Doing so might not gain much performance benefit, especially if you have small database or are already using an optimal RAID configuration for your drives, but multiple files can give you added flexibility in two important ways.

First, if you need to restore a database from a backup because of a disk crash, the new database must contain the same number of files as the original. For example, if your original database consists of one large 1.2 TB file, you need to restore it to a database with one file of that size. If you don't have another 1.2 TB drive immediately available, you can't restore the database. If, however, you originally created the database on several smaller files, you have added flexibility during a restoration. You might be more likely to have several 500 GB drives available than one large 1.2 TB drive.

Second, spreading the database onto multiple files, even on the same drive, gives you the flexibility of easily moving the database onto separate drives if you modify your hardware configuration in the future. (See the later section "Moving or copying a database" for details.)

Objects with space allocated to them—namely, tables and indexes—are created in a particular filegroup. (They can also be created on a partition scheme, which is a collection of filegroups. Chapter 8, "Special storage," discusses partitioning and partition schemes.) If the filegroup (or partition scheme) isn't specified, objects are created in the default filegroup. When you add space to objects stored in a particular filegroup, the data is stored in a *proportional fill* manner, which means that if you have one file in a filegroup with twice as much free space as another, the first file will have two *extents* (units of space) allocated from it for each extent allocated from the second file. (Later, the section "Space allocation" talks about extents in more detail.) Creating all your files to be the same size is recommended to avoid the issues of proportional fill.

You can also use filegroups to allow backups of parts of the database. Because a table is created on a single filegroup, you can choose to back up just a certain set of critical tables by backing up the filegroups in which you placed those tables. You can also restore individual files or filegroups in two ways.

- You can do a partial restore of a database and restore only a subset of filegroups, which must always include the primary filegroup. The database goes online as soon as the primary filegroup is restored, but only objects created on the restored filegroups are available. Partial restore of just a subset of filegroups can be a solution to allow very large databases (VLDBs) to be available within a mandated time window.

- If you have a failure of a subset of the disks on which you created your database, you can restore backups of the filegroups on those disks on top of the existing database. This method of restoring also requires that you have log backups, which are discussed in more detail in Chapter 5.

A FILEGROUP CREATION example

This example creates a database named *sales* with three filegroups:

- The primary filegroup, with the files salesPrimary1 and salesPrimary2. The FILEGROWTH increment for both of these files is specified as 100 MB.

- A filegroup named SalesGroup1, with the files salesGrp1File1 and salesGrp1Fi1e2.

- A filegroup named SalesGroup2, with the files salesGrp2File1 and salesGrp2Fi1e2.

```
CREATE DATABASE Sales
ON PRIMARY
( NAME = salesPrimary1,
FILENAME =
    'C:\Program Files\Microsoft SQL Server\MSSQL11.MSSQLSERVER\MSSQL\DATA\salesPrimary1.
mdf',
SIZE = 1000, MAXSIZE = 5000,
FILEGROWTH = 1000 ),
( NAME = salesPrimary2,
FILENAME =
    'C:\Program Files\Microsoft SQL Server\MSSQL11.MSSQLSERVER\MSSQL\DATA\salesPrimary2.
ndf',
SIZE = 1000, MAXSIZE = 5000,
FILEGROWTH = 1000 ),
FILEGROUP SalesGroup1
( NAME = salesGrp1Fi1e1,
FILENAME =
    'C:\Program Files\Microsoft SQL Server\MSSQL11.MSSQLSERVER\MSSQL\DATA\salesGrp1Fi1e1.
ndf',
SIZE = 500, MAXSIZE = 3000,
FILEGROWTH = 500 ),
( NAME = salesGrp1Fi1e2,
FILENAME =
    'C:\Program Files\Microsoft SQL Server\MSSQL11.MSSQLSERVER\MSSQL\DATA\salesGrp1Fi1e2.
ndf',
SIZE = 500, MAXSIZE = 3000,
FILEGROWTH = 500 ),
FILEGROUP SalesGroup2
( NAME = salesGrp2Fi1e1,
FILENAME =
    'C:\Program Files\Microsoft SQL Server\MSSQL11.MSSQLSERVER\MSSQL\DATA\salesGrp2Fi1e1.
ndf',
SIZE = 1000, MAXSIZE = 50000,
FILEGROWTH = 5000 ),
( NAME = salesGrp2Fi1e2,
FILENAME =
    'C:\Program Files\Microsoft SQL Server\MSSQL11.MSSQLSERVER\MSSQL\DATA\salesGrp2Fi1e2.
ndf',
SIZE = 1000, MAXSIZE = 50000,
FILEGROWTH = 500 )
LOG ON
( NAME = 'Sales_log',
FILENAME =
    'C:\Program Files\Microsoft SQL Server\MSSQL11.MSSQLSERVER\MSSQL\DATA\saleslog.ldf',
SIZE = 500MB, MAXSIZE = 2500MB,
FILEGROWTH = 500MB );
```

Filestream filegroups

Chapter 1, "SQL Server 2012 architecture and configuration," briefly mentions filestream storage during a discussion on configuration options. You can create filestream filegroups when you create a database, just like you can regular filegroups, but you must specify that the filegroup is for filestream data by using the phrase CONTAINS FILESTREAM.

Unlike regular filegroups, each filestream filegroup can contain only one file reference, and that file is specified as an operating system folder, not a specific file. The path up to the last folder must exist, and the last folder must not exist. So in the following example, the path C:\Data must exist, but the Reviews_FS subfolder can't exist when you execute the CREATE DATABASE statement. Also unlike regular filegroups, no space is preallocated to the filegroup, and you don't specify size or growth information for the file within the filegroup. The file and filegroup grow as data is added to tables that are created with filestream columns.

```
CREATE DATABASE MyMovieReviews
ON
PRIMARY
  ( NAME = Reviews_data,
    FILENAME = 'c:\data\Reviews_data.mdf'),
FILEGROUP MovieReviewsFSGroup1 CONTAINS FILESTREAM
  ( NAME = Reviews_FS,
    FILENAME = 'c:\data\Reviews_FS')
LOG ON  ( NAME = Reviews_log,
    FILENAME = 'c:\data\Reviews_log.ldf');
GO
```

If you run this code (after enabling filestream storage, as described in Chapter 1), you should see a Filestream.hdr file and a $FSLOG folder in c:\Data\Reviews_FS. *Filestream.hdr* file is a *FILESTREAM* container header file, which shouldn't be modified or removed. For existing databases, you can add a filestream filegroup using ALTER DATABASE, as covered in the next section. All data in all columns placed in the MovieReviewsFSGroup1 is maintained and managed with individual files created in the Reviews_FS folder. Chapter 8 talks more about the file organization within this folder during a discussion on special storage formats.

SQL Server 2012 expands the possibilities of Filestream data to let you use Windows applications to manage the file data stored in SQL Server. When a database is enabled for filestream with a filestream filegroup, you can create FileTables that hold data and metadata from Windows files. The FileTable feature lets an application integrate its storage and data management components, and provides integrated SQL Server services, including full-text search and semantic search, over the unstructured data and the metadata describing that data. Chapter 8 discusses how SQL Server manages the FileTable feature and the FileTable data.

Altering a database

You can use the ALTER DATABASE statement to change a database's definition in one of the following ways:

- By changing the name of the database.

- By adding one or more new data files to the database. If you want, you can put these files in a user-defined filegroup. All files added in a single ALTER DATABASE statement must go in the same filegroup.

- By adding one or more new log files to the database.

- By removing a file or a filegroup from the database. You can do this only if the file or filegroup is completely empty. Removing a filegroup removes all the files in it.

- By adding a new filegroup to a database. (Adding files to those filegroups must be done in a separate ALTER DATABASE statement.)

- By modifying an existing file in one of the following ways:

  - By increasing the value of the SIZE property.

  - By changing the MAXSIZE or FILEGROWTH property.

  - By changing the logical name of a file by specifying a NEWNAME property. The value of NEWNAME is then used as the NAME property for all future references to this file.

  - By changing the FILENAME property for files, which can effectively move the files to a new location. The new name or location doesn't take effect until you restart SQL Server. For *tempdb*, SQL Server automatically creates the files with the new name in the new location; for other databases, you must move the file manually after stopping your SQL Server instance. SQL Server then finds the new file when it restarts.

  - By marking the file as OFFLINE. You should set a file to OFFLINE when the physical file has become corrupted and the file backup is available to use for restoring. (You also can mark the whole database as OFFLINE, which you read about shortly in a discussion about database properties.) Marking a file as OFFLINE allows you to indicate that you don't want SQL Server to recover that particular file when it is restarted.

- By modifying an existing filegroup in one of the following ways:

  - By marking the filegroup as READONLY so that updates to objects in the filegroup aren't allowed. The primary filegroup can't be made READONLY.

  - By marking the filegroup as READWRITE, which reverses the READONLY property.

- By marking the filegroup as the default for the database.

- By changing the filegroup's name.

- By changing one or more database options. (Database options are covered later in this chapter.)

The ALTER DATABASE statement can make only one of the changes described each time it is executed. Note that you can't move a file from one filegroup to another.

ALTER DATABASE examples

The following examples demonstrate some of the changes that you can make using the ALTER DATABASE command.

This example increases the size of a database file:

```
USE master
GO
ALTER DATABASE Test1
MODIFY FILE
( NAME = 'test1dat3',
SIZE = 2000MB);
```

The following example needs three *ALTER DATABASE* statements to create a new filegroup in a database, add two 500 MB files to the filegroup, and make the new filegroup the default:

```
ALTER DATABASE Test1
ADD FILEGROUP Test1FG1;
GO
ALTER DATABASE Test1
ADD FILE
( NAME = 'test1dat4',
FILENAME =
    'C:\Program Files\Microsoft SQL Server\MSSQL11.MSSQLSERVER\MSSQL\DATA\t1dat4.ndf',
SIZE = 500MB,
MAXSIZE = 1000MB,
FILEGROWTH = 50MB),
( NAME = 'test1dat5',
FILENAME =
    'C:\Program Files\Microsoft SQL Server\MSSQL11.MSSQLSERVER\MSSQL\DATA\t1dat5.ndf',
SIZE = 500MB,
MAXSIZE = 1000MB,
FILEGROWTH = 50MB)
TO FILEGROUP Test1FG1;
GO
ALTER DATABASE Test1
MODIFY FILEGROUP Test1FG1 DEFAULT;
GO
```

Databases under the hood

A database consists of user-defined space for the permanent storage of user objects such as tables and indexes. This space is allocated in one or more operating system files.

Databases are divided into logical pages (of 8 KB each), and within each file the pages are numbered contiguously from 0 to N, with the value N being determined by the file size. You can refer to any page by specifying a database ID, a file ID, and a page number.

When you use the ALTER DATABASE command to enlarge a file, the new space is added to the end of the file—that is, the first page of the newly allocated space is page $N + 1$ on the file you're enlarging. When you shrink a database by using the DBCC SHRINKDATABASE or DBCC SHRINKFILE command, pages are removed starting at the highest-numbered page in the database (at the end) and moving toward lower-numbered pages. This ensures that page numbers within a file are always contiguous.

When you create a new database using the CREATE DATABASE command, it receives a unique database ID, and you can see a row for the new database in the *sys.databases* view. The rows returned in *sys.databases* include basic information about each database, such as its name, *database_id*, and creation date, as well as the value for each database option that the ALTER DATABASE command can set. Later in the chapter, you learn more about database options.

Space allocation

Space in a database is used for storing tables and indexes. That space is managed in units called *extents*. An extent is made up of eight logically contiguous pages (or 64 KB of space). To make space allocation more efficient, SQL Server 2012 doesn't allocate entire extents to tables with small amounts of data. SQL Server 2012 has two types of extents.

- *Uniform extents* are owned by a single object. All eight pages in the extent can be used only by the owning object.

- *Mixed extents* are shared by up to eight objects.

SQL Server allocates pages for a new table or index from mixed extents. When the table or index grows to eight pages, all future allocations use uniform extents.

When a table or index needs more space, SQL Server needs to find available space to be allocated. If the table or index is still less than eight pages total, SQL Server must find a mixed extent with space available. If the table or index is eight pages or larger, SQL Server must find a free uniform extent.

SQL Server uses two special types of pages to record which extents have been allocated and for which type of use (mixed or uniform) the extent is available.

- *Global Allocation Map (GAM) pages* record which extents have been allocated for any type of use. A GAM has a bit for each extent in the interval it covers. If the bit is 0, the corresponding extent is in use; if the bit is 1, the extent is free. After the header and other overhead are accounted for, about 8,000 bytes, or 64,000 bits, are available on the page, so each GAM can cover about 64,000 extents, or almost 4 GB of data. This means that one GAM page exists in a file for every 4 GB of file size.

■ *Shared Global Allocation Map (SGAM) pages* record which extents are now used as mixed extents and have at least one unused page. Just like a GAM, each SGAM covers about 64,000 extents, or almost 4 GB of data. The SGAM has a bit for each extent in the interval it covers. If the bit is 1, the extent being used is a mixed extent and has free pages; if the bit is 0, the extent isn't being used as a mixed extent, or it's a mixed extent whose pages are all in use.

Table 3-2 shows the bit patterns that each extent has set in the GAM and SGAM pages, based on its current use.

TABLE 3-2 Bit settings in GAM and SGAM pages

Current use of extent	GAM bit setting	SGAM bit setting
Free, not in use	1	0
Uniform extent or full mixed extent	0	0
Mixed extent with free pages	0	1

Several tools are available for actually examining the bits in the GAMs and SGAMs. In Chapter 6, which starts looking at data page structures in detail, you see how to use the DBCC PAGE command to view the contents of a SQL Server database page in a query window. Because the page numbers of the GAMs and SGAMs are known, you can just look at page 2 or 3. If you use *DBCC PAGE* with format 3, which gives the most details, you see output that displays which extents are allocated and which aren't. Example 3-1 shows the last section of the output using DBCC PAGE with format 3 for the first GAM page of my AdventureWorks database.

```
(1:0)        - (1:24256)   =     ALLOCATED

(1:24264)    -             = NOT ALLOCATED

(1:24272)    - (1:29752)   =     ALLOCATED

(1:29760)    - (1:30168)   = NOT ALLOCATED

(1:30176)    - (1:30240)   =     ALLOCATED

(1:30248)    - (1:30256)   = NOT ALLOCATED

(1:30264)    - (1:32080)   =     ALLOCATED

(1:32088)    - (1:32304)   = NOT ALLOCATED
```

EXAMPLE 3-1 GAM page contents indicating allocation status of extents in a file.

This output indicates that all extents up through the one that starts on page 24,256 are allocated. This corresponds to the first 189 MB of the file. The extent starting at 24,264 isn't allocated, but the next 5,480 pages are allocated.

If SQL Server needs to find a new, completely unused extent, it can use any extent with a corresponding bit value of 1 in the GAM page. If it needs to find a mixed extent with available space (one or more free pages), it finds an extent with a value in the SGAM of 1 (which always has a value in the GAM of 0). If no mixed extents have available space, it uses the GAM page to find a whole new extent to allocate as a mixed extent, and uses one page from that. If no free extents are available at all, the file is full.

SQL Server can locate the GAMs in a file quickly because a GAM is always the third page in any database file (that is, page 2); an SGAM is the fourth page (that is, page 3). Another GAM appears every 511,230 pages after the first GAM on page 2, and another SGAM appears every 511,230 pages after the first SGAM on page 3. Page 0 in any file is the File Header page, and only one exists per file. Page 1 is a Page Free Space (PFS) page. Chapter 6 explains more about how individual pages within a table look and tells you about the details of PFS pages. For now, because this is a discussion about space allocation, you see how to keep track of which pages belong to which tables.

Index Allocation Map (IAM) pages keep track of the extents in a 4 GB section of a database file used by an allocation unit. An *allocation unit* is a set of pages belonging to a single partition in a table or index and comprises pages of one of three storage types: pages holding regular in-row data, pages holding Large Object (LOB) data (which includes the new SQL Server 2012 columnstore indexes), or pages holding row-overflow data. Chapters 6 and 7 cover regular in-row storage; Chapter 8 covers LOB, row-overflow storage, columnstore indexes, and partitions.

For example, a table on four partitions with all three types of data (in-row, LOB, and row-overflow) has at least 12 IAM pages. Again, because a single IAM page covers only a 4 GB section of a single file, multiple IAM pages are created if the partition spans files, or if the file is more than 4 GB in size and the partition uses pages in more than one 4 GB section.

An IAM page also contains a 96-byte page header, like all other pages, followed by an IAM page header, which contains eight page-pointer slots. Finally, an IAM page contains a set of bits that map a range of extents onto a file, which doesn't necessarily have to be the same file that the IAM page is in. The header has the address of the first extent in the range mapped by the IAM. The eight page-pointer slots contain pointers to up to eight pages belonging to the relevant object contained in mixed extents; only the first IAM for an object has values in these pointers. When an object takes up more than eight pages, all its additional extents are uniform extents, which means that an object never needs more than eight pointers to pages in mixed extents. If rows (and then pages) are deleted from a table, or if the table wasn't empty when first created, the table can actually use fewer than eight of these pointers. Each bit of the bitmap represents an extent in the range, whether or not the extent is allocated to the object owning the IAM. If a bit is on, the relative extent in the range is allocated to the object owning the IAM; if a bit is off, the relative extent isn't allocated to the object owning the IAM.

For example, if the bit pattern in the first byte of the IAM is 1100 0000, the first and second extents in the range covered by the IAM are allocated to the object owning the IAM, and extents 3 through 8 aren't allocated to the object owning the IAM.

IAM pages are allocated as needed for each object and are located randomly in the database file. Each IAM covers a possible range of about 512,000 pages.

The *sys.system_internals_allocation_units* internal system view has a *first_iam_page* column that points to the first IAM page for an allocation unit. All IAM pages for that allocation unit are linked in a chain, with each IAM page containing a pointer to the next in the chain. You can find out more about IAMs and allocation units in Chapters 5, 6, and 7 in the discussions on object and index storage.

In addition to GAMs, SGAMs, and IAMs, a database file has three other types of special allocation pages.

- *Page Free Space (PFS)* pages keep track of how each particular page in a file is used. The second page (page 1) of a file is a PFS page, as is every 8,088th page thereafter. Chapter 6 covers PFS pages.

- A *Differential Changed Map (DIFF)* on the seventh page (page 6) keeps track of which extents in a file have been modified since the last full database backup.

- A *Minimal Logging Changed Map (ML)* on the eighth page (page 7) is used when an extent in the file is used in a minimally or bulk-logged operation.

Chapter 5 covers these last two kinds of pages when discussing the internals of backup and restore operations.

Like GAM and SGAM pages, DIFF and ML map pages have 1 bit for each extent in the section of the file they represent. They occur at regular intervals—every 511,230 pages.

You can use *DBCC PAGE* to view the details of IAM, PFS, DIFF, and ML pages. Later chapters show you more examples of the output of this command as you learn more about the different types of allocation pages.

Setting database options

You can set several dozen options, or properties, for a database to control certain behavior within that database. Some options must be set to ON or OFF, some must be set to one of a list of possible values, and others are enabled by just specifying their name. By default, all the options that require ON or OFF have an initial value of OFF unless the option was set to ON in the *model* database. All databases created after an option is changed in *model* have the same values as *model*. You can easily change the value of some of these options by using Management Studio. You can use the *ALTER DATABASE* command to set all of them directly.

The *sys.databases* catalog view lists the current values of all the options. This view also contains other useful information, such as database ID, creation date, and the database owner's Security ID (SID). The following query retrieves some of the most important columns from *sys.databases* for the four databases that exist on a new default installation of SQL Server:

```
SELECT name, database_id, suser_sname(owner_sid) as owner,
    create_date, user_access_desc, state_desc
FROM sys.databases
WHERE database_id <= 4;
```

The query produces this output, although the created dates may vary:

```
name    database_id owner create_date              user_access_desc state_desc
------  ----------- ----- ------------------------ ---------------- ----------
master  1           sa    2003-04-08 09:13:36.390  MULTI_USER       ONLINE
tempdb  2           sa    2012-02-24 18:36:09.250  MULTI_USER       ONLINE
model   3           sa    2003-04-08 09:13:36.390  MULTI_USER       ONLINE
msdb    4           sa    2011-11-04 22:38:12.077  MULTI_USER       ONLINE
```

The *sys.databases* view contains a number and a name for the *user_access* and *state* information. Selecting all columns from *sys.databases* would show you that the *user_access_desc* value of MULTI_USER has a corresponding *user_access* value of 0, and the *state_desc* value of ONLINE has a *state* value of 0. SQL Server Books Online shows the complete list of number and name relationships for the columns in *sys.databases*.

These are just two of the database options displayed in the *sys.databases* view. The complete list of database options is divided into seven main categories: state options, cursor options, auto options, parameterization options, SQL options, database recovery options, and external access options. Specific technologies in which SQL Server can participate also have options, including database high availability, Service Broker activities, change tracking, database encryption, and snapshot isolation. Some options, particularly the SQL options, have corresponding SET options that you can toggle on or off for a particular connection. Be aware that your application interface may enable some of these SET options by default, so applications act as though the corresponding database option has already been set.

Table 3-3 lists the options, by category. Options listed on a single line and values separated by vertical bars (|) are mutually exclusive. The following sections go into more detail on four of the option categories.

TABLE 3-3 Database options, by category

Category	Options
State options	*SINGLE_USER	RESTRICTED_USER	MULTI_USER* *OFFLINE	ONLINE	EMERGENCY* *READ_ONLY	READ_WRITE*
Cursor options	*CURSOR_CLOSE_ON_COMMIT { ON	OFF }* *CURSOR_DEFAULT { LOCAL	GLOBAL }*
Auto options	*AUTO_CLOSE { ON	OFF }* *AUTO_CREATE_STATISTICS { ON	OFF }* *AUTO_SHRINK { ON	OFF }* *AUTO_UPDATE_STATISTICS { ON	OFF }* *AUTO_UPDATE_STATISTICS_ASYNC { ON	OFF }*
Parameterization options	*DATE_CORRELATION_OPTIMIZATION { ON	OFF }* *PARAMETERIZATION { SIMPLE	FORCED }*

Category	Options
SQL options	*ANSI_NULL_DEFAULT { ON	OFF }* *ANSI_NULLS { ON	OFF }* *ANSI_PADDING { ON	OFF }* *ANSI_WARNINGS { ON	OFF }* *ARITHABORT { ON	OFF }* *CONCAT_NULL_YIELDS_NULL { ON	OFF }* *NUMERIC_ROUNDABORT { ON	OFF }* *QUOTED_IDENTIFIER { ON	OFF }* *RECURSIVE_TRIGGERS { ON	OFF }*
Database recovery options	*RECOVERY { FULL	BULK_LOGGED	SIMPLE }* *TORN_PAGE_DETECTION { ON	OFF }* *PAGE_VERIFY { CHECKSUM	TORN_PAGE_DETECTION	NONE }* *TARGET_RECOVERY_TIME = target_recovery_time {SECONDS	MINUTES}*
External access options	*DB_CHAINING { ON	OFF }* *TRUSTWORTHY { ON	OFF }* *CONTAINMENT = { NONE	PARTIAL }* *DEFAULT_FULLTEXT_LANGUAGE = { <lcid>	language_name	language_alias}* *DEFAULT_LANGUAGE = { <lcid>	language_name	language_alias}* *NESTED_TRIGGERS = {OFF	ON}* *TRANSFORM_NOISE_WORDS = {OFF	ON}* *TWO_DIGIT_YEAR_CUTOFF = {1753, ..., 2049, ..., 9999}*
High availability options	*PARTNER { = 'partner_server' }* *	FAILOVER* *	FORCE_SERVICE_ALLOW_DATA_LOSS* *	OFF* *	RESUME* *	SAFETY { FULL	OFF }* *	SUSPEND* *	TIMEOUT integer* *WITNESS { = 'witness_server' }	OFF }* *HADR {AVAILABILITY_GROUP = group_name	OFF}* *	SUSPEND	RESUME*
Service Broker options	*ENABLE_BROKER	DISABLE_BROKER* *NEW_BROKER* *ERROR_BROKER_CONVERSATIONS* *HONOR_BROKER_PRIORITY { ON	OFF }*
Change Tracking options	*CHANGE_TRACKING {= ON	= OFF}* *AUTO_CLEANUP = {ON	OFF}* *	CHANGE_RETENTION = retention_period {DAYS	HOURS	MINUTES}*
Database Encryption option	*ENCRYPTION {ON	OFF}*
Snapshot Isolation options	*ALLOW_SNAPSHOT_ISOLATION {ON	OFF }* *READ_COMMITTED_SNAPSHOT {ON	OFF }*
Filestream option	*NON_TRANSACTED ACCESS = {OFF	READ_ONLY	FULL }* *	DIRECTORY_NAME = <directory_name>*

State options

The state options control who can use the database and for what operations. Usability has three aspects:

- **User access state** determines which users can use the database.

- **Status state** determines whether the database is available to anybody for use.

- **Updateability state** determines what operations can be performed on the database.

You control each aspect by using the ALTER DATABASE command to enable an option for the database. None of the state options uses the keywords ON and OFF to control the state value.

SINGLE_USER | RESTRICTED_USER | MULTI_USER

These three options describe the user access property of a database. They are mutually exclusive; setting any one of them unsets the others. To set one of these options for your database, simply use the option name. For example, to set the *AdventureWorks* database to single-user mode, use the following command:

```
ALTER DATABASE AdventureWorks SET SINGLE_USER;
```

A database in SINGLE_USER mode can have only one connection at a time. A database in RESTRICTED_USER mode can have connections only from users who are considered "qualified"—those who are members of the dbcreator or sysadmin server role or the db_owner role for that database. The default for a database is MULTI_USER mode, which means anyone with a valid user name in the database can connect to it. If you attempt to change a database's state to a mode incompatible with the current conditions—for example, if you try to change the database to SINGLE_USER mode when other connections exist—the behavior of SQL Server is determined by the TERMINATION option you specify. (Termination options are covered shortly.)

To determine which user access value is set for a database, you can examine the *sys.databases* catalog view, as shown here:

```
SELECT USER_ACCESS_DESC FROM sys.databases
WHERE name = '<name of database>';
```

This query returns *MULTI_USER*, *SINGLE_USER*, or *RESTRICTED_USER*.

OFFLINE | ONLINE | EMERGENCY

You use these three mutually exclusive options to describe the status of a database. The default for a database is ONLINE. As with the user access options, when you use ALTER DATABASE to put the database in one of these modes, you don't specify a value of ON or OFF; you just use the name of the option. When a database is set to OFFLINE, it's closed and shut down cleanly and marked as offline. The database can't be modified while it's offline. A database can't be put into OFFLINE mode if any connections exist in the database. Whether SQL Server waits for the other connections to terminate or generates an error message is determined by the TERMINATION option specified.

The following code sample shows how to set a database's status value to OFFLINE and how to determine the status of a database:

```
ALTER DATABASE AdventureWorks SET OFFLINE;

SELECT state_desc from sys.databases
WHERE name = 'AdventureWorks';
```

As shown in the preceding query, you can determine the current status of a database by examining the *state_desc* column of the *sys.databases* view. This column can return status values other than OFFLINE, ONLINE, and EMERGENCY, but those values can't be set directly using ALTER DATABASE. (You can explicitly set a database to *EMERGENCY* mode with DBCC commands, as discussed in Chapter 14.) A database can have the status value RESTORING while it's in the process of being restored from a backup. It can have the status value RECOVERING during a restart of SQL Server. The recovery process is done on one database at a time, and until SQL Server finishes recovering a database, the database has a status of RECOVERING. If the recovery process can't be completed for some reason (most likely because one or more of the log files for the database is unavailable or unreadable), SQL Server gives the database the status of RECOVERY_PENDING. Your databases can also be put into RECOVERY_PENDING mode if SQL Server runs out of either log or data space during rollback recovery, or if SQL Server runs out of locks or memory during any part of the startup process. Chapter 5 goes into more detail about the difference between restore recovery and startup recovery.

If all the needed resources, including log files, are available, but corruption is detected during recovery, the database may be put in the *SUSPECT* state. A database is completely unavailable if it's in the SUSPECT state, and you won't even see the database listed if you run *sp_helpdb*. However, you can still see the status of a suspect database by looking at the *state_desc* column in the *sys.databases* view. In many cases, you can make a suspect database available for read-only operations by setting its status to EMERGENCY mode. If you really have lost one or more of the log files for a database, EMERGENCY mode allows you to access the data while you copy it to a new location. When you move from RECOVERY_PENDING to EMERGENCY, SQL Server shuts down the database and then restarts it with a special flag that allows it to skip the recovery process. Skipping recovery can mean you have logically or physically inconsistent data: missing index rows, broken page links, or incorrect metadata pointers. By putting your database specifically in EMERGENCY mode, you are acknowledging that the data might be inconsistent but you want access to it anyway.

READ_ONLY | READ_WRITE

These mutually exclusive options describe a database's ability to be updated. The default is READ_WRITE. As with the user access options, when you use ALTER DATABASE to put the database in one of these modes, you don't specify a value of ON or OFF; you just use the name of the option.

When the database is in READ_WRITE mode, any user with the appropriate permissions can carry out data modification operations. However, in READ_ONLY mode, no INSERT, UPDATE, or DELETE operations can be executed. Also, because no modifications are done when a database is in READ_ONLY mode, automatic recovery isn't run on this database when SQL Server is restarted, and no locks need to be acquired during any SELECT operations. Shrinking a database in READ_ONLY mode isn't possible.

A database can't be put into READ_ONLY mode if any connections are made to the database. Whether SQL Server waits for the other connections to terminate or generates an error message is determined by the TERMINATION option specified.

The following code shows how to set a database's updatability value to READ_ONLY and how to determine the updatability of a database:

```
ALTER DATABASE AdventureWorks SET READ_ONLY;
SELECT name, is_read_only FROM sys.databases
WHERE name = 'AdventureWorks';
```

When READ_ONLY is enabled for database, the is_read_only column returns 1; otherwise, it returns 0 for a READ_WRITE database.

Termination options

As just mentioned, several state options can't be set when a database is in use or is in use by an unqualified user. You can specify how SQL Server should handle this situation by indicating a termination option in the ALTER DATABASE command. You can have SQL Server wait for the situation to change, generate an error message, or terminate the connections of unqualified users. The termination option determines the behavior of SQL Server in the following situations.

- When you attempt to change a database to SINGLE_USER and it has more than one current connection

- When you attempt to change a database to RESTRICTED_USER and unqualified users are currently connected to it

- When you attempt to change to OFFLINE a database that has current connections to it

- When you attempt to change to READ_ONLY a database that has current connections to it

The default behavior of SQL Server in any of these situations is to wait indefinitely. The following TERMINATION options change this behavior.

- ***ROLLBACK AFTER integer [SECONDS]***   This option causes SQL Server to wait for the specified number of seconds and then break unqualified connections. Incomplete transactions are rolled back. When the transition is to SINGLE_USER mode, all connections are unqualified except the one issuing the ALTER DATABASE statement. When the transition is to RESTRICTED_USER mode, unqualified connections are those of users who aren't members of the db_owner fixed database role or the dbcreator and sysadmin fixed server roles.

- ***ROLLBACK IMMEDIATE***   This option breaks unqualified connections immediately. All incomplete transactions are rolled back. Keep in mind that although the connection may be broken immediately, the rollback might take some time to complete. All work done by the transaction must be undone so for certain operations, such as a batch update of millions of rows or a large index rebuild, you can be in for a long wait. Unqualified connections are the same as those described previously.

- **NO_WAIT** This option causes SQL Server to check for connections before attempting to change the database state and causes the ALTER DATABASE statement to fail if certain connections exist. If the database is being set to SINGLE_USER mode, the ALTER DATABASE statement fails if any other connections exist. If the transition is to RESTRICTED_ USER mode, the ALTER DATABASE statement fails if any unqualified connections exist.

The following command changes the user access option of the *AdventureWorks* database to SINGLE_USER and generates an error if any other connections to the database exist:

```
ALTER DATABASE AdventureWorks SET SINGLE_USER WITH NO_WAIT;
```

Cursor options

The cursor options control the behavior of server-side cursors defined using one of the following T-SQL commands for defining and manipulating cursors: DECLARE, OPEN, FETCH, CLOSE, and DEAL-LOCATE.

- **CURSOR_CLOSE_ON_COMMIT {ON | OFF}** When this option is set to ON, any open cursors are closed (in compliance with SQL-92) when a transaction is committed or rolled back. If OFF (the default) is specified, cursors remain open after a transaction is committed. Rolling back a transaction closes any cursors except those defined as INSENSITIVE or STATIC.

- **CURSOR_DEFAULT {LOCAL | GLOBAL}** When this option is set to LOCAL and cursors aren't specified as GLOBAL when they are created, the scope of any cursor is local to the batch, stored procedure, or trigger in which it was created. The cursor name is valid only within this scope. The cursor can be referenced by local cursor variables in the batch, stored procedure, or trigger, or by a stored procedure output parameter. When this option is set to GLOBAL and cursors aren't specified as LOCAL when they are created, the scope of the cursor is global to the connection. The cursor name can be referenced in any stored procedure or batch executed by the connection.

Auto options

The auto options affect actions that SQL Server might take automatically. All these options are Boolean options, with a value of ON or OFF.

- **AUTO_CLOSE** When this option is set to ON, the database is closed and shut down cleanly when the last user of the database exits, thereby freeing any resources. All file handles are closed, and all in-memory structures are removed so that the database isn't using any memory. When a user tries to use the database again, it reopens. If the database was shut down cleanly, the database isn't initialized (reopened) until a user tries to use the database the next time SQL Server is restarted.

The AUTO_CLOSE option is handy for personal SQL Server databases because it allows you to manage database files as normal files. You can move them, copy them to make backups, or even email them to other users. However, don't use this option for databases accessed by an application that repeatedly makes and breaks connections to SQL Server. The overhead of closing and reopening the database between each connection hurts performance.

- **AUTO_SHRINK**   When this option is set to ON, all of a database's files are candidates for periodic shrinking. Both data files and log files can be automatically shrunk by SQL Server. The only way to free space in the log files so that they can be shrunk is to back up the transaction log or set the recovery model to SIMPLE. The log files shrink at the point that the log is backed up or truncated. This option is never recommended.

- **AUTO_CREATE_STATISTICS**   When this option is set to ON (the default), the SQL Server Query Optimizer creates statistics on columns referenced in a query's *WHERE*, *ON*, *GROUP BY*, or *DISTINCT* clauses. Adding statistics improves query performance because the SQL Server Query Optimizer can better determine how to evaluate a query.

- **AUTO_UPDATE_STATISTICS**   When this option is set to ON (the default), existing statistics are updated if the data in the tables has changed. SQL Server keeps a counter of the modifications made to a table and uses it to determine when statistics are outdated. When this option is set to OFF, existing statistics aren't automatically updated. (They can be updated manually.) Chapter 7 and Chapter 11, "The Query Optimizer," discuss statistics in more detail.

> **Note** Chapter 12 discusses in more detail the preceding two statistics options, as well as AUTO_UPDATE_STATISTICS_ASYNC and the PARAMETERIZATION options.

SQL options

The SQL options control how various SQL statements are interpreted. The default for all these Boolean options is OFF for SQL Server, but many tools, such as Management Studio, and many programming interfaces, such as Open Database Connectivity (ODBC), enable certain session-level options that override the database options and make it appear as though the ON behavior is the default.

- **ANSI_NULL_DEFAULT**   When this option is set to ON, columns comply with the ANSI SQL-92 rules for column nullability. That is, if you don't specifically indicate whether a column in a table allows NULL values, NULLs are allowed. When this option is set to OFF, newly created columns don't allow NULLs if no nullability constraint is specified.

- **ANSI_NULLS**   When this option is set to ON, any comparisons with a NULL value result in UNKNOWN, as specified by the ANSI-92 standard. If this option is set to OFF, comparisons of non-Unicode values to NULL result in a value of TRUE if both values being compared are NULL.

- **ANSI_PADDING** When this option is set to ON, strings being compared with each other are set to the same length before the comparison takes place. When this option is OFF, no padding takes place.

- **ANSI_WARNINGS** When this option is set to ON, errors or warnings are issued when conditions such as division-by-zero or arithmetic overflow occur.

- **ARITHABORT** When this option is set to ON, a query is terminated when an arithmetic overflow or division-by-zero error is encountered during the execution of a query. When this option is OFF, the query returns NULL as the result of the operation.

- **CONCAT_NULL_YIELDS_NULL** When this option is set to ON, concatenating two strings results in a NULL string if either string is NULL. When this option is set to OFF, a NULL string is treated as an empty (zero-length) string for the purposes of concatenation.

- **NUMERIC_ROUNDABORT** When this option is set to ON, an error is generated if an expression results in loss of precision. When this option is OFF, the result is simply rounded. The setting of ARITHABORT determines the severity of the error. If ARITHABORT is OFF, only a warning is issued and the expression returns a NULL. If ARITHABORT is ON, an error is generated and no result is returned.

- **QUOTED_IDENTIFIER** When this option is set to ON, identifiers such as table and column names can be delimited by double quotation marks, and literals must then be delimited by single quotation marks. All strings delimited by double quotation marks are interpreted as object identifiers. Quoted identifiers don't have to follow the T-SQL rules for identifiers when QUOTED_IDENTIFIER is ON. They can be keywords and can include characters not normally allowed in T-SQL identifiers, such as spaces and dashes. You can't use double quotation marks to delimit literal string expressions; you must use single quotation marks. If a single quotation mark is part of the literal string, it can be represented by two single quotation marks (''). This option must be set to ON if reserved keywords are used for object names in the database. When it is OFF, identifiers can't be in quotation marks and must follow all T-SQL rules for identifiers.

- **RECURSIVE_TRIGGERS** When this option is set to ON, triggers can fire recursively, either directly or indirectly. Indirect recursion occurs when a trigger fires and performs an action that causes a trigger on another table to fire, thereby causing an update to occur on the original table, which causes the original trigger to fire again. For example, an application updates table T1, which causes trigger *Trig1* to fire. *Trig1* updates table T2, which causes trigger *Trig2* to fire. *Trig2* in turn updates table T1, which causes *Trig1* to fire again. Direct recursion occurs when a trigger fires and performs an action that causes the same trigger to fire again. For example, an application updates table T3, which causes trigger *Trig3* to fire. *Trig3* updates table T3 again, which causes trigger *Trig3* to fire again. When this option is OFF (the default), triggers can't be fired recursively.

Database recovery options

The database option RECOVERY (FULL, BULK_LOGGED, or SIMPLE) determines how much recovery can be done on a SQL Server database. It also controls how much information is logged and how much of the log is available for backups. Chapter 5 covers this option in more detail.

Two other options also apply to work done when a database is recovered. You can set the TORN_PAGE_DETECTION option to ON or OFF in SQL Server 2012, but that particular option will go away in a future version. The recommended alternative is to set the PAGE_VERIFY option to a value of TORN_PAGE_DETECTION or CHECKSUM (so TORN_PAGE_DETECTION should now be considered a value, rather the name of an option).

The PAGE_VERIFY options discover damaged database pages caused by disk I/O path errors, which can cause database corruption problems. The I/O errors themselves are generally caused by power failures or disk failures that occur when a page is being written to disk.

- **CHECKSUM**   When PAGE_VERIFY is set to CHECKSUM, SQL Server calculates a checksum over the contents of each page and stores the value in the page header when a page is written to disk. When the page is read from disk, a checksum is recomputed and compared with the value stored in the page header. If the values don't match, error message 824 (indicating a checksum failure) is reported.

- **TORN_PAGE_DETECTION**   Setting the PAGE_VERIFY option to *TORN_PAGE_DETECTION* causes a bit to be flipped for each 512-byte sector in a database page (8 KB) whenever the page is written to disk. It allows SQL Server to detect incomplete I/O operations caused by power failures or other system outages. A bit in the wrong state when the page is later read by SQL Server means that the page was written incorrectly (a "torn page" has been detected). Although SQL Server database pages are 8 KB, disks perform I/O operations using 512-byte sectors. Therefore, 16 sectors are written per database page. A torn page can occur if the system crashes (for example, because of power failure) between the time the operating system writes the first 512-byte sector to disk and the completion of the 8 KB I/O operation. When the page is read from disk, the torn bits stored in the page header are compared with the actual page sector information. Unmatched values indicate that only part of the page was written to disk. In this situation, error message 824 (indicating a torn-page error) is reported. Torn pages are typically detected by database recovery if it is truly an incomplete write of a page. However, other I/O path failures can cause a torn page at any time.

- **NONE (No Page Verify Option)**   You can specify that that neither the CHECKSUM nor the TORN_PAGE_DETECTION value be generated when a page is written, and these values won't be verified when a page is read.

Both checksum and torn-page errors generate error message 824, which is written to both the SQL Server error log and the Windows event log. For any page that generates an 824 error when read, SQL Server inserts a row into the system table *suspect_pages* in the *msdb* database. (SQL Server Books Online has more information on "Understanding and Managing the suspect_pages Table.")

SQL Server retries any read that fails with a checksum, torn page, or other I/O error four times. If the read is successful in any one of those attempts, a message is written to the error log and the command that triggered the read continues. If the attempts fail, the command fails with error message 824.

You can "fix" the error by restoring the data or potentially rebuilding the index if the failure is limited to index pages. If you encounter a checksum failure, you can run DBCC CHECKDB to determine the type of database page or pages affected. You should also determine the root cause of the error and correct the problem as soon as possible to prevent additional or ongoing errors. Finding the root cause requires investigating the hardware, firmware drivers, BIOS, filter drivers (such as virus software), and other I/O path components. You can find more information about DBCC CHECKDB errors and how to handle them in Chapter 14.

A new recovery option in SQL Server 2012 is *TARGET_RECOVERY_TIME*, which allows optimum checkpoint frequency to be controlled at the database level. Chapter 5 covers this option during a discussion on checkpoints and the recovery interval.

Other database options

Of the other categories of database options, three more are covered in later chapters. The external access options that involve contained databases are discussed in Chapter 4, "Special databases." The Filestream access options, introduced in Chapter 1, are discussed in Chapter 8. The snapshot isolation options are discussed in Chapter 13, "Transactions and concurrency." All others are beyond the scope of this book.

Understanding database security

Security is a huge topic that affects almost every action of every SQL Server user, including administrators and developers, and it deserves an entire book of its own. However, some areas of the SQL Server security framework are crucial to understanding how to work with a database or with any objects in a SQL Server database, so the topic can't be left completely untouched in this book.

SQL Server manages a hierarchical collection of entities. The most prominent of these entities are the SQL Server instance and databases in the instance. Underneath the database level are objects. Each entity below the instance level is owned by individuals or groups of individuals. The SQL Server security framework controls access to the entities within a SQL Server instance. Like any resource manager, the SQL Server security model has two parts: authentication and authorization.

Authentication is the process by which the SQL Server validates and establishes the identity of an individual who wants to access a resource. *Authorization* is the process by which SQL Server decides whether a given identity is allowed to access a resource.

This section covers the basic issues of database access and then describes the metadata where information on database access is stored. You also read about the concept of schemas and describe how they are used to access objects.

The following two terms form the foundation for describing security control in SQL Server 2012.

- **Securable**   This is an entity on which permissions can be granted. Securables include databases, schemas, and objects.

- **Principal**   This entity can access securables. A *primary principal* represents a single user (such as a SQL Server login or a Windows login); a *secondary principal* represents multiple users (such as a role or a Windows group).

Database access

Authentication is performed at two different levels in SQL Server. First, anyone who wants to access any SQL Server resource must be authenticated at the server level, unless they are connecting to a contained database. SQL Server 2012 security provides two basic methods for authenticating logins: Windows authentication and SQL Server authentication. In Windows authentication, SQL Server login security is integrated directly with Windows security, allowing the operating system to authenticate SQL Server users. In SQL Server authentication, an administrator creates SQL Server login accounts within SQL Server, and any user connecting to SQL Server must supply a valid SQL Server login name and password.

Windows authentication uses *trusted connections,* which rely on the impersonation feature of Windows. Through impersonation, SQL Server can handle the security context of the Windows user account initiating the connection and test whether the SID has a valid privilege level. Any available network libraries support Windows impersonation and trusted connections when connecting to SQL Server.

SQL Server can use Kerberos to support mutual authentication between the client and the server, as well as to pass a client's security credentials between computers so that work on a remote server can proceed using the credentials of the impersonated client. With Windows 2008 or later, SQL Server uses Kerberos and delegation to support Windows authentication as well as SQL Server authentication.

The authentication method (or methods) used by SQL Server is determined by its security mode. SQL Server can run in one of two security modes: Windows authentication mode (which uses only Windows authentication) and mixed mode (which can use either Windows authentication or SQL Server authentication, as chosen by the client). When you connect to an instance of SQL Server configured for Windows authentication mode, you can't supply a SQL Server login name, and your Windows user name determines your level of access to SQL Server.

One advantage of Windows authentication has always been that it allows SQL Server to take advantage of the security features of the operating system, such as password encryption, password aging, and minimum and maximum length restrictions on passwords. When running on Windows 2008 or later, SQL Server authentication can also take advantage of Windows password policies. Look at the ALTER LOGIN command in Books Online for the full details. Also note that if you choose Windows authentication during setup, the default SQL Server *sa* login is disabled. If you switch to mixed mode after setup, you can enable the *sa* login using the ALTER LOGIN command. You can change the authentication mode in Management Studio by right-clicking the server name, choosing Properties, and then selecting the security page. Under Server Authentication, select the new server authentication mode, as shown in Figure 3-2.

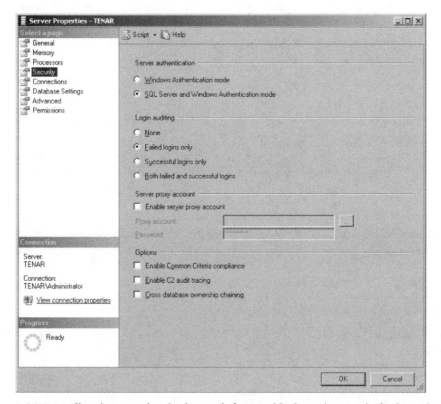

FIGURE 3-2 Choosing an authentication mode for your SQL Server instance in the Server Properties sheet.

Under mixed mode, Windows-based clients can connect via Windows authentication, and connections that don't come from Windows clients or that come across the Internet can connect via SQL Server authentication. Also, when a user connects to an instance of SQL Server that has been installed in mixed mode, the connection can always supply a SQL Server login name explicitly. This allows a connection to be made using a login name distinct from the user name in Windows.

All login names, whether from Windows or SQL Server authentication, can be seen in the *sys. server_principals* catalog view, which also contains a SID for each server principal. If the principal is a Windows login, the SID is the same one that Windows uses to validate the user's access to Windows resources. The view contains rows for server roles, Windows groups, and logins mapped to certificates and asymmetric keys, but those principals aren't discussed here.

Database security

Logon names can be database owners, as seen in the *sys.databases* view, which has a column for the SID of the login that owns the database. Databases are one the very few resources owned by login names. As you'll see, most objects within a database are owned by database principals.

The SID used by a principal determines which databases that principal has access to. Each database has a sys.database_principals catalog view, which you can think of as a mapping table that maps login names to users in that particular database. Although a login name and a user name can have the same value, they are separate things.

Database users come in four types. A database user can map to a SQL Server login; the two most common types are a user that maps to a SQL Server login and one that maps to a Windows login. You can also have a database user who doesn't map to any login; this is used for impersonation purposes to have a user to be the owner of objects, who never actually uses the database. SQL Server 2012 added a fourth type of user, which is a user *without* a login. With this type of access, you can connect directly to one specific database, using a password, and have access to only that database. This type of user is available only in contained databases, which are discussed in Chapter 4.

The following query shows the mapping of users in the *AdventureWorks2012* database to login names, and it also shows the default schema (discussed shortly) for each database user. A *LEFT JOIN* is used because (as mentioned in the preceding paragraph), not all users have corresponding login names.

```
SELECT s.name as [Login Name], d.name as [User Name],
    default_schema_name as [Default Schema]
  FROM sys.database_principals d
    LEFT JOIN sys.server_principals s
  ON s.sid = d.sid
  WHERE d.type_description = 'SQL_USER';
```

The *AdventureWorks2012* database provides these results:

```
Login Name User Name           Default Schema
---------- ------------------- --------------
sa         dbo                 dbo
NULL       guest               guest
NULL       INFORMATION_SCHEMA  NULL
sue        sue                 sue
```

Note that the login *sue* has the same value for the user name in this database. Other databases that *sue* has access to are not guaranteed to use the same user name. The login name *sa* has the user name *dbo*. This special login name is used by the *sa* login, by all logins in the sysadmin role, and by whatever login is listed in *sys.databases* as the owner of the database. Within a database, users, not logins, own objects, and users, not logins, are granted permissions. The preceding results also indicate the default schema for each user in my *AdventureWorks* database. In this case, the default schema is the same as the user name, but that doesn't have to be the case, as you'll see in the next section.

Databases vs. schemas

In the ANSI SQL-92 standard, a schema is defined as a collection of database objects that are owned by a single user and form a single namespace. A *namespace* is a set of objects that can't have duplicate names. For example, two tables can have the same name only if they are in separate schemas, so no two tables in the same schema can have the same name. You can think of a schema as a container of objects. (In the context of database tools, a *schema* also refers to the catalog information that describes the objects in a schema or database. In SQL Server Analysis Services, a schema is a description of multidimensional objects such as cubes and dimensions.)

Principals and schemas

A CREATE SCHEMA statement existed prior to SQL Server 2005, but it effectively did nothing because an implicit relationship between users and schemas could be changed or removed. In fact, that relationship was so close, many users of these earlier versions of SQL Server were unaware that users and schemas are different things. Every user was the owner of a schema with the same name as the user. If you created a user *sue*, for example, SQL Server 2000 created a schema called *sue*, which was *sue*'s default schema.

In SQL Server 2012, users and schemas are two separate things. To understand the difference between users and schemas, think of the following: Permissions are granted to users, but objects are placed in schemas.

The statement *GRANT CREATE TABLE TO sue* refers to the user *sue*. Suppose that *sue* then creates a table, as follows:

```
CREATE TABLE mytable (col1 varchar(20));
```

This table is placed in *sue*'s default schema, which may be the schema *sue*. If another user wants to retrieve data from this table, he can issue this statement:

```
SELECT col1 FROM sue.mytable;
```

In this statement, *sue* refers to the schema that contains the table.

Primary and secondary principals can own schemas. Although every object in a SQL Server 2012 database is owned by a user, you never reference an object by its owner; you reference it by the schema in which it is contained. In most cases, the owner of the schema is the same as the owner of all objects within the schema. The metadata view *sys.objects* contains a column called *principal_id*, which contains the user_id of an object's owner if it isn't the same as the owner of the object's schema. Also, a user is never added to a schema; schemas contain objects, not users. For backward compatibility, if you execute the *sp_adduser* or *sp_grantdbaccess* procedure to add a user to a database, SQL Server 2012 creates both a user and a schema of the same name and makes the schema the default for the new user. However, you should get used to using the new DDL CREATE USER and CREATE SCHEMA statements because *sp_adduser* and *sp_grantdbaccess* have been deprecated. When you create a user, you can specify a default schema if you want, but the default for the default schema is the *dbo* schema.

Default schemas

When you create a new database in SQL Server 2012, several schemas are included in it, including dbo, INFORMATION_SCHEMA, and guest. Every database also has a schema called sys, which provides a way to access all the system tables and views. Finally, every fixed database role except public has a schema of the same name in SQL Server 2012.

Users can be assigned a default schema that might or might not exist when the user is created. A user can have at most one default schema at any time. As mentioned earlier, if no default schema is specified for a user, the default schema for the user is dbo. A user's default schema is used for name resolution during object creation or object reference. If you haven't specifically assigned a default schema to a user before that user creates objects, SQL Server tries to create the new objects in the dbo schema rather than in a schema owned by the user creating the object. The user might not have permission to create objects in the dbo schema, even if that is the user's default schema. To avoid confusion, in SQL Server 2012 you should always specify the schema name for all object access as well as object management.

 Note When a login in the sysadmin role creates an object with a single part name, the schema is always *dbo*. However, a sysadmin can explicitly specify an alternate schema in which to create an object.

To create an object in a schema, you must satisfy the following conditions.

- The schema must exist.

- The user creating the object must have permission to create the object (through CREATE TABLE, CREATE VIEW, CREATE PROCEDURE, and so on), either directly or through role membership.

- The user creating the object must be the owner of the schema or a member of the role that owns the schema, or the user must have ALTER rights on the schema or have the ALTER ANY SCHEMA permission in the database.

Moving or copying a database

You might need to move a database before performing maintenance on your system, after a hardware failure, or when you replace your hardware with a newer, faster system. Copying a database is a common way to create a secondary development or testing environment. You can move or copy a database by using a technique called detach and attach or by backing up the database and restoring it in the new location.

Detaching and reattaching a database

You can detach a database from a server by using a simple stored procedure. Detaching a database requires that no one is using the database. If you find existing connections that you can't terminate, you can use the ALTER DATABASE command and set the database to SINGLE_USER mode using one of the termination options that breaks existing connections. Detaching a database ensures that no in-complete transactions are in the database and that no dirty pages exist for this database in memory. If these conditions can't be met, the detach operation fails. After the database is detached, the entry for it is removed from the *sys.databases* catalog view and from the underlying system tables.

Here is the command to detach a database:

```
EXEC sp_detach_db <name of database>;
```

After the database is detached, from the perspective of SQL Server, it's as though you had dropped it. No metadata for the database remains within the SQL Server instance, and the only trace of it might be if your msdb database contained backup-and-restore history for the database that hadn't yet been deleted. However, the history of when backups and restores were done would provide no informa-tion about the structure or content of the database. If you are planning to reattach the database later, recording the properties of all the files that were part of the database is a good idea.

> **Note** The DROP DATABASE command also removes all traces of the database from your instance, but dropping a database is more severe than detaching. SQL Server makes sure that no one is connected to the database before dropping it, but it doesn't check for dirty pages or open transactions. Dropping a database also removes the physical files from the operating system, so unless you have a backup, the database is really gone.

To attach a database, you can use the CREATE DATABASE command with the FOR ATTACH option. (A stored procedure, sp_attach_db, is available, but it's deprecated and not recommended in SQL Server 2012.) The CREATE DATABASE command gives you control over all the files and their place-ment; it also isn't limited to only 16 files like sp_attach_db is. CREATE DATABASE has no such limit—in fact, you can specify up to 32,767 files and 32,767 file groups for each database. The syntax summary for the *CREATE DATABASE* command showing the attach options is shown here:

```
CREATE DATABASE database_name
    ON <filespec> [ ,...n ]
    FOR { ATTACH
        | ATTACH_REBUILD_LOG }
```

Note that only the primary file is required to have a *<filespec>* entry because the primary file contains information about the location of all other files. If you'll be attaching existing files with a different path than when the database was first created or last attached, you must have additional *<filespec>* entries. In any event, all the data files for the database must be available, whether or not they are specified in the CREATE DATABASE command. If the database has multiple log files, they must all be available.

However, if a read/write database has a single log file that's currently unavailable and if the database was shut down with no users or open transactions before the attach operation, FOR ATTACH rebuilds the log file and updates information about the log in the primary file. If the database is read-only, the primary file can't be updated, so the log can't be rebuilt. Therefore, when you attach a read-only database, you must specify the log file or files in the FOR ATTACH clause.

Alternatively, you can use the FOR ATTACH_REBUILD_LOG option, which specifies that the database be created by attaching an existing set of operating system files. This option is limited to read/write databases. If one or more transaction log files are missing, the log is rebuilt. A *<filespec>* entry must specify the primary file. Also, if the log files are available, SQL Server uses those files rather than rebuild the log files, so FOR ATTACH_REBUILD_LOG functions as though you used FOR ATTACH.

If your transaction log is rebuilt by attaching the database, using FOR ATTACH_REBUILD_LOG breaks the log backup chain. You should consider making a full backup after performing this operation.

You typically use FOR ATTACH_REBUILD_LOG when you copy a read/write database with a large log to another server where the copy is used mostly or exclusively for read operations and therefore requires less log space than the original database.

Although the documentation says that you should use CREATE DATABASE FOR ATTACH only on databases previously detached using sp_detach_db, sometimes following this recommendation isn't necessary. If you shut down the SQL Server instance, the files are closed, just as though you had detached the database. However, you aren't guaranteed that all dirty pages from the database were written to disk before the shutdown. This shouldn't cause a problem when you attach such a database if the log file is available. The log file has a record of all completed transactions, and a full recovery is performed when the database is attached to ensure that the database is consistent. One benefit of using the sp_detach_db procedure is that SQL Server knows that the database was shut down cleanly, and the log file doesn't have to be available to attach the database. SQL Server builds a new log file for you. This can be a quick way to shrink a log file that has become much larger than you would like, because the new log file that sp_attach_db creates for you would be the minimum size—less than 1 MB.

Backing up and restoring a database

You can also use backup and restore to move a database to a new location, as an alternative to detach and attach. One benefit of this method is that the database doesn't need to come offline at all because backup is a completely online operation. Because this book isn't a how-to guide for database administrators, you should refer to the bibliography in the companion content for several excellent book recommendations about the mechanics of backing up and restoring a database and to learn best practices for setting up a backup-and-restore plan for your organization. Nevertheless, some issues relating to backup-and-restore processes can help you understand why one backup plan might be better suited to your needs than another, so Chapter 5 discusses backup and restore briefly. Most of these issues involve the role of the transaction log in backup-and-restore operations.

Understanding compatibility levels

Each new version of SQL Server includes many new features, most of which require new keywords and also change certain behaviors that existed in earlier versions. To provide maximum backward compatibility, Microsoft enables you to set the compatibility level of a database running on a SQL Server 2012 instance to one of the following modes: 110 (for SQL Server 2012), 100 (for SQL Server 2008), or 90 (for SQL Server 2005). All newly created databases in SQL Server 2012 have a compatibility level of 110 unless you change the level for the *model* database. A database that has been upgraded or attached from an older version has its compatibility level set to the version from which the database was upgraded.

All the examples and explanations in this book assume that you're using a database in 110 compatibility mode, unless otherwise noted. If you find that your SQL statements behave differently from the ones in this book, you should first verify that your database is in 110 compatibility mode by executing this command:

```
SELECT compatibility_level FROM sys.databases
WHERE name = '<database name>';
```

To change to a different compatibility level, use the ALTER DATABASE command:

```
ALTER DATABASE <database name>
SET COMPATIBILITY_LEVEL = <compatibility-level>;
```

Note The compatibility-level options are intended to provide a transition period while you're upgrading a database or an application to SQL Server 2012. You should try to change your applications so that compatibility options aren't needed because Microsoft doesn't guarantee that these options will continue to work in future versions of SQL Server.

Not all changes in behavior from older versions of SQL Server can be duplicated by changing the compatibility level. For the most part, the differences have to do with whether new reserved keywords and new syntax are recognized, and they don't affect how your queries are processed internally. For example, if you change to compatibility level 90, you don't disallow the use of your *columnstore* indexes or ignore the new database options. But because the word MERGE was a new reserved keyword in SQL Server 2008 (compatibility level 100), by setting your compatibility level to 90, you can create a table called MERGE without using any special delimiters—or a table that you already have in a SQL Server 2005 database continues to be accessible if the database stays in the 90 compatibility level.

For a complete list of the behavioral differences between the compatibility levels and the new reserved keywords, see the documentation for *ALTER DATABASE Compatibility Level*.

Conclusion

A database is a collection of objects such as tables, views, and stored procedures, and one SQL Server instance can contain many databases. Every database has its own transaction log; integrity constraints among objects keep a database logically consistent.

Databases are stored in operating system files in a one-to-many relationship. Each database has at least one file for data and one file for the transaction log. You can increase and decrease the size of databases and their files easily, either manually or automatically.

CHAPTER 4

Special databases

Kalen Delaney and Benjamin Nevarez

Chapter 3, "Databases and database files," introduced databases as a collection of objects such as tables, views, and stored procedures and discussed decisions that someone creating a new SQL Server database would have to make. This chapter covers some special databases, such as the SQL Server system databases, as well as database snapshots and the concept of contained databases. The system databases *master*, *model*, *msdb*, *tempdb*, and the resource database are installed on every instance of SQL Server, and this chapter explains the purpose of each. Because *tempdb* is critical for optimal functioning and performance of SQL Server, this chapter goes deeper into its internals. Database snapshots—an Enterprise Edition feature that allows you to create a point-in-time, read-only copy of any database—is also covered. Finally, another kind of "special" database is the partially contained database. This new feature in SQL Server 2012 is a first step toward full containment whose purpose is to minimize application dependency on instance-level objects and to help identify cross-database dependencies.

System databases

A new SQL Server installation always includes four databases: *master*, *model*, *tempdb*, and *msdb*. It also contains a fifth, "hidden" database that you never see using any of the normal SQL commands that list all your databases. This database is referred to as the *resource database*, but its actual name is *mssqlsystemresource*.

Understanding the master database

The *master* database is composed of system tables that keep track of the server installation as a whole and all other databases that are subsequently created. Although every database has a set of system catalogs that maintain information about objects that the database contains, the *master* database has system catalogs that keep information about system-wide configuration settings, endpoints, logins, databases on the current instance, database files and usage, and the definitions of linked servers.

System objects such as procedure, view, and function definitions aren't stored in the master database; they are kept in the resource database, as explained later in this section.

The *master* database is critical to your system, so always keep a current backup copy of it. Operations such as creating another database, changing configuration values, and modifying login accounts all make modifications to *master*, so you should always back up *master* after performing such actions.

Understanding the model database

The *model* database is simply a template database. Every time you create a new database, SQL Server makes a copy of *model* to form the basis of the new database. If you want every new database to start out with certain objects or permissions, you can put them in *model* so that all new databases inherit them. You can also change most properties of the *model* database by using the *ALTER DATABASE* command, and those property values then are used by any new database you create.

Introducing the tempdb database

The *tempdb* database is used as a workspace. Unique among SQL Server databases, it's re-created—not recovered—every time SQL Server is restarted. It's used for temporary tables explicitly created by users, for worktables that hold intermediate results created internally by SQL Server during query processing and sorting, for maintaining row versions used in snapshot isolation and certain other operations, and for materializing static cursors and the keys of keyset cursors. Because the *tempdb* database is re-created, any objects or permissions that you create in it are lost the next time you start your SQL Server instance. Alternatively, you can create the object in the *model* database, from which *tempdb* is copied.

> **Tip** Any objects that you create in the *model* database also are added to any new databases you create subsequently. If you want objects to exist only in *tempdb,* you can create a startup stored procedure that creates the objects every time your SQL Server instance starts.

Because *tempdb* database sizing and configuration is critical for optimal functioning and performance of SQL Server, the database is covered in more detail in its own section later in this chapter.

Understanding the resource database

As mentioned, the hidden *mssqlsystemresource* database is usually referred to as the *resource database*. Executable system objects, such as system stored procedures and functions, are stored here. Microsoft created this database to allow very fast and safe upgrades. If no one can get to this database, no one can change it, and you can upgrade to a new service pack that introduces new system objects by simply replacing the resource database with a new one. Keep in mind that you can't see this database using any of the normal means for viewing databases, such as selecting from *sys.databases* or executing *sp_helpdb*. It also won't show up in the system databases tree in the Object Explorer pane of SQL Server Management Studio, and it doesn't appear in the drop-down list of databases accessible from your query windows. However, this database still needs disk space.

You can see the files in your default *binn* directory by using Microsoft Windows Explorer. My data directory is at C:\Program Files\Microsoft SQL Server\MSSQL11.MSSQLSERVER\MSSQL\Binn; I can see a file called mssqlsystemresource.mdf, which is 40 MB in size, and mssqlsystemresource.ldf, which is 0.5 MB. The created and modified date for both of these files is the date that the code for the current build was frozen. It should be the same date that you see when you run *SELECT @@version*. For SQL Server 2012, the RTM build, this is 11.0.2100.60.

If you absolutely need to "see" the contents of *mssqlsystemresource*, you can do so by using a couple of methods. The easiest, if you just want to see what's there, is to stop SQL Server, make copies of the two files for the resource database, restart SQL Server, and then attach the copied files to create a database with a new name. You can do this by using Object Explorer in Management Studio or by using the *CREATE DATABASE FOR ATTACH* syntax to create a clone database:

```
CREATE DATABASE resource_copy
ON (NAME = data, FILENAME = 'C:\data\mssqlsystemresource_copy.mdf'),
   (NAME = log, FILENAME = 'C:\data\mssqlsystemresource_copy.ldf')
    FOR ATTACH;
```

SQL Server treats this new *resource_copy* database like any other user database, and it doesn't treat the objects in it as special in any way. If you want to change anything in the resource database, such as the text of a supplied system stored procedure, changing it in *resource_copy* obviously doesn't affect anything else on your instance. However, if you start your SQL Server instance in single-user mode, you can make a single connection to this instance, and that connection can use the *mssqlsystemresource* database. Starting an instance in single-user mode isn't the same thing as setting a database to single-user mode. For details on how to start SQL Server in single-user mode, see the *SQL Server Books Online* entry for the *sqlservr.exe* application.

Understanding the msdb database

The *msdb* database is used by the SQL Server Agent service and other companion services, which perform scheduled activities such as backups and replication tasks, and the Service Broker, which provides queuing and reliable messaging for SQL Server. In addition to backups, objects in *msdb* support jobs, alerts, log shipping, policies, database mail, and recovery of damaged pages. When you aren't actively performing these activities on this database, you can generally ignore *msdb* (but you might take a peek at the backup history and other information kept there).

You can think of the *msdb* tables as another form of system table: Just as you can never directly modify system tables, you shouldn't directly add data to or delete data from tables in *msdb* unless you really know what you're doing or are instructed to do so by a SQL Server technical support engineer. In older versions of SQL Server, you could actually drop the *msdb* database; your SQL Server instance was still usable, but obviously you couldn't maintain any backup history, and you couldn't define tasks, alerts, or jobs or set up replication. An undocumented traceflag still allows you to drop the *msdb* database, but because the default *msdb* database is so small, I recommend leaving it alone even if you think you might never need it.

Moving system databases

You might need to move system databases as part of a planned relocation or scheduled maintenance operation. If you move a system database and later rebuild the *master* database, you must move that system database again because the rebuild operation installs all system databases to their default location. The steps for moving *tempdb*, *model*, and *msdb* are slightly different than for moving the *master* database.

> **Note** In SQL Server 2012, the *mssqlsystemresource* database can't be moved. If you move the files for this database, you won't be able to restart your SQL Server service.

Here are the steps for moving an undamaged system database (other than the master database):

1. For each file in the database to be moved, use the *ALTER DATABASE* command with the *MODIFY FILE* option to specify the new physical location.

2. Stop the SQL Server instance.

3. Physically move the files.

4. Restart the SQL Server instance.

5. Verify the change by running the following query:

```
SELECT name, physical_name AS CurrentLocation, state_desc
FROM sys.master_files
WHERE database_id = DB_ID(N'<database_name>');
```

If the system database needs to be moved because of a hardware failure, the solution is a bit more problematic because you might not have access to the server to run the *ALTER DATABASE* command. Follow these steps to move a damaged system database (other than the *master* database or the resource database):

1. Stop the instance of SQL Server if it has been started.

2. Start the instance of SQL Server in *master-only* recovery mode (by specifying *traceflag 3608*) by entering one of the following commands at the command prompt:

```
-- If the instance is the default instance:
NET START MSSQLSERVER /f /T3608

-- For a named instance:
NET START MSSQL$instancename /f /T3608
```

/f indicates that the instance of SQL Server starts with minimal configuration.

3. For each file in the database to be moved, use the *ALTER DATABASE* command with the *MODIFY FILE* option to specify the new physical location. You can use either Management Studio or the *SQLCMD* utility.

4. Exit Management Studio or the *SQLCMD* utility.

5. Stop the instance of SQL Server.

6. Physically move the file or files to the new location.

7. Restart the instance of SQL Server without traceflag 3608. For example, run *NET START MSSQLSERVER*.

8. Verify the change by running the following query:

```
SELECT name, physical_name AS CurrentLocation, state_desc
FROM sys.master_files
WHERE database_id = DB_ID(N'<database_name>');
```

Moving the master database

Full details on moving the *master* database can be found in *SQL Server Books Online,* but the steps are summarized here. The biggest difference between moving this database and moving other system databases is that you must go through the SQL Server Configuration Manager.

To move the *master* database, followw these steps.

1. Open the SQL Server Configuration Manager. Right-click the desired instance of SQL Server, choose Properties, and then click the Startup Parameters tab.

2. Edit the Startup Parameters values to point to the new directory location for the *master* database data and log files and click Update. If you want, you can also move the SQL Server error log files. The parameter value for the data file must follow the *–d* parameter, the value for the log file must follow the *–l* parameter, and the value for the error log must follow the *–e* parameter, as shown here:

```
-dE:\Data\master.mdf
-lE:\Data\mastlog.ldf
-eE:\Data\LOG\ERRORLOG
```

3. Stop the instance of SQL Server and physically move the files for to the new location.

4. Restart the instance of SQL Server.

5. Verify the file change for the *master* database by running the following query:

```
SELECT name, physical_name AS CurrentLocation, state_desc
FROM sys.master_files
WHERE database_id = DB_ID('master');
```

Finally, if you are also changing your drive letters or folders, you need to verify and perhaps change the location of the SQL Server Agent error log file and the configured database default locations setting. The Database default locations setting is defined on Server Properties | Database Settings.

The tempdb database

In some ways, the *tempdb* database is just like any other database, but it has some unique behaviors. Not all of them are relevant to the topic of this chapter, so some references will be made to other chapters where you can find additional information.

As mentioned previously, the biggest difference between *tempdb* and all the other databases in your SQL Server instance is that *tempdb* is re-created rather than recovered every time SQL Server is restarted. You can think of *tempdb* as a workspace for temporary user objects and internal objects explicitly created by SQL Server itself.

Every time *tempdb* is re-created, it inherits most database options from the model database. However, the recovery model isn't copied because *tempdb* always uses simple recovery, which is discussed in detail in Chapter 5, "Logging and recovery." Certain database options can't be set for *tempdb*, such as *OFFLINE* and *READONLY*. You also can't drop the *tempdb* database.

In the simple recovery model, the *tempdb* database's log is constantly being truncated and can never be backed up. No recovery information is needed because every time SQL Server is started, *tempdb* is completely re-created; any previous user-created temporary objects—that is, all your tables and data—disappear.

Logging for *tempdb* is also different than for other databases. (Chapter 5 covers normal logging.) Many people assume that *tempdb* has no logging, but this isn't true. Operations within *tempdb* are logged so that transactions on temporary objects can be rolled back, but the records in the log contain only enough information to roll back a transaction, not to recover (or redo) it.

As mentioned earlier, recovery is run on a database as one of the first steps in creating a snapshot. You can't recover *tempdb*, so you can't create a snapshot of it, which means that you can't run *DBCC CHECKDB* using a snapshot (or, in fact, most of the DBCC validation commands). Another difference with running DBCC in *tempdb* is that SQL Server skips all allocation and catalog checks. Running *DBCC CHECKDB* (or *CHECKTABLE*) in *tempdb* acquires a Shared Table lock on each table as it is checked. (Locking is discussed in Chapter 13, "Transactions and concurrency.")

Objects in tempdb

Three types of objects are stored in *tempdb*: user objects, internal objects, and the version store, used primarily for snapshot isolation.

User objects

All users have the privileges to create and use local and global temporary tables that reside in *tempdb*. (Local and global temporary table names have the # or ## prefix, respectively. However, by default, users don't have the privileges to use *tempdb* and then create tables there, unless the table name is prefaced with # or ##.) You can easily grant the privileges in an autostart procedure that runs each time the SQL Server instance is restarted.

Other user objects that need space in *tempdb* include table variables and table-valued functions. The user objects created in *tempdb* are in many ways treated just like user objects in any other database: Space must be allocated for them when they are populated, and the metadata needs to be managed. You can see user objects by examining the system catalog views, such as *sys.objects*, and information in the *sys.partitions* and *sys.allocation_units* views enable you to see how much space is taken up by user objects. Chapter 6, "Table storage"; Chapter 7, "Indexes: internals and management"; and Chapter 8, "Special storage," discuss these views.

Internal objects

Internal objects in *tempdb* aren't visible using the normal tools, but they still take up space from the database. They aren't listed in the catalog views because their metadata is stored only in memory. The three basic types of internal objects are work tables, work files, and sort units.

Work tables are created by SQL Server during the following operations:

- Spooling, to hold intermediate results during a large query

- Working with XML or other large object (LOB) data type variables

- Processing SQL Service Broker objects

- Working with static or keyset cursors

Work files are used when SQL Server is processing a query that uses a hash operator, either for joining or aggregating data. Although hashing works by building a hash table in memory, it can use *tempdb* space if not enough memory is available, which can also become a performance problem.

Sort units are created when a sort operation takes place, and this occurs in many situations in addition to a query containing an *ORDER BY* clause. SQL Server uses sorting to build an index, and it might use sorting to process queries involving grouping. In some cases, a merge join might require that SQL Server sort the data before performing the join. Sort units are created in *tempdb* to hold the data as it is being sorted. SQL Server can also create sort units in user databases in addition to *tempdb*, particularly when creating indexes. As you'll see in Chapter 7, when you create or rebuild an index, you have the choice to do the sort in the current user database or in *tempdb,* specified by the *SORT_IN_TEMPDB* option, which is *OFF* by default.

Keep in mind that some other SQL Server features can create internal objects by indirectly performing the previous operations. For example, *DBCC CHECKDB* uses work tables to hold intermediate results of sort operations, and Database Mail or event notifications both rely on Service Broker.

Version store

The version store supports technology for row-level versioning of data. Older versions of updated rows are kept in *tempdb* in the following situations:

- When an *AFTER* trigger is fired (versions aren't generated by *INSTEAD OF* triggers)

- When a Data Modification Language (DML) command is executed in a database that allows snapshot transactions, either snapshot isolation or read-committed snapshot isolation (RCSI)

- When multiple active result sets (MARS) are invoked from a client application

- During online index builds or rebuilds when the index has concurrent DML

Chapter 13 discusses versioning and snapshot transactions in detail.

Optimizations in tempdb

Because *tempdb* is used for many internal operations, you have to take care in monitoring and managing it. The next sections present some best practices and monitoring suggestions. In this section, I tell you about some of the internal optimizations in SQL Server that allow *tempdb* to manage objects much more efficiently.

Logging optimizations

As you know, every operation that affects your user database in any way is logged. In *tempdb*, however, this isn't entirely true. For example, with logging update operations, only the original data (the "before" image) is logged, not the new values (the "after" image). The commit operations and committed log records also aren't flushed to disk synchronously in *tempdb*, making these transactions faster than they are in user databases.

Allocation and caching optimizations

Many allocation optimizations are used in all databases, not just *tempdb*. However, *tempdb* is most likely the database in which the greatest number of new objects are created and dropped during production operations, so the impact on *tempdb* is greater than on user databases. In SQL Server, allocation pages are accessed very efficiently to determine where free extents are available; you should see far less contention on the allocation pages than in older versions of the product. SQL Server also has a very efficient search algorithm for finding an available single page from mixed extents. When a database has multiple files, SQL Server has a very efficient proportional fill algorithm that allocates space to multiple data files, proportional to the amount of free space available in each file so that all the files fill up at about the same time.

Another optimization specific to *tempdb* prevents you from having to allocate any new space for some objects. If a work table is dropped, one IAM page and one extent are saved (for a total of nine pages), so deallocating and then reallocating the space isn't necessary if the same work table needs to be created again. This dropped work table cache isn't very big and has room for only 64 objects. If a work table is truncated internally and the query plan that uses that worktable is still in the plan cache, again the first IAM page and the first extent are saved. For these truncated tables, the number of objects that can be cached isn't limited; it depends only on the available memory space.

User objects in *tempdb* can also have some of their space cached if they are dropped. For a small table of less than 8 MB, dropping a user object in *tempdb* causes one IAM page and one extent to be saved. However, if the table has had any additional DDL performed, such as creating indexes or constraints, or if the table was created using dynamic SQL, no caching is done.

For a large table, the entire drop is performed as a deferred operation. Deferred drop operations are in fact used in every database as a way to improve overall throughput because a thread doesn't need to wait for the drop to complete before proceeding with its next task. Like the other allocation optimizations available in all databases, the deferred drop probably provides the most benefit in *tempdb*, where tables are most likely to be dropped during production operations. A background thread eventually cleans up the space allocated for dropped tables, but until then, the allocated space remains. You can detect this space by looking at the *sys.allocation_units* system view for rows with a *type* value of 0, which indicates a dropped object; you also can see that the *container_id* column is 0, which indicates that the allocated space doesn't really belong to any object.

Best practices

By default, your *tempdb* database is created on only one data file. You will probably find that multiple files give you better I/O performance and less contention on the global allocation structures (the GAM, SGAM, and PFS pages). Contention and the optimal number of files are covered in more detail in the next section. No matter how many files you have, they should be on the fastest disks you can afford. One log file should be sufficient, and that should also be on a fast disk.

To determine the optimum size of your *tempdb*, you must test your own applications with your data volumes, but knowing when and how *tempdb* is used can help you make preliminary estimates. Database maintenance activities such as *DBCC CHECKDB* or rebuilding indexes with the *SORT_IN_ TEMPDB* option can greatly affect *tempdb* size as well. Keep in mind that only one *tempdb* exists for each SQL Server instance, so one badly behaving application can affect all other users in all other applications. Chapter 13 explains how to determine the size of the version store. All these factors affect the space needed for your *tempdb*. Finally, Chapter 14, "DBCC internals," looks at how the DBCC consistency checking commands use *tempdb* and how to determine the *tempdb* space requirements.

Database options for *tempdb* should rarely be changed, and some options aren't applicable to *tempdb*. In particular, *tempdb* ignores the autoshrink option. In any case, shrinking *tempdb* isn't recommended unless your workload patterns have changed significantly. If you do need to shrink your *tempdb*, you're probably better off shrinking each file individually. Keep in mind that the files might not be able to shrink if any internal objects or version store pages need to be moved. The best way to shrink *tempdb* is to *ALTER* the database, change the file sizes, and then stop and restart SQL Server so that *tempdb* is rebuilt to the desired size. You should allow your *tempdb* files to autogrow only as a last resort and only to prevent errors due to running out of room. Don't rely on autogrow to manage the size of your *tempdb* files. Autogrow causes a delay in processing when you can probably least afford it, although the impact is somewhat less if you use instant file initialization. You should determine the optimum size of *tempdb* through testing and planning so that *tempdb* can start with as much space as it needs and won't have to grow while your applications are running. Also, autogrow is temporary for *tempdb*; when SQL Server is restarted, *tempdb* is created using its configured size.

Here are some tips for making optimum use of your *tempdb*. The next section elaborates on recommendations to avoid or minimize *tempdb* contention and later chapters explain why the other suggestions are considered best practices:

- Take advantage of *tempdb* object caching—for example, by avoiding additional DDL statements after the object is created, as explained earlier.

- Keep your transactions short, especially those that use snapshot isolation, MARS, or triggers.

- Avoid page allocation and deallocation by keeping columns to be updated at a fixed size rather than a variable size (which can implement the *UPDATE* as a *DELETE* followed by an *INSERT*).

- Don't mix long and short transactions from different databases (in the same instance) if versioning is being used.

tempdb contention

Because contention is one of the most common *tempdb* issues, this section explains what the problem is and how to avoid or minimize it. Contention, which exists in two different flavors, DML and DDL, can occur when *tempdb* is heavily used and can negatively affect the performance of the entire SQL Server instance. DML contention is related to the allocation and deallocation of pages for *INSERT*, *UPDATE*, and *DELETE* operations happening on *tempdb* temporary objects. However, DDL contention occurs in system catalog tables when a high number of user objects, like temporary tables or table variables, are created or dropped.

DML contention is the most common; DDL contention is briefly discussed at the end of this section.

DML contention

Every time a new object is created in *tempdb*, SQL Server must allocate two pages: an Index Allocation Map (IAM) page and the first page for the object. To do this, SQL Server needs to access the Page Free Space (PFS) and Shared Global Allocation Map (SGAM) pages in *tempdb*. As explained in Chapter 3 (and discussed in more detail in Chapter 6), PFS pages keep track of which database pages are available to hold new data. The first PFS page is the second page of a file (Page 1). The first SGAM page is the fourth page in a file (Page 3) and records which extents are now used as mixed extents and have at least one unused page. When *INSERT*, *UPDATE*, and *DELETE* operations are performed on *tempdb*, latches are held on the PFS and SGAM pages and can cause contention when many allocations or deallocations occur at the same time. So under a heavy load when many temporary tables are being created and updated, the PFS and SGAM pages need to be accessed and updated, leading to latch contention.

One way to see whether you have DML contention on *tempdb* is to look for waits on resource "2:1:1" and "2:1:3" on the sysprocesses system table or the *sys.dm_os_waiting_tasks* DMV, as explained later. Notice that a PFS page can also be found every 8,088 pages or about 64 MB, and a SGAM every 511,232 pages or almost 4 GB of data. The allocation and caching optimizations mentioned earlier also help minimize contention.

You can peek into the allocation and deallocation of pages process with *tempdb* by looking at the allocation ring buffer, which you can inspect by using the undocumented traceflag 1106. Be careful not to use this traceflag in a production environment, because it can affect the performance of the SQL Server instance. You can run this in your test environment:

```
DBCC TRACEON(1106, -1);
```

The script in Listing 4-1, adapted from one presented at the PASS Summit 2011 conference by Bob Ward, shows you how.

LISTING 4-1 Inspecting the allocation ring buffer

```
DECLARE @ts_now bigint;
SELECT @ts_now=cpu_ticks/(cpu_ticks/ms_ticks)
FROM sys.dm_os_sys_info;
SELECT record_id,
DATEADD(ms, -1 * (@ts_now - [timestamp]), GETDATE()) as event_time,
CASE
    WHEN event = 0 THEN 'Allocation Cache Init'
    WHEN event = 1 THEN 'Allocation Cache Add Entry'
    WHEN event = 2 THEN 'Allocation Cache RMV Entry'
    WHEN event = 3 THEN 'Allocation Cache Reinit'
    WHEN event = 4 THEN 'Allocation Cache Free'
    WHEN event = 5 THEN 'Truncate Allocation Unit'
    WHEN event = 10 THEN 'PFS Alloc Page'
    WHEN event = 11 THEN 'PFS Dealloc Page'
    WHEN event = 20 THEN 'IAM Set Bit'
    WHEN event = 21 THEN 'IAM Clear Bit'
    WHEN event = 22 THEN 'GAM Set Bit'
    WHEN event = 23 THEN 'GAM Clear Bit'
    WHEN event = 24 THEN 'SGAM Set Bit'
    WHEN event = 25 THEN 'SGAM Clear Bit'
    WHEN event = 26 THEN 'SGAM Set Bit NX'
    WHEN event = 27 THEN 'SGAM Clear Bit NX'
    WHEN event = 28 THEN 'GAM Zap Extent'
    WHEN event = 40 THEN 'Format IAM Page'
    WHEN event = 41 THEN 'Format Page'
    WHEN event = 42 THEN 'Reassign IAM Page'
    WHEN event = 50 THEN 'Worktable Cache Add IAM'
    WHEN event = 51 THEN 'Worktable Cache Add Page'
    WHEN event = 52 THEN 'Worktable Cache RMV IAM'
    WHEN event = 53 THEN 'Worktable Cache RMV Page'
    WHEN event = 61 THEN 'IAM Cache Destroy'
    WHEN event = 62 THEN 'IAM Cache Add Page'
    WHEN event = 63 THEN 'IAM Cache Refresh Requested'
    ELSE 'Unknown Event'
END as event_name,
session_id as s_id,
page_id,
```

```
allocation_unit_id as au_id
FROM
(
SELECT
xml_record.value('(./Record/@id)[1]', 'int') AS record_id,
xml_record.value('(./Record/SpaceMgr/Event)[1]', 'int') AS event,
xml_record.value('(./Record/SpaceMgr/SpId)[1]', 'int') AS session_id,
xml_record.value('(./Record/SpaceMgr/PageId)[1]', 'varchar(100)') AS page_id,
xml_record.value('(./Record/SpaceMgr/AuId)[1]', 'varchar(100)') AS allocation_unit_id,
timestamp
FROM
    (
    SELECT timestamp, convert(xml, record) as xml_record
    FROM sys.dm_os_ring_buffers
    WHERE ring_buffer_type = N'RING_BUFFER_SPACEMGR_TRACE'
    ) AS the_record
) AS ring_buffer_record
-- WHERE session_id = 52
ORDER BY record_id;
```

> **Note** This script works in SQL Server 2012 only, but you can update it to run in previous versions of SQL Server by using the *RING_BUFFER_ALLOC_TRACE* ring buffer instead and replacing the *SpaceMgr* element with *ALLOC*. You can find a similar script at the knowledge base article at *http://support.microsoft.com/kb/947204*.

When you run the script the first time, you get no output records. On a different session, run a simple statement like this to create activity on a temporary table:

```
CREATE TABLE #test (name varchar(20))
INSERT INTO #test VALUES ('Test')
```

Running the allocation ring buffer script again results in output similar to this:

record_id	event_name	s_id	page_id	au_id
1406	Allocation Cache Init	58	0:0	5709:2560
1407	PFS Alloc Page	58	1:287	5709:2560
1408	GAM Clear Bit	58	1:296	99:0
1409	SGAM Set Bit	58	1:296	99:0
1410	PFS Alloc Page	58	1:296	99:0
1411	Format IAM Page	58	1:296	5709:2560
1412	Format Page	58	1:287	5709:2560

The sample output includes the first page allocated to the object, 1:287, the first IAM page, 1:296, plus some other additional information.

> **Note** You should see only about a dozen events. If you see many events, you can filter by session_id by uncommenting the *WHERE* session_id section and specifying a session ID.

Don't forget to disable the traceflag before continuing:

```
DBCC TRACEOFF(1106, -1);
```

To detect DML contention, you can use any of the following queries, which look for *PAGELATCH* waits on *tempdb*, as indicated by the database ID 2 and the *waitresource* and *resource_description* columns.

```
SELECT * FROM sysprocesses
WHERE lastwaittype LIKE 'PAGE%LATCH%' AND waitresource LIKE '2:%';

SELECT * from sys.dm_os_waiting_tasks
WHERE wait_type LIKE 'PAGE%LATCH%'
  AND resource_description LIKE '2:%';
```

You can also track the *sqlserver.latch_suspend_end* event in extended events filtering on *database_id = 2* in SQL Server 2012.

The *waitresource* and *resource_description* column, for the purpose of latch resource owner, is defined as

```
<db-id>:<file-id>:<page-in-file>
```

in which *<db-id>* is always 2 for *tempdb* and *<file-id>* and *<page-in-file>* are the file ID and page number respectively.

lastwaittype and *wait_type* are the name of the wait type. This section is interested only on the *PAGELATCH* wait type.

To see how it works so you can be ready to identify it in a real environment, you can easily simulate some *PAGELATCH* contention using the *ostress* utility, which you can download as part of the RML Utilities at *http://www.microsoft.com/download/en/details.aspx?id=8161*.

For example, copy the following two statements into a file and name it *query.sql*:

```
CREATE TABLE #test (id int, name char(7000));
INSERT INTO #test VALUES (1, 'Hello');
```

Then run the following on a command-line prompt:

```
ostress -n1000 -iquery.sql -q
```

In this command, *-n* means the number of connections processing each query, *-i* indicates the file containing the SQL statements to be executed, and *−q* means quiet mode, which is used to suppress all query output.

> **Note** These are the minimum parameters needed. Type **ostress** for a list of other available parameters, including some you might want to use for this test, such as *-S, -E, -P,* or *−U.*

On a test environment with a default *tempdb* configuration, you might see some output similar to this:

Spid	kpid	blocked	waittype	waittime	lastwaittype	waitresource
59	12404	0	0x0033	9	PAGELATCH_UP	2:1:1
91	12320	568	0x0033	29	PAGELATCH_UP	2:1:1
92	1020	0	0x0000	0	PAGELATCH_SH	2:1:1
93	8104	0	0x0000	0	PAGELATCH_SH	2:1:1
117	7288	568	0x0033	31	PAGELATCH_UP	2:1:1
132	12528	0	0x0000	0	PAGELATCH_SH	2:1:1

As mentioned, this section is focused on *PAGELATCH*, not *PAGEIOLATCH* waits. Latches are short-term lightweight synchronization objects. *PAGELATCH* waits are used to synchronize access to buffer pages; *PAGEIOLATCH* is used for disk-to-memory transfers, and a high number of these waits typically suggest disk I/O subsystem issues.

> **More info** To find out how to troubleshoot *PAGEIOLATCH* and other waits, read the "SQL Server Waits and Queues" white paper at *http://technet.microsoft.com/library/Cc966413*.

After you find out that you have a DML contention problem in your environment, how do you fix it? To avoid or minimize DML contention on *tempdb*, you can follow one or more of the following recommendations.

- Although doing so might not always be possible, you can try to identify the queries that make heavy use of *tempdb* to try to minimize that use.

- You can increase the number of data files used for *tempdb*, as explained in the next section. Having multiple files reduces contention by splitting the latch contention over multiple allocation bitmaps, because each data file has its own PFS, GAM, and SGAM pages.

- You can consider using traceflag 1118, which forces uniform extent allocations instead of mixed page allocations and, by doing that, reduces SGAM contention. When traceflag 1118 is enabled, only one extent is allocated from a GAM page, rather than potentially 8 pages from a SGAM page. However, due to some optimizations, such as the cache of temporary tables mentioned previously, this traceflag might not be required so much in the latest SQL Server versions. Notice, too, that this is an instance-level configuration, so it affects not only *tempdb* but also every database on the instance.

Despite some published recommendations, the optimal number of files for *tempdb* can be difficult to estimate and depends on several factors, such as *tempdb* usage, workload, and degree of contention. An initial recommendation is to start with a number of data files equal to the number of logical processors (or cores) assigned to SQL Server. But for systems with a high number of processors (for example, 16 or more), just a quarter or half the number of files might be enough. However, if after following these initial recommendations contention isn't reduced, you might have to increase the number of data files.

Also, having all the files the same size is equally important for the proportional fill algorithm introduced earlier: its round-robin algorithm chooses a different file for each consecutive page allocation. If files aren't the same size, this algorithm tries to use the largest file more than the other files, defeating the purpose of using multiple files. If you look at this from another angle, note that having too many data files can also create performance problems as the work necessary to do the round-robin allocation can reduce performance and increase management overhead.

DDL contention

DDL contention relates to system catalog tables and occurs when a high number of user objects are created or dropped. As mentioned previously, user objects in *tempdb* include local and global temporary tables and table variables. System catalog tables don't keep metadata for internal objects. To monitor DDL contention, use the performance counters Temp Tables Creation Rate and Temp Tables for Destruction on SQL Server:General Statistics. Fixing DDL contention requires identifying these queries and minimizing the creation of these temporary tables and table variables.

tempdb space monitoring

Because *tempdb* is used by the entire instance, proactively monitoring space usage in *tempdb* is a very important task. Quite a few tools, stored procedures, and system views report on object space usage, as discussed in chapters 6, 7, and 8. However, SQL Server has three DMVs that you can use to monitor the space usage in t*empdb: sys.dm_db_file_space_usage, sys.dm_db_session_space_usage*, and *sys.dm_db_task_space_usage*, which provide information at the file, session, and task levels, respectively. You can use these DMVs to track the total number of pages allocated for both user and internal objects. In addition to the scope, some other major differences between these DMVs are as follows.

- *sys.dm_db_file_space_usage* also returns version store information, tracking the number of pages in uniform extents allocated to the version store (versions are never stored in mixed extents). Although a session can actually generate versions, the version store is a global resource; no version store information is kept at the session or task level. Versions can't be removed when the session ends.

- Unlike in previous versions of SQL Server, in SQL Server 2012 *sys.dm_db_file_space_usage* can now be used for any database in the instance, not only tempdb. tempdb-only properties are shown as NULL for other databases. The *sys.dm_db_task_space_usage* and *sys.dm_db_session_space_usage* DMVs currently return information only for *tempdb*.

One interesting way to understand how these DMVs work is by producing some activity on *tempdb* while looking at their output at the same time. You can try the following exercise, which uses these three DMVs to monitor the number of pages allocated and deallocated on internal objects at the database data file, session, and task level, respectively. Open a query window in Management Studio and execute the following code:

```
USE AdventureWorks2012;
GO

CREATE TABLE dbo.SalesOrderDetail(
```

```
        SalesOrderID int,
        SalesOrderDetailID int,
        CarrierTrackingNumber nvarchar(25),
        OrderQty smallint,
        ProductID int,
        SpecialOfferID int,
        UnitPrice money,
        UnitPriceDiscount money,
        LineTotal numeric(38, 6),
        rowguid uniqueidentifier,
        ModifiedDate datetime);
GO
INSERT INTO dbo.SalesOrderDetail
SELECT * FROM Sales.SalesOrderDetail;
GO 80
```

Open a second window and use the following code. To help on filtering the output, replace the session_id value with the corresponding value of the session used by the first window as shown in Management Studio.

```
USE tempdb;
GO
SELECT * FROM sys.dm_db_file_space_usage;

SELECT * FROM sys.dm_db_task_space_usage
WHERE session_id = 52;

SELECT * FROM sys.dm_db_session_space_usage
WHERE session_id = 52;
```

Go back to the first window and be ready to run the following statement:

```
CREATE CLUSTERED INDEX PK_SalesOrderID
on dbo.SalesOrderDetail(SalesOrderID, SalesOrderDetailID)
WITH (SORT_IN_TEMPDB = ON);
```

This statement creates an index on a big table and, because the *SORT_IN_TEMPDB* option is specified, uses a *tempdb* internal object to store temporary sort results. Keep in mind that in some cases you might need to adjust the size of the dbo.SalesOrderDetail table by changing the value of *N* in the *GO N* statement as needed for two reasons.

- To make sure that you, in fact, create activity on *tempdb* (depending on the amount of memory available on your system, *tempdb* space might not be required as the sort could be performed entirely in memory)

- So that the *CREATE INDEX* statement can run for a reasonable amount of time—say, a couple of minutes—so you can look at the DMVs while the allocation and deallocation of pages is happening

Now run the *CREATE INDEX* statement in one window and monitor the pages allocated and deallocated by continually running the DMVs on the second window. Assuming that no other significant activity is occurring in *tempdb* when the *CREATE INDEX* operation is running, initially the sum of *internal_objects_alloc_page_count* at the task level (for *exec_contextid > 0*, if the task is running in parallel) is the same as the *internal_object_reserved_page_count* at the file level, as shown in the following snapshots.

- *sys.dm_db_file_space_usage* partial output:

```
database_id    file_id   internal_object_reserved_page_count
2              1         101280
```

- *sys.dm_db_task_space_usage* partial output:

```
session_id  exec_context_id  internal_objects_alloc_page_count
52          0                352
52          1                27200
52          2                15520
52          3                27392
52          4                31168
```

Notice that while the *CREATE INDEX* statement is running, *internal_objects_alloc_page_count* in *sys.dm_db_session_space_usage* shows 0, because the number of pages isn't shown until the task is completed. As pages are being deallocated and no longer reserved (before the end of the *CREATE INDEX* operation), they are shown both in unallocated_extent_page_count and internal_objects_dealloc_page_count, at the file and task level, respectively.

Finally, when the *CREATE INDEX* operation is completed, *internal_objects_alloc_page_count* in *sys.dm_db_session_space_usage* shows some value around to 122,624 for this example, which is also the maximum value reached on both internal_object_reserved_page_count and *internal_objects_alloc_page_count* at the file and task level DMVs, respectively. Being familiar with this output can help you to better troubleshoot problems when they appear on a real system.

To clean up after running the exercise, run this command:

```
DROP TABLE dbo.SalesOrderDetail;
```

Database snapshots

SQL Server 2012 Enterprise Edition supports a feature called database snapshots, which allow you to create a point-in-time, read-only copy of a database. In fact, you can create multiple snapshots of the same source database at different points in time. The actual space needed for each snapshot is typically much less than the space required for the original database because the snapshot stores only pages that have changed, as is discussed shortly.

Database snapshots allow you to do the following:

- Turn a mirrored database into a reporting database. You can't read from a mirrored database, but you can create a snapshot of this database and read from it.

- Generate reports without blocking or being blocked by production operations.

- Protect against administrative or user errors.

- Temporarily back up before doing major updates on a database. You can use the snapshot to revert the database to the state that it was when the snapshot was taken. Keep in mind that database snapshots aren't a substitute for your backup and restore strategy, are still dependent on the source database, and aren't redundant storage.

You'll probably think of more ways to use snapshots as you gain experience with them.

Note As of SQL Server 2012, database mirroring is a deprecated feature that won't be supported in a future version of SQL Server. Microsoft instead recommends using AlwaysOn Availability Groups.

Creating a database snapshot

The mechanics of snapshot creation are straightforward—you simply specify an option for the *CREATE DATABASE* command. Object Explorer doesn't provide a graphical interface for creating a database snapshot, so you must use the T-SQL syntax. (After creation, a database snapshot is viewable from the Database Snapshot node of the SQL Server Management Studio Object Explorer.) When you create a snapshot, you must include each data file from the source database in the *CREATE DATABASE* command, with the original logical name and a new physical name and path. No other properties of the files can be specified, and no log file is used.

Here is the syntax to create a snapshot of the *AdventureWorks2012* database, putting the snapshot files in the *C:\Data* directory:

```
CREATE DATABASE AdventureWorks_snapshot ON
( NAME = N'AdventureWorks2012_Data',
  FILENAME =
  N'C:\Data\AdventureWorks_snapshot.mdf')
AS SNAPSHOT OF AdventureWorks2012;
```

Each file in the snapshot is created as a sparse file, which is a feature of the NTFS file system. (Don't confuse sparse files with sparse columns which is a feature introduced with SQL Server 2008.) Initially, a sparse file contains no user data, and disk space for user data hasn't been allocated to it. As data is written to the sparse file, NTFS allocates disk space gradually. A sparse file can potentially grow very large. Sparse files grow in 64 KB increments; thus, the size of a sparse file on disk is always a multiple of 64 KB.

The snapshot files contain only the data that has changed from the source. For every file, SQL Server creates a bitmap that's kept in cache, with a bit for each page of the file indicating whether that page has been copied to the snapshot. Every time a page in the source is updated, SQL Server checks the bitmap for the file to see whether the page has already been copied and, if it hasn't, it's copied at that time. This operation is called a *copy-on-write operation*.

Figure 4-1 shows a database with a snapshot that contains 10 percent of the data (one page) from the source.

Percent copied 10%

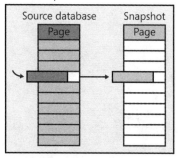

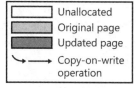

FIGURE 4-1 A database snapshot that contains one page of data from the source database.

When a process reads from the snapshot, it first accesses the bitmap to see whether the page it wants is in the snapshot file or still on the source. Figure 4-2 shows read operations from the same database as in Figure 4-1. Nine of the pages are accessed from the source database, and one is accessed from the snapshot because it has been updated on the source. When a process reads from a database snapshot, no locks are taken no matter what isolation level you are in. This is true whether the page is read from the sparse file or from the source database. This is one big advantage of using database snapshots.

Percent copied 10%

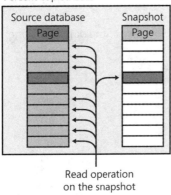

Read operation
on the snapshot

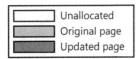

FIGURE 4-2 Read operations from a database snapshot, reading changed pages from the snapshot, and un-changed pages from the source database.

As mentioned earlier, the bitmap is stored in cache, not with the file itself, so it's always readily available. When SQL Server shuts down or the database is closed, the bitmaps are lost and need to be reconstructed at database startup. SQL Server determines whether each page is in the sparse file as it's accessed, and then records that information in the bitmap for future use.

The snapshot reflects the point in time when the *CREATE DATABASE* command is issued—that is, when the creation operation commences. SQL Server checkpoints the source database and records a synchronization Log Sequence Number (LSN) in the source database's transaction log. As you'll see in Chapter 5, during a discussion about the transaction log, the LSN helps determine a specific point in time in a database. SQL Server then runs recovery on the snapshot so that any uncommitted transactions are rolled back. So although the sparse file for the snapshot starts out empty, it might not stay that way for long. If transactions are in progress at the time the snapshot is created, the recovery process has to undo uncommitted transactions before the snapshot database can be usable, so the snapshot contains the original versions of any page in the source that contains modified data. You can do the following test to see this behavior. First, create a new table in *AdventureWorks2012*:

```
USE AdventureWorks2012;
GO
CREATE TABLE t1 (id int);
```

Open a new transaction:

```
BEGIN TRANSACTION;
INSERT INTO t1 VALUES (1);
```

Then create a new database snapshot, as explained before. At this moment, the SQL Server error log shows the following:

```
1 transactions rolled back in database 'AdventureWorks_snapshot' (8). This is an informational
message only. No user action is required.
```

Snapshots can be created only on NTFS volumes because they are the only volumes that support the sparse file technology. If you try to create a snapshot on a FAT or FAT32 volume, you'll get an error like one of the following:

```
Msg 1823, Level 16, State 2, Line 1
A database snapshot cannot be created because it failed to start.
```

```
Msg 5119, Level 16, State 1, Line 1
Cannot make the file "E:\AW_snapshot.MDF" a sparse file. Make sure the file system supports
sparse files.
```

The first error is basically the generic failure message; the second message provides more detail about why the operation failed. As of now, SQL Server isn't supported in the new Windows Server 2012 Resilient File System (ReFS). According to Microsoft, support might be added in the future.

Understanding space used by database snapshots

You can find out the number of bytes that each sparse file of the snapshot is now using on disk by looking at the Dynamic Management Function *sys.dm_io_virtual_file_stats*, which returns the current number of bytes in a file in the *size_on_disk_bytes* column. This function takes *database_id* and *file_id* as parameters. The database ID of the snapshot database and the file IDs of each of its sparse files are displayed in the *sys.master_files* catalog view, where you can also see the *is_sparse* column, which is always 1 for database snapshots. You can also view the size in Windows Explorer by right-clicking the file name and looking at the properties (see Figure 4-3). The Size value is the maximum size, and the Size On Disk should be the same value that you see using *sys.dm_io_virtual_file_stats*. The maximum size should be about the same size the source database was when the snapshot was created.

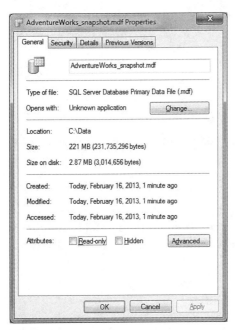

FIGURE 4-3 The snapshot file's Properties sheet in Windows Explorer, showing the current size of the sparse file as the size on disk.

Because you can have multiple snapshots for the same database, you need to make sure that you have enough disk space available. The snapshots start out relatively small, but as the source database is updated, each snapshot grows. Allocations to sparse files are made in fragments called *regions*, in units of 64 KB. When a region is allocated, all the pages are zeroed out except the one page that has changed. Then, space is available for seven more changed pages in the same region, and a new region isn't allocated until those seven pages are used.

You could overcommit your storage, meaning that under normal circumstances, you can have many times more snapshots than you have physical storage for, but if the snapshots grow, the physical volume might run out of space. When the physical volume runs out of space, the write operations to the source can't copy the before image of the page to the sparse file. The snapshots that can't write their pages out are marked as suspect and are unusable, but the source database continues operating normally. "Fixing" a suspect snapshot is impossible; you must drop the snapshot database.

Note Storage can become overcommitted when running online *DBCC CHECKDB* and related commands, which use a hidden snapshot during processing. You have no control of the placement of the hidden snapshot that the commands use—they're placed on the same volume that the files of the parent database reside on. If this happens, the DBCC uses the source database and acquires table locks. You can read much more detail of the internals of the DBCC commands and how they use database snapshots in Chapter 14.

Finally, the performance of the database snapshots depends on several factors, such as the system's I/O capabilities, the number of the database snapshots, and the number of pages that are updated for the first time.

Managing your snapshots

If any snapshots exist on a source database, the source database can't be dropped, detached, or restored. You can basically replace the source database with one of its snapshots by reverting the source database to the way it was when a snapshot was made. You do this by using the *RESTORE* command:

```
RESTORE DATABASE AdventureWorks2012
FROM DATABASE_SNAPSHOT = 'AdventureWorks_snapshot';
```

During the revert operation, both the snapshot and the source database are unavailable and marked as "In restore." If an error occurs during the revert operation, the operation tries to finish reverting when the database starts again. Keep in mind that the revert operation also overwrites the old transaction log file and rebuilds it, changing some of its properties like size or file growth.

You can't revert to a snapshot if multiple snapshots exist, so you should first drop all snapshots except the one you want to revert to. Dropping a snapshot is like using any other *DROP DATABASE* operation. When the snapshot is deleted, all NTFS sparse files are also deleted.

Keep in mind these additional considerations regarding database snapshots:

- Snapshots can't be created for the *model*, *master*, or *tempdb* databases. (Internally, snapshots can be created to run the online DBCC checks on the *master* database, but they can't be created explicitly.)

- A snapshot inherits the security constraints of its source database, and because it is read-only, you can't change the permissions.

- If you drop a user from the source database, the user is still in the snapshot.

- Snapshots can't be backed up or restored, but backing up the source database works normally; it's unaffected by database snapshots.

- Snapshots can't be attached or detached.

- Full-text indexing and *FILESTREAM* filegroups aren't supported on database snapshots.

Partially contained databases

One main problem faced when moving databases between instances of SQL Server is the application dependency on instance-level objects or objects defined on some other user databases that typically are left behind and need to be identified and moved manually. These instance-level objects could be logins, linked servers, jobs, and so on. Objects defined outside the database are usually tables accessed on other user databases in the same instance. SQL Server 2012 introduces *partially contained databases*, which is a first step toward full contained databases. In full contained databases, everything required for the application to work is contained in the database without outside dependencies. Although a limited functionality is available in SQL Server 2012, full containment is expected in a future version of SQL Server.

Partially contained databases in SQL Server 2012 include three major features, which are explained in more detail in this section:

- In SQL Server 2012, a new kind of user—a contained user—can be authenticated at the database level instead of at the instance level.

- Contained databases introduce the concept of the *catalog collation*. Some changes to database collations having the purpose of removing some dependencies from the instance and *tempdb* collations.

- SQL Server 2012 separates contained and uncontained entities and provides mechanisms to identify the entities contained in the database from the entities outside it.

Contained databases can also pose security threats that the SQL Server administrator needs to understand, as is explained later. Also, features such as replication, change data capture, and change tracking aren't available on partially contained databases.

Configuring a contained database

Contained databases need to be enabled at the instance level using the contained database authentication option:

```
EXEC sp_configure 'contained database authentication', 1;
RECONFIGURE;
GO
```

When this configuration is set, you can configure individual databases as contained by using the new *CONTAINMENT* option of the *ALTER* and *CREATE DATABASE* statements:

```
CREATE DATABASE MyDB CONTAINMENT = PARTIAL;
```

Current options are *PARTIAL* and *NONE* (the default). *NONE* means that it's a non-contained database. *PARTIAL* configures the database as a contained database and fails if the database is configured for replication, change data capture, or change tracking.

Creating contained users

When a database is configured as contained, contained users can be created and granted permissions within it. Two kinds of contained users can be created: a Windows principal (either a Windows user or a Windows group) and a contained database user with password. You can also grant instance-level logins permissions to a contained database by mapping them to users, but because that creates an instance dependency, it's not recommended. The benefit of contained users is that no login needs to be created at the instance level, because the authentication information is contained in the database and is automatically moved as the database is moved. Contained users are especially important in high-availability and disaster recovery scenarios such as AlwaysOn Availability groups, because they allow to failover a database to another SQL Server instance without needing to manually add any logins or having to worry about their login SIDs (security identifiers). For example, the following statement creates a new contained user named accounting:

```
USE MyDB;
GO
CREATE USER accounting WITH PASSWORD = 'a9j3uf@dc';
```

Contained users are allowed only on contained databases. Trying to create a contained user on a non-contained database returns the following error message:

```
Msg 33233, Level 16, State 1, Line 1
You can only create a user with a password in a contained database.
```

Contained users require the contained database name to be specified at connection time—for example, as part of the connection string. With Management Studio, that means selecting Options in the Connect to Database Engine window, choosing the Connection Properties tab, and manually typing the database name (see Figure 4-4).

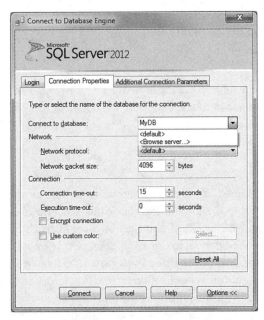

FIGURE 4-4 Connecting as a contained user.

Selecting <default> for a default database or <Browse server ...> to list existing databases doesn't work for a contained user, and the error message shown in Figure 4-5 is returned.

FIGURE 4-5 Error when browsing for database as a contained user.

You can use the *sp_migrate_user_to_contained* stored procedure to help you convert database users mapped to SQL Server logins to contained users. Refer to *Books Online* for more details.

The diagram in Figure 4-6, taken from the Microsoft SQL Server Security blog, illustrates the new database authentication method in SQL Server 2012.

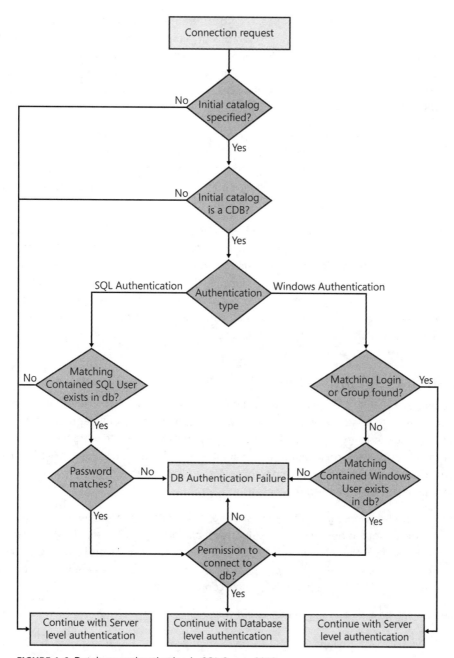

FIGURE 4-6 Database authentication in SQL Server 2012.

As shown in Figure 4-6, in addition to the server-level authentication available in all previous versions, SQL Server now supports database-level authentication which, as indicated previously, requires a contained user and the contained database name to be specified as the initial catalog at connection time.

Because contained users move the authentication process from the instance to the database level, a SQL Server administrator needs to understand a few security concerns. One of the most important security concerns is that, as users can now be created at the database level, individuals with the *ALTER ANY USER* database permission can create contained database users and, by consequence, provide access to the instance without the knowledge of the SQL Server administrator. Therefore, administrators should periodically audit users on contained databases.

Also, individuals with the *ALTER ANY DATABASE* permission can change the containment setting of a database—for example, from *NONE* to *PARTIAL*—and then again be able to create contained users without the knowledge of the administrator (provided that the instance is configured for contained databases, as explained previously). A similar scenario could happen with an administrator attaching a contained database, especially if he is unaware of the contained status.

Finally, an intentional or accidental denial of service is possible for a login when a contained user is created with the same name as an existing login and the existing login tries to connect to the contained database. So a best practice is to make sure that no contained users are created having the same name as an existing login. Weaker passwords than the current password policy might be possible when attaching a contained database as passwords aren't checked. Forcing a password reset after attaching the database can be a solution to this security issue. Some other security concerns might be possible; refer to *Books Online* for more details.

Understanding database collation changes

Contained databases introduce several changes to database collations, whose purpose is to remove some dependence from the instance and *tempdb* collations. As discussed in Chapter 6, collations provide sorting rules, case sensitivity, and accent sensitivity properties for character data types such as char and varchar. They apply not only to data stored in tables but also to all text used in SQL Server, including variable names, metadata, and temporary objects. Collation behavior in contained databases varies from that in non-contained databases.

A known problem when working with databases with collation different from the one of the SQL Server instance is the use of temporary tables. Temporary tables are stored in *tempdb*, which usually has the same collation as the SQL Server instance. To understand what the problem is, start by creating a new database with a *Finnish_Swedish_CI_AS* collation in an instance where the collation is *SQL_Latin1_General_CP1_CI_AS*. Note that this is a non-contained database.

Create the new database by running the following statement:

```
CREATE DATABASE Test COLLATE Finnish_Swedish_CI_AS;
```

Then create a regular and a temporary table:

```
USE Test;
GO
CREATE TABLE table1 (col1 varchar(40));
GO
CREATE TABLE #table2 (col1 varchar(40));
GO
```

The regular table has the same collation as the hosting database, whereas the temporary table uses the collation of *tempdb*. Trying to join both tables results in an error:

```
SELECT * FROM table1 t1 JOIN #table2 t2
ON t1.col1 = t2.col1;
```

The following error message is returned:

```
Msg 468, Level 16, State 9, Line 2
```

```
Cannot resolve the collation conflict between "SQL_Latin1_General_CP1_CI_AS" and "Finnish_
Swedish_CI_AS" in the equal to operation.
```

You can run the following code to verify that, in fact, the collations for both tables are different:

```
USE Test;
GO
SELECT name, collation_name
FROM sys.columns
WHERE name = 'col1';
USE tempdb;
GO
SELECT name, collation_name
FROM sys.columns
WHERE name = 'col1';
```

The first *SELECT* returns *Finnish_Swedish_CI_AS*; the second shows *SQL_Latin1_General_CP1_CI_AS*. This is no longer a problem with contained databases in which the temporary tables are created using the same collation as the contained database. To test it, drop the temporary table, configure *Test* as a contained database, and create a new temporary table:

```
DROP TABLE #table2;
GO
USE master;
GO
ALTER DATABASE Test SET CONTAINMENT = PARTIAL;
GO
USE Test;
GO
CREATE TABLE #table2 (col1 varchar(40));
GO
```

Running the previous query again joins both tables without error. You can also run the previous query to verify that both the standard and temporary tables are now using the same collation—in this case, *Finnish_Swedish_CI_AS*.

SQL Server 2012 also introduces the concept of catalog collation, used by system metadata and transient objects. Catalog collation is always *Latin1_General_100_CI_AS_WS_KS_SC* in all contained databases and can't be changed. Similar to the case shown earlier, in which temporary tables are created using the same collation as the contained database, catalog collation also helps reduce dependencies on the instance and *tempdb* collation.

However, some more complex scenarios regarding collation might exist when a session crosses contained and non-contained databases. In that case, the behavior is determined by the database collation in which the batch begins. For more details about this scenario, refer to *Books Online*.

Detecting uncontained features

SQL Server 2012 provides a couple of methods to help detect uncontained features in your databases: the sys.dm_db_uncontained_entities DMV and the database_uncontained_usage extended event. These methods work with both contained and uncontained databases. The sys.dm_db_uncontained_ entities DMV helps identify static uncontained entities. You can use the database_uncontained_usage extended event to detect uncontained entities at runtime, including those using dynamic SQL or triggered from client-side code. However, only code being executed is identified by this extended event, so this must be monitored for enough time.

The following example using the sys.dm_db_uncontained_entities DMV creates a few uncontained objects: a user mapped to a login, a stored procedure referencing a table in *AdventureWorks2012*, a stored procedure referencing a non-existing object, and a view using an instance-level system view:

```
CREATE LOGIN User1 WITH PASSWORD = 'ab@3cd';
GO
CREATE USER User1 FOR LOGIN User1;
GO
CREATE PROCEDURE proc1;
AS
SELECT * FROM AdventureWorks2012.Sales.SalesOrderDetail;
GO
CREATE PROCEDURE proc2;
AS
SELECT * FROM non_existing_table;
GO
CREATE VIEW view1;
AS
SELECT * FROM sys.linked_logins;
```

Next, run the following query:

```
SELECT class_desc, major_id, statement_type as s_type, feature_name, feature_type_name
FROM sys.dm_db_uncontained_entities;
```

You should see the following output:

```
class_desc          major_id   s_type feature_name                        feature_type_name
OBJECT_OR_COLUMN    245575913  SELECT Server or Database Qualified Name   T-SQL Syntax
OBJECT_OR_COLUMN    261575970  SELECT Deferred Name Resolution            Unknown Containment
                                                                          Behavior
OBJECT_OR_COLUMN    277576027  SELECT linked_logins                       System View
DATABASE_PRINCIPAL  5          NULL   Database Principal                  Database Entity
ROUTE               65536      NULL   Route                               Database Entity
```

The output lists the entities just created: both stored procedures and the view, showed under class_desc as *OBJECT_OR_COLUMN* (which you could identify by using the major_id column as described later), and the user mapped to a login, showed as *DATABASE_PRINCIPAL*. The object from the AdventureWorks2012 database referenced by proc1 is described as Server or Database Qualified Name, whereas the *non_existing_table* object referenced in proc2 is shown as Deferred Name Resolution. An additional entity of class *ROUTE* is shown. Routes are objects used by the service broker to determine where to deliver messages. By default, each database contains the *AutoCreatedLocal* route, which specifies that messages for any service that doesn't have an explicit route are delivered within the SQL Server instance.

Objects with more than one uncontained entity are listed only once, for the first entity found. You can use the major_id column to get additional information about the object, but this information is located in different catalog views depending of class_desc—for example, sys.database_principals. principal_id for the class 4 or *DATABASE_PRINCIPAL*, or *object_id* for *OBJECT_OR_COLUMN*. The DMV also includes the columns *statement_line_number, statement_offset_begin*, and *statement_offset_end*, which can be used to find out the specific part of the code including the uncontained feature.

Conclusion

Although a typical SQL Server installation has many databases, it always includes the following three: *master, model*, and *tempdb*. An installation also includes *msdb,* but that database can be removed. (Removing *msdb* requires a special traceflag and is rarely recommended.) A SQL Server instance also includes the *mssqlsystemresource* database, which can't be seen using the normal tools. Also, as of SQL Server 2005, you can take database snapshots, which are a read-only view of a user database and are required to reside on the same instance as the source database. Finally, contained databases, a new feature with SQL Server 2012, can be a very useful feature for database portability, which allows you to easily move user databases between instances of SQL Server.

CHAPTER 5

Logging and recovery

Kalen Delaney

C hapter 3, "Databases and database files," covered the data files that hold information in a Microsoft SQL Server database. Every database also has at least one file that stores its transaction log. Chapter 3 referred to SQL Server transaction logs and log files but didn't really go into detail about how a log file is different from a data file and exactly how SQL Server uses its log files. This chapter explains the structure of SQL Server log files and how they're managed when transaction information is logged. You will learn about how SQL Server log files grow and when and how a log file can be reduced in size. Finally, you see how log files are used during SQL Server backup and restore operations and how your database's recovery model affects them.

Transaction log internals

The transaction log records changes made to the database and stores enough information to allow SQL Server to recover the database. The recovery process takes place every time a SQL Server instance is started, and it can take place every time SQL Server restores a database or a log from backup. Recovery is the process of reconciling the data files and the log. Any changes to the data that the log indicates have been committed must appear in the data files, and any changes not marked as committed must not appear in the data files. The log also stores information needed to roll back an operation if SQL Server receives a request to roll back a transaction from the client (using the ROLLBACK TRAN command) or if an error, such as a deadlock, generates an internal rollback.

Physically, the transaction log is one or more files associated with a database at the time the database is created or altered. Operations that perform database modifications write records in the transaction log that describe the changes made (including the page numbers of the data pages modified by the operation), any added or removed data values, information about the transaction that the modification was part of, and the date and time of the beginning and end of the transaction. SQL Server also writes log records when certain internal events happen, such as checkpoints. Each log record is labeled with a log sequence number (LSN) that's guaranteed to be unique. All log entries that are part of the same transaction are linked so that all parts of a transaction can be located easily for both undo activities (as with a rollback) and redo activities (during system recovery).

The Buffer Manager guarantees that the transaction log is written before the changes to the database are written. (This is called write-ahead logging.) This guarantee is possible because SQL Server keeps track of its current position in the log by means of the LSN. Every time a page is changed, the LSN corresponding to the log entry for that change is written into the header of the data page. Dirty pages can be written to the disk only when the LSN on the page is less than or equal to the LSN for the last record written to the log. The Buffer Manager also guarantees that log pages are written in a specific order, making it clear which log blocks must be processed after a system failure, regardless of when the failure occurred.

Log records for a transaction are written to disk before the commit acknowledgement is sent to the client process, but the actual changed data might not have been physically written out to the data pages. Although the writes to the log are asynchronous, at commit time the thread must wait for the writes to complete to the point of writing the commit record in the log for the transaction. (SQL Server must wait for the commit record to be written so that it knows the relevant log records are safely on the disk.) Writes to data pages are completely asynchronous. That is, writes to data pages need only be posted to the operating system, and SQL Server can check later to see that they were completed. They don't have to be completed immediately because the log contains all the information needed to redo the work, even in the event of a power failure or system crash before the write completes. The system would be much slower if it had to wait for every I/O request to complete before proceeding.

Logging involves demarcating the beginning and end of each transaction (and savepoints, if a transaction uses them). Between the beginning and ending demarcations is information about the changes made to the data. This information can take the form of the actual "before and after" data, or it can refer to the operation performed so that those values can be derived. The end of a typical transaction is marked with a commit record, which indicates that the transaction must be reflected in the database's data files or redone if necessary. A transaction aborted during normal runtime (not system restart) due to an explicit rollback or something like a resource error (for example, an out-of-memory error) actually undoes the operation by applying changes that undo the original data modifications. The records of these changes are written to the log and marked as "compensation log records."

As mentioned earlier, both recovery types have the goal of making sure that the log and the data agree. A restart recovery runs every time SQL Server is started. The process runs on each database because each database has its own transaction log. Your SQL Server error log reports the progress of restart recovery, and for each database, the error log tells you how many transactions were rolled forward and how many were rolled back. This type of recovery is sometimes referred to as crash recovery because a crash or other unexpected stopping of the SQL Server service requires the recovery process to be run when the service is restarted. If the service was shut down cleanly with no open transactions in any database, only minimal recovery is necessary on system restart. In SQL Server 2012, restart recovery can be run on multiple databases in parallel, each handled by a different thread.

The other type of recovery, restore recovery (or media recovery), is run by request when a restore operation is executed. This process makes sure that all committed transactions in the backup of the transaction log are reflected in the data and that any incomplete transactions don't show up in the data. Restore recovery is discussed in more detail later in this chapter.

Both recovery types must deal with two situations: when transactions are recorded as committed in the log but not yet written to the data files, and when changes to the data files don't correspond to committed transactions. These two situations can occur because committed log records are written to the log files on disk every time a transaction commits. Changed data pages are written to the data files on disk completely asynchronously, every time a checkpoint occurs in a database. As mentioned in Chapter 1, "SQL Server 2012 architecture and configuration," data pages can also be written to disk at other times, but the regularly occurring checkpoint operations give SQL Server a point at which all changed (or dirty) pages are known to have been written to disk. Checkpoint operations also write log records from transactions in progress to disk because the cached log records are also considered to be dirty.

If the SQL Server service stops after a transaction commits but before the data is written out to the data pages, when SQL Server starts and runs recovery, the transaction must be rolled forward. SQL Server essentially redoes the transaction by reapplying the changes indicated in the transaction log. All transactions that need to be redone are processed first (even though some of them might need to be undone later during the next phase). This is called the redo phase of recovery.

If a checkpoint occurs before a transaction is committed, it writes the uncommitted changes out to disk. If the SQL Server service then stops before the commit occurs, the recovery process finds the changes for the uncommitted transactions in the data files, and it has to roll back the transaction by undoing the changes reflected in the transaction log. Rolling back all the incomplete transactions is called the undo phase of recovery.

Note This chapter refers to recovery as a system startup function, which is its most common role by far. However, recovery is also run during the final step of restoring a database from backup or attaching a database, and can also be forced manually. Also, recovery is run when creating a database snapshot, during database mirroring synchronization, or when failing over to a database mirror.

Later, this chapter covers some special issues related to recovery during a database restore. These include the three recovery models that you can set using the ALTER DATABASE statement and the ability to place a named marker in the log to indicate a specific point to recover to. The following discussion deals with recovery in general, whether it's performed when the SQL Server service restarts or when a database is being restored from a backup.

Phases of recovery

During recovery, only changes that occurred or were in progress since the last checkpoint are evaluated to determine whether they need to be redone or undone. Any transactions that completed before the last checkpoint, either by being committed or rolled back, are accurately reflected in the data pages, and no additional work needs to be done for them during recovery.

The recovery algorithm has three phases, which center around the last checkpoint record in the transaction log. Figure 5-1 illustrates the three phases.

- **Phase 1: Analysis** The first phase is a forward pass starting at the last checkpoint record in the transaction log. This pass determines and constructs a dirty page table (DPT) consisting of pages that might have been dirty at the time SQL Server stopped. An active transaction table is also built that consists of uncommitted transactions at the time SQL Server stopped.

- **Phase 2: Redo** This phase returns the database to the state it was in at the time the SQL Server service stopped. The starting point for this forward pass is the start of the oldest uncommitted transaction. The minimum LSN in the DPT is the first time SQL Server expects to have to redo an operation on a page, but it needs to redo the logged operations starting all the way back at the start of the oldest open transaction so that the necessary locks can be acquired. (Prior to SQL Server 2005, just allocation locks needed to be reacquired. In SQL 2005 and later, all locks for those open transactions need to be reacquired.)

- **Phase 3: Undo** This phase uses the list of active transactions (uncommitted at the time SQL Server stopped) found in Phase 1 (Analysis). It rolls each of these active transactions back individually. SQL Server follows the links between entries in the transaction log for each transaction. Any uncommitted transaction at the time SQL Server stopped is undone so that the database reflects none of the changes.

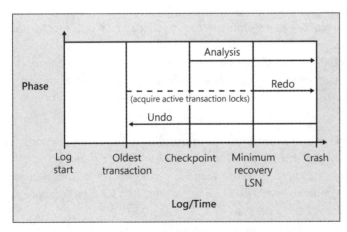

FIGURE 5-1 The three phases of the SQL Server recovery process.

SQL Server uses the log to keep track of the data modifications that were made, as well as any locks applied to the objects being modified. This allows SQL Server to support a feature called fast recovery when SQL Server is restarted (Enterprise and Developer editions only). With fast recovery, the database is available as soon as the redo phase is finished. The same locks acquired during the original modification can be reacquired to keep other processes from accessing the data that needs to have its changes undone; all other data in the database remains available. Fast recovery can't be done during media recovery, but it is used by database mirroring recovery, which uses a hybrid of media recovery and restart recovery.

Also, SQL Server uses multiple threads to process the recovery operations on the different databases simultaneously, so databases with higher ID numbers don't have to wait for all databases with lower ID numbers to be completely recovered before their own recovery process starts.

Page LSNs and recovery

Every database page has an LSN in the page header that reflects the location in the transaction log of the last log entry that modified a row on that page. Each log record that represents changes to a data page has two LSNs associated with it. In addition to the LSN for the actual log record, it keeps track of the LSN that was on the data page before the change recorded by this log record. During a redo operation of transactions, the LSN for each log record is compared to the page LSN of the data page that the log entry modified. If the page LSN is equal to the *previous* page LSN in the log record, the operation indicated in the log entry is redone. If the LSN on the page is equal to or higher than the *actual* LSN for this log record, SQL Server skips the REDO operation. Figure 5-2 illustrates these two possibilities. The LSN on the page can't be between the previous and current values for the log record.

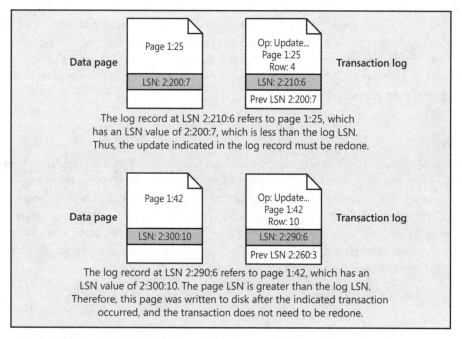

FIGURE 5-2 Comparing LSNs to decide whether to process the log entry during recovery.

Because recovery finds the last checkpoint record in the log (plus transactions that were still active at the time of the checkpoint) and proceeds from there, recovery time is short, and all changes committed before the checkpoint can be purged from the log or archived. Otherwise, recovery can take a long time and transaction logs can become unreasonably large. A transaction log can't be truncated before the point of the earliest transaction that's still open, no matter how many checkpoints have occurred since the transaction started and how many other transactions have started or completed. If a transaction remains open, the log must be preserved because it's still not clear whether the transaction is done or ever will be done. The transaction might ultimately need to be rolled back or rolled forward.

 Note Truncating of the transaction log is a logical operation and merely marks parts of the log as no longer needed so the space can be reused. Truncation isn't a physical operation and doesn't reduce the size of the transaction log files on disk. To reduce the physical size, a shrink operation must be performed.

Some SQL Server administrators have noted that the transaction log seems unable to be truncated, even after the log is backed up. This problem often results from a user opening a transaction and then forgetting about it. For this reason, from an application development standpoint, you should ensure that transactions are kept short. Another possible reason for an inability to truncate the log relates to a table being replicated using transactional replication when the replication log reader hasn't processed all the relevant log records yet. This situation is less common, however, because typically a latency of only a few seconds occurs while the log reader does its work. You can use DBCC OPENTRAN to look for the earliest open transaction or the oldest replicated transaction not yet processed and then take corrective measures (such as killing the offending process or running the sp_repldone stored procedure to allow the replicated transactions to be purged). Chapter 13, "Transactions and concurrency," discusses the problems with transaction management and some possible solutions. The next section covers shrinking the log.

Log reading

Although the log contains a record of every change made to a database, it's not intended to be used as an auditing tool. The transaction log enables SQL Server to guarantee recoverability in case of statement or system failure and to allow a system administrator to take backups of the changes to a SQL Server database. If you want to keep a readable record of changes to a database, you have to do your own auditing. You can do this by creating a trace of SQL Server activities, using SQL Server Profiler (which has been deprecated in SQL Server 2012) or one of the newer tracing or auditing mechanisms, such as Extended Events, which are discussed in Chapter 2, "The SQLOS."

Note Some third-party tools can read the transaction log, show you all the operations that have taken place in a database, and allow you to roll back any of those operations. The developers of these tools spent tens of thousands of hours looking at byte-level dumps of the transaction log files and correlating that information with the output of an undocumented DBCC LOG command. As soon as they had a product on the market, Microsoft started working with them, which made their lives a bit easier in subsequent releases. However, no such tools are available for SQL Server 2012 as this writing, and none have been announced.

Although you might assume that reading the transaction log directly would be interesting or even useful, it's usually just too much information. If you know in advance that you want to keep track of what your server running SQL Server is doing, you're much better off using one of the available tracing or auditing tools with the appropriate filter to capture just the information that is useful to you.

The log cache

Just like data pages are written to the data cache before they are written to disk, SQL Server caches log records before they are physically written. The log cache contains up to 128 entries on 64-bit systems or 32 entries on 32-bit systems. Each entry can maintain a buffer to store the log records before they get written to disk as a single block. The block can be anywhere from 512 bytes to 60 KB, but the buffer has to allow for the largest potential block so is always 60 KB. The number of actual buffers allocated depends on the actual workload and the performance of the log disk. As the log buffers are written to disk, SQL Server can reuse the buffer. If writes are taking longer, more buffers might need to be allocated. If the writes complete quickly, fewer buffers are needed. Outstanding log writes are capped at 4 MB at any one time, so if your workload is generating large log blocks, you have fewer buffers allocated than a workload that generates a lot of smaller log blocks.

SQL Server 2012 introduces another structure to manage the cached log blocks called the log pool. The log pool is a hash table hashed on the block ID and the database ID. (Earlier, you saw that a LSN is composed of three parts and looks like this: 2:200:7. The first two parts are the log block, and the third part is the record within the block.) The log pool allows SQL Server to access sets of log records needed for different technologies that need access to the log. For example, the replication agents need access to the set of replicated transactions, the mirroring and replica managers need access to the transactions to be propagated to the mirrors or replicas, and so on. If you search the list of Dynamic Management Objects (DMVs), you should see seven of them have to do with log pools. Although the actual cached log blocks have a global hash table, each database has to manage its own log, so the metadata refers to log pool managers that manage their own log records plus a free pool of log buffers for that database.

Changes in log size

No matter how many physical files have been defined for the transaction log, SQL Server always treats the log as one contiguous stream. For example, when the DBCC SHRINKDATABASE command determines how much the log can be shrunk, it doesn't consider the log files separately but instead determines the shrinkable size based on the entire log.

Understanding virtual log files

The transaction log for any database is managed as a set of virtual log files (VLFs) whose size is determined internally by SQL Server based on the total size of all log files and the growth increment used when enlarging the log. When a log file is first created, it always has between 2 and 16 VLFs. If the file size is 1 MB or less, SQL Server divides the size of the log file by the minimum VLF size (31 * 8 KB) to determine the number of VLFs. If the log file size is between 1 MB and 64 MB, SQL Server splits the log into four VLFs. If the log file is greater than 64 MB but less than or equal to 1 GB, eight VLFs are created. If the size is more than 1 GB, 16 VLFs are created. When the log grows, the same formula is used to determine how many new VLFs to add. A log always grows in units of entire VLFs and can be shrunk only to a VLF boundary. Figure 5-3 illustrates a physical log file, along with several VLFs.

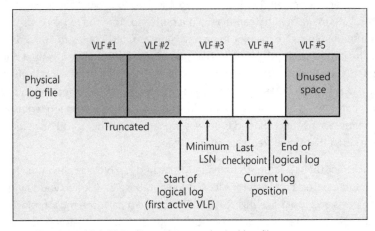

FIGURE 5-3 Multiple VLFs that make up a physical log file.

A VLF can be in one of four states.

- **Active** The active portion of the log begins at the minimum LSN representing an active transaction. The active portion of the log ends at the last LSN written. Any VLFs that contain any part of the active log are considered active VLFs. Figure 5-3 shows two active VLFs.

- **Recoverable** The portion of the log preceding the oldest active transaction is needed only to maintain a sequence of log backups for restoring the database to a former state.

- **Reusable** If transaction log backups aren't being maintained or you've already backed up the log, VLFs before the oldest active transaction aren't needed and can be reused. Truncating or backing up the transaction log changes recoverable VLFs into reusable VLFs.

- **Unused** One or more VLFs at the physical end of the log files might not have been used yet if not enough logged activity has taken place.

> **Note** For the purpose of determining which VLFs are reusable, active transactions include more than just open transactions. The earliest active transaction might be a transaction marked for replication that hasn't yet been processed, the beginning of a log backup operation, or the beginning of an internal diagnostic scan that SQL Server performs periodically. If transactions are marked for replication and haven't yet been processing by the Log Reader, they are considered active, as are transactions that haven't yet been copied to a database mirror or replica.

Observing virtual log files

You can observe the same key properties of virtual log files by executing the undocumented command DBCC LOGINFO. If you don't specify a parameter, the command must be run in the database for which you want information. Alternatively, you could specify a database name in parentheses. DBCC LOGINFO returns one row for each VLF. Listing 5-1 shows the result of running this command in my *AdventureWorks2012* database. Eight rows are returned, but not all columns are shown here.

LISTING 5-1 Viewing VLFs

```
FileId   FileSize        StartOffset     FSeqNo      Status      CreateLSN
--------  --------------  --------------  ----------  ----------  --------------------
2         458752          8192            42          2           0
2         458752          466944          41          0           0
2         458752          925696          43          2           0
2         712704          1384448         44          2           0
2         4194304         2097152         47          2           44000000085601161
2         4194304         6291456         46          2           44000000085601161
2         4194304         10485760        40          2           44000000085601161
2         4194304         14680064        0           0           44000000085601161
```

The number of rows shows how many VLFs are in the database. The *FileId* column indicates which of the log's physical files contains the VLF; my *AdventureWorks2008R2* database has only one physical log file. FileSize and StartOffset are indicated in bytes, so you can see that the first VLF starts after 8192 bytes (the number of bytes in a page). The first physical page of a log file contains header information, not log records, so the VLF is considered to start on the second page. The *FileSize* column is actually redundant for most rows because the size value can be computed by subtracting the StartOffset values for two successive VLFs. The rows are listed in physical order, but that's not always the order in which the VLFs have been used. The use order (logical order) is reflected in the column called *FSeqNo* (which stands for File Sequence Number).

In Listing 5-1, you can see that the rows are listed in physical order according to the *StartOffset*, but the logical order doesn't match. The *FSeqNo* values indicate that the seventh VLF is actually the first one in use (logical) order; the last one in use order is the fifth VLF in physical order. The *FSeqNo* values don't start a 0 or 1 because they change to the next value in sequence when a VLF is reused; if a database has been in use for a while, all the lower numbers will have been replaced, probably multiple times. Even if you create a brand new database, you should see that the *FSeqNo* values don't start at 0 or 1. Because a new database is copied from model, the lowest *FSeqNo* value is one more than the maximum value used in your *model* database.

The *Status* column indicates whether the VLF is reusable. A status of 2 means that it's either active or recoverable; a status of 0 indicates that it's reusable or completely unused. (A completely unused VLF has a *FSeqNo* value of 0, as in the eighth row of Listing 5-1.) As mentioned earlier, truncating or backing up the transaction log changes recoverable VLFs into reusable VLFs, so a status of 2 changes to a status of 0 for all VLFs that don't include active log records. In fact, one way to tell which VLFs are active is if those that still have a status of 2 after a log backup or truncation contain records from active transactions. VLFs with a status of 0 can be reused for new log records, and the log doesn't need to grow to keep track of the activity in the database. On the other hand, if all the VLFs in the log have a status of 2, SQL Server needs to add new VLFs to the log to record new transaction activity.

One last column shown in Listing 5-1 is called *CreateLSN*. That column lists the current LSN value at the time the VLF was added to the transaction log. A CreateLSN value of 0 means that the VLF was part of the original log file created when the database was created. You can also tell how many VLFs were added in any one operation by noticing which VLFs have the same value for CreateLSN. In Listing 5-1, the *CreateLSN* values indicate that the log file grew only once, and four new VLFs were added at the same time.

You might wonder whether it's better to have just a few large VLFs or many smaller VLFs. Not one easy answer is available, of course. If you have larger VLFs, your log space is harder to manage, because you might have just a few active log records in the VLF, but the entire VLF would be considered active and would never be reusable. Smaller VLFs make managing the size of the log that you want easier, but too many VLFs cause additional overhead. No ideal size or ideal number exists for VLFs. Try to keep your VLFs less than 1 GB in size, which can require that you create your initial log in chunks. So rather than create a 32 GB log, which would have 16 VLFs of 2 GB each, you can create it as an 8 GB file, and then alter its size three times to add 8 GB more each time. That gives you 32 GB, but the VLFs are 512 MB (half a gigabyte) each.

Although keeping the size of the VLFs smaller than 1 GB is more important than worrying about the number of VLFs, having too many VLFs causes overhead, as mentioned earlier. Each time your SQL Server starts up, each VLF is examined, and during certain operations that affect the log, the header of each active VLF needs to be examined. If possible, try to keep the number of VLFs to no more than a few hundred, with possibly 1,000 as an upper limit. In SQL Server 2012, you receive a warning message in your error log if SQL Server finds a lot of VLFs when it is running restart recovery. Initially, the developers thought they would return the message if you had more than 1,000 VLFs, but they reconsidered. The message is now generated if a database has more than 10,000 VLFs. However, as of the

RTM version of SQL Server 2012, the developers haven't updated the error message. So you receive the following message in your error log when you have more than 10,000 VLFs:

```
Database <database name> has more than 1000 virtual log files which is excessive. Too many
virtual log files can cause long startup and backup times. Consider shrinking the log and using
a different growth increment to reduce the number of virtual log files.
```

Using multiple log files

This chapter mentioned earlier that SQL Server treats multiple physical log files as though they were one sequential stream. This means that all VLFs in one physical file are used before any VLFs in the second file are used. If you have a well-managed log that's regularly backed up or truncated, you might never use any log files other than the first one. If none of the VLFs in multiple physical log files is available for reuse when a new VLF is needed, SQL Server adds new VLFs to each physical log file in round-robin fashion.

You can actually see the order of usage of different physical files by examining the output of DBCC LOGINFO. The first column is the file_id of the physical file. If you can capture the output of DBCC LOGINFO into a table, you can then sort it in a more useful way. The following code creates a table called *sp_LOGINFO* that can hold the output of DBCC LOGINFO. Because the table is created in the master database and starts with the characters *sp_*, it can be accessed and modified in any database.

```
USE master
GO
IF EXISTS (SELECT 1 FROM sys.tables
                        WHERE name = 'sp_LOGINFO')
        DROP TABLE sp_loginfo;
GO
CREATE TABLE sp_LOGINFO
(RecoveryUniteID int,
 FileId tinyint,
 FileSize bigint,
 StartOffset bigint,
 FSeqNo int,
 Status tinyint,
 Parity tinyint,
 CreateLSN numeric(25,0) );
GO
```

The following code creates a new database called *TWO_LOGS* and then copies a large table from the *AdventureWorks2012* sample database into *TWO_LOGS*, causing the log to grow:

```
USE Master
GO
IF EXISTS (SELECT * FROM sys.databases
                        WHERE name = 'TWO_LOGS')
    DROP DATABASE TWO_LOGS;
GO
CREATE DATABASE TWO_LOGS
  ON PRIMARY
  (NAME = Data ,
    FILENAME =
```

```
        'C:\Program Files\Microsoft SQL Server\MSSQL11.MSSQLSERVER\MSSQL\DATA\TWO_LOGS.mdf'
            , SIZE = 100 MB)
    LOG ON
    (NAME = TWO_LOGS1,
        FILENAME =
        'C:\Program Files\Microsoft SQL Server\MSSQL11.MSSQLSERVER\MSSQL\DATA\TWO_LOGS1.ldf'
            , SIZE = 5 MB
                , MAXSIZE = 2 GB),
    (NAME = TWO_LOGS2,
        FILENAME =
        'C:\Program Files\Microsoft SQL Server\MSSQL11.MSSQLSERVER\MSSQL\DATA\TWO_LOGS2.ldf'
            , SIZE = 5 MB);
GO
```

If you run DBCC LOGINFO, notice that it returns VLFs sorted by *FileID* and, initially, the file sequential number values (*FSeqNo*) are also in order:

```
USE TWO_LOGS
GO
DBCC LOGINFO;
GO
```

Now you can insert some rows into the database by copying from another table:

```
SELECT * INTO Orders
    FROM AdventureWorks2012.Sales.SalesOrderDetail;
GO
```

If you run DBCC LOGINFO again, notice that after the SELECT INTO operation, even though each FileID has many more rows, the output is still sorted by *FileID*, and *FSeqNo* values aren't related at all. Instead, you can save the output of DBCC LOGINFO in the *sp_loginfo* table and sort it by *FSeqNo*:

```
TRUNCATE TABLE sp_LOGINFO;
INSERT INTO sp_LOGINFO
    EXEC ('DBCC LOGINFO');
GO
-- Unused VLFs have a Status of 0, so the CASE forces those to the end
SELECT FileId, StartOffset, FSeqNo, Status, CreateLSN FROM sp_LOGINFO
ORDER BY CASE FSeqNo WHEN 0 THEN 9999999 ELSE FSeqNo END;
GO
```

The output of the SELECT is shown here:

```
FileId StartOffset          FSeqNo       Status CreateLSN
------ -------------------- ----------- ------ ----------------
2      8192                 43          0      0
2      1253376              44          0      0
2      2498560              45          0      0
2      3743744              46          0      0
3      8192                 47          0      0
3      1253376              48          0      0
3      2498560              49          0      0
3      3743744              50          0      0
2      5242880              51          0      50000000247200092
2      5496832              52          0      50000000247200092
3      5242880              53          0      51000000035600288
3      5496832              54          0      51000000035600288
2      5767168              55          0      53000000037600316
2      6021120              56          0      53000000037600316
3      5767168              57          0      56000000010400488
3      6021120              58          0      56000000010400488
2      6356992              59          0      58000000007200407
2      6610944              60          0      58000000007200407
3      6356992              61          0      60000000025600218
3      6610944              62          0      60000000025600218
2      7012352              63          0      62000000023900246
2      7266304              64          0      62000000023900246
3      7012352              65          0      64000000037100225
3      7266304              66          0      64000000037100225
2      7733248              67          0      66000000037600259
2      7987200              68          0      66000000037600259
2      8241152              69          0      66000000037600259
3      7733248              70          0      68000000035500288
3      7987200              71          0      68000000035500288
3      8241152              72          0      68000000035500288
2      8519680              73          0      71000000037300145
2      8773632              74          0      71000000037300145
2      9027584              75          0      71000000037300145
3      8519680              76          0      75000000018700013
3      8773632              77          2      75000000018700013
3      9027584              0           0      75000000018700013
```

Now notice that after the first eight initial VLFs are used (the ones with a *CreateLSN* value of 0), the VLFs alternate between the physical files. Because of the amount of log growth each time, several new VLFs are created, first from FileID 2 and then from FileID 3. The last VLF added to FileID 3 hasn't been used yet.

So you really have no reason to use multiple physical log files if you have done thorough testing and have determined the optimal size of your database's transaction log. However, if you find that the log needs to grow more than expected and if the volume containing the log doesn't have sufficient free space to allow the log to grow enough, you might need to create a second log file on another volume.

Understanding automatic truncation of virtual log files

SQL Server assumes that you're not maintaining a sequence of log backups if any of the following is true:

- You have configured the database to truncate the log regularly by setting the recovery model to SIMPLE.

- You have never taken a full database backup.

- You haven't taken a full database backup since switching the database to FULL or BULK_LOGGED recovery model from SIMPLE recovery model.

Under any of these circumstances, the database is considered to be in autotruncate mode. SQL Server truncates the database's transaction log every time it gets "full enough" (as explained shortly).

Remember that truncation means that all log records prior to the oldest active transaction are invalidated and all VLFs not containing any part of the active log are marked as reusable. It doesn't imply shrinking of the physical log file. Also, if your database is a publisher in a replication scenario, the oldest open transaction could be a transaction marked for replication that hasn't yet been replicated.

"Full enough" means that more log records exist than can be redone in a reasonable amount of time during system startup—the recovery interval. You can change the recovery interval manually by using the sp_configure stored procedure or by using SQL Server Management Studio, as discussed in Chapter 1, or by setting the TARGET_RECOVERY_TIME for your database, as mentioned in Chapter 3. However, letting SQL Server autotune this value is best. In most cases, this recovery interval value is set to one minute. By default, sp_configure shows zero minutes (and TARGET_RECOVERY_TIME shows zero seconds), meaning that SQL Server autotunes the value. SQL Server bases its recovery interval on the estimate that 10 MB worth of transactions can be recovered in one minute.

The actual log truncation is invoked by the checkpoint process, which is usually sleeping and is awakened only on demand. Each time a user thread calls the log manager, the log manager checks the log size. If the size exceeds the amount of work that can be recovered during the recovery interval (either for the server or for the database), the checkpoint thread is woken up. The thread checks the database and then truncates the inactive portion of the log.

Also, if the log ever gets to 70 percent full while the database is in autotruncate mode, the log manager wakes the thread to force a checkpoint. Growing the log is much more expensive than truncating it, so SQL Server truncates the log whenever it can.

> **Note** If the log manager is never needed, the checkpoint process won't be invoked and the truncation never happens. If you have a database in autotruncate mode, for which the transaction log has VLFs with a status of 2, you don't see the status change to 0 until some logging activity is required in the database.

If the log is regularly truncated, SQL Server can reuse space in the physical file by cycling back to an earlier VLF when it reaches the end of the physical log file. In effect, SQL Server recycles the space in the log file that's no longer needed for recovery or backup purposes. My *AdventureWorks2008R2* database is in this state because a full database backup has never been made.

Maintaining a recoverable log

If a log backup sequence is being maintained, the part of the log before the minimum LSN can't be overwritten until those log records have actually been backed up. The VLF status stays at 2 until the log backup occurs. After the log backup, the status changes to 0 and SQL Server can cycle back to the beginning of the file. Figure 5-4 depicts this cycle, simplified. As you can see from the FSeqNo values in the earlier output from the *AdventureWorks2008R2* database, SQL Server doesn't always reuse the log files in their physical sequence.

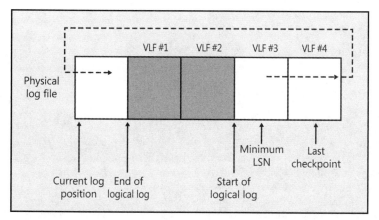

FIGURE 5-4 The active portion of the log cycling back to the beginning of the physical log file.

> **Note** If a database isn't in autotruncate mode and you aren't performing regular log backups, your transaction log is never truncated. If you are doing only full database backups, you must truncate the log manually to keep it at a manageable size.

The easiest way to tell whether a database is in autotruncate mode is by using the sys.database_recovery_status catalog view and looking in the column called last_log_backup_lsn. If that column value is null, the database is in autotruncate mode.

You can actually observe the difference between a database that's in autotruncate mode and a database that isn't by running the simple script in Listing 5-2. This script creates a new database called *newdb*, creates a new table in that database, inserts three records, and then updates those records 1,000 times. Each update is an individual transaction, and each one is written to the transaction log. However, note that the log doesn't grow at all, and the number of VLFs doesn't increase even after 3,000 update records are written. Although the number of VLFs doesn't change, you see that the *FSeqNo* values change. Log records are being generated, and as each VLF is reused, it gets a new *FSeqNo* value.

LISTING 5-2 Observing a database in auto truncate mode

```
USE master;
IF EXISTS (SELECT * FROM sys.databases WHERE name = 'newdb')
    DROP DATABASE newdb;
GO
CREATE DATABASE newdb;
GO
USE newdb;
-- First look at the VLFs for the newdb database
DBCC LOGINFO;
-- Now verify that newdb is in auto truncate mode
SELECT last_log_backup_lsn
FROM master.sys.database_recovery_status
WHERE database_id = db_id(' newdb ');
GO
CREATE TABLE newtable (a int);
GO
INSERT INTO newtable VALUES (10);
INSERT INTO newtable VALUES (20);
INSERT INTO newtable VALUES (30);
GO
SET NOCOUNT ON
DECLARE @counter int;
SET @counter = 1 ;
WHILE @counter < 1000 BEGIN
    UPDATE newtable SET a = a + 1;
    SET @counter = @counter + 1;
END;
```

Now make a backup of the *newdb* database after making sure that the database isn't in the SIMPLE recovery model. Recovery models are discussed in more detail later in this chapter, but for now, you can just make sure that newdb is in the appropriate recovery model by executing the following command:

```
ALTER DATABASE newdb SET RECOVERY FULL;
```

You can use the following statement to make the backup, substituting the path shown with the path to your SQL Server installation, or the path to any backup location:

```
BACKUP DATABASE newdb to disk =
    'c:\Program Files\Microsoft SQL Server\MSSQL.1\MSSQL\backup\newdb.bak';
```

As soon as you make the full backup, verify that the database isn't in autotruncate mode, again by looking at the *database_recovery_status* view:

```
SELECT last_log_backup_lsn
FROM master.sys.database_recovery_status
WHERE database_id = db_id('newdb');
```

This time, you should get a non-null value for *last_log_backup_lsn* to indicate that log backups are expected. Run the update script in Listing 5-2 again, starting with the DECLARE statement. You should see that the physical log file has grown to accommodate the added log records and more VLFs. The initial space in the log couldn't be reused because SQL Server assumed that you were saving that information for transaction log backups.

Now you can try to shrink the log down again. The first thing that you need to do is truncate it, which you can do by setting the recovery model to SIMPLE as follows:

```
ALTER DATABASE newdb SET RECOVERY SIMPLE;
```

If you then issue the following command, or if you issue the DBCC SHRINKDATABASE command for the *newdb* database, SQL Server shrinks the log file:

```
DBCC SHRINKFILE (2);
```

At this point, you should notice that the physical size of the log file has been reduced. If a log is truncated without any shrink command issued, SQL Server marks the space used by the truncated records as available for reuse but doesn't change the size of the physical file.

In SQL Server 7.0, where this log architecture was first introduced, running the preceding commands exactly as specified didn't always shrink the physical log file. The log file didn't shrink because the active part of the log was located at the end of the physical file. Physical shrinking can take place only from the end of the log; the active portion is never shrinkable. To remedy this situation, you had to enter some dummy transactions after truncating the log to force the active part of the log to move around to the beginning of the file. In versions later than SQL Server 7.0, this process is unnecessary. If a shrink command has already been issued, truncating the log internally generates a series of NO-OP (or dummy) log records that force the active log to move from the physical end of the file. Shrinking happens as soon as the log is no longer needed.

Automatically shrinking the log

Remember that truncating isn't the same thing as shrinking. A database should be truncated so that it's the most shrinkable, and if the log is in autotruncate mode and the autoshrink option is set, the log is physically shrunk at regular intervals.

If a database has the autoshrink option on, an autoshrink process kicks in every 30 minutes (as discussed in Chapter 3, "Databases and database files") and determines the size to which the log should be shrunk. The log manager accumulates statistics on the maximum amount of log space used in the 30-minute interval between autoshrink processes. The autoshrink process marks the shrink-point of the log as 125 percent of the maximum log space actually used or the minimum size of the log, whichever is larger. (Minimum size is the creation size of the log or the size to which it has been manually increased or decreased.) The log then shrinks to that size whenever it gets the chance, which is when it gets truncated or backed up.

You can have autoshrink without having the database in autotruncate mode, although you can't guarantee that the log actually shrinks. For example, if the log is never backed up, none of the VLFs are marked as reusable, so no shrinking can take place.

Note Putting a database in autoshrink mode is never recommended, because the overhead involved in shrinking data files can be enormous. The preceding paragraph was included to explain what SQL Server does when this option is enabled, if people on your team don't follow best practices. This option should be removed in a future version.

Be aware that just because a database is in autotruncate mode, you can't guarantee that the log won't grow. (You can be sure of the opposite—that if a database isn't in autotruncate mode, the log will grow.) Autotruncate means only that VLFs considered recoverable are marked as reusable at regular intervals, but VLFs in an active state aren't affected. If you have a long-running transaction (which might be a transaction that someone forgot to commit), all VLFs that contain any log records since that long-running transaction started are considered active and can never be reused. One uncommitted transaction can mean the difference between a very manageable transaction log size and a log that uses more disk space than the database itself and continues to grow.

Viewing the log file size

You can see the current size of the log file for all databases, as well as the percentage of the log file space that has been used, by running the command DBCC SQLPERF('logspace'). However, because it's a DBCC command, filtering the rows to get just the rows for a single database is difficult. Instead, you can use the dynamic management view *sys.dm_os_performance_counters* and retrieve the percentage full for each database's log:

```
SELECT instance_name as [Database],
       cntr_value as "LogFullPct"
FROM sys.dm_os_performance_counters
WHERE counter_name LIKE 'Percent Log Used%'
    AND instance_name not in ('_Total', 'mssqlsystemresource')
    AND cntr_value > 0;
```

The final condition is needed to filter out databases that have no log file size reported. This includes any database that's unavailable because it hasn't been recovered or is in a suspect state, as well as any database snapshots, which have no transaction log.

Database backup and restore

As you probably know by now, this book isn't intended to be a how-to book for database administrators. The bibliography in the companion content lists several excellent books that can teach you the mechanics of making database backups and restoring databases, and can offer best practices for setting up a backup-and-restore plan for your organization. Nevertheless, some important issues relating to backup and restore processes can help you understand why one backup plan might be better suited to your needs than another. Most of these issues involve the role the transaction log plays in backup and restore operations, so this section discusses the main ones.

Understanding the types of backups

No matter how much fault tolerance you have implemented on your database system, it is no replacement for regular backups. Backups can provide a solution to accidental or malicious data modifications, programming errors, and natural disasters (if you store backups in a remote location). If you opt for the fastest possible speed for data file access at the cost of fault tolerance, backups provide insurance in case your data files are damaged. Backups are also the preferred way to manage the copying of databases to other machines or other instances.

If you're using a backup to restore lost data, the amount of potentially recoverable data depends on the type of backup. SQL Server 2012 has four main types of backups (and a couple of variations on those types).

- **Full backup**   This type of backup copies all the pages from a database onto a backup device, which can be a local or network disk file, or a local tape drive.

- **Differential backup**   This type of backup copies only the extents that changed since the last full backup was made. The extents are copied onto a specified backup device. SQL Server can tell quickly which extents need to be backed up by examining the bits on the Differential Changed Map (DIFF) pages for each data file in the database. DIFF pages are big bitmaps, with one bit representing an extent in a file, just like the Global Allocation Map (GAM) and Shared Global Allocation Map (SGAM) pages discussed in Chapter 3. Each time a full backup is made, all bits in the DIFF are cleared to 0. When any page in an extent is changed, the bit in the DIFF page corresponding to that extent is changed to 1.

- **Log backup**   In most cases, this type of backup copies all log records that have been written to the transaction log since the last log backup was made. However, the exact behavior of the BACKUP LOG command depends on your database's recovery model setting. (Recovery models are discussed shortly.)

- **File and filegroup backup**   This type of backup is intended to increase flexibility in scheduling and media handling compared to full backups, in particular for very large databases. File and filegroup backups are also useful for large databases that contain data with varying update characteristics—meaning, some filegroups allow both read and write operations, whereas some are read-only.

A full backup can be performed while your database is in use. This is considered a "fuzzy" backup—that is, it's not an exact image of the state of the database at any particular point in time. The backup threads just copy extents, and if other processes need to make changes to those extents while the backup is in progress, they can do so.

To maintain consistency for either full, differential, or file backups, SQL Server records the current log sequence number (LSN) at the time the backup starts and again at the time the backup ends. This allows the backup to capture the relevant parts of the log as well. The relevant part starts with the oldest active transaction at the time of the first recorded LSN and ends with the second recorded LSN.

As mentioned earlier, what gets recorded with a log backup depends on the recovery model you are using. So before you learn about log backup in detail, you need to read about recovery models.

Understanding recovery models

As explained in Chapter 3 in a discussion on database options, the RECOVERY option has three possible values: FULL, BULK_LOGGED, and SIMPLE. The value that you choose determines the size of your transaction log, the speed and size of your transaction log backups (or whether you can make log backups at all), as well as the degree to which you are at risk of losing committed transactions in case of media failure.

Minimally logged operations

Before looking at the details of the three recovery models, you need to consider a concept called minimal logging. Minimally logged operations are ones that don't write every single individual row because doing so modifies the transaction log. At a minimum, enough information has to be logged when a minimally logged operation is performed to allow SQL Server to rollback a transaction that has failed. Even when SQL Server logs the changed data, it doesn't actually write it to the log in the sequence that it was changed. These minimally logged operations include the following.

- **SELECT INTO**   This command always creates a new table in the default filegroup.

- **Bulk import operations**   These include the *BULK INSERT* command and the *bcp* executable.

- **INSERT INTO . . . SELECT**   This command is used in the following situations.

  - When data is selected using the OPENROWSET(BULK. . .) function.

  - When more than an extent's worth of data is being inserted into a table without nonclustered indexes and the TABLOCK hint is used. If the destination table is empty, it can have a clustered index. If the destination table is already populated, it can't. (This option can be useful to create a new table in a nondefault filegroup with minimal logging. The SELECT INTO command doesn't allow specifying a filegroup.)

- **Partial updates**   Columns having a large value data type receive partial updates (as discussed in Chapter 8, "Special storage").

- **.WRITE**   This clause is used in the UPDATE statement when inserting or appending new data.

- **WRITETEXT and UPDATETEXT**   These statements are used when inserting or appending new data into LOB data columns (text, ntext, or image). Minimal logging isn't used in these cases when existing data is updated.

- **Index operations**   These include the following.

  - CREATE INDEX, including indexes on views

  - ALTER INDEX REBUILD or DBCC DBREINDEX

- DROP INDEX, in which the creation of the new heap is minimally logged, but the page deallocation is always fully logged

Exactly what gets written to the log when a minimally logged operation is performed depends on your recovery model. In general, minimal logging doesn't mean the same thing as no logging, nor does it minimize logging for all operations. It's a feature that minimizes the amount of logging for the operations described earlier, and if you have a high-performance I/O subsystem, performance likely improves as well. But on lower-end machines, minimally logged operations can be slower than fully logged operations.

FULL recovery model

The FULL recovery model provides the least risk of losing work in the case of a damaged data file. If a database is in this mode, all operations are fully logged. This means that in addition to logging every row added with the INSERT operation, removed with the DELETE operation, or changed with the UPDATE operation, for minimally logged operations SQL Server writes to the transaction log a copy of every page added to a table or index. . If you experience a media failure for a database file and need to recover a database that was in the FULL recovery model and you've been making regular transaction log backups preceded by a full database backup, you can restore to any specified point in time up to the time of the last log backup. Also, if your log file is available after the failure of a data file, you can restore up to the last transaction committed before the failure. SQL Server 2012 also supports a feature called log marks, which allows you to place reference points in the transaction log. If your database is in FULL recovery mode, you can choose to recover to one of these log marks.

As mentioned, the CREATE INDEX and ALTER INDEX REBUILD commands are minimally logged operations, and in the FULL recovery model, SQL Server copies all the new index pages to the transaction log. This means that when you restore from a transaction log backup that includes index creations, the recovery operation is much faster than the original index creation, because the index doesn't have to be rebuilt—all the index pages have been captured as part of the log backup. The same logging is done when you use the ALTER INDEX command to rebuild an index. (Prior to SQL Server 2000, SQL Server logged only that an index had been built, so when you restored from a log backup, the entire index would have to be rebuilt.) Also, SELECT INTO is a minimally logged operation. You should be aware of the following cases in which certain minimally logged operations write every row to the transaction log in FULL recovery.

- If you are building or rebuilding an index in ONLINE mode, SQL Server writes every new index row to the log. (Chapter 7, "Indexes: internals and management," covers ONLINE index operations.)

- If you are performing a SELECT INTO operation that creates a new table with an IDENTITY column, SQL Server writes a log record for every row as the identity value is generated.

So in general, the FULL recovery model sounds great, right? As always, it has tradeoffs. The biggest tradeoff is that the size of your transaction log files can be enormous, so it can take much longer to make log backups than with releases prior to SQL Server 2000.

BULK_LOGGED recovery model

If you never perform any of the minimally logged operations listed earlier, you should notice no difference between a database in FULL recovery model and a database in BULK_LOGGED recovery model. The only difference is when you perform one of the minimally logged operations.

When you execute one of these minimally logged operations in a database in BULK_LOGGED recovery, SQL Server logs only that the operation occurred and logs information about space allocations. Every data file in a SQL Server 2012 database has at least one special page called a minimally logged map (ML map) page, which is managed much like the GAM and SGAM pages discussed in Chapter 3 and the DIFF pages mentioned earlier in this chapter. Each bit on an ML map page represents an extent; a bit set to 1 means that this extent has been changed by a minimally logged operation since the last transaction log backup. An ML map page is located on the eighth page of every data file and every 511,230 pages thereafter. All bits on an ML map page are reset to 0 every time a log backup occurs.

Because of the reduced logging for minimally logged operations, the operations themselves can potentially be carried out much faster than in the FULL recovery model. However, the speed improvement isn't guaranteed. The only guarantee with minimally logged operations in BULK_LOGGED recovery is that the log itself is smaller.

As you might have guessed, exceptions are expected. In particular, just like for FULL recovery, if you are performing a SELECT INTO operation that creates a new table with an IDENTITY column, SQL Server writes a log record for every row as the identity value is being generated. So this happens not only in FULL recovery but also in BULK_LOGGED.

Minimally logged operations might actually be slower in BULK_LOGGED recovery than in FULL recovery in certain cases. Although minimal logging doesn't have as many log records to write, and the logs aren't as big (because they don't contain the full page image), with minimal logging in BULK_LOGGED recovery, SQL Server forces the changed data pages to be flushed to disk as soon as the minimally logged operations finishes, before the transaction commits. This forced flushing of the data pages can be very expensive, especially when the I/O for these pages is random. You can contrast this to operations in FULL recovery, in which disk writing doesn't happen until a checkpoint occurs, which always uses sequential I/O and is asynchronous with the operations that created the log records. If you don't have a fast I/O subsystem, it can become very noticeable that minimal logging is slower than full logging.

The BULK_LOGGED recovery model allows you to restore a database completely in case of media failure and gives you the best performance and least log space usage for certain minimally logged operations. In FULL recovery mode, these operations are fully logged (all the changed data is written to the log), but in BULK_LOGGED recovery mode, they are logged only minimally. This can be much more efficient than normal logging because in general, when you write data to a user database, you must write it to disk twice: once to the log and once to the database itself. This is because the database system uses an undo/redo log so that it can roll back or redo transactions when needed.

As mentioned earlier, having your database in BULK_LOGGED recovery and not having actually performed any minimally logged operations is no different from being in FULL recovery. You can restore your database to any point in time or to a named log mark because the log contains a full sequential record of all changes to your database.

The tradeoff to having a smaller log comes during the backing up of the log. In addition to copying the contents of the transaction log to the backup media, SQL Server scans the ML map pages and backs up all the modified extents along with the transaction log. The log file itself stays small, but because the log backup can be many times larger, it takes more time and might take up a lot more space than in the FULL recovery model. The time it takes to restore a log backup made in the BULK_LOGGED recovery model is similar to the time it takes to restore a log backup made in the FULL recovery model. The operations don't have to be redone; all the information necessary to recover all data and index structures is available in the log backup.

SIMPLE recovery model

The SIMPLE recovery model offers the simplest backup-and-restore strategy. In fact, the logging that takes place in SIMPLE recovery is exactly the same as the logging in BULK_LOGGED recovery. The difference in SIMPLE recovery is that your transaction log is truncated whenever a checkpoint occurs, which happens at regular, frequent intervals. Therefore, the only types of backups that can be made are those that don't require log backups. These types of backups are full database backups, differential backups, partial full and differential backups, and filegroup backups for read-only filegroups. You get an error if you try to back up the log while in SIMPLE recovery. Because the log isn't needed for backup purposes, sections of it can be reused as soon as all the transactions that it contains are committed or rolled back, and the transactions are no longer needed for recovery from server or transaction failure. In fact, as soon as you change your database to SIMPLE recovery model, the log is truncated.

Keep in mind that SIMPLE logging doesn't mean the same thing as no logging. What's "simple" is your backup strategy, because you never need to worry about log backups. However, all operations are logged in SIMPLE recovery, just like in the BULK_LOGGED model. A log for a database in SIMPLE recovery might not grow as much as the log for a database in FULL because the minimally logged operations also are minimally logged in SIMPLE recovery. This also doesn't mean you don't have to worry about the size of the log in SIMPLE recovery. As in any recovery model, log records for active transactions can't be truncated, and neither can log records for any transaction that started after the oldest open transaction. So if you have large or long-running transactions, you still might need lots of log space.

Switching recovery models

The recommended method for changing your database recovery model is to use the ALTER DATABASE command:

```
ALTER DATABASE <database_name>
    SET RECOVERY [FULL | BULK_LOGGED | SIMPLE]
```

To see what recovery model your database is in, you can inspect the *sys.databases* view. For example, this query returns the recovery model and the state of the *AdventureWorks2008R2* database:

```
SELECT name, database_id, suser_sname(owner_sid) as owner ,
       state_desc, recovery_model_desc
FROM sys.databases
WHERE name = 'AdventureWorks2008R2'
```

When created, a database starts in whatever recovery model is used by the *model* database on the instance. If you're using SQL Server 2012 Standard or Enterprise edition, the model database starts in FULL recovery model, so all your new databases also begin in FULL recovery. You can change the recovery model of the model database just like you do for any user database—by using the ALTER DATABASE command.

To make best use of your transaction log, you can switch between FULL and BULK_LOGGED recovery without worrying about your backup scripts failing. You might want to switch between FULL and BULK_LOGGED recovery if you usually operate in FULL recovery but occasionally need to perform a minimally logged operation quickly. You can change to BULK_LOGGED and pay the price later when you back up the log; the backup simply takes longer and is larger.

You can't easily switch to and from SIMPLE recovery if you're trying to maintain a sequence of log backups. Switching *into* SIMPLE is no problem, but when you switch back to FULL or BULK_LOGGED, you need to plan your backup strategy and be aware that you have no log backups up to that point. So when you use the ALTER DATABASE command to change from SIMPLE to FULL or BULK_LOGGED, you should first make a complete database backup for the change in behavior to be complete. Remember that in SIMPLE recovery, your transaction log is truncated at regular intervals. This recovery model isn't recommended for production databases, where you need maximum transaction recoverability. The only time that SIMPLE recovery is really useful is in test and development situations or for small databases that are primarily read-only. FULL or BULK_LOGGED is recommended for your production databases, and you can switch between those models whenever you need to.

Choosing a backup type

If you're responsible for creating the backup plan for your data, you need to choose not only a recovery model, but also the kind of backup to make. You've read about the three main types: full, differential, and log. In fact, you can use all three types together. To accomplish any type of full restore of a database, you must make a full database backup occasionally to use as a starting point for other types of backups. Also, you can choose among a differential backup, a log backup, or a combination of both. Here are the characteristics of these last two types, which can help you decide between them.

A differential backup

- Is faster if your environment includes many changes to the same data. It backs up only the most recent change, whereas a log backup captures every individual update.

- Captures the entire B-tree structures for new indexes, whereas a log backup captures each individual step in building the index.

- Is cumulative. When you recover from a media failure, only the most recent differential backup needs to be restored because it contains all the changes since the last full database backup.

A log backup

- Allows you to restore to any point in time because it is a sequential record of all changes.

- Can be made after the database media fails, as long as the log is available. This allows you to recover right up to the point of the failure. The last log backup (called the tail of the log) must specify the WITH NO_TRUNCATE option in the *BACKUP LOG* command if the database itself is unavailable.

- Is sequential and discrete. Each log backup contains completely different log records. When you use a log backup to restore a database after a media failure, all log backups must be applied in the order that they were made.

Remember that backups can be created as compressed backups, as briefly discussed in Chapter 1. This can greatly reduce the amount of time and space required to actually create the backup (full, differential, or log) on the backup device. The algorithm for compressing backups varies greatly from the algorithms used for row or page data compression; Chapter 8 elaborates on the differences.

Restoring a database

How often you make each type of backup determines two things: how fast you can restore a database and how much control you have over which transactions are restored. Consider the schedule in Figure 5-5, which shows a database fully backed up on Sundays. The log is backed up daily, and a differential backup is made on Tuesdays and Thursdays. A drive failure occurs on a Friday. If the failure doesn't include the log files, or you've mirrored them or protected them in some other way, you should back up the tail of the log with the NO_TRUNCATE option.

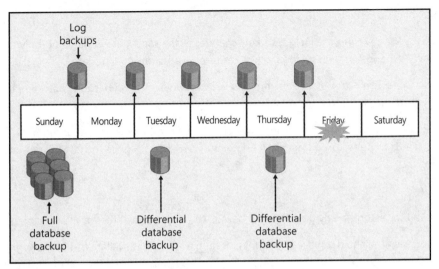

FIGURE 5-5 The combined use of log and differential backups, which reduces total restore time.

 Warning If you are operating in BULK_LOGGED recovery mode, backing up the log also backs up any data changed with a minimally logged operation, so you might need to have more than just the log file available to back up the tail of the log. You also need to have available any filegroups containing data inserted by a minimally logged operation.

To restore this database after a failure, you must start by restoring the full backup made on Sunday. This does two things: It copies all the data and index extents, as well as all the log blocks, from the backup media to the database files, and it applies all the transactions in the log. You must determine whether incomplete transactions are rolled back. You can opt to recover the database by using the WITH RECOVERY option of the RESTORE command to roll back any incomplete transactions and open the database for use. No further restoring can be done. If you choose not to roll back incomplete transactions by specifying the WITH NORECOVERY option, the database is left in an inconsistent state and can't be used.

If you choose WITH NORECOVERY, you can then apply the next backup. In the scenario depicted in Figure 5-5, you would restore the differential backup made on Thursday, which would copy all the changed extents back into the data files. The differential backup also contains the log records spanning the time the differential backup was being made, so you have to decide whether to recover the database. Complete transactions are always rolled forward, but you determine whether incomplete transactions are rolled back.

After the differential backup is restored, you must restore, in sequence, all the log backups made after the differential backup is made. This includes the tail of the log backed up after the failure if you could make this last backup.

Note Restore recovery (media recovery) is similar to restart recovery, which is described earlier in this chapter, but it is a redo-only operation. It includes an analysis pass to determine how much work might need to be done, and then a roll-forward pass to redo completed transactions and return the database to the state it was in when the backup was complete. Unlike restart recovery, with restore recovery you have control over when the rollback pass is done. It shouldn't be done until all the rolling forward from all the backups has been applied. When a RESTORE WITH RECOVERY is specified after the redo pass, the database is restarted and SQL Server runs a restart recovery to undo incomplete transactions. Also, SQL Server might need to make some adjustments to metadata after the recovery is complete, so no access to the database is allowed until all phases of recovery are finished. In other words, you don't have the option to use "fast" recovery as part of a RESTORE.

Backing up and restoring files and filegroups

SQL Server 2012 allows you to back up individual files or filegroups, which can be useful in environments with extremely large databases. You can choose to back up just one file or filegroup each day, so the entire database doesn't have to be backed up as often. This also can be useful when you have an isolated media failure on a single drive and think that restoring the entire database would take too long.

Keep in mind these details about backing up and restoring files and filegroups.

- Individual files and filegroups with the read-write property can be backed up only when your database is in FULL or BULK_LOGGED recovery model because you must apply log backups after you restore a file or filegroup, and you can't make log backups in SIMPLE recovery. Read-only filegroups and the files in them can be backed up in SIMPLE recovery.

- You can restore individual file or filegroup backups from a full database backup.

- Immediately before restoring an individual file or filegroup, you must back up the transaction log. You must have an unbroken chain of log backups from the time the file or filegroup backup was made.

- After restoring a file or filegroup backup, you must restore all transaction log backups made between the time you backed up the file or filegroup and the time you restored it. This guarantees that the restored files are in sync with the rest of the database.

Suppose that you back up filegroup FG1 at 10 a.m. on Monday. The database is still in use, and changes happen to data in FG1 and transactions are processed that change data in both FG1 and other filegroups. You back up the log at 4 p.m. More transactions are processed that change data in both FG1 and other filegroups. At 6 p.m., a media failure occurs and you lose one or more of the files that make up FG1.

To restore, you must first back up the tail of the log containing all changes that occurred between 4 p.m. and 6 p.m. The tail of the log is backed up using the special WITH NO_TRUNCATE option, but you can also use the NORECOVERY option. When backing up the tail of the log WITH NORECOVERY, the database is put into the RESTORING state and can prevent an accidental background change from interfering with the restore sequence.

You can then restore FG1 using the RESTORE DATABASE command, specifying just filegroup FG1. Your database isn't in a consistent state because the restored FG1 has changes only through 10 a.m., and the rest of the database has changes through 6 p.m. However, SQL Server knows when the last change was made to the database because each page in a database stores the LSN of the last log record that changed that page. When restoring a filegroup, SQL Server makes a note of the maximum LSN in the database. You must restore log backups until the log reaches at least the maximum LSN in the database, and you don't reach that point until you apply the 6 p.m. log backup.

Performing partial backups

Partial backups can be based either on full or differential backups, but they don't contain all the filegroups. Partial backups contain all the data in the primary filegroup and all the read-write file-groups. In addition, you can specify that any read-only files also be backed up. If the entire database is marked as read-only, a partial backup contains only the primary filegroup. Partial backups are par-ticularly useful for very large databases (VLDBs) using the SIMPLE recovery model because they allow you to back up only specific filegroups, even without having log backups.

Restoring pages

SQL Server 2012 also allows you to restore individual pages. When SQL Server detects a damaged page, it marks it as suspect and stores information about the page in the *suspect_pages* table in the *msdb* database. Damaged pages can be detected when activities such as the following take place.

- A query needs to read a page.

- DBCC CHECKDB or DBCC CHECKTABLE is being run.

- BACKUP or RESTORE is being run.

- You are trying to repair a database with DBCC DBREPAIR.

Several types of errors can require a page to be marked as suspect and entered into the suspect_pages table. These can include checksum and torn page errors, as well as internal consistency prob-lems, such as a bad page ID in the page header. The event_type column in the suspect_pages table indicates the reason for the status of the page, which usually reflects the reason the page has been entered into the suspect_pages table. SQL Server Books Online lists the following possible values for the *event_type* column:

event_type value	Description
1	823 error caused by an operating system CDC error or 824 errors other than a bad checksum or a torn page (for example, a bad page ID).
2	Bad checksum.
3	Torn page.
4	Restored. (The page was restored after it was marked as bad.)
5	Repaired. (DBCC repaired the page.)
7	Deallocated by DBCC.

Some errors recorded in the *suspect_pages* table might be transient errors, such as an I/O error that occurs because a cable has been disconnected. Rows can be deleted from the *suspect_pages* table by someone with the appropriate permissions, such as someone in the *sysadmin* server role. Also, not all errors that cause a page to be inserted in the *suspect_pages* table require that the page be restored. A problem that occurs in cached data, such as in a nonclustered index, might be resolved by rebuilding the index. If a *sysadmin* drops a nonclustered index and rebuilds it, the corrupt data, although fixed, isn't indicated as fixed in the *suspect_pages* table.

Page restore is intended specifically to replace pages that have been marked as suspect because of an invalid checksum or a torn write. Although multiple database pages can be restored at the same time, you aren't expected to be replacing a large number of individual pages. If you do have many damaged pages, you should probably consider a full file or database restore. Also, you should probably try to determine the cause of the errors; if you discover a pending device failure, you should do your full file or database restore to a new location. Log restores must be done after the page restores to bring the new pages up-to-date with the rest of the database. Just as with file restore, the log backups are applied to the database files containing a page that is being recovered.

In an online page restore, the database is online for the duration of the restore, and only the data being restored is offline. Note that not all damaged pages can be restored with the database online.

Note Online page restore is allowed only in SQL Server 2012 Enterprise Edition. Offline page restore is available in all editions.

SQL Server Books Online lists the following basic steps for a page restore:

1. Obtain the page IDs of the damaged pages to be restored. A checksum or torn write error returns the page ID, which is the information needed for specifying the pages. You can also get page IDs from the *suspect_pages* table.

2. Start a page restore with a full, file, or filegroup backup that contains the page or pages to be restored. In the *RESTORE DATABASE* statement, use the PAGE clause to list the page IDs of all pages to be restored. The maximum number of pages that can be restored in a single file is 1,000.

3. Apply any available differentials required for the pages being restored.

4. Apply the subsequent log backups.

5. Create a new log backup of the database that includes the final LSN of the restored pages—that is, the point at which the last restored page was taken offline. The final LSN, set as part of the first restore in the sequence, is the redo target LSN. Online roll-forward of the file containing the page can stop at the redo target LSN. To learn the current redo target LSN of a file, see the *redo_target_lsn* column of *sys.master_files*.

6. Restore the new log backup. When this new log backup is applied, the page restore is complete and the pages are usable. All bad pages are affected by the log restore; all other pages have a more recent LSN in their page header, and no redo is needed. Also, no UNDO phase is needed for page-level restore.

Performing a partial restore

SQL Server 2012 lets you do a partial restore of a database in emergency situations. Despite the description and syntax looking similar to file and filegroup backup and restore, a partial restore is very different. With file and filegroup restore, you start with a complete database and replace one or more files or filegroups with previously backed up versions. With a partial database restore, you don't start with a full database; you restore individual filegroups, which must include the primary filegroup containing all the system tables, to a new location. Any filegroups that you don't restore are treated as offline when you attempt to refer to data stored on them. You can then restore log backups or differential backups to bring the data in those filegroups to a later point in time. This allows you the option of recovering the data from a subset of tables after an accidental deletion or modification of table data. You can use the partially restored database to extract the data from the lost tables and copy it back into your original database.

Restoring with standby

In normal recovery operations, you have the choice of either running recovery to roll back incomplete transactions or not running recovery at all. If you run recovery, no further log backups can be restored and the database is fully usable. If you don't run recovery, the database is inconsistent and SQL Server won't let you use it at all. You have to choose one or the other because of the way log backups are made.

For example, in SQL Server 2012, log backups don't overlap—each log backup starts where the previous one ended. Consider a transaction that makes hundreds of updates to a single table. If you back up the log during the update and then after it, the first log backup has the beginning of the transaction and some of the updates, and the second log backup has the remainder of the updates and the commit. Suppose that you then need to restore these log backups after restoring the full database. If you run recovery after restoring the first log backup, the first part of the transaction is rolled back. If you then try to restore the second log backup, it starts in the middle of a transaction, and SQL Server won't have information about what the beginning of the transaction was. You certainly can't recover transactions from this point because their operations might depend on this update that you've partially lost. SQL Server, therefore, doesn't allow any more restoring to be done. The alternative isn't to run recovery to roll back the first part of the transaction and instead to leave the transaction incomplete. SQL Server takes into account that the database is inconsistent and doesn't allow any users into the database until you finally run recovery on it.

What if you want to combine the two approaches? Being able to restore one log backup and look at the data before restoring more log backups would be nice, particularly if you're trying to do a point-in-time recovery, but you won't know what the right point is. SQL Server provides an option called STANDBY that allows you to recover the database and still restore more log backups. If you re-store a log backup and specify WITH STANDBY = '<some filename>', SQL Server rolls back incomplete transactions but keeps track of the rolled-back work in the specified file, which is known as a *standby file*. The next restore operation reads the contents of the standby file and redoes the operations that were rolled back, and then it restores the next log. If that restore also specifies WITH STANDBY, incomplete transactions again are rolled back, but a record of those rolled-back transactions is saved. Keep in mind that you can't modify any data if you've restored WITH STANDBY (SQL Server generates an error message if you try), but you can read the data and continue to restore more logs. The final log must be restored WITH RECOVERY (and no standby file is kept) to make the database fully usable.

Conclusion

In addition to one or more data files, every database in a SQL Server instance has one or more log files that keep track of changes to that database. (Remember that database snapshots don't have log files because no changes are ever made directly to a snapshot.) SQL Server uses the transaction log to guarantee consistency of your data, at both a logical and a physical level. Also, administrators can back up the transaction log to make restoring a database more efficient. Administrators or database owners can also set a database's recovery model to determine the level of detail stored in the transaction log.

CHAPTER 6

Table storage

Kalen Delaney

This chapter starts with a basic introduction to tables and then continues into some very detailed examinations of their internal structures. Simply put, a *table* is a collection of data about a specific *entity* (a person, place, or thing) with a discrete number of named *attributes* (for example, quantity or type). Tables are at the heart of Microsoft SQL Server and the relational model in general. In SQL Server, a table is often referred to as a *base table* to emphasize where data is stored. Calling it a base table also distinguishes it from a *view*, a virtual table that's an internal query referencing one or more base tables or other views.

Attributes of a table's data (such as color, size, quantity, order date, and supplier's name) take the form of named *columns* in the table. Each instance of data in a table is represented as a single entry, or *row* (formally called a *tuple*). In a true relational database, each row in a table is unique and has a unique identifier called a *primary key*. (SQL Server, in accordance with the ANSI SQL standard, doesn't require you to make a row unique or declare a primary key. However, because both concepts are central to the relational model, implementing them is always recommended.)

Most tables have some relationship to other tables. For example, in a typical order-entry system, the *orders* table has a *customer_number* column for keeping track of the customer number for an order, and *customer_number* also appears in the *customer* table. Assuming that *customer_number* is a unique identifier, or primary key, of the *customer* table, a foreign key relationship is established by which *orders* and *customer* tables can subsequently be joined.

So much for the 30-second database design primer. You can find plenty of books that discuss logical database and table design, but this isn't one of them. Presumably you already understand basic relational database theory and design and generally know what your tables will look like. The rest of this chapter discusses the internals of tables in SQL Server 2012.

Table creation

To create a table, SQL Server uses the ANSI SQL standard *CREATE TABLE* syntax. SQL Server Management Studio provides a front-end, fill-in-the-blank table designer that can sometimes make your job easier. Ultimately, the SQL syntax is always sent to SQL Server to create a table, no matter what interface you use. This chapter emphasizes direct use of the Data Definition Language (DDL) rather than discussing the GUI tools. You should keep all DDL commands in a script so that later you can easily rerun them to re-create the table. (Even if you use one of the friendly front-end tools, the ability to re-create the table later is critical.) Management Studio and other front-end tools can create and save operating system files using the SQL DDL commands necessary to create any object. DDL is essentially source code, and you should treat it as such. Keep a backup copy. You should also consider keeping these files under version control, using a source control product such as Microsoft's Visual Studio Team Foundation Server.

At the basic level, creating a table requires little more than knowing what you want to name it, what columns it contains, and what range of values (domain) each column can store. The following is the basic syntax for creating the *customer* table in the *dbo* schema, with three fixed-length character (*char*) columns. (Note that this table definition isn't necessarily the most efficient way to store data because it always requires 46 bytes per entry for data plus a few bytes of overhead, regardless of the actual length of the data.)

```
CREATE TABLE dbo.customer
(
name           char(30),
phone          char(12),
emp_id         char(4)
);
```

This example shows each column on a separate line for readability. As far as the SQL Server parser is concerned, white spaces created by tabs, carriage returns, and the spacebar are identical. From the system's standpoint, the following *CREATE TABLE* example is identical to the preceding one, but it's harder to read from a user's standpoint:

```
CREATE TABLE customer (name char(30), phone char(12), emp_id char(4));
```

Naming tables and columns

A table is always created within one schema of one database. Tables also have owners, but unlike with versions of SQL Server prior to 2005, the table owner name isn't used to access the table. The schema is used for all object access. Normally, a table is created in the default schema of the user who is creating it, but the *CREATE TABLE* statement can specify the schema in which the object is to be created. A user can create a table only in a schema for which the user has *ALTER* permissions. Any user in the sysadmin, db_ddladmin, or db_owner roles can create a table in any schema. A database can contain multiple tables with the same name, as long as the tables are in different schemas. The full name of a table has three parts, in the following form:

> *database_name.schema_name.table_name*

The first two parts of the three-part name specification have default values. The default for the *database_name* is whatever database context in which you're currently working. The *schema_name* actually has two possible defaults when querying. If no schema name is specified when you reference an object, SQL Server first checks for an object in your default schema. If your default schema has no such object, SQL Server checks to see whether the *dbo* schema has an object of the specified name.

Note To access a table or other object in a schema other than your default or *dbo* schema, you must include the schema name along with the table name. In fact, you should get in the habit of always including the schema name when referring to any object in SQL Server 2012. Not only does this remove any possible confusion about which schema you are interested in but it can lead to some performance benefits.

The *sys* schema is a special case. For compatibility views, such as *sysobjects,* SQL Server accesses the object in the *sys* schema before any object you might have created with the same name. Obviously, it's not a good idea to create an object of your own called *sysobjects* because you will never be able to access it. Compatibility views can also be accessed through the *dbo* schema, so the objects *sys.sysobjects* and *dbo.sysobjects* are the same. For catalog views and Dynamic Management Objects, you must specify the *sys* schema to access the object.

You should make column names descriptive and because you'll use them repeatedly, you should avoid wordiness. The name of the column (or any object in SQL Server, such as a table or a view) can be whatever you choose, as long as it conforms to the SQL Server rule for regular identifiers: It must consist of a combination of 1 through 128 letters; digits; or the symbols #, $, @, or _. Alternatively, you can use a delimited identifier that includes any characters you like (discussed in more detail shortly).

In some cases, you can access a table using a four-part name, in which the first part is the name of the SQL Server instance. However, you can refer to a table using a four-part name only if the SQL Server instance has been defined as a linked server. You can read more about linked servers in *SQL Server Books Online*.

Avoiding reserved keywords

Certain reserved keywords, such as *TABLE, CREATE, SELECT,* and *UPDATE,* have special meaning to the SQL Server parser, and collectively they make up the SQL language implementation. You should avoid using reserved keywords for your object names. In addition to the SQL Server reserved keywords, the SQL-92 standard has its own list of reserved keywords. In some cases, this list is more restrictive than the SQL Server list; in other cases, it's less restrictive. The *SQL Server Books Online* page for "Reserved Keywords" documents the Transact-SQL reserved keywords. It also shows the ODBC reserved keyword list, which is the same as the SQL-92 reserved keyword list.

Watch out for the SQL-92 reserved keywords. Some of the words aren't reserved keywords in SQL Server—yet—but they might become reserved keywords in a future SQL Server version. If you use a SQL-92 reserved keyword, you might end up having to alter your application before upgrading it if the word becomes a SQL Server reserved keyword.

Using delimited identifiers

You can't use keywords in your object names unless you use a delimited identifier. In fact, if you use a delimited identifier, not only can you use keywords as identifiers but you can also use any other string as an object name—whether or not it follows the rules for identifiers. They include spaces and other nonalphanumeric characters that normally aren't allowed. Two types of delimited identifiers exist.

- Bracketed identifiers, which are delimited by square brackets ([*object name*])

- Quoted identifiers, which are delimited by double quotation marks (*"object name"*)

You can use bracketed identifiers in any environment, but to use quoted identifiers, you must enable a special option using *SET QUOTED_IDENTIFIER ON*. If you turn on *QUOTED_IDENTIFIER*, double quotes are interpreted as referencing an object. To delimit string or date constants, you must use single quotes.

Now look at some examples. Because *column* is a reserved keyword, the first statement that follows is illegal in all circumstances. The second statement is illegal unless *QUOTED_IDENTIFIER* is on. The third statement is legal in any circumstance:

```
CREATE TABLE dbo.customer(name char(30), column char(12), emp_id char(4));

CREATE TABLE dbo.customer(name char(30), "column" char(12), emp_id char(4));

CREATE TABLE dbo.customer(name char(30), [column] char(12), emp_id char(4));
```

The SQL Native Client ODBC driver and SQL Native Client OLE DB Provider for SQL Server automatically set *QUOTED_IDENTIFIER* to *ON* when connecting. You can configure this in ODBC data sources, ODBC connection attributes, or OLE DB connection properties. You can determine whether this option is on or off for your session by executing the following query:

```
SELECT quoted_identifier
FROM sys.dm_exec_sessions
WHERE session_id = @@spid;
```

A result value of 1 indicates that *QUOTED_IDENTIFIER* is *ON*. If you're using Management Studio, you can check the setting by running the preceding command in a query window or by choosing Options from the Tools menu and then expanding the Query Execution/SQL Server node and examining the ANSI properties information, as shown in Figure 6-1.

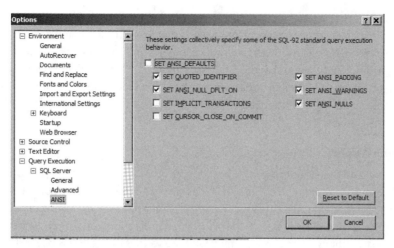

FIGURE 6-1 Examining the ANSI properties for a connection in Management Studio.

> **Tip** Technically, you can use delimited identifiers with all object and column names, so you never have to worry about reserved keywords. However, I don't recommend this. Many third-party tools for SQL Server don't handle quoted identifiers well, and they can make your code difficult to read. Using quoted identifiers might also make upgrading to future versions of SQL Server more difficult.

Rather than use delimited identifiers to protect against reserved keyword problems, you should simply adopt some simple naming conventions. For example, you can precede column names with the first few letters of the table name and an underscore. This naming style makes the column or object name more readable and also greatly reduces your chances of encountering a keyword or reserved word conflict.

Understanding naming conventions

Many organizations and multiuser development projects adopt standard naming conventions, which is generally a good practice. For example, assigning a standard moniker of *cust_id* to represent a customer number in every table clearly shows that all the tables share common data. If an organization instead uses several monikers in the tables to represent a customer number, such as *cust_id*, *cust_num*, *customer_number*, and *customer_#*, it won't be as obvious that these monikers represent common data.

One naming convention is the Hungarian-style notation for column names. Hungarian-style notation is a widely used practice in C programming, whereby variable names include information about their data types. This notation uses names such as *sint_nn_custnum* to indicate that the *custnum* column is a small integer (*smallint* of 2 bytes) and is NOT NULL (doesn't allow nulls). Although this practice makes good sense in C programming, it defeats the data type independence that SQL Server provides; therefore, I recommend against using it.

Choosing a data type

SQL Server provides many data types, most of which are straightforward. Choosing the appropriate data type is simply a matter of mapping the domain of values you need to store to the corresponding data type. In choosing data types, you want to avoid wasting storage space while allowing enough space for a sufficient range of possible values over the life of your application. Discussing the details about all the possible considerations when programming with the various data types is beyond the scope of this book. For the most part, this chapter covers just some of the basic issues related to dealing with the various data types.

The decision about what data type to use for each column depends primarily on the nature of the data the column holds and the operations you want to perform on the data. The five basic data type categories in SQL Server 2012 are numeric, character, date and time, Large Object (LOB), and miscellaneous. SQL Server 2012 also supports a variant data type called *sql_variant*. Values stored in a *sql_variant* column can be of almost any data type. Chapter 8, "Special storage," discusses LOB columns because their storage format is different from that of other data types discussed in this chapter. This section examines some of the issues related to storing data of different data types.

Numeric data types

You should use numeric data types for data on which you want to perform numeric comparisons or arithmetic operations. Your main decisions are the maximum range of possible values you want to be able to store and the accuracy you need. The tradeoff is that data types that can store a greater range of values take up more space.

Numeric data types can also be classified as either exact or approximate. Exact numeric values are guaranteed to store exact representations of your numbers. Approximate numeric values have a far greater range of values, but the values aren't guaranteed to be stored precisely. The greatest range of values that exact numeric values can store data is −10∧38 + 1 to 10∧38 −1. Unless you need numbers with greater magnitude, I recommend that you not use the approximate numeric data types.

The exact numeric data types can be divided into two groups: integers and decimals. Integer types range in size from 1 to 8 bytes, with a corresponding increase in the range of possible values. The *money* and *smallmoney* data types are included frequently among the integer types because internally they are stored in the same way. For the *money* and *smallmoney* data types, it is understood that the rightmost four digits are after the decimal point. For the other integer types, no digits come after the decimal point. Table 6-1 lists the integer data types along with their storage size and range of values.

TABLE 6-1 Range and storage requirements for integer data types

Data type	Range	Storage (bytes)
bigint	-2^{63} to $2^{63}-1$	8
int	-2^{31} to $2^{31}-1$	4
smallint	-2^{15} to $2^{15}-1$	2
tinyint	0 to 255	1
money	−922,337,203,685,477.5808 to 922,337,203,685,477.5807, with accuracy of one ten-thousandth of a monetary unit	8
smallmoney	−214,748.3648 to 214,748.3647, with accuracy of one ten-thousandth of a monetary unit	4

The decimal and numeric data types allow a high degree of accuracy and a large range of values. For those two synonymous data types, you can specify a *precision* (the total number of digits stored) and a *scale* (the maximum number of digits to the right of the decimal point). The maximum number of digits that can be stored to the left of the decimal point is precision minus scale—that is, subtract the scale from precision to get the number of digits. Two different decimal values can have the same precision and very different ranges. For example, a column defined as decimal (8,4) can store values from −9,999.9999 to 9,999.9999; a column defined as decimal (8,0) can store values from −99,999,999 to 99,999,999.

Table 6-2 shows the storage space required for decimal and numeric data based on the defined precision.

TABLE 6-2 Storage requirements for decimal and numeric data types

Precision	Storage (bytes)
1 to 9	5
10 to 19	9
20 to 28	13
29 to 38	17

SQL Server 2005 SP2 added a feature to allow decimal data to be stored in a variable amount of space. This can be useful when you have some values that need a high degree of precision, but most of the values in the column need only a few bytes, or are 0 or NULL. Unlike *varchar*, *vardecimal* isn't a data type, but rather a table property set by using the *sp_tableoption* procedure (in SQL Server 2005, it must also be enabled for the database). In SQL Server 2008 and SQL Server 2012, all databases except *master*, *model*, *tempdb*, and *msdb* always allow tables to have the *vardecimal storage format* property enabled.

Although the vardecimal storage format can reduce the storage size of the data, using it comes at the cost of adding CPU overhead. After the *vardecimal* property is enabled for a table, all *decimal* data in the table is stored as variable-length data. This includes all indexes on *decimal* data and all log records that include *decimal* data.

Changing the value of the *vardecimal storage format* property of a table is an offline operation, and SQL Server exclusively locks the table being modified until all the decimal data is converted to the new format. Because the vardecimal storage format has been deprecated, this chapter won't describe the details of the internal storage for *vardecimal* data. For new development, I recommend that you use SQL Server's compression capabilities to minimize your storage requirement for data that requires a variable number of bytes. Chapter 8 discusses data compression.

Date and time data types

SQL Server 2012 supports six data types for storing date and time information. The *datetime* and *smalldatetime* data types have been available since the very first version, and four new types were added in SQL Server 2008: *date, time, datetime2,* and *datetimeoffset*. The difference between these types is the range of possible dates, the number of bytes needed for storage, whether both date and time are stored (or just the date or just the time), and whether time zone information is incorporated into the stored value. Table 6-3, taken from *SQL Server 2012 Books Online*, shows the range and storage requirements for each of the date and time data types.

TABLE 6-3 SQL Server date and time data types range and storage requirements

Type	Format	Range	Accuracy	Storage size (bytes)	User-defined fractional second precision
time	*hh:mm:ss [.nnnnnnn]*	00:00:00.0000000 through 23:59:59.9999999	100 nanoseconds	3 to 5	Yes
date	*YYYY-MM-DD*	0001-01-01 through 9999-12-31	1 day	3	No
smalldatetime	*YYYY-MM-DD hh:mm:ss*	1900-01-01 through 2079-06-06	1 minute	4	No
datetime	*YYYY-MM-DD hh:mm:ss [.nnn]*	1753-01-01 through 9999-12-31	0.00333 second	8	No
datetime2	*YYYY-MM-DD hh:mm:ss [.nnnnnnn]*	0001-01-01 00:00:00.0000000 through 9999-12-31 23:59:59.9999999	100 nanoseconds	6 to 8	Yes
datetimeoffset	*YYYY-MM-DD hh:mm:ss [.nnnnnnn] [+|-]hh:mm*	0001-01-01 00:00:00.0000000 through 9999-12-31 23:59:59.9999999 (in UTC)	100 nanoseconds	8 to 10 (2 bytes for time zone data)	Yes

If no date is supplied, the default of January 1, 1900, is assumed; if no time is supplied, the default of 00:00:00.000 (midnight) is assumed.

Note If you're new to SQL Server date and time data, you might be surprised that for the original *datetime* data type, the earliest possible date that could be stored was January 1, 1753. This was done for historical reasons and started with the original Sybase specification for the *datetime* data type. In what is sometimes referred to as the Western world, modern time has used two calendars: Julian and Gregorian. These calendars were a number of days apart (depending on which century you look at), so when a culture that used the Julian calendar moved to the Gregorian calendar, they dropped between 10 to 13 days from the calendar. Great Britain made this shift in 1752, and in that year, September 2 was followed by September 14. Sybase decided not to store dates earlier than 1753 because the date arithmetic functions would be ambiguous. However, other countries made the change at other times, and in Turkey, the calendar wasn't shifted until 1927.

Internally, values for all date and time data types are stored completely differently from how you enter them or how they are displayed. Dates and times are always stored as two separate components: a date component and a time component.

For the original *datetime* data types, *datetime* and *smalldatetime*, the data is stored internally as two separate components. For *datetime* values, the data is stored as two 4-byte values: the first (for the date) being the number of days before or after the base date of January 1, 1900, and the second (for the time) being the number of clock ticks after midnight, with each tick representing 3.33 milliseconds, or 1/300 of a second. You can actually see these two parts if you convert a *datetime* value to a binary string of 8 hexadecimal bytes. For *smalldatetime* values, each component is stored in 2 bytes. The date is stored as the number of days after January 1, 1900, and the time is stored as the number of minutes after midnight.

The following example shows how to see the component parts of the current date and time, stored in a variable of type *datetime*, retrieved using the parameterless system function *CURRENT_TIMESTAMP*. The first *CONVERT* operation shows the full hexadecimal byte string that stores the *datetime* value. The second *CONVERT* displays the first 4 bytes converted to an integer; the third *CONVERT* displays the second 4 bytes converted to an integer. Storing current date and time in a local variable ensures that the same value is being used for all the *CONVERT* operations.

```
DECLARE @today datetime
SELECT @today = CURRENT_TIMESTAMP
SELECT @today AS [CURRENT TIMESTAMP];
SELECT CONVERT (varbinary(8), @today) AS [INTERNAL FORMAT];
SELECT CONVERT (int, SUBSTRING (CONVERT (varbinary(8), @today), 1, 4))
       AS [DAYS AFTER 1/1/1900];
SELECT CONVERT (int, SUBSTRING (CONVERT (varbinary(8), @today), 5, 4))
       AS [TICKS AFTER MIDNIGHT];
```

These are the results when the code runs on March 14, 2012:

```
CURRENT TIMESTAMP
----------------------
2012-03-14 15:00:45.043

INTERNAL FORMAT
------------------
0x0000A01400F76609

DAYS AFTER 1/1/1900
-------------------
40980

TICKS AFTER MIDNIGHT
--------------------
16213513
```

When adding new *date* and *time* data types in SQL Server 2008, Microsoft changed the internal representation of dates and times completely. Dates are now stored as a 3-byte positive number, representing the number of days after January 1, 0001. For the *datetimeoffset* type, an additional 2 bytes are used to store a time offset, in hours and minutes, from UTC. Note that although internally the base date for the new date and data types is January 1, 0001, when SQL Server is interpreting a date value where the actual date isn't specified, January 1, 1900, is the default. For example, if you try to insert the string '01:15:00' into a *datetime2* column, SQL Server interprets this as a time of 1:15 on January 1, 1900.

All the new types that contain time information (*time*, *datetime2*, and *datetimeoffset*) allow you to specify the precision of the time component by following the data type name with a number between 1 and 7 indicating the desired scale. The default, if no scale is specified, is to assume a scale of 7. Table 6-4 shows what each possible scale value means in terms of the precision and storage requirement of the stored data values.

TABLE 6-4 Scale values for time data with storage requirements and precision

Specified scale	Result (precision, scale)	Column length (bytes)	Fractional seconds (precision)
None	(16,7)	5	7
(0)	(8,0)	3	0–2
(1)	(10,1)	3	0–2
(2)	(11,2)	3	0–2
(3)	(12,3)	4	3–4
(4)	(13,4)	4	3–4
(5)	(14,5)	5	5–7
(6)	(15,6)	5	5–7
(7)	(16,7)	5	5–7

For a quick look at what the information in Table 6-4 means, you can run the following three conversions:

```
SELECT CAST(CURRENT_TIMESTAMP AS time);
SELECT CAST(CURRENT_TIMESTAMP AS time(2));
SELECT CAST(CURRENT_TIMESTAMP AS time(7));
```

The following are my results. Note that the scale value determines the number of decimal digits and that the value for *time* is identical to *time*(7):

```
17:39:43.0830000
17:39:43.08
17:39:43.0830000
```

Internally, the time is computed using the following formula, assuming *H* represents hours, *M* represents minutes, *S* represents seconds, *F* represents fractional sections, and *D* represents scale (number of decimal digits):

$$(((H * 60) + M) * 60 + S) * 10^D + F$$

For example, the value 17:39:43.08, with *time(2)* format, would be stored internally as

$$(((17 * 60) + 39) * 60 + 43) * 10^2 + 083, \text{ or } 6358383$$

The same time, stored as *time*(7), would be

$$(((17 * 60) + 39) * 60 + 43) * 10^7 + 083, \text{ or } 635830000083$$

Later in the section "Internal storage," you see what this data looks like when stored in a data row.

SQL Server 2012 provides dozens of functions for working with *date* and *time* data, as well as dozens of different formats that can be used for interpreting and displaying date and time values. Covering date and time data in that level of detail is beyond the scope of this book. However, the most important thing to understand about these types is that what you see isn't what's actually stored on disk. The on-disk format, whether you're using the old *datetime* and *smalldatetime* types or any of the new types, is completely unambiguous, but it's not very user-friendly. You need to be sure to provide input data in an unambiguous format. For example, the value '3/4/48' is *not* unambiguous. Does it represent March 4 or April 3, and is the year 1948, 2048, or perhaps 48 (almost 2,000 years ago)? The ISO 8601 format is an international standard with unambiguous specification. Using this format, March 4, 1948, could be represented as 19480304 or 1948-03-04. However, because SQL Server's interpretation of 1948-03-04 can vary based on your *SET DATEFORMAT* settings and the default collation, I recommend using 19480304 (in general, formatted as yyyymmdd).

Character data types

Character data types come in four varieties. They can be fixed-length or variable-length strings of single-byte characters (*char* and *varchar*) or fixed-length or variable-length strings of Unicode characters (*nchar* and *nvarchar*). Unicode character strings need two bytes for each stored character; use them when you need to represent characters that can't be stored in the single-byte characters that are sufficient for storing most of the characters in the English and European alphabets. Single-byte character strings can store up to 8,000 characters, and Unicode character strings can store up to 4,000 characters. You should know the type of data that you are dealing with to decide between single-byte and double-byte character strings. Keep in mind that the catalog view *sys.types* reports the length in number of bytes, not in number of characters. In SQL Server 2005 and later, you can also define a variable-length character string with a *max* length. Columns defined as *varchar(max)* are treated as normal variable-length columns when the actual length is less than or equal to 8,000 bytes, and they are treated as a large object value (mentioned later in this section and covered in detail in Chapter 8) when the actual length is greater than 8,000 bytes.

Deciding whether to use a variable-length or fixed-length data type is a more difficult decision, and it isn't always straightforward or obvious. As a general rule, variable-length data types are most appropriate when you expect significant variation in the size of the data for a column and when the data in the column won't be changed frequently.

Using variable-length data types can yield important storage savings. It can sometimes result in a minor performance loss but at other times can result in improved performance. A row with variable-length columns requires special offset entries to be maintained internally. These entries keep track of the actual column length. Calculating and maintaining the offsets requires slightly more overhead than does a pure fixed-length row, which needs no such offsets. This task requires a few addition and subtraction operations to maintain the offset value. However, the extra overhead of maintaining these offsets is generally inconsequential, and this alone wouldn't make a significant difference on most, if any, systems.

Another potential performance issue with variable-length fields is the cost of increasing the size of a row on a page that's almost full. If a row with variable-length columns uses only part of its maximum length and is later updated to a longer length, the enlarged row might not fit on the same page any more. If the table has a clustered index, the row must stay in the same position relative to the other rows, so the solution is to split the page and move some of the rows from the page with the enlarged row onto a newly linked page—a potentially expensive operation. Chapter 7, "Indexes: internals and management," describes the details of page splitting and moving rows. If the table has no clustered index, the row can move to a new location and leave a forwarding pointer in the original location. Later, this chapter examines forwarding pointers.

Looking at this from another angle, using variable-length columns can sometimes improve performance because it can allow more rows to fit on a page. But the efficiency results from more than simply requiring less disk space. A data page for SQL Server is 8 KB (8,192 bytes), of which 8,096 bytes are available to store data. (The rest is for internal use to keep track of structural information about the page and the object to which it belongs.) One I/O operation brings back the entire page. If you can fit 80 rows on a page, a single I/O operation brings back 80 rows. But if you can fit 160 rows on a page, one I/O operation is essentially twice as efficient. In operations that scan for data and return many adjacent rows, this can amount to a significant performance improvement. The more rows you can fit per page, the better your I/O and cache-hit efficiency is.

Consider a simple customer table. Suppose that you could define it in two ways: fixed-length and variable-length, as shown in Listings 6-1 and 6-2. If you want to create these tables for yourself, you can use any database, but these listings include a reference to a database called testdb. As a best practice, don't create them in a system database other than tempdb.

LISTING 6-1 A customer table with all fixed-length columns

```
USE testdb;
GO

CREATE TABLE customer_fixed
(
 cust_id        smallint    NOT NULL,
 cust_name      char(50)    NULL,
 cust_addr1     char(50)    NULL,
 cust_addr2     char(50)    NULL,
 cust_city      char(50)    NULL,
 cust_state     char(2)     NULL,
 cust_postcode  char(10)    NULL,
 cust_phone     char(20)    NULL,
 cust_fax       char(20)    NULL,
 cust_email     char(30)    NULL,
 cust_URL       char(100)   NULL
 );
 GO
```

LISTING 6-2 A customer table with variable-length columns

```
USE testdb;
GO

CREATE TABLE customer_var
(
 cust_id        smallint       NOT NULL,
 cust_name      varchar(50)            NULL,
 cust_addr1     varchar(50)    NULL,
 cust_addr2     varchar(50)    NULL,
 cust_city      varchar(50)    NULL,
 cust_state     char(2)        NULL,
 cust_postcode  varchar(10)    NULL,
 cust_phone     varchar(20)    NULL,
 cust_fax       varchar(20)    NULL,
 cust_email     varchar(30)            NULL,
 cust_URL       varchar(100)   NULL
 );
 GO
```

Columns that contain addresses, names, or URLs all have data with length that varies significantly. Look at the differences between choosing fixed-length columns and choosing variable-length columns. In Listing 6-1, which uses all fixed-length columns, every row uses 384 bytes for data, regardless of the number of characters actually inserted in the row. SQL Server also needs an additional 10 bytes of overhead for every row in this table, so each row needs a total of 394 bytes for storage. Say that even though the table must accommodate addresses and names up to the specified size, the average row is only half the maximum size.

In Listing 6-2, assume that for all the variable-length (*varchar*) columns, the average entry is actually only about half the maximum. Instead of a row length of 394 bytes, the average length is 224 bytes. This length is computed as follows.

- The *smallint* and *char(2)* columns total 4 bytes.

- The *varchar* columns' maximum total length is 380, half of which is 190 bytes.

- A 2-byte overhead exists for each of nine *varchar* columns, for 18 bytes.

- Add 2 more bytes for any row with one or more variable-length columns.

- These rows also require the same 10 bytes of overhead that the fixed-length rows from Listing 6-1 require, regardless of the presence of variable-length fields.

So the total is 4 + 190 + 18 + 2 + 10 = 224. (Later, this chapter discusses the actual meaning of each of these bytes of overhead.)

In the fixed-length example in Listing 6-1, you always fit 20 rows on a data page (8,096/394, discarding the remainder). In the variable-length example in Listing 6-2, you can fit an average of 36 rows per page (8,096/224). The table using variable-length columns consumes about half as many pages in storage, a single I/O operation retrieves almost twice as many rows, and a page cached in memory is twice as likely to contain the row you want.

> **More info** You need additional overhead bytes for each row if you are using snapshot isolation. Chapter 13, "Transactions and concurrency," discusses this concurrency option, as well as the extra row overhead needed to support it. Additional bytes also might be needed for other special SQL Server features.

When you choose column lengths, don't be wasteful—but don't be cheap, either. Allow for future needs, and realize that if the additional length doesn't change how many rows fit on a page, the additional size is free anyway. Consider again the examples in Listings 6-1 and 6-2. The *cust_id* is declared as a *smallint*, meaning that its maximum positive value is 32,767 (unfortunately, SQL Server doesn't provide any unsigned *int* or unsigned *smallint* data types), and it consumes 2 bytes of storage. Although 32,767 customers might seem like a lot to a new company, the company might be surprised by its own success and find in a couple of years that the 32,767 size is too limited.

The database designers might regret that they tried to save 2 bytes and didn't simply make the data type an *int*, using 4 bytes but with a maximum positive value of 2,147,483,647. They'll be especially disappointed if they realize they didn't really save any space. If you compute the rows-per-page calculations just discussed, increasing the row size by 2 bytes, you'll see that the same number of rows still fit on a page. The additional 2 bytes are free; they were simply wasted space before. They never cause fewer rows per page in the fixed-length example, and they'll rarely cause fewer rows per page even in the variable-length case.

So which strategy wins: potentially better update performance, or more rows per page? Like most questions of this nature, no one answer is right; it depends on your application. If you understand the tradeoffs, you can make the best choice. Now that you know the issues, this general rule merits repeating: Variable-length data types are most appropriate when you expect significant variation in the size of the data for that column and when the column won't be updated frequently.

Character data collation

For many data types, the rules to compare and sort are straightforward. No matter whom you ask, 12 is always greater than 11, and even if people write dates in different ways, August 20, 2012, is never the same as August 21, 2011. But for character data, this principle doesn't apply. Most people would sort *csak* before *cukor*, but in an Hungarian dictionary, they come in the opposite order. Also, is *STREET* equal to *Street* or not? Finally, how are characters with diacritic marks, such as accents or umlauts, sorted?

Because different users have different preferences and needs, character data in SQL Server are always associated with a *collation*. A collation is a set of rules that defines how character data is sorted and compared, and how language-dependent functions such as *UPPER* and *LOWER* work. The collation also determines the character repertoire for the single-byte data types: *char*, *varchar*, and *text*. Metadata in SQL Server—that is, names of tables, variables, and so forth—are also subject to collation rules.

Determining which collation to use   You can define which collation to use at several levels in SQL Server. When you create a table, you can define the collation for each character column. If you don't supply a collation, the database collation is used.

The database collation also determines the collation for the metadata in the database. So in a database with a case-insensitive collation, you can use *MyTable* or *MYTABLE* to refer to a table created with the name *mytable*, but in a database with a case-sensitive collation, you must refer to it as *mytable*. The database collation also determines the collation for string literals and for data in character variables. One exception is temporary tables, which use the collation of the tempdb database unless your database is marked as "Partially Contained." (The tempdb database and contained databases are discussed in Chapter 4, "Special databases.")

You can specify the database collation when you create a database. If you don't, the server collation is used. Under some fairly restricted circumstances, the *ALTER DATABASE* statement permits you to change the database collation. (Basically, if you have any CHECK constraints in the database, you can't change the collation.) This rebuilds the system tables to reflect the new collation rules in the metadata. However, columns in user tables are left unchanged, and you need to change these yourself. For details on all restrictions, read the *ALTER DATABASE* topic in *SQL Server Books Online*.

The server collation is used by the system databases *master*, *model*, *tempdb*, and *msdb*, except as in the case mentioned above for temporary tables created by partially contained databases. The resource database, on the other hand, always has the same collation, Latin1_General_CI_AI. The server collation is also the collation for variable names, so on a server with a case-insensitive collation, @a and @A are the same variable, but they are two different ones if the server collation is case-sensitive. You select the server collation at setup.

Finally, you can use the *COLLATE* clause to force the collation in an expression. One situation in which you need to do this is when the same expression includes two columns with different collations. This results in a *collation conflict*, and SQL Server requires you to resolve it with the *COLLATE* clause.

Viewing available collations   To see the available collations, you can run the query

```
SELECT * FROM fn_helpcollations();
```

When running this query on a SQL Server 2012 instance, the result contains 3,885 collations. Other collations are deprecated and aren't listed by fn_helpcollations.

Collations fall into two main groups: Windows collations and SQL Server collations. SQL Server collations are mainly former collations retained for compatibility reasons. Nevertheless, the collation SQL_Latin1_General_CP1_CI_AS is one of the most commonly used ones because it's the default collation when you install SQL Server on a machine with English (United States) as the system locale.

Working with Windows collations   Windows collations take their definition from Microsoft Windows. SQL Server doesn't query Windows for collation rules; instead, the SQL Server team has copied the collation definitions into SQL Server. The collations in Windows typically are modified with new releases of Windows to adapt to changes in the Unicode standard, and because collations determine in which order data appear in indexes, SQL Server can't accept that the definition of a collation changes because you move a database to a different Windows version.

Anatomy of a collation name   Windows collations come in families, with 34 collations in each family. All collations in the same family start with the same *collation designator*, which indicates which language or group of languages the collation family supports.

The collation designator is followed by tokens that indicate the nature of the collation. The collation can be a binary collation, in which case the token is BIN or BIN2. For the other 32 collations, the tokens are CI/CS to indicate case sensitivity/insensitivity, AI/AS to indicate accent sensitivity/insensitivity, KS to indicate kanatype sensitivity, WS to indicate width sensitivity, and SC to indicate that the collation supports supplementary characters.

If CI is part of the collation name, the strings *smith* and *SMITH* are equal, but they are different if CS is in the name. Likewise, if the collation is AI, *cote*, *coté*, *côte*, and *côté* are all equal, but in an AS collation, they are different. Kanatype relates to Japanese text only, and in a kanatype-sensitive collation, katakana and hiragana counterparts are considered different. Width sensitivity refers to East Asian languages for which both half-width and full-width forms of some characters exist. KI and WI tokens don't exist, but insensitivity to kanatype and width is implied if KS and WS are absent.

Supplementary characters can be used to store Unicode characters with a codepoint value that can't fit in 2 bytes. These characters with codepoint values larger than 0xFFFF are stored in two consecutive 16-bit words called surrogate pairs. A string stored in an *nchar(20)* column always uses 40 bytes of storage. However, if you are using an SC collation, some of the characters might need the usual 2 bytes, but some can be supplementary characters and need 4 bytes. This is because an SC collation can host the full range of Unicode, which is 2^{21} characters. So the *nchar(20)* might be able to store only 10 characters. Because each character takes the bytes it needs, the result is between 10 and 20 characters in each column.

The following are some examples of collation names:

- **Latin1_General_CI_AS** A case-insensitive, accent-sensitive collation for Western European languages such as English, German, and Italian

- **Finnish_Swedish_CS_AS** A case-sensitive and accent-sensitive collation for Finnish and Swedish

- **Japanese_CI_AI_KS_WS_SC** A collation that's insensitive to case and accent, sensitive to kanatype and width differences, and supports supplementary characters

- **Turkish_BIN2** A binary collation for Turkish

Different versions of the same collation A collation designator might include a version number that indicates to which SQL Server version the collation was added. The lack of a version number means that the collation was one of the original collations in SQL Server 2000; 90 indicates that the collation was added in SQL Server 2005; and 100 means that it was added in SQL Server 2008.

SQL Server 2008 added new collations for languages and language groups for which a collation already existed. So now Latin1_General and Latin1_General_100, Finnish_Swedish and Finnish_Swedish_100, and other collation pairs exist. These additions reflect the changes in Windows. The old collations are based on the collations in Windows 2000, and the new_100 collations are based on the collations in Windows 2008.

> **Caution** If you plan to access your SQL Server 2012 instance as a linked server from SQL Server 2005, you should avoid using the _100 collations. If you try to access such a column from SQL Server 2005, you get the error message, "An invalid tabular data stream (TDS) collation was encountered."

The single-byte character types These character data types—*char*, *varchar*, and *text*—can represent only 255 possible characters, and the *code page* of the collation determines which 255 characters are available. In most code pages, the characters from 32 to 127 are always the same, taken from the ASCII standard, and remaining characters are selected to fit a certain language area. For instance, CP1252, also known as Latin-1, supports Western European languages such as English, French, Swedish, and others. CP1250 is for the Cyrillic script, CP1251 is for Eastern European languages, and so on.

When it comes to other operations—sorting, comparing, lower/upper, and so on—in a Windows collation, the rules are exactly the same for the single-byte data types and the double-byte Unicode data types. One exception is that in a binary collation, sorting is done by character codes, and the order in the single-byte code page can be different from the order in Unicode. For instance, in a Polish collation, *char(209)* prints Ń (a capital N with an acute accent), whereas *unicode(N'Ń')* prints 323, which is the code point in Unicode for this character. (The code points in Unicode agree with the code points in Latin-1 but apply only to the range 160-255.) Microsoft has added some extra characters to its version of Latin-1. One example of this is the euro (€) character, which is *char(128)* in a collation based on CP1252 but in Unicode, code point 128 is a nonprinting character, and *unicode(N'€')* prints 8364.

Some collations don't map to a single-byte code page. You can use these collations only with Unicode data types. For instance, if you run the code

```
CREATE TABLE NepaleseTest
    (col1 char(5) COLLATE Nepali_100_CI_AS NOT NULL);
```

you get the following error message:

```
Msg 459, Level 16, State 2, Line 1
Collation 'Nepali_100_CI_AS' is supported on Unicode data types only and cannot be applied
to char, varchar or text data types.
```

To view the code page for a collation, you can use the *collationproperty* function, as in this example:

```
SELECT collationproperty('Latin1_General_CS_AS', 'CodePage');
```

This returns 1252. For a collation that supports Unicode only, you get 0 in return. (If you get NULL back, you have misspelled the collation name or the word *CodePage*.)

You can't use Unicode-only collations as the server collation.

Sort order The collation determines the sort order. A Windows collation that's insensitive (such as case or accents) also applies to the sort order. For instance, in a case-insensitive collation, differences in case don't affect how the data is sorted. In a sensitive collation, case, accent, kanatype, and width affect the sorting, but only with a secondary weight—that is, these properties affect the sorting only when no other differences exist.

To illustrate this, consider this table:

```
CREATE TABLE #words (word    nvarchar(20) NOT NULL,
                     wordno tinyint PRIMARY KEY CLUSTERED);
INSERT #words
    VALUES(N'cloud',  1), (N'CSAK',    6), (N'cukor',   11),
          (N'Oblige', 2), (N'Opera',   7), (N'Öl',      12),
          (N'résumé', 3), (N'RESUME',  8), (N'RÉSUMÉ',  13),
          (N'resume', 4), (N'resumes', 9), (N'résumés', 14),
          (N'ŒIL',    5), (N'œil',    10);
```

To examine how a collation works, use the following query. Start by looking at the commonly used collation Latin1_General_CI_AS:

```
WITH collatedwords (collatedword, wordno) AS (
   SELECT word COLLATE Latin1_General_CI_AS, wordno
   FROM    #words
)
SELECT collatedword, rank = dense_rank() OVER(ORDER BY collatedword),
       wordno
```

```
FROM    collatedwords
ORDER  BY collatedword;
```

When I ran the query, I got this result:

```
collatedword   rank   wordno
-------------- ------ ------
cloud          1      1
CSAK           2      6
cukor          3      11
Oblige         4      2
ŒIL            5      5
œil            5      10
Öl             6      12
Opera          7      7
RESUME         8      8
resume         8      4
résumé         9      3
RÉSUMÉ         9      13
resumes        10     9
résumés        11     14
```

The *rank* column gives the ranking in the sort order. You can see that for the words that vary only in case, the ranking is the same. You can also see from the output that sometimes the uppercase version comes first, and sometimes the lowercase version comes first. This is something that is entirely arbitrary, and it's perfectly possible that you might see a different order for these pairs if you run the query yourself.

If the collation is changed to Latin1_General_CS_AS, this is the result:

```
collatedword   rank   wordno
-------------- ------ ------
cloud          1      1
CSAK           2      6
cukor          3      11
Oblige         4      2
œil            5      10
ŒIL            6      5
Öl             7      12
Opera          8      7
resume         9      4
RESUME         10     8
résumé         11     3
RÉSUMÉ         12     13
resumes        13     9
résumés        14     14
```

All entries now have a different ranking. The lowercase forms come before the uppercase forms when no other difference exists because in Windows collations, lowercase always has a lower secondary weight than uppercase.

Now see what happens with a different language. Here's a test for the collation Hungarian_CI_AI:

```
collatedword    rank    wordno
-------------   ------  ------
cloud           1       1
cukor           2       11
CSAK            3       6
Oblige          4       2
ŒIL             5       5
œil             5       10
Opera           6       7
Öl              7       12
RÉSUMÉ          8       13
RESUME          8       8
résumé          8       3
resume          8       4
resumes         9       9
résumés         9       14
```

The words *CSAK* and *öl* now sort after *cukor* and *Opera*. This is because in the Hungarian alphabet, CS and Ö are letters on their own. You can also see that in this CI_AI collation, all four forms of *résumé* have the same rank.

In these examples, the data type for the column was *nvarchar,* but if you change the table to use *varchar* and rerun the examples, you get the same results.

Character ranges and collations   The sort order applies not only to *ORDER BY* clauses but also to operators such as > and ranges in *LIKE* expressions. For instance, note the following code:

```
SELECT * FROM #words
WHERE word COLLATE Latin1_General_CI_AS > 'opera';
SELECT * FROM #words
WHERE word COLLATE Latin1_General_CS_AS > 'opera';
```

The first *SELECT* lists six words, whereas the second lists seven (because in a case-sensitive collation, *Opera* is > *opera*).

If you are used to character ranges from regular expressions in other languages, you might fall into the following trap when trying to select the words that start with an uppercase letter:

```
SELECT * FROM #words WHERE word LIKE '[A-Z]%';
```

But even with a case-sensitive collation, this code usually lists all 14 words. (In some languages, Ö sorts as a separate letter after *Z,* so it doesn't fall into the specified range.) The range *A–Z* is also subject to the collation rules. This also has another consequence. If you change *cloud* to *aloud* in the list, *SELECT* now returns only 13 rows in a case-sensitive collation because *a* sorts before *A;* the range *A–Z* doesn't include *a.*

As you can see, this can be a bit confusing. Be very careful when using ranges with character data. If you need to do so, make sure that you really test the edge cases to ensure that you don't exclude any data inadvertently.

Binary collations   In a binary collation, no secondary weights exist, and characters sort by their code points in the character set. So with Latin1_General_BIN2 in the previous example, you get

```
collatedword    rank    wordno
--------------  ------  ------
CSAK            1       6
Oblige          2       2
Opera           3       7
RESUME          4       8
RÉSUMÉ          5       13
cloud           6       1
cukor           7       11
resume          8       4
resumes         9       9
résumé          10      3
résumés         11      14
Öl              12      12
ŒIL             13      5
œil             14      10
```

Now the words with the uppercase first letters *C*, *O*, and *R* come before those with the lowercase *c*, *o*, and *r*, as they do in the ASCII standard. *Öl* and the two forms of *œil* have code points beyond the first 127 ASCII codes and therefore come at the end of the list.

Because binary collations are based on the code points and might be different in the single-byte code page and in Unicode, the order can be different for single-byte and Unicode data types. For instance, if you change the data type in #*words* to *varchar* and run the example with Latin1_General_BIN2 again, notice that *Öl* now comes last.

As you recall from the previous discussion, two types of binary collations exist: BIN and BIN2. Of these, the BIN collations are earlier collations, and if you need to use a binary collation in new development, you should use a BIN2 collation. To understand the difference between the two, we need to look at a Unicode string in its binary representation. For instance, consider

```
SELECT convert(varbinary, N'ABC');
```

This code returns 0x410042004300. The ASCII code for *A* is 65, or 41 in hexadecimal. In Unicode, *A* is U+0041 (Unicode characters are often written as U+nnnn, where nnnn is the code point in hexadecimal notation), but converted to *varbinary*, it appears as 4100. This is because PC architecture is *little endian*, which means that the least significant byte is stored first. (The reason for this is beyond the scope of this book to explain.)

Therefore, to sort *nvarchar* data by their code points properly, SQL Server shouldn't just look at the byte string but should also swap each word to get the correct code points. This is exactly what the BIN2 collations do. The older BIN collations perform this swap only for the first character, and then perform a byte-per-byte comparison for remaining characters. To illustrate the difference between the two types of binary collations and also true byte-sort, here is an example that uses the characters *Z* (U+005A) and *Ń* (N with grave accent; U+0143):

```
SELECT n, str, convert(binary(6), str) AS bytestr,
       row_number() OVER(ORDER BY convert(varbinary, str))
          AS bytesort,
       row_number() OVER(ORDER BY str COLLATE Latin1_General_BIN)
          AS collate_BIN,
       row_number() OVER(ORDER BY str COLLATE Latin1_General_BIN2)
          AS collate_BIN2
FROM  (VALUES(1, N'ZZZ'), (2, N'ZŃŃ'), (3, N'ŃZZ'), (4, N'ŃŃŃ '))
       AS T(n, str)
ORDER BY n;
```

Here is the result:

```
n           str    bytestr           bytesort   collate_BIN   collate_BIN2
----------- ------ ----------------- ---------- ------------- ------------
1           ZZZ    0x5A005A005A00    4          2             1
2           ZŃŃ    0x5A0043014301    3          1             2
3           ŃZZ    0x43015A005A00    2          4             3
4           ŃŃŃ    0x430143014301    1          3             4
```

You can see that in the *collate_BIN2* column, the rows are numbered according to their code points in Unicode. In the *bytesort* column, however, they are numbered in reverse order because the least significant byte in the character code takes precedence. Finally, in the *collate_BIN* column, the two entries that start with *Z* are sorted first, but in reverse order regarding *collate_BIN2*.

Working with SQL Server collations   The group of SQL Server collations (known as *SQL collations* for short) is much smaller than the Windows collations. In total, of the 76 SQL collations, only one is deprecated.

A SQL collation uses two different rule sets: one for single-byte data types and one for Unicode data types. The rules for single-byte data types are defined by SQL Server itself and derive from the days when SQL Server didn't support Unicode. When you work with Unicode data, a SQL collation uses the same rules as the matching Windows collation. To see which Windows collation a certain SQL collation matches, you can view the *description* column in the output from *fn_helpcollations()*.

The name of a SQL collation always starts with *SQL_* followed by a language indicator, similar to the name of a Windows collation. Likewise, names for SQL collations include *CI/CS* and *AI/AS* to indicate case and accent sensitivity. Some binary SQL collations also exist. In contrast to names for

Windows collations, SQL collations always include the code page for single-byte characters in the name. For some reason, though, CP1252, Windows Latin-1, appears as CP1 in the names.

Many SQL collations relate to American National Standards Institute (ANSI) code pages—that is, code pages used by non-Unicode Windows applications. However, SQL collations also exist for the OEM code pages CP437 and CP850—that is, code pages used in the command-line window. Even EBCDIC (Extended Binary Coded Decimal Interchange Code) has a few SQL collations.

Sort orders With a SQL collation, you can get different results depending on the data type. For instance, in the earlier example with the 14 words, if it's run with *word* as *nvarchar* and with the commonly used SQL collation SQL_Latin1_General_CP1_CI_AS, the result is the same as when Latin1_General_CI_AS is used. But if you change *word* to be *varchar*, you get this result:

```
collatedword    rank    wordno
--------------  ------  ------
ŒIL             1       5
œil             2       10
cloud           3       1
CSAK            4       6
cukor           5       11
Oblige          6       2
Öl              7       12
Opera           8       7
RESUME          9       8
resume          9       4
résumé          10      3
RÉSUMÉ          10      13
resumes         11      9
résumés         12      14
```

Now the two forms of *œil* come first and have different ranks, despite the collation being case-insensitive. In this collation, a few accented letters sort as though they were punctuation characters. (The others are *Š*, *Ÿ*, and *Ž*.) Other differences in SQL_Latin1_General_CP1_CI_AS between the single-byte and Unicode data types include how punctuation characters are sorted. However, as long as your data mainly consists of the digits 0–9 and the English letters A–Z, these differences likely aren't significant to you.

Tertiary collations Just like Windows collations, SQL collations have primary and secondary weights, but the similarities don't stop there. Of the SQL collations, 32 also have *tertiary weights*. With one exception, the tertiary collations are all case-insensitive. The tertiary weight gives preference to uppercase, so when everything else is equal in the entire *ORDER BY* clause, uppercase words sort first. In some tertiary collations, this is indicated by *pref* appearing in the name, whereas in other tertiary collations, this is implicit. You find the full list of tertiary collations in *SQL Server Books Online* in the topic for the built-in function *TERTIARY_WEIGHTS*.

Studying the tertiary collations involves a different table with different words:

```
CREATE TABLE #prefwords
        (word    char(3) COLLATE SQL_Latin1_General_Pref_CP1_CI_AS
                        NOT NULL,
         wordno int NOT NULL PRIMARY KEY NONCLUSTERED,
         tert    AS tertiary_weights(word));
CREATE CLUSTERED INDEX word_ix ON #prefwords (word);
--CREATE INDEX tert_ix on #prefwords(word, tert)
go
INSERT #prefwords (word, wordno)
    VALUES ('abc', 1), ('abC', 4), ('aBc', 7),
           ('aBC', 2), ('Abc', 5), ('ABc', 8),
           ('AbC', 3), ('ABC', 6);
go
SELECT word, wordno, rank = dense_rank() OVER (ORDER BY word),
       rowno = row_number() OVER (ORDER BY word)
FROM   #prefwords
ORDER  BY word--, wordno;
```

The output from this query is

word	wordno	rank	rowno
ABC	6	1	8
ABc	8	1	6
AbC	3	1	7
Abc	5	1	5
aBC	2	1	4
aBc	7	1	3
abC	4	1	2
abc	1	1	1

Notice that all words have the same rank; nevertheless, uppercase letters consistently come before lowercase. Also, in the *rowno* column, rows are numbered in opposite order, which is likely to be by chance. That is, the tertiary weight affects only the *ORDER BY* at the end of the query, but not the *ORDER BY* for the *dense_rank* and *row_number* functions.

Now, if you look at the query plan for this query, you find a Sort operator, which is surprising, considering the clustered index on *word*. If you go one step back in the plan, you find a Compute Scalar operator, and if you press F4, you can see that this operator defines [Expr1005] = Scalar Operator(tertiary_weights([tempdb].[dbo].[#prefwords].[word])); if you look at the Sort operator, you see that it sorts by *word* and Expr1005. That is, the tertiary weight isn't stored in the index but is computed at runtime.

This is where the function *TERTIARY_WEIGHTS* comes in. This function accepts parameters of the types *char, varchar,* and *text* and returns a non-NULL value if the input value isn't from a tertiary collation. *SQL Server Books Online* suggests that you can add a computed column with this function and then add an index on the character column and the computed column, like the *tert_ix* in the previous script. If you uncomment the creation of *tert_ix* in the previous script and also comment out the *rank* and *rowno* columns from the *SELECT* statement, you see a plan without any Sort operator. Thus, the *TERTIARY_WEIGHTS* function can help improve performance with tertiary collations.

Now see what happens if *wordno* is uncommented from the *ORDER BY* clause, so that the query now reads as follows:

```
SELECT word, wordno
FROM   #prefwords
ORDER  BY word, wordno;
```

This is the output:

```
word    wordno
------  ------
abc     1
aBC     2
AbC     3
abC     4
Abc     5
ABC     6
aBc     7
ABc     8
```

That is, the tertiary weight matters only when no other difference appears in the entire *ORDER BY* clause. Needless to say, the query plan again includes the Sort operator.

Collations defined during SQL Server setup   When you install SQL Server, you need to select a server collation. This choice is important because if you make an incorrect selection, you can't easily change this later. You essentially have to reinstall SQL Server.

SQL Server Setup provides a default collation, and this is always a CI_AS collation—that is, a collation sensitive to accents but insensitive to case, kanatype, and width.

Setup selects the collation designator for the default collation from the *system locale*—that is, the locale that applies on the system level, which might be different from the regional settings for your own Windows user. The default is always a Windows collation, except in one very notable case: Isf your system locale is English (United States), the default is SQL_Latin1_General_CP1_CI_AS. The reason for this seemingly odd default is backward compatibility.

When different versions of the same language exist, the default depends on whether your system locale existed in previous versions of Windows or was added in Windows 2008. So, for instance, for English (United Kingdom) and German (Germany) the default is Latin1_General_CI_AS, whereas for English (Singapore) and Swahili (Kenya) the default is Latin1_General_100_CI_AS. Again, the reason for this variation is backward compatibility. For the full list of default collations, see the topic "Collation Settings in Setup" in *SQL Server Books Online*.

Although Setup suggests a default collation, that this default is the best for your server is far from certain. You should make a conscious, deliberate decision. If you install a server to run a third-party product, you should consult the vendor's documentation to see whether it has any recommendations or requirements for the application. If you plan to migrate databases from an earlier version of SQL Server, you should probably select the same collation for the new server as for your existing server. As noted earlier, if you plan to access the server as a linked server from SQL Server 2005, you should avoid the _100 collations.

Another thing to be aware of is that your Windows administrator might have installed a U.S. English version of Windows, leaving the system locale as English (United States) even if the local language is something else. If this is the case on your server, and you don't pay attention when you install SQL Server, you can end up with a collation that doesn't fit well with the language in your country.

Some languages have multiple appropriate choices. For instance, for German, the default is Latin1_General_CI_AS, but you can also use any of the German_Phonebook collations (in which ä, ö, and ü sort as *ae*, *oe*, and *ue*).

Running the Installation Wizard   When you run the Installation Wizard for SQL Server 2012, you need to be observant because the collation selection isn't on a page of its own but appears on a second tab on the Server Configuration window. You'll have to watch carefully because the collation selection isn't displayed when you get to the Server Configuration window. You'll see a screen asking for information about the service accounts to use. When you select the Collation tab on that screen, you see something like Figure 6-2.

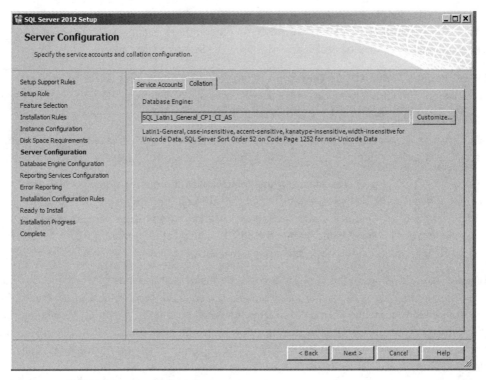

FIGURE 6-2 Setting the server configuration.

If you choose to customize your collation and click the Customize button, you can use an option button to select whether to use a Windows collation or a SQL collation. If you select a Windows collation, you can select the Collation Designator from a drop-down list. Below that are check boxes to select case sensitivity and other features. The Binary choice gives you a BIN collation, whereas

Binary-Code Point gives you a BIN2 collation. If you select to use a SQL collation, a single list box lists all SQL collations.

Performance considerations   Does the choice of collation affect performance? Yes, but in many cases only marginally, and your most important criteria should be to choose the collation that best meets your users' needs. However, the collation can have quite drastic effects in a few situations.

Generally, binary collations give you the best performance, but in most applications, they don't give a very good user experience.

As long as you work with *varchar* data, the SQL collations perform almost equally well. The SQL collations include rules for only the 255 characters in the code page covered by the collation. A Windows collation always works with the full rules of Unicode internally, even for single-byte data. Thus, the internal routines for SQL collations are far less complex than those for Unicode.

The Windows collations have some differences between collation families in which some are faster than others. A special case is the case-insensitive Latin1_General and Latin1_General_100 collations, which appear to perform better than any other collation family when you work with Unicode data. Contrary to what you might expect, case-sensitive collations don't give better performance; instead, their rate is a few percentage points slower in many operations. Again, this isn't something that you should pay too much attention to. If your users expect to see data sorted according to, say, the Danish alphabet, you have no reason to select Latin1_General_CI_AS just because it operates a little faster. What's the point of a faster operation that doesn't do what your users need? Also, keep in mind that a typical query includes so many other components that the effect of the collation is likely to be lost in the noise.

A trap with SQL Server collations   The collation really does matter in a few situations. Consider the following:

```
SELECT col FROM tbl WHERE indexedcol = @value;
```

For this query, the collation doesn't have much impact as long as the column and *@value* have the same data type. Also, the column having a Unicode data type and *@value* as *char* or *varchar* isn't considered an issue. However, the column as single-byte and *@value* as Unicode becomes an issue because of the data-type precedence rules in SQL Server. The *char* and *varchar* data types have lower precedence than *nchar* and *nvarchar*, so the column is converted to the type of the value, which has ramifications for how the index can be used.

If the column has a Windows collation, SQL Server can still perform an index seek operation, albeit with a more complex filter, so compared to a query without conversion, you can expect the execution time to double or triple. However, this query becomes really problematic when the column has a SQL collation. The index doesn't serve any purpose after the conversion because in a SQL collation, the rules are entirely different for single-byte and Unicode data. SQL Server can at best scan the index. In a big table, performance can be drastically affected, with execution times that are 100 or 1,000 times more than for a properly written query. Thus, if you opt to use a SQL collation, you need to watch that you don't mix *varchar* and *nvarchar* casually.

Another case where the collation can make a huge difference is when SQL Server has to look at almost all characters in the strings. For instance, look at the following:

```
SELECT COUNT(*) FROM tbl WHERE longcol LIKE '%abc%';
```

This might execute 10 times faster or more with a binary collation than a nonbinary Windows collation. Also, with *varchar* data, this executes up to seven or eight times faster with a SQL collation than with a Windows collation. If you have a *varchar* column, you can speed this up by forcing the collation as follows:

```
SELECT COUNT(*) FROM tbl
WHERE longcol COLLATE SQL_Latin1_General_CP_CI_AS LIKE '%abc%';
```

If your column is *nvarchar*, you have to force a binary collation instead, but that would be possible only if users can accept a case-sensitive search.

The same considerations apply to the functions *CHARINDEX* and *PATINDEX*.

Special data types

This section on data types ends by showing you a few additional data types that you might find useful.

Binary data types The *binary* and *varbinary* data types are used to store bit strings. The values are entered and displayed using their hexadecimal (hex) representation, which is indicated by a prefix of 0x. So a hex value of 0x270F corresponds to a decimal value of 9,999 and a bit string of 0010011100001111. In hex, each two displayed characters represent a byte, so the value of 0x270F represents 2 bytes. You need to decide whether you want your data to be fixed or variable length, and you can use some of the same considerations discussed previously for deciding between *char* and *varchar* to make your decision. The maximum length of *binary* or *varbinary* data is 8,000 bytes.

bit data type The *bit* data type can store a 0 or a 1 and can consume only a single bit of storage space. However, if a table has only 1 bit column, that column will take up a whole byte. Up to 8 bit columns are stored in a single byte.

LOB data types SQL Server 2012 allows you to define columns with the *max* attribute: *varchar(max)*, *nvarchar(max)*, and *varbinary(max)*. If the number of bytes actually inserted into these columns exceeds the maximum of 8,000, these columns are stored using a special storage format for LOB data. The special storage format is the same one used for the data types *text*, *ntext*, and *image*, but because those types will be discontinued in a future version of SQL Server, using the variable-length data types with the *max* specifier is recommended for all new development. The *varchar(max)* (or *text*) data type can store up to $2^{31} - 1$ non-Unicode characters; *nvarchar(max)* (or *ntext*) can store up to $2^{30} - 1$ (half as many) Unicode characters; and *varbinary(max)* (or *image*) can store up to $2^{31} - 1$ bytes of binary data. Also, *varbinary(max)* data can be stored as filestream data. Chapter 8 covers filestream data in more detail, as well as the storage structures for LOB data.

cursor data type   This data type can hold a reference to a cursor. Although you can't declare a column in a table to be of type *cursor*, this data type can be used for output parameters and local variables. I've included the *cursor* data type in this list only for completeness; this chapter won't cover any more about it.

rowversion data type   This data type is a synonym for what was formerly called a *timestamp*. When using the *timestamp* data type name, many people might assume that the data has something to do with dates or times, but it doesn't. A column of type *rowversion* holds an internal sequence number that SQL Server automatically updates every time the row is modified. The value of any *rowversion* column is actually unique within an entire database, and a table can have only one column of type *rowversion*. Any operation that modifies any *rowversion* column in the database generates the next sequential value. The actual value stored in a *rowversion* column is seldom important by itself. The column detects whether a row has been modified since the last time it was accessed by determining whether the *rowversion* value has changed.

sql_variant data type   This data type allows a column to hold values of any data type except *text*, *ntext*, *image*, *XML*, user-defined data types, variable-length data types with the *max* specifier, or *rowversion* (*timestamp*). The internal storage of *sql_variant* data is described later in this chapter.

Spatial data types   SQL Server 2012 provides two data types for storing spatial data: *geometry* and *geography*. The *geometry* data type supports planar, or Euclidean (flat-earth), data and conforms to the Open Geospatial Consortium (OGC) Simple Features for SQL Specification version 1.1.0. The *geography* data type stores ellipsoidal (round-earth) data, such as Global Positioning Satellite (GPS) latitude and longitude coordinates. These data types have their own methods for accessing and manipulating the data, as well as their own special extended index structures, which vary from the normal SQL Server indexes. Any further discussion of the access methods and storage of spatial data is beyond the scope of this book.

table data type   The *table* data type stores the result of a function and can be used as the data type of local variables. Columns in tables can't be of type *table*.

xml data type   This type lets you store XML documents and fragments in a SQL Server database. You can use the *xml* data type as a column type when you create a table or as the data type for variables, parameters, and the return value of a function. XML data has its own methods for retrieval and manipulation, but this book doesn't go into detail on how to work with it.

uniqueidentifier data type   This data type is sometimes referred to as a globally unique identifier (GUID) or universal unique identifier (UUID). A GUID or UUID is a 128-bit (16-byte) value generated in a way that, for all practical purposes, guarantees uniqueness among every networked computer in the world. It's becoming an important way to identify data, objects, software applications, and applets in distributed systems. The way the *uniqueidentifier* data type is generated and manipulated has some very interesting aspects.

The T-SQL language supports the system functions *NEWID* and *NEWSEQUENTIALID*, which you can use to generate *uniqueidentifier* values. A column or variable of data type *uniqueidentifier* can be initialized to a value in one of the following ways:

- Using the system-supplied function *NEWID* or *NEWSEQUENTIALID* as a default value

- Using a string constant in the following form (32 hexadecimal digits separated by hyphens): *xxxxxxxx-xxxx-xxxx-xxxx-xxxxxxxxxxxx* (each *x* is a hexadecimal digit in the range 0 through 9 or *a* through *f*)

This data type can be quite cumbersome to work with, and the only operations allowed against a *uniqueidentifier* value are comparisons (=, <>, <, >, <=, >=) and checking for NULL. However, using this data type internally can offer several advantages.

One reason to use the *uniqueidentifier* data type is that the values generated by *NEWID* or *NEWSEQUENTIALID* are guaranteed to be globally unique for any machine on a network because the last 6 bytes of a *uniqueidentifier* value make up the node number for the machine. When the SQL Server machine doesn't have an Ethernet/Token-Ring (IEEE 802.x) address, it has no node number; as a result, the generated GUID is guaranteed to be unique among all GUIDs generated on that computer. However, another computer without an Ethernet/Token-Ring address could possibly generate the identical GUID. The GUIDs generated on computers with network addresses are guaranteed to be globally unique.

The primary reason why SQL Server needed a way to generate a GUID was for use in merge replication, in which identifier values for the same table could be generated on any one of many different SQL Server machines. A way was needed to determine whether two rows really were the same row, and no two rows not referring to the same entity would have the same identifier. Using GUID values provides that functionality. Two rows with the same GUID value must indicate that they really are the same row.

The difference between the *NEWSEQUENTIALID* and the *NEWID* functions is that *NEWSEQUENTIALID* creates a GUID that is greater than any GUID previously generated by this function on a specified computer and can be used to introduce a sequence to your GUID values. This turns out to increase greatly the scalability of systems using merge replication. If the *unqiueidentifer* values are being used as the clustered key for the replicated tables, the new rows are then inserted in random disk pages. (You'll see the details in Chapter 7, when clustered indexes are discussed in detail.) If the machines involved are performing a large number of I/O operations, the nonsequential GUID generated by the *NEWID* function results in many random B-tree lookups and inefficient insert operations. The new function, *NEWSEQUENTIALID*, which is a wrapper around the Windows function *UuidCreateSequential*, does some byte scrambling and creates an ordering to the generated UUID values.

The list of *uniqueidentifier* values can't be exhausted. This isn't the case with other data types frequently used as unique identifiers. In fact, SQL Server uses this data type internally for row-level merge replication. A *uniqueidentifier* column can have a special property called *ROWGUIDCOL*; at most, one *uniqueidentifier* column can have this property per table. The *ROWGUIDCOL* property can be specified as part of the column definition in *CREATE TABLE* and *ALTER TABLE ADD COLUMN*, or it can be added or dropped for an existing column using *ALTER TABLE ALTER COLUMN*.

You can reference a *uniqueidentifier* column with the *ROWGUIDCOL* property using the keyword *ROWGUIDCOL* in a query. This is similar to referencing an identity column using the *IDENTITYCOL* keyword. The *ROWGUIDCOL* property doesn't imply any automatic value generation, and if automatic value generation is needed, the *NEWSEQUENTIALID* function should be defined as the default column value. You can have multiple *uniqueidentifier* columns per table, but only one of them can have the *ROWGUIDCOL* property. You can use the *uniqueidentifier* data type for whatever reason you come up with, but if you're using one to identify the current row, an application must have a generic way to ask for it without needing to know the column name. That's what the *ROWGUIDCOL* property does.

The NULL problem

The issue of whether to allow NULL has become a heated debate for many in the industry, and the discussion here might outrage a few people. However, my intention isn't to engage in a philosophical debate. Pragmatically, dealing with NULL brings added complexity to the storage engine because SQL Server keeps a special bitmap in every row to indicate which nullable columns actually are NULL. If NULLs are allowed, SQL Server must decode this bitmap for every row accessed. Allowing NULL also adds complexity in application code, which can often lead to bugs. You must always add special logic to account for the case of NULL.

As the database designer, you might understand the nuances of NULL and three-valued logic in aggregate functions when you do joins and when you search by values. Also, you must also consider whether your development staff really understands how to work with NULLs. If possible, you should use all NOT NULL columns and define *default* values for missing or unknown entries (and possibly make such character columns *varchar* if the default value is significantly different in size from the typical entered value).

In any case, declaring NOT NULL or NULL explicitly is good practice when you create a table. If no such declaration exists, SQL Server assumes NOT NULL. (In other words, no NULLs are allowed.) This might surprise many of you who assume that the default for SQL Server is to allow NULLs. The reason for this misconception is that most of the tools and interfaces for working with SQL Server enable a session setting that makes allowing NULLs the default. However, you can set the default to allow NULLs by using a session setting or a database option, which, as just mentioned, is what most tools and interfaces already do. If you script your DDL and then run it against another server that has a different default setting, you get different results if you don't declare NULL or NOT NULL explicitly in the column definition.

Several database options and session settings can control the behavior of SQL Server regarding NULL values. You can set database options using the *ALTER DATABASE* command, as Chapter 3, "Databases and database files," showed you. You also can enable session settings for one connection at a time using the *SET* command.

Note The database option *ANSI_null_default* corresponds to the two session settings *ANSI_NULL_DFLT_ON* and *ANSI_NULL_DFLT_OFF*. When the *ANSI_null_default* database option is false (the default setting for SQL Server), new columns created with the *ALTER TABLE* and *CREATE TABLE* commands are, by default, NOT NULL if the nullability status of the column isn't explicitly specified. *SET ANSI_NULL_DFLT_OFF* and *SET ANSI_NULL_DFLT_ON* are mutually exclusive options that indicate whether the database option should be overridden. When set to *ON*, each option forces the opposite option off. Neither option, when off, turns the opposite option on; it only discontinues the current on setting.

You use the function *GETANSINULL* to determine the default nullability for your current session. This function returns 1 when new columns allow null values and the column or data type nullability wasn't defined explicitly when the table was created or altered. I strongly recommend declaring NULL or NOT NULL explicitly when you create a column. This removes all ambiguity and ensures that you're in control of how the table is built, regardless of the default nullability setting.

CONCAT_NULL_YIELDS_NULL is both a database option and a session setting. When *CONCAT_NULL_YIELDS_NULL* is on, concatenating a NULL value with a string yields a NULL result. For example, *SELECT 'abc' + NULL* yields NULL. When *SET CONCAT_NULL_YIELDS_NULL* is off, concatenating a NULL value with a string yields the string itself. In other words, the NULL value is treated as an empty string. For example, *SELECT 'abc' + NULL* yields *abc*. If the session-level setting isn't specified, the value of the database option applies.

ANSI_NULLS is also a database option and a session setting. When this option is set to *ON*, all comparisons to a NULL value evaluate to UNKNOWN. When it's set to *OFF*, comparisons of values to a NULL value evaluate to TRUE if both values are NULL. Also, when this option is set to *ON*, your code must use the condition *IS NULL* to determine whether a column has a NULL value. When this option is set to *OFF*, SQL Server allows = *NULL* as a synonym for *IS NULL* and <> *NULL* as a synonym for *IS NOT NULL*.

A fourth session setting is *ANSI_DEFAULTS*. Setting this to *ON* is a shortcut for enabling both *ANSI_NULLS* and *ANSI_NULL_DFLT_ON*, as well as other session settings not related to NULL handling. The SQL Server ODBC driver and the SQL Server OLE DB provider automatically set *ANSI_DEFAULTS* to *ON*. You can change the *ANSI_NULLS* setting when you define your data source name (DSN). You should be aware that the tool you are using to connect to SQL Server might set certain options *ON* or *OFF*.

The following query shows the values for all the *SET* options in your current session, and if you have *VIEW SERVER STATE* permission, you can change or remove the *WHERE* clause to return information about other sessions as follows:

```
SELECT * FROM sys.dm_exec_sessions
WHERE session_id = @@spid;
```

As you can see, you can configure and control the treatment and behavior of NULL values in several ways, and you might think that keeping track of all the variations would be impossible. If you try to control every aspect of NULL handling separately within each individual session, you can cause immeasurable confusion and even grief. However, most of the issues become moot if you follow a few basic recommendations:

- Never allow NULL values in your tables.

- Include a specific NOT NULL qualification in your table definitions.

- Don't rely on database properties to control the behavior of NULL values.

If you must use NULLs in some cases, you can minimize problems by always following the same rules, and the easiest rules to follow are the ones that ANSI already specifies.

Also, certain database designs allow for NULL values in a large number of columns and in a large number of rows. SQL Server 2008 introduced the concept of sparse columns, which reduce the space requirements for NULL values at the cost of more overhead to retrieve NOT NULL values. So the biggest benefit from sparse columns is found when a large percentage of your data is NULL. Chapter 8 discusses sparse column storage.

You need to be aware of a couple other storage considerations when allowing your columns to be NULL. For fixed-length columns (not defined to be sparse), the column always uses the full defined length, even when storing NULL. For example, a column defined as *char(200)* always uses 200 bytes whether it's NULL or not. Variable-length columns are different and don't take up any space for the actual data storage of NULLs. However, that doesn't mean no space is required at all, as you'll see later in this chapter when the internal storage mechanisms are described.

User-defined data types

A user-defined data type (UDT) provides a convenient way to guarantee consistent use of underlying native data types for columns known to have the same domain of possible values. Perhaps your database stores various phone numbers in many tables. Although no single, definitive way exists to store phone numbers, consistency is important in this database. You can create a *phone_number* UDT and use it consistently for any column in any table that keeps track of phone numbers to ensure that they all use the same data type. Here's how to create this UDT:

```
CREATE TYPE phone_number FROM varchar(20) NOT NULL;
```

And here's how to use the new UDT when you create a table:

```
CREATE TABLE customer
(
cust_id             smallint        NOT NULL,
cust_name           varchar(50)     NOT NULL,
cust_addr1          varchar(50)     NOT NULL,
cust_addr2          varchar(50)     NOT NULL,
cust_city           varchar(50)     NOT NULL,
cust_state          char(2)         NOT NULL,
cust_postal_code    varchar(10)     NOT NULL,
cust_phone          phone_number    NOT NULL,
cust_fax            varchar(20)     NOT NULL,
cust_email          varchar(30)     NOT NULL,
cust_web_url        varchar(100)    NOT NULL
);
```

When the table is created, internally the *cust_phone* data type is known to be *varchar(20)*. Notice that both *cust_phone* and *cust_fax* are *varchar(20)*, although *cust_phone* has that declaration through its definition as a UDT.

Information about the columns in your tables is available through the catalog view *sys.columns*, which the section "Internal storage" looks at in more detail. For now, a basic query shows you two columns in *sys.columns*, one containing a number representing the underlying system data type and one containing a number representing the data type used when creating the table. The following query selects all the rows from *sys.columns* and displays the *column_id*, the column name, the data type values, and the maximum length, and then displays the results:

```
SELECT column_id, name, system_type_id, user_type_id,
       type_name(user_type_id) as user_type_name, max_length
FROM sys.columns
WHERE object_id=object_id('customer');
```

column_id	type_name	system_type_id	user_type_id	user_type_name	max_length
1	cust_id	52	52	smallint	2
2	cust_name	167	167	varchar	50
3	cust_addr1	167	167	varchar	50
4	cust_addr2	167	167	varchar	50
5	cust_city	167	167	varchar	50
6	cust_state	175	175	char	2
7	cust_postal_code	167	167	varchar	10
8	cust_phone	167	257	phone_number	20
9	cust_fax	167	167	varchar	20
10	cust_email	167	167	varchar	30
11	cust_web_url	167	167	varchar	100

You can see that both the *cust_phone* and *cust_fax* columns have the same *system_type_id* value, although the *cust_phone* column shows that the *user_type_id* is a UDT (*user_type_id* = 257). The type is resolved when the table is created and the UDT can't be dropped or changed as long as a table is now using it. When declared, a UDT is static and immutable, so no inherent performance penalty occurs in using a UDT instead of the native data type.

The use of UDTs can make your database more consistent and clear. SQL Server implicitly converts between compatible columns of different types (either native types or UDTs of different types).

Currently, UDTs don't support the notion of subtyping or inheritance, nor do they allow a *DEFAULT* value or a CHECK constraint to be declared as part of the UDT itself. These powerful object-oriented concepts will likely make their way into future versions of SQL Server. These limitations notwithstanding, UDT functionality is a dynamic and often underused feature of SQL Server.

IDENTITY property

Providing simple counter-type values for tables that don't have a natural or efficient primary key is common. Columns such as *cust_id* are usually simple counter fields. The *IDENTITY* property makes generating unique numeric values easy. *IDENTITY* isn't a data type; it's a column property that you can declare on a whole-number data type such as *tinyint, smallint, int, bigint,* or *numeric/decimal* (with which only a scale of zero makes any sense). Each table can have only one column with the *IDENTITY* property. The table's creator can specify the starting number (seed) and the amount that this value increments or decrements. If not otherwise specified, the seed value starts at 1 and increments by 1, as shown in this example:

```
CREATE TABLE customer
(
cust_id      smallint        IDENTITY   NOT NULL,
cust_name    varchar(50)     NOT NULL
);
```

To find out which seed and increment values were defined for a table, you can use the *IDENT_SEED(tablename)* and *IDENT_INCR(tablename)* functions. Look at this statement:

```
SELECT IDENT_SEED('customer'), IDENT_INCR('customer')
```

It produces the following result for the *customer* table because values weren't declared explicitly and the default values were used:

```
1  1
```

This next example explicitly starts the numbering at 100 (seed) and increments the value by 20:

```
CREATE TABLE customer
(
cust_id      smallint        IDENTITY(100, 20)  NOT NULL,
cust_name    varchar(50)     NOT NULL
);
```

The value automatically produced with the *IDENTITY* property is normally unique, but that isn't guaranteed by the *IDENTITY* property itself, nor are the *IDENTITY* values guaranteed to be consecutive. (Later, this section expands on the issues of nonunique and nonconsecutive *IDENTITY* values.) For efficiency, a value is considered used as soon as it's presented to a client doing an *INSERT* operation. If that client doesn't ultimately commit the *INSERT*, the value never appears, so a break occurs in the consecutive numbers. An unacceptable level of serialization would exist if the next number couldn't be parceled out until the previous one was actually committed or rolled back. (And even then, as soon as a row was deleted, the values would no longer be consecutive. Gaps are inevitable.)

Note If you need exact sequential values without gaps, *IDENTITY* isn't the appropriate feature to use. Instead, you should implement a *next_number*-type table in which you can make the operation of bumping the number contained within it part of the larger transaction (and incur the serialization of queuing for this value).

To temporarily disable the automatic generation of values in an identity column, you use the *SET IDENTITY_INSERT tablename* ON option. In addition to filling in gaps in the identity sequence, this option is useful for tasks such as bulk-loading data in which the previous values already exist. For example, if you're loading a new database with customer data from your previous system, you might want to preserve the previous customer numbers for existing data but have new rows automatically assigned a customer number using *IDENTITY*. The *SET* option was created exactly for cases like this.

Because the *SET* option allows you to determine your own values for an *IDENTITY* column, the *IDENTITY* property alone doesn't enforce uniqueness of a value within the table. Although *IDENTITY* generates a unique number if *IDENTITY_INSERT* has never been enabled, the uniqueness isn't guaranteed after you use the *SET* option. To enforce uniqueness (which you'll almost always want to do when using *IDENTITY*), you should also declare a UNIQUE or PRIMARY KEY constraint on the column. If you insert your own values for an identity column (using *SET IDENTITY_INSERT*), when automatic generation resumes, the next value is the next incremented value (or decremented value) of the highest value that exists in the table, whether it was generated previously or explicitly inserted.

 Tip If you use the *bcp* utility for bulk-loading data, be aware of the *-E* (uppercase) parameter if your data already has assigned values that you want to keep for a column that uses the *IDENTITY* property. You can also use the T-SQL *BULK INSERT* command with the *KEEPIDENTITY* option. For more information, refer to *SQL Server Books Online* for *bcp* and *BULK INSERT*.

The keyword *IDENTITYCOL* automatically refers to the specific column in a table that has the *IDENTITY* property, whatever its name. If that column is *cust_id*, you can refer to the column as *IDENTITYCOL* without knowing or using the column name, or you can refer to it explicitly as *cust_id*. For example, the following two statements work identically and return the same data:

```
SELECT IDENTITYCOL FROM customer;
SELECT cust_id FROM customer;
```

The column name returned to the caller is *cust_id*, not *IDENTITYCOL*, in both cases.

When inserting rows, you must omit an identity column from the column list and VALUES section. (The only exception is when the *IDENTITY_INSERT* option is on.) If you do supply a column list, you must omit the column for which the value is supplied automatically. Here are two valid *INSERT* statements for the *customer* table shown previously:

```
INSERT customer VALUES ('ACME Widgets');
INSERT customer (cust_name) VALUES ('AAA Gadgets');
```

Selecting these two rows produces this output:

```
cust_id    cust_name
-------    ---------
1          ACME Widgets
2          AAA Gadgets
```

In applications, immediately knowing the value produced by *IDENTITY* for subsequent use is sometimes desirable. For example, a transaction might first add a new customer and then add an order for that customer. To add the order, you probably need to use the *cust_id*. Rather than select the value from the *customer* table, you can simply select the special system function @@*IDENTITY*, which contains the last identity value used by that connection. It doesn't necessarily provide the last value inserted in the table, however, because another user might have subsequently inserted data. If multiple *INSERT* statements are carried out in a batch on the same or different tables, the variable has the value for the last statement only. Also, if an *INSERT* trigger fires after you insert the new row, and if that trigger inserts rows into a table with an identity column, @@*IDENTITY* doesn't have the value inserted by the original *INSERT* statement. To you, it might look like you're inserting and then immediately checking the value, as follows:

```
INSERT customer (cust_name) VALUES ('AAA Gadgets');
SELECT @@IDENTITY;
```

However, if a trigger were fired for the *INSERT*, the value of @@*IDENTITY* might have changed.

You might find two other functions useful when working with identity columns: *SCOPE_IDENTITY* and *IDENT_CURRENT*. *SCOPE_IDENTITY* returns the last identity value inserted into a table in the same scope, which could be a stored procedure, trigger, or batch. So if you replace @@*IDENTITY* with the *SCOPE_IDENTITY* function in the preceding code snippet, you can see the identity value inserted into the *customer* table. If an *INSERT* trigger also inserted a row that contained an identity column, it would be in a different scope, like this:

```
INSERT customer (cust_name) VALUES ('AAA Gadgets');
SELECT SCOPE_IDENTITY();
```

In other cases, you might want to know the last identity value inserted in a specific table from any application or user. You can get this value by using the *IDENT_CURRENT* function, which takes a table name as an argument:

```
SELECT IDENT_CURRENT('customer');
```

This doesn't always guarantee that you can predict the next identity value to be inserted because another process could insert a row between the time you check the value of *IDENT_CURRENT* and the time you execute your *INSERT* statement.

You can't define the *IDENTITY* property as part of a UDT, but you can declare the *IDENTITY* property on a column that uses a UDT. A column that has the *IDENTITY* property must always be declared NOT NULL (either explicitly or implicitly); otherwise, error number 8147 results from the *CREATE TABLE* statement and *CREATE* won't succeed. Likewise, you can't declare the *IDENTITY* property and a *DEFAULT* on the same column. To check that the current identity value is valid based on the current maximum values in the table, and to reset it if an invalid value is found (which should never be the case), use the *DBCC CHECKIDENT(tablename)* statement.

Identity values are fully recoverable. If a system outage occurs while an insert activity is taking place with tables that have identity columns, the correct value is recovered when SQL Server restarts. SQL Server does this during the checkpoint processing by flushing the current identity value for all tables. For activity beyond the last checkpoint, subsequent values are reconstructed from the transaction log during the standard database recovery process. Any inserts into a table that have the *IDENTITY* property are known to have changed the value, and the current value is retrieved from the last *INSERT* statement (post-checkpoint) for each table referenced in the transaction log. The net result is that when the database is recovered, the correct current identity value is also recovered.

In rare cases, the identity value can become out of sync. If this happens, you can use the *DBCC CHECKIDENT* command to reset the identity value to the appropriate number. Also, the *RESEED* option to this command allows you to set a new starting value for the identity sequence. See *SQL Server Books Online* for complete details.

Sequence object

SQL Server 2012 introduces an alternative to the *IDENTITY* property that lets you share an incremental sequence of values across multiple tables. A sequence can be created on any connection, and then that connection or any other can generate the next available value in the sequence by referencing *NEXT VALUE FOR* the sequence object. Every time *NEXT VALUE FOR* the sequence object is referenced, the next value is in the sequence is returned.

A *SEQUENCE* is an object with a specific name in a specific schema, with the following properties.

- **Datatype**   The data type can be any integer type, which includes *tinyint, smallint, int, bigint, decimal*, or *numeric* with a scale of 0 and any user-defined type that is based on one of the integer types. The default is *bigint*.

- **Starting value**   This value is the first one returned by the sequence object. It must be less than or equal to the maximum value and greater than or equal to the minimum value. The default value is the same as the minimum value for an ascending sequence and the same as the maximum value for a descending sequence.

- **Increment**   The increment determines how the next value of the sequence object is determined. If an increment is possible, it's added to the previous value every time *NEXT VALUE FOR* the sequence object is referenced. If the increment is negative, it's subtracted from the previous value every time *NEXT VALUE FOR* the sequence object is referenced. The increment can't be 0, and the default value is 1.

- **Minimum value**   The minimum is the lower bound for the sequence object and the default is the minimum supported by the data type.

- **Maximum value**   The maximum is the upper bound for the sequence object and the default is the maximum supported by the data type.

- **Cycle property**   The keyword *CYCLE* allows you to indicate that the sequence object values should restart from the minimum (for ascending sequences) or maximum (for descending sequences) when the minimum or maximum is exceeded, instead of generating an error. The default is *NO CYCLE*.

- **Cache value**   You can reduce the number of disk I/Os required to generate sequence numbers and increase performance by specifying a number of sequence values to be cached. When *CACHE* is specified, it should be followed by a number of values to cache; the default is determined internally by SQL Server and isn't predictable. The downside of using cached sequence values is that unexpected SQL Server shutdowns can result in the loss of cached values that haven't been used. SQL Server doesn't store all the cached values; instead, it stores the current value and the maximum value in the cached set. On a controlled shutdown, the maximum value can be replaced by whatever maximum was actually reached. With an uncontrolled shutdown, SQL Server thinks it has already used all the cached values, and the next sequence object will be greater than the maximum value stored.

Sequence values and shutdown events

Here's a concrete example adapted from *SQL Server Books Online*: If a new sequence is created with a starting value of 1 and a cache size of 25, when the first value is referenced, values 1 through 25 are made available from memory. The maximum cached value (25) is written to disk and stored in a system table. When all 25 numbers are used, the next request (for number 26) causes the cache to be allocated again. The new last cached value (50) is written to disk.

If a controlled shutdown occurs after you use 32 numbers, the next available sequence number in memory (33) is written to disk, replacing the previously stored value of 50. Then, when SQL Server restarts and a new sequence number is needed, the starting number is read from the system tables (33). Then 25 new numbers (33-58) are allocated to memory and the next available number (59) is written to disk.

If an *unexpected* shutdown occurred, perhaps due to a power failure, after 32 numbers were used, the sequence would restart with the number read from disk (50) that had not been updated to 33. Values from 33 to 50 would be lost. This functionality can leave gaps but guarantees that the same value is never issued twice for a single sequence object unless it's defined as *CYCLE* or manually restarted.

Most properties of a sequence object can be modified, and the sequence can be restarted by using the *ALTER SEQUENCE* command. You can read the details in *Books Online*.

Here are few code examples for clarification. This batch creates a sequence object called MySequence and then creates two tables:

```
CREATE SEQUENCE dbo.MySequence
    AS INT
    MINVALUE 1
    NO MAXVALUE
    START WITH 1
    NO CYCLE
    CACHE 25;

CREATE TABLE dbo.Customers
(
    CustomerID INT PRIMARY KEY,
    EMail      VARCHAR(320) NOT NULL UNIQUE
);

CREATE TABLE dbo.Orders
(
    OrderID    INT PRIMARY KEY,
    CustomerID INT NOT NULL FOREIGN KEY
                     REFERENCES dbo.Customers(CustomerID)
);
GO
```

The next batch declares two variables and then inserts into both tables. Every time that either variable is used, the *NEXT VALUE FOR* the sequence object is activated:

```
DECLARE @CustomerID INT = NEXT VALUE FOR dbo.MySequence;
DECLARE     @OrderID    INT = NEXT VALUE FOR dbo.MySequence;

INSERT dbo.Customers(CustomerID, EMail)
    SELECT @CustomerID, 'Ken@books.com';

INSERT dbo.Orders(OrderID, CustomerID)
    SELECT @OrderID, @CustomerID;

SELECT * FROM dbo.Customers;
SELECT * FROM dbo.Orders;
GO
```

You can also directly access the *NEXT VALUE FOR* the sequence object in an *INSERT*, an *UPDATE*, or a variable assignment:

```
INSERT dbo.Customers(CustomerID, EMail)
    SELECT NEXT VALUE FOR dbo.MySequence, 'Sue@books.com';
```

SQL Server 2012 includes a stored procedure called sp_sequence_get_range to generate multiple sequence values at the same time. You supply the sequence object name and the number of values desired as input. The procedure returns the first and last values in the range, as well as the minimum, maximum, and increment values defined for the sequence object.

The benefit of sequence objects over identity values is that the sequence object can be used by any table or at any time you need a sequential value. You're still not guaranteed no gaps because values can be lost due to SQL Server rollbacks or crashes. Also, the *NEXT VALUE FOR* your sequence object can be accessed without having the value used anywhere. For example, you could simply *SELECT* the sequence values repeatedly, without inserting them into a table. The following batch generates 50 sequential values but doesn't save them:

```
SELECT NEXT VALUE FOR dbo.MySequence;
GO 50
```

Metadata is available on all sequences in a database in the sys.sequences view. A specific permission called *CREATE SEQUENCE* can be granted to users, and any user with *ALTER SCHEMA* or *CONTROL SCHEMA* rights can create a sequence.

Internal storage

This section describes how SQL Server actually stores table data. It also explores the basic system metadata that keeps track of data storage information. Although you can use SQL Server effectively without understanding the internals of data storage, a detailed knowledge of how SQL Server stores data helps you develop efficient applications.

When you create a table, one or more rows are inserted into a number of system tables to manage that table. SQL Server provides catalog views built on top of the system tables that allow you to explore their contents. At minimum, you can see metadata for your new table in the *sys.tables*, *sys.indexes*, and *sys.columns* catalog views. When you define the new table with one or more constraints, you also can see information in the *sys.check_constraints*, *sys.default_constraints*, *sys.key_constraints*, or *sys.foreign_keys* view. For every table created, a single row that contains the name, object ID, and ID of the schema containing the new table (among other items) is available through the *sys.tables* view. Remember that the *sys.tables* view inherits all the columns from *sys.objects* (which shows information relevant to all types of objects) and then includes additional columns pertaining only to tables. The *sys.columns* view shows you one row for each column in the new table, and each row contains information such as the column name, data type, and length. Each column receives a column ID, which initially corresponds to the order in which you specified the columns when you created the table—that is, the first column listed in the *CREATE TABLE* statement has a column ID of 1, the second column has a column ID of 2, and so on. Listing 6-3 shows the rows returned by the *sys.tables* and *sys.columns* views when you create a table. (Not all columns are shown for each view.)

LISTING 6-3 Basic catalog information stored after a table Is created

```
CREATE TABLE dbo.employee (
            emp_lname   varchar(15)   NOT NULL,
            emp_fname   varchar(10)   NOT NULL,
            address     varchar(30)   NOT NULL,
            phone       char(12)      NOT NULL,
            job_level   smallint      NOT NULL
)
```

sys.tables	object_id	name		schema_id	type_desc	
	917578307	employee		1	UsER_TABLE	

sys.columns	object_id	column_id	name	system_type_id	max_length
	917578307	1	emp_lname	167	15
	917578307	2	emp_fname	167	10
	917578307	3	address	167	30
	917578307	4	phone	175	12
	917578307	5	job_level	52	2

> **Note** Gaps can appear in the column ID sequence if the table is altered to drop columns. However, the information schema view (*INFORMATION_SCHEMA.COLUMNS*) gives you a value called *ORDINAL_POSITION* because the ANSI SQL standard demands it. The ordinal position is the order in which the column is listed when you use *SELECT* * on the table. So the *column_id* isn't necessarily the ordinal position of that column.

The sys.indexes catalog view

In addition to *sys.columns* and *sys.tables*, the *sys.indexes* view returns at least one row for each table. In versions of SQL Server prior to SQL Server 2005, the *sysindexes* table contains all the physical storage information for both tables and indexes, which are the only objects that actually use storage space. The *sysindexes* table has columns to keep track of the space used by all tables and indexes, the physical location of each index root page, and the first page of each table and index. (In Chapter 7, you'll see more about root pages and what the "first" page actually means.) In SQL Server 2012, the compatibility view *sys.sysindexes* contains much of the same information, but it's incomplete because of changes in the storage organization introduced in SQL Server 2005. The *sys.indexes* catalog view contains only basic property information about indexes, such as whether the index is clustered or nonclustered, unique or nonunique, and other properties, as discussed in Chapter 7. To get all the storage information in SQL Server 2012, you have to look at two other catalog views in addition to *sys.indexes*: *sys.partitions* and *sys.allocation_units* (or alternatively, the undocumented *sys.system_internals_allocation_units*). The basic contents of these views are discussed shortly, but you first should focus on *sys.indexes*.

You might be aware that if a table has a clustered index, the table's data is actually considered part of the index, so the data rows are actually index rows. For a table with a clustered index, SQL Server has a row in *sys.indexes* with an *index_id* value of 1, and the *name* column in *sys.indexes* contains the name of the index. The name of the table associated with the index can be determined from the *object_id* column in *sys.indexes* using the *object_id* function. If a table has no clustered index, the data itself isn't organized, and such a table is called a *heap*. A heap in *sys.indexes* table has an *index_id* value of 0, and the *name* column contains NULL.

Every additional index has a row in *sys.indexes* with an *index_id* value between 2 and 250 or between 256 and 1,005. (The values 251 – 255 are reserved.) Because as many as 999 nonclustered indexes can be on a single table and only 1 row is available for the heap or clustered index, every table has between 1 and 1,000 rows in the *sys.indexes* view for relational indexes. A table can have additional rows in *sys.indexes* for XML indexes. Metadata for XML indexes is available in the *sys.xml_indexes* catalog view, which inherits columns from the *sys.indexes* view. (Chapter 9, "Special indexes," discusses XML indexes detail.)

Two main features in SQL Server 2012 make using more than one catalog view to keep track of storage information most efficient. First, SQL Server can store a table or index on multiple partitions, so the space used by each partition, as well as the partition's location, must be kept track of separately. Second, table and index data can be stored in three different formats, which are regular row data, row-overflow data, and LOB data. Both row-overflow data and LOB data can be part of an index, so each index has to keep track of its special format data separately. So each table can have multiple indexes, each table and index can be stored on multiple partitions, and each partition needs to keep track of data in up to three formats. Chapter 7 discusses indexes; Chapter 8 discusses the storage of row-overflow data and LOB data, as well as partitioned tables and indexes.

Data storage metadata

Each heap and index has a row in *sys.indexes*, and each table and index in a SQL Server 2012 database can be stored on multiple partitions. The *sys.partitions* view contains one row for each partition of each heap or index. Every heap or index has at least one partition, even if you haven't specifically partitioned the structure, but one table or index can have up to 15,000 partitions. So a one-to-many relationship exists between *sys.indexes* and *sys.partitions*. The *sys.partitions* view contains a column called *partition_id* as well as the *object_id* and *index_id*, so you can join *sys.indexes* to *sys.partitions* on the *object_id* and *index_id* columns to retrieve all the partition ID values for a particular table or index. The term used in SQL Server 2012 to describe a subset of a table or index on a single partition is *hobt*, which stands for Heap Or B-Tree and is pronounced (you guessed it) "hobbit." (As explained in Chapter 1, "SQL Server 2012 architecture and configuration," a B-tree is the storage structure used for indexes.) The *sys.partitions* view includes a column called *hobt_id*, and in SQL Server 2012, a one-to-one relationship always exists between *partition_id* and *hobt_id*. In fact, you can see that these two columns in the *sys.partitions* table always have the same value.

Each partition (whether for a heap or an index) can have three types of rows, each stored on its own set of pages. These types are called *in-row data pages* (for "regular" data or index information), *row-overflow data pages*, and *LOB data pages*. A set of pages of one particular type for one particular partition is called an *allocation unit*, so the final catalog view you need to learn about is *sys.allocation_units*. This view contains one, two, or three rows per partition because each heap or index on each partition can have as many as three allocation units. Regular in-row pages always have an allocation unit, but LOB data and row-overflow data also might have an allocation unit. Figure 6-3 shows the relationship between *sys.indexes*, *sys.partitions*, and *sys.allocation_units*.

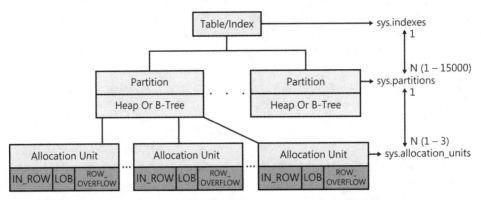

FIGURE 6-3 The relationship between *sys.indexes*, *sys.partitions*, and *sys.allocation_units*.

Catalog view queries

Now look at a specific example now to see information in these three catalog views. First, create the table shown earlier in Listing 6-3. You can create it in any database, but either use *tempdb*, so the table is dropped automatically the next time you restart your SQL Server instance, or create a new database just for testing. Many of the examples in this chapter assume a database called *testdb*.

```
CREATE TABLE dbo.employee(
          emp_lname   varchar(25)  NOT NULL,
          emp_fname   varchar(15)  NOT NULL,
          address     varchar(100) NOT NULL,
          phone       char(12)     NOT NULL,
          job_level   smallint     NOT NULL
);
```

This table has one row in *sys.indexes* and one in *sys.partitions*, as you can see when you run the following queries. Only a few columns from *sys.indexes* are included here, but because *sys.partitions* has only six columns, all have been retrieved:

```
SELECT object_id, name, index_id, type_desc
FROM sys.indexes
WHERE object_id=object_id(N'dbo.employee');

SELECT *
FROM sys.partitions
WHERE object_id=object_id(N'dbo.employee');
```

Here are my results (yours might vary slightly because your ID values are probably different):

object_id	name	index_id	type_desc
5575058	NULL	0	HEAP

partition_id	object_id	index_id	partition_number	hobt_id	rows
72057594038779904	5575058	0	1	72057594038779904	0

Each row in the *sys.allocation_units* view has a unique *allocation_unit_id* value. Each row also has a value in the column called *container_id* that can be joined with *partition_id* in *sys.partitions*, as shown in this query:

```
SELECT object_name(object_id) AS name,
    partition_id, partition_number AS pnum,  rows,
    allocation_unit_id AS au_id, type_desc AS age_type_desc,
    total_pages AS pages
FROM sys.partitions p JOIN sys.allocation_units a
   ON p.partition_id = a.container_id
WHERE object_id=object_id(N'dbo.employee');
```

Again, this simple table shows only one row because it has only one partition, no nonclustered indexes, and only one type of data (*IN_ROW_DATA*). Here is the result:

name	partition_id	pnum	rows	au_id	page_type_desc	pages
employee	72057594038779904	1	0	72057594043301888	IN_ROW_DATA	0

Now add some new columns to the table that need to be stored on other types of pages. You can store *varchar* data on row-overflow pages if the total row size exceeds the maximum of 8,060 bytes. By default, text data is stored on text pages. For *varchar* data stored on row-overflow pages and for text data, the row itself has additional overhead to store a pointer to the off-row data. Chapter 8 looks at the details of row-overflow and text data storage, although they are mentioned later in this section, and *ALTER TABLE* is discussed at the end of this chapter, but for now you should look at the additional rows in *sys.allocation_units*:

```
ALTER TABLE dbo.employee ADD resume_short varchar(8000);
ALTER TABLE dbo.employee ADD resume_long text;
```

Running the preceding query, which joins *sys.partitions* and *sys.allocation_units*, results in the following three rows:

name	partition_id	pnum	rows	au_id	page_type_desc	pages
employee	72057594038779904	1	0	72057594043301888	IN_ROW_DATA	0
employee	72057594038779904	1	0	72057594043367424	ROW_OVERFLOW_DATA	0
employee	72057594038779904	1	0	72057594043432960	LOB_DATA	0

You might also want to add an index or two and check the contents of these catalog views again. Notice that just adding a clustered index doesn't change the number of rows in *sys.allocation_units*, but it does change the *partition_id* numbers because the entire table is rebuilt internally when you create a clustered index. Adding a nonclustered index adds at least one more row to *sys.allocation_ units* to keep track of the pages for that index. The following query joins all three views—*sys.indexes*, *sys.partitions*, and *sys.allocation_units*—to show you the table name, index name and type, page type, and space usage information for the *dbo.employee* table:

```
SELECT convert(char(8),object_name(i.object_id)) AS table_name,
    i.name AS index_name, i.index_id, i.type_desc as index_type,
    partition_id, partition_number AS pnum, rows,
    allocation_unit_id AS au_id, a.type_desc as page_type_desc,
```

```
      total_pages AS pages
FROM sys.indexes i JOIN sys.partitions p
      ON i.object_id = p.object_id AND i.index_id = p.index_id
   JOIN sys.allocation_units a
      ON p.partition_id = a.container_id
WHERE i.object_id=object_id(N'dbo.employee');
```

Because no data has been inserted into this table, you should notice that the values for rows and pages are all 0. During the discussion on actual page structures, you'll insert data into your tables so that you can look at the internal storage of the data at that time.

The queries run so far don't provide any information about the location of pages in the various allocation units. SQL Server 2000 provided the *sysindexes* table, which contains three columns that indicate where data is located: *first*, *root*, and *firstIAM*. These columns are still available in SQL Server 2012 (with slightly different names: *first_page*, *root_page*, and *first_iam_page*), but they can be seen only in an undocumented view called *sys.system_internals_allocation_units*. This view is identical to *sys.allocation_units* except for the addition of these three additional columns, so you can replace *sys.allocation_units* with *sys.system_internals_allocation_units* in the preceding allocation query and add these three extra columns to the select list. Keep in mind that as an undocumented object, this view is for internal use only and is subject to change (as are other views starting with *system_internals*). Forward compatibility isn't guaranteed.

Data pages

Data pages are the structures that contain user data that has been added to a database's tables. As mentioned earlier, data pages come in three varieties, each of which stores data in a different format. SQL Server has pages for in-row data, pages for row-overflow data, and pages for LOB data. As with all other types of pages in SQL Server, data pages have a fixed size of 8 KB, or 8,192 bytes. They consist of three major components: the page header, data rows, and the row offset array, as shown in Figure 6-4.

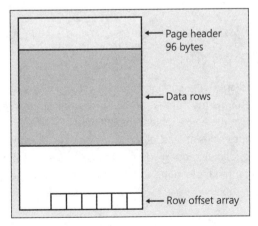

FIGURE 6-4 The structure of a data page.

Page header

As you can see in Figure 6-4, the page header occupies the first 96 bytes of each data page (leaving 8,096 bytes for data, row overhead, and row offsets). Table 6-5 lists some of the information shown when we examine the page header.

TABLE 6-5 Information available by examining the page header

Field	Meaning
pageID	The file number and page number of this page in the database
nextPage	The file number and page number of the next page if this page is in a page chain
prevPage	The file number and page number of the previous page if this page is in a page chain
Metadata: ObjectId	The ID of the object to which this page belongs
Metadata: PartitionId	The ID of the partition that this page is part of
Metadata: AllocUnitId	The ID of the allocation unit that contains this page
LSN	The Log Sequence Number (LSN) corresponding to the last log entry that changed this page
slotCnt	The total number of slots (rows) used on this page
Level	The level of this page in an index (always 0 for leaf pages)
indexId	The index ID of this page (always 0 for data pages)
freeData	The byte offset of the first free space on this page
Pminlen	The number of bytes in fixed-length portion of rows
freeCnt	The number of free bytes on the page
reservedCnt	The number of bytes reserved by all transactions
Xactreserved	The number of bytes reserved by the most recently started transaction
tornBits	A bit string containing 1 bit per sector for detecting torn page writes (or checksum information if *torn_page_detection* isn't on)
flagBits	A 2-byte bitmap that contains additional information about the page

Data rows for in-row data

Following the page header is the area in which the table's actual data rows are stored. The maximum size of a single data row is 8,060 bytes of in-row data. Rows can also have row-overflow and LOB data stored on separate pages. The number of rows stored on a given page varies depending on the table structure and on the data being stored. A table with all fixed-length columns always can store the same number of rows per page; variable-length rows can store as many rows as will fit based on the actual length of the data entered. Keeping the row length shorter allows more rows to fit on a page, thus reducing I/O and increasing the likelihood that needed data can stay in cache.

Row offset array

The row offset array is a block of 2-byte entries, each indicating the offset on the page at which the corresponding data row begins. Every row has a 2-byte entry in this array (as discussed earlier, when you read about the 10 overhead bytes needed by every row). Although these bytes aren't stored in the row with the data, they do affect the number of rows that fit on a page.

The row offset array indicates the logical order of rows on a page. For example, if a table has a clustered index, SQL Server stores the rows in the order of the clustered index key. This doesn't mean the rows are physically stored on the page in the order of the clustered index key. Rather, slot 0 in the offset array refers to the first row in the clustered index key order, slot 1 refers to the second row, and so forth. As you'll see shortly when you examine an actual page, the physical location of these rows can be anywhere on the page.

Examining data pages

You can view the contents of a data page by using the *DBCC PAGE* command, which allows you to view the page header, data rows, and row offset table for any given page in a database. Only system administrators can use *DBCC PAGE*. However, because you typically don't need to view the contents of a data page, you can't find information about *DBCC PAGE* in the SQL Server documentation. Nevertheless, in case you want to use it, here's the syntax:

```
DBCC PAGE ({dbid | dbname}, filenum, pagenum[, printopt])
```

The *DBCC PAGE* command includes the parameters shown in Table 6-6. The code and results in Listing 6-4 show sample output from *DBCC PAGE* with a *printopt* value of 1. Note that *DBCC TRACEON(3604)* instructs SQL Server to return the results to the client. Without this traceflag, no output is returned for the *DBCC PAGE* command.

TABLE 6-6 Parameters of the *DBCC PAGE* command

Parameter	Description
Dbid	The ID of the database containing the page
Dbname	The name of the database containing the page
Filenum	The file number containing the page
Pagenum	The page number within the file
Printopt	An optional print option; takes one of these values: 0 Default; prints the buffer header and page header 1 Prints the buffer header, page header, each row separately, and the row offset table 2 Prints the buffer and page headers, the page as a whole, and the offset table 3 Prints the buffer header, page header, each row separately, and the row offset table; each row is followed by each of its column values listed separately

LISTING 6-4 Code and sample output from *DBCC PAGE* with a *printopt* value of 1

```
DBCC TRACEON(3604);

GO
DBCC PAGE (pubs, 1, 266, 1);
GO

PAGE: (1:266)

BUFFER:
  BUF @0x0000000300557440
```

```
bpage = 0x00000002F1DE0000          bhash = 0x0000000000000000          bpageno = (1:266)
bdbid = 7                           breferences = 0                     bcputicks = 0
bsampleCount = 0                    bUse1 = 16442                       bstat = 0x9
blog = 0x15a                        bnext = 0x0000000000000000

PAGE HEADER:
Page @0x00000002F1DE0000

m_pageId = (1:266)                  m_headerVersion = 1                 m_type = 1
m_typeFlagBits = 0x0                m_level = 0                         m_flagBits = 0x200
m_objId (AllocUnitId.idObj) = 84    m_indexId (AllocUnitId.idInd) = 256
Metadata: AllocUnitId = 72057594043432960
Metadata: PartitionId = 72057594039042048
Metadata: ObjectId = 245575913      m_prevPage = (0:0)                  Metadata: IndexId = 1
pminlen = 24                        m_slotCnt = 23                      m_nextPage = (0:0)
m_freeData = 2136                   m_reservedCnt = 0                   m_freeCnt = 6010
m_xactReserved = 0                  m_xdesId = (0:0)                    m_lsn = (30:373:2)
m_tornBits = -551612808             DB Frag ID = 1                      m_ghostRecCnt = 0

Allocation Status

GAM (1:2) = ALLOCATED           SGAM (1:3) = NOT ALLOCATED
PFS (1:1) = 0x60 MIXED_EXT ALLOCATED   0_PCT_FULL                          DIFF (1:6) = CHANGED
ML (1:7) = NOT MIN_LOGGED

DATA:

Slot 0, Offset 0x631, Length 88, DumpStyle BYTE

Record Type = PRIMARY_RECORD        Record Attributes =   NULL_BITMAP VARIABLE_COLUMNS
Record Size = 88
Memory Dump @0x00000000156FA631

0000000000000000:   30001800 34303820 3439362d 37323233 43413934   0...408 496-7223CA94
0000000000000014:   303235ff 09000000 05003300 38003f00 4e005800   025ÿ    .....3.8.?.N.X.
0000000000000028:   3137322d 33322d31 31373657 68697465 4a6f686e   172-32-1176WhiteJohn
000000000000003C:   736f6e31 30393332 20426967 67652052 642e4d65   son10932 Bigge Rd.Me
0000000000000050:   6e6c6f20 5061726b                              nlo Park

Slot 1, Offset 0xb8, Length 88, DumpStyle BYTE

Record Type = PRIMARY_RECORD        Record Attributes =   NULL_BITMAP VARIABLE_COLUMNS
Record Size = 88
Memory Dump @0x00000000156FA0B8

0000000000000000:   30001800 34313520 3938362d 37303230 43413934   0...415 986-7020CA94
0000000000000014:   363138ff 09000000 05003300 38004000 51005800   618ÿ    .....3.8.@.Q.X.
0000000000000028:   3231332d 34362d38 39313547 7265656e 4d61726a   213-46-8915GreenMarj
000000000000003C:   6f726965 33303920 36337264 2053742e 20233431   orie309 63rd St. #41
0000000000000050:   314f616b 6c616e64                              10akland

Slot 2, Offset 0x110, Length 85, DumpStyle BYTE

Record Type = PRIMARY_RECORD        Record Attributes =   NULL_BITMAP VARIABLE_COLUMNS
Record Size = 85
Memory Dump @0x00000000156FA110
```

```
0000000000000000:    30001800 34313520 3534382d 37373233 43413934    0...415 548-7723CA94
0000000000000014:    373035ff 09000000 05003300 39003f00 4d005500    705ÿ      .....3.9.?.M.U.
0000000000000028:    3233382d 39352d37 37363643 6172736f 6e436865    238-95-7766CarsonChe
000000000000003C:    72796c35 38392044 61727769 6e204c6e 2e426572    ryl589 Darwin Ln.Ber
0000000000000050:    6b656c65 79                                     keley
```

Slot 3, Offset 0x522, Length 93, DumpStyle BYTE

Record Type = PRIMARY_RECORD   Record Attributes = NULL_BITMAP VARIABLE_COLUMNS
Record Size = 93
Memory Dump @0x00000000156FA522

```
0000000000000000:    30001800 34303820 3238362d 32343238 43413935    0...408 286-2428CA95
0000000000000014:    313238ff 09000000 05003300 3a004100 55005d00    128ÿ      .....3.:.A.U.].
0000000000000028:    3236372d 34312d32 3339344f 274c6561 72794d69    267-41-23940'LearyMi
000000000000003C:    63686165 6c323220 436c6576 656c616e 64204176    chael22 Cleveland Av
0000000000000050:    2e202331 3453616e 204a6f73 65                    . #14San Jose
```

Slot 4, Offset 0x374, Length 86, DumpStyle BYTE

Record Type = PRIMARY_RECORD   Record Attributes = NULL_BITMAP VARIABLE_COLUMNS
Record Size = 86
Memory Dump @0x00000000156FA374

```
0000000000000000:    30001800 34313520 3833342d 32393139 43413934    0...415 834-2919CA94
0000000000000014:    363039ff 09000000 05003300 3b003f00 4f005600    609ÿ      .....3.;.?.O.V.
0000000000000028:    3237342d 38302d39 33393153 74726169 67687444    274-80-9391StraightD
000000000000003C:    65616e35 34323020 436f6c6c 65676520 41762e4f    ean5420 College Av.O
0000000000000050:    616b6c61 6e64                                   akland
```

Slot 5, Offset 0x7ff, Length 89, DumpStyle BYTE

Record Type = PRIMARY_RECORD   Record Attributes = NULL_BITMAP VARIABLE_COLUMNS
Record Size = 89
Memory Dump @0x00000000156FA7FF

```
0000000000000000:    30001800 39313320 3834332d 30343632 4b533636    0...913 843-0462KS66
0000000000000014:    303434fe 09000000 05003300 38003f00 51005900    044þ      .....3.8.?.Q.Y.
0000000000000028:    3334312d 32322d31 37383253 6d697468 4d65616e    341-22-1782SmithMean
000000000000003C:    64657231 30204d69 73736973 73697070 69204472    der10 Mississippi Dr
0000000000000050:    2e4c6177 72656e63 65                             .Lawrence
```

Slot 6, Offset 0x60, Length 88, DumpStyle BYTE

Record Type = PRIMARY_RECORD   Record Attributes = NULL_BITMAP VARIABLE_COLUMNS
Record Size = 88
Memory Dump @0x00000000156FA060

```
0000000000000000:    30001800 34313520 3635382d 39393332 43413934    0...415 658-9932CA94
0000000000000014:    373035ff 09000000 05003300 39004000 50005800    705ÿ      .....3.9.@.P.X.
0000000000000028:    3430392d 35362d37 30303842 656e6e65 74416272    409-56-7008BennetAbr
000000000000003C:    6168616d 36323233 20426174 656d616e 2053742e    aham6223 Bateman St.
0000000000000050:    4265726b 656c6579                               Berkeley
```

Slot 7, Offset 0x478, Length 82, DumpStyle BYTE

Record Type = PRIMARY_RECORD   Record Attributes = NULL_BITMAP VARIABLE_COLUMNS

```
Record Size = 82
Memory Dump @0x00000000156FA478

0000000000000000:   30001800 34313520 3833362d 37313238 43413934    0...415 836-7128CA94
0000000000000014:   333031ff 09000000 05003300 37003a00 49005200    301ÿ      .....3.7.:.I.R.
0000000000000028:   3432372d 31372d32 33313944 756c6c41 6e6e3334    427-17-2319DullAnn34
000000000000003C:   31302042 6c6f6e64 65205374 2e50616c 6f20416c    10 Blonde St.Palo Al
0000000000000050:   746f                                            to
```

Slot 8, Offset 0x57f, Length 81, DumpStyle BYTE

Record Type = PRIMARY_RECORD   Record Attributes =   NULL_BITMAP VARIABLE_COLUMNS
Record Size = 81
Memory Dump @0x00000000156FA57F

```
0000000000000000:   30001800 37303720 3933382d 36343435 43413935    0...707 938-6445CA95
0000000000000014:   343238ff 09000000 05003300 3d004100 4b005100    428ÿ      .....3.=.A.K.Q.
0000000000000028:   3437322d 32372d32 33343947 72696e67 6c657362    472-27-2349Gringlesb
000000000000003C:   79427572 74504f20 426f7820 37393243 6f76656c    yBurtPO Box 792Covel
0000000000000050:   6f                                              o
```

Slot 9, Offset 0x73e, Length 95, DumpStyle BYTE

Record Type = PRIMARY_RECORD   Record Attributes =   NULL_BITMAP VARIABLE_COLUMNS
Record Size = 95
Memory Dump @0x00000000156FA73E

```
0000000000000000:   30001800 34313520 3538352d 34363230 43413934    0...415 585-4620CA94
0000000000000014:   313330ff 09000000 05003300 3b004300 52005f00    130ÿ      .....3.;.C.R._.
0000000000000028:   3438362d 32392d31 3738364c 6f636b73 6c657943    486-29-1786LocksleyC
000000000000003C:   6861726c 656e6531 38204272 6f616477 61792041    harlene18 Broadway A
0000000000000050:   762e5361 6e204672 616e6369 73636f              v.San Francisco
```

Slot 10, Offset 0x5d0, Length 97, DumpStyle BYTE

Record Type = PRIMARY_RECORD   Record Attributes =   NULL_BITMAP VARIABLE_COLUMNS
Record Size = 97
Memory Dump @0x00000000156FA5D0

```
0000000000000000:   30001800 36313520 3239372d 32373233 544e3337    0...615 297-2723TN37
0000000000000014:   323135fe 09000000 05003300 39004400 58006100    215þ      .....3.9.D.X.a.
0000000000000028:   3532372d 37322d33 32343647 7265656e 654d6f72    527-72-3246GreeneMor
000000000000003C:   6e696e67 73746172 32322047 72617962 61722048    ningstar22 Graybar H
0000000000000050:   6f757365 2052642e 4e617368 76696c6c 65          ouse Rd.Nashville
```

Slot 11, Offset 0x79d, Length 98, DumpStyle BYTE

Record Type = PRIMARY_RECORD   Record Attributes =   NULL_BITMAP VARIABLE_COLUMNS
Record Size = 98
Memory Dump @0x00000000156FA79D

```
0000000000000000:   30001800 35303320 3734352d 36343032 4f523937    0...503 745-6402OR97
0000000000000014:   333330ff 09000000 05003300 41004900 59006200    330ÿ      .....3.A.I.Y.b.
0000000000000028:   3634382d 39322d31 38373242 6c6f7463 6865742d    648-92-1872Blotchet-
000000000000003C:   48616c6c 73526567 696e616c 64353520 48696c6c    HallsReginald55 Hill
0000000000000050:   7364616c 6520426c 2e436f72 76616c6c 6973        sdale Bl.Corvallis
```

Slot 12, Offset 0x4ca, Length 88, DumpStyle BYTE

Record Type = PRIMARY_RECORD   Record Attributes = NULL_BITMAP VARIABLE_COLUMNS
Record Size = 88
Memory Dump @0x00000000156FA4CA

```
0000000000000000:    30001800 34313520 3933352d 34323238 43413934    0...415 935-4228CA94
0000000000000014:    353935ff 09000000 05003300 3b004000 4c005800    595ÿ        .....3.;.@.L.X.
0000000000000028:    3637322d 37312d33 32343959 6f6b6f6d 6f746f41    672-71-3249YokomotoA
000000000000003C:    6b696b6f 33205369 6c766572 2043742e 57616c6e    kiko3 Silver Ct.Waln
0000000000000050:    75742043 7265656b                               ut Creek
```

Slot 13, Offset 0x689, Length 94, DumpStyle BYTE

Record Type = PRIMARY_RECORD   Record Attributes = NULL_BITMAP VARIABLE_COLUMNS
Record Size = 94
Memory Dump @0x00000000156FA689

```
0000000000000000:    30001800 36313520 3939362d 38323735 4d493438    0...615 996-8275MI48
0000000000000014:    313035ff 09000000 05003300 3f004400 55005e00    105ÿ        .....3.?.D.U.^.
0000000000000028:    3731322d 34352d31 38363764 656c2043 61737469    712-45-1867del Casti
000000000000003C:    6c6c6f49 6e6e6573 32323836 20437261 6d20506c    lloInnes2286 Cram Pl
0000000000000050:    2e202338 36416e6e 20417262 6f72                 . #86Ann Arbor
```

Slot 14, Offset 0x219, Length 82, DumpStyle BYTE

Record Type = PRIMARY_RECORD   Record Attributes = NULL_BITMAP VARIABLE_COLUMNS
Record Size = 82
Memory Dump @0x00000000156FA219

```
0000000000000000:    30001800 32313920 3534372d 39393832 494e3436    0...219 547-9982IN46
0000000000000014:    343033ff 09000000 05003300 3b004100 4e005200    403ÿ        .....3.;.A.N.R.
0000000000000028:    3732322d 35312d35 34353544 65467261 6e63654d    722-51-5454DeFranceM
000000000000003C:    69636865 6c332042 616c6469 6e672050 6c2e4761    ichel3 Balding Pl.Ga
0000000000000050:    7279                                            ry
```

Slot 15, Offset 0x31c, Length 88, DumpStyle BYTE

Record Type = PRIMARY_RECORD   Record Attributes = NULL_BITMAP VARIABLE_COLUMNS
Record Size = 88
Memory Dump @0x00000000156FA31C

```
0000000000000000:    30001800 34313520 3834332d 32393931 43413934    0...415 843-2991CA94
0000000000000014:    363039fe 09000000 05003300 3b003f00 51005800    609þ        .....3.;.?.Q.X.
0000000000000028:    3732342d 30382d39 39333153 7472696e 67657244    724-08-9931StringerD
000000000000003C:    69726b35 34323020 54656c65 67726170 68204176    irk5420 Telegraph Av
0000000000000050:    2e4f616b 6c616e64                               .Oakland
```

Slot 16, Offset 0x41f, Length 89, DumpStyle BYTE

Record Type = PRIMARY_RECORD   Record Attributes = NULL_BITMAP VARIABLE_COLUMNS
Record Size = 89
Memory Dump @0x00000000156FA41F

```
0000000000000000:    30001800 34313520 3335342d 37313238 43413934    0...415 354-7128CA94
0000000000000014:    363132ff 09000000 05003300 3d004400 52005900    612ÿ        .....3.=.D.R.Y.
0000000000000028:    3732342d 38302d39 3339314d 61634665 61746865    724-80-9391MacFeathe
```

```
000000000000003C:    72537465 61726e73 34342055 706c616e 64204874    rStearns44 Upland Ht
0000000000000050:    732e4f61 6b6c616e 64                            s.Oakland
```

Slot 17, Offset 0x3ca, Length 85, DumpStyle BYTE

Record Type = PRIMARY_RECORD   Record Attributes = NULL_BITMAP VARIABLE_COLUMNS
Record Size = 85
Memory Dump @0x00000000156FA3CA

```
0000000000000000:    30001800 34313520 3533342d 39323139 43413934    0...415 534-9219CA94
0000000000000014:    363039ff 09000000 05003300 39003e00 4e005500    609ÿ      .....3.9.>.N.U.
0000000000000028:    3735362d 33302d37 3339314b 61727365 6e4c6976    756-30-7391KarsenLiv
000000000000003C:    69613537 3230204d 6341756c 65792053 742e4f61    ia5720 McAuley St.Oa
0000000000000050:    6b6c616e 64                                     kland
```

Slot 18, Offset 0x26b, Length 92, DumpStyle BYTE

Record Type = PRIMARY_RECORD   Record Attributes = NULL_BITMAP VARIABLE_COLUMNS
Record Size = 92
Memory Dump @0x00000000156FA26B

```
0000000000000000:    30001800 33303120 3934362d 38383533 4d443230    0...301 946-8853MD20
0000000000000014:    383533ff 09000000 05003300 3b004100 53005c00    853ÿ      .....3.;.A.S.\.
0000000000000028:    3830372d 39312d36 36353450 616e7465 6c657953    807-91-6654PanteleyS
000000000000003C:    796c7669 61313935 36204172 6c696e67 746f6e20    ylvia1956 Arlington
0000000000000050:    506c2e52 6f636b76 696c6c65                      Pl.Rockville
```

Slot 19, Offset 0x6e7, Length 87, DumpStyle BYTE

Record Type = PRIMARY_RECORD   Record Attributes = NULL_BITMAP VARIABLE_COLUMNS
Record Size = 87
Memory Dump @0x00000000156FA6E7

```
0000000000000000:    30001800 34313520 3833362d 37313238 43413934    0...415 836-7128CA94
0000000000000014:    333031ff 09000000 05003300 39003f00 4e005700    301ÿ      .....3.9.?.N.W.
0000000000000028:    3834362d 39322d37 31383648 756e7465 72536865    846-92-7186HunterShe
000000000000003C:    72796c33 34313020 426c6f6e 64652053 742e5061    ryl3410 Blonde St.Pa
0000000000000050:    6c6f2041 6c746f                                 lo Alto
```

Slot 20, Offset 0x2c7, Length 85, DumpStyle BYTE

Record Type = PRIMARY_RECORD   Record Attributes = NULL_BITMAP VARIABLE_COLUMNS
Record Size = 85
Memory Dump @0x00000000156FA2C7

```
0000000000000000:    30001800 37303720 3434382d 34393832 43413935    0...707 448-4982CA95
0000000000000014:    363838fe 09000000 05003300 3b004200 4c005500    688þ      .....3.;.B.L.U.
0000000000000028:    3839332d 37322d31 3135384d 63426164 64656e48    893-72-1158McBaddenH
000000000000003C:    65617468 65723330 31205075 746e616d 56616361    eather301 PutnamVaca
0000000000000050:    76696c6c 65                                     ville
```

Slot 21, Offset 0x1c0, Length 89, DumpStyle BYTE

Record Type = PRIMARY_RECORD   Record Attributes = NULL_BITMAP VARIABLE_COLUMNS
Record Size = 89
Memory Dump @0x00000000156FA1C0

```
0000000000000000:   30001800 38303120 3832362d 30373532 55543834   0...801 826-0752UT84
0000000000000014:   313532ff 09000000 05003300 39003d00 4b005900   152ÿ       .....3.9.=.K.Y.
0000000000000028:   3839392d 34362d32 30333552 696e6765 72416e6e   899-46-2035RingerAnn
000000000000003C:   65363720 53657665 6e746820 41762e53 616c7420   e67 Seventh Av.Salt
0000000000000050:   4c616b65 20436974 79                           Lake City
```

Slot 22, Offset 0x165, Length 91, DumpStyle BYTE

Record Type = PRIMARY_RECORD   Record Attributes = NULL_BITMAP VARIABLE_COLUMNS
Record Size = 91
Memory Dump @0x00000000156FA165

```
0000000000000000:   30001800 38303120 3832362d 30373532 55543834   0...801 826-0752UT84
0000000000000014:   313532ff 09000000 05003300 39003f00 4d005b00   152ÿ       .....3.9.?.M.[.
0000000000000028:   3939382d 37322d33 35363752 696e6765 72416c62   998-72-3567RingerAlb
000000000000003C:   65727436 37205365 76656e74 68204176 2e53616c   ert67 Seventh Av.Sal
0000000000000050:   74204c61 6b652043 697479                       t Lake City
```

OFFSET TABLE:

Row - Offset
22 (0x16) - 357 (0x165)
21 (0x15) - 448 (0x1c0)
20 (0x14) - 711 (0x2c7)
19 (0x13) - 1767 (0x6e7)
18 (0x12) - 619 (0x26b)
17 (0x11) - 970 (0x3ca)
16 (0x10) - 1055 (0x41f)
15 (0xf) - 796 (0x31c)
14 (0xe) - 537 (0x219)
13 (0xd) - 1673 (0x689)
12 (0xc) - 1226 (0x4ca)
11 (0xb) - 1949 (0x79d)
10 (0xa) - 1488 (0x5d0)
9 (0x9) - 1854 (0x73e)
8 (0x8) - 1407 (0x57f)
7 (0x7) - 1144 (0x478)
6 (0x6) - 96 (0x60)
5 (0x5) - 2047 (0x7ff)
4 (0x4) - 884 (0x374)
3 (0x3) - 1314 (0x522)
2 (0x2) - 272 (0x110)
1 (0x1) - 184 (0xb8)
0 (0x0) - 1585 (0x631)
```

As you can see, the output from *DBCC PAGE* is divided into four main sections: *BUFFER*, *PAGE HEADER*, *DATA*, and *OFFSET TABLE* (really, the offset array). The *BUFFER* section shows information about the buffer for the given page. A *buffer* in this context is the in-memory structure that manages a page, and the information in this section is relevant only when the page is in memory.

The *PAGE HEADER* section in the output from *DBCC PAGE* displays the data for all the header fields on the page. (Table 6-5 shows the meaning of most of these fields.) The *DATA* section contains information for each row. Using *DBCC PAGE* with a *printopt* value of 1 or 3 indicates the slot position
```

of each row, the offset of the row on the page, and the length of the row. The row data is divided into three parts.

- The left column indicates the byte position within the row where the displayed data occurs.

- The middle section contains the actual data stored on the page, displayed in five columns of eight hexadecimal digits each.

- The rightmost column contains an ASCII character representation of the data. Only character data is readable in this column, although some of the other data might be displayed.

The *OFFSET TABLE* section shows the contents of the row offset array at the end of the page. In the output from *DBCC PAGE*, you can see that this page contains 23 rows, with the first row (indicated by Slot 0) beginning at offset 1585 (0x631). The first row physically stored on the page is actually row 6, with an offset in the row offset array of 96. *DBCC PAGE* with a *printopt* value of 1 displays the rows in slot number order, even though, as you can see by the offset of each of the slots, it isn't the order in which the rows physically exist on the page. If you use *DBCC PAGE* with a *printopt* value of 2, you see a dump of all 8,096 bytes of the page (after the header) in the order they are stored on the page.

The structure of data rows

A table's data rows have the general structure shown in Figure 6-5 (as long as the data is stored in uncompressed form). This format is called the FixedVar format because the data for all fixed-length columns is stored first, followed by the data for all variable-length columns. Table 6-7 shows the information stored in each FixedVar row. (Chapter 8 shows the format of rows stored in a different format, used when the data on the page is compressed.)

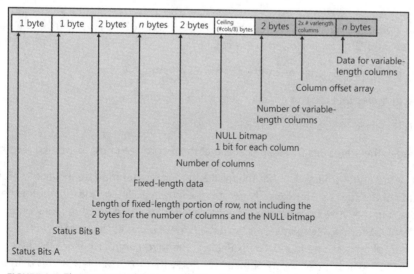

FIGURE 6-5 The structure of data rows in FixedVar format.

TABLE 6-7 Information stored in a table's data rows

Information	Mnemonic	Size
Status Bits A	*TagA*	1 byte
Status Bits B	*TagB*	1 byte
Fixed-length size	*Fsize*	2 bytes
Fixed-length data	*Fdata*	Fsize – 4
Number of columns	*Ncol*	2 bytes
NULL bitmap (1 bit for each column in the table; a 1 indicates that the corresponding column is NULL or that the bit is unused.)	*Nullbits*	Ceiling (*Ncol* / 8)
Number of variable-length columns stored in row	*VarCount*	2 bytes
Variable column offset array	*VarOffset*	2 * *VarCount*
Variable-length data	*VarData*	*VarOff[VarCount]* - (*Fsize* + 4 + Ceiling (*Ncol* / 8) + 2 * *VarCount*)

Status Bits A contains a bitmap indicating row properties. The bits have the following meanings:

- **Bit 0** This indicates special versioning information. In SQL Server 2012, this is always 0.

- **Bits 1 through 3** Taken as a 3-bit value, 0 (000) indicates a primary record, 1(001) indicates a forwarded record, 2 (010) indicates a forwarding stub, 3 (011) indicates an index record, 4(100) indicates a BLOB fragment or row-overflow data, 5(101) indicates a ghost index record, 6 (110) indicates a ghost data record, and 7 (111) indicates a ghost version record. (Later in this chapter, the section "Moving rows" covers forwarded records; Chapter 7 discusses ghost records.)

- **Bit 4** This indicates that a NULL bitmap exists. In SQL Server 2012, a NULL bitmap is always present, even if no NULLs are allowed in any column.

- **Bit 5** This indicates that variable-length columns exist in the row.

- **Bit 6** This indicates that the row contains versioning information.

- **Bit 7** This isn't used in SQL Server 2012.

The only bit used in the Status Bits B field indicates that the record is a ghost forwarded record.

You can see in Figure 6-5 and Table 6-7 that the third and fourth bytes indicate the length of the fixed-length portion of the row. As Figure 6-5 shows, it is the length excluding the 2 bytes for the number of columns, and the NULL bitmap, which is variable length depending on the total number of columns in the table. Another way to interpret the data in these bits is as the location in the row where the number of columns can be found. For example, if the third and fourth bytes (bytes 2–3) contain the value 0x0016, which is decimal 22, it means not only that the row has 22 bytes before the value for number of columns but also that the value for the number of columns can be found at byte 22. In some of the figures in this chapter and later ones, bytes 2–3 can be identified as the position to find the number of columns.

Within each block of fixed-length or variable-length data, the data is stored in the column order in which the table was created. For example, suppose a table is created with the following command:

```
CREATE TABLE Test1
(
Col1 int                NOT NULL,
Col2 char(25)           NOT NULL,
Col3 varchar(60)        NULL,
Col4 money              NOT NULL,
Col5 varchar(20)        NOT NULL
);
```

The fixed-length data portion of this row contains the data for *Col1*, followed by the data for *Col2*, followed by the data for *Col4*. The variable-length data portion contains the data for *Col3*, followed by the data for *Col5*. For rows that contain only fixed-length data, the following is true.

- The first hexadecimal digit of the first byte of the data row is 1, indicating that no variable-length columns exist. (The first hexadecimal digit comprises bits 4 through 7; bits 6 and 7 are always 0, and if no variable-length columns exist, bit 5 is also 0. Bit 4 is always 1, so the value of the four bits is displayed as 1.)

- The data row ends after the NULL bitmap, which follows the fixed-length data (that is, the shaded portion shown in Figure 6-5 won't exist in rows with only fixed-length data).

- The total length of every data row is the same.

A data row with any variable-length columns has a column offset array with a 2-byte entry for each non-NULL variable-length column, indicating the position within the row where the column ends. (The terms *offset* and *position* aren't exactly interchangeable. Offset is 0-based, and position is 1-based. A byte at an offset of 7 is in the eighth byte position in the row.) Storing variable-length columns with a NULL value involves some special issues, as discussed later in the section "NULLS and variable-length columns."

How to find a physical page

Before examining specific data, you need to look at something else first. The examples that follow use the *DBCC PAGE* command to examine the physical database pages. To run this command, you need to know what page numbers are used to store rows for a table. As mentioned previously, a value for *first_page* was stored in an undocumented view called *sys.system_internals_allocation_units*, which is almost identical to the *sys.allocation_units* view. First, you need to create a table (used in the following section) and insert a single row into it:

```
USE testdb;
CREATE TABLE Fixed
(
Col1 char(5)    NOT NULL,
Col2 int        NOT NULL,
Col3 char(3)    NULL,
Col4 char(6)    NOT NULL
);
INSERT Fixed VALUES ('ABCDE', 123, NULL, 'CCCC');
```

The following query yields the value for *first_page* in the *Fixed* table:

```
SELECT object_name(object_id) AS name,
    rows, type_desc as page_type_desc,
    total_pages AS pages, first_page
FROM sys.partitions p  JOIN sys.system_internals_allocation_units a
    ON p.partition_id = a.container_id
WHERE object_id=object_id(N'dbo.Fixed');
RESULTS:
name   rows   page_type_desc   pages   first_page
-----  ----   --------------   -----   --------------
Fixed  1      IN_ROW_DATA      2       0xCF0400000100
```

You can then take the value of *first_page* from the preceding *sys.system_internals_allocation_units* output (0xCF0400000100) and convert it to a file and page address. (The value that you get for *first_page* most likely is different from the one I got.) In hexadecimal notation, each set of two hexadecimal digits represents a byte. First, swap the bytes had to be swapped to get 00 01 00 00 04 CF. The first two groups represent the 2-byte file number; the last four groups represent the page number. So the file is 0x0001, which is 1, and the page number is 0x000004CF, which is 1231 in decimal.

Unless you particularly enjoy playing with hexadecimal conversions, you might want to use one of three other options for determining the actual page numbers associated with your SQL Server tables.

Creating a function to perform the conversion

You can use the following function to convert a 6-byte hexadecimal page number value (such as 0xCF0400000100) to a *file_number:page_number* format:

```
CREATE FUNCTION convert_page_nums (@page_num binary(6))
    RETURNS varchar(11)
AS
  BEGIN
    RETURN(convert(varchar(2), (convert(int, substring(@page_num, 6, 1))
          * power(2, 8)) +
              (convert(int, substring(@page_num, 5, 1)))) + ':' +
                convert(varchar(11),
  (convert(int, substring(@page_num, 4, 1)) * power(2, 24)) +
  (convert(int, substring(@page_num, 3, 1)) * power(2, 16)) +
  (convert(int, substring(@page_num, 2, 1)) * power(2, 8)) +
  (convert(int, substring(@page_num, 1, 1)))) )
  END;
```

You can then execute this *SELECT* to call the function:

```
SELECT dbo.convert_page_nums(0xCF0400000100);
```

You should get back the result 1:1231.

You could also use the function in the previous *SELECT* to return the formatted page number:

```
SELECT object_name(object_id) AS name,
    rows, type_desc as page_type_desc,
    total_pages AS pages, first_page,
```

```
        dbo.convert_page_nums(first_page) AS page_number_formatted
FROM sys.partitions p  JOIN sys.system_internals_allocation_units a
    ON p.partition_id = a.container_id
WHERE object_id=object_id(N'dbo.Fixed');
```

 Warning SQL Server doesn't guarantee that the *first_page* column in *sys.system_internals_ allocation_units* always indicates the first page of a table. (The view is undocumented, after all.) You should find that *first_page* is reliable until you begin to perform deletes and updates on the data in the table.

Using the sys.dm_db_database_page_allocations DMV

You can use another undocumented metadata object called *sys.dm_db_database_page_allocations* to determine actual page numbers. Because most of the information returned is relevant only to indexes, this function isn't discussed in detail until Chapter 7. However, for a sneak preview, you can run the following *SELECT* and note the values in the first two columns of output in the row where *page_type_desc = 'data_page'*:

```
SELECT allocated_page_file_id, allocated_page_page_id, page_type_desc
    FROM sys.dm_db_database_page_allocations
    (db_id('testdb'), object_id('Fixed'), NULL, NULL, 'DETAILED');
```

If you weren't in *testdb*, you could replace *testdb* with the name of whatever database you were in when you created this table. The values for allocated_page_file_id and allocated_page_page_id should be the same values you used when you converted the hexadecimal string for the *first_page* value. In this example, the *allocated_page_file_id* value is 1 and the *allocated_page_page_id* value is 1231. So those are the values to use when calling *DBCC PAGE*.

Using the sys.fn_PhysLocFormatter function

Another method for obtaining file and page number information involves using an undocumented function, *sys.fn_PhysLocFormatter*, with an undocumented value, *%%physloc%%*, to return the physical row location in your result rows along with data values from a table. This can be useful if you want to find which page in a table contains a particular value. You can use *sys.dm_db_database_page_allocations* to find all pages in a table but not specifically the pages containing a particular row. However, *sys.fn_PhysLocFormatter* can show you only data pages for the data that is returned in a *SELECT* statement. This method can't be used to get page numbers of index pages or other special types of pages that are covered in Chapters 7 and 8. You can use this function to get the pages used by the data in the table *Fixed*, as follows:

```
SELECT sys.fn_PhysLocFormatter (%%physloc%%) AS RID, * FROM Fixed;
GO
```

Here are my results:

```
RID            Col1    Col2            Col3   Col4
------------   ------- -------------   ------ ------
(1:1231:1 )    ABCDE   123             NULL   CCCC
```

As soon as you have the *FileID* and *PageID* values, you can use *DBCC PAGE*. For a larger table, you could use *sys.fn_PhysLocFormatter* to get the pages only for the specific rows returned by the conditions in the *WHERE* clause.

Caution The *%%physloc%%* value isn't understood by the relational engine, which means that if you use *%%physloc%%* in a *WHERE* clause, SQL Server has to examine every row to see which ones are on the page indicated by *%%physloc%%*. It can't use *%%physloc%%* to find the row. Another way of looking at this is that *%%physloc%%* can be returned as output to report on a physical row location, but can't be used as input to find a particular location in a table. The *%%physloc%%* value was introduced as a debugging feature by the SQL Server product development team and isn't intended to be used (or supported) in production applications.

Storage of fixed-length rows

Now look at the simpler case of an all fixed-length row using the table built in the preceding section:

```
CREATE TABLE Fixed
(
Col1 char(5)      NOT NULL,
Col2 int          NOT NULL,
Col3 char(3)      NULL,
Col4 char(6)      NOT NULL
);
```

When this table is created, you should be able to execute the following queries against the *sys. indexes* and *sys.columns* views to receive the information similar to the results shown:

```
SELECT object_id, type_desc,
    indexproperty(object_id, name, 'minlen') as min_row_len
    FROM sys.indexes where object_id=object_id(N'Fixed');

SELECT  column_id, name, system_type_id, max_length as max_col_len
FROM sys.columns
WHERE object_id=object_id(N'Fixed');
RESULTS:
object_id       type_desc    minlen
------------    -----------  -------
53575229        HEAP         22
```

column_id	name	system_type_id	max_length
1	Col1	175	5
2	Col2	56	4
3	Col3	175	3
4	Col4	175	6

Note The *sysindexes* compatibility view contains columns called *minlen* and *xmaxlen*, which store the minimum and maximum length of a row. In SQL Server 2012, these values aren't available in any of the catalog views, but you can get them by using undocumented parameters to the *indexproperty* function. As with all undocumented features, keep in mind that they're not supported by Microsoft, and future compatibility isn't guaranteed.

For tables containing only fixed-length columns, the value returned for *minlen* by the *indexproperty* function equals the sum of the column lengths (from *sys.columns.max_length*) plus 4 bytes. It doesn't include the 2 bytes for the number of columns or the bytes for the NULL bitmap.

To look at a specific data row in this table, you must first insert a new row. If you didn't insert this row in the preceding section, insert it now:

```
INSERT Fixed VALUES ('ABCDE', 123, NULL, 'CCCC');
```

Figure 6-6 shows this row's actual contents on the data page.

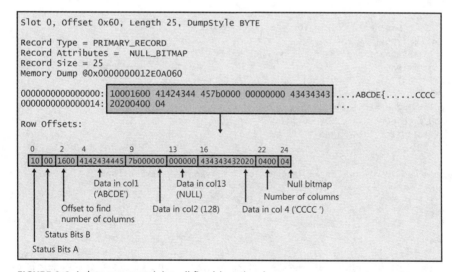

FIGURE 6-6 A data row containing all fixed-length columns.

To get the page contents, run the *DBCC PAGE* command, using the file and page number obtained with one of the methods described previously:

```
DBCC PAGE(testdb, 1, 1231, 1);
```

Reading the output of *DBCC PAGE* takes a bit of practice. First, note that the output shows the data rows in groups of 4 bytes at a time. The shaded area in Figure 6-6 has been expanded to show the bytes in a more readable form.

The first byte is Status Bits A, and its value (0x10) indicates that only bit 4 is on, and because bit 5 isn't on, you know the row has no variable-length columns. The second byte in the row (Status Bits B) is unused. The third and fourth bytes (1600) indicate the length of the fixed-length fields, which is also the column offset in which the *Ncol* value can be found. (As a multibyte numeric value, this information is stored in a byte-swapped form, so the value is really 0x0016, which translates to 22.) To know where in the row between offsets 4 and 22 each column actually is located, you need to know the offset of each column. In SQL Server 2000, the *syscolumns* system table has a column indicating the offset within the row. Although you can still select from the compatibility view called *syscolumns* in SQL Server 2012, the results you get back aren't reliable. The offsets can be found in an undocumented view called *sys. system_internals_partition_columns* that you can then join to *sys.partitions* to get the information about the referenced objects and join to *sys.columns* to get other information about each column.

The query in Listing 6-5 returns basic column information, including the offset within the row for each column. This same query is used for other tables later in this chapter.

LISTING 6-5 Column detail query

```
SELECT c.name AS column_name, column_id, max_inrow_length,
        pc.system_type_id, leaf_offset
 FROM sys.system_internals_partition_columns pc
    JOIN sys.partitions p
      ON p.partition_id = pc.partition_id
    JOIN sys.columns c
        ON column_id = partition_column_id
          AND c.object_id = p.object_id
WHERE p.object_id=object_id(N'Fixed');

RESULTS:
column_name    column_id    max_inrow_length    system_type_id    leaf_offset
-----------    ---------    ----------------    --------------    -----------
Col1           1            5                   175               4
Col2           2            4                   56                9
Col3           3            3                   175               13
Col4           4            6                   175               16
```

So now you can find the data in the row for each column simply by using the offset value in the preceding results: The data for column *Col1* begins at offset 4, the data for column *Col2* begins at offset 9, and so on. As an *int*, the data in *Col2* (7b000000) must be byte-swapped to give the value 0x0000007b, which is equivalent to 123 in decimal.

Notice that the 3 bytes of data for *Col3* are all zeros, representing an actual NULL in the column. Because the row has no variable-length columns, the row ends 3 bytes after the data for column *Col4*.

The 2 bytes starting right after the fixed-length data at offset 22 (0400, which is byte-swapped to yield 0x0004) indicate that four columns are in the row. The last byte is the NULL bitmap. The value of 0x04 is 00000100 is in binary, and bits are shown from high order to low order. The low-order 4 bits represent the four columns in the table, 0100, which indicates that only the third column actually IS NULL. The high-order 4 bits are 0000 because those bits are unused. The NULL bitmap must have a multiple of 8 bits, and if the number of columns isn't a multiple of 8, some bits are unused.

Storage of variable-length rows

Now look at the somewhat more complex case of a table with variable-length data. Each row has three *varchar* columns and two fixed-length columns:

```
CREATE TABLE Variable
(
Col1 char(3)       NOT NULL,
Col2 varchar(250)  NOT NULL,
Col3 varchar(5)    NULL,
Col4 varchar(20)   NOT NULL,
Col5 smallint      NULL
);
```

When this table is created, you should be able to execute the queries in Listing 6-6 against the *sys.indexes*, *sys.partitions*, *sys.system_internals_partition_columns*, and *sys.columns* views to receive the information similar to the results shown at the bottom of the listing.

LISTING 6-6 Obtaining column metadata

```
SELECT object_id, type_desc,
    indexproperty(object_id, name, 'minlen') as minlen
    FROM sys.indexes where object_id=object_id(N'Variable');

SELECT  name, column_id, max_inrow_length, pc.system_type_id, leaf_offset
  FROM sys.system_internals_partition_columns pc
    JOIN sys.partitions p
        ON p.partition_id = pc.partition_id
    JOIN sys.columns c
        ON column_id = partition_column_id AND c.object_id = p.object_id
WHERE p.object_id=object_id(N'Variable');

RESULTS:
object_id    type_desc    minlen
-----------  -----------  -----------
69575286     HEAP         9
```

column_name	column_id	max_inrow_length	system_type_id	leaf_offset
Col1	1	3	175	4
Col2	2	250	167	-1
Col3	3	5	167	-2
Col4	4	20	167	-3
Col5	5	2	52	7

Now you can insert a row into the table as follows:

```
INSERT Variable VALUES
    ('AAA', REPLICATE('X', 250), NULL, 'ABC', 123);
```

The *REPLICATE* function is used here to simplify populating a column; this function builds a string of 250 Xs to be inserted into *Col2*.

Figure 6-7 shows the details of this row as stored on the page in the *DBCC PAGE* output. (Note that not all 250 Xs are shown in *Col2*.) You can find the location of the fixed-length columns by using the *leaf_offset* value in *sys.system_internals_partition_columns* in the query results in Listing 6-6. In this table, *Col1* begins at offset 4 and *Col5* begins at offset 7. Variable-length columns aren't shown in the query output with a specific byte offset because the offset can be different in each row. Instead, the row itself holds the ending position of each variable-length column within that row in a part of the row called the *Column Offset Array*. The query output shows that *Col2* has an *leaf_offset* value of –1, which means that *Col2* is the first variable-length column; an offset for *Col3* of –2 means that *Col3* is the second variable-length column, and an offset of –3 for *Col4* means that *Col4* is the third variable-length column.

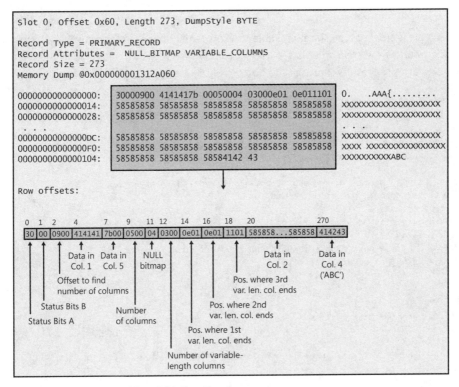

FIGURE 6-7 A data row with variable-length columns.

To find the variable-length columns in the data row itself, you first locate the column offset array in the row. Right after the 2-byte field indicating the total number of columns (0x0500) and the NULL bitmap with the value 0xe4 is another 2-byte field with the value 0x0300 (or 3, decimal) indicating that three variable-length fields exist. Next comes the column offset array. Three 2-byte values indicate the ending position of each of the three variable-length columns: 0x0e01 is byte-swapped to 0x010e, so the first variable byte column ends at position 270. The next 2-byte offset is also 0x0e01, so that column has no length and has nothing stored in the variable data area. Unlike with fixed-length fields, if a variable-length field has a NULL value, it takes no room in the data row. SQL Server distinguishes between a *varchar* containing NULL and an empty string by determining whether the bit for the field is 0 or 1 in the NULL bitmap. The third 2-byte offset is 0x1101, which, when byte-swapped, gives us 0x0111. This means the row ends at position 273 (and is 273 bytes long).

The total storage space needed for a row depends on numerous factors. Variable-length columns add more overhead to a row, and their actual size is probably unpredictable. Even for fixed-length columns, the number of overhead bytes can change depending on the number of columns in the table. The example shown earlier in Listing 6-1 illustrates that 10 bytes of overhead exist if a row contains all fixed-length columns. For that table, 10 is the correct number. The size of the NULL bitmap needs to be long enough to store a bit for every column in the row. In Listing 6-1, the table has 11 columns, so the NULL bitmap needs to be 2 bytes. In the examples illustrated by Figure 6-6 and Listing 6-7, the tables have fewer than eight columns, so the NULL bitmaps need only a single byte. Don't forget that the total row overhead must also include the 2 bytes for each row in the row offset table at the bottom of the page.

NULLS and variable-length columns

As mentioned previously, fixed-length columns are always the same length, even if the column contains NULL. For variable-length columns, NULLs don't take any space in the variable-length data part of the row. However, as you saw in Listing 6-7, a 2-byte column offset entry still exists for each variable-length column, so you can't say that they take no space at all. However, if a zero-length value is stored at the end of the list of variable-length data columns, SQL Server doesn't store any information about it and doesn't include the 2 bytes in the column offset array.

For example, the following table allows NULLs in each of its character columns, and the columns are all variable length. The only fixed-length column is the integer identity column:

```
CREATE TABLE dbo.null_varchar
    (
     id INT PRIMARY KEY IDENTITY(1,1),
     col1 VARCHAR(10) NULL,
     col2 VARCHAR(10) NULL,
     col3 VARCHAR(10) NULL,
     col4 VARCHAR(10) NULL,
     col5 VARCHAR(10) NULL,
```

```
        col6 VARCHAR(10) NULL,
        col7 VARCHAR(10) NULL,
        col8 VARCHAR(10) NULL,
        col9 VARCHAR(10) NULL,
        col10 VARCHAR(10) NULL
    );
GO
```

Insert four rows into this table. The first row has a single character in the last *varchar* column and NULLs in all the others. The second has a single character in the first *varchar* column and NULLs in all the others. The third has a single character in the last *varchar* column and empty strings in all the others. The fourth has a single character in the first *varchar* column and empty strings in all the others:

```
SET NOCOUNT ON
INSERT INTO null_varchar(col10)
    SELECT 'a';
INSERT INTO null_varchar(col1)
    SELECT 'b';
INSERT INTO null_varchar
    SELECT '','','','','','','','','','c';
INSERT INTO null_varchar
    SELECT 'd','','','','','','','','','';
GO
```

Now you can use *sys.dm_db_database_page_allocations* and *DBCC PAGE* (as shown previously) to look at the page containing these four rows. Here is the first row (with the column offset array bold-faced):

```
Slot 0, Offset 0x60, Length 35, DumpStyle BYTE
Record Type = PRIMARY_RECORD
Record Attributes = NULL_BITMAP VARIABLE_COLUMNS
Record Size = 35
Memory Dump @0x0000000012E0A060
0000000000000000:   30000800 01000000 0b00fe03 0a002200 22002200  0........þ...".".".
0000000000000014:   22002200 22002200 22002200 230061             ".".".".".".#.a
```

The column offset array has nine entries with the value (after byte-swapping) of hex 22, or decimal 22, and one entry with the decimal value 23. The value of 22 for the first nine positions indicates that data ends in the same position as the column offset array ends, and SQL Server determines that this means those nine columns are empty (meaning either NULL or an empty string). By looking at the NULL bitmap, in positions 11 and 12, you see *fe03*, which is hex *03fe* after byte-swapping. In binary, this is 0000001111111110. The column positions are shown from right to left. This table has only 11 columns, so the last 5 bits in the NULL bitmap are ignored. The rest of the string indicates the first and last columns aren't NULL, but all the other columns are NULL.

The 10th value in the column offset array is hex 23, or decimal 19, which means that data ends at offset 19, which contains the ASCII code hex 61, representing *a*.

Here is the second row (with the column offset array boldfaced):

```
Slot 1, Offset 0x83, Length 17, DumpStyle BYTE
Record Type = PRIMARY_RECORD
Record Attributes = NULL_BITMAP VARIABLE_COLUMNS
Record Size = 17
Memory Dump @0x0000000012E0A083
0000000000000000:   30000800 02000000 0b00fc07 01001100 62       0.........ü....b
```

Note several important differences between this row and the preceding one. First, the column offset array contains only a single value, which is the ending position for the first variable-length column. The 1100 bytes are byte-swapped to 0011 and converted to 17 decimal, which is the offset where the ASCII code for *b* (that is, hex 62) is located. Immediately preceding the column offset array is the 2-byte value indicating the number of variable-length columns. The first row had a hex value of 000a here, indicating 10 variable-length columns. The second row has 0001, which means only one of the variable-length columns is actually stored in the row. We just saw that zero-length columns prior to columns containing data do use the column offset array, but in this case, because all the zero-length columns are after the last non-NULL, only the non-NULL column is represented here. If you look at the NULL bitmap, you'll see *fc07*, which is hex *07fc* after byte-swapping. In binary, this is 0000011111111100, indicating that the first two columns aren't NULL, but all the rest are.

If you look at the rows containing empty strings instead of NULLs, the output should be exactly the same, except for the NULL bitmap. Here is the third row (slot 2) and the fourth row (slot 3), with the NULL bitmaps boldfaced:

```
Slot 2, Offset 0x94, Length 35, DumpStyle BYTE
Record Type = PRIMARY_RECORD
Record Attributes = NULL_BITMAP VARIABLE_COLUMNS
Record Size = 35
Memory Dump @0x0000000012E0A060
0000000000000000:   30000800 01000000 0b000000 0a002200 22002200  0.........þ...".".".
0000000000000014:   22002200 22002200 22002200 230063           ".".".".".#.a

Slot 3, Offset 0xb7, Length 17, DumpStyle BYTE
Record Type = PRIMARY_RECORD
Record Attributes =  NULL_BITMAP VARIABLE_COLUMNS
Record Size = 17
Memory Dump @0x0000000012E0A083
0000000000000000:   30000800 02000000 0b000000 01001100 64       0.........ü.....b
```

For both the third and fourth rows, the NULL bitmap is all zeros, indicating that none of the columns is NULL. The first and third rows vary only in the actual character value stored and in the NULL bitmap. The second and fourth rows vary in the same way.

If you insert a row with all NULLs in the *varchar* columns, the row storage changes a bit more. Here is what it would look like:

```
Slot 4, Offset 0xc8, Length 12, DumpStyle BYTE
Record Type = PRIMARY_RECORD
Record Attributes = NULL_BITMAP
Record Size = 12
Memory Dump @0x66B4C0C8
00000000:   10000800 05000000 0b000000 †††††††††††.......
```

This row looks just like an all fixed-length row and ends right after the NULL bitmap. Bit 5 in the first byte (Status Bits A) has been set to 0 to indicate that no variable-length columns are stored in this row.

Storage of date and time data

The storage of date and time data types was described earlier in this chapter, and now that you've had some practice looking at the actual on-disk storage, you can look at some date and time data. The following table stores all the different data and time data types in a single row, and all the different possible scales for time data. (Remember that *datetime2* and *datetimeoffset* can also indicate a scale for the time component, but the time values look no different than the time values stored with the simple *time* data type.) The table also includes single-column character values, which is used just so the other values can be found easily in the single row of hex data that *DBCC PAGE* produces:

```
CREATE TABLE times (
        a char(1),
        dt1 datetime,
        b char(1),
        sd smalldatetime,
        c char(1),
        dt2 datetime2,
        d char(1),
        dt date,
        e char(1),
        dto datetimeoffset,
        f char(1),
        t time,
        g char(1),
        t0 time(0),
        h char(1),
        t1 time(1),
        i char(1),
        t2 time(2),
        j char(1),
        t3 time(3),
        k char(1),
        t4 time(4),
        l char(1),
```

```
         t5 time(5),
         m char(1),
         t6 time(6),
         n char(1),
         t7 time(7));
GO
```

Now insert one one-row data, with the same time value provided for each date or time column. The data types that need a date component assume a default date of January 1, 1900:

```
INSERT INTO times
SELECT
      'a', '01:02:03.123',
      'b', '01:02:03.123',
      'c', '01:02:03.123',
      'd', '01:02:03.123',
      'e', '01:02:03.123',
      'f', '01:02:03.123',
      'g', '01:02:03.123',
      'h', '01:02:03.123',
      'i', '01:02:03.123',
      'j', '01:02:03.123',
      'k', '01:02:03.123',
      'l', '01:02:03.123',
      'm', '01:02:03.123',
      'n', '01:02:03.123';
```

Here is the *DBCC PAGE* output for this row. The single-character column data is boldfaced to use as dividers:

```
00000000:  10005800 61090b11 00000000 00623e00 00006330..X.a .......b>.†..c0
00000014:  7c27ab08 5b950a64 5b950a65 307c27ab 085b950a |'".[?.d[?.e0|'".[?.
00000028:  00006630 7c27ab08 678b0e00 686f9100 6958ae05 ..f0|'". g?..ho?.iX®.
0000003C:  6a73cf38 006b7e1a 38026cec 08311600 6d3859ea  jsÏ8.k~.8.lì.1..m8Yê
00000050:  dd006e30 7c27ab08 1c000000 0000        Ý.n0|'".......
```

Table 6-8 shows the translation into decimal format for each of these values.

TABLE 6-8 Translation of various date and time values

Column name	Data type and bytes used	Value stored in row	Byte-swapped date	Time (hex)	Decimal values date	Time (decimal)
dt1	*datetime -8-*	090b110000000000	00 00 00 00	00 110b 09	0	1116937
sd	*smalldatetime -4-*	3e000000	00 00	00 3e	0	62
dt2	*datetime2 -8-*	307c27ab085b950a	0a 95 5b	08 ab 277c 30	693595	37231230000
dt	*date -3-*	5b950a	0a 95 5b	(none)	693595	(none)
dto	*datetime offset -10-*	307c27ab085b950a00 00	0a 95 5b	08 ab 277c 30	693595	37231230000
t	*time -5-*	307c27ab08	(none)	08 ab 277c 30	(none)	37231230000
t0	*time(0) -3-*	8b0e00	(none)	00 0e 8b	(none)	3723
t1	*time(1) -3-*	6f9100	(none)	00 91 6f	(none)	37231

Column name	Data type and bytes used	Value stored in row	Byte-swapped date	Time (hex)	Decimal values date	Time (decimal)
t2	time(2) -3-	58ae05	(none)	05 ae 58	(none)	372312
t3	time(3) -4-	73cf3800	(none)	00 38cf 73	(none)	3723123
t4	time(4) -4-	7e1a3802	(none)	02 381a 7e	(none)	37231230
t5	time(5) -5-	ec08311600	(none)	00 16 3108 ec	(none)	372312300
t6	time(6) -5-	3859eadd00	(none)	00 dd ea59 38	(none)	3723123000
t7	time(7) -5-	307c27ab08	(none)	08 ab 277c 30	(none)	37231230000

Here are some points to notice;

- For the *datetime* and *smalldatetime* data types, the date value is stored as 0, meaning that the date is the base of January 1, 1900. For the other types that store a date, the date value is stored as 693595, which represents the number of days after the internal base date of January 1, 0001. To compute the corresponding date, you can use the *dateadd* function:

```
SELECT DATEADD(dd, 693595, CAST('0001/1/1' AS datetime2));
```

This returns the value '1900-01-01' 00:00:00.00', which is the default when no date is specified.

- The fractional seconds component is the last *N* digits of the time component, where *N* is the scale of the time data, as listed in the table definition. So for the *time(7)* value, the fractional seconds are .1230000; for *time(4)*, the fractional seconds are .1230; for *time(1)* value, the fractional seconds are .1; and the *time(0)* value has no fractional sections.

- Whatever remains in the time portion after the appropriate number of digits is removed for the fractional seconds is the hours, minutes, and seconds value. Because the same time value was used for all the columns in the table, the time values all start with the same four digits: 3723. Previously, you saw the formula for converting a time value to an integer; here is the reverse, using the modulo operator (%) and integer division. SQL Server uses the following conversions to determine the hours, minutes, and seconds from 3723:

```
SELECT hours = (3723 / 60) / 60;
SELECT minutes = (3723 / 60) % 60;
SELECT seconds = 3723 % 60;

RESULT:
hours
----------
1

minutes
----------
2

seconds
----------
3
```

- The column storing *datetimeoffset* data has 2 extra bytes to store the *timezone* offset. Two bytes are needed because the offset is stored as the number of hours and minutes (1 byte for each) from Coordinated Universal Time (UTC).

Storage of sql_variant data

The *sql_variant* data type provides support for columns that contain any or all of the SQL Server base data types except LOBs and variable-length columns with the *max* qualifier, *rowversion* (*timestamp*), XML, and the types that can't be defined for a column in a table, namely *cursor* and *table*. For instance, a column defined as *sql_variant* can contain a *smallint* value in some rows, a *float* value in others, and a *char* value in the remainder.

This feature was designed to support what appears to be semistructured data in products sitting above SQL Server. This semistructured data exists in conceptual tables with a fixed number of columns of known data types and one or more optional columns whose type might not be known in advance. An example is email messages in Microsoft Office Outlook and Microsoft Exchange. With the *sql_variant* data type, you can pivot a conceptual table into a real, more compact table with sets of property-value pairs. For a graphical example, the conceptual table shown in Table 6-9 has three rows of data. The fixed columns exist in every row. Each row can also have values for one or more of the three different properties, which have different data types.

TABLE 6-9 A conceptual table with an arbitrary number of columns and data types

Row	Fixed columns	Property 1	Property 2	Property 3
row -1	XXXXXX	value-11		value -13
row -2	YYYYYY	value-22		
row -3	ZZZZZZ	value-31	value-32	

This can be pivoted into Table 6-10, where the fixed columns are repeated for each different property that appears with those columns. The column called *value* can be represented by *sql_variant* data and be a different data type for each different property.

TABLE 6-10 Semistructured data stored using the sql_variant data type

Fixed columns	Property	Value
XXXXXX	property-1	value-11
XXXXXX	property-3	value-13
YYYYYY	property-2	value-22
ZZZZZZ	property-1	value-31
ZZZZZZ	property-2	value-32

Internally, columns of type *sql_variant* are always considered variable length. Their storage structure depends on the data type, but the first byte of every *sql_variant* field always indicates the actual data type being used in that row.

The following creates a simple table with a *sql_variant* column and inserts a few rows into it so that you can observe the structure of the *sql_variant* storage:

```
USE testdb;
GO
CREATE TABLE variant (a int, b sql_variant);
GO
INSERT INTO variant VALUES (1, 3);
INSERT INTO variant VALUES (2, 3000000000);
INSERT INTO variant VALUES (3, 'abc');
INSERT INTO variant VALUES (4, current_timestamp);
```

SQL Server decides what data type to use in each row based on the data supplied. For example, the *3* in the first *INSERT* is assumed to be an integer. In the second *INSERT*, the *3000000000* is larger than the biggest possible integer, so SQL Server assumes a decimal with a precision of 10 and a scale of 0. (It could have used a *bigint*, but that would need more storage space.) You can now use sys.dm_db_database_page_allocations to find the first page of the table and use *DBCC PAGE* to see its contents, as follows:

```
SELECT allocated_page_file_id, allocated_page_page_id, page_type_desc
    FROM sys.dm_db_database_page_allocations
        (db_id('testdb'), object_id('variant'), NULL, NULL, 'DETAILED');
-- (I got a value of file 1, page 2508 for the data page in this table)
GO
DBCC TRACEON (3604);
DBCC PAGE (testdb, 1, 2508, 1);
```

In Listing 6-7, you can see the contents of the four rows. This section won't go into the details of every single byte because most are the same as what you've already examined.

LISTING 6-7 Rows containing sql_variant data

```
DATA:

Slot 0, Offset 0x60, Length 21, DumpStyle BYTE

Record Type = PRIMARY_RECORD        Record Attributes =  NULL_BITMAP VARIABLE_COLUMNS
Record Size = 21
Memory Dump @0x00000000185CA060

0000000000000000:    30000800 01000000 02000001 00150038 01030000  0..............8....
0000000000000014:    00

Slot 1, Offset 0x75, Length 24, DumpStyle BYTE

Record Type = PRIMARY_RECORD        Record Attributes =  NULL_BITMAP VARIABLE_COLUMNS
Record Size = 24
Memory Dump @0x00000000185CA075

0000000000000000:    30000800 02000000 02000001 0018006c 010a0001  0..............l....
0000000000000014:    005ed0b2                                      .^Ð²

Slot 2, Offset 0x8d, Length 26, DumpStyle BYTE
```

```
Record Type = PRIMARY_RECORD          Record Attributes =  NULL_BITMAP VARIABLE_COLUMNS
Record Size = 26
Memory Dump @0x00000000185CA08D


0000000000000000:   30000800 03000000 02000001 001a00a7 01401f08  0..............§.@..
0000000000000014:   d0003461 6263                                 Ð.4abc

Slot 3, Offset 0xa7, Length 25, DumpStyle BYTE

Record Type = PRIMARY_RECORD          Record Attributes =  NULL_BITMAP VARIABLE_COLUMNS
Record Size = 25
Memory Dump @0x00000000185CA0A7


0000000000000000:   30000800 04000000 02000001 0019003d 0192a7f9  0..............=.'§ù
0000000000000014:   0013a000 00                                   .. ..

OFFSET TABLE:

Row - Offset
3 (0x3) - 167 (0xa7)
2 (0x2) - 141 (0x8d)
1 (0x1) - 117 (0x75)
0 (0x0) - 96 (0x60)
```

The difference between the three rows starts at bytes 13 and 14, which indicate the position where the first variable-length column ends. Because only one variable-length column exists, this is also the length of the row. The *sql_variant* data begins at byte 15. Byte 15 is the code for the data type, and is shaded in each row. You can find the codes in the *system_type_id* column of the *sys.types* catalog view. Listing 6-8 reproduces the relevant part of that view.

LISTING 6-8 Datatypes and their ID values

```
system_type_id   name
---------------- ----------------------
34               image
35               text
36               uniqueidentifier
40               date
41               time
42               datetime2
43               datetimeoffset
48               tinyint
52               smallint
56               int
58               smalldatetime
59               real
60               money
61               datetime
62               float
98               sql_variant
99               ntext
104              bit
106              decimal
108              numeric
122              smallmoney
```

```
127            bigint
165            varbinary
167            varchar
173            binary
175            char
189            timestamp
231            nvarchar
231            sysname
239            nchar
240            hierarchyid
240            geometry
240            geography
241            xml
```

In the variant table, the first row uses data type hex 38 (which is 56 decimal and *int*), the second uses hex 6C (which is 108 decimal, which is numeric), the third uses hex A7 hex (which is 167 decimal and *varchar*), and the last row uses data type hex 3D hex (which is 61 decimal and *datetime*). Following the byte for data type is a byte representing the version of the *sql_variant* format, and that is always 1 in SQL Server 2012. One of the following four sets of bytes can come after the version:

- For numeric and decimal: 1 byte for the precision and 1 byte for the scale

- For strings: 2 bytes for the maximum length and 4 bytes for the collation ID

- For *binary* and *varbinary*: 2 bytes for the maximum length

- For all other types: no extra bytes

These bytes are then followed by the actual data in the *sql_variant* column.

Constraints

Constraints provide a powerful yet easy way to enforce the data integrity in your database. Constraints are also called *declarative data integrity* because they are part of the actual table definition. This is in contrast to *programmatic data integrity*, which uses stored procedures or triggers.

Data integrity comes in three forms.

- **Entity integrity** ensures that a table has a primary key. In SQL Server 2012, you can guarantee entity integrity by defining PRIMARY KEY or UNIQUE constraints or by building unique indexes. Alternatively, you can write a trigger to enforce entity integrity, but this is usually far less efficient.

- **Domain integrity** ensures that data values meet certain criteria. In SQL Server 2012, domain integrity can be guaranteed in several ways. Choosing appropriate data types can ensure that a data value meets certain conditions—for example, that the data represents a valid date. Other approaches include defining CHECK or FOREIGN KEY constraints or writing a trigger. You can also consider DEFAULT constraints as an aspect of enforcing domain integrity.

- **Referential integrity** enforces relationships between two tables: a referenced table and a referencing table. SQL Server allows you to define FOREIGN KEY constraints to enforce referential integrity, as well as write triggers for enforcement. Referential integrity enforcement always has two sides. If data is updated or deleted from the referenced table, referential integrity ensures that any data in the referencing table that refers to the changed or deleted data is handled in some way. On the other side, if data is updated or inserted into the referencing table, referential integrity ensures that the new data matches a value in the referenced table.

This section briefly describes some of the internal aspects of managing constraints. The five types of constraints are PRIMARY KEY, UNIQUE, FOREIGN KEY, CHECK, and DEFAULT.

You might also sometimes see the *IDENTITY* property and the nullability of a column described as constraints. You shouldn't consider these attributes to be constraints; instead, think of them as properties of a column, for two reasons.

- Each constraint has its own row in the *sys.objects* catalog view, but *IDENTITY* and nullability information isn't available in *sys.objects*, only in *sys.columns* and *sys.identity_columns*. So you can think of these properties as more like data types, which are also viewable through *sys.columns*.

- When you use the *SELECT INTO* command to make a copy of a table, all column names and data types are copied, as well as *IDENTITY* information and column nullability, but constraints *aren't* copied to the new table. So you can think of *IDENTITY* and nullability as being more a part of the actual table structure than the constraints are.

Constraint names and catalog view information

The following simple *CREATE TABLE* statement, which includes a primary key on the table, creates a PRIMARY KEY constraint along with the table, and the constraint has a very cryptic-looking name:

```
CREATE TABLE customer
(
cust_id     int         IDENTITY  NOT NULL  PRIMARY KEY,
cust_name   varchar(30) NOT NULL
);
```

If you don't supply a constraint name in the *CREATE TABLE* or *ALTER TABLE* statement that defines the constraint, SQL Server comes up with a name for you. The constraint produced from the preceding simple statement has a name very similar to the nonintuitive name *PK__customer__3BD0198E35BCFE0A*. (The hexadecimal number at the end of the name most likely is different for a *customer* table that you create.) All types of single-column constraints use this naming scheme, as is explained shortly. The advantage of explicitly naming your constraint rather than using the system-generated name is greater clarity. The constraint name is used in the error message for any constraint violation, so creating a name such as *CUSTOMER_PK* probably makes more sense to users than a name such as *PK__customer__0856260D*. You should choose your own constraint names if such error messages are visible to your users. The first two characters (*PK*) show the constraint type—*PK* for PRIMARY KEY, *UQ* for UNIQUE, *FK* for FOREIGN KEY, *CK* for CHECK, and *DF* for DEFAULT. Next are two underscore characters, which serve as a separator.

> **Tip** You might be tempted to use one underscore to conserve characters and to avoid having to truncate as much. However, it's common to use a single underscore in a table name or a column name, both of which appear in the constraint name. Using two underscore characters distinguishes the kind of a name it is and where the separation occurs.

> **Note** Constraint names are schema-scoped, which means they all share the same namespace and hence must be unique within a schema. Within a schema, you can't have two tables with the same name for any of their constraints.

Next is the table name (*customer*), which is limited to 116 characters for a PRIMARY KEY constraint and slightly fewer characters for all other constraint names. All constraints other than PRIMARY KEY and UNIQUE have two more underscore characters for separation, followed by the next sequence of characters, which is the column name. The column name is truncated to five characters if necessary. If the column name has fewer than five characters, the length of the table name portion can be slightly longer.

Finally, the hexadecimal representation of the object ID for the constraint comes after another separator. This value is used in the *object_id* column of the *sys.objects* catalog view. Because object names are limited to 128 characters in SQL Server 2012, the total length of all portions of the constraint name must also be less than or equal to 128.

Several catalog views contain constraint information. They all inherit the columns from the *sys. objects* view and include additional columns specific to the type of constraint.

- *sys.key_constraints*

- *sys.check_constraints*

- *sys.default_constraints*

- *sys.foreign_keys*

The *parent_object_id* column, which indicates which object contains the constraint, is actually part of the base *sys.objects* view, but for objects that have no "parent," this column is 0.

Constraint failures in transactions and multiple-row data modifications

Many bugs occur in application code because developers don't understand how the failure of a constraint affects a user-declared multiple-statement transaction. The biggest misconception is that any error, such as a constraint failure, automatically aborts and rolls back the entire transaction. On the contrary, after an error is raised, the transaction needs either to proceed and ultimately commit, or to roll back. This feature provides the developer with the flexibility to decide how to handle errors. (The semantics are also in accordance with the ANSI SQL-92 standard for COMMIT behavior.)

Because many developers have handled transaction errors incorrectly and because it can be tedious to add an error check after every command, SQL Server includes a SET option called XACT_ABORT that causes SQL Server to abort a transaction if it encounters any error during the transaction. The default setting is OFF, which is consistent with ANSI-standard behavior.

A final comment about constraint errors and transactions: A single data modification statement (such as an UPDATE statement) that affects multiple rows is automatically an atomic operation, even if it's not part of an explicit transaction. If such an UPDATE statement finds 100 rows that meet the criteria of the WHERE clause but one row fails because of a constraint violation, no rows are updated. Chapter 13 discusses implicit and explicit transactions a bit more.

The order of integrity checks

The modification of a given row fails if any constraint is violated or a trigger rolls back the operation. As soon as a failure occurs in a constraint, the operation is aborted, subsequent checks for that row aren't performed, and no triggers fire for the row. Hence, the order of these checks can be important, as the following list shows:

1. Defaults are applied as appropriate.

2. NOT NULL violations are raised.

3. CHECK constraints are evaluated.

4. FOREIGN KEY checks of referencing tables are applied.

5. FOREIGN KEY checks of referenced tables are applied.

6. The UNIQUE and PRIMARY KEY constraints are checked for correctness.

7. Triggers fire.

Altering a table

SQL Server 2012 allows existing tables to be modified in several ways. By using the ALTER TABLE command, you can make the following types of changes to an existing table.

- Change the data type or the NULL property of a single column.

- Add one or more new columns, with or without defining constraints for those columns.

- Add one or more constraints.

- Drop one or more constraints.

- Drop one or more columns.

- Enable or disable one or more constraints (applies only to CHECK and FOREIGN KEY constraints).

- Enable or disable one or more triggers.

- Rebuild a table or a partition to change the compression settings or remove fragmentation. (Fragmentation is discussed in Chapter 7; Chapter 8 discusses compression.)

- Change the lock escalation behavior of a table. (Chapter 13 discusses locks and lock escalation.)

Changing a data type

By using the *ALTER COLUMN* clause of *ALTER TABLE*, you can modify the data type or the *NULL* property of an existing column. But be aware of the following restrictions.

- The modified column can't be a *text*, *image*, *ntext*, or *rowversion* (*timestamp*) column.

- If the modified column is the *ROWGUIDCOL* for the table, only *DROP ROWGUIDCOL* is allowed; no data type changes are allowed.

- The modified column can't be a computed or replicated column.

- The modified column can't have a PRIMARY KEY or FOREIGN KEY constraint defined on it.

- The modified column can't be referenced in a computed column.

- The modified column can't have the type changed to *timestamp*.

- If the modified column participates in an index, the only type changes that are allowed are increasing the length of a variable-length type (for example, *varchar(10)* to *varchar(20)*), changing nullability of the column, or both.

- If the modified column has a UNIQUE or CHECK constraint defined on it, the only change allowed is altering the length of a variable-length column. For a UNIQUE constraint, the new length must be greater than the old length.

- If the modified column has a default defined on it, the only changes allowed are increasing or decreasing the length of a variable-length type, changing nullability, or changing the precision or scale.

- The old type of the column should have an allowed implicit conversion to the new type.

- The new type always has *ANSI_PADDING* semantics if applicable, regardless of the current setting.

- If conversion of an old type to a new type causes an overflow (arithmetic or size), the *ALTER TABLE* statement is aborted.

Here's the syntax, followed by an example, of the *ALTER COLUMN* clause of the *ALTER TABLE* statement:

```
ALTER TABLE table-name ALTER COLUMN column-name
     { type_name [ ( prec [, scale] ) ] [COLLATE <collation name> ]
        [ NULL | NOT NULL ]
        |   {ADD | DROP} {ROWGUIDCOL | PERSISTED}  }

/* Example: Change the length of the emp_lname column in the employee
   table from varchar(15) to varchar(30) */
ALTER TABLE employee
   ALTER COLUMN emp_name varchar(30);
```

Adding a new column

You can add a new column, with or without specifying column-level constraints. If the new column doesn't allow NULLs, isn't an identity column, and isn't a *rowversion* (or *timestamp* column), the new column must have a default constraint defined (unless no data is in the table yet). SQL Server populates the new column in every row with a NULL, the appropriate identity or *rowversion* value, or the specified default. If the newly added column is nullable and has a default constraint, the existing rows of the table aren't filled with the default value, but rather with NULL values. You can override this restriction by using the *WITH VALUES* clause so that the existing rows of the table are filled with the specified default value.

> **Note** In SQL Server 2012 Enterprise Edition, adding a NOT NULL column with a default value is performed as a metadata-only operation when the default value is a constant. The existing rows in the table aren't updated during the operation; instead, SQL Server stores the default value in the metadata of the table and accesses the value as needed during query processing.

Adding, dropping, disabling, or enabling a constraint

You can use *ALTER TABLE* to add, drop, enable, or disable a constraint. The trickiest part of using *ALTER TABLE* to manipulate constraints is that the word *CHECK* can be used in three different ways.

- To specify a *CHECK* constraint.

- To defer the checking of a newly added constraint. The following example adds a constraint to validate that *cust_id* in *orders* matches a *cust_id* in *customer*, but you don't want the constraint applied to existing data:

```
ALTER TABLE orders
   WITH NOCHECK
   ADD FOREIGN KEY (cust_id) REFERENCES customer (cust_id);
```

Note Rather than use *WITH NOCHECK*, this example could use *WITH CHECK* to force the constraint to be applied to existing data, but that's unnecessary because it's the default behavior.

- To enable or disable a constraint. This example enables all constraints on the *employee* table:

```
ALTER TABLE employee
    WITH CHECK CHECK CONSTRAINT ALL;
```

 Note When enabling an existing constraint, the default is to *not* validate the existing data, so *WITH CHECK* is needed to override that. The second *CHECK* indicates that now the constraint is enabled.

The only types of constraints that you can disable are CHECK and FOREIGN KEY constraints. Disabling them tells SQL Server not to validate new data as it is added or updated. Use caution when disabling and re-enabling constraints, however. If a constraint was part of the table when the table was created or was added to the table using the *WITH CHECK* option, SQL Server knows that the data conforms to the data integrity requirements of the constraint. The SQL Server Query Optimizer can then take advantage of this knowledge in some cases. For example, if you have a constraint that requires *col1* to be greater than 0, and then an application submits a query looking for all rows where *col1* < 0, if the constraint has always been in effect, the Optimizer knows that no rows can satisfy this query and the plan is a very simple plan. However, if the constraint has been disabled and re-enabled without using the *WITH CHECK* option, you aren't guaranteed that some of the data in the table will meet the integrity requirements. You might not have any data less than or equal to 0, but the Optimizer can't know that when it's devising the plan; all the Optimizer knows is that the constraint can't be trusted. The catalog views *sys.check_constraints* and *sys.foreign_keys* each have a column called *is_not_trusted*. If you re-enable a constraint and don't use the *WITH CHECK* option to tell SQL Server to revalidate all existing data, the *is_not_trusted* column is set to 1.

Although you can't use *ALTER TABLE* to disable or enable a PRIMARY KEY or UNIQUE constraint, you can use the *ALTER INDEX* command to disable the associated index. Chapter 7 discusses *ALTER INDEX* in more detail. You can use *ALTER TABLE* to drop PRIMARY KEY and UNIQUE constraints, but you need to be aware that dropping one of these constraints automatically drops the associated index. In fact, the only way to drop those indexes is by altering the table to remove the constraint.

 Note You can't use *ALTER TABLE* to modify a constraint definition. You must use *ALTER TABLE* to drop the constraint and then use *ALTER TABLE* to add a new constraint with the new definition.

Dropping a column

You can use *ALTER TABLE* to remove one or more columns from a table. However, you can't drop the following columns:

- A replicated column

- A column used in an index

- A column used in a CHECK, FOREIGN KEY, UNIQUE, or PRIMARY KEY constraint

- A column associated with a default defined using the *DEFAULT* keyword or bound to a default object

- A column to which a rule is bound

You can drop a column using the following syntax:

```
ALTER TABLE table-name
    DROP COLUMN column-name [, next-column-name]...
```

 Note Notice the syntax difference between dropping a column and adding a new column. The word *COLUMN* is required when dropping a column but not when you add a new column to a table.

Internals of altering tables

Not all the *ALTER TABLE* variations require SQL Server to change every row when the *ALTER TABLE* command is issued. SQL Server can carry out an *ALTER TABLE* command in three basic ways.

- It might need to change only metadata.

- It might need to examine all the existing data to ensure that it's compatible with the change but needs to make changes only to metadata.

- It might need to change every row physically.

In many cases, SQL Server can just change the metadata (primarily the data seen through *sys. columns*) to reflect the new structure. In particular, the data isn't touched when a column is dropped, when a new column is added and NULL is assumed as the new value for all rows, when the length of a variable-length column is increased, or when a non-nullable column is changed to allow NULLs. That data isn't touched when a column is dropped means that the disk space of the column isn't reclaimed. You might have to reclaim the disk space of a dropped column when the row size of a table approaches or exceeds its limit. You can reclaim space by creating or re-creating a clustered index on the table using *ALTER INDEX*, as you'll see in Chapter 7, or by rebuilding the table using *ALTER TABLE*, as you'll see in Chapter 8.

Some changes to a table's structure require that the data be examined but not modified. For example, when you change the nullability property to disallow NULLs, SQL Server must first ensure that the existing rows have no NULLs. A variable-length column can be shortened when all the existing data is within the new limit, so the existing data must be checked. If any rows have data longer than the new limit specified in *ALTER TABLE*, the command fails. Be aware that for a huge table, this can take some time. Changing a fixed-length column to a shorter type, such as changing an *int* column to *smallint* or changing a *char(10)* to *char(8)*, also requires examining all the data to verify that all existing values can be stored in the new type. However, even though the new data type takes up fewer bytes, the rows on the physical pages aren't modified. If you have created a table with an *int* column, which needs 4 bytes in each row, all rows will use the full 4 bytes. After altering the table to change the *int* to *smallint*, you are restricted in the range of data values you can insert, but the rows continue to use 4 bytes for each value, instead of the 2 bytes that *smallint* requires. You can verify this by using the *DBCC PAGE* command. Changing a *char(10)* to *char(8)* displays similar behavior, and the rows continue to use 10 bytes for that column, but the data inserted is restricted to be no more than 8 bytes long. It's not until the table is rebuilt that the *char(10)* columns are actually re-created to become *char(8)*.

Other changes to a table's structure require SQL Server to change every row physically; as it makes the changes, it has to write the appropriate records to the transaction log, so these changes can be extremely resource-intensive for a large table. One example of this type of change is changing the data type of a column to a new type with a different internal storage representation.

Another negative side effect of altering tables happens when a column is altered to increase its length. In this case, the old column isn't actually replaced; instead, a new column is added to the table, and *DBCC PAGE* shows you that the old data is still there. You can explore the page dumps for this situation on your own, but you can see some of this unexpected behavior just by looking at the column offsets using the column detail query shown earlier in Listing 6-5.

First, create a table with all fixed-length columns, including a *smallint* in the first position:

```
CREATE TABLE change
(col1 smallint, col2 char(10), col3 char(5));
```

Now look at the column offsets:

```
SELECT c.name AS column_name, column_id, max_inrow_length, pc.system_type_id, leaf_offset
  FROM sys.system_internals_partition_columns pc
    JOIN sys.partitions p
      ON p.partition_id = pc.partition_id
    JOIN sys.columns c
        ON column_id = partition_column_id
          AND c.object_id = p.object_id
WHERE p.object_id=object_id('change');

RESULTS:
column_name   column_id   max_inrow_length   system_type_id  leaf_offset
-------------  -----------  ------------------  --------------  -----------
col1          1            2                   52              4
col2          2            10                  175             6
col3          3            5                   175             16
```

Now change *smallint* to *int*:

```
ALTER TABLE change
    ALTER COLUMN col1 int;
```

Finally, run the column detail query from Listing 6-5 again to see that *col1* now starts much later in the row and that no column starts at offset 4 immediately after the row header information. This new column creation due to an *ALTER TABLE* takes place even before any data has been placed in the table:

```
column_name   column_id   max_inrow_length   system_type_id   leaf_offset
-----------   ---------   ----------------   --------------   -----------
col1          1           4                  56               21
col2          2           10                 175              6
col3          3           5                  175              16
```

Another drawback to the behavior of SQL Server in not actually dropping the old column is that the row size is now more severely limited. The row size now includes the old column, which is no longer usable or visible (unless you use *DBCC PAGE*). For example, if you create a table with a couple of large fixed-length character columns, as shown here, you can then ALTER the *char(2000)* column to be *char(3000)*:

```
CREATE TABLE bigchange
(col1 smallint, col2 char(2000), col3 char(1000));

ALTER TABLE bigchange
    ALTER COLUMN col2 char(3000);
```

At this point, the row lengths should be just over 4,000 bytes because of a 3,000-byte column, a 1,000-byte column, and a *smallint*. However, if you try to add another 3,000-byte column, it fails:

```
ALTER TABLE bigchange
    ADD col4 char(3000);

Msg 1701, Level 16, State 1, Line 1
Creating or altering table 'bigchange' failed because the minimum row size
would be 9009, including 7 bytes of internal overhead. This exceeds the
maximum allowable table row size of 8060 bytes.
```

However, just creating a table with two 3,000-byte columns and a 1,000-byte column doesn't cause any problems:

```
CREATE TABLE nochange
(col1 smallint, col2 char(3000), col3 char(1000), col4 char(3000));
```

Note that you can't *ALTER* a table to rearrange the logical column order or to add a new column in a particular position in the table. A newly added column always gets the next highest *column_id* value. When you execute *SELECT* * on a table or look at the metadata with *sp_help*, the columns are always returned in *column_id* order. If you need a different order, you have several options.

- Don't use *SELECT* *; always *SELECT* a list of columns in the order that you want to have them returned.

- Create a view on the table that *SELECT*s the columns in the order you want them and then you can *SELECT* * from the view or run *sp_help* on the view.

- Create a new table, copy the data from the old table, drop the old table, and rename the new table to the old name. Don't forget to re-create all constraints, indexes, and triggers.

You might think that Management Studio Table Designer can create a script to add a new column in a particular position or rearrange the column order, but this isn't true. In the background, the tool is actually using the preceding third option and creating a completely new table with all new indexes, constraints, and triggers. If you wonder why running a script to simply add a new column to an existing (large) table is taking a long time, this is probably the reason.

 Note You can configure whether the Table Designer can save changes to a table that require a *DROP* and *CREATE* from the Tools/Options menu. The default, fortunately, is to prevent saving such a change.

Heap modification internals

You've seen how SQL Server stores data in a heap. Now you can look at what SQL Server actually does internally when your heap data is modified. Modifying data in an index, which includes a table with a clustered index, is a completely separate topic and is covered in detail in Chapter 7. As a rule of thumb, you should almost always have a clustered index on a table. In some cases you might be better off with a heap, such as when the most important factor is the speed of *INSERT* operations, but until you do thorough testing to establish that you have such a situation, having a clustered index is better than having no organization to your data at all. In Chapter 7, you'll see the benefits and trade-offs of clustered and nonclustered indexes and examine some guidelines for their use. For now, you'll look only at how SQL Server deals with the data modifications on tables without clustered indexes.

Allocation structures

Chapter 3 mentioned a special kind of allocation page called a Page Free Space (PFS) page and indicated that its use was relating to how data is stored on a page. PFS pages are particularly useful when SQL Server is performing data modification operations on a heap. Because these special pages keep track of how much space is free on each data page, *INSERT* operations in a heap know where space is available for the new data and *UPDATE* operations know where a row can be moved. PFS pages contain 1 byte for each page in an 8,088-page range of a file. This is much less dense than GAMs, SGAMs, and IAMs, which contain one bit per extent. Figure 6-8 shows the structure of a byte on a PFS page. Only the last three bits are used to indicate the page fullness, and four of the other five bits each have a meaning.

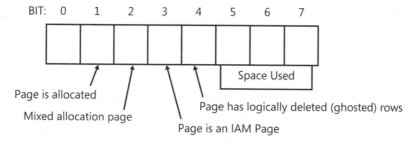

Possible values for the three bits indicating space used:

- 000 = 0: Page is empty
- 001 = 1: Page is 1–50% full
- 010 = 2: Page is 51–80% full
- 011 = 3: Page is 81–95% full
- 100 = 4: Page is 96–100% full

FIGURE 6-8 Meaning of the bits in a PFS byte.

The bits are interpreted this way:

- **Bit 1** indicates whether the page is actually allocated. For example, a uniform extent can be allocated to an object, but all pages in the extent might not be allocated. To tell which pages within an allocated extent are actually used, SQL Server needs to look at this bit in the appropriate byte in the PFS page.

- **Bit 2** indicates whether the corresponding page is from a mixed extent.

- **Bit 3** indicates that this page is an IAM page. Remember that IAM pages aren't located at known locations in a file.

- **Bit 4** indicates that this page contains ghost records. As you'll see, SQL Server uses a background cleanup thread to remove ghost records, and these bits on the PFS pages help SQL Server find those pages that need to be cleaned up. (Ghost records show up only in indexes or when using row-level versioning, so they aren't discussed further in this chapter, but are discussed in Chapters 7 and 13.)

- **Bits 5 through 7** are taken as a 3-bit value. The values 0 to 4 indicate the page fullness, as follows:

    - **0** The page is empty.

    - **1** The page is 1–50 percent full.

    - **2** The page is 51–80 percent full.

    - **3** The page is 81–95 percent full.

    - **4** The page is 96–100 percent full.

PFS pages are at known locations within each data file. The second page (page 1) of a file is a PFS page, as is every 8,088th page thereafter, which would be page 8088, page 16176, and so on.

Inserting rows

When inserting a new row into a table, SQL Server must determine where to put it. When a table has no clustered index—that is, when the table is a heap—a new row is always inserted wherever room is available in the table. You've seen how IAMs and the PFS pages keep track of which extents in a file already belong to a table and which of the pages in those extents have space available. Even without a clustered index, space management is quite efficient. If no pages with space are available, SQL Server tries to find unallocated pages from existing uniform extents that already belong to the object. If none exists, SQL Server must allocate a whole new extent to the table. Chapter 3 discussed how the GAMs and SGAMs are used to find extents available to be allocated to an object.

Deleting rows

When you delete rows from a table, you have to consider what happens to both the data pages and the index pages. Remember that the data is actually the leaf level of a clustered index, and deleting rows from a table with a clustered index happens the same way as deleting rows from the leaf level of a nonclustered index. Deleting rows from a heap is managed differently, as is deleting from node pages of an index.

Deleting rows from a heap

SQL Server 2012 doesn't reorganize space on a page automatically when a row is deleted. As a performance optimization, the compaction doesn't occur until a page needs additional contiguous space for inserting a new row. You can see this in the example, which deletes a row from the middle of a page and then inspects that page using *DBCC PAGE*:

```
USE testdb;
GO

CREATE TABLE smallrows
(
    a int identity,
    b char(10)
);
GO

INSERT INTO smallrows
    VALUES ('row 1');
INSERT INTO smallrows
    VALUES ('row 2');
INSERT INTO smallrows
    VALUES ('row 3');
INSERT INTO smallrows
    VALUES ('row 4');
INSERT INTO smallrows
    VALUES ('row 5');
```

```
GO

SELECT allocated_page_file_id, allocated_page_page_id, page_type_desc
    FROM sys.dm_db_database_page_allocations
        (db_id('testdb'), object_id('smallrows'), NULL, NULL, 'DETAILED');
-- Note the file ID and page ID values from the row for the data page
--  and use those values with DBCC PAGE (I got FileID 1 and PageID 4536)

DBCC TRACEON(3604);
GO
DBCC PAGE(testdb, 1, 280,1);
```

The following is the output from *DBCC PAGE*:

```
DATA:

Slot 0, Offset 0x60, Length 21, DumpStyle BYTE

Record Type = PRIMARY_RECORD          Record Attributes =  NULL_BITMAP
Record Size = 21

Memory Dump @0x0000000018BFA060

0000000000000000:   10001200 01000000 726f7720 31202020 20200200  ........row 1      ..
0000000000000014:   00                                                              .

Slot 1, Offset 0x75, Length 21, DumpStyle BYTE

Record Type = PRIMARY_RECORD          Record Attributes =  NULL_BITMAP
Record Size = 21

Memory Dump @0x0000000018BFA075

0000000000000000:   10001200 02000000 726f7720 32202020 20200200  ........row 2      ..
0000000000000014:   00                                                              .

Slot 2, Offset 0x8a, Length 21, DumpStyle BYTE

Record Type = PRIMARY_RECORD          Record Attributes =  NULL_BITMAP
Record Size = 21

Memory Dump @0x0000000018BFA08A

0000000000000000:   10001200 03000000 726f7720 33202020 20200200  ........row 3      ..
0000000000000014:   00                                                              .

Slot 3, Offset 0x9f, Length 21, DumpStyle BYTE

Record Type = PRIMARY_RECORD          Record Attributes =  NULL_BITMAP
Record Size = 21

Memory Dump @0x0000000018BFA09F

0000000000000000:   10001200 04000000 726f7720 34202020 20200200  ........row 4      ..
0000000000000014:   00                                                              .
```

```
Slot 4, Offset 0xb4, Length 21, DumpStyle BYTE

Record Type = PRIMARY_RECORD          Record Attributes =  NULL_BITMAP
Record Size = 21

Memory Dump @0x0000000018BFA0B4

0000000000000000:    10001200 05000000 726f7720 35202020 20200200   ........row 5     ..
0000000000000014:    00                                                               .

OFFSET TABLE:

Row - Offset
4 (0x4) - 180 (0xb4)
3 (0x3) - 159 (0x9f)
2 (0x2) - 138 (0x8a)
1 (0x1) - 117 (0x75)
0 (0x0) - 96 (0x60)
```

Now delete the middle row (*WHERE a = 3*) and look at the page again:

```
DELETE FROM smallrows
WHERE a = 3;
GO

DBCC PAGE(testdb, 1, 280,1);
GO
```

The following is the output from the second execution of *DBCC PAGE*:

```
DATA:

Slot 0, Offset 0x60, Length 21, DumpStyle BYTE

Record Type = PRIMARY_RECORD          Record Attributes =  NULL_BITMAP
Record Size = 21

Memory Dump @0x00000000144DA060

0000000000000000:    10001200 01000000 726f7720 31202020 20200200   ........row 1     ..
0000000000000014:    00                                                               .

Slot 1, Offset 0x75, Length 21, DumpStyle BYTE

Record Type = PRIMARY_RECORD          Record Attributes =  NULL_BITMAP
Record Size = 21

Memory Dump @0x00000000144DA075

0000000000000000:    10001200 02000000 726f7720 32202020 20200200   ........row 2     ..
0000000000000014:    00                                                               .

Slot 3, Offset 0x9f, Length 21, DumpStyle BYTE

Record Type = PRIMARY_RECORD          Record Attributes =  NULL_BITMAP
Record Size = 21
```

```
Memory Dump @0x00000000144DA09F

0000000000000000:    10001200 04000000 726f7720 34202020 20200200   ........row 4     ..
0000000000000014:    00                                                          .
```

Slot 4, Offset 0xb4, Length 21, DumpStyle BYTE

Record Type = PRIMARY_RECORD   Record Attributes = NULL_BITMAP
Record Size = 21

```
Memory Dump @0x00000000144DA0B4

0000000000000000:    10001200 05000000 726f7720 35202020 20200200   ........row 5     ..
0000000000000014:    00                                                          .
```

OFFSET TABLE:

```
Row - Offset
4 (0x4) - 180 (0xb4)
3 (0x3) - 159 (0x9f)
2 (0x2) - 0 (0x0)
1 (0x1) - 117 (0x75)
0 (0x0) - 96 (0x60)
```

Note that in the heap, the row offset array at the bottom of the page shows that the third row (at slot 2) is now at offset 0 (which means no row is using slot 2), and the row using slot 3 is at its same offset as before the delete. No data on the page is moved when the *DELETE* occurs. The row doesn't show up in the page when you use *printopt* 1 or 3 for *DBCC PAGE*. However, if you dump the page with *printopt* 2, you still see the bytes for "row 3." They aren't physically removed from the page, but the 0 in the row offset array indicates that the space isn't used now and can be used by a new row.

In addition to space on pages not being reclaimed, empty pages in heaps frequently can't be reclaimed. Even if you delete all the rows from a heap, SQL Server doesn't mark the empty pages as unallocated, so the space isn't available for other objects to use. The dynamic management view (DMV) *sys.dm_db_partition_stats* still shows the space as belonging to the heap table and sys.dm_db_database_page_allocations shows the is_allocated column with a value of 0 and the page_type_desc column as NULL. One way to avoid this problem is to request a table lock when the delete is being performed (Chapter 13 looks at lock hints). If this problem has already occurred and you are showing more space belonging to a table than it really has, you can rebuild the table using the *ALTER TABLE...REBUILD* command, or you can build a clustered index on the table to reorganize the space and then drop the index (if desired).

Reclaiming pages

When the last row is deleted from a data page, the entire page is deallocated. The exception is if the table is a heap, as discussed previously. (If the page is the only one remaining in the table, it isn't deallocated.) Deallocation of a data page results in the deletion of the row in the index page that pointed to the deallocated data page. Index pages are deallocated if an index row is deleted (which, again, might occur as part of a delete/insert update strategy), leaving only one entry in the index page. That entry is moved to its neighboring page, and then the empty page is deallocated.

Updating rows

SQL Server can update rows in several different ways: automatically and invisibly choosing the fastest update strategy for the specific operation. In determining the strategy, SQL Server evaluates the number of rows affected, how the rows are accessed (via a scan or an index retrieval, and via which index), and whether changes to the index keys will occur. Updates can happen either in place, by just changing one column's value to a new value in the original row, or as a delete followed by an insert. Updates also can be managed by the query processor or by the storage engine. This section examines only whether the update happens in place or whether SQL Server treats it as two separate operations: delete the old row and insert a new row.

Moving rows

What happens if a row has to move to a new location in the table? In SQL Server 2012, this can happen for a couple of different reasons. Chapter 7 looks at the structure of indexes and shows that the value in a table's clustered index column (or columns) determines the location of the row. So, if the value of the clustered key is changed, the row most likely has to move within the table.

If it still has the same row locator—in other words, the clustering key for the row stays the same— no nonclustered indexes have to be modified. If a table has no clustered index—in other words, if it's a heap—a row might move because it no longer fits on the original page. This can happen whenever a row with variable-length columns is updated to a new, larger size so that it no longer fits in the original location. As you'll see when Chapter 7 covers index structures, every nonclustered index on a heap contains pointers to the data rows that are the actual physical location of the row, including the file number, page number, and row number. So that the nonclustered indexes don't all have to be updated just because a row moves to a different physical location, SQL Server leaves a forwarding pointer in the original location when a row has to move.

Consider an example to see these forwarding pointers. You'll create a table that's much like the one created for *DELETE* operations, but this table has two columns of variable length. After populating the table with five rows to fill the page, you'll update one of the rows to make its third column much longer. The row no longer fits on the original page and has to move. You can use *sys.dm_db_ database_page_allocations* to get the page numbers used by the table as shown in Listing 6-9.

LISTING 6-9 Creating a forwarded record

```
USE testdb;
GO
DROP TABLE bigrows;
GO
CREATE TABLE bigrows
(   a int IDENTITY ,
    b varchar(1600),
    c varchar(1600));
GO
```

```
INSERT INTO bigrows
    VALUES (REPLICATE('a', 1600), '');
INSERT INTO bigrows
    VALUES (REPLICATE('b', 1600), '');
INSERT INTO bigrows
    VALUES (REPLICATE('c', 1600), '');
INSERT INTO bigrows
    VALUES (REPLICATE('d', 1600), '');
INSERT INTO bigrows
    VALUES (REPLICATE('e', 1600), '');
GO
UPDATE bigrows
SET c = REPLICATE('x', 1600)
WHERE a = 3;
GO


SELECT allocated_page_file_id, allocated_page_page_id, page_type_desc
    FROM sys.dm_db_database_page_allocations
        (db_id('testdb'), object_id('bigrows'), NULL, NULL, 'DETAILED');
-- Note the file ID and page ID values from the rows that are for data pages
--    and use those values with DBCC PAGE (I got file ID 1 and
--    page ID values of 286 and 277.

DBCC TRACEON(3604);
GO
DBCC PAGE(testdb, 1, 286, 1);
GO
```

The following doesn't show the entire output from the *DBCC PAGE* command, but it does shows what appears in the slot where the row with a = 3 formerly appeared:

```
Slot 2, Offset 0xcfe, Length 9, DumpStyle BYTE
Record Type = FORWARDING_STUB          Record Attributes =
Memory Dump @0x61ADDFEB
00000000:    04150100 00010000 00†††††††††††††††††††.........
```

The value of 4 in the first byte means that this is just a forwarding stub. The 00000115 in the next 4 bytes is the page number to which the row has been moved. Because this is a hexadecimal value, you need to convert it to 277 decimal. The next group of 4 bytes tells you that the page is at slot 0, file 1. In fact, file 1 page 277 was the second data page that the output of sys.dm_db_database_page_allocations reported. If you then use *DBCC PAGE* to look at that page, page 277, you can see what the forwarded record looks like, and you can see that the Record Type indicates *FORWARDED_RECORD*.

Managing forward pointers

Forward pointers allow you to modify data in a heap without worrying about having to make drastic changes to the nonclustered indexes. If a forwarded row must move again, the original forwarding pointer is updated to point to the new location. You'll never end up with a forwarding pointer pointing to another forwarding pointer. Also, if the forwarded row shrinks enough to fit in its original place, the record might move back to its original place (if that page still has room), and the forward pointer would be eliminated.

Currently, when a forward pointer is created, it stays there forever—with only a few exceptions. The first exception is the case already mentioned, in which a row shrinks and returns to its original location. Another exception is when the entire database shrinks. The bookmarks are actually reassigned when a file is shrunk. The shrink process never generates forwarding pointers. For pages removed by the shrink process, any forwarded rows or stubs they contain are effectively "unforwarded." Other cases in which the forwarding pointers are removed are the obvious ones: if the forwarded row is deleted or if a clustered index is built on the table so that it's no longer a heap. Lastly, you can remove forwarding pointers by rebuilding the heap with the *ALTER TABLE* command:

```
ALTER TABLE bigrows REBUILD ;
```

> **More info** To get a count of forward records in a table, you can look at the output from the *sys.dm_db_index_physical_stats* function, which is discussed in Chapter 7.

Updating in place

In SQL Server 2012, updating a row in place is the rule rather than the exception. This means that the row stays in exactly the same location on the same page and only the bytes affected are changed. Also, the log contains a single record for each such updated row unless the table has an update trigger on it or is marked for replication. In these cases, the update still happens in place, but the log contains a delete record followed by an insert record.

In cases where a row can't be updated in place, the cost of a not-in-place update is minimal because of the way the nonclustered indexes are stored and because of the use of forwarding pointers, as described previously. In fact, you can have a not-in-place update for which the row stays on the original page. Updates happen in place if a heap is being updated (and no forwarding pointer is required), or if a table with a clustered index is updated without any change to the clustering keys. You can also get an update in place if the clustering key changes but the row doesn't need to move at all. For example, if you have a clustered index on a last-name column containing consecutive key values of *Abolrous*, Bechynsky, and *Charney*, you might want to update Bechynsky to *Belishky*. Because the row stays in the same location even after the clustered index key changes, SQL Server performs this as an update in place. On the other hand, if you update *Abolrous* to *Burk*, the update can't occur in place, but the new row might stay on the same page.

Updating not in place

If your update can't happen in place because you're updating clustering keys, the update occurs as a delete followed by an insert. In some cases, you'll get a hybrid update; some of the rows are updated in place and some aren't. If you're updating index keys, SQL Server builds a list of all rows that need to change as both a *DELETE* and an *INSERT* operation. This list is stored in memory, if it's small enough, and is written to *tempdb* if necessary. This list is then sorted by key value and operator (*DELETE* or *INSERT*). If the index whose keys are changing isn't unique, the *DELETE* and *INSERT* steps are then applied to the table. If the index is unique, an additional step is carried out to collapse *DELETE* and *INSERT* operations on the same key into a single update operation.

More info The Query Optimizer determines whether this special *UPDATE* method is appropriate, and this internal optimization, called *Split/Sort/Collapse*, is described in detail in Chapter 11, "The Query Optimizer."

Conclusion

Tables are at the heart of relational databases in general and SQL Server in particular. This chapter looked at the internal storage issues of various data types—in particular, comparing fixed-length and variable-length data types. You saw that SQL Server 2012 provides multiple options for storing variable-length data, including data that's too long to fit on a single data page, and you saw that it's simplistic to think that using variable-length data types is either always good or always bad. SQL Server provides user-defined data types for support of domains, as well as the *IDENTITY* property and the SEQUENCE object to allow you to obtain auto-sequenced numeric values. You also saw how data is physically stored in data pages, and you queried some of the metadata views that provide information from the underlying (and inaccessible) system tables. SQL Server also provides constraints, which offer a powerful way to ensure your data's logical integrity.

CHAPTER 7

Indexes: internals and management

Kalen Delaney

M icrosoft SQL Server doesn't have a configuration option or a knob that allows you to make it run faster—no panacea. However, indexes—when created and designed appropriately—are probably the closest thing to a panacea. The right index, created for the right query, can reduce query execution time from hours down to seconds. You have absolutely no other way to see these kinds of gains; adding hardware or tweaking configuration options often give only marginal gains. What about indexes can make a query request drop from millions of I/Os to only a few? And does just any index improve performance? Unfortunately, great performance doesn't just happen; all indexes aren't equal, nor will just any index improve performance. In fact, over-indexing can be worse than under-indexing. You can't just "index every column" and expect SQL Server to improve.

So, how do you know how to create the best indexes? The answer isn't easy and requires multiple pieces: knowing your data, knowing your workload, and knowing how SQL Server works. SQL Server involves multiple components: index internals, statistics, query optimization, and maintenance. This chapter focuses on index internals and maintenance, expanding on these topics to suggest best practices for index creation and optimal indexing strategies. By knowing how SQL Server physically stores indexes as well as how the storage engine accesses and manipulates these physical structures, you are better equipped to create the *right* indexes for your workload.

SQL Server 2012 provides two completely different kinds of storage for indexes.

- Indexes can be stored in a special tree structure, known as a B-tree.

- Each index column can be stored in its own segment, in a structure called a columnstore index.

Understanding the details of the storage structures will help prepare you for Chapter 10, "Query execution," and Chapter 11, "The Query Optimizer," because then you can visualize the choices (in physical structures) from which SQL Server can choose the optimal query plans and why some structures are more effective than others for certain queries.

This chapter is split into multiple sections. The first section explains B-tree index usage and concepts, as well as index storage internals. In that section, you learn how indexes are organized on disk and how they are used for data retrieval. The second section dives into what happens when data is modified—both how it happens and how SQL Server guarantees consistency. In that section, you also learn the potential effects of data modifications on B-tree indexes, such as fragmentation. The third section discusses index management and maintenance. The last section describes columnstore indexes, added in SQL Server 2012, which are stored and managed completely differently than B-tree indexes.

Overview

Think of the indexes you might see in your everyday life—those in books and other documents. Suppose that you're trying to create an index in SQL Server using the *CREATE INDEX* statement and you're using two SQL Server references to find out how to write the statement. One reference is the (hypothetical) *Microsoft SQL Server Transact-SQL Language Reference Manual*, referred to here as the "T-SQL Reference." Assume that the T-SQL Reference is just an alphabetical list of all the SQL Server keywords, commands, procedures, and functions. The other reference is this book: *Microsoft SQL Server 2012 Internals*. You can find information quickly in either book about indexes, even though the two books are organized differently.

In the T-SQL Reference, all the commands and keywords are organized alphabetically. You know that *CREATE INDEX* is near the front with all the other *CREATE* statements, so you can just ignore most of the rest of the book. Keywords and phrases are shown at the top of each page to tell you what commands are on that page. Thus, you can flip through just a few pages quickly and end up at a page that has *CREATE DATABASE* on it, and you know that *CREATE INDEX* appears shortly thereafter. Now, if you flipped forward and came to *CREATE VIEW* without passing *CREATE INDEX*, you'd know that *CREATE INDEX* was missing from the book, because the commands and keywords are organized alphabetically. (Of course, this is just an example—*CREATE INDEX* would certainly be in the T-SQL Reference.)

Next, you try to find *CREATE INDEX* in *Microsoft SQL Server 2012 Internals*. This book is *not* ordered alphabetically by commands and keywords, but the index at the back of this book has all its entries organized alphabetically. So, again, you can use the fact that *CREATE INDEX* is near the front of the alphabet and find it quickly. However, unlike in the T-SQL Reference, when you find the words *CREATE INDEX*, you won't see nice, neat examples right in front of you. The index only gives you pointers—it tells you what pages to look at. In fact, it might list many pages in the book. Also, if you look up *CREATE TABLE* in the book's index, you might find dozens of pages listed. Finally, if you look up the *sp_addumpdevice* stored procedure (a completely deprecated command), you won't find it in the index at all because it's not described in this book.

The first example, with the book's contents actually being ordered, is analogous to using a clustered index; the second example, with the need to look up the actual page referenced in the index into the book, is analogous to a nonclustered index. If a table has a clustered index, you can say that the table is clustered and its data is logically stored in the clustering key order, just as the T-SQL Reference has all the main topics in order. When you find the data you're looking for, your search is complete. In a nonclustered index, the index is a completely separate structure from the data itself. After you find what you're looking for in the index, you might have to follow some sort of reference pointer to get to the actual data. Although a nonclustered index in SQL Server is very much like the index in the back of a book, it's not exactly the same. Also, if your nonclustered index is a columnstore index, it's actually very different, as you'll see in the last section of this chapter.

SQL Server B-tree indexes

In SQL Server, most indexes are organized using a B-tree structure (see Figure 7-1). In fact, in this chapter, any reference to any kind of index without qualifying it indicates a B-tree index. The term *B-tree* stands for "balanced tree," and SQL Server uses a special kind called B+ trees (pronounced "b-plus trees"). The difference between B-trees and B+ trees isn't really relevant for this discussion of the way SQL Server indexes are managed, so the difference will be ignored. Index structures are referred to as simply B-trees. Unlike a normal tree, B-trees are always inverted, with their root (a single page) at the top and their leaf level at the bottom. The existence of intermediate levels depends on multiple factors. *B-tree* is an overloaded term used in different ways by different people—either to mean the entire index structure or just the non-leaf levels. In this book, the term *B-tree* means the entire index structure.

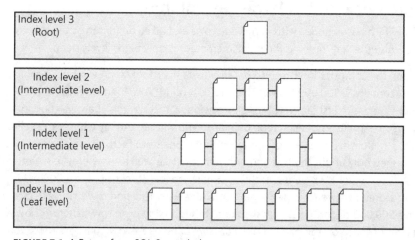

FIGURE 7-1 A B-tree for a SQL Server index.

What's interesting about B-trees in SQL Server is how they are constructed and what each level contains. Structurally, indexes might change a small amount based on whether multiple CPUs are used to create or rebuild them (as explained in more detail later in the section "MAXDOP"), but for the most part, the size and width of the tree are based on the definition of the index and the number and size of rows in the table. A few examples, starting with the general terms and definitions, will show this.

First, indexes have two primary components: a leaf level and one or more non-leaf levels. The non-leaf levels are interesting to understand and discuss, but simply put, they're used for navigation (mostly for navigating to the leaf level). However, the first intermediate level is also used in fragmentation analysis and to drive read-aheads during large range scans of the index.

To understand these structures, look at the leaf level in generic terms—meaning that these basic concepts apply to both clustered and nonclustered indexes. The leaf level of an index contains an *entry* for every row of the table, and these entries are stored in index key order. Later, this chapter gets specific on what's in an index entry. This section focuses on traditional indexes and those created without filters. (*Filtered indexes* are a feature added in SQL Server 2008, which will be described later in the chapter.)

Non-leaf levels exist to help navigate to a row at the leaf level, but the architecture is rather straightforward. Each non-leaf level stores an entry for every page of the level below—and levels are added until the index builds up to a root of one page. Each higher non-leaf level in the index—that is, farther away from the leaf level—is smaller than the one below it because each row at a level contains only the minimum key value that can be on each page of the level below, plus a pointer to that page. In other words, each non-leaf level of an index has one row for each page of the level below. Although you might think that this could result in many levels (that is, a tall tree), the limitation on the size of the key (which has a maximum of 900 bytes or 16 columns, whichever comes first) in SQL Server helps to keep the number of levels in an index tree relatively small.

Example 1: An index with a large key column

In the first example—which has an index with fairly wide rows and a key definition at the maximum size—the tree size of this index (at the time the index is created) is only eight levels deep.

To see this tree (and the computations used to determine its size), look at an example in which the leaf level of the index contains 1,000,000 "rows." The quotes around "rows" indicate that these aren't necessarily data rows—these are just leaf-level rows of *any* index. Later in this chapter—during a discussion on the physical structures of each type of index—you will see exactly what leaf-level rows are and how they are structured. However, for this example, you need to focus on an abstract "index" in which you're concerned only about the leaf and non-leaf levels, as well as how they're structured within the confines of SQL Server 8 KB pages. In this example, the leaf-level rows are 4,000 bytes, which means you can store only two rows per page. For a table with 1 million rows, the leaf level of the index would have 500,000 pages. Relatively speaking, this is a fairly wide row structure; however, you aren't wasting a lot of space on the page. If the leaf-level page had two 3,000-byte rows, you'd still fit only two rows per page, but then you'd have 2,000 bytes of wasted space. (This would be an example of internal fragmentation, which is discussed later in the "Fragmentation" section.)

Now, why are these just "rows" and not specifically data rows? This leaf level *could* be the leaf level for a clustered index (therefore data rows) *or* these leaf-level rows could be rows in a nonclustered index that uses *INCLUDE* to add non-key columns to the leaf level of the index. When *INCLUDE* is used, leaf-level pages can contain rows wider than the 900-byte or 16-column key maximum (again, this chapter explains later why this can be beneficial). In this example, the leaf level of this index would be 4 GB in size (500,000 pages of 8 KB each) at the time it's created. This structure, depending on its definition, could become larger—and possibly very fragmented—if a lot of new data is added. However—and again depending on its definition—you can control how fragmented this index becomes when data is volatile (a topic discussed further in later sections). In this case, the leaf level of the index is large because of "row" width. And, using the maximum of 900 bytes means that you can fit only eight (8,096 bytes per page/900 bytes per row) rows per non-leaf level page. However, by using this maximum, the resulting tree (up to a root of one page) would be *relatively* small and result only in eight levels. In fact, improving scalability is the primary reason for the limit to an index key of 900 bytes or 16 columns—whichever comes first.

- Root page of non-leaf level (Level 7) = 2 rows = 1 page (8 rows per page)

- Intermediate non-leaf level (Level 6) = 16 rows = 2 pages (8 rows per page)

- Intermediate non-leaf level (Level 5) = 123 rows = 16 pages (8 rows per page)

- Intermediate non-leaf level (Level 4) = 977 rows = 123 pages (8 rows per page)

- Intermediate non-leaf level (Level 3) = 7,813 rows = 977 pages (8 rows per page)

- Intermediate non-leaf level (Level 2) = 62,500 rows = 7,813 pages (8 rows per page)

- Intermediate non-leaf level (Level 1) = 500,000 rows = 62,500 pages (8 rows per page)

- Leaf level (Level 0) = 1,000,000 rows = 500,000 pages (2 rows per page)

Example 2: An index with a very narrow key column

An index with a smaller key size would scale even faster. Imagine the same leaf-level pages (1 million rows at 2 rows per page) but with a smaller index key and therefore a smaller row size in the non-leaf levels (including some space for overhead) of only 20 bytes; you can fit 404 rows per non-leaf-level page.

- Root page of non-leaf level (Level 3) = 4 rows = 1 page (404 rows per page)

- Intermediate non-leaf level (Level 2) = 1,238 rows = 4 pages (404 rows per page)

- Intermediate non-leaf level (Level 1) = 500,000 rows = 1,238 pages (404 rows per page)

- Leaf level (Level 0) = 1,000,000 rows = 500,000 pages (2 rows per page)

For this second example, not only is the initial index only four levels but it also can add 130,878,528 rows (the maximum possible number of rows is 404*404*404*2—or 131,878,528—minus the number of rows that already exist: 1 million) before it would require another level. Think of it like this: The root page currently allows 404 entries, but only 4 are stored, and the existing non-leaf levels aren't 100 percent full. This maximum is only theoretical, but without any other factors—such as fragmentation—a four-level tree could seek into a table with more than 131 million rows (again, with this small index key size). This means that a lookup into this index that uses the tree to navigate down to the corresponding row requires only four I/Os. Also, because the trees are balanced, finding any record requires the same amount of resources. Retrieval speed is consistent because the index has the same depth throughout. An index can become fragmented—and pages can become less dense—but these trees don't become unbalanced. This is something you look at later, in a discussion on index maintenance.

Memorizing all the math used to show these examples isn't critical, but understanding the true scalability of indexes, especially with reasonably created keys, means you will likely create more effective indexes—that is, more efficient, with narrower keys. Also, SQL Server has tools to help you see the actual structures—no math required. Most importantly, the size of an index and the number of levels depend on three things: the index definition, whether the base table has a clustered index, and the number of pages in the leaf level of the indexes. The number of leaf-level pages is directly tied to both row size and the number of rows in the table. This doesn't mean that the goal when defining indexes is to have only very narrow indexes; in fact, extremely narrow indexes usually have fewer uses than slightly wider indexes. It just means that you should understand the implications of different indexing choices and decisions. Also, features such as *INCLUDE* and filtered indexes can profoundly affect the index in both size and usefulness. However, knowing how SQL Server works and the internal structures of indexes are a large part of finding the right balance between having too many and too few indexes and, most importantly, of having the right indexes.

Tools for analyzing indexes

To help you understand index structures fully, this section uses a few tools whose appropriate use you need to get a feel for. This section also focuses on an overview of the options for execution, as well as some tips and tricks. The details on analyzing various aspects of the output can be found throughout this chapter.

Using the dm_db_index_physical_stats DMV

One of the most useful functions that you can use to determine table structures is *sys.dm_db_index_physical_stats*. This DMV can provide insight into whether your table has a clustered index, how many nonclustered indexes exist, and whether your table (and each index) has row-overflow or Large Object (LOB) data. Most importantly, it can expose to you the entire structure and its state of health. This particular DMV requires five parameters, all with defaults. If you set all the parameters to their defaults and don't filter the rows or the columns, the function returns 21 columns of data for (almost) every level of every index on every table on every partition in every database of the current SQL Server instance. You would request that information as follows:

```
SELECT * FROM sys.dm_db_index_physical_stats (NULL, NULL, NULL, NULL, NULL);
```

When executed on a very small SQL Server instance, with only the *AdventureWorks2012*, *pubs*, and *Northwind* databases in addition to the system databases, more than 600 rows are returned. Obviously, 21 columns and 600 rows is too much output to illustrate here, so you should play with this command to get some experience. However, more than likely you don't actually want to see every index on every table in every database (although that can have some benefits on smaller instances, such as a development instance). To distill this DMV to a more targeted execution, consider the parameters.

- **database_id** The first parameter must be specified as a number, but you can embed the *DB_ID* function as a parameter if you want to specify the database by name. If you specify

NULL (the default), the function returns information about all databases. If the database ID is *NULL*, the next three parameters must also be *NULL* (their default value).

- **object_id**   The second parameter is the object ID, which must also be a number, not a name. Again, the *NULL* default means that you want information about all objects; in that case, the next two parameters, *index_id* and *partition_id*, must also be *NULL*. Just as for the database ID, you can use an embedded function (*OBJECT_ID*) to get the object ID if you know the object name. Note that if you're executing this from a different database than your current database, you should use a three-part object name with the *OBJECT_ID* function, including the database name and the schema name.

- **index_id**   The third parameter allows you to specify the index ID from a particular table. Again, the default of *NULL* indicates that you want all the indexes. A handy fact to remember here is that the clustered index on a table always has an *index_id* of 1.

- **partition_number**   The fourth parameter indicates the partition number, and *NULL* means that you want information for all the partitions. Remember that if you haven't explicitly created a table or index on a partition scheme, SQL Server internally considers it to be built on a single partition.

- **mode**   The fifth and last parameter is the only one for which the default *NULL* doesn't result in returning the most information. This parameter indicates the level of information that you want returned (and therefore directly affects the speed of execution) when querying this function. When the function is called, SQL Server traverses the page chains for the allocated pages for the specified partitions of the table or index. Unlike *DBCC SHOWCONTIG* in SQL Server 2000, which usually requires a shared (S) table lock, *sys.dm_db_index_physical_stats* (and *DBCC SHOWCONTIG* in SQL Server 2005) requires only an Intent-Shared (IS) table lock, which is compatible with most other kinds of locks, as discussed in Chapter 13, "Transactions and concurrency." Valid inputs are DEFAULT, *NULL*, *LIMITED*, *SAMPLED*, and *DETAILED*. The default is *NULL*, which corresponds to *LIMITED* (and can also be requested by specifying the mode *DEFAULT*). Here is what the latter three values mean:

  - **LIMITED**   This mode is the fastest and scans the smallest number of pages. For an index, it scans only the first non-leaf (or intermediate) level of the index. For a heap, a scan is avoided by using the table's Index Allocation Maps (IAMs) and then the associated Page Free Space (PFS) pages to define the allocation of the table. This enables SQL Server to obtain details about fragmentation in page order (more on this later in the chapter), but not page density or other details that can be calculated only from reading the leaf-level pages. In other words, it's fast but not quite as detailed. More specifically, this corresponds to the *WITH FAST* option of the now-deprecated *DBCC SHOWCONTIG* command.

  - **SAMPLED**   This mode returns physical characteristics based on a 1 percent sample of all pages in the index or heap, plus the page order from reading the pages at the first intermediate level. However, if the index has less than 10,000 pages total, SQL Server converts *SAMPLED* to *DETAILED*.

- **DETAILED** This mode scans all pages and returns all physical characteristics (both page order and page density) for all levels of the index. This is incredibly helpful when analyzing a small table but can take quite a bit of time for larger tables. It could also essentially "flush" your buffer pool if the index being processed is larger than the buffer pool.

Be careful when using the built-in *DB_ID* or *OBJECT_ID* functions. If you specify an invalid name or simply misspell the name, you don't receive an error message and the value returned is *NULL*. However, because *NULL* is a valid parameter, SQL Server assumes that this is what you meant to use. For example, to see all the previously described information, but only for the *AdventureWorks2012* database, you might mistype the name as follows:

```
SELECT * FROM sys.dm_db_index_physical_stats
        (DB_ID ('AdventureWorks2011'), NULL, NULL, NULL, NULL);
```

No *AdventureWorks2011* database exists, so the *DB_ID* function returns *NULL*, as though you had called the function with all *NULL* parameters. No error or warning is given.

You could guess from the number of rows returned that you made an error, but if you have no idea how much output to expect, the error might not be immediately obvious. *SQL Server Books Online* suggests that you can avoid this issue by capturing the IDs into variables and error-checking the values in the variables before calling the *sys.dm_db_index_physical_stats* function, as shown in Listing 7-1.

LISTING 7-1 Using variables to specify the object with *sys.dm_db_index_physical_stats*

```
DECLARE @db_id SMALLINT;
DECLARE @object_id INT;

SET @db_id = DB_ID (N'AdventureWorks2012');
SET @object_id = OBJECT_ID (N'AdventureWorks2012.Person.Address');

IF (@db_id IS NULL OR @object_id IS NULL)
BEGIN
    IF @db_id IS NULL
    BEGIN
        PRINT N'Invalid database';
    END;
    ELSE IF @object_id IS NULL
    BEGIN
        PRINT N'Invalid object';
    END
END
ELSE
SELECT *
FROM sys.dm_db_index_physical_stats
    (@db_id, @object_id, NULL, NULL, NULL);
```

Another more insidious problem is that the *OBJECT_ID* function is called based on your current database, before any call to the *sys.dm_db_index_physical_stats* function is made. So if you are in the *AdventureWorks2012* database but want information from a table in the *pubs* database, you could try running the following code:

```
SELECT *
FROM sys.dm_db_index_physical_stats
     (DB_ID (N'pubs'), OBJECT_ID (N'dbo.authors'), NULL, NULL, NULL);
```

However, because the current database (*AdventureWorks2012*) doesn't have a dbo.authors table, @*object_id* is passed as *NULL*, and you get all the information from all the objects in *pubs*.

If an object with the same name exists in two databases, the problem might be even harder to detect. If *AdventureWorks2012* had a *dbo.authors* table, the ID for that table would be used to try to retrieve data from the *pubs* database—and it's unlikely that the *authors* table has the same ID even if it exists in both databases. SQL Server returns an error if the ID returned by *object_id()* doesn't match any object in the specified database, but if does match the object ID for another table, the details for *that* table are produced, potentially causing even more confusion. The following script shows the error:

```
USE AdventureWorks2012;
GO

CREATE TABLE dbo.authors
    (ID CHAR(11), name varchar(60));
GO

SELECT *
FROM sys.dm_db_index_physical_stats
     (DB_ID (N'pubs'), OBJECT_ID (N'dbo.authors'), NULL, NULL, NULL);
```

When you run the preceding *SELECT*, the *dbo.authors* ID is determined based on the current environment, which is still *AdventureWorks2012*. But when SQL Server tries to use that ID (which doesn't exist) in *pubs*, the following error is generated:

```
Msg 2573, Level 16, State 40, Line 1
Could not find table or object ID 295672101. Check system catalog.
```

The best solution is to fully qualify the table name, either in the call to the *sys.dm_db_index_physical_stats* function itself or, as in the code sample shown in Listing 7-1, to use variables to get the ID of the fully qualified table name. If you write wrapper procedures to call the *sys.dm_db_index_physical_stats* function, you can concatenate the database name onto the object name before retrieving the object ID, thereby avoiding the problem. Because the output of this function is a bit cryptic, you might find it beneficial to write your own procedure to access this function and return the information in a way that's more user-friendly.

In summary, this function is incredibly useful for determining the size and health of your indexes; however, you need to know how to work with it to get only the specific information in which you're interested. But even for a subset of tables or indexes, and with careful use of the available parameters, you still might get more data back than you want. Because *sys.dm_db_index_physical_stats* is a table-valued function, you can add your own filters to the results being returned. For example, you can choose to look at the results for just the nonclustered indexes. Using the available parameters, your only choices are to see all the indexes or only one particular index. If you make the third parameter *NULL* to specify all indexes, you can then add a filter in a *WHERE* clause to indicate that you want only nonclustered index rows (*WHERE index_id > 1*). Note that although a *WHERE* clause can limit the number of rows returned, it won't necessarily limit the tables and indexes analyzed.

Using sys.dm_db_database_page_allocations

The *sys.dm_db_database_page_allocations function* introduced in Chapter 6, "Table storage," is undocumented but extremely useful. In SQL Server 2012 it replaces the command *DBCC IND*, which is also undocumented but widely used. Both are safe to use on production systems. The function has five parameters, which are very similar to the parameters for *sys.dm_db_index_physical_stats: database_id, object_id, index_id, partition_number,* and *mode.* The only difference is that the mode parameter only has two values: *LIMITED* and *DETAILED.*

Table 7-1 describes the columns in the result set. Note that all page references have the file and page component conveniently split between two columns, so you don't have to do any conversion. Also note that the description information indicates which values aren't available if *LIMITED* mode is used.

TABLE 7-1 Column descriptions for *sys.dm_db_database_page_allocations*

Column name	Description
database_id	Contains the ID of the database for which the command is run.
object_id	Contains the object ID of the object for which the extent is allocated.
index_id	Contains the index ID of the object for which the extent is allocated.
rowset_id	Contains the rowset ID of the object for which the extent is allocated.
allocation_unit_id	Contains the allocation unit ID of the object for which the extent is allocated.
allocation_unit_type	Contains the type of allocation unit for which the extent is allocated. One of: 1, 2, 3.
allocation_unit_type_desc	Contains a textual description of the allocation unit type. One of: *IN_ROW_DATA (1), LOB_DATA (2), ROW_OVERFLOW_DATA (3).*
data_clone_id	For internal use only.
clone_state	For internal use only.
clone_state_desc	For internal use only.
extent_file_id	The file ID of the extent to which the page is allocated.
extent_page_id	The first page ID in the extent to which the page is allocated.
allocated_page_iam_file_id	The file ID of the IAM page that tracks this allocated page. *NULL* if the page is an IAM page.
allocated_page_iam_page_id	The page ID of the IAM page that tracks this allocated page. *NULL* if the page is an IAM page.
allocated_page_file_id	The file ID of the page allocated from the extent described by *extent_file_id* and *extent_page_id.*
allocated_page_page_id	The page ID of the page allocated from the extent described by *extent_file_id* and *extent_page_id.*
is_allocated	1 if the page in the specified extent is allocated, 0 if it's not.
is_iam_page	1 if the page allocated is an IAM page, 0 if it's not.
is_mixed_extent_allocation	1 if the page is allocated from a mixed extent, 0 if it's allocated from a uniform extent.
has_ghost_records	1 if the page contains ghost records, 0 if it doesn't contain ghosts.
page_free_space_percent	For pages allocated to heap and *ROW_OVERFLOW_DATA* or *LOB_DATA* allocation units, contains a string indicating how full the page is. Not valid for pages allocated to other allocation units. If the allocation unit isn't a heap, *ROW_OVERFLOW_DATA* or *LOB_DATA,* this field is *NULL.* One of: 0, 50, 80, 95, 100.

Column name	Description
page_type	The page type of the page in the index or heap. This value is non-NULL only when *DETAILED* mode is used. One of: 1, 2, 3, 4, 10.
page_type_desc	The type of page in the table. This value is non-NULL only when *DETAILED* mode is used. One of: DATA_PAGE (1), INDEX_PAGE (2), TEXT_MIX_PAGE (3), TEXT_TREE_PAGE (4), IAM_PAGE (10).
page_level	The level of the index in which this page resides. Is non-NULL only when *DETAILED* mode is used, and when the page exists in an index.
next_page_file_id	The file ID of the next page pointed to by the current allocated page. The value is non-NULL only when *DETAILED* mode is used.
next_page_page_id	The page ID of the next page pointed to by the current allocated page. The value is non-NULL only when *DETAILED* mode is used.
previous_page_file_id	The file ID of the previous page pointed to by the current allocated page. The value is non-NULL only when *DETAILED* mode is used.
previous_page_page_id	The page ID of the previous page pointed to by the current allocated page. The value is non-NULL only when *DETAILED* mode is used.
is_page_compressed	Indicates whether the page in question is page-compressed. The value is non-NULL only when *DETAILED* mode is used.
has_ghost_records	Indicates whether the page contains any deleted rows that still remain on the page as ghost records. The value is non-NULL only when *DETAILED* mode is used.

The function returns a row for every page used or allocated for whatever databases, objects, indexes, and partitions are specified.

Chapter 6 describes some return values because they are equally relevant to heaps. When dealing with indexes, you also can look at the *index_id* column, which is 0 for a heap, 1 for pages of a clustered index, and a number between 2 and 1,005 for the pages of a nonclustered index. In SQL Server 2012, a table can have up to 1,000 total indexes (one clustered and 999 nonclustered). Although 1,005 is higher than would be expected—2–1,000 would be sufficient for 999 nonclustered indexes—the range of nonclustered index IDs skips 251–255 because 255 had special meaning in earlier releases (it was used for the LOB values in a table) and 251–254 were unused. To simplify any backward-compatibility issues, this range (251–255) still isn't used.

The *page_level* value allows you to see at what level of the index tree a page is located, with a value of 0 meaning the leaf level. The highest value for any particular index is, therefore, the root page of that index, and you should be able to verify that the root page is the same value you get from the *sys.system_internals_allocation_units* view in the *root_page* column. Four columns indicate the page linkage at each level of each index (in *DETAILED* mode only). Each page has a file ID and page ID for the next page and a file ID and page ID for the previous page. Of course, for the root pages, all these values are 0. You can also determine the first page by finding a page with zeros for the previous page, and you can find the last page because it has zeros for the next page. Because the output of the *sys.dm_db_database_page_allocations* function is too wide to display on a book page, and because it's likely that you want to reorder the result set or limit the columns returned, the output isn't reproduced here. I will use this function in many examples in this chapter, with a filtered set of rows and/or columns.

Understanding B-tree index structures

As discussed earlier in this chapter, B-tree index structures are divided into two basic components of the index: the leaf level and the non-leaf level(s). The details in this section can help you better understand what's specifically stored within these portions of your indexes and how they vary based on index type.

Clustering key dependency

The leaf level of a clustered index contains the data, not just the index keys. So the answer to the question, "What else is in the leaf level of a clustered index besides the key value?" is "Everything else"—that is, all the columns of every row in the table are in the leaf level of a clustered index. Another way to say this is that when a clustered index is created, the data becomes the leaf level of the clustered index. At the time a clustered index is created, data in the table is moved to new pages and ordered by the clustering key. When created, a clustered index is maintained logically rather than physically. This order is maintained through a doubly linked list called a *page chain*. The order of pages in the page chain, and the order of rows on the data pages, is based on the definition of the clustered index. Deciding on which column(s) to cluster is an important performance consideration. Note that although heap pages do have pointers to next and previous pages, the ordering is arbitrary and doesn't represent any ordering in the table itself.

Because the actual page chain for the data pages can be ordered in only one way, a table can have only one clustered index. In general, most tables perform better when the table is clustered. However, the clustering key needs to be chosen carefully. Also, to choose an appropriate clustering key, you must understand how the clustered index works, as well as the internal dependencies on the clustering key (especially as far as the nonclustered indexes are concerned).

The dependencies of the nonclustered indexes on the clustering key have been in SQL Server since the storage engine was redesigned in SQL Server 7.0. It all starts with how rows are identified (and looked up) when using a nonclustered index to reference a corresponding row within the table. If a table has a clustered index, rows are identified (and looked up by) their clustering key. If the table doesn't have a clustered index, rows are identified (and looked up by) their physical row identifier (RID), described in more detail later in this chapter. This process of looking up corresponding data rows in the base table is known as a *bookmark lookup*, which is named after the analogy that nonclustered indexes reference a place within a book, as a bookmark does.

Nonclustered indexes contain only the data as defined by the index. When looking up a row within a nonclustered index, you often need to go to the actual data row for additional data that's not part of the nonclustered index definition. To retrieve this additional data, you must look into the table for that data. This section focuses only on how the bookmark lookup is performed when a table is clustered.

First, all clustered indexes must be unique so that nonclustered index entries can point to exactly one specific row. Consider the problem that would occur if a table were clustered by a nonunique value of last name. If a nonclustered index existed on a unique value, such as social security number, and a query looked into the index for a specific social security number of 123-45-6789 and found that its clustering key was 'Smith,' then if multiple rows with a last name of Smith existed, the question would be—which one? How would the specific row with a Social Security number of 123-45-6789 be located efficiently?

For a clustering key to be used effectively, all nonclustered index entries must refer to exactly one row. Because that pointer is the clustering key in SQL Server, the clustering key must be unique. If you build a clustered index without specifying the *UNIQUE* keyword, SQL Server guarantees uniqueness internally by adding a hidden uniquifier column to the rows when necessary.

 Note In *SQL Server Books Online*, the word *uniquifier* is written as *uniqueifier*; however, the internal tools—such as *DBCC PAGE*—spell it as it's spelled here.

This uniquifier is a 4-byte integer value added to the data row when the row's clustering key isn't unique. After it's added, it becomes part of the clustering key, meaning that it's duplicated in every nonclustered index. You can see whether a specific row has this extra value when you review the actual structure of index rows, as you will see later in this chapter.

Second, if a clustering key is used to look up the corresponding data rows from a nonclustered index into the clustered index (the data), the clustering key is the most overly duplicated data in a table; all the columns that make up the clustering key are included in every nonclustered index, in addition to being in the actual data row. As a result, the width of the clustering key is important. Consider a clustered index with a 64-byte clustering key on a table with 12 nonclustered indexes and 1 million rows. Without counting internal and structural overhead, the overhead required just to store the clustering key (to support the lookup) in every nonclustered index is 732 MB, compared with only 92 MB if the clustering key were only 8 bytes and only 46 MB if the clustering key were only 4 bytes. Although this is just a rough estimate, it shows that you waste a lot of space (and potentially buffer pool memory) if you have an overly wide clustering key. However, it's not just about space alone; this also translates into performance and efficiency of your nonclustered indexes. And, in general, you don't want your nonclustered indexes to be unnecessarily wide.

Third, because the clustering key is the most redundant data within your entire table, you should be sure to choose a non-volatile clustering key. If a clustering key changes, it can have multiple negative effects.

- It can cause record relocation within the clustered index, which can cause page splits and fragmentation (discussed in more detail later in this chapter).

- It causes every nonclustered index to be modified so that the value of the clustering key is correct for the relevant nonclustered index rows. This wastes time and space, causes fragmentation which then requires maintenance, and adds unnecessary overhead to every modification of the column(s) that make up the clustering key.

Three attributes—unique, narrow, and static—also (but not always) apply to a well-chosen primary key, and because you can have only one primary key (and only one clustering key), SQL Server uses a unique clustered index to enforce a primary key constraint when no index type is defined in the primary key definition. However, this isn't always known by the table's creator. Also, if the primary key doesn't adhere to these criteria—for example, when the primary key is chosen from the data's natural key, which, for example, is a wide, 100-byte combination of seven columns that's unique only when combined—using a clustered index to enforce uniqueness and duplicating the entire 100-byte combination of columns in every nonclustered index can have very negative side effects. So, for some unsuspecting database developers, a very wide clustering key might have been created for them because of these defaults. The good news is that you can define the primary key to be nonclustered and easily create a clustered index on a different column (or set of columns); however, you have to know when—and how—to do this.

Finally, a table's clustering key should also be chosen so as to minimize fragmentation for inserts (fragmentation is discussed in more detail later in this chapter) if you plan to perform many random inserts into the table. Although only the logical order of a clustered index is maintained after it's created, this maintenance causes overhead. If rows consistently need to enter the table at random entry points—for example, inserts into a table ordered by last name—that table's logical order is slightly more expensive to maintain than a table that's always adding rows to the end of the table—for example, inserts into a table ordered by order number, which is (or should be) an ever-increasing identity column.

More details of the internals of indexes are reviewed later in the chapter, but to summarize the discussion thus far, the clustering key should be chosen not only based on table usage—and, it's really hard to say "always" or "never" with regard to the clustering key—but also on the internal dependencies that SQL Server has on the clustering key. The following are examples of good clustering keys.

- A single column key defined with an ever-increasing identity column (for example, a 4-byte *int* or an 8-byte *bigint*).

- A composite key defined with an ever-increasing date column (first), followed by a second column that uniquely identifies the rows—like an identity column. This can be very useful for date-based partitioned tables and tables where the data is inserted in increasing date-based order as it offers an additional benefit for range queries on date. Examples of this include a 12-byte composite key composed of *SalesDate* (8 bytes) and *SalesNumber* (4-byte *int*) or, a date column that doesn't include time.

- A GUID column can be used successfully as a clustering key because it's clearly unique, relatively narrow (16 bytes wide), and likely to be static. However, as a clustering key, a GUID is appropriate only when it follows an ever-increasing pattern. Some GUIDs—depending on how they're generated—might cause a tremendous amount of fragmentation. If the GUID is generated outside SQL Server (like in a client application) or generated inside SQL Server using the *NEWID()* function, fragmentation reduces the effectiveness of this column as a clustering key. If possible, consider using the *NEWSEQUENTIALID()* function instead (for ever-increasing GUIDs) or choosing a different clustering key. If you still want to use a GUID as a primary key and it's not ever-increasing, you can make it a nonclustered index instead of a clustered index.

In summary, choosing a clustering key involves no absolutes; only general best practices work well for most tables. However, if a table has only one index—and no nonclustered indexes—the nonclustered index dependencies on the clustering key are no longer relevant. However, most tables will likely have at least a few nonclustered indexes, and most tables perform better with a clustered index. As a result, a clustered index with a well-chosen clustering key is always the first step to better performance. The second step is "finding the right balance" in your nonclustered indexes by choosing appropriate—and usually a relatively minimal number of—nonclustered indexes.

Nonclustered B-tree indexes

As shown earlier, all indexes have two primary components: the leaf level and the non-leaf level(s). For a clustered index, the leaf level *is* the data. For a nonclustered index, the leaf level is a separate and additional structure that has a copy of some of the data. Specifically, a nonclustered index depends on its definition to form the leaf level. The leaf level of a nonclustered index consists of the index key (according to the definition of the index), any included columns (using the *INCLUDE* feature added in SQL Server 2005), and the data row's bookmark value (either the clustering key if the table is clustered or the physical RID if the table is a heap). A nonclustered index has exactly the same number of rows as rows in the table, unless a filter predicate is used when the index is defined. Filtered indexes were added in SQL Server 2008 and are discussed in more detail later in this chapter.

The nonclustered index can be used in two ways: to help point to the data (similar to an index in the back of a book, by using bookmark lookups, as discussed earlier) or to answer a query directly. When a nonclustered index has all the data as requested by the query, this is known as *query cover-ing*, and the index is called a *covering index*. When a nonclustered index covers a query, the nonclustered index can be used to answer a query directly and a bookmark lookup (which can be expensive for a nonselective query) can be avoided. This can be one of the most effective ways to improve range query performance.

The bookmark lookup of a row occurs when a nonclustered index doesn't have all the data required by the query, but the query is driven by a predicate that the index can help to find. If a table has a clustered index, the nonclustered index is used to drive the query to find the corresponding data row by using the clustering key. If the table is a heap—in other words, it has no clustered index—the lookup value is an 8-byte RID, which is an actual row locator in the form *FileID:PageID:SlotNumber*. This 8-byte row identifier breaks down into 2 bytes for the *FileID*, 4 bytes for the *PageID*, and 2 bytes for the *SlotNumber*. You will see exactly how these lookup values are used when you review data access later in this chapter.

The presence or absence of a nonclustered index doesn't affect how the data pages are organized, so you're not restricted to having only one nonclustered index per table, as is the case with clustered indexes. In SQL Server 2012, each table can include as many as 999 nonclustered indexes, but you'll usually want to have far fewer than that.

In summary, nonclustered indexes don't affect the base table; however, the base table's structure—either a heap or a table with a clustered index—affects the structure of your nonclustered indexes.

This is something to consider and understand if you want to minimize wasted overhead and achieve the best performance.

Constraints and indexes

As mentioned earlier, an unsuspecting database developer might have created a clustered index unintentionally by having defined a PRIMARY KEY constraint in his table. The idea for using constraints comes from relational theory, in which a table has entity identifiers defined (to understand table relationships and help join tables in a normalized schema). When constraints are defined on a table in SQL Server, both PRIMARY KEY and UNIQUE KEY constraints can enforce certain aspects of entity integrity within the database.

For a PRIMARY KEY constraint, SQL Server enforces

- that all the columns involved in the PRIMARY KEY don't allow NULL values

- that the PRIMARY KEY value is unique within the table

If any of the columns allow NULL values, the PRIMARY KEY constraint can't be created. To enforce uniqueness, SQL Server creates a UNIQUE index on the columns that make up the PRIMARY KEY constraint. The default index type, if not specified, is a unique clustered index.

For a UNIQUE constraint, SQL Server allows the columns that make up the constraint to allow NULLs, but it doesn't allow all key columns to be NULL for more than one row. To enforce uniqueness for the constraint, SQL Server creates a unique index on the columns that make up the constraint. The default index type, if not specified, is a unique nonclustered index.

When you declare a PRIMARY KEY or UNIQUE constraint, the underlying index structure that's created is the same as though you had used the *CREATE INDEX* command directly. However, usage and features have some differences. For example, a constraint-based index can't have other features added (such as included columns or filters, which are discussed later in this chapter), but a UNIQUE index can have these features while still enforcing uniqueness over the key definition of the index. Also, when referencing a UNIQUE index—which doesn't support a constraint—through a FOREIGN KEY constraint, you can't reference indexes with filters. However, an index that doesn't use filters or an index that uses included columns can be referenced. These powerful options can minimize the total number of indexes and yet still create a reference with a FOREIGN KEY constraint.

The names of the indexes built to support these constraints are the same as the constraint names. Concerning internal storage and how these indexes work, unique indexes created using the *CREATE INDEX* command are no different from indexes created to support constraints. The Query Optimizer makes decisions based on the presence of the unique index rather than on whether the column was declared as a constraint. In other words, *how* the index was created is irrelevant to the Query Optimizer.

Index creation options

For creating B-tree indexes, the *CREATE INDEX* command is relatively straightforward:

```
CREATE [ UNIQUE ] [ CLUSTERED | NONCLUSTERED ] INDEX index_name
  ON <object> ( column [ ASC | DESC ] [ ,...n ] )
    [ INCLUDE ( column_name [ ,...n ] ) ]
    [ WHERE <filter_predicate> ]
```

The required parts of an index are the index name, the key definition, and the table on which this index is defined. An index can have non-key columns included in the leaf level of the index, using *INCLUDE*. An index can be defined over the entire rowset of the table—which is the default—or, they can be limited to only the rows as defined by a filter, using WHERE <filter_predicate>. (SQL Server 2008 introduced the ability to filter indexes.) Both of these are discussed as the physical structures of nonclustered indexes are analyzed.

However, *CREATE INDEX* provides some additional options for specialized purposes. You can add a WITH clause to the *CREATE INDEX* command:

```
[WITH
([FILLFACTOR = fillfactor]
[[,] [PAD_INDEX] = { ON | OFF }]
[[,] DROP_EXISTING = { ON | OFF }]
[[,] IGNORE_DUP_KEY = { ON | OFF }]
[[,] SORT_IN_TEMPDB = { ON | OFF }]
[[,] STATISTICS_NORECOMPUTE  = { ON | OFF }]
[[,] ALLOW_ROW_LOCKS = { ON | OFF }]
[[,] ALLOW_PAGE_LOCKS = { ON | OFF }]
[[,] MAXDOP = max_degree_of_parallelism]
[[,] ONLINE = { ON | OFF }]
[[,]DATA_COMPRESSION = { NONE | ROW | PAGE}
    [ ON PARTITIONS ( { <partition_number_expression> | <range> }
    [ , ...n ] ) ]
```

The *FILLFACTOR*, *PAD_INDEX*, *DROP_EXISTING*, *SORT_IN_TEMPDB*, and *ONLINE* index creation options are predominantly defined and used for index maintenance. To use them appropriately, you must better understand the physical structures of indexes as well as how data modifications work. Later in this chapter, the section "Managing index structures" covers these options in detail. Chapter 8, "Special storage," covers the *DATA_COMPRESSION* option—and compression in general. The remaining options are described here.

IGNORE_DUP_KEY

You can ensure the uniqueness of an index key by defining it as UNIQUE or by defining a PRIMARY KEY or UNIQUE constraint. If an *UPDATE* or *INSERT* statement would affect multiple rows, or if even one row is found that would cause duplicates of keys defined as unique, the entire statement is aborted and no rows are affected. Alternatively, when you create a UNIQUE index, you can use the *IGNORE_DUP_KEY* option so that a duplicate key error on a multiple-row *INSERT* won't cause the entire statement to be rolled back. The nonunique row is discarded, and all other rows are inserted.

IGNORE_DUP_KEY doesn't allow the uniqueness of the index to be violated; instead, it makes a violation in a multiple-row data modification nonfatal to all the nonviolating rows.

STATISTICS_NORECOMPUTE

The *STATISTICS_NORECOMPUTE* option determines whether the statistics on the index should be updated automatically. Every index maintains a histogram representing the distribution of values for the leading column of the index. Among other things, the Query Optimizer uses these statistics to determine the usefulness of a particular index when choosing a query plan. As data is modified, the statistics become increasingly out of date, and this can lead to less-than-optimal query plans if the statistics aren't updated. Chapter 3, "Databases and database files," and Chapter 12, "Plan caching and recompilation," discuss in more detail the database option *AUTO_UPDATE_STATISTICS*, which enables all statistics in a database to be updated automatically when needed.

In general, the database option should be enabled. However, you can use the *STATISTICS_ NORECOMPUTE* option to set a specific statistic or index to not update automatically. Adding this clause overrides an *ON* value for the *AUTO_UPDATE_STATISTICS* database option. If the database option is set to *OFF*, you can't override that behavior for a particular index, and in that case, all statistics in the database must be updated manually using *UPDATE STATISTICS* or *sp_updatestats*. To see if the statistics for a given table are set to update automatically, as well as the last time they were updated, use *sp_autostats <table_name>*.

MAXDOP

The *MAXDOP* option controls the maximum number of processors that can be used for index creation. It can override the server configuration option *max degree of parallelism* for index building.

Allowing multiple processors to be used for index creation can greatly enhance the performance of index build operations. Like it does with other parallel operations, the Query Optimizer determines at runtime the actual number of processors to use, based on the system's current load. The *MAXDOP* value sets only a maximum. Multiple processors can be used for index creation only when you run SQL Server Enterprise or SQL Server Developer editions. Also, when used, each processor builds an equal-sized chunk of the index in parallel. When this occurs, the tree might not be perfectly balanced, and the math used to determine the theoretical minimum number of required pages varies from the actual number, because each parallel thread builds a separate tree. After each thread is completed, the trees are essentially concatenated. SQL Server can use any extra page space that's reserved during this parallel process for later modifications.

Index placement

A final clause in the *CREATE INDEX* command allows you to specify the placement of the index:

```
[ ON { partition_scheme_name ( column_name )
      | filegroup_name } ]
```

You can specify that an index should be either placed on a particular filegroup or partitioned according to a predefined partition scheme. By default, if no filegroup or partition scheme is specified, the index is placed on the same filegroup as the base table. Chapter 3 discusses filegroups; Chapter 8 discusses table and index partitioning.

Physical index structures for B-trees

Index pages for B-tree indexes have almost the same structure as data pages, except they store index rows instead of data rows. Like with all other types of pages in SQL Server, index pages use a fixed size of 8 KB, or 8,192 bytes. Index pages also have a 96-byte header, and an offset array at the end of the page has 2 bytes for each row to indicate the offset of that row on the page. A nonclustered index can have all three allocation units associated with it: *IN_ROW_DATA*, *ROW_OVERFLOW_DATA*, and *LOB_DATA*, as mentioned in Chapter 6 and discussed in detail in Chapter 8. Each index has a row in the *sys.indexes* catalog view, with an *index_id* value of either 1 (for a clustered index) or a number between 2 and 250 or between 256 and 1005 (indicating a nonclustered index). Remember that SQL Server has reserved values between 251 and 255.

Index row formats

Index rows are structured just like data rows, with two main exceptions.

- An index row can't have *SPARSE* columns. If a *SPARSE* column is used in an index definition (and indexes have some limitations on where a *SPARSE* columns can be used, so as it can't be used in a PRIMARY KEY), the column is created in the index row as though it hadn't been defined as *SPARSE*.

- If a clustered index is created and the index isn't defined as unique, the duplicated key values include a uniquifier.

Index and data rows have a couple other structure differences. An index row doesn't use the *TagB* or *Fsize* row header values. In place of the *Fsize* field, which indicates where the fixed-length portion of a row ends, the page header *pminlen* value is used to decode an index row. The *pminlen* value indicates the offset at which the fixed-length data portion of the row ends. If the index row has no variable-length or nullable columns, that is the end of the row. Only if the index row has nullable columns are the field called *Ncol* and the null bitmap both present. The *Ncol* field contains a value indicating how many columns are in the index row; this value is needed to determine how many bits are in the null bitmap. Data rows have an *Ncol* field and null bitmap whether or not any columns allow NULL, but index rows have only a null bitmap and an *Ncol* field if NULLs are allowed in any of the columns of the index. Table 7-2 shows the meaning of the bytes in an index row.

TABLE 7-2 Information stored in an index row

Information	Mnemonic	Size
Status Bits A	*TagA* Some of the relevant bits are as follows: **Bits 1 through 3** Taken as a 3-bit value. 0 indicates a primary record, 3 an index record, and 5 a ghost index record. (Ghost records are discussed later in this chapter.) **Bit 4** Indicates that a NULL bitmap exists. **Bit 5** Indicates that variable-length columns exist in the row.	1 byte
Fixed-length data	*Fdata*	*pminlen*—1
Number of columns	*Ncol*	2 bytes
NULL bitmap (1 bit for each column in the table; a 1 indicates that the corresponding column is NULL)	*Nullbits*	Ceiling (*Ncol* / 8)
Number of variable-length columns; only present if > 0	*VarCount*	2 bytes
Variable column offset array; only present if *VarCount* > 0	*VarOffset*	2 * *VarCount*
Variable-length data, if any	*VarData*	

The specific column data stored in an index row depends on the type of index and the level in which that index row is located.

Clustered index structures

The leaf level of a clustered index is the data itself. When a clustered index is created, the data is copied and ordered based on the clustering key (as discussed earlier in this chapter). The row structure of a clustered index is no different from the row structure of a heap, except in one case: when the clustering key isn't defined with the *UNIQUE* attribute. In this case, SQL Server must guarantee uniqueness internally, and to do this, each duplicate row requires an additional uniquifier value.

As mentioned earlier, if your clustered index isn't created with the *UNIQUE* property, SQL Server adds a 4-byte integer to make each nonunique key value unique. Because the clustering key is used to identify the base rows being referenced by nonclustered indexes (the bookmark lookup), each row in a clustered index needs to be referenced in a unique way.

SQL Server adds the uniquifier only when necessary—that is, when duplicate keys are added to the table. Suppose that you create a small table with all fixed-length columns and then add a clustered, nonunique index to the table:

```
USE AdventureWorks2012;
GO

CREATE TABLE Clustered_Dupes
    (Col1 CHAR(5)    NOT NULL,
     Col2 INT        NOT NULL,
     Col3 CHAR(3)    NULL,
     Col4 CHAR(6)    NOT NULL);
GO

CREATE CLUSTERED INDEX Cl_dupes_col1 ON Clustered_Dupes(col1);
```

Now look at an interesting piece of information in the metadata. The compatibility view sysindexes includes a *keycnt* column, which doesn't exist in the catalog view sys.indexes. However, an undocumented argument to the indexproperty function called *keycnt80* returns the same information—namely, the number of key columns defined for an index. If you use that function to look at the row in *sys.indexes* view for this table, you should notice something unexpected:

```
SELECT index_id, keycnt = indexproperty(object_id, name, 'keycnt80'), name
FROM sysindexes
WHERE id = OBJECT_ID ('Clustered_Dupes');

RESULT:
index_id  keycnt name
--------  ------ --------------
1         2      Cl_dupes_col1
```

The *keycnt* column has a value of 2. If this index had the *UNIQUE* property, the *keycnt* value would be 1. The *keycnt* value of 2 indicates that the uniquifier column is part of the index key.

Non-leaf level(s) of a clustered index

To navigate to the leaf level of an index, a B-tree is created, which includes the data rows in the leaf level. Each row in the non-leaf levels has one entry for every page of the level below (later, this chapter delves more into what this specifically looks like with each index type), and this entry includes an index key value and a 6-byte pointer to reference the page. In this case, the page pointer is in the format of 2 bytes for the *FileID* and 4 bytes for the *PageNumberInTheFile*. SQL Server doesn't need an 8-byte RID because the slot number doesn't need to be stored. The index key part of the entry always indicates the first value that could be on the pointed-to page. If the index key is defined in ASC (ascending) sequence, the first value is the minimum value; if the index key is defined in DESC (descending) sequence, the first value is the maximum value. Note that they don't necessarily indicate the *actual* first value, just the first *possible* value for the page (as when the row with the lowest or highest key value on a page is deleted, the index row in the level above isn't updated).

Analyzing a clustered index structure

To better understand how the clustered index is stored as well as traversed, you should review specific structures created in a sample database called *IndexInternals.* For this example, you review an *Employee* table created with a clustered index on the PRIMARY KEY.

> **Note** The *IndexInternals* sample database is available for download. A few tables already exist in this database. Review the *EmployeeCaseStudy-TableDefinition.sql* script to see the table definitions, and then move to the *EmployeeCaseStudy-AnalyzeStructures.sql* script to analyze the structures. A backup of this database and a zip file containing the solution can be found in the companion content.

Here is the table definition for the *Employee* table as it already exists within the *IndexInternals* database:

```
CREATE TABLE Employee
    (EmployeeID      INT           NOT NULL      IDENTITY PRIMARY KEY,
    LastName         NCHAR(30)     NOT NULL,
    FirstName        NCHAR(29)     NOT NULL,
    MiddleInitial    NCHAR(1)      NULL,
    SSN              CHAR(11)      NOT NULL,
    OtherColumns     CHAR(258)     NOT NULL      DEFAULT 'Junk');
GO
```

The *Employee* table was created using a few deviations from normal best practices to make the structures somewhat predictable (for example, easier math and easier visualization). First, all columns have fixed widths even if when data values vary. Not all columns should be variable just because the data values vary, but when your column is over 20 characters and your data varies (and isn't overly volatile), it's best to consider variable-width character columns rather than fixed-width columns, to save space and for better *INSERT* performance. (*UPDATE* performance can be compromised, especially when updates make the variable-width column larger.) This is covered in more detail later in the section on fragmentation. In these specific tables, fixed-width columns are used to ensure a predictable row size and to help with better visualizing the data structures.

In this case, and including overhead, the data rows of the *Employee* table are exactly 400 bytes per row (using a filler column called *OtherColumns*, which adds 258 bytes of junk at the end of the data row). A row size of 400 bytes means that you can fit 20 rows per data page: 8,096 bytes per page/400 bytes per row = 20.24, which translates into 20 rows per page because the *IN_ROW* portion of the data row can't span pages. To calculate how large the tables are, you need to know how many rows these tables contain. In the *IndexInternals* database, this table has already been set up with exactly 80,000 rows. At 20 rows per page, this table requires 4,000 data pages to store its 80,000 rows.

To investigate the *Employee* table further, use *sys.dm_db_index_physical_stats* to determine the number of pages within the table, as well as the number of levels within the indexes. You can confirm the index structures using the DMV to see the number of levels as well as the number of pages within each level:

```
SELECT index_depth AS D
    , index_level AS L
    , record_count AS 'Count'
    , page_count AS PgCnt
    , avg_page_space_used_in_percent AS 'PgPercentFull'
    , min_record_size_in_bytes AS 'MinLen'
    , max_record_size_in_bytes AS 'MaxLen'
    , avg_record_size_in_bytes AS 'AvgLen'
FROM sys.dm_db_index_physical_stats
    (DB_ID ('IndexInternals')
    , OBJECT_ID ('IndexInternals.dbo.Employee')
    , 1, NULL, 'DETAILED');
GO
```

```
RESULT:
D   L   Count   PgCnt   PgPercentFull         MinLen  MaxLen  AvgLen
--- --- ------- ------- -------------------   ------- ------- ------
3   0   80000   4000    99.3081294786261      400     400     400
3   1   4000    7       91.7540400296516      11      11      11
3   2   7       1       1.09957993575488      11      11      11
```

The clustered index for this table has a leaf level of 4,000 pages, which is as expected, provided that it has 80,000 rows at 20 rows per page. From the *MinLen* (*min_record_size_in_bytes*) column, you can see the row length in the leaf level is 400 bytes; however, the row length of the non-leaf levels is only 11 bytes. This structure is easily broken down as 4 bytes for the integer column (*EmployeeID*) on which the clustered index is defined, 6 bytes for the page pointer, and 1 byte for row overhead. Only 1 byte is needed for overhead because the index row contains only fixed-width columns, and none of those columns allow NULLs; therefore, you don't need a NULL bitmap in the index pages. You also can see that the first level above the leaf level has 4,000 rows because level 1 has a *Count* (*record_count*) of 4,000. In fact, level 1 has only seven pages, shown as *PgCnt* (*page_count*); in level 2, you can see that *Count* shows as 7. This refers to when this chapter explained that each level up the tree contains a pointer for every page of the level below it. If a level has 4,000 pages, the next level up has 4,000 rows. You can see a more detailed version of this structure in Figure 7-2.

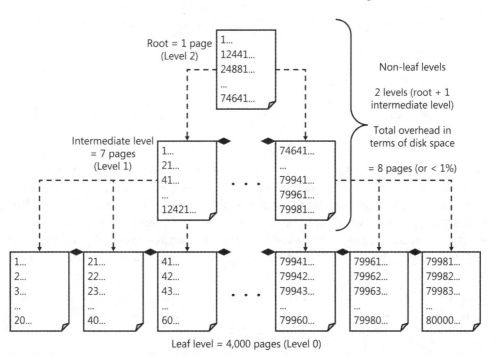

FIGURE 7-2 Page details for multiple index levels.

To understand both traversal as well as linkage further, you can use the *sys.dm_db_database_page_allocations* function to see which pages contain rows from which index level, as well as which pages precede and follow various pages in all levels of the index. Note that the code in Listing 7-2 selects just a subset of the columns and specifies parameters to indicate only pages from the clustered index of the Employee table in the IndexInternals database.

LISTING 7-2 Listing the pages from the IndexInternals.dbo.Employee table

```
SELECT page_level as Level, allocated_page_file_id as PageFID,
       allocated_page_page_id as PagePID,
       previous_page_file_id as PrevPageFID, previous_page_page_id as PrevPagPID,
       next_page_file_id as NextPageFID, next_page_page_id NextPagePID
FROM sys.dm_db_database_page_allocations(db_id('IndexInternals'),
                                object_id('dbo.Employee'), 1, null, 'DETAILED')
ORDER BY page_level DESC, previous_page_page_id;
GO
```

```
RESULT (abbreviated):
Level      PageFID PagePID     PrevPageFID PrevPagePID NextPageFID NextPagePID
---------- ------- ----------- ----------- ----------- ----------- -----------
2          1       234         0           0           0           0
1          1       232         0           0           1           233
1          1       233         1           232         1           235
1          1       235         1           233         1           236
1          1       236         1           235         1           237
1          1       237         1           236         1           238
1          1       238         1           237         1           239
1          1       239         1           238         0           0

0          1       168         0           0           1           169
0          1       169         1           168         1           170
<snip>
0          1       4230        1           4229        1           4231
0          1       4231        1           4230        0           0

NULL       1       157         0           0           0           0
```

Because this table was created when the database was empty and because the clustered index was built after loading the data into a staging area (this is solely a separate location used for temporarily storing data—in this case, a different filegroup), this table's clustered index could use a completely contiguous range of pages within file 1. However, they aren't completely contiguous from the root down because indexes are built from the leaf level up to the root as the rows are ordered for each of the levels. The most important thing to understand, however, is navigation. Consider the following query:

```
SELECT e.*
FROM dbo.Employee AS e
WHERE e.EmployeeID = 27682;
```

To find all the data for a row with an *EmployeeID* of 27682 (remember, this is the clustering key value), SQL Server starts at the root page and navigates down to the leaf level. Based on the output shown previously, the root page is page 234 in *FileID* 1; you can see this because the root page is the only page at the highest index level (*IndexLevel* = 2). To analyze the root page, you need to use *DBCC PAGE* with output style 3—and make sure that the query window in SQL Server Management Studio is set to return grid results. Output style 3 means that the tabular set of a non-leaf page is returned to the grid results, separating the rows from the page header, which is returned to the messages window:

```
DBCC PAGE (IndexInternals, 1, 234, 3);
GO
```

RESULT:

FileId	PageId	Row	Level	ChildFileId	ChildPageId	EmployeeID (key)	KeyHashValue
1	234	0	2	1	232	NULL	NULL
1	234	1	2	1	233	12441	NULL
1	234	2	2	1	235	24881	NULL
1	234	3	2	1	236	37321	NULL
1	234	4	2	1	237	49761	NULL
1	234	5	2	1	238	62201	NULL
1	234	6	2	1	239	74641	NULL

By reviewing the output from *DBCC PAGE* for the root page, you can see the *EmployeeID* values at the start of each "child page" in the *EmployeeID* (key) column. Because these are based on ordered rows in the level below, you need to find only the appropriate range. For the third page, you can see a low value of 24881, and for the fourth page, a low value of 37321. So if the value 27682 exists, it would have to be in the index area defined by this particular range. For navigational purposes, you must navigate down the tree using page (*ChildPageId*) 235 in *FileID* (*ChildFileId*) 1. To see this page's contents, you can again use *DBCC PAGE* with output style 3:

```
DBCC PAGE (IndexInternals, 1, 235, 3);
GO
```

RESULT (abbreviated):

FileId	PageId	Row	Level	ChildFileId	ChildPageId	EmployeeID (key)	KeyHashValue
1	235	0	1	1	1476	24881	NULL
...							
1	235	139	1	1	1615	27661	NULL
1	235	140	1	1	1616	27681	NULL
1	235	141	1	1	1617	27701	NULL
...							
1	235	621	1	1	2097	3730	NULL

Finally, if a row with an *EmployeeID* of 27682 exists, it must be on page 1616 of *FileID* 1. You can see if it is:

```
DBCC TRACEON(3604);
GO
DBCC PAGE (IndexInternals, 1, 1616, 3);
GO
```

Because this page is data page, the output doesn't come back in a tabular format. You see each data row individually, followed by a list of each column value in that row.

```
...
Slot 1 Column 1 Offset 0x4 Length 4 Length (physical) 4
EmployeeID = 27682

Slot 1 Column 2 Offset 0x8 Length 60 Length (physical) 60
LastName = Arbariol

Slot 1 Column 3 Offset 0x44 Length 58 Length (physical) 58
FirstName = Burt

Slot 1 Column 4 Offset 0x7e Length 2 Length (physical) 2
MiddleInitial = R

Slot 1 Column 5 Offset 0x80 Length 11 Length (physical) 11
SSN = 123-45-6789

Slot 1 Column 6 Offset 0x8b Length 258 Length (physical) 258
OtherColumns = Junk
...
```

 Note *DBCC PAGE* returns all the details for the page—that is, the header and all data rows. This condensed output shows only the column values from output style 3 for the *EmployeeID* value of interest (27682). The header and all other rows have been removed.

By having traversed the structure for a row, you have reviewed two things: the index internals and the process by which a single data row can be found using a clustering key value. This method is used when performing a bookmark lookup from a nonclustered index to retrieve the data when the table is clustered. To understand fully how nonclustered indexes are used, you also need to know how a nonclustered index is stored and how it's traversed to get to the data.

Nonclustered index structures

The leaf-level contents of a nonclustered index depend on many factors: the definition of the non-clustered index key, the base table's structure (either a heap or a clustered index), the existence of any nonclustered index features such as included columns or filtered indexes, and whether the nonclus-tered index is defined as unique.

To best understand nonclustered indexes, you should continue looking at the *IndexInternals* data-base. This time, however, you review nonclustered indexes on two tables: the *Employee* table, which is clustered by the PRIMARY KEY constraint on the *EmployeeID* column, and the *EmployeeHeap* table, which doesn't have a clustered index. The *EmployeeHeap* table is a copy of the *Employee* table but uses a nonclustered PRIMARY KEY constraint on the *EmployeeID* column instead of a clustered one. This is the first structure to examine.

Nonclustered index rows on a heap

The *EmployeeHeap* table has exactly the same definition and data as the *Employee* table used in the prior example. Here is the *EmployeeHeap* table definition:

```
CREATE TABLE EmployeeHeap
    (EmployeeID      INT        NOT NULL      IDENTITY PRIMARY KEY NONCLUSTERED,
    LastName        NCHAR(30)  NOT NULL,
    FirstName       NCHAR(29)  NOT NULL,
    MiddleInitial   NCHAR(1)   NULL,
    SSN             CHAR(11)   NOT NULL,
    OtherColumns    CHAR(258)  NOT NULL      DEFAULT 'Junk');
GO
```

As with the *Employee* table, the data rows of *EmployeeHeap* are exactly 400 bytes per row, and with 80,000 rows, this table also requires 4,000 data pages. To see the physical size of the data, you can use the *sys.dm_db_index_physical_stats* function discussed at the beginning of this chapter. To confirm that this table is exactly the same (in data) as the leaf level of the clustered index, use the DMV to see the number of pages, as well as the row length for the index with an *index_id* of 0 (the third parameter to the DMV):

```
SELECT index_depth AS D
    , index_level AS L
    , record_count AS 'Count'
    , page_count AS PgCnt
    , avg_page_space_used_in_percent AS 'PgPercentFull'
    , min_record_size_in_bytes AS 'MinLen'
    , max_record_size_in_bytes AS 'MaxLen'
    , avg_record_size_in_bytes AS 'AvgLen'
FROM sys.dm_db_index_physical_stats
    (DB_ID ('IndexInternals')
    , OBJECT_ID ('IndexInternals.dbo.EmployeeHeap')
    , 0, NULL, 'DETAILED');
GO
```

```
RESULT:
D   L   Count  PgCnt  PgPercentFull       MinLen  MaxLen  AvgLen
--- --- ------ ------ ------------------- ------- ------- ------
1   0   80000  4000   99.3081294786261    400     400     400
```

For the *EmployeeHeap* table, all constraints are created using nonclustered indexes. As mentioned, the PRIMARY KEY is created as a nonclustered index on the *EmployeeID* column and a UNIQUE KEY is defined with a nonclustered index on the *SSN* column.

To determine what's in the leaf level of a nonclustered index built on a heap, first review the structure of the nonclustered index as shown by *sys.dm_db_index_physical_stats*. For nonclustered indexes, you supply the specific index ID for parameter 3. To see the index ID used for each index, you could use a query against *sys.indexes*. Assuming that the index on EmployeeID had an *index_id* value of 2, you could run the query shown in Listing 7-3.

LISTING 7-3 Examining the size of a nonclustered index on a heap

```
SELECT index_depth AS D
    , index_level AS L
    , record_count AS 'Count'
    , page_count AS PgCnt
    , avg_page_space_used_in_percent AS 'PgPercentFull'
    , min_record_size_in_bytes AS 'MinLen'
    , max_record_size_in_bytes AS 'MaxLen'
```

```
            , avg_record_size_in_bytes AS 'AvgLen'
FROM sys.dm_db_index_physical_stats
    (DB_ID ('IndexInternals')
    , OBJECT_ID ('IndexInternals.dbo.EmployeeHeap')
    , 2, NULL, 'DETAILED');
GO


RESULT:
D    L    Count   PgCnt   PgPercentFull        MinLen   MaxLen   AvgLen
---  ---  ------  ------- ------------------   -------  -------  ------
2    0    80000   149     99.477291821102      13       13       13
2    1    149     1       23.9065974796145     11       11       11
```

In the result shown in Listing 7-3, the leaf level of the nonclustered index (level 0) shows a record count of 80,000 (based on 80,000 rows in the table) and a minimum, maximum, and average length of 13 (the fixed-width index rows). This breaks down very clearly and easily: The nonclustered index is defined on the *EmployeeID* column (an integer of 4 bytes); the table is a heap, so the data row's bookmark (the physical RID) is 8 bytes; and because this is a fixed-width row with no columns that allow NULL values, the row overhead is 1 byte (4 + 8 + 1 = 13 bytes). To see the data stored more specifically, you can use use *sys.dm_db_database_page_allocations* to determine relevant page numbers:

```
SELECT page_level as Level, allocated_page_file_id as PageFID,
       allocated_page_page_id as PagePID,
       previous_page_file_id as PrevPageFID, previous_page_page_id as PrevPagPID,
       next_page_file_id as NextPageFID, next_page_page_id NextPagePID
FROM sys.dm_db_database_page_allocations(db_id('IndexInternals'),
                            object_id('dbo.EmployeeHeap'), 2, null, 'DETAILED')
ORDER BY page_level DESC, previous_page_page_id;
GO


RESULT (abbreviated):
Level        PageFID PagePID      PrevPageFID PrevPagePID NextPageFID NextPagePID
----------   ------- -----------  ----------- ----------- ----------- -----------
1            1       8608         0           0           0           0

0            1       8544         0           0           1           8545
0            1       8545         1           8544        1           8546
...
0            1       8755         1           8754        1           8756
0            1       8756         1           8755        0           0

NULL         1       254          0           0           0           0
```

The root page is on page 8608 of *FileID* 1. Leaf-level pages are labeled with a Level of 0, so the first page of the leaf level is on page 8544 of *FileID* 1. To review the data on this page, you can use *DBCC PAGE* with output style 3. (To save space, the output for this leaf-level index page shows only the first 8 rows and the last 3 rows, out of 539 rows.)

```
DBCC PAGE (IndexInternals, 1, 8544, 3);
GO
```

```
RESULT (abbreviated):
FileId PageId    Row     Level   EmployeeID (key) HEAP RID             KeyHashValue
------ --------- ------- ------- ---------------- -------------------- ----------------
1      8544      0       0       1                0xF500000001000000   (010086470766)
1      8544      1       0       2                0xF500000001000100   (020068e8b274)
1      8544      2       0       3                0xF500000001000200   (03000d8f0ecc)
1      8544      3       0       4                0xF500000001000300   (0400b4b7d951)
1      8544      4       0       5                0xF500000001000400   (0500d1d065e9)
1      8544      5       0       6                0xF500000001000500   (06003f7fd0fb)
1      8544      6       0       7                0xF500000001000600   (07005a186c43)
1      8544      7       0       8                0xF500000001000700   (08000c080f1b)
...
1      8544      536     0       537              0xD211000001001000   (190098ec2ef0)
1      8544      537     0       538              0xD211000001001100   (1a0076439be2)
1      8544      538     0       539              0xD211000001001200   (1b001324275a)
```

From the output of *DBCC PAGE*, you can see that the leaf-level page of a nonclustered index on a heap has the index key column value (in this case, the *EmployeeID*), plus the actual data row's RID. The final value displayed is called *KeyHashValue*, which isn't actually stored in the index row. (The values you get back for the *KeyHashValue* might be slightly different than the ones shown.) It's a fixed-length string derived using a hash formula on all key columns. This value is used to represent the row in certain other tools. One such tool discussed in Chapter 13 is the *sys.dm_tran_locks* DMV that shows the locks being held. When a lock is held on an index row, the list of locks displays *KeyHashValue* to indicate which key (or index row) is locked.

The following function converts the RID to the *FileID:PageID:SlotNumber* format:

```
CREATE FUNCTION convert_RIDs (@rid BINARY(8))
    RETURNS VARCHAR(30)
AS
    BEGIN
    RETURN (
        CONVERT (VARCHAR(5),
            CONVERT(INT, SUBSTRING(@rid, 6, 1)
            + SUBSTRING(@rid, 5, 1)) )
        + ':' +
        CONVERT(VARCHAR(10),
            CONVERT(INT, SUBSTRING(@rid, 4, 1)
            + SUBSTRING(@rid, 3, 1)
            + SUBSTRING(@rid, 2, 1)
            + SUBSTRING(@rid, 1, 1)) )
        + ':' +
        CONVERT(VARCHAR(5),
            CONVERT(INT, SUBSTRING(@rid, 8, 1)
            + SUBSTRING(@rid, 7, 1)) ) )
    END;
GO
```

With this function, you can find out the specific page number on which a row resides. For example, a row with an *EmployeeID* of 6 has a hexadecimal RID of 0xF500000001000500:

```
SELECT dbo.convert_RIDs (0xF500000001000500);
GO

RESULT:
1:245:5
```

This function converts the page number to 1:245:5, which is composed of *FileID* 1, *PageID* 245, and *SlotNumber* 5. To view this specific page, you can use *DBCC PAGE* and then review the data on slot 5 (to see if this is, in fact, the row with *EmployeeID* of 6):

```
DBCC PAGE (IndexInternals, 1, 245, 3);
GO

Slot 5 Column 1 Offset 0x4 Length 4 Length (physical) 4
EmployeeID = 6

Slot 5 Column 2 Offset 0x8 Length 60 Length (physical) 60
LastName = Anderson

Slot 5 Column 3 Offset 0x44 Length 58 Length (physical) 58
FirstName = Dreaxjktgvnhye

Slot 5 Column 4 Offset 0x7e Length 2 Length (physical) 2
MiddleInitial =

Slot 5 Column 5 Offset 0x80 Length 11 Length (physical) 11
SSN = 123-45-6789

Slot 5 Column 6 Offset 0x8b Length 258 Length (physical) 258
OtherColumns = Junk
...
```

In this case, you've seen the structure of a nonclustered index row in the leaf level of the non-clustered index, as well as how a bookmark lookup is performed using the heap's RID from the nonclustered index to the heap.

For navigation, consider the following query:

```
SELECT e.*
FROM dbo.EmployeeHeap AS e
WHERE e.EmployeeID = 27682;
```

Because this table is a heap, only nonclustered indexes can be used to navigate this data efficiently. In this case, *EmployeeID* also has a nonclustered index. The first step is to go to the root page (as shown in the *DBCC IND* output earlier, the root page is page 8608 of *FileID* 1):

```
DBCC PAGE (IndexInternals, 1, 8608, 3);
GO

RESULT:
FileId  PageId  Row     Level ChildFileId ChildPageId EmployeeID (key)  KeyHashValue
------- ------  ------- ----- ----------- ----------- ----------------- ------------
1       8608    0       1     1           8544        NULL              NULL
1       8608    1       1     1           8545        540               NULL
```

...

1	8608	49	1	1	8593	26412	NULL
1	8608	50	1	1	8594	26951	NULL
1	8608	51	1	1	8595	27490	NULL
1	8608	52	1	1	8596	28029	NULL
1	8608	53	1	1	8597	28568	NULL
1	8608	54	1	1	8598	29107	NULL
...							
1	8608	147	1	1	8755	79234	NULL
1	8608	148	1	1	8756	79773	NULL

The *EmployeeID* column in this output shows a low value of 27490 for the child page 8595 in *FileID* 1; also, the next page has a low value of 28029. So if an *EmployeeID* of 27682 exists, it would have to be in the index area defined by this particular range. Next, you must navigate down the tree using page (*ChildPageId*) 8595 in *FileID* (*ChildFileId*) 1. To see this page's contents, you can again use *DBCC PAGE* with output style 3:

```
DBCC PAGE (IndexInternals, 1, 8595, 3);
GO
```

```
RESULT:
```

FileId	PageId	Row	Level	EmployeeID (key)	HEAP RID	KeyHashValue
1	8595	0	0	27490	0x1617000001000900	(6200aa3b160b)
1	8595	1	0	27491	0x1617000001000A00	(6300cf5caab3)
...						
1	8595	191	0	27681	0x2017000001000000	(2100fcdaf887)
1	8595	192	0	27682	0x2017000001000100	(220012754d95)
1	8595	193	0	27683	0x2017000001000200	(23007712f12d)
...						
1	8595	538	0	28028	0x3117000001000700	(7c00b4675dbf)

Note The output returns 539 rows. This condensed output shows the first two rows, the last row, and then three rows surrounding the value of interest (27682).

From this point, you know how the navigation continues. SQL Server translates the data row's RID into the format of *FileID:PageID:SlotNumber* and proceeds to look up the corresponding data row in the heap.

Nonclustered index rows on a clustered table

For nonclustered indexes on a table with a clustered index, the leaf-level row structure is similar to that of a nonclustered index on a heap. The leaf level of the nonclustered index contains the index key and the bookmark lookup value (the clustering key). However, if the nonclustered index key has some columns in common with the clustering key, SQL Server stores the common columns only once in the nonclustered index row. For example, if the key of your clustered index is *EmployeeID* and you have a nonclustered index on (*Lastname, EmployeeID, SSN*), the index rows don't store the value of *EmployeeID* twice. In fact, the number of columns and the column order don't matter. For this example (as it's not generally a good practice to have a wide clustering key), imagine a clustering key defined on columns *b*, *e*, and *h*. The following nonclustered indexes would have these column(s) added to make up the nonclustered index leaf-level rows (the columns—if any—that are added to the leaf level of the nonclustered index are italicized and boldfaced):

Nonclustered index key	Nonclustered leaf-level row
A	a, *b*, *e*, *h*
c, h, e	c, h, e, *b*
E	e, *b*, *h*
H	h, *e*, *b*
b, c, d	b, c, d, *e*, *h*

To review the physical structures of a nonclustered index created on a clustered table, look at the UNIQUE constraint on the *SSN* column of the *Employee* table:

```
-- Add the NONCLUSTERED UNIQUE KEY on SSN for Employee
ALTER TABLE Employee
    ADD CONSTRAINT EmployeeSSNUK
        UNIQUE NONCLUSTERED (SSN);
GO
```

To gather information on the data size and number of levels, use the *sys.dm_db_index_physical_stats* DMV. However, before you can use the DMV, you need the specific index ID that you could get by querying *sys.indexes*:

```
SELECT name AS IndexName, index_id
FROM sys.indexes
WHERE [object_id] = OBJECT_ID ('Employee');
GO


RESULT:
IndexName          index_id
---------------- --------
EmployeePK         1
EmployeeSSNUK      2
```

Now use that value to look at the information about the index levels:

```
SELECT index_depth AS D
    , index_level AS L
    , record_count AS 'Count'
    , page_count AS PgCnt
    , avg_page_space_used_in_percent AS 'PgPercentFull'
    , min_record_size_in_bytes AS 'MinLen'
    , max_record_size_in_bytes AS 'MaxLen'
    , avg_record_size_in_bytes AS 'AvgLen'
FROM sys.dm_db_index_physical_stats
    (DB_ID ('IndexInternals')
    , OBJECT_ID ('IndexInternals.dbo.Employee')
    , 2, NULL, 'DETAILED');
GO
```

```
RESULT:
D   L        Count    PgCnt    PgPercentFull     MinLen   MaxLen   AvgLen
--  -------  -------  -------  ----------------  -------  -------  ------
2   0        80000    179      99.3661106992834  16       16       16
2   1        179      1        44.2055843834939  18       18       18
```

In this case, the leaf level of the nonclustered index (level 0) shows a record count of 80,000 (the table has 80,000 rows) and a minimum, maximum, and average length of 16 (the fixed-width index rows). This breaks down very clearly and easily; the nonclustered index is defined on the *SSN* column (a fixed-width character column of 11 bytes); the table has a clustering key of *EmployeeID* so the data row's bookmark (the clustering key) is 4 bytes; and because this row is a fixed-width row with no columns that allow NULL values, the row overhead is 1 byte (11 + 4 + 1 = 16 bytes). To see the data stored more specifically, you can use *sys.dm_db_database_page_allocations* to review the leaf-level pages of this index:

```
SELECT page_level as Level, allocated_page_file_id as PageFID,
       allocated_page_page_id as PagePID,
       previous_page_file_id as PrevPageFID, previous_page_page_id as PrevPagPID,
       next_page_file_id as NextPageFID, next_page_page_id NextPagePID
FROM sys.dm_db_database_page_allocations(db_id('IndexInternals'),
                                object_id('dbo.Employee'), 2, null, 'DETAILED')
ORDER BY page_level DESC, previous_page_page_id;
GO
```

```
RESULT (abbreviated):
Level       PageFID  PagePID     PrevPageFID PrevPagePID NextPageFID NextPagePID
----------  -------  ----------  ----------- ----------- ----------- -----------
1           1        4328        0           0           0           0

0           1        4264        0           0           1           4265
0           1        4265        1           4264        1           4266
...
0           1        4505        1           4504        1           4506
0           1        4506        1           4505        0           0

NULL        1        158         0           0           0           0
```

The root page is on page 4328 of *FileID* 1. Leaf-level pages are labeled with an *Level* of 0, so the first page of the leaf level is on page 4264 of *FileID* 1. To review the data on this page, you can use *DBCC PAGE* with format 3:

```
DBCC PAGE (IndexInternals, 1, 4264, 3);
GO
```

```
RESULT (abbreviated):
FileId PageId      Row    Level  SSN (key)    EmployeeID  KeyHashValue
------ ----------- ------ ------ -----------  ----------- ----------------
1      4264        0      0      000-00-000A  31101       (fd00604642ee)
1      4264        1      0      000-00-000B  22669       (fb00de40fee1)
1      4264        2      0      000-00-000C  18705       (0101d993da83)
...
1      4264        446    0      013-00-000L  44969       (ff00355b1727)
1      4264        447    0      013-00-000M  7176        (03012415a3e8)
1      4264        448    0      013-00-000N  11932       (f100f75a17a4)
```

From the output of *DBCC PAGE*, you can see that the leaf-level page of a nonclustered index on a clustered table has actual column values for both the index key (in this case, the *SSN* column) and the data row's bookmark, which in this case is the *EmployeeID*. This is an actual value, copied into the leaf level of the nonclustered index. Had the clustering key been wider, the leaf level of the nonclustered index also would have been wider.

For navigation, review the following query:

```
SELECT e.*
FROM dbo.Employee AS e
WHERE e.SSN = '123-45-6789';
```

To find all the data for a row with a *SSN* of 123-45-6789, SQL Server starts at the root page and navigates down to the leaf level. Based on the output shown earlier, the root page is in page 4328 of *FileID* 1 (you can see this because the root page is the only page at the highest index level (*IndexLevel* = 1). You could perform the same analysis as before and follow the navigation through the B-tree, but that part is left as an optional exercise for you.

Nonunique nonclustered index rows

You now know that the leaf level of a nonclustered index must have a bookmark because from the leaf level, you want to be able to find the actual data row. The non-leaf levels of a nonclustered index need only help you traverse down to pages at the lower levels. For a unique nonclustered index (such as in the previous examples of PRIMARY KEY and UNIQUE constraint indexes), the non-leaf level rows contain only the nonclustered index key values and the child-page pointer. However, if the index is *not* unique, the non-leaf level rows contain the nonclustered index key values, the child-page pointer, and the bookmark value. In other words, the bookmark value is added to the nonclustered index key in a nonunique, nonclustered index to guarantee uniqueness (as the bookmark, by definition, must be unique).

Keep in the mind that for the purposes of creating the index rows, SQL Server doesn't care whether the keys in the nonunique index actually contain duplicates. If the index isn't defined to be unique, even if all the values are unique, the non-leaf index rows always contain the bookmark.

You can easily see this by creating the three indexes in Listing 7-4 to review both their leaf and non–leaf level row sizes.

LISTING 7-4 Comparing the size of the leaf-level rows of three indexes

```
CREATE NONCLUSTERED INDEX TestTreeStructure
ON Employee (SSN);
GO

CREATE UNIQUE NONCLUSTERED INDEX TestTreeStructureUnique1
ON Employee (SSN);
GO

CREATE UNIQUE NONCLUSTERED INDEX TestTreeStructureUnique2
ON Employee (SSN, EmployeeID);
GO
```

```
SELECT si.[name] AS iname
    , index_depth AS D
    , index_level AS L
    , record_count AS 'Count'
    , page_count AS PgCnt
    , avg_page_space_used_in_percent AS 'PgPercentFull'
    , min_record_size_in_bytes AS 'MinLen'
    , max_record_size_in_bytes AS 'MaxLen'
    , avg_record_size_in_bytes AS 'AvgLen'
FROM sys.dm_db_index_physical_stats
    (DB_ID ('IndexInternals')
    , OBJECT_ID ('IndexInternals.dbo.Employee')
    , NULL, NULL, 'DETAILED') ps
    INNER JOIN sys.indexes si
        ON ps.[object_id] = si.[object_id]
            AND ps.[index_id] = si.[index_id]
WHERE ps.[index_id] > 2;
GO
```

```
RESULT:
iname                      D L Count PgCnt PgPercentFull     MinLen MaxLen AvgLen
------------------------   - - ----- ----- ----------------- ------ ------ ------
TestTreeStructure          2 0 80000 179   99.3661106992834  16     16     16
TestTreeStructure          2 1 179   1     53.0516431924883  22     22     22
TestTreeStructureUnique1   2 0 80000 179   99.3661106992834  16     16     16
TestTreeStructureUnique1   2 1 179   1     44.2055843834939  18     18     18
TestTreeStructureUnique2   2 0 80000 179   99.3661106992834  16     16     16
TestTreeStructureUnique2   2 1 179   1     53.0516431924883  22     22     22
```

Notice that the leaf level (level 0) of all three indexes is identical in all columns: *Count* (*record_count*), *PgCnt* (*page_count*), *PgPercentFull* (*avg_space_used_in_percent*), and all three length columns. For the non-leaf level of the indexes (which are very small), you can see that the lengths vary; for the first (*TestTreeStructure*) and the third (*TestTreeStructureUnique2*), the non-leaf levels are identical. The first index has the *EmployeeID* added because it's the clustering key (therefore the bookmark). The third index has *EmployeeID* already in the index—it doesn't need to be added again. However, in the first index, because it wasn't defined as unique, SQL Server had to add the clustering key all the way up the tree. For the second index—which was unique on *SSN* alone—SQL Server didn't include *EmployeeID* all the way up the tree. If you're interested, you can continue to analyze these structures using *sys.dm_db_database_page_allocations* and *DBCC PAGE* to view the physical row structures further.

Nonclustered index rows with included columns (using INCLUDE)

For all nonclustered indexes so far, the focus has been on the physical aspects of indexes created by constraints or indexes created to test physical structures. None of my examples have approached the limits of index key size, which are 900 bytes or 16 columns, whichever comes first. These limits exist to help ensure index tree scalability as well as traditionally curb the maximum number of columns that can be indexed.

In some cases, adding columns in an index allows SQL Server to eliminate the bookmark lookup when accessing data for a range query, a concept called *covering indexes*. A covering index is a nonclustered index in which all the information needed to satisfy a query can be found in the leaf level, so SQL Server doesn't have to access the data pages at all. This can be a powerful tool for optimizing some of your more complex range-based queries.

Rather than add columns to the nonclustered index key and make the tree deeper, you can add columns for a covering index to the index rows without it becoming part of the key by using the *IN-CLUDE* syntax. It's a very simple addition to your *CREATE INDEX* command:

```
CREATE [UNIQUE] [CLUSTERED | NONCLUSTERED] INDEX index_name
  ON table_name (column_name [ASC | DESC][,...n])
    [ INCLUDE ( column_name [ ,...n ] ) ]
```

The columns listed after the keyword *INCLUDE* allow you to exceed the 900-byte or 16-key column limits in the leaf level of a nonclustered index. The included columns appear only in the leaf level and don't affect the sort order of the index rows in any way. In certain situations, SQL Server can silently add an included column to your indexes—for example, when an index is created on a partitioned table and no *ON filegroup* or *ON partition_scheme_name* is specified.

Nonclustered index rows with filters (filtered indexes)

By default, the leaf level of a nonclustered index contains one index row for every row of data in the table, in logical order based on the index key definition. SQL Server 2008 first included the capability of adding a filter predicate to your nonclustered index definition. This way, SQL Server can create nonclustered index rows only for data that matches your predicate, thus limiting the size of the nonclustered index. This can be extremely useful if you have one of the following situations.

- When a column contains mostly NULL values and where queries retrieve only the rows where the data is NOT NULL. This is especially useful when combined with *SPARSE* columns.

- When a column contains only a limited number of interesting values or you want to enforce uniqueness only for a set of values. For example, what if you wanted to allow NULL values for the *SSN* column of the *Employee* table? Using a constraint, SQL Server allows only a single row to be NULL. However, by using a filtered index, you can create a unique index over only the rows where the *SSN* isn't NULL. The syntax would look like the following:

  ```
  CREATE UNIQUE NONCLUSTERED INDEX SSN_NOT_NULLs
  ON Employee (SSN)
  WHERE SSN IS NOT NULL;
  ```

- When queries retrieve only a particular range of data and you want to add indexes to this data but not the entire table. For example, you have a table partitioned by month that covers three years' worth of data (2012, 2011, and 2010) and a team wants to heavily analyze data in the fourth quarter of 2011. Rather than create wider nonclustered indexes for all your data, you can create indexes (possibly using *INCLUDE* as well) that focus only on

  ```
  WHERE SalesDate >= '20111001' AND SalesDate < '20120101';
  ```

The leaf level of a nonclustered index created with a filter contains an index row only for keys that match the filter definition. Also, the column on which the filter is defined doesn't need to be part of the key, or even in an included column; however, that can help make the index more useful for certain queries. You can use *sys.dm_db_database_page_allocations*, *DBCC PAGE*, and the other previously mentioned DMVs to review the size and structure for indexes with filters.

Indexes on computed columns and indexed views

Without indexes, views and computed columns are purely logical. The data involved has no physical storage. A computed column isn't stored with the table data; it's recomputed every time a row is accessed (unless the computed column is marked as PERSISTED). A view doesn't save any data; it instead saves a *SELECT* statement that's executed every time the data in the view is accessed. With these indexes on views and computed columns, SQL Server actually materializes what was only logical data into the physical leaf level of an index.

Before you can create indexes on either computed columns or views, certain prerequisites must be met. The biggest issue is that SQL Server must be able to guarantee that given the identical base table data, the same values are always returned for any computed columns or for the rows in a view (that is, the computed columns and views are *deterministic*). To guarantee that the same values are always generated, these indexes have three categories of requirements.

- A number of session-level options must be set to a specific value.

- The functions that can be used within the computed column or view definition have some restrictions.

- The tables on which the view is based must meet certain criteria. (This requirement applies only to indexed views.)

SET options

The following seven *SET* options can affect the resulting value of an expression or predicate, so you must set them as shown to create indexed views or indexes on computed columns:

```
SET CONCAT_NULL_YIELDS_NULL ON
SET QUOTED_IDENTIFIER ON
SET ANSI_NULLS ON
SET ANSI_PADDING ON
SET ANSI_WARNINGS ON
SET NUMERIC_ROUNDABORT OFF
```

Notice that all the options have to be *ON* except *NUMERIC_ROUNDABORT*, which has to be *OFF*. The *ARITHABORT* option must be set to *ON*, but setting *ANSI_WARNINGS* to *ON* automatically sets *ARITHABORT* to *ON*, so you don't need to set it separately.

If any of these options isn't set as specified, you get an error message when you try to create an indexed view or an index on a computed column. Also, if you've already created one of these indexes, after which you change the *SET* option settings, and then attempt to modify data in the computed column or table on which the index is based, you get an error. If you issue a *SELECT* that normally should use the index, and if the *SET* options don't have the values indicated, the index is ignored but no error is generated.

You can determine whether the *SET* options are set appropriately in a couple of ways before you create one of these indexes. You can use the function *SESSIONPROPERTY* to test the settings for your current connection. A returned value of 1 means that the setting is *ON*; a 0 means that it's *OFF*. The following example checks the current session setting for the option *NUMERIC_ROUNDABORT*:

```
SELECT SESSIONPROPERTY ('NUMERIC_ROUNDABORT');
```

Alternatively, you can use the *sys.dm_exec_sessions* DMV to check the *SET* options for any connection. The following query returns the values for five of the previously discussed six *SET* options for the current session:

```
SELECT quoted_identifier, arithabort, ansi_warnings,
       ansi_padding, ansi_nulls, concat_null_yields_null
FROM sys.dm_exec_sessions
WHERE session_id = @@spid;
```

Unfortunately, *NUMERIC_ROUNDABORT* isn't included in the *sys.dm_exec_sessions* DMV results. You can't see the setting for that value for any other connections except the current one, using the *SESSIONPROPERTY* function.

Permissible functions

Any function is either *deterministic* or *nondeterministic*. If the function returns the same result every time it's called with the same set of input values, it's deterministic. If it can return different results when called with the same set of input values, it's nondeterministic. For the purposes of indexes, a function is considered deterministic if it always returns the same values for the same input values when all the *SET* options have the required settings. Any function used in a computed column's definition or used in the *SELECT* list or *WHERE* clause of an indexable view must be deterministic.

 More info *SQL Server Books Online* contains a complete list of which supplied functions are deterministic and which are nondeterministic. Some functions can be either deterministic or nondeterministic, depending on how they are used; *SQL Server Books Online* also describes these functions.

The list of nondeterministic functions might seem quite restrictive, but SQL Server must be able to guarantee that the values stored in the index are consistent. In some cases, the restrictions might be overly cautious, but the downside of being not cautious enough would be that your indexed views or indexes on computed columns are meaningless. The same restrictions apply to functions you use in your own user-defined functions (UDFs)—that is, your own functions can't be based on any nondeterministic built-in function. You can verify the determinism property of any function by using the *OBJECTPROPERTY* function:

```
SELECT OBJECTPROPERTY (object_id('<function_name>'), 'IsDeterministic')
```

Even if a function is deterministic, if it contains *float* or *real* expressions, the result of the function might vary with different processors depending on the processor architecture or microcode version. Expressions or functions containing values of the data type *float* or *real* are therefore considered to be *imprecise*. To guarantee consistent values even when moving a database from one machine to another (by detaching and attaching, or by performing backup and restore), imprecise values can be used only in key columns of indexes if they are physically stored in the database and not recomputed. An imprecise value can be used if it's the value of a stored column in a table or if it's a computed column marked as persisted. The section "Indexes on computed columns" covers persisted columns in more detail.

Schema binding

To create an indexed view, a requirement on the table itself is that the definition of any underlying object's schema can't change. To prevent a change in schema definition, the *CREATE VIEW* statement allows the *WITH SCHEMABINDING* option. When you specify *WITH SCHEMABINDING*, the *SELECT* statement that defines the view must include the two-part names (*schema.object*) of all referenced tables. You can't drop the table or alter the columns that participate in a view created with the *WITH SCHEMABINDING* clause unless you've dropped that view or changed it so that it's no longer schema-bound. Otherwise, SQL Server raises an error. If any of the tables on which the view is based are owned by someone other than the user creating the view, the view creator doesn't automatically have the right to create the view with schema binding because that would restrict the table's owner from making changes to her own table. A user must be granted REFERENCES permission on a table to create a view with schema binding on that table. You will see an example of schema binding shortly.

Indexes on computed columns

SQL Server allows you to build indexes on deterministic, precise (and persisted imprecise) computed columns where the resulting data type is otherwise indexable. This means that the column's data type can't be any of the LOB data types (such as *text, varchar(max)*, or *XML*). Such a computed column can be an index key, included column, or part of a PRIMARY KEY or UNIQUE constraint. When you create an index on computed columns, the six previously mentioned *SET* options must first have the correct values set.

Here's an example with an incorrect setting for *ANSI_NULLS*:

```
SET ANSI_NULLS OFF;
GO
CREATE TABLE t1 (a INT, b as 2*a);
GO
CREATE INDEX i1 ON t1 (b);
GO
```

Because one of the *SET* options doesn't have the correct value when the table is created, you get this message when you try to create the index:

```
Server: Msg 1935, Level 16, State 1, Line 2
Cannot create index. Object 't1' was created with the following SET options off:
    'ANSI_NULLS'.
```

If more than one option has an incorrect value, the error message would report them all.

Here's an example that creates a table with a nondeterministic computed column:

```
CREATE TABLE t2 (a INT, b DATETIME, c AS DATENAME(MM, b));
GO
CREATE INDEX i2 ON t2 (c);
GO
```

When you try to create the index on the computed column *c*, you get this error:

```
Msg 2729, Level 16, State 1, Line 1
Column 'c' in table 't2' cannot be used in an index or statistics or as a partition
    key because it is nondeterministic.
```

Column *c* is nondeterministic because the month value of *DATENAME()* can have different values depending on the language you're using.

Using the COLUMNPROPERTY function

You can check the value *IsDeterministic* with the column property function to determine whether a computed column is deterministic before you create an index on that column (or on a view). If you specify this value, the *COLUMNPROPERTY* function returns 1 if the column is deterministic and 0 otherwise. The result is undefined for columns that are neither computed columns nor columns in a view, so you should consider checking the *IsComputed* value before you check the *IsDeterministic* value. The following example detects that column *c* in table *t2* in the previous example is nondeterministic:

```
SELECT COLUMNPROPERTY (OBJECT_ID('t2'), 'c', 'IsDeterministic');
```

The value 0 is returned, which means that column *c* is nondeterministic. Note that the *COLUMNPROPERTY* function requires an object ID for the first argument and a column name for the second argument.

The *COLUMNPROPERTY* function also has a value of *IsIndexable*. That's probably the easiest to use for a quick check, but it won't give you the reason if the column isn't indexable. For that, you should check these other properties.

Implementation of a computed column

If you create an index on a computed column, that column is no longer a virtual column in the table. The computed value physically exists in the leaf level of the index, which might contain the actual rows of the table if the index is clustered. Updates to the columns on which the computed column is based also update the computed column in the table itself. For example, in the *t1* table created previously, if you insert a row with the value 10 in column *a*, the row is created with both the values 10 and 20 in the actual data row. If you then update the 10 to 15, the second column is updated automatically to 30.

Persisted columns

The ability to mark a computed column as *PERSISTED* allows storage of computed values in a table, even before you build an index. In fact, this feature was added to the product to allow columns of computed values based on underlying table columns of the imprecise (or approximate) types *float* and *real* to have indexes built on them. The alternative, when you want an index on such a column, would be to drop and re-create the underlying column defining it as a precise (or exact) data type, such as numeric or decimal. Rebuilding a large table can involve an enormous amount of overhead, so that solution shouldn't be your first choice.

For example, in the *Northwind* database, the *Order Details* table has a column called *Discount* of type *real*. The following code adds a computed column called *Final* that shows the total price for an item after the discount is applied. The statement to build an index on *Final* fails because the resulting column involving the *real* value is imprecise and not persisted:

```
USE Northwind;
GO
ALTER TABLE [Order Details]
    ADD Final AS
     (Quantity * UnitPrice) - Discount * (Quantity * UnitPrice);
GO
CREATE INDEX OD_Final_Index on [Order Details](Final);
GO


Error Message:
Msg 2799, Level 16, State 1, Line 1
Cannot create index or statistics 'OD_Final_Index' on table 'Order Details'
    because the computed column 'Final' is imprecise and not persisted. Consider removing
    column from index or statistics key or marking computed column persisted.
```

Without persisted computed columns, the only way to create an index on a computed column containing the final price would be to drop the *Discount* column from the table and redefine it as an exact numeric data type. Any existing indexes on *Discount* also would have to be dropped and then rebuilt. With persisted computed columns, all you need to do is drop the computed column (a metadata-only operation) and then redefine it as a persisted computed column. You can then build the index on the column:

```
ALTER TABLE [Order Details]
    DROP COLUMN Final;
GO
ALTER TABLE [Order Details]
    ADD Final AS
    (Quantity * UnitPrice) - Discount * (Quantity * UnitPrice) PERSISTED;
GO
CREATE INDEX OD_Final_Index on [Order Details](Final);
```

When determining whether you have to use the *PERSISTED* option, use the *COLUMNPROPERTY* function and the *IsPrecise* property to determine whether a deterministic column is precise:

```
SELECT COLUMNPROPERTY (OBJECT_ID ('Order Details'), 'Final', 'IsPrecise');
```

You can also use persisted computed columns when you define partitions. A computed column used as the partitioning column must be explicitly marked as *PERSISTED*, whether it's precise or imprecise. Chapter 8 looks at partitioning.

Indexed views

Indexed views in SQL Server are similar to what other products call *materialized views*. One of the most important benefits of indexed views is the ability to materialize summary aggregates of large tables. Consider a customer table containing rows for several million U.S.-based customers, from which you want information regarding customers in each state. You can create a view based on a *GROUP BY* query, grouping by state and containing the count of orders per state. Normal views are only named, saved queries and don't store the results. Every time the view is referenced, the aggregation to produce the grouped results must be re-executed. When you create an index on the view, the aggregated data is stored in the leaf level of the index. So instead of millions of customer rows, your indexed view has only 50 rows—one for each state, plus maybe a couple more for territories and the District of Columbia. Your aggregate reporting queries can then be processed using the indexed views without having to scan the underlying, large tables.

The first index you must build on a view is a clustered index. Because the clustered index contains all the data at its leaf level, this index actually does the materialization of the view. The view's data is physically stored at the leaf level of the clustered index.

Additional requirements

In addition to the requirement that all functions used in the view must be deterministic, and that the required *SET* options must be set to the appropriate values, the view definition can't contain any of the following.

- *TOP*
- LOB columns
- *DISTINCT*
- *MIN, MAX, COUNT(*), COUNT(<expression>), STDEV, VARIANCE, AVG*
- *SUM* on a nullable expression
- A derived table
- The *ROWSET* function
- Another view (you can reference only base tables)

- *UNION*

- Subqueries, OUTER joins, or self-joins

- Full-text predicates (*CONTAINS, FREETEXT*)

- *COMPUTE, COMPUTE BY*

- *ORDER BY*

Also, if the view definition contains *GROUP BY*, the *SELECT* list must include the aggregate *COUNT_BIG (*)*. *COUNT_BIG* returns a *BIGINT*, which is an 8-byte integer. A view that contains *GROUP BY* can't contain *HAVING, CUBE, ROLLUP*, or *GROUP BY ALL*. Also, all *GROUP BY* columns must appear in the *SELECT* list. Note that if your view contains both *SUM* and *COUNT_BIG (*)*, you can compute the equivalent of the *AVG* aggregate function even though *AVG* isn't allowed in indexed views. Although these restrictions might seem severe, remember that they apply to the view definitions, not to the queries that might use the indexed views.

To verify that you've met all the requirements, you can use the *OBJECTPROPERTY* function's *IsIndexable* property. The following query tells you whether you can build an index on a view called *Product Totals*:

```
SELECT OBJECTPROPERTY (OBJECT_ID ('Product_Totals'), 'IsIndexable');
```

A returned value of 1 means you've met all requirements and can build an index on the view.

Creating an indexed view

The first step in building an index on a view is to create the view itself. Here's an example from the *AdventureWorks2012* database:

```
USE AdventureWorks2012;
GO
CREATE VIEW Vdiscount1
WITH SCHEMABINDING
AS SELECT SUM (UnitPrice*OrderQty) AS SumPrice
    , SUM (UnitPrice * OrderQty * (1.00 - UnitPriceDiscount))
        AS SumDiscountPrice
    , COUNT_BIG (*) AS Count
    , ProductID
FROM Sales.SalesOrderDetail
GROUP BY ProductID;
```

Notice the *WITH SCHEMABINDING* clause and the specification of the schema name (*Sales*) for the table. At this point, it's a normal view—a stored *SELECT* statement that uses no storage space. In fact, if you look at the data in *sys.dm_db_partition_stats* for this view, notice that no rows are returned:

```
SELECT si.name AS index_name,
    ps.used_page_count, ps.reserved_page_count, ps.row_count
FROM sys.dm_db_partition_stats AS ps
    JOIN sys.indexes AS si
        ON ps.[object_id] = si.[object_id]
WHERE ps.[object_id] = OBJECT_ID ('dbo.Vdiscount1');
```

To create an indexed view, you must first create a *unique clustered index*. The clustered index on a view contains all the data that makes up the view definition. This statement defines a unique clustered index for the view:

```
CREATE UNIQUE CLUSTERED INDEX VDiscount_Idx ON Vdiscount1 (ProductID);
```

After the indexed view is created, rerun the previous *SELECT* statement to see the pages materialized by the index on the view:

```
RESULT:
index_name      used_page_count    reserved_page_count   row_count
--------------  -----------------  -------------------   ---------
VDiscountIdx    4                  4                     266
```

Data that comprises the indexed view is persistent, with the indexed view storing the data in the clustered index's leaf level. You could construct something similar by using temporary tables to store the data you're interested in. But a temporary table is static and doesn't reflect changes to underlying data. In contrast, SQL Server automatically maintains indexed views, updating information stored in the clustered index whenever anyone changes data that affects the view.

After you create the unique clustered index, you can create multiple nonclustered indexes on the view. You can determine whether a view is indexed by using the *OBJECTPROPERTY* function's *IsIndexed* property. For the *Vdiscount1* indexed view, the following statement returns a 1, which means the view is indexed:

```
SELECT OBJECTPROPERTY (OBJECT_ID ('Vdiscount1'), 'IsIndexed');
```

When a view is indexed, metadata about space usage and location is available through the catalog views, just as for any other index.

Using an indexed view

One of the most valuable benefits of indexed views is that your queries don't have to reference a view directly to use the index on the view. Consider the *Vdiscount1* indexed view. Suppose that you issue the following *SELECT* statement:

```
SELECT ProductID, total_sales = SUM (UnitPrice * OrderQty)
FROM  Sales.SalesOrderDetail
GROUP BY ProductID;
```

The Query Optimizer recognizes that the precomputed sums of all the *UnitPrice * OrderQty* values for each *ProductID* are already available in the index for the *Vdiscount1* view. The Query Optimizer evaluates the cost of using that indexed view in processing the query, and the indexed view very likely is used to access the information required to satisfy this query; the *Sales.SalesOrderDetail* table might never be touched at all.

Note Although you can create indexed views in any edition of SQL Server 2012, for the Query Optimizer to consider using them even when they aren't referenced in the query, the engine edition of SQL Server 2012 must be Enterprise, Developer, or Evaluation.

Just because you have an indexed view doesn't mean the Query Optimizer always chooses it for the query's execution plan. In fact, even if you reference the indexed view directly in the *FROM* clause, the Query Optimizer might access the base table directly instead. To make sure that an indexed view in your *FROM* clause isn't expanded into its underlying *SELECT* statement, you can use the *NOEXPAND* hint in the *FROM* clause. (As with any hint, you'll need to verify that the *NOEXPAND* hint actually does improve performance before making it part of your production code.) Some of the internals of index selection, query optimization, and indexed view usage are discussed in more detail in Chapter 11, "The Query Optimizer."

In addition to the B-tree indexes discussed in this section, SQL Server also supports several other kinds of indexes. Columnstore indexes, new in SQL Server 2012, are covered at the end of this chapter. Spatial indexes, full-text indexes, semantic indexes, and XML indexes are covered in Chapter 9, "Special indexes."

Data modification internals

You've seen how SQL Server stores data and index information; now you can look at what SQL Server actually does internally when your data is modified. You've seen how clustered indexes define logical order to your data and how a heap is nothing more than a collection of unordered pages. You've seen how nonclustered indexes are structures stored separately from the data and how that data is a copy of the actual table's data, defined by the index definition. Also, as a rule of thumb, you should always have a clustered index on a table. This section reviews how SQL Server deals with the existence of indexes when processing data modification statements.

 More info The SQL Customer Advisory Team published a white paper in mid-2007 that compares various table structures and essentially supports the recommendation of always having a clustered index in a table; see *http://www.microsoft.com/technet/prodtechnol/sql/ bestpractice/clusivsh.mspx*. Although that paper was written for SQL Server 2005 and the specific values and percent improvement percentages might have changed, the conclusions still apply.

Note that for every *INSERT, UPDATE,* and *DELETE* operation on a table, the equivalent operation also happens to every nonclustered index on the table (with some exceptions for *UPDATE*). The mechanisms described in this section apply equally to clustered and nonclustered indexes. Any modifications to the table are made to the heap or clustered index first, then to each nonclustered index in turn.

In SQL Server 2012, the exception to this rule is filtered indexes, in which the filter predicate means that the filtered nonclustered index leaf level might not have a matching row for the table row being modified. When changes are made to the table, the filtered index predicate is evaluated to determine whether it's necessary to apply the same operation to the filtered nonclustered index.

Inserting rows

When inserting a new row into a table, SQL Server must determine where to put the data, as well as insert a corresponding row into each nonclustered index. Each operation follows the same pattern: Modify the appropriate data page (based on whether the table has a clustered index) and then insert the corresponding index rows into the leaf level of each nonclustered index.

When a table has no clustered index—that is, when the table is a heap—a new row is always inserted wherever room is available in the table. In Chapter 3, you learned how IAMs keep track of which extents in a file already belong to a table; in Chapter 6, you saw how the PFS pages indicate which pages in those extents have available space. If no pages with space are available, SQL Server tries to find unallocated pages from existing uniform extents that already belong to the object. If none exists, SQL Server must allocate a whole new extent to the table. Chapter 3 discussed how the Global Allocated Maps (GAMs) and Shared Global Allocation Maps (SGAMs) are used to find extents available to be allocated to an object. So, although locating space in which to do an *INSERT* is relatively efficient using the PFS and IAM, because the location of a row (on *INSERT*) isn't defined, determining where to place a row within a heap is usually less efficient than if the table has a clustered index.

For an *INSERT* into a table with a clustered index and for index rows being inserted into nonclustered indexes, the row (regardless of whether it's a data row or an index row) always has a specific location within the index where it must be inserted, based on the value the new row has for the index key columns. An *INSERT* occurs either when the new row is the direct result of an *INSERT* or when it's the result of an *UPDATE* statement that causes the row to move or an index key column to change. When a row has to move to a new page, the *UPDATE* statement is internally executed using a *DELETE* followed by an *INSERT* (the *DELETE/INSERT* strategy). New rows are inserted based on their index key position, and SQL Server splices in a new page via a page split if the current leaf level (a data page if this is the clustered index or an index page if this is a nonclustered index) has no room. Because the index dictates a particular ordering for the rows in the leaf level of the index, every new row has a specific location where it belongs. If no room is available for the new row on the page where it belongs, a new page must be allocated and linked into the B-tree. If possible, this new page is allocated from the same extent as the other pages to which it's linked. If the extent is already full, which is usually the case, a new extent (eight pages or 64 KB) is allocated to the object. As described in Chapter 3, SQL Server uses the GAM pages to find an available extent.

Splitting pages

After SQL Server finds the new page, the original page must be split; half the rows (the first half based on the slot array on the page) are left on the original page, and the other half are moved to the new page, or as close to a 50/50 split as possible. In some cases, SQL Server finds that even after the split, not enough room is available for the new row, which, because of variable-length fields, could potentially be much larger than any of the existing rows on the pages. As part of the split, SQL Server must add a corresponding entry for every new page into the parent page of the level above. One row is added if only a single split is needed. However, if the new row still won't fit after a single split, multiple new pages and additions can potentially be made to the parent page. Suppose that SQL Server tries to insert a new row with 8,000 bytes on a page with 32 rows on it. It splits the page once, and the new 8,000-byte row won't fit. Even after a second split, the new row won't fit. Eventually, SQL Server recognizes that the new row can't fit on a page with any other rows, so it allocates a new page to hold only the new row. Quite a few splits occur, resulting in many new pages and many new rows on the parent page.

An index tree is always searched from the root down, so during an *INSERT* operation, it's split on the way down. This means that while the index is being searched on an *INSERT*, the index is protected in anticipation of possibly being updated. The protection mechanism is a latch, which you can think of as something like a lock. (Locks are discussed in detail in Chapter 13.) A latch is acquired while a page is being read from or written to disk and protects the physical integrity of the contents of the page. Latches are also acquired during physical manipulation of a page, such as during a split operation. A parent node is latched (and protected) until the child node's needed split(s) is complete and no further updates to the parent node are required from the current operation. Then the parent latch can be released safely.

Before the latch on a parent node is released, SQL Server determines whether the page can accommodate another two rows; if not, it splits the page. This occurs only if the page is being searched with the objective of adding a row to the index. The goal is to ensure that the parent page always has room for the row or rows that result from a child page splitting. (Occasionally, this results in pages being split that don't need to be—at least not yet. In the long run, it's a performance optimization that helps to minimize deadlocks in an index and allows for free space to be added for future rows that might require it.) The type of split depends on the type of page being split: a root page of an index, an intermediate index page, or a leaf-level page. Also, when a split occurs, it's committed independently of the transaction that caused the page to split, using special internal transactions called *system transactions*. Therefore, even if the *INSERT* transaction is rolled back, the split isn't rolled back.

Splitting the root page of an index

If the root page of an index needs to be split for a new index row to be inserted, two new pages are allocated to the index. All rows from the root are split between these two new pages, and the new index row is inserted into the appropriate place on one of these pages. The original root page is still the root, but now it has only two rows on it, pointing to each of the newly allocated pages. Keeping the original root page means that an update to the index metadata in the system catalogs (which contains a pointer to the index root page) is avoided. A root-page split creates a new level in the index. Because indexes are usually only a few levels deep and typically very scalable, this type of split doesn't occur often.

Splitting an intermediate index page

An intermediate index page split is accomplished simply by locating the midpoint of the index keys on the page, allocating a new page, and then copying the lower half of the old index page into the new page. A new row is added to the index page in the level above the page that split, corresponding to the newly added page. Again, this doesn't occur often, although it's much more common than splitting the root page.

Splitting a leaf-level page

A leaf-level page split is the most interesting and potentially common case, and it's probably the only split that you, as a developer or DBA, should be concerned with. The mechanism is the same for splitting clustered index data pages or nonclustered index leaf-level index pages.

Data pages split only under *INSERT* activity and only when a clustered index exists on the table. Although splits are caused only by *INSERT* activity, that activity can be a result of an *UPDATE* statement, not just an *INSERT* statement. As you're about to learn, if the row can't be updated in place or at least on the same page, the update is performed as a *DELETE* of the original row followed by an *INSERT* of the new version of the row. The insertion of the new row can cause a page to split.

Splitting a leaf-level (data or index) page is a complicated operation. Much like an intermediate index page split, it's accomplished by locating the midpoint of the index keys on the page, allocating a new page, and then copying half of the old page into the new page. It requires that the index manager determine the page on which to locate the new row and then handle large rows that don't fit on either the old page or the new page. When a data page is split, the clustered index key values don't change, so the nonclustered indexes aren't affected.

Now look at what happens to a page when it splits. The following script creates a table with large rows—so large, in fact, that only five rows fit on a page. After the table is created and populated with five rows, you find its first (and only, in this case) page by using the *sys.dm_db_database_page_allocations* function, finding the information for the data page, and then using *DBCC PAGE* to look at the page contents. Because you don't need to see all 8,020 bytes of data on the page, you look at only the slot array at the end of the page and then see what happens to those rows when you insert a sixth row, as shown in Listing 7-5.

LISTING 7-5 Examining a page after a split

```
USE AdventureWorks2012;
GO

CREATE TABLE bigrows
(
    a int  primary key,
    b varchar(1600)
);
GO

/* Insert five rows into the table */
INSERT INTO bigrows
    VALUES (5, REPLICATE('a', 1600));
```

```
INSERT INTO bigrows
    VALUES (10, replicate('b', 1600));
INSERT INTO bigrows
    VALUES (15, replicate('c', 1600));
INSERT INTO bigrows
    VALUES (20, replicate('d', 1600));
INSERT INTO bigrows
    VALUES (25, replicate('e', 1600));
GO


SELECT allocated_page_file_id as PageFID, allocated_page_page_id as PagePID,
FROM sys.dm_db_database_page_allocations(db_id('AdventureWorks2012'),
    object_id('dbo.bigrows'), null, null, 'DETAILED')
WHERE page_type = 1;;
GO


RESULTS: (Your page number may be different.)
PageFID PagePID
------- -----------
1       23816


DBCC TRACEON(3604);
GO
DBCC PAGE(AdventureWorks2012, 1, 23816, 1);
GO
```

Here is the slot array from the *DBCC PAGE* output:

```
Row - Offset
4 (0x4) - 6556 (0x199c)
3 (0x3) - 4941 (0x134d)
2 (0x2) - 3326 (0xcfe)
1 (0x1) - 1711 (0x6af)
0 (0x0) - 96 (0x60)
```

Now insert one more row and look at the slot array again:

```
INSERT INTO bigrows
    VALUES (22, REPLICATE('x', 1600));
GO
DBCC PAGE (AdventureWorks2012, 1, 23816, 1);
GO
```

The displayed page contains the first half of the rows from the original page because the newly allocated page always contains the second half of the rows, but the new row value can be inserted on either page depending on the value of its index keys. In this example, the new row, with a clustered key value of 22, would have been inserted in the second half of the page, between the last two values of 20 and 25. So when this page split occurs, the first three rows stay on page 23816, the original page. You can inspect the page header to find the location of the next page, which contains the new row, or you can run the earlier query to execute the sys.*dm_db_database_pages_allocated* function.

The page number is indicated by the *m_nextPage* field. This value is expressed as a *file number:page number* pair, in decimal, so you can easily use it with the *DBCC PAGE* command. In this case, *m_nextPage* returned a value of 1:23820. You can use *DBCC PAGE* to look at the page that's indicated as the next page:

```
DBCC PAGE (AdventureWorks2012, 1, 23820, 1);
```

Here's the slot array after the *INSERT* for the second page:

```
Row - Offset
2 (0x2) - 1711 (0x6af)
1 (0x1) - 3326 (0xcfe)
0 (0x0) - 96 (0x60)
```

Note that after the page split, three rows are on the page: the last two original rows, with keys of 20 and 25, and the new row, with a key of 22. If you examine the actual data on the page, notice that the new row is at slot position 1, even though the row itself is physically the last one on the page. Slot 1 (with value 22) starts at offset 3326; slot 2 (with value 25) starts at offset 1711. The clustered key ordering of the rows is indicated by the slot number of the row, not by the physical position on the page. If a table has a clustered index, the row at slot 1 always has a key value less than the row at slot 2 and greater than the row at slot 0. Only the slot numbers are rearranged, not the data. This is an optimization, so only a small number of offsets are rearranged instead of the entire page's contents. That rows in an index are always stored in the exact same physical order as their keys is a myth—in fact, SQL Server can store the rows anywhere on a page so long as the slot array provides the correct logical ordering.

Page splits are expensive operations, involving updates to multiple pages (the page being split, the new page, the page that used to be the *m_nextPage* of the page being split, and the parent page), all of which are fully logged. As such, you want to minimize the frequency of page splits in your production system, especially during peak usage times. You can avoid negatively affecting performance by minimizing splits. You often can minimize splits by choosing a better clustering key (one where new rows are inserted at the end of the table, rather than randomly, as with a GUID clustering key) or, especially when splits are caused by update to variable-width columns, by reserving some free space on pages using the *FILLFACTOR* option when you're creating or rebuilding the indexes. You can use this setting to your advantage during your least busy operational hours by periodically rebuilding (or reorganizing) the indexes with the desired *FILLFACTOR*. That way, the extra space is available during peak usage times, and you save the overhead of splitting then. Later, this chapter discusses the pros and cons of various maintenance options.

Deleting rows

When you delete rows from a table, you have to consider what happens both to the data pages and the index pages. Remember that the data is actually the leaf level of a clustered index, and deleting rows from a table with a clustered index happens the same way as deleting rows from the leaf level of a nonclustered index. Deleting rows from a heap is managed differently, as is deleting from non-leaf pages of an index.

Deleting rows from a heap

SQL Server 2012 doesn't automatically compact space on a page when a row is deleted. As a performance optimization, the compaction doesn't occur until a page needs additional contiguous space for inserting a new row. You can see this in Listings 7-6 and 7-7, which delete a row from the middle of a page and then inspects that page by using *DBCC PAGE*.

LISTING 7-6 Deleting a row from a heap

```
USE AdventureWorks2012;
GO
IF object_id('dbo.smallrows') IS NOT NULL
    DROP TABLE dbo.smallrows;
GO
CREATE TABLE dbo.smallrows
(
    a int identity,
    b char(10)
);
GO

INSERT INTO dbo.smallrows
    VALUES ('row 1');
INSERT INTO dbo.smallrows
    VALUES ('row 2');
INSERT INTO dbo.smallrows
    VALUES ('row 3');
INSERT INTO dbo.smallrows
    VALUES ('row 4');
INSERT INTO dbo.smallrows
    VALUES ('row 5');
GO

SELECT allocated_page_file_id as PageFID, allocated_page_page_id as PagePID,
FROM sys.dm_db_database_page_allocations(db_id('AdventureWorks2012'),
    object_id('dbo.smallrows'), null, null, 'DETAILED');
WHERE page_type = 1;

Results:
PageFID PagePID
------- -----------
1       23821

DBCC TRACEON(3604);
GO
DBCC PAGE(AdventureWorks2012, 1, 23821,1);
```

Listing 7-7 shows the output.

LISTING 7-7 Examining a page before deleting

```
DATA:

Slot 0, Offset 0x60, Length 21, DumpStyle BYTE

Record Type = PRIMARY_RECORD        Record Attributes =  NULL_BITMAP
Record Size = 21

Memory Dump @0x000000001514A060

0000000000000000:    10001200 01000000 726f7720 31202020 20200200  ..........row 1      ..
0000000000000014:    00                                                              .

Slot 1, Offset 0x75, Length 21, DumpStyle BYTE

Record Type = PRIMARY_RECORD        Record Attributes = NULL_BITMAP
Record Size = 21

Memory Dump @0x000000001514A075

0000000000000000:    10001200 02000000 726f7720 32202020 20200200  ........row 2      ..
0000000000000014:    00                                                              .

Slot 2, Offset 0x8a, Length 21, DumpStyle BYTE

Record Type = PRIMARY_RECORD        Record Attributes = NULL_BITMAP
Record Size = 21

Memory Dump @0x000000001514A08A

0000000000000000:    10001200 03000000 726f7720 33202020 20200200  .........row 3      ..
0000000000000014:    00                                                              .

Slot 3, Offset 0x9f, Length 21, DumpStyle BYTE

Record Type = PRIMARY_RECORD        Record Attributes = NULL_BITMAP
Record Size = 21

Memory Dump @0x000000001514A09F

0000000000000000:    10001200 04000000 726f7720 34202020 20200200  .........row 4      ..
0000000000000014:    00                                                              .

Slot 4, Offset 0xb4, Length 21, DumpStyle BYTE

Record Type = PRIMARY_RECORD        Record Attributes = NULL_BITMAP
Record Size = 21

Memory Dump @0x000000001514A0B4

0000000000000000:    10001200 05000000 726f7720 35202020 20200200  ........row 5      ..
0000000000000014:    00                                                              .

OFFSET TABLE:
```

```
Row - Offset
4 (0x4) - 180 (0xb4)
3 (0x3) - 159 (0x9f)
2 (0x2) - 138 (0x8a)
1 (0x1) - 117 (0x75)
0 (0x0) - 96 (0x60)
```

Now delete the middle row (*WHERE a = 3*) and look at the page again:

```
DELETE FROM dbo.smallrows
WHERE a = 3;
GO


DBCC PAGE(AdventureWorks2012, 1, 23821, 1);
GO
```

Listing 7-8 shows the output from the second execution of *DBCC PAGE*.

LISTING 7-8 Examining the page after deleting a row

```
DATA:

Slot 0, Offset 0x60, Length 21, DumpStyle BYTE

Record Type = PRIMARY_RECORD          Record Attributes = NULL_BITMAP
Record Size = 21

Memory Dump @0x000000001514A060

0000000000000000:   10001200 01000000 726f7720 31202020 20200200   ........row 1    ..
0000000000000014:   00                                                          .

Slot 1, Offset 0x75, Length 21, DumpStyle BYTE

Record Type = PRIMARY_RECORD          Record Attributes = NULL_BITMAP
Record Size = 21

Memory Dump @0x000000001514A075

0000000000000000:   10001200 02000000 726f7720 32202020 20200200   ........row 2    ..
0000000000000014:   00                                                          .

Slot 3, Offset 0x9f, Length 21, DumpStyle BYTE

Record Type = PRIMARY_RECORD          Record Attributes = NULL_BITMAP
Record Size = 21

Memory Dump @0x000000001514A09F

0000000000000000:   10001200 04000000 726f7720 34202020 20200200   ........row 4    ..
0000000000000014:   00                                                          .

Slot 4, Offset 0xb4, Length 21, DumpStyle BYTE

Record Type = PRIMARY_RECORD          Record Attributes = NULL_BITMAP
```

```
Record Size = 21

Memory Dump @0x000000001514A0B4

0000000000000000:    10001200 05000000 726f7720 35202020 20200200   ........row 5      ..
0000000000000014:    00                                             .
```

OFFSET TABLE:

```
Row - Offset
4 (0x4) - 180 (0xb4)
3 (0x3) - 159 (0x9f)
2 (0x2) - 0 (0x0)
1 (0x1) - 117 (0x75)
0 (0x0) - 96 (0x60)
```

By using *DBCC PAGE* with style 1 on a heap, the row doesn't show up in the page itself—only in the slot array. The slot array at the bottom of the page shows that the third row (at slot 2) is now at offset 0 (which means no row is really using slot 2), and the row using slot 3 is at its same offset as before the *DELETE*. The data on the page is *not* compacted.

In addition to space on pages not being reclaimed, empty pages in heaps frequently can't be reclaimed. Even if you delete all the rows from a heap, SQL Server doesn't mark the empty pages as unallocated, so the space isn't available for other objects to use. The function *sys.dm_db_database_page_allocations* still shows the space as belonging to the heap.

Deleting rows from a B-tree

In the leaf level of an index, either clustered or nonclustered, rows are marked as *ghost records* when they are deleted. This means that the row stays on the page, but a bit is changed in the row header to indicate that the row is really deleted (a *ghost*). The page header also reflects the number of ghost records on a page. Ghost records are used for several purposes. They can be used to make rollbacks much more efficient; if the row hasn't been removed physically, all SQL Server has to do to roll back a *DELETE* is to change the bit indicating that the row is a ghost. It's also a concurrency optimization for key-range locking (discussed in Chapter 13), along with other locking modes. Ghost records also are used to support row-level versioning (also discussed in Chapter 13).

Ghost records are cleaned up sooner or later, depending on the load on your system, and sometimes they are cleaned up before you have a chance to inspect them. A background thread called the *ghost-cleanup thread* removes ghost records that are no longer needed to support active transactions or any other feature. In the code shown in Listing 7-9, if you perform the *DELETE* and then wait a minute or two to run *DBCC PAGE*, the ghost record might really disappear. That is why you look at the page number for the table before you run the *DELETE*, so you can execute the *DELETE* and the *DBCC PAGE* with a single click from the query window. To guarantee that the ghost record isn't cleaned up, you can put the *DELETE* into a user transaction and not commit or roll back the transaction before examining the page. The ghost-cleanup thread doesn't clean up ghost records that are part of an active transaction. Alternatively, you can use the undocumented trace flag 661 to disable ghost cleanup to ensure consistent results when running tests such as in this script. As usual, keep in mind that undocumented trace flags aren't guaranteed to continue to work in any future release or service pack, and no support is available for them. Also, be sure to turn off the trace flag when you're done with your testing. You can also force SQL Server to clean up the ghost records. The procedure *sp_clean_db_free_space* removes all ghost records from an entire database (as long as they aren't part of an uncommitted transaction), and the procedure *sp_clean_db_file_free_space* does the same for a single file of a database.

The code in Listing 7-9 builds the same table used in the previous *DELETE* example, but this time, the table has a primary key declared, which means a clustered index is built. The data is the leaf level of the clustered index, so when the row is removed, it's marked as a ghost.

LISTING 7-9 Deleting a row from a table with a clustered index

```
USE AdventureWorks2012;
GO
IF object_id('dbo.smallrows') IS NOT NULL
     DROP TABLE dbo.smallrows;
GO
CREATE TABLE dbo.smallrows
(
    a int IDENTITY PRIMARY KEY,
    b char(10)
);
GO
INSERT INTO dbo.smallrows
    VALUES ('row 1');
INSERT INTO dbo.smallrows
    VALUES ('row 2');
INSERT INTO dbo.smallrows
    VALUES ('row 3');
INSERT INTO dbo.smallrows
    VALUES ('row 4');
INSERT INTO dbo.smallrows
    VALUES ('row 5');
GO
SELECT allocated_page_file_id as PageFID, allocated_page_page_id as PagePID,
FROM sys.dm_db_database_page_allocations(db_id('AdventureWorks2012'),
                                  object_id('dbo.smallrows'), null, null, 'DETAILED')

Results:
PageFID PagePID
------- -----------
1       4568

DELETE FROM dbo.smallrows
WHERE a = 3;
GO
DBCC TRACEON(3604);
DBCC PAGE(AdventureWorks2012, 1, 4568, 1);
GO
```

Listing 7-10 shows the output from *DBCC PAGE*.

LISTING 7-10 Examining a page with a ghost record

```
PAGE HEADER:
Page @0x00000002DA6F4000

m_pageId = (1:24116)              m_headerVersion = 1            m_type = 1
m_typeFlagBits = 0x0             m_level = 0                    m_flagBits = 0x0
m_objId (AllocUnitId.idObj) = 411   m_indexId (AllocUnitId.idInd) = 256
Metadata: AllocUnitId = 72057594064863232
Metadata: PartitionId = 72057594058047488
Metadata: ObjectId = 823673982    m_prevPage = (0:0)            Metadata: IndexId = 1
pminlen = 18                      m_slotCnt = 5                 m_nextPage = (0:0)
m_freeData = 201                  m_reservedCnt = 0             m_freeCnt = 7981
m_xactReserved = 0                m_xdesId = (0:5658)           m_lsn = (76:374:2)
m_tornBits = 0                    DB Frag ID = 1                m_ghostRecCnt = 1

Allocation Status

GAM (1:2) = ALLOCATED            SGAM (1:3) = ALLOCATED
PFS (1:16176) = 0x68 MIXED_EXT ALLOCATED    0_PCT_FULL
DIFF (1:6) = CHANGED
ML (1:7) = NOT MIN_LOGGED

DATA:

Slot 0, Offset 0x60, Length 21, DumpStyle BYTE

Record Type = PRIMARY_RECORD       Record Attributes = NULL_BITMAP
Record Size = 21

Memory Dump @0x0000000018C3A060

0000000000000000:    10001200 01000000 726f7720 31202020 20200200   ........row 1
0000000000000014:    00                                              .

Slot 1, Offset 0x75, Length 21, DumpStyle BYTE

Record Type = PRIMARY_RECORD       Record Attributes = NULL_BITMAP
Record Size = 21

Memory Dump @0x0000000018C3A075

0000000000000000:    10001200 02000000 726f7720 32202020 20200200   ........row 2
0000000000000014:    00                                              .

Slot 2, Offset 0x8a, Length 21, DumpStyle BYTE

Record Type = GHOST_DATA_RECORD    Record Attributes = NULL_BITMAP
Record Size = 21

Memory Dump @0x0000000018C3A08A

0000000000000000:    1c001200 03000000 726f7720 33202020 20200200   ........row 3
0000000000000014:    00                                              .

Slot 3, Offset 0x9f, Length 21, DumpStyle BYTE
```

```
Record Type = PRIMARY_RECORD          Record Attributes = NULL_BITMAP      Record Size = 21

Memory Dump @0x0000000018C3A09F

0000000000000000:   10001200 04000000 726f7720 34202020 20200200  ........row 4
0000000000000014:   00                                                 .

Slot 4, Offset 0xb4, Length 21, DumpStyle BYTE

Record Type = PRIMARY_RECORD          Record Attributes = NULL_BITMAP
Record Size = 21

Memory Dump @0x0000000018C3A0B4

0000000000000000:   10001200 05000000 726f7720 35202020 20200200  ........row 5
0000000000000014:   00                                                 .

OFFSET TABLE:

Row - Offset
4 (0x4) - 180 (0xb4)
3 (0x3) - 159 (0x9f)
2 (0x2) - 138 (0x8a)
1 (0x1) - 117 (0x75)
0 (0x0) - 96 (0x60)
```

Note that the row still shows up in the page itself (using *DBCC PAGE* style 1) because the table has a clustered index. Also, you can experiment using different output styles to see how both a heap and a clustered index work with ghosted records, but you still see empty slots, *GHOST_DATA_RECORD* types, or both for clarification. The header information for the row shows that this is really a ghost record. The slot array at the bottom of the page shows that the row at slot 2 is still at the same offset and that all rows are in the same location as before the deletion. Also, the page header gives us a value (*m_ghostRecCnt*) for the number of ghost records in the page. To see the total count of ghost records in a table, use the *sys.dm_db_index_physical_stats* function.

> **More info** A detailed discussion of the ghost cleanup mechanism and an examination of the transaction logging involved are available at Paul Randal's blog. See the blog post at *http://www.SQLskills.com/BLOGS/PAUL/post/Inside-the-Storage-Engine-Ghost-cleanup-in-depth.aspx*.

Deleting rows in the non-leaf levels of an index

When you delete a row from a table, all nonclustered indexes must be maintained because every nonclustered index has a pointer to the row that's now gone. Rows in index non-leaf pages aren't ghosted when deleted, but just as with heap pages, the space isn't compacted until new index rows need space in that page.

Reclaiming pages

When the last row is deleted from a data page, the entire page is deallocated by the ghost cleanup background thread. The exception is if the table is a heap, as discussed earlier. (If the page is the only one remaining in the table, it isn't deallocated.) Deallocation of a data page results in the deletion of the row in the index page that pointed to the deallocated data page. Non-leaf index pages are deallocated if an index row is deleted (which, again, for an update might occur as part of a *DELETE/INSERT* strategy), leaving only one entry in the index page. That entry is moved to its neighboring page if space is available, and then the empty page is deallocated.

The discussion so far has focused on the page manipulation necessary for deleting a single row. If multiple rows are deleted in a single *DELETE* operation, you must be aware of some other issues. The issues of modifying multiple rows in a single query are the same for *INSERT*s, *UPDATE*s, and *DELETE*s and are discussed later in this chapter.

Updating rows

SQL Server updates rows in multiple ways, automatically and invisibly choosing the fastest update strategy for the specific operation. In determining the strategy, SQL Server evaluates the number of rows affected, how the rows are accessed (via a scan or an index retrieval, and via which index), and whether changes to the index keys occur. Updates can happen either in place, by just changing one column's value to a new value in the original row, or as a *DELETE* followed by an *INSERT*. Updates also can be managed by the query processor or by the storage engine.

This section examines only whether the update happens in place or whether SQL Server treats it as two separate operations: delete the old row and insert a new row. The question of whether the update is controlled by the query processor or the storage engine is actually relevant to all data modification operations, not just updates, so a separate section looks at that.

Moving rows

What happens if a table row needs to move to a new location? This can happen because a row with variable-length columns is updated to a new, larger size so that it no longer fits on the original page. It can also happen when the clustered or nonclustered index column(s) change because rows are logically ordered by the index key. For example, if you have a clustered index on *lastname*, a row with a *lastname* value of *Abercrombie* is stored near the beginning of the table. If the *lastname* value is then updated to *Zischka*, this row has to move to near the end of the table.

Earlier in this chapter, you looked at the structure of indexes and saw that the leaf level of nonclustered indexes contains a row locator, or bookmark, for every single row in the table. If the table has a clustered index, that row locator is the clustering key for that row. So if—and only if—the clustered index key is being updated, modifications are required in every nonclustered index (with the possible exception of filtered nonclustered indexes). Keep this in mind when you decide on which columns to build your clustered index. It's a great idea to cluster on a nonvolatile column, such as an identity.

If a row moves because it no longer fits on the original page, it still has the same row locator (in other words, the clustering key for the row stays the same), and no nonclustered indexes have to be modified. This is true even if the table is moved to a new physical location (filegroup or partitioning scheme). Nonclustered indexes are updated only if the clustering key changes, and moving the physical location of a table row doesn't change its clustering key.

In the discussion of index internals, you also saw that if a table has no clustered index—in other words, if it's a heap—the row locator stored in the nonclustered index is actually the physical location of the row. If a row in a heap moves to a new page, the row leaves a forwarding pointer in the original location. This is a performance optimization, so that the nonclustered indexes won't need to be changed; they still refer to the original location, and from there, they are directed to the new location. In this case, if the table moves to a new location (filegroup or partitioning scheme), the nonclustered indexes are updated because the physical location of all records in the heap must change, thus invalidating the prior row locators in the nonclustered indexes.

Look at the query in Listing 7-11, which creates a table very similar to the one created for doing inserts, except this table has a third column of variable length. After you populate the table with five rows, which fill the page, you update one of the rows to make its third column much longer. The row no longer fits on the original page and has to move. You can then use the *sys.dm_db_database_page_allocations* function to get the page numbers used by the table.

LISTING 7-11 Creating a forwarding stub

```
USE AdventureWorks2012;
GO
IF object_id('dbo.bigrows') IS NOT NULL DROP TABLE bigrows;
GO
CREATE TABLE dbo.bigrows
(   a int IDENTITY ,
    b varchar(1600),
    c varchar(1600));
GO
INSERT INTO TABLE dbo.bigrows
    VALUES (REPLICATE('a', 1600), '');
INSERT INTO TABLE dbo.bigrows
    VALUES (REPLICATE('b', 1600), '');
INSERT INTO TABLE dbo.bigrows
    VALUES (REPLICATE('c', 1600), '');
INSERT INTO TABLE dbo.bigrows
    VALUES (REPLICATE('d', 1600), '');
INSERT INTO TABLE dbo.bigrows
    VALUES (REPLICATE('e', 1600), '');
GO
UPDATE TABLE dbo.bigrows
SET c = REPLICATE('x', 1600)
WHERE a = 3;
GO

SELECT allocated_page_file_id as PageFID, allocated_page_page_id as PagePID,
FROM sys.dm_db_database_page_allocations(db_id('AdventureWorks2012'),
    object_id('dbo.bigrows'), null, null, 'DETAILED');

RESULTS:
PageFID PagePID
```

```
-------  -----------
1        2252
1        4586

DBCC TRACEON(3604);
GO
DBCC PAGE(AdventureWorks2012, 1, 2252, 1);
GO
```

The entire output from the *DBCC PAGE* command isn't shown here, but you can see what appears in the slot where the row with *a = 3* formerly appeared:

```
Slot 2, Offset 0x1feb, Length 9, DumpStyle BYTE
Record Type = FORWARDING_STUB        Record Attributes =
Memory Dump @0x61ADDFEB
00000000:   04ea1100 00010000 00†††††††††††††††††††.........
```

The value of 4 in the first byte means that this is just a forwarding stub. The 0011ea in the next 3 bytes is the page number to which the row has been moved. Because this is a hexadecimal value, you need to convert it to 4586 decimal. The next group of 4 bytes tells us that the page is at slot 0, file 1. (Of course, if you run this code, you might get different file and page number values, but when you translate them to decimal you should see the same results that you got for the second data page when looking at the *sys.dm_db_database_page_allocations* function above. You can see that the second page (*PagePID*) in my output was 4586.) If you then use *DBCC PAGE* to look at that page 4586, you can see what the forwarded record looks like.

Managing forwarding pointers

Forwarding pointers allow you to modify data in a heap without worrying about having to make drastic changes to the nonclustered indexes. If a row that has been forwarded must move again, the original forwarding pointer is updated to point to the new location. You never end up with a forwarding pointer pointing to another forwarding pointer. Also, if the forwarded row shrinks enough to fit in its original place, the record might move back to its original place—if room is still available on that page—and the forwarding pointer would be eliminated.

When you rebuild a table with the *ALTER TABLE* command, all data is moved to new pages and any forwarded records become regular data rows. A future version of SQL Server might include some mechanism for performing a physical reorganization of the data in a heap, which would get rid of forwarding pointers without a complete rebuild. (Note that forwarding pointers exist only in heaps, and that the *ALTER INDEX* option to reorganize an index won't do anything to heaps.) You can defragment a nonclustered index on a heap, but not the table itself.

Currently, when a forwarding pointer is created, it stays there until the row is deleted or the table is rebuilt—with only a few exceptions. The first exception is the case already mentioned, in which a row shrinks and returns to its original location. The second exception is when the entire database shrinks. The bookmarks are actually reassigned when a file is shrunk. The shrink process never generates forwarding pointers. For pages that were removed because of the shrink process, any forwarded rows or stubs they contain are effectively "unforwarded." Other cases in which the forwarding pointers are removed are the obvious ones: if the forwarded row is deleted or if a clustered index is built on the table so that it's no longer a heap.

To get a count of forwarded records in a table, you can look at the output from the *sys.dm_db_index_physical_stats* function.

Updating in place

In SQL Server 2012, updating a row in place is the rule rather than the exception. This means that the row stays in exactly the same location on the same page, and only the bytes affected are changed. Also, the log contains a single record for each update in-place operation unless the table has an update trigger on it or is marked for replication. In these cases, the update still happens in place, but the log contains a *DELETE* record followed by an *INSERT* record if any of the index key columns are updated.

In cases where a row can't be updated in place, the cost of a not-in-place update is minimal because of the way the nonclustered indexes are stored and because of the use of forwarding pointers. In fact, you can have an update not in place for which the row stays on the original page. Updates happen in place if a heap is being updated (and enough space is available on the page) or if a table with a clustered index is updated without any change to the clustering keys. You can also get an update in place if the clustering key changes but the row doesn't need to move at all. For example, if you have a clustered index on a *lastname* column containing consecutive key values of *Abolrous*, Bechynsky, and *Charney*, you might want to update *Bechynsky* to *Belishky*. Because the row stays in the same location even after the clustered index key changes, SQL Server performs this as an update in place. On the other hand, if you update *Abolrous* to *Burk*, the update can't occur in place, but the new row might stay on the same page.

Updating not in place

If your update can't happen in place because you're updating clustering keys, the update occurs as a *DELETE* followed by an *INSERT*. In some cases, you get a hybrid update: Some of the rows are updated in place and some aren't. If you're updating index keys, SQL Server builds a list of all the rows that need to change as both a *DELETE* and an *INSERT* operation. This list is stored in memory, if it's small enough, and is written to *tempdb* if necessary. This list is then sorted by key value and operator (*DELETE* or *INSERT*). If the index whose keys are changing isn't unique, the *DELETE* and *INSERT* steps are then applied to the table. If the index is unique, an additional step is carried out to collapse *DELETE* and *INSERT* operations on the same key into a single *UPDATE* operation.

Table-level vs. index-level data modification

So far this chapter has discussed only the placement and index manipulation necessary for modifying either a single row or a few rows with no more than a single index. If you are modifying multiple rows in a single operation (*INSERT, UPDATE*, or *DELETE*) or by using *BCP* or the *BULK INSERT* command and the table has multiple indexes, you must be aware of some other issues. SQL Server offers two strategies for maintaining all the indexes that belong to a table: table-level modification and index-level modification. The Query Optimizer chooses between them based on its estimate of the anticipated execution costs for each strategy.

Table-level modification is sometimes called *row-at-a-time*, and index-level modification is sometimes called *index-at-a-time*. In table-level modification, all indexes are maintained for each row as that row is modified. If the update stream isn't sorted in any way, SQL Server has to do a lot of random index accesses, one access per index per update row. If the update stream is sorted, it can't be sorted in more than one order, so nonrandom index accesses can occur for at most one index.

In index-level modifications, SQL Server gathers all the rows to be modified and sorts them for each index. In other words, you have as many sort operations as you have indexes. Then, for each index, the updates are merged into the index, and each index page is never accessed more than once, even if multiple updates pertain to a single index leaf page.

Clearly, if the update is small—say, less than a handful of rows—and the table and its indexes are sizable, the Query Optimizer usually considers table-level modification the best choice. Most OLTP operations use table-level modification. On the other hand, if the update is relatively large, table-level modifications require a lot of random I/O operations and might even read and write each leaf page in each index multiple times. In that case, index-level modification offers much better performance. The amount of logging required is the same for both strategies.

You can determine whether your updates were done at the table level or the index level by inspecting the query execution plan. If SQL Server performs the update at the index level, you see a plan produced that contains an *UPDATE* operator for each of the affected indexes. If SQL Server performs the update at the table level, you see only a single *UPDATE* operator in the plan.

Logging

Standard *INSERT*, *UPDATE*, and *DELETE* statements are always logged to ensure atomicity, and you can't disable logging of these operations. The modification must be known to be safely on disk in the transaction log (write-ahead logging) before the commit of the statement or transaction can be acknowledged to the calling application. Page allocations and deallocations, including those done by *TRUNCATE TABLE*, are also logged. As you saw in Chapter 5, "Logging and recovery," certain operations can be minimally logged when your database is in the *BULK_LOGGED* recovery mode, but even then, information about allocations and deallocations is written to the log, as is the fact that a minimally logged operation has been executed.

Locking

Any data modification must always be protected with some form of exclusive lock. For the most part, SQL Server makes all the locking decisions internally; a user or programmer doesn't need to request a particular kind of lock. Chapter 10, "Query execution," explains the different types of locks and their compatibility. However, because locking is closely tied to data modification, you should always be aware of the following points:

- Every type of data modification performed in SQL Server requires some form of exclusive lock. For most data modification operations, SQL Server considers row locking as the default, but if many locks are required, SQL Server can lock pages or even the whole table.

- Update locks can be used to signal the intention to do an update, and they are important for avoiding deadlock conditions. But ultimately, the update operation requires that an exclusive lock be performed. The update lock serializes access to ensure that an exclusive lock can be acquired, but the update lock isn't sufficient by itself.

- Exclusive locks must always be held until the end of a transaction in case the transaction needs to be undone—unlike shared locks, which can be released as soon as the scan moves off the page, such as when the *READ COMMITTED* isolation is in effect.

- If a full table scan must be used to find qualifying rows for an *UPDATE* or a *DELETE*, SQL Server must inspect every row to determine the row to modify. Other processes that need to find individual rows are blocked even if they ultimately modify different rows. Without inspecting the row, SQL Server has no way of knowing whether the row qualifies for the modification. If you're modifying only a subset of rows in the table as determined by a *WHERE* clause, be sure to have indexes available to allow SQL Server to access the needed rows directly so it doesn't have to scan every row in the table.

Fragmentation

Fragmentation is a general term used to describe various effects that can occur in indexes because of data modifications. The two general types of fragmentation are internal and external.

Internal fragmentation (often called *physical fragmentation* or *page density*) means that index pages have wasted space, both at the leaf and non-leaf levels. This can occur because of any or all of the following:

- Page splits (described earlier) leaving empty space on the page that was split and the newly allocated page

- *DELETE* operations that leave pages less than full

- Row sizes that contribute to under-full pages (for instance, a fixed-width, 5,000-byte data record in a clustered index leads to 3,000 wasted bytes per clustered index data page)

Internal fragmentation means the index is taking more space than necessary, leading to increased disk space usage, more pages to read to process the data, and more memory used to hold the pages in the buffer pool. Sometimes internal fragmentation can be advantageous, because it allows more rows to be inserted on pages without *causing* page splits. Deliberate internal fragmentation can be achieved using the *FILLFACTOR* and *PAD_INDEX* options, which are described in the next section.

External fragmentation (often called *logical fragmentation* or *extent fragmentation*) means the pages or extents comprising the leaf level of a clustered or nonclustered index aren't in the most efficient order. The most efficient order is where the logical order of the pages and extents (as defined by the index keys, following the next-page pointers from the page headers) is the same as the physical order of the pages and extents within the data file(s). In other words, the index leaf-level page that has the row with the next index key is also the next physically contiguous page in the data file. This is separate from fragmentation at the *file-system* level, where the actual data files can be composed of several physical sections.

External fragmentation is caused by page splits and reduces the efficiency of ordered scans of part of a clustered or nonclustered index. The more external fragmentation exists, the less likely the storage engine can perform efficient prereading of the pages necessary for the scan.

The methods of detecting and removing fragmentation are discussed in the next section.

Managing B-tree index structures

SQL Server maintains your indexes automatically, ensuring that the correct rows are there. As you add new rows, it automatically inserts them into the correct position in a table with a clustered index and adds new leaf-level rows to your nonclustered indexes that point to the new data rows. When you remove rows, SQL Server automatically deletes the corresponding leaf-level rows from your nonclustered indexes. Rows added to or removed from heaps also require that any nonclustered index indexes be adjusted.

So, although your indexes continue to contain all the correct index rows in the B-tree to help SQL Server find the rows you are looking for, you might still occasionally need to perform maintenance operations on your indexes, especially to deal with fragmentation in its various forms. Also, several properties of indexes can be changed.

Dropping indexes

One of the biggest differences between managing indexes created with the *CREATE INDEX* command and indexes that support constraints is in how you can drop the index. The *DROP INDEX* command allows you to drop only indexes that were built with the *CREATE INDEX* command. To drop indexes that support constraints, you must use *ALTER TABLE* to drop the constraint. Also, to drop a PRIMARY KEY or UNIQUE constraint that has any FOREIGN KEY constraints referencing it, you must first drop the FOREIGN KEY constraint. This can leave you with a window of vulnerability if your goal is to drop indexes and immediately rebuild them, perhaps with a new *fillfactor*. Although the FOREIGN KEY constraint is gone, an *INSERT* statement can add a row to the table that violates your referential integrity.

One way to avoid this problem is to use *ALTER INDEX*, which allows you to drop and rebuild one or all of your indexes on a table in a single statement without requiring the auxiliary step of removing FOREIGN KEY constraints. Alternatively, you can use the *CREATE INDEX* command with the *DROP_EXISTING* option if you want to rebuild existing indexes without having to drop and re-create them in two steps. Although you can normally use *CREATE INDEX* with *DROP_EXISTING* to redefine the properties of an index—such as the key columns or included columns, or whether the index is unique—if you use *CREATE INDEX* with *DROP_EXISTING* to rebuild an index that supports a constraint, you can't make these kinds of changes. The index must be re-created with the same columns, in the same order, and the same values for uniqueness and clustering.

Using the ALTER INDEX command

The *ALTER INDEX* command allows you to use a single command to invoke various kinds of index changes that in previous versions required an eclectic collection of different commands, including *sp_indexoption*, *DBCC DBREINDEX*, and *DBCC INDEXDEFRAG*. Rather than use individual commands or procedures for each different index maintenance activity, you can use *ALTER INDEX* to handle all of them. For a complete description of all the options to *ALTER INDEX*, see the *SQL Server Books Online* topic "ALTER INDEX."

Basically, you can make four types of changes using *ALTER INDEX*, three of which have corresponding options that you can specify when you create an index using *CREATE INDEX*.

Rebuilding an index

Rebuilding the index replaces the *DBCC DBREINDEX* command and can be thought of as replacing the *DROP_EXISTING* option to the *CREATE INDEX* command. However, this option also allows indexes to be moved or partitioned. A new option allows indexes to be rebuilt online in the same way you can create indexes online (as mentioned earlier in the section "Index creation options"). Online index building and rebuilding is discussed shortly.

Disabling an index

Disabling an index makes it completely unavailable, so it can't be used for finding rows for any operations. Disabling the index also means that it won't be maintained as changes to the data are made.

You can disable one index or all indexes with a single command. No *ENABLE* option is available. Because no maintenance is performed while an index is disabled, indexes must be completely rebuilt to make them useful again. Re-enabling, which can take place either online or offline, is done with the *REBUILD* option to *ALTER INDEX*. This feature was introduced mainly for the internal purposes of SQL Server when applying upgrades and service packs, but disabling an index has a few interesting uses.

- You can use it if you want to ignore the index temporarily for troubleshooting purposes.

- Rather than drop nonclustered indexes before loading data, you can disable them. However, you can't disable the clustered index and continue to work with the table. If you disable the clustered index on a table, the table's data is unavailable because the leaf level of the clustered index *is* the data. Disabling the clustered index essentially disables the table. However, if your data is going to be loaded in clustered index order (for an ever-increasing clustering key) so that all new data goes to the end of the table, disabling the nonclustered indexes can help to improve load performance. After the data is loaded, you can rebuild the nonclustered indexes without having to supply the entire index definition. All the metadata is saved while the index is disabled.

Changing index options

Most options that you can specify during a *CREATE INDEX* operation can also be specified with the *ALTER INDEX* command: *ALLOW_ROW_LOCKS*, *ALLOW_PAGE_LOCKS*, *IGNORE_DUP_KEY*, *FILLFACTOR*, *PAD_INDEX*, *STATISTICS_NORECOMPUTE*, *MAXP_DOP*, and *SORT_IN_TEMPDB*. The *IGNORE_DUP_KEY* option was described earlier in the section "Index creation options."

FILLFACTOR and PAD_INDEX   *FILLFACTOR*, probably the most commonly used of these options, lets you reserve some space on each leaf page of an index. In a clustered index, because the leaf level contains the data, you can use *FILLFACTOR* to control how much space to leave in the table itself. By reserving free space, you can later avoid the need to split pages to make room for a new entry. An important fact about *FILLFACTOR* is that the value isn't maintained; it indicates only how much space is reserved with the existing data at the time the index is built or rebuilt. If you need to, you can use the *ALTER INDEX* command to rebuild the index and reestablish the original *FILLFACTOR* specified. If you don't specify a new *FILLFACTOR* when using *ALTER INDEX*, the previously used *FILLFACTOR* is used.

  FILLFACTOR should always be specified index by index. If *FILLFACTOR* isn't specified, the server-wide default is used. The value is set for the server via the *sp_configure* procedure with the *fillfactor* option. This configuration value is 0 by default (and is the same as 100), which means that leaf pages of indexes are made as full as possible. *Not* changing this serverwide setting is a best practice. *FILLFACTOR* applies only to the index's leaf pages. In specialized and high-use situations, you might want to reserve space in the intermediate index pages to avoid page splits there, too. You can do this by specifying the *PAD_INDEX* option, which instructs SQL Server to use the same *FILLFACTOR* value at all levels of the index. Just as for *FILLFACTOR*, *PAD_INDEX* is applicable only when an index is created (or re-created).

  When you create a table that includes PRIMARY KEY or UNIQUE constraints, you can specify whether the associated index is clustered or nonclustered, and you can also specify the *fillfactor*. Because the *fillfactor* applies only at the time the index is created, and because no data exists when you first create the table, it might seem that specifying the *fillfactor* at that time is completely useless. However, if you decide to rebuild your indexes after the table is populated and if no new *fillfactor* is specified, the original value is used. You can also specify a *fillfactor* when you use *ALTER TABLE* to add a PRIMARY KEY or UNIQUE constraint to a table; if the table already contains data, the *fillfactor* value is applied when you build the index to support the new constraint.

DROP_EXISTING   The *DROP_EXISTING* option specifies that a given index should be dropped and rebuilt as a single transaction. This option is particularly useful when you rebuild clustered indexes. Normally, when a developer drops a clustered index, SQL Server must rebuild every nonclustered index to change its bookmarks to RIDs instead of the clustering keys. Then, if a developer builds (or rebuilds) a clustered index, SQL Server must again rebuild all nonclustered indexes to update the bookmarks. The *DROP_EXISTING* option of the *CREATE INDEX* command allows a clustered index to be rebuilt without having to rebuild the nonclustered indexes twice. If you're creating the index on exactly the same keys that it had previously, the nonclustered indexes don't need to be rebuilt. If you are changing the key definition, the nonclustered indexes are rebuilt only once, after the clustered index is rebuilt. Rather than use the *DROP_EXISTING* option to rebuild an existing index, you can use the *ALTER INDEX* command.

SORT_IN_TEMPDB   The *SORT_IN_TEMPDB* option allows you to control where SQL Server performs the sort operation on the key values needed to build an index. The default is that SQL Server uses space from the filegroup on which the index is to be created. While the index is being built, SQL Server scans the data pages to find the key values and then builds leaf-level index rows in internal sort buffers. When these sort buffers are filled, they are written to disk. If the *SORT_IN_TEMPDB* option is specified, the sort buffers are allocated from *tempdb*, so much less space is needed in the source database. If you don't specify *SORT_IN_TEMPDB*, not only does your source database require enough free space for the sort buffers and a copy of the index (or the data, if a clustered index is being built), but the disk heads for the database also need to move back and forth between the base table pages and the work area where the sort buffers are stored. If, instead, your *CREATE INDEX* command includes the *SORT_IN_TEMPDB* option, performance can be greatly improved if your *tempdb* database is on a separate physical disk from the database you're working with.

You can optimize head movement because two separate heads read the base table pages and manage the sort buffers. You can speed up index creation even more if your *tempdb* database is on a faster disk than your user database and you use the *SORT_IN_TEMPDB* option.

Reorganizing an index

Reorganizing an index is the only change that doesn't have a corresponding option in the *CREATE INDEX* command. The reason is that when you create an index, nothing is available to reorganize. The *REORGANIZE* option replaces the *DBCC INDEXDEFRAG* command and removes some of the fragmentation from an index, but it's not guaranteed to remove all the fragmentation, just as *DBCC INDEXDEFRAG* might not remove all the fragmentation (in spite of its name). Before discussing removing fragmentation, you must first look at detecting fragmentation in the next section.

Detecting fragmentation

As you've already seen in numerous examples, the output of *sys.dm_db_index_physical_stats* returns a row for each level of an index. However, when a table is partitioned, it effectively treats each partition as a table, so this DMV actually returns a row for each level of each partition of each index. For a small index with only in-row data (no row-overflow or LOB pages) and only the one default partition, you might get only two or three rows back (one for each index level). But if multiple partitions and additional allocation units are available for the row-overflow and LOB data, you might see many more rows. For example, a clustered index on a table containing row-overflow data, built on 11 partitions and being two levels deep, have 33 rows (2 levels × 11 partitions + 11 partitions for the *row_overflow* allocation units) in the fragmentation report returned by *sys.dm_db_index_physical_stats*.

Earlier, the section "Tools for analyzing indexes" details the input parameters and the output results, but the following columns provide fragmentation information that's not obvious.

- **Forwarded_record_count**   Forwarded records (discussed earlier in the section "Data modification internals") are possible only in a heap and occur when updates cause a row with variable-length columns to increase in size so that it no longer fits in its original location. If a table has many forwarded records, scanning the table can be very inefficient.

- **Ghost_Record_Count and version_ghost_record_count** Ghost records are rows that physically still exist on a page but logically have been removed, as discussed in the section "Data modification internals." Background processes in SQL Server clean up ghost records, but until that happens, no new records can be inserted in their place. So if many ghost records exist, your table has the drawback of much internal fragmentation—that is, the table is spread out over more pages and takes longer to scan—but none of the advantages (the pages have no room to insert new rows to avoid external fragmentation). A subset of ghost records is measured by *version_ghost_record_count*. This value reports the number of rows that have been retained by an outstanding Snapshot isolation transaction. These aren't cleaned up until all relevant transactions have been committed or rolled back. Chapter 13 covers Snapshot isolation.

Removing fragmentation

If fragmentation becomes too severe and affects query performance, you have several options for removing it. You might also wonder how severe is too severe. First, fragmentation isn't always a bad thing. The biggest performance penalty from having fragmented data arises when your application needs to perform an ordered scan on the data. The more the logical order varies from the physical order, the greater the cost of scanning the data. If, on the other hand, your application needs only one or a few rows of data, it doesn't matter whether the table or index data is in logical order or is physically contiguous, or whether it's spread all over the disk in totally random locations. If you have a good index to find the rows you are interested in, SQL Server can find one or a few rows very efficiently, wherever they happen to be physically located.

If you are doing ordered scans of an index (such as table scans on a table with a clustered index or a leaf-level scan of a nonclustered index) and if your *avg_fragmentation_in_percent* value is between 10 and 25, you should reorganize your index to remove the fragmentation. As you'll see shortly, reorganizing an index (also called *defragging*) compacts the leaf-level pages back to their originally specified *fillfactor* and then rearranges the pages at the leaf level to correct the logical fragmentation, using the same pages that the index originally occupied. No new pages are allocated, so this operation is much more space-efficient than rebuilding the index.

If the *avg_fragmentation_in_percent* value is greater than 25, you should consider completely rebuilding your index. Rebuilding an index means that a whole new set of pages is allocated for it. This removes almost all fragmentation, but it's not guaranteed to eliminate it completely. If the free space in the database is itself fragmented, you might not be able to allocate enough contiguous space to remove all gaps between extents. Also, if other work is going on that needs to allocate new extents while your index is being rebuilt, the extents allocated to the two processes can end up being interleaved.

Defragmentation is designed to remove logical fragmentation from the leaf level of an index while keeping the index online and as available as possible. When defragmenting an index, SQL Server acquires an Intent-Exclusive lock on the index B-tree. Exclusive page locks are taken on individual pages only while those pages are being manipulated, as you see later in this chapter during the discussion on the defragmentation algorithm. The *ALTER INDEX* command initiates defragmentation. The general form of the command to remove fragmentation is as follows:

```
ALTER INDEX { index_name | ALL }
   ON <object>
     REORGANIZE
           [ PARTITION = partition_number ]
           [ WITH ( LOB_COMPACTION = { ON | OFF } ) ]
```

As you can see, *ALTER INDEX* with the *REORGANIZE* option supports partitioned indexes, so you can choose to defragment just one particular partition (the default is to defragment all the partitions). It also allows you to control whether the LOB data is affected by the defragmenting.

As mentioned earlier, every index is created with a specific *fillfactor*. The initial *fillfactor* value is stored with the index metadata, so when defragmenting is requested, SQL Server can inspect this value. During defragmentation, SQL Server attempts to reestablish the initial *fillfactor* if it's greater than the current *fillfactor* on a leaf-level page. Defragmentation is designed to compact data, and this can be done by putting more rows per page and increasing the fullness percentage of each page. SQL Server might end up then removing pages from the index after the defragmentation. If the current *fillfactor* is greater than the initial *fillfactor*, SQL Server can't *reduce* the fullness level of a page by moving rows out of it. The compaction algorithm inspects adjacent pages (in logical order) to see whether room is available to move rows from the second page to the first. The process very efficiently looks at a sliding window of eight logically consecutive pages. It determines whether enough rows can be moved around within the eight pages to allow a single page to be emptied and removed, and moves rows only if this is the case.

As mentioned earlier, when reorganizing and index you can opt to compact LOB pages. The default is *ON*. Reorganizing a specified clustered index compacts all LOB columns contained in the clustered index before it compacts the leaf pages. Reorganizing a nonclustered index compacts all LOB columns that are non-key (*INCLUDE*d) columns in the index.

LOB compaction finds low-density extents—those that are used at less than 75 percent. It moves pages out of these low-density uniform extents and places the data from them in available space in other uniform extents already allocated to the LOB allocation unit. This functionality allows much better use of disk space, which can be wasted with low-density LOB extents. No new extents are allocated, either during this compaction phase or during the next phase.

The second phase of the reorganization operation actually moves data to new pages in the in-row allocation unit with the goal of having the logical order of data match the physical order. The index is kept online because only two pages at a time are processed in an operation similar to a heapsort or smoothsort (the details of which are beyond the scope of this book). The following example is a simplification of the actual process of reorganization.

Consider an index on a column of *datetime* data. Monday's data logically precedes Tuesday's data, which precedes Wednesday's data, which precedes Thursday's data, and so on. If, however, Monday's data is on page 88, Tuesday's is on page 50, Wednesday's is on page 100, and Thursday's is on page

77, the physical and logical ordering doesn't match in the slightest, which is logical fragmentation. When defragmenting an index, SQL Server determines the first physical page belonging to the leaf level (page 50, in this case) and the first logical page in the leaf level (page 88, which holds Monday's data) and swaps the data on those two pages, using one additional new page as a temporary storage area. After this swap, the first logical page with Monday's data is on page 50, the lowest-numbered physical page. After each page swap, all locks and latches are released and the key of the last page moved is saved. The next iteration of the algorithm uses the saved key to find the next logical page— Tuesday's data, which is now on page 88. The next physical page is 77, which holds Thursday's data. So another swap is made to place Tuesday's data on page 77 and Thursday's on page 88. This process continues until no more swaps need to be made. Note that no defragmenting is done for pages on mixed extents.

You need to be aware of some restrictions on using the REORGANIZE option. Certainly, if the index is disabled, it can't be defragmented. Also, because the process of removing fragmentation needs to work on individual pages, you get an error if you try to reorganize an index that has the option ALLOW_PAGE_LOCKS set to OFF. Reorganization can't happen if a concurrent online index is built on the same index or if another process is concurrently reorganizing the same index.

You can observe the progress of each index's reorganization in the sys.dm_exec_requests DMV in the percent_complete column. The value in this column reports the percentage completed in one index's reorganization. If you are reorganizing multiple indexes in the same command, you might see the value go up and down as each index is defragmented in turn.

Rebuilding an index

You can completely rebuild an index in several ways. You can use a simple combination of DROP IN-DEX followed by CREATE INDEX, but this method is probably the least preferable. In particular, if you are rebuilding a clustered index in this way, all the nonclustered indexes must be rebuilt when you drop the clustered index. This nonclustered index rebuilding is necessary to change the row locators in the leaf level from the clustered key values to row IDs. Then, when you rebuild the clustered index, all the nonclustered indexes must be rebuilt. Also, if the index supports a PRIMARY KEY or UNIQUE constraint, you can't use the DROP INDEX command at all—unless you first drop all the FOREIGN KEYs. Although this is possible, it's not preferable.

Better solutions are to use the ALTER INDEX command or to use the DROP_EXISTING clause along with CREATE INDEX. As an example, here are both methods for rebuilding the PK_TransactionHistory_TransactionID index on the Production.TransactionHistory table:

```
ALTER INDEX PK_TransactionHistory_TransactionID
        ON Production.TransactionHistory REBUILD;

CREATE UNIQUE CLUSTERED INDEX PK_TransactionHistory_TransactionID
        ON Production.TransactionHistory
            (TransactionDate, TransactionID)
        WITH DROP_EXISTING;
```

Although the *CREATE* method requires knowing the index schema, it's actually more powerful and offers more options that you can specify. You can change the columns that make up the index, change the uniqueness property, or change a nonclustered index to clustered, as long as a clustered index isn't already on the table. You can also specify a new filegroup or a partition scheme to use when rebuilding. Note that if you do change the clustered index key properties, all nonclustered indexes must be rebuilt, but only once (not twice, as would happen if you executed *DROP INDEX* followed by *CREATE INDEX*).

When using the *ALTER INDEX* command to rebuild a clustered index, the nonclustered indexes never need to be rebuilt just as a side effect because you can't change the index definition at all. However, you can specify *ALL* instead of an index name and request that all indexes be rebuilt. Another advantage of the *ALTER INDEX* method is that you can specify just a single partition to be rebuilt—if, for example, the fragmentation report from *sys.dm_db_index_physical_stats* shows fragmentation in just one partition or a subset of the partitions.

Online index building

The default behavior of either method of rebuilding an index is that SQL Server takes an exclusive lock on the index, so it's completely unavailable while the index is being rebuilt. If the index is clustered, the entire table is unavailable; if the index is nonclustered, the table uses a shared lock, which means no modifications can be made but other processes can *SELECT* from the table. Of course, they can't take advantage of the index you're rebuilding, so the query might not perform as well as it should.

SQL Server 2012 provides the option to rebuild one or all indexes online. The *ONLINE* option is available with both *ALTER INDEX* and *CREATE INDEX*, with or without the *DROP_EXISTING* option. Note that it can't be used with XML indexes or indexes on local temp tables. Here's the syntax for building the preceding index, but doing it online:

```
ALTER INDEX PK_TransactionHistory_TransactionID
        ON Production.TransactionHistory REBUILD WITH (ONLINE = ON);
```

The online build works by maintaining two copies of the index simultaneously: the original (the source) and the new one (the target). The target is used only for writing any changes made while the rebuild is going on. All reading is done from the source, and modifications are applied to the source as well. SQL Server row-level versioning is used, so anyone retrieving information from the index can read consistent data. Figure 7-3 (taken from *SQL Server Books Online*) illustrates the source and target, showing three phases that the build process goes through. For each phase, the illustration describes what kind of access is allowed, what is happening in the source and target tables, and what locks are applied.

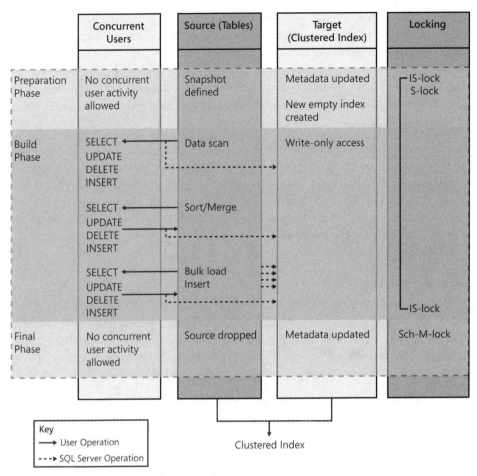

Concurrent Users	Source (Tables)	Target (Clustered Index)	Locking
Preparation Phase No concurrent user activity allowed	Snapshot defined	Metadata updated New empty index created	⌐ IS-lock S-lock
Build Phase SELECT UPDATE DELETE INSERT	Data scan	Write-only access	
SELECT UPDATE DELETE INSERT	Sort/Merge		
SELECT UPDATE DELETE INSERT	Bulk load Insert		└ IS-lock
Final Phase No concurrent user activity allowed	Source dropped	Metadata updated	Sch-M-lock

Key
→ User Operation
- - -▶ SQL Server Operation

Clustered Index

FIGURE 7-3 The structures and phases of online index building.

The actual processes might vary slightly depending on whether the index is being built initially or being rebuilt and whether the index is clustered or nonclustered.

Here are the steps involved in rebuilding a nonclustered index:

1. A Shared lock (S-lock) is taken on the index, which prevents any data modification queries, and an Intent-Shared lock (IS-lock) is taken on the table.

2. The index is created with the same structures as the original and marked as write-only.

3. The Shared lock is released on the index, leaving only the Intent-Shared lock on the table.

4. A versioned scan (discussed in detail in Chapter 13) is started on the original index, which means modifications made during the scan are ignored. The scanned data is copied to the target.

5. All subsequent modifications write to both the source and the target. Reads use only the source.

6. The scan of the source and copy to the target continues while normal operations are performed. SQL Server uses a proprietary method for reconciling obvious problems, such as a record being deleted before the scan has inserted it into the new index.

7. The scan completes.

8. A Schema-Modification lock (Sch-M-lock)—the strictest of all types of locks—is taken to make the table completely unavailable.

9. The source index is dropped, metadata is updated, and the target index is made to be read-write.

10. The Schema-Modification lock is released.

Building a new nonclustered index involves exactly the same steps except no target index is used, so the versioned scan is done on the base table, and write operations need to maintain only the target index rather than both indexes. A clustered index rebuild works exactly like a nonclustered rebuild, as long as no schema change is made (a change of index keys or uniqueness property).

A build of new clustered index, or a rebuild of a clustered index with a schema change, has a few more differences. First, an intermediate mapping index is used to translate between the source and target physical structures. Also, all existing nonclustered indexes are rebuilt one at a time after a new base table has been built. For example, creating a clustered index on a heap with two nonclustered indexes involves the following steps:

1. Create a new write-only clustered index.

2. Create a new nonclustered index based on the new clustered index.

3. Create another new nonclustered index based on the new clustered index.

4. Drop the heap and the two original nonclustered indexes.

Before the operation completes, SQL Server is maintaining six structures at the same time. Online index building isn't really considered a performance enhancement because an index can actually be built faster offline, and all these structures don't need to be maintained simultaneously. Online index building is an availability feature—you can rebuild indexes to remove all fragmentation or re-establish a *fillfactor* even if your data must be fully available at all times.

> **Note** The ability to perform online index operations involves two exceptions.
>
> If the index contains a LOB column, online index operations aren't available. This means that if the table contains a LOB column, the clustered index can't be rebuilt online. Online operations are prevented only if a nonclustered index specifically includes a LOB column.
>
> A single partition of a clustered or nonclustered index can't be rebuilt online.

Columnstore indexes

SQL Server 2012 introduces a new feature called *columnstore indexes*, which are part of a new family of technologies called xVelocity, all focused on optimizing in-memory processing. Columnstore indexes completely change the way data is organized and managed and don't use the familiar B-tree structure (described early in this chapter). Columnstore indexes store each column individually using a special kind of compression called Vertipaq compression, which is also used in Analysis Services and Power Pivot.

Columnstore indexes are particularly beneficial in data warehouse systems in which your queries are accessing most, if not all, of the rows in a very large table, but only referencing a subset of the columns. In fact, even if your queries need most of the columns in most of the rows, a columnstore index would still most likely be useful because of the special Vertipaq compression algorithm, as well as a new processing technique called batch processing, which allows much more data to be retrieved and operated on much more efficiently than with a normal B-tree index, in which the information is stored in rows. The new technology allowing data to be managed by columns in a columnstore is an alternative to the B-tree structure which manages data in rowstores.

The performance value of columnstore indexes usually isn't seen unless you have a very large fact table, with at least 10 million rows of data, running on a system with more than four processors. The next section describes the creation and storage of columnstore indexes and the metadata available to examine them.

Creation of columnstore indexes

Creating a columnstore index is very similar syntactically to creating a nonclustered B-tree index, but most of the index options aren't allowed. The only options available are *DROP_EXISTING* and *MAXDOP*. You can specify a filegroup or partition scheme on which to place the index. If neither a filegroup nor a partition scheme is specified, the table is stored on the same filegroup or partition scheme as the underlying table.

Columnstore indexes have some restrictions on the allowable data types. Basically all common business data types are supported, although some have a limitation in the actual length. The following data types aren't allowed in a columnstore index:

- *binary* and *varbinary*

- *ntext*, *text*, and *image*

- *varchar(max)* and *nvarchar(max)*

- *uniqueidentifier*

- *rowversion* (and *timestamp*)

- *sql_variant*

- *decimal* (and *numeric*) with precision greater than 18 digits

- *datetimeoffset*, with scale greater than 2

- CLR types (*hierarchyid* and *spatial* types)

- *xml*

A columnstore index also can't include any *SPARSE* columns, computed columns, or included columns; it can't be clustered or unique; and it can't be created on an indexed view. The index can't be compressed using normal page or row compression, as the Vertipaq compression replaces that. However, the table on which the columnstore index is built can be compressed using row or page compression.

The act of creating a columnstore index can take a substantial amount of memory, based on the number of columns, the data types of the index columns, and the number of processors used, such as the DOP. You can use the following formula to get a rough idea of the amount of memory SQL Server requests a memory grant before starting to build the index:

```
Memory grant request in MB =
  [(4.2 * Number of columns in the columnstore index) + 68] * DOP +
     (Number of character columns in the columnstore index * 34)
```

Notice that the memory grant doesn't depend on the number of rows in the table because the columnstore index is built and stored in segments consisting of about a million rows each. Each segment can be built separately, so the total number doesn't increase the amount of memory required. You should also be aware that by default, SQL Server limits queries to only 25 percent of the available memory. This is configurable using SQL Server's Resource Governor (discussed in Chapter 2, "The SQLOS"). If you get an error about lack of memory immediately on starting to create your columnstore index, such as 8657 or 8658, or errors about running out of memory after execution begins, such as 701 or 802, you might need to adjust the memory available to queries in the default workload group, which contains any queries not specified to be in a different workload group. So if you haven't set up Resource Governor at all, chances are that all queries are in the default workload group, and each of them is limited to 25 percent of the available memory. You can change this setting to 75 percent with the following commands:

```
ALTER WORKLOAD GROUP [DEFAULT] WITH (REQUEST_MAX_MEMORY_GRANT_PERCENT=75);
ALTER RESOURCE GOVERNOR RECONFIGURE;
```

After reading about the storage of columnstore indexes, you'll see a specific example of creating and examining a columnstore index.

Storage of columnstore indexes

As mentioned, columnstore indexes, which are typically wide composite indexes, aren't stored as rows, but as columns. Each index column is stored separately in a set of structures called *segments*. Each segment stores up to about one million values (actually 2^{20} or 1,048,576 values) from a single partition. SQL Server tries to put the full 2^{20} values in each segment, leaving a final segment with whatever rows remain. For example, if a table has exactly 10 million rows, each column in a columnstore index could have nine segments of 1,048,576 values and one of 562,816 values. In fact, because the index is usually built in parallel, with each thread processing its own subset of rows, multiple segments might have fewer than the full 1,048,576 values.

After the columns are broken into segments, all the columns for the same set of rows are combined in a row group. Within each row group, SQL Server applies its Vertipaq compression technology, which encodes the values and then rearranges the rows within the segment to give the best compression results. Figure 7-4 illustrates the encoding and conversion of a set of values for multiple index columns into several segments.

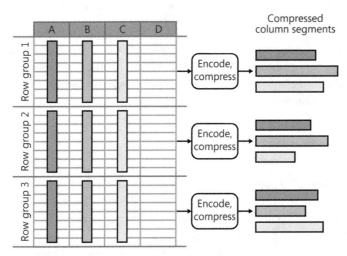

FIGURE 7-4 Transforming columnstore index columns into segments.

The table in Figure 7-4 has been divided into three row groups, in which three of the four columns from the table are defined as part of the columnstore index. You end up with nine compressed column segments, three segments for each of the three columns (A, B, and C in Figure 7-4).

The encoding of values is done to enable the compression to work more efficiently, with all the values converted to a 64-bit integer value. SQL Server uses two types of encoding: dictionary based and value based. Dictionary encoding converts a set of distinct values into a set of sequential numbers, which then serve as ID values into a dictionary. The dictionary is an array stored separately from the column segments, in a similar structure to the segments. A metadata view called *sys.column_store_dictionaries* is available. For a given partition, a column in a columnstore index can have one primary dictionary (shared among segments) and 0 or more secondary dictionaries, with each segment having no more than one. The reason for secondary dictionaries is to cap the size of each dictionary and help reduce the memory requirements when building or scanning the index. Secondary dictionaries are only used for string columns.

For exact numeric data types, when too many distinct values exist to make dictionary encoding worthwhile (that is, not enough duplication of values), SQL Server uses value-based encoding. The value-based encoding applies to integer and decimal data and converts the range of values (from the minimum value in the segment to the maximum value in the segment) to a distinct set of values in a smaller range.

For decimal data types, the smallest possible positive exponent is chosen so that all values in a segment can be converted into integers. For example, for values 0.8, 11.22, and 3.141, the exponent would be 3 (1000) and the converted integers would be 800, 11220, and 3141.

For integer data, the smallest possible negative exponent is chosen so that the distance between the min and the max values in a segment is reduced as much as possible (without losing precision). For example, for values 900, 1100, and 2345000, the exponent would be –2 (1/100) and the converted integer numbers would be 9, 11, and 23450.

When the exponent is chosen and applied to all the values, the base is set to the min integer in that segment. Each value in the segment is then adjusted by subtracting the base from the value. For the preceding decimal example, the base would be 800 and the final encoded values would be 0, 10420, and 2341. For the integer example, the base would be 9 and the final encoded values would be 0, 2, and 23441. The exponent chosen is stored in the *sys.column_store_segments* view in the column called magnitude, and the view stores the base in the *base_id* column. (Details are in the section "Columnstore index metadata.")

Each individual segment will contain more data than can fit on a single SQL Server page, so segments are stored as BLOBs, using the same storage format that SQL Server uses to store *text*, *image*, *ntext*, *varchar(max)*, and *varbinary(max)* data.

To create a table with a columnstore index, use the AdventureWorksDW2012 database that you can download from Microsoft and also find on the book's companion website. The code in Listing 7-12 makes a copy of the *FactInternetSales* table called *FactInternetSalesBig*, and then copies the *FactInternetSalesBig* table into itself nine times, doubling the size each time. It also changes the value of the *RevisionNumber* column each time it copies the table, so the value indicates on which iteration the row was added. Then it modifies the value of the *SalesOrderNumber* column by appending the *RevisionNumber* value, so that the combination of *SalesOrderNumber* and *SalesOrderLineNumber* is unique across the entire table. (Note that this script could take a while to run, depending on the resources available on your machine. On my laptops, it usually takes between 10 and 30 minutes.)

LISTING 7-12 Creating a table with a columnstore index

```
USE AdventureWorksDW2012
GO
IF  object_id('dbo.FactInternetSalesBig') IS NOT NULL
    DROP TABLE dbo.FactInternetSalesBig;
GO
CREATE TABLE dbo.FactInternetSalesBig (
   ProductKey int NOT NULL,
   OrderDateKey int NOT NULL,
   DueDateKey int NOT NULL,
   ShipDateKey int NOT NULL,
   CustomerKey int NOT NULL,
   PromotionKey int NOT NULL,
   CurrencyKey int NOT NULL,
   SalesTerritoryKey int NOT NULL,
   SalesOrderNumber nvarchar(20) NOT NULL,
   SalesOrderLineNumber tinyint NOT NULL,
   RevisionNumber tinyint NOT NULL,
```

```
        OrderQuantity smallint NOT NULL,
        UnitPrice money NOT NULL,
        ExtendedAmount money NOT NULL,
        UnitPriceDiscountPct float NOT NULL,
        DiscountAmount float NOT NULL,
        ProductStandardCost money NOT NULL,
        TotalProductCost money NOT NULL,
        SalesAmount money NOT NULL,
        TaxAmt money NOT NULL,
        Freight money NOT NULL,
        CarrierTrackingNumber nvarchar(25) NULL,
        CustomerPONumber nvarchar(25) NULL,
        OrderDate datetime NULL,
        DueDate datetime NULL,
        ShipDate datetime NULL
)
GO

INSERT INTO dbo.FactInternetSalesBig
SELECT * FROM dbo.FactInternetSales;
GO

IF  object_id('dbo.RevisionNumberValue') IS NOT NULL
    DROP TABLE dbo.RevisionNumberValue;
GO
CREATE TABLE RevisionNumberValue (RevisionNumber tinyint);
INSERT INTO RevisionNumberValue SELECT 1;
GO

-- Make sure everything between this comment and the GO 9 is run as a single batch
DECLARE @RevisionNumber tinyint;
SELECT @RevisionNumber = RevisionNumber + 1 FROM RevisionNumberValue;
SELECT @RevisionNumber as RevisionNumber;
INSERT INTO dbo.FactInternetSalesBig WITH (TABLOCK)
    SELECT ProductKey
        ,OrderDateKey
        ,DueDateKey
        ,ShipDateKey
        ,CustomerKey
        ,PromotionKey
        ,CurrencyKey
        ,SalesTerritoryKey
        ,SalesOrderNumber  + cast (@RevisionNumber as nvarchar(4))
        ,SalesOrderLineNumber
        ,@RevisionNumber
        ,OrderQuantity
        ,UnitPrice
        ,ExtendedAmount
        ,UnitPriceDiscountPct
        ,DiscountAmount
        ,ProductStandardCost
        ,TotalProductCost
        ,SalesAmount
```

```
            ,TaxAmt
            ,Freight
            ,CarrierTrackingNumber
            ,CustomerPONumber
            ,OrderDate
            ,DueDate
            ,ShipDate
    FROM dbo.FactInternetSalesBig;
UPDATE RevisionNumberValue SET RevisionNumber = RevisionNumber + 1;
GO 9

SELECT COUNT(*) FROM FactInternetSalesBig;
GO
```

The table will have 30,923,776 rows in it. Now build the columnstore index on all 26 columns in the table:

```
CREATE NONCLUSTERED COLUMNSTORE INDEX csi_FactInternetSalesBig
ON dbo.FactInternetSalesBig (
    ProductKey,
    OrderDateKey,
    DueDateKey,
    ShipDateKey,
    CustomerKey,
    PromotionKey,
    CurrencyKey,
    SalesTerritoryKey,
    SalesOrderNumber,
    SalesOrderLineNumber,
    RevisionNumber,
    OrderQuantity,
    UnitPrice,
    ExtendedAmount,
    UnitPriceDiscountPct,
    DiscountAmount,
    ProductStandardCost,
    TotalProductCost,
    SalesAmount,
    TaxAmt,
    Freight,
    CarrierTrackingNumber,
    CustomerPONumber,
        OrderDate,
    DueDate,
    ShipDate
);
GO
```

The companion material for this book contains the preceding code to build this table and columnstore index, as well as code to build a unique clustered index on the table and partition it into five partitions. Chapter 8 briefly revisits this columnstore index example, so you can explore the difference in the metadata after the table is partitioned.

Columnstore index metadata

As mentioned in the preceding section, each segment in a columnstore index is stored as a LOB, just like SQL Server's *varchar(max)* and *varbinary(max)* datatypes (when they are stored outside the data row). All the LOBs together for one columnstore index are stored in a LOB allocation unit for the index, which you can see when you examine the *sys.allocation_units* catalog view, as in the query shown in Listing 7-13. The results are shown at the end.

LISTING 7-13 Displaying the allocation units for a table with a columnstore index

```
SELECT index_id, rows, data_compression_desc, type_desc, total_pages
FROM sys.partitions p
    JOIN sys.allocation_units au
        ON p.partition_id = au.container_id
WHERE OBJECT_NAME(object_id) = 'FactInternetSalesBig';
GO
```

```
index_id  rows      data_compression_desc type_desc    total_pages
--------- --------- --------------------- ------------ -----------
0         30923776  NONE                  IN_ROW_DATA  749490
5         30923776  COLUMNSTORE           IN_ROW_DATA  0
5         30923776  COLUMNSTORE           LOB_DATA     117906
```

The query returns one row for the base table, which is a heap and has no row-overflow or LOB columns. The columnstore index has two rows, even though all the index storage is in the LOB_DATA allocation unit. Every partition has an *IN_ROW_DATA* allocation unit assigned, even if (as shown in Listing 7-13) no pages are allocated to it. The *data_compression_desc* value of *COLUMNSTORE* is a new value for this column in *sys.partitions* that indicates that the compression for columnstore indexes is a different type of compression that SQL Server previously had available. Chapter 8 covers the other possible values for *data_compression_desc* during a discussion on data compression. Notice in Listing 7-13 that even though the columnstore index contains all the columns from the base table, the total number of pages needed for the columnstore index is only about 15 percent of the number of pages needed for the table.

The most useful metadata for examining your columnstore indexes is a new catalog view called *sys.column_store_segments*, which returns one row per segment per column per partition for all columnstore indexes in a database (see Table 7-3).

TABLE 7-3 Column descriptions for *sys.column_store_segments*

Column name	Description
partition_id	The partition ID for this partition of this index, unique within a database.
column_id	The ID of the column within the columnstore index.
segment_id	ID of the segment for this column of the index. The first segment has ID 0.
version	The version of the column segment format. For SQL Server 2012 this value is 1.

Column name	Description
encoding_type	The type of encoding used for this segment. One of: 1: Value encoding 2: Dictionary encoding of non-strings 3: Dictionary encoding of string values 4: No encoding, the actual value is stored
row_count	The number of rows in the row group.
has_nulls	1 if the segment has any null values.
base_id	Base value id if encoding type 1 is being used. If encoding type 1 isn't being used, base_id is set to 1.
Magnitude	Magnitude if encoding type 1 is being used. If encoding type 1 isn't being used, magnitude is set to 1.
primary_dictionary_id	ID of primary dictionary.
secondary_dictionary_id	ID of secondary dictionary. Returns -1 if no secondary dictionary exists.
min_data_id	The minimum value occurring in this segment of this column.
max_data_id	The maximum value occurring in this segment of this column.
null_value	Value used to represent nulls.
on_disk_size	The size of the segment in bytes.

In my columnstore index, the 30+ million rows were split into 41 row groups. Depending on the exact plan chosen when you built your index and the number of degree of parallelism used, you might get a different number of row groups. Most of the row groups have the full 1,048,576 values in each segment, but several of them don't. The index has 26 columns, but because it needs a way to identify the row in the table to which each columnstore index row belongs, and the table doesn't have a clustered index, a 27th column is introduced containing the RID, just as regular nonclustered indexes point to the table row with the RID. So my index has 41 row groups for 27 columns, or 1,107 rows in *sys.column_store_segments*.

Notice that the *sys.column_store_segments* view contains columns indicating the minimum and maximum value in each segment. These values aren't required to overlap, but in most cases they will. If the columnstore index is built on a table with a clustered index, values might overlap less for the clustered index column in the columnstore index, but all the other columns will still have overlapping values. However, because each segment for each column has some knowledge of the values, for certain predicates SQL Server can determine that none of the rows in one or more segments satisfies the predicate and performs "segment elimination" as the query is executed. (Chapter 10 describes query plans for accessing data through a columnstore index.)

To give you some idea of the kinds of information you can get from *sys.column_store_segments*, you can run the query in Listing 7-14, which should give you the results shown at the end.

LISTING 7-14 Displaying the columns in the columnstore index

```
SELECT s.column_id, col_name(ic.object_id, ic.column_id) as column_name,
    count(*) as segment_count
FROM sys.column_store_segments s join sys.partitions p
    ON s.partition_id = p.partition_id
```

```
        LEFT JOIN sys.index_columns ic
            ON p.object_id = ic.object_id AND p.index_id = ic.index_id
                AND s.column_id = ic.index_column_id
    WHERE object_name(p.object_id) = 'FactInternetSalesBig'
    GROUP BY s.column_id,  col_name(ic.object_id, ic.column_id)
    ORDER by s.column_id;
    GO


    column_id    column_name              segment_count
    ----------   ----------------------   -------------
    1            ProductKey               41
    2            OrderDateKey             41
    3            DueDateKey               41
    4            ShipDateKey              41
    5            CustomerKey              41
    6            PromotionKey             41
    7            CurrencyKey              41
    8            SalesTerritoryKey        41
    9            SalesOrderNumber         41
    10           SalesOrderLineNumber     41
    11           RevisionNumber           41
    12           OrderQuantity            41
    13           UnitPrice                41
    14           ExtendedAmount           41
    15           UnitPriceDiscountPct     41
    16           DiscountAmount           41
    17           ProductStandardCost      41
    18           TotalProductCost         41
    19           SalesAmount              41
    20           TaxAmt                   41
    21           Freight                  41
    22           CarrierTrackingNumber    41
    23           CustomerPONumber         41
    24           OrderDate                41
    25           DueDate                  41
    26           ShipDate                 41
    27           NULL                     41
```

The only way to map a row in *sys.column_store_segments* to an object is by using the *partition_id* column to join to *sys.partitions*, which has an *object_id* column. You also need to join to *sys.index_columns* to map columns in the index to columns in the table. A *LEFT JOIN* is needed so that you can get the extra column for the RID. It shows up with a NULL column name. Also note that the *column_id* value in the *sys.column_store_segments* view is the *column_id* in the columnstore index, which might not be the same as the *column_id* in the underlying table. The join of *sys.column_store_segments* with the view *sys.index_columns* matches the *column_id* in *sys.column_store_segments* with the *index_column_id* in *sys.index_columns*. Then, the corresponding *column_id* in the *sys.index_columns* view is the *column_id* in the table (*FactInternetSalesBig*).

Next is a query that provides the number of rows in each segment, but because each column has the same number of rows in each segment, the query is filtered on only a single column:

```
SELECT segment_id, sum(row_count)
FROM sys.column_store_segments s join sys.partitions p
    ON  s.partition_id = p.partition_id
```

```
        JOIN sys.index_columns ic
            ON p.object_id = ic.object_id AND p.index_id = ic.index_id
                AND s.column_id = ic.index_column_id
WHERE object_name(p.object_id) = 'FactInternetSalesBig' and index_column_id = 1
GROUP BY  segment_id;
GO
```

The last query, in Listing 7-15, shows the minimum and maximum values for one particular column—in this case, the *OrderDateKey* column, with the results shown at the end.

LISTING 7-15 Displaying information about each segment for one column

```
SELECT segment_id, min_data_id, max_data_id
FROM sys.column_store_segments s join sys.partitions p
        ON s.partition_id = p.partition_id
  LEFT JOIN sys.index_columns ic
        ON p.object_id = ic.object_id AND p.index_id = ic.index_id
            AND s.column_id = ic.index_column_id
WHERE object_name(p.object_id) = 'FactInternetSalesBig'
        AND col_name(ic.object_id, ic.column_id) = 'OrderDateKey'
ORDER by segment_id;
GO
```

segment_id	row_count	min_data_id	max_data_id
0	1048576	20050701	20080731
1	1048576	20050701	20080731
2	1048576	20050701	20080731
3	1048576	20050701	20080731
4	1048576	20050701	20080731
5	1048576	20050701	20080731
6	1048576	20050701	20080731
7	1048576	20050701	20080731
8	1048576	20050701	20080731
9	1048576	20050701	20080731
10	1048576	20050701	20080731
11	1048576	20050701	20080731
12	1048576	20050701	20080731
13	1048576	20050701	20080731
14	1048576	20050701	20080731
15	1048576	20050701	20080731
16	1048576	20050701	20080731
17	1048576	20050701	20080731
18	294103	20050701	20080731
19	1048576	20050701	20080731
20	1048576	20050701	20080731
21	344114	20050701	20080731
22	1048576	20050701	20080731
23	1048576	20050701	20080731
24	1048576	20050701	20080731
25	1048576	20050701	20080731
26	287568	20050701	20080731
27	310490	20050701	20080731
28	267256	20050701	20080731
29	311833	20050701	20080731
30	301248	20050701	20080731

31	283065	20050701	20080731
32	194672	20050701	20080731
33	196186	20050701	20080731
34	135472	20050707	20080731
35	140182	20050701	20080731
36	363584	20050701	20080731
37	523826	20050701	20080731
38	755275	20050701	20080731
39	1048576	20050701	20080731
40	502	20080223	20080227

Several upcoming chapters revisit columnstore indexes. Chapter 8 shows you metadata for a columnstore index that has a clustered index and is partitioned. Chapter 10 discusses query plans for queries using columnstore indexes. Chapter 11 looks at how the Query Optimizer works with columnstore index information and discusses some best practices for working with columnstore indexes, particularly that as soon as a table has a columnstore index, the data in the table can't be updated.

 Note In November 2012, Microsoft announced that in the next major release of SQL Server, columnstore indexes will be able to have clustered indexes and will be updatable. Knowing that these enhancements are coming might encourage you to start working with columnstore indexes now in SQL Server 2012 and allow you to start planning for how you'll use them in later versions.

Conclusion

This chapter discussed index concepts, index internals, special index structures, data modifications, and index management. You looked at the new SQL Server 2012 technology called *columnstore indexes* and described how their storage is different from other nonclustered indexes. This chapter covered many best practices along the way and, although performance tuning wasn't the primary goal, the more you know about how indexes work internally, the more optimal structures you can create. Finally, by understanding how SQL Server organizes indexes on disk, you can be more adept at troubleshooting problems and managing changes within your database.

Special storage

Kalen Delaney

E arlier chapters discussed the storage of "regular rows" for both data and index information. (Chapter 7, "Indexes: internals and management," also looked at a completely different way of storing indexes: using columnstores, which aren't stored in rows at all.) Chapter 6, "Table storage," explained that regular rows are in a format called *FixedVar*. SQL Server provides ways of storing data in another format, called Column Descriptor (CD). It also can store special values in either the *FixedVar* or CD format that don't fit on the regular 8 KB pages.

This chapter describes data that exceeds the typical row size limitations and is stored as either row-overflow or Large Object (LOB) data. You'll learn about two additional methods for storing data on the actual data pages, introduced in Microsoft SQL Server 2008: one that uses a new type of complex column with a regular data row (sparse columns), and one that uses the new CD format (compressed data). This chapter also discusses FILESTREAM data, a feature introduced in SQL Server 2008 that allows you to access data from operating system files as though it were part of your relational tables, and FileTables, a new feature in SQL Server 2012 that allows you to create a table containing both FILESTREAM data and Windows file attribute metadata.

Finally, this chapter covers the ability of SQL Server to separate data into partitions. Although this doesn't change the data format in the rows or on the pages, it does change the metadata that keeps track of what space is allocated to which objects.

Large object storage

SQL Server 2012 has two special formats for storing data that doesn't fit on the regular 8 KB data page. These formats allow you to store rows that exceed the maximum row size of 8,060 bytes. As discussed in Chapter 6, this maximum row size value includes several bytes of overhead stored with the row on the physical pages, so the total size of all the table's defined columns must be slightly less than this amount. In fact, the error message that you get if you try to create a table with more bytes than the allowable maximum is very specific. If you execute the following *CREATE TABLE* statement with column definitions that add up to exactly 8,060 bytes, you'll get the error message shown here:

```
USE testdb;
GO
CREATE TABLE dbo.bigrows_fixed
(    a char(3000),
     b char(3000),
     c char(2000),
     d char(60) ) ;
```

```
Msg 1701, Level 16, State 1, Line 1
Creating or altering table 'bigrows' failed because the minimum row size would be 8067,
including 7 bytes of internal overhead. This exceeds the maximum allowable table row size of
8060 bytes.
```

In this message, you can see the number of overhead bytes (7) that SQL Server wants to store with the row itself. An additional 2 bytes is used for the row-offset information at the end of the page, but those bytes aren't included in this total.

Restricted-length large object data (row-overflow data)

One way to exceed this size limit of 8,060 bytes is to use variable-length columns because for variable-length data, SQL Server 2005 and later versions can store the columns in special row-overflow pages, as long as all the fixed-length columns fit into the regular in-row size limit. So you need to look at a table with all variable-length columns. Notice that although my example uses all *varchar* columns, columns of other data types can also be stored on row-overflow data pages. These other data types include *varbinary*, *nvarchar*, and *sqlvariant* columns, as well as columns that use CLR user-defined data types. The following code creates a table with rows whose maximum defined length is much longer than 8,060 bytes:

```
USE testdb;
CREATE TABLE dbo.bigrows
  (a varchar(3000),
   b varchar(3000),
   c varchar(3000),
   d varchar(3000) );
```

In fact, if you ran this *CREATE TABLE* statement in SQL Server 7.0, you would get an error, and the table wouldn't be created. In SQL Server 2000, the table was created, but you got a warning that inserts or updates might fail if the row size exceeds the maximum.

With SQL Server 2005 and later, not only could the preceding *dbo.bigrows* table be created, but you also could insert a row with column sizes that add up to more than 8,060 bytes with a simple *INSERT*:

```
INSERT INTO dbo.bigrows
    SELECT REPLICATE('e', 2100), REPLICATE('f', 2100),
      REPLICATE('g', 2100),  REPLICATE('h', 2100);
```

To determine whether SQL Server is storing any data in row-overflow data pages for a particular table, you can run the following allocation query from Chapter 5, "Logging and recovery":

```
SELECT object_name(object_id) AS name,
    partition_id, partition_number AS pnum,  rows,
    allocation_unit_id AS au_id, type_desc as page_type_desc,
    total_pages AS pages
FROM sys.partitions p  JOIN sys.allocation_units a
  ON p.partition_id = a.container_id
WHERE object_id=object_id('dbo.bigrows');
```

This query should return output similar to that shown here:

```
name     partition_id      pnum rows au_id              page_type_desc    pages
----     ----------------  ---- ---- ----------------   ----------------  -----
bigrows  72057594039238656 1    1    72057594043957248  IN_ROW_DATA       2
bigrows  72057594039238656 1    1    72057594044022784  ROW_OVERFLOW_DATA 2
```

You can see that there are two pages for the one row of regular in-row data and two pages for the one row of row-overflow data. Alternatively, you can use the *sys.dm_db_database_page_allocations* function and see the four pages individually:

```
SELECT allocated_page_file_id as PageFID, allocated_page_page_id as PagePID,
       object_id as ObjectID, partition_id AS PartitionID,
       allocation_unit_type_desc as AU_type, page_type as PageType
FROM sys.dm_db_database_page_allocations
       (db_id('testdb'), object_id('bigrows'), null, null, 'DETAILED');
```

You should see the four rows, one for each page, looking similar to the following:

```
PageFID PagePID   ObjectID   PartitionID AU_type            PageType
------- --------- ---------- ----------- ------------------ ----------
1       303       1653580929 1           IN_ROW_DATA        10
1       302       1653580929 1           IN_ROW_DATA        1
1       297       1653580929 1           ROW_OVERFLOW_DATA  10
1       296       1653580929 1           ROW_OVERFLOW_DATA  3
```

Of course, your actual ID values will be different, but the *AU*-type and *PageType* values should be the same, and you should have four rows returned indicating four pages belong to the *bigrows* table. Two pages are for the row-overflow data, and two are for the in-row data. As you saw in Chapter 7, the *PageType* values have the following meanings.

- *PageType* = 1, Data page

- *PageType* = 2, Index page

- *PageType* = 3, LOB or row-overflow page, *TEXT_MIXED*

- *PageType* = 4, LOB or row-overflow page, *TEXT_DATA*

- *PageType* = 10, IAM page

You learn more about the different types of LOB pages in the next section, "Unrestricted-length large object data."

You can see one data page and one IAM page for the in-row data, and one data page and one IAM page for the row-overflow data. With the results from *sys.dm_db_database_page_allocations*, you could then look at the page contents with *DBCC PAGE*. On the data page for the in-row data, you would see three of the four *varchar* column values, and the fourth column would be stored on the data page for the row-overflow data. If you run *DBCC PAGE* for the data page storing the in-row data (page 1:302 in the preceding output), notice that it isn't necessarily the fourth column in the column order that is stored off the row. (I won't show you the entire contents of the rows because the single row fills almost the entire page.) Look at the in-row data page using *DBCC PAGE* and notice the column with e, the column with g, and the column with h. The column with f has moved to the new row. In the place of that column, you can see the bytes shown here:

```
65020000 00010000 00c37f00 00340800 00280100 00010000 0067
```

Included are the last byte with *e* (ASCII code hexadecimal 65) and the first byte with *g* (ASCII code hexadecimal 67), and in between are 24 other bytes (boldfaced). Bytes 16 through 23 (the 17th through the 24th bytes) of those 24 bytes are treated as an 8-byte numeric value: 2801000001000000 (bold italic). You need to reverse the byte order and break it into a 2-byte hex value for the slot number, a 2-byte hex value for the file number, and a 4-byte hex value for the page number. So the slot number is 0x0000 for slot 0 because this overflowing column is the first (and only) data on the row-overflow page. You have 0x0001 (or 1) for the file number and 0x00000128 (or 296) for the page number. You saw these the same file and page numbers when using *sys.dm_db_database_page_allocations*.

Table 8-1 describes the first 16 bytes in the row.

TABLE 8-1 The first 16 bytes of a row-overflow pointer

Bytes	Hex value	Decimal value	Meaning
0	0x02	2	Type of special field: 1 = LOB2 = overflow
1–2	0x0000	0	Level in the B-tree (always 0 for overflow)
3	0x00	0	Unused
4–7	0x00000001	1	Sequence: a value used by optimistic concurrency control for cursors that increases every time a LOB or overflow column is updated
8–11	0x00007fc3	32707	Timestamp: a random value used by *DBCC CHECKTABLE* that remains unchanged during the lifetime of each LOB or overflow column
12–15	0x00000834	2100	Length

SQL Server stores variable-length columns on row-overflow pages only under certain conditions. The determining factor is the row length itself. How full the regular page is into which SQL Server is trying to insert the new row doesn't matter; SQL Server constructs the row as usual and stores some of its columns on overflow pages only if the row itself needs more than 8,060 bytes.

Each column in the table is either completely on the row or completely off the row. This means that a 4,000-byte variable-length column can't have half its bytes on the regular data page and half on a row-overflow page. If a row is less than 8,060 bytes and the page on which SQL Server is trying to insert the row has no room, regular page-splitting algorithms (described in Chapter 7) are applied.

One row can span many row-overflow pages if it contains many large variable-length columns. For example, you can create the table *dbo.hugerows* and insert a single row into it as follows:

```
CREATE TABLE dbo.hugerows
    (a varchar(3000),
     b varchar(8000),
     c varchar(8000),
     d varchar(8000));

INSERT INTO dbo.hugerows
    SELECT REPLICATE('a', 3000), REPLICATE('b', 8000),
        REPLICATE('c', 8000),  REPLICATE('d', 8000);
```

Substituting *hugerows* for *bigrows* for the allocation query shown earlier yields the following results:

```
name      partition_id       pnum rows au_id              page_type_desc     pages
--------  -----------------  ---- ---- -----------------  -----------------  -----
hugerows  72057594039304192  1    1    72057594044088320  IN_ROW_DATA        2
hugerows  72057594039304192  1    1    72057594044153856  ROW_OVERFLOW_DATA  4
```

The output shows four pages for the row-overflow information, one for the row-overflow IAM page, and three for the columns that didn't fit in the regular row. The number of large variable-length columns that a table can have isn't unlimited, although it is quite large. A table is limited to 1,024 columns, which can be exceeded when you are using sparse columns, as discussed later in this chapter. However, another limit is reached before that. When a column must be moved off a regular page onto a row-overflow page, SQL Server keeps a pointer to the row-overflow information as part of the original row, which you saw in the *DBCC* output earlier as 24 bytes, and the row still needs 2 bytes in the column-offset array for each variable-length column, whether or not the variable-length column is stored in the row. So 308 turns out to be the maximum number of overflowing columns you can have, and such a row needs 8,008 bytes just for the 26 overhead bytes for each overflowing column in the row.

> **Note** Just because SQL Server can store many large columns on row-overflow pages doesn't mean that doing so is always a good idea. This capability does allow you more flexibility in the organization of your tables, but you might pay a heavy performance price if many additional pages need to be accessed for every row of data. Row-overflow pages are intended to be a solution in the situation where most rows fit completely on your data pages and you have row-overflow data only occasionally. By using row-overflow pages, SQL Server can handle the extra data effectively, without requiring a redesign of your table.

In some cases, if a large variable-length column shrinks, it can be moved back to the regular row. However, for efficiency, if the decrease is just a few bytes, SQL Server doesn't bother checking. Only when a column stored in a row-overflow page is reduced by more than 1,000 bytes does SQL Server even consider checking to see whether the column can now fit on the regular data page. You can observe this behavior if you previously created the *dbo.bigrows* table for the earlier example and inserted only the one row with 2,100 characters in each column.

The following update reduces the size of the first column by 500 bytes and reduces the row size to 7,900 bytes, which should all fit on one data page:

```
UPDATE bigrows
SET a = replicate('a', 1600);
```

However, if you rerun the allocation query, you'll still see two row-overflow pages: one for the row-overflow data and one for the IAM page. Now reduce the size of the first column by more than 1,000 bytes and rerun the allocation query:

```
UPDATE bigrows
SET a = 'aaaaa';
```

You should see only three pages for the table now, because there is no longer a row-overflow data page. The IAM page for the row-overflow data pages hasn't been removed, but you no longer have a data page for row-overflow data.

Keep in mind that row-overflow data storage applies only to columns of variable-length data, which are defined as no longer than the usual variable-length maximum of 8,000 bytes per column. Also, to store a variable-length column on a row-overflow page, you must meet the following conditions.

- All the fixed-length columns, including overhead bytes, must add up to no more than 8,060 bytes. (The pointer to each row-overflow column adds 24 bytes of overhead to the row.)

- The actual length of the variable-length column must be more than 24 bytes.

- The column must not be part of the clustered index key.

If you have single columns that might need to store more than 8,000 bytes, you should use either LOB (*text*, *image*, or *ntext*) columns or the *MAX* data types.

Unrestricted-length large object data

If a table contains the deprecated LOB data types (*text*, *ntext*, or *image* types), by default the actual data isn't stored on the regular data pages. Like row-overflow data, LOB data is stored in its own set of pages, and the allocation query shows you pages for LOB data as well as pages for regular in-row data and row-overflow data. For LOB columns, SQL Server stores a 16-byte pointer in the data row that indicates where the actual data can be found. Although the default behavior is to store all the LOB data off the data row, SQL Server allows you to change the storage mechanism by setting a table option to allow LOB data to be stored in the data row itself if it is small enough. Note that no database or server setting is available to control storing small LOB columns on the data pages; it's managed as a table option.

The 16-byte pointer points to a page (or the first of a set of pages) where the data can be found. These pages are 8 KB in size, like any other page in SQL Server, and individual *text*, *ntext*, and *image* pages aren't limited to storing data for only one occurrence of a *text*, *ntext*, or *image* column. A *text*, *ntext*, or *image* page can hold data from multiple columns and from multiple rows; the page can even have a mix of *text*, *ntext*, and *image* data. However, one *text* or *image* page can hold only *text* or *image* data from a single table. (Even more specifically, one *text* or *image* page can hold only *text* or *image* data from a single partition of a table, which should become clear when partitioning metadata is discussed at the end of this chapter.)

The collection of 8 KB pages that make up a LOB column aren't necessarily located next to each other. The pages are logically organized in a B-tree structure, so operations starting in the middle of the LOB string are very efficient. The structure of the B-tree varies slightly depending on whether the amount of data is less than or more than 32 KB. (See Figure 8-1 for the general structure.) B-trees were discussed in detail when describing indexes in Chapter 7.

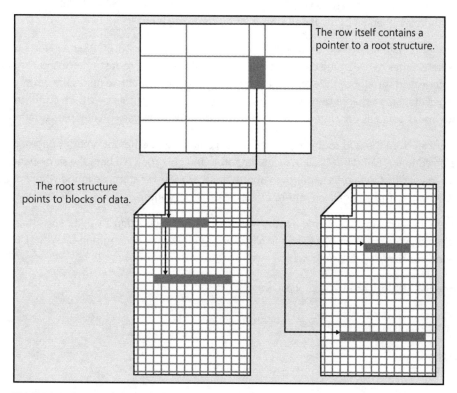

FIGURE 8-1 A text column pointing to a B-tree that contains the blocks of data.

Note Although the acronym LOB can be expanded to mean "large object," these two terms will be used in this chapter to mean two different things. LOB is used only when referring to the data using the special storage format shown in Figure 8-1. The term *large object* is used when referring to any method for storing data that might be too large for a regular data page. This includes row-overflow columns, the actual LOB data types, the *MAX* data types, and FILESTREAM data.

If the amount of LOB data is less than 32 KB, the text pointer in the data row points to an 84-byte text root structure. This forms the root node of the B-tree structure. The root node points to the blocks of *text*, *ntext*, or *image* data. Although the data for LOB columns is arranged logically in a B-tree, both the root node and the individual blocks of data are spread physically throughout LOB pages for the table. They're placed wherever space is available. The size of each block of data is determined by the size written by an application. Small blocks of data are combined to fill a page. If the amount of data is less than 64 bytes, it's all stored in the root structure.

If the amount of data for one occurrence of a LOB column exceeds 32 KB, SQL Server starts building intermediate nodes between the data blocks and the root node. The root structure and the data blocks are interleaved throughout the *text* and *image* pages. The intermediate nodes, however, are stored in pages that aren't shared between occurrences of *text* or *image* columns. Each page storing intermediate nodes contains only intermediate nodes for one *text* or *image* column in one data row.

SQL Server can store the LOB root and the actual LOB data on two different types of pages. One of these, referred to as *TEXT_MIXED*, allows LOB data from multiple rows to share the same pages. However, when your text data gets larger than about 40 KB, SQL Server starts devoting whole pages to a single LOB value. These pages are referred to as *TEXT_DATA* pages.

You can see this behavior by creating a table with a *text* column, inserting a value of less than 40 KB and then one greater than 40 KB, and finally examining information returned by *sys.dm_db_ database_page_allocations* (see Listing 8-1).

LISTING 8-1 Storing LOB data on two types of pages

```
IF OBJECT_ID('textdata') IS NOT NULL
    DROP TABLE textdata;
GO
CREATE TABLE textdata
 (bigcol text);
GO
INSERT INTO textdata
    SELECT REPLICATE(convert(varchar(MAX), 'a'), 38000);
GO
SELECT allocated_page_file_id as PageFID, allocated_page_page_id as PagePID,
       object_id as ObjectID, partition_id AS PartitionID,
       allocation_unit_type_desc as AU_type, page_type as PageType
FROM sys.dm_db_database_page_allocations(db_id('testdb'), object_id('textdata'),
                                  null, null, 'DETAILED');

GO
```

```
INSERT INTO textdata
    SELECT REPLICATE(convert(varchar(MAX), 'a'), 41000);
GO
SELECT allocated_page_file_id as PageFID, allocated_page_page_id as PagePID,
       object_id as ObjectID, partition_id AS PartitionID,
       allocation_unit_type_desc as AU_type, page_type as PageType
FROM sys.dm_db_database_page_allocations(db_id('testdb'), object_id('textdata'),
                                         null, null, 'DETAILED');
GO
```

The *INSERT* statements in Listing 8-1 convert a string value into the data type *varchar(MAX)* because this is the only way to generate a string value longer than 8,000 bytes. (The next section discusses *varchar(MAX)* in more detail.) The first time you select from *sys.dm_db_database_page_allocations*, you should have *PageType* values of 1, 3, and 10. The second time after data greater than 40 KB in size is inserted, you should also see *PageType* values of 4. *PageType* 3 indicates a *TEXT_MIXED* page, and *PageType* 4 indicates a *TEXT_DATA* page.

Storing LOB data in the data row

If you store all your LOB data type values outside your regular data pages, SQL Server needs to perform additional page reads every time you access that data, just as it does for row-overflow pages. In some cases, you might notice a performance improvement by allowing some of the LOB data to be stored in the data row. You can enable a table option called *text in row* for a particular table by setting the option to *'ON'* (including the single quotation marks) or by specifying a maximum number of bytes to be stored in the data row. The following command enables up to 500 bytes of LOB data to be stored with the regular row data in a table called *employee*:

```
EXEC sp_tableoption employee, 'text in row', 500;
```

Notice that the value is in bytes, not characters. For *ntext* data, each character needs 2 bytes so that any *ntext* column is stored in the data row if it's less than or equal to 250 characters. When you enable the *text in row* option, you never get just the 16-byte pointer for the LOB data in the row, as is the case when the option isn't *'ON'*. If the data in the LOB field is more than the specified maximum, the row holds the root structure containing pointers to the separate chunks of LOB data. The minimum size of a root structure is 24 bytes, and the possible range of values that *text in row* can be set to is 24 to 7,000 bytes. (If you specify the option *'ON'* instead of a specific number, SQL Server assumes the default value of 256 bytes.)

To disable the *text in row* option, you can set the value to either *'OFF'* or 0. To determine whether a table has the *text in row* property enabled, you can inspect the *sys.tables* catalog view as follows:

```
SELECT name, text_in_row_limit
FROM sys.tables
WHERE name = 'employee';
```

This *text_in_row_limit* value indicates the maximum number of bytes allowed for storing LOB data in a data row. If a 0 is returned, the *text in row* option is disabled.

Now create a table very similar to the one that looks at row structures, but change the *varchar(250)* column to the *text* data type. You'll use almost the same *INSERT* statement to insert one row into the table:

```
CREATE TABLE HasText
(
Col1 char(3)      NOT NULL,
Col2 varchar(5)   NOT NULL,
Col3 text         NOT NULL,
Col4 varchar(20)  NOT NULL
);

INSERT HasText VALUES
    ('AAA', 'BBB', REPLICATE('X', 250), 'CCC');
```

Now use the allocation query to find the basic information for this table and look at the *sys.dm_db_database_page_allocations* information for this table (see Listing 8-2).

LISTING 8-2 Finding basic information for the HasText table

```
SELECT convert(char(7), object_name(object_id)) AS name,
    partition_id, partition_number AS pnum,  rows,
    allocation_unit_id AS au_id, convert(char(17), type_desc) as page_type_desc,
  total_pages AS pages
FROM sys.partitions p  JOIN sys.allocation_units a
  ON p.partition_id = a.container_id
WHERE object_id=object_id('dbo.HasText');

SELECT allocated_page_file_id as PageFID, allocated_page_page_id as PagePID,
      object_id as ObjectID, partition_id AS PartitionID, allocation_unit_type_desc as AU_Type,
      page_type as PageType
FROM sys.dm_db_database_page_allocations(db_id('testdb'),
      object_id('textdata'), null, null, 'DETAILED')
```

name	partition_id	pnum	rows	au_id	page_type_desc	pages
HasText	72057594039435264	1	1	72057594044350464	IN_ROW_DATA	2
HasText	72057594039435264	1	1	72057594044416000	LOB_DATA	2

PageFID	PagePID	ObjectID	PartitionID	AU_Type	PageType
1	2197	133575514	72057594039435264	LOB data	3
1	2198	133575514	72057594039435264	LOB data	10
1	2199	133575514	72057594039435264	In-row data	1
1	2200	133575514	72057594039435264	In-row data	10

You can see two LOB pages (the LOB data page and the LOB IAM page) and two pages for the in-row data (again, the data page and the IAM page). The data page for the in-row data is 2199, and the LOB data is on page 2197. The following output shows the data section from running *DBCC PAGE* on page 2199. The row structure is very similar to the row structure shown in Chapter 6, in Figure 6-6, except for the text field itself. Bytes 21 to 36 are the 16-byte text pointer, and you can see the value 9508 starting at offset 29. When the bytes are reversed, it becomes 0x0895, or 2197 decimal, which is the page containing the text data, as you saw in the output in Listing 8-2.

```
DATA:

Slot 0, Offset 0x60, Length 40, DumpStyle BYTE

Record Type = PRIMARY_RECORD     Record Attributes = NULL_BITMAP VARIABLE_COLUMNS
Record Size = 40
Memory Dump @0x625BC060

00000000:   30000700 41414104 00600300 15002580 28004242 †0...AAA..`....%. (.BB
00000014:   420000e1 07000000 00950800 00010001 00434343 †B..á.....?..   CCC
```

FIGURE 8-2 A row containing a text pointer.

Now let's enable text data in the row, for up to 500 bytes:

```
EXEC sp_tableoption HasText, 'text in row', 500;
```

Enabling this option doesn't force the text data to be moved into the row. You have to update the text value to actually force the data movement:

```
UPDATE HasText
SET col3 = REPLICATE('Z', 250);
```

If you run *DBCC PAGE* on the original data page, notice that the text column of 250 *z*'s is now in the data row, and that the row is practically identical in structure to the row containing *varchar* data that you saw in Figure 6-6.

> **Note** Although enabling *text in row* doesn't move the data immediately, disabling the option does. If you turn off *text in row*, the LOB data moves immediately back onto its own pages, so you must be sure not to turn this off for a large table during heavy operations.

A final issue when working with LOB data and the *text in row* option is dealing with the situation in which *text in row* is enabled but the LOB is longer than the maximum configured length for some rows. If you change the maximum length for *text in row* to 50 for the *HasText* table you've been working with, this also forces the LOB data for all rows with more than 50 bytes of LOB data to be moved off the page immediately, just as when you disable the option completely:

```
EXEC sp_tableoption HasText, 'text in row', 50;
```

However, setting the limit to a smaller value is different from disabling the option in two ways. First, some of the rows might still have LOB data that is under the limit, and for those rows, the LOB data is stored completely in the data row. Second, if the LOB data doesn't fit, the information stored in the data row itself isn't simply the 16-byte pointer, as it would be if *text in row* were turned off. Instead, for LOB data that doesn't fit in the defined size, the row contains a root structure for a B-tree that points to chunks of the LOB data. As long as the *text in row* option isn't *'OFF'* (or 0), SQL Server never stores the simple 16-byte LOB pointer in the row. It stores either the LOB data itself (if it fits) or the root structure for the LOB data B-tree.

A root structure is at least 24 bytes long (which is why 24 is the minimum size for the *text in row* limit), and the meaning of the bytes is similar to the meaning of the 24 bytes in the row-overflow pointer. The main difference is that no length is stored in bytes 12–15. Instead, bytes 12–23 constitute a link to a chunk of LOB data on a separate page. If multiple LOB chucks are accessed via the root, multiple sets of 12 bytes can be here, each pointing to LOB data on a separate page.

As indicated earlier, when you first enable *text in row*, no data movement occurs until the text data is actually updated. The same is true if the limit is increased—that is, even if the new limit is large enough to accommodate the LOB data that was stored outside the row, the LOB data isn't moved onto the row automatically. You must update the actual LOB data first.

Keep in mind that even if the amount of LOB data is less than the limit, the data isn't necessarily stored in the row. You're still limited to a maximum row size of 8,060 bytes for a single row on a data page, so the amount of LOB data that can be stored in the actual data row might be reduced if the amount of non-LOB data is large. Also, if a variable-length column needs to grow, it might push LOB data off the page so as not to exceed the 8,060-byte limit. Growth of variable-length columns always has priority over storing LOB data in the row. If no variable-length *char* fields need to grow during an update operation, SQL Server checks for growth of in-row LOB data, in column offset order. If one LOB needs to grow, others might be pushed off the row.

Finally, you should be aware that SQL Server logs all movement of LOB data, which means that reducing the limit of or turning *'OFF'* the *text in row* option can be a very time-consuming operation for a large table.

Although large data columns using the LOB data types can be stored and managed very efficiently, using them in your tables can be problematic. Data stored as *text*, *ntext*, or *image* can't always be manipulated with the usual data-manipulation commands and, in many cases, you need to resort to using the operations *readtext*, *writetext*, and *updatetext*, which require dealing with byte offsets and data-length values. Prior to SQL Server 2005, you had to decide whether to limit your columns to a maximum of 8,000 bytes or to deal with your large data columns by using different operators than you used for your shorter columns. Starting with version 2005, SQL Server provides a solution that gives you the best of both worlds, as you'll see in the next section.

Storing MAX-length data

SQL Server 2005 and later versions give you the option of defining a variable-length field with the *MAX* specifier. Although this functionality is frequently described by referring only to *varchar(MAX)*, the *MAX* specifier can also be used with *nvarchar* and *varbinary*. You can indicate the *MAX* specifier instead of an actual size when you use one of these types to define a column, variable, or parameter. By using the *MAX* specifier, you leave it up to SQL Server to determine whether to store the value as a regular *varchar*, *nvarchar*, or *varbinary* value or as a LOB. In general, if the actual length is 8,000 bytes or less, the value is treated as though it were one of the regular variable-length data types, including possibly overflowing onto row-overflow pages. However, if the *varchar(MAX)* column does need to spill off the page, the extra pages required are considered LOB pages and show the *IAM_chain_type* LOB when examined using *DBCC IND*. If the actual length is greater than 8,000 bytes, SQL Server stores and treats the value exactly as though it were *text*, *ntext*, or *image*. Because variable-length columns with the *MAX* specifier are treated either as regular variable-length columns or as LOB columns, no special discussion of their storage is needed.

The size of values specified with *MAX* can reach the maximum size supported by LOB data, which is currently 2 GB. By using the *MAX* specifier, however, you are indicating that the maximum size should be the maximum the system supports. If you upgrade a table with a *varchar(MAX)* column to a future version of SQL Server, the MAX length becomes whatever the new maximum is in the new version.

> **Tip** Because the *MAX* data types can store LOB data as well as regular row data, you are recommended to use these data types in future development in place of the *text*, *ntext*, or *image* types, which Microsoft has indicated will be removed in a future version.

Appending data into a LOB column

In the storage engine, each LOB column is broken into fragments of a maximum size of 8,040 bytes each. When you append data to a large object, SQL Server finds the append point and looks at the current fragment where the new data will be added. It calculates the size of the new fragment (including the newly appended data). If the size is more than 8,040 bytes, SQL Server allocates new large object pages until a fragment is left that is less than 8,040 bytes, and then it finds a page that has enough space for the remaining bytes.

When SQL Server allocates pages for LOB data, it has two allocation strategies:

- For data that is less than 64 KB in size, it randomly allocates a page. This page comes from an extent that is part of the large object IAM, but the pages aren't guaranteed to be continuous.

- For data that is more than 64 KB in size, it uses an append-only page allocator that allocates one extent at a time and writes the pages continuously in the extent.

From a performance standpoint, writing fragments of 64 KB at a time is beneficial. Allocating 1 MB in advance might be beneficial if you know that the size will be 1 MB, but you also need to take into account the space required for the transaction log. If you a create a 1 MB fragment first with any random contents, SQL Server logs the 1 MB, and then all the changes are logged as well. When you perform large object data updates, no new pages need to be allocated, but the changes still need to be logged.

As long as the large object values are small, they can be in the data page. In this case, some pre-allocation might be a good idea so that the large object data doesn't become too fragmented. A general recommendation might be that if the amount of data to be inserted into a large object column in a single operation is relatively small, you should insert a large object value of the final expected value, and then replace substrings of that initial value as needed. For larger sizes, try to append or insert in chunks of 8 * 8,040 bytes. This way, a whole extent is allocated each time, and 8,040 bytes are stored on each page.

If you do find that your large object data is becoming fragmented, you can use *ALTER INDEX RE-ORGANIZE* to defragment that data. In fact, this option (*WITH LOB_COMPACTION*) is on by default, so you just need to make sure that you don't set it to *'OFF'*.

FILESTREAM and FileTable data

Although the flexible methods that SQL Server uses to store large object data in the database give you many advantages over data stored in the file system, they also have many disadvantages. Some of the benefits of storing large objects in your database include the following.

- Transactional consistency of your large object data can be guaranteed.

- Your backup and restore operations include the large object data, allowing you integrated, point-in-time recovery of your large objects.

- All data can be stored using a single storage and query environment.

Some of the disadvantages of storing large objects in your database include the following.

- Large objects can require a very large number of buffers in cache.

- The upper limit on the size of any large object value is 2 GB.

- Updating large objects can cause extensive database fragmentation.

- Database files can become extremely large.

- Read or write streaming operations from *varchar(MAX)* and *varbinary(MAX)* columns are significantly slower than streaming from NTFS files.

SQL Server allows you to manage file system objects as though they were part of your database to provide the benefits of having large objects in the database while minimizing the disadvantages. The data stored in the file system can be FILESTREAM or FileTable data. As you start evaluating whether FILESTREAM or FileTable data is beneficial for your applications, consider both the benefits and the drawbacks. Some benefits of both FILESTREAM and FileTable data include the following.

- The large object data is stored in the file system but rooted in the database as a 48-byte file pointer value in the column that contains the FILESTREAM data.

- The large object data is accessible through both Transact-SQL (T-SQL) and the NTFS streaming APIs, which can provide great performance benefits.

- The large object size is limited only by the NTFS volume size, not the old 2 GB limit for large object data stored within a database.

FILESTREAM data has the following additional benefits.

- The large object data is kept transactionally consistent with structured data.

- Databases containing FILESTREAM data can participate in the SQL Server 2012 AlwaysOn availability groups.

FileTable data has these additional benefits.

- The data is available through any Wind32 application without any modification of the application.

- FileTables allow you to support a hierarchy of directories and files.

Some drawbacks of using FILESTREAM or FileTable data include the following.

- Database snapshots can't include the FILESTREAM filegroups, so the FILESTREAM data is unavailable. A *SELECT* statement in a database snapshot that requests a FILESTREAM column generates an error.

- SQL Server can't encrypt FILESTREAM data natively.

Because the FileTable feature is built on top of the FILESTREAM technology, I'll first tell you about FILESTREAM (which was introduced in SQL Server 2008) and then about what has been added in SQL Server 2012 to enable FileTables.

Enabling FILESTREAM data for SQL Server

The capability to access FILESTREAM data must be enabled both outside and inside your SQL Server instance, as mentioned in Chapter 1 when discussing configuration. Through the SQL Server Configuration Manager, you must enable T-SQL access to FILESTREAM data, and if that has been enabled, you can also enable file I/O streaming access. If file I/O streaming access is allowed, you can allow remote clients to have access to the streaming data if you want. When the SQL Server Configuration Manager is opened, make sure that you have selected SQL Server Services in the left pane. In the right pane, right-click the SQL instance that you want to configure and select Properties from the drop-down menu. The Properties sheet has six tabs, including one labeled *FILESTREAM*. You can see the details of the FILESTREAM tab of the SQL Server Properties sheet in Figure 8-3.

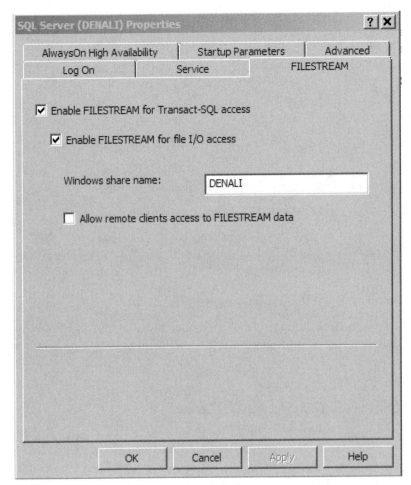

FIGURE 8-3 Configuring a SQL Server instance to allow FILESTREAM access.

After the server instance is configured, you need to use *sp_configure* to set your SQL Server instance to the level of FILESTREAM access that you require. Three values are possible.

- 0 (the default) means that no FILESTREAM access is allowed.

- 1 means that you can use T-SQL to access FILESTREAM data.

- 2 means that you can use both T-SQL and the Win32 API for FILESTREAM access.

As with all configuration options, don't forget to run the *RECONFIGURE* command after changing a setting:

```
EXEC sp_configure 'filestream access level', 2; RECONFIGURE;
```

Creating a FILESTREAM-enabled database

To store FILESTREAM data, a database must have at least one filegroup that was created to allow FILESTREAM data. When creating a database, a filegroup that allows FILESTREAM data is specified differently from a filegroup containing row data in several different ways.

- The path specified for the FILESTREAM filegroup must exist only up to the last folder name. The last folder name must not exist but is created when SQL Server creates the database.

- The *size* and *filegrowth* properties don't apply to FILESTREAM filegroups.

- If no FILESTREAM-containing filegroup is specified as *DEFAULT*, the first FILESTREAM-containing filegroup listed is the default. (Therefore, you have one default filegroup for row data and one default filegroup for FILESTREAM data.)

Look at the following code, which creates a database called *MyFilestreamDB* with two FILESTREAM-containing filegroups. The path c:\Data2 must exist, but it must not contain either the *filestream1* or the *filestream2* folders:

```
CREATE DATABASE  MyFilestreamDB  ON  PRIMARY
    (NAME = N'Rowdata1', FILENAME = N'c:\data\Rowdata1.mdf' , SIZE = 2304KB ,
    MAXSIZE = UNLIMITED, FILEGROWTH = 1024KB ),
FILEGROUP FileStreamGroup1 CONTAINS FILESTREAM DEFAULT( NAME = FSData1,
    FILENAME = 'c:\Data2\FileStreamGroup1'),
FILEGROUP FileStreamGroup2 CONTAINS FILESTREAM ( NAME = FSData2,
    FILENAME = 'c:\Data2\FileStreamGroup2')
LOG ON
    (NAME = N'FSDBLOG', FILENAME = N'c:\data\FSDB_log.ldf' , SIZE = 1024KB ,
    MAXSIZE = 2048GB , FILEGROWTH = 10%);
```

When the preceding *MyFilestreamDB* database is created, SQL Server creates the two folders, *FileStreamGroup1* and *FileStreamGroup2*, in the C:\Data2 directory. These folders are referred to as the FILESTREAM *containers*. Initially, each container contains an empty folder called $FSLOG and a header file called filestream.hdr. As tables are created to use FILESTREAM space in a container, a folder for each partition or each table containing FILESTREAM data is created in the container.

An existing database can be altered to have a FILESTREAM filegroup added, and then a subsequent *ALTER DATABASE* command can add a file to the FILESTREAM filegroup. Note that you can't add FILESTREAM filegroups to the *master*, *model*, and *tempdb* databases.

Creating a table to hold FILESTREAM data

To specify that a column is to contain FILESTREAM data, it must be defined as type *varbinary(MAX)* with a *FILESTREAM* attribute. The database containing the table must have at least one filegroup defined for FILESTREAM. Your table creation statement can specify which filegroup its FILESTREAM data is stored in, and if none is specified, the default FILESTREAM filegroup is used. Finally, any table that has FILESTREAM columns must have a column of the *uniqueidentifier* data type with the *ROWGUIDCOL* attribute specified. This column must not allow NULL values and must be guaranteed to be unique by specifying either the UNIQUE or PRIMARY KEY single-column constraint. The

ROWGUIDCOL column acts as a key that the *FILESTREAM* agent can use to locate the actual row in the table to check permissions, obtain the physical path to the file, and possibly lock the row if required.

Now look at the files that are created within the container. When created in the *MyFilestreamDB* database, the following table adds several folders to the *FileStreamGroup1* container:

```
CREATE TABLE MyFilestreamDB.dbo.Records
(
        [Id] [uniqueidentifier] ROWGUIDCOL NOT NULL UNIQUE,
        [SerialNumber] INTEGER UNIQUE,
        [Chart_Primary] VARBINARY(MAX) FILESTREAM NULL,
        [Chart_Secondary] VARBINARY(MAX) FILESTREAM NULL)
FILESTREAM_ON FileStreamGroup1;
```

Because this table is created on *FileStreamGroup1*, the container located at C:\Data2\ FileStreamGroup1 is used. One subfolder is created within *FileStreamGroup1* for each table or partition created in the *FileStreamGroup1* filegroup, and those filenames are GUIDs. Each file has a subfolder for each column within the table or partition which holds FILESTREAM data, and again, the names of those subfolders are GUIDs. Figure 8-4 shows the structure of the files on my disk right after the *MyFilestreamDB.dbo.Records* table is created. The *FileStreamGroup2* folder has only the $FSLOG subfolder, and no subfolders for any tables. The *FileStreamGroup1* folder has a GUID-named subfolder for the *dbo.Records* table and, within that, a GUID-named subfolder for each of the two *FILESTREAM* columns in the table. No files exist except for the original filestream.hdr file. Files aren't added until FILESTREAM data is actually inserted into the table.

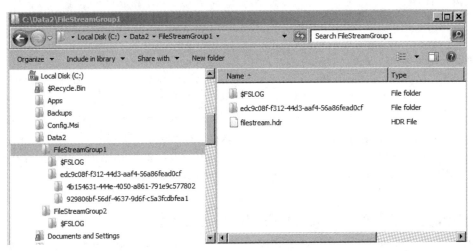

FIGURE 8-4 The operating system file structure after creating a table with two FILESTREAM data columns.

Warning When the table is dropped, the folders, subfolders, and files they contain are *not* removed from the file system immediately. Instead, they are removed by a Garbage Collection thread, which fires regularly as well as when the SQL Server service stops and re-starts. You can delete the files manually, but be careful: You might delete folders for a column or table that still exists in the database, even while the database is online. Subsequent access to that table generates an error message containing the text "Path not found."

You might think that SQL Server would prevent any file that is part of the database from being deleted. However, to absolutely prevent the file deletions, SQL Server has to hold open file handles for every single file in all the FILESTREAM containers for the entire data-base, and for large tables that wouldn't be practical.

Manipulating FILESTREAM data

FILESTREAM data can be manipulated with either T-SQL or the Win32 API. When using T-SQL, you can process the data exactly as though it were *varbinary(MAX)*. Using the Win32 API requires that you first obtain the file path and current transaction context. You can then open a WIN32 handle and use it to read and write the large object data. All the examples in this section use T-SQL; you can get the details of Win32 manipulation from *SQL Server Books Online*.

As you add data to the table, files are added to the subfolders for each column. *INSERT* operations that fail with a runtime error (for example, due to a uniqueness violation) still create a file for each FILESTREAM column in the row. Although the row is never accessible, it still uses file system space.

Inserting FILESTREAM data

You can insert data by using regular T-SQL *INSERT* statements. You must insert FILESTREAM data by using the *varbinary(MAX)* data type but can convert any string data in the *INSERT* state-ment. The following statement adds one row to the *dbo.Records* table, created earlier with two FILESTREAM columns. The first FILESTREAM column gets a 90,000-byte character string converted to *varbinary(MAX)*, and the second FILESTREAM column gets an empty binary string.

```
USE MyFileStreamDB
INSERT INTO dbo.Records
    SELECT newid (), 24,
      CAST (REPLICATE (CONVERT(varchar(MAX), 'Base Data'), 10000)
                      AS varbinary(max)),
      0x;
```

First, the nine-character string *Base Data* to *varchar(MAX)* is converted because a regular string value can't be more than 8,000 bytes. The *REPLICATE* function returns the same data type as its first parameter, so that first parameter should be unambiguously a large object. Replicating the 9-byte string 10,000 times results in a 90,000-byte string, which is then converted to *varbinary(MAX)*. Notice that a value of 0x is an empty binary string, which isn't the same as a NULL. Every row that has a non-NULL value in a FILESTREAM column has a file, even for zero-length values.

Figure 8-5 shows what your file system should look like after running the preceding code to create a database with two FILESTREAM containers and create a table with two *FILESTREAM* columns, and then inserting one row into that table. In the left pane, you can see the two FILESTREAM containers, *FileStreamGroup1* and *FileStreamGroup2*.

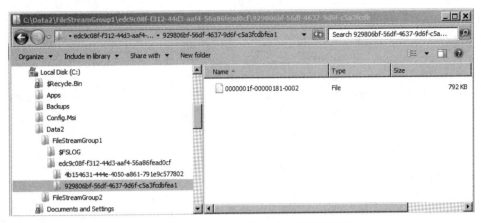

FIGURE 8-5 The operating system file structure after inserting FILESTREAM data.

The *FileStreamGroup1* container has a folder with a GUID name for the *dbo.Records* table that I created, and that folder container has two folders, with GUID names, for the two columns in that table. The right pane shows the file containing the actual data inserted into one of the columns.

Updating FILESTREAM data

Updates to FILESTREAM data are always performed as a *DELETE* followed by an *INSERT*, so you see a new row in the directory for the column(s) updated. Also, the T-SQL "chunked update," specified with the *.WRITE* clause, isn't supported. So any update to FILESTREAM data results into SQL Server creating a new copy of the FILESTREAM data file. I recommend that you use file-system streaming access for manipulation (both inserts and updates) of your FILESTREAM data.

When a FILESTREAM value is set to NULL, the FILESTREAM file associated with that value is deleted when the Garbage Collection thread runs. (Garbage collection is discussed later in this chapter.) The Garbage Collection thread also cleans up old versions of the FILESTREAM files after an *UPDATE* creates a new file.

Deleting FILESTREAM data

When a row is deleted through the use of a *DELETE* or a *TRUNCATE TABLE* statement, any FILESTREAM file associated with the row is deleted. However, deletion of the file isn't synchronous with row deletion. The file is deleted by the *FILESTREAM* Garbage Collection thread. This is also true for *DELETE*s that are generated as part of an *UPDATE*, as mentioned in the preceding section paragraph.

Note The *OUTPUT* clause for data manipulation operations (*INSERT, UPDATE, DELETE,* and *MERGE*) is supported in the same way it is for column modifications. However, you need to be careful if you are using the *OUTPUT* clause to insert into a table with a *varbinary(MAX)* column instead without the *FILESTREAM* specifier. If the FILESTREAM data is larger than 2 GB, the insert of FILESTREAM data into the table can result in a runtime error.

Manipulating FILESTREAM data and transactions

FILESTREAM data manipulation is fully transactional. However, you need to be aware that when you are manipulating FILESTREAM data, not all isolation levels are supported. Also, some isolation levels are supported for T-SQL access but not for file-system access. Table 8-2 indicates which isolation levels are available in which access mode.

TABLE 8-2 Isolation levels supported with FILESTREAM data manipulation

Isolation level	T-SQL access	File-system access
Read uncommitted	Supported	Not supported
Read committed	Supported	Supported
Repeatable read	Supported	Not supported
Serializable	Supported	Not supported
Read committed snapshot	Supported	Supported
Snapshot	Supported	Supported

If two processes trying to access the same *FILESTREAM* datafile are in incompatible modes, the file-system APIs fail with an *ERROR_SHARING_VIOLATION* message rather than just block, as would happen when using T-SQL. As with all data access, readers and writers within the same transaction can never get a conflict on the same file but unlike non-FILESTREAM access, two write operations within the same transaction can end up conflicting with each other when accessing the same file, unless the file handle has been previously closed. You can read much more about transactions, isolation levels, and conflicts in Chapter 13, "Transactions and concurrency."

Logging FILESTREAM changes

As mentioned previously, each *FILESTREAM* filegroup has a $FSLOG folder that keeps track of all FILESTREAM activity that touches that filegroup. The data in this folder is used when you perform transaction log backup and restore operations in the database (which include the *FILESTREAM* filegroup) and also during the recovery process.

The $FSLOG folder primarily keeps track of new information added to the FILESTREAM filegroup. A file gets added to the log folder to reflect each of the following.

- A new table containing FILESTREAM data is created.

- A *FILESTREAM* column is defined.

- A new row is inserted containing non-NULL data in the *FILESTREAM* column.

- A *FILESTREAM* value is updated.

- A *COMMIT* occurs.

Here are some examples.

- If you create a table containing two *FILESTREAM* columns, four files are added to the $FSLOG folder—one for the table, two for the columns, and one for the implied *COMMIT*.

- If you insert a single row containing FILESTREAM data in an autocommit transaction, two files are added to the $FSLOG folder—one for the *INSERT* and one for the *COMMIT*.

- If you insert five rows in an explicit transaction, six files are added to the $FSLOG folder.

Files aren't added to the $FSLOG folder when data is deleted or when a table is truncated or dropped. However, the SQL Server transaction log keeps track of these operations, and a new metadata table contains information about the removed data.

Using garbage collection for FILESTREAM data

The FILESTREAM data can be viewed as serving as the live user data, as well as the log of changes to that data, and as row versions for snapshot operations (discussed in Chapter 13). SQL Server needs to make sure that the FILESTREAM data files aren't removed if they might possibly be needed for any backup or recovery needs. In particular, for log backups, all new FILESTREAM content must be backed up because the transaction log doesn't contain the actual FILESTREAM data, and only the FILESTREAM data has the redo information for the actual FILESTREAM contents. In general, if your database isn't in the SIMPLE recovery mode, you need to back up the log twice before the Garbage Collector can remove unneeded data files from your *FILESTREAM* folders.

Consider this example: You can start with a clean slate by dropping and re-creating the *My-FilestreamDB* database. A *DROP DATABASE* statement immediately removes all the folders and files because now doing any subsequent log backups isn't possible. The script in Listing 8-3 recreates the database and creates a table with just a single *FILESTREAM* column. Finally, the script inserts three rows into the table and backs up the database. If you inspect the *FileStreamGroup1* container, you see that the folder for the columns contains three files for the three rows.

LISTING 8-3 Dropping and recreating a database

```
USE master;
GO
DROP DATABASE MyFilestreamDB;
GO
CREATE DATABASE  MyFilestreamDB  ON  PRIMARY
     (NAME = N'Rowdata1', FILENAME = N'c:\data\Rowdata1.mdf' , SIZE = 2304KB ,
      MAXSIZE = UNLIMITED, FILEGROWTH = 1024KB ),

FILEGROUP FileStreamGroup1 CONTAINS FILESTREAM DEFAULT( NAME = FSData1,
     FILENAME = 'c:\Data2\FileStreamGroup1'),
FILEGROUP FileStreamGroup2 CONTAINS FILESTREAM ( NAME = FSData2,
```

```
         FILENAME = 'c:\Data2\FileStreamGroup2')
    LOG ON
        (NAME = N'FSDBLOG', FILENAME = N'c:\data\FSDB_log.ldf' , SIZE = 1024KB ,
         MAXSIZE = 2048GB , FILEGROWTH = 10%);
GO
USE MyFilestreamDB;
GO
CREATE TABLE dbo.Records
(
        Id [uniqueidentifier] ROWGUIDCOL NOT NULL UNIQUE,
        SerialNumber INTEGER UNIQUE,
        Chart_Primary VARBINARY(MAX) FILESTREAM NULL
)
FILESTREAM_ON FileStreamGroup1;
GO
INSERT INTO dbo.Records
    VALUES (newid(), 1,
            CAST (REPLICATE (CONVERT(varchar(MAX), 'Base Data'),
                   10000) as varbinary(max))),
        (newid(), 2,
            CAST (REPLICATE (CONVERT(varchar(MAX), 'New Data'),
                   10000) as    varbinary(max))),
        (newid(), 3, 0x);
GO
BACKUP DATABASE MyFileStreamDB to disk = 'C:\backups\FBDB.bak';
GO
```

Now delete one of the rows, as follows:

```
DELETE dbo.Records
WHERE SerialNumber = 2;
GO
```

Now inspect the files on disk, and you still see three files.

Back up the log and run a checkpoint. Note that on a real system, enough changes would probably be made to your data that your database's log would get full enough to trigger an automatic *CHECKPOINT*. However, during testing, when you aren't putting much into the log at all, you have to force the *CHECKPOINT*:

```
BACKUP LOG  MyFileStreamDB to disk = 'C:\backups\FBDB_log.bak';
CHECKPOINT;
```

Now if you check the FILESTREAM data files, you still see three rows. Wait five seconds for garbage collection, and you'll still see three rows. You need to back up the log and then force another *CHECKPOINT*:

```
BACKUP LOG  MyFileStreamDB to disk = 'C:\backups\FBDB_log.bak';
CHECKPOINT;
```

Now within a few seconds, you should see one of the files disappear. The reason you need to back up the log twice before the physical file is available for garbage collection is to make sure that the file space isn't reused by other FILESTREAM operations while it still might be needed for restore purposes.

You can run some additional tests of your own. For example, if you try dropping the *dbo.Records* table, notice that you again have to perform two log backups and *CHECKPOINTs* before SQL Server removes the folders for the table and the column.

> **Note** SQL Server 2012 provides a new procedure called *sp_filestream_force_garbage_collection*, which forces the garbage collection of unneeded FILESTREAM files. If the garbage collection of unneeded files seems to be delayed frequently, and you want to force removal of these files, you could schedule regularly executions of this procedure. The procedure takes database name as a parameter and optionally takes a logical name of a FILESTREAM container as a second parameter. If the first parameter is missing, the current database is assumed. If the second parameter is missing, garbage collection is performed on all FILESTREAM containers in the database.

Exploring metadata with FILESTREAM data

Within your SQL Server tables, the storage required for FILESTREAM isn't particularly complex. In the row itself, each FILESTREAM column contains a file pointer that is 48 bytes in size. Even if you look at a data page with the *DBCC PAGE* command, not much more information about the file is available. However, SQL Server does provide a new function to translate the file pointer to a path name. The function is actually a method applied to the column name in the table. So the following code returns a UNC name for the file containing the actual column's data in the row inserted previously:

```
SELECT Chart_Primary, Chart_Primary.PathName()
FROM dbo.Records
WHERE SerialNumber = 3;
GO
```

The UNC value returned looks like this:

```
\\<server_name>\<share_name>\v1\<db_name>\<object_schema>\<table_name>\<column_name>\<GUID>
```

Keep in mind the following points about using the *PathName* function.

- The function name is case-sensitive, even on a server that's not case-sensitive, so it always must be entered as *PathName*.

- The default *share_name* is the service name for your SQL Server instance (so for the default instance, it is MSSQLSERVER). By using the SQL Server Configuration Manager, you can right-click your SQL Server instance and choose Properties. The *FILESTREAM* tab of the SQL Server Properties sheet allows you to change the *share_name* to another value of your choosing.

- The *PathName* function can take an optional parameter of 0, 1, or 2, with 0 being the default. The parameter controls only how the *server_name* value is returned; all other values in the UNC string are unaffected. Table 8-3 shows the meanings of the different values.

TABLE 8-3 Parameter values for the *PathName* function

Value	Description
0	Returns the server name converted to BIOS format; for example, \\SERVERNAME\MSSQLSERVER\v1\MyFilestream\dbo\Records\Chart_Primary\A73F19F7-38EA-4AB0-BB89-E6C545DBD3F9
1	Returns the server name without conversion; for example, \\ServerName\MSSQLSERVER\v1\MyFilestream\Dbo\Records\Chart_Primary\A73F19F7-38EA-4AB0-BB89-E6C545DBD3F9
2	Returns the complete server path; for example, \\ServerName.MyDomain.com\MSSQLSERVER\v1\MyFilestream\Dbo\Records\Chart_Primary\A73F19F7-38EA-4AB0-BB89-E6C545DBD3F9

Other metadata gives you information about your FILESTREAM data.

- *sys.database_files* returns a row for each of your FILESTREAM files. These files have a *type* value of 2 and a *type_desc* value of *FILESTREAM*.

- *sys.filegroups* returns a row for each of your FILESTREAM filegroups. These files have a *type* value of FD and a *type_desc* value of *FILESTREAM_DATA_FILEGROUP*.

- *sys.data_spaces* returns one row for each data space, which is either a filegroup or a partition scheme. Filegroups holding FILESTREAM data are indicated by the type *FD*.

- *sys.tables* has a value in the column for *filestream_data_space_id*, which is the data space ID for either the FILESTREAM filegroup or the partition scheme that the FILESTREAM data uses. Tables with no FILESTREAM data have NULL in this column.

- *sys.columns* has a value of 1 in the *is_filestream* column for columns with the *filestream* attribute.

The older metadata, such as the system procedure *sp_helpdb <database_name>* or *sp_help <object_name>*, doesn't show any information about FILESTREAM data.

Earlier, this chapter mentioned that rows or objects that are deleted don't generate files in the $FSLOG folder, but data about the removed data is stored in a system table. No metadata view allows you to see this table; you can observe it only by using the dedicated administrator connection (DAC). You can look in a view called *sys.internal_tables* for an object with *TOMBSTONE* in its name. Then, by using the DAC, you can look at the data inside the *TOMBSTONE* table. If you rerun the preceding script but don't back up the log, you can use the following code:

```
USE MyFilestreamDB;
GO
SELECT name FROM sys.internal_tables
WHERE name like '%tombstone%';

-- I see the table named: filestream_tombstone_2073058421
-- Reconnect using DAC, which puts us in the master database
USE MyFileStreamDB;
GO
SELECT * FROM sys.filestream_tombstone_2073058421;
GO
```

If this table is empty, the login SQL Server and the $FSLOG are in sync, and all unneeded files have been removed from the FILESTREAM containers on disk.

Creating a FileTable

FileTable storage, introduced in SQL Server 2012, allows you to create special user tables that have a predefined schema and to extend the capabilities of FILESTREAM data discussed earlier. The two most important extensions are that FileTables allow full support and compatibility with Win32 applications and support the hierarchical namespace of directories and files. Each row in a FileTable table represents an operating system file or directory in a hierarchical structure and contains attributes about the file or directory, such as created date, modified, date, and the name of the file or directory.

The first step in creating a FileTable is to make sure that the database supports FILESTREAM data with at least one FILESTREAM filegroup. Also, the database option to allow *NON_TRANSACTED_ ACCESS* must be set to either *FULL* or *READ_ONLY*, and a directory name must be supplied for use by Windows applications as part of the share name when accessing the FileTable files. These options can be supplied as part of the initial *CREATE DATABASE* operation, or the database can be altered to include these options:

```
ALTER DATABASE MyFilestreamDB
SET FILESTREAM ( NON_TRANSACTED_ACCESS = FULL, DIRECTORY_NAME = N'FileTableData' );
```

By setting *NON_TRANSACTED_ACCESS* to something other than *NONE*, you are enabling FileTable storage within the database. SQL Server 2012 provides a new catalog view, called *sys.database_ filestream_options*, to examine each database's readiness for storing FileTable data. The following query selects from that view showing only rows where non-transacted access has been allowed. A value of 0 for *NON_TRANSACTED_ACCESS* means the feature wasn't enabled, 1 means it has been enabled for *READ_ONLY*, and 2 means it has been enabled for *FULL* access.

```
SELECT DB_NAME(database_id) as DBNAME,  non_transacted_access_desc, directory_name
FROM sys.database_filestream_options
WHERE non_transacted_access > 0;
```

Enabling the *NON_TRANSACTED_ACCESS* to the *MyFilestreamDB* as shown in the preceding *ALTER* statement would produce the following results:

```
DB_NAME              non_transacted_access_desc     directory_name
---------------      --------------------------     ----------------
MyFilestreamDB       FULL                           FileTableData
```

After the database is properly configured for FileTable access, you can create a FileTable with a very simple *CREATE TABLE* statement. Because the schema is predefined, all you do is specify a name for your FileTable and a directory name in which all the files stored in this FileTable can be found in the operating system. Optionally, you can also specify a collation for the data in the files stored in the FileTable, but if none is specified, the default database collation is used.

```
CREATE TABLE Documents AS Filetable
    WITH (Filetable_Directory = 'DocumentsData');
```

At this point, you can look at the Windows share that is now available by allowing your database *NON_TRANSACTED_ACCESS*. You can see this by opening Windows Explorer on the server machine and navigating to either \\127.0.0.1 or \\<your machine name>. Along with whatever other shares have been set up on the machine, you should see a share for your SQL Server instance name, or *mssqlserver* if your instance is the default instance. You can open up the share and see a directory named *FiletableData*, and when you open the directory, you should see the table name *DocumentsData*. Figure 8-6 shows you what this structure looks like on my machine, for a SQL Server 2012 instance called denali. (In SQL Server 2008 and 2008 R2, you also saw share names for your SQL Server instances that have been configured to allow FILESTREAM access. However, attempting to access the share directly will result in an error.)

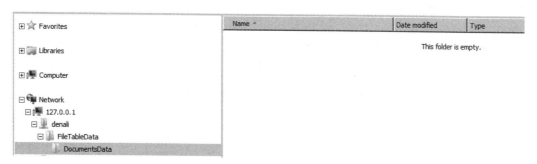

FIGURE 8-6 The FileTable share containing no files.

While exploring the operating system files, you can also revisit the *Data2* folder (which was the default FILESTREAM container for the database), which you saw earlier in the FILESTREAM data discussion, and see that a GUID now exists for one more table containing FILESTREAM data and one FILESTREAM column in that table.

As mentioned, the FileTable data is completely available through the share to all Windows applications, including Windows Explorer. You can copy a file from anywhere on your system and paste it into the share. Figure 8-7 shows the share now containing a copy of one of my errorlog files.

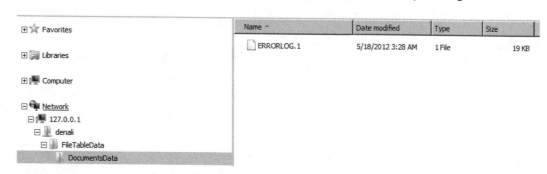

FIGURE 8-7 The FileTable share after inserting one file.

When a SQL Server instance is enabled for FILESTREAM access, SQL Server installs a component called an NTFS filter driver. When a Windows application interacts with a FileTable share, the interaction is intercepted by the NTFS filter driver and is redirected to SQL Server to allow these changes that you make to the share, such as inserting a new file, to be reflected in the table inside SQL Server. From SQL Server Management Studio, I can also *SELECT* from my Documents table, and see that it now has one row in it, to reflect the file that was added to it through Windows.

Some of the columns are returned, but the wide output prevents showing all the columns:

Table 8-4 lists all the column names available in the FileTable.

TABLE 8-4 Predefined columns in a FileTable

File attribute name	Type	Description
stream_id	[uniqueidentifier] rowguidcol	A unique ID for the FILESTREAM data.
file_stream	varbinary(max) filestream	Contains the FILESTREAM data.
Name	nvarchar(255)	The file or directory name.
path_locator	hierarchyid	The position of this node in the hierarchical FileNamespace. Primary key for the table.
parent_path_locator	hierarchyid	The *hierarchyid* of the containing directory. *parent_path_locator* is a persisted computed column.
file_type	nvarchar(255)	Represents the type of the file. This column can be used as the *TYPE COLUMN* when you create a full-text index. file_type is a persisted computed column based on the file extension.
cached_file_size	bigint	The size in bytes of the FILESTREAM data. *cached_file_size* is a persisted computed column.
creation_time	datetime2(4) not null	The date and time that the file was created.
last_write_time	datetime2(4) not null	The date and time that the file was last updated.
last_access_time	datetime2(4) not null	The date and time that the file was last accessed.
is_directory	bit not null	Indicates whether the row represents a directory. This value is calculated automatically, and can't be set.
is_offline	bit not null	Offline file attribute.
is_hidden	bit not null	Hidden file attribute.
is_readonly	bit not null	Read-only file attribute.
is_archive	bit not null	Archive attribute.

File attribute name	Type	Description
is_system	bit not null	System file attribute.
is_temporary	bit not null	Temporary file attribute.

You can see that many of these column names correspond to attributes that you can see for all your files through Windows Explorer.

> **Note** All application access to your FileTable data is through the FileTable share. The FILESTREAM container is the actual physical storage of the FILESTREAM data, and only database administrators need to be aware of this location. The FILESTREAM containers are backed up when a database containing FILESTREAM data is backed up.

Considering performance for FILESTREAM data

Although a thorough discussion of performance tuning and troubleshooting is beyond the scope of this book, I want to provide you with some basic information about setting up your system to get high performance from FILESTREAM data. Paul Randal, one of the co-authors of this book, has written a white paper on FILESTREAM that you can access on the MSDN site at *http://msdn.microsoft.com/en-us/library/cc949109.aspx*. (This white paper is also available on this book's companion website, *http://www.SQLServerInternals.com/companion*.) This section just briefly mentions some of the main points Paul makes regarding what you can do to get good performance. All these suggestions are explained in much more detail in the white paper.

- Make sure that you're storing the right-sized data in the right way. Jim Gray (et al) published a research paper several years ago titled "To BLOB or Not to BLOB: Large Object Storage in a Database or a Filesystem?" that gives recommendations for when to store data outside the database. To summarize the findings, large object data smaller than 256 KB should be stored in a database, and data that's 1 MB or larger should be stored in the file system. For data between these two values, the answer depends on other factors, and you should test your application thoroughly. The key point here is that you won't get good performance if you store lots of relatively small large objects using FILESTREAM.

- Use an appropriate RAID level for the NTFS volume that hosts the FILESTREAM data container. For example, don't use RAID 5 for a write-intensive workload.

- Use an appropriate disk technology. SCSI is usually faster than SATA/IDE because SCSI drives usually have higher rotational speeds, which help them have lower latency and seek times. However, SCSI drives are also more expensive.

- Whichever disk technology you choose, if it is SATA, ensure that it supports NCQ, and if SCSI, ensure that it supports CTQ. Both of these allow the drives to process multiple, interleaved I/Os concurrently.

- Separate the data containers from each other, and separate the containers from other database data and log files. This avoids contention for the disk heads.

- Defragment the NTFS volume, if needed, before setting up FILESTREAM, and defragment periodically to maintain good scan performance.

- Turn off 8.3 name generation on the NTFS volume by using the command-line *fsutil* utility. This is an order-N algorithm that must check that the new name generated doesn't collide with any existing names in the directory. Note, however, that this slows down insert and update performance a lot.

- Use *fsutil* to turn off tracking of last access time.

- Set the NTFS cluster size appropriately. For larger objects greater than 1 MB in size, use a cluster size of 64 KB to help reduce fragmentation.

- A partial update of FILESTREAM data creates a new file. Batch lots of small updates into one large update to reduce churn.

- When streaming the data back to the client, use a server message block (SMB) buffer size of approximately 60 KB or multiples thereof. This helps keep the buffers from getting overly fragmented, because Transmission Control Protocol/Internet Protocol (TCP/IP) buffers are 64 KB.

Taking these suggestions into consideration and performing thorough testing of your application can give you great performance when working with very large data objects.

Summarizing FILESTREAM and FileTable

When you configure a SQL Server instance to support FILESTREAM storage, you are allowing Windows files to be accessed and manipulated as data in any SQL Server table. When you configure a database with FILESTREAM filegroups to have non-transacted access, you are allowing FileTables to be created in the database. A FileTable builds on the FILESTREAM capability by providing a table whose rows not only contain the Windows file contents but also all the Windows file properties. These files are accessible through the FileTable share and can be manipulated through any Windows application.

Keep in mind that the FileTable structure is predefined and can't be altered. If you want to add your own attributes along with the files in a FileTable, you can create another table with your user-defined attributes and a foreign key reference to the FileTable column *path_locator*, which is the primary key of the FileTable.

Detailed information about how to work with this FileTable data through a Windows application is beyond the scope of this book. The goal of this section was to present some of the storage internals of the FILESTREAM data and FileTables, and well as to give you an idea of how SQL Server works with these constructs.

Sparse columns

This section looks at another special storage format, added in SQL Server 2008. Sparse columns are ordinary columns that have an optimized storage format for NULL values. Sparse columns reduce the space requirements for NULL values, allowing you to have many more columns in your table definition, as long as most of them are NULL. Using sparse columns requires more overhead to store and retrieve non-NULL values.

Sparse columns are intended to be used for tables storing data describing entities with many possible attributes, in which most of the attributes will be NULL for most rows. For example, a content management system such as Microsoft Windows SharePoint Services might need to keep track of many different types of data in a single table. Because different properties apply to different subsets of rows in the table, only a small subset of the columns is populated with values for each row. Another way of looking at this is that for any particular property, only a subset of rows has a value for that property. Sparse columns allow you to store a very large number of possible columns for a single row. For this reason, the Sparse Columns feature is sometimes also referred to as the *wide-table* feature.

Management of sparse columns

You shouldn't consider defining a column as *SPARSE* unless at least 90 percent of the rows in the table are expected to have NULL values for that column. This limit isn't enforced, however, and you can define almost any column as SPARSE. Sparse columns save space on NULL values.

The Sparse Columns feature allows you to have far more columns that you ever could before. The limit is now 30,000 columns in a table, with no more than 1,024 of them being non-sparse. (Computed columns are considered non-sparse.) Obviously, not all 30,000 columns could have values in them. The number of populated columns you can have depends on the bytes of data in the row. Sparse columns optimize the storage size for NULL values, which take no space at all for sparse columns, unlike non-sparse columns, which do need space even for NULLs. (As you saw in Chapter 6, a fixed-length NULL column always uses the whole column width, and a variable-length NULL column uses at least two bytes in the column offset array.)

Although the sparse columns themselves take no space, some fixed overhead is needed to allow for sparse columns in a row. As soon as you define even one column with the *SPARSE* attribute, SQL Server adds a sparse vector to the end of the row. We'll see the actual structure of this sparse vector in the section "Physical storage," later in this chapter, but to start, you should be aware that even with sparse columns, the maximum size of a data row (excluding LOB and row-overflow) remains at 8,060, including overhead bytes. Because the sparse vector includes additional overhead, the maximum number of bytes for the rest of the rows decreases. Also, the size of all fixed-length non-NULL sparse columns in a row is limited to 8,023 bytes.

Creating a table

Creating a table with sparse columns is very straightforward, as you can just add the attribute *SPARSE* to any column of any data type except *text*, *ntext*, *image*, *geography*, *geometry*, *timestamp*, or any user-defined data type. Also, sparse columns can't include the *IDENTITY*, *ROWGUIDCOL*, or *FILESTREAM* attributes. A sparse column can't be part of a clustered index or part of the primary key. Tables containing sparse columns can't be compressed, either at the row level or the page level. (The next section discusses compression in detail.) A few other restrictions are enforced, particularly if you are partitioning a table with sparse columns, so you should check the documentation for full details.

The examples in this section are necessarily very simple because it would be impractical to print code examples with enough columns to make sparse columns really useful. The following example shows the creation of two very similar tables: one that doesn't allow sparse columns and another that does. I attempt to insert the same rows into each table. Because a row allowing sparse columns has a smaller maximum length, it fails when trying to insert a row that the table with no sparse columns has no problem with:

```
USE testdb;
GO
IF OBJECT_ID('test_nosparse') IS NOT NULL
    DROP TABLE test_nosparse;
GO
CREATE TABLE test_nosparse
(
  col1 int,
  col2 char(8000),
  col3 varchar(8000)
);
GO
INSERT INTO test_nosparse
        SELECT null, null, null;
INSERT INTO test_nosparse
        SELECT 1, 'a', 'b';
GO
```

These two rows can be inserted with no error. Now, build the second table:

```
IF OBJECT_ID('test_sparse') IS NOT NULL
    DROP TABLE test_sparse;
GO

CREATE TABLE test_sparse
(
 col1 int SPARSE,
 col2 char(8000) SPARSE,
 col3 varchar(8000) SPARSE
);
GO

INSERT INTO test_sparse
        SELECT NULL, NULL, NULL;
INSERT INTO test_sparse
        SELECT 1, 'a', 'b';
GO
```

The second *INSERT* statement generates the following error:

```
Msg 576, Level 16, State 5, Line 2
Cannot create a row that has sparse data of size 8046 which is greater than the
allowable maximum sparse data size of 8023.
```

Although the second row inserted into the *test_sparse* table looks just like a row that was inserted successfully into the *test_nosparse* table, internally it's not. The total of the sparse columns is 4 bytes for the *int*, plus 8,000 bytes for the *char* and 24 bytes for the row-overflow pointer, which is greater than the 8,023-byte limit.

Altering a table

You can alter tables to convert a non-sparse column into a sparse column, or vice versa. Be careful, however, because if you are altering a very large row in a table with no sparse columns, changing one column to be sparse reduces the number of bytes of data that are allowed on a page. This can result in an error being thrown in cases where an existing column is converted into a sparse column. For example, the following code creates a table with large rows, but the *INSERT* statements, with or without NULLs, are accepted. However, when you try to make one of the columns *SPARSE*—even a relatively small column like the 8-byte *datetime* column—the extra overhead makes the existing rows too large and the *ALTER* fails:

```
IF OBJECT_ID('test_nosparse_alter') IS NOT NULL
    DROP TABLE test_nosparse_alter;
GO
GO
CREATE TABLE test_nosparse_alter
(
c1 int,
c2 char(4020) ,
c3 char(4020) ,
c4 datetime
);
GO
INSERT INTO test_nosparse_alter SELECT NULL, NULL, NULL, NULL;
INSERT INTO test_nosparse_alter SELECT 1, 1, 'b', GETDATE();
GO
ALTER TABLE test_nosparse_alter
  ALTER COLUMN c4 datetime SPARSE;
```

This error is received:

```
Msg 1701, Level 16, State 1, Line 2
Creating or altering table 'test_nosparse_alter' failed because the minimum row size
would be 8075, including 23 bytes of internal overhead. This exceeds the maximum
allowable table row size of 8060 bytes.
```

In general, you can treat sparse columns just like any other column, with only a few restrictions. In addition to the restrictions mentioned earlier on the data types that can't be defined as *SPARSE*, you need to keep in mind the following limitations.

- A sparse column can't have a default value.

- A sparse column can't be bound to a rule.

- Although a computed column can refer to a sparse column, a computed column can't be marked as *SPARSE*.

- A sparse column can't be part of a clustered index or a unique primary key index. However, both persisted and non-persisted computed columns that refer to sparse columns can be part of a clustered key.

- A sparse column can't be used as a partition key of a clustered index or heap. However, a sparse column can be used as the partition key of a nonclustered index.

Except for the requirement that sparse columns can't be part of the clustered index or primary key, building indexes on sparse columns has no other restrictions. However, if you're using sparse columns the way they are intended to be used and the vast majority of your rows have NULL for the sparse columns, any regular index on a sparse column is very inefficient and might have limited usefulness. Sparse columns are really intended to be used with filtered indexes, which are discussed in Chapter 7.

Column sets and sparse column manipulation

If sparse columns are used as intended, only a few columns in each row have values, and your *INSERT* and *UPDATE* statements are relatively straightforward. For *INSERT* statements, you can specify a column list and then specify values only for those few columns in the column list. For *UPDATE* statements, values can be specified for just a few columns in each row. The only time you need to be concerned about how to deal with a potentially very large list of columns is if you are selecting data without listing individual columns—that is, using a *SELECT* *. Good developers know that using *SELECT* * is never a good idea, but SQL Server needs a way of dealing with a result set with potentially thousands (or tens of thousands) of columns. The mechanism to help deal with *SELECT* * is a construct called *COLUMN_SET,* which is an untyped XML representation that combines multiple columns of a table into a structured output. You can think of a *COLUMN_SET* as a nonpersisted computed column because the *COLUMN_SET* isn't physically stored in the table. In this release of SQL Server, the only possible *COLUMN_SET* contains all the sparse columns in the table. Future versions might allow us to define other *COLUMN_SET* variations.

A table can only have one *COLUMN_SET* defined, and when a table has a *COLUMN_SET* defined, *SELECT* * no longer returns individual sparse columns. Instead, it returns an XML fragment containing all the non-NULL values for the sparse columns. For example, the code in Listing 8-4 builds a table containing an identity column, 25 sparse columns, and a column set.

LISTING 8-4 Building a table with an identity column, sparse columns, and a column set

```
USE testdb;
GO
IF EXISTS (SELECT * FROM sys.tables WHERE name = 'lots_of_sparse_columns')
            DROP TABLE lots_of_sparse_columns;
GO
```

```
CREATE TABLE lots_of_sparse_columns
(ID int IDENTITY,
 col1 int SPARSE,
 col2 int SPARSE,
 col3 int SPARSE,
 col4 int SPARSE,
 col5 int SPARSE,
 col6 int SPARSE,
 col7 int SPARSE,
 col8 int SPARSE,
 col9 int SPARSE,
 col10 int SPARSE,
 col11 int SPARSE,
 col12 int SPARSE,
 col13 int SPARSE,
 col14 int SPARSE,
 col15 int SPARSE,
 col16 int SPARSE,
 col17 int SPARSE,
 col18 int SPARSE,
 col19 int SPARSE,
 col20 int SPARSE,
 col21 int SPARSE,
 col22 int SPARSE,
 col23 int SPARSE,
 col24 int SPARSE,
 col25 int SPARSE,
 sparse_column_set XML COLUMN_SET FOR ALL_SPARSE_COLUMNS);
 GO
```

Next, values are inserted into 3 of the 25 columns, specifying individual column names:

```
INSERT INTO lots_of_sparse_columns (col4, col7, col12)  SELECT 4,6,11;
```

You can also insert directly into the *COLUMN_SET*, specifying values for columns in an XML fragment. The capability to update the *COLUMN_SET* is another feature that differentiates *COLUMN_SET*s from computed columns:

```
INSERT INTO lots_of_sparse_columns (sparse_column_set)
            SELECT '<col8>42</col8><col17>0</col17><col22>30000</col22>';
```

Here are my results when I run *SELECT* * from this table:

```
SELECT * FROM lots_of_sparse_columns;
Results:
ID      sparse_column_set
-------  --------------------------------------------------
1       <col4>4</col4><col7>6</col7><col12>11</col12>
2       <col8>42</col8><col17>0</col17><col22>30000</col22>
```

You can still select from individual columns, either instead of or in addition to selecting the entire *COLUMN_SET*. So the following *SELECT* statements are both valid:

```
SELECT ID, col10, col15, col20
    FROM lots_of_sparse_columns;
SELECT *, col11
    FROM lots_of_sparse_columns;
```

Keep the following points in mind if you decide to use sparse columns in your tables.

- When defined, the *COLUMN_SET* can't be altered. To change a *COLUMN_SET*, you must drop and re-create the *COLUMN_SET* column.

- A *COLUMN_SET* can be added to a table that doesn't include any sparse columns. If sparse columns are later added to the table, they appear in the column set.

- A *COLUMN_SET* is optional and isn't required to use sparse columns.

- Constraints or default values can't be defined on a *COLUMN_SET*.

- Distributed queries aren't supported on tables that contain *COLUMN_SET*s.

- Replication doesn't support *COLUMN_SET*s.

- The Change Data Capture feature doesn't support *COLUMN_SET*s.

- A *COLUMN_SET* can't be part of any kind of index. This includes XML indexes, full-text indexes, and indexed views. A *COLUMN_SET* also can't be added as an included column in any index.

- A *COLUMN_SET* can't be used in the filter expression of a filtered index or filtered statistics.

- When a view includes a *COLUMN_SET*, the *COLUMN_SET* appears in the view as an XML column.

- XML data has a size limit of 2 GB. If the combined data of all the non-NULL sparse columns in a row exceeds this limit, the operation produces an error.

- Copying all columns from a table with a *COLUMN_SET* (using either *SELECT * INTO* or *INSERT INTO SELECT **) doesn't copy the individual sparse columns. Only the *COLUMN_SET*, as data type XML, is copied.

Physical storage

At a high level, you can think of sparse columns as being stored much as they are displayed using the *COLUMN_SET*—that is, as a set of (column-name, value) pairs. So if a particular column has no value, it's not listed and no space at all is required. If a column has a value, not only does SQL Server need to store that value but it also needs to store information about which column has that value. As a result, non-NULL sparse columns take more space than their NULL counterparts. To see the difference graphically, you can compare Tables 8-5 and 8-6.

Table 8-5 represents a table with non-sparse columns. You can see a lot of wasted space when most of the columns are NULL. Table 8-6 shows what the same table looks like if all the columns except the ID are defined as *SPARSE*. All that is stored are the names of all the non-NULL columns and their values.

TABLE 8-5 Representation of a table defined with non-sparse columns, with many NULL values

ID	sc1	sc2	sc3	sc4	sc5	sc6	sc7	sc8	sc9
1	1								9
2		2		4					
3						6	7		
4	1				5				
5				4				8	
6			3						9
7					5		7		
8		2						8	
9			3			6			

TABLE 8-6 Representation of a table defined with sparse columns, with many NULL values

ID	<sparse columns>
1	(sc1,sc9)(1,9)
2	(sc2,sc4)(2,4)
3	(sc6,sc7)(6,7)
4	(sc1,sc5)(1,5)
5	(sc4,sc8)(4,8)
6	(sc3,sc9)(3,9)
7	(sc5,sc7)(5,7)
8	(sc2,sc8)(2,8)
9	(sc3,sc6)(3,6)

SQL Server keeps track of the physical storage of sparse columns with a structure within a row called a *sparse vector*. Sparse vectors are present only in the data records of a base table that has at least one sparse column declared, and each data record of these tables contains a sparse vector. A sparse vector is stored as a special variable-length column at the end of a data record. It's a special system column, and no metadata about this column appears in *sys.columns* or any other view. The sparse vector is stored as the last variable-length column in the row. The only thing after the sparse vector would be versioning information, used primarily with Snapshot isolation, as is discussed in Chapter 13. The NULL bitmap has no bit for the sparse vector column (if a sparse vector exists, it's never NULL), but the count in the row of the number of variable-length columns includes the sparse vector. You might want to revisit Figure 6-5 in Chapter 6 at this time to familiarize yourself with the general structure of data rows.

Table 8-7 lists the meanings of the bytes in the sparse vector.

TABLE 8-7 Bytes in a sparse vector

Name	Number of bytes	Meaning
Complex Column Header	2	Value of 05 indicates that the complex column is a sparse vector.
Sparse Column Count	2	Number of sparse columns.
Column ID Set	2 * the number of sparse columns	Two bytes for the column ID of each column in the table with a value stored in the sparse vector.
Column Offset Table	2 * the number of sparse columns	Two bytes for the offset of the ending position of each sparse column.
Sparse Data	Depends on actual values	Data

Now look at the bytes of a row containing sparse columns. First, build a table containing two sparse columns, and populate it with three rows:

```
USE testdb;
GO
IF OBJECT_ID ('sparse_bits') IS NOT NULL
                DROP TABLE sparse_bits;
GO
CREATE TABLE sparse_bits
(
c1 int IDENTITY,
c2 varchar(4),
c3 char(4) SPARSE,
c4 varchar(4) SPARSE
);
GO
INSERT INTO sparse_bits SELECT 'aaaa', 'bbbb', 'cccc';
INSERT INTO sparse_bits SELECT 'dddd', null, 'eeee';
INSERT INTO sparse_bits SELECT 'ffff', null, 'gg';
GO
```

Now you can use *sys.dm_db_database_page_allocations* to find the page number for the data page storing these three rows and then use *DBCC PAGE* to look at the bytes on the page:

```
SELECT allocated_page_file_id as PageFID, allocated_page_page_id as PagePID,
     object_id as ObjectID, partition_id AS PartitionID,
     allocation_unit_type_desc as AU_type, page_type as PageType
FROM sys.dm_db_database_page_allocations
     (db_id('testdb'), object_id('sparse_bits'), null, null, 'DETAILED');
-- The output indicated that the data page for my table was on page 289;
DBCC TRACEON(3604);
DBCC PAGE(testdb, 1, 289, 1);
```

Only the output for the first data row, which is spread over three lines of *DBCC PAGE* output, is shown here:

```
00000000:   30000800 01000000 02000002 00150029 80616161 0.............).aaa
00000014:   61050002 00030004 00100014 00626262 62636363 a           bbbbccc
00000020:   63                                            c
```

The boldfaced bytes are the sparse vector. You can find it easily because it starts right after the last non-sparse variable-length column, which contained *aaaa*, or 61616161, and continues to the end of the row. Figure 8-8 translates the sparse vector according to the meanings from Table 8-7. Don't forget that you need to byte-swap numeric fields before translating. For example, the first two bytes are 05 00, which need to be swapped to get the hex value 0x0005. Then you can convert it to decimal.

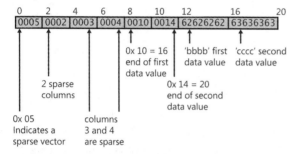

FIGURE 8-8 Interpretation of the actual bytes in a sparse vector.

You can apply the same analysis to the bytes in the other two rows on the page. Here are some things to note:

- No information about columns with NULL values appears in the sparse vector.

- No difference exists in storage between fixed-length and variable-length strings within the sparse vector. However, that doesn't mean you should use the two interchangeably. A sparse *varchar* column that doesn't fit in the 8,060 bytes can be stored as row-overflow data; a sparse *char* column can't be.

- Because only 2 bytes are used to store the number of sparse columns, this sets the limit on the maximum number of sparse columns.

- The 2 bytes for the complex column header indicate that there might be other possibilities for complex columns. At this time, the only other type of complex column that can be stored is one storing a back-pointer, as SQL Server does when it creates a forwarded record. (Chapter 6 briefly discussed forwarded records when discussing updates to heaps.)

Metadata

Very little extra metadata is needed to support sparse columns. The catalog view *sys.columns* contains two columns to keep track of sparse columns in your tables: *is_sparse* and *is_column_set*. Each column has only two possible values, 0 or 1.

Corresponding to these column properties in *sys.columns*, the property function *COLUMNPROP-ERTY()* also has the following properties related to sparse columns: *IsSparse* and *IsColumnSet*.

To inspect all tables with "sparse" in their name and determine which of their columns are *SPARSE*, which are column sets, and which are neither, you can run the following query:

```
SELECT OBJECT_NAME(object_id) as 'Table', name as 'Column', is_sparse, is_column_set
FROM sys.columns
WHERE OBJECT_NAME(object_id) like '%sparse%';
```

To see just the table and column names for all *COLUMN_SET* columns, you can run the following query:

```
SELECT OBJECT_NAME(object_id) as 'Table', name as 'Column'
FROM sys.columns
WHERE COLUMNPROPERTY(object_id, name, 'IsColumnSet') = 1;
```

Storage savings with sparse columns

The sparse column feature is designed to save you considerable space when most of your values are NULL. In fact, as mentioned earlier, columns that aren't NULL but are defined as *SPARSE* take up more space than if they weren't defined as *SPARSE* because the sparse vector has to store a couple of extra bytes to keep track of them. To start to see the space differences, you can run the script in Listing 8-5, which creates four tables with relatively short, fixed-length columns. Two have sparse columns and two don't. Rows are inserted into each table in a loop, which inserts 100,000 rows. One table with sparse columns is populated with rows with NULL values, and the other is populated with rows that aren't NULL. One table with no sparse columns is populated with rows with NULL values; the other is populated with rows that aren't NULL.

LISTING 8-5 Saving space with sparse columns

```
USE testdb;
GO
SET NOCOUNT ON;
GO

IF OBJECT_ID('sparse_nonulls_size') IS NOT NULL
            DROP TABLE sparse_nonulls_size;
GO
CREATE TABLE sparse_nonulls_size
(col1 int IDENTITY,
 col2 datetime SPARSE,
 col3 char(10) SPARSE
 );
GO
IF OBJECT_ID('nonsparse_nonulls_size') IS NOT NULL
            DROP TABLE nonsparse_nonulls_size;
GO
GO
CREATE TABLE nonsparse_nonulls_size
(col1 int IDENTITY,
```

```
 col2 datetime,
 col3 char(10)
 );
GO
IF OBJECT_ID('sparse_nulls_size') IS NOT NULL
                DROP TABLE sparse_nulls_size;
GO
GO
CREATE TABLE sparse_nulls_size
(col1 int IDENTITY,
 col2 datetime SPARSE,
 col3 char(10) SPARSE
 );
GO
IF OBJECT_ID('nonsparse_nulls_size') IS NOT NULL
                DROP TABLE nonsparse_nulls_size;
GO
GO
CREATE TABLE nonsparse_nulls_size
(col1 int IDENTITY,
 col2 datetime,
 col3 char(10)
 );
GO
DECLARE @num int
SET @num = 1
WHILE @num < 100000
BEGIN
  INSERT INTO sparse_nonulls_size
        SELECT GETDATE(), 'my message';
  INSERT INTO nonsparse_nonulls_size
        SELECT GETDATE(), 'my message';
  INSERT INTO sparse_nulls_size
        SELECT NULL, NULL;
  INSERT INTO nonsparse_nulls_size
        SELECT NULL, NULL;
  SET @num = @num + 1;
END;
GO
```

Now look at the number of pages in each table. The following metadata query looks at the number of data pages in the *sys.allocation_units* view for each of the four tables:

```
SELECT object_name(object_id) as 'table with 100K rows', data_pages
FROM sys.allocation_units au
    JOIN sys.partitions p
        ON p.partition_id = au.container_id
WHERE object_name(object_id) LIKE '%sparse%size';
```

And here are my results:

```
table with 100K rows     data_pages
----------------------- ----------
sparse_nonulls_size      610
nonsparse_nonulls_size   402
sparse_nulls_size        169
nonsparse_nulls_size     402
```

Note that the smallest number of pages is required when the table has NULL sparse columns. If the table has no sparse columns, the space usage is the same whether or not the columns have NULLs because the data was defined as fixed length. This space requirement is more than twice as much as needed for the sparse columns with NULL. The worst case is if the columns have been defined as *SPARSE* but have no NULL values.

Of course, the previous examples are edge cases, where *all* the data is either NULL or non-NULL, and is of all fixed-length data types. So although you can say that sparse columns require more storage space for non-NULL values than is required for identical data that's not declared as *SPARSE*, the actual space savings depends on the data types and the percentage of rows that are NULL. Table 8-8—reprinted from *SQL Server Books Online*—shows the space usage for each data type. The NULL Percentage column indicates what percent of the data must be NULL to achieve a net space savings of 40 percent.

TABLE 8-8 Storage requirements for sparse columns

Data type	Storage bytes when not SPARSE	Storage bytes when SPARSE and bot NULL	NULL percentage
Fixed-length data types			
Bit	0.125	5	98 percent
Tinyint	1	5	86 percent
Smallint	2	6	76 percent
Int	4	8	64 percent
Bigint	8	12	52 percent
Real	4	8	64 percent
Float	8	12	52 percent
smallmoney	4	8	64 percent
Money	8	12	52 percent
smalldatetime	4	8	64 percent
Datetime	8	12	52 percent
uniqueidentifier	16	20	43 percent
Date	3	7	69 percent
Precision-dependent–length data types			
datetime2(0)	6	10	57 percent
datetime2(7)	8	12	52 percent
time(0)	3	7	69 percent
time(7)	5	9	60 percent
datetimeoffset(0)	8	12	52 percent
datetimeoffset (7)	10	14	49 percent
decimal/numeric(1,s)	5	9	60 percent
decimal/numeric(38,s)	17	21	42 percent

Data type	Storage bytes when not SPARSE	Storage bytes when SPARSE and bot NULL	NULL percentage
Data-dependent–length data types			
sql_variant	Varies		
varchar or char	2+avg. data	4+avg. data	60 percent
nvarchar or nchar	2+avg. data	4+avg. data	60 percent
varbinary or binary	2+avg. data	4+avg. data	60 percent
Xml	2+avg. data	4+avg. data	60 percent
hierarchyId	2+avg. data	4+avg. data	60 percent

The general recommendation is that you should consider using sparse columns when you anticipate that they provide a space savings of at least 20 to 40 percent.

Data compression

SQL Server provides the capability of data compression, a feature introduced in SQL Server 2008 and available in the Enterprise edition only. Compression can reduce the size of your tables by exploiting existing inefficiencies in the actual data. These inefficiencies can be grouped into two general categories.

- The first category relates to storage of individual data values when they are stored in columns defined using the maximum possible size. For example, a table might need to define a *quantity* column as *int* because occasionally you could be storing values larger than 32,767, which is the maximum *smallint* value. However, *int* columns always need 4 bytes, and if most of your *quantity* values are less than 100, those values could be stored in *tinyint* columns, which need only 1 byte of storage. The Row Compression feature of SQL Server can compress individual columns of data to use only the actual amount of space required.

- The second type of inefficiency in the data storage occurs when the data on a page contains duplicate values or common prefixes across columns and rows. This inefficiency can be minimized by storing the repeating values only once and then referencing those values from other columns. The Page Compression feature of SQL Server can compress the data on a page by maintaining entries containing common prefixes or repeating values. Note that when you choose to apply page compression to a table or index, SQL Server always also applies Row Compression.

Vardecimal

SQL Server 2005 SP2 introduced a simple form of compression, which could be applied only to columns defined using the *decimal* data type. (Keep in mind that the data type *numeric* is completely equivalent to *decimal*, and anytime I mention *decimal*, it also means *numeric*.) In SQL Server 2005, the option must be enabled at both the database level (using the procedure *sp_db_vardecimal_storage_format*) and at the table level (using the procedure *sp_tableoption*). In SQL Server 2008, SQL Server

2008 R2, and SQL Server 2012, all user databases are enabled automatically for the vardecimal storage format, so vardecimal must be enabled only for individual tables. Like data compression, which this section looks at in detail, the vardecimal storage format is available only in SQL Server Enterprise edition.

In SQL Server 2005, when both of these stored procedures were run, *decimal* data in the tables enabled for vardecimal were stored differently. Rather than be treated as fixed-length data, *decimal* columns are stored in the variable section of the row and use only the number of bytes required. (Chapter 6 looked at the difference between fixed-length data and variable-length data storage.) In addition to all the table partitions that use the vardecimal format for all *decimal* data, all indexes on the table automatically use the vardecimal format.

Decimal data values are defined with a precision of between 1 and 38 and, depending on the defined precision, they use between 5 and 17 bytes. Fixed-length *decimal* data uses the same number of bytes for every row, even if the actual data could fit into far fewer bytes. When a table doesn't use the vardecimal storage format, every entry in the table consumes the same number of bytes for each defined decimal column, even if the value of a row is 0, NULL, or some value that can be expressed in a smaller number of bytes, such as the number 3. When vardecimal storage format is enabled for a table, the *decimal* columns in each row use the minimum amount of space required to store the specified value. Of course, as you saw in Chapter 6, every variable-length column has 2 bytes of additional overhead associated with it, but when storing very small values in a column defined as *decimal* with a large precision, the space saving can more than make up for those additional 2 bytes. For vardecimal storage, both NULLs and zeros are stored as zero-length data and use only the 2 bytes of overhead.

Although SQL Server 2012 supports the vardecimal format, I recommend that you use row compression when you want to reduce the storage space required by your data rows. Both the table option and the database option for enabling vardecimal storage have been deprecated.

Row compression

You can think of row compression as an extension of the vardecimal storage format. In many situations, SQL Server uses more space than needed to store data values, and without the Row Compression feature, the only control you have is to use a variable-length data type. Any fixed-length data types always use the same amount of space in every row of a table, even if space is wasted.

As mentioned earlier, you can declare a column as type *int* because occasionally you might need to store values greater than 32,767. An *int* needs 4 bytes of space, no matter what number is stored, even if the column is NULL. Only character and binary data can be stored in variable-length columns (and, of course, decimal, when that option is enabled). Row compression allows integer values to use only the amount of storage space required, with the minimum being 1 byte. A value of 100 needs only a single byte for storage, and a value of 1,000 needs 2 bytes. The storage engine also includes an optimization that allows zero and NULL to use no storage space for the data itself.

Later, this section provides the details about compressed data storage. Starting in SQL Server 2008 R2, row compression also can compress Unicode data. Rather than each Unicode character always be stored in two bytes, if the character needs only a single byte, it is stored only in a single byte.

Enabling row compression

You can enable compression when creating a table or index, or when using the *ALTER TABLE* or *ALTER INDEX* command. Also, if the table or index is partitioned, you can choose to compress just a subset of the partitions. (You'll look at partitioning later in this chapter.)

The script in Listing 8-6 creates two copies of the *dbo.Employees* table in the *AdventureWorks2012* database. When storing row-compressed data, SQL Server treats values that can be stored in 8 bytes or fewer (that is, short columns) differently than it stores data that needs more than 8 bytes (long columns). For this reason, the script updates one of the rows in the new tables so that none of the columns in that row contains more than 8 bytes. The *Employees_rowcompressed* table is then enabled for row compression, and the *Employees_uncompressed* table is left uncompressed. A metadata query examining pages allocated to each table is executed against each table so that you can compare the sizes before and after row compression.

LISTING 8-6 Comparing two tables to show row compression

```
USE AdventureWorks2012;
GO
IF OBJECT_ID('Employees_uncompressed') IS NOT NULL
               DROP TABLE Employees_uncompressed;
GO
GO
SELECT e.BusinessEntityID, NationalIDNumber, JobTitle,
       BirthDate, MaritalStatus, VacationHours,
       FirstName, LastName
  INTO Employees_uncompressed

  FROM HumanResources.Employee e
    JOIN Person.Person p
        ON e.BusinessEntityID = p.BusinessEntityID;
GO
UPDATE Employees_uncompressed
SET NationalIDNumber = '1111',
        JobTitle = 'Boss',
        LastName = 'Gato'
WHERE FirstName = 'Ken'
AND LastName = 'Sánchez';
GO
ALTER TABLE dbo.Employees_uncompressed
   ADD CONSTRAINT EmployeeUn_ID
       PRIMARY KEY (BusinessEntityID);
GO
SELECT OBJECT_NAME(object_id) as name,
        rows, data_pages, data_compression_desc
FROM sys.partitions p JOIN sys.allocation_units au
        ON p.partition_id = au.container_id
WHERE object_id = object_id('dbo.Employees_uncompressed');

IF OBJECT_ID('Employees_rowcompressed') IS NOT NULL
               DROP TABLE Employees_rowcompressed;
GO
SELECT BusinessEntityID, NationalIDNumber, JobTitle,
        BirthDate, MaritalStatus, VacationHours,
```

```
        FirstName, LastName
    INTO Employees_rowcompressed
    FROM dbo.Employees_uncompressed
GO
ALTER TABLE dbo.Employees_rowcompressed
    ADD CONSTRAINT EmployeeR_ID
        PRIMARY KEY (BusinessEntityID);
GO
ALTER TABLE dbo.Employees_rowcompressed
REBUILD WITH (DATA_COMPRESSION = ROW);
GO
SELECT OBJECT_NAME(object_id) as name,
        rows, data_pages, data_compression_desc
FROM sys.partitions p JOIN sys.allocation_units au
        ON p.partition_id = au.container_id
WHERE object_id = object_id('dbo.Employees_rowcompressed');
GO
```

The *dbo.Employees_rowcompressed* table is referred to again later in this section, or you can examine it on your own as the details of compressed row storage are covered.

Now you can start looking at the details of row compression, but keep these points in mind:

- Row compression is available only in SQL Server 2008, SQL Server 2008 R2, and SQL Server 2012 Enterprise and Developer editions.

- Row compression doesn't change the maximum row size of a table or index.

- Row compression can't be enabled on a table with any columns defined as *SPARSE*.

- If a table or index has been partitioned, row compression can be enabled on all the partitions or on a subset of the partitions.

New row format

Chapter 6 looked at the format for storing rows that has been used since SQL Server 7.0 and is still used in SQL Server 2012 if you haven't enabled compression. That format is referred to as the *FixedVar* format because it has a fixed-length data section separate from a variable-length data section. A completely new row format was introduced in SQL Server 2008 for storing compressed rows, and this format is referred to as CD format. The term *CD*, which stands for "column descriptor," refers to every column having description information contained in the row itself.

You might want to re-examine Figure 6-6 in Chapter 6 as a reminder of what the *FixedVar* format looks like and compare it to the new CD format. Figure 8-9 shows an abstraction of the CD format. It's difficult to be as specific as Figure 6-6 is because except for the header, the number of bytes in each region is completely dependent on the data in the row.

Header	CD Region	Short Data Region	Long Data Region	Special Information

FIGURE 8-9 General structure of a CD record.

Each of these sections is described in detail.

Header   The row header is always a single byte and roughly corresponds to what Chapter 6 referred to as Status Bits A. The bits have the following meanings.

- **Bit 0**   This bit indicates the type of record; it's 1 for the new CD record format.

- **Bit 1**   This bit indicates that the row contains versioning information.

- **Bits 2 through 4**   Taken as a 3-bit value, these bits indicate what kind of information is stored in the row. The possible values are as follows:

  000 Primary record

  001 Ghost empty record

  010 Forwarding record

  011 Ghost data record

  100 Forwarded record

  101 Ghost forwarded record

  110 Index record

  111 Ghost index record

- **Bit 5**   This bit indicates that the row contains a long data region (with values greater than 8 bytes in length).

- **Bits 6 and 7**   These bits are not used in SQL Server 2012.

The CD region   The CD region is composed of two parts. The first part is either 1 or 2 bytes, indicating the number of short columns. If the most significant bit of the first byte is set to 0, it's a 1-byte field with a maximum value of 127. If a table has more than 127 columns, the most significant bit is 1, and SQL Server uses 2 bytes to represent the number of columns, which can be up to 32,767.

Following the 1 or 2 bytes for the number of columns is the CD array, which uses 4 bits for each column in the table to represent information about the length of the column. Four bits can have 16 different possible values, but in SQL Server 2012, only 13 of them are used.

- 0 (0x0) indicates that the corresponding column is NULL.

- 1 (0x1) indicates that the corresponding column is a 0-byte short value.

- 2 (0x2) indicates that the corresponding column is a 1-byte short value.

- 3 (0x3) indicates that the corresponding column is a 2-byte short value.

- 4 (0x4) indicates that the corresponding column is a 3-byte short value.

- 5 (0x5) indicates that the corresponding column is a 4-byte short value.

- 6 (0x6) indicates that the corresponding column is a 5-byte short value.

- 7 (0x7) indicates that the corresponding column is a 6-byte short value.

- 8 (0x8) indicates that the corresponding column is a 7-byte short value.

- 9 (0x9) indicates that the corresponding column is an 8-byte short value.

- 10 (0xa) indicates that the corresponding column is long data value and uses no space in the short data region.

- 11 (0xb) is used for columns of type bit with the value of 1. The corresponding column takes no space in the short data region.

- 12 (0xc) indicates that the corresponding column is a 1-byte symbol, representing a value in the page dictionary. (Later, the section "Page compression" talks about the dictionary).

The short data region   The short data region doesn't need to store the length of each short data value because that information is available in the CD region. However, if table has hundreds of columns, accessing the last columns can be expensive. To minimize this cost, columns are grouped into clusters of 30 columns each and at the beginning of the short data region is an area called the short data cluster array. Each array entry is a single-byte integer and indicates the sum of the sizes of all the data in the previous cluster in the short data region, so that the value is basically a pointer to the first column of the cluster. The first cluster of short data starts right after the cluster array, so no cluster offset is needed for it. A cluster might not have 30 data columns, however, because only columns with a length less than or equal to 8 bytes are stored in the short data region.

As an example, consider a row with 64 columns, and columns 5, 10, 15, 20, 25, 30, 40, 50, and 60 are long data, and the others are short. The CD region contains the following.

- A single byte containing the value 64, the number of columns in the CD region.

- A CD array of 4 * 64 bits, or 32 bytes, containing information about the length of each column. It has 55 entries with values indicating an actual data length for the short data, and 8 entries of 0xa, indicating long data.

The short data region contains the following.

- A short data cluster offset array containing the two values, each containing the length of a short data cluster. In this example, the first cluster, which is all the short data in the first 30 columns, has a length of 92, so the 92 in the offset array indicates that the second cluster starts 92 bytes after the first. The number of clusters can be calculated as (Number of columns − 1) /30. The maximum value for any entry in the cluster array is 240, if all 30 columns were short data of 8 bytes in length.

- All the short data values.

Figure 8-10 illustrates the CD region and the short data region with sample data for the row described previously. The CD array is shown in its entirety, with a symbol indicating the length of each of the 64 values. (So the depiction of this array can fit on a page of this book, the actual data values aren't shown.) The first cluster has 24 values in the short data region (6 are long values), the second cluster has 27 (3 are long), and the third cluster has the remaining 4 columns (all short).

CD Region		Short Data Region				
Number of columns	CD array --64 4-bit values ('a' indicates long column)	Length of short data in each 30-column cluster (N–1)/30 values	Three clusters of actual data			
N = 64	3285a4358a6543a3456a6666a5463a 254372644a745269277a463495736a 5433	92	106	24 values	27 values	4 values

FIGURE 8-10 The CD region and short data region in a CD record.

To locate the entry for a short column value in the short data region, the short data cluster array is first examined to determine the start address of the containing cluster for the column in the short data region.

The long data region   Any data in the row longer than 8 bytes is stored in the long data region. This includes complex columns, which don't contain actual data but instead contain information necessary to locate data stored off the row. This can include large object data and row overflow data pointers. Unlike short data, where the length can be stored simply in the CD array, long data needs an actual offset value to allow SQL Server to determine the location of each value. This offset array looks very similar to the offset array discussed in Chapter 6 for the *FixedVar* records.

The long data region is composed of three parts: an offset array, a long data cluster array, and the long data.

The offset array is composed of the following.

- **A 1-byte header in which currently only the first two bits are used**   Bit 0 indicates whether the long data region contains any 2-byte offset values. Currently, this value is always 1, because all offsets are always 2 bytes. Bit 1 indicates whether the long data region contains any complex columns.

- **A 2-byte value indicating the number of offsets to follow**   The most significant bit in the first byte of the offset value indicates whether the corresponding entry in the long data region is a complex column. The rest of the bits/bytes in the array entry store the ending offset value for the corresponding entry in the long data region.

Similar to the cluster array for the short data, the long data cluster array is used to limit the cost of finding columns near the end of a long list of columns. It has one entry for each 30-column cluster (except the last one). Because the offset of each long data column is already stored in the offset array, the cluster array just needs to keep track of how many of the long data values are in each cluster. Each value is a 1-byte integer representing the number of long data columns in that cluster. Just as for the short data cluster, the number of entries in the cluster array can be computed as (Number of columns in the table – 1)/30.

Figure 8-11 illustrates the long data region for the row described previously, with 64 columns, nine of which are long. Values for the offsets aren't included for space considerations. The long data cluster array has two entries indicating that six of the values are in the first cluster and two are in the second. The remaining values are in the last cluster.

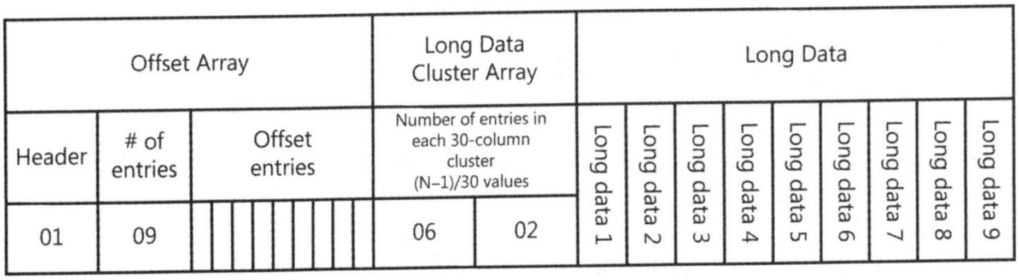

Offset Array			Long Data Cluster Array		Long Data								
Header	# of entries	Offset entries	Number of entries in each 30-column cluster (N–1)/30 values		Long data 1	Long data 2	Long data 3	Long data 4	Long data 5	Long data 6	Long data 7	Long data 8	Long data 9
01	09		06	02									

FIGURE 8-11 The long data region of a CD record.

Special information   The end of the row contains three optional pieces of information. The existence of any or all of this information is indicated by bits in the 1-byte header at the very beginning of the row.

- **Forwarding pointer**   This value is used when a heap contains a forwarding stub that points to a new location to which the original row has been moved. Chapter 6 discussed forwarding pointers. The forwarding pointer contains three header bytes and an 8-byte row ID.

- **Back pointer**   This value is used in a row that has been forwarded to indicate the original location of the row. It's stored as an 8-byte Row ID.

- **Versioning info**   When a row is modified under one of the snapshot-based isolation levels, SQL Server adds 14 bytes of versioning information to the row. Chapter 13 discusses row versioning and Snapshot isolation.

Now look at the actual bytes in two of the rows in the *dbo.Employees_rowcompressed* table created earlier in Listing 8-6. The *DBCC PAGE* command gives additional information about compressed rows and pages. In particular, before the bytes for the row are shown, *DBCC PAGE* displays the CD array. For the first row returned on the first page in the *dbo.Employees_rowcompressed* table, all the columns contain short data. The row has the data values shown here:

BusinessEntityID	NationalIDNumber	JobTitle	BirthDate	MaritalStatus	VacationHours	FirstName	LastName
1	1111	Boss	1963-03-02	S	99	Ken	Gato

For short data, the CD array contains the actual length of each of the columns, and you can see the following information for the first row in the *DBCC PAGE* output:

```
CD array entry = Column 1 (cluster 0, CD array offset 0): 0x02 (ONE_BYTE_SHORT)
CD array entry = Column 2 (cluster 0, CD array offset 0): 0x06 (FIVE_BYTE_SHORT)
CD array entry = Column 3 (cluster 0, CD array offset 1): 0x06 (FIVE_BYTE_SHORT)
CD array entry = Column 4 (cluster 0, CD array offset 1): 0x04 (THREE_BYTE_SHORT)
CD array entry = Column 5 (cluster 0, CD array offset 2): 0x02 (ONE_BYTE_SHORT)
CD array entry = Column 6 (cluster 0, CD array offset 2): 0x02 (ONE_BYTE_SHORT)
CD array entry = Column 7 (cluster 0, CD array offset 3): 0x04 (THREE_BYTE_SHORT)
CD array entry = Column 8 (cluster 0, CD array offset 3): 0x06 (FIVE_BYTE_SHORT)
```

So the first column has a CD code of 0x02, which indicates a 1-byte value, and, as you can see in the data row, is the integer 1. The second column contains a 5-byte value and is the Unicode string 1111. Notice that compressed Unicode strings are always an odd number of bytes. This is how SQL Server determines that the string has actually been compressed, because an uncompressed Unicode string—which needs 2 bytes for each character—will always be an even number of bytes. Because the Unicode string has an even number of characters, SQL Server adds a single byte 0x01 as a terminator. In Figure 8-12, which shows the *DBCC PAGE* output for the row contents, you can see that three strings have the 0x01 terminator to make their length odd: '1111', 'Boss', and 'Gato'. I'll leave it to you to inspect the codes for the remaining columns.

```
01086246 22648131 31313110 426f7373 1079ef0a    ..bF"d.1111.Boss.yï.
53e34b65 6e476174 6f10                          SāKenGato.
```

Row Expansion:

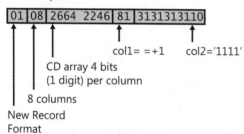

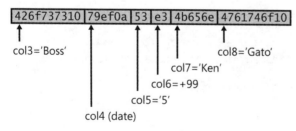

FIGURE 8-12 A compressed row with eight short data columns.

Now look at a row with some long columns. The 22nd row on the page (Slot 21) has three long columns in the data values shown here:

BusinessEntityID	NationalIDNumber	JobTitle	BirthDate	MaritalStatus	VacationHours	FirstName	LastName
22	95958330	Marketing Specialist	1981-06-21	S	45	Sariya	Harnpadoungsataya

The CD array for this row looks like the following:

```
CD array entry = Column 1 (cluster 0, CD array offset 0): 0x02 (ONE_BYTE_SHORT)
CD array entry = Column 2 (cluster 0, CD array offset 0): 0x0a (LONG)
CD array entry = Column 3 (cluster 0, CD array offset 1): 0x0a (LONG)
CD array entry = Column 4 (cluster 0, CD array offset 1): 0x04 (THREE_BYTE_SHORT)
CD array entry = Column 5 (cluster 0, CD array offset 2): 0x02 (ONE_BYTE_SHORT)
CD array entry = Column 6 (cluster 0, CD array offset 2): 0x02 (ONE_BYTE_SHORT)
CD array entry = Column 7 (cluster 0, CD array offset 3): 0x08 (SEVEN_BYTE_SHORT)
CD array entry = Column 8 (cluster 0, CD array offset 3): 0x0a (LONG)
```

Figure 8-13 shows the bytes that *DBCC PAGE* returns for this data row. The bytes in the long data region are boldfaced.

```
Record Memory Dump
000000001492A57A:    2108a24a 22a89697 090b53ad 53617269 79611001    !.¢J"¨—  .SSariya..
000000001492A58E:    03000900 1e002f00 39353935 38333330 104d6172    .. .../.95958330.Mar
000000001492A5A2:    6b657469 6e672053 70656369 616c6973 74104861    keting Specialist.Ha
000000001492A5B6:    726e7061 646f756e 67736174 617961                rnpadoungsataya
```

FIGURE 8-13 A compressed row with five short data columns and three long.

Notice the following in the first part of the row, before the long data region.

- The first byte in the row is 0x21, indicating that not only is this row in the new CD record format, but also that the row contains a long data region.

- The second byte indicates eight columns in the table, just as for the first row.

- The following 4 bytes for the CD array has three values of *a*, which indicate long values not included in the short data region.

- The short data values are listed in order after the CD array and are as follows:

  - The *BusinessEntityID* is 1 byte, with the value 0x96, or +22.

  - The *Birthdate* is 3 bytes.

  - The *MaritalStatus* is 1 byte, with the value 0x0053, or 'S'.

  - The *VacationHours* is 1 byte, with the value 0xad, or +45.

  - The *FirstName* is 7 bytes, with the value 53617269796110 or *'Sariya'*.

The Long Data Region Offset Array is 8 bytes long, as follows.

- The first byte is 0x01, which indicates that the row-offset positions are 2 bytes long.

- The second byte is 0x03, which indicates three columns in the long data region.

- The next 6 bytes are the 2-byte offsets for each of the three values. Notice that the offset refers to position the column ends with the Long Data area itself.

  - The first 2-byte offset is 0x0009, which indicates that the first long value is 9 bytes long.

  - The second 2-byte offset is 001e, or 30, which indicates that the second long value ends 21 bytes after the first. The second value is *Marketing Specialist*, which is a 21-byte string.

  - The third 2-byte offset is 0x002f, or 47, which indicates the third value, *Harnpadoungsataya*, ends 17 bytes after the second long value.

Fewer than 30 columns means no Long Data Cluster Array, but the data values are stored immediately after the Long Data Region Offset Array.

Because of space constraints, this chapter won't show you the details of a row with multiple column clusters (that is, more than 30 columns), but you should have enough information to start exploring such rows on your own.

Page compression

In addition to storing rows in a compressed format to minimize the space required, SQL Server 2012 can compress whole pages by isolating and reusing repeating patterns of bytes on the page.

Unlike row compression, page compression is applied only after a page is full, and only if SQL Server determines that compressing the page saves a meaningful amount of space. (You'll find out what that amount is later in this section.) Keep the following points in mind when planning for page compression.

- Page compression is available only in the SQL Server 2008, SQL Server 2008 R2, and SQL Server 2012 Enterprise and Developer editions.

- Page compression always includes row compression—that is, if you enable page compression for a table, row compression is automatically enabled.

- When compressing a B-tree, only the leaf level can be page compressed. For performance reasons, the node levels are left uncompressed.

- If a table or index has been partitioned, page compression can be enabled on all the partitions or on a subset of the partitions.

The code in Listing 8-7 makes another copy of the *dbo.Employees* table and applies page compression to it. It then captures the page location and linkage information from *DBCC IND* for the three tables: *dbo.Employees_uncompressed*, *dbo.Employees_rowcompressed*, and *dbo. Employees_pagecompressed*. The code then uses the captured information to report on the number of data pages in each of the three tables.

LISTING 8-7 Applying page compression to a table

```
USE AdventureWorks2012;
GO
IF OBJECT_ID('Employees_pagecompressed') IS NOT NULL
            DROP TABLE Employees_pagecompressed;
GO
SELECT BusinessEntityID, NationalIDNumber, JobTitle,
       BirthDate, MaritalStatus, VacationHours,
       FirstName, LastName
  INTO Employees_pagecompressed
  FROM dbo.Employees_uncompressed
GO
ALTER TABLE dbo.Employees_pagecompressed
   ADD CONSTRAINT EmployeeP_ID
       PRIMARY KEY (BusinessEntityID);
GO
ALTER TABLE dbo.Employees_pagecompressed
REBUILD WITH (DATA_COMPRESSION = PAGE);
GO
SELECT OBJECT_NAME(object_id) as name,
                 rows, data_pages, data_compression_desc
FROM sys.partitions p JOIN sys.allocation_units au
              ON p.partition_id = au.container_id
WHERE object_id = object_id('dbo.Employees_pagecompressed');
GO

SELECT object_name(object_id) as Table_Name, count(*) as Page_Count
FROM sys.dm_db_database_page_allocations(db_id('AdventureWorks2012'), null, null, null,
'DETAILED')
WHERE object_name(object_id) like ('Employees%compressed')
AND page_type_desc = 'DATA_PAGE'
GROUP BY object_name(object_id);
```

If you run this script, notice in the output that row compression reduced the size of this small table from five pages to three, and then page compression further reduced the size from three pages to two.

SQL Server can perform two different operations to try to compress a page by using common values: *column prefix compression* and *dictionary compression*.

Column prefix compression

As the name implies, column prefix compression works on data columns in the table being compressed, but it looks only at the column values on a single page. For each column, SQL Server chooses a common prefix that can be used to reduce the storage space required for values in that column. The longest value in the column that contains that prefix is chosen as the *anchor value*. Each column is then stored—not as the actual data value, but as a delta from the anchor value. Suppose that you have the following character values in a column of a table to be page-compressed:

```
DEEM
DEE
FFF
DEED
DEE
DAN
```

SQL Server might note that DEE is a useful common prefix, so *DEED* is chosen as the anchor value. Each column would be stored as the difference between its value and the anchor value. This difference is stored as a two-part value: the number of characters from the anchor to use and the additional characters to append. So *DEEM* is stored as <3><M>, meaning the value uses the first three characters from the common prefix and appends a single character, *M*, to it. *DEED* is stored as an empty string (but not null) to indicate it matched the prefix exactly. *DEE* is stored as <3>, with the second part empty, because no additional characters can be appended. The list of column values is replaced by the values shown here:

```
DEEM -> <3><M>
DEE  -> <3><>
FFF  -> <><FFF>
DEED -> <><>
DEE  -> <3><>
DAN  -> <1><AN>
```

Keep in mind that the compressed row is stored in the CD record format, so the CD array value has a special encoding to indicate the value is actually NULL. If the replacement value is <><>, and the encoding doesn't indicate NULL, the value matches the prefix exactly.

SQL Server applies the prefix detection and value replacement algorithm to every column and creates a new row called an *anchor record* to store the anchor values for each column. If no useful prefix can be found, the value in the anchor record is NULL, and then all the values in the column are stored just as they are.

Figure 8-14 shows an image of six rows in a table page compression, and then shows the six rows after the anchor record has been created and the substitutions have been made for the actual data values.

Original Data		
ABCD	DEEM	ABC
ABD	DEE	DEE
ABC	FFF	GHI
AAN	DEED	HHH
NULL	DEE	KLM
ADE	DAN	NOP

Data After Column Prefix Compression		
Anchor Record		
ABCD	DEED	NULL
<><>	<3><M>	ABC
<2><D>	<3><>	DEE
<3><>	<><FFF>	GHI
<1><AN>	<><>	HHH
NULL	<3><>	KLM
<1><DE>	<1><AN>	NOP

FIGURE 8-14 Before and after column prefix compression.

Dictionary compression

After prefix compression is applied to every column individually, the second phase of page compression looks at all values on the page to find duplicates in any column of any row, even if they have been encoded to reflect prefix usage. You can see in the bottom part of Figure 8-16 that two of the values occur multiple times: <3><> occurs three times and <1><AN> occurs twice. The process of detecting duplicate values is data type–agnostic, so values in completely different columns could be the same in their binary representation. For example, a 1-byte character is represented in hex as 0x54, and it would be seen as a duplicate of the 1-byte integer 84, which is also represented in hex as 0x54. The dictionary is stored as a set of symbols, each of which corresponds to a duplicated value on the data page. After the symbols and data values are determined, each occurrence of one of the duplicated values is replaced by the symbol. SQL Server recognizes that the value actually stored in the column is a symbol and not a data value by examining the encoding in the CD array. Values which have been replaced by symbols have a CD array value of 0xc. Figure 8-15 shows the data from Figure 8-14 after replacing the five values with symbols.

Dictionary of Symbols: [S1] = <1><AN> [S2] = <3><>		
<><>	<3><M>	ABC
<2><D>	[S2]	DEE
[S2]	<><FFF>	GHI
[S1]	<><>	HHH
NULL	[S2]	KLM
<1><DE>	[S1]	NOP

FIGURE 8-15 A page compressed with dictionary compression.

Not every page in a compressed table has both an anchor record for prefixes and a dictionary. If no useful prefix values are available, the page might have just a dictionary. If no values repeat often enough that replacing them with symbols saves space, the page might have just an anchor record. Of course, some pages might have neither an anchor record nor a dictionary if the data on the page has no patterns at all.

Physical storage

When a page is compressed, only one main structural change occurs. SQL Server adds a hidden row right after the page header (at byte offset 96, or 0x60) called the compression information (CI) record. Figure 8-16 shows the structure of the CI record.

Header	PageModCount	Offsets	Anchor Record	Dictionary

FIGURE 8-16 Structure of a CI record.

The CI record doesn't have an entry in the slot array for the page, but it's always at the same location. Also, a bit in the page header indicates that the page is page-compressed, so SQL Server looks for the CI record. If you use *DBCC PAGE* to dump a page, the page header information contains a value called *m_typeFlagBits*. If this value is 0x80, the page is compressed.

You can run the following script to use the *sys.dm_db_database_page_allocations* function to find the page ID (PID) of the first page and the file ID (FID) of the first page for each of the three tables that you've been exploring. You can use this information to examine the page with *DBCC PAGE*. Notice that only the page for *Employees_pagecompressed* has the *m_typeFlagBits* value set to 0x80.

```
USE AdventureWorks2012;
GO
SELECT object_name(object_id) as Table_Name, allocated_page_file_id as First_Page_FID,
       allocated_page_page_id as First_Page_PID
```

```
FROM sys.dm_db_database_page_allocations(db_id('AdventureWorks2012'),
        null, null, null, 'DETAILED')
WHERE object_name(object_id) like ('Employees%compressed')
AND page_type_desc = 'DATA_PAGE'
AND previous_page_page_id  IS NULL;
```

Using *DBCC PAGE* to look at a page-compressed page does provide information about the contents of the CI record, and you'll look at some of that information after examining what each section means.

Header   The header is a 1-byte value keeping track of information about the CI. Bit 0 indicates the version, which in SQL Server 2012 is always 0. Bit 1 indicates whether the CI has an anchor record, and bit 2 indicates whether the CI has a dictionary. The rest of the bits are unused.

PageModCount   The *PageModCount* value keeps track of the changes to this particular page and is used when determining whether the compression on the page should be reevaluated, and a new CI record built. The next section, "Page compression analysis," talks more about how this value is used.

Offsets   The offsets contain values to help SQL Server find the dictionary. It contains a value indicating the page offset for the end of the anchor record and a value indicating the page offset for the end of the CI record itself.

Anchor Record   The anchor record looks exactly like a regular CD record on the page, including the record header, the CD array, and both a short data area and a long data area. The values stored in the data area are the common prefix values for each column, some of which might be NULL.

Dictionary   The dictionary area is composed of three sections.

- A 2-byte field containing a numeric value representing the number of entries in the dictionary

- An offset array of 2-byte entries, indicating the end offset of each dictionary entry relative to the start of the dictionary data section

- The actual dictionary data entries

Remember that each dictionary entry is a byte string that is replaced in the regular data rows by a symbol. The symbol is simply an integer value from 0 to N. Also, remember that the byte strings are data type–independent—that is, they are just bytes. After SQL Server determines what recurring values are stored in the dictionary, it sorts the list first by data length, then by data value, and then assigns the symbols in order. So suppose that the values to be stored in the dictionary are these:

```
0x 53 51 4C
0x FF F8
0x DA 15 43 77 64
0x 34 F3 B6 22 CD
0x 12 34 56
```

Table 8-9 shows the sorted dictionary, along with the length and symbol for each entry.

TABLE 8-9 Values in a page compression dictionary

Value	Length	Symbol
0x FF F8	2 bytes	0
0x 12 34 56	3 bytes	1
0x 53 51 4C	3 bytes	2
0x 34 F3 B6 22 CD	4 bytes	3
0x DA 15 43 77 64	4 bytes	4

The dictionary area would then resemble Figure 8-17.

Header	Offsets	Dictionary
5	02 00	0x FF F8
	05 00	0x 12 34 56
	08 00	0x 53 51 4C
	0D 00	0x 34 F3 B6 22 CD
	12 00	0x DA 15 43 77 64

FIGURE 8-17 Dictionary area in a compression information record.

Note that the dictionary never actually stores the symbol values. They are stored only in the data records that need to use the dictionary. Because they are simply integers, they can be used as an index into the offset list to find the appropriate dictionary replacement value. For example, if a row on the page contains the dictionary symbol [2], SQL Server looks in the offset list for the third entry, which in Figure 8-17 ends at offset 0800 from the start of the dictionary. SQL Server then finds the value that ends at that byte, which is 0x 53 51 4C. If this byte string was stored in a *char* or *varchar* column—that is, a single-byte character string—it would correspond to the character string *SQL*.

Earlier in this chapter, you saw that the *DBCC PAGE* output displays the CD array for compressed rows. For compressed pages, *DBCC PAGE* shows the CI record and details about the anchor record within it. Also, with format 3, *DBCC PAGE* shows details about the dictionary entries. When I captured the *DBCC PAGE* in format 3 for the first page of my *Employees_pagecompressed* table and copied it to a Microsoft Office Word document, it needed 384 pages. Needless to say, I won't show you all that output (just copying the CI record information required 10 pages, which is still too much to show in this book). You can explore the output of *DBCC PAGE* for the tables with compressed pages on your own.

Page compression analysis

This section covers some of the details regarding how SQL Server determines whether to compress a page and what values it uses for the anchor record and the dictionary. Row compression is always performed when requested, but page compression depends on the amount of space that can be saved. However, the actual work of compressing the rows has to wait until after page compression is performed. Because both types of page compression—prefix substitution and dictionary symbol substitution—replace the actual data values with encodings, the row can't be compressed until SQL Server determines what encodings will replace the actual data.

When page compression is first enabled for a table or partition, SQL Server goes through every full page to determine the possible space savings. (Any pages that aren't full aren't considered for compression.) This compression analysis actually creates the anchor record, modifies all the columns to reflect the anchor values, and generates the dictionary. Then it compresses each row. If the new compressed page can hold at least five more rows, or 25 percent more rows than the current page (whichever is larger), the compressed page replaces the uncompressed page. If compressing the page doesn't result in this much savings, the compressed page is discarded.

When determining what values to use for the anchor record on a compressed page, SQL Server needs to look at every byte in every row, one column at a time. As it scans the column, it also keeps track of possible dictionary entries that can be used in multiple columns. The anchor record values can be determined for each column in a single pass—that is, by the time all the bytes in all the rows for the first column are examined once, SQL Server has determined the anchor record value for that column or has determined that no anchor record value will save sufficient space.

As SQL Server examines each column, it collects a list of possible dictionary entries. As discussed earlier, the dictionary contains values that occur enough times on the page so that replacing them with a symbol is cost-effective in terms of space. For each possible dictionary entry, SQL Server keeps track of the value, its size, and the count of occurrences. If (size_of_data_value -1) * (count-1) -2 is greater than zero, it means the dictionary replacement saves space, and the value is considered eligible for the dictionary. Because the dictionary symbols are single-byte integers, SQL Server tries can't store more than 255 entries in the dictionary on any page, so if more dictionary entries might be used based on the data on the page, they are sorted by number of occurrences during the analysis, and only the most frequently occurring values are used in the dictionary.

CI record rebuilding

If a table is enabled for either page or row compression, new rows are always compressed before they are inserted into the table. However, the CI record containing the anchor record and the dictionary is rebuilt on an all-or-nothing basis—that is, SQL Server doesn't just add some new entry to the dictionary when new rows are inserted. SQL Server evaluates whether to rebuild the CI record when the page has been changed a sufficient number of times. It keeps track of changes to each page in the *PageModCount* field of the CI record, and that value is updated every time a row is inserted, updated, or deleted.

If a full page is encountered during a data modification operation, SQL Server examines the *PageModCount* value. If the *PageModCount* value is greater than 25 or the value *PageModCount/*

<number of rows on the page> is greater than 25 percent, SQL Server applies the compression analysis as it does when it first compresses a page. Only when recompressing the page makes room for at least five more rows (or 25 percent more rows than the current page) does the new compressed page replace the old page.

Page compression in a B-tree and page compression in a heap each have important differences.

Compression of B-tree pages   For B-trees, only the leaf level is page compressed. When inserting a new row into a B-tree, if the compressed row fits on the page, it is inserted, and nothing more is done. If it doesn't fit, SQL Server tries to recompress the page, according to the conditions described in the preceding section. A successful recompression means that the CI record changed, so the new row must be recompressed and then SQL Server tries to insert it into the page. Again, if it fits, it is simply inserted; if the new compressed row doesn't fit on the page, even after possibly recompressing the page, the page needs to be split. When splitting a compressed page, the CI record is copied to a new page exactly as is, except that the *PageModCount* value is set to 25. This means that the first time the page gets full, it gets a full analysis to determine whether it should be recompressed. B-tree pages are also checked for possible recompression during index rebuilds (either online or offline) and during shrink operations.

Compression of heap pages   Pages in a heap are checked for possible compression only during rebuild and shrink operations. Also, if you drop a clustered index on a table so that it becomes a heap, SQL Server runs compression analysis on any full pages. To make sure that the *RowID* values stay the same, heaps aren't recompressed during typical data modification operations. Although the *Page-ModCount* value is maintained, SQL Server never tries to recompress a page based on the *PageMod-Count* value.

Compression metadata

An enormous amount of metadata information relating to data compression doesn't exist. The catalog view *sys.partitions* has a *data_compression* column and a *data_compression_desc* column. The *data_compression* column has possible values of 0, 1, 2, and 3 corresponding to *data_compression_desc* values of *NONE*, *ROW*, *PAGE*, and *COLUMNSTORE*. (Only *ROW* and *PAGE* compression are discussed here.) Keep in mind that although row compression is always performed if enabled, page compression isn't. Even if *sys.partitions* indicates that a table or partition is page compressed, that just means that page compression is enabled. Each page is analyzed individually, and if a page isn't full, or if compression won't save enough space, the page isn't compressed.

You can also inspect the dynamic management function *sys.dm_db_index_operational_stats*. This table-valued function returns the following compression-related columns.

- ***page_compression_attempt_count***   The number of pages evaluated for *PAGE*-level compression for specific partitions of a table, index, or indexed view. This includes pages that weren't compressed because significant savings couldn't be achieved.

- ***page_compression_success_count***   The number of data pages that were compressed by using *PAGE* compression for specific partitions of a table, index, or indexed view.

SQL Server also provides a stored procedure called *sp_estimate_data_compression_savings,* which can give you some idea of whether compression provides a large space savings. This procedure samples up to 5,000 pages of the table and creates an equivalent table with the sampled pages in *tempdb.* Using this temporary table, SQL Server can estimate the new table size for the requested compression state (*NONE, ROW,* or *PAGE*). Compression can be evaluated for whole tables or parts of tables, including heaps, clustered indexes, nonclustered indexes, indexed views, and table and index partitions.

Keep in mind that the result is only an estimate and your actual savings can vary widely based on the fill factor and the size of the rows. If the procedure indicates that you can reduce your row size by 40 percent, you might not actually get a 40 percent space savings for the whole table. For example, if you have a row that's 8,000 bytes long and you reduce its size by 40 percent, you still can fit only one row on a data page, and your table still needs the same number of pages.

Running *sp_estimate_data_compression_savings* might yield results that indicate that the table will grow. This can happen when many rows in the table use almost the whole maximum size of the data types, and the addition of the overhead needed for the compression information is more than the savings from compression.

If the table is already compressed, you can use this procedure to estimate the size of the table (or index) if it were to be uncompressed.

Performance issues

The main motivation for compressing your data is to save space with extremely large tables, such as data warehouse fact tables. A second goal is to increase performance when scanning a table for reporting purposes, because far fewer pages need to be read. Keep in mind that compression comes at a cost: You see a tradeoff between the space savings and the extra CPU overhead to compress the data for storage and then uncompress the data when it needs to be used. On a CPU-bound system, you might find that compressing your data can actually slow down your system considerably.

Page compression provides the most benefit for I/O-bound systems, with tables for which the data is written once and then read repeatedly, as in the situations mentioned in the preceding paragraph: data warehousing and reporting. For environments with heavy read and write activity, such as online transaction processing (OLTP) applications, you might want to consider enabling row compression only and avoid the costs of analyzing the pages and rebuilding the CI record. In this case, the CPU overhead is minimal. In fact, row compression is highly optimized so that it's visible only at the storage engine layer. The relational engine (query processor) doesn't need to deal with compressed rows at all. The relational engine sends uncompressed rows to the storage engine, which compresses them if required. When returning rows to the relational engine, the storage engine waits as long as it can before uncompressing them. In the storage engine, comparisons can be done on compressed data, as internal conversions can convert a data type to its compressed form before comparing to data in the table. Also, only columns requested by the relational engine need to be uncompressed, as opposed to uncompressing an entire row.

Compression and logging   In general, SQL Server logs only uncompressed data because the log needs to be read in an uncompressed format. This means that logging changes to compressed records has a greater performance impact because each row needs to be uncompressed and decoded (from the anchor record and dictionary) before writing to the log. This is another reason compression gives you more benefit on primarily read-only systems, where logging is minimal.

SQL Server writes compressed data to the log in a few situations. The most common situation is when a page is split. SQL Server writes the compressed rows as it logs the data movement during the split operation.

Compression and the version store   Chapter 13 covers the version store during a discussion about Snapshot isolation, but I want to mention briefly here how the version store interacts with compression. SQL Server can write compressed rows to the version store, and the version store processing can traverse older versions in their compressed form. However, the version store doesn't support page compression, so the rows in the version store can't contain encodings of the anchor record prefixes and the page dictionary. So anytime any row from a compressed page needs to be versioned, the page must be uncompressed first.

The version store is used for both varieties of Snapshot isolation (full snapshot and read-committed snapshot) and is also used for storing the before-and-after images of changed data when triggers are fired. (These images are visible in the logical tables *inserted* and *deleted*.) Keep this in mind when evaluating the costs of compression. Snapshot isolation has lots of overhead already, and adding page compression into the mix affects performance even more.

Backup compression

Chapter 1, "SQL Server 2012 architecture and configuration," briefly mentioned backup compression when discussing configuration options. It's worth repeating that the algorithm used for compressing backups is very different than the database compression algorithms discussed in this chapter. Backup compression uses an algorithm very similar to zipping, where it's just looking for patterns in the data. Even after tables and indexes are compressed by using the data compression techniques, they still can be compressed further by using the backup compression algorithms.

Page compression looks only for prefix patterns and can still leave other patterns uncompressed, including common suffixes. Page compression eliminates redundant strings, but in most cases plenty of strings aren't redundant, and string data compresses very well using zip-type algorithms.

Also, a fair amount of space in a database constitutes overhead, such as unallocated slots on pages and unallocated pages in allocated extents. Depending on whether Instant File Initialization was used, and what was on the disk previously if it was, the background data can actually compress very well.

Thus, making a compressed backup of a database that has many compressed tables and indexes can provide additional space savings for the backup set.

Table and index partitioning

As you've already seen when looking at the metadata for table and index storage, partitioning is an integral feature of SQL Server space organization. Figure 6-3 in Chapter 6 illustrated the relationship between tables and indexes, partitions, and allocation units. Tables and indexes that are built without any reference to partitions are considered to be stored on a single partition. One of the more useful metadata objects for retrieving information about data storage is the *sys.dm_db_partition_stats* dynamic management view, which combines information found in *sys.partitions*, *sys.allocation_units* and *sys.indexes*.

A partitioned object is split internally into separate physical units that can be stored in different locations. Partitioning is invisible to the users and programmers, who can use T-SQL code to select from a partitioned table exactly the same way they select from a nonpartitioned table. Creating large objects on multiple partitions improves the manageability and maintainability of your database system and can greatly enhance the performance of activities such as purging historic data and loading large amounts of data. In SQL Server 2000, partitioning was available only by manually creating a view that combines multiple tables—a functionality that's referred to as *partitioned* views. SQL Server 2005 introduced built-in partitioning of tables and indexes, which has many advantages over partitioned views, including improved execution plans and fewer prerequisites for implementation.

This section focuses primarily on physical storage of partitioned objects and the partitioning metadata. Chapter 11, "The Query Optimizer," examines query plans involving partitioned tables and partitioned indexes.

Partition functions and partition schemes

To understand the partitioning metadata, you need a little background into how partitions are defined, using an example based on the SQL Server samples. You can find my *Partition.sql* script on the companion website. This script defines two tables, *TransactionHistory* and *TransactionHistoryArchive*, along with a clustered index and two nonclustered indexes on each. Both tables are partitioned on the *TransactionDate* column, with each month of data in a separate partition. Initially, *TransactionHistory* has 12 partitions and *TransactionHistoryArchive* has two.

Before you create a partitioned table or index, you must define a partition function, which is used to define the partition boundaries logically. When a partition function is created, you must specify whether the partition should use a *LEFT*-based or *RIGHT*-based boundary point. Simply put, this defines whether the boundary value itself is part of the left-hand or right-hand partition. Another way to consider this is to ask this question: Is it an upper boundary of one partition (in which case it goes to the *LEFT*), or a lower boundary point of the next partition (in which case it goes to the *RIGHT*)? The number of partitions created by a partition function with *n* boundaries will be *n*+1. Here is the partition function being used for this example:

```
CREATE PARTITION FUNCTION [TransactionRangePF1] (datetime)
AS RANGE RIGHT FOR VALUES ('20111001', '20111101', '20111201',
            '20120101', '20120201', '20120301', '20120401',
            '20120501', '20120601', '20120701', '20120801');
```

Notice that the table name isn't mentioned in the function definition because the partition function isn't tied to any particular table. The *TransactionRangePF1* function divides the data into 12 partitions because 11 *datetime* boundaries exist. The keyword *RIGHT* specifies that any value that equals one of the boundary points goes into the partition to the right of the endpoint. So for this function, all values less than October 1, 2011 go in the first partition and values greater than or equal to October 1, 2011 and less than November 1, 2011 go in the second partition. *LEFT* (the default) could also have been specified, in which case the value equal to the endpoint goes in the partition to the left. After you define the partition function, you define a partition scheme, which lists a set of filegroups onto which each range of data is placed. Here is the partition schema for my example:

```
CREATE PARTITION SCHEME [TransactionsPS1]
AS PARTITION [TransactionRangePF1]
TO ([PRIMARY], [PRIMARY], [PRIMARY]
, [PRIMARY], [PRIMARY], [PRIMARY]
, [PRIMARY], [PRIMARY], [PRIMARY]
, [PRIMARY], [PRIMARY], [PRIMARY]);
GO
```

To avoid having to create 12 files and filegroups, I have put all the partitions on the *PRIMARY* filegroup, but for the full benefit of partitioning, you should probably have each partition on its own filegroup. The *CREATE PARTITION SCHEME* command must list at least as many filegroups as partitions, but it can list one more filegroup, which is considered the "next used" filegroup. If the partition function splits, the new boundary point is added in the filegroup used next. If you don't specify an extra filegroup at the time you create the partition scheme, you can alter the partition scheme to set the next-used filegroup before modifying the function.

As you've seen, the listed filegroups don't have to be unique. In fact, if you want to have all the partitions on the same filegroup, as I have here, you can use a shortcut syntax:

```
CREATE PARTITION SCHEME [TransactionsPS1]
AS PARTITION [TransactionRangePF1]
ALL TO ([PRIMARY]);
GO
```

Note that putting all the partitions on the same filegroup is usually done just for the purpose of testing your code.

Additional filegroups are used in order as more partitions are added, which can happen when a partition function is altered to split an existing range into two. If you don't specify extra filegroups at the time you create the partition scheme, you can alter the partition scheme to add another filegroup.

The partition function and partition scheme for a second table are shown here:

```
CREATE PARTITION FUNCTION [TransactionArchivePF2] (datetime)
AS RANGE RIGHT FOR VALUES ('20110901');
GO

CREATE PARTITION SCHEME [TransactionArchivePS2]
AS PARTITION [TransactionArchivePF2]
TO ([PRIMARY], [PRIMARY]);
GO
```

The script then creates two tables and loads data into them. I will not include all the details here. To partition a table, you must specify a partition scheme in the *CREATE TABLE* statement. I create a table called *TransactionHIstory* that includes this line as the last part of the *CREATE TABLE* statement as follows:

```
ON [TransactionsPS1] (TransactionDate)
```

The second table, *TransactionHistoryArchive*, is created using the *TransactionsPS2* partitioning scheme. The script then loads data into the two tables, and because the partition scheme has already been defined, each row is placed in the appropriate partition as the data is loaded. After the tables are loaded, you can examine the metadata.

Metadata for partitioning

Figure 8-18 shows most of the catalog views for retrieving information about partitions. Along the left and bottom edges, you can see the *sys.tables*, *sys.indexes*, *sys.partitions*, and *sys.allocation_units* catalog views that were discussed earlier in this chapter.

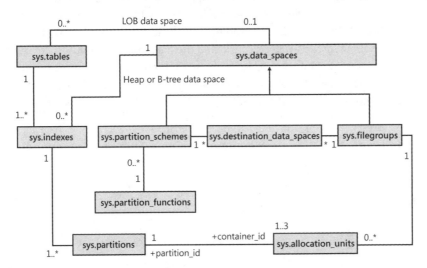

FIGURE 8-18 Catalog views containing metadata for partitioning and data storage.

Some of the queries use the undocumented *sys.system_internals_allocation_units* view instead of *sys.allocation_units* to retrieve page address information. The following are the most relevant columns of each of these views.

- **sys.data_spaces** has a primary key called *data_space_id*, which is either a partition ID or a filegroup ID. Each filegroup has one row, and each partition scheme has one row. One column in *sys.data_spaces* specifies to which type of data space the row refers. If the row refers to a partition scheme, *data_space_id* can be joined with *sys.partition_schemes.data_space_id*. If the row refers to a filegroup, *data_space_id* can be joined with *sys.filegroups.data_space_id*. The *sys.indexes* view also has a *data_space_id* column to indicate how each heap or B-tree stored in *sys.indexes* is stored. So, if you know that a table is partitioned, you can join it directly with *sys.partition_schemes* without going through *sys.data_spaces*. Alternatively, you can use the following query to determine whether a table is partitioned by replacing *dboTransactionHistoryArchive* with the name of the table in which you're interested:

```
SELECT DISTINCT object_name(object_id) as TableName,
            ISNULL(ps.name, 'Not partitioned') as PartitionScheme
    FROM (sys.indexes i LEFT  JOIN sys.partition_schemes ps
                ON (i.data_space_id = ps.data_space_id))
    WHERE (i.object_id = object_id(dbo.TransactionHistoryArchive'))
            AND   (i.index_id IN (0,1));
```

- **sys.partition_schemes** has one row for each partition scheme. In addition to the *data_space_id* and the name of the partition scheme, it has a *function_id* column to join with *sys.partition_functions*.

- **sys.destination_data_spaces** is a linking table because *sys.partition_schemes* and *sys.filegroups* are in a many-to-many relationship with each other. For each partition scheme, there is one row for each partition. The partition number is in the *destination_id* column, and the filegroup ID is stored in the *data_space_id* column.

- **sys.partition_functions** contains one row for each partition function, and its primary key *function_id* is a foreign key in *sys.partition_schemes*.

- **sys.partition_range_values** (not shown) has one row for each endpoint of each partition function. Its *function_id* column can be joined with *sys.partition_functions*, and its *boundary_id* column can join with either *partition_id* in *sys.partitions* or with *destination_id* in *sys.destination_data_spaces*.

These views have other columns not mentioned here, and additional views provide additional information, such as the columns and their data types that the partitioning is based on. However, the preceding information should be sufficient to understand Figure 8-18 and the view shown in Listing 8-8. This view returns information about each partition of each partitioned table. The *WHERE* clause filters out partitioned indexes (other than the clustered index), but you can change that condition if you desire. I first create a function to return an index name, with an object ID and an index ID given, so that the view can easily return any index names. When selecting from the view, you can add your own *WHERE* clause to find information about just the table you're interested in.

LISTING 8-8 View returning data about each partition of each partitioned table

```
CREATE FUNCTION dbo.index_name (@object_id int, @index_id tinyint)
RETURNS sysname
AS
BEGIN
  DECLARE @index_name sysname
  SELECT @index_name = name FROM sys.indexes
    WHERE object_id = @object_id and index_id = @index_id
  RETURN(@index_name)
END;
```

```
GO
CREATE VIEW Partition_Info AS
  SELECT OBJECT_NAME(i.object_id) as ObjectName,
    dbo.INDEX_NAME(i.object_id,i.index_id) AS IndexName,
    object_schema_name(i.object_id) as SchemaName,
    p.partition_number as PartitionNumber, fg.name AS FilegroupName, rows as Rows,
    au.total_pages as TotalPages,
    CASE boundary_value_on_right
        WHEN 1 THEN 'less than'
        ELSE 'less than or equal to'
    END as 'Comparison'
    , rv.value as BoundaryValue,
    CASE WHEN ISNULL(rv.value, rv2.value) IS NULL THEN 'N/A'
    ELSE
      CASE
        WHEN boundary_value_on_right = 0 AND rv2.value IS NULL
          THEN 'Greater than or equal to'
        WHEN boundary_value_on_right = 0
          THEN 'Greater than'
        ELSE 'Greater than or equal to' END + ' ' +
          ISNULL(CONVERT(varchar(15), rv2.value), 'Min Value')
            + ' ' +
            +
          CASE boundary_value_on_right
            WHEN 1 THEN 'and less than'
              ELSE 'and less than or equal to'
              END + ' ' +
              + ISNULL(CONVERT(varchar(15), rv.value),
                        'Max Value')
        END as 'TextComparison'
  FROM sys.partitions p
    JOIN sys.indexes i
      ON p.object_id = i.object_id and p.index_id = i.index_id
    LEFT JOIN sys.partition_schemes ps
      ON ps.data_space_id = i.data_space_id
    LEFT JOIN sys.partition_functions f
      ON f.function_id = ps.function_id
    LEFT JOIN sys.partition_range_values rv
      ON f.function_id = rv.function_id
          AND p.partition_number = rv.boundary_id
    LEFT JOIN sys.partition_range_values rv2
      ON f.function_id = rv2.function_id
          AND p.partition_number - 1= rv2.boundary_id
    LEFT JOIN sys.destination_data_spaces dds
      ON dds.partition_scheme_id = ps.data_space_id
          AND dds.destination_id = p.partition_number
    LEFT JOIN sys.filegroups fg
      ON dds.data_space_id = fg.data_space_id
    JOIN sys.allocation_units au
      ON au.container_id = p.partition_id
WHERE i.index_id <2 AND au.type =1;
```

The *LEFT JOIN* operator is needed to get all the partitions because the *sys.partition_range_values*
view has a row only for each boundary value, not for each partition. *LEFT JOIN* gives the last partition
with a boundary value of NULL, which means that the value of the last partition has no upper limit. A

derived table groups together all the rows in *sys.allocation_units* for a partition, so the space used for all the types of storage (in-row, row-overflow, and LOB) is aggregated into a single value. This query uses the preceding view to get information about my *TransactionHistory* table's partitions:

```
SELECT ObjectName, PartitionNumber, Rows, TotalPages, Comparison, BoundaryValue
FROM Partition_Info
WHERE ObjectName = 'TransactionHistory' AND SchemaName = 'dbo'
ORDER BY ObjectName, PartitionNumber ;
```

Here are my results for the *TransactionHistory* object:

Object_Name	Partitionnumber	Rows	Totalpages	Comparison	BoundaryValue
TransactionHistory	1	11155	89	Less than	2011-10-01
TransactionHistory	2	9339	74	Less than	2011-11-01
TransactionHistory	3	10169	81	Less than	2011-12-01
TransactionHistory	4	12181	97	Less than	2012-01-01
TransactionHistory	5	9558	74	Less than	2012-02-01
TransactionHistory	6	10217	81	Less than	2012-03-01
TransactionHistory	7	10703	89	Less than	2012-04-01
TransactionHistory	8	10640	89	Less than	2012-05-01
TransactionHistory	9	12508	90	Less than	2012-06-01
TransactionHistory	10	12585	97	Less than	2012-07-01
TransactionHistory	11	3380	33	Less than	2012-08-01
TransactionHistory	12	1008	17	Less than	NULL

This view contains details about the boundary point of each partition, as well as the filegroup that each partition is stored on, the number of rows in each partition, and the amount of space used. It also contains a few additional columns that aren't shown here, just to keep the output from being too wide. In particular, I didn't return the *FilegroupName* value, because in my example, all the partitions are on the same filegroup. Anytime your partitions are on different filegroups, you most likely will want to see that value for each partition. Note that although the comparison indicates that the values in the partitioning column for the rows in a particular partition are less than the specified value, you should assume that it also means that the values are greater than or equal to the specified value in the preceding partition. However, this view doesn't provide information about where in the particular filegroup the data is located. The next section looks at a metadata query that provides location information.

Note If a partitioned table contains FILESTREAM data, you should partition the FILESTREAM data by using the same partition function as the non-FILESTREAM data. Because the regular data and the FILESTREAM data are on separate filegroups, the FILESTREAM data needs its own partition scheme. However, the partition scheme for the FILESTREAM data can use the same partition function to make sure the same partitioning is used for both FILESTREAM and non-FILESTREAM data.

The sliding window benefits of partitioning

One of the main benefits of partitioning your data is that you can move data from one partition to another as a metadata-only operation; the data itself doesn't have to move. As mentioned earlier, this isn't intended to be a complete how-to guide to SQL Server 2012 partitioning; instead, it's a description of the internal storage of partitioning information.

 Note For a complete description of designing, setting up, and managing partitioned tables and indexes, read Ron Talmage's white paper at *http://msdn.microsoft.com/en-us/library/dd578580.aspx*.

To understand the internals of rearranging partitions, you need to look at additional partitioning operations.

The main operation you use when working with partitions is the *SWITCH* option to the *ALTER TABLE* command. This option allows you to

- Assign a table as a partition of an already-existing partitioned table

- Switch a partition from one partitioned table to another

- Reassign a partition to form a single table

In all these operations, no data is moved. Instead, the metadata is updated in the *sys.partitions* and *sys.system_internals_allocation_units* views to indicate that a particular allocation unit now is part of a partition in a different object. For example, the following query returns information about each allocation unit in the first two partitions of the *TransactionHistory* and *TransactionHistoryArchive* tables, including the number of rows, the number of pages, the type of data in the allocation unit, and the page where the allocation unit starts:

```
SELECT convert(char(25),object_name(object_id)) AS name,
    rows, convert(char(15),type_desc) as page_type_desc,
    total_pages AS pages, first_page, index_id, partition_number
FROM sys.partitions p JOIN sys.system_internals_allocation_units a
    ON p.partition_id = a.container_id
WHERE (object_id=object_id('[dbo].[TransactionHistory]')
  OR object_id=object_id('[dbo].[TransactionHistoryArchive]'))
  AND index_id = 1 AND partition_number <= 2;
```

Here is the data I get back. (I left out the *page_type_desc* because all the rows are of type *IN_ROW_DATA*.)

name	rows	pages	first_page	index_id	partition_number
TransactionHistory	11155	89	0xD81B00000100	1	1
TransactionHistory	9339	74	0xA82200000100	1	2
TransactionHistoryArchive	89253	633	0x981B00000100	1	1
TransactionHistoryArchive	0	0	0x000000000000	1	2

Now you can move one of the partitions. The ultimate goal is to add a new partition to *TransactionHistory* to store a new month's worth of data and to move the oldest month's data into *TransactionHistoryArchive*. The partition function used by my *TransactionHistory* table divides the data into 12 partitions, and the last one contains all dates greater than or equal to August 1, 2012. You can alter the partition function to put a new boundary point in for September 1, 2012, so the last partition is split. Before doing that, you must ensure that the partition scheme using this function knows what filegroup to use for the newly created partition. With this command, some data movement occurs and all data from the last partition of any tables using this partition scheme is moved to a new allocation unit. Refer to *SQL Server Books Online* for complete details about each of the following commands:

```
ALTER PARTITION SCHEME TransactionsPS1
NEXT USED [PRIMARY];
GO


ALTER PARTITION FUNCTION TransactionRangePF1()
SPLIT RANGE ('20120901');
GO
```

Next, you can do something similar for the function and partition scheme used by *TransactionHistoryArchive*. In this case, add a new boundary point for October 1, 2011:

```
ALTER PARTITION SCHEME TransactionArchivePS2
NEXT USED [PRIMARY];
GO


ALTER PARTITION FUNCTION TransactionArchivePF2()
SPLIT RANGE ('20111001');
GO
```

Now move all data from *TransactionHistory* with dates earlier than October 1, 2011, to the second partition of *TransactionHistoryArchive*. However, the first partition of *TransactionHistory* technically has no lower limit; it includes everything earlier than October 1, 2011. The second partition of *TransactionHistoryArchive* does have a lower limit, which is the first boundary point, or September 1, 2011. To *SWITCH* a partition from one table to another, you must guarantee that all the data to be moved meets the requirements for the new location, so you need to add a *CHECK* constraint that guarantees that no data in *TransactionHistory* is earlier than September 1, 2011. After adding the *CHECK* constraint, I run the *ALTER TABLE* command with the *SWITCH* option to move the data in partition 1 of *TransactionHistory* to partition 2 of *TransactionHistoryArchive*. (For testing purposes, you could try leaving out the next step that adds the constraint and try just executing the *ALTER TABLE/ SWITCH* command. You get an error message. After that, you can add the constraint and run the *ALTER TABLE/SWITCH* command again.)

```
ALTER TABLE [dbo].[TransactionHistory]
ADD CONSTRAINT [CK_TransactionHistory_DateRange]
CHECK ([TransactionDate] >= '20110901');
GO
ALTER TABLE [dbo].[TransactionHistory]
SWITCH PARTITION 1
TO [dbo].[TransactionHistoryArchive] PARTITION 2;
GO
```

Now run the metadata query that examines the size and location of the first two partitions of each table:

```
SELECT convert(char(25),object_name(object_id)) AS name,
    rows, convert(char(15),type_desc) as page_type_desc,
    total_pages AS pages, first_page, index_id, partition_number
FROM sys.partitions p JOIN sys.system_internals_allocation_units a
    ON p.partition_id = a.container_id
WHERE (object_id=object_id('[dbo].[TransactionHistory]')
  OR object_id=object_id('[dbo].[TransactionHistoryArchive]'))
  AND index_id = 1 AND partition_number <= 2;
```

```
RESULTS:
name                     rows    pages       first_page        index_id     partition_number
-------------------      ------- ----------  --------------    -----------  ----------------
TransactionHistory       0       0           0x000000000000    1            1
TransactionHistory       9339    74          0xA82200000100    1            2
TransactionHistoryAr     89253   633         0x981B00000100    1            1
TransactionHistoryAr     11155   89          0xD81B00000100    1            2
```

Notice that the second partition of *TransactionHistoryArchive* now has exactly the same information that the first partition of *TransactionHistory* had in the first result set. It has the same number of rows (11,155), the same number of pages (89), and the same starting page (0xD81B00000100, or file 1, page 7,128). No data was moved; the only change was that the allocation unit starting at file 1, page 7,128 isn't recorded as belonging to the second partition of the *TransactionHistoryArchive* table.

Although my partitioning script created the indexes for the partitioned tables by using the same partition scheme used for the tables themselves, this isn't always necessary. An index for a partitioned table can be partitioned using the same partition scheme or a different one. If you don't specify a partition scheme or filegroup when you build an index on a partitioned table, the index is placed in the same partition scheme as the underlying table, using the same partitioning column. Indexes built on the same partition scheme as the base table are called *aligned indexes*.

However, an internal storage component is associated with automatically aligned indexes. As mentioned earlier, if you build an index on a partitioned table and don't specify a filegroup or partitioning scheme on which to place the index, SQL Server creates the index using the same partitioning scheme that the table uses. However, if the partitioning column isn't part of the index definition, SQL Server adds the partitioning column as an extra included column in the index. If the index is clustered, adding an included column isn't necessary because the clustered index already contains all the columns. Another case in which SQL Server doesn't add an included column automatically is when you create a unique index, either clustered or nonclustered. Because unique partitioned indexes require that the partitioning column is contained in the unique key, a unique index for which you haven't explicitly included the partitioning key isn't partitioned automatically.

Partitioning a columnstore index

To end this section, look at an example that combines partitioning with columnstore indexes, which Chapter 7 described. If you still have the *dbo.FactInternetSalesBig* table, you can follow the examples here.

First, create a very simple partition function and partition scheme. The partition function splits the data into five partitions, which eventually are mapped to the *SalesTerritoryKey* column of the big table. Then define a partition scheme that puts all the partitions on the PRIMARY filegroup:

```
USE AdventureWorksDW2012
GO
CREATE PARTITION FUNCTION [PF_TerritoryKey](int) AS RANGE LEFT FOR VALUES (2, 4, 6, 8)
GO
CREATE PARTITION SCHEME [PS_TerritoryKey] AS PARTITION [PF_TerritoryKey] ALL TO ([PRIMARY]);
GO
```

Now you can rebuild the clustered index to use this partitioning scheme, but you should get an error message initially, because if a table has a columnstore index, it must be partitioned aligned with the table. So you have to drop the columnstore index before you can rebuild the clustered index, and then you can rebuild the columnstore index using the same partitioning scheme.

```
DROP INDEX dbo.FactInternetSalesBig.csi_FactInternetSalesBig;
GO
CREATE CLUSTERED INDEX clus_FactInternetSalesBig ON  dbo.FactInternetSalesBig
(SalesTerritoryKey)
ON  PS_TerritoryKey (SalesTerritoryKey)
GO
```

Now you can rebuild the columnstore index on the same partitioning scheme, as shown in Listing 8-9.

LISTING 8-9 Rebuilding the columnstore index on the same partitioning scheme

```
CREATE NONCLUSTERED COLUMNSTORE INDEX csi_FactInternetSalesBig
ON dbo.FactInternetSalesBig (
    ProductKey,
    OrderDateKey,
    DueDateKey,
    ShipDateKey,
    CustomerKey,
    PromotionKey,
    CurrencyKey,
    SalesTerritoryKey,
    SalesOrderNumber,
    SalesOrderLineNumber,
    RevisionNumber,
    OrderQuantity,
    UnitPrice,
    ExtendedAmount,
    UnitPriceDiscountPct,
    DiscountAmount,
    ProductStandardCost,
    TotalProductCost,
    SalesAmount,
    TaxAmt,
    Freight,
    CarrierTrackingNumber,
    CustomerPONumber
) ON PS_TerritoryKey (SalesTerritoryKey)
GO
```

To explore my partitions, you can re-create the *Partition_Info* view from Listing 8-8 in the *AdventureWorksDW2012* database. Then you can determine how many rows are in each partition by looking at just a couple of columns from that view:

```
select PartitionNumber, Rows from Partition_Info
where ObjectName = 'FactInternetSalesBig';
GO
```

Here are my results:

```
PartitionNumber  Rows
---------------  --------------------
1                4618240
2                6289920
3                3921408
4                5725696
5                10368512
```

Now that you have a columnstore index, you can also use the metadata view that Chapter 7 explored—namely, *sys.column_store_segments*. The following query groups by column to show you the total number of segments in the table. If you run this query, you'll see 24 rows indicating 24 columns. The index had only 23 columns defined, but because the clustered index wasn't unique, the uniquifier is added as a column. The result of this query also shows 41 total segments:

```
-- GROUP BY COLUMN
SELECT s.column_id,  col_name(ic.object_id, ic.column_id) as column_name,    count(*) as segment_
count
FROM sys.column_store_segments s join sys.partitions p on s.partition_id = p.partition_id
   LEFT JOIN sys.index_columns ic
        ON p.object_id = ic.object_id AND p.index_id = ic.index_id
        AND s.column_id = ic.index_column_id
WHERE object_name(p.object_id) = 'FactInternetSalesBig'
GROUP BY s.column_id,  col_name(ic.object_id, ic.column_id), object_name(p.object_id)
ORDER by 1;
GO
```

Because of the boundary values used, not every partition has exactly the same number of rows, as you saw in the data from the *Partition_Info* view. Each partition could have a different number of segments, and the following query shows how many segments are created for each partition:

```
SELECT   partition_number, count( segment_id) as NumSegments, sum(row_count) as NumRows
FROM sys.column_store_segments s join sys.partitions p on s.partition_id = p.partition_id
   JOIN sys.index_columns ic
        ON p.object_id = ic.object_id AND p.index_id = ic.index_id
        AND s.column_id = ic.index_column_id
WHERE object_name(p.object_id) = 'FactInternetSalesBig' and index_column_id = 2
GROUP BY partition_number WITH ROLLUP;
GO
```

The results show that partition 5 has more than 10 million rows and 12 segments, whereas partitions 1 and 3 each have only six segments. The grand totals produced by the *ROLLUP* clause, show the 41 total segments, and that the total number of rows in the table is 30923776.

```
partition_number  NumSegments  NumRows
----------------  -----------  ----------
1                 6            4618240
2                 8            6289920
3                 6            3921408
4                 9            5725696
5                 12           10368512
NULL              41           30923776
```

Conclusion

This chapter looked at how SQL Server stores data that doesn't use the typical *FixedVar* record format and data that doesn't fit into the usual 8 KB data page.

This chapter discussed row-overflow and large object data, which is stored on its own separate pages, and FILESTREAM data, which is stored outside SQL Server, in files in the file system. You also read about FileTables, which allow FILESTREAM data to be accessed and manipulated through SQL Server tables.

Some special storage capabilities in SQL Server 2012 require that you look at row storage in a completely different way. Sparse columns allow you to have very wide tables of up to 30,000 columns, as long as most of those columns are NULL in most rows. Each row in a table containing sparse columns has a special descriptor field that provides information about which columns are non-NULL for that particular row.

This chapter also described the row storage format used with compressed data. Data can be compressed at either the row level or the page level, and the rows and pages themselves describe the data that is contained therein. This type of row format is referred to as the CD format.

Finally, you looked at partitioning of tables and indexes. Although partitioning doesn't really require a special format for your rows and pages, it does require accessing the metadata in a special way.

CHAPTER 9

Special indexes

Bob Beauchemin

S QL Server indexes, as discussed in Chapter 7, "Indexes: internals and management," are B-tree indexes. The leaf node level of a B-tree always contains columns and rows, where the actual "data" for the index resides. The key range information that's used for index key traversal is stored above the leaf level in the intermediate and root nodes. Looking at just the leaf nodes, you can divide the data columns into key columns and non-key columns. In a clustered index, the clustering key is the key column(s), and the rest of the data columns in the table are non-key columns. In a nonclustered index definition, the key columns appear after the table in the *CREATE INDEX* statement. Every nonclustered index also contains a copy of the clustering key, except in the case of heaps (tables without a clustering key that contain a row-id instead of a clustering key). You can include non-key columns in a nonclustered index by using the *INCLUDE* clause of *CREATE INDEX*. You can use the *INCLUDE* clause to help cover the non-key needs of a particular query rather than incur random IOs against the clustered index.

Indexes can also include persisted computed columns as either key columns or non-key columns. These columns aren't the actual data, but can be derived from the actual data. An example of a persisted computed column is one that's based on a known formula or method using one or more of the table's columns as input. Another property of nonclustered indexes is that they typically contain one row in the index for each row in the table in which the nonclustered index's key values are non-NULL. If the authors table has 23 rows, a nonclustered index on the table will also contain 23 leaf-node rows. The exception to this is the filtered index, introduced in SQL Server 2008, in which only some rows from the table are represented in the index—that is, those rows that satisfy the filter.

This chapter looks at the special indexes and points out the similarities and differences between them and "regular" indexes. You'll also see how they are used in unique ways to optimize queries over special data types, including XML documents, text documents, and spatial data. This chapter covers four types of indexes that are used to index special kinds of data: XML indexes, spatial indexes, full-text indexes, and semantic indexes.

Special indexes vs. ordinary indexes

The means of creating, maintaining, and using special indexes seem, at first glance, to be significantly different from "ordinary" indexes, but when you have a chance to inspect these indexes, you'll find that they are really implemented by using internal tables and ordinary B-tree indexes on the internal tables. Internal tables are similar in concept to what's referred to as "side-tables" in some other databases' extender technologies, but you can't use the internal tables directly. You can list the internal tables in a particular database by using the query

```
SELECT * FROM sys.internal_tables;
```

Running this query against a newly created database shows tables that are used for service broker built-in queues, as well as some tables that implement the filestream, filetable, and change tracking features. Some of these tables exist whether or not you're using the corresponding feature.

By looking at the special indexes' corresponding internal tables (you can inspect the contents only by using the DAC, or Dedicated Administrator Connection), you can see that they break a few of the rules of typical nonclustered indexes.

Special indexes can—and usually do—contain more than one row for each row in the base table. XML indexes, for example, contain one row for each node in the XML column. If the base table contains one row and the XML value in that row contains 42 XML elements, 10 XML attributes, and 30 text nodes, the XML index will contain 82 rows for one "base table" row.

Special indexes don't contain the actual indexed columns from the base table. They usually consist almost entirely of computed columns, although they do usually contain a copy of the clustering key to enable joining back to the base table just as nonclustered indexes do when using a *key lookup*. For example, the columns of a spatial index contain the following elements.

- **CellID** is computed by using the *Hilbert space-filling curve* algorithm for the spatial cells that each row intersects with.

- **Cell_Attributes** identifies a spatial relationship that can exist between the spatial feature and the cell.

- **SRID** represents the spatial reference identifier of the feature in the base table.

The spatial index also contains the clustering key, but *not* the spatial column value itself. Except for the clustering key, the other columns are persisted computed columns with values derived from the spatial column. As another example, one of the full-text index's internal tables is actually an inverted index, in which the one index row per keyword might contain references to multiple base table rows.

You use the special indexes with special T-SQL query constructs. XML indexes are used with XQuery methods on the XML data type, and full-text indexes are used only with special T-SQL functions and predicates. Spatial indexes are used only with queries using particular spatial methods.

XML indexes

SQL Server 2005 marked the introduction of the native XML data type and the inclusion of the XQuery language as part of SQL Server. XQuery is a declarative query language that can be parsed, algebrized, and optimized similar to the way that the SQL language can. Although many of the same rules apply to XML and XQuery as apply to relational data, XQuery has some different rules and constructs than SQL. For example, relational sets are unordered, so an *ORDER BY* clause is required if you want to return rows in order, but XQuery mandates that the results be returned in document order. XML indexes exist to optimize XQuery as SQL indexes exist to optimize SQL queries.

> **Note** In SQL Server 2012 SP1, Microsoft introduced an entirely different type of XML indexing with a different implementation: the Selective XML Index. Because of the release timing of this feature, this book doesn't cover it.

Creating and maintaining XML indexes

Because XML indexes are somewhat different from relational indexes, you need to understand their implementation before you can see how to use them for maximum effectiveness. SQL Server supports four different types of XML indexes: a single "primary" XML index and three different types of "secondary" XML indexes. However, the primary XML index isn't strictly an index on the original form of XML.

You must create a primary XML index before creating any secondary XML indexes. To create a primary XML index, use the XML index–specific DDL statement, *CREATE PRIMARY XML INDEX*. This statement designates the table and XML data-type column to use. A simple *CREATE PRIMARY XML INDEX* DDL statement would look like this:

```
CREATE PRIMARY XML INDEX invoiceidx ON xmlinvoice(invoice);
```

You create a secondary XML index by using the primary XML index, so a simple DDL statement to create a secondary XML index would look like this:

```
CREATE XML INDEX invpathidx ON xmlinvoices(invoice)
 USING XML INDEX invoiceidx FOR PATH;
```

The table on which the XML index is created must have a primary key, and the table's primary key must be its clustering key. This primary/clustering key can contain up to 15 columns. XML indexing exists completely separately from "ordinary" relational indexing—that is, an XML index must be created on an XML data type column, and relational indexes can't be created on an XML data type column. You can, however, use an XML data type column in a full-text index.

You aren't limited to one XML column per table, so if a table contains more than one XML data type column, you can create an XML index or set of XML indexes on each XML column. You can create a maximum of 249 XML indexes per table in addition to the 999 nonclustered indexes allowed. Multiple XML primary indexes on a single XML column aren't allowed. XML indexes can be created only on XML data type columns in a table. You can't create an XML index on an XML column defined in an indexed view, on a table variable with XML columns, on XML data-type variables, or on a computed XML column. To create an XML index, the *SET* option settings must be the same as those required for indexed views.

You can use the following index options with XML indexes:

- *PAD_INDEX*

- *FILLFACTOR*

- *SORT_IN_TEMPDB*

- *ALLOW_ROW_LOCKS* and *ALLOW_PAGE_LOCKS*

XML indexes don't support online index rebuild. The *ONLINE=ON* option, if specified, causes an error. The *IGNORE_DUP_KEY* option also has no meaning for XML indexes. Although *MAXDOP* is syntactically supported for XML indexes, they are always built using a single processor (the equivalent of *MAXDOP = 1)*. The *COMPRESSION* keyword can't be specified for an XML index. The *filegroup* designation and partitioning information for the base table also apply to the XML indexes, and you can't specify filegroup or partitioning information separately for an XML index.

Primary XML index

The primary XML index on an XML column is a clustered index on an internal table known as the node table that users can't use directly from their T-SQL statements. The primary XML index is a B-tree and its usefulness is because of the way that the optimizer creates a plan for the entire query. Although the optimizer can operate on the entire XML column as though it is a blob, when you need to execute XML queries, decomposing the XML into relational columns and rows is often more useful. The primary XML index contains one row for each node in the XML instance, which you can validate by inspecting the internal table. By creating an example primary XML index when executing the DDL shown in Listing 9-1, you can see the columns that the primary XML index contains. First, create a database to use with the XML index examples, create a table containing a XML data type column, and populate the table with a number of rows.

LISTING 9-1 Creating a table with an XML column and a PRIMARY XML INDEX

```
CREATE DATABASE xmltest
go
USE xmltest
go

-- create the table
-- the clustering key must be the primary key of the table
-- to enable XML index creation
CREATE TABLE xmlinvoice (
  invoiceid INT IDENTITY PRIMARY KEY,
  invoice XML
);
GO
-- Insert some sample XML documents
-- run the sample script provided with the downloads to create additional rows
-- additional rows elided, run code example to produce all six rows
INSERT INTO xmlinvoice VALUES('
<Invoice InvoiceID="1000" dept="hardware">
   <CustomerName>Jane Smith</CustomerName>
   <LineItems>
```

```
      <LineItem>
          <Sku>134</Sku>
          <Description>Gear</Description>
          <Price>9.95</Price>
      </LineItem>
   </LineItems>
</Invoice>');
GO

-- create the primary XML index
CREATE PRIMARY XML INDEX invoiceidx ON xmlinvoice(invoice);
GO

-- display XML index information
-- sys.xml_indexes inherits from sys.indexes
SELECT * FROM sys.xml_indexes;

-- display the columns in the primary XML index (on the internal node table)
-- one row of metadata per column
SELECT * FROM sys.columns c
JOIN sys.indexes i ON i.object_id = c.object_id
WHERE i.name = 'invoiceidx'
AND i.type = 1;
```

Table 9-1 shows the column information (one column per row in the query results) that this statement produces. Some terms require further explanation, which is provided later in this chapter.

TABLE 9-1 Columns in the node table

Column name	Column description	Data type
id	node identifier in *ordpath* format	VARBINARY(900)
nid	node name (tokenized)	INTEGER
Tagname	tag name	NVARCHAR(4000)
Taguri	tag uri	NVARCHAR(4000)
Tid	node data type (tokenized)	INTEGER
value	first portion of the node value	SQL_VARIANT
Lvalue	long node value (pointer)	NVARCHAR(MAX)
lvaluebin	long node value in binary (pointer)	VARBINARY(MAX)
Hid	path (tokenized)	VARCHAR(900)
xsinil	is it NULL (xsi:nil)	BIT
xsitype	does it use xsi:type	Bit
pk1...n	primary key columns of the base table	Depends on PK data type

This internal table contains a multicolumn clustered index on the id and 1-to-n primary key (pk1... pkn) columns of the base table.

The name of the internal table that comprises the XML index is based on the *OBJECT_ID* of the base table, followed by the *index_id* of the XML index in *sys.indexes*. The XML index's *index_id* begins numbering with 256000. For example, a primary XML index created on a table with an *OBJECT_ID* of 245575913—that is, the first XML index created in the database—would be named *xml_index_nodes_245575913_256000*.

The *sys.indexes* table has two entries for an XML index. The XML index is listed as an index under the base table's *OBJECT_ID* in *sys.indexes* as index type = 3 (XML), in addition to being listed as an index over the internal table as index_type = 1. You can see these with the following query:

```
SELECT * FROM sys.indexes
WHERE name = 'invoiceidx';
```

To obtain the size of the primary XML index, you can execute the following query that uses the internal table *OBJECT_ID*:

```
SELECT SCHEMA_NAME(itab.schema_id) AS schema_name
    ,itab.name AS internal_table_name
    ,idx.name AS index_name
    ,p.*
    ,au.*
FROM sys.internal_tables AS itab
JOIN sys.indexes AS idx
-- JOIN to the clustered index
ON itab.object_id = idx.object_id AND idx.index_id = 1
JOIN   sys.partitions AS p
ON p.object_id = idx.object_id AND p.index_id = idx.index_id
JOIN   sys.allocation_units AS au
ON au.container_id =
    CASE au.type
        WHEN 2 THEN p.partition_id
        ELSE p.hobt_id
    END
WHERE idx.name = 'invoiceidx'
ORDER BY itab.name, idx.index_id;
```

The primary XML index has 11 columns (as shown earlier in Table 9-1) in addition to the base table's primary key, which can be a multicolumn key; it contains enough data to execute any XQuery. The query processor uses the primary XML index (if it's the only existing XML index) to execute almost every XQuery. Although having the primary XML index is a vast improvement over creating a large portion of it again during each query (as described later in the chapter), the size of the node table is usually around three times that of the XML data type in the base table. The actual size of the XML index depends on the XML instances in the XML column. If they contain many tags and small values, more rows are created in the primary XML index and the index size is relatively larger. Few tags and large values mean that fewer rows are created in the primary XML index, and the index size is closer to the data size. Take this into consideration when planning disk space. This is because the node table contains explicit representations of information (such as the path and node number) that's a different representation of information (computed columns) inherent in the structure of the XML document itself.

The node identifier is represented by a node numbering system that's optimized for operations on the document structure (such as parent-child relationship and the relative order of nodes in the document) and insertion of new nodes. This node numbering system is known as ORDPATH. One reason for numbering all the nodes are to maintain document order and structural integrity in the query result. These aren't requirements of relational systems, but are requirements in XML. Using the ORDPATH numbering system makes satisfying these requirements easier for the query engine. The ORDPATH format contains document order and structure information. For further details on ORD-PATH, see the white paper "ORDPATHs: Insert-Friendly XML Node Labels" by Patrick and Elizabeth O'Neil and others (*http://www.cs.umb.edu/~poneil/ordpath.pdf*). Notice that the path portion of the *HIERARCHYID* data type, introduced in SQL Server 2008, also uses ORDPATH.

Secondary XML indexes

After the primary XML index is created, you can create three additional kinds of secondary XML indexes: *PATH*, *PROPERTY*, and *VALUE*. Secondary XML indexes are entirely optional, and you can create them in any order. The secondary XML indexes assist in certain types of XQuery processing, as discussed later. For example, you can create a *PATH* secondary index using the earlier primary XML index like this:

```
CREATE XML INDEX invpathidx ON xmlinvoice(invoice)
 USING XML INDEX invoiceidx FOR PATH
```

Secondary XML indexes are actually nonclustered indexes on the node table. The *PATH* index, for example, is a typical nonclustered index on the *HID* and *VALUE* columns of the node table. The *PROPERTY* index is nonclustered index on the *pk*, *HID*, and *VALUE*) columns, and the *VALUE* index is a nonclustered index on the *VALUE* and *HID* columns. To see the key columns for all the indexes on the node table in index order, you can execute this query:

```
SELECT i.name AS indexname, c.name AS colname, ic.*
FROM sys.index_columns ic
JOIN sys.columns c
ON ic.column_id = c.column_id AND ic.object_id = c.object_id
JOIN sys.indexes i
ON ic.object_id = i.object_id AND ic.index_id = i.index_id
WHERE ic.object_id =
    (SELECT object_id FROM sys.indexes
     WHERE name = 'invoiceidx' AND type = 1)
ORDER BY index_id, key_ordinal;
```

Secondary XML indexes also contain an entry in *sys.indexes* as a "type=3" or XML index, just like the primary XML index does. You can query XML index-specific information for using *sys.xml_indexes*, which inherits most of its information from *sys.indexes* and adds XML index-specific information.

Using XQuery in SQL Server: internals

You use XQuery in SQL Server through a series of built-in SQL methods on the XML data type. Introduced in SQL Server 2005, the XML data type is a native type that can be used as a column in a table, as procedure parameters, or as T-SQL variables. The built-in methods can be used with any instance of the XML data type. Table 9-2 lists the five methods, their signatures, and what they do.

TABLE 9-2 XML data type functions

Name	Signature	Usage
exist	bit = X.exist(string xquery)	Checks for existence of nodes. Returns 1 if any output returned from query; otherwise, returns 0,
value	scalar = X.value(string xquery, string SQL type)	Returns a SQL scalar value from a query cast to specified SQL data type.
query	XML = X.query(string xquery)	Returns an XML data type instance from query.
nodes	X.nodes(string xquery)	Table-value function used for XML to relational decomposition. Returns one row for each node that matches the query.
modify	X.modify(string xml-dml)	A mutator method that changes the XML value in place.

Notice that each method requires an XQuery expression (or an XML DML expression, in the case of *modify*) as a *(N)VARCHAR* SQL input parameter. Each method is used as a part of an "ordinary" SQL statement, as in the following examples.

```
SELECT invoice.query('
    (: XQuery program :)
    declare namespace pmt="urn:www-payco-com:payments";
    for $invitem in //Invoice
    return
      <pmt:Payment>
        <pmt:InvoiceID> {data($invitem/@InvoiceID)} </pmt:InvoiceID>
        <pmt:CustomerName>
            {data($invitem/CustomerName)}
        </pmt:CustomerName>
        <pmt:PayAmt>
            {data(sum($invitem/LineItems/LineItem/Price))}
        </pmt:PayAmt>
      </pmt:Payment>
  ') AS xmldoc
FROM xmlinvoice;

-- Extract a value from XML data type and use in a SQL predicate
SELECT invoiceid
    FROM xmlinvoice
    -- XML.value must return a scalar value (XML singleton or empty sequence)
    WHERE invoice.value('
        (: XQuery program :)
        sum(//Invoice/LineItems/LineItem/Price)
    ',
    -- SQL data type
    'money') > 10.00;
```

SQL Server includes an XQuery processor as well as a SQL query processor. Because XQuery always occurs as part of a SQL query (SQL Server doesn't process standalone XQuery statements), a SQL query containing an XML data type method and XQuery is evaluated in stages:

1. The SQL and XQuery portions of the query both go through a static phase. For the SQL part of the query, the static phase includes a SQL parser, static type-checking (using SQL metadata), and algebrization/optimization, which Chapter 11, "The Query Optimizer," covers. The XQuery portion of the query goes through a similar static phase, including an XQuery parser,

static type checking (using an optional XML schema collection, if available) and algebrization/ optimization.

2. At this stage, you have both a SQL query tree and an XQuery query tree. These trees are combined, followed by static optimization of the combined logical and physical tree.

3. Runtime optimization of the entire tree is performed, using relational indexes and XML indexes and producing a query plan for execution.

Although the combined query plan can contain some XQuery-specific iterators (as explained later in the chapter), the XQuery portion of the plan or the optimizations that take place during its optimization provide no direct visibility. Whereas direct visibility into the query optimizations considered during plan creation is available in an aggregated form using the DMV *sys.dm_exec_query_transformation_stats*, no XML-specific transformations are surfaced in this DMV. For additional information about XQuery optimization and processing, read the white paper "XQuery Implementation in a Relational Database System" by Shankar Pal and others.

Understanding how a query plan uses an XML index

Now that you've seen what the XML indexes consist of in terms of columns and rows, look at how they are useful with particular kinds of XML queries, starting with how SQL Server actually executes a SQL query that contains an XML data type method.

When an SQL-with-XML query is executed against a table containing an XML data type column, the query must process every XML instance in every row. At the top level, such a query can be executed in two ways.

■ Select the rows in the base table (that is, the relational table that contains the XML data type column) that qualify first, and then use XQuery to process each XML instance. This is known as *top-down* query processing.

■ Process all XML instances by using the XQuery first, and then join the rows that qualify to the base table. This is known as *bottom-up* query processing.

The SQL Server query optimizer analyzes both the XQuery pieces and relational pieces of the query as a single entity, and creates a single query plan that encompasses and best optimizes the entire SQL statement.

If you've created only the primary XML index, it's almost always used in each step of the XQuery portion of the query plan. Using the primary XML index to process the query is better in almost every case. If a primary XML index isn't available, a table-valued function is used to evaluate the query, as shown in Figure 9-1 of the query plan for an *exist()* query:

```
SELECT * FROM xmlinvoice
WHERE invoice.exist('/Invoice[@InvoiceID = "1003"]') = 1;
```

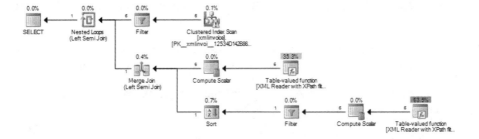

FIGURE 9-1 Query plan when no XML indexes exist, using the XML *exist()* method.

When the primary XML index is in place, the optimizer chooses which indexes to use. If you have all three secondary indexes, four choices are available:

- Index scan or seek on the primary XML index

- Index scan or seek on node table's *PATH* index

- Index scan or seek on node table's *PROPERTY* index

- Index scan or seek on node table's *VALUE* index

The primary XML index is clustered (data is stored) in XML document order, which makes it ideal for processing subtrees. Much of the work in XML queries consists of processing subtrees or assembling an answer by using subtrees, so the clustered index on the node table is most frequently used. Figure 9-2 shows an example of how the same query plan looks after only the primary XML index is created.

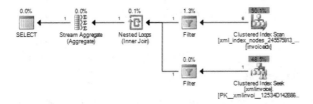

FIGURE 9-2 Query plan for the same query as Figure 9-1, but after defining a primary XML index.

Notice that the XQuery portion of the plan (at the bottom) and the base table portion of the plan (at the top) are joined with a *LEFT OUTER JOIN* because, like in a SQL query with an *EXIST* clause, the XQuery exist method is looking only for the existence of a node in the document, not how many nodes should be returned.

Contrast this with a query that uses the *query()* method:

```
SELECT invoice.query('/Invoice//LineItem') AS line_item_xml
FROM xmlinvoice;
```

Figure 9-3 shows what a query plan looks like without an XML index.

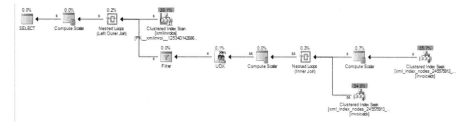

FIGURE 9-3 Query plan when a PRIMARY XML INDEX exists, using the XML *query()* method.

The SQL portion of the query (top row) is executed first, filtering out the rows in which the XML column *IS NULL*. Then, the XQuery portion of the query is executed. Without an XML index, you must use an [*Xml Reader with XPath Filter*] iterator to determine which nodes qualify and to select the *LineItem* nodes, as well as an [*Xml Reader*] to select each node that qualifies (in this case, all nodes under and including the qualifying *LineItem* node). To select and process the information in the XQuery portion, the XML document BLOB must produce a node table for the relevant path.

As an aside, not all columns in the node table are required when using [*Xml Reader*], but almost all of them are. By looking at relative cost of the plan steps in the query plan in Figure 9-3, you can see that the [*Xml Reader*] step constitutes 99 percent of the query plan resources. After the rows (nodes) are fetched, the output of [*Xml Reader with XPath Filter*] is joined with the [*Xml Reader*] output, and the XML document (produced by the *query()* method) is serialized with an XML-specific *UDX* iterator of type *XML SERIALIZER*. That information uses a *LEFT OUTER JOIN* to join with the base table information, because all rows are returned, even of the XQuery portion of the query returns no rows or the XML column is *NULL*.

When the XML primary index is added, the query plan improves dramatically to a plan cost of .0117017 versus 1232.25 (look at the Estimated Subtree Cost of the *SELECT* iterator for both plans) because simple range seeks are performed using the XML index instead of a runtime serialization of the node table. The general shape of the query plan remains the same.

> **Note** The query plan cost for the non-indexed plan is artificially high because, without an XML index, the optimzer can't estimate how many rows will satisfy the XQuery predicate. The optimizer blindly estimates 200 rows returned from [*Xml Reader with XPath Filter*] and 900 rows returned from the [*Xml Reader*] step. The actual counts of rows are 8 and 56, respectively. The query plan using the XML index can correctly evaluate the number of rows to be returned.

Although query plans for SQL/XQuery *SELECT* statements are vastly improved when using an XML index, the plan for an *INSERT* statement is much more expensive when XML indexes are present, because the parsing done by [*Xml Reader*] must be done for all nodes as part of the *INSERT*. The corresponding *INSERT* plan costs are 0.01000024 (no XML index) versus 72.4162 (with a primary XML index). So you pay a heavy price for maintenance of the node table at *INSERT* time.

Using secondary XML indexes

The *PATH*, *PROPERTY*, and *VALUE* XML indexes are more special purpose and are meant to help specific queries. This section continues with examples that use the *exist()* and *query()* methods on the XML data type.

The *PATH* XML index is built on the Path ID (*HID*) and *VALUE* columns of the primary XML index. Because it contains both paths and values, if you need the value (for comparison) by using the path, it's a good "covering" index, as shown in this query:

```
-- this only uses path index if value index is not available
SELECT * FROM xmlinvoice
WHERE invoice.exist('/Invoice/@InvoiceID[. = "1003"]') = 1;
```

You need to have two conditions for the *PATH* index to be useful.

- You need the path to the node you're using.

- The path shouldn't contain predicates or wildcards.

Knowing both the path and value enables index seeks into the *PATH* index. The following example uses the *PATH* index to determine which rows contain *InvoiceID* 1003 and the primary XML index to find the *Invoice* node serialize its value as output.

```
SELECT invoice.query('/Invoice[@InvoiceID = "1003"]')
FROM xmlinvoice;
```

The *PROPERTY* index contains the primary key of the base table (*pk1*), Path ID (*HID*), and *VALUE*, in that order. Because it also contains the primary key of the base table, it helps for searching multiple-valued properties in the same XML instance. Even though all the *Invoice* documents have the same specific structure, this isn't known to the XQuery processor; therefore, every attribute and subelement is considered part of a property bag (set of name-value pairs). You'll see later that typing the XML by using an XML schema lessens the number of unknown property bags the processor has and the structure is known through the schema. In the preceding example, the *PROPERTY* index is used to scan for *CustomerName* elements under *Invoice*, and *CustomerName* is considered part of a property bag of subelements. Even when attributes are used in predicates, property *CustomerName* is useful. In the following example, the *PROPERTY* index is used to search by *Invoice* elements anywhere in the document they occur:

```
SELECT * FROM xmlinvoice
WHERE invoice.exist('//Invoice/@InvoiceID[. = "1003"]') = 1;
```

In queries like this one, the *PROPERTY* index is preferred over the path index if both are available because the *PATH* isn't very selective.

The *VALUE* index contains the same index columns as the *PATH* index—*VALUE* and Path ID (*HID*)—but in the reverse order. Because it contains the value before the path, it's useful for expressions that contain both path wildcards and values, such as the following:

```
-- uses value index if the search value "Mary Weaver" is more selective than the path
SELECT * FROM xmlinvoice
WHERE invoice.exist('/Invoice/CustomerName/text()[. = "Mary Weaver"]') = 1;
```

Note that, if the preferred type of secondary XML index isn't available, an alternate secondary index or the primary XML index can be used. In the preceding example, if the *VALUE* secondary index isn't available, the query processor might decide to use the primary XML index. If the *PROPERTY* secondary index isn't available, the processor often uses a two-step process combining *PATH* and the primary XML index. Sometimes a two-step process is used even with the *PROPERTY* index. Adding another step (such as *JOIN*) to the query plan almost always results in a slower query.

So far, you've been using only the *exist()* method on the XML data type, using a single path and predicate. Things work approximately the same way with the other XML methods. The query method can use node construction (production of new XML nodes in the output) in addition to node selection. Construction is optimized by using a special tag named *Desc* that can be seen in the query plan. Any part of the XQuery that requires selection, however, will use the same subset of the plan as you've been seeing. Keep in mind that any index observations are made with specific sets of data and your results can vary.

Working with XML indexes and schema-validated columns

When an XML *SCHEMA COLLECTION* validates the XML data type column, the order and structure of the documents and the cardinality of each subelement might be known at query compilation time. This provides the query optimizer with more opportunities to optimize the query. You can specify an XML schema for invoices in a schema collection named *invoice_xsd* and restrict the XML column to contain only documents (the XML data type can ordinarily contain documents or fragments), and it would look like this:

```
-- create the table, must have primary key
CREATE TABLE xmlinvoice2(
  invoiceid INTEGER IDENTITY PRIMARY KEY,
  invoice XML(DOCUMENT invoice_xsd)
)
GO
```

When you issue the same queries against a schema-valid column, three major changes seem to occur in query plan and index usage.

- **More bottom-up type queries**   Because of the XML schema, the number of nodes that need to be searched for a specific document is known, and is sometimes fewer than the number of documents (rows) in the table. When this occurs, a bottom-up query filters away more of the data.

- **Greater use of the *VALUE* secondary index, instead of *PROPERTY* and *PATH***   Because of the schema, the processor knows that a specific element occurs in only one place in the document, and also that the type of values that the *VALUE* index is more important and useful. Filtering can be done in one step instead of two. This is similar to the query optimizer understanding the cardinality of a standard data set based on a provided predicate.

- **More efficient scans**   If an element is defined as a numeric or integral data type, scans for a numeric range—for example, *LineItems* priced between $5 and $10—can be done more efficiently. No separate step consisting of data type conversion is required.

As an example of the greater usage of *VALUE* index, the following query changes from a top-down query with a two-step (sub)plan using the *PROPERTY* index and a clustered node table index, to a bottom-up query with a one-step (sub)plan using the *VALUE* index:

```
SELECT *
FROM xmlinvoice
WHERE invoice.exist('/Invoice/CustomerName[. = "Mary Weaver"]') = 1;
```

The *DOCUMENT* qualifier infers the cardinality of 1 for the top-level element. *DOCUMENT* means that the column must contain a document with a single XML root element (no fragments); this is used for data validation and static type inference. However, a predicate expression that starts with *//Invoice* is optimized differently (uses *VALUE* index) than one that starts with */Invoice* (uses *PATH* index). The performance of the two, however, will likely be close.

Using XML-specific information in query plans

Because the primary XML index is taking up three times the space of the XML content in the data type, if you could choose only one secondary XML index, which one would you choose? The answer really depends on your workload. The good news is that because SQL and XQuery are combined to yield a single query plan, ordinary plan analysis (via any of the Showplan methods, including Figure Showplan in SQL Server Management Studio) works just as well for XML indexes as with relational indexes. You create the index and observe the effect on the query plan. A few caveats exist, however: First, you can't force index query hints on XML indexes for the purpose of comparing different index strategies for performance. Also, although all four XML indexes on an XML column are used for query optimization and are "ordinary" relational indexes, the Database Tuning Advisor doesn't suggest XML indexes.

When reading a Showplan for a SQL/XQuery query, you need to recognize a couple of new XQuery-specific iterators.

- **Table-Valued Function [*XML Reader with XPath Filter*]**   This item refers to the on-the-fly creation of a rowset, having the node table format (the node table isn't actually created) for the XQuery portion of the query. You'll see this only when doing queries on an XML column when no XML indexes exist.

- **Table-Valued Function [*XML Reader*]**   This item is similar to [*XML Reader with XPath Filter*], except that all the relevant XML data is used. No XPath predicate exists.

- ***UDX***   This item refers to five internal operators for XQuery processing. The name of each operator can be found in the "Name" property if you bring up the Properties window (note that this doesn't show up in the "hover-over" query step information). The operators are as follows.

  - *Serializer UDX* serializes the query result as XML.

  - *TextAdd UDX* evaluates the XQuery *string()* function.

  - *Contains UDX* evaluates the XQuery *contains()* function.

  - *Data UDX* evaluates the XQuery *data()* function.

  - *Check UDX* validates XML being inserted.

Spatial indexes

Spatial data was introduced in SQL Server 2008, and SQL Server 2012 dramatically expands support for it. Spatial data is multidimensional and is meant to represent objects (also called *spatial features*) in multidimensional space. SQL Server supports two different spatial data types: *GEOMETRY* (Euclidean geometry) and *GEOGRAPHY* (spherical geometry). The *GEOMETRY* data type is also used when dealing with projected coordinate systems—that is, a coordinate system derived from projecting a portion of the earth on to a flat grid. These types are implemented natively in SQL Server as .NET classes. Spatial operations on these data types are implemented as methods or properties of the type. SQL Server supports spatial indexes over either the *GEOMETRY* or *GEOGRAPHY* data types.

The B-trees that SQL Server uses for indexes are linear in nature, but spatial data is (at least) two-dimensional (latitude-longitude or X-Y coordinates). This means that to index spatial data effectively, you need to either use a multidimensional index or find a mechanism to coerce multidimensional spatial data into a linear form and use a B-tree index. SQL Server takes the latter approach by breaking down spatial space via *tessellation* (tiling, *http://en.wikipedia.org/wiki/Tessellation*), and then numbering the tessellated areas (cells) using the Hilbert space-filling curve.

Before focusing on the details of the spatial indexing implementation, you should first explore the purpose of spatial indexing. Unlike other SQL Server indexes, where the index is used to provide locality of reference over a specific value or values and the index data itself is used to provide the projection (covering index), spatial indexes are used to limit the number of rows when performing expensive computations.

Purpose of spatial indexes

Suppose that you have a spatial data set (table) containing 5 million points of interest for restaurants in the United States. You're trying to find restaurants within a 5-mile radius of New York City, where you're staying in a hotel and doing a web search. The way you would accomplish this programmatically is with the spatial data type's *STDistance()* method. If you have an index on the state column of the points-of-interest table, you don't need to waste time doing an *STDistance()* 5 miles from New York City for all the points in Wisconsin, for example. New York and New Jersey are the only states that it makes sense to use. The query optimizer could eliminate most of the states, but only if you phrase your query in terms of them—for example, *WHERE state IN ('NY', 'NJ')*. The state index is unaware of the spatial relationship between the states. New York state is rather large and has many neighboring states. In some locations in New York state, you could search Connecticut, Vermont, or Pennsylvania, or even Quebec or Ontario in Canada. The point of a spatial index is to eliminate most of the rows—that is, it's used as a first-order filter—before computing *STDistance()* on the remaining rows.

When using the *GEOMETRY* data type, a bounding box is drawn around the area that the spatial index covers. The reason should be obvious: When using *GEOMETRY*, specification of the bounding box is crucial to the usefulness of the index because a plane is unbounded in all directions. The bounding box should cover all the spatial features in the spatial data set (table) to be effective. With the *GEOGRAPHY* index, the entire globe (typically, earth) is always indexed. Then the area is broken down into a grid of smaller areas by means of tessellation. With the *GEOMETRY* data type, these areas are rectangles. With *GEOGRAPHY*, the entire earth is broken into two halves (hemispheres) along the equator, both halves are flattened, and the resulting areas are combined and tessellated. Because you're tessellating a sphere, these tessellated areas (called *cells*) aren't rectangular.

Next, you need to decide on the density of the tessellated cells. To consider again the state index analogy for a minute, using the 5-mile radius search, the state index isn't granular enough to eliminate most points, and a county index would be better. So the density (number of cells per square mile) of the spatial index matters. SQL Server tessellates the area in the hierarchical, multilevel manner. SQL Server has four cell tessellation levels, and the density of each can be specified in the *CREATE SPATIAL INDEX* DDL statement. The choice of grid-size is 4x4 (low), 8x8 (medium), or 16x16 (high) for each level. So a grid-size of low at each level (all-low or LLLL grid) would tessellate the bounding box into 4 to the 4th power—that is, 256x256 cells, where a high (all-high or HHHH grid) at each level index would produce 65536x65536 cells. The four-level variable-density grid is specified by specifying *GEOMETRY_GRID* or *GEOGRAPHY_GRID* and specifying the density levels in the DDL statement. The default is an all-medium index—that is, 4096x4096 total cells. The density choice usually depends on the type of spatial objects you're indexing; for example, an all-high (HHHH grid) is almost always preferable for indexing point data. Such an index might not be as useful for polygon or LineString data. Figure 9-4 shows the four levels for an all-low grid (LLLL, 4x4 at each level).

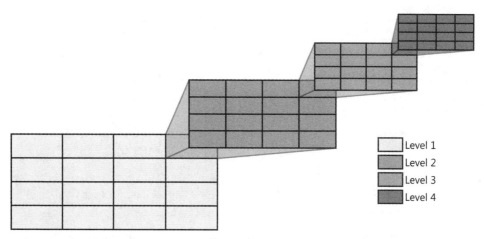

FIGURE 9-4 Visualizing a four-level, 4x4 grid spatial index.

In SQL Server 2012, Microsoft responded to requests for an "all-purpose default index" that would produce good results with any kind of spatial data set. As a result, a new gridding specification was invented, the eight-level grid with grid levels of HLLLLLLL. This grid is specified as *GEOMETRY_AUTO_GRID* or *GEOGRAPHY_AUTO_GRID* in the DDL. In SQL Server 2012, the auto-grid specification is the default.

Grid size matters because not all spatial data sets contain only points. For larger features, because the spatial index consists of one row-per-cell, the grid density directly affects the number of cells needed to cover each spatial feature (row in a table). For example, if the spatial features were states (polygon objects) instead of points, the state of Rhode Island (the smallest state by area in the United States) would have an all-high (HHHH) *GEOGRAPHY_GRID* spatial index overlapping 7368 cells, a *GEOGRAPHY_AUTO_GRID* overlapping over 8192 cells, and an all-low (LLLL) *GEOGRAPHY_GRID* spatial index overlapping only 2 cells.

To limit the number of rows in the spatial index, you can specify a *CELLS_PER_OBJECT* value in the *CREATE SPATIAL INDEX* DDL statement. The default for *CELLS_PER_OBJECT* is 16 for *GEOMETRY_GRID* or *GEOGRAPHY_GRID*, 8 for *GEOMETRY_AUTO_GRID*, and 12 for *GEOGRAPHY_AUTO_GRID*. You can specify values from 1 to 8192. So how does *CELLS_PER_OBJECT* and grid density reconcile if *CELLS_PER_OBJECT* has more cells than it can hold?

During creation of the spatial index, decomposition of a spatial feature (row) into cells (spatial index rows) is accomplished one hierarchy level at a time, from least dense to most dense. Three rules are used.

- **Covering optimization rule**   If a spatial feature completely covers a cell of the coarsest grid level (such as level 1, in a HHHH grid), you don't need to keep cells for lower grid-levels (in this case, levels 2, 3, and 4) and tessellation stops at the coarsest grid level for that cell.

- **Deepest cell optimization rule**   If a cell is partially covered at level 4 and as well as at levels 1, 2, and 3, only the deepest cell—that is, the level 4 cell—needs be kept.

- **Cells-per-object optimization rule** The tessellation is performed from coarsest to finest (that is, from level 1 to level 4), and if the number of cells at level 2 exceeds the CELLS_PER_OBJECT, level 3 and level 4 tessellations aren't performed for this spatial feature.

To summarize the spatial index definition in terms of DDL, you can specify the

- **Bounding box** For *GEOMETRY* spatial indexes only.

- **Tessellation scheme** *GEOMETRY_GRID* or *GEOMETRY_AUTO_GRID* for *GEOMETRY*, *GEOGRAPHY_GRID* or *GEOGRAPHY_AUTO_GRID* for *GEOGRAPHY*.

- **Cell density** For *GEOMETRY_GRID* and *GEOGRAPHY_GRID* (*manual grids*) only. Each cell has four levels of density, and *LOW*, *MEDIUM*, or *HIGH* is specified for each level. For the *AUTO_GRID* schemes, the cell density is fixed at HLLLLLLL.

- ***CELLS_PER_OBJECT*** For all spatial indexes. You can specify values from 1 to 8192.

In addition to the spatial-specific parameters for a spatial index, you can specify "typical" index-specific SQL Server parameters, including the following:

- *ON [FILEGROUP]*

- *PAD_INDEX*

- *FILL_FACTOR*

- *SORT_IN_TEMPDB*

- *STATISTICS_RECOMPUTE*

- *DROP_EXISTING*

- *MAXDOP*

- *ALLOW_PAGE_LOCKS*

Also, the series of set options required for creating a spatial index is the same as the options required for an indexed view. SQL Server 2012 adds support for index compression of spatial indexes (restricted to SQL Server Enterprise edition), so you can specify either *PAGE COMPRESSION* or *ROW COMPRESSION*; the default compression type is *NONE*. Using compression with spatial indexes is effective. My cursory tests obtained between 25 percent to 40 percent reduction in size with ROW *COMPRESSION* and 50 percent to 90 percent reduction in size with PAGE *COMPRESSION*. Queries that use a compressed spatial index run, using about the same (in some cases, less) CPU and elapsed time as the same queries using uncompressed spatial indexes. Because spatial indexes can be quite large—depending on the *CELLS_PER_OBJECT* and density settings and the makeup of the spatial data set being indexed—compression of spatial indexes is a space-saving choice and can potentially boost performance for very large indexes.

Spatial indexes must always specify *ONLINE=OFF*, because Online Index rebuild isn't supported. If the *IGNORE_DUP_KEY=ON* option is specified, an error is raised. If a spatial index is created on a partitioned table, the spatial index is partitioned using the table's partition scheme by default. You can create a spatial index on a single spatial column, but multiple spatial indexes (up to 249) on a single column are supported. This is useful when you want indexes with different densities or *CELLS_PER_OBJECT* specification. Finally, you need to have a primary key, which must also be the table's clustering key and can contain up to 15 columns. You can create a maximum of 249 spatial indexes per table in addition to the 999 nonclustered indexes allowed. You can't create a spatial index on an indexed view.

The following DDL creates a spatial index for a geometry data type column named *shape*, using a grid density of *HIGH* at each level, a bounding box that covers the spatial features, and a specification of 1024 *CELLS_PER_OBJECT*.

```
CREATE SPATIAL INDEX [idx_geom_census_hhhh] ON dbo.Census( shape)
USING GEOMETRY_GRID
WITH (BOUNDING_BOX =(17, -180, 72, -60),
GRIDS = (LEVEL_1 = HIGH, LEVEL_2 = HIGH, LEVEL_3 = HIGH,LEVEL_4 = HIGH),
CELLS_PER_OBJECT = 1024);
```

Composition of the spatial index

Now that you've created a spatial index on the census table in the census database, what does it look like? The spatial index is an internal table, and you can use the *select * from sys.internal_tables* query to locate it. The spatial index internal tables have an naming convention of *extended_index_[object_id_ of_base_table]_[ordinal _starting_at384000]*. The first spatial index is ordinal 384000; additional spatial indexes on the same table simply add 1 to the last ordinal.

Analogous to XML indexes are two entries in *sys.indexes* for a spatial index. The spatial index is listed as an index under the base table's *OBJECT_ID* in *sys.indexes* as *index_type* = 4 (Spatial), in addition to being listed as an index over the internal table as *index_type* = 1.

Two additional metadata views provide additional information specific to spatial indexes. *Sys.spatial_indexes* inherits from *sys.indexes* and adds the *spatial_index_type, spatial_index_type_ description* and *tessellation_scheme columns*. The *sys.spatial_index_tessellations* metadata view provides the rest of the spatial index information, including *bounding_box, grid_density* and *CELLS_PER_OBJECT*. As with the XML index, you can obtain space information by querying through the internal table metadata view; for spatial indexes, that always provides compression information. By executing the following query, you can see that the spatial index comprises the columns shown in Table 9-3.

```
SELECT * FROM sys.columns c
 JOIN sys.indexes i ON i.object_id = c.object_id
 WHERE i.name = ' idx_geom_census_hhhh'
 AND i.type = 1;
```

TABLE 9-3 Columns in the spatial index

Column name	Column description	Data type
Cell_Id	Hilbert number of the cell	Binary(5)
Cell_Attributes	Enumeration	Smallint
SRID (not in auto-grid indexes)	Spatial reference identifier	Int
pk0...n	Primary key(s) of the base table	Depends on key column(s) data type

This internal table contains a multicolumn clustered index on the *cell_id* and 1-to-n primary key *(pk1...pkn)* columns of the base table.

The *AUTO_GRID* spatial index in SQL Server 2012 gives slightly different names to the columns in the internal table (which are opaque to the programmer). The first two columns are named *Id* and *Attr* respectively, and the table has no *SRID* column. SQL Server spatial indexes use the *SRID* column to optimize the condition that a spatial data type method executed via two different *SRIDs* (for example, *@a.STIntersects(@b)*, where *@a* and *@b* are spatial features with different *SRIDs*) always returns *NULL*. *SRID* is the spatial reference identifier property of the spatial feature. For more information on *SRIDs*, refer to *SQL Server Books Online*.

For *GEOMETRY_GRID* and *GEOGRAPHY_GRID*, the *Cell_id* is a binary field encoded as L1.L2.L3.L4.D, where L1-L4 represents the cell number. (Remember that the lowest grid density is 16x16 = 256 cells, so with four grid levels, cell *2.4.12.1*—at level 4—would equate to *02 04 0C 01 04*.) The cell *2.4.12* at level 3 would equate to *02 04 0C 00 03*, noting that level number (3) would be used to distinguish between a cell at level 3 and cell 0 at level 4. The encoding for the *AUTO_GRID Cell_id* is slightly different because the density is fixed and eight grid levels are supported. The encoding uses the whole topmost byte for the first level (which is high-density) and half of one byte for each of the next seven grid levels (which are low-density), and then encodes level-number-plus-one in the last half byte. So the cell *2.4.12* at level 3 would be *02 4C 00 00 04*, and cell *0.0.0.0.0.0.0.0* at level 8 would be *00 00 00 00 09*. Notice that the *Cell_id* for the *AUTO_GRID* still occupies 5 bytes, like the *Cell_id* for *GEOMETRY_GRID* and *GEOGRAPHY_GRID*.

Whereas the *Cell_id* provides a primary filter for the spatial query, the *Cell_Attributes* column provides an additional internal filter. This column is an enumeration and can have the following values.

- **0** The spatial feature "touches" inside or outside the cell's border within floating-point precision.

- **1** The spatial feature partially covers the cell.

- **2** The spatial feature completely covers the cell.

The internal filter refers to the optimization that, if you're attempting to see whether A intersects B, or if either A or B completely covers the cell and the other feature partially or completely covers the cell, no computation needs to be done. The answer to "does A intersect B?" is always true.

Remember that the spatial index is only a primary filter; it doesn't actually produce the rowset that is the answer. Instead, it produces "candidate rows." The primary filter can produce false positives (because when the expensive *STIntersects()* query runs, the false positives are eliminated) but never false negatives, because *STIntersects()* is never run on rows eliminated by the primary filter.

How a spatial query uses a spatial index

Spatial queries use spatial indexes only for certain spatial predicates. The spatial index is only used with queries that contain the following spatial predicates.

- *geometry1.STContains(geometry2) = 1*

- *geometry1.STDistance(geometry2) < number*

- *geometry1.STDistance(geometry2) <= number*

- *geometry1.STEquals(geometry2) = 1*

- *geometry1.STIntersects(geometry2) = 1*

- *geometry1.STOverlaps(geometry2) = 1*

- *geometry1.STTouches(geometry2) = 1*

- *geometry1.STWithin(geometry2) = 1*

> **Note** In either form of *STDistance()* predicate, for geography, at least one geography argument (*geography1* or *geography2*) must specify a geography instance that represents a point. Otherwise, the spatial index isn't used. To use the spatial index, each of these methods is rewritten in terms of *STIntersects()* for the purpose of eliminating rows in the primary filter.

The query optimizer chooses whether to use a spatial index and, if more than one spatial index exists, which spatial index to use. Inside the query processor are three internal query optimizations that involve rewriting the query plan to use spatial indexes, as mentioned in *sys.dm_exec_query_transformation_stats*.

- *SpatialIntersectFilterOverGridIndex*

- *SpatialJointoApply*

- *SpatialNearestNeighbor*

The nearest neighbor optimization is new in SQL Server 2012. The *SpatialIntersectFilterOverGridIndex* and *SpatialJoinToApply* optimizations refer to cases where a table and a variable or two tables containing spatial columns are being joined by using one of these predicates. The query optimizer doesn't always choose the correct spatial index; if multiple spatial indexes exist, you can also use table hints or query hints to choose a spatial index.

How to ensure that your spatial index is being used

Use of a spatial index with a large or complex spatial dataset can mean the difference between a query that takes minutes to execute and sub-second execution. You can use an index hint as a last resort. If the spatial index isn't being used, you can resort to the following query rewrite hints.

- Make the query as uncomplicated as possible. Don't try to combine *STIntersects()* with a call to *STBuffer()*, *MakeValid()*, or other nested spatial method calls or subqueries. Use multiple statements, if needed.

- Don't use a string version (using spatial well-known text) directly in a spatial query or as a parameter to a stored procedure using a spatial data type. The optimizer needs the spatial form or the parameter for estimation and index determination, not the string form.

- Use a stored procedure or *sp_executesql* around the spatial query to ensure that the query optimizer "knows" the parameter value when it's creating the query plan. This is known as *parameter sniffing*. The parameter value must be known at beginning of the batch or on entry to a stored procedure or *sp_executesql*.

- If you're using client code, be sure to use a parameterized query that passes the value in *SqlParameterCollection*. Database APIs change this query into a call that uses *sp_executesql*.

- Check the query plan (an actual or estimated plan will work) to ensure that the index is being used. The Spatial Index step in the query plan is easy to locate, as you'll see later in this chapter.

Listing 9-2 shows an example that uses the *zipcodes* table from the *census* sample database to illustrate different ways of phrasing the query.

LISTING 9-2 Phrasing the query in different ways

```
-- does not always (pre-2008 SP1) use the spatial index without a hint
DECLARE @latlonPoint geometry = geometry::Parse('POINT (45.518066 -122.767464)');
SELECT a.id, a.shape.STAsText()
FROM zipcodes a
WHERE a.shape.STIntersects(@latlonPoint)=1;
go
-- this does use the spatial index without using a hint
DECLARE @latlonPoint geometry = geometry::Parse('POINT (45.518066 -122.767464)');
EXECUTE sp_executesql
N'SELECT a.id, a.shape.STAsText()
FROM zipcodes a
WHERE a.shape.STIntersects(@latlonPoint)=1', N'@latlonPoint geometry', @latlonPoint;
go
-- so does this
CREATE PROCEDURE find_zipcode (@g geometry)
AS
SELECT a.id, a.shape.STAsText()
FROM zipcodes a
WHERE a.shape.STIntersects(@g)=1;
go
DECLARE @latlonPoint geometry = geometry::Parse('POINT (45.518066 -122.767464)');
EXECUTE find_zipcode @latlonPoint;
```

To summarize, using a stored procedure or parameterized query with *sp_executesql* is better to allow the query processor to have the best chance of using the spatial index.

Spatial query plans and spatial indexes

All query plans that use spatial indexes follow roughly the same pattern for the spatial part of the query. An as example, the following spatial query produces the plan shown in Figure 9-5.

```
DECLARE @latlonPoint geometry = geometry::Parse('POINT (45.518066 -122.767464)');
EXECUTE sp_executesql
N'SELECT a.id, a.shape.STAsText()
FROM zipcodes a
WHERE a.shape.STIntersects(@latlonPoint)=1',
N'@latlonPoint geometry', @latlonPoint;
```

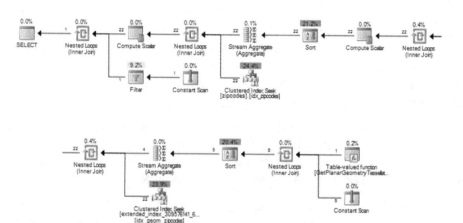

FIGURE 9-5 Query plan that uses a spatial index.

Now you can go over the spatial part of the query plan, iterator by iterator. Starting at the top right iterator, the table-valued function [*GetPlanarGeometryTessellation_Varbinary*] is invoked to tessellate the side of the spatial join that doesn't use the index. Note that SQL Server can use only one spatial index on one table in a query plan, even if both tables have a spatial index. The other table or spatial feature (known as the query sample) is tessellated, and a set of cells is produced. This is the same internal tessellation routine that's used to create a spatial index. If the geometry data type is used, the bounding box is set up to match the spatial index's bounding box.

When *GEOMETRY_GRID* or *GEOGRAPHY_GRID* is used, the grid levels are set to match the spatial index and *MAX_CELLS* is hardcoded to 1024 cells per object. When the *AUTO_GRID*s are used, *MAX_CELLS* can be hinted with the *SPATIAL_WINDOW_MAX_CELLS* query hint. The default *MAX_CELLS* parameter is 512 for *GEOMETRY* and 768 for *GEOGRAPHY*. Higher values make the spatial index steps more efficient but slower. Lower values make the spatial index steps faster, but more time is spent in the secondary filter because of potentially poorer index efficiency, with the optimum somewhere in between. For denser spatial index in the table or variable (query sample), a higher number should give better execution time; for sparser spatial data, a lower number should give better execution time. Values from 1 to 8192 are permitted. Using the *SPATIAL_WINDOW_MAX_CELLS* hint doesn't guarantee that the spatial index will be used.

The tessellation iterator returns a set of *cell_id* and *cell_attributes* columns, but before using these to seek into the spatial index, all the descendant cells and ancestor cells must be retrieved. All descendant cells are part of the same index range seek on the spatial index, which is accomplished by creating a table with five rows with a *ConstantScan* operator, using the *getdescendantlimitforspatialbinary* and *getancestorforspatialbinary* internal functions. Notice that these routines are similar to the routines used in XML query plans to get descendants of selected XML nodes—that is, the hierarchical nature of the spatial index levels is used in the calculations. An *Inner Join (nested loops inner join,* in this case) gets all the descendant and ancestor cells, and then the set of cells is sorted and grouped to remove duplicates. You now have your input to the spatial index step.

The spatial index is accessed with the sets of cells produced by all the previous steps using a range seek. The range seek predicates are based on the set of cells produced by the input query sample (*JOIN*ed table, in this case) >= *getdescendantlimitforspatialbinary* and <= *getancestorforspatialbinary.* This is known as the primary filter step. The output from the inner join that uses the spatial index is the set of candidate cells. The set at this point contains the primary key or keys (of the spatial table) and the *cell_attributes* for each candidate cell. The *cell_attributes* column is converted to a *tinyint data type.* The rows are then sorted and grouped by primary key(s).

Now that you have a set and candidate cells sorted by primary key(s), you need to join back to the base table for each cell (row) to obtain the spatial column to apply the *STIntersect()* operation. This is done with a seek on the clustered index. In this case, because you're doing only 22 seeks, a *Nested Loop* join is used. The key column, spatial column, and *cell_attribute* column are returned.

The *Filter* iterator implements the secondary filter (*STIntersects()*) by applying the *STIntersects()* spatial operator to each row. Before the expensive spatial operation is performed, the *cell_attribute* is consulted to see whether the filter can return just "true" because one or both sides overlap an entire cell (see the earlier description of *cell_attributes*). Note that although 22 candidate rows are chosen, only one row actually satisfies the spatial predicate. That one row is returned as the answer.

To wrap up the description of this query plan that uses a spatial index, notice that the effectiveness of the spatial index is based on how many rows it eliminates. If many candidate cells are available, the join back to the base table by the primary cell is much more expensive, as is the actually spatial calculation (*STIntersects()* in this case). If a large percentage of the rows survive the primary filter, an entire scan of the base table would be necessary. In this case, using a scan and filter on all rows might be cheaper. Also, the more processors are available for the scan and filter, the less likely the spatial index will be chosen. Finally, because NULL values in a spatial column slow down spatial index queries, you should use default values instead, if at all possible.

If the same spatial column has more than one spatial index, the query optimizer doesn't have enough information to choose effectively which spatial index to use. In this case, hinting the more effective spatial index would be necessary, if this can be determined based on input.

Nearest neighbor optimization in SQL Server 2012

The nearest neighbor query is one of the most common queries against spatial data. The common use case is in a mapping application that, given the user's current location, wants to return a screen's worth of nearest points of interest (such as closest restaurants). The obvious way to phrase the spatial query for a TOP 10 restaurant query, given a *STDistance()* method on the geography data column, would be

```
DECLARE @me geography = 'POINT (-121.626 47.8315)';
SELECT TOP(10) Location, Description, Location.STDistance(@me) AS distance
FROM [spatial_table]
ORDER BY distance;
```

Unfortunately in pre-SQL Server 2012 versions, this query doesn't use the spatial index, and the performance of such a query is slow. Attempting to hint the spatial index results in Error Msg 8622:

```
Query processor could not produce a query plan because of the hints defined in this query.
Resubmit the query without specifying any hints and without using SET FORCEPLAN.
```

SQL Server 2012 includes a new query optimization in its engine that allows use of the spatial index in a nearest neighbor query. To use the spatial index, the query must contain a predicate that refers to *STDistance()*:

```
...FROM [spatial_table]
WHERE Location.STDistance(@me) < 1000 -- 'where-distance' query
ORDER BY distance;
```

The predicate doesn't necessarily have to include a maximum distance, like in the preceding example, but it can be something as unobtrusive as

```
...FROM [spatial_table]
WHERE Location.STDistance(@me) IS NOT NULL -- 'where is not null' query
ORDER BY distance;
```

This uses the spatial index without hinting, with the resulting order of magnitude increase in speed. As an example, the following query produces the plan shown in Figure 9-6.

```
CREATE PROCEDURE dbo.Top5LimitDistance (@g1 geography)
AS
SELECT TOP(5) SpatialLocation.ToString(), City
FROM Person.Address
WHERE SpatialLocation.STDistance(@g1) < 100000
ORDER BY SpatialLocation.STDistance(@g1)
GO

DECLARE @g geography = 'POINT(-121.626 47.8315)';
EXECUTE dbo.Top5LimitDistance @g;
GO
```

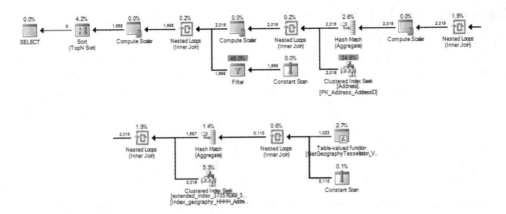

FIGURE 9-6 Query plan showing the SQL Server 2012 nearest neighbor optimization.

The nearest neighbor optimization happens after all the rows are selected, so that portion of the query plan is identical to the spatial index query plan in the preceding *JOIN* example. A *TOP N Sort* iterator, using the spatial predicate in the *ORDER BY* clause (*ORDER BY SpatialLocation. STDistance(@g)*, in this case), eliminates the superfluous rows.

You can, however, rewrite the nearest neighbor query by using a numbers table that was used prior to SQL Server 2012. This query rewrite might, in some cases, produce better results than the nearest neighbor optimization, as shown in Figure 9-7.

```
DECLARE @start FLOAT = 1000;
DECLARE @g geography = 'POINT(-121.626 47.8315)';
WITH NearestPoints AS
(
    SELECT TOP(5) SpatialLocation.ToString() loc, City, SpatialLocation.STDistance(@g) as dist, n
    FROM dbo.numbers
    JOIN Person.Address T with (index=Index_geography_HHHH_Address)
    ON T.SpatialLocation.STDistance(@g) < @start*POWER(2,dbo.numbers.n)
    ORDER BY dbo.numbers.n
)
SELECT * FROM NearestPoints
ORDER BY n, dist;
```

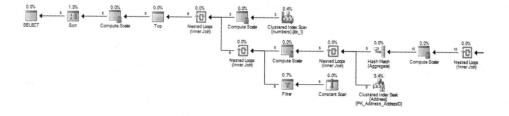

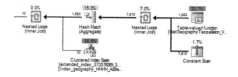

FIGURE 9-7 Query plan for an alternate way to do nearest neighbor queries (it doesn't use the nearest neighbor optimization).

Notice that with this type of query rewrite, you must hint the spatial index. So how does this algorithm do against the new, automatic spatial index use plan? The plan cost for this simple example where I tried this out is as follows:

- Query rewrite and hint: 0.517

- SQL Server 2012 with *WHERE* and *distance*: 4.06683

- SQL Server 2012 with *WHERE ... IS NOT NULL*: 14.7

However, the differences in query plans that involve spatial don't always seem to be relevant because the query optimizer sometimes underestimates the big difference that using the spatial index will make. Both the SQL Server 2012 nearest neighbor optimization and the query rewrite yield sub-second responses, compared to 10 seconds or so responses when not using the index. So instead, try comparing I/O or worker time for the optimization versus the rewrite.

- Query rewrite and hint: 1x worker time/reads/clrtime

- SQL Server 2012 with *WHERE* and *distance*: 10x worker time/reads/clrtime

- SQL Server 2012 with *WHERE ... IS NOT NULL*: 3x worker time/reads/clrtime

Apparently, even though the query is far less straightforward to write and the spatial index needs to be hinted, the numbers table query rewrite method wins in this case.

Spatial index diagnostic stored procedures

The spatial index definition provides a series of parameters, including auto-grid versus four-level density-specific grid, 83 different density choices, and a great range of CELLS_PER_OBJECT specifications. Unfortunately, spatial index selection isn't among the recommendations supported by the Database Tuning Advisor program. This leaves the spatial index author with little to go by but intuition when attempting to determine the index parameter specification. However, SQL Server does provide a set of system stored procedures and functions that allow you to deduce the effectiveness of a single spatial index and query sample combination. You can use these procedures, along with a couple of common-sense best practices at the end of this section, to choose the best spatial index parameters.

The information that the spatial index procedures provide consists of three main categories.

- Information about the index itself

- Information about the query sample

- The efficiency of the query index when used against the query sample

Because queries can use a spatial index against only one side of a spatial query, the term *query sample* refers to the side of the spatial query (individual spatial feature or spatial column in a table) that doesn't use the spatial index. That sample must be tessellated during the query.

Each spatial data type has a set of spatial index diagnostic procedures. The *sp_help_spatial_geometry_index* and *sp_help_spatial_geography_index* system procedures output information as columns, and the *sp_help_spatial_geometry_index_xml* and *sp_help_spatial_geography_index_xml* output XML. Each procedure takes a table name, index name, and sample query. An option for verbose or basic properties is also available. First, you should walk through a problem to see how to interpret the output.

Suppose that you are trying to decide between an index with all-high (known as HHHH) and all-medium (known as MMMM) density to run a query similar to the following:

```
DECLARE @geometry geometry =
 geometry::STGeomFromText('POLYGON((500000 300000,500000 340000,540000 340000,540000
300000,500000 300000))', 0);
EXECUTE sp_executesql
N'select * from spatial_table where LOCATION.STIntersects(@g) = 1', N'@g geometry', @geometry
```

You would create (or have the customer create) both indexes and run the procedure against each one, using the sample query. Here's example code to analyze the "all-medium" spatial index:

```
CREATE SPATIAL INDEX [idx_mmmm] ON dbo.spatial_table(spatial_column)
USING GEOMETRY_GRID
WITH (BOUNDING_BOX =(0, 0, 1000000, 1000000),
GRIDS = (LEVEL_1 = MEDIUM,LEVEL_2 = MEDIUM,LEVEL_3 = MEDIUM,LEVEL_4 = MEDIUM),
CELLS_PER_OBJECT = 1024);
go

Declare @geometry geometry =
 geometry::STGeomFromText('POLYGON((500000 300000,500000 340000,540000 340000,540000
```

```
300000,500000 300000))', 0)
DECLARE @x xml;
EXEC sp_help_spatial_geometry_index_xml 'dbo.spatial_table', 'idx_mmmm', 1, @geometry, @x
output;
SELECT @x -- copy output and save as an XML file
GO
```

The XML output produced would look something like Listing 9-3.

LISTING 9-3 Output of the *sp_help_geometry_index_xml* system stored procedure

```
<Base_Table_Rows>511650</Base_Table_Rows>
<Bounding_Box_xmin>4.100000000000000e+005</Bounding_Box_xmin>
<Bounding_Box_ymin>3.580000000000000e+004</Bounding_Box_ymin>
<Bounding_Box_xmax>9.450000000000000e+005</Bounding_Box_xmax>
<Bounding_Box_ymax>3.800000000000000e+005</Bounding_Box_ymax>
<Grid_Size_Level_1>64</Grid_Size_Level_1>
<Grid_Size_Level_2>64</Grid_Size_Level_2>
<Grid_Size_Level_3>64</Grid_Size_Level_3>
<Grid_Size_Level_4>64</Grid_Size_Level_4>
<Cells_Per_Object>16</Cells_Per_Object>
<Total_Primary_Index_Rows>1965865</Total_Primary_Index_Rows>
<Total_Primary_Index_Pages>6827</Total_Primary_Index_Pages>
<Average_Number_Of_Index_Rows_Per_Base_Row>3</Average_Number_Of_Index_Rows_Per_Base_Row>
<Total_Number_Of_ObjectCells_In_Level0_In_Index>20</Total_Number_Of_ObjectCells_In_Level0_In_
Index>
<Total_Number_Of_ObjectCells_In_Level2_For_QuerySample>24</Total_Number_Of_ObjectCells_In_
Level2_For_QuerySample>
<Total_Number_Of_ObjectCells_In_Level2_In_Index>6</Total_Number_Of_ObjectCells_In_Level2_In_
Index>
<Total_Number_Of_ObjectCells_In_Level3_For_QuerySample>834</Total_Number_Of_ObjectCells_In_
Level3_For_QuerySample>
<Total_Number_Of_ObjectCells_In_Level3_In_Index>19436</Total_Number_Of_ObjectCells_In_Level3_In_
Index>
<Total_Number_Of_ObjectCells_In_Level4_For_QuerySample>163</Total_Number_Of_ObjectCells_In_
Level4_For_QuerySample>
<Total_Number_Of_ObjectCells_In_Level4_In_Index>1946403</Total_Number_Of_ObjectCells_In_Level4_
In_Index>
<Total_Number_Of_Interior_ObjectCells_In_Level2_For_QuerySample>24</Total_Number_Of_Interior_
ObjectCells_In_Level2_For_QuerySample>
<Total_Number_Of_Interior_ObjectCells_In_Level3_For_QuerySample>647</Total_Number_Of_Interior_
ObjectCells_In_Level3_For_QuerySample>
<Total_Number_Of_Interior_ObjectCells_In_Level4_For_QuerySample>96</Total_Number_Of_Interior_
ObjectCells_In_Level4_For_QuerySample>
<Total_Number_Of_Intersecting_ObjectCells_In_Level2_In_Index>6</Total_Number_Of_Intersecting_
ObjectCells_In_Level2_In_Index>
<Total_Number_Of_Intersecting_ObjectCells_In_Level3_For_QuerySample>187</Total_Number_Of_
Intersecting_ObjectCells_In_Level3_For_QuerySample>
<Total_Number_Of_Intersecting_ObjectCells_In_Level3_In_Index>18021</Total_Number_Of_
Intersecting_ObjectCells_In_Level3_In_Index>
<Total_Number_Of_Intersecting_ObjectCells_In_Level4_For_QuerySample>67</Total_Number_Of_
Intersecting_ObjectCells_In_Level4_For_QuerySample>
<Total_Number_Of_Intersecting_ObjectCells_In_Level4_In_Index>1893267</Total_Number_Of_
Intersecting_ObjectCells_In_Level4_In_Index>
<Total_Number_Of_Border_ObjectCells_In_Level0_In_Index>20</Total_Number_Of_Border_ObjectCells_
In_Level0_In_Index>
```

```
<Total_Number_Of_Border_ObjectCells_In_Level3_In_Index>1415</Total_Number_Of_Border_ObjectCells_
In_Level3_In_Index>
<Total_Number_Of_Border_ObjectCells_In_Level4_In_Index>53136</Total_Number_Of_Border_
ObjectCells_In_Level4_In_Index>
<Interior_To_Total_Cells_Normalized_To_Leaf_Grid_Percentage>1.801159496425824e-001</Interior_To_
Total_Cells_Normalized_To_Leaf_Grid_Percentage>
<Intersecting_To_Total_Cells_Normalized_To_Leaf_Grid_Percentage>1.257059231880523e-001</
Intersecting_To_Total_Cells_Normalized_To_Leaf_Grid_Percentage>
<Border_To_Total_Cells_Normalized_To_Leaf_Grid_Percentage>9.969417812716937e+001</Border_To_
Total_Cells_Normalized_To_Leaf_Grid_Percentage>
<Average_Cells_Per_Object_Normalized_To_Leaf_Grid>1.041708198964136e-001</Average_Cells_Per_
Object_Normalized_To_Leaf_Grid>
<Average_Objects_PerLeaf_GridCell>9.599617253607010e+000</Average_Objects_PerLeaf_GridCell>
<Number_Of_SRIDs_Found>1</Number_Of_SRIDs_Found>
<Width_Of_Cell_In_Level1>8.359375000000000e+003</Width_Of_Cell_In_Level1>
<Width_Of_Cell_In_Level2>1.306152343750000e+002</Width_Of_Cell_In_Level2>
<Width_Of_Cell_In_Level3>2.040863037109375e+000</Width_Of_Cell_In_Level3>
<Width_Of_Cell_In_Level4>3.188848495483398e-002</Width_Of_Cell_In_Level4>
<Height_Of_Cell_In_Level1>5.378125000000000e+003</Height_Of_Cell_In_Level1>
<Height_Of_Cell_In_Level2>8.403320312500000e+001</Height_Of_Cell_In_Level2>
<Height_Of_Cell_In_Level3>1.313018798828125e+000</Height_Of_Cell_In_Level3>
<Height_Of_Cell_In_Level4>2.051591873168945e-002</Height_Of_Cell_In_Level4>
<Area_Of_Cell_In_Level1>2.877296875000000e+009</Area_Of_Cell_In_Level1>
<Area_Of_Cell_In_Level2>4.495776367187500e+007</Area_Of_Cell_In_Level2>
<Area_Of_Cell_In_Level3>7.024650573730469e+005</Area_Of_Cell_In_Level3>
<Area_Of_Cell_In_Level4>1.097601652145386e+004</Area_Of_Cell_In_Level4>
<CellArea_To_BoundingBoxArea_Percentage_In_Level1>1.562500000000000e+000</CellArea_To_
BoundingBoxArea_Percentage_In_Level1>
<CellArea_To_BoundingBoxArea_Percentage_In_Level2>2.441406250000000e-002</CellArea_To_
BoundingBoxArea_Percentage_In_Level2>
<CellArea_To_BoundingBoxArea_Percentage_In_Level3>3.814697265625000e-004</CellArea_To_
BoundingBoxArea_Percentage_In_Level3>
<CellArea_To_BoundingBoxArea_Percentage_In_Level4>5.960464477539063e-006</CellArea_To_
BoundingBoxArea_Percentage_In_Level4>
<Number_Of_Rows_Selected_By_Primary_Filter>2931</Number_Of_Rows_Selected_By_Primary_Filter>
<Number_Of_Rows_Selected_By_Internal_Filter>2666</Number_Of_Rows_Selected_By_Internal_Filter>
<Number_Of_Times_Secondary_Filter_Is_Called>265</Number_Of_Times_Secondary_Filter_Is_Called>
<Number_Of_Rows_Output>2779</Number_Of_Rows_Output>
<Percentage_Of_Rows_NotSelected_By_Primary_Filter>9.942714746408677e+001</Percentage_Of_Rows_
NotSelected_By_Primary_Filter>
<Percentage_Of_Primary_Filter_Rows_Selected_By_Internal_Filter>9.095871716137836e+001</
Percentage_Of_Primary_Filter_Rows_Selected_By_Internal_Filter>
<Internal_Filter_Efficiency>9.593378913278158e+001</Internal_Filter_Efficiency>
<Primary_Filter_Efficiency>9.481405663596043e+001</Primary_Filter_Efficiency>
```

Note The counts in this example are taken from a SQL Server 2008 invocation of this procedure. SQL Server 2012 currently contains a bug in this stored procedure that produces slightly higher—and technically incorrect—counts, although the general concepts (figuring out which spatial index parameters are optimal) still apply.

The most useful data is contained in the "Number of rows selected by ... filter" properties and filter efficiency properties. In this case, they were as follows:

- High-density index:

  Number_Of_Rows_Selected_By_Primary_Filter   2931

  Number_Of_Rows_Selected_By_Internal_Filter   2399

  Number_Of_Times_Secondary_Filter_Is_Called   532

- Medium-density index:

  Number_Of_Rows_Selected_By_Primary_Filter   2931

  Number_Of_Rows_Selected_By_Internal_Filter   2666

  Number_Of_Times_Secondary_Filter_Is_Called   265

Notice that "primary filter" in this case is the spatial index in question. The goal is to have the rows selected by the primary or internal filter rather than run the secondary filter (the actual *STIntersects()* operation). Note that false positives can result, but not false negatives, and the actual number of rows returned wasn't 2931 but 2779.

The best way to judge the effectiveness of the index, however, is with the property *Internal_Filter_Efficiency* or *Primary_Filter_Efficiency*. *Internal_Filter_Efficiency*, for example, showed the high-density index at 86 percent and the medium-density index at 96 percent. Clearly, the medium-density index is a better choice for this query. Also, looking at the statistics on the index itself shows that the medium-density index is a smaller index with fewer rows and index rows per base row. The figures were as follows:

- High density:

  Total_Primary_Index_Rows   5273534

  Average_Number_Of_Index_Rows_Per_Base_Row 10

- Medium density:

  Total_Primary_Index_Rows   1965865

  Average_Number_Of_Index_Rows_Per_Base_Row 3

A *Total_Number_Of_ObjectCells_In_Level0_For_QuerySample* property tells you whether the index can be used. Level 0 indicates that the query sample you've chosen is outside the bounds of the bounding box. A non-zero value indicates that you should adjust the bounding box on a geometry index, because all Level 0 cells can't be eliminated by either the primary or secondary filter.

The spatial index diagnostic procedures' most enlightening pieces of information have to do with the filter counts and efficiencies reported at the end of the set of columns or XML document output.

But what are these filters exactly and what do the results mean? The procedure output refers to three filters:

- Primary filter
- Internal filter
- Secondary filter

Remember also that the point of a spatial index is to reduce the number of *Intersect* operations (or other operations covered by the spatial index) actually performed by using tiling. The "secondary filter" in this case is the *STIntersects* operation itself. Now, if you think of the primary filter as filtering 100 polygons out of 10,000, the query would still have to process an *Intersects* operation on the 100 polygons to actually see if they qualify. But suppose that the index and query sample both *completely* cover a cell, or the index completely covers the cell and the query sample touches it. You know that because the cell qualifies for *STIntersects*, you don't need to run *Intersect* on the query sample for that combination. That's the internal filter.

Now look at some sample output. In this case, the index was over a geography column that contains only points. The query sample is a polygon.

```
Base_Table_Rows                                  511650
Number_Of_Rows_Selected_By_Primary_Filter        2931
Number_Of_Rows_Selected_By_Internal_Filter       2666
Number_Of_Times_Secondary_Filter_Is_Called       265
Number_Of_Rows_Output                             2779
```

This means that you start with 511650 rows in the table. Using the index (primary filter) eliminates all but 2931 of them. The internal filter determines that 2666 are true hits, not false positive. They have to run *Intersect* 265 times (2931 - 2666) times. Because the number of rows returned is 2779, some false positives occurred. Using the method *Filter()* instead of *STIntersect()* just means returning all the rows selected by the primary filter (2931).

Finally, remember that a *GEOGRAPHY* index has no bounding box, so no part of the rows or query sample can be outside the index. With *GEOMETRY*, some of the rows or query samples can be outside the bounding box. This means that with *GEOGRAPHY*, *Rows_Selected_By_Primary_Filter* must be greater than or equal to the *Number_Of_Rows_Output*. With *GEOMETRY*, *Number_Of_Rows_Output* also can be greater than *Rows_Selected_By_Primary_Filter*.

The procedures report some raw numbers and some derived numbers. The formula used to compute these numbers is documents. Suppose that:

N = Number of rows in the table

O = Number of rows output

P = Number of rows selected by primary filter (by the index)

S = Number of rows selected by internal filter (by the index optimizations)

Then:

P-S = *Number_Of_Times_Secondary_Filter_Is_Called* (number of times the expensive operation ran)

(N-P)/N = *Percentage_Of_Rows_NotSelected_By_Primary_Filter*

S/P = *Percenage_Of_Primary_Filter_Rows_Selected_By_internal_Filter*

S/O = *Internal_Filter_Efficiency_%*

O/P = *Primary_Filter_Efficiency_%*

Now, see how you would choose the query sample procedure parameter in common spatial index use cases. The query sample is a singleton *GEOMETRY* or *GEOGRAPHY*; it can't contain multiple values. It maps most closely when your query is something like the following:

```
SELECT ... FROM tablea a
WHERE a.geog.STIntersects(@g)=1;
```

In this case, *@g* is your query sample, and *Number_Of_Output_Rows* is the number of rows the query returns. But what if you have a conditional query or query that has more than one row as output, like the following?

```
SELECT ...
FROM tablea a
JOIN tableb b
ON a.id = @someid AND b.geog.STIntersects(a.geog)=1;
```

In this case, you could specify your query sample like this:

```
DECLARE @my_query_sample geography = (select geog from tablea a where a.id = @someid);
```

To produce a representative singleton, you could use

```
SELECT @my_query_sample = a.geog
FROM tablea a, tableb b
WHERE a.id = @someid AND b.geog.STIntersects(a.geog)=1;
```

Now realize that you will have to perform this operation (represented by the output) against an aggregate of all the rows that actually satisfy the spatial join. To understand this better, you can work an example query that uses a spatial join, to answer the question, "Which spatial index is a better candidate for a spatial index usage in this spatial join?" This join is looking at two tables with spatial columns, *zipcodes* and *points*, to determine which postal codes intersect with which points. A *WHERE* clause limits *zipcodes* to postal codes in the state of Oregon (*'OR'*):

```
SELECT a.zipcode, b.point
FROM zipcodes a, points b
WHERE a.zipcode IN (SELECT zipcode FROM zipcodes WHERE state = 'OR')
AND a.geog.STIntersects(b.geog)=1;
```

So, which index on which spatial table is the best one to use? Oregon has 430 postal codes. Your table has 1000 points. You have an index on *zipcodes* and one on *points*. Remember that *STIntersects()* is commutative (*a.geog.STIntersects(b.geog) = b.geog.STIntersects(a.geog)*). Which index is "better"? Notice that the query returns one column from *zipcodes* and one column from *points*, so you can't just use *STUnion()* to join all the Oregon postal codes together. You'd get the same points that way but have no idea which postal code goes with which point. So your choices are as follows.

- Use a representative query sample for *zipcodes* in Oregon, analyze the spatial index on the point table, and realize that you will do this "query" over an aggregate of 430 rows:

```
DECLARE @my_query_sample geography =
  (SELECT TOP(1) geog FROM zipcodes a
    WHERE a.zipcode IN (SELECT zipcode FROM zipcodes WHERE state = 'OR') );
```

- Use a representative query sample for the point table, analyze the spatial index on the *zipcode* table, and realize that you will do this "query" over an aggregate of 1,000 rows:

```
DECLARE @my_query_sample geography = (SELECT TOP(1) geog FROM points);
```

Be aware that doing 430 or 1,000 seeks against the spatial index might keep the query optimizer from choosing that plan with the spatial index. You could also declare your query sample like this:

```
DECLARE @geog geography;
SELECT @geog = a.geog -- or @geog = b.geog
FROM zipcodes a, points b
WHERE a.zipcode IN (SELECT zipcode FROM zipcodes WHERE state = 'OR')
AND a.geog.STIntersects(b.geog)=1
```

But that still will give you one representative combination point or postal code as a query sample (for example, *@geog* is still a singleton). If all your points are in Oregon, it will produce a similar analytic output, and if all your points aren't in Oregon, specifying it that way might be better. But then you would have to know how many points in Oregon to deduce how many seeks, and you can't check the output against *Number_Of_Rows_Returned* because you don't know which row it actually chose.

If you need just points, not *zipcode-point* combinations, you could use a spatial *geography::UnionAggregate* of all the *zipcodes* in Oregon and run the query that way. The spatial analysis procedures give you a 1-1 mapping against that query. Alternatively, you can use a *state* table rather than a *zipcode* table. Of course, this assumes that postal codes don't overlap multiple states.

Finally, you get detailed information about the index. Some, but not all, of the information is available in the spatial index metadata, but having this information in the stored procedure output is also handy.

- **Bounding Box dimensions** are for geography but are always -180, -90, 180, and 90.

- *GridLevelSize* is at four levels.

- *Cells_Per_Object* is the maximum tessellated cells per row as specified in DDL.

- **Page and row counts** are for the spatial index.

- **Average number of cells per base row** determines how many of the *Cells_Per_Object* were actually used.

- **Geography** means *Height, Width, and Area* of a cell are always the same.

- ***CellAreaToBoundingBox* percentage** is at 4 levels.

- ***SRIDs*** should be the total found.

The most interesting is likely the info about the number of cells in each level (including level0 of the bounding box). Any levels that are 0 rows don't appear in the XML output. You get info for the following.

- Number of object cells for index

- Number of interior cells

- Number of intersecting cells

- Number of border cells

This information, which summarizes *cell_attribute* counts in the internal table, constitutes the internal filter.

Diagnostics with the SQL Server 2012 spatial functions

The primary purpose of *sp_help_spatial_geometry_histogram* and *sp_help_spatial_geography_histogram* (both new in SQL Server 2012) is to understand data distribution and help determine, in general, what type of spatial index and spatial index hint you can use to get optimum performance. The results from these system procedures could be put into a table and saved as a high-level histogram or used to provide an in-depth analysis to suggest grid resolutions when using *GEOMETRY_GRID* or *GEOGRAPHY_GRID*.

Looking at spatial data visually is a good way to start solving a spatial indexing problem. Although spatial index diagnostic stored procedures can yield many numeric statistics about the index and its usage, this might be a tedious way to choose the best spatial index. Using these system stored procedures can provide a quick way to visualize the gridding produced by different spatial index parameters. When the grid information is *UNION*ed with the underlying spatial data set to be indexed, the spatial index programmer can use this visual representation to select appropriate spatial index parameters just by looking at the results.

You could also choose to define multiple spatial indexes on a single spatial column and, because the spatial data isn't uniformly distributed, decide which spatial index and *SPATIAL_WINDOW_MAX_CELLS* value to use query by query. A good example of this might be if you have different data densities in your base table for different counties in the United States. Because the states vary greatly in size, you might want to use different spatial indexes and *SPATIAL_WINDOW_MAX_CELLS*, depending on which state you were working with. You could also pre-join the spatial data to the output of the histogram stored procedures to record which index hints to use and use dynamic SQL to execute these queries.

Full-text indexes

Full-text indexes have been included in SQL Server since SQL Server 7.0, although they have changed drastically in implementation over the last few releases. In SQL Server 2008, the data structures for full-text search were brought into the database; before then, the full-text search indexes were run in instances of Microsoft Search Server. In SQL Server 2008, the index itself resides in the database as a set of internal tables, and most of the indexing and processing is done inside the SQL Server process. This section concentrates on the SQL Server 2012 implementation, which is similar to the SQL Server 2008 implementation with a number of performance enhancements and some additional features.

As opposed to XML and spatial data, full-text search is an optional component of SQL Server. It must be specifically installed to be used. Installing the full-text search component not only allows you to create full-text indexes but also installs a set of components needed for indexing and querying.

- The full-text search daemon launcher service (*MSSQLFDLauncher*) launches the process (FDHOST.exe) that hosts word breakers and filters.

- A series of language-specific processors (word breakers and stemmers) is used not only to populate the full-text index itself but also to parse the sets of words or phrases in a full-text predicate.

- A default set of language-specific stoplists is used in full-text index processing and with full-text predicates to eliminate noise words.

- A default (empty placeholder) set of language-specific thesaurus files is referenced by specifying the *THESAURUS* keyword in a full-text search query or by using a *FREETEXT* query. You also can use word substitution and specify word equivalences when searching.

- A series of processors for different document formats (filters) allows processing of different types of documents, such as XML files.

- You can search property lists. A full-text index can use a list of document properties (extended properties) to search on. No search property lists are provided; they must be manually created through DDL.

Each full-text search component (except for the service) can be extended with third-party or user-defined extensions.

First, look at how to create a full-text index. Full-text indexes reside in full-text catalogs. In SQL Server 2005 and earlier, full-text catalogs existed outside the database in separate files; in SQL Server 2008 and later, you can think of full-text catalogs as containers for sets of full-text indexes. Performing maintenance on a full-text catalog performs that operation on all the full-text indexes contained within it. You create a full-text catalog with the *CREATE FULLTEXT CATALOG DDL* statement, as follows:

```
CREATE FULLTEXT CATALOG ft
WITH ACCENT_SENSITIVITY = ON
AS DEFAULT;
```

This statement specifies a name for the catalog (*ft*, in this case), whether it's considered the default full-text catalog for that database, and whether all the catalog's full-text indexes are considered to be accent-sensitive. Now that the database has a full-text catalog, you can create full-text indexes within it.

You can create one full-text index per table or indexed view. The full-text index definition can refer to a specific full-text catalog or use the *DEFAULT* catalog, if it exists. The full-text index can index data in one or more columns of the following data types: *VARCHAR*, *NVARCHAR*, *CHAR*, *NCHAR*, and *VARBINARY(MAX)*. For backward compatibility, *TEXT*, *NTEXT*, and *IMAGE* data types can also be used. To create a full-text index, you specify the following.

- **Columns and column-based DDL keywords** The column-based DDL keywords include the *LANGUAGE* to use when creating the index on the column. Although you can specify a different *LANGUAGE* column by column, your full-text queries must use a single language (implicitly or explicitly) or an error will occur. The *STATISTICAL_SEMANTICS* keyword is used to enable Semantic Search feature by column, as covered in more detail in the section on semantic indexes at the end of this chapter.

- *TYPE COLUMN* If the column is a *VARBINARY(MAX)* column, an additional *TYPE_COLUMN* can be specified for that column. The *TYPE_COLUMN* indicates, per row, the type of document to be indexed. The appropriate filter is then used by row. Columns that aren't *VARBINARY* or columns without a *TYPE_COLUMN* specification use the parser for .txt documents.

- **Key index specification** The key index specification must refer to a unique key on the table. The key doesn't need to be clustering or primary. The default key index is the column (if it exists) that contains the *ROWGUIDCOL* property. Using a key index in the *INTERGRAL* series of data types—for example, *INTEGER* rather than the *UNIQUEIDENTIFIER* data type—is best for performance. It also changes the full-text index's internal structure and implementation slightly.

- *FILEGROUP* **specification** The *FILEGROUP* specification can be specified or default to the table's *DEFAULT FILEGROUP*. For a partitioned table, the full-text index uses the table's primary file group.

- *STOPLIST* **and** *SEARCHPROPERTY LIST* **specifications** Full-text indexes can specify a stoplist (other than the default) as well as a search property list. A default exists for the stoplist, but not for the default search property list. You can also specify that no stoplist be used.

- **Change tracking type** As opposed to other types of indexes that always stay transactionally in sync with the base table, full-text indexes are built asynchronously from the base table. You can choose between initial population and updating mechanisms. The updating mechanisms and initial population is specified by the change tracking keyword in *CREATE FULLTEXT INDEX* and can be changed in *ALTER FULLTEXT INDEX*.

You can populate a full-text index at creation time or manually populate it later. You can specify *NO POPULATION* (at creation time) only when you specify *CHANGE_TRACKING = OFF* in the *CREATE FULLTEXT INDEX* DDL statement. The other choices on the *CREATE FULLTEXT INDEX* DDL statement are *CHANGE_TRACKING=MANUAL* and *CHANGE_TRACKING=AUTO*. *CHANGE_TRACKING=AUTO*, the default, is the closest to the way other indexes work. However, even *AUTO* change tracking populates and refreshes full-text index rows asynchronously from DML or the DDL that triggers the population and doesn't comprise part of the *INSERT*, *UPDATE*, and *DELETE* query plan. However, transactional guarantees are available in some aspects.

A row is guaranteed to either be part of the full-text index or not. The full-text index guarantees that rows aren't partially indexed.

Rows aren't missed from processing as part of the full-text index population.

Here's an example DDL for creating a full-text index:

```
CREATE FULLTEXT INDEX ON dbo.Documents
    (file_stream TYPE COLUMN file_type LANGUAGE 1033)
          KEY INDEX DocumentsFt
          ON ft
WITH SEARCH PROPERTY LIST = DocumentProperties,
    CHANGE_TRACKING = AUTO,
    STOPLIST = SYSTEM;
```

This DDL statement creates a full-text index on the *dbo.Documents* table. This full-text index is contained within the *ft* full-text catalog. A single column of data type *VARBINARY(MAX)*, named *file_stream*, is indexed using language 1033 (US English). Because different kinds of documents can appear in the *file_stream* column, the *TYPE COLUMN* (named *file_type*) contains a document suffix that indicates which filter to use per row. The key index column (which must be a unique, single, non-nullable column) is named *DocumentsFt*. The full-text index uses the default system stoplist, and a search property list named *DocumentProperties*. The *CHANGE_TRACKING* parameter indicates that the full-text index is built when the DDL executes and is kept up to date automatically as rows are inserted, updated, and deleted.

Internal tables created by the full-text index

Creating a full-text index creates a set of internal tables, which are visible in the *sys.internal_tables* metadata view and are suffixed with the object ID of the base table. Note that the word *docid* is used in the names of many of the tables; a full-text index's *docid* refers to the key column of each row, if the key column is an integer. If the key column isn't an integer, an additional table—the *docid* map table—is present. If the key column is an integer, no *docidmap* internal table is available. The following sections provide short descriptions of each internal table, its column layout, and indexes.

ifts_comp_fragment_[t_objectid]_[ordinal]

This is the full-text inverted index. Multiple fragment tables can constitute the inverted index, with each fragment having a unique ordinal. It contains full-text keyword and property information and indicates which documents contain each keyword/property. Table 9-4 lists the columns.

TABLE 9-4 Columns of *ifts_comp_fragment_[t_objectid]_[ordinal]*

Column name	Column description	Data type
keyword	Keyword in binary format	VARBINARY(128)
Colid	Column ID (in base table)	INT
Pid	Unused	INT
docidmax	Maximum document ID where keyword appears	BIGINT
dupseq	The sequence number if this keyword has more than one row (duplicate rows)	INT
docidmin	Minimum document ID where key appears	BIGINT
lvl1cnt	Document count (number of documents in which the keyword appears)	BIGINT
complv1	Binary encoding of document IDs in which the keyword appears	VARBINARY(1024)
complv2	Binary encoding of offset in words in each document in which the keyword occurs	VARBINARY(1024)
comppid	Compressed encoding of the property ID that contains this occurrence of the keyword	VARBINARY(1024)

This internal table contains a multicolumn clustered index on the *keyword, colid, pid, docidmax,* and *dupseq* columns.

fulltext_index_docidstatus_[t_objectid]

This table tracks pending changes that need to be applied to the full-text index, including deletes and retries. For change-tracked full-text indexes, this table also tracks inserts and updates. Rows are removed from this table when indexing is complete. Some of this information can be retrieved using the *sp_fulltext_pendingchanges* system procedure. Table 9-5 lists the columns.

TABLE 9-5 Columns of *fulltext_index_docidstatus_[t_objectid]*

Column name	Column description	Data type
Docid	Document ID number	BIGINT
Status	Document Status	TINYINT
Ts	TimeStamp column	ROWVERSION
retry_count	Retry count	TINYINT

This internal table contains a clustered index on the *docid* column, and nonclustered indexes on the *status, docid, ts,* and *status* columns.

fulltext_docidfilter_[t_objectid]

This table tracks the timestamp of the latest version of the fragment that contains up-to-date information for a given *document_id*. It also tracks deleted *document_id*s. Full-text index population maintains this table. Having many entries in the *docidfilter* table negatively affects query performance because each *document_id* returned by the full-text index execution engine needs to be verified against the filter table. Master Merge clears all the rows from the table and improves performance. Table 9-6 lists the columns.

TABLE 9-6 Columns of *fulltext_docidfilter_[t_objectid]*

Column name	Column description	Data type
Docid	Document ID number	BIGINT
Status	Document Status	TINYINT
Ts	TimeStamp column	ROWVERSION

This internal table contains a multicolumn clustered index on the *docid* and *ts* columns.

fulltext_indexeddocid_[t_objectid]

Rows appear in this table after their contents are indexed. If a row in the base table is subsequently deleted, the entry for that row is removed from this table, although the information isn't removed from the fragment table. This table is used to improve performance during indexing. It has just one column: *docid*, which uses a *BIGINT* data type for the document ID number. This internal table also contains a clustered index on the *docid* column.

fulltext_avdl_[t_objectid]

This internal table keeps track of the average document length and document count for each full-text indexed column. The information is used by the ranking algorithm. Table 9-7 lists the columns.

TABLE 9-7 Columns of *fulltext_avdl_[t_objectid]*

Column name	Column description	Data type
Colid	Column ID (in base table)	INT
Pid	Property id (used for internal tracking)	INT
doc_cnt	Count of documents	BIGINT
ave_doc_len	Average Document Length	INT

This internal table contains a multicolumn clustered index on the *colid* and *pid* columns.

fulltext_index_docidmap_[t_objectid]

This table is used to correlate document IDs and full-text search index keys. It's not created if the full-text index key is an integral data type. The information in this internal table can be retrieved exactly by the system stored procedure *sp_fulltext_keymappings*. Table 9-8 lists the columns.

TABLE 9-8 Columns of *fulltext_index_docidmap_[t_objectid]*

Column name	Column description	Data type
Docid	Document ID number	BIGINT
Ftkey	Full-text key value	Same data type as full-text key

This internal table contains a clustered index on the *docid* column and a nonclustered index on the *ftkey* column.

Other internal tables

In addition to the internal tables that comprise the full-text index, internal tables are used with the thesaurus metadata tables (*fulltext_thesaurus_phrase_table*, *fulltext_thesaurus_state_table* and *fulltext_thesaurus_metadata_table*). These internal tables are mostly used as a cache in *tempdb* for the thesaurus files. They are rebuilt automatically during thesaurus queries or during explicit calling of the *sp_fulltext_load_thesaurus_file* system procedure. Because a thesaurus exists per instance and per language, the thesaurus internal tables exist in *tempdb* rather than user databases.

Associated data about related full-text objects such as property lists and stoplists is kept in system tables in SQL Server 2012 and surfaced through metadata views. System stopword list information is available in *sys.fulltext_system_stopwords*.

Full-text index metadata views

The information about full-text indexes is kept entirely in *sys.fulltext_indexes*. Unlike XML and spatial indexes, you can't find full-text index information in *sys.indexes*. This metadata table contains not only properties for the full-text index but also information about the status of the full-text index's population (known as the *crawl*) pertaining to that index. It also contains information about a full-text index's associated property list and stoplist. Unlike XML and spatial indexes, a full-text index can't span filegroups, so the filegroup is listed here as well. A full-text index can contain data from multiple columns, which are listed in *sys.fulltext_columns* rather than *sys.columns*. The *sys.fulltext_indexes* metadata table contains the ID of the full-text catalog to which it belongs. Also, a somewhat redundant *sys. fulltext_index_catalog_usages* metadata table contains *fulltext_index*, *table*, and *catalog* columns.

Although the data for full-text indexes and associated tables is actually stored in internal tables, the data is surfaced through the following dynamic management functions.

- *sys.dm_fts_index_keywords*

- *sys.dm_fts_index_keywords_by_document*

- *sys.dm_fts_index_keywords_by_property*

Full-text index creation

Full-text indexes are built and maintained by a background process known as an index population (or crawl). Index population occurs partially in the database engine and partially in a separate FDHOST. exe executable. Creation and termination of FDHOST.exe is controlled by the Filter Daemon Launcher (FDLauncher.exe) Windows service. The crawl uses the full-text gatherer thread in the engine (sqlservr. exe) to fetch the content and pass it to the FDHOST process using shared memory. The reasoning behind using a separate Windows process for full-text search indexing is that third parties can build word breakers and filters. This separation offers protection to the database engine in the event of poorly designed word breakers and filters.

The crawl process splits the table into *N* ranges during its initialization by using statistics on the internal table, and creates a work item for each range. The number of tasks to use in the crawl is based on the number of processors available. Document content from the base table is passed to FDHOST. exe in batches.

Inside the FDHOST.exe process, the appropriate filter component for the document type processes the content and presents it to the language-specific word breaker component. The word "breaker" breaks the content into words according to language-specific rules, ignoring the stopwords specified in the stopword list. After the word "breaker" produces keywords; it passes them to both the full-text index writer and the semantic index builder if *STATISTICAL_SEMANTICS* is specified in the *CREATE FULLTEXT INDEX* DDL statement. The full-text index writer and semantic index builder components reside in database engine (sqlservr.exe). You can track the index-building progress by using dynamic management views (more on this later, in the "Full-text status metadata and diagnostic information" section).

The words are recorded in the fragment table (table named *ifts_comp_fragment_[t_objectid]_ [ordinal]* whose columns are defined in Table 9-4), along with the position of the word in the document. That a document contains a specific keyword is recorded in the fragment table's *complv1* field, and the word position is recorded in the *complv2* field. Notice that the word position includes stopwords in the position count, even though these aren't indexed, and the word position is a position-based ordinal, not the character position in the document. The information in these two fields is encoded in a compressed binary format. If a *SEARCH_PROPERTY_LIST* is specified for the full-text index and this keyword appears as a property, the property IDs are also recorded in the *comppid* column. The fragment table(s) comprises the inverted index.

The documents are processed sequentially in batches. The *docid* status table records status information while the document is being processed, including any retries. When a document has been completely processed, a row with its *docid* is added to the *indexeddocid* table. Errors are recorded in the error log at [SQLServerInstance location]\MSSQL\Log, with names that begin with SQLFT. You can get additional information about the full-text crawl process and information about parsing properties by turning on trace flag 7603, which is documented in *SQL Server Books Online*.

A full-text index build might produce more than one fragment. Because gathering information from multiple fragments slows down queries, at the end of a complete full-text index build, a master merge step is performed to consolidate all the fragments. Although the master merge is a memory-intensive and CPU-intensive process, you can control the amount of resources that are used with instance–level configuration parameters, as explained in the next two sections.

Maintenance of a full-text index

As mentioned earlier, building and maintaining a full-text index is expensive. As a result, you have greater control via DDL as to how a full-text index is built originally and how a full-text index is maintained. A special *ALTER FULLTEXT INDEX* DDL statement even has its own set of options. A full-text index consists of multiple fragments, which you can reorganize for better performance. However, this operation, known as a *master merge*, is quite expensive itself. Full-text indexes are never updated when they are created. Instead, changes are recorded in a separate fragment and additional information in the *fulltext_docidfilter* internal table is used to determine which version of each row to use during a full-text query and a master merge.

How a full-text index is maintained, and what options you have for maintaining it, depends on the *CHANGE_TRACKING* specification. This specification is originally chosen with the *CREATE FULLTEXT INDEX* DDL statement, and you have the following options.

- *AUTO* change tracking is the default and specifies that changes in the base table are automatically propagated to the full-text index. Remember, however, that this process isn't transactionally consistent.

- *MANUAL* change tracking does keep a list of which *docid* values have changed, but doesn't propagate changes in the base table to the full-text index. You must manually do this using the *ALTER FULLTEXT INDEX* DDL statement.

- Turning change tracking *OFF* doesn't keep its list of which *docid* values have changed; you must manually build or rebuild the index. When you create a full-text index with change tracking off, you can also specify *NO POPULATION* to postpone the building of the index.

So what options does *ALTER FULLTEXT INDEX* provide for maintaining the index? You have three choices to specify in the *START POPULATION* clause.

- **START FULL POPULATION** specifies that every row of the base table be processed. This is equal to a complete rebuild.

- **START UPDATE POPULATION** specifies that changes to the base table be processed. This doesn't reprocess all the rows. This option works with full-text indexes for which *MANUAL* change tracking is specified.

- **START INCREMENTAL POPULATION** specifies that changes made to the base table since the last incremental population be processed. This option can be used only when *MANUAL* change tracking is specified and the base table contains a timestamp (SQL Server data type *ROWVERSION*) column. If the base table has no timestamp column, this is equal to *FULL POPULATION*.

Because full-text index building and maintenance is an expensive process and can take resources away from other parts of the database engine, you can *STOP* a full-text index operation with *ALTER FULLTEXT INDEX*. You can also *PAUSE* and *RESUME* full-text operation, if the operation is a full population. Update and incremental populations can't be paused or resumed. You can also *DISABLE* a full-text index. When a full-text index is disabled, the gatherer doesn't gather full-text information and change tracking is turned off until the full-text index is re-enabled with *ALTER FULLTEXT INDEX...ENABLE*.

Each full-text index fragment contains a timestamp that records when it was built. Updates or row deletions won't update or delete the fragment's information in place. Therefore, full-text queries need to read information from multiple fragments, collate the inverted index information, and discard obsolete entries for rows that have subsequently been updated. Because this can degrade query performance, you can rebuild the entire index with *ALTER FULLTEXT INDEX...START FULL POPULATION* or reconstruct all the full-text indexes in a particular catalog with *ALTER FULLTEXT CATALOG...REBUILD*. Using *ALTER FULLTEXT INDEX...START FULL POPULATION* will end with a master merge, and you can specifically perform a master merge on all the full-text indexes in a particular catalog with *ALTER FULLTEXT CATALOG...REORGANIZE*. A master merge merges all the fragments into a single fragment per index and removes obsolete entries. The degree of parallelism for master merge can be controlled by the system stored procedure and parameter *sp_fulltext_service 'master_merge_dop'*. When this argument isn't specified, the service uses the lesser of 4 or the number of available CPUs or CPU cores.

Full-text status metadata, configuration, and diagnostic information

Because full-text indexes live in catalogs and all the full-text indexes can be rebuilt with a master merge (individually or per catalog), a dynamic management view (DMV) exists for catalog information: *sys.dm_fts_active_catalogs*. This DMV provides information on counts of the number of indexes being populated (auto, manual, and incremental/full population). This DMV also contains a number of obsolete columns.

Because full-text indexing is a dynamic and resource-intensive process, many dynamic management views provide information about the progress and status of full-text indexing, including the following.

- **sys.dm_fts_index_population** provides information about populations now in progress. Not only is status and population type information provided but also number of ranges into which the population has been parallelized and number of outstanding batches.

- **sys.dm_fts_population_ranges** provides information about ranges.

- **sys.dm_fts_outstanding_batches** provides information about index batches.

- **sys.dm_fts_memory_pools** provides information for the full-text gatherer.

- **sys.dm_fts_memory_buffers** lists buffers now being used for a crawl.

You can control the amount of resources allocated to full-text search crawl per instance by using *sp_configure*. The options *ft_crawl_bandwidth (max)* and *ft_crawl_bandwidth (min)* apply to the size of all full-text memory buffers, and *ft_notify_bandwidth (max)* and *ft_notify_bandwidth (min)* apply to the size of a pool of small memory buffers (this configuration option is being deprecated). The instance level option *Max fulltext search crawl range* applies to the number of partitions (CPUs) used for full-text indexing.

In addition to the DMVs, information is available per full-text index by using the property functions *FULLTEXTCATALOGPROPERTY, FULLTEXTSERVICEPROPERTY, OBJECTPROPERTYEX* (for full-text index information, this property function takes a table object id parameter), *COLUMNPROPERTYEX, INDEXPROPERTYEX, DATABASEPROPERTYEX,* and *SERVERPROPERTYEX.*

Extended events can be used to trace crawl and master merge processing. Events are included for the following.

- *full_text_crawl_started*

- *full_text_crawl_stopped*

- *full_text_full_update_instead_of_partial_update*

- *full_text_reorganize_start*

- *full_text_reorganize_progress*

How a full-text index is used in a query

Full-text indexes support four specific T-SQL query constructs. Two are used in predicates in SQL statements and two are full-text rowset functions. The *CONTAINS* and *FREETEXT* operator are used in a *WHERE* clause, similar in concept to the T-SQL *LIKE* operator, but they go beyond simple pattern matching. The *CONTAINS* operator can perform a full-text search on one or more of the columns specified in full-text indexing, and uses a special syntax that allows *CONTAINS* to look for the following.

- A word or phrase

- The prefix of a word or phrase (* wildcard)

- A word near another word (*NEAR*)

- A word inflectionally generated from another (*INFLECTIONAL*)

- A word that is a synonym of another word using a thesaurus (*THESAURUS*)

- A document property using property lists (*PROPERTY*)

You can give weighting to a term with *CONTAINS*, using the *ISABOUT* clause, and use the *AND, AND NOT,* and *OR* logical operators in full-text search *CONTAINS* grammar to combine search grammar constructs. *ISABOUT* is a vector-space query in traditional information retrieval terminology, using the *Jaccard* coefficient.

The *FREETEXT* predicate takes a string of words to match. Unlike the *CONTAINS* predicate, *FREETEXT* has no specific grammar, but it automatically uses the engine to break the string into individual words, generate inflectional forms of the words, and use expansions and replacements from the thesaurus.

CONTAINSTABLE and FREETEXTTABLE are full-text functions that a return a rowset consisting of two columns: full-text key and a ranking. One major difference between full-text functions and table valued functions is that full-text functions can't be "cross applied" with other tables. The ranking for FREETEXTTABLE is done according to the OKAPI BM25 ranking function. The ranking for CONTAINSTABLE uses a simpler algorithm, with special considerations if a NEAR clause is specified or ISABOUT is specified to provide weighting of terms. The table returned can be used to join with the base table. CONTAINSTABLE and FREETEXTTABLE are usually used with the TOP clause for further optimization.

A full-text query plan

Unlike all other indexes, full-text predicates and functions require a full-text index to be useable. The SQL Server query optimizer doesn't make an index selection or usage choice, as it does with XML and spatial indexes. With the CONTAINS and FREETEXT predicates, the full-text portion of the query is done completely in a streaming full-text system function, FulltextMatch, which returns a table of docids to the next query step, as shown in Figure 9-8. No visibility into the FulltextMatch function is provided by the query plan; the five parameters to the function always have the values 0,1,0,NULL,NULL. The FulltextMatch iterator is usually costed by the query optimizer, based on statistics on the internal tables. The CONTAINSTABLE and FREETEXTTABLE full-text functions are also implemented by using the FulltextMatch function. The output from the iterator in this case contains the columns docid and score. When CONTAINSTABLE and FREETEXTTABLE contain the top_n_by_rank parameter, the TOP N rows by score are selected in the FulltextMatch function, and the SQL query plan contains a TOP iterator.

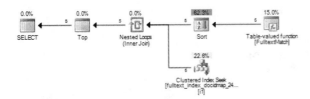

FIGURE 9-8 Query plan for a full-text query using the CONTAINSTABLE full-text search function (plan uses the fulltext index).

Here's an example, using the CONTAINSABLE full-text function with the top_n_by_rank parameter, which uses the weighted search look for the words "performance", "data", and "record". Each search word is given a different ranking (specified by the "weight" keyword) and the query returns the top five results, as shown in Figure 9-8.

```
SELECT * FROM CONTAINSTABLE(documents, *,
    'ISABOUT (performance weight (.8), data weight (.4), record weight (.2) )',5);
```

	KEY	RANK
1	1F290F3E-8AC8-E111-8882-000C298732FD	170
2	34290F3E-8AC8-E111-8882-000C298732FD	159
3	29290F3E-8AC8-E111-8882-000C298732FD	141
4	32290F3E-8AC8-E111-8882-000C298732FD	133
5	18290F3E-8AC8-E111-8882-000C298732FD	130

FIGURE 9-9 Output of the fulltext query corresponding to the plan shown in Figure 9-8.

Although almost all processing for a full-text query occurs in the database engine process (as of SQL Server 2008), the full-text predicates and function do have to communicate with the *FDHOST* process to parse the input to the predicates or functions. In addition to using the language-specific word breaker, the stemmer component also lives in the *FDHOST* process. After wordbreaking and—if required by the full-text syntax—stemming, control is returned to the database process. A dynamic management function, *sys.dm_fts_parser*, can provide visibility into this process and return a table describing the results of the parse.

SQL Server 2008 introduced an optimization for full-text index key columns that are *INT* or *BIGINT*. Where the full-text index key column is *INT* or *BIGINT*, no *docidmap* table is created when the full-text index is. Better yet, this optimization does away with the *docidmap* lookup step in the query plan, which adds another *JOIN* to every full-text search query. Removing this *JOIN* produces a plan that results in improved performance.

Extended event information for full-text queries

In SQL Server 2012, two new extended events provide quite a bit of visibility into the *FulltextMatch* streaming table-valued function shown in the query plan. These events are *full_text_exec_query_stats* and *full_text_query_recompile*.

Parsing the full-text portion of the query (*CONTAINS*, *CONTAINSTABLE*, *FREETEXT*, and *FREETEXTTABLE*) produces a full-text internal execution tree. This is similar to a "plan" for executing that part of the query—that is, it's a plan for the *Fulltext_Match* query plan iterator (represented as an XML element in the trace). The *fulltext_exec_query_stats* event provides an XML document that describes the query execution tree, similar to the way you can obtain an XML document for a query plan. The *Fulltext_Match* iterator can be recompiled similar to the way a SQL query plan can.

For this simple full-text query using *CONTAINTABLE,*

```
-- single term, all columns
SELECT * from CONTAINSTABLE(documents, *, 'data');
```

the following information is produced:

```
<Root FragmentSelectionTimestamp="0x0000021b79" QueryHandle="1048949072" IsParallel="false">
 <Scalar Name="ContainsTableSSERank" InclusiveTime="0ms" RowCount="111">
  <Filter Name="SingleFragmentDocidFilter" InclusiveTime="0ms" RowCount="111"
   FilterTableStrategy="Scan" SetRangeCalls="1">
   <Aggregate Name="Level1Batch Aggregate" InclusiveTime="0ms" RowCount="111">
    <Fragment Keyword="data" InclusiveTime="0ms" RowCount="124">
```

```
        <PhysicalRead InclusiveTime="0ms" RowCount="18" Scans="1" LogicalReads="6"
PhysicalReads="0"
              ReadAheads="0" LobLogicalReads="0" LobPhysicalReads="0" LobReadAheads="0" />
        <Decompression InclusiveTime="0ms" RowCount="124" />
      </Fragment>
    </Aggregate>
  </Filter>
 </Scalar>
</Root>
```

The *RootFragment* element contains a query handle (the plan handles are reused in subsequent full-text queries) and an *IsParallel* indicator. Full-text queries, including the *Fulltext Match* function, can be executed in parallel, based on the number of rows to be processed. Rows can be processed in batches for performance, as indicated in the *SetWidthLevel2Batch* element.

Each fragment keyword has an XML *Fragment* element for each full-text keyword fragment. Each node provides row counts, and timings (*InclusiveTime*), as well as approximate information on scans and page reads. A subnode indicates timings and rowcounts for decompression of the index fragment.

In between the *RootFragment* and *Fragment* nodes are full-text operators, including *Scalar*, *Filter*, *Aggregate*, and *MergeUnion*. These can be connected by *AND* and *OR* operators and occur as nested XML elements, the same way as SQL query plans represent their iterators. Some common iterators (although this might not be an inclusive list) include the following.

- **TopNByRank** is used in *FREETEXT/CONTAINSTABLE* with the *TOP* operand.

- **MergeUnion Merger Type HeapMerger** is a top-level iterator used with *OR* or *FREETEXT* query processing.

- **ContainsTableSSERank** is used with *CONTAINSTABLE* queries.

- **ContainsTableSSERankForNear** is used with *CONTAINSTABLE* queries containing the *NEAR* operator.

- **CDocidRankWtToDocidRankAdaptor** is used to apply weighting to ranking.

- **FreeTextSSETermRank** is used with *FREETEXT* queries.

- **IsAboutSSESum** is used with the *ISABOUT* construct.

- **Filter-For-Pid-Level1** is used for queries with search properties.

- **SingleFragmentDocidFilter** is used in filters with scalar values.

- **SingleFragmentSeekFilter** provides implementation of filters with scalar values.

- **Scalars** provides information about which full-text function was used.

- **Filters** indicates the filters used by the full-text function.

- **Aggregates** provides information about aggregates used in implementing the full-text operation.

Notice that some iterations include SSE as part of the name. This refers to the use of Streaming SIMD Extensions instruction set extensions by full-text search in SQL Server 2012.

Using these statistics, along with the *fulltext_query_recompile* event, which fires whenever the full-text query portion of the plan is recompiled, can help with troubleshooting and can help you gain insight into the full-text query process.

Semantic indexes

Semantic Search—a new feature in SQL Server 2012—uses the full-text keywords returned from FDHOST.exe process as input and builds on that index to enable new searching scenarios over unstructured data. Semantic search does searches on the *meaning* of the document, analogous to the way that full-text search searches on the keywords contained in the document.

Because the indexes for Semantic Search are built using the same input as full-text search, no semantic index–specific DDL or index processing is separate from the full-text search processing. You specify the *STATISTICAL_SEMANTICS* keyword column by column in the *CREATE FULLTEXT INDEX* or *ALTER FULLTEXT INDEX* DDL, as reflected in the *sys.fulltext_index_columns* metadata view. Here's an example, modifying the full-text index created earlier:

```
CREATE FULLTEXT INDEX ON dbo.Documents
  (file_stream TYPE COLUMN file_type LANGUAGE 1033 STATISTICAL_SEMANTICS)
        KEY INDEX DocumentsFt ON ft
WITH SEARCH PROPERTY LIST = DocumentProperties,
   CHANGE_TRACKING = AUTO,
   STOPLIST = SYSTEM;
```

The Semantic Search feature requires that a *SemanticsDB* database be installed. This database is available on the installation media with the SQL Server product but isn't installed by default. It can also be downloaded separately from the SQL Server 2012 Feature Pack, available on the web. You can use an ordinary *CREATE DATABASE...FOR ATTACH* DDL statement to install the *SemanticsDB* database. When the *SemanticsDB* is installed, it needs to be registered with the Semantic Search engine, using the *sp_fulltext_semantic_register_language_statistics_db* system stored procedure. It can also be unregistered by using the system procedure *sp_fulltext_semantic_unregister_language_statistics_db*. You can't customize or provide your own version of the *SemanticsDB*.

The Semantic Search feature is provided for a subset of languages that full-text search supports. The system metadata view, *sys.fulltext_semantic_languages*, lists the supported languages. The metadata view *sys.fulltext_semantic_language_statistics_database* provides information about the version and registration date of the active *SemanticsDB*.

The semantic database consists of a single public table named *version*, for version control, and a series of internal tables comprised of language models. A single internal table, the *sys.language_model_mapping_table*, contains *LCID* (locale ID) and *LMID* (language model ID) pairs. This table provides a lookup into the language model tables, named *language_model_[LMID]*. The language model tables consist of the columns listed in Table 9-9.

TABLE 9-9 Columns in the language model tables

Column name	Column description	Data type
word_id	Word ID number	INT
Word	Keyphrase (encoded)	BINARY(16)
Logprob	The log(probability) that the word occurs in text in that language	TINYINT

The language model table is used to provide input to the semantic index.

Semantic indexing occurs in two phases, along with full-text indexing.

- In phase 1, the full-text keyword index and the semantic key phrase index are populated in parallel at the same time. The data required to index document similarity is also extracted at this time.

- In phase 2, the semantic Document Similarity Index is populated. This index depends on both indexes that were populated in phase 1.

The progress of the semantic index can be tracked, using new information in existing full-text index DMVs or new semantic Search–specific DMVs. The full-text search DMV, *sys.dm_fts_index_population*, contains a status field that can reflect that a semantic population (phase 1) is now in progress. A new DMV, *sys.dm_fts_semantic_similarity_population*, provides semantic index-specific population information (phase 2). The new DMV *sys.dm_db_fts_index_physical_stats* provides size information about semantic as well as full-text indexes. The extended event *fulltext_semantic_document_language* can be used to track the language used for each document by semantic indexing during a full-text crawl with *statistical_semantics* enabled. Note that in SQL Server 2012 Semantic Search, only single-word "key phrases" are supported. Also, singular and plural forms of the same word are indexed as separate key phrases.

Two semantic indexes are always built as internal tables if *STATISTICAL_SEMANTICS* is enabled: the Tag Index (TI) and the Document Similarity Index (DSI). Tables 9-10 and 9-11 list the columns.

TABLE 9-10 Columns for *ti_[t_objectid]*

Column name	Column description	Data type
doc_id	Document ID number	BIGINT
cid	Column ID (in base table)	INT
Weight	Weighting for number of times word appears in the document	REAL
Phrase	Keyphrase	VARBINARY(128)

This internal table contains a multicolumn clustered index on the *doc_id*, *cid*, *weight*, and *phrase* columns, and a single nonclustered index on the *phrase*, *weight*, *doc_id*, and *cid* columns.

TABLE 9-11 Columns for *dsi_[t_objectid]*

Column name	Column description	Data type
doc_id	Document ID number	BIGINT
cid	Column ID (in base table)	INT
Weight	Weighting for how similar the document pair is	REAL
doc_id_related	Related document ID	BIGINT
cid_related	Related column ID	INT

This internal table contains a multicolumn clustered index on the *doc_id*, *cid*, *weight*, *doc_id_related*, and *cid_related* columns and a single nonclustered index on the *doc_id_related*, *cid_related*, *weight*, *doc_id*, and *cid* columns.

The *TI* contains a row for each key phrase, per document and per column. This index is used to summarize documents of varying lengths, including possibly very long documents, into their top keywords and phrases. When a user uses full-text search to identify documents, he can follow up with a query of the Tag Index to obtain a keyword summary, rather than read the entirety of each matching document. The weighting value identifies the relative importance of that particular phrase in the document and is calculated based on a variation of the *TF-ITF* algorithm returning the log of probability. The Tag Index algorithm compares the relative number of times the phrase appears in the document compared to the frequency with which that phrase appears in the language model, using n-grams (unigrams in SQL Server 2012). The algorithm is independent of the set of documents (known as a *corpus*) and scales linearly, which is a particular advantage when using a large set of documents. A maximum number of phrases (100, at time of this writing) are kept per document, based on relative weighting, number of occurrences, and document size. This ensures scalability, even if the document is very large.

The rowset function *SEMANTICKEYPHRASETABLE* provides the contents of the Tag Index. *SEMANTICKEYPHRASETABLE* can also specify a specific document of specific columns to provide the rows from the *TI* more granularly. When using *SEMANTICKEYPHRASETABLE*, the results are almost always joined back to the base table to obtain information beyond the *docids*.

The following query uses *SEMANTICKEYPHRASETABLE* to obtain key phrases that were extracted from the document DataCompression.pdf. The results are sorted most relevant to least relevant, with the range for the score column from 0 to 1. Notice that, because the full-text index in the *Documents* table is a *UNIQUEIDENTIFIER* data type (that is, not an *INTEGER*), an extra *JOIN* with the *docid_map* table is required, as mentioned earlier in the section on full-text indexes. Figure 9-10 shows the query plan.

```
DECLARE @Title as NVARCHAR(1000);
DECLARE @DocID as UNIQUEIDENTIFIER;
SET @Title = 'DataCompression.pdf';
SELECT @DocID = stream_id FROM Documents WHERE name = @Title;

SELECT name, document_key, keyphrase, score
FROM SEMANTICKEYPHRASETABLE (Documents, *, @DocID)
INNER JOIN Documents ON stream_id = document_key
ORDER BY score DESC;
```

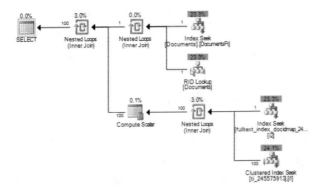

FIGURE 9-10 Query plan using semantic search tag index with the *SEMANTICKEYPHRASETABLE* function.

	name	document_key	keyphrase	score
1	DataCompression.pdf	18290F3E-8AC8-E111-8882-000C298732FD	compressed	1
2	DataCompression.pdf	18290F3E-8AC8-E111-8882-000C298732FD	compression	1
3	DataCompression.pdf	18290F3E-8AC8-E111-8882-000C298732FD	cpu	1
4	DataCompression.pdf	18290F3E-8AC8-E111-8882-000C298732FD	data	1
5	DataCompression.pdf	18290F3E-8AC8-E111-8882-000C298732FD	page	1
6	DataCompression.pdf	18290F3E-8AC8-E111-8882-000C298732FD	table	0.9934
7	DataCompression.pdf	18290F3E-8AC8-E111-8882-000C298732FD	sql	0.9674109
8	DataCompression.pdf	18290F3E-8AC8-E111-8882-000C298732FD	clustered	0.9227936
9	DataCompression.pdf	18290F3E-8AC8-E111-8882-000C298732FD	partition	0.902344
10	DataCompression.pdf	18290F3E-8AC8-E111-8882-000C298732FD	compressing	0.8877496
11	DataCompression.pdf	18290F3E-8AC8-E111-8882-000C298732FD	compress	0.8860195
12	DataCompression.pdf	18290F3E-8AC8-E111-8882-000C298732FD	row	0.8461081

FIGURE 9-11 Output of the semantic search query using *SEMANTICKEYPHRASETABLE*.

The Document Similarity Index (DSI) provides a row for each pair of related documents, along with a per-document-pair similarity rating (weight). This index is built on top of the Tag Index. The *TOP N* matching phrases for each set of document pairs is calculated using an algorithm known as *cosine similarity*. Out of the original *TOP N* pairs, only ten are kept, based on descending cosine similarity weighting.

The internal table that comprises the Document Similarity Index is used by the rowset function *SEMANTICSIMILARITYTABLE*, through a direct join with this table. The weighting value is calculated by a variation of the cosine similarity algorithm.

The following query uses the *SEMANTICSIMILARITYTABLE* to obtain documents that are semantically similar to the DataCompression.pdf document. In this case, *semantically similar* means that both documents contain keywords that don't occur often in "typical" language usage. The statistical frequency of keywords in "typical" language usage is defined in the semantic database tables. These are returned in order, most relevant first, as shown in Figure 9-12.

```
/* Get similar documents for Data Compression Paper */
DECLARE @Title as NVARCHAR(1000);
DECLARE @DocID as UNIQUEIDENTIFIER;

SET @Title = 'DataCompression.pdf';
SELECT @DocID = stream_id FROM Documents WHERE name = @Title;

SELECT @Title AS SourceTitle, name AS MatchedTitle, stream_id, score
FROM SEMANTICSIMILARITYTABLE (Documents, *, @DocID)
INNER JOIN Documents ON stream_id = matched_document_key
ORDER BY score DESC;
```

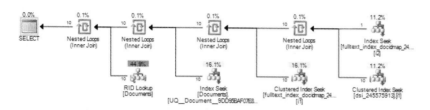

FIGURE 9-12 Query plan using semantic search document similarity index with the *SEMANTICSIMILARITYTABLE* function.

Figure 9-13 shows the query output13. Notice that, even without a *TOP* clause, only the ten rows with the highest scores are returned.

	SourceTitle	MatchedTitle	stream_id	score
1	DataCompression.pdf	PartTableAndIndexStrat.docx	4A290F3E-8AC8-E111-8882-000C298732FD	0.3282307
2	DataCompression.pdf	ScaleUpDWinSQL2008.docx	57290F3E-8AC8-E111-8882-000C298732FD	0.3274468
3	DataCompression.pdf	Fast_Track_Configuration_Guide.docx	36290F3E-8AC8-E111-8882-000C298732FD	0.3260192
4	DataCompression.pdf	Columnstore Indexes for Fast DW QP SQL Server 11...	2D290F3E-8AC8-E111-8882-000C298732FD	0.3254797
5	DataCompression.pdf	Tuning_CDC.doc	22290F3E-8AC8-E111-8882-000C298732FD	0.3117937
6	DataCompression.pdf	FastTrackImpl.doc	1C290F3E-8AC8-E111-8882-000C298732FD	0.3063217
7	DataCompression.pdf	FTRARefConfigGuide.docx	38290F3E-8AC8-E111-8882-000C298732FD	0.3038685
8	DataCompression.pdf	DataLoadPerfGuide.docx	19290F3E-8AC8-E111-8882-000C298732FD	0.2992353
9	DataCompression.pdf	IndexedViews2008.pdf	3D290F3E-8AC8-E111-8882-000C298732FD	0.2970308
10	DataCompression.pdf	WhyNotSybaseASE.docx	77290F3E-8AC8-E111-8882-000C298732FD	0.2854296

FIGURE 9-13 Output of the query using the *SEMANTICSIMILARITYTABLE* function.

SEMANTICSIMILARITYDETAILSTABLE takes two documents as input and performs a self-join using the Tag Index rows for each document. An *InnerJoin* is performed to return the set of keywords that apply to both documents. A built-in scalar operator then calculates a similarity on the fly, given the two weight values for documents that qualify. The set of documents is then sorted by the results of this function.

The following query investigates why the two documents DataCompression.pdf and ScaleUpDWin-SQL2008.docx are semantically similar using the *SEMANTICSIMILARITYDETAILSTABLE* function, and returns the key phrases that are most similar in relevance in order, most similar first. Notice that, in SQL Server 2012, only unigrams are returned, as shown in Figure 9-14.

```
DECLARE @SourceTitle as NVARCHAR(1000);
DECLARE @MatchedTitle as NVARCHAR(1000);
DECLARE @SourceDocID as UNIQUEIDENTIFIER;
DECLARE @MatchedDocID as UNIQUEIDENTIFIER;

SET @SourceTitle = 'DataCompression.pdf';
SET @MatchedTitle = 'ScaleUpDWinSQL2008.docx';
SELECT @SourceDocID = stream_id FROM Documents WHERE name = @SourceTitle;
SELECT @MatchedDocID = stream_id FROM Documents WHERE name = @MatchedTitle;

SELECT @SourceTitle AS SourceTitle, @MatchedTitle AS MatchedTitle, keyphrase, score
FROM SEMANTICSIMILARITYDETAILSTABLE(
Documents, file_stream, @SourceDocID, file_stream, @MatchedDocID)
ORDER BY score DESC;
```

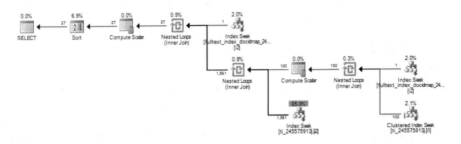

FIGURE 9-14 Query plan using semantic search tag index with the *SEMANTICSIMILARITYDETAILSTABLE* function.

In this function, the query plan consists of a self-join of the Tag Index table based on the same phrase being present in both documents. Figure 9-15 shows the first part of the query output.

	Source Title	Matched Title	keyphrase	score
1	DataCompression.pdf	ScaleUpDWinSQL2008.docx	sql	0.7682468
2	DataCompression.pdf	ScaleUpDWinSQL2008.docx	cpu	0.4313935
3	DataCompression.pdf	ScaleUpDWinSQL2008.docx	compression	0.3693292
4	DataCompression.pdf	ScaleUpDWinSQL2008.docx	data	0.3586714
5	DataCompression.pdf	ScaleUpDWinSQL2008.docx	table	0.336091
6	DataCompression.pdf	ScaleUpDWinSQL2008.docx	server	0.3269899
7	DataCompression.pdf	ScaleUpDWinSQL2008.docx	query	0.3148932
8	DataCompression.pdf	ScaleUpDWinSQL2008.docx	compressed	0.3064148
9	DataCompression.pdf	ScaleUpDWinSQL2008.docx	clustered	0.28418
10	DataCompression.pdf	ScaleUpDWinSQL2008.docx	cpus	0.2822624

FIGURE 9-15 Output of the query using the *SEMANTICSIMILARITYDETAILSTABLE* function.

All functions supported by semantic search eventually return full-text search key values. There-fore, just as with full-text search, if the full-text search key isn't *INT* or *BIGINT*, an additional *docidmap* lookup (two lookups in the case of *SEMANTICSIMILARITYDETAILSTABLE*) is required. This can be seen in the preceding query plans.

Conclusion

This chapter has explored four different types of special index: XML, spatial, full text, and semantic. Although they are built, maintained, and used a bit differently than their "ordinary" SQL index counterparts, by looking at the internal tables that comprise these indexes and query plans that use them, you can deduce (for the most part) that they aren't so different from clustered and nonclustered indexes using computed columns after all.

Query execution

Craig Freedman and Benjamin Nevarez

The SQL Server query processor consists of two components: the query optimizer and the query execution engine. The query optimizer is responsible for generating good query plans. The query execution engine takes the query plans generated by the query optimizer and, as its name suggests, runs them. Query execution involves many functions, including using the storage engine to retrieve and update data from tables and indexes and implementing operations such as joins and aggregation.

This chapter focuses on understanding query behavior by examining the details of your query execution plans. It explains how the SQL Server query processor works, beginning with the basics of query plans and working toward progressively more complex examples.

Introducing query processing and execution

To better understand the factors that affect query performance, to understand how to spot potential performance problems with a query plan, and ultimately to learn how to use query optimizer hints to tune individual query plans, we first need to understand how the SQL Server query processor executes queries. This section introduces iterators, one of the most fundamental query execution concepts; discusses how to read and understand query plans; explores some of the most common query execution operators; and shows how SQL Server combines these operators to execute even the most complex queries.

Iterators

SQL Server breaks queries down into a set of fundamental building blocks called operators or iterators. Each iterator implements a single basic operation such as scanning data from a table, updating data in a table, filtering or aggregating data, or joining two data sets. In all, a few dozen such primitive iterators are available. Iterators can have no children; have one, two, or more children; and can be combined into trees called query plans. By building appropriate query plans, SQL Server can execute any SQL statement. In practice, certain statements frequently have many valid query plans. The query optimizer's job is to find the best (for example, the cheapest or fastest) query plan for a particular statement.

An iterator reads input rows either from a data source such as a table or from its children (if it has any) and produces output rows, which it returns to its parent. The output rows that an iterator produces depend on the operation that the iterator performs. All versions of SQL Server traditionally use a row-at-a-time model—that is, operators process only one row at a time. This approach is now called row-based processing and will be discussed throughout most of this chapter. A new processing approach introduced with SQL Server 2012, called batch-mode processing, uses operators that can process batches of rows at a time and will be explained at the end of this chapter in the section "Columnstore indexes and batch processing."

In the row-based model, all iterators implement the same set of core methods. For example, the Open method tells an iterator to prepare to produce output rows, the GetRow method requests an iterator to produce a new output row, and the Close method indicates that the iterator's parent is through requesting rows. Because all iterators implement the same methods, iterators are independent of one another. That is, an iterator doesn't need specialized knowledge of its children (if any) or parent. Consequently, iterators can be easily combined in many different ways and into many different query plans.

When SQL Server executes a query plan, control flows down the query tree. That is, SQL Server calls the methods Open and GetRow on the iterator at the root of the query tree, and these methods propagate down through the tree to the leaf iterators. Data flows (or, more accurately, is pulled up) the tree when one iterator calls another iterator's GetRow method.

To understand how iterators work, look at an example. Most examples in this chapter, including the following, are based on an extended version of the *Northwind* database called *Northwind2*. You can download a script to build *Northwind2* from the book's companion website. Consider this query:

```
SELECT COUNT(*) FROM [Orders]
```

The simplest way to execute this query is to scan each row in the *Orders* table and count the rows. SQL Server uses two iterators to achieve this result: one to scan the rows in the *Orders* table and another to count them, as illustrated in Figure 10-1.

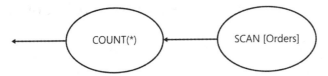

FIGURE 10-1 Iterators for basic *COUNT(*)* query.

To execute this query plan, SQL Server calls Open on the root iterator in the plan, which in this example is the *COUNT(*)* iterator. The *COUNT(*)* iterator performs the following tasks in the Open method:

1. It calls *Open* on the scan iterator, which readies the scan to produce rows.

2. It calls *GetRow* repeatedly on the scan iterator, counting the rows returned, and stopping only when *GetRow* indicates that it has returned all the rows.

3. It calls *Close* on the scan iterator to indicate that it has finished getting rows.

Note *COUNT(*)* is actually implemented by the stream aggregate iterator, which is described in more detail later in this chapter.

By the time the *COUNT(*)* iterator returns from *Open*, it has already calculated the number of rows in the *Orders* table. To complete execution, SQL Server calls *GetRow* on the *COUNT(*)* iterator and returns this result. Technically, SQL Server calls *GetRow* on the *COUNT(*)* iterator one more time because it doesn't know that the *COUNT(*)* iterator produces only a single row until it tries to retrieve a second row. In response to the second *GetRow* call, the *COUNT(*)* iterator returns that it has reached the end of the result set. The *COUNT(*)* iterator neither cares nor needs to know that it's counting rows from a scan iterator. It will count rows from any subtree that SQL Server puts below it, regardless of how simple or complex the subtree might be.

Properties of iterators

Three important properties of iterators can affect query performance and are worth special attention: memory consumption, nonblocking vs. blocking, and dynamic cursor support.

Memory consumption

All iterators require some small fixed amount of memory to store state, perform calculations, and so forth. SQL Server doesn't track this fixed memory or try to reserve this memory before executing a query. When SQL Server caches an executable plan, it caches this fixed memory so that it doesn't need to allocate it again and to speed up subsequent executions of the cached plan.

However, some iterators, referred to as memory-consuming iterators, require additional memory to execute. This additional memory is used to store row data. The amount of memory required by a memory-consuming operator is generally proportional to the number of rows processed. To ensure that the server doesn't run out of memory and that queries containing memory-consuming iterators don't fail, SQL Server estimates how much memory these queries need and reserves a memory grant before executing such a query.

Memory-consuming iterators can affect performance in a few ways.

- Queries with memory-consuming iterators might have to wait to acquire the necessary memory grant and can't begin execution if the server is executing other such queries and doesn't have enough available memory. This waiting can directly affect performance by delaying execution.

- If too many queries are competing for limited memory resources, the server might suffer from reduced concurrency and/or throughput. This impact generally isn't a major issue for data warehouses but is undesirable in Online Transaction Processing (OLTP) systems.

- If a memory-consuming iterator requests too little memory, it might need to spill data to disk during execution. Spilling can significantly affect query and system performance adversely because of the extra I/O overhead. Moreover, if an iterator spills too much data, it can run out of disk space on *tempdb* and fail.

The primary memory-consuming iterators are sort, hash join, and hash aggregation.

Nonblocking vs. blocking iterators

Iterators can be classified into two categories.

- **Iterators that consume input rows and produce output rows at the same time (in the GetRow method)** These iterators are often referred to as nonblocking.

- **Iterators that consume all input rows (generally in the Open method) before producing any output rows** These iterators are often referred to as "blocking" or "stop-and-go."

The compute scalar iterator is a simple example of a nonblocking iterator. It reads an input row, computes a new output value using the input values from the current row, immediately outputs the new value, and continues to the next input row.

The sort iterator is a good example of a blocking iterator. The sort can't determine the first output row until it has read and sorted all input rows. (The last input row could be the first output row; the sort can't know without first consuming every row.)

Blocking iterators often, but not always, consume memory. For example, as just noted, sort is both memory consuming and blocking. However, the COUNT(*) example, which was used to introduce the concept of iterators, doesn't consume memory and yet is blocking. It's not possible to know the number of rows without reading and counting them all.

If an iterator has two children, the iterator might be blocking with respect to one and nonblocking with respect to the other. Hash join (discussed later in this chapter) is a good example of such an iterator.

Nonblocking iterators are generally optimal for OLTP queries for which response time is important. They are often especially desirable for TOP N queries in which N is small. Because the goal is to return the first few rows as quickly as possible, avoiding blocking iterators can help; otherwise, those iterators might process more data than necessary before returning the first rows. Nonblocking iterators can also be useful when evaluating an EXISTS subquery, which again helps avoid processing more data than necessary to conclude that at least one output row exists.

Dynamic cursor support

The iterators used in a dynamic cursor query plan have special properties. Among other things, a dynamic cursor plan must be able to return a portion of the result set on each fetch request, must be able to scan forward or backward, and must be able to acquire scroll locks as it returns rows. To support this functionality, an iterator must be able to save and restore its state, must be able to scan forward or backward, must process one input row for each output row it produces, and must be non-blocking. Not all iterators have all these properties, however.

For a query to be executed using a dynamic cursor, the optimizer must be able to find a query plan that uses only iterators that support dynamic cursors. Finding such a plan is not always possible. Consequently, some queries can't be executed using a dynamic cursor. For example, queries that include a GROUP BY clause inherently violate the one input row for each output row requirement. Thus, such queries can never be executed using a dynamic cursor.

Reading query plans

To better understand what the query processor is doing, we need a way to look at query plans. SQL Server has several different ways of displaying a query plan; these techniques are collectively referred to as "the showplan options."

SQL Server supports three showplan options: graphical, text, and XML. Each showplan option outputs the same query plan. The difference between these options is how the information is formatted, the level of detail included, how to read it, and how to use it.

Graphical plans

The graphical showplan option uses visually appealing icons that correspond to the iterators in the query plan. The tree structure of the query plan is clear. Arrows represent the data flow between the iterators. ToolTips provide detailed help, including a description of and statistical data on each iterator; this includes estimates of the number of rows generated by each operator (that is, the cardinality estimates), the average row size, and the cost of the operator. The Management Studio Properties sheet includes even more detailed information about each operator and about the overall query plan. For example, the Properties sheet lists the SET options (such as ARITHABORT and ANSI_NULLS) used during the plan's compilation, parameter and variable values used during optimization and at execution time, thread-level execution statistics for parallel plans, the degree of parallelism for parallel plans, the size of the memory grant (if any), the size of the cached query plan, requested and actual cursor types, information on missing indexes, and compilation time (both elapsed and CPU time) and memory. Some available data varies from plan type to plan type and from operator to operator.

Generally, graphical plans give a good view of the big picture, which makes them especially useful for beginners and even for experienced users who simply want to browse plans quickly. However, some query plans are so large that they can only be viewed either by scaling the graphics down to a point where the icons are hard to read or by scrolling in two dimensions.

We can generate graphical plans using Management Studio in SQL Server. Management Studio also supports saving and reloading graphical plans in files with an .sqlplan extension. In fact, the contents of an .sqlplan file are really just an XML plan, and the same information is available in both graphical and XML plans.

Text plans

The text showplan option represents each iterator on a separate line. SQL Server uses indentation and vertical bars (| characters) to show the child–parent relationship between the iterators in the query tree. Arrows aren't used explicitly, but data always flows up the plan from a child to a parent. After you understand how to read it, text plans are often easier to read—especially when big plans are involved. Two types of text plans are available: SET SHOWPLAN_TEXT ON, which displays just the query plan, and SET SHOWPLAN_ALL ON, which displays the query plan as well as most of the same estimates and statistics included in the graphical plan ToolTips window and Properties sheet.

XML plans

SQL Server 2005 introduced the XML showplan option. It brings together many of the best features of text and graphical plans. The ability to nest XML elements makes XML a much more natural choice than text for representing the tree structure of a query plan. XML plans comply with a published XSD schema (at *http://schemas.microsoft.com/sqlserver/2004/07/showplan/showplanxml.xsd*) and, unlike text and graphical plans, are easy to search and process programmatically using any standard XML tools. You can even save XML plans in a SQL Server XML column, index them, and query them using the built-in SQL Server XQuery functionality. Moreover, while compared with text plans, the native XML format is more challenging to read directly; as noted previously, Management Studio can save graphical showplan output as XML plan files (with the .sqlplan extension) and can load XML plan files (again with the .sqlplan extension) and display them graphically.

XML plans contain all the information available in both graphical or text plans, and are also the basis for the USE PLAN query hint discussed in Chapter 11, "The Query Optimizer," and Chapter 12, "Plan caching and recompilation."

The XML plan follows a hierarchy of a batch element, a statement element, and a query plan element (<*QueryPlan*>). If a batch or procedure contains multiple statements, the XML plan output for that batch or procedure will contain multiple query plans. Within the query plan element is a series of relational operator elements (<*RelOp*>). Each iterator has one relational operator element in the query plan, and these elements are nested according to the tree structure of the query plan. Similar to the other showplan options, each relational operator element includes cost estimates and statistics, as well as some operator-specific information.

Estimated vs. actual query plans

We can ask SQL Server to output a plan (for any showplan option—graphical, text, or XML) with or without actually running a query.

A query plan generated without executing a query is referred to as the "estimated execution plan" because SQL Server might choose to recompile the query (recompiles can occur for various reasons) and might generate a different query plan at execution time. The estimated execution plan is useful for a variety of purposes, such as viewing the query plan of a long-running query without waiting for it to complete; viewing the query plan for an insert, update, or delete statement without altering the state of the database or acquiring any locks; or exploring the effect of various optimization hints on a query plan without actually running the query. The estimated execution plan includes cardinality, row size, cost estimates, and—new in SQL Server 2012—estimated execution mode, which is covered later in this chapter.

> **Tip** The estimated costs reported by the optimizer are intended as a guide to compare the anticipated relative cost of various operators within a single query plan or the relative cost of two different plans. These unitless estimates aren't meant to be interpreted in any absolute sense such as milliseconds or seconds.

A query plan generated after executing a query is referred to as the *actual execution plan*. The actual execution plan includes the same information as the estimated execution plan plus the actual row counts and the actual number of executions for each operator. Comparing the estimated and actual row counts can help us identify cardinality estimation errors, which might lead to other plan issues.

> **Tip** The actual execution plan includes the same cost estimates as the estimated execution plan. Although SQL Server actually executes the query plan while generating the actual execution plan, these cost estimates are still the same estimates generated by the optimizer and don't reflect the actual execution cost.

Several Transact-SQL commands are available to collect showplan option output when running ad hoc queries from SQL Server Management Studio or from the SQLCMD command-line utility. These commands enable you to collect both text and XML plans, as well as estimated and actual plans. Table 10-1 lists all the available SET commands to enable showplan options.

TABLE 10-1 SET commands for displaying query plans

	Command	Execute query?	Include estimated row counts & stats	Include actual row counts & stats
Text Plan	SET SHOWPLAN_TEXT ON	No	No	No
	SET SHOWPLAN_ALL ON	No	Yes	No
	SET STATISTICS PROFILE ON	Yes	Yes	Yes
XML Plan	SET SHOWPLAN_XML ON	No	Yes	No
	SET STATISTICS PROFILE XML	Yes	Yes	Yes

We can also collect query plan information using Extended Events, and XML plans using Dynamic Management Views (DMVs). These options are especially useful when analyzing applications in which you don't have access to the source code. The DMVs that contain plan information are discussed in Chapter 12.

Query plan display options

To compare the various ways of viewing query plans, consider the following query:

```
DECLARE @Country nvarchar(15)
SET @Country = N'USA'
SELECT O.[CustomerId], MAX(O.[Freight]) AS MaxFreight
FROM [Customers] C JOIN [Orders] O
  ON C.[CustomerId] = O.[CustomerId]
WHERE C.[Country] = @Country
GROUP BY O.[CustomerId]
OPTION (OPTIMIZE FOR (@Country = N'UK'))
```

Figure 10-2 shows the graphical plan for this query.

FIGURE 10-2 A graphical execution plan.

Don't be too concerned yet with understanding how the operators in this query plan actually function. Later, this chapter delves into the details of the various operators. For now, simply observe how SQL Server combines the individual operators together in a tree structure. Notice that the clustered index scans are leaf operators and have no children, the sort and stream aggregate operators have one child each, and the merge join operator has two children. Also, notice how the data flows as shown by the arrows from the leaf operators on the right side of the plan to the root of the tree on the left side of the plan.

Figure 10-3 shows the ToolTip information, and Figure 10-4 shows the Properties sheet from the actual (runtime) plan for the merge join operator. The ToolTip window and Properties sheet show additional information about the operator, such as the optimizer's cost and cardinality estimates, the actual number of output rows, and the execution mode.

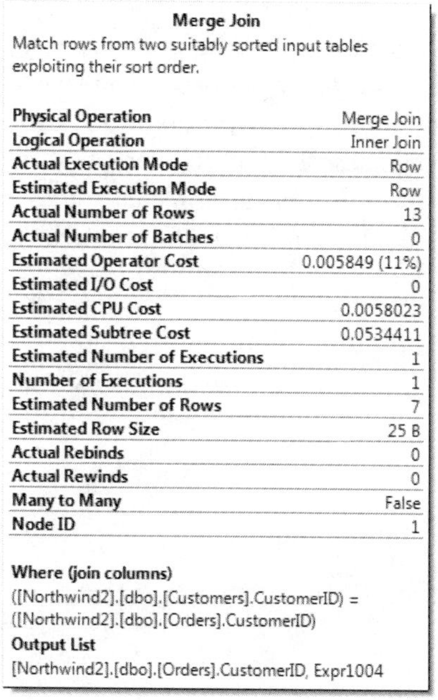

Merge Join
Match rows from two suitably sorted input tables exploiting their sort order.
Physical Operation Merge Join
Logical Operation Inner Join
Actual Execution Mode Row
Estimated Execution Mode Row
Actual Number of Rows 13
Actual Number of Batches 0
Estimated Operator Cost 0.005849 (11%)
Estimated I/O Cost 0
Estimated CPU Cost 0.0058023
Estimated Subtree Cost 0.0534411
Estimated Number of Executions 1
Number of Executions 1
Estimated Number of Rows 7
Estimated Row Size 25 B
Actual Rebinds 0
Actual Rewinds 0
Many to Many False
Node ID 1
Where (join columns)
([Northwind2].[dbo].[Customers].CustomerID) = ([Northwind2].[dbo].[Orders].CustomerID)
Output List
[Northwind2].[dbo].[Orders].CustomerID, Expr1004

FIGURE 10-3 ToolTip for merge join operator in a graphical plan.

Properties
Merge Join
Misc
Actual Execution Mode Row
Actual Number of Batches 0
Actual Number of Rows 13
Actual Rebinds 0
Actual Rewinds 0
Description Match rows from
Estimated CPU Cost 0.0058023
Estimated Execution Mode Row
Estimated I/O Cost 0
Estimated Number of Executions 1
Estimated Number of Rows 7
Estimated Operator Cost 0.005849 (11%)
Estimated Rebinds 0
Estimated Rewinds 0
Estimated Row Size 25 B
Estimated Subtree Cost 0.0534411
Logical Operation Inner Join
Many to Many False
Node ID 1
Number of Executions 1
Output List [Northwind2].[db
Parallel False
Physical Operation Merge Join
Residual [Northwind2].[db
Actual Number of Batches
Actual number of Batches output by this operator.

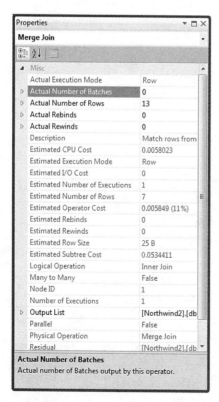

FIGURE 10-4 Properties sheet for merge join operator.

Figure 10-5 shows the Properties sheet for the *SELECT* icon at the root of the plan. Notice that it includes query-wide information such as the *SET* options used during compilation, the compilation time and memory, the cached plan size, the degree of parallelism, the memory grant, the parameter and variable values used during compilation and execution, and the query and query plan hashes. The meaning of these fields as part of the XML plan example is described shortly. Keep in mind that a variable and a parameter are very different elements, and Chapter 12 discusses the difference in detail. However, the various query plans that we will examine use the term parameter to refer to either variables or parameters.

FIGURE 10-5 Properties sheet for *SELECT* at the top of a query plan.

Now consider the same query plan by looking at the output of *SET SHOWPLAN_TEXT ON*. Here, the text plan shows only the query plan:

```
|--Merge Join(Inner Join, MERGE:([O].[CustomerID])=([C].[CustomerID]), RESIDUAL:(...))
   |--Stream Aggregate(GROUP BY:([O].[CustomerID])
      DEFINE:([Expr1004]=MAX([O].[Freight])))
   |   |--Sort(ORDER BY:([O].[CustomerID] ASC))
   |      |--Clustered Index Scan(OBJECT:([Orders].[PK_Orders] AS [O]))
   |--Clustered Index Scan(OBJECT:([Customers].[PK_Customers] AS [C]),
      WHERE:([C].[Country]=[@Country]) ORDERED FORWARD)
```

Note This and all other text plan examples in this chapter have been edited for brevity and improved clarity. For example, the database and schema names of objects are removed from all plans. In some cases, lines are wrapped where they usually aren't wrapped in the output.

Notice that although no icons or arrows are used, this view of the plan has precisely the same operators and tree structure as the graphical plan. Recall that each line represents one operator—the equivalent of one icon in the graphical plan—and the vertical bars (the | characters) link each operator to its parent and children.

The output of *SET SHOWPLAN_ALL ON* includes the same plan text but, as noted earlier, also includes additional information including cardinality and cost estimates. The *SET STATISTICS PROFILE ON* output includes actual row and operator execution counts, in addition to all the other information.

Finally, Listing 10-1 shows a highly abbreviated version of the SET STATISTICS XML ON output for the same query plan. Notice that the same set of operators are used in the XML version of the plan as in the graphical and text versions. Also observe that the child operators are nested within the parent operator's XML element. For example, the merge join has two children, so two relational operator elements are nested within the merge join's relational operator element.

LISTING 10-1 Abbreviated SET STATISTICS XML output

```
<StmtSimple StatementText=
   "SELECT O.[CustomerId], MAX(O.[Freight]) as MaxFreight
   FROM [Customers] C JOIN [Orders] O
      ON C.[CustomerId] = O.[CustomerId
   WHERE C.[Country] = @Country
   GROUP BY O.[CustomerId]
   OPTION (OPTIMIZE FOR (@Country = N'UK'))"...>
 <StatementSetOptions ANSI_NULLS="false" ANSI_PADDING="false" ANSI_WARNINGS="false"
ARITHABORT="true"
               CONCAT_NULL_YIELDS_NULL="false" NUMERIC_ROUNDABORT="false"     QUOTED_
IDENTIFIER="false"/>
 <QueryPlan DegreeOfParallelism="1" MemoryGrant="1024" CachedPlanSize="24"
        CompileTime="68" CompileCPU="9" CompileMemory="392">
  <RelOp NodeId="1" PhysicalOp="Merge Join" LogicalOp="Inner Join"...>
   <Merge ManyToMany="false">
    <RelOp NodeId="2" PhysicalOp="Stream Aggregate" LogicalOp="Aggregate"...>
     <StreamAggregate>
      <RelOp NodeId="3" PhysicalOp="Sort" LogicalOp="Sort"...>
       <MemoryFractions Input="1" Output="1" />
       <Sort Distinct="false">
        <RelOp NodeId="4" PhysicalOp="Clustered Index Scan"
                  LogicalOp="Clustered Index Scan"...>
         <IndexScan Ordered="false" ForcedIndex="false" ForcedScan="false" NoExpandHint="false">
          <Object Database="[Northwind2]" Schema="[dbo]" Table="[Orders]"
                  Index="[PK_Orders]" Alias="[O]" IndexKind="Clustered"/>
         </IndexScan>
        </RelOp>
```

```
      </Sort>
     </RelOp>
    </StreamAggregate>
   </RelOp>
   <RelOp NodeId="8" PhysicalOp="Clustered Index Scan"
             LogicalOp="Clustered Index Scan"...>
    <IndexScan Ordered="true" ScanDirection="FORWARD" ForcedIndex="false"
NoExpandHint="false" …>
      <Object Database="[Northwind2]" Schema="[dbo]" Table="[Customers]"
              Index="[PK_Customers]" Alias="[C]" IndexKind="Clustered" />
      <Predicate>
       <ScalarOperator ScalarString="[Northwind2].[dbo].[Customers].[Country]
                        as [C].[Country]=[@Country]">
       </ScalarOperator>
      </Predicate>
     </IndexScan>
    </RelOp>
   </Merge>
  </RelOp>
  <ParameterList>
   <ColumnReference Column="@Country" ParameterCompiledValue="N'UK'"
        ParameterRuntimeValue="N'USA'" />
  </ParameterList>
 </QueryPlan>
</StmtSimple>
```

Some other elements are worth pointing out.

■ The *<StmtSimple>* element includes a StatementText attribute that, as you might expect, includes the original statement text (truncated up to 4,000 characters). Depending on the statement type, another element (such as *<StmtCursor>*) can replace the *<StmtSimple>* element.

■ The *<StatementSetOptions>* element includes attributes for the various SET options.

■ The *<QueryPlan>* element includes the following attributes:

● **DegreeOfParallelism**　The number of threads per operator for a parallel plan. A value of
0 or 1 indicates a serial plan. This example is a serial plan.

● **MemoryGrant**　The total memory granted to run this query in kilobyte (KB) units. This
query was granted 1024 KB.

● **CachedPlanSize**　The amount of plan cache memory (in KB) consumed by this query plan.

● **CompileTime and CompileCPU**　The elapsed and CPU time (in milliseconds) used to
compile this plan.

● **CompileMemory**　The amount of memory (in KB) used while compiling this query.

■ The *<QueryPlan>* element also includes a <ParameterList> element, which includes the compile time and runtime values for each parameter and variable. This example has just the one @
Country variable.

- The *<RelOp>* element for each memory-consuming operator (in this example, just the sort) includes a *<MemoryFractions>* element, which indicates the portion of the total memory grant used by that operator. Two fractions are available: The input fraction refers to the portion of the memory grant used while the operator is reading input rows, and the output fraction refers to the portion of the memory grant used while the operator is producing output rows. Generally, during the input phase of an operator's execution, it must share memory with its children; during the output phase of an operator's execution, it must share memory with its parent. Because the sort is the only memory-consuming operator in the plan in this example, it uses the entire memory grant. Thus, the fractions are both one.

Although each relational operator element has been truncated from the output in Listing 10-1, each includes additional attributes and elements with all the estimated and runtime statistics available in the graphical and text query plan examples:

```
<RelOp NodeId="1" PhysicalOp="Merge Join" LogicalOp="Inner Join"
        EstimateRows="7" EstimateIO="0" EstimatedExecutionMode="Row"
        EstimateCPU="0.0058023" AvgRowSize="25"
        EstimatedTotalSubtreeCost="0.0534411" Parallel="false"
        EstimateRebinds="0" EstimateRewinds="0">
  <RunTimeInformation>
   <RunTimeCountersPerThread Thread="0" ActualRows="13"
          ActualEndOfScans="1" ActualExecutions="1" />
  </RunTimeInformation>
  ...
</RelOp>
```

Note Most examples in this chapter display the query plan in text format, obtained with *SET SHOWPLAN_TEXT ON*. Text format is more compact and easier to read than XML format and also includes more detail than screen shots of plans in graphical format. However, in some cases observing the "shape" of a query plan is important, and you will see some examples of graphical plans. If you prefer to see plans in a format other than the one supplied in this chapter, you can download the code for this chapter's queries from the companion website and display the plans in the format of your choosing by using your own installation of SQL Server.

Analyzing plans

To really understand query plans and really be able to spot, fix, or work around problems with query plans requires a solid understanding of the query operators that make up these plans. Overall, too many operators are available to discuss them in one chapter. Moreover, you can combine these operators into query plans in innumerable ways. Thus, this section focuses on understanding the most common query operators—the most basic building blocks of query execution—and give some insight into when and how SQL Server uses them to construct a variety of interesting query plans. Specifically, this section looks at scans and seeks, joins, aggregations, unions, a selection of subquery plans, and parallelism. After you understand how these basic operators and plans work, breaking down and understanding much bigger and more complex query plans is possible.

Scans and seeks

Scans and seeks are the iterators that SQL Server uses to read data from tables and indexes. These iterators are among the most fundamental ones that SQL Server supports. They appear in nearly every query plan. Understanding the difference between scans and seeks is important: A scan processes an entire table or the entire leaf level of an index, whereas a seek efficiently returns rows from one or more ranges of an index based on a predicate.

First look at an example of a scan. Consider the following query:

```
SELECT [OrderId] FROM [Orders] WHERE [RequiredDate] = '1998-03-26'
```

The *RequiredDate* column has no index. As a result, SQL Server must read every row of the *Orders* table; evaluate the predicate on *RequiredDate* for each row; and if the predicate is true (that is, if the row qualifies), return the row.

To maximize performance, SQL Server evaluates the predicate in the scan iterator whenever possible. However, if the predicate is too complex or too expensive, SQL Server might evaluate it in a separate filter iterator. The predicate appears in the text plan with the *WHERE* keyword or in the XML plan with the *<Predicate>* tag. Here is the text plan for the preceding query:

```
|--Clustered Index Scan(OBJECT:([Orders].[PK_Orders]),
  WHERE:([Orders].[RequiredDate]='1998-03-26'))
```

Figure 10-6 illustrates a scan.

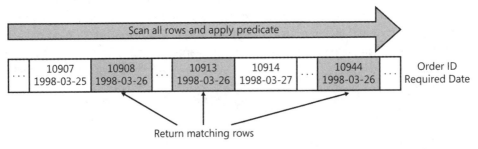

FIGURE 10-6 A scan operation, which examines all rows in all pages of a table.

Because a scan touches every row in the table whether or not it qualifies, the cost is proportional to the total number of rows in the table. Thus, a scan is an efficient strategy if the table is small or if many of the rows qualify for the predicate. However, if the table is large, and most of the rows do not qualify, a scan touches many more pages and rows and performs many more I/Os than is necessary.

Now look at an example of an index seek. Suppose that we have a similar query, but this time the predicate is on the *OrderDate* column on which we do have an index:

```
SELECT [OrderId] FROM [Orders] WHERE [OrderDate] = '1998-02-26'
```

This time, SQL Server can use the index to navigate directly to those rows that satisfy the predicate. In this case, the predicate is referred to as a seek predicate. In most cases, SQL Server doesn't need to evaluate the seek predicate explicitly; the index ensures that the seek operation returns only rows that qualify. The seek predicate appears in the text plan with the *SEEK* keyword or in the XML plan with the *<SeekPredicates>* tag. Here is the text plan for this example:

```
|--Index Seek(OBJECT:([Orders].[OrderDate]),
    SEEK:([Orders].[OrderDate]=CONVERT_IMPLICIT(datetime,[@1],0)) ORDERED FORWARD)
```

 Note SQL Server autoparameterized the query by substituting the parameter *@1* for the literal date.

Figure 10-7 illustrates an index seek.

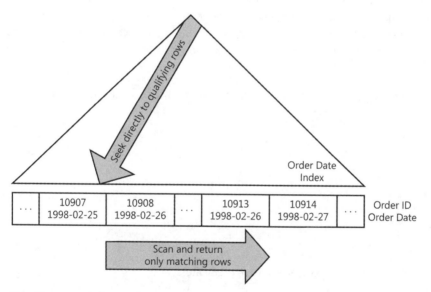

FIGURE 10-7 An index seek, which starts at the root and navigates to the leaf to find qualifying rows.

Because a seek touches only rows that qualify and pages that contain these qualifying rows, the cost is proportional to the number of qualifying rows and pages rather than to the total number of rows in the table. Thus, a seek is generally a more efficient strategy when using a highly selective seek predicate—that is, if a seek predicate eliminates a large fraction of the table.

SQL Server distinguishes between scans and seeks as well as between scans on heaps (a table with no clustered index), scans on clustered indexes, and scans on nonclustered indexes. Table 10-2 shows how all the valid combinations appear in plan output.

TABLE 10-2 Scan and seek operators as they appear in a query plan

	Scan	Seek
Heap	Table scan	
Clustered index	Clustered index scan	Clustered index seek
Nonclustered index	Index scan	Index seek

Seekable predicates and covered columns

Before SQL Server can perform an index seek, it must determine whether the keys of the index are suitable for evaluating a predicate in the query. A predicate that might be used as the basis for an index seek is referred to as a "seekable predicate." SQL Server must also determine whether the index contains or "covers" the set of the columns that are referenced by the query. The following discussion explains how to determine which predicates are seekable, which predicates aren't seekable, and which columns an index covers.

Single-column indexes

Determining whether a predicate can be used to seek on a single-column index is fairly straightforward. SQL Server can use single-column indexes to answer most simple comparisons including equality and inequality (greater than, less than, and so on) comparisons. More-complex expressions, such as functions over a column and *LIKE* predicates with a leading wildcard character, generally prevent SQL Server from using an index seek.

Suppose that column *Col1* has a single-column index. We can use this index to seek on these predicates.

- [Col1] = 3.14

- [Col1] > 100

- [Col1] BETWEEN 0 AND 99

- [Col1] LIKE 'abc%'

- [Col1] IN (2, 3, 5, 7)

However, we can't use the index to seek on these predicates.

- ABS([Col1]) = 1

- [Col1] + 1 = 9

- [Col1] LIKE '%abc'

Composite indexes

Composite, or multicolumn, indexes are slightly more complex. With a composite index, the order of the keys matters. It determines the sort order of the index and affects the set of seek predicates that SQL Server can evaluate using the index.

For an easy way to visualize why order matters, think about a phone book. A phone book is similar to an index with the keys (last name, first name). The contents of the phone book are sorted by last name, and we can easily look people up if we know their last names. However, if we have only a first name, getting a list of people with that name is very difficult. We would need another phone book sorted on first name.

In the same way, if we have an index on two columns, we can use only the index to satisfy a predicate on the second column if we have an equality predicate on the first column. Even if we can't use the index to satisfy the predicate on the second column, we might be able to use it on the first column. In this case, we introduce a "residual" predicate for the predicate on the second column. This predicate is evaluated just like any other scan predicate.

Consider using a two-column index on columns *Col1* and *Col2* to seek on any of the predicates that worked on the single-column index. The two-column index also can be used to seek on the following additional predicates.

- [Col1] = 3.14 AND [Col2] = 'pi'

- [Col1] = 'xyzzy' AND [Col2] <= 0

For the next set of examples, use the index to satisfy the predicate on column *Col1*, but not on column *Col2*. In these cases, column Col2 needs a residual predicate.

- [Col1] > 100 AND [Col2] > 100

- [Col1] LIKE 'abc%' AND [Col2] = 2

Finally, we can't use the index to seek on the next set of predicates because we can't seek even on column *Col1*. These cases require a different index—that is, one in which column *Col2* is the leading column—or require a scan with a predicate.

- [Col2] = 0

- [Col1] + 1 = 9 AND [Col2] BETWEEN 1 AND 9

- [Col1] LIKE '%abc' AND [Col2] IN (1, 3, 5)

Identifying index keys

In most cases, the index keys are the set of columns that you specify in the CREATE INDEX statement. However, when you create a nonunique, nonclustered index on a table with a clustered index, you append the clustered index keys to the nonclustered index keys if they're not explicitly part of the nonclustered index keys. You can seek on these implicit keys as though you specified them explicitly.

Covered columns   The heap or clustered index for a table (often called the "base table") contains (or "covers") all columns in the table. Nonclustered indexes, however, contain (or cover) only a subset of the columns in the table. By limiting the set of columns stored in a nonclustered index, SQL Server can store more rows on each page, which saves disk space and improves the efficiency of seeks and scans by reducing the number of I/Os and the number of pages touched. Nevertheless, a scan or seek of an index can only return the columns that the index covers.

Each nonclustered index covers the key columns that were specified when it was created. Also, if the base table is a clustered index, each nonclustered index on this table covers the clustered index keys whether or not they are part of the nonclustered index's key columns. Starting with SQL Server 2005, we can also add nonkey columns to a nonclustered index by using the *INCLUDE* clause of the *CREATE INDEX* statement. Unlike index keys, order isn't relevant for included columns.

Example of index keys and covered columns   Suppose that you have this schema:

```
CREATE TABLE T_heap (a int, b int, c int, d int, e int, f int);
CREATE INDEX T_heap_a ON T_heap (a);
CREATE INDEX T_heap_bc ON T_heap (b, c);
CREATE INDEX T_heap_d ON T_heap (d) INCLUDE (e);
CREATE UNIQUE INDEX T_heap_f ON T_heap (f);

CREATE TABLE T_clu (a int, b int, c int, d int, e int, f int);
CREATE UNIQUE CLUSTERED INDEX T_clu_a ON T_clu (a);
CREATE INDEX T_clu_b ON T_clu (b);
CREATE INDEX T_clu_ac ON T_clu (a, c);
CREATE INDEX T_clu_d ON T_clu (d) INCLUDE (e);
CREATE UNIQUE INDEX T_clu_f ON T_clu (f);
```

Table 10-3 shows the key columns and covered columns for each index.

TABLE 10-3 Key columns and covered columns in a set of nonclustered indexes

Index	Key columns	Covered columns
T_heap_a	a	a
T_heap_bc	b, c	b, c
T_heap_d	d	d, e
T_heap_f	f	f
T_clu_a	a	a, b, c, d, e, f
T_clu_b	b, a	a, b
T_clu_ac	a, c	a, c
T_clu_d	d, a	a, d, e
T_clu_f	f	a, f

Notice that the key columns for each nonclustered index on *T_clu* include the clustered index key column *a* with the exception of *T_clu_f*, which is a unique index. *T_clu_ac* includes column *a* explicitly as the first key column of the index, and so the column appears in the index only once and is used as the first key column. Because the other indexes don't explicitly include column *a*, the column is merely appended to the end of the list of keys.

Bookmark lookup

We've just seen how SQL Server can use an index seek to efficiently retrieve data that matches a predicate on the index keys. However, we also know that nonclustered indexes don't cover all the columns in a table. Consider a query with a predicate on a nonclustered index key that selects columns not covered by the index. If SQL Server performs a seek on the nonclustered index, it will miss some of the required columns. Alternatively, if it performs a scan of the clustered index (or heap), it will get all the columns, but will touch every row of the table and the operation will be less efficient. Look at the following query:

```
SELECT [OrderId], [CustomerId] FROM [Orders] WHERE [OrderDate] = '1998-02-26'
```

This query is identical to the query used earlier to illustrate an index seek, but this time the query selects two columns: *OrderId* and *CustomerId*. The nonclustered index *OrderDate* covers only the *OrderId* column (which also happens to be the clustering key for the *Orders* table in the *Northwind2* database).

SQL Server has a solution for this problem. For each row that it fetches from the nonclustered index, it can look up the value of the remaining columns (for instance, the *CustomerId* column in the example) in the clustered index. This operation is called a *bookmark lookup*. A bookmark is a pointer to the row in the heap or clustered index. SQL Server stores the bookmark for each row in the nonclustered index precisely so that it can always navigate from the nonclustered index to the corresponding row in the base table.

Figure 10-8 illustrates a bookmark lookup from a nonclustered index to a clustered index.

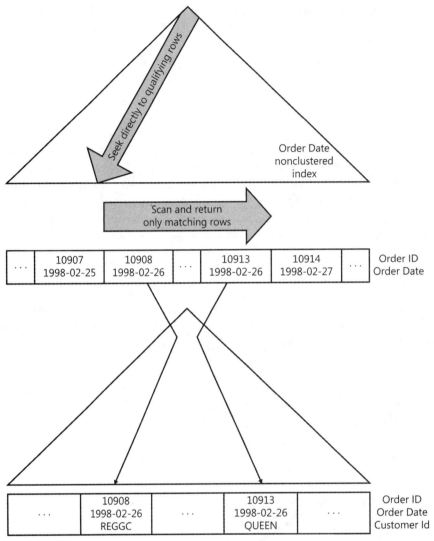

FIGURE 10-8 A bookmark lookup, using the information from the nonclustered index leaf level to find the row in the clustered index.

The resulting plan for this query uses a nested loops join (the behavior of this operator is discussed later in this chapter) combined with a clustered index seek if the base table is a clustered index, or a RID (row ID) lookup if the base table is a heap. You can tell that a clustered index seek is a bookmark lookup by the *LOOKUP* keyword in text plans or by the attribute *Lookup="true"* in XML plans. The text plan is shown next:

```
|--Nested Loops(Inner Join, OUTER REFERENCES:([Orders].[OrderID]))
   |--Index Seek(OBJECT:([Orders].[OrderDate]),
     SEEK:([Orders].[OrderDate]='1998-02-26') ORDERED FORWARD)
   |--Clustered Index Seek(OBJECT:([Orders].[PK_Orders]),
     SEEK:([Orders].[OrderID]=[Orders].[OrderID]) LOOKUP ORDERED FORWARD)
```

In a graphical plan, SQL Server uses the Key Lookup icon to make the distinction between a typical clustered index seek and a bookmark lookup very clear. Figure 10-9 illustrates the graphical execution plan.

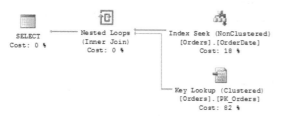

FIGURE 10-9 Graphical plan for index seek and bookmark lookup.

Bookmark lookup can be used with heaps as well as with clustered indexes, as shown earlier. A bookmark lookup on a heap still uses a nested loops join, but instead of a clustered index seek, SQL Server uses a *RID* lookup operator. A *RID* lookup operator includes a seek predicate on the heap bookmark, but a heap isn't an index, and a *RID* lookup isn't an index seek.

Bookmark lookup isn't a cheap operation. Assuming (as is commonly the case) that no correlation exists between the nonclustered and clustered index keys, each bookmark lookup performs a random I/O into the clustered index or heap. Random I/Os are very expensive. When comparing various plan alternatives, including scans, seeks, and seeks with bookmark lookups, the optimizer must decide whether it's cheaper to perform more sequential I/Os and touch more rows using an index scan (or an index seek with a less selective predicate) that covers all required columns, or to perform fewer random I/Os and touch fewer rows using a seek with a more selective predicate and a bookmark lookup. Because random I/Os are so much more expensive than sequential I/Os, the cutoff point beyond which a clustered index scan becomes cheaper than an index seek with a bookmark lookup generally involves a surprisingly small percentage of the total table—often just a few percent of the total rows.

> **Tip** In some cases, you can introduce a better plan option by creating a new index or by adding one or more included columns to an existing index to eliminate a bookmark lookup or change a scan into a seek. You add columns using the *INCLUDE* clause of the *CREATE INDEX* statement. Of course, whenever you create new indexes or add included columns to an existing index, you do consume additional disk space and you do make it more expensive to search and update the index. Thus, you must balance the frequency and importance of the queries that benefit from the new index against the queries or updates that are slower.

Joins

SQL Server supports three physical join operators: nested loops join, merge join, and hash join. The bookmark lookup example showed a nested loops join. The following sections take a detailed look at how each join operator works, explain what logical join types each operator supports, and discuss the performance trade-offs of each join type.

Before we get started, one common myth needs to be put to rest. No "best" join operator exists, and no join operator is inherently good or bad. We can't draw any conclusions about a query plan merely from the presence of a particular join operator. Each join operator performs well in the right circumstances and poorly in the wrong circumstances. The description of each join operator will include its strengths and weaknesses and the conditions and circumstances under which it performs well.

Nested loops join

The nested loops join is the simplest and most basic join algorithm. It compares each row from one table (known as the *outer table*) to each row from the other table (known as the *inner table*), looking for rows that satisfy the join predicate.

 Note The terms inner and outer are overloaded; their meanings must be inferred from context. *Inner table* and *outer table* refer to the inputs to the join; *inner join* and *outer join* refer to the semantics of the logical join operations.

The following pseudocode shows the nested loops join algorithm:

```
for each row R1 in the outer table
  for each row R2 in the inner table
    if R1 joins with R2
       return (R1, R2)
```

The nesting of the loops in this algorithm gives the nested loops join its name.

The total number of rows compared, and thus the cost of this algorithm, is proportional to the size of the outer table multiplied by the size of the inner table. Because this cost grows quickly as the size of the input tables grow, in practice the optimizer tries to minimize cost by reducing the number of inner rows that must be processed for each outer row.

Consider this query:

```
SELECT O.[OrderId]
FROM [Customers] C JOIN [Orders] O ON C.[CustomerId] = O.[CustomerId]
WHERE C.[City] = N'London'
```

Executing this query results in the following query plan:

```
Rows Executes
46  1     |--Nested Loops(Inner Join, OUTER REFERENCES:([C].[CustomerID]))
6   1          |--Index Seek(OBJECT:([Customers].[City] AS [C]),
                  SEEK:([C].[City]=N'London') ORDERED FORWARD)
46  6          |--Index Seek(OBJECT:([Orders].[CustomerID] AS [O]),
                  SEEK:([O].[CustomerID]=[C].[CustomerID]) ORDERED FORWARD)
```

Unlike most examples in this chapter, this plan was generated using *SET STATISTICS PROFILE ON* to show the number of rows and executions for each operator. The outer table in this plan is *Customers*; the inner table is *Orders*. Hence, according to the nested loops join algorithm, SQL Server begins by seeking on the *Customers* table. The join takes one customer at a time and performs an index seek on the *Orders* table for each customer. Because the table has six customers, it executes the index seek on the *Orders* table six times. Notice that the index seek on the *Orders* table depends on the CustomerId, which comes from the *Customers* table. Each of the six times that SQL Server repeats the index seek on the *Orders* table, *CustomerId* has a different value. Thus, each of the six executions of the index seek varies and returns different rows.

CustomerId is referred to as a correlated parameter. If a nested loops join has correlated parameters, those parameters appear in the plan as OUTER REFERENCES. This type of nested loops join in which an index seek depends on a correlated parameter is often referred to as an index join. An index join is possibly the most common type of nested loops join. In fact, in SQL Server, as this chapter has shown, a bookmark lookup is simply an index join between a nonclustered index and the base table.

The prior example illustrated two important techniques that SQL Server uses to boost the performance of a nested loops join: correlated parameters and, more importantly, an index seek based on those correlated parameters on the inner side of the join. Another performance optimization not seen here is the use of a lazy spool on the inner side of the join. A lazy spool caches and can reaccess the results from the inner side of the join. A lazy spool is especially useful when correlated parameters have many duplicate values and when the inner side of the join is relatively expensive to evaluate. By using a lazy spool, SQL Server can avoid recomputing the inner side of the join multiple times with the same correlated parameters. Later, this chapter shows some examples of spools, including lazy spools.

Not all nested loops joins have correlated parameters. A simple way to get a nested loops join without correlated parameters is with a cross join, which matches all rows of one table with all rows of the other table. Implementing a cross join with a nested loops join involves scanning and joining every row of the inner table to every row of the outer table. The set of inner table rows doesn't change depending on which outer table row is processed. Thus, with a cross join, no correlated parameters can be used.

In some cases, if we don't have a suitable index or don't have a join predicate that's suitable for an index seek, the optimizer might generate a query plan without correlated parameters. The rules for determining whether a join predicate is suitable for use with an index seek are identical to the rules for determining whether any other predicate is suitable for an index seek. Consider the following query, which returns the number of employees who were hired after each other employee:

```
SELECT E1.[EmployeeId], COUNT(*)
FROM [Employees] E1 JOIN [Employees] E2
  ON E1.[HireDate] < E2.[HireDate]
GROUP BY E1.[EmployeeId]
```

Because the *HireDate* column has no index, this query generates a simple nested loops join with a predicate but without any correlated parameters and without an index seek:

```
|--Compute Scalar(DEFINE:([Expr1004]=CONVERT_IMPLICIT(int,[Expr1007],0)))
   |--Stream Aggregate(GROUP BY:([E1].[EmployeeID]) DEFINE:([Expr1007]=Count(*)))
      |--Nested Loops(Inner Join, WHERE:([E1].[HireDate]<[E2].[HireDate]))
         |--Clustered Index Scan(OBJECT:([Employees].[PK_Employees] AS [E1]))
         |--Clustered Index Scan(OBJECT:([Employees].[PK_Employees] AS [E2]))
```

Don't be concerned with the aggregation. The purpose of this example is to illustrate the behavior of the nested loops join. Aggregation is discussed later in this chapter.

Now consider the following identical query that has been rewritten to use a *CROSS APPLY*:

```
SELECT E1.[EmployeeId], ECnt.Cnt
FROM [Employees] E1 CROSS APPLY
(
    SELECT COUNT(*) Cnt
    FROM [Employees] E2
    WHERE E1.[HireDate] < E2.[HireDate]
) ECnt
```

Although these two queries are identical and will always return the same results, the plan for the query with CROSS APPLY uses a nested loops join with a correlated parameter:

```
|--Nested Loops(Inner Join, OUTER REFERENCES:([E1].[HireDate]))
   |--Clustered Index Scan(OBJECT:([Employees].[PK_Employees] AS [E1]))
   |--Compute Scalar(DEFINE:([Expr1004]=CONVERT_IMPLICIT(int,[Expr1007],0)))
      |--Stream Aggregate(DEFINE:([Expr1007]=Count(*)))
         |--Clustered Index Scan (OBJECT:([Employees].[PK_Employees] AS [E2]),
            WHERE:([E1].[HireDate]<[E2].[HireDate]))
```

 Tip This example demonstrates that in some cases, small changes to a query—even re-writes that don't change the semantics of the query—can yield substantially different query plans. In particular, in some cases, a *CROSS APPLY* can induce the optimizer to generate a correlated nested loops join, which might or might not be desirable.

Join predicates and logical join types   The nested loops join is one of the most flexible join methods. It supports all join predicates including equijoin (equality) predicates and inequality predicates.

The nested loops join supports the following logical join operators.

- Inner join

- Left outer join

- Cross join

- Cross apply and outer apply

- Left semi-join and left anti-semi-join

The nested loops join doesn't support the following logical join operators.

- Right and full outer join

- Right semi-join and right anti-semi-join

To understand why the nested loops join doesn't support right outer or semi-joins, first look at how to extend the nested loops join algorithm to support left outer and semi-joins. The following pseudocode for a left outer join needs only two extra lines (shown in bold) to extend the inner join algorithm:

```
for each row R1 in the outer table
  begin
    for each row R2 in the inner table
      if R1 joins with R2
        output (R1, R2)
      if R1 did not join
        output (R1, NULL)
  end
```

This algorithm keeps track of whether a particular outer row is joined. If after exhausting all inner rows we find that a particular inner row didn't join, we can output it as a NULL extended row. We can write similar pseudocode for a left semi-join or left anti-semi-join.

> **Note** A semi-join or anti-semi-join returns one-half of the input information—that is, columns from one of the joined tables. So rather than output (R1, R2) as the previous pseudocode shows, a left semi-join outputs just R1. Moreover, a semi-join returns each row of the outer table once, at most. Thus, after finding a match and outputting a specific row R1, a left semi-join moves immediately to the next outer row. A left anti-semi-join returns a row from R1 if it does *not* match with R2.

Now consider how to support a right outer join. In this case, we want to return pairs (R1, R2) for rows that join and pairs (NULL, R2) for rows of the inner table that don't join. The problem is that the inner table is scanned multiple times—once for each row of the outer join. The same inner rows multiple might be encountered times during these multiple scans. At what point can we conclude that a particular inner row hasn't or won't join? Moreover, if an index join is used, some inner rows might not be encountered at all but should also be returned for an outer join. Further analysis uncovers similar problems for right semi-joins and right anti-semi-joins.

Fortunately, because right outer join commutes into left outer join, and right semi-join commutes into left semi-join, SQL Server can use the nested loops join for right outer and semi-joins. However, although these transformations are valid, they might affect performance. When the optimizer transforms a right join into a left join, it also switches the outer and inner inputs to the join. Recall that to use an index join, the index needs to be on the inner table. By switching the outer and inner inputs to the table, the optimizer also switches the table on which we need an index to be able to use an index join.

Full outer joins The nested loops join can't directly support full outer join. However, the optimizer can transform [Table1] FULL OUTER JOIN [Table2] into [Table1] LEFT OUTER JOIN [Table2] UNION ALL [Table2] LEFT ANTI-SEMI-JOIN [Table1]. Basically, this transforms the full outer join into a left outer join—which includes all pairs of rows from *Table1* and *Table2* that join and all rows of *Table1* that don't join—then adds back the rows of *Table2* that don't join using an anti-semi-join. Suppose that we have two customer tables and that each customer table has different customer IDs. We want to merge the two lists while keeping track of the customer IDs from each table. We want the result to include all customers, whether or not a customer appears in both lists or in just one list. We can generate this result with a full outer join. Make the rather unrealistic assumption that two customers with the same name are indeed the same customer.

```
CREATE TABLE [Customer1] ([CustomerId] int PRIMARY KEY, [Name] nvarchar(30))
CREATE TABLE [Customer2] ([CustomerId] int PRIMARY KEY, [Name] nvarchar(30))

SELECT C1.[Name], C1.[CustomerId], C2.[CustomerId]
FROM [Customer1] C1 FULL OUTER JOIN [Customer2] C2
   ON C1.[Name] = C2.[Name]
```

The plan for this query demonstrates the transformation in action:

```
|--Concatenation
   |--Nested Loops(Left Outer Join, WHERE:([C1].[Name]=[C2].[Name]))
   |  |--Clustered Index Scan(OBJECT:([Customer1].[PK_Customer1] AS [C1]))
   |  |--Clustered Index Scan(OBJECT:([Customer2].[PK_Customer2] AS [C2]))
   |--Compute Scalar(DEFINE:([C1].[CustomerId]=NULL, [C1].[Name]=NULL))
      |--Nested Loops(Left Anti Semi Join, WHERE:([C1].[Name]=[C2].[Name]))
         |--Clustered Index Scan(OBJECT:([Customer2].[PK_Customer2] AS [C2]))
         |--Clustered Index Scan(OBJECT:([Customer1].[PK_Customer1] AS [C1]))
```

The concatenation operator implements the *UNION ALL*. This operator is covered in a bit more detail when unions are discussed later in this chapter.

Costing The complexity or cost of a nested loops join is proportional to the size of the outer input multiplied by the size of the inner input. Thus, a nested loops join generally performs best for relatively small input sets. The inner input doesn't need to be small, but if it's large, including an index on a highly selective join key helps.

In some cases, a nested loops join is the only join algorithm that SQL Server can use. SQL Server must use a nested loops join for cross joins as well as for some complex cross applies and outer applies. Moreover, as we are about to see, with one exception, a nested loops join is the only join algorithm that SQL Server can use without at least one equijoin predicate. In these cases, the optimizer must choose a nested loops join regardless of cost.

 Note Merge join supports full outer joins without an equijoin predicate. This unusual scenario is discussed in the next section.

Merge join

Now look at merge join. Unlike the nested loops join, which supports any join predicate, the merge join requires at least one equijoin predicate. Moreover, the inputs to the merge join must be sorted on the join keys. For example, for a join predicate [Customers].[CustomerId] = [Orders].[CustomerId], the *Customers* and *Orders* tables must both be sorted on the *CustomerId* column.

The merge join works by simultaneously reading and comparing the two sorted inputs one row at a time. At each step, it compares the next row from each input. If the rows are equal, it outputs a joined row and continues. If the rows aren't equal, it discards the lesser of the two inputs and continues. Because the inputs are sorted, any row that the join discards must be less than any of the remaining rows in either input and, as a result, can never join. A merge join doesn't necessarily need to scan every row from both inputs. As soon as it reaches the end of either input, the merge join stops scanning.

The algorithm is expressed in the following pseudocode:

```
get first row R1 from input 1
get first row R2 from input 2
while not at the end of either input
  begin
    if R1 joins with R2
      begin
        output (R1, R2)
        get next row R2 from input 2
      end
    else if R1 < R2
      get next row R1 from input 1
    else
      get next row R2 from input 2
  end
```

Unlike the nested loops join, in which the total cost might be proportional to the *product* of the number of rows in the input tables, with a merge join each table is read at most once, and the total cost is proportional to the *sum* of the number of rows in the inputs. Thus, merge join is often a better choice for larger inputs.

One-to-many vs. many-to-many merge join The previous pseudocode implements a one-to-many merge join. After it joins two rows, it discards R2 and moves to the next row of input 2. This presumes that it will never find another row from input 1 that will ever join with the discarded row. In other words, input 1 can't have any duplicates. However, input 2 can have duplicates because it didn't discard the current row from input 1.

Merge join can also support many-to-many merge joins. In this case, it must keep a copy of each row from input 2 whenever it joins two rows. This way, if it later finds a duplicate row from input 1, it can play back the saved rows. However, if it finds that the next row from input 1 isn't a duplicate, it can discard the saved rows. The merge join saves these rows in a worktable in *tempdb*. The amount of required disk space depends on the number of duplicates in input 2.

A one-to-many merge join is always more efficient than a many-to-many merge join because it doesn't need a worktable. To use a one-to-many merge join, the optimizer must be able to determine that one of the inputs consists strictly of unique rows. Typically, this means that either the input has a unique index or the plan has an explicit operator (perhaps a sort distinct or a group by) to ensure that the input rows are unique.

Sort merge join vs. index merge join   SQL Server can get sorted inputs for a merge join in two ways: It can explicitly sort the inputs using a sort operator or it can read the rows from an index. In general, a plan using an index to achieve sort order is cheaper than a plan using an explicit sort.

Join predicates and logical join types   Merge joins support multiple equijoin predicates as long as the inputs are sorted on all the join keys. The specific sort order doesn't matter as long as both inputs are sorted in the same order. For example, for a join predicate T1.[Col1] = T2.[Col1] and T1.[Col2] = T2.[Col2], we can use a merge join as long as tables *T1* and *T2* are both sorted either on (Col1, Col2) or on (Col2, Col1).

Merge joins also support residual predicates. Consider the join predicate T1.[Col1] = T2.[Col1] and T1.[Col2] > T2.[Col2]. Although the inequality predicate can't be used as part of a merge join, the equijoin portion of this predicate can be used to perform a merge join (presuming both tables are sorted on [Col1]). For each row pair that joins on the equality portion of predicate, the merge join can apply the inequality predicate. If the inequality evaluates to true, the join returns the row; if not, it discards the row.

Merge joins support all outer and semi-join variations. For instance, to implement an outer join, a merge join simply needs to track whether each row has joined. Rather than discard a row that hasn't joined, it can NULL extend it and output it as appropriate. Notice that unlike the inner join case, in which a merge join can stop as soon as it reaches the end of either input, for an outer (or anti-semi-) join the merge join must scan to the end of whichever input it's preserving. For a full outer join, it must scan to the end of both inputs.

Merge joins support a special case for full outer join. In some cases, the optimizer generates a merge join for a full outer join, even without an equijoin predicate. This join is equivalent to a many-to-many merge join in which all rows from one input join with all rows from the other input. As with any other many-to-many merge join, SQL Server builds a worktable to store and play back all rows from the second input. SQL Server supports this plan as an alternative to the previously discussed transformation used to support full outer join with nested loops join.

Examples   Because merge joins require that input rows be sorted, the optimizer is most likely to choose a merge join when an index returns rows in that sort order. The following query simply joins the *Orders* and *Customers* tables:

```
SELECT O.[OrderId], C.[CustomerId], C.[ContactName]
FROM [Orders] O JOIN [Customers] C
  ON O.[CustomerId] = C.[CustomerId]
```

Because no predicates exist other than the join predicates, both tables must be scanned in their entirety. Moreover, the *CustomerId* column of both tables has covering indexes. Thus, the optimizer chooses a merge join plan:

```
|--Merge Join(Inner Join, MERGE:([C].[CustomerID])=([O].[CustomerID]), RESIDUAL:(...))
   |--Clustered Index Scan(OBJECT:([Customers].[PK_Customers] AS [C]), ORDERED FORWARD)
   |--Index Scan(OBJECT:([Orders].[CustomerID] AS [O]), ORDERED FORWARD)
```

We can tell that this join is one to many by the absence of the *MANY-TO-MANY* keyword in the query plan. The *CustomerId* column of the *Customers* table has a unique index—actually, a primary key. Thus, the optimizer knows that this table won't have duplicate *CustomerId* values and chooses the one-to-many join.

For a unique index to enable a one-to-many join, we must be joining on all the key columns of the unique index. Joining on a subset of the key columns isn't enough because the index guarantees only uniqueness on the entire set of key columns.

Now consider a slightly more complex example. The following query returns a list of orders that are shipped to cities different from the city on file for the customer who placed the order:

```
SELECT O.[OrderId], C.[CustomerId], C.[ContactName]
FROM [Orders] O JOIN [Customers] C
   ON O.[CustomerId] = C.[CustomerId] AND O.[ShipCity] <> C.[City]
ORDER BY C.[CustomerId]
```

The *ORDER BY* clause encourages the optimizer to choose a merge join. (This point will be explained in a moment.) Here is the query plan:

```
|--Merge Join(Inner Join, MERGE:([C].[CustomerID])=([O].[CustomerID]),
   RESIDUAL:(... AND [O].[ShipCity]<>[C].[City]))
      |--Clustered Index Scan(OBJECT:([Customers].[PK_Customers] AS [C]), ORDERED FORWARD)
      |--Sort(ORDER BY:([O].[CustomerID] ASC))
                  |--Clustered Index Scan(OBJECT:([Orders].[PK_Orders] AS [O]))
```

This new plan has a couple of points worth noting.

- Because this query needs the *ShipCity* column from the *Orders* table for the extra predicate, the optimizer can't use a scan of the *CustomerId* index, which doesn't cover the extra column, to get rows from the Orders table sorted by the *CustomerId* column. Instead, the optimizer chooses to scan the clustered index and sort the results. The *ORDER BY* clause requires that the optimizer add this sort either before the join, as in this example, or after the join. By performing the sort before the join, the plan can take advantage of the merge join. Moreover, the merge join preserves the input order, so the data doesn't need to be sorted again after the join.

 Note Technically, the optimizer could decide to use a scan of the *CustomerId* index along with a bookmark lookup, but because it's scanning the entire table, the bookmark lookup would be prohibitively expensive.

- This merge join demonstrates a residual predicate: *O.[ShipCity] <> C.[City]*. The optimizer can't use this predicate as part of the join's merge keys because it's an inequality. However, as the example shows, as long as at least one equality predicate exists, SQL Server can use the merge join.

Hash join

Hash join is the third physical join operator. Hash joins do the heavy lifting when dealing with physical join operators. Although nested loops joins work well with relatively small data sets, and merge joins help with moderately sized data sets, hash joins excel at performing the largest joins. Hash joins parallelize and scale better than any other join and are great at minimizing response times for data warehouse queries.

Hash joins share many characteristics with merge joins. Like merge joins, hash joins require at least one equijoin predicate, support residual predicates, and support all outer and semi-joins. Unlike merge joins, hash joins don't require ordered input sets and, although they do support full outer joins, require an equijoin predicate.

The hash join algorithm executes in two phases known as *build* and *probe*. During the build phase, it reads all rows from the first input (often called the left or build input), hashes the rows on the equijoin keys, and creates or builds an in-memory hash table. During the probe phase, it reads all rows from the second input (often called the right or probe input), hashes these rows on the same equijoin keys, and looks or probes for matching rows in the hash table. Because hash functions can lead to collisions (two different key values that hash to the same value), the hash join typically must check each potential match to ensure that it really joins. Here is pseudocode for this algorithm:

```
for each row R1 in the build table
  begin
    calculate hash value on R1 join key(s)
    insert R1 into the appropriate hash bucket
  end
for each row R2 in the probe table
  begin
    calculate hash value on R2 join key(s)
    for each row R1 in the corresponding hash bucket
      if R1 joins with R2
        output (R1, R2)
  end
```

Unlike the nested loops and merge joins, which immediately begin flowing output rows, the hash join is blocking on its build input. That is, it must read and process its entire build input before it can return any rows. Moreover, unlike the other join methods, the hash join requires a memory grant to store the hash table. Thus, SQL Server can run a limited number of concurrent hash joins at any specific time. Although these characteristics and restrictions generally aren't a problem for data warehouses, they are undesirable for most OLTP applications.

 Note A sort merge join does require a memory grant for the sort operator(s), but doesn't require a memory grant for the merge join.

Memory and spilling   Before a hash join begins execution, SQL Server tries to estimate how much memory it will need to build its hash table. It uses the cardinality estimate for the size of the build input along with the expected average row size to estimate the memory requirement. To minimize the memory required by the hash join, the optimizer chooses the smaller of the two tables as the build table. SQL Server then tries to reserve sufficient memory to ensure that the hash join can successfully store the entire build table in memory.

If SQL Server grants the hash join less memory than it requests or if the estimate is too low, the hash join might run out of memory during the build phase. If the hash join runs out of memory, it begins spilling a small percentage of the total hash table to disk (to a workfile in *tempdb*). The hash join keeps track of which buckets of the hash table are still in memory and which ones have been spilled to disk. As it reads each new row from the build table, it checks to see whether it hashes to an in-memory or an on-disk bucket. If it hashes to an in-memory bucket, it proceeds as usual. If it hashes to an on-disk bucket, it writes the row to disk. This process of running out of memory and spilling buckets to disk can repeat multiple times until the build phase is complete.

The hash join performs a similar process during the probe phase. For each new row from the probe table, it checks to see whether it hashes to an in-memory or an on-disk bucket. If it hashes to an in-memory bucket, it probes the hash table, produces any appropriate joined rows, and discards the row. If it hashes to an on-disk bucket, it writes the row to disk. After the join completes the first pass of the probe table, it returns one by one to any buckets that spilled, reads the build rows back into memory, reconstructs the hash table for each bucket, and then reads the corresponding probe bucket and completes the join. If while processing spilled sets of buckets the hash join again runs out of memory, the process simply repeats. The number of times that the hash join repeats this algorithm and spills the same data is referred to as the *recursion level*. After a set number of recursion levels, if the hash join continues to spill, it switches to a special "bailout" algorithm that, although less efficient, is guaranteed to complete eventually.

Left deep vs. right deep vs. bushy hash join trees   The shape and order of joins in a query plan can significantly affect the performance of the plan. The shape of a query plan is so important that the terms for the most common shapes—left deep, right deep, and bushy—are based on the physical appearance of the query plan (see Figure 10-10).

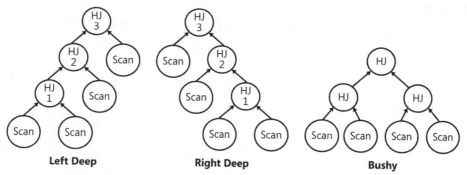

FIGURE 10-10 Three common shapes for query plans involving joins.

The shape of the join tree is particularly interesting for hash joins because it affects the memory consumption.

In a left deep tree, the output of one hash join is the build input to the next hash join. Because hash joins consume their entire build input before moving to the probe phase, in a left deep tree only adjacent pairs of hash joins are active at the same time. For example, for the left deep example in Figure 10-10, SQL Server begins by building the hash table for HJ1. When HJ1 begins probing, HJ2 begins building its hash table. When HJ1 is done probing, SQL Server can release the memory used by its hash table. Only then does HJ2 begin probing and HJ3 begin building its hash table. Thus, HJ1 and HJ3 are never active at the same time and can share the same memory grant. The total memory requirement is the maximum of the memory needed by any two adjacent joins—that is, HJ1 and HJ2 or HJ2 and HJ3.

In a right deep tree, the output of one hash join is the probe input to the next hash join. All the hash joins build their complete hash tables before any begin the probe phase of the join. All the hash joins are active at the same time and can't share memory. When SQL Server does begin the probe phase of the join, the rows flow up the entire tree of hash joins without blocking. Thus, the total memory requirement is the sum of the memory needed by all three joins.

Examples   The following query is nearly identical to the earlier merge join example except that one additional column, the *OrderDate* column, is selected from the *Orders* table:

```
SELECT O.[OrderId], O.[OrderDate], C.[CustomerId], C.[ContactName]
FROM [Orders] O JOIN [Customers] C
   ON O.[CustomerId] = C.[CustomerId]
```

Because the *CustomerId* index on the *Orders* table doesn't cover the *OrderDate* column, we need a sort to use a merge join. The second merge join example showed this outcome earlier, but this time an *ORDER BY* clause isn't used. Thus, the optimizer chooses the following hash join plan:

```
|--Hash Match(Inner Join, HASH:([C].[CustomerID])=([O].[CustomerID]), RESIDUAL:(...))
   |--Clustered Index Scan(OBJECT:([Customers].[PK_Customers] AS [C]))
   |--Clustered Index Scan(OBJECT:([Orders].[PK_Orders] AS [O]))
```

Summary of join properties

Table 10-4 summarizes the characteristics of the three physical join operators.

TABLE 10-4 Characteristics of the three join algorithms

	Nested loops join	Merge join	Hash join
Best for...	Relatively small inputs with an index on the inner table on the join key.	Medium to large inputs with indexes to provide order on the equijoin keys and/or where order is required after the join.	Data warehouse queries with medium to large inputs. Scalable parallel execution.
Concurrency	Supports large numbers of concurrent users.	Many-to-one join with order provided by indexes (rather than explicit sorts) supports large numbers of concurrent users.	Best for small numbers of concurrent users.
Stop and go	No	No	Yes (build input only)
Equijoin required	No	Yes (except for full outer join)	Yes
Outer and semi-joins	Left joins only (full outer joins via transformation)	All join types	All join types
Uses memory	No	No (might require sorts that use memory)	Yes
Uses tempdb	No	Yes (many-to-many join only)	Yes (if join runs out of memory and spills)
Requires order	No	Yes	No
Preserves order	Yes (outer input only)	Yes	No
Supports dynamic cursors	Yes	No	No

Aggregations

SQL Server supports two physical operators for performing aggregations: stream aggregate and hash aggregate operators.

Scalar aggregation

Scalar aggregates are queries with aggregate functions in the select list and no GROUP BY clause. Scalar aggregates always return a single row. SQL Server always implements scalar aggregates using the stream aggregate operator.

First consider a trivial example:

```
SELECT COUNT(*) FROM [Orders]
```

This query produces the following plan:

```
|--Compute Scalar(DEFINE:([Expr1003]=CONVERT_IMPLICIT(int,[Expr1004],0)))
   |--Stream Aggregate(DEFINE:([Expr1004]=Count(*)))
      |--Index Scan(OBJECT:([Orders].[OrderDate]))
```

The stream aggregate operator just counts the number of input rows and returns this result. The stream aggregate actually computes the count ([Expr1004]) as a BIGINT. The compute scalar is needed to convert this result to the expected output type of INT. Notice that a scalar stream aggregate is one of the only examples of a nonleaf operator that can produce an output row even with an empty input set.

You can easily see how to implement other simple scalar aggregate functions such as *MIN*, *MAX*, and *SUM*. A single-stream aggregate operator can calculate multiple scalar aggregates at the same time:

```
SELECT MIN([OrderDate]), MAX([OrderDate]) FROM [Orders]
```

Here's the query plan with a single-stream aggregate operator:

```
|--Stream Aggregate(DEFINE:([Expr1003]=MIN([Orders].[OrderDate]),
  [Expr1004]=MAX([Orders].[OrderDate])))
   |--Index Scan(OBJECT:([Orders].[OrderDate]))
```

Notice that SQL Server doesn't need to convert the result for the *MIN* and *MAX* aggregates because the data types of these aggregates are computed based on the data type of the OrderDate column.

Some aggregates such as *AVG* are actually calculated from two other aggregates such as *SUM* and *COUNT*:

```
SELECT AVG([Freight]) FROM [Orders]
```

Notice that the compute scalar operator in the plan computes the average from the sum and count:

```
|--Compute Scalar(DEFINE:([Expr1003]=CASE WHEN [Expr1004]=(0)
  THEN NULL
  ELSE [Expr1005]/CONVERT_IMPLICIT(money,[Expr1004],0)
  END))
   |--Stream Aggregate(DEFINE:([Expr1004]=COUNT_BIG([Orders].[Freight]),
     Expr1005]=SUM([Orders].[Freight])))
      |--Clustered Index Scan(OBJECT:([Orders].[PK_Orders]))
```

The *CASE* expression is needed to make sure that SQL Server doesn't attempt to divide by zero.

Although *SUM* doesn't need to be computed per se, it still needs the count:

```
SELECT SUM([Freight]) FROM [Orders]
```

Notice that the *CASE* expression in this query plan uses the *COUNT* to ensure that *SUM* returns NULL instead of zero if no rows exist:

```
|--Compute Scalar(DEFINE:([Expr1003]=CASE WHEN [Expr1004]=(0)
  THEN NULL
  ELSE [Expr1005]
  END))
   |--Stream Aggregate(DEFINE:([Expr1004]=COUNT_BIG([Orders].[Freight]),
```

```
[Expr1005]=SUM([Orders].[Freight])))
    |--Clustered Index Scan(OBJECT:([Orders].[PK_Orders]))
```

Scalar distinct   Now look at what happens if a *DISTINCT* keyword is added to a scalar aggregate. Consider this query to compute the number of distinct cities to which orders have been shipped:

```
SELECT COUNT(DISTINCT [ShipCity]) FROM [Orders]
```

This query produces this query plan:

```
|--Compute Scalar(DEFINE:([Expr1003]=CONVERT_IMPLICIT(int,[Expr1006],0)))
   |--Stream Aggregate(DEFINE:([Expr1006]=COUNT([Orders].[ShipCity])))
      |--Sort(DISTINCT ORDER BY:([Orders].[ShipCity] ASC))
         |--Clustered Index Scan(OBJECT:([Orders].[PK_Orders]))
```

Because the query must count only rows that have a unique value for the *ShipCity* column, SQL Server adds a sort distinct operator to eliminate rows with duplicate *ShipCity* values. Sort distinct is one of the common methods used by SQL Server to eliminate duplicates. Removing duplicate rows after sorting the input set is easy because the duplicates are then next to one another. SQL Server can use other methods to eliminate duplicates, as explained shortly. Other than the addition of the sort operator, this plan is the same as the *COUNT(*)* plan with which the discussion of aggregation began.

Not all distinct aggregates require duplicate elimination. For example, MIN and MAX behave identically with and without the distinct keyword. The minimum and maximum values of a set remain the same whether or not the set includes duplicate values. For example, this query gets the same plan as the previous *MIN/MAX* query, but without the *DISTINCT* keyword:

```
SELECT MIN(DISTINCT [OrderDate]), MAX(DISTINCT [OrderDate]) FROM [Orders]
```

For a unique index, SQL Server also can skip the duplicate elimination because the index guarantees that no duplicates exist. For example, the following query is identical to the simple *COUNT(*)* query with which this discussion began:

```
SELECT COUNT(DISTINCT [OrderId]) FROM [Orders]
```

Multiple distinct   Consider this query:

```
SELECT COUNT(DISTINCT [ShipAddress]), COUNT(DISTINCT [ShipCity])
FROM [Orders]
```

As we've seen, SQL Server can compute *COUNT(DISTINCT [ShipAddress])* by eliminating rows that have duplicate values for the *ShipAddress* column. Similarly, SQL Server can compute *COUNT(DISTINCT [ShipCity])* by eliminating rows that have duplicate values for the *ShipCity* column. But considering that these two sets of rows are different, how can SQL Server compute both at the same time? The answer is that it can't. It must first compute one aggregate result, then the other, and then it must combine the two results into a single output row:

```
|--Nested Loops(Inner Join)
   |--Compute Scalar(DEFINE:([Expr1003]=CONVERT_IMPLICIT(int,[Expr1009],0)))
   |   |--Stream Aggregate(DEFINE:([Expr1009]=COUNT([Orders].[ShipAddress])))
   |      |--Sort(DISTINCT ORDER BY:([Orders].[ShipAddress] ASC))
   |         |--Clustered Index Scan(OBJECT:([Orders].[PK_Orders]))
   |--Compute Scalar(DEFINE:([Expr1004]=CONVERT_IMPLICIT(int,[Expr1010],0)))
      |--Stream Aggregate(DEFINE:([Expr1010]=COUNT([Orders].[ShipCity])))
         |--Sort(DISTINCT ORDER BY:([Orders].[ShipCity] ASC))
            |--Clustered Index Scan
               (OBJECT:([Orders].[PK_Orders]))
```

The two inputs to the nested loops join compute the two counts from the original query. One of the inputs removes duplicates and computes the count for the *ShipAddress* column; the other input removes duplicates and computes the count for the *ShipCity* column. The nested loops join has no join predicate; it's a cross join. Because both inputs to the nested loops join each produce a single row—they are both scalar aggregates—the result of the cross join is also a single row. The cross join just serves to "glue" the two columns of the result into a single row.

If different columns have more than two distinct aggregates, the optimizer just uses more than one cross join. The optimizer also uses this type of plan for a mix of nondistinct and distinct aggregates. In that case, the optimizer uses a single cross join input to calculate all the nondistinct aggregates.

Stream aggregation

Now that we've seen how to compute scalar aggregates, look at how SQL Server computes general-purpose aggregates that involve a *GROUP BY* clause. Begin by looking closer at how stream aggregation works.

The algorithm Stream aggregate relies on data arriving sorted by the *GROUP BY* column(s). Like a merge join, if a query includes a *GROUP BY* clause with more than one column, the stream aggregate can use any sort order that includes all the columns. For example, a stream aggregate can group on columns *Col1* and *Col2* with data sorted on (Col1, Col2) or on (Col2, Col1). As with merge join, the sort order might be delivered by an index or by an explicit sort operator. The sort order ensures that sets of rows with the same value for the *GROUP BY* columns will be adjacent to one another.

Here's pseudocode for the stream aggregate algorithm:

```
clear the current aggregate results
clear the current group by columns
for each input row
  begin
    if the input row does not match the current group by columns
      begin
        output the current aggregate results (if any)
        clear the current aggregate results
        set the current group by columns to the input row
      end
    update the aggregate results with the input row
  end
```

For example, to compute a *SUM*, the stream aggregate considers each input row. If the input row belongs to the current group (that is, the *group by* columns of the input row match the *group by* columns of the previous row), the stream aggregate updates the current *SUM* by adding the appropriate value from the input row to the running total. If the input row belongs to a new group (that is, the *group by* columns of the input row don't match the *group by* columns of the previous row), the stream aggregate outputs the current *SUM*, resets the *SUM* to zero, and starts a new group.

Simple examples Consider the following query that counts the number of orders shipped to each address:

```
SELECT [ShipAddress], [ShipCity], COUNT(*)
FROM [Orders]
GROUP BY [ShipAddress], [ShipCity]
```

Here is the plan for this query:

```
|--Compute Scalar(DEFINE:([Expr1003]=CONVERT_IMPLICIT(int,[Expr1006],0)))
   |--Stream Aggregate(GROUP BY: ([Orders].[ShipCity], [Orders].[ShipAddress])
     DEFINE:([Expr1006]=Count(*)))
     |--Sort(ORDER BY:([Orders].[ShipCity] ASC, [Orders].[ShipAddress] ASC))
     |--Clustered Index Scan(OBJECT:([Orders].[PK_Orders]))
```

This plan is basically the same as the one used for the scalar aggregate queries, except that SQL Server needs to sort the data before it aggregates. Think of the scalar aggregate as one big group containing all the rows. Thus, for a scalar aggregate, the rows don't need to be sorted into different groups.

Stream aggregate preserves the input sort order. Suppose that the previous query is extended with an *ORDER BY* clause that sorts the results on the *GROUP BY* keys:

```
SELECT [ShipAddress], [ShipCity], COUNT(*)
FROM [Orders]
GROUP BY [ShipAddress], [ShipCity]
ORDER BY [ShipAddress], [ShipCity]
```

The resulting plan still has only the one sort operator (below the stream aggregate):

```
|--Compute Scalar(DEFINE:([Expr1003]=CONVERT_IMPLICIT(int,[Expr1006],0)))
   |--Stream Aggregate(GROUP BY:([Orders].[ShipAddress],[Orders].[ShipCity])
     DEFINE:([Expr1006]=Count(*)))
     |--Sort(ORDER BY:([Orders].[ShipAddress] ASC, [Orders].[ShipCity] ASC))
        |--Clustered Index Scan(OBJECT:([Orders].[PK_Orders]))
```

However, notice that the sort columns are reversed from the first example. Previously, whether SQL Server sorted on the *ShipAddress* or *ShipCity* column first didn't matter. Now because the query includes an *ORDER BY* clause, the optimizer chooses to sort on the *ShipAddress* column first to avoid needing a second sort operator following the stream aggregate.

If we have an appropriate index, the plan doesn't need a sort operator at all. Consider the following query, which counts orders by customer (instead of shipping address):

```
SELECT [CustomerId], COUNT(*)
FROM [Orders]
GROUP BY [CustomerId]
```

The new plan uses an index on the *CustomerId* column to avoid sorting:

```
|--Compute Scalar(DEFINE:([Expr1003]=CONVERT_IMPLICIT(int,[Expr1006],0)))
  |--Stream Aggregate(GROUP BY:([Orders].[CustomerID])
       DEFINE:([Expr1006]=Count(*)))
   |--Index Scan(OBJECT:([Orders].[CustomerID]), ORDERED FORWARD)
```

Select distinct   If we have an index to provide order, SQL Server can also use the stream aggregate to implement *SELECT DISTINCT*. (If we don't have an index to provide order, the optimizer can't use a stream aggregate without adding a sort. In this case, the optimizer can just use the sort distinct directly; using a stream aggregate isn't necessary.) *SELECT DISTINCT* is essentially the same as *GROUP BY* on all selected columns with no aggregate functions. For example, the following,

```
SELECT DISTINCT [CustomerId] FROM [Orders]
```

can also be written as follows:

```
SELECT [CustomerId] FROM [Orders] GROUP BY [CustomerId]
```

Both queries use the same plan:

```
|--Stream Aggregate(GROUP BY:([Orders].[CustomerID]))
  |--Index Scan(OBJECT:([Orders].[CustomerID]), ORDERED FORWARD)
```

Notice that the stream aggregate has a *GROUP BY* clause, but no defined columns.

Distinct aggregates   SQL Server implements distinct aggregates for queries with a *GROUP BY* clause identically to the way it implements distinct scalar aggregates. In both cases, a distinct aggregate needs a plan that eliminates duplicates before aggregating. Suppose that we want to find the number of distinct customers served by each employee:

```
SELECT [EmployeeId], COUNT(DISTINCT [CustomerId])
FROM [Orders]
GROUP BY [EmployeeId]
```

This query results in the following plan:

```
|--Compute Scalar(DEFINE:([Expr1003]=CONVERT_IMPLICIT(int,[Expr1006],0)))
   |--Stream Aggregate(GROUP BY:([Orders].[EmployeeID])
       DEFINE:([Expr1006]=COUNT([Orders].[CustomerID])))
     |--Sort(DISTINCT ORDER BY:([Orders].[EmployeeID] ASC,[Orders].[CustomerID] ASC))
        |--Clustered Index Scan(OBJECT:([Orders].[PK_Orders]))
```

However, we just saw how SQL Server can use an aggregate to eliminate duplicates. SQL Server can also use an aggregate to implement distinct aggregates without the sort distinct. To see such a plan, we need to create a non-unique two-column index. For this example, you create a temporary index on the *EmployeeId* and *CustomerId* columns of the *Orders* table:

```
CREATE INDEX [EmployeeCustomer] ON [Orders] (EmployeeId, CustomerId)
```

Now, the plan looks as follows:

```
|--Compute Scalar(DEFINE:([Expr1003]=CONVERT_IMPLICIT(int,[Expr1006],0)))
   |--Stream Aggregate(GROUP BY:([Orders].[EmployeeID])
      DEFINE:([Expr1006]=COUNT([Orders].[CustomerID])))
     |--Stream Aggregate(GROUP BY:([Orders].[EmployeeID], [Orders].[CustomerID]))
        |--Index Scan(OBJECT:([Orders].[EmployeeCustomer]), ORDERED FORWARD)
```

Notice that the optimizer has replaced the sort distinct with a stream aggregate. This plan is possible because, as in the previous *SELECT DISTINCT* example, an index provides order on the columns over which we need to eliminate duplicates. We need to drop the temporary index before continuing:

```
DROP INDEX [Orders].[EmployeeCustomer]
```

Multiple distincts   Finally, look at how SQL Server implements a mix of nondistinct and distinct aggregates (or multiple distinct aggregates) in a single *GROUP BY* query. Suppose that we want to find the total number of orders taken by each employee, as well as the total number of distinct customers served by each employee:

```
SELECT [EmployeeId], COUNT(*), COUNT(DISTINCT [CustomerId])
FROM [Orders]
GROUP BY [EmployeeId]
```

Like with the earlier scalar aggregate with multiple distincts example, SQL Server can't compute the two aggregates at the same time. Instead, it must compute each aggregate separately. However, unlike the scalar aggregate example, the GROUP BY clause means that each aggregate returns multiple rows. The resulting plan is shown next:

```
|--Compute Scalar(DEFINE:([Expr1003]=CONVERT_IMPLICIT(int,[globalagg1008],0)))
   |--Compute Scalar(DEFINE:([Expr1004]=CONVERT_IMPLICIT(int,[Expr1011],0)))
      |--Stream Aggregate(GROUP BY:([Orders].[EmployeeID])
         DEFINE:([Expr1011]=COUNT([Orders].[CustomerID]),[globalagg1008]=SUM([partiala
gg1007])))
         |--Stream Aggregate(GROUP BY:([Orders].[EmployeeID], [Orders].[CustomerID])
            DEFINE:([partialagg1007]=Count(*)))
            |--Sort(ORDER BY:([Orders].[EmployeeID] ASC, [Orders].[CustomerID] ASC))
               |--Clustered Index Scan(OBJECT:([Orders].[PK_Orders]))
```

The resulting plan is very simple, starting with a sort by EmployeeID and CustomerID. The first stream aggregate operator groups the records by EmployeeID and CustomerID, counting the number of records on each group, and sending the resulting 464 records to the next stream aggregate. The second stream aggregate will now group by EmployeeID, performing additional count and sum operations and producing the final nine records. Figure 10-11 shows the graphical plan for the query.

FIGURE 10-11 Graphical plan showing stream aggregation to compute multiple distinct aggregates.

Hash aggregation

The other aggregation operator, hash aggregate, is similar to hash join. It doesn't require (or pre-serve) sort order, requires memory, and is blocking—that is, it doesn't produce any results until it has consumed its entire input. Hash aggregate excels at efficiently aggregating very large data sets and, in parallel plans, scales better than stream aggregate.

Here is pseudocode for the hash aggregate algorithm:

```
for each input row
  begin
    calculate hash value on group by column(s)
    check for a matching row in the hash table
    if matching row not found
      insert a new row into the hash table
    else
      update the matching row with the input row
  end
output all rows in the hash table
```

Although stream aggregate computes just one group at a time, hash aggregate computes all the groups simultaneously. Like a hash join, a hash aggregate uses a hash table to store these groups. With each new input row, it checks the hash table to see whether the new row belongs to an existing group. If it does, it simply updates the existing group. If it doesn't, it creates a new group. Because the input data is unsorted, any row can belong to any group. Thus, a hash aggregate can't output any results until it finishes processing every input row.

Memory and spilling   As with hash join, the hash aggregate requires memory. Before executing a query with a hash aggregate, SQL Server uses cardinality estimates to estimate how much memory it needs to execute the query. A hash join stores each build row, so the total memory requirement is proportional to the number and size of the build rows. The number of rows that join and the output cardinality of the join have no effect on the memory requirement of the join. A hash aggregate, how-ever, stores only one row for each group, so the total memory requirement is actually proportional to the number and size of the output groups or rows. Fewer unique values of the *group by* column(s) and fewer groups mean that a hash aggregate needs less memory. More unique values of the *group by* column(s) and more groups mean that a hash aggregate needs more memory.

Like a hash join, if a hash aggregate runs out of memory, it must begin spilling rows to a workfile in *tempdb*. The hash aggregate spills one or more buckets, including any partially aggregated results along with any additional new rows that hash to the spilled buckets. After the hash aggregate finishes processing all input rows, it outputs the completed in-memory groups and repeats the algorithm by reading back and aggregating one set of spilled buckets at a time. By dividing the spilled rows into multiple sets of buckets, the hash aggregate reduces the size of each set and thus reduces the risk that the algorithm will need to repeat many times.

Although duplicate rows are a potential problem for hash join because they lead to skew in the size of the different hash buckets and make it difficult to divide the work into small uniform portions, duplicates can be quite helpful for hash aggregates because they collapse into a single group.

Examples   The optimizer tends to favor hash aggregation for tables with more rows, fewer groups, no *ORDER BY* clause or other reason to sort, and no index that produces sorted rows. For example, the original stream aggregate example grouped the *Orders* table on the *ShipAddress* and *ShipCity* columns. This query produces 94 groups from 830 orders. Now consider the following essentially identical query, which groups the *Orders* table on the *ShipCountry* column:

```
SELECT [ShipCountry], COUNT(*)
FROM [Orders]
GROUP BY [ShipCountry]
```

The *ShipCountry* column has only 21 unique values. Because a hash aggregate requires less memory as the number of groups decreases, and a sort requires memory proportional to the number of input rows, this time the optimizer chooses a plan with a hash aggregate:

```
|--Compute Scalar(DEFINE:([Expr1003]=CONVERT_IMPLICIT(int,[Expr1006],0)))
   |--Hash Match(Aggregate, HASH:([Orders].[ShipCountry]), RESIDUAL:(...)
        DEFINE:([Expr1006]=COUNT(*)))
      |--Clustered Index Scan(OBJECT:([Orders].[PK_Orders]))
```

Notice that the hash aggregate hashes on the *group by* column. (The residual predicate from the hash aggregate—which has been edited out of the previous text plan to save space—is used to compare rows in the hash table to input rows in case of a hash value collision.) Also observe that with the hash aggregate no sort is needed. However, suppose that we explicitly request a sort using an *ORDER BY* clause in the query:

```
SELECT [ShipCountry], COUNT(*)
FROM [Orders]
GROUP BY [ShipCountry]
ORDER BY [ShipCountry]
```

Because of the explicit *ORDER BY* clause, the plan must include a sort, thus the optimizer chooses a stream aggregate plan:

```
|--Compute Scalar(DEFINE:([Expr1003]=CONVERT_IMPLICIT(int,[Expr1006],0)))
   |--Stream Aggregate(GROUP BY:([Orders].[ShipCountry]) DEFINE:([Expr1006]=Count(*)))
     |--Sort(ORDER BY:([Orders].[ShipCountry] ASC))
       |--Clustered Index Scan(OBJECT:([Orders].[PK_Orders]))
```

If the table gets big enough and the number of groups remains small enough, eventually the optimizer will decide that using the hash aggregate and sorting after the aggregation are cheaper. For example, the *Northwind2* database includes a *BigOrders* table, which includes the same data from the original *Orders* table repeated five times. The *BigOrders* table has 4,150 rows compared to the 830 rows in the original *Orders* table. However, if the preceding query is repeated against the *BigOrders* table, the same 21 groups still result:

```
SELECT [ShipCountry], COUNT(*)
FROM [BigOrders]
GROUP BY [ShipCountry]
ORDER BY [ShipCountry]
```

As the following plan shows, the optimizer concludes that using the hash aggregate and sorting 21 rows are better than sorting 4,150 rows and using a stream aggregate:

```
|--Sort(ORDER BY:([BigOrders].[ShipCountry] ASC))
  |--Compute Scalar(DEFINE:([Expr1004]=CONVERT_IMPLICIT(int,[Expr1007],0)))
    |--Hash Match(Aggregate, HASH:([BigOrders].[ShipCountry]),
      RESIDUAL:(...) DEFINE:([Expr1007]=COUNT(*)))
      |--Clustered Index Scan(OBJECT:([BigOrders].[OrderID]))
```

Figure 10-12 shows the graphical plan for this query. Notice the sort is performed as the last operation because the hash aggregation didn't require that the data be sorted earlier.

FIGURE 10-12 Graphical plan with hash aggregation and sorting.

Distinct   Just like a stream aggregate, a hash aggregate can be used to implement distinct operations. Suppose that we want just a list of distinct countries to which orders have been shipped:

```
SELECT DISTINCT [ShipCountry] FROM [Orders]
```

Just as the optimizer chose a hash aggregate when grouping on the *ShipCountry* column, it also chooses a hash aggregate for this query:

```
|--Hash Match(Aggregate, HASH:([Orders].[ShipCountry]), RESIDUAL:(...))
  |--Clustered Index Scan(OBJECT:([Orders].[PK_Orders]))
```

Finally, hash aggregate can be used to implement distinct aggregates, including multiple distincts. The basic idea is the same as for stream aggregate. SQL Server computes each aggregate separately and then joins the results. Suppose that for each country to which orders have been shipped, we want to find both the number of employees who've taken orders and the number of customers who've placed orders that were shipped to that country. For the optimizer to choose a plan with a hash aggregate, this query needs to run against a much larger table than was used for other examples. The *Northwind2* database includes a *HugeOrders* table, which includes the same data from the original *Orders* table repeated 25 times.

```
SELECT [ShipCountry], COUNT(DISTINCT [EmployeeId]), COUNT(DISTINCT [CustomerId])
FROM [HugeOrders]
GROUP BY [ShipCountry]
```

The following query plan has several interesting features:

```
|--Compute Scalar(DEFINE:([HugeOrders].[ShipCountry]=[HugeOrders].[ShipCountry]))
  |--Hash Match(Inner Join, HASH:([HugeOrders].[ShipCountry])=
    ([HugeOrders].[ShipCountry]),RESIDUAL:(...))
    |--Compute Scalar(DEFINE:([HugeOrders].[ShipCountry]=[HugeOrders].[ShipCountry]))
    |   |--Compute Scalar(DEFINE:([Expr1005]=CONVERT_IMPLICIT(int,[Expr1012],0)))
    |      |--Hash Match(Aggregate, HASH:([HugeOrders].[ShipCountry]),RESIDUAL:(...)
            DEFINE:([Expr1012]=COUNT([HugeOrders].[CustomerID])))
```

```
|       |--Hash Match(Aggregate,HASH:([HugeOrders].[ShipCountry],
|         [HugeOrders].[CustomerID]),RESIDUAL:(...))
|           |--Clustered Index Scan (OBJECT:([HugeOrders].[OrderID]))
|--Compute Scalar(DEFINE:([HugeOrders].[ShipCountry]=
|  [HugeOrders].[ShipCountry]))
|--Compute Scalar(DEFINE:([Expr1004]=CONVERT_IMPLICIT(int,[Expr1013],0)))
  |--Stream Aggregate (GROUP BY:([HugeOrders].[ShipCountry])
   DEFINE:([Expr1013]=COUNT([HugeOrders].[EmployeeID])))
     |--Sort(ORDER BY:([HugeOrders].[ShipCountry]))
       |--Hash Match(Aggregate,HASH:([HugeOrders].[ShipCountry],
         [HugeOrders].[EmployeeID]),RESIDUAL:(...))
         |--Clustered Index Scan (OBJECT:([HugeOrders].[OrderID]))
```

- This plan shows that SQL Server can mix hash aggregates and stream aggregates in a single plan. In fact, this plan uses both a hash aggregate and a stream aggregate in the computation of *COUNT(DISTINCT [EmployeeId])*. The hash aggregate eliminates duplicate values from the *EmployeeId* column; the sort and stream aggregate computes the counts. Although SQL Server could use a sort distinct and eliminate the hash aggregate, the sort would require more memory.

- SQL Server uses a pair of hash aggregates to compute *COUNT(DISTINCT [Customer-Id])*. This portion of the plan works exactly like the earlier distinct example that used two stream aggregates. The bottommost hash aggregate eliminates duplicate values from the CustomerId column, whereas the topmost computes the counts.

- Because the hash aggregate doesn't return rows in any particular order, SQL Server can't use a merge join without introducing another sort. Instead, the optimizer chooses a hash join for this plan.

Figure 10-13 shows the graphical plan.

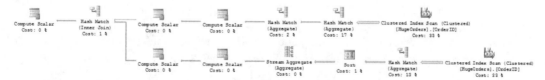

FIGURE 10-13 Graphical plan showing hash aggregation and a hash join to compute multiple distinct aggregates.

Unions

Two types of union queries are available: *UNION ALL* and *UNION*. A *UNION ALL* query simply combines the results from two or more different queries and returns the results. For example, this simple *UNION ALL* query returns a list of all employees and customers:

```
SELECT [FirstName] + N' ' + [LastName], [City], [Country] FROM [Employees]
UNION ALL
SELECT [ContactName], [City], [Country] FROM [Customers]
```

The plan for this query uses the concatenation operator:

```
|--Concatenation
  |--Compute Scalar(DEFINE:([Expr1003]=([Employees].[FirstName] + N' ')+
    [Employees].[LastName]))
  |    |--Clustered Index Scan(OBJECT:([Employees].[PK_Employees]))
  |--Clustered Index Scan(OBJECT:([Customers].PK_Customers]))
```

The concatenation operator simply executes each of its inputs—it might have more than two—one at a time and returns the results from each input. Any employees who also happen to be customers will be returned twice by this query.

Now consider the following similar query, which outputs a list of all cities and countries in which employees and/or customers are located:

```
SELECT [City], [Country] FROM [Employees]
UNION
SELECT [City], [Country] FROM [Customers]
```

Because this query uses *UNION* rather than *UNION ALL*, the query plan must eliminate duplicates. The optimizer uses the same concatenation operator as in the prior plan, but adds a sort distinct to eliminate duplicates:

```
|--Sort(DISTINCT ORDER BY:([Union1006] ASC, [Union1007] ASC))
  |--Concatenation
    |--Clustered Index Scan(OBJECT:([Employees].[PK_Employees]))
    |--Clustered Index Scan(OBJECT:([Customers].[PK_Customers]))
```

Another essentially identical alternative plan is to replace the sort distinct with a hash aggregate. A sort distinct requires memory proportional to the number of input rows before the duplicates are eliminated; a hash aggregate requires memory proportional to the number of output rows after the duplicates are eliminated. Thus, a hash aggregate requires less memory than the sort distinct when many duplicates occur, and the optimizer is more likely to choose a hash aggregate when it expects many duplicates. Consider the following query, which combines data from the *Orders* and *BigOrders* tables to generate a list of all countries to which orders have shipped:

```
SELECT [ShipCountry] FROM [Orders]
UNION
SELECT [ShipCountry] FROM [BigOrders]
```

Here is the query plan, which shows the hash distinct:

```
|--Hash Match(Aggregate, HASH:([Union1007]), RESIDUAL:(...))
  |--Concatenation
    |--Clustered Index Scan(OBJECT:([Orders].[PK_Orders]))
    |--Clustered Index Scan(OBJECT:([BigOrders].[OrderID]))
```

Next, suppose that we want to find a list of all employees and customers sorted by name. We know that if we can create appropriate indexes on the *Employees* and *Customers* tables, we can get a sorted list of employees or customers. See what happens if we create both indexes and run a *UNION ALL* query with an *ORDER BY* clause. For this example, we need to create a new table with a subset of the columns from the *Employees* table, as well as create two new indexes. The following script creates the new table and indexes along with the test query:

```
SELECT [EmployeeId], [FirstName] + N' ' + [LastName] AS [ContactName],
  [City], [Country]
INTO [NewEmployees]
FROM [Employees]

ALTER TABLE [NewEmployees] ADD CONSTRAINT [PK_NewEmployees] PRIMARY KEY ([EmployeeId])
CREATE INDEX [ContactName] ON [NewEmployees]([ContactName])
CREATE INDEX [ContactName] ON [Customers]([ContactName])

SELECT [ContactName] FROM [NewEmployees]
UNION ALL
SELECT [ContactName] FROM [Customers]
ORDER BY [ContactName]
```

Here is the query plan:

```
|--Merge Join(Concatenation)
  |--Index Scan(OBJECT:([NewEmployees].[ContactName]), ORDERED FORWARD)
  |--Index Scan(OBJECT:([Customers].[ContactName]), ORDERED FORWARD)
```

Notice that instead of a concatenation operator, we get a merge join (concatenation) operator. The merge join (concatenation) or merge concatenation operator isn't really a join at all. It's implemented by the same iterator as the merge join, but it actually performs a *UNION ALL* (just like a regular concatenation operator) while preserving the order of the input rows. Like a merge join, a merge concatenation requires that input data be sorted on the merge key (in this case, the *ContactName* column from the two input tables). By using the order-preserving merge concatenation operator instead of the non-order–preserving concatenation operator, the optimizer avoids the need to add an explicit sort to the plan. Figure 10-14 shows the graphical plan.

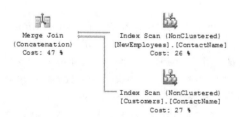

FIGURE 10-14 Graphical plan showing a merge concatenation.

The merge join operator can implement both *UNION ALL*, as just shown, and *UNION*. For example, try repeating the previous query as a *UNION* without the *ORDER BY*. In other words, we want to eliminate duplicates, but we aren't interested in whether the results are sorted.

```
SELECT [ContactName] FROM [NewEmployees]
UNION
SELECT [ContactName] FROM [Customers]
```

The new plan still uses a merge join operator:

```
|--Merge Join(Union)
  |--Stream Aggregate(GROUP BY:([NewEmployees].[ContactName]))
  |   |--Index Scan(OBJECT:([NewEmployees].[ContactName]), ORDERED FORWARD)
  |--Stream Aggregate(GROUP BY:([Customers].[ContactName]))
     |--Index Scan(OBJECT:([Customers].[ContactName]), ORDERED FORWARD)
```

This time the plan has a merge join (union) or merge union operator. The merge union eliminates duplicate rows that appear in both of its inputs; it does *not* eliminate duplicate rows from either individual input. That is, if a name appears in both the *NewEmployees* and the *Customers* tables, the merge union will eliminate that duplicate name. However, if a name appears twice in the *NewEmployees* table or twice in the *Customers* table, the merge union by itself does *not* eliminate it. Thus, the optimizer has also added stream aggregates above each index scan to eliminate any duplicates from the individual tables. As discussed earlier, aggregation operators can be used to implement distinct operations. Figure 10-15 shows the graphical plan.

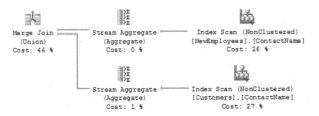

FIGURE 10-15 Graphical plan showing a merge union operation.

Before continuing, you can drop the extra table and indexes created just for this example:

```
DROP TABLE [NewEmployees]
DROP INDEX [Customers].[ContactName]
```

SQL Server can use one additional operator to perform a *UNION*. The hash union operator is similar to a hash aggregate with two inputs. A hash union builds a hash table on its first input and eliminates duplicates from it just like a hash aggregate. It then reads its second input and, for each row, probes its hash table to see whether the row is a duplicate of a row from the first input. If the row isn't a duplicate, the hash union returns it. Because the hash union doesn't insert rows from the second input into the hash table, it doesn't eliminate duplicates that appear only in its second input. To use a hash union, the optimizer either must explicitly eliminate duplicates from the second input or must know that the second input has no duplicates.

Hash unions are rare. To see an example of a hash union, we need to create a large table with big rows but many duplicates. The script in Listing 10-2 creates two tables. The first table, *BigTable*, has 100,000 rows, and each row includes a char(1000) column, but all the rows have the same value for the *Dups* column. The second table, *SmallTable*, has a uniqueness constraint to guarantee no duplicates.

LISTING 10-2 Hash union example

```
CREATE TABLE [BigTable] ([PK] int PRIMARY KEY, [Dups] int, [Pad] char(1000))
CREATE TABLE [SmallTable] ([PK] int PRIMARY KEY, [NoDups] int UNIQUE, [Pad] char(1000))

SET NOCOUNT ON
DECLARE @i int
SET @i = 0
BEGIN TRAN
WHILE @i < 100000
BEGIN
  INSERT [BigTable] VALUES (@i, 0, NULL)
  SET @i = @i + 1
  IF @i % 1000 = 0
  BEGIN
    COMMIT TRAN
    BEGIN TRAN
  END
END
COMMIT TRAN

SELECT [Dups], [Pad] FROM [BigTable]
UNION
SELECT [NoDups], [Pad] FROM [SmallTable]
```

The optimizer chooses a hash union for this query. The hash union is a good choice for eliminating the many duplicates from the *BigTable* table. Moreover, because of the uniqueness constraint on the *NoDups* column of the *SmallTable* table, eliminating duplicates from this input isn't necessary to use it with a hash union.

> **Note** On a machine with multiple processors or multiple cores, the optimizer might choose a substantially different parallel plan that doesn't include a hash union. If this happens, append an *OPTION (MAXDOP 1)* hint to the query, and you should get the intended plan. The *OPTION (MAXDOP 1)* query hint forces SQL Server to choose a serial plan for the query. Later, this chapter discusses parallelism; Chapters 11 and 12 discuss hints, including this one.

```
|--Hash Match(Union)
  |--Clustered Index Scan(OBJECT:([BigTable].[PK_BigTable]))
  |--Clustered Index Scan(OBJECT:([SmallTable].[PK_SmallTable]))
```

Figure 10-16 shows the graphical plan showing the hash union.

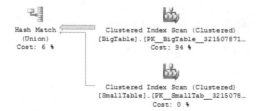

FIGURE 10-16 Graphical plan showing a hash union operation.

Advanced index operations

Earlier, this chapter discussed index scans and seeks. You might have noticed that all the index seek examples so far have involved simple predicates of the form *<column> <comparison operator> <expression>*. For instance, the very first example was *[OrderDate] = '1998-02-26'*. Now look at how SQL Server uses indexes to execute queries with *AND*'ed and *OR*'ed predicates. (*AND*'ed and *OR*'ed predicates are often referred to as "conjuctions" and "disjunctions," respectively.) Specifically, look at dynamic index seeks, index unions, and index intersections.

Dynamic index seeks

Consider the following query with a simple IN list predicate:

```
SELECT [OrderId]
FROM [Orders]
WHERE [ShipPostalCode] IN (N'05022', N'99362')
```

We have an index on the *ShipPostalCode* column, and because this index covers the *OrderId* column, this query results in a simple index seek:

```
|--Index Seek(OBJECT:([Orders].[ShipPostalCode]), SEEK:([Orders].[ShipPostalCode]=N'05022'
  OR [Orders].[ShipPostalCode]=N'99362') ORDERED FORWARD)
```

Notice that the *IN* list is logically identical to the *OR*'ed predicate in the index seek. SQL Server executes an index seek with *OR*'ed predicates by performing two separate index seek operations. First, the server executes an index seek with the *predicate [ShipPostalCode] = N'05022'* and then it executes a second index seek with the *predicate [ShipPostalCode] = N'99362'*.

Now consider the following identical query, which uses variables in place of constants:

```
DECLARE @SPC1 nvarchar(20), @SPC2 nvarchar(20)
SELECT @SPC1 = N'05022', @SPC2 = N'99362'
SELECT [OrderId]
FROM [Orders]
WHERE [ShipPostalCode] IN (@SPC1, @SPC2)
```

We might expect this query to result in a simple index seek as well. However, we instead get the following more complex plan:

```
|--Nested Loops(Inner Join, OUTER REFERENCES:([Expr1009],[Expr1010], [Expr1011]))
  |--Merge Interval
  |   |--Sort(TOP 2, ORDER BY:([Expr1012] DESC, [Expr1013] ASC,
  |      [Expr1009] ASC, [Expr1014] DESC))
  |   |--Compute Scalar (DEFINE:([Expr1012]=((4)&[Expr1011]) = (4) AND
  |      NULL = [Expr1009],[Expr1013]=(4)&[Expr1011],[Expr1014]=(16)&[Expr1011]))
  |   |--Concatenation
  |      |--Compute Scalar(DEFINE:([@SPC2]=[@SPC2], [@SPC2]=[@SPC2],
[Expr1003]=(62)))
  |         |--Constant Scan
  |      |--Compute Scalar(DEFINE:([@SPC1]=[@SPC1],
  |         [@SPC1]=[@SPC1], [Expr1006]=(62)))
  |         |--Constant Scan
  |
```

```
|--Index Seek(OBJECT:([Orders].[ShipPostalCode]), SEEK:([Orders].[ShipPostalCode] >
[Expr1009] AND [Orders].[ShipPostalCode] < [Expr1010]) ORDERED FORWARD)
```

We don't get the index seek that we expect because the optimizer doesn't know the values of the variables at compile time and therefore can't be sure whether they will have different values or the same value at runtime. If the variables have different values, the original simple index seek plan is valid. However, if the variables have the same value, the original plan isn't valid. It would seek to the same index key twice and thus return each row twice. Obviously, this result would be incorrect because the query should return each row only once.

The more complex plan works by eliminating duplicates from the *IN* list at execution time. The two constant scans and the concatenation operator generate a "constant table" with the two *IN* list values. Then the plan sorts the parameter values, and the merge interval operator eliminates the duplicates (which, because of the sort, will be adjacent to one another). Finally, the nested loops join executes the index seek once for each unique value. You can see the graphical plan for this query in Figure 10-17.

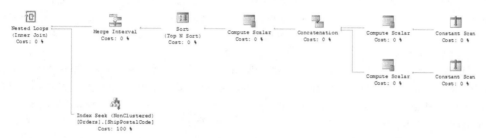

FIGURE 10-17 Graphical plan for a query with a dynamic seek for variables in an *IN* list.

You might be wondering why SQL Server needs the merge interval operator. Why can't the plan just use a sort distinct to eliminate any duplicate values? To answer this question, consider a slightly more complex query:

```
DECLARE @OD1 datetime, @OD2 datetime
SELECT @OD1 = '1998-01-01', @OD2 ='1998-01-04'
SELECT [OrderId]
FROM [Orders]
WHERE [OrderDate] BETWEEN @OD1 AND DATEADD(day, 6, @OD1)
  OR [OrderDate] BETWEEN @OD2 AND DATEADD(day, 6, @OD2)
```

This query returns orders placed within one week of either of two dates. The query plan is nearly identical to the plan for the *IN* list query:

```
|--Nested Loops(Inner Join, OUTER REFERENCES:([Expr1011],[Expr1012],[Expr1013]))
  |--Merge Interval
  |   |--Sort(TOP 2, ORDER BY:([Expr1014] DESC, [Expr1015] ASC,
  |      [Expr1011] ASC, [Expr1016] DESC))
  |      |--Compute Scalar(DEFINE:([Expr1014]=((4)&[Expr1013]) = (4)
  |         AND NULL = [Expr1011], [Expr1015]=(4)&[Expr1013],
  |         [Expr1016]=(16)&[Expr1013]))
  |         |--Concatenation
  |            |--Compute Scalar(DEFINE:([@OD1]=[@OD1],
  |               [ConstExpr1003]=dateadd(day,(6),[@OD1]),
```

```
            [Expr1007]=(22)|(42)))
  |             |--Constant Scan
  |         |--Compute Scalar(DEFINE:([@OD2]=[@OD2],
  |             [ConstExpr1004]=dateadd(day,(6),[@OD2]),[Expr1010]=(22)|(42)))
  |         |--Constant Scan
  |--Index Seek(OBJECT:([Orders].[OrderDate]),SEEK:([Orders].[OrderDate] > [Expr1011] AND
     [Orders].[OrderDate] < [Expr1012]) ORDERED FORWARD)
```

Again, the plan includes a pair of constant scans and a concatenation operator. However, this time, rather than return discrete values from an *IN* list, the constant scans return ranges. Unlike the prior example, eliminating duplicates is no longer sufficient. Now the plan needs to handle ranges that aren't duplicates but do overlap. The sort ensures that ranges that might overlap are next to one another and the merge interval operator collapses overlapping ranges. In the example, the two date ranges (1998-01-01 to 1998-01-07 and 1998-01-04 to 1998-01-10) do in fact overlap, and the merge interval collapses them into a single range (1998-01-01 to 1998-01-10).

These plans are referred to as *dynamic index seeks* because the range(s) that SQL Server actually fetches aren't statically known at compile time and are determined dynamically during execution. Dynamic index seeks and the merge interval operator can be used for both *OR*'ed and *AND*'ed predicates, although they are most common for *OR*'ed predicates. *AND*'ed predicates can generally be handled by using one of the predicates, preferably the most selective predicate, as the seek predicate and then applying all remaining predicates as residuals. Recall that with *OR*'ed predicates we want the *union* of the set of rows that matches *any* of the predicates, whereas with *AND*'ed predicates we want the *intersection* of the set of rows that matches *all* the predicates.

Index unions

We've just seen how SQL Server can use an index seek even if we have an *OR*'ed predicate. Now consider a slightly different query that *OR*'s predicates on two different columns:

```
SELECT [OrderId]
FROM [Orders]
WHERE [OrderDate] BETWEEN '1998-01-01' AND '1998-01-07'
  OR [ShippedDate] BETWEEN '1998-01-01' AND '1998-01-07'
```

This query returns orders that were either placed or shipped during the first week of 1998. We have indexes on both the *OrderDate* and the *ShippedDate* columns, but each index can be used to satisfy only one of the two predicates. If SQL Server uses the index on the *OrderDate* column to find orders placed during the first week of 1998, it might miss orders that weren't placed but did ship during this week. Similarly, if it uses the index on the *ShippedDate* column to find orders shipped during the first week of 1998, it might miss orders that were placed but didn't ship during this week.

SQL Server has two strategies that it can use to execute a query such as this one. One option is to use a clustered index scan (or table scan) and apply the entire predicate to all rows in the table. This strategy is reasonable if the predicates aren't very selective and if the query will end up returning many rows. However, if the predicates are reasonably selective and if the table is large, the clustered index scan strategy isn't very efficient. The other option is to use both indexes. This plan looks like the following:

```
|--Sort(DISTINCT ORDER BY:([Orders].[OrderID] ASC))
   |--Concatenation
      |--Index Seek(OBJECT:([Orders].[OrderDate]),
         SEEK:([Orders].[OrderDate] >= '1998-01-01' AND
         [Orders].[OrderDate] <= '1998-01-07')
         ORDERED FORWARD)
      |--Index Seek(OBJECT:([Orders].[ShippedDate]),
         SEEK:([Orders].[ShippedDate] >= '1998-01-01' AND
         [Orders].[ShippedDate] <= '1998-01-07')
         ORDERED FORWARD)
```

The optimizer effectively rewrote the query as a union:

```
SELECT [OrderId]
FROM [Orders]
WHERE [OrderDate] BETWEEN '1998-01-01' AND '1998-01-07'
UNION
SELECT [OrderId]
FROM [Orders]
WHERE [ShippedDate] BETWEEN '1998-01-01' AND '1998-01-07'
```

By using both indexes, this plan gets the benefit of the index seek—namely that it only retrieves rows that satisfy the query predicates—yet avoids missing any rows, as might happen if it used only one of the two indexes. However, by using both indexes, the plan might generate duplicates if, as is likely in this example, any of the orders were both placed and shipped during the first week of 1998. To ensure that the query plan doesn't return any rows twice, the optimizer adds a sort distinct. This type of plan is referred to as an index union.

The manual rewrite is valid only because the *OrderId* column is unique, which ensures that the *UNION* doesn't eliminate more rows than it should. However, even if we don't have a unique key and can't manually rewrite the query, the optimizer always has an internal unique "relational key" for each row (the same key that it uses to perform bookmark lookups) and thus can always perform this transformation.

Now consider the following nearly identical query:

```
SELECT [OrderId]
FROM [Orders]
WHERE [OrderDate] = '1998-01-01'
  OR [ShippedDate] = '1998-01-01'
```

The only difference between this query and the prior one is that this query has equality predicates on both columns. Specifically, we're searching for orders that were either placed or shipped on the first day of 1998. Yet, this query yields the following plan:

```
|--Stream Aggregate(GROUP BY:([Orders].[OrderID]))
   |--Merge Join(Concatenation)
      |--Index Seek(OBJECT:([Orders].[OrderDate]),
         SEEK:([Orders].[OrderDate]='1998-01-01') ORDERED FORWARD)
      |--Index Seek(OBJECT:([Orders].[ShippedDate]),
         SEEK:([Orders].[ShippedDate]='1998-01-01') ORDERED FORWARD)
```

Instead of the concatenation and sort distinct operators, we now have a merge concatenation and a stream aggregate. Because we have equality predicates on the leading column of each index, the index seeks return rows sorted on the second column (the *OrderId* column) of each index. Because index seeks return sorted rows, this query is suitable for a merge concatenation. Moreover, because the merge concatenation returns rows sorted on the merge key (the *OrderId* column), the optimizer can use a stream aggregate instead of a sort to eliminate duplicates. This plan is generally a better choice because the sort distinct uses memory and could spill data to disk if it runs out of memory, whereas the merge concatenation and stream aggregate don't use memory.

SQL Server didn't use the merge concatenation in the prior example because the predicates were inequalities. The inequalities mean that the index seeks in that example returned rows sorted by the *OrderDate* and the *ShippedDate* columns. Because the rows weren't sorted by the *OrderId* column, the optimizer couldn't use the merge concatenation without explicit sorts.

Although the previous examples involve only two predicates and two indexes, SQL Server can use index union with any number of indexes, just as we can write a *UNION* query with any number of inputs.

A union only returns the columns that are common to all its inputs. In each of the preceding index union examples (whether based on concatenation and sort distinct, merge union, or hash union), the only column that the indexes have in common is the clustering key *OrderId*. Thus, the union can only return the *OrderId* column. If we ask for other columns, the plan must perform a bookmark lookup. This is true even if one index in the union covers the extra columns. Consider the following query, which is identical to the previous query but selects the *OrderDate* and *ShippedDate* columns in addition to the *OrderId* column:

```
SELECT [OrderId], [OrderDate], [ShippedDate]
FROM [BigOrders]
WHERE [OrderDate] = '1998-01-01'
  OR [ShippedDate] = '1998-01-01'
```

 Note This example uses the *BigOrders* table because the optimizer tends to favor simply scanning the entire table rather than performing a bookmark lookup for smaller tables.

Here is the query plan showing the bookmark lookup:

```
|--Nested Loops(Inner Join, OUTER REFERENCES:([Uniq1002],[BigOrders].[OrderID]))
   |--Stream Aggregate(GROUP BY:([BigOrders].[OrderID], [Uniq1002]))
   |    |--Merge Join(Concatenation)
   |        |--Index Seek(OBJECT:([BigOrders].[OrderDate]),
   |           SEEK:([BigOrders].[OrderDate]='1998-01-01')
            ORDERED FORWARD)
   |        |--Index Seek(OBJECT:([BigOrders].[ShippedDate]),
   |           SEEK:([BigOrders].[ShippedDate]='1998-01-01')
            ORDERED FORWARD)
   |--Clustered Index Seek(OBJECT:([BigOrders].[OrderID]),
      SEEK:([BigOrders].[OrderID]=[BigOrders].[OrderID] AND [Uniq1002]=[Uniq1002])
      LOOKUP ORDERED FORWARD)
```

Index intersections

We've just seen how SQL Server can convert *OR*'ed predicates into a union query and use multiple indexes to execute this query. SQL Server can also use multiple indexes to execute queries with *AND*'ed predicates. Consider the following query:

```
SELECT [OrderId]
FROM [Orders]
WHERE [OrderDate] = '1998-02-26'
  AND [ShippedDate] = '1998-03-04'
```

This query is looking for orders that were placed on February 26, 1998, and were shipped on March 4, 1998. We have indexes on both the *OrderDate* and the *ShippedDate* columns, and we can use both indexes. Here is the query plan:

```
|--Merge Join(Inner Join, MERGE:([Orders].[OrderID])=([Orders].[OrderID]), RESIDUAL:(...))
  |--Index Seek(OBJECT:([Orders].[ShippedDate]),
    SEEK:([Orders].[ShippedDate]='1998-03-04')
    ORDERED FORWARD)
  |--Index Seek(OBJECT:([Orders].[OrderDate]),
    SEEK:([Orders].[OrderDate]='1998-02-26')
    ORDERED FORWARD)
```

This plan is very similar to the index union plan with the merge union operator, except that this time we have an actual join. Note that the merge join implements an inner join logical operation. It's really a join this time; it's not a union. The optimizer has effectively rewritten this query as a join (although the explicit rewrite doesn't get the same plan):

```
SELECT O1.[OrderId]
FROM [Orders] O1 JOIN [Orders] O2
  ON O1.[OrderId] = O2.[OrderId]
WHERE O1.[OrderDate] = '1998-02-26'
  AND O2.[ShippedDate] = '1998-03-04'
```

This query plan is referred to as an index intersection. Just as an index union can use different operators depending on the plan, so can index intersection. Like in the merge union example, the first index intersection example uses a merge join because as a result of the equality predicates, the two index seeks return rows sorted on the *OrderId* column. Now consider the following query that searches for orders that match a range of dates:

```
SELECT [OrderId]
FROM [BigOrders]
WHERE [OrderDate] BETWEEN '1998-02-01' AND '1998-02-04'
  AND [ShippedDate] BETWEEN '1998-02-09' AND '1998-02-12'
```

Note Again, the larger *BigOrders* table is used because the optimizer favors a simple clustered index scan over a hash-join-based index intersection for the smaller table.

The inequality predicates mean the index seeks no longer return rows sorted by the *OrderId* column; therefore, SQL Server can't use a merge join without first sorting the rows. Rather than sort, the optimizer chooses a hash join:

```
|--Hash Match(Inner Join, HASH:([BigOrders].[OrderID], [Uniq1002])=([BigOrders].[OrderID],
[Uniq1002]), RESIDUAL:(...))
  |--Index Seek(OBJECT:([BigOrders].[OrderDate]),
    SEEK:([BigOrders].[OrderDate] >= '1998-02-01' AND
    [BigOrders].[OrderDate] <= '1998-02-04')
    ORDERED FORWARD)
  |--Index Seek(OBJECT:([BigOrders].[ShippedDate]),
    SEEK:([BigOrders].[ShippedDate] >= '1998-02-09' AND
    [BigOrders].[ShippedDate] <= '1998-02-12')
    ORDERED FORWARD)
```

Just like an index union, SQL Server can use index intersection plans with more than two tables. Each additional table simply adds one more join to the query plan.

Unlike an index union, which can only deliver those columns that all the indexes have in common, an index intersection can deliver all the columns covered by any of the indexes. A bookmark lookup isn't needed. For example, the following query, which selects the *OrderDate* and *ShippedDate* columns in addition to the *OrderId* column, uses the same plan as the similar example that selected just the *OrderId* column:

```
SELECT [OrderId], [OrderDate], [ShippedDate]
FROM [Orders]
WHERE [OrderDate] = '1998-02-26'
  AND [ShippedDate] = '1998-03-04'
```

Subqueries

Subqueries are powerful tools that enable you to write far more expressive and complex queries. Many different types of subqueries and many different ways to use subqueries are available. A complete discussion of subqueries could fill an entire chapter, if not an entire book. This section provides an introductory look at subqueries.

Subqueries are essentially joins. However, as we'll see, some subqueries generate more complex joins or use some fairly unusual join features.

Before considering specific examples, you can look at the different ways to classify subqueries. Subqueries can be categorized in three ways.

- **Noncorrelated vs. correlated subqueries** A noncorrelated subquery has no dependencies on the outer query, can be evaluated independently of the outer query, and returns the same result for each row of the outer query. A correlated subquery does have a dependency on the outer query. It can only be evaluated in the context of a row from the outer query and might return a different result for each row of the outer query.

- **Scalar vs. multirow subqueries** A scalar subquery returns or is expected to return a single row (that is, a scalar), whereas a multirow subquery might return a set of rows.

- **The clause of the outer query in which the subquery appears** Subqueries can be used in nearly any context, including the *SELECT* list and the *FROM*, *WHERE*, *ON*, and *HAVING* clauses of the main query.

Noncorrelated scalar subqueries

To begin the subject of subqueries, you can look at some simple noncorrelated scalar subqueries. The following query returns a list of orders in which the freight charge exceeds the average freight charge for all orders:

```
SELECT O1.[OrderId], O1.[Freight]
FROM [Orders] O1
WHERE O1.[Freight] >
  (
  SELECT AVG(O2.[Freight])
  FROM [Orders] O2
  )
```

Notice that we could extract the calculation of the average freight charge and execute it as a completely independent query. As a result, this subquery is noncorrelated. Also, notice that this subquery uses a scalar aggregate and thus returns exactly one row. So, this subquery is also a scalar subquery. Look over the query plan:

```
|--Nested Loops(Inner Join, WHERE:([O1].[Freight]>[Expr1004]))
  |--Compute Scalar(DEFINE:([Expr1004]=CASE WHEN [Expr1011]=(0)
    THEN NULL
    ELSE
    [Expr1012]/CONVERT_IMPLICIT(money,[Expr1011],0) END))
  |     |--Stream Aggregate(DEFINE:([Expr1011]=COUNT_BIG([O2].[Freight]),
  |       [Expr1012]=SUM([O2].[Freight])))
  |         |--Clustered Index Scan
  |           (OBJECT:([Orders].[PK_Orders] AS [O2]))
  |--Clustered Index Scan(OBJECT:([Orders].[PK_Orders] AS [O1]))
```

As you might expect, SQL Server executes this query by first calculating the average freight on the outer side of the nested loops join. The calculation requires a scan of the *Orders* table (alias [O2]). Because this calculation yields precisely one row, SQL Server then executes the scan on the *Orders* table (alias [O1]) on the inner side of the join exactly once. The average freight result calculated by the subquery (and stored in [Expr1004]) is used to filter the rows from the second scan.

Now look at another noncorrelated scalar subquery, this time to find those orders placed by a specific customer who's selected by name:

```
SELECT O.[OrderId]
FROM [Orders] O
WHERE O.[CustomerId] =
  (
  SELECT C.[CustomerId]
  FROM [Customers] C
  WHERE C.[ContactName] = N'Maria Anders'
  )
```

Notice that this time the subquery doesn't have a scalar aggregate to guarantee that it returns exactly one row. Moreover, the *ContactName* column has no unique index, so this subquery can actually return multiple rows. However, because the subquery is used in the context of an equality predicate, it's a scalar subquery and must return a single row. If we have two customers with the name "Maria Anders" (which we don't), this query must fail. SQL Server ensures that the subquery returns at most one row by counting the rows with a stream aggregate and then adding an assert operator to the plan:

```
|--Nested Loops(Inner Join, OUTER REFERENCES:([Expr1006]))
  |--Assert(WHERE:(CASE WHEN [Expr1005]>(1) THEN (0) ELSE NULL END))
  |   |--Stream Aggregate(DEFINE:([Expr1005]=Count(*),
  |       [Expr1006]=ANY([C].[CustomerID])))
  |       |--Clustered Index Scan (OBJECT:([Customers].[PK_Customers] AS [C]),
  |           WHERE:([C].[ContactName]=N'Maria Anders'))
  |--Index Seek(OBJECT:([Orders].[CustomerID] AS [O]),
    SEEK:([O].[CustomerID]=[Expr1006])
    ORDERED FORWARD)
```

If the assert operator finds that the subquery returned more than one row—that is, if [Expr1005]>(1) is true—it raises the following error:

```
Msg 512, Level 16, State 1, Line 1
Subquery returned more than 1 value. This is not permitted when the
subquery follows =, !=, <, <= , >, >= or when the subquery
is used as an expression.
```

Note that SQL Server uses the assert operator to check many other conditions such as constraints (check, referential integrity, and so on), the maximum recursion level for common table expressions (CTEs), warnings for duplicate key insertions to indexes built with the IGNORE_DUP_KEY option, and more.

The ANY aggregate is a special internal-only aggregate that, as its name suggests, returns any row. Because this plan raises an error if the scan of the Customers table returns more than one row, the ANY aggregate has no real effect. The plan could as easily use the MIN or MAX aggregates and get the same result. However, some aggregate is necessary because the stream aggregate expects each output column either to be aggregated or in the GROUP BY clause (which is empty in this case). This is the same reason the following query doesn't compile:

```
SELECT COUNT(*), C.[CustomerId]
FROM [Customers] C
WHERE C.[ContactName] = N'Maria Anders'
```

If you try to execute this query, you get the following error:

```
Msg 8120, Level 16, State 1, Line 1
Column 'Customers.CustomerID' is invalid in the select list because
it is not contained in either an aggregate function or the
GROUP BY clause.
```

The assert operator isn't inherently expensive and is relatively harmless in this simple example, but it does limit the set of transformations available to the optimizer, which might result in an inferior plan in some cases. Often, creating a unique index or rewriting the query eliminates the assert operator and improves the query plan. For example, as long as we aren't concerned that two customers might have the same name, the previous query can be written as a simple join:

```
SELECT O.[OrderId]
FROM [Orders] O JOIN [Customers] C
  ON O.[CustomerId] = C.[CustomerId]
WHERE C.[ContactName] = N'Maria Anders'
```

This query produces a much simpler join plan:

```
|--Nested Loops(Inner Join, OUTER REFERENCES:([C].[CustomerID]))
  |--Clustered Index Scan(OBJECT:([Customers].[PK_Customers] AS [C]),
     WHERE:([C].[ContactName]=N'Maria Anders'))
  |--Index Seek(OBJECT:([Orders].[CustomerID] AS [O]),
     SEEK:([O].[CustomerID]=[C].[CustomerID]) ORDERED FORWARD)
```

Although writing this query as a simple join is the best option, consider what happens if a unique index is created on the ContactName column:

```
CREATE UNIQUE INDEX [ContactName] ON [Customers] ([ContactName])

SELECT O.[OrderId]
FROM [Orders] O
WHERE O.[CustomerId] =
  (
  SELECT C.[CustomerId]
  FROM [Customers] C
  WHERE C.[ContactName] = N'Maria Anders'
  )
DROP INDEX [Customers].[ContactName]
```

Because of the unique index, the optimizer knows that the subquery can produce only one row, eliminates the now unnecessary stream aggregate and assert operators, and converts the query into a join:

```
|--Nested Loops(Inner Join, OUTER REFERENCES:([C].[CustomerID]))
  |--Index Seek(OBJECT:([Customers].[ContactName] AS [C]),
     SEEK:([C].[ContactName]=N'Maria Anders') ORDERED FORWARD)
  |--Index Seek(OBJECT:([Orders].[CustomerID] AS [O]),
     SEEK:([O].[CustomerID]=[C].[CustomerID]) ORDERED FORWARD)
```

Correlated scalar subqueries

Now that we've seen how SQL Server evaluates a simple noncorrelated subquery, you can explore what happens with a correlated scalar subquery. The following query is similar to the first subquery, but this time it returns those orders in which the freight charge exceeds the average freight charge for all previously placed orders:

```
SELECT O1.[OrderId]
FROM [Orders] O1
WHERE O1.[Freight] >
  (
  SELECT AVG(O2.[Freight])
  FROM [Orders] O2
  WHERE O2.[OrderDate] < O1.[OrderDate]
  )
```

This time SQL Server can't execute the subquery independently. Because of the correlation on the *OrderDate* column, the subquery returns a different result for each row from the main query. Recall that with the noncorrelated subquery, SQL Server evaluated the subquery first and then executed the main query. This time SQL Server evaluates the main query first and then evaluates the subquery once for each row from the main query:

```
|--Filter(WHERE:([O1].[Freight]>[Expr1004]))
   |--Nested Loops(Inner Join, OUTER REFERENCES:([O1].[OrderDate]))
     |--Clustered Index Scan(OBJECT:([Orders].[PK_Orders] AS [O1]))
       |--Index Spool(SEEK:([O1].[OrderDate]=[O1].[OrderDate]))
       |--Compute Scalar(DEFINE:([Expr1004]=
         CASE WHEN [Expr1011]=(0)
         THEN NULL
         ELSE [Expr1012]
         /CONVERT_IMPLICIT(money,[Expr1011],0) END))
         |--Stream Aggregate (DEFINE:([Expr1011]=
           COUNT_BIG([O2].[Freight]),[Expr1012]=SUM([O2].[Freight])))
         |--Index Spool(SEEK:([O2].[OrderDate] <[O1].[OrderDate]))
         |--Clustered Index Scan
         (OBJECT:([Orders].[PK_Orders] AS [O2]))
```

This plan isn't as complicated as it looks. Figure 10-18 shows the graphical plan. The index spool immediately above the scan of [O2] is an eager index spool or index-on-the-fly spool. It builds a temporary index on the OrderDate column of the Orders table. It's called an eager spool because it "eagerly" loads its entire input set and builds the temporary index as soon as it's opened.

FIGURE 10-18 Graphical plan showing two index spool operations: one lazy and one eager.

The index makes subsequent evaluations of the subquery more efficient because the *Order-Date* column has a predicate. The stream aggregate computes the average freight charge for each execution of the subquery. The index spool above the stream aggregate is a lazy index spool. It merely caches subquery results. If it encounters any *OrderDate* a second time, it returns the cached result rather than recomputing the subquery. It's called a *lazy spool* because it "lazily" loads results on demand only. Finally, the filter at the top of the plan compares the freight charge for each order to the subquery result ([Expr1004]) and returns those rows that qualify.

> **Note** We can determine the types of spools more easily from the complete SHOWPLAN_ALL output or from the graphical plan. The logical operator for the spool indicates whether each spool is an eager or lazy spool. The spools are there strictly for performance. The optimizer decides whether to include them in the plan based on its cost estimates. If the optimizer doesn't expect many duplicate values for the *OrderDate* column or many rows at all from the outer side of the join, it might eliminate the spools. For example, if you try the same query with a selective filter on the main query such as *O1.[ShipCity] = N'Berlin'*, the spools go away.

We've already seen how a nested loops join executes its inner input once for each row from its outer input. In most cases, each execution of the inner input proceeds completely independently of any prior executions. However, spools are special. A spool, such as the lazy index spool in the previous example, is designed to optimize the case in which the inner side of the join executes with the same correlated parameter(s) multiple times. Thus, for a spool, distinguishing between executions with the same correlated parameter(s), or *rewinds*, and executions with different correlated parameters, or *rebinds*, is useful. Specifically, a *rewind* is defined as an execution with the same correlated parameter(s) as the immediately preceding execution, whereas a rebind is defined as an execution with different correlated parameters than the immediately preceding execution.

A rewind results in the spool playing back a cached result, while a rebind results in the spool "binding" new correlated parameter values and loading a new result. A regular (nonindex) lazy spool only caches one result set at a time. Thus, a regular spool truncates and "reloads" its worktable on each rebind. A lazy index spool, such as the spool in the previous plan, accumulates results and doesn't truncate its worktable on a rebind.

We can see the estimated and actual number of rewinds and rebinds using *SET STATISTICS XML ON* or using the graphical plan. The statistics XML for the lazy index spool follow. As you might expect, the sum of the number of rewinds and rebinds is the same as the total number of executions:

```
<RelOp NodeId="3" PhysicalOp="Index Spool" LogicalOp="Lazy Spool"...
EstimateRebinds="827.89" EstimateRewinds="1.11028">
  <RunTimeInformation>
    <RunTimeCountersPerThread Thread="0" ActualRows="830" ActualRebinds="480"
        ActualRewinds="350"
        ActualEndOfScans="0"
        ActualExecutions="830" />
  </RunTimeInformation>
</RelOp>
```

Figure 10-19 shows the ToolTip from the graphical plan, showing the same information as in this XML fragment.

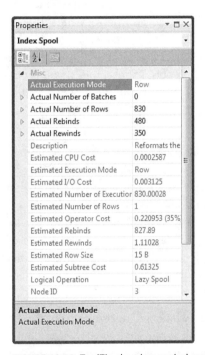

FIGURE 10-19 ToolTip showing rewind and rebind information.

Rewinds and rebinds are counted the same way for index and nonindex spools. As described earlier, a reexecution is counted as a rewind only if the correlated parameter(s) remain the same as the immediately before execution and is counted as a rebind if the correlated parameter(s) change from the prior execution. This is true even for reexecutions, in which the same correlated parameter(s) were encountered in an earlier (although not immediately prior) execution. However, because lazy index spools such as the one in this example retain results for all prior executions and all previously encountered correlated parameter values, the spool might treat some reported rebinds as rewinds. In other words, by failing to account for correlated parameter(s) that were seen before the most recent execution, the query plan statistics might overreport the number of rebinds for an index spool.

Next, look at another example of a correlated scalar subquery. Suppose that we want to find those orders for which the freight charge exceeds the average freight charge for all orders placed by the same customer:

```
SELECT O1.[OrderId], O1.[Freight]
FROM [Orders] O1
WHERE O1.[Freight] >
  (
  SELECT AVG(O2.[Freight])
  FROM [Orders] O2
  WHERE O2.[CustomerId] = O1.[CustomerId]
  )
```

This query is very similar to the previous one, yet a substantially different plan results:

```
|--Nested Loops(Inner Join)
  |--Table Spool
  |   |--Segment
  |      |--Sort(ORDER BY:([O1].[CustomerID] ASC))
  |         |--Clustered Index Scan (OBJECT:([Orders].[PK_Orders] AS [O1]),
  |            WHERE:([O1].[CustomerID] IS NOT NULL))
  |--Nested Loops(Inner Join, WHERE:([O1].[Freight]>[Expr1004]))
    |--Compute Scalar(DEFINE:([Expr1004]=
    |         CASE WHEN [Expr1012]=(0)
    |         THEN NULL
    |         ELSE [Expr1013]
    |         /CONVERT_IMPLICIT(money,[Expr1012],0)
    |         END))
    |  |--Stream Aggregate(DEFINE:([Expr1012]=
    |     COUNT_BIG([O1].[Freight]),[Expr1013]=SUM([O1].[Freight])))
    |  |--Table Spool
    |--Table Spool
```

Again, this plan isn't as complicated as it looks; Figure 10-20 shows the graphical plan. The outer side of the topmost nested loops join sorts the rows of the clustered index scan by the *CustomerId* column. The segment operator breaks the rows into groups (or segments) with the same value for the *CustomerId* column. Because the rows are sorted, sets of rows with the same *CustomerId* value will be consecutive. Next, the table spool—a segment spool—reads and saves one of these groups of rows that share the same *CustomerId* value.

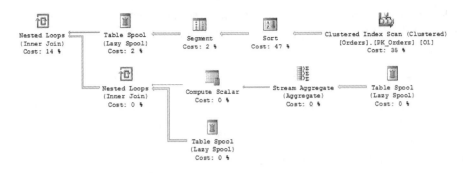

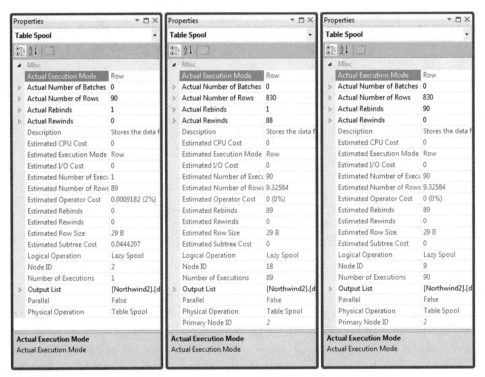

Properties ▾ □ ×		Properties ▾ □ ×		Properties ▾ □ ×	
Table Spool ▾		**Table Spool** ▾		**Table Spool** ▾	
▲ Misc		▲ Misc		▲ Misc	
Actual Execution Mode	Row	Actual Execution Mode	Row	Actual Execution Mode	Row
▷ Actual Number of Batches	0	▷ Actual Number of Batches	0	▷ Actual Number of Batches	0
▷ Actual Number of Rows	90	▷ Actual Number of Rows	830	▷ Actual Number of Rows	830
▷ Actual Rebinds	1	▷ Actual Rebinds	1	▷ Actual Rebinds	90
▷ Actual Rewinds	0	▷ Actual Rewinds	88	▷ Actual Rewinds	0
Description	Stores the data f	Description	Stores the data f	Description	Stores the data f
Estimated CPU Cost	0	Estimated CPU Cost	0	Estimated CPU Cost	0
Estimated Execution Mode	Row	Estimated Execution Mode	Row	Estimated Execution Mode	Row
Estimated I/O Cost	0	Estimated I/O Cost	0	Estimated I/O Cost	0
Estimated Number of Exect	1	Estimated Number of Exect	90	Estimated Number of Exect	90
Estimated Number of Rows	89	Estimated Number of Rows	9.32584	Estimated Number of Rows	9.32584
Estimated Operator Cost	0.0009182 (2%)	Estimated Operator Cost	0 (0%)	Estimated Operator Cost	0 (0%)
Estimated Rebinds	0	Estimated Rebinds	89	Estimated Rebinds	89
Estimated Rewinds	0	Estimated Rewinds	0	Estimated Rewinds	0
Estimated Row Size	29 B	Estimated Row Size	29 B	Estimated Row Size	29 B
Estimated Subtree Cost	0.0444207	Estimated Subtree Cost	0	Estimated Subtree Cost	0
Logical Operation	Lazy Spool	Logical Operation	Lazy Spool	Logical Operation	Lazy Spool
Node ID	2	Node ID	18	Node ID	9
Number of Executions	1	Number of Executions	89	Number of Executions	90
▷ Output List	[Northwind2].[d	▷ Output List	[Northwind2].[d	▷ Output List	[Northwind2].[d
Parallel	False	Parallel	False	Parallel	False
Physical Operation	Table Spool	Physical Operation	Table Spool	Physical Operation	Table Spool
		Primary Node ID	2	Primary Node ID	2
Actual Execution Mode		**Actual Execution Mode**		**Actual Execution Mode**	
Actual Execution Mode		Actual Execution Mode		Actual Execution Mode	

FIGURE 10-20 Graphical plan showing a segment spool with two secondary spools.

When the spool finishes loading a group of rows, it returns a single row for the entire group. (Note that a segment spool is the only type of spool that exhibits this behavior of returning only a single row regardless of how many input rows it reads.) At this point, the topmost nested loops join executes its inner input. The two leaf-level table spools—secondary spools—replay the group of rows that the original segment spool saved. The graphical plan illustrates the relationship between the secondary and primary spools by showing that the Primary Node ID for each of the secondary spools is the same as the Node ID for the primary segment spool. (In this example, the primary spool's Node ID is 2.) The stream aggregate computes the average freight for each group of rows (and, thus, for each *CustomerId* value). The result of the stream aggregate is a single row. The inner of the two nested loops compares each spooled row (which again consists of rows with the same *CustomerId* value) against this average and returns those rows that qualify. Finally, the segment spool truncates its worktable and repeats the process beginning with reading the next group of rows with the next *CustomerId* value.

By using the segment spool, the optimizer creates a plan that needs to scan the *Orders* table only one time. A spool such as this one that replays the same set of rows in different places within the plan is referred to as a common subexpression spool. Note that not all common subexpression spools are segment spools.

> **Note** The spool is a segment spool because it appears immediately above a segment operator in the plan. As in the earlier example, we can find more information about the spools and other operators in this plan from *SHOWPLAN_ALL*, *SHOWPLAN_XML*, or the graphical plan. *SHOWPLAN_XML* and the graphical plan provide the richest information including the *group by* column for the segment operator and the primary spool's Node ID for each secondary spool.

Finally, suppose that we want to compute the order with the maximum freight charge placed by each customer:

```
SELECT O1.[OrderId], O1.[Freight]
FROM [Orders] O1
WHERE O1.[Freight] =
  (
  SELECT MAX(O2.[Freight])
  FROM [Orders] O2
  WHERE O2.[CustomerId] = O1.[CustomerId]
  )
```

This query is similar to the previous two queries, but again a very different and surprisingly simple plan results:

```
|--Top(TOP EXPRESSION:((1)))
  |--Segment
    |--Sort(ORDER BY:([O1].[CustomerID] DESC, [O1].[Freight] DESC))
      |--Clustered Index Scan
        (OBJECT:([Orders].[PK_Orders] AS [O1]),
         WHERE:([O1].[Freight] IS NOT NULL AND
         [O1].[CustomerID] IS NOT NULL))
```

This plan sorts the *Orders* table by the *CustomerId* and *Freight* columns. As in the previous example, the segment operator breaks the rows into groups or segments with the same value for the *CustomerId* column. The top operator is a segment top. Unlike a typical top, which returns the top *N* rows for the entire input set, a segment top returns the top *N* rows for each group. The top is also a "top with ties." A top with ties returns more than *N* rows if the *N*th row has any duplicates or ties. In this query plan, because the sort ensures that the rows with the maximum freight charge are ordered first within each group, the top returns the row or rows with the maximum freight charge from each group. This plan is very efficient because it processes the *Orders* table only once and, unlike the previous plan, doesn't need a spool.

Note As with the segment spool, the top is a segment top because it appears immediately above a segment operator. We can also tell that the top is a top with ties by checking SHOWPLAN_ALL, SHOWPLAN_XML, or the graphical plan.

Removing correlations

The SQL Server query optimizer can remove correlations from many subqueries including scalar and multirow queries. If the optimizer can't remove correlations from a subquery, it must execute the subquery plan on the inner side of a nested loops join. However, by removing correlations, the optimizer can transform a subquery into a regular join and consider more plan alternatives with different join orders and join types. For example, the following query uses a noncorrelated subquery to return orders placed by customers who live in London:

```
SELECT O.[OrderId]
FROM [Orders] O
WHERE O.[CustomerId] IN
  (
  SELECT C.[CustomerId]
  FROM [Customers] C
  WHERE C.[City] = N'London'
  )
```

We can easily write the same query using a correlated subquery:

```
SELECT O.[OrderId]
FROM [Orders] O
WHERE EXISTS
  (
  SELECT *
  FROM [Customers] C
  WHERE C.[CustomerId] = O.[CustomerId]
    AND C.[City] = N'London'
  )
```

One query includes a noncorrelated subquery; the other includes a correlated subquery. However, the optimizer generates the same plan for both queries:

```
|--Nested Loops(Inner Join, OUTER REFERENCES:([C].[CustomerID]))
  |--Index Seek(OBJECT:([Customers].[City] AS [C]),
    SEEK:([C].[City]=N'London')
    ORDERED FORWARD)
  |--Index Seek(OBJECT:([Orders].[CustomerID] AS [O]),
    SEEK:([O].[CustomerID]= [C].[CustomerID])
    ORDERED FORWARD)
```

In the second query, the optimizer removes the correlation from the subquery so that it can scan the *Customers* table first (on the outer side of the nested loops join). If the optimizer didn't remove the correlation, the plan would need to scan the *Orders* table first to generate a *CustomerId* value before it could scan the *Customers* table.

For a more complex example of subquery decorrelation, consider the following query, which outputs a list of orders along with the freight charge for each order and the average freight charge for all orders by the same customer:

```
SELECT O1.[OrderId], O1.[Freight],
(
  SELECT AVG(O2.[Freight])
  FROM [Orders] O2
  WHERE O2.[CustomerId] = O1.[CustomerId]
  ) Avg_Freight
FROM [Orders] O1
```

We might expect that a correlated *SELECT* list subquery, such as the one used in this query, must be evaluated exactly once for each row from the main query. However, as the following plan illustrates, the optimizer can remove the correlation from this query:

```
|--Compute Scalar(DEFINE:([Expr1004]=[Expr1004]))
  |--Hash Match(Right Outer Join,HASH:([O2].[CustomerID])=([O1].[CustomerID]),
    RESIDUAL:(...))
    |--Compute Scalar(DEFINE:([Expr1004]=CASE WHEN [Expr1013]=(0)
      THEN NULL
      ELSE [Expr1014]
      /CONVERT_IMPLICIT(money,[Expr1013],0)
      END))
    |    |--Stream Aggregate(GROUP BY:([O2].[CustomerID])
          DEFINE:([Expr1013]=COUNT_BIG([O2].[Freight]),
              [Expr1014]=SUM([O2].[Freight])))
    |      |--Sort(ORDER BY:([O2].[CustomerID] ASC))
    |        |--Clustered Index Scan
            (OBJECT:([Orders].[PK_Orders] AS [O2]))
    |--Clustered Index Scan(OBJECT:([Orders].[PK_Orders] AS [O1]))
```

This plan first computes the average freight charge for all customers and then joins this result with the *Orders* table. It computes the average freight charge for each customer exactly once, regardless of the number of orders placed by that customer. Had the optimizer not removed the correlation, the plan would have had to compute the average freight charge for each customer separately for each order placed by that customer. For example, if a customer placed three orders, the plan would have computed the average freight charge for that customer three times. Clearly, the plan with the decorrelated subquery is more efficient. However, if the main query has a sufficiently selective predicate, the correlated plan does become more efficient and the optimizer will select it.

In addition to computing the average freight charges only once per customer, by removing the correlation, the optimizer is free to use any join operator. For example, this plan uses a hash join. The join itself is a right outer join. The outer join guarantees that the plan returns all orders, even those that might have a NULL value for the *CustomerId* column. An inner join would discard such rows because NULLs never join.

Subqueries in CASE expressions

Usually, SQL Server evaluates *CASE* expressions like any other scalar expression, often using a compute scalar operator. In the absence of any subqueries, a *CASE* expression is really nothing remarkable. However, you can use subqueries in the *WHEN*, *THEN*, and *ELSE* clauses of a *CASE* expression. SQL Server uses some slightly more exotic join functionality, which we haven't seen yet, to evaluate *CASE* expressions with subqueries. To see how these plans work, use the following script to set up an artificial scenario:

```
CREATE TABLE [MainTable] ([PK] int PRIMARY KEY, [Col1] int, [Col2] int, [Col3] int)
CREATE TABLE [WhenTable] ([PK] int PRIMARY KEY, [Data] int)
CREATE TABLE [ThenTable] ([PK] int PRIMARY KEY, [Data] int)
CREATE TABLE [ElseTable] ([PK] int PRIMARY KEY, [Data] int)

INSERT [MainTable] VALUES (1, 11, 101, 1001)
INSERT [MainTable] VALUES (2, 12, 102, 1002)
INSERT [WhenTable] VALUES (11, NULL)
INSERT [ThenTable] VALUES (101, 901)
INSERT [ElseTable] VALUES (102, 902)
SELECT M.[PK],
  CASE WHEN EXISTS (SELECT * FROM [WhenTable] W WHERE W.[PK] = M.[Col1])
    THEN (SELECT T.[Data] FROM [ThenTable] T WHERE T.[PK] = M.[Col2])
    ELSE (SELECT E.[Data] FROM [ElseTable] E WHERE E.[PK] = M.[Col3])
  END AS Case_Expr
FROM [MainTable] M

DROP TABLE [MainTable], [WhenTable], [ThenTable], [ElseTable]
```

Semantically, this query scans table *MainTable* and for each row checks whether table *WhenTable* has a matching row. If a match is found, it looks up an output value in table *ThenTable*; otherwise, it looks up an output value in table *ElseTable*. To show precisely what's happening, the script also adds a few rows of data. *MainTable* has two rows: one matches a row in *WhenTable*, and the other doesn't. Thus, one row results in a lookup from *ThenTable*; the other row results in a lookup from *ElseTable*. Finally, *ThenTable* includes rows that match both *MainTable* rows; *ElseTable* is empty. Although *ElseTable* is empty, the query still outputs all rows from *MainTable*, including the row that doesn't have a match in *WhenTable*. This row simply outputs NULL for the result of the *CASE* expression. Here is the output of the query:

```
PK Case_Expr
---------- -----------
1  901
2  NULL
```

And here is the query plan:

```
Rows Executes
0    0    |--Compute Scalar(DEFINE:([Expr1011]=CASE WHEN [Expr1012]
              THEN [T].[Data] ELSE [E].[Data] END))
2    1        |--Nested Loops(Left Outer Join, PASSTHRU:([Expr1012]),
                  OUTER REFERENCES:([M].[Col3]))
2    1            |--Nested Loops(Left Outer Join,PASSTHRU:(IsFalseOrNull [Expr1012]),
                      OUTER REFERENCES:([M].[Col2]))
```

```
2  1      |   |--Nested Loops(Left Semi Join,
                   OUTER REFERENCES:([M].[Col1]),DEFINE:([Expr1012] = [PROBE
VALUE]))
2  1      |   |   |--Clustered Index Scan (OBJECT:([MainTable].[PK_MainTable]
                   AS [M]))
1  2      |   |   |--Clustered Index Seek(OBJECT:([WhenTable].[PK_WhenTable]
                   AS [W]),SEEK:([W].[PK]=[M].[Col1]))
1  1      |   |--Clustered Index Seek (OBJECT:([ThenTable].[PK_ThenTable] AS [T]),
                   SEEK:([T].[PK]=[M].[Col2]))
0  1      |--Clustered Index Seek (OBJECT:([ElseTable].[PK_ElseTable] AS [E]),
                   SEEK:([E].[PK]=[M].[Col3]))
```

As we might expect, this query plan begins by scanning *MainTable*, which returns two rows. Next, the plan executes the *WHEN* clause of the *CASE* expression. The plan implements the *EXISTS* subquery using a left semi-join with *WhenTable*. SQL Server frequently uses semi-joins to evaluate *EXISTS* subqueries because the semi-join merely checks whether a row from one input joins with or matches any row from the other input. However, a typical semi-join (or anti-semi-join) only returns rows for matches (or nonmatches). In this case, the query must return all rows from *MainTable*, regardless of whether these rows have a matching row in *WhenTable*. Thus, the semi-join can't simply discard a row from *MainTable* just because *WhenTable* has no matching row.

The solution is a special type of semi-join with a *PROBE* column. This semi-join returns all rows from MainTable whether or not they match and sets the *PROBE* column (in this case, [Expr1012]) to true or false to indicate whether it found a matching row in *WhenTable*. Because the semi-join doesn't actually return a row from *WhenTable*, there's no way to determine whether the semi-join found a match without the *PROBE* column.

Next, depending on the value of the *PROBE* column, the query plan needs to look for a matching row in either *ThenTable* or *ElseTable*. However, the query plan must look in only one of the two tables; it can't look in both. The plan uses a special type of nested loops join to ensure that it performs only one of the two lookups. This nested loops join has a special predicate known as a *PASSTHRU* predicate. The join evaluates the *PASSTHRU* predicate on each outer row. If the *PASSTHRU* predicate evaluates to true, the join immediately returns the outer row without executing its inner input. If the *PASSTHRU* predicate evaluates to false, the join proceeds as usual and tries to join the outer row with an inner row.

> **Note** In this example, the query plan could execute both subqueries (for the *THEN* and *ELSE* clauses of the *CASE* expression) and then discard any unnecessary results. However, besides being inefficient, in some cases executing the extra subqueries could cause the query plan to fail. For example, if one of the scalar subqueries joined on a nonunique column, it could return more than one row, which would result in an error. It would be incorrect for the plan to fail while executing an unnecessary operation.

The plan actually has two nested loops joins with *PASSTHRU* predicates: one to evaluate the *THEN* clause subquery and one to evaluate the *ELSE* clause subquery. The *PASSTHRU* predicate for the first (bottommost) join tests the condition *IsFalseOrNull [Expr1012]*. The *IsFalseOrNull* function simply inverts the Boolean *PROBE* column. For each *MainTable* row, if the semi-join finds a matching row, the *PROBE* column ([Expr1012]) is true, the *PASSTHRU* predicate evaluates to false, and the join evaluates the index seek on *ThenTable*. However, if the semi-join doesn't find a matching row, the *PROBE* column is false, the *PASSTHRU* predicate evalutes to true, and the join returns the *MainTable* row without evaluating the index seek on *ThenTable*. The *PASSTHRU* predicate for the next (topmost) join tests the opposite condition to determine whether to perform the index seek on *ElseTable*. Thus, the plan executes exactly one of the two index seeks for each *MainTable* row.

To see the behavior of the *PASSTHRU* predicates, notice that while the *MainTable* scans and each join returns two rows, the plan executes the index seeks on *ThenTable* and *ElseTable* only once. A *PASSTHRU* predicate is the only scenario in which the number of rows on the outer side of a nested loops join doesn't precisely match the number of executes on the inner side.

Also notice how the query plan uses outer joins because the *THEN* or *ELSE* subqueries aren't guaranteed to actually return any rows. In fact, in this example, the index seek on *ElseTable* is executed for one of the *MainTable* rows, yet it returns no rows. The outer join simply returns a NULL, and the query still returns the *MainTable* row. If the query plan had used an inner join, it would have incorrectly discarded the *MainTable* row.

This example demonstrates a *CASE* expression with a single *WHEN* clause. SQL Server supports *CASE* expressions with multiple *WHEN* clauses and multiple *THEN* clause subqueries in the same way. The *PASSTHRU* predicates merely get progressively more complex to ensure that only one of the *THEN* clauses (or the *ELSE* clause) is actually executed.

Parallelism

SQL Server can execute queries using multiple CPUs simultaneously; this capability is referred to as parallel query execution. Parallel query execution can be used to reduce the response time of (that is, speed up) a large query. It can also be used to a run a bigger query (one that processes more data) in about the same amount of time as a smaller query (that is, scale up) by increasing the number of CPUs used in processing the query.

Although parallelism can be used to reduce the response time of a single query, this speedup comes at a cost: It increases the overhead associated with executing a query. Although this overhead is relatively small, it does make parallelism inappropriate for small queries (for OLTP queries, for example) in which the overhead would dominate the total execution time, and the goal is to run the maximum number of concurrent queries and to maximize the overall throughput of the system. SQL Server does generally scale well; however, if we compare the same query running serially—that is, without parallelism and on a single CPU—and in parallel on two CPUs, we will typically find that the parallel execution time is more than half the serial execution time. Again, this effect is caused by the parallelism overhead.

Parallelism is primarily useful on servers running a relatively small number of concurrent queries. On this type of server, parallelism can enable a small set of queries to keep many CPUs busy. Servers running many concurrent queries (such as an OLTP system) don't need parallelism to keep the CPUs busy; the mere fact that we have so many queries to execute can keep the CPUs busy. As already discussed, running these queries in parallel would just add overhead that would reduce the overall throughput of the system.

SQL Server parallelizes queries by horizontally partitioning the input data into approximately equal-sized sets, assigning one set to each CPU, and then performing the same operation (such as aggregate, join, and so on) on each set. Suppose that SQL Server decides to use two CPUs to execute a hash aggregate that happens to be grouping on an integer column. The server creates two threads (one for each CPU). Each thread executes the same hash aggregate operator. SQL Server might partition the input data by sending rows in which the *GROUP BY* column is odd to one thread and rows in which the *GROUP BY* column is even to the other thread, as shown in Figure 10-21. As long as all rows that belong to one group are processed by one hash aggregate operator and one thread, the plan produces the correct result.

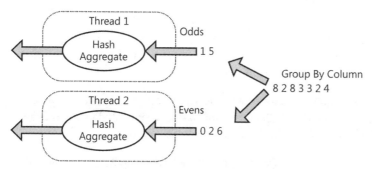

FIGURE 10-21 Executing an aggregate query on two threads.

This method of parallel query execution is both simple and scales well. In the previous example, both hash aggregate threads execute independently. The two threads don't need to communicate or coordinate their work in any way. To increase the degree of parallelism (DOP), SQL Server can simply add more threads and adjust the partitioning function. In practice, SQL Server uses a hash function to distribute rows for a hash aggregate. The hash function handles any data type, any number of *GROUP BY* columns, and any number of threads.

This method of parallelism isn't the same as "pipeline" parallelism in which multiple unrelated operators run concurrently in different threads. Although SQL Server frequently places different operators in different threads, the primary reason for doing so is to allow repartitioning of the data as it flows from one operator to the next. With pipeline parallelism, the degree of parallelism and the total number of threads would be limited to the number of operators.

The query optimizer decides whether to execute a query in parallel. For the optimizer even to consider a parallel plan, the following criteria must be met.

- SQL Server must be running on a multiprocessor, multicore, or hyperthreaded machine.

- The process affinity configuration must allow SQL Server to use at least two processors. Process affinity replaces the 'affinity mask' and 'affinity64 mask' sp_configure options and can be set through the use of the ALTER SERVER CONFIGURATION statement that's covered on Chapter 2, "The SQLOS."

- The *max degree of parallelism* advanced configuration option must be set to zero (the default) or to more than one. (The following section discusses this option in more detail). The MAX_DOP configuration for Resource Governor must also allow the use of parallel plans. Chapter 2 also covers the Resource Governor.

- The estimated cost to run a serial plan for a query is higher than the value set in cost threshold for parallelism.

As with most other decisions, the choice of whether to choose a serial or a parallel plan is cost-based. A complex and expensive query that processes many rows is more likely to result in a parallel plan than a simple query that processes very few rows. Although you rarely need to, you can also adjust the *cost threshold for parallelism* advanced configuration setting to raise or lower the threshold above which the optimizer considers parallel plans.

Degree of parallelism (DOP)

The degree of parallelism (DOP) isn't part of the cached compiled plan and might change with each execution. SQL Server decides the DOP at the start of execution as follows:

1. If the query includes a *MAXDOP N* query hint, SQL Server sets the maximum DOP for the query to *N* or to the number of available processors if *N* is zero (limited by the process affinity and *MAX_DOP* Resource Governor configurations, as explained earlier).

2. If the query doesn't include a *MAXDOP N* query hint, SQL Server sets the maximum DOP to the setting of the *max degree of parallelism* advanced configuration option. As with the *MAXDOP N* query hint, if this option is set to zero (the default), SQL Server sets the maximum DOP to the number of available processors (again, limited by the process affinity and *MAX_DOP* Resource Governor configurations).

3. SQL Server calculates the maximum number of concurrent threads that it needs to execute the query plan (as shown momentarily, this number can exceed the DOP) and compares this result to the number of available threads. If not enough threads are available, SQL Server reduces the DOP, as necessary. In the extreme case, SQL Server switches the parallel plan back to a serial plan. A serial plan runs with just the single connection thread, so it can always execute. When the DOP is fixed, SQL Server reserves sufficient threads to ensure that the query can execute without running out of threads. This process is similar to how SQL Server acquires a memory grant for memory-consuming queries. The principal difference is that a query might wait to acquire a memory grant, but never waits to reserve threads.

The *max worker threads* advanced configuration option determines the maximum number of threads available to SQL Server for system activities, as well as for parallel query execution. The default setting for this option, 0, enables SQL Server to automatically configure the number of worker threads at startup. It's set higher for systems with more processors. It's also set higher for 64-bit servers than for 32-bit servers. You rarely need to change the setting of this option.

As noted earlier, the number of threads used by a query might exceed the DOP. If you check *sys.dm_os_tasks* while running a parallel query, you might see more threads than the DOP. The number of threads might exceed the DOP because if SQL Server needs to repartition data between two operators, it places them in different threads. The DOP only determines the number of threads per operator, not the total number of threads per query plan. As with the memory grant computation, when SQL Server computes the maximum number of threads that a query plan might consume, it does take blocking or stop-and-go operators into account. The operators above and below a blocking operator are never executed at the same time and thus can share both memory and threads. When a query runs with a particular DOP, SQL Server also limits the number of schedulers used by that query to the selected DOP. That is, all threads used by the query are assigned to the same set of DOP schedulers, and the query uses only DOP CPUs, regardless of the total number of threads.

Parallelism operator (also known as exchange)

The actual partitioning and movement of data between threads is handled by the parallelism (or exchange) iterator. Although it's unique in many respects, the parallelism iterator implements the same interfaces like any other iterator. Most of the other iterators don't need to be aware that they are executing in parallel. The optimizer simply places appropriate parallelism iterators in the plan and it runs in parallel.

The exchange iterator is unique in that it's really two iterators: a producer and a consumer. SQL Server places the producer at the root of a query subtree (often called a branch). The producer reads input rows from its subtree, assembles the rows into packets, and routes these packets to the appropriate consumer(s). SQL Server places the consumer at the leaf of the next query subtree. The consumer receives packets from its producer(s), removes the rows from these packets, and returns the rows to its parent iterator. For example, as Figure 10-22 illustrates, a repartition exchange running at DOP2 consists of two producers and two consumers:

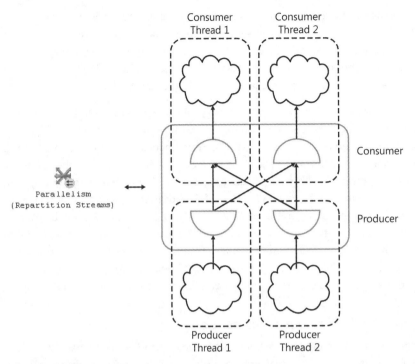

FIGURE 10-22 A repartition exchange running on two CPUs.

Although the data flow between most iterators is pull-based (an iterator calls *GetRow* on its child when it's ready for another row), the data flow in between an exchange producer and consumer is push-based. That is, the producer fills a packet with rows and "pushes" it to the consumer. This model allows the producer and consumer threads to execute independently. SQL Server does have flow control to prevent a fast producer from flooding a slow consumer with excessive packets.

Exchanges can be classified in three different ways.

- By the number of producer and consumer threads

- By the partitioning function used by the exchange to route rows from a producer thread to a consumer thread

- According to whether the exchange preserves the order of the input rows

Table 10-5 shows how to classify exchanges based on the number of producer and/or consumer threads. The number of threads within each parallel "zone" of a query plan is the same and is equal to the DOP. Thus, an exchange might have exactly one producer or consumer thread if it's at the beginning or end of a serial zone within the plan or it might have exactly DOP producer or consumer threads.

TABLE 10-5 Types of parallelism exchange operators

Type	# Producer threads	# Consumer threads
Gather streams	DOP	1
Repartition streams	DOP	DOP
Distribute streams	1	DOP

A gather streams exchange is often called a *start parallelism* exchange because the operators above it run serially while the operators below it run in parallel. The root exchange in any parallel plan is always a gather exchange because the results of any query plan must ultimately be funneled back to the single connection thread to be returned to the client. A distribute streams exchange is often called a *stop parallelism* exchange. It's the opposite of a gather streams exchange. The operators above a distribute streams exchange run in parallel, whereas the operators below it run serially.

Table 10-6 shows how to classify exchanges based on the type of partitioning. Partitioning type only makes sense for a repartition or a distribute streams exchange. The only way to route rows in a gather exchange is to use the single consumer thread.

TABLE 10-6 Types of partitioning for executing parallel queries

Partitioning type	Description
Broadcast	Send all rows to all consumer threads.
Hash	Determine where to send each row by evaluating a hash function on one or more columns in the row.
Round robin	Send each packet of rows to the next consumer thread in sequence.
Demand	Send the next row to the next consumer that asks for a row. This partition type is the only type of exchange that uses a pull rather than a push model for data flow. Demand partitioning is used only to distribute partition ids in parallel plans with partitioned tables.
Range	Determine where to send each row by evaluating a range function on one column in the row. Range partitioning is used only by certain parallel index build and statistics-gathering plans.

Finally, exchanges can be broken down into merging (or order preserving) and nonmerging (or non-order–preserving) exchanges. The consumer in a merging exchange ensures that rows from multiple producers are returned in a sorted order. (The rows must already be in this sorted order at the producer; the merging exchange doesn't actually sort.) A merging exchange makes sense only for a gather or a repartition streams exchange; a distribute streams exchange has only one producer, only one stream of rows, and nothing to merge at each consumer.

SQL Server commonly uses merging exchanges in plans for queries with *ORDER BY* clauses or in plans with parallel stream aggregate or merge join operators. However, merging exchanges are generally more expensive than, and don't scale as well as, nonmerging exchanges. A merging exchange can't return rows until it has received rows from every input; even then, a merging exchange must returns rows in sorted order. If some inputs to a merging exchange include rows that are much later in the sort order than rows from the other inputs, the exchange can't return the rows that sort later. The inputs returning the rows that sort later might get too far ahead of the other inputs and be forced to wait while the other inputs "catch up." The higher the DOP (that is, the more threads), the more likely that some of the inputs will be forced to wait for other inputs.

In some extreme cases, merging exchanges might lead to intra-query "parallel deadlocks." For a query plan to be susceptible to a parallel deadlock, it must include at least two merging exchanges separated by order-preserving operators; a parallel merge join above a pair of merging exchanges or a merging exchange above index seek with multiple ranges. Although parallel deadlocks don't cause a query to fail, they can lead to serious performance degradations. Parallel deadlocks were a far more common problem in SQL Server 2000, but improvements in recent versions have resolved this problem in all but a few very rare scenarios. To check for a parallel deadlock, use the *sys.dm_os_waiting_tasks* DMV. If all threads associated with a session are blocked on the CXPACKET wait type, you have a parallel deadlock. Generally, the only solution to a parallel deadlock is to reduce the DOP, force a serial plan, or alter the query plan to eliminate the merging exchanges.

In light of these performance issues, the optimizer costs parallel plans with merging exchanges fairly high and tries to avoid choosing a plan with merging exchanges as the DOP increases.

SQL Server includes all the previous properties in all three query plan varieties (graphical, text, and XML). Moreover, in graphical query plans, you can also tell at a glance which operators are running in parallel (that is, which operators are between a start exchange and a stop exchange) by looking for a little parallelism symbol on the operator icons, as illustrated in Figure 10-23.

Clustered Index Scan
Serial Scan

Clustered Index Scan
Parallel Scan

FIGURE 10-23 Clustered index scan operator icon with and without parallelism.

The rest of this subsection looks at how a few of the operators discussed earlier in this chapter behave in parallel plans. Because most operators neither need to know nor care whether they are executing in parallel and can be parallelized merely by placing them below a start exchange, we will look primarily at the handful of operators whose behavior is interesting in the context of parallelism.

Parallel scan

The scan operator is one of the few operators that is parallel "aware." The threads that compose a parallel scan work together to scan all rows in a table. Rows or pages aren't assigned beforehand to a particular thread. Instead, the storage engine dynamically hands out pages or ranges of rows to threads. A parallel page supplier coordinates access to the pages or rows of the table. The parallel page supplier ensures that each page or range of rows is assigned to exactly one thread, so it's processed exactly once.

At the beginning of a parallel scan, each thread requests a set of pages or a range of rows from the parallel page supplier. The threads then begin processing their assigned pages or rows and begin returning results. When a thread finishes with its assigned set of pages, it requests the next set of pages or the next range of rows from the parallel page supplier.

This algorithm has a couple of advantages.

- It's independent of the number of threads. SQL Server can add and remove threads from a parallel scan, and it automatically adjusts. If the number of threads doubles, each thread processes (approximately) half as many pages. And, if the I/O system can keep up, the scan runs twice as fast.

- It's resilient to skew or load imbalances. If one thread runs slower than the other threads, that thread simply requests fewer pages, whereas the other faster threads pick up the extra work. The total execution time degrades smoothly. Compare this scenario to what would happen if SQL Server statically assigned pages to threads: The slow thread would dominate the total execution time.

Start with a simple example. Parallel plans require fairly big tables; if the tables are too small, the optimizer concludes that a serial plan is perfectly adequate. The following script creates two tables. Each table has 250,000 rows and, thanks to the fixed-length *char(200)* column, well over 6,500 pages.

```
CREATE TABLE [HugeTable1]
  (
  [Key] int,
  [Data] int,
  [Pad] char(200),
  CONSTRAINT [PK1] PRIMARY KEY ([Key])
  )

SET NOCOUNT ON
DECLARE @i int
BEGIN TRAN
SET @i = 0
WHILE @i < 250000

BEGIN
  INSERT [HugeTable1] VALUES(@i, @i, NULL)
  SET @i = @i + 1
  IF @i % 1000 = 0
  BEGIN
    COMMIT TRAN
    BEGIN TRAN
  END
END
COMMIT TRAN

SELECT [Key], [Data], [Pad]
INTO [HugeTable2]
FROM [HugeTable1]

ALTER TABLE [HugeTable2]
ADD CONSTRAINT [PK2] PRIMARY KEY ([Key])
```

Now try the simplest possible query:

```
SELECT [Key], [Data]
FROM [HugeTable1]
```

Despite the large table, this query results in a serial plan:

```
|--Clustered Index Scan(OBJECT:([HugeTable1].[PK1]))
```

We don't get a parallel plan because parallelism is really about speeding up queries by applying more CPUs to the problem. The cost of this query is dominated by the cost of reading pages from disk (which is mitigated by readahead rather than parallelism) and returning rows to the client. The query uses relatively few CPU cycles and, in fact, would probably run slower if SQL Server parallelized it.

Now suppose that we add a fairly selective predicate to the query:

```
SELECT [Key], [Data]
FROM [HugeTable1]
WHERE [Data] < 1000
```

This query results in a parallel plan:

```
|--Parallelism(Gather Streams)
   |--Clustered Index Scan(OBJECT:([HugeTable1].[PK1]),
      WHERE:([HugeTable1].[Data]<CONVERT_IMPLICIT(int,[@1],0)))
```

Because the *Data* column doesn't have an index, SQL Server can't perform an index seek and must evaluate the predicate for each row. By running this query in parallel, SQL Server distributes the cost of evaluating the predicate across multiple CPUs. (In this case, the predicate is so cheap that it probably doesn't make much difference whether the query runs in parallel.)

The exchange in this plan doesn't return the rows in any particular order. It simply returns the rows in whatever order it receives them from its producer threads. Now observe what happens if an *ORDER BY* clause is added to the query:

```
SELECT [Key], [Data]
FROM [HugeTable1]
WHERE [Data] < 1000
ORDER BY [Key]
```

The optimizer recognizes a clustered index that can return rows sorted by the *Key* column. To exploit this index and avoid an explicit sort, the optimizer adds a merging or order-preserving exchange to the plan:

```
|--Parallelism(Gather Streams, ORDER BY:([HugeTable1].[Key] ASC))
   |--Clustered Index Scan(OBJECT:([HugeTable1].[PK1]),
      WHERE:([HugeTable1].[Data]<CONVERT_IMPLICIT(int,[@1],0)) ORDERED FORWARD)
```

We can identify the merging exchange by the *ORDER BY* clause in the query plan. This clause indicates the order in which the exchange returns the rows.

Load balancing

As noted earlier, the parallel scan algorithm dynamically allocates pages to threads. We can devise an experiment to see this effect in action. Consider this query:

```
SELECT MIN([Data]) FROM [HugeTable1]
```

This query scans the entire table, but because of the aggregate it uses a parallel plan. The aggregate also ensures that the query returns only one row. Without it, the execution time of this query would be dominated by the cost of returning rows to the client. This overhead could alter the results of the experiment.

```
|--Stream Aggregate(DEFINE:([Expr1003]=MIN([partialagg1004])))
  |--Parallelism(Gather Streams)
    |--Stream Aggregate(DEFINE:([partialagg1004]=MIN([HugeTable1].[Data])))
      |--Clustered Index Scan(OBJECT:([HugeTable1].[PK1]))
```

Before proceeding with the experiment, notice that this plan includes two stream aggregates instead of the usual one in a serial plan. The bottommost aggregate is referred to as a local or partial aggregate. The local aggregate computes the minimum value of the *Data* column within each thread. The topmost aggregate is referred to as a global aggregate. The global aggregate computes the minimum of the local minimums. Local aggregation improves query performance in two ways. First, it reduces the number of rows flowing through the exchange. Second, it enables parallel execution of the aggregate. Because this query computes a single result row (recall that it's a scalar aggregate) without the local aggregate, all the scanned rows would have to be processed by a single thread. SQL Server can use local aggregation for both stream and hash aggregates, for most built-in and many user-defined aggregate functions, and for both scalar aggregates (like in this example) and grouping aggregates. In the case of grouping aggregates, the benefits of local aggregation increase as the number of groups decreases. The smaller the number of groups, the more work the local aggregate can actually perform.

Returning to the experiment, by using *SET STATISTICS XML ON* we can run the previous query and see exactly how many rows each thread processes. (The same information is also visible with graphical showplan in the Properties sheet.) Here is an excerpt of the XML output on a two-processor system:

```
<RelOp NodeId="3" PhysicalOp="Clustered Index Scan" LogicalOp="Clustered Index Scan"...>
 <RunTimeInformation>
  <RunTimeCountersPerThread Thread="1" ActualRows="124986"... />
  <RunTimeCountersPerThread Thread="2" ActualRows="125014"... />
  <RunTimeCountersPerThread Thread="0" ActualRows="0"... />
 </RunTimeInformation>
</RelOp>
```

Notice that both threads (threads 1 and 2) processed approximately half the rows. (Thread 0 is the coordinator or main thread. It executes only the portion of the query plan above the topmost exchange, so don't expect it to process any rows for operators executed in a parallel portion of the query plan.)

Now repeat the experiment, but this time run an expensive serial query at the same time. This cross join query will run for a very long time and use plenty of CPU cycles. The *OPTION (MAXDOP 1)* query hint forces SQL Server to execute this query in serial. Chapters 11 and 12 discuss this and other hints in more detail.

```
SELECT MIN(T1.[Key] + T2.[Key])
FROM [HugeTable1] T1 CROSS JOIN [HugeTable2] T2
OPTION (MAXDOP 1)
```

This serial query runs with a single thread and consumes cycles from only one of the two schedulers. While it's running, try running the parallel scan query again. Here is the statistics XML output for the second run:

```
<RelOp NodeId="3" PhysicalOp="Clustered Index Scan" LogicalOp="Clustered Index Scan"...>
 <RunTimeInformation>
  <RunTimeCountersPerThread Thread="1" ActualRows="54232"... />
  <RunTimeCountersPerThread Thread="2" ActualRows="195768"... />
  <RunTimeCountersPerThread Thread="0" ActualRows="0"... />
 </RunTimeInformation>
</RelOp>
```

This time, thread 1 processed more than 75 percent of the rows while thread 2, which was busy executing the serial plan, processed fewer than 25 percent of the rows. The parallel scan automatically balanced the work across the two threads. Because thread 1 had more free cycles (it wasn't competing with the serial plan), it requested and scanned more pages.

 Caution If you try this experiment, don't forget to terminate the serial query when you are done! Otherwise, it will continue to run and waste cycles for a very long time.

The same load balancing that we just observed applies equally whether a thread is slowed down because of an external factor (such as the serial query in this example) or because of an internal factor. For example, if it costs more to process some rows than others, we will see the same behavior.

Parallel nested loops join

SQL Server parallelizes a nested loops join by distributing the outer rows (that is, the rows from the first input) randomly among the nested loops join threads. For example, if two threads are running a nested loops join, SQL Server sends about half of the rows to each thread. Each thread then runs the inner side (that is, the second input) of the nested loops join for its set of rows as though it were running serially. That is, for each outer row assigned to it, the thread executes its inner input using that row as the source of any correlated parameters. In this way, the threads can run independently. SQL Server doesn't add exchanges to or parallelize the inner side of a nested loops join.

Here is a simple example of a parallel nested loops join:

```
SELECT T1.[Key], T1.[Data], T2.[Data]
FROM [HugeTable1] T1 JOIN [HugeTable2] T2
  ON T1.[Key] = T2.[Key]
WHERE T1.[Data] < 500
```

Now analyze the *STATISTICS PROFILE* output for this plan:

```
Rows Executes
500  1   |--Parallelism(Gather Streams)
500  2     |--Nested Loops(Inner Join, OUTER REFERENCES:([T1].[Key], [Expr1004])
                      WITH UNORDERED PREFETCH)
500  2       |--Clustered Index Scan (OBJECT:([HugeTable1].[PK1] AS [T1]),
             WHERE:([T1].[Data]<(500)))
500  500     |--Clustered Index Seek (OBJECT:([HugeTable2].[PK2] AS [T2]),
              SEEK:([T2].[Key]=[T1].[Key])
              ORDERED FORWARD)
```

This plan has only one exchange (in other words, parallelism operator). Because this exchange is at the root of the query plan, all operators in this plan—the nested loops join, the table scan, and the clustered index seek—execute in each thread. The lack of an index on the *Data* column of *Huge-Table1* forces the clustered index scan and the use of a residual predicate to evaluate T1.[Data] < 500. Because *HugeTable1* has 250,000 rows, the scan is expensive and, as in the previous examples, the optimizer chooses a parallel scan of *HugeTable1*. The scan of *HugeTable1* is not immediately below an exchange (in other words, a parallelism operator). In fact, it's on the outer side of the nested loops join, and it's the nested loops join that is below the exchange. Nevertheless, because the scan is on the outer side of the join and because the join is below a start (in other words, a gather) exchange, SQL Server performs a parallel scan of *HugeTable1*. Because a parallel scan assigns pages to threads dynamically, the scan distributes the *HugeTable1* rows among the threads. It doesn't matter which rows it distributes to which threads.

Because SQL Server ran this query with DOP 2 on my system, notice that two executes occurred each for the clustered index scan of *HugeTable1* and for the join (both of which are in the same thread). Moreover, the scan and join both return a total of 500 rows, although we can't tell from this output how many rows each thread returned. We can (and momentarily will) determine this information using statistics XML output.

Next, the join executes its inner side (in this case, the clustered index seek on *HugeTable2*) for each of the 500 outer rows. Here is where things get a little tricky. Although each of the two threads contains an instance of the clustered index seek iterator, and even though the seek is below the join, which is below the exchange, the seek is on the *inner* side of the join, so the seek does *not* use a parallel scan. Instead, the two seek instances execute independently of one another on two different outer rows and two different correlated parameters. As in a serial plan, we see 500 executes of the index seek: one for each row on the outer side of the join. With only one exception (addressed later in the chapter), no matter how complex the inner side of a nested loops join is, we always execute it as a serial plan just as in this simple example.

Round-robin exchange

In the previous example, SQL Server relies on the parallel scan to distribute rows uniformly among the threads. In some cases, SQL Server must add a round-robin exchange to distribute the rows. (Recall that a round-robin exchange sends each subsequent packet of rows to the next consumer thread in a fixed sequence.) Here is one such example:

```
SELECT T1_Top.[Key], T1_Top.[Data], T2.[Data]
FROM
  (
  SELECT TOP 100 T1.[Key], T1.[Data]
  FROM [HugeTable1] T1
  ORDER BY T1.[Data]
  ) T1_Top,
  [HugeTable2] T2
WHERE T1_Top.[Key] = T2.[Key]
```

Here is the corresponding plan:

```
|--Parallelism(Gather Streams)
  |--Nested Loops(Inner Join, OUTER REFERENCES:([T1].[Key],
    [Expr1004]) WITH UNORDERED PREFETCH)
    |--Parallelism(Distribute Streams, RoundRobin Partitioning)
    |  |--Top(TOP EXPRESSION:((100)))
    |    |--Parallelism(Gather Streams, ORDER BY:([T1].[Data] ASC))
    |      |--Sort(TOP 100, ORDER BY:([T1].[Data] ASC))
    |        |--Clustered Index Scan (OBJECT:([HugeTable1].[PK1] AS [T1]))
    |--Clustered Index Seek(OBJECT:([HugeTable2].[PK2] AS [T2]), SEEK:([T2].[Key]=[T1].[Key])
ORDERED FORWARD)
```

The main difference between this plan and the plan from the original example is that this plan includes a top-100 rows iterator. The top iterator can only be correctly evaluated in a serial plan thread. (It can't be split among multiple threads or we might end up with too few or too many rows.) Thus, SQL Server must add a stop (that is, a distribute streams) exchange above the top iterator and can't use the parallel scan to distribute the rows among the join threads. Instead, SQL Server parallelizes the join by having the stop exchange use round-robin partitioning to distribute the rows among the join threads.

Parallel nested loops join performance

The parallel scan has one major advantage over the round-robin exchange. A parallel scan automatically and dynamically balances the workload among the threads; a round-robin exchange doesn't. As the previous parallel scan example demonstrates, if we have a query in which one thread is slower than the others, the parallel scan might help compensate.

Both the parallel scan and a round-robin exchange might fail to keep all join threads busy if too many threads and too few pages and/or rows are available to be processed. Some threads might get no rows to process and end up idle. This problem can be more pronounced with a parallel scan because it doles out multiple pages at one time to each thread while the exchange distributes one packet (equivalent to one page) of rows at one time.

To see this problem in the previous original parallel nested loops join example, check the statistics XML output:

```
<RelOp NodeId="1" PhysicalOp="Nested Loops" LogicalOp="Inner Join"...>
  <RunTimeInformation>
    <RunTimeCountersPerThread Thread="2" ActualRows="0"... />
    <RunTimeCountersPerThread Thread="1" ActualRows="500"... />
    <RunTimeCountersPerThread Thread="0" ActualRows="0"... />
  </RunTimeInformation>
</RelOp>
```

This output shows that all the join's output rows are processed by thread 1. The problem is that the clustered index scan of *HugeTable1* has a residual predicate T1.[Data] < 500, which is true for the first 500 rows in the table and false for the remaining rows. The first few pages of the table containing the first 500 rows are all assigned to the first thread.

In this example, it's not a big problem because the inner side of the join is fairly cheap and contributes a small percentage of the overall cost of the query (with the clustered index scan of *HugeTable1* contributing a much larger percentage of the cost). However, this problem could be more significant if the inner side of the query were more expensive.

Inner-side parallel execution

This chapter noted earlier that with one exception, SQL Server always executes the inner side of a parallel nested loops join as a serial plan. The exception occurs when the optimizer knows that the outer input to the nested loops join is guaranteed to return only a single row and when the join has no correlated parameters. That is, the inner side of the join is guaranteed to run exactly once and can be run independently of the outer side of the join. In this case, if the join is an inner join, the inner side of the join might include a parallel scan. Moreover, in some rare scenarios, if the join is an outer or semi-join, it might be executed in a serial zone (below a stop exchange), and the inner side of the join might include exchanges.

Consider this query:

```
SELECT T1.[Key], T1.[Data], T2.[Key]
FROM [HugeTable1] T1 JOIN [HugeTable2] T2
  ON T1.[Data] = T2.[Data]
WHERE T1.[Key] = 0
```

This query yields the following plan:

```
|--Parallelism(Gather Streams)
  |--Nested Loops(Inner Join, WHERE:([T1].[Data]=[T2].[Data]))
    |--Parallelism(Distribute Streams, Broadcast Partitioning)
    |  |--Clustered Index Seek (OBJECT:([HugeTable1].[PK1] AS [T1]),
    |      SEEK:([T1].[Key]=(0)) ORDERED FORWARD)
    |--Clustered Index Scan(OBJECT:([HugeTable2].[PK2] AS [T2]))
```

The equality predicate *T1.[Key] = 0* ensures that the clustered index seek of *HugeTable1* returns exactly one row. Notice that the plan includes a broadcast exchange, which delivers this single row to each instance of the nested loops join. In this plan, the clustered index scan of *HugeTable2* uses a parallel scan—that is, all instances of this scan cooperatively scan *HugeTable2* exactly once. If this plan used a serial scan of *HugeTable2*, each scan instance would return the entire contents of *HugeTable2* that, in conjunction with the broadcast exchange, would result in the plan returning each row multiple times. Figure 10-24 shows the graphical plan for this query, along with the ToolTip indicating that a broadcast exchange is being used.

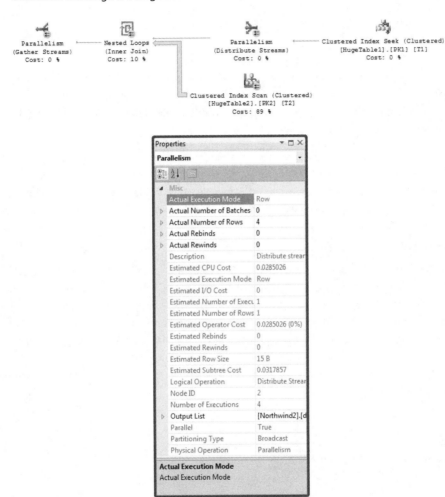

FIGURE 10-24 A parallel plan using a broadcast exchange.

Parallel merge join

SQL Server parallelizes merge joins by distributing both sets of input rows among the individual merge join threads using hash partitioning. If two input rows join, they have the same values for the join key and therefore hash to the same merge join thread. Unlike the parallel plan examples so far, merge join also requires that its input rows be sorted. In a parallel merge join plan, as in a serial merge join plan, SQL Server can use an index scan to deliver rows to the merge join in the correct sort order. However, in a parallel plan, SQL Server must also use a merging exchange to preserve the order of the input rows.

Although, as discussed previously, the optimizer tends to favor plans that don't require a merging exchange; including an *ORDER BY* clause in a join query can encourage such a plan. Consider the following query:

```
SELECT T1.[Key], T1.[Data], T2.[Key]
FROM [HugeTable1] T1 JOIN [HugeTable2] T2
  ON T1.[Key] = T2.[Data]
ORDER BY T1.[Key]
```

The optimizer chooses the following query plan:

```
|--Parallelism(Gather Streams, ORDER BY:([T1].[Key] ASC))
  |--Merge Join(Inner Join, MERGE:([T1].[Key])=([T2].[Data]), RESIDUAL:(...))
    |--Parallelism(Repartition Streams, Hash Partitioning,
      PARTITION COLUMNS:([T1].[Key]), ORDER BY:([T1].[Key] ASC))
    | |--Clustered Index Scan (OBJECT:([HugeTable1].[PK1] AS [T1]), ORDERED FORWARD)
    |--Sort(ORDER BY:([T2].[Data] ASC))
      |--Parallelism(Repartition Streams, Hash Partitioning,
        PARTITION COLUMNS:([T2].[Data]))
        |--Clustered Index Scan (OBJECT:([HugeTable2].[PK2] AS [T2]))
```

This plan includes three exchanges, including two merging exchanges. Two of the exchanges are hash partitioning exchanges and are placed below the merge join. These exchanges ensure that any input rows that might potentially join are delivered to the same merge join thread. The first merge join input uses a merging exchange, and the clustered index scan of *HugeTable1* delivers the input rows sorted on the join key. The second merge join input uses a nonmerging exchange. The clustered index scan of *HugeTable2* doesn't deliver input rows sorted on the join key. Instead, a sort occurs between the merge join and the exchange. By placing the exchange below the sort, the optimizer avoids the need to use a merging exchange. The final exchange is the start exchange at the top of the plan. This exchange returns the rows in the order required by the *ORDER BY* clause on the query and takes advantage of the property that the merge join output rows in the same order as it inputs them

Parallel hash join

SQL Server uses one of two different strategies to parallelize a hash join. One strategy uses hash partitioning just like a parallel merge join; the other strategy uses broadcast partitioning and is often called a broadcast hash join.

Hash partitioning

The more common strategy for parallelizing a hash join involves distributing the build rows (in other words, the rows from the first input) and the probe rows (in other words, the rows from the second input) among the individual hash join threads using hash partitioning. As in the parallel merge join case, if two input rows join, they are guaranteed to hash to the same hash join thread. After the data is hash partitioned among the threads, the hash join instances all run completely independently on their respective data sets. Unlike merge joins, hash joins don't require that input rows be delivered in any particular order and, as a result, don't require merging exchanges. The absence of any interthread dependencies ensures that this strategy scales extremely well as the DOP increases.

For an example of a parallel hash join, consider the following simple query:

```
SELECT T1.[Key], T1.[Data], T2.[Key]
FROM [HugeTable1] T1 JOIN [HugeTable2] T2
 ON T1.[Data] = T2.[Data]
```

SQL Server executes this query using the following plan:

```
|--Parallelism(Gather Streams)
  |--Hash Match(Inner Join, HASH:([T1].[Data])=([T2].[Data]), RESIDUAL:(...))
    |--Parallelism(Repartition Streams, Hash Partitioning,
      PARTITION COLUMNS:([T1].[Data]))
    | |--Clustered Index Scan (OBJECT:([HugeTable1].[PK1] AS [T1]))
    |--Parallelism(Repartition Streams, Hash Partitioning,
      PARTITION COLUMNS:([T2].[Data]))
        |--Clustered Index Scan (OBJECT:([HugeTable2].[PK2] AS [T2]))
```

Broadcast partitioning

Consider what happens if SQL Server tries to parallelize a hash join using hash partitioning, but only a small number of rows exist on the build side of the hash join. Fewer rows than hash join threads means that some threads might receive no rows at all. In this case, those threads would have no work to do during the probe phase of the join and would remain idle. Even if more rows are available than threads, the presence of duplicate key values and/or skew in the hash function means that some threads might receive and process many more rows than other threads.

To reduce the risk of skew problems, when the optimizer estimates that the number of build rows is relatively small, it might choose to broadcast these rows to all the hash join threads. Because all build rows are broadcast to all hash join threads, in a broadcast hash join, which threads process which probe rows doesn't matter. Each probe row can be sent to any thread and if it can join with any build rows, it will.

For example, the following query includes a very selective predicate:

```
SELECT T1.[Key], T1.[Data], T2.[Key]
FROM [HugeTable1] T1 JOIN [HugeTable2] T2
  ON T1.[Data] = T2.[Data]
WHERE T1.[Key] < 100
```

Because of the selective predicate, the optimizer chooses a broadcast hash join plan:

```
|--Parallelism(Gather Streams)
      |--Hash Match(Inner Join, HASH:([T1].[Data])=([T2].[Data]), RESIDUAL:(…))
            |--Bitmap(HASH:([T1].[Data]), DEFINE:([Bitmap1004]))
            |     |--Parallelism(Distribute Streams, Broadcast Partitioning)
            |           |--Clustered Index Seek(OBJECT:([HugeTable1].[PK1] AS [T1]),
            |                 SEEK:([T1].[Key] < (100)) ORDERED FORWARD)
            |--Clustered Index Scan(OBJECT:([HugeTable2].[PK2] AS [T2]),
                  WHERE:(PROBE([Bitmap1004],[HugeTable2].[Data] as [T2].[Data],N'[IN ROW]')))
```

The exchange above the clustered index seek of *HugeTable1* is now a broadcast exchange, whereas the exchange above the clustered index scan of *HugeTable2* is gone. This plan doesn't need an exchange above the scan of *HugeTable2* because the parallel scan automatically distributes the pages and rows of *HugeTable2* among the hash join threads. This result is similar to how the parallel scan distributed rows among nested loops join threads for the parallel nested loops join, as discussed earlier. The plan also includes a bitmap operator, which will be explained in the next section. Similar to the parallel nested loops join, if the probe input of a broadcast hash join has a serial zone (for example, caused by a top operator), the query can use a round-robin exchange to redistribute the rows.

Although broadcast hash joins do reduce the risk of skew problems, they aren't suitable for all scenarios. In particular, broadcast hash joins use more memory than their hash-partitioned counterparts. Because a broadcast hash join means SQL Server sends every build row to every hash join thread, if the number of threads doubles, the amount of memory consumed also doubles. Thus, a broadcast hash join requires memory that is proportional to the degree of parallelism, whereas a hash-partitioned parallel hash join requires the same amount of memory regardless of the degree of parallelism.

Bitmap filtering

Now, look at the following query:

```
SELECT T1.[Key], T1.[Data], T2.[Key]
FROM [HugeTable1] T1 JOIN [HugeTable2] T2
  ON T1.[Data] = T2.[Data]
WHERE T1.[Key] < 10000
```

The predicate T1.[Key] < 10000 eliminates 96 percent of the build rows from *HugeTable1*. It also indirectly eliminates 96 percent of the rows from *HugeTable2* because they no longer join with rows from *HugeTable1*. Having a way to eliminate these rows from *HugeTable2* much earlier without the overhead of passing the rows through the exchange and into the hash join would be nice. The bitmap operator provides just such a mechanism:

```
|--Parallelism(Gather Streams)
     |--Hash Match(Inner Join, HASH:([T1].[Data])=([T2].[Data]), RESIDUAL:(…))
          |--Bitmap(HASH:([T1].[Data]), DEFINE:([Bitmap1004]))
          |    |--Parallelism(Repartition Streams, Hash Partitioning,
          |         PARTITION COLUMNS:([T1].[Data]))
          |         |--Clustered Index Seek(OBJECT:([HugeTable1].[PK1] AS [T1]),
          |              SEEK:([T1].[Key] < (10000)) ORDERED FORWARD)
          |--Parallelism(Repartition Streams, Hash Partitioning,
               PARTITION COLUMNS:([T2].[Data]))
               |--Clustered Index Scan(OBJECT:([HugeTable2].[PK2] AS [T2]),
                    WHERE:(PROBE([Bitmap1004],[Northwind2].[dbo].[HugeTable2].[Data] as [T2].
                    [Data],N'[IN ROW]')))
```

As its name suggests, the bitmap operator builds a bitmap. Just like the hash join, the bitmap operator hashes each row of *HugeTable1* on the join key and sets the corresponding bit in the bitmap. When the scan of *HugeTable1* and the hash join build are complete, SQL Server transfers the bitmap to the probe side of the join, typically to the exchange operator. However, when the filter is based on an integer column, as in the example, the filter can be pushed down directly to the base table or index—in this case, to the clustered index scan operator. This scan uses the bitmap as a filter; notice the *WHERE* clause in the plan. Even further, the *IN ROW* parameter on the *WHERE* clause means that the filter was pushed down to the storage engine. The storage engine hashes each row of *HugeTable2* on the join key and tests the corresponding bit in the bitmap. If the bit is set, the row might join, and the storage engine passes it along to the query processor. If the bit isn't set, the row can't join and the storage engine discards it.

This strategy is called "semi-join reduction" and relies on the fact that only the records from the second table that qualify for the join with the first table are processed. SQL Server bitmap filters are based on bloom filters, originally conceived by Burton Bloom in 1970. Other semi-join reduction technologies such as bitmap indexes have been used by other database vendors.

Although somewhat rarer, some parallel merge joins also use a bitmap operator. To use the bitmap operator, a merge join must have a sort on its left input. The optimizer adds the bitmap operator below the sort. Recall that a merge join processes both inputs concurrently. Without the sort, building the bitmap on one input before beginning to process the other input wouldn't be possible. However, because the sort is blocking, the plan can build a bitmap on the left input before the merge join begins processing its right input.

Inserts, updates, and deletes

Data modification (*INSERT, UPDATE, DELETE*, and *MERGE*) statements could be the subject of an entire chapter. This section provides just a brief overview of data modification statement plans. For more information about how SQL Server processes data modification operations, see Chapter 11.

Data modification plans consist of two sections: a "read cursor" and a "write cursor." The read cursor determines which rows will be affected by the data modification statement. The read cursor works like a regular *SELECT* statement. All the material about understanding queries discussed in this chapter, including the discussion of parallelism, applies equally well to the read cursor of a data modification plan. The write cursor executes the actual *INSERTS, UPDATES, DELETES*, or *MERGES*. The write cursor, which can get extremely complex, also executes other side effects of the data modification such as nonclustered index maintenance, indexed view maintenance, referential integrity constraint validation, and cascading actions. The write cursor is implemented using many of the same operators that were already discussed. However, unlike the read cursor, with which we can often affect performance by rewriting the query or by using hints (some of which are discussed in Chapters 11 and 12), we have comparatively little control over the write cursor, query plan, and performance. Short of creating or dropping indexes or constraints, we can't control the list of indexes that must be maintained and constraints that must be validated. Also note that the write cursor is never executed using parallelism.

Consider the following *UPDATE* statement, which changes the shipper for orders shipped to London. This statement is guaranteed to violate the foreign key constraint on the *ShipVia* column and will fail.

```
UPDATE [Orders]
SET [ShipVia] = 4
WHERE [ShipCity] = N'London'
```

This statement uses the following query plan:

```
|--Assert(WHERE:(CASE WHEN [Expr1023] IS NULL THEN (0) ELSE NULL END))
  |--Nested Loops(Left Semi Join, OUTER REFERENCES:([Orders].[ShipVia]),
    DEFINE:([Expr1023] = [PROBE VALUE]))
    |--Clustered Index Update(OBJECT:([Orders].[PK_Orders]),
      OBJECT:([Orders].[ShippersOrders]),
      SET:([Orders].[ShipVia] = [Expr1019]))
    |   |--Compute Scalar(DEFINE:([Expr1021]=[Expr1021]))
    |      |--Compute Scalar(DEFINE:([Expr1021]=CASE WHEN [Expr1003]
    |              THEN (1)
    |              ELSE (0) END))
    |        |--Compute Scalar(DEFINE:([Expr1019]=(4)))
    |          |--Compute Scalar(DEFINE:([Expr1003]=
    |            CASE WHEN [Orders].[ShipVia] = (4)
    |            THEN (1) ELSE (0) END))
    |            |--Top(ROWCOUNT est 0)
    |              |--Clustered Index Scan
    |                (OBJECT:([Orders].[PK_Orders]),
    |                WHERE:([Orders].[ShipCity]=N'London') ORDERED)
    |--Clustered Index Seek(OBJECT:([Shippers].[PK_Shippers]),
      SEEK:([Shippers].[ShipperID]=[Orders].[ShipVia]) ORDERED FORWARD)
```

The read cursor for this plan consists solely of the clustered index scan of the *Orders* table, whereas the write cursor consists of the entire remainder of the plan. The write cursor includes a clustered index update operator, which updates two indexes on the *Orders* table: the *PK_Orders* clustered index and the *ShippersOrders* nonclustered index. The write cursor also includes a join with the Shippers table and an assert operator, which validate the foreign key constraint on the *ShipVia* column.

Understanding data warehouses

A data warehouse is a decision support system for business decision making, designed to execute queries from users as well as reporting and analytical applications. It's also structurally different from an OLTP system, which focuses on operational transaction processing (we'll look at some of these differences in a just a moment). Because of these different purposes, both systems also have different workloads: A data warehouse usually must support complex and large queries, compared with the typically small transactions of an OLTP system.

Another main difference between OLTP databases and data warehouses is the degree of normalization found in them. An OLTP system uses normalized data, usually at a third normal form, while a data warehouse uses a denormalized dimensional model. An OLTP normalized model helps remove data redundancies, focus on data integrity, and benefit update operations because data needs to be updated in one place only. Otherwise, a data warehouse dimensional model is more appropriate for ad hoc complex queries, and will usually have fewer tables and require fewer joins.

Dimensional data modeling on data warehouses relies on the use of fact and dimension tables. Fact tables contain facts or numerical measures of the business, which can participate in calculations, whereas dimension tables are the attributes or descriptions of the facts. Fact tables also usually have foreign keys to link them to the primary keys of the dimension tables.

Data warehouses also usually follow star and snowflake schema structures. A star schema contains a fact table and a single table for each dimension. Snowflake schemas are similar to star schemas to the extent that they also have a fact table, but dimension tables can also be normalized, and each dimension can have more than one table. Fact tables are typically huge and can store millions or billions of rows, compared to dimension tables, which are significantly smaller. The size of data warehouse databases tends to range from hundreds of gigabytes to terabytes.

Queries that join a fact table to dimension tables are called star join queries. SQL Server includes special optimizations for star join queries (which we'll look at shortly), can automatically detect star and snowflake schemas, and can reliably identify fact and dimension tables. This is significant because sometimes, to avoid the overhead of constraint enforcement during updates, data warehouse implementations don't explicitly define foreign key constraints. In these cases, the query optimizer might need to rely on heuristics to detect star schemas.

One such heuristic is to consider the largest table of the star join query as the fact table (which also must have a specified minimum size, currently defined as 100 pages). The second heuristic requires that all the joins in a star join query need to be inner joins and use equality predicates on a single column. Notice also that even in the rare case where a dimension table is incorrectly chosen as a fact table through the use of these heuristics, the query optimizer will still select a valid plan that will return the correct data, although it might not be an efficient one.

Regarding optimizations for star join queries, the use of Cartesian (or cross) products of the dimension tables with multicolumn index lookups on a fact table is interesting to consider. Although cross products are avoided during the regular optimization process because they can generate huge intermediate results, they can be used for data warehouse queries involving small dimension tables. As the rows of the cross product are being generated, they are immediately used to look up on a multicolumn index without requiring a lot of memory for the intermediate results.

In "Optimizing Star Join Queries for Data Warehousing in Microsoft SQL Server," published in the *Proceedings of the 2008 IEEE 24th International Conference on Data Engineering*, Cesar Galindo-Legaria (and others) defined three different approaches to optimizing star join queries based on the selectivity of the fact table, as shown next. As mentioned previously, selectivity is a measure of the number of records that are estimated to be returned by a query, with smaller numbers represent higher selectivity (fewer rows).

For highly selective queries that return up to 10 percent of the rows in the fact table, the query optimizer can produce a plan with nested loops joins, index seeks and bookmark lookups. For medium selectivity queries, which return anywhere from 10 to 75 percent of the records in the fact table, SQL Server might recommend hash joins with bitmap filters in combination with fact table scans or fact table range scans. Finally, for the least selective queries, processing more than 75 percent of the fact table, the query optimizer mostly will recommend regular hash joins with fact table scans. The choice of these operators and plans isn't surprising for the highly and least selective queries, because it's their standard usage, as explained earlier in this chapter. What is new is the choice of hash joins and bitmap filtering for medium selectivity queries, as discussed next.

Bitmap filtering is an optimization for star join queries that was introduced with SQL Server 2008 and is available only in the Enterprise, Developer, and Evaluation editions. It's referred to as optimized bitmap filtering to differentiate it from the standard bitmap filtering that was already available in previous versions of SQL Server and was covered in the preceding section. Optimized bitmap filtering improves the performance of star join queries by removing unnecessary rows from processing early in the query plan, so that subsequent operators have fewer rows to process. In this case, it filters rows from the fact table to avoid additional join processing.

Optimized bitmap filtering works with hash joins that, as shown earlier, use two inputs, the smaller of which (the build table) is being completely read into memory. Optimized bitmap filtering takes advantage of a hash join having to process the build input anyway, so as SQL Server processes the build table, it creates a bitmap representation of the join key values found. Because SQL Server can reliably detect fact and dimension tables, and the latter are the smaller of the two, the build input on which the bitmap is based will be a dimension table. This bitmap representation of the dimension table will be used to filter the second input of the hash join, the probe input, which in this case will be the fact table. This basically means that only the rows in the fact table that qualify for the join to the dimension table will be processed.

Next is an example of optimized bitmap filtering. Run the following query:

```
USE AdventureWorksDW2012;
GO
SELECT *
FROM dbo.FactInternetSales AS f
JOIN dbo.DimProduct AS p ON f.ProductKey = p.ProductKey
JOIN dbo.DimCustomer AS c ON f.CustomerKey = c.CustomerKey
WHERE p.ListPrice > 50 AND c.Gender = 'M';
```

Note You might not get the plan shown earlier on a test system with a limited number of logical processors. At the end of this section are a couple of alternatives that you can try on a test environment to simulate a system with a larger number of processors.

Because this plan is too big to show here, Figure 10-25 includes only a section. This part of the plan shows one bitmap operator, in this case processing the rows from the DimProduct table, which is the build input of a hash join at the left of the bitmap operator. This bitmap operator is identified as Opt_Bitmap1007, as you can verify in the operator's Properties sheet, and the Opt_ prefix indicates that optimized bitmap filtering is, in fact, being used. This bitmap is later being applied by a clustered index scan operator to help remove the nonqualifying rows of the FactInternetSales table (the rows of the fact table that don't join the DimProduct table). You can verify this in the operator tooltip or properties as shown in Figure 10-26.

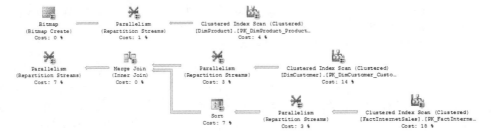

FIGURE 10-25 A bitmap filtering example.

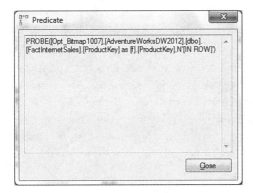

FIGURE 10-26 FactInternetSales clustered index scan predicate.

Bitmap filtering can significantly improve the performance of data warehouse queries by pushing the filters down into the scan of the fact table early in the query plan, so subsequent operators have fewer rows to process.

Finally, if you can't get the plan shown earlier on a test system with a limited number of logical processors, you can simulate that your SQL Server 2012 instance has access to more processors by using two possible undocumented alternatives. Keep in mind that these two choices are only for testing and shouldn't be used on a production system. The first choice is the DBCC OPTIMIZER_WHATIF statement that you can use with the CPUs parameter, as in the following example to simulate a system with eight processors:

```
DBCC OPTIMIZER_WHATIF(CPUs, 8)
```

After running the previous statement, the query optimizer produces plans as in a system with eight processors. This command affects only your current session that you can reset to the state it was before by using the ResetAll parameter.

```
DBCC OPTIMIZER_WHATIF(ResetAll)
```

You can also use the Status parameter to see the current configuration; to see the output of this command you also need to run *DBCC TRACEON(3604)* first. Keep in mind that all these parameters are case sensitive.

```
DBCC OPTIMIZER_WHATIF(Status)
```

The second solution is to use the *–P* SQL Server startup parameter. To implement it, open Configuration Manager, right-click your SQL Server service, select Properties, select the Startup Parameters tab, and add a parameter such as *-P8*, for example, to simulate eight processors. Click OK and restart the instance. Don't forget to remove this startup parameter and restart your instance again when you finish your testing. A limitation of this alternative, compared with the DBCC *OPTIMIZER_WHATIF* statement, is that it has global impact and requires instance restart.

Using columnstore indexes and batch processing

Columnstore indexes, a new feature in SQL Server 2012, were introduced in Chapter 7, "Indexes: internals and management," and touched on again in Chapter 8, "Special storage." This section shows you the query processing aspect of the technology. As explained at the beginning of this chapter, the standard query processing mode in all versions of SQL Server uses a row-at-a-time model; operators process only one row at a time. Columnstore indexes are complemented with a new vector-based query execution capability with operators that can process batches of rows at a time. In addition to the I/O performance improvements, the new query processing capabilities also provide some benefits because columnstore indexes are compressed and typical data warehouse queries use only 10 to 15 percent of the columns of a table (saving 85 to 90 percent in disk I/O). Batch processing alone provides performance benefits by reducing the overhead of data movement between operators along with the fact that these new processing algorithms are also optimized for the latest generation of processors. Segment elimination is used as well because eliminating segments based on metadata alone is extremely effective. To take benefit of the columnstore indexes technology, you need only to create an index on fact tables and probably also large dimension tables (with more than 10 million rows); changing the queries or anything else on the application isn't needed.

Columnstore indexes are a great solution for data warehouse scenarios and aren't intended to replace row processing, which is the best solution for OLTP scenarios. The query optimizer will decide when to use a columnstore index and when to use the other type of data access, such as a B-tree index or a heap. The query optimizer will also choose the processing mode depending on the case— for example, batch operations for the expensive parts of a query processing a large number of rows or row-based operators for OLTP queries. Batch processing is only possible when columnstore indexes are available. Plans might also have a combination of operators running in both batch and row modes, but the expensive parts of the query should be performed in batch mode, something that you can verify on the execution plan, for example, while troubleshooting performance problems.

Several existing operators can now run either in row mode or batch mode: hash join, hash aggregate, project, and filter. The same is true for the new columnstore index scan operator. A new operator, batch hash table build, can run in batch mode only. Batch operators require batches of rows as their input, same as row operators require single rows. Plans can have groups of operators in batch mode along with groups of operators in row mode, but the query processor will try to minimize the number of these conversions because exchanging data between batch and row format can be a performance problem. Batch plans can also make use of optimized bitmap filters, which can help push down predicates all the way to the storage engine, to filter out data from the fact table as early as possible. Different from B-tree indexes, no optimizer statistics are created with columnstore indexes; the query optimizer will instead rely on the statistics of the base table.

Finally, a plan might switch from batch to row processing dynamically if the system doesn't have enough memory or threads, and sometimes this could be evidence of a performance problem. You can detect it by looking at the plan and comparing the estimated against the actual execution mode or by using the *batch_hash_table_build_bailout* extended event. Memory problems are the most common cause as the hash tables used by batch mode processing are required to fit in memory and, if not enough memory is available at runtime, SQL Server might dynamically switch the operation back to row mode, where standard hash tables can be used. Memory limitations can be caused by bad cardinality estimations, so you might consider verifying and updating the statistics for your tables. However, an estimated parallel plan switching to serial can show that the system didn't have enough threads.

So now look at some examples and examine the generated execution plans, this time using the AdventureWorksDW2012 database. Start by creating a columnstore index on the *FactInternetSales* fact table by running the following statements:

```
USE AdventureWorksDW2012;
GO
CREATE NONCLUSTERED COLUMNSTORE INDEX csi_FactInternetSales
ON dbo.FactInternetSales
(
    ProductKey,
    OrderDateKey,
    DueDateKey,
    ShipDateKey,
    CustomerKey,
    PromotionKey,
    CurrencyKey,
    SalesTerritoryKey,
    SalesOrderNumber,
    SalesOrderLineNumber,
    RevisionNumber,
    OrderQuantity,
    UnitPrice,
    ExtendedAmount,
    UnitPriceDiscountPct,
    DiscountAmount,
    ProductStandardCost,
    TotalProductCost,
    SalesAmount,
    TaxAmt,
    Freight,
    CarrierTrackingNumber,
    CustomerPONumber,
    OrderDate,
    DueDate,
    ShipDate
);
```

Then we can run a typical star join query. The following query is joining the *FactInternetSale* fact table with the *DimDate* dimension table, grouping on *MonthNumberOfYear* and aggregating data on the *SalesAmount* column to get the total of sales by month for the calendar year 2005:

```
SELECT d.MonthNumberOfYear,
    SUM(SalesAmount) AS TotalSales
FROM dbo.FactInternetSales AS f
    JOIN dbo.DimDate AS d
    ON f.OrderDateKey = d.DateKey
WHERE CalendarYear = 2005
GROUP BY d.MonthNumberOfYear;
```

This will produce the plan shown in Figure 10-27.

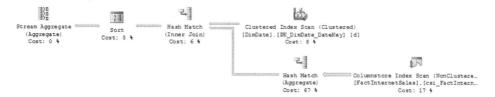

FIGURE 10-27 Plan using columnstore index scan operator.

At this moment, you might notice that although the plan is using the columnstore index we just created, the columnstore index scan operator properties, as shown in Figure 10-28, show that it's really running in the row execution mode.

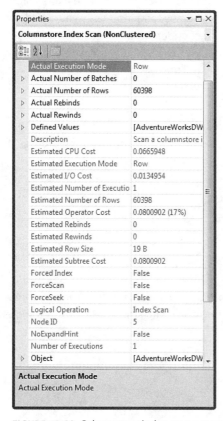

FIGURE 10-28 Columnstore index scan properties.

In fact, all operators in the plan are running under the row execution mode. Although the *Storage* property on the columnstore index scan operator is *ColumnStore*, it doesn't mean that batch algorithms had to be used. The query optimizer will only select batch execution mode with expensive operations and large amounts of data. You can drop the columnstore index before continuing.

```
DROP INDEX csi_FactInternetSales ON dbo.FactInternetSales;
```

Now test with a bigger table with millions of records. By the way, if you don't have disk space for millions of records or don't want to wait to create those big tables, you can use a trick with the undocumented *ROWCOUNT* and *PAGECOUNT* options of the *UPDATE STATISTICS* statement. For example, you can run the following statement to create a copy of the *FactInternetSales* table:

```
SELECT * INTO dbo.FactInternetSalesCopy
FROM dbo.FactInternetSales;
```

Run the following statement:

```
UPDATE STATISTICS FactInternetSalesCopy WITH ROWCOUNT = 10000000, PAGECOUNT = 1000000;
```

The *UPDATE STATISTICS* statement will update the page and row count in the catalog views and the query optimizer will use this information to generate a plan according to this data. You can use this procedure to inspect the execution plans created by the query optimizer. Keep in mind that as an undocumented statement, it shouldn't be used in a production environment and most likely you would want to drop the updated table after you finish testing (you can also consider using the *DBCC UPDATEUSAGE* statement to correct the page and row count, but dropping the table is safer). After you finish testing with the *FactInternetSalesCopy* table, you can drop it by running the following statement:

```
DROP TABLE dbo.FactInternetSalesCopy;
```

This exercise uses the table and columnstore index created in Chapter 7. The table name is dbo. FactInternetSalesBig and has more than 30 million rows. Update your query to use this table as shown here:

```
SELECT d.MonthNumberOfYear,
    SUM(SalesAmount) AS TotalSales
FROM dbo.FactInternetSalesBig AS f
    JOIN dbo.DimDate AS d
    ON f.OrderDateKey = d.DateKey
WHERE CalendarYear = 2005
GROUP BY d.MonthNumberOfYear;
```

Running the star join query again will give you a totally different plan, this time running some operators in parallel and, more important, some operators in the batch mode. Figure 10-29 shows the graphical plan.

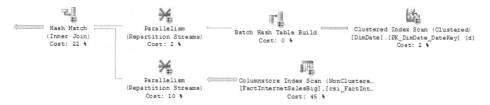

FIGURE 10-29 Plan using batch processing.

The plan shows the new operators columnstore index scan and batch hash table build, both running in batch mode. The properties of these operators show the number of batches processed as well. The purpose of the batch hash table build operator is to read the *DimDate* dimension table to build the hash table that will be used by the hash join operator on its left, which is also running in batch mode. The batch hash table build operator always runs in batch mode and it can accept its input either in batches or rows. Something not directly obvious in the graphical plan is that, while reading the dimension table, the batch hash table build operator also builds a bitmap using the join key *DateKey*, which is later used to filter out rows on the probe side input, which in this case is the columnstore index scan on the fact table. The bitmap is identified as *Opt_Bitmap1006*, and both operations are denoted in boldface in the following text plan. By using this bitmap filter, this join predicate can be pushed down to the columnstore index scan where rows with no match can be eliminated earlier in the plan.

```
|--Stream Aggregate(GROUP BY:([d].[MonthNumberOfYear]) DEFINE:([Expr1005]=SUM([partiala
gg1007])))
     |--Sort(ORDER BY:([d].[MonthNumberOfYear] ASC))
          |--Parallelism(Gather Streams)
               |--Hash Match(Partial Aggregate, HASH:([d].[MonthNumberOfYear])
                    DEFINE:([partiawlagg1007]=SUM([FactInternetSalesBig].[SalesAmount] as [f].
[SalesAmount])))
                    |--Hash Match(Inner Join, HASH:([d].[DateKey])=([f].[OrderDateKey]))
                         |--Parallelism(Repartition Streams, Hash Partitioning,
                              PARTITION COLUMNS:([d].[DateKey]))
                         |    |--Batch Hash Table Build(DEFINE:([Opt_Bitmap1006]))
                         |         |--Clustered Index Scan(OBJECT:([DimDate].[PK_DimDate_
DateKey] AS [d]),
                                        WHERE:([DimDate].[CalendarYear] as [d].
[CalendarYear]=(2005)))
                         |--Parallelism(Repartition Streams, Hash Partitioning,
                              PARTITION COLUMNS:([f].[OrderDateKey]))
                              |--Index Scan(OBJECT:([FactInternetSalesBig].[csi_
FactInternetSalesBig] AS [f]),
                                   WHERE:(PROBE([Opt_Bitmap1006],[FactInternetSalesBig].
[OrderDateKey] as [f].[OrderDateKey])))
```

Adding new data

The most noticeable limitation of columnstore indexes, at least on the SQL Server 2012 release, is that tables containing these indexes are non-updatable. This means no *INSERT*, *UPDATE*, *DELETE*, or *MERGE* operations are allowed in the table as soon as a columnstore index is created. This might look like a big disadvantage, but remember that this technology is targeted at data warehouses that are already read-only most of the time and might receive data only on a nightly batch job. Three common workarounds to this limitation, which Microsoft has said will go away in a future release of SQL Server, are to do the following.

- **Drop/disable, create/rebuild the columnstore index.** In some scenarios, you might be able to simply just drop or disable the columnstore index, add the new data, or update existing data, and then create or rebuild the index again.

- **Use partition switching.** Many implementations are currently using partitioning to take benefit of partition switching in which you can instantly add large amounts of data to a table by using a metadata-only operation. Columnstore indexes can be added to this scenario. For example, you can load new data into a staging table, create a partition-aligned columnstore index on the staging table, and switch the staging table into an empty partition of the main table.

- **Use *UNION ALL*.** In this scenario, you can have a fact table with a columnstore index and a second table, with the same schema, as a regular updatable table. You can use the regular table to perform daily update operations and query both tables using *UNION ALL* to combine their data as a single table. You also can optionally use the partition switching method described before to move this data into the columnstore periodically (for example, nightly).

This last example shows you how *UNION ALL* works and how you need to make sure that it's working properly by inspecting its plan. Suppose that we now use *FactInternetSales* as an updatable table and *FactInternetSalesBig* as the table containing the columnstore index. Then we create a view that concatenates both the updatable table and the non-updateable fact table:

```
CREATE VIEW vFactInternetSales
AS
SELECT * FROM dbo.FactInternetSales
UNION ALL
SELECT * FROM dbo.FactInternetSalesBig;
```

Now, we are ready to run the following star join query using the view just created:

```
SELECT d.MonthNumberOfYear,
    SUM(SalesAmount) AS TotalSales
FROM dbo.vFactInternetSales AS f
    JOIN dbo.DimDate AS d
    ON f.OrderDateKey = d.DateKey
WHERE CalendarYear = 2005
GROUP BY d.MonthNumberOfYear;
```

This code produces the plan shown in Figure 10-30. This time, we see a more complicated plan that basically consists of two sections: a section running in row mode to process the data on the updatable table FactInternetSales, and a section mostly running in batch mode to process the data on FactInternetSalesBig table containing the columnstore index. The section running in batch mode is very similar to the previous example. The main point to verify in this kind of plan, especially when troubleshooting performance problems, is to make sure that the expensive part of the plan is in fact being executed in batch mode.

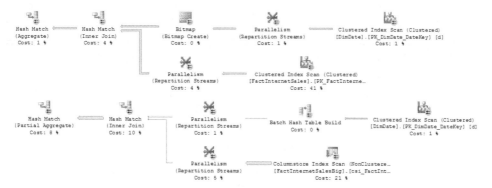

FIGURE 10-30 *UNION ALL* plan.

To clean up, you can drop the view:

```
DROP VIEW vFactInternetSales;
```

Hints

Finally, sometimes the query optimizer won't give you a good execution plan. As with previous versions of SQL Server, you still can choose to use a hint to force any index in the cases where the query optimizer isn't giving you a good execution plan. This can happen, for example, when the query optimizer is choosing a columnstore index when it shouldn't or when you want to force a columnstore index when it's not being selected. You can use the new *IGNORE_NONCLUSTERED_COLUMNSTORE_INDEX* hint to ask the query optimizer to avoid using any columnstore index, as shown next:

```
SELECT d.MonthNumberOfYear,
    SUM(SalesAmount) AS TotalSales
FROM dbo.FactInternetSalesBig AS f
    JOIN dbo.DimDate AS d
    ON f.OrderDateKey = d.DateKey
WHERE CalendarYear = 2005
GROUP BY d.MonthNumberOfYear
OPTION (IGNORE_NONCLUSTERED_COLUMNSTORE_INDEX);
```

You can also force the use of a columnstore index by using the existing *INDEX* hint, as shown in the following example:

```
SELECT d.MonthNumberOfYear,
    SUM(SalesAmount) AS TotalSales
FROM dbo.FactInternetSalesBig AS f WITH (INDEX(csi_FactInternetSalesBig))
    JOIN dbo.DimDate AS d
    ON f.OrderDateKey = d.DateKey
WHERE CalendarYear = 2005
GROUP BY d.MonthNumberOfYear;
```

Conclusion

This chapter explained the basics of query processing in SQL Server. It introduced iterators—the fundamental building blocks of query processing—and discussed how to view query plans in three different formats: text, graphical, and XML. You learned about many of the most common iterators, including the iterators that implement scans and seeks, joins, and aggregation. You looked at more complex query plans including dynamic index seeks, index unions and intersection, and various sub-query examples. You also explored how the query processor implements parallel query execution. All the query plans that SQL Server supports are built from these and other basic operators. The chapter closed with a section explaining data warehousing, optimized bitmap filters, and the new columnstore indexes and batch processing introduced with SQL Server 2012.

Most of the time, the SQL Server query processor works extremely well. The optimizer generally chooses satisfactory query plans, and most applications work well without any special tuning. However, sometimes your queries won't performing optimally. The more you understand about what actually happens during query execution, the better you can detect when a plan isn't optimal and when it has room for improvement.

The Query Optimizer

Conor Cunningham

The Query Optimizer in Microsoft SQL Server 2012 determines the query plan to be executed for a specific SQL statement. Because the Query Optimizer doesn't have a lot of exposed features, it's not as widely understood as some of the other components in the SQL Server Engine. This chapter describes the Query Optimizer and how it works. After reading this chapter, you should understand the high-level optimizer architecture and be able to conclude why a particular plan was selected by the Query Optimizer. By extension, you should be able to troubleshoot problem query plans in cases when the Query Optimizer might not select the desired query plan and how to affect that selection.

This chapter is split into two sections. The first section explains the basic mechanisms of the Query Optimizer, including the high-level structures that are used and how they define the set of alternatives considered for each plan. The second section discusses specific areas in the Query Optimizer and how they fit into this framework. It explains how indexes are selected, how statistics are used, and how to understand update plans.

Overview

Figure 11-1 shows the basic compilation "pipeline" for a single query.

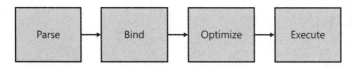

FIGURE 11-1 Query processor pipeline.

When a query is compiled, the SQL statement is first *parsed* into an equivalent tree representation. For queries with valid SQL syntax, the next stage performs a series of validation steps on the query, generally called *binding,* where the columns and tables in the tree are compared to database metadata to ensure that those columns and tables exist and are visible to the current user. This stage also performs semantic checks on the query to ensure that it's valid, such as making sure that the columns bound to a *GROUP BY* operation are valid. After the query tree is bound and is determined to be a valid query, the Query Optimizer takes the query and starts evaluating different possible query plans. The Query Optimizer performs this search, selects the query plan to be executed, and then returns it to the system to execute. The *execution* component runs the query plan and returns the query results.

The SQL Server 2012 Query Optimizer has a number of additional features that extend this diagram to make it more useful for database developers and database administrators (DBAs). For example, query plans are cached because they are expensive to produce and are often used repeatedly. Old query plans are recompiled if the underlying data has changed sufficiently. SQL Server also supports the T-SQL language, which means that batches of multiple statements can be processed in one request to the SQL Server Engine. The Query Optimizer doesn't consider batch compilation or workload analysis, so this chapter focuses on what happens in a single query's compilation.

Understanding the tree format

When you submit a SQL query to the query processor, the SQL string is parsed into a tree representation. Each node in the tree represents a query operation to be performed. For example, each table in the *FROM* clause has its own operator. A *WHERE* clause is also represented in a separate operator. Joins are represented with operators that have one input for each table. For example, the query *SELECT * FROM Customers C INNER JOIN Orders O on C.cid = O.cid WHERE O.date = '2008-11-06'* might be represented internally, as shown in Figure 11-2.

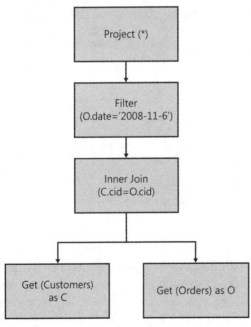

FIGURE 11-2 Query tree format example.

The query processor actually uses different tree formats throughout the compilation process. For example, the Query Optimizer converts a tree from a logical description of the desired result (as discussed earlier) to a plan with real physical operators that can be executed. Perhaps the most obvious place where this selection happens is when the Query Optimizer selects a join algorithm, converting a logical join (such as an *INNER JOIN*) into a physical join (a hash join, merge join, or nested loops join). Most tree formats are pretty close to each other. In many examples in this chapter, execution plans are used to describe specific optimizations performed by the Query Optimizer in earlier, internal tree formats.

Understanding optimization

So far, this chapter has discussed only the basic transformation from a logical query tree into an equivalent physical query plan. Another major job of the Query Optimizer is to find an *efficient* query plan. Usually, a query can be evaluated in many ways, and some plans are often much slower than others. The speed difference between these two plans is significant; selecting the wrong query plan can cause a database application to perform so slowly that it appears broken to the user. Therefore, that the Query Optimizer selects an efficient plan is very important.

At first, you might think that every SQL query would have an "obvious" best plan, and the Query Optimizer should just select it as quickly as it can. Unfortunately, finding an optimal query plan is actually a much more difficult algorithmic problem for SQL Server. Consider the following SQL query:

```
SELECT * FROM A
INNER JOIN B ON (A.a = B.b)
INNER JOIN C ON (A.a = C.c)
INNER JOIN D ON (A.a = D.d)
INNER JOIN E ON (A.a = E.e)
INNER JOIN F ON (A.a = F.f)
INNER JOIN G ON (A.a = G.g)
INNER JOIN H ON (A.a = H.h)
```

This query has many possible implementation plans because inner joins can be computed in different orders. Actually, if you use this same pattern to add more tables into this query, the query would have so many possible plan choices that considering them all isn't feasible. Because inner joins can be evaluated in any order (ABCD..., ABDC..., ACBD...,) and in different topologies, such as [(A join B) join (B join C)], the number of possible query plans for this query is actually greater than $N!$ [N x $(N-1)$ x $(N-2)$ x ...]. As the number of tables in a query increases, the set of alternatives to consider quickly grows to be larger than what any computer can count. The storage of all possible query plans also becomes a problem. In 32-bit Intel x86-based machines, SQL Server usually has a maximum of about 1.6 GB of memory that can be used to compile a query, and storing every possible alternative in memory might not be possible. Even if a computer could store all these alternatives, the user might not want to wait that long to enumerate all those possible choices. The Query Optimizer solves this problem using heuristics and statistics to guide those heuristics, and this chapter describes these concepts.

Many people believe that the job of the Query Optimizer is to select the absolute best query plan for a certain query. You can now see that the scope of the problem makes this impossible; if you can't consider every plan shape, proving that a plan is optimal is difficult. However, the Query Optimizer *can* find a "good enough" plan quickly, and often this is the optimal performing plan or very close to it.

Search space and heuristics

The Query Optimizer uses a framework to search and compare many different possible plan alternatives efficiently. This framework allows SQL Server to consider complex, nonobvious ways to implement a certain query. Keeping track of all these different alternatives to find a plan to run efficiently isn't easy. The search framework of SQL Server contains several components that help it perform its job efficiently and reliably. Although largely internal, these components are described in this section to give you a better idea about how a query is optimized and how to better design your applications to take advantage of its capabilities.

Rules

The Query Optimizer is a search framework. The Query Optimizer considers transformations of a specific query tree from the current state to a different, equivalent state that's also stored in memory. In the framework used in SQL Server, the transformations are done via *rules*, which are very similar to the mathematical theorems you likely learned in school. For example, you know that *A INNER JOIN B* is equivalent to *B INNER JOIN A* because both queries return the same result for all possible table data sets. This is a form of commutativity in which this operation can be performed in any order and yield the same result—or, in the case of databases, return the same set of rows. (In regular integer arithmetic, commutativity means that (1+2) is equivalent to (2+1).) Rules are matched to tree patterns and are then applied if they are suitable to generate new alternatives (which then can lead to more rule matching). These rules form the basis of how the Query Optimizer works, and they also help encode some of the heuristics necessary to perform the search in a reasonable amount of time.

The Query Optimizer has different kinds of rules.

- Rules that heuristically rewrite a query tree into a new shape are called *substitution rules*.

- Rules that consider mathematical equivalences are called *exploration rules*. These rules generate new tree shapes but can't be directly executed.

- Rules that convert logical trees into physical trees to be executed are called *implementation rules*.

The best of these generated physical alternatives from implementation rules is eventually output by the Query Optimizer as the final query execution plan.

Properties

The search framework collects information about the query tree in a format that can make it easier for rules to work. Called *properties*, these structures collect information from subtrees to help make decisions about what rules can be processed at a higher point in a tree. For example, one property used in SQL Server is the set of columns that make up a unique key on the data. Consider the following query:

```
SELECT col1, col2, MAX(col3) FROM Table1 GROUP BY col1, col2;
```

This query is represented internally as a tree, as shown in Figure 11-3.

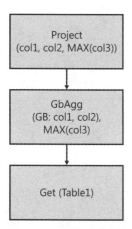

FIGURE 11-3 *GROUP BY* tree example.

If the columns (*col1, col2*) make up a unique key on table *groupby*, doing grouping isn't necessary at all because each group has exactly one row. The *MAX()* of a set of size one is the element itself. So, writing a rule that removes the *groupby* from the query tree completely is possible. Figure 11-4 shows this rule in action.

```
CREATE TABLE groupby (col1 int, col2 int, col3 int);
ALTER TABLE groupby ADD CONSTRAINT unique1 UNIQUE(col1, col2);
SELECT col1, col2, MAX(col3) FROM groupby GROUP BY col1, col2;
```

FIGURE 11-4 Query plan with aggregate operation removed.

By looking at the final query plan, you can see that the Query Optimizer performs no grouping operation, even though the query uses a *GROUP BY*. The properties collected during optimization enable this rule to perform a tree transformation to make the resulting query plan complete more quickly.

SQL Server also collects many properties during optimization. As is done in most modern compilers, the Query Optimizer collects domain constraint information about each column referenced in the query. The Query Optimizer collects information from predicates, join conditions, partitioning information, and check constraints to reason about how all these predicates can be used to optimize the query. One useful application of this scalar property is in *contradiction detection*. The Query Optimizer can determine whether the query is written in such a way as to never return any rows at all. When the Query Optimizer detects a contradiction, it rewrites the query to remove the portion of the query containing the contradiction. Figure 11-5 shows an example of a contradiction detected during optimization.

```
CREATE TABLE DomainTable(col1 int);
GO
SELECT *
FROM DomainTable D1
INNER JOIN DomainTable D2
ON D1.col1=D2.col1
WHERE D1.col1 > 5 AND D2.col1 < 0;
```

SELECT   Constant Scan
Cost: 0 %   Cost: 100 %

FIGURE 11-5 Query plan simplified via contradiction.

The final query plan doesn't even reference the table at all; it's replaced with a special Constant Scan operator that doesn't access the storage engine and, in this case, returns zero rows. This means that the query runs faster, consumes less memory, and doesn't need to acquire locks against the resources referenced in the section containing the contradiction when being executed.

> **Note** In this chapter, I've tried to create examples that you can run so that you can see for yourself how the system operates based on experiments. Unfortunately, in some cases, different features interact in a way that makes showing exactly how one feature operates in isolation is difficult. In this example, I added a join to avoid another optimization, called *trivial plan*, that sometimes overrides contradiction detection. Because features change from release to release, you should use these examples only to explore the current state of the Query Optimizer. How the internals of the Query Optimizer will work from release to release isn't guaranteed, so you shouldn't try to build detailed knowledge of the Query Optimizer into your application.

Like with rules, both logical and physical properties are available.

- **Logical properties** cover things like the output column set, key columns, and whether or not a column can output any nulls. These apply to all equivalent logical and all physical plan fragments. When an exploration rule is evaluated, the resulting query tree shares the same logical properties as the original tree used by the rule.

- **Physical properties** are specific to a single plan, and each plan operator has a set of physical properties associated with it. One common physical property is whether the result is sorted. This property would influence whether the Query Optimizer looks for an index to deliver that desired sort. Another physical property is the set of columns from a table that a query can read. This drives decisions such as whether a secondary index is sufficient to return all the needed columns in a query or whether each matching row also needs a base table lookup.

Storage of alternatives: the Memo

Earlier, this chapter mentioned that the storage of all the alternatives considered during optimization could be large for some queries. The Query Optimizer contains a mechanism to avoid storing duplicate information, thus saving memory (and time) during the compilation process. The structure is called the *Memo*, and one of its purposes is to find previously explored subtrees and avoid reoptimizing those areas of the plan. It exists for the life of one optimization.

The Memo works by storing equivalent trees in *groups*. If you were to execute each subtree in a group, every alternative in that subtree would return the same logical result. Conceptually, each operator from the original query tree starts in its own group, meaning that groups reference other groups rather than reference other operators directly while stored in the Memo. This model is used to avoid storing trees more than once during query optimization and enables the Query Optimizer to avoid searching the same possible plan alternatives more than once.

In addition to storing equivalent alternatives, groups also store properties structures. Alternatives rooted in the same group have equivalent logical and scalar properties. Logical properties are actually called *group properties* in SQL Server, even when not being stored in the Memo. So every alternative in a group should have the same output columns, key columns, possible partitionings, and so on. Because computing these properties is expensive, this structure also helps avoid unnecessary work during optimization.

The Memo stores all considered plans. For large queries, the Memo might contain many thousands of groups and many alternatives within each group. Combined, this represents a huge number of alternatives. Although most queries don't consume large amounts of memory during optimization, large data warehouse queries could possibly consume all memory on a machine during optimization. If the Query Optimizer is about to run out of memory while searching the set of plans, it contains logic to pick a "good enough" query plan rather than run out of memory.

After the Query Optimizer finishes searching for a plan, it goes through the Memo, starting at the root, to select the best alternative from each group that satisfies the query's requirements. These operators are assembled into the final query plan and are then transformed into a format that the query execution component in SQL Server can understand. This final tree transformation does contain a small number of runtime optimization rewrites, but it's very close to the showplan output generated for the query plan.

An example of how the Memo works is shown later in this chapter, during the examination of the Query Optimizer's architecture and pipeline.

Operators

SQL Server 2012 has around 40 logical operators and even more physical operators. Some operators are extremely common, such as Join or Filter. Others are harder to find, such as Segment, Sequence Project, and UDX. Traditionally, operators in SQL Server follow the model shown in Figure 11-6.

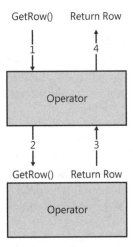

GetRow()   Return Row

1   4

Operator

2   3

GetRow()   Return Row

Operator

FIGURE 11-6 SQL Server operator data flow model.

This "row-based" model works by requesting rows from one or more children and then producing rows to return to the caller. The caller can be another operator or can be sent to the user if it's the uppermost operator in the query tree. Each operator returns one row at a time, meaning that the caller must call for each row. The uniformity in this design allows operators to be combined in many different ways. It also allows new operators to be added to the system without major changes to the Query Optimizer, such as the property framework, that help the Query Optimizer select a query plan.

Note SQL Server 2012 also introduces a new, "batch-based" operator model that's used for some data warehouse queries. Although this model varies in important ways from the row-based approach, the core optimization problem is the same. Later, the section "Data warehousing" covers batch-model operations and their differences.

So that everyone gets the most out of this chapter, I'll cover a few of the more rare and exotic operators here and will reference them later. This way, you get an idea of how your query is represented in the system.

Compute Scalar: Project

The Compute Scalar, called a *Project* in the Query Optimizer, is a simple operator that attempts to declare a set of columns, compute some value, or perhaps restrict columns from other operators in the query tree. These operators correspond to the *SELECT* list in the SQL language; they aren't actually overly interesting to the Query Optimizer because the Query Optimizer doesn't need to do much with them. The Query Optimizer ends up moving them around the query tree during optimization, trying to separate them from the rest of the Query Optimizer logic that deals with join order, index selection, and other optimizations.

Compute Sequence: Sequence Project

Compute Sequence, known as a *Sequence Project* in the Query Optimizer, is somewhat similar to a Compute Scalar in that it computes a new value to be added into the output stream. The key difference is that this works on an ordered stream and contains state that is preserved from row to row. Ranking functions use this operator, for example. Compute Sequence is implemented using a different physical operation and imposes additional restrictions on how the Query Optimizer can reorder this expression. This operator is usually seen in the ranking and windowing functions.

semi-join

The term *semi-join* comes from academic database literature, and it describes an operator that performs a join but returns only values from one of its inputs. The query processor uses this internal mechanism to handle most subqueries. SQL Server represents subqueries such as *EXISTS <subselect>* or *IN <subselect>* in this manner because it simplifies reason about the set of possible transformations for the query and because the runtime implementation of a semi-join and a regular join are similar. Contrary to popular belief, a subquery isn't always executed and cached in a temporary table; it's treated much like a regular join. In fact, the Query Optimizer has transformation rules that can transform regular joins to semi-joins and vice-versa.

One common misconception is that using subqueries is inherently incorrect. Like most generalizations, this isn't true. Often, a subquery is the most natural way to represent what you want in SQL, and that's why it's part of the SQL language. Sometimes a subquery is blamed for a poorly indexed table, missing statistics, or a predicate written in a way that's too obtuse for the Query Optimizer to figure out how to use its domain constraint property framework. You *can* have too many subqueries in a system, especially if they are duplicated many times in the sazxszme query. So if your company's development practices specify, "No subqueries," examine your system closely; subqueries are usually blamed for many other problems that might lie right under the surface.

Listing 11-1 is an example of where a subquery would be appropriate. Suppose that you need to ask a sales tracking system for a store to show you all customers who have placed an order in the last 30 days so that you can send them a thank-you email. Figures 11-7, 11-8, and 11-9 show the query plans for the three different approaches to try to submit queries to answer this question.

LISTING 11-1 Common errors in writing subquery plans

```
CREATE TABLE Customers(custid int IDENTITY, name NVARCHAR(100));
CREATE TABLE Orders (orderid INT IDENTITY, custid INT, orderdate DATE, amount MONEY);
INSERT INTO Customers(name) VALUES ('Conor Cunningham');
INSERT INTO Customers(name) VALUES ('Paul Randal');
INSERT INTO Orders(custid, orderdate, amount) VALUES (1, '2008-08-12', 49.23);
INSERT INTO Orders(custid, orderdate, amount) VALUES (1, '2008-08-14', 65.00);
INSERT INTO Orders(custid, orderdate, amount) VALUES (2, '2008-08-12', 123.44);

-- Let's find out customers who have ordered something in the last month

-- Semantically wrong way to ask the question - returns duplicate names
SELECT name FROM Customers C INNER JOIN Orders O ON C.custid = O.custid WHERE
DATEDIFF("m", O.orderdate, '2008-08-30') < 1
```

```
-- and then people try to "fix" by adding a distinct
SELECT DISTINCT name
FROM
Customers C
INNER JOIN
Orders O
ON C.custid = O.custid
WHERE DATEDIFF("m", O.orderdate, '2008-08-30') < 1;
-- this happens to work, but it is fragile, hard to modify, and it is usually not done properly.

-- the subquery way to write the query returns one row for each matching Customer
SELECT name
FROM Customers C
WHERE
EXISTS (
SELECT 1
FROM Orders O
WHERE C.custid = O.custid AND DATEDIFF("m", O.orderdate, '2008-08-30') < 1
);
-- note that the subquery plan has a cheaper estimated cost result
-- and should be faster to run on larger systems
```

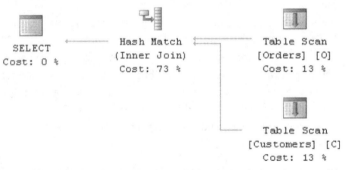

FIGURE 11-7 Query plan using an *INNER JOIN* instead of a subquery (the section commented with "Semantically wrong way to ask the question - returns duplicate names").

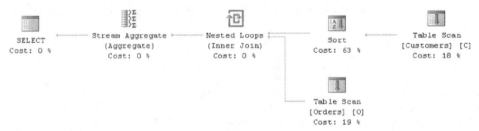

FIGURE 11-8 Query plan using *DISTINCT* and *INNER JOIN* instead of a subquery (the section commented with "try to 'fix' by adding a distinct").

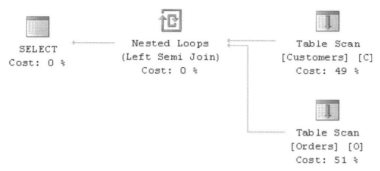

FIGURE 11-9 Query plan using subquery.

In this last query plan, the matching rows from the *Customers* table are kept and directly returned to the user through the left semi-join operator.

> **Note** The left and right semi-joins have to do with which child's rows are preserved in the operation. Unfortunately for anyone confused as to the meaning of these operators, the plan representation in SQL Server Management Studio and in previous tools is transposed. The "left" child is the top child and the "right" child is the bottom child in the transposed form.

Apply

Since SQL Server 2005, *CROSS APPLY* and *OUTER APPLY* represent a special kind of subquery in which a value from the left input is passed as a parameter to the right child. Sometimes called a *correlated nested loops join,* it represents passing a parameter to a subquery. The most common application for this feature is to do an index lookup join, as shown in Listing 11-2 and Figure 11-10.

LISTING 11-2 Example of *APPLY* query

```
CREATE TABLE idx1(col1 INT PRIMARY KEY, col2 INT);
CREATE TABLE idx2(col1 INT PRIMARY KEY, col2 INT);
GO
SELECT *
FROM idx1
CROSS APPLY (
    SELECT *
    FROM idx2
    WHERE idx1.col1=idx2.col1
  ) AS a;
```

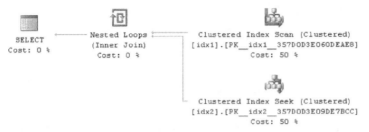

FIGURE 11-10 *APPLY* query plan.

This query is logically equivalent to an *INNER JOIN*, and Figure 11-11 demonstrates that the resulting query plan is identical in SQL Server 2012.

```
SELECT * FROM idx1 INNER JOIN idx2
ON idx1.col1=idx2.col1;
```

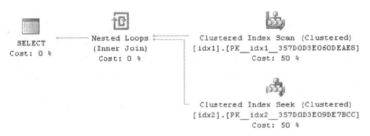

FIGURE 11-11 *INNER JOIN* query generates a nested loop and seek plan.

In both cases, a value from the outer table is referenced as an argument to the seek on the inner table. Notice that a standard inner join also can generate a seek, which means that the Query Optimizer considers turning a *JOIN* into an *APPLY* as part of the optimization process. Although the example shown here is so simple that you wouldn't need to write the query that way, this syntax is useful in more complex scenarios. First, dynamic management views (DMVs, including an example discussed later in the section "Plan hinting") have a common pattern in which a value is passed to a management function by using a cross apply. Second, in rare, very complex cases, the Query Optimizer's rule engine can't rewrite a simple inner join to get an index seek. In those cases, rewriting the query to use *CROSS APPLY* is useful to pass a parameter down past an opaque operator manually. The semantics of a query can change as a result of a rewrite like this, so be very sure that you understand the semantics of your query when considering a rewrite like this.

The Apply operator is almost like a function call in a procedural language. For each row from the outer (left) side, some logic on the inner (right) side is evaluated and zero or more rows are returned for that invocation of the right subtree. The Query Optimizer can sometimes remove the correlation and convert an Apply into a more general join, and in those cases other joins can sometimes be reordered to explore different plan choices.

Spools

SQL Server has a number of different, specialized spools, each one highly tuned for some scenario. Conceptually, they all do the same thing—they read all the rows from the input, store them in memory or spill it to disk, and then allow operators to read the rows from this cache. Spools exist to make a copy of the rows, and this can be important for transactional consistency in some update plans and to improve performance by caching a complex subexpression to be used multiple times in a query.

The most exotic spool operation is called a *common subexpression*. This spool can be written once and then read by multiple, different children in the query. It's currently the only operator that can have multiple parents in the final query plan. This spool shows up multiple times in the showplan output and is actually the *same* operator. Common subexpression spools have only one client at a time. So, the first instance populates the spool, and each later reference reads from this spool in sequence. The first reference has children, whereas later references appear in the query plan as leaves of the query tree.

Common subexpression spools are used most frequently in wide update plans, described later in this chapter. However, they are also used in windowed aggregate functions, special aggregates that don't have to collapse the rows like a regular aggregate computation. Listing 11-3 and Figure 11-12 show how a common subexpression spool is used to store the intermediate query input and then use it multiple times as inputs to other parts of the query tree. The initial table spool reads values from *window1*, and the later branches in the tree supply the spooled rows to multiple branches.

LISTING 11-3 Aggregate with OVER clause uses common subexpression spool

```
CREATE TABLE window1(col1 INT, col2 INT);
GO
DECLARE @i INT=0;
WHILE @i<100
BEGIN
INSERT INTO window1(col1, col2) VALUES (@i/10, rand()*1000);
SET @i+=1;
END;

SELECT col1, SUM(col2) OVER(PARTITION BY col1) FROM window1;
```

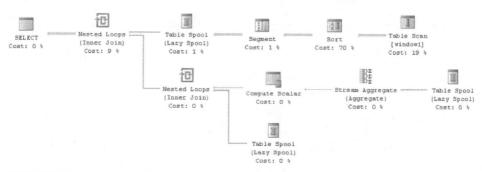

FIGURE 11-12 Query plan containing common subexpression spool.

Exchange

The Exchange operator is used to represent parallelism in query plans. This can be seen in the show-plan as a Gather Streams, Repartition Streams, or Distribute Streams operation, based on whether it's collecting rows from threads or distributing rows to threads, respectively. Several row distribution algorithms exist, and each operator has a preferred algorithm based on its context in a query. In SQL Server, parallelism exists in zones where the system tries to speed up by using additional CPUs. Figure 11-13 demonstrates a query in which multiple threads scan a table in parallel.

```
      SELECT          Parallelism          Table Scan
      Cost: 0 %     (Gather Streams)       [exchange]
                        Cost: 0 %          Cost: 100 %
```

FIGURE 11-13 Exchange operator in query plan.

 Note You can find descriptions for other SQL Server operators online at *http://technet.microsoft.com/en-us/library/ms191158.aspx.*

Optimizer architecture

The Query Optimizer contains many optimization phases that each perform different functions. The different phases help the Query Optimizer perform the highest-value operations earliest in the optimization process.

The major phases in the optimization of a query, as shown in Figure 11-14, are as follows:

- Simplification
- Trivial plan
- Auto-stats create/update
- Exploration/implementation (phases)
- Convert to executable plan

```
|                                                          |
|                                                          |
Simplification  Trivial Plan  Auto-Stats   Stage 0  Stage 1  Stage 2   Convert to
                                                                       Executable
                                           Exploration                    Plan
```

FIGURE 11-14 Query Optimizer pipeline.

Before optimization

The SQL Server query processor performs several steps before the actual optimization process begins. These transformations help shape the tree into a form that's easier for the Optimizer to optimize. View expansion is one major preoptimization activity. When a query is compiled that references a view, the text of the view is read from the server's metadata and parsed. One consequence of this design choice is that a query that references a view many times gets this view expanded many times before it's optimized. Coalescing adjacent *UNION* operations is another preoptimization transformation that's performed to simplify the tree. This converts the syntactic two-child form of *UNION [ALL]*, *INTERSECT [ALL]*, and *EXCEPT [ALL]* into a single operator that can have more than two children. This rewrite simplifies the tree structure and enables the Query Optimizer to write rules to affect *UNION*s more easily. For example, grouping *UNION* operations makes the task of removing duplicate rows easier and more efficient.

Simplification

Early in optimization, the tree is normalized in the Simplification phase to convert the tree from a form linked closely to the user syntax into one that helps later processing. For example, the Query Optimizer detects semantic contradictions in the query and removes them by rewriting the query into a simpler form. Also, the rewrites performed during Simplification make subsequent operations such as index matching, computed column matching, and statistics generation easier to perform correctly.

The Simplification phase also performs a number of other tree rewrites, including the following.

- Grouping joins together and picking an initial join order, based on cardinality data for each table

- Finding contradictions in queries that can allow portions of a query not to be executed

- Performing the necessary work to rewrite *SELECT* lists to match computed columns

Earlier in this chapter, you saw a contradiction detection example in Figure 11-5.

Trivial plan/auto-parameterization

The main optimization path in SQL Server is a very powerful cost-based model of a query's execution time. As databases and queries over those databases have become larger and more complex, this model has enabled SQL Server to solve bigger and bigger business problems. The fixed startup cost for running this model can be expensive for applications that don't try to perform complex operations. Making a single path that spans from the smallest to the largest queries can be challenging because the requirements and specifications are vastly different.

To be able to satisfy small query applications well, SQL Server uses a fast path to identify queries where cost-based optimization isn't needed. Generally, this code identifies cases in which a query doesn't have any cost-based choices to make. This means that only one plan is available to execute or an obvious best plan can be identified. In these cases, the Query Optimizer directly generates the best plan and returns it to the system to be executed. For example, the query *SELECT col1 FROM Table1* for a table without any indexes has a straightforward best plan choice: read the rows from the base table heap and return them to the user, as seen in Figure 11-15.

```
CREATE TABLE Table1 (col1 INT, col2 INT);
SELECT col1 FROM Table1;
```

```
  SELECT          ◄────────  Table Scan
  Cost: 0 %                   [Table1]
                            Cost: 100 %
```

FIGURE 11-15 Trivial plan example: table scan.

The SQL Server query processor actually takes this concept one step further. When simple queries are compiled and optimized, the query processor attempts to rewrite them into an equivalent parameterized query instead. If the plan is determined to be trivial, the parameterized query is turned into an executable plan. Then, future queries that have the same shape except for constants in well-known locations in the query text just run the existing compiled query and avoid going through the Query Optimizer at all. This speeds up applications with small queries on SQL Server significantly.

```
SELECT col1 FROM Table1 WHERE col2 = 5;
SELECT col1 FROM Table1 WHERE col2 = 6;
```

The text of these queries in the following procedure cache shows only one query plan, and it's parameterized.

```
SELECT text
    FROM sys.dm_exec_query_stats AS qs
    CROSS APPLY sys.dm_exec_sql_text(qs.sql_handle) AS st
WHERE st.text LIKE '%Table1%';

----------------------------------------
(@1 tinyint)SELECT [col1] FROM [Table1] WHERE [col2]=@1
```

If you examine the XML plan for this query plan, notice the (boldfaced) indication that this query was a trivial plan. The other choice is full, meaning that cost-based optimization was performed:

```
... <StmtSimple ... StatementOptmLevel="TRIVIAL"> ...
```

Because XML plan output is verbose, most of it has been omitted for space.

Limitations

SQL Server 7.0 introduced trivial plan optimization. Whereas each version of SQL Server has slightly different rules, all versions have queries that skip the trivial plan stage completely and perform only regular optimization activities. Using more complex features can disqualify a query from being considered trivial because those features always have a cost-based plan choice or are too difficult to identify as trivial. Examples of query features that cause a query not to be considered trivial include Distributed Query, Bulk Insert, XPath queries, queries with joins or subqueries, queries with hints, some cursor queries, and queries over tables containing filtered indexes.

SQL Server 2005 added another feature, *forced parameterization*, to auto-parameterize queries more aggressively. This feature parameterizes all constants, ignoring cost-based considerations. This feature is most useful for an application in which the SQL is generated (and you can't make it generate parameterized queries) and the resulting query plans are almost always identical (or the plans perform similarly even if they vary). Specifically, this feature is worth considering when the application queries can't be changed by the DBA in charge of the server.

The benefit of this feature is that it can reduce compilations, compilation time, and the number of plans in the procedure cache. All these things *can* improve system performance. On the other hand, this feature can reduce performance when different parameter values would cause different plans to be selected. These values are used in the Query Optimizer's cardinality and property framework to decide how many rows to return from each possible plan choice, and forced parameterization blocks these optimizations. So if you think your application would benefit from using forced parameterization, perform some experiments to see whether the application works better. Chapter 12, "Plan caching and recompilation," goes into more detail on the various parameterization options.

The Memo: exploring multiple plans efficiently

The core structure of the Query Optimizer is the Memo. This structure helps store the result of all the rules run in the Query Optimizer, and it also helps guide the search of possible plans to find a good plan quickly and to avoid searching a subtree more than once. This speeds up the compilation process and reduces the memory requirements. In effect, this allows the Query Optimizer to run more advanced optimizations compared to other optimizers without a similar mechanism. Although this structure is internal to the Query Optimizer, this section describes its basic operations so that you can better understand the way the Query Optimizer selects a plan.

The Memo stores operators from a query tree and uses logical pointers to represent that tree's edges. Consider the query *SELECT * FROM (A INNER JOIN B ON A.a=B.b) AS D INNER JOIN C ON D.c=C.c,* which can be drawn as a tree, as shown in Figure 11-16. Figure 11-17 shows the same query stored in the Memo.

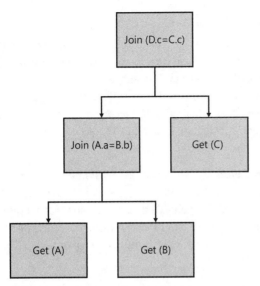

FIGURE 11-16 Tree of a three-table join.

```
(Root) Group 4:
        0 Join 3 2
Group 3:
        0 Join 0 1
Group 2:
        0 Table C
Group 1:
        0 Table B
Group 0:
        0 Table A
```

FIGURE 11-17 Initial Memo layout for a three-table join.

The Memo consists of a series of *groups*. When the Memo is first populated, each operator is put into its own group. The references between operators are changed to be references to other groups in the Memo. In this model, storing multiple alternatives that yield the same result in the same group in the Memo is possible. With this change, searching for the best subtree independently of what exists in higher-level groups in the Memo is possible. Logical properties are stored within each memo group, and every additional entry in a group can share the property structure for that group with the initial alternative.

One type of alternative explored by the Query Optimizer is *join associativity*. [(A join B) join C)] is equivalent to [A join (B join C)]. Figure 11-18 describes the updated Memo structure after the Query Optimizer considers this transformation. (The boldfaced sections are new.)

```
Group 5:
        0 Join 1 2
(Root) Group 4:
        1 Join 0 5
        0 Join 3 2
Group 3:
        0 Join 0 1
Group 2:
        0 Table C
Group 1:
        0 Table B
Group 0:
        0 Table A
```

FIGURE 11-18 Three-table Memo, after the join associativity rule is applied.

Notice how the new alternative fits into a structure. (B join C) wasn't previously in the Memo, so a new group is created that then references the existing groups for B and C. This representation saves a lot of memory when considering multiple possible query plans, and enables the Query Optimizer to know whether it has previously considered a section of the search space so it can avoid redoing that work. (A join C) would be another valid alternative, even though it's not shown.

Rules are the mechanisms that allow the Memo to explore new alternatives during the optimization process. The join associativity example is implemented as an optimization rule that matches a specific pattern and then creates a new alternative that's equivalent to the first one (returns the same result for that portion of the query). The result of a rule, by definition, can go into the same group as the root of the original pattern.

An optimization search pass is split into two parts. In the first part of the search, exploration rules match logical trees and generate new, equivalent alternative logical trees that are inserted into the Memo. Implementation rules run next, generating physical trees from the logical trees. After a physical tree is generated, it's evaluated by the costing component to determine the cost for this query tree. The resulting cost is stored in the Memo for that alternative. When all physical alternatives and their costs are generated for all groups in the Memo, the Query Optimizer finds the one query tree in the Memo that has the lowest cost and then copies that into a standalone tree. The selected physical tree is very close to the showplan form of the tree.

The optimization process is optimized further by using multiple search passes, separating the rules based on cost and how likely they are to be useful. Each of three phases runs a set of exploration and implementation rules. The phases are configured to make small queries optimize quickly and to make more expensive queries consider more aggressive rewrite rules that can take longer to compile. For example, index matching is performed in the first phase, whereas the matching of index view generally isn't performed until a later phase. The Query Optimizer can quit optimization at the end of a phase if a sufficiently good plan has been found. This calculation is done by comparing the estimated cost of the best plan found so far against the actual time spent optimizing so far. If the current best plan is still very expensive, another phase is run to try to find a better plan. This model allows the Query Optimizer to generate plans efficiently for a wide range of workloads.

By the end of the search, the Query Optimizer has selected a single plan to be returned to the system. This plan is copied from the Memo into a separate tree format that can be stored in the Procedure Cache. During this process, a few small, physical rewrites are performed. Finally, the plan is copied into a new piece of contiguous memory and is stored in the procedure cache.

Statistics, cardinality estimation, and costing

The Query Optimizer uses a model with estimated costs of each operator to determine which plan to choose. The costs are based on statistical information used to estimate the number of rows processed in each operator. By default, statistics are generated automatically during the optimization process to help generate these cardinality estimates. The Query Optimizer also determines which columns need statistics on each table.

When a set of columns is identified as needing statistics, the Query Optimizer tries to find a pre-existing statistics object for that column. If it doesn't find one, the system samples the table data to create a new statistics object. If one already exists, it's examined to determine whether the sample was recent enough to be useful for the compilation of the current query. If it's considered out of date, a new sample is used to rebuild the statistics object. This process continues for each column where statistics are needed.

Both auto-create and auto-update statistics are enabled by default. In practice, most people leave these flags enabled and get good behavior from the Query Optimizer. However, you can disable the creation and update behavior of statistics:

```
ALTER DATABASE ... SET AUTO_CREATE_STATISTICS {ON | OFF }
ALTER DATABASE ... SET AUTO_UPDATE_STATISTICS {ON | OFF }
```

These commands modify the behavior for auto-create and auto-update statistics, respectively, for all tables in a database. If automatic creation or updating of statistics is disabled, the Query Optimizer returns a warning in the showplan output when compiling a query where it thinks it needs this information. In this mode of operation, the DBA is responsible for keeping the statistics objects up to date in the system.

Controlling the auto-update behavior of individual statistics objects using hints on specific operations is also possible:

```
CREATE INDEX ... WITH (STATISTICS_NORECOMPUTE = ON)
CREATE STATISTICS ... WITH (NORECOMPUTE)
```

Although these settings are usually left enabled, some reasons for disabling the creation or update behavior of statistics, include the following.

- The database has a maintenance window when the DBA decides to update statistics explicitly rather than have these objects update automatically during the day. This is often because the DBA has reason to believe that the Query Optimizer might choose a poor plan if the statistics are changed.

- The database table is very large, and the time to update the statistics automatically is too high.

- The database table has many unique values, and the sample rate used to generate statistics isn't high enough to capture all the statistical information needed to generate a good query plan. The DBA likely uses a maintenance window to update statistics manually at a higher sample rate than the default (which varies based on the table size).

- The database application has a short query timeout defined and doesn't want automatic statistics to cause a query to require noticeably more time than average to compile because it could cause that timeout to abort the query.

This last scenario manifests in a subtle manner that can break your applications. If a query in an online transaction processing (OLTP) application was set with a small timeout of a few seconds, this is generally sufficient to compile all queries (even with automatic statistics). However, as the database table grows, the time to sample the table to create or update statistics grows. Eventually, the total time to perform this operation reaches the query timeout. Because each query is compiled as part of a user transaction, a timeout forces the transaction to abort and roll back. When the next query against that table is compiled, the timeout is hit again and the whole query rolls back. This unfortunately causes applications to fail unexpectedly because the query now will never complete.

To address this functionality, SQL Server 2005 introduced a feature called *asynchronous statistics update*, or *ALTER DATABASE...SET AUTO_UPDATE_STATISTICS_ASYNC {ON | OFF}*. This allows the statistics update operation to be performed on a background thread in a different transaction context. The benefit to this model is that it avoids the repeating rollback issue. The original query continues and uses out-of-date statistical information to compile the query and return it to be executed. When the statistics are updated, plans based on those statistics objects are invalidated and are recompiled on their next use.

Statistics design

Statistics are stored in the system metadata and are composed primarily of a *histogram* (a representation of the data distribution for a column). Don't confuse the word *statistics* with the word *histogram*. Other elements in the statistics object include some header information (including the number of rows sampled when the object was created), *trie trees* (a representation of the data distribution for string columns), and density information (which tracks information about average data distributions across one or more columns).

Statistics can be created over most, but not all, data types in SQL Server 2012. As a general rule, data types that support comparisons (such as >, =, and so on) support the creation of statistics. The Query Optimizer doesn't need to reason about distributions if these aren't comparable in the language. Examples of data types in which statistics aren't supported include old-style BLOBs (such as *image*, *text*, and *ntext*) and some of the newer user-defined data type (UDT)–based types when they aren't byte-order comparable.

Also, SQL Server supports statistics on computed columns. This allows the Query Optimizer to make cardinality estimates over expressions, such as *col1 + col2*, or some of the more complex types, such as the geography type, where the primary use case is to run a function on the UDT rather than compare the UDT directly.

The following code creates statistics on a persisted computed column created on a function of an otherwise noncomparable UDT. When this UDT method is used in later queries, the Query Optimizer can use this statistic to estimate cardinality more accurately.

```
CREATE TABLE geog(col1 INT IDENTITY, col2 GEOGRAPHY);
INSERT INTO geog(col2) VALUES (NULL);
INSERT INTO geog(col2) VALUES (GEOGRAPHY::Parse('LINESTRING(0 0, 0 10, 10 10, 10 0, 0 0)'));
ALTER TABLE geog ADD col3 AS col2.STStartPoint().ToString() PERSISTED;
CREATE STATISTICS s2 ON geog(col3);
DBCC SHOW_STATISTICS('geog', 's2');
```

Statistics can be enumerated by querying the system metadata using the following code. Figure 11-19 shows the results.

```
SELECT o.name AS tablename, s.name AS statname
FROM sys.stats s INNER JOIN sys.objects o ON s.object_id = o.object_id;
```

	tablename	statname
86	Customers	_WA_Sys_00000001_00551192
87	Customers	_WA_Sys_00000002_00551192
88	Orders	_WA_Sys_00000003_014935...
89	Orders	_WA_Sys_00000002_014935...
90	idx1	PK__idx1__357D0D3E060DE...
91	idx2	PK__idx2__357D0D3E09DE7...
92	idx2	i1
93	geog	s2
94	queue_me...	queue_clustered_index
95	queue_me...	queue_secondary_index
96	queue_me...	queue_clustered_index
97	queue_me...	queue_secondary_index
98	queue_me...	queue_clustered_index

FIGURE 11-19 Query output listing statistics objects.

When identified, the statistics object can be viewed using the *DBCC SHOW_STATISTICS* command, as shown in Figure 11-20.

DBCC SHOW_STATISTICS(exchange,_WA_Sys_00000004_4C0144E4)

Name	Updated	Rows	Rows Sampled	Steps	Density	Average key length	String Index	Filter Expression	Unfiltered Rows
_WA_Sys_00000004_4C0144E4	Nov 27 2008 9:49AM	60000	8264	185	0.703127	4	NO	NULL	60000

All density	Average Length	Columns
0.0001049208	4	col4

	RANGE_HI_KEY	RANGE_ROWS	EQ_ROWS	DISTINCT_RANGE_ROWS	AVG_RANGE_ROWS
1	0	0	1	0	1
2	23	102.4228	28.55033	22	4.65559
3	80	321.9001	20.53245	52	6.17722
4	119	263.3728	20.53245	38	6.930864
5	161	226.7933	20.53245	41	5.531543
6	192	204.8455	20.53245	30	6.828184
7	229	146.3182	20.53245	29	5.028785
8	268	219.4774	20.53245	38	5.77572
9	319	314.5842	20.53245	50	6.291684
10	357	234.1092	28.55033	34	6.80407
11	396	182.8978	20.53245	38	4.819702
12	423	190.2137	28.55033	26	7.315812
13	467	197.5296	28.55033	33	6.052347
14	521	336.5319	20.53245	53	6.349659
15	567	314.5842	20.53245	45	6.99076
16	621	270.6887	20.53245	50	5.377159
17	672	256.0569	35.93245	45	5.68644
18	699	139.0023	20.53245	22	6.31407
19	743	204.8455	28.55033	38	5.398066
20	780	182.8978	11.53645	36	5.080494
21	828	292.6365	20.53245	47	6.226308
22	867	197.5296	20.53245	36	5.46
23	911	219.4774	28.55033	38	5.783642
24	938	131.6864	20.53245	26	5.152974
25	1001	270.6887	20.53245	50	5.377159

FIGURE 11-20 *DBCC SHOW_STATISTICS* output.

After the Query Optimizer determines that it needs either to create a new statistics object or update an existing out-of-date one, the system creates an internal query to generate a new statistics object. Figure 11-21 shows the query that builds the statistics object in the SQL Server Profiler output.

```
Showplan All For Query Compile                          Micr

StmtText                                                 StmtId
--------                                                 ------
Stream Aggregate(DEFINE:([Expr1004]=STATMAN([s1].[dbo].[trace].[col1])))   0
  |--Sort(ORDER BY:([s1].[dbo].[trace].[col1] ASC))                        0
     |--Table Scan(OBJECT:([s1].[dbo].[trace]))                            0
```

FIGURE 11-21 SQL Profiler showplan output for histogram generation.

> **Note** *STATMAN* is a special internal aggregate function that works like other aggregate functions in the system: Many rows are consumed by a streaming group by operator and are passed to the *STATMAN* aggregate. It generates a BLOB that stores the histogram, density information, and any trie trees created during this operation. When finished, the statistics BLOB is stored in the database metadata and is used by queries—including the one that issued the command originally, except in the case of asynchronous statistics update.

The Optimizer samples database pages to generate statistics, including all rows from each sampled page. For small tables, all pages are sampled—meaning that rows are considered when building the histogram. For larger tables, a smaller and smaller percentage of pages are sampled. So that the histogram remains a reasonable size, it's limited to 200 total steps. If it examines more than 200 unique values while building the histogram, the Query Optimizer uses logic to try to reduce the number of steps based on an algorithm that preserves as much distribution information as possible. Because histograms are most useful for capturing the non-uniform data distributions of a system, they try to preserve the information that captures the most frequent values and how much more frequent those values are than the least frequent values in the data.

Density/frequency information

In addition to a histogram, the Query Optimizer keeps track of the number of unique values for a set of columns. When combined with the total number of rows viewed when creating the table, this can calculate the average number of duplicate values in the column. This information, called the *density information*, is stored in the statistics object. Density is calculated by the formula 1/*frequency*, with *frequency* being the average number of duplicates for each value in a table. This information is also returned when *DBCC SHOW_STATISTICS* is called. For multicolumn statistics, the *statistics* object stores density information for each combination of columns (in the order that they were specified in the *CREATE STATISTICS* statement) in the *statistics* object. This stores information about the number of duplicate *sets* of values.

The code in Listing 11-4 creates a two-column table with 30,000 rows.

LISTING 11-4 Multicolumn statistics

```
CREATE TABLE MULTIDENSITY (col1 INT, col2 INT);
go
DECLARE @i INT;
SET @i=0;
WHILE @i < 10000
BEGIN
    INSERT INTO MULTIDENSITY(col1, col2) VALUES (@i, @i+1);
    INSERT INTO MULTIDENSITY(col1, col2) VALUES (@i, @i+2);
    INSERT INTO MULTIDENSITY(col1, col2) VALUES (@i, @i+3);
    set @i+=1;
END;
GO
-- create multi-column density information
CREATE STATISTICS s1 ON MULTIDENSITY(col1, col2);
GO
```

In *col1* are 10,000 unique values, each duplicated three times. In *col2* are actually 10,002 unique values. For the multicolumn density, each set of (*col1*, *col2*) in the table is unique. Figure 11-22 shows the data stored for the multicolumn statistics object.

```
DBCC SHOW_STATISTICS ('MULTIDENSITY', 's1')
```

	Name	Updated	Rows	Rows Sampled	Steps	Density
1	s1	Nov 27 2008 10:16AM	30000	30000	3	0.3333333

	All density	Average Length	Columns
1	0.0001	4	col1
2	3.333333E-05	8	col1, col2

FIGURE 11-22 Multicolumn density information in the statistics object.

The density information for *col1* is 0.0001. 1/0.0001 = 10,000, which is the number of unique values of *col1*. The density information for (*col1, col2*) is about 0.00003 (the numbers are stored as floating points and are imprecise).

Now examine the cardinality estimates for the *GROUP BY* operation using *GROUP BY* lists that match the density information in Figure 11-23. The actual and estimated cardinalities match up exactly for this query:

```
SET STATISTICS PROFILE ON
SELECT COUNT(*) AS CNT FROM MULTIDENSITY GROUP BY col1
```

	Rows	Executes	StmtText	EstimateRows
1	10000	1	SELECT COUNT(*) AS CNT FROM MULTIDENSITY GROUP ...	10000
2	0	0	I-Compute Scalar(DEFINE:([Expr1004]=CONVERT_IMPLICIT([...	10000
3	10000	1	I-Hash Match(Aggregate, HASH:([s1].[dbo].[MULTIDENSI...	10000
4	30000	1	I-Table Scan(OBJECT:([s1].[dbo].[MULTIDENSITY]))	30000

FIGURE 11-23 *STATISTICS PROFILE* output for the hash aggregate.

Note The columns from the *STATISTICS PROFILE* output have been reordered to show the *EstimateRows* column for the Hash Match implementing the *GROUP BY* operation.

For a query grouping over both columns, you can see that the estimate matches up with the value seen in the density calculation. The *STATISTICS PROFILE* output in Figure 11-24 shows that this changes the estimate to 30,000 rows.

```
SET STATISTICS PROFILE ON
SELECT COUNT(*) AS CNT FROM MULTIDENSITY GROUP BY col1, col2
```

Rows	Executes	StmtText	EstimateRows
30000	1	SELECT COUNT(*) AS CNT FROM MULTIDENSITY GROUP ...	30000
0	0	I-Compute Scalar(DEFINE:([Expr1004]=CONVERT_IMPLICIT([...	30000
30000	1	I-Hash Match(Aggregate, HASH:([s1].[dbo].[MULTIDENSI...	30000
30000	1	I-Table Scan(OBJECT:([s1].[dbo].[MULTIDENSITY]))	30000

FIGURE 11-24 *STATISTICS PROFILE* output for a two-column aggregate.

The Query Optimizer must perform an additional step when calculating an operator's output cardinality. Because statistics are usually created before compilation of the query that uses them and are often only samples of the data, the values stored in the statistics object don't usually match the exact count of rows at the time the query is compiled. So the Query Optimizer uses these two values to calculate the fraction of rows that should qualify in the operation. This is then scaled to the actual number of values in the table at the time the query is compiled.

The Query Optimizer doesn't expose exactly how each part of the cardinality estimate is computed. However, if you find that a query has estimates that vary widely from what actually happens when you run the query, the statistics profile feature can help you identify whether the Query Optimizer has bad information. You might need to update statistics to capture new data in the table, create statistics with a higher sample rate, or otherwise make sure that the information used during compilation is accurate. Although SQL Server does this automatically in most cases, this is often a good way to find and fix problems with poor plan selection.

Filtered statistics

SQL Server 2008 introduced the Filtered Index and Filtered Statistics features. The statistics object is created over a subset of the rows in a table based on a filter predicate. Creating a filtered index auto-creates a matching filtered statistics object that matches the behavior of nonfiltered indexes. This information is exposed through the *sys.stats* metadata view shown in Figure 11-25.

```
SELECT * FROM SYS.STATS
```

	object_id	name	stats_id	auto_created	user_created	no_recompute	has_filter	filter_definition
95	26157...	s1	2	0	1	0	0	NULL
96	26157...	_WA_Sys_00000002_0F975522	3	1	0	0	0	NULL
97	26157...	s3	4	0	1	0	1	([col2]>(5))
98	19930...	queue_clustered_index	1	0	0	0	0	NULL

FIGURE 11-25 A *filter_definition* expression in SQL Server Statistics.

Filtered statistics are used in a manner that's similar to traditional statistics; the set of columns on which distributions are needed is determined early in query compilation. The set of filter predicates defined on the table for the query must be a subset of the *filter_definition* of the statistics object for the statistic to be considered. If multiple such statistics exist, the one with the tightest bounds is used.

Filtered statistics can avoid a common problem in cardinality estimation in which estimates become skewed because of data correlation between columns. For example, if you create a table called *CARS*, you might have a column called *MAKE* and a column called *MODEL*. The following table shows that multiple models of cars are made by Ford.

CAR_ID	MAKE	MODEL
1	Ford	F-150
2	Ford	Taurus
3	BMW	M3

Also, assume that you want to run a query like the following:

```
SELECT * FROM CARS WHERE MAKE='Ford' AND MODEL='F-150';
```

When the query processor tries to estimate the selectivity for each condition in an *AND* clause, it usually assumes that each condition is independent. This allows the selectivity of each predicate to be multiplied together to form the total selectivity for the complete *WHERE* clause. For this example, it would be

2/3 * 1/3 = 2/9

The actual selectivity is really 1/3 for this query because every F-150 is a Ford. This kind of estimation error can be large in some data sets. Detecting statistical correlations like this is a very computationally expensive problem, so the default behavior is to assume *independence*, even though that might introduce some amount of error into the cardinality estimation process.

Filtered Statistics solves this problem by capturing the conditional probability for the *MODEL* column when the *MAKE* value is *Ford*. Although using this solution requires many statistics objects, it can be effective to fix the most important cases in an application in which cardinality estimation error is causing poorly performing plans to be chosen by the Query Optimizer, especially when the *WHERE* clause has a relatively small number of distinct values.

In addition to the Independence assumption, the Query Optimizer contains other assumptions that are used both to simplify the estimation process and to be consistent in how estimates are made across all operators. Another assumption in the Query Optimizer is Uniformity. This means that if a range of values is being considered but the values aren't known, they are assumed to be uniformly distributed over the range in which they exist. For example, if a query has an *IN* list with different parameters for each value, the values of the parameters aren't assumed to be grouped. The final assumption in the Query Optimizer is Containment. This says that if a range of values is being joined with another range of values, the default assumption is that that query is being asked because those ranges overlap and qualify rows. Without this assumption, many common queries would be underestimated and poor plans would be chosen.

String statistics

SQL Server 2005 introduced a feature to improve cardinality estimation for strings called *String Statistics* or *trie trees*. SQL Server histograms can have up to 200 steps, or unique values, to store information about the overall distribution of a table. Although this works well for many numeric types, the string data types often have many more unique values as well as numerous functions that depend more heavily on a deeper statistical understanding of the type, such as *LIKE*. Two hundred unique values often isn't sufficient to provide accurate cardinality estimates for strings, and storing lots of strings outside the table can use a lot of space. Trie trees were created to store efficiently a sample of the strings in a column.

The trie tree isn't documented, but it generally work as follows. The trie tree for a column containing the following values is shown in Figure 11-26.

ABC
AAA
ABCDEF
ADAD
BBB

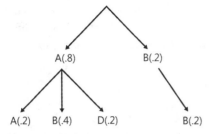

FIGURE 11-26 Example of a trie tree.

SQL Server actually stores a *sample* of the strings in the column, and its size is bound not to take up too much space. SQL Server also has some idea of the relative frequency for each substring listed in the trie tree. Overall, this provides the ability to store far more than 200 unique substrings' worth of frequency information.

Cardinality estimation details

During optimization, each operator in the query is evaluated to estimate the number of rows processed by that operator. This helps the Query Optimizer make proper tradeoffs based on the costs of different query plans. This process is done bottom up, with the base table cardinalities and statistics being used as input to tree nodes above it. This process continues all the way up the query tree, and the estimated number of rows returned from a query in showplan information is based on this calculation.

Listing 11-5 shows a sample used to explain how the cardinality derivation process works. This query is represented in the query processor, using the tree shown in Figure 11-27.

LISTING 11-5 Cardinality estimation sample

```
CREATE TABLE Table3(col1 INT, col2 INT, col3 INT);
GO
SET NOCOUNT ON;
BEGIN TRANSACTION;
DECLARE @i INT=0;
WHILE @i< 10000
BEGIN
INSERT INTO Table3(col1, col2, col3) VALUES (@i, @i,@i % 50);
SET @i+=1;
END;
COMMIT TRANSACTION;
GO
SELECT col1, col2 FROM Table3 WHERE col3 < 10;
```

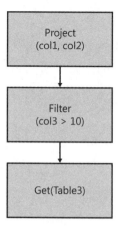

FIGURE 11-27 Example of a logical query tree for cardinality estimation.

For this query, the Filter operator requests statistics on each column participating in the predicate (*col3* in this query). The request is passed down to *Table3*, where an appropriate statistics object is created or updated. That statistics object is then passed to the filter to determine the operator's selectivity. *Selectivity* is the fraction of rows that are expected to be qualified by the predicate and then returned to the user. Selectivity is used (instead of merely counting the number of matching values in a statistics histogram) to scale the estimate from the sample to the current row count properly because the current row count can vary from when the statistics object was created, and the statistics object might be over only a sample of the rows.

When the selectivity for an operator is computed, it's multiplied by the current number of rows for the query. The selectivity of this filter operation is based on the histogram loaded for column *col3*, as shown in Figure 11-28.

	Name	Updated	Rows	Rows Sampled	Steps	Density	Average key length	String Index	Filter Expression	Unfiltered Rows
1	_WA_Sys_00000003_108B795B	Nov 27 2008 10:30AM	10000	10000	50	0	4	NO	NULL	10000

	All density	Average Length	Columns
1	0.02	4	col3

	RANGE_HI_KEY	RANGE_ROWS	EQ_ROWS	DISTINCT_RANGE_ROWS	AVG_RANGE_ROWS
1	0	0	200	0	1
2	1	0	200	0	1
3	2	0	200	0	1
4	3	0	200	0	1
5	4	0	200	0	1
6	5	0	200	0	1
7	6	0	200	0	1
8	7	0	200	0	1
9	8	0	200	0	1
10	9	0	200	0	1
11	10	0	200	0	1

FIGURE 11-28 Using a histogram to estimate cardinality.

This example uses a synthetic data distribution so that you can follow the computations more easily. The distribution on *col3* is uniformly distributed from 0 to 49, and 10/50 values are less than 10, or 20 percent of the rows. Therefore, the selectivity of this filter in the query is 0.2, and the calculation of the number of rows resulting from the filter is as follows:

(# rows in operator below) * (selectivity of this operator)

10000 * 0.2 = 2000 rows

You can validate this computation by looking at the showplan information for the query shown in Figure 11-29.

Misc	
Defined Values	[s1].[dbo].[Table3].col1, [s1].[dbo].[Table.
Description	Scan rows from a table.
Estimated CPU Cost	0.0110785
Estimated I/O Cost	0.0232035
Estimated Number of Executions	1
Estimated Number of Rows	2000
Estimated Operator Cost	0.034282 (100%)

FIGURE 11-29 Operator row estimate for cardinality example.

The estimate for the operator is taken by looking at the histogram, counting the number of sampled rows matching the criteria (in this case, 10 histogram steps with 200 equal rows are required for values that match the filter condition). Then, the number of qualifying rows (2,000) is normalized against the number of rows sampled when the histogram was created (10,000) to create the selectivity for the operator (0.2). This is then multiplied by the current number of rows in the table (10,000) to get the estimated query output cardinality. The cardinality estimation process is continued for any other filter conditions, and the results are usually just multiplied to estimate the total selectivity for each condition.

One other interesting aspect of the histogram is *RANGE_ROWS*, *DISTINCT_RANGE_ROWS*, and *AVG_RANGE_ROWS*. Because histograms are limited to 200 steps, some values being queried might not be represented in the histogram steps. These values are represented in the *RANGE* values and are counts of rows between the step values. For query conditions that don't match one of the equal (EQ) rows in the histogram, values in the range are assumed to be uniformly distributed over the domain between the two bounding histogram steps. The fraction is determined from this assumption and is used to generate the selectivity, as in the previous examples.

Although most operators work using a mechanism similar to Filter, some other operators need additional mechanisms to make good cardinality estimates. For example, *GROUP BY* doesn't actually try to determine which slices of a histogram should be used to estimate the operator's selectivity. Instead, it needs to determine the number of unique values over a set of columns, as shown in Figure 11-30. This information can be estimated by looking at the histogram, but another mechanism in the statistics object can help perform this calculation quickly. When the histogram has enough information to use each histogram step to estimate cardinality, the optimizer does so. When this is not the case, the density information is used to make a generic estimate instead (visible through *DBCC SHOW_STATISTICS*). In this case, the density information shows .02 for *col3* in the histogram, although the example is simple enough that the individual steps are used to determine that 10 distinct values exist, and therefore the cardinality estimate is 10 for this query.

```
SELECT COUNT(*) FROM Table3 WHERE col3 < 10 GROUP BY col3;
```

	Misc	
	Build Residual	[s1].[dbo].[Table3].[col3] = [s1].[dbo].[Tab
⊞	Defined Values	[Expr1007] = Scalar Operator(COUNT(*))
	Description	Use each row from the top input to build a
	Estimated CPU Cost	0.0834958
	Estimated I/O Cost	0
	Estimated Number of Executions	1

FIGURE 11-30 *GROUP BY* cardinality estimate.

This is a representation of the average number of duplicates for any value in the table. In other words, this tells you how to compute the number of groups by using the total number of rows. For this simple *GROUP BY* query, the estimate of rows is (1/0.02)*(10,000/10,000) = 50, which matches the number of groups you would expect from the creation script:

```
GROUP BY Selectivity = (1/density)
GROUP BY Card. Estimate = (Input operator) * (selectivity)
```

When a multicolumn statistics object is created, it computes density information for the sets of columns being evaluated in the order of the statistics object. So a statistics object created on (*col1, col2, col3*) has density information stored for ((*col1*), (*col1, col2*), and (*col1, col2, col3*)). This can be used to compute the cardinality estimate for a query over that table doing *GROUP BY col1*; *GROUP BY col1, col2*; or *GROUP BY col1, col2, col3*. You can see this computation in the results of *DBCC SHOW_STATISTICS* in Figure 11-31.

```
CREATE TABLE Table4(col1 int, col2 int, col3 int)
GO
DECLARE @i int=0
WHILE @i< 10000
BEGIN
INSERT INTO Table4(col1, col2, col3) VALUES (@i % 5, @i % 10,@i % 50);
SET @i+=1
END
CREATE STATISTICS s1 on Table4(col1, col2, col3)
DBCC SHOW_STATISTICS (Table4, s1)
```

	All density	Average Length	Columns
1	0.2	4	col1
2	0.1	8	col1, col2
3	0.02	12	col1, col2, col3

FIGURE 11-31 Multicolumn density information.

> **Note** Because SQL Server doesn't automatically create statistics for multicolumn cases like this except in index creation; I created the statistics object manually for this example.

Multicolumn density information is important because it captures correlation data between columns in the same table. By default, if every column were assumed to be completely independent, you would expect a large number of different groups to be returned because each column added to the grouping columns would add more and more uniqueness (and less and less selectivity for the *GROUP BY* operator). However, in this case, you can see that the selectivity of the *GROUP BY* is the same as in the previous example: 50 groups. The data captured in the multicolumn density can be used to get this cardinality estimation to be more accurate.

If a similar table is created with random data in the first two columns, the density looks quite different, as shown in Figure 11-32. This would imply that every combination of *col1*, *col2*, and *col3* is actually unique in that case. By examining the various inputs into the cardinality estimation process, you can determine whether the plan used reasonable information during the compilation process.

	All density	Average Length	Columns
1	0.01	4	col1
2	0.0001579031	8	col1, col2
3	0.0001009387	12	col1, col2, col3

FIGURE 11-32 Multicolumn density for random data distribution.

Cardinality estimation involves many, many more details than this chapter can cover. Most details change somewhat from release to release, and most aren't exposed or documented enough to make trying to follow the exact computation useful. Understanding the statistics and cardinality estimation mechanism is still very useful, so you can perform plan debugging and hinting (as explained later in this chapter).

Limitations

The cardinality estimation of SQL Server is usually very good. Unfortunately, making a model that is perfect for every query for all applications is very difficult. Although most of these are internal details, some of them are interesting to know about, so you can understand that the calculations explained earlier in this section don't work perfectly in every query.

- **Multiple predicates in an operator**   The selectivities of multiple predicates are multiplied during cardinality estimation to determine the resulting estimate for the whole operator. This means that the predicates are assumed to be statistically independent. In practice, most data has some statistical dependencies between columns. As the number of predicates in the query increases, the Query Optimizer actually doesn't directly multiply all the selectivities, and it assumes that these different predicates are related. So the selectivity of an operator with many predicates may be greater than you might expect.

- **Deep query trees**   The process of tree-based cardinality estimation is good, but it also means that any errors lower in the query tree are magnified as the calculation proceeds higher up the query tree to more and more operators. Eventually, the error introduced in all these computations overwhelms the value of using histograms to compute cardinality estimates. As a result, very deep query trees eventually stop using histograms for the higher tree portions and may use simpler heuristics to make cardinality estimates to avoid assuming information on data that's very likely to be invalid.

- **Less common operators**   The Query Optimizer uses many operators. Most of the common operators have extremely deep support developed over multiple versions of the product. Some of the lesser-used operators, however, don't necessarily have the same depth of support for every single scenario. So if you're using an infrequent operator or one that has only recently been introduced, it might not provide cardinality estimates that are as good as most core operators. In these cases, double-checking the estimates using *SET STATISTICS PROFILE ON* is worthwhile to see whether the estimates are close to what's expected. In many cases where the estimates are incorrect, the impact is often mitigated because specialized operators don't always have many plan choices, and the impact of an error in cardinality estimation might be reduced.

Costing

The process of estimating cardinality is done using the logical query trees. *Costing* is the process of determining how much time each potential plan choice will require to run, and it's done separately for each physical plan considered. Because the Query Optimizer considers multiple different physical plans that return the same results, this makes sense. Costing is the component that picks between hash joins and loops joins or between one join order and another.

The idea behind costing is actually quite simple. Using the cardinality estimates and some additional information about the average and maximum width of each column in a table, it can determine how many rows fit on each database page. This value is then translated into a number of disk reads that a query requires to complete. The total costs for each operator are then added to determine the total query cost, and the Query Optimizer can select the fastest (lowest-cost) query plan from the set of considered plans during optimization.

In practice, costing isn't this simple. Sequential I/Os have a cost difference because rotating media disk blocks are stored sequentially on disk and therefore don't require waiting to move the disk head to a new track or even waiting for a complete rotation of the disk platter, and random I/Os, where neither of these conditions is guaranteed to be true. Also, some queries are large enough that the data can be read into memory and read multiple times during a query. These additional reads often can read the page from the memory-based page buffer pool, avoiding the need to read from disk at all. Even further, some queries might take more memory than is available in the server for the query— in this case, the costing component needs to determine that some pages get evicted from the buffer pool and must be reread, either randomly or sequentially. The Optimizer uses logic to consider all these conditions, and the process of determining the actual cost for an operator can take a while to calculate. All these considerations help make sure that SQL Server does the best job possible to select a good query plan for each query.

To make the Query Optimizer more consistent, the development team used several assumptions when creating the costing model.

- A query is assumed to start with a cold cache. This means that the query processor assumes that each initial I/O for a query requires reading from disk. In a very small number of cases (usually small, OLTP queries), this might cause the Query Optimizer to pick a slightly slower plan that optimizes for the number of initial I/Os required to complete the query. The cold-cache assumption is a simplification that allows the query processor to generate plans more consistently, but it's a (small) difference between the mathematical model used to compare plans and reality.

- Random I/Os are assumed to be evenly dispersed over the set of pages in a table or index. If a nonindexed base table (a heap) has 100 disk pages and the query is doing 100 random bookmark-based lookups from a nonclustered index into that heap, the Query Optimizer assumes that 100 random I/Os occur in the query against that heap because it assumes that each target row is on a separate page. Like the statistical column correlation example earlier in the chapter, this assumption also doesn't always hold. The actual set of rows could be clustered physically on the same pages (perhaps they were all inserted at the same time and thus ended up on adjacent pages), and it might require only five I/Os to read the rows of interest. In this case, the Query Optimizer would overcost this query. This also rarely happens, but knowing this is valuable to understand that the mathematical model used for costing is just that—a model. In the rare cases when the model doesn't work properly, query hints can be used to help force a different query plan.

The Query Optimizer has other assumptions built into its costing model. One assumption relates to how the client reads the query results. Costing assumes every query reads every row in the query result. However, some clients read only a few rows and then close the query. For example, if you are using an application that shows you pages of rows onscreen at a time, that application can read 40 rows even though the original query might have returned 10,000 rows. If the Query Optimizer knows the number of rows the user will consume, it can optimize for the number in the plan selection process to pick a faster plan. Typically, this causes the Query Optimizer to switch from using operators such as hash join (which has a larger startup cost at the beginning of a query) to nested loops joins (which have a lower startup cost but a higher per-row cost).

SQL Server exposes a hint called *FAST N* for just this case. If a user typically reads only a subset of the rows in a query, it can pass *OPTION (FAST N)* to the query to tell the Query Optimizer to cost the query for returning *N* rows instead of the whole result set. The example in Listing 11-6 demonstrates the *FAST N* hint, which selects a hash join without the *FAST N* hint. Figure 11-33 shows that a loop join is picked when the hint is applied.

LISTING 11-6 *FAST N* example

```
CREATE TABLE A(col1 INT);
CREATE CLUSTERED INDEX i1 ON A(col1);
GO
SET NOCOUNT ON;
BEGIN TRANSACTION;
DECLARE @i INT=0;
WHILE @i < 10000
BEGIN
INSERT INTO A(col1) VALUES (@i);
SET @i+=1;
END;
COMMIT TRANSACTION;
GO
```

```
SELECT A1.* FROM A as A1 INNER JOIN A as A2 ON A1.col1=A2.col1;
SELECT A1.* FROM A as A1 INNER JOIN A as A2 ON A1.col1=A2.col1 OPTION (FAST 1);
```

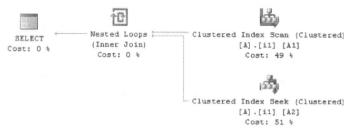

FIGURE 11-33 Loops join plan (with *FAST 1* hint).

Index selection

Index selection is one of the most important aspects of query optimization. The basic idea behind index matching is to take predicates from a *WHERE* clause, join condition, or other limiting operation in a query and to convert that operation so that it can be performed against an index. Two basic operations can be performed against an index.

- Seek for a single value or a range of values on the index key

- Scan the index forward or backward

For seek, the initial operation starts at the root of a B-tree and navigates down the tree to a desired location in the index based on the index keys. When completed, the query processor can iterate over all rows that match the predicate or until the last value in the range is found. Because leaves in a B-tree are linked in SQL Server, scanning rows in order using this structure is possible after the intermediate B-tree nodes are traversed.

The job of the Query Optimizer is to figure out which predicates can be applied to the index to return rows as quickly as possible. Some predicates can be applied to an index, whereas others can't. For example, the query *SELECT col1, PKcol FROM MyTable WHERE col1=2* has one predicate in the form of <column> = <constant>. This pattern can be matched to a seek operation if that column has an index. The resulting alternative that is generated is to perform a seek against the nonclustered index and to return the rows that match, if any. Figure 11-34 demonstrates a basic seek plan generated by the Query Optimizer.

```
CREATE TABLE idxtest2(col2 INT, col3 INT, col4 INT);
CREATE INDEX i2 ON idxtest2(col2, col3);

SELECT col2, col3 FROM idxtest2 WHERE col2=5
```

FIGURE 11-34 Index seek plan.

The Query Optimizer can also apply compound predicates against multicolumn indexes, as long as the operation can be converted into starting and ending index keys. Figure 11-35 shows a multicolumn seek plan, and you can see the predicates used if you look at the properties for this operator in Management Studio.

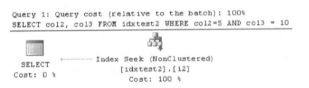

FIGURE 11-35 Multicolumn index seek plan.

Predicates that can be converted into an index operation are often called *sargable*, or "search-ARGument-able." This means that the form of the predicate can be converted into an index operation. Predicates that can never match or don't match the selected index are called *non-sargable predicates*. Predicates that are non-sargable would be applied after any index seek or range scan operations so that the query can return rows that match all predicates. Making things somewhat confusing is that SQL Server usually evaluates non-sargable predicates within the seek/scan operator in the query tree. This is a performance optimization; if this weren't done, the series of steps performed would be as follows:

1. Seek Operator: Seek to a key in an index's B-tree.

2. Latch the page.

3. Read the row.

4. Release the latch on the page.

5. Return the row to the filter operator.

6. Filter: Evaluate the non-sargable predicate against the row. If it qualifies, pass the row to the parent operator. Otherwise, repeat step 2 to get the next candidate row.

This is slower than optimal because returning the row to a different operator requires loading in a different set of instructions and data to the CPU. By keeping the logic in one place, the overall CPU cost of evaluating the query goes down. The actual operation in SQL Server looks like this:

1. Seek Operator: Seek to a key in an index's B-tree.

2. Latch the page.

3. Read the row.

4. Apply the non-sargable predicate filter. If the row doesn't pass the filter, repeat step 3. Otherwise, continue to step 5.

5. Release the latch on the page.

6. Return the row.

This is called *pushing non-sargable predicates* (the predicate is pushed from the filter into the seek/scan). It's a physical optimization but can show up in queries that process many rows.

Not all predicates can be evaluated in the seek/scan operator. Because the latch operation prevents other users from even looking at a page in the system, this optimization is reserved for predicates that are very cheap to perform. This is called *non-pushable, non-sargable predicates*. Examples include the following.

- Predicates on large objects (including *varbinary(max), varchar(max), nvarchar(max)*)

- Common language runtime (CLR) functions

- Some T-SQL functions

Predicate sargability is an important consideration in database application design. One reason systems can perform poorly is that the application against the database is written in such a way as to make predicates non-sargable. In many cases, this is avoidable if the issue is identified early enough, and fixing this one issue can sometimes increase database application performance by an order of magnitude.

SQL Server considers many formulations when trying to apply indexes against sargable predicates in a query. For *AND* conditions (*WHERE col1=5 AND col2=6 AND...*), SQL Server tries to do the following:

1. Use a list of required seek equality columns, seek inequality columns, and columns needed to satisfy the query but without predicates to attempt to find an index that exactly matches the request. If such an index exists, use it.

2. Try to find a set of indexes to satisfy the equality conditions and perform an inner join for all such indexes.

3. If step 2 didn't cover all required columns, consider joins with any other indexes based on the set of columns in the indexes included so far in the solution.

4. Perform a join back to the base table to get any remaining columns.

In all cases, the costs of each solution are considered and the solution is returned only if it's believed to be least-cost. So a solution that joins many indexes together is used only if it's believed to cost less than a scan of all rows in the base table. Second, this algorithm is performed locally in the query tree. Even if the Query Optimizer generates a specific alternative using this process, it might not ultimately be part of the final query plan. Costing is used to determine the cheapest complete query plan. Thus, this isn't a rule-based mechanism for selecting indexes; it's a heuristic that is part of a broader costing infrastructure to help choose efficient query plans.

Filtered indexes

SQL Server 2008 and later versions can create indexes with simple predicates that restrict the set of rows included in the index. At first glance, the Filtered Indexes feature is a subset of the functionality already contained in indexed views. Nevertheless, this feature exists for good reasons.

- Indexed views are more expensive to use and maintain than filtered indexes.

- The matching capability of the Indexed View feature isn't supported in all editions of SQL Server.

- A number of different SQL Server users had scenarios that were just slightly more complex than the regular index feature, so they weren't really interested in moving to a full indexed view solution.

So although indexed views are still a very useful feature, they tend to be more useful for the more classical relational query precomputation scenarios.

Filtered Indexes are created using a new *WHERE* clause on a *CREATE INDEX* statement. Listing 11-7 demonstrates how to create an index and how it can be used in a query. Figures 11-36 and 11-37 show the resulting query plans for a query when the filtered index is covering and when it's not, respectively.

LISTING 11-7 Filtered index example

```
CREATE TABLE testfilter1(col1 INT, col2 INT);
go
DECLARE @i INT=0;
SET NOCOUNT ON;
BEGIN TRANSACTION;
WHILE @i < 40000
BEGIN
INSERT INTO testfilter1(col1, col2) VALUES (rand()*1000, rand()*1000);
SET @i+=1;
END;
COMMIT TRANSACTION;
go

CREATE INDEX i1 ON testfilter1(col2) WHERE col2 > 800;

SELECT col2 FROM testfilter1 WHERE col2 > 800;
SELECT col2 FROM testfilter1 WHERE col2 > 799;
```

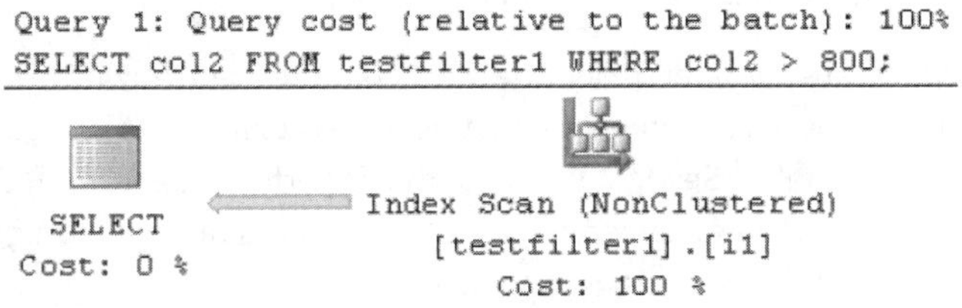

FIGURE 11-36 Filtered index used in query plan.

```
Query 1: Query cost (relative to the batch): 100%
SELECT col2 FROM testfilter1 WHERE col2 > 799;
```

```
   SELECT                 Table Scan
   Cost: 0 %              [testfilter1]
                          Cost: 100 %
```

FIGURE 11-37 Filtered index not used because of noncovering filter condition.

The cost of the first select query is 0.0141293, whereas the second query has an estimated cost of 0.112467. The filtered index benefits from having fewer rows and is also narrower than the base table, so it also has fewer pages. When you know specific constraints that are used on queries with large tables in which space is an issue, this kind of index can be quite useful.

SQL Server imposes a number of restrictions on the scalar constructs that can be used to formulate the filter in the *CREATE INDEX* command. These are based largely on what the Query Optimizer's domain property framework can use easily when matching indexes. As a result, some of the more complex pieces of the system aren't supported in this release because matching these indexes efficiently is impossible.

Filtered indexes can handle several scenarios.

- Not all data fits easily into the relational database model with a small, fixed set of columns that are set for every row. Often, some fields are used only occasionally, resulting in many NULL entries for that column. A traditional index stores many NULLs and wastes a lot of storage space. Updates to the table have to maintain this index for every row.

- If you are querying a table with a small number of distinct values and are using a multicolumn predicate in which some of the elements are fixed, you can create a filtered index to speed up this specific query. This might be useful for a regular report run only for your boss; it speeds up a small set of queries without slowing down updates as much for everyone else.

- As shown in Listing 11-7, the index can be used when an expensive query on a large table has a known query condition.

Indexed views

Traditional, nonindexed views have been used for goals such as simplifying SQL queries, abstracting data models from user models, and enforcing user security. From an optimization perspective, SQL Server doesn't do much with these views because they are expanded, or in-lined, before optimization begins. This gives the Query Optimizer opportunities to optimize queries globally, but it also makes it difficult for the Query Optimizer to consider plans that perform the view evaluation first, and then process the rest of the query. Arbitrary tree matching is a computationally complex problem, and the feature set of views is too large to perform this operation efficiently.

Note Matching of indexed views is supported only in SQL Server 2012 Enterprise Edition.

The Indexed Views feature allows SQL Server to expose some of the benefits of view materialization while retaining the benefits of global reasoning about query operations. SQL Server exposes a *CREATE INDEX* command on views that creates a materialized form of the query result. The resulting structure is physically identical to a table with a clustered index. Nonclustered indexes also are supported on this structure. The Query Optimizer can use this structure to return results more efficiently to the user. The Query Optimizer contains logic to use this index both in cases when the original query text referenced the view explicitly as well as in cases when the user submits a query that uses the same components as the view (in any equivalent order). Actually, the query processor expands indexed views early in the query pipeline and always uses the same matching code for both cases. The *WITH (NOEXPAND)* hint tells the query processor not to expand the view definition.

The example in Listing 11-8 uses three different paths to get SQL Server to match the view. Figures 11-38, 11-39, and 11-40 show the plans for the matches.

LISTING 11-8 Indexed view matching examples

```
-- Create two tables for use in our indexed view
CREATE TABLE table1(id INT PRIMARY KEY, submitdate DATETIME, comment NVARCHAR(200));
CREATE TABLE table2(id INT PRIMARY KEY IDENTITY, commentid INT, product NVARCHAR(200));
GO
-- submit some data into each table
INSERT INTO table1(id, submitdate, comment) VALUES (1, '2008-08-21', 'Conor Loves Indexed
Views');
INSERT INTO table2(commentid, product) VALUES (1, 'SQL Server');
GO
-- create a view over the two tables
CREATE VIEW dbo.v1 WITH SCHEMABINDING AS
SELECT t1.id, t1.submitdate, t1.comment, t2.product FROM dbo.table1 t1 INNER JOIN dbo.table2 t2
ON t1.id=t2.commentid;
go
-- indexed the view
CREATE UNIQUE CLUSTERED INDEX i1 ON v1(id);

-- query the view directly --> matches
SELECT * FROM dbo.v1;
-- query the statement used in the view definition --> matches as well
SELECT t1.id, t1.submitdate, t1.comment, t2.product
FROM dbo.table1 t1 INNER JOIN dbo.table2 t2
    ON t1.id=t2.commentid;
-- query a logically equivalent statement used in the view definition that
-- is written differently --> matches as well
SELECT t1.id, t1.submitdate, t1.comment, t2.product
FROM dbo.table2 t2 INNER JOIN dbo.table1 t1 ON t2.commentid=t1.id;
```

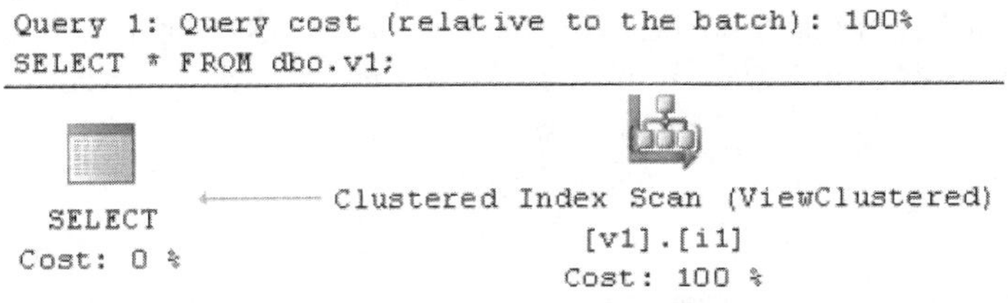

Query 1: Query cost (relative to the batch): 100%
SELECT * FROM dbo.v1;

SELECT
Cost: 0 %

Clustered Index Scan (ViewClustered)
[v1].[i1]
Cost: 100 %

FIGURE 11-38 A direct reference match of an indexed view.

```
Query 1: Query cost (relative to the batch): 100%
SELECT t1.id, t1.submitdate, t1.comment, t2.product F
```

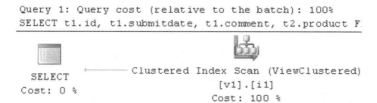

```
SELECT          ←——— Clustered Index Scan (ViewClustered)
Cost: 0 %                      [v1].[i1]
                            Cost: 100 %
```

FIGURE 11-39 An indexed view match when the query is a match to the view definition.

```
Query 1: Query cost (relative to the batch): 100%
SELECT t1.id, t1.submitdate, t1.comment, t2.product F
```

```
SELECT          ←——— Clustered Index Scan (ViewClustered)
Cost: 0 %                      [v1].[i1]
                            Cost: 100 %
```

FIGURE 11-40 An indexed view match when the query isn't an exact match to the view definition.

In some cases, the Query Optimizer doesn't match the view. Remember that indexed views are inserted into the Memo and evaluated against other plan choices. Although they are often the best plan choice, this isn't always the case. In Listing 11-9, the Query Optimizer can detect logical contradictions between the view definition and the query that references the view. Figure 11-41 shows the query plan that directly references the base table instead of the view.

LISTING 11-9 Example when an index view isn't matched

```
CREATE TABLE table3(col1 INT PRIMARY KEY IDENTITY, col2 INT);
INSERT INTO table3(col2) VALUES (10);
INSERT INTO table3(col2) VALUES (20);
INSERT INTO table3(col2) VALUES (30);
GO
-- create a view that returns values of col2 > 20
CREATE VIEW dbo.v2 WITH SCHEMABINDING AS
SELECT t3.col1, t3.col2 FROM dbo.table3 t3 WHERE t3.col2 > 20;
GO
-- materialize the view
CREATE UNIQUE CLUSTERED INDEX i1 ON v2(col1);
GO

-- now query the view and filter the results to have col2 values equal to 10.
-- The optimizer can detect this is a contradiction and avoid matching the indexed view
-- (the trivial plan feature can "block" this optimization)
SELECT * FROM dbo.v2 WHERE col2 = CONVERT(INT, 10);
```

```
Query 1: Query cost (relative to the batch): 100%
SELECT * FROM dbo.v2 WHERE col2 = CONVERT(INT, 10);
```

```
SELECT          ←——— Clustered Index Scan (Clustered)
Cost: 0 %           [table3].[PK__table3__357D0D3E595B4…
                            Cost: 100 %
```

FIGURE 11-41 A query plan when Indexed View isn't matched.

Note The predicate in this example is *[v1].[dbo].[table3].[col2] as [t3].[col2]=[@1] AND [v1]. [dbo].[table3].[col2] as [t3].[col2]>(20)*. Although I've tried to make the examples in this chapter as simple as possible, the Query Optimizer uses logic here to detect that I have made this query example *too* simple. As a result, it has treated it like a trivial plan and auto-parameterized it for use by all future queries like this one that vary only by the constant (10). Although the intricacies of trivial plans aren't formally documented and are subject to change with each release, Figure 11-42 shows what could happen when you modify the query slightly to avoid the trivial plan feature (in my case, I used a query hint, but that's not shown in the code).

```
Query 1: Query cost (relative to the batch): 100%
SELECT * FROM dbo.v2 WHERE col2 = CONVERT(INT, 10)
```

```
   SELECT              Constant Scan
   Cost: 0 %           Cost: 100 %
```

FIGURE 11-42 A Constant Scan plan because of non-trivial plan contradiction detection.

This plan is a zero-row scan because the Query Optimizer recognizes that *col2* = 10 and *col2* > 20 never return rows. This query plan doesn't even try to scan *table3* or *v2*.

Tip Unfortunately, in other cases the Query Optimizer doesn't recognize an indexed view, even when it would be a good plan choice. Often, these cases deal with complex interactions between high-level features within the query processor (such as computed column matching and the algorithm to explore join orders). Although SQL Server does provide some information through warnings and showplans that can help you see the behaviors of the system at this level, it requires a lot of internal knowledge to understand fully. If you happen to find yourself in a case where you believe that the indexed view should match but doesn't, consider the *WITH (NOEXPAND)* hint to force the query processor to pick that indexed view. This usually is enough to get the plan to include the indexed view.

SQL Server also supports matching indexed views in cases beyond exact matches of the query text to the view definition. It also supports using an indexed view for inexact matches in which the definition of the view is broader than the query submitted by the user. SQL Server then applies residual filters, projections (columns in the select list), and even aggregates to use the view as a partial precomputation of the query result.

The code in Listing 11-10 demonstrates view matching for both filter and projection residuals. It creates a view that has more rows and more columns than the final query, but the indexed view is still matched by the Query Optimizer. Figure 11-43 shows the resulting query plan.

LISTING 11-10 Indexed view matching example (a subset of rows and columns)

```
-- base table
CREATE TABLE basetbl1 (col1 INT, col2 INT, col3 BINARY(4000));
CREATE UNIQUE CLUSTERED INDEX i1 ON basetbl1(col1);
GO
-- populate base table
SET NOCOUNT ON;
DECLARE @i INT =0;
WHILE @i < 50000
BEGIN
INSERT INTO basetbl1(col1, col2) VALUES (@i, 50000-@i);
SET @i+=1;
END;
GO
-- create a view over the 2 integer columns
CREATE VIEW dbo.v2 WITH SCHEMABINDING AS
SELECT col1, col2 FROM dbo.basetbl1;
GO
-- index that on col2 (base table is only indexed on col1)
CREATE UNIQUE CLUSTERED INDEX iv1 on dbo.v2(col2);

-- the indexed view still matches for both a restricted
-- column set and a restricted row set
SELECT col1 FROM dbo.basetbl1 WHERE col2 > 2500;
```

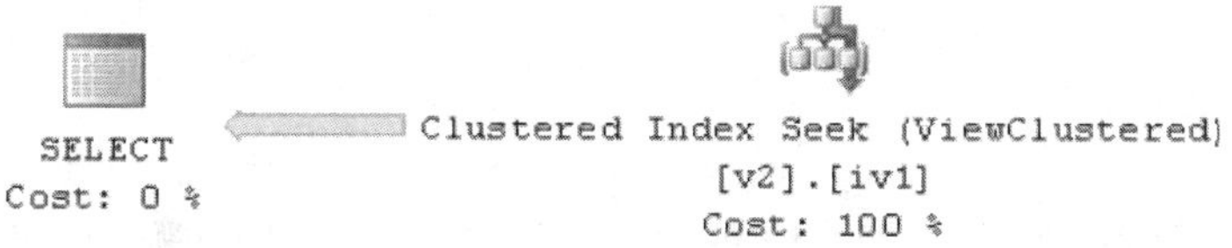

FIGURE 11-43 An indexed view matched for a subset of rows and columns.

The projection isn't explicitly listed as a separate Compute Scalar operator in this query because SQL Server 2012 has special logic to remove projections that don't compute an expression. The filter operator in the index matching code is translated into an index seek against the view. If you modify the query to compute an expression, Figure 11-44 demonstrates the residual Compute Scalar added to the plan.

```
SELECT col1 + 1 FROM dbo.basetbl1 WHERE col2 > 2500 AND col1 > 10;
```

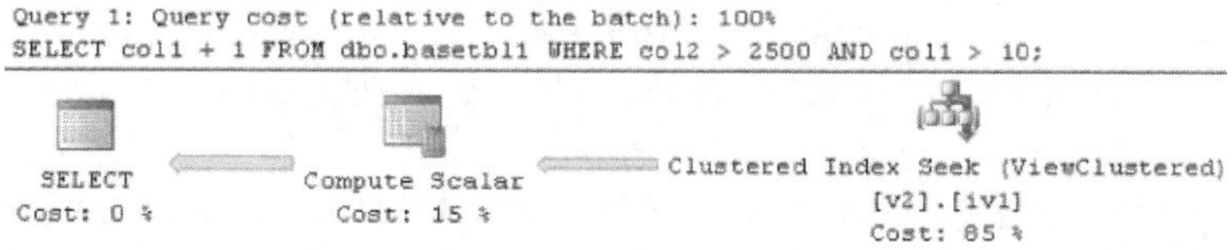

FIGURE 11-44 Compute Scalar, needed only when computing new values.

Like all options considered by the Query Optimizer, indexed view alternatives are generated and stored in the Memo and are compared by using costing equations against other possible plans. Alternatives including partial matches also cost the residual operations, which means that an indexed view plan can be generated but not picked when the Query Optimizer considers other plans to have lower costs.

Indexed views are maintained as part of the update processing for tables on which the view is based. This ensures that the view provides a consistent result if it's selected by the Query Optimizer for any query plan. Because some query operations are incompatible with this design guarantee, SQL Server places some restrictions on the set of supported constructs in indexed views to ensure that the view can be created, matched, and updated as efficiently as possible. The description of the restrictions in *SQL Server Books Online* is long and detailed, which can make understanding the higher-level rules very difficult.

For updating indexed views, the core question behind the restrictions is, "Can the query processor compute the necessary changes to the indexed view clustered and nonclustered indexes without having to recompute the whole indexed view?" If it can, the query processor *can* perform these changes efficiently as part of the maintenance of the base tables that are referenced in the view. This property is relatively easy for filters, projections (compute scalar), and inner joins on keys. Operators that destroy or create data are more difficult to maintain, so these are often restricted from use in indexed views.

Later in this chapter, the "Updates" section discusses how indexed views are represented in update plans.

Partitioned tables

As SQL Server is used to store more and more data, management of very large databases becomes a bigger concern for DBAs. First, the time to perform operations such as an index rebuild grows with the data size, and eventually this can affect system availability. Second, the size of large tables makes performing operations difficult because the system is often strained for resources, such as temp space, log space, and physical memory. Table and index partitioning can help you manage large databases better and minimize downtime.

Physically, partitioned tables and indexes are really *N* tables or indexes that store a fraction of the rows. When comparing this to their nonpartitioned equivalents, the difference in the plan is often that the partitioned case requires iterating over a list of tables or a list of indexes to return all the rows. In SQL Server 2005, this was represented using an *APPLY* operator, which is essentially a nested loops join. In the SQL Server 2005 representation, a special table of partition IDs was passed in as parameters to the query execution component in a join to iterate over each partition. Although this works well in most cases, some important scenarios didn't work well with this model. For example, a restriction in parallel query plans requires that the parallel table or index scan feature (in which multiple threads read rows from a table at the same time to improve performance) didn't work on the inner side of a nested loops join, and this couldn't be fixed easily or efficiently. Unfortunately, this is the majority case for table partitioning. Also, the *APPLY* representation enabled join collocation, where two tables partitioned in the same way can be joined very efficiently. Unfortunately, this turned out to be less common in practice than was foreseen when the feature was originally designed. For reasons like this, the representation was refined further in SQL Server 2008.

SQL Server represents partitioning in most cases by storing the partitions within the operator that accesses the partitioned table or index. This provides a number of benefits, such as enabling parallel scans to work properly. It also removed a number of other differences between partitioned and non-partitioned cases in the Query Optimizer that manifested themselves as missed performance optimizations. This should simplify deploying partitioning in applications that started out as nonpartitioned.

The following code includes the example to show this new design. Figure 11-45 shows the resulting query plan for SQL Server 2012 over partitioned tables.

```
CREATE PARTITION FUNCTION pf2008(date) AS RANGE RIGHT
        FOR VALUES ('2012-10-01', '2012-11-01', '2012-12-01');
CREATE PARTITION SCHEME ps2012 AS PARTITION pf2012 ALL TO ([PRIMARY]);

CREATE TABLE ptnsales(saledate DATE, salesperson INT, amount MONEY) ON ps2012(saledate);
INSERT INTO ptnsales (saledate, salesperson, amount) VALUES ('2012-10-20', 1, 250.00);
INSERT INTO ptnsales (saledate, salesperson, amount) VALUES ('2012-11-05', 2, 129.00);
INSERT INTO ptnsales (saledate, salesperson, amount) VALUES ('2012-12-23', 2, 98.00);
INSERT INTO ptnsales (saledate, salesperson, amount) VALUES ('2012-10-3', 1, 450.00);

SELECT * FROM ptnsales WHERE (saledate) NOT BETWEEN '2012-11-01' AND '2012-11-30';
```

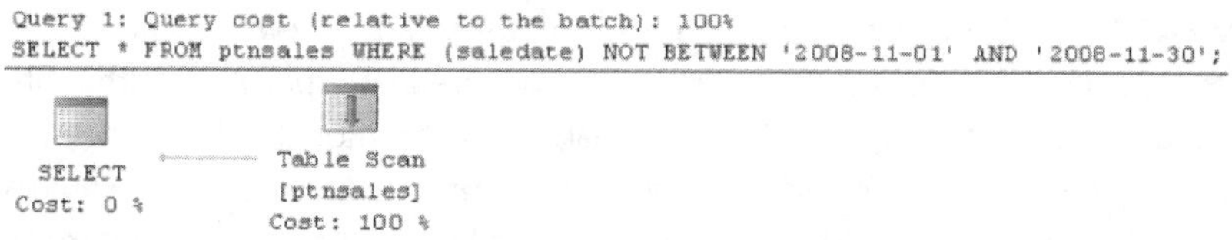

Query 1: Query cost (relative to the batch): 100%
SELECT * FROM ptnsales WHERE (saledate) NOT BETWEEN '2008-11-01' AND '2008-11-30';

SELECT
Cost: 0 %

Table Scan
[ptnsales]
Cost: 100 %

FIGURE 11-45 Query plan for the SQL Server partitioning model.

You can see that the base case doesn't require an extra join with a Constant Scan. This makes the query plans look like the nonpartitioned cases more often, which should make understanding the query plans easier.

One benefit of this model is that getting parallel scans over partitioned tables is now possible. The following example creates a large partitioned table and then performs a *COUNT(*)* operation that generates a parallel scan. In SQL Server, some aggregate functions can be split into two parts, with one part executed in the same thread as the table. This can speed up execution time in large queries and minimize the number of rows that need to be passed from thread to thread. Listing 11-11 demonstrates how SQL Server 2012 generates parallel scans over partitioned tables to compute aggregates. Figure 11-46 shows the resulting query plan.

LISTING 11-11 Partitioned parallel scan example

```
CREATE PARTITION FUNCTION pfparallel(INT) AS RANGE RIGHT FOR VALUES (100, 200, 300);
CREATE PARTITION SCHEME psparallel AS PARTITION pfparallel ALL TO ([PRIMARY]);
GO
CREATE TABLE testscan(randomnum INT, value INT, data BINARY(3000)) ON psparallel(randomnum);
GO
SET NOCOUNT ON;
BEGIN TRANSACTION;
DECLARE @i INT=0;
WHILE @i < 100000
BEGIN
INSERT INTO testscan(randomnum, value) VALUES (rand()*400, @i);
SET @i+=1;
END;
COMMIT TRANSACTION;
GO
-- now let's demonstrate a parallel scan over a partitioned table in SQL Server 2012
SELECT COUNT(*) FROM testscan;
```

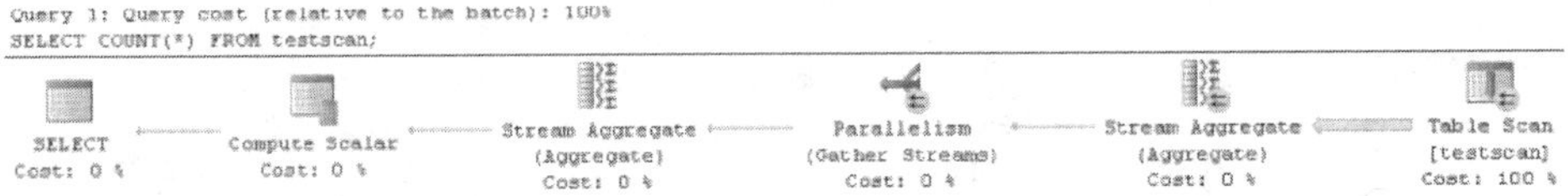

FIGURE 11-46 Parallel scan on partitioned tables in SQL Server 2012.

SQL Server 2005 had limitations on how parallel queries could be executed against partitioned tables. The use of the *APPLY* operator to scan each partition interacted poorly with some other restrictions in the system to allow SQL Server 2005 to run only one thread per partition. Although this allowed the query to run in parallel when scanning many partitions, this model didn't work well when the query accessed a single partition. When accessing a single partition, only one thread could access the partition, essentially ignoring the Parallel Scan feature. Unfortunately, one core reason for SQL Server range partitioning is to access the most current partition in a date range. The *APPLY* model also made it difficult to handle partition skew (in which one partition is much larger than others) efficiently. Although SQL Server 2005 would consider the size of the largest partition when costing a query using this pattern, it still has one thread finishing later than the other threads.

The Query Optimizer has improved the end-to-end experience in partitioned table plan generation. The ability to represent partitioned table access in the same manner as nonpartitioned access guarantees that the performance differences between partitioned and nonpartitioned tables are minimized. Specifically, the set of considered parallel plan options is much more consistent. The query execution component can adjust dynamically between using one thread per partition and using multiple threads per partition, which should allocate threads to finish processing a query more efficiently.

In SQL Server, join collocation is still represented by using the apply/nested loops join, but other cases use the traditional representation. This works with other features within the query processor to guarantee that they behave the same as nonpartitioned tables. The following example builds on the last example to demonstrate that joining two tables with the same partitioning scheme can be done using the collocated join technique. The scenarios for this remain the same as in SQL Server 2005—cases in which you want to join two partitioned tables or indexes together. Often, this would be a fact table and a large dimension table index that is partitioned in the same manner as the fact table. Figure 11-47 shows a per-partitioned join example when the original SQL Server 2005 partitioning logic is still visible.

```
-- SQL Server join collocation uses the constant scan + apply model
SELECT * FROM testscan t1 INNER JOIN testscan t2 ON t1.randomnum=t2.randomnum;
```

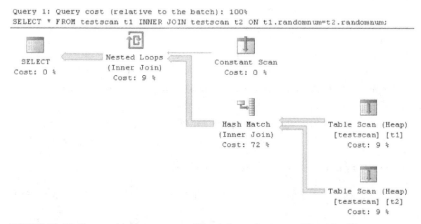

Query 1: Query cost (relative to the batch): 100%
SELECT * FROM testscan t1 INNER JOIN testscan t2 ON t1.randomnum=t2.randomnum;

FIGURE 11-47 Query plan for a per-partition join against a partitioned table.

The partitioned table implementation in SQL Server 2012 does have a quirk that's worth noting because it might surprise you at first. If you look closely at the showplan output in Figure 11-48 for this last query plan, notice that this partitioned table heap scan has a seek predicate.

⊞ Output List	[s1].[dbo].[testscan].randomnum, [s1].[dbo].[testscan].value, [s1].[dbo].[testscan].data
Parallel	False
Partitioned	True
Physical Operation	Table Scan
Scan Direction	FORWARD
⊞ Seek Predicates	Seek Keys[1]: Prefix PtnId1001 = Scalar Operator([Expr1008])
TableCardinality	100000

FIGURE 11-48 Seek predicate for partitioned heaps.

Although SQL Server 2005 exposed the partition ID within the query plan, SQL Server 2008 and later versions largely hide that from view. It's still in the query plan, but is much more closely tied to indexing in most cases. Every partitioned access structure in SQL Server 2008 and later versions is modeled as an index in which the first column is the partitioning column. Because the partitioning ID (derived from the partitioning key) is needed to perform seeks anyway, this actually matches the effective behavior seen in SQL Server 2005. The only quirk is that partitioned heaps now appear to have an index. You can see this in the properties from the previous example.

Partition-aligned index views

SQL Server 2008 and later allows for partition-aligned index views that can survive across *SWITCH* operations. In SQL Server 2005, these views had to be dropped before a *SWITCH* could be performed, and this hampered the ability to keep a system running as a production system while the indexed views were disabled and rebuilt. Now, partitioned tables—especially in large data warehouses—have a way to maintain a database while keeping it fully available.

Windowing functions

SQL Server 2012 introduces a new kind of spool associated with windowing functions. Windowing functions can compute moving averages and running totals, and the Window Spool operator is specially crafted for this kind of scenario. Spools can work in different ways. The most traditional query processing spool algorithm operates by consuming all rows from its input operators in the query tree before returning rows to the client. Other spools can cache rows as they flow through the operator (lazy spooling) for more efficient reuse later in the query. For the windowing functions, a new operator was created that spools rows based on the active windows of an ordered stream computation.

The Window Spool works as follows:

- It consumes all rows from its input and stores them in the spool (in memory if small enough, paging to disk if not).

- For each row in the spool, it outputs all rows stored in the spool (expanding the rows processed by a factor of *N*).

- An aggregate (*GROUP BY*) operator sits above the spool and converts the *N* rows into one row.

At the end of the computation, the output of these operators should match the total spooled rows. When SQL Server determines that the row count is small enough to allow in-memory processing, it uses in-memory processing. Otherwise, the spool spills to disk as necessary to satisfy requests to read rows multiple times.

The new syntax allows for functions that compute data over a stream of inputs and return a row for each input row. The following example shows how this capability can be used to compute 200-day moving averages for stock price history (a common calculation in the financial services industry used to determine stock movement variability compared to its historical moving average). Figure 11-49 displays the results. This query runs over a table that stores daily closing price quotes for stocks and is picking a single stock for the moving average computation.

```
SELECT    dateid,
          quote,
          AVG(quote) OVER(ORDER BY dateid ROWS BETWEEN 200 PRECEDING AND CURRENT ROW)
          AS avg200day
FROM stockquote
WHERE stockid=1
ORDER BY dateid;
```

Query 1: Query cost (relative to the batch): 100%
INSERT INTO update1 (col2, col3) VALUES (2, 3);

T-SQL			
INSERT	Clustered Index Insert	Compute Scalar	Constant Scan
Cost: 0 %	[update1].[PK__update1__357D0D3E1A1_	Cost: 0 %	Cost: 0 %
	Cost: 100 %		

FIGURE 11-49 200-day moving average computation result.

Like ranking functions, this allows a per-row calculation to be performed for each input row. Figure 11-50 shows the main pattern used in these queries.

Query 1: Query cost (relative to the batch): 100%
UPDATE update1 SET col2 = 5;

T-SQL			
UPDATE	Clustered Index Update	Top	Clustered Index Scan (Clustered)
Cost: 0 %	[update1].[PK__update1__357D0D3E1A1_	Cost: 0 %	[update1].[PK__update1__357D0D3E1A1_
	Cost: 75 %		Cost: 25 %

FIGURE 11-50 Windowing function query plan operators.

The Segment and Compute Scalar operators—used internally as part of the Window Spool—compute group boundaries and row counts, respectively. For this specific example, notice that the query plan in SQL Server 2012 has two Window Spools (and the associated other operators). This is used when computing fixed-size windows and is a technical limitation that might be removed in future releases of the product.

Data warehousing

SQL Server contains a number of special optimizations that speed the execution of data warehouse queries. A *data warehouse* is a large database that usually has one large fact table and a number of smaller dimension tables that contain detail information referenced by the fact table. These are typically called *star schema* or *snowflake schema* (*snowflake* applies to dimension tables that reference other dimension tables). These kinds of schemas are often used to store large amounts of raw data that is then processed to help discover information to help a company learn something about its business.

Data warehouses often try to make each row in the fact table as small as possible because the table is so large. Large data, such as strings, is moved to dimension tables to reduce in-row space. Fact tables are usually so large that the use of nonclustered indexes is limited because of the large storage requirements to store these structures. Dimension tables are often indexed. This pattern doesn't match a typical transaction processing system, in which each table is accessed based on the queries used against the system.

When you're optimizing queries against data warehouses, don't scan the fact table more than necessary because this is usually the largest single contributor to execution time. SQL Server can recognize star and snowflake schemas and apply special optimizations to improve query performance. First, SQL Server orders joins differently in data warehouses to try to perform as many limiting operations against the dimension tables as possible *before* performing a scan of the fact table. This can even include performing full cross products between dimension tables to eliminate scans of the fact table.

SQL Server also contains special bitmap operators that help reduce data movement across threads in parallel queries when using the star join pattern. This is a physical optimization in which a hash of information from the dimension tables used in the query is computed and stored in the bitmap. Bitmaps from each dimension are combined (which is also efficient to compute). Finally, the combined bitmap is used when scanning the fact table to pre-filter the rows that need to be materialized into memory and copied to different threads when executing a parallel query plan. These bitmaps are applied by using a probe filter applied as a non-sargable predicate to the fact table. This is somewhat like a special on-the-fly index, created just for data warehouse queries of this pattern. Figure 11-51 shows the most common query plan shape used for Star Join queries.

FIGURE 11-51 Bitmap operator example query plan.

SQL Server 2012 introduces significant changes in the space of relational data warehouse processing. First is a new kind of index called a columnstore. Second is a new query execution model called Batch Mode. Together, these two improvements can significantly improve runtime for data warehouse queries that use the star join pattern. Because this new functionality has limitations, customers will need to design their applications specifically to work within the defined restrictions to realize the performance benefits that it delivers. The following sections explain details of the new model.

Columnstore indexes

Columnstores in SQL Server 2012 are nonclustered indexes that use less space than a traditional B-tree index in SQL Server. They are intended to be created on the fact table of a data warehouse (and potentially also on large dimension tables). They achieve space savings by ignoring the standard practice of physically collocating all the column data for an index together for each row. Instead, they collocate values from each column together. Because the typical star join query reads only a subset of the columns from a table, this can reduce the I/O requirements to satisfy a query. Because I/O can dominate large data warehouse query performance, this can improve the response times from these queries when a small fraction of the data is being accessed.

The Sales fact table in Figure 11-52 conceptually shows how data is stored in different types of indexes. In traditional indexes, data is stored sequentially per row, aligned with the horizontal rectangle in Figure 11-52. In the columnstore index, data is stored sequentially per column. Typical rotating storage retrieves data most quickly based on how it's stored sequentially. When the user issues a data warehouse query that needs only a subset of the columns, the column orientation allows for the query to access only the needed data without having to skip unneeded columns. This reduces the I/O requirements for many data warehouse queries and improves overall performance.

Date	DepartmentID	ProductID	SalesAmt
12/21/2011	1	23	1000.00
12/21/2011	1	125	120.00
12/21/2011	2	3	3000.00

Date	DepartmentID	ProductID	SalesAmt
12/21/2011	1	23	1000.00
12/21/2011	1	125	120.00
12/21/2011	2	3	3000.00

FIGURE 11-52 Column orientation versus row orientation highlighted in a Sales fact table,

Also, fact table data is often highly repetitive, so opportunities exist to use compression to further reduce storage requirements (which further improves scan time on the primary cost in a data warehouse star join query). Because scans are the primary access pattern, space savings can be gained by leveraging run-length compression techniques. For example, if the data in the fact table for DepartmentID 23 is sorted by DepartmentID, you can just capture that 527 instances exist of DepartmentID 23 rather than store it 527 times. This type of index doesn't work for index seeks to random rows to find nonclustered attributes because sometimes that "row" has no specific storage for every column value, but this tradeoff is a good one in the data warehouse domain because B-tree indexes are rarely nonclustered, anyway. Different compression techniques are used for each data type to maximize space savings. For example, strings have a side "dictionary" in which each string is given a synthetic ID to never store the same string more than once. Numerous compression techniques are applied within the columnstore index over multiple columns to deliver additional storage savings, compared to a regular B-tree index using row and/or page compression.

From the perspective of the Query Optimizer, having a significantly smaller index reduces the I/O cost to read the fact table and process the query. In traditional (non-columnstore) indexes, data warehouse configurations are designed so that the dimension tables fit into buffer pool memory, but the fact table doesn't. Also, the page replacement algorithms for the buffer pool bias toward keeping dimension table pages (because they are frequently referenced in most data warehouse queries), whereas fact table pages aren't often kept in the buffer pool—because they don't fit and because they are always candidates to be replaced as the newest pages with the lowest hit counts in the buffer. Therefore, reducing the size of the fact table often directly reduces the largest cost of queries in these systems because they are frequently doing full scans of the fact table on every query. In some cases, the column-oriented storage model and compression might be sufficient to allow the columnstore index for some fact tables to fit into memory on 64-bit machines, allowing a completely cached scan of all tables in the query. Avoiding I/O greatly improves the performance of these kinds of queries. In all cases, buying enough RAM for 64-bit hardware to get the dimension tables to fit in memory makes sense, as does provisioning enough RAM, when possible, to store a fact table in memory when using a columnstore index.

Batch mode processing

The next innovation added in SQL Server 2012 relates to how data warehouse queries are processed in memory by the Query Execution component. Batch-based query processing has several key differences from traditional row-based techniques for queries that need to process many rows. The changes made for this new execution model significantly reduce the CPU requirements to execute each query. This allows for additional performance gains over the traditional row-based mode, but these benefits are most visible when processing many rows, and the techniques aren't supported for every possible query operator in SQL Server 2012.

Although data warehouse queries do use a lot of I/O, most modern hardware configurations invest in storage subsystems that improve I/O performance. For example, customers often buy many disk drives and multiple controllers so that the overall I/O throughput is significantly improved. Although this is a great way to improve query performance, the eventual result is that the CPU is the "next" bottleneck that prevents further performance gains. Often, data warehouse queries are bottlenecked on the CPU *because* they have well-tuned storage subsystems. Improving CPU performance is therefore also necessary to improve data warehouse query performance even when using columnstore indexes because the dominant cost is the CPU, especially if the fact table doesn't need to be scanned from disk.

The batch execution model improves CPU performance in multiple ways. First, it reduces the number of CPU instructions needed to process each row, often by a factor of 10 or more. As a result, if you have fewer instructions, you can finish more quickly. Not all CPU instructions take the same number of cycles to execute, however. Memory access instructions cause the CPU to "block" while waiting for data to be copied from main memory. Depending on the machine, this can take hundreds of clock cycles. The batch execution model specifically implements techniques that greatly reduce the number of blocking memory references required to execute a query, allowing the system to finish queries much more quickly than would be otherwise possible with the traditional row-based model.

Grouping rows for repeated operations

In batch mode, data is processed in groups of rows instead of one row at a time. The number of rows per group depends on the query's row width and is designed to try to keep each batch around the right size to fit into the internal caches of a CPU core. Modern CPUs have multilayered cache hierarchies and can run significantly more quickly if programs are written to maximize the number of operations that can be performed solely within the CPU. Even operations such as reading a value from main memory is far more expensive than reading from the CPU's own registers, and this performance gap has been increasing over successive generations of CPU architectures. The batch-based approach helps structure the program code and user data to minimize the number of times that a CPU core needs to talk to other parts of the system (memory, disk, network, or other CPU cores). For queries that process significant numbers of rows, sending groups of rows reduces the cases where the CPU stalls waiting for memory accesses to return.

Whereas the row-based processing engine in SQL Server didn't needlessly copy data between two operators in a query tree, the architecture did copy data values as part of its model. The batch-based engine eschews data copies and attempts, whenever possible, to avoid copying data values at all. This way, the same data values remain in the CPU's cache as each batch flows through the operators in the query tree. Rather than copy data values, the batch data structures are annotated so that most common copy operations are replaced or otherwise optimized. For example, the batch structure keeps a bit to track whether a filter operation has invalidated a row, as shown in Figure 11-53. Rather than copy the batch to remove the filtered rows, these rows remain in the batch but are ignored by later operators. In this manner, data copying can be avoided to reduce overall processing time.

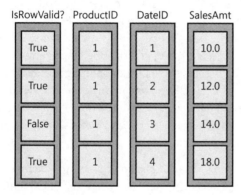

FIGURE 11-53 Bitmap to track row validity when executing filters.

For example, a filter operation that evaluates *WHERE intcol = 0"* can see the data for *intcol* for all rows in the batch sequentially. This allows the CPU core to quickly perform the filter on each row with a minimum of instructions and data movement. To avoid recopying the batch, filters are further optimized to record their results in a special bitmap to determine whether the rows were filtered. Later operations would process only values in which the rows have the right bit value enabled.

Auditing the number of batches used in each operator is possible in the query using the Actual XML Showplan. In the properties for each operator, determining whether an operation worked in batch is possible by looking at the "Actual Execution Mode" to see whether it has the value "Batch". If it does, an "Actual Number of Batches" entry describes how many batches were used to execute this query. Some operators, specifically Exchange, won't execute in batch mode or report batch counts. You can examine operators above/below this operator in the tree to determine how many batches were processed by the query for these operators. Figure 11-54 shows an example.

Columnstore Index Scan (NonClustered)
Scan a columnstore index, entirely or only a range.

Physical Operation	Columnstore Index Scan
Logical Operation	Index Scan
Actual Execution Mode	Batch
Estimated Execution Mode	Batch
Storage	ColumnStore
Actual Number of Rows	36403751
Actual Number of Batches	76258

FIGURE 11-54 Showplan output for Actual Number of Batches.

Column orientation within batches

Like the columnstore index, data within batches is allocated by column instead of by row (although the actual representations vary for purely technical reasons). This difference might seem trivial, but it significantly affects system performance. This allocation model allows some operations to be performed more quickly. Continuing the filter example, a filter in a row-based processing model would have to call down to its child operator to get each row. This code could require the CPU cache to load new instructions and new data from main memory. In the batch model, the instructions to execute the filter instructions will likely be in memory already because this operation is being performed on a set of rows within a batch. In effect, using "tighter" loops enables the CPU to optimize these operations more effectively, reducing the average number of CPU stalls waiting on memory accesses. Although any particular batch might still need to load data or code from main memory when it starts executing, the batch model allows this cost to be amortized over a set of rows whose size is optimized for the CPU's cache size.

In addition to the benefits from executing tighter loops, you can further optimize the average cases seen in data warehouse queries. Fact tables often have many repeating data values (dimension tables are created because of the data deduplication that can occur). When processing a query, the query processor can determine whether all values of a specific column are the same. If they are, the system can just store each value once instead of once per row. This simple run-length compression technique allows operations, such as filter or aggregation (*GROUP BY*), to compute a value once and avoid many CPU cycles. This technique can further reduce the average per-row cost to execute queries. Figure 11-55 shows an example of the memory savings in the batch structure.

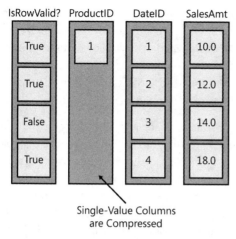

Single-Value Columns
are Compressed

FIGURE 11-55 Per-column compression representation.

Data encoding

The third major difference in the batch model is that data is stored within memory using a probabilistic representation to further reduce the number of times the CPU core needs to access memory that isn't already in the CPU's internal caches. Because each CPU register (on modern CPUs) can store 64-bit values, operations perform more quickly on values that fit within this register because these can be run with a single CPU instruction. For example, a 64-bit nullable *int* field technically takes 64 bits for the data and another 1 bit for the null bit (65 total bits). Rather than store this in two CPU registers, the user data is encoded during query processing so that the most common values (including 0 and NULL) for 64-bit fields are stored within the main 64-bit word, and uncommon fields (such as the highest and lowest values) are stored outside the main 64-bit storage with a special encoding so that SQL Server can determine when the data is in-batch vs. out-of-batch. Figure 11-56 shows an example of how this is represented in the batch execution engine.

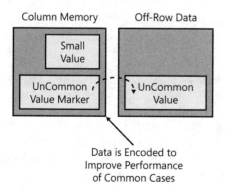

Data is Encoded to
Improve Performance
of Common Cases

FIGURE 11-56 Uncommon data stored outside of the main batch.

Out-of-batch values process more slowly than in-row values. Although this representation does require that the data be transformed before it's returned to the client, that cost is often far less than the cost of extra CPU instructions and memory accesses that would otherwise be required. Each supported data type has such encoding to allow efficient processing within the CPU core. Strings are stored using a special dictionary, and the lookup key into that dictionary is used for most processing (which separates the operations that require copying strings efficiently).

With a different in-memory representation for most scalar data, re-implementing core logic from the expression service becomes necessary and give the opportunity to further reduce the per-row query computation cost. For data that fits nicely into a 64-bit register, often some expressions (+, -, *, /, etc.) can be performed with a single CPU instruction. For each batch, computations are further segmented into different computation passes over the batch data based on the number of instructions required to perform the operation for each kind of encoded data. If SQL Server can tell that some arithmetic operations can be performed quickly if they never cause a CPU arithmetic overflow, those operations can be done first before a later pass over the remaining values with a slower method that checks for overflow. In the worst case, batch processing falls back to use the traditional row-based expression evaluation engine if the expression isn't supported by an efficient batch-based execution algorithm or if the data is stored out-of-row. In this way, SQL Server 2012 reduces the average per-row CPU cost to evaluate a query in each operator.

Logical database design best practices

Traditional data warehouse design patterns already place focus on reducing the maximum size of each column in the fact table to reduce the I/O cost to evaluate queries and/or enable larger table cardinalities to be efficiently supported. Columnstore indexes and batch processing contain restrictions that will extend these guidelines as follows when using SQL Server for customers who want to take advantage of the new functionality.

- You need to determine whether each column needs to support NULLs. If the column can be declared as NOT NULL, this helps batch processing fit values more easily into a CPU register.

- You must design data warehouses to use the supported set of data types. Generally, this precludes many types that don't fit within a CPU register or that require functionality that can't be optimized, such as CLR data types.

- Data uniqueness must be enforced elsewhere, either through a constraint or in a UNIQUE (B-tree) index in the physical database design.

Although later releases of SQL Server might loosen some of these restrictions, doing the up-front work in the data warehouse design to take advantage of what's possible on modern CPU hardware will provide performance advantages. You can find a complete list of columnstore guidelines for SQL Server 2012 at *http://msdn.microsoft.com/en-us/library/gg492088(v=SQL.110).aspx.*

Plan shape

Batch processing is used only in parallel query plans that match the star join pattern in SQL Server 2012. Some changes to parallelism when using the batch model have been made that have important differences from prior releases. In traditional, row model–based parallelism, the query plan uses Exchange operators to represent thread boundaries. When an operator ran in parallel, a static determination was made to send parts of the data to one thread, parts to another thread, and so on. For example, a hash join might run one thread with data starting with values A-J, another thread with values starting on K–M, and so on. When this distribution to threads wasn't done evenly, queries could be stuck waiting on the last thread to finish. In the row model, the typical parallel query plan would therefore use 1 + (# of zones) * (degree of parallelism) threads to execute a query.

Figure 11-57 shows how the per-thread hash tables are created in a parallel query. Note that this shows how data is distributed when creating the hash tables; the actual join with the second table is done as a later step (not shown, but it distributes data to threads similarly).

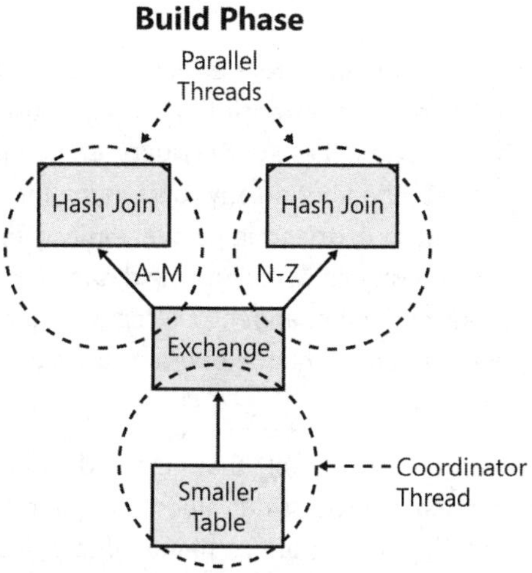

FIGURE 11-57 Row model hash join build example.

Batch-based execution uses a significantly different approach in which threads aren't statically allocated to portions of a query plan. Instead, each operator has groups of work to be performed on batches that sit in queues. Threads take work from various queues and perform the work required for that operator. A steady queue of work needs to be done in various parts of the query tree, so threads migrate to where the data is being processed. This usually means that fewer threads are required to execute queries, especially more complex ones. Figure 11-58 shows how this model interacts with the hash join operator in batch mode. Another difference from the prior model is that the operators themselves control parallelism within each operator rather than have multiple instances of each operator (one per thread in a statically allocated zone). Because operators create work at the unit of a batch, this allows for threads to cluster to whichever operators need work right now. This separation from the physical thread could be thought of as the introduction of work queues on each operator, in which threads are dynamically assigned to do work on non-empty queues during the execution of the query. The atomic unit of work in this model is a batch.

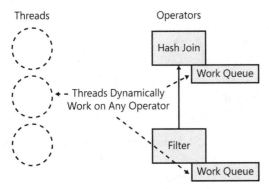

FIGURE 11-58 Batch mode parallelism distribution model.

The next difference in the batch model relates to how cross-thread dependencies are handled. When the Optimizer considers query plans, care must be taken in some transformations because they affect how a query can be executed in parallel during the execution phase of the query. Some operations are naturally parallelizable, such as filter; you can evaluate the filter on any row independently of any other row, so the operation can be performed on different threads and in parallel easily. Others require more care to parallelize. For example, the row-model hash join partitions the data from each join input by value on the join key such that N threads could work independently. Effectively, it creates N hash tables over subsections of the domain. The *Redistribute* Exchange operator does this work within traditional query plans.

The batch model approach for hash joins uses a single, shared hash table that's created and used in separate phases. Each build phase thread works independently, processing values and determining where in the hash table they would go. Later, these independent results are combined into a single, read-only hash table. During the probe phase, the data from the larger hash join input is used to seek into the hash table to determine the existence of matching rows. This approach allows multiple threads read from the hash table concurrently and independently because it's read-only during the processing of the join. This approach reduces cross-thread data movement and cross-thread coordination compared to prior techniques. Generally, SQL Server considers ways to maximize parallelism and minimize cross-thread coordination to improve the performance of star join queries.

Query plans using batch processing have a few differences from the row model.

- Any star join pattern that uses batch processing also has a row mode section at the top of the query and an Exchange operator between the two plan regions. This technical limitation exists in SQL Server 2012 and might be removed in later releases, but it's not a problem and should be expected.

- The batch mode sections of query plans in SQL Server 2012 also have exchanges between every operator. The batch model doesn't require cross-thread data movement, and exchanges usually aren't executed, but they exist in the plan only for a special case in batch processing related to how memory management works in query execution. Queries in SQL Server begin executing by estimating how much memory they need, and then reserving it. This reservation is used for operations, such as hash joins, that need to allocate memory during execution. Although this estimate is usually sufficient, sometimes a query can underestimate the memory requirement. Rather than fail the query, SQL Server 2012 abandons the batch-based execution strategy and falls back to a row-based approach when this happens. This technical limitation will likely be removed in later releases, as well. When reading the operators in a query plan, look closely at whether the operator is listed as being a batch mode operator; customers will want to validate this key attribute that they are running with the optimized code path.

Taken in total, the typical desired shape for data warehouse star join plans in SQL Server 2012 will be as follows.

- Join all dimension tables before a single scan of the fact table.

- Use hash joins for all these joins.

- Create bitmaps for each dimension and use them to scan the fact table.

- Use *GROUP BY* both at the top (row-based) and pushed down toward the source operations (local aggregates in batch mode).

- Use parallelism for the entire batch section of the query.

Figure 11-59 shows the common query plan shape for batch execution plans in this scenario.

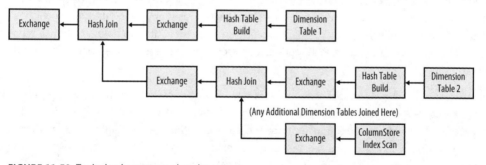

FIGURE 11-59 Typical columnstore plan shape.

When batch processing is used in a query, it usually outperforms the row-based approach, often by a significant amount (10x improvement is possible).

Columnstore limitations and workarounds

As a new feature, columnstores do have nontrivial limitations in SQL Server 2012. One limitation is that tables must be marked as read-only as long as the columnstore exists. In other words, you can't perform *INSERT, UPDATE, DELETE,* or *MERGE* operations on the table while the columnstore index is active. Although this seems like a significant limitation at first, in practice it's not that bad. If you remember that this feature targets data warehouses, these applications are already effectively read-only during regular operations with updates done in batches at night.

With such a pattern, the index can potentially be dropped and re-created each evening around the daily extract, transform, and load (ETL) operation. Even when this isn't true, most large fact tables use table partitioning to manage the data volume. You can load a partition of data at a time because the *SWITCH PARTITION* operation is compatible with the columnstore index. The use of partitioning allows data to be loaded in a closer-to-real-time model, with no downtime of the index on the fact table. Finally, you can use a *UNION ALL* view over the fact table containing a columnstore index and a regular read-write table. Inserts can be performed on the regular read-write table, enabling customers to add data during the day while still getting most of the benefits of the columnstore index. These workarounds should give customers flexibility to use the columnstore index in SQL Server 2012 in various scenarios.

The other columnstore restrictions in SQL Server 2012 relate to data types and which operations block the use of batch processing. Columnstore indexes support data types that are commonly used in data warehouses. Some of the more complex data types, including *varchar(max)*, *nvarchar(max)*, CLR types, and other types not often found in fact tables are restricted from using columnstore indexes. Although the set of supported types might be somewhat expanded in future releases, these restrictions exist to improve the performance of data warehouses and that data types would be added to this set is unlikely unless you had a compelling reason related to data warehouse scenarios. Therefore, the database designer/architect must carefully select the data types when creating the data warehouse.

Because most of the literature related to data warehouses encourages care in selecting the data types to be used in fact tables to reduce row width, the restrictions for columnstore indexes should be largely compatible with existing industry norms in this space. Some users might need to adjust their schemas on types such as decimal, which has an upper-precision boundary; this allows the common cases to fit within the 64-bit CPU registers in the format used to process queries.

Updates

Updates are an interesting area within query processing. In addition to many of the challenges faced while optimizing traditional *SELECT* queries, update optimization also considers physical optimizations such as how many indexes need to be touched for each row, whether to process the updates one index at a time or all at once, and how to avoid unnecessary deadlocks while processing changes as quickly as possible. The Optimizer contains several features specific to updates that help make queries complete as quickly as possible. This section discusses a number of these optimizations.

The term *update processing* actually includes all top-level commands that change data, such as *INSERT, UPDATE, DELETE,* and *MERGE.* As you see in this section, SQL Server treats these commands almost identically. Every update query in SQL Server is composed of the same basic operations.

- It determines what rows are changed (inserted, updated, deleted, merged).

- It calculates the new values for any changed columns.

- It applies the change to the table and any nonclustered index structures.

Figure 11-60 shows how *INSERT* works using this pattern.

```
CREATE TABLE update1 (col1 INT PRIMARY KEY IDENTITY, col2 INT, col3 INT);
INSERT INTO update1 (col2, col3) VALUES (2, 3);
```

Query 1: Query cost (relative to the batch): 100%
INSERT INTO update1 (col2, col3) VALUES (2, 3);

INSERT Cost: 0 %	Clustered Index Insert [update1].[PK__update1__357D0D3E1A1.. Cost: 100 %		Compute Scalar Cost: 0 %	Constant Scan Cost: 0 %

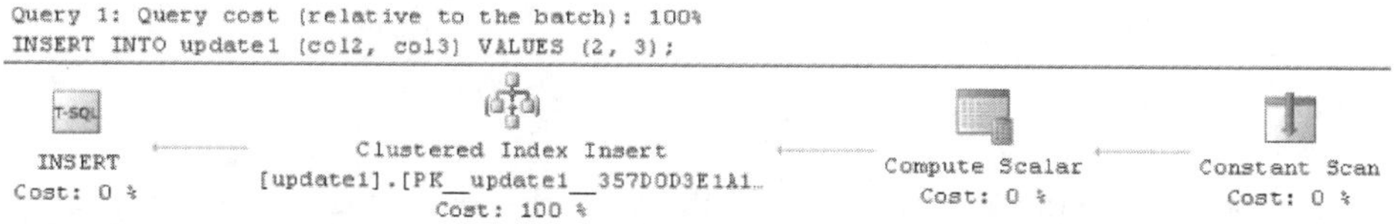

FIGURE 11-60 Basic *INSERT* query plan.

The *INSERT* query uses a special operator called a *Constant Scan* that, in relational algebra, generates rows without reading them from a table. If you are inserting a row into a table, it doesn't really have an existing table, so this operator creates a row for the insert operator to process. The *Compute Scalar* operation evaluates the values to be inserted. In the example, these are constants, but they could be arbitrary scalar expressions or scalar subqueries. Finally, the insert operator physically updates the primary key-clustered index.

Figure 11-60 shows how *UPDATE* plans are represented.

```
UPDATE update1 SET col2 = 5;
```

Query 1: Query cost (relative to the batch): 100%
UPDATE update1 SET col2 = 5;

UPDATE Cost: 0 %	Clustered Index Update [update1].[PK__update1__357D0D3E1A1.. Cost: 75 %	Top Cost: 0 %	Clustered Index Scan (Clustered) [update1].[PK__update1__357D0D3E1A1.. Cost: 25 %

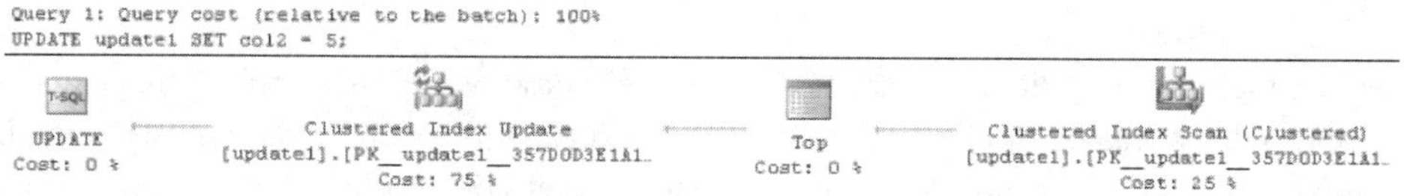

FIGURE 11-61 *UPDATE* query plan.

The *UPDATE* query reads values from the clustered index, performs a *Top* operation, and then updates the same clustered index. The *Top* operation is actually a placeholder for processing *ROWCOUNT* and does nothing unless you've executed a *SET ROWCOUNT N* operation in your session. Note that SQL Server 2012 removed ROWCOUNT Top processing for INSERT, UPDATE, and DELETE commands, and the Top operator won't appear in the plans when trying the examples on this version of the product. Prior versions do include them, so the code kept the longer plan shapes to avoid confusion when running the examples on legacy versions of the product. Also note that in the example, the *UPDATE* command doesn't modify the key of the clustered index, so the row in the index doesn't need to be moved. Finally, an operator doesn't seem to be available to calculate the new value 5 for *col2*. This obviously isn't true—it *is* handled, but a physical optimization is available to collapse this command into the Update operator for processing. If you examine the properties of the Update operator in Figure 11-61, notice that the query has also been auto-parameterized and the target value is supplied directly into the Update.

Figure 11-62 shows the *DELETE* query plan pattern. The *DELETE* query is very similar to the *UPDATE* query—the only real difference is that the row is deleted at the end. The only material difference is that the *WHERE* clause is used as a condition to the source table's seek operation.

```
DELETE FROM update1 WHERE col3 = 10;
```

```
Query 1: Query cost (relative to the batch): 100%
DELETE FROM update1 WHERE col3 = 10;
```

T-SQL	Clustered Index Delete	Top	Clustered Index Scan (Clustered)
DELETE	[update1].[PK__update1__357D0D3E1A1...	Top	[update1].[PK__update1__357D0D3E1A1...
Cost: 0 %	Cost: 75 %	Cost: 0 %	Cost: 25 %

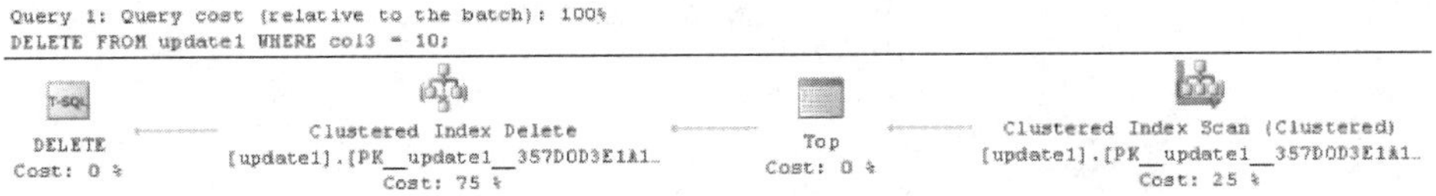

FIGURE 11-62 *DELETE* query plan.

SQL Server generates different plans based on the physical layout of tables, indexes, and other secondary structures. In a very similar example that doesn't have a primary key-clustered index, notice that the resulting plan shape changes (see Figure 11-63).

```
CREATE TABLE update2 (col1 INT, col2 INT, col3 INT);
INSERT INTO update2 (col2, col3) VALUES (2, 3);
```

```
Query 1: Query cost (relative to the batch): 100%
INSERT INTO update2 (col2, col3) VALUES (2, 3);
```

T-SQL	Table Insert
INSERT	[update2]
Cost: 0 %	Cost: 100 %

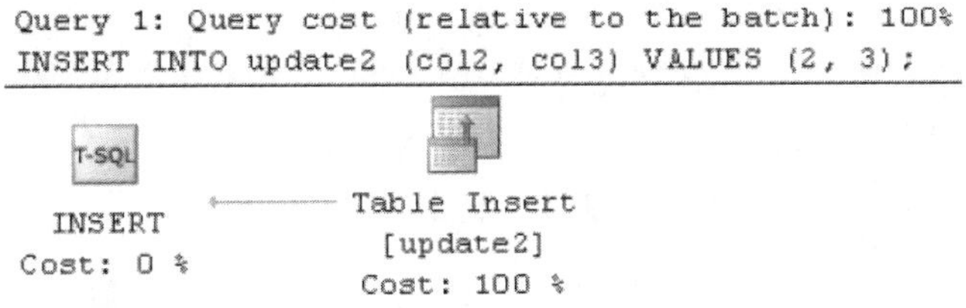

FIGURE 11-63 Simple *INSERT* query plan.

When the table is a heap (it has no clustered index), a special optimization occurs that can collapse the operations into a smaller form. This is called a *simple update* (the word *update* is used generically here to refer to insert, update, delete, and merge plans), and it's obviously faster. This single operator does all the work to insert into a heap, but it doesn't support every feature in Update.

Figure 11-64 shows how inserts work against tables with multiple indexes.

```
CREATE TABLE update3 (col1 INT, col2 INT, col3 INT);
CREATE INDEX i1 ON update3(col1);
CREATE INDEX i2 ON update3(col2);
CREATE INDEX i3 ON update3(col3);

INSERT INTO update3(col1, col2, col3) VALUES (1, 2, 3);
```

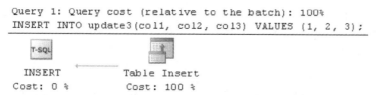

```
Query 1: Query cost (relative to the batch): 100%
INSERT INTO update3(col1, col2, col3) VALUES (1, 2, 3);
```

INSERT ← Table Insert
Cost: 0 %   Cost: 100 %

FIGURE 11-64 All-in-one *INSERT* query plan.

This query needs to update all the indexes because a new row has been created. However, Figure 11-64 shows that the plan has only the one operator. If you look at the properties for this operator in Management Studio, as shown in Figure 11-65, you can see that it actually updates all indexes in one operator. This is another one of the physical optimizations done to improve the performance of common update scenarios. This kind of insert is called an *all-in-one* or a *per-row* insert.

Object	[s1].[dbo].[update3], [s1].[dbo].[update3].[i1]
[1]	[s1].[dbo].[update3]
[2]	[s1].[dbo].[update3].[i1]
[3]	[s1].[dbo].[update3].[i2]
[4]	[s1].[dbo].[update3].[i3]

FIGURE 11-65 Multiple indexes updated by a single operator.

By using the same table, you can try an *UPDATE* command to update some, but not all, of the indexes. Figure 11-66 shows the resulting query plan.

```
UPDATE update3 SET col2=5, col3=5;
```

```
Query 1: Query cost (relative to the batch): 100%
UPDATE update3 SET col2=5, col3=5;
```

UPDATE ← Table Update ← Compute Scalar ← Compute Scalar ← Top ← Table Scan [update3]
Cost: 0 %   Cost: 90 %   Cost: 0 %   Cost: 0 %   Cost: 0 %   Cost: 10 %

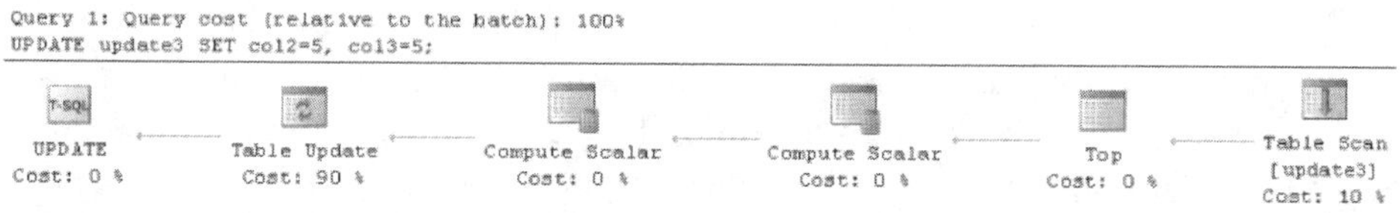

FIGURE 11-66 A query plan that modifies only some of the indexes on a table.

Now things are becoming a bit more complex. The query scans the heap in the Table Scan operator, performs the *ROWCOUNT Top (in versions before SQL Server 2012)*, performs two Compute Scalars, and then performs a Table Update. If you examine the properties for the Table Update, notice that it lists only indexes *i2* and *i3* because the Query Optimizer can statically determine that this command won't change *i1*. One of the Compute Scalars calculates the new values for the columns. The other is yet another physical optimization that helps compute whether each row needs to modify each and every index.

SQL Server contains logic to handle non-updating updates. In this case, the user calls for an update but actually submits the existing value for the row. The Query Optimizer can recognize this case and avoid some internal steps, such as logging changes, when a value is updated to the same value. Because a number of prepackaged SQL applications and tools allow users to retrieve a row, modify some columns, and then write a complete update for all columns back to the database (not just the columns that changed), this actually turned out to be a needed and useful way to speed up queries.

This optimization isn't always applied; SQL Server uses logic to speculate how likely and useful this optimization is, but it does reduce write traffic and log traffic in the cases when it applies.

Halloween Protection

Halloween Protection describes a feature of relational databases that's used to provide correctness in update plans. The need for the solution is best described by explaining what happens in a naïve implementation of an update plan. One simple way to perform an update is to have an operator that iterates through a B-tree index and updates each value that satisfies the filter. This works fine as long as the operator assigns a value to a constant or to a value that doesn't apply to the filter. However, if the query attempts more complex operations such as increasing each value by 10%, in some cases the iterator can see rows that have already been processed earlier in the scan because the previous update moved the row ahead of the cursor iterating through the B-tree.

Not every query needs to worry about this problem, but it is an issue for some shapes of query plans. The typical protection against this problem is to scan all the rows into a buffer, and then process the rows from the buffer. In SQL Server, this is usually implemented by using a spool or a Sort operator, each of which has certain guarantees about reading all input rows before producing output rows to the next operator in the query tree. SQL Server can also use a special form of the Compute Scalar operator to provide Halloween Protection (see *http://en.wikipedia.org/wiki/Halloween_Problem*) in certain limited cases, but the showplan has no public information to indicate that this is happening (other than an extra Compute Scalar being in the plan). In all cases, the copy protects against updating the same row twice.

Split/Sort/Collapse

SQL Server contains a physical optimization called *Split/Sort/Collapse*, which is used to make wide update plans more efficient. The feature examines all the change rows to be changed in a batch and determines the net effect that these changes would have on an index. Unnecessary changes are avoided, which can reduce the I/O requirements to complete the query. This change also allows a single linear pass to be made to apply changes to each index, which is more efficient than a series of random I/Os. Figure 11-67 shows the resulting query plan.

```
CREATE TABLE update5(col1 INT PRIMARY KEY);
INSERT INTO update5(col1) VALUES (1), (2), (3);
UPDATE update5 SET col1=col1+1;
```

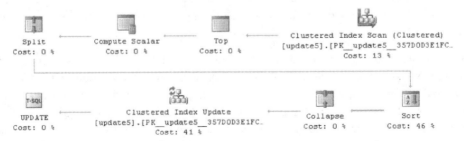

FIGURE 11-67 Split/Sort/Collapse *UPDATE* query plan.

This query is modifying a clustered index that has three rows with values 1, 2, and 3. After this query, you would expect the rows to have the values 2, 3, and 4. Rather than modify three rows, you can determine that you can just delete 1 and insert 4 to make the changes to this query. For this trivial example, you can avoid the modification of one row, but for larger tables, this savings can be substantial.

This optimization is implemented using an internal column called the *action column*. It contains a value to represent whether each row is an *INSERT, UPDATE, DELETE*, or *MERGE*. The action column is used by the Update operator to determine what change should be applied to the index. Although the showplan shows different names for this Update operator based on the submitted query, it's the same operator internally and is modified by the action column. Unfortunately, you can't see the values of this column because it's only a construct within the query processor.

The action column is also used by the query processor to help determine the net changes to be applied to an index. It's also used by the Split/Sort/Collapse logic to determine the next change to the index. Now walk through what happens in each step. Before the split, the row data is shown in Table 11-1.

TABLE 11-1 Pre-split update data representation

Action	Old Value	New Value
UPDATE	1	2
UPDATE	2	3
UPDATE	3	4

Split converts each *UPDATE* into one *DELETE* and one *INSERT*. Immediately after the split, the rows appear as shown in Table 11-2.

TABLE 11-2 Post-split data representation

Action	Value
DELETE	1
INSERT	2
DELETE	2
INSERT	3
DELETE	3
INSERT	4

The Sort sorts on (value, action), in which *DELETE* sorts before *INSERT*. After the sort, the rows appear as shown in Table 11-3.

TABLE 11-3 Post-sort data representation

Action	Value
DELETE	1
DELETE	2
INSERT	2
DELETE	3
INSERT	3
INSERT	4

The Collapse operator looks for (*DELETE, INSERT*) pairs for the same value and removes them. In this example, it replaces the *DELETE* and *INSERT* rows with *UPDATE* for the rows with the values 2 and 3. The *UPDATE* reduces the number of B-tree maintenance operations necessary, and the storage engine is written not to log anything for B-tree updates to the same value (locks are still taken, however, for correctness). Table 11-4 shows the final form of the rows, after the collapse.

TABLE 11-4 Post-collapse data representation

Action	Value
DELETE	1
UPDATE	2
UPDATE	3
INSERT	4

The result is the net change that needs to be made to the index. Technically, each index also contains a primary key reference or heap row identifier, and even the rows missing from Table 11-4 are actually updated to fix the reference to the heap or clustered index. Log traffic is still reduced from the regular update path, and the I/O ordering benefits are also gained.

Although the Split/Sort/Collapse logic is a performance optimization, it also helps avoid false failures when modifying a unique index (such as this primary key). If the original plan were to be executed without Split/Sort/Collapse, it would try to change the row with value 1 to 2. This would conflict with the existing row that has value 2 in the index. Although this could be avoided for this query by iterating backward over the rows, picking a single scan order to avoid this issue isn't always possible. Split/Sort/Collapse allows SQL Server to support queries such as this example without returning an error.

Merge

SQL Server contains a special type of update operation called *MERGE*. *MERGE* is a hybrid of the other update operations and can be used to perform conditional changes to a table. The business value of this operation is that it can collapse multiple T-SQL operations into a single query. This simplifies the code you have to write to modify tables, it improves performance, and it really helps operations against large tables whose size could make multistep operations effectively too slow to be useful.

Now that you've seen how the other update operations are handled, you might have figured out that *MERGE* actually isn't a difficult extension of the action column techniques used in the other operations. Like the other queries, the source data is scanned, filtered, and modified. However, in the case of *MERGE*, the set of rows to be changed is then joined with the target source to determine what should be done with each row. Based on this join, the action column for each row is modified to tell the *STREAM UPDATE* operation what to do with each row.

In Listing 11-12, an existing table is going to be updated with new data, some of which might already exist in the table. Therefore, *MERGE* is used to determine only the set of rows that are missing. Figure 11-69 shows the resulting *MERGE* query plan.

LISTING 11-12 A *MERGE* example

```
CREATE TABLE AnimalsInMyYard(sightingdate DATE, Animal NVARCHAR(200));
GO
INSERT INTO AnimalsInMyYard(sightingdate, Animal) VALUES ('2012-08-12', 'Deer');
INSERT INTO AnimalsInMyYard(sightingdate, Animal) VALUES ('2012-08-12', 'Hummingbird');
INSERT INTO AnimalsInMyYard(sightingdate, Animal) VALUES ('2012-08-13', 'Gecko');
GO
CREATE TABLE NewSightings(sightingdate DATE, Animal NVARCHAR(200));
GO
INSERT INTO NewSightings(sightingdate, Animal) VALUES ('2012-08-13', 'Gecko');
INSERT INTO NewSightings(sightingdate, Animal) VALUES ('2012-08-13', 'Robin');
INSERT INTO NewSightings(sightingdate, Animal) VALUES ('2012-08-13', 'Dog');
GO

-- insert values we have not yet seen - do nothing otherwise
MERGE AnimalsInMyYard A USING NewSightings N
    ON (A.sightingdate = N.sightingdate AND A.Animal = N.Animal)
WHEN NOT MATCHED
    THEN INSERT (sightingdate, Animal) VALUES (sightingdate, Animal);
```

Query 1: Query cost (relative to the batch): 100%
MERGE AnimalsInMyYard A USING NewSightings N ON (A.sightingdate = N.sightingdate AND
    A.Animal = N.Animal) WHEN NOT MATCHED THEN INSERT (sightingdate, Animal)
    VALUES (sightingdate, Animal);

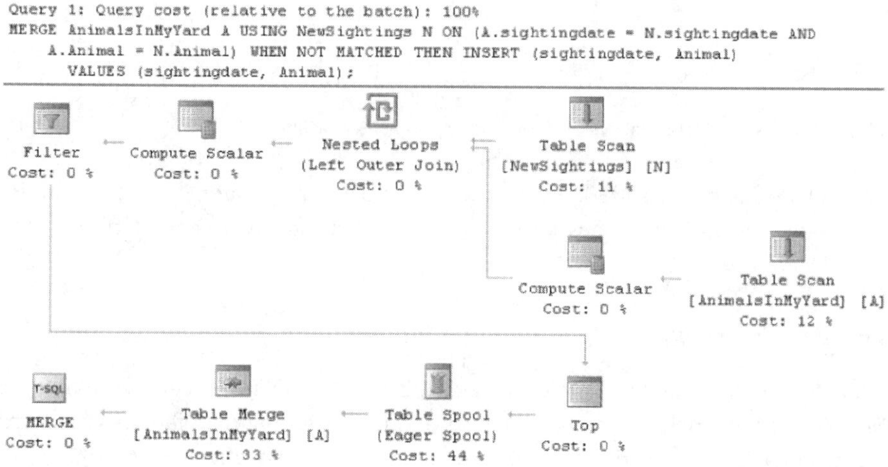

FIGURE 11-68 *MERGE* query plan.

Because *MERGE* plans tend to get a bit large, I'll split this one into pieces and discuss each portion of it. Figure 11-69 shows the first part of the plan.

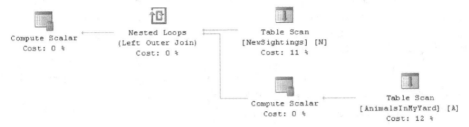

FIGURE 11-69 *MERGE* plan: initial join to find preexisting rows.

First, the source table *NewSightings* is read, and the query processor performs a probe into the target table *AnimalsInMyYard* to see whether the row is already there. The Compute Scalar underneath the left outer join exists merely to add a column that is 1 if the value was matched and, because of the nature of how left outer joins work, returns a value of NULL if no matching row matches the source table row. The Compute Scalar above the join generates the *Action* column:

```
[Action1008] = Scalar Operator(ForceOrder(CASE WHEN [TrgPrb1006] IS NOT NULL THEN NULL ELSE (4)
END))
```

In the upper half of this plan (see Figure 11-70), the filter eliminates rows that have a null action (Predicate: *[Action1008] IS NOT NULL*) because this *MERGE* statement only has one action (having multiple operations within a single *MERGE* statement is possible). The spool provides Halloween Protection, which means that it consumes all rows from its inputs before attempting to write values back into the *AnimalsInMyYard* table. Table *MERGE* is really just an Update operation, but the showplan output has been changed to avoid confusion.

FIGURE 11-70 *MERGE* plan: Update, Halloween Protection spool, and row filter.

Take care when deciding to use *MERGE*. Although it's a powerful operator, it's also easily misused. *MERGE* is best-suited for OLTP workloads with small queries that use a two-query pattern, like this:

Check for whether a row exists.

If it doesn't exist, *INSERT*.

Using a non-*MERGE* statement to write your *INSERT*, *UPDATE*, or *DELETE* query is often better. The readability benefits will help future maintenance, and the performance differences seen using *MERGE* are substantial in key scenarios but often don't manifest at all in others. You can test your own scenario to see whether it makes your workload improve.

Wide update plans

SQL Server also has special optimization logic to speed the execution of large batch changes to a table. If a query is changing a large percentage of a table, SQL Server can create a plan that avoids modifying each B-tree with many individual updates. Instead, it can generate a per-index plan that determines all the rows that need to be changed, sorts them into the order of the index, and then applies the changes in a single pass through the index. This approach can be noticeably more efficient than updating each row individually. These plans are called *per index* or *wide update* plans, as you see in their plan shape.

The following code demonstrates a wide update plan. Figure 11-71 shows the resulting plan.

```
CREATE TABLE dbo.update6(col1 INT PRIMARY KEY, col2 INT, col3 INT);
CREATE INDEX i1 ON update6(col2);
GO
CREATE VIEW v1 WITH SCHEMABINDING AS SELECT col1, col2 FROM dbo.update6;
GO
CREATE UNIQUE CLUSTERED INDEX i1 ON v1(col1);
UPDATE update6 SET col1=col1 + 1;
```

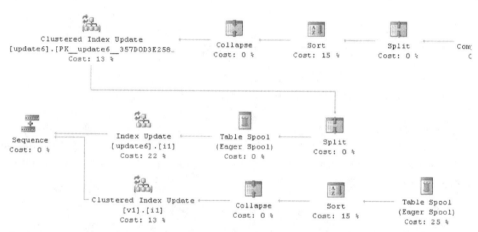

FIGURE 11-71 Wide update query plan (truncated).

Because this is complicated, the plan is split into smaller sections so that it can fit on this page and not be as overwhelming.

Figure 11-72 shows the first portion of the query plan, and it works just like the previous example: The set of net changes is applied to the clustered index. This set is a superset of all the nonclustered indexes because a clustered index includes all columns.

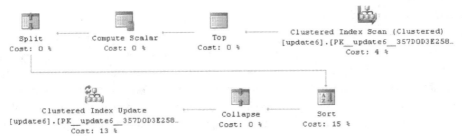

FIGURE 11-72 Clustered index update section of wide update plan.

Figure 11-73 shows the next part of the query plan. The section of the first branch above the clustered index update does numerous things. The spool in this plan is a common subexpression spool (described earlier in the chapter). This broadcasts rows to allow each index to use this data as input. The Sequence operator doesn't change or modify data; it's designed to process the first input first, the second input second, and so on. This drives the processing of the rows in a wide update plan. Finally, because this set of rows can have multiple clients that each perform Split/Sort/Collapse, SQL Server has an optimization to perform the split once instead of N times by doing it on the first branch.

FIGURE 11-73 Updated rows split and stored in a multiread spool.

Finally, the second branch reads the previous spooled and split rows, sorts them for this index, collapses them, and performs the net change to this index. Figure 11-74 shows this portion of the plan. If the query had additional indexes to update, they could be applied as additional branches in the query that would be processed in order.

FIGURE 11-74 One nonclustered index branch in a wide update plan.

Note Wide update plans are the most general and fully functional form of update plan in SQL Server, and architecturally any plan can be executed as a wide update plan in SQL Server. Some features, such as indexed views and query notifications, are updated using only wide update plans. Because some optimizations available in SQL Server are limited to more traditional feature sets, be aware that using some features forces SQL Server to use wide update plans. In most cases, this doesn't matter to your application, but it could matter in systems with small amounts of data that perform many updates.

Non-updating updates

UPDATE operations have a number of special optimizations to improve performance for common scenarios. For example, a common programming paradigm for updating a row against a database is as follows:

1. Run a *SELECT* query that retrieves a row from the database and copies the values into the client or mid-tier layer:

   ```
   SELECT col1, col2, col3, ... FROM Table WHERE primarykey = <constant>
   ```

2. Allow the user to update some columns selectively.

3. When the client is finished modifying the row, attempt to write the values back to the server:

   ```
   UPDATE Table SET col1=@p1, col2=@p2, col3=@p3 ... WHERE primarykey = constant AND col1 =
   originalcol1value AND col2 = originalcol2value AND col3 = originalcol3value AND ...
   ```

This pattern provides a functional but not optimal concurrency control without requiring the server to hold locks on the base table. Also, the database programmer generally implements only one *UPDATE* query that can handle any set of modified columns and just passes the original values in the *SET* list to avoid having to deal with many query plans.

SQL Server uses update logic that can determine the set of indexes to maintain based on the columns in the *SET* list of an *UPDATE*. By default, however, the pattern described here would cause SQL Server to update all indexes for each *UPDATE*, even if only one column value actually changed. To avoid this problem, SQL Server implements a feature called *Non-Updating Updates*, which can dynamically detect unchanged values and avoid updates to unchanged indexes. Although the query plan still references each index, it avoids the work to write unneeded values.

This optimization isn't performed in all cases; some logic is used to try to apply it to scenarios where it seems most likely to improve performance. This optimization is transparent to the user, although you can see it as additional filters in some query plans.

Sparse column updates

SQL Server provides a feature called *sparse columns* that supports creating more columns in a table than were previously supported, as well as creating rows that were technically greater than the size of a database page. The primary use case for the feature is flexible-schema systems in which users can create columns dynamically. Often these columns are mostly NULL but have some rows in which a value is defined. This pattern is also largely independent for each sparse column, meaning that a specific row potentially has a few but usually not many non-NULL sparse column values.

Sparse columns are stored in a complex column in a regular data row, as described in Chapter 8, "Special storage." When working with the sparse column data, SQL Server must interpret the complex columns to determine which columns actually have values. To modify sparse columns, rows are read, new values are computed, and then rows are written. The main difference is that sparse columns require a bit more work to read and modify.

Partitioned updates

Updating partitioned tables is somewhat more complicated than nonpartitioned equivalents. Instead of a single physical table (heap) or B-tree, the query processor has to handle one heap or B-tree *per partition*. It needs to figure out where each row belongs, and rows can move between partitions in some update plans. Also, each index can be partitioned using a separate partition function. Even indexed views can be partitioned, and they too can be partitioned differently than the other access paths associated with a table. Luckily, partitioned update plans in SQL Server are an extension of the update plan shapes already discussed in this chapter. So this section discusses only how those plans vary when using partitioning.

In the description of *SELECT* plans over partitioned tables earlier in this chapter, recall that the partitioning ID was represented within the query processor as a virtual leading column on every access method (heap or index). Partitioned table updates also use this representation, which makes the plans look a lot like the plans to update indexes. This leading column also appears in some of the other operators used in update plans, such as the Split/Sort/Collapse operators. The following examples demonstrate how partitioning fits into these plans.

The first example creates a partitioned table and then inserts a single row into it. Figure 11-75 shows the plan.

```
CREATE PARTITION FUNCTION pfinsert(INT) AS RANGE RIGHT FOR VALUES (100, 200, 300);
CREATE PARTITION SCHEME psinsert AS PARTITION pfinsert ALL TO ([PRIMARY]);
go
CREATE TABLE testinsert(ptncol INT, col2 INT) ON psinsert(ptncol);
go
INSERT INTO testinsert(ptncol, col2) VALUES (1, 2);
```

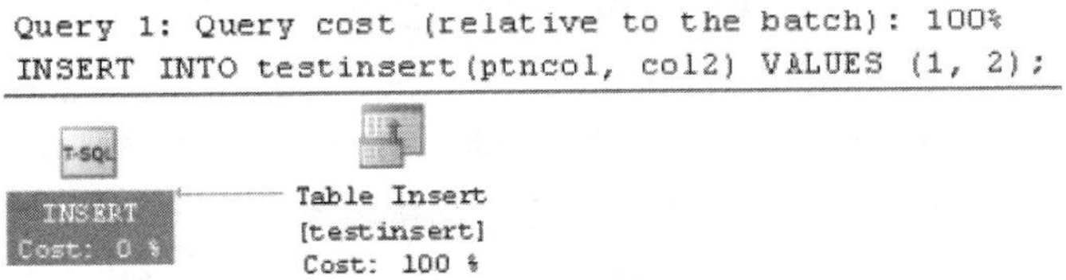

FIGURE 11-75 Partitioned insert: single partition.

Looking at the query plan, notice that this matches the behavior you would expect from a nonpartitioned table. It has a single operator that just inserts into the table. Internally, however, the Query Execution operator must determine which partition needs to be updated, load that partition, and set the appropriate value. By looking at the properties for the *INSERT* operator, you can see (in Figure 11-76) the partitioning-specific logic that makes this happen. First, *Expr1005* is computed to determine the target partition to use, and you can see the partition boundaries passed to an internal function called *RangePartitionNew*. In the *Predicate* section, the extra *Expr1005* computed value is used to set the *PtnId1001* column, which is the virtual partition ID column that's exposed in the system to support partitioning. The rest of the *Predicate* list supports setting values for the regular columns *ptncol* and *col2*.

⊟ **Misc**	
⊞ **Defined Values**	[Expr1005] = Scalar Operator(RangePartitionNew([@1],(1),(100),(200),(300)))
Description	Insert input rows into the table specified in Argument field.
Estimated CPU Cost	0.000001
Estimated I/O Cost	0.01
Estimated Number of Executi	1
Estimated Number of Rows	1
Estimated Operator Cost	0.0100022 (100%)
Estimated Rebinds	0
Estimated Rewinds	0
Estimated Row Size	9 B
Estimated Subtree Cost	0.0100022
Logical Operation	Insert
Node ID	0
⊞ **Object**	[s1].[dbo].[testinsert]
⊞ **Output List**	
Parallel	False
Partitioned	True
Physical Operation	Table Insert
Predicate	[s1].[dbo].[testinsert].[ptncol] = [@1],[s1].[dbo].[testinsert].[col2] = [@2],[PtnId1001] = RaiseIfNullInsert([Expr1005]

FIGURE 11-76 Partition selection computation in the query plan.

The query processor can load the partition necessary to modify each row dynamically. If you insert multiple rows in a single statement, you can see in Figure 11-77 how the query processor supports updating each row properly.

```
INSERT INTO testinsert(ptncol, col2) VALUES (5, 10),(105,25);
```

```
Query 1: Query cost (relative to the batch): 100%
INSERT INTO testinsert(ptncol, col2) VALUES (5, 10),(105,25);
```

```
  T-SQL                                                                                  
 INSERT  ←——  Table Insert  ←——  Compute Scalar  ←——     Top      ←——  Constant Scan
Cost: 0 %     [testinsert]          Cost: 0 %            Cost: 0 %         Cost: 0 %
              Cost: 100 %
```

FIGURE 11-77 Dynamic partition computation in insert plans.

This query attempts to insert two rows, and the query plan uses the Constant Scan operator to represent this. The Compute Scalar operator runs the partitioning function to determine the target partition of each row, as shown in Figure 11-78.

Defined Values	[Expr1007] = Scalar Operator(RangePartitionNew([Union1005],(1),(100),(200),(300)))

FIGURE 11-78 Range partitioning computation in showplan output.

Furthermore, the Table Insert operator uses this computed scalar (see Figure 11-79) and for each row changes to the right partition, if necessary.

⊟ Predicate	
⊟ ScalarOperator	Scalar Operator([s1].[dbo].[testinsert].[ptncol] = [Union1005],[s1].[dbo].[testinsert].[col2] = [Union1006],[PtnId100
⊞ Item	
ScalarString	[s1].[dbo].[testinsert].[ptncol] = [Union1005],[s1].[dbo].[testinsert].[col2] = [Union1006],[PtnId1001] = [Expr1007]

FIGURE 11-79 Using a range partition to determine insert target partition.

Note Compute Scalar exists in this two-row plan and not in the first example for reasons connected purely to implementation. These factors aren't necessary to understand the plans, nor do they materially affect the performance of the plans when they are run.

Changing partitions can be a somewhat expensive operation, especially when many of the rows in the table are being changed in a single statement. The Split/Sort/Collapse logic can also be used to reduce the number of partition switches that happen, improving runtime performance. In the following example, a large number of rows are inserted into the partitioned table, and the Query Optimizer chooses to sort on the virtual partition ID column before inserting to reduce the number of partition switches at run time. Figure 11-80 shows the Sort optimization in the query plan.

```
CREATE TABLE #nonptn(ptncol INT, col2 INT)
DECLARE @i int = 0
WHILE @i < 10000
BEGIN
INSERT INTO #nonptn(ptncol) VALUES (RAND()*1000)
SET @i+=1
END
GO
INSERT INTO testinsert SELECT * FROM #nonptn;
```

```
Query 1: Query cost (relative to the batch): 100%
INSERT INTO testinsert SELECT * FROM #nonptn;
```

INSERT Cost: 0 %	Table Insert [testinsert] Cost: 21 %	Sort Cost: 75 %	Top Cost: 0 %	Compute Scalar Cost: 0 %	Table Scan [#nonptn] Cost: 4 %

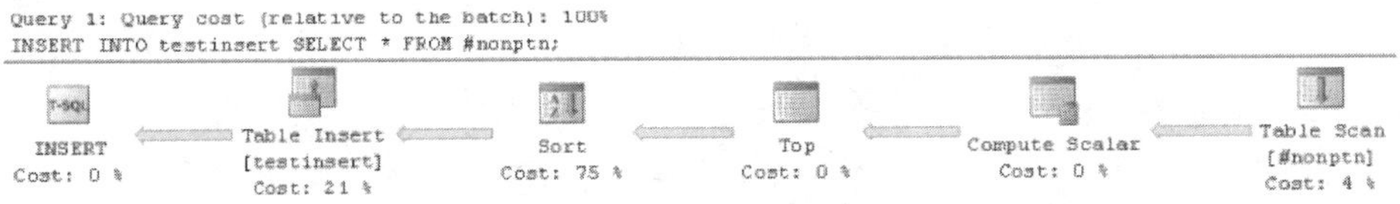

FIGURE 11-80 Sort optimization to reduce partition switching.

The sort has an ordering requirement, as shown in Figure 11-81, which is derived from the call to the partitioning function in the Compute Scalar earlier in the plan, just like the previous example.

⊞ Order By   Expr1009 Ascending

FIGURE 11-81 Ordering requirement for partitioned insert sort optimization.

Updates to partitioned tables are more complex because they can move rows. However, they follow the same principles as updates. The key property to understand is that the query processor must read each row, determine the change to that row, compute the target partition for that row, and then perform the change. This can include deleting the partition from one B-tree and inserting it into another. This matches closely with the Split/Sort/Collapse idea for batch updates, but for partitioned updates, it can happen even for smaller changes.

Locking

SQL Server contains a number of tricks and optimizations to improve the overall performance and throughput of updates within the system. Whereas much of the Query Optimizer is agnostic to locking, several targeted features and locking modes in updates improve concurrency (and avoid deadlock errors). One special locking mode is called a U (for update) lock. This special lock type is compatible with other S (shared) locks but incompatible with other U locks. In many of the plan shapes used in Update queries, SQL Server has two different operators accessing the same access method. The first is the source table, and it is only reading. The second is the update itself. If only a shared (S) lock were taken in the read operator, multiple users could run queries at the same time, could both acquire S locks for a row, and then could deadlock because neither could upgrade the lock to an exclusive (X) lock when the update operator later saw the row. To prevent this, the U lock is compatible with other S locks but not with other U locks. This prevents other potential writers from reading a row, which then avoids the deadlock.

The following code demonstrates how to examine the locking behavior of an update query plan. Figure 11-82 shows the query plan used in this example, and Figure 11-83 shows the locking output from *sp_lock*.

```
CREATE TABLE lock(col1 INT, col2 INT);
CREATE INDEX i2 ON lock(col2);
INSERT INTO lock (col1, col2) VALUES (1, 2);
INSERT INTO lock (col1, col2) VALUES (10, 3);

SET TRANSACTION ISOLATION LEVEL REPEATABLE READ;
BEGIN TRANSACTION;
UPDATE lock SET col1 = 5 WHERE col1 > 5;
EXEC sp_lock;
ROLLBACK;
```

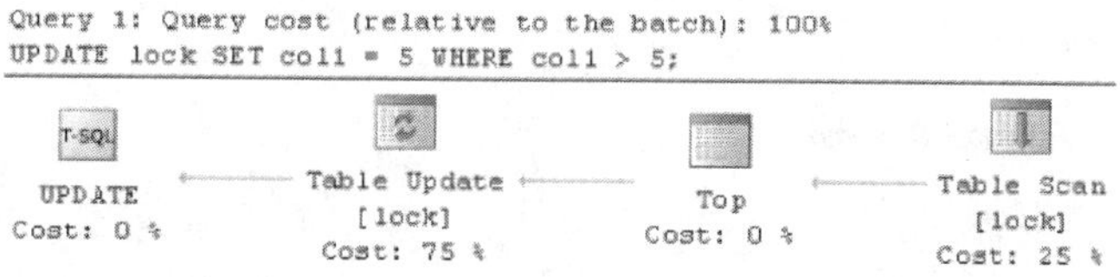

```
Query 1: Query cost (relative to the batch): 100%
UPDATE lock SET col1 = 5 WHERE col1 > 5;
```

T-SQL		Table Update			Top			Table Scan	
UPDATE		[lock]						[lock]	
Cost: 0 %		Cost: 75 %			Cost: 0 %			Cost: 25 %	

FIGURE 11-82 The update plan used in the locking example.

	spid	dbid	ObjId	IndId	Type	Resource	Mode	Status
1	52	21	0	0	DB		S	GRANT
2	52	1	1131151075	0	TAB		IS	GRANT
3	52	21	693577509	0	PAG	1:75676	IX	GRANT
4	52	21	693577509	0	RID	1:75676:1	X	GRANT
5	52	21	693577509	0	TAB		IX	GRANT

FIGURE 11-83 The *sp_lock* output for the update plan.

Using a higher isolation mode with a user-controlled (non-auto-commit) transaction allows you to examine the final locking state of each object in the query. In this case, you can see that the row (*Resource 1:75676:1*) was locked with an X lock. This lock started as a U lock and was promoted to an X lock by the *UPDATE*.

You can run a slightly different query that shows that the locks vary based on the query plan selected. Figure 11-84 shows a seek-based update plan. In the second example, the U lock is taken by the nonclustered index, whereas the base table contains the X lock. So, this U lock protection works only when going through the same access paths because it's taken on the first access path in the query plan. Figure 11-85 shows the locking behavior of this query.

```
BEGIN TRANSACTION;
UPDATE lock SET col1 = 5 WHERE col2 > 2;
EXEC sp_lock;
```

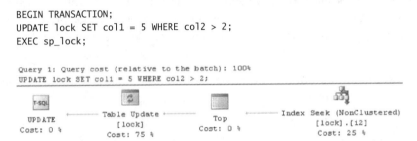

FIGURE 11-84 Locking behavior of an update plan with a seek.

	spid	dbid	ObjId	IndId	Type	Resource	Mode	Status
1	52	21	0	0	DB		S	GRANT
2	52	21	693577509	2	KEY	(a0004dc87aeb)	U	GRANT
3	52	1	1131151075	0	TAB		IS	GRANT
4	52	21	693577509	2	PAG	1:75678	IU	GRANT
5	52	21	693577509	0	PAG	1:75676	IX	GRANT
6	52	21	693577509	0	RID	1:75676:1	X	GRANT
7	52	21	693577509	0	TAB		IX	GRANT

FIGURE 11-85 The *sp_lock* output for a seek-based update plan.

Partition-level lock escalation

Locking behavior usually isn't the domain of the Query Optimizer. Although the Query Optimizer does try to generate plans that minimize locking conflicts, it's largely agnostic to the locking interactions of plans. The Query Optimizer uses a lot of logic to implement partitioning, including logic to prune unnecessary partitions from query plans so that they aren't touched. One great addition in the SQL Server 2008 product is *partition–level lock escalation*, which allows the database to avoid lock escalation to the table-level for partitioned tables. When combined with pruning, this feature provides a powerful way to improve application concurrency, especially when queries over large, partitioned tables can take a long time to execute. The following command can enable the functionality:

```
ALTER TABLE TableName SET (LOCK_ESCALATION = AUTO);
```

Chapter 13, "Transactions and concurrency," discusses locking in detail.

Distributed query

SQL Server includes a feature called *Distributed Query*, which accesses data on different SQL Server instances, other database sources, and non-database tabular data such as Microsoft Office Excel files or comma-separated text files. Distributed Query is based on the OLE DB interfaces, and most OLE DB providers are feature-rich enough to be used by the Distributed Query feature. Because multiple sources can be referenced within a single query, it's an effective mechanism to interact with data from multiple sources without writing a lot of special-case code.

Distributed Query supports several distinct use cases.

- You can use Distributed Query to move data from one source to another. Although it's not a complete ETL tool like SQL Server Integration Services, it's often a very easy way to copy a table from one server instance to another. For example, if a company's financial reporting group wanted a copy of the sales figures for each month, you could write a query to copy the data from the SQL Server instance servicing the Sales team to another instance in the Financial Reporting group.

- You can use Distributed Query to integrate nontraditional sources into a SQL Server query. Because non-database data such as Active Directory Domain Services, Microsoft Exchange Server, and a number of third-party sources have OLE DB providers, you can write queries to gather information from those sources and to then use the power of the SQL language to ask rich questions of that data that might not be supported by the source of that data.

- You can use Distributed Query for reporting. Because multiple sources can be queried in a single query, you can use Distributed Query to gather data into a single source and generate reports (which can be surfaced through Reporting Services, if desired).

- You can use Distributed Query for scale-out scenarios. SQL Server supports a special *UNION ALL* view called a *Distributed Partitioned View (DPV)*. This view stitches together distinct portions of a single range, each stored on a different SQL Server instance. Exceptionally large tables can be stored on different servers, and queries can be directed to access only the subset necessary to satisfy a particular query. The Distributed Query feature covers a number of scenarios and can help make solving those scenarios much easier.

Distributed Query is implemented within the Query Optimizer's plan-searching framework. With the exception of pass-through queries, which aren't modified during optimization, distributed queries initially are represented by using the same operators as regular queries. Each base table represented in the Query Optimizer tree contains metadata collected from the remote source, using OLE DB metadata interfaces such as OLE DB schema rowsets. The information collected is very similar to the information that the query processor collects for local tables, including column data, index data, and statistics.

One additional piece of collected information includes data about what SQL grammar constructs the remote source supports, which are used later in optimization. After metadata is collected, the Query Optimizer derives special property data for each operator that manipulates remote information. This property determines whether generating a SQL statement is possible to represent the whole query subtree that can be sent directly to the remote data source. Some operators, such as Filter and Project, can be remoted easily; others can be performed only locally, such as the streaming table-valued function operator used to implement portions of the XQuery feature in SQL Server.

SQL Server performs exploration rules to transform query trees into forms that might allow the server to remote larger trees. For example, SQL Server attempts to group all remote tables from the same source together in a single subtree and splits aggregates into local forms that can be remoted. During this process, some of the more advanced rules in SQL Server are disabled if they are known to generate alternatives that prevent subtree remoting. Although SQL Server doesn't maintain specific costing models for each remote source, the feature is designed to remote large subtrees to that source in the hopes of moving the least amount of data between servers. This usually provides a close-to-optimal query plan.

This example creates a linked server to point to a remote SQL Server instance. Then, it uses the four-part name syntax to generate a query that can be completely remoted to the remote source (see Figure 11-86).

```
EXEC sp_addlinkedserver 'remote', N'SQL Server';
go
SELECT * FROM remote.Northwind.dbo.customers WHERE ContactName = 'Marie Bertrand';
```

FIGURE 11-86 A fully remoted Distributed Query.

As you can see, this relatively simple query was essentially completely remoted by the Query Optimizer. The properties information for the Remote Query node contains the query text that's executed on the remote server. The results are brought back to the local server and returned to the user.

The generated query, shown here, is somewhat more verbose than the text submitted originally, but this is necessary to ensure that the semantics of the remoted query match the local query text exactly:

```
SELECT "Tbl1002"."CustomerID" "Col1004","Tbl1002"."CompanyName" "Col1005",
"Tbl1002"."ContactName" "Col1006","Tbl1002"."ContactTitle" "Col1007","Tbl1002"."Address"
"Col1008","Tbl1002"."City" "Col1009","Tbl1002"."Region" "Col1010","Tbl1002".
"PostalCode" "Col1011","Tbl1002"."Country" "Col1012","Tbl1002"."Phone" "Col1013","Tbl1002"."Fax"
"Col1014" FROM "Northwind"."dbo"."customers" "Tbl1002" WHERE "Tbl1002"."ContactName"=N'Marie
Bertrand';
```

Because the OLE DB model has a rich, cursor-based update model, using SQL Server to update remote data sources is possible via regular *UPDATE* statements. These plans look identical to the local plans discussed in this chapter, except that the top-level Update operation is specific to the remote source. Because the storage engine model in SQL Server is originally based on the OLE DB interfaces, the mechanisms for performing local and remote updates are actually very similar. When a whole update query can be remoted—because the property information for every operator determines that the remote source can support an *UPDATE* statement that's semantically equivalent to performing the operation locally through the exposed OLE DB interfaces—SQL Server can and will generate complete remote *INSERT*, *UPDATE*, and *DELETE* statements to be performed on the remote server. You should examine any query that you think can be completely remoted to ensure that it actually can be. In some cases, a specific grammar construct or intrinsic function that's unnecessary in the query blocks it from being completely remoted.

The Distributed Query feature, introduced in SQL Server 7.0, has some limitations that you should consider when designing scenarios that use it.

- The feature relies on the remote providers to supply very detailed cardinality and statistical information to SQL Server so that it can use this knowledge to compare different query plans. Because most OLE DB providers don't provide much statistical information, this can limit the quality of query plans generated by the Query Optimizer. Also, because Microsoft isn't actively extending OLE DB, some providers aren't actively maintained.

- Not every feature in SQL Server is supported via the remote query mechanism, such as some XML and UDT-based functionality. SQL Server 2012 doesn't have a native mechanism to support querying managed adaptors written for the CLR runtime.

- The costing model used within SQL Server is good for general use but sometimes generates a plan that's substantially slower than optimal. Unfortunately, the impact of not remoting a query in the Distributed Query feature is larger than in the local case because more work needs to be done to move rows from a remote source. Care should be taken when using the feature to test out the functionality before you put it into production. Pregenerating pass-through queries for common, expensive queries might be useful to ensure they are always remoted properly.

Extended indexes

This chapter, in earlier versions, used to contain an overview of non–B-tree indexes supported in SQL Server, including full-text, XML, and spatial indexes. Chapter 9, "Special indexes," is now dedicated to providing in-depth information on these topics.

Plan hinting

A lot of misinformation exists about query hints, and often the misuse of hints can cause the creation of global policies for or against the use of hints in queries. One goal of this chapter is to give DBAs and developers the tools they need to have a different kind of conversation about the design, implementation, and maintenance of SQL Server applications. This section explains query hints and when to use them.

Earlier, this chapter discussed some of the problems that the engineering team faced with Query Optimizer. The complexity of some algorithms involved in optimizing SQL queries is high enough that exploring every possible query plan for every query that can be sent to the system is impossible.

Latency restrictions in statistics gathering and mathematical modeling issues in cardinality estimation also place some limits on the powers of the Query Optimizer, considering the current computational powers of processors today. The reality is that the Query Optimizer can't generate a perfect plan for some queries.

That being said, the Query Optimizer actually does an amazing job on most queries. Many years of very smart thinking have gone into the development of this component, and the result is a system that almost always finds a very good query plan very quickly. This is accomplished through a number of smart algorithms, heuristics, and an understanding of common scenarios. Each release of the product gets better and can handle more and more scenarios.

When people ask me about hints, I first ask them about their application. Many people don't realize that the application's design has a huge impact on whether hints are appropriate or necessary. If your database schema has a classic, third-normal form set of data tables and your queries are all written using an understanding of the American National Standards Institute (ANSI) SQL grammar, SQL Server likely will do a reasonable job on your query without any modification. As you push the system and stress the design in different directions, you can find areas where the algorithms and heuristics in the product start not working as well. For example, if you have huge variations in data distribution or have an application that relies on the statistical correlation of column values to select a great plan, sometimes you might not get a join order that's near optimal for your query. So before you consider hints, make sure that you can understand how your application is designed, specifically around what kinds of things make your application not look like a common database application.

If you have identified a poorly performing query that's important to your application and have an idea why the Query Optimizer could be having trouble, you can consider whether a hint will help this application. I usually tell people not to use a hint unless they have a good reason, which means that the standard behavior of the system is unacceptable for your business and a better plan choice is acceptable. So, if you know that a particular join order or index selection yields deadlocks with the other queries in your system, you should consider using a hint; locking isn't a factor in how the Query Optimizer optimizes queries, and each query is effectively optimized independently of the others in the system.

Now, some database development teams can impose rules such as "No hints," or "Always force this index on this table when doing a *SELECT*." This doesn't mean that they are wrong—often, these kinds of rules exist for very good reasons. I urge you to read through this chapter and make sure that you have a conversation with your DBA about the reasons for each rule. When you are building a new feature and changing a database application, using a hint or altering these development practices might be completely appropriate. The goal of this section is to help you understand the purpose of each hint, with the hope that this lets you see the situations when it might be appropriate (or inappropriate) to use a hint.

Query and table hints are, in almost all cases, requirements given by the query author to the Query Optimizer when generating a query plan. So, if a hint can't be satisfied, the Query Optimizer actually returns an error and doesn't return a plan at all. Locking hints are an exception—these are sometimes ignored to preserve the correctness of data manipulation operations necessary for the system to work properly. The name is somewhat misleading, but this behavior allows you to modify the query and know that you had an impact on the query generation process.

This section describes how most of the query or table hints fit within the context of the Query Optimizer's architecture, including situations where it might be appropriate to use hints.

Debugging plan issues

Determining when to use a hint requires an understanding of the workings of the Query Optimizer and how it might not be making a correct decision, and then an understanding of how the hint might change the plan generation process to address the problem. For more than half of the problems Microsoft typically sees in support calls about query plans, issues with incorrect cardinality estimates are the primary cause of a poor plan choice. In other words, a better cardinality estimate yields an acceptable plan choice. You should research cardinality issues first when you have concerns about plan quality because such issues are the most common.

In other cases, more complex issues around costing, physical data layout, lock escalation, memory contention, or other issues can be factors in performance degradation. This section explains how to identify cardinality estimation errors and then use hints to correct poor plan choices because these are usually something that can be fixed without buying new hardware or otherwise altering the host machine.

The primary tool to identify cardinality estimation errors is the statistics profile output in SQL Server. When enabled, this mode generates the *actual* cardinalities for each query operator in the plan. These can be compared against the Query Optimizer's estimated cardinalities to find any differences. Because cardinality estimation is performed from the bottom of the tree upward (right to left in the showplan's graphical display), errors propagate. Usually, the location of the lowest error indicates where to consider hints.

Other tools exist to track down performance issues with query plans. Using *SET STATISTICS TIME ON* is a good way to determine runtime information for a query. SQL Profiler is a great tool for tracking deadlocks and other system-wide issues that can be captured by tracing. *DBCC MEMORYSTATUS* is an excellent tool to find out what components in the system are causing memory pressure within SQL Server. Most of these tools fall outside the scope of this chapter, although they can be helpful for some plan issues.

Figure 11-87 shows a query run against one of the catalog views to see how each operator's estimated and actual cardinalities match up.

```
SET STATISTICS PROFILE ON;
SELECT * FROM sys.objects;
```

	Rows	Executes	StmtText	EstimateRows	EstimateExecutions
1	91	1	SELECT * FROM sys.objects;	91	NULL
2	91	1	|-Nested Loops(Left Outer Join, OUTER REFEREN...	91	1
3	91	1	|-Nested Loops(Left Outer Join, OUTER REFER...	91	1
4	91	1	| |-Filter(WHERE:(has_access('CO',[s1].[sys].[sy...	91	1
5	0	0	| | |-Compute Scalar(DEFINE:([Expr1006]=CO...	91	1
6	91	1	| | |-Clustered Index Scan(OBJECT:([s1].[sy...	91	1
7	0	91	| |-Clustered Index Seek(OBJECT:([s1].[sys].[sys...	1	91
8	91	91	|-Clustered Index Seek(OBJECT:([mssqlsystemres...	1	91

FIGURE 11-87 Statistics profile output.

> **Note** The *EstimateRows* and *EstimateExecutions* columns have been moved from the actual output order for display in Figure 11-87. Although the estimation for this query is perfect, estimates commonly vary from the actual cardinalities, especially as queries become more complex. Usually, you want them to be close enough that the plan choice won't change, which is almost always less than an order of magnitude off by the top of the tree. Also, note that the *EstimateRows* number is the average per execution, whereas *Rows* is merely total rows. You can divide *Rows* by *Executes* to get the numbers to be comparable.

Looking at the statistics profile output to find an error can help identify where the Query Optimizer has used bad information to make a decision. Usually, updating statistics with fullscan can help isolate whether this is an issue with out-of-date or undersampled statistics. If the Query Optimizer makes a poor decision even with up-to-date statistics, this might mean that the Query Optimizer has an out-of-model condition. For example, a strong data correlation between two columns in a query can cause errors in the cardinalities seen in the query. When an out-of-model condition is identified as being the cause of a poor plan choice, hints are the mechanism to correct the plan choice and to use a better query plan.

{HASH | ORDER} GROUP

SQL Server has two possible implementations for *GROUP BY* (and *DISTINCT*).

- It can be implemented by sorting the rows and then grouping adjacent rows with the same grouping values.

- It can hash each group into a different memory location.

When one of these options is specified, it's implemented by turning off the implementation rule for the other physical operator. This applies to all *GROUP BY* operations within a query, including those from views within the query.

Many data warehouse queries have a common pattern of a number of joins followed by an aggregate operation. If the estimates for the number of rows returned in the joins section are in error, the estimated size for the aggregate operation can be substantially incorrect. If it's underestimated, a sort and a stream aggregate can be chosen. Because memory is allocated to each operator based on the estimated cardinality estimates, an underestimation could cause the sort to spill to disk. In a case like this, hinting a hash algorithm might be a good option. Similarly, if memory is scarce or more distinct grouping values are available than expected, perhaps using a stream aggregate would be more appropriate. This hint is a good way to affect system performance, especially in larger queries and in situations when many queries are being run at once on a system.

{MERGE | HASH | CONCAT} UNION

Many people incorrectly use *UNION* in queries when they likely want to use *UNION ALL*, perhaps because it's the shorter command. *UNION ALL* is a faster operation, in general because it takes rows from each input and simply returns them all. *UNION* must compare rows from each side and ensure that no duplicates are returned. Essentially, *UNION* performs a *UNION ALL* and then a *GROUP BY* operation over all output columns. In some cases, the Query Optimizer can determine that the output columns contain a key that's unique over both inputs and can convert the *UNION* to a *UNION ALL*, but in general, making sure that you're asking the right query is worthwhile. These three hints apply only to *UNION*.

Now, assuming that you have the right operation, you can pick from among three join patterns, and these hints let you specify which one to use. This example shows the *MERGE UNION* hint:

```
CREATE TABLE t1 (col1 INT);
CREATE TABLE t2 (col1 INT);
go
INSERT INTO t1(col1) VALUES (1), (2);
INSERT INTO t2(col1) VALUES (1);

SELECT * FROM t1
UNION
SELECT * FROM t2
OPTION (MERGE UNION);
```

As you can see, each hint forces a different query plan pattern.

- With common input sizes, *MERGE UNION* is useful.

- *CONCAT UNION* is best at low-cardinality plans (one sort).

- *HASH UNION* works best when a small input can be used to make a hash table against which the other inputs can be compared.

UNION hinting is done for roughly the same reasons as *GROUP BY* hinting. Both operations are commonly used near the top of a query definition, and they have the potential to suffer if an error occurs in cardinality estimation in a query with many joins. Typically, one either hints to the *HASH* operator to address cardinality underestimation or hints to the *CONCAT* operator to address overestimation.

FORCE ORDER, {LOOP | MERGE | HASH} JOIN

Join order and algorithm hints are common techniques to fix poor plan choices. When estimating the number of rows that qualify a join, the best algorithm depends on factors such as the cardinality of the inputs, the histograms over those inputs (which are used to make estimates about how many rows qualify the join condition), the available memory to store data in memory such as hash tables, and what indexes are available (which can speed up loop join scenarios). If the cardinality or histograms aren't representative of the input, a poor join order or algorithm can result. Also, correlations in data across joins can be extremely difficult to model with current technologies; even filtered statistics work only within a single table.

> **Tip** If the statistics profile output demonstrates that the cardinality estimates were substantially incorrect, the join order can be forced by rewriting the query into the order you want to see for the tables in the output plan. This modifies how the Query Optimizer sets the initial join order and then disables rules that reorder joins. When the new query is hinted, you should time it to ensure that the plan is faster than the original. Also, as your data changes, you need to reexamine these hints regularly to make sure that the plan you have forced is still appropriate; you are essentially saying "I know better than the Query Optimizer," which is the equivalent of performing all the maintenance on your own car.

Places where I've seen these hints be appropriate in the past are as follows.

- Small, OLTP-like queries where locking is a concern.

- Larger data-warehouse systems with many joins, complex data correlations, and enough of a fixed query pattern that you can reason about the join order in ways that make sense for all queries. For example, "I am happy if I access dimension tables in this order first, then the fact table, and everything is a hash join."

- Systems that extend beyond traditional relational application design and use some engine features often enough to change query performance materially. Examples might include using SQL as a document store with Full-Text or XQuery components that are mixed with traditional relational components or using Distributed Queries against a remote provider that doesn't surface statistical information to the SQL Server query processor.

Unfortunately, no semi-join–specific implementation hints are exposed in SQL Server 2012, although they can be indirectly affected by the other join hints.

INDEX=<indexname> | <indexid>

The *INDEX=<indexname>* | *<indexid>* hint has been in SQL Server for many releases and is very effective in forcing the Query Optimizer to use a specific index when compiling a plan. The primary scenario where this is interesting is in an OLTP application where you want to force a plan to avoid scans. Remember that the Query Optimizer tries to generate a plan using only this index first, but it also adds joins to additional indexes for a table if the index you have forced isn't covering for the query (meaning that the query uses only columns contained in the index key, the table's primary key, or listed as an *INCLUDED* column in the referenced index). You would generally use a query filter predicate to generate a seek against the index, but this hint is also valid for index scans if you use indexes to narrow row widths to improve query execution time. A second scenario where this would be useful is in a plan developed on one server for use on another, such as a test to deployment server or an independent software vendor (ISV) who creates a plan for an application and then ships this application to customers to deploy on their own SQL Server instance.

FORCESEEK

This hint was added in SQL Server 2008 and has since been extended. It tells the Query Optimizer that it needs to generate a seek predicate when using an index. In a few cases, the Query Optimizer can determine that an index scan is better than a seek when compiling the query. For example, if a query is compiled while the table is almost empty, the storage engine can store all the existing rows in one page in an index. In this case, a scan is faster than a seek in terms of I/O because the storage engine supports scanning from the leaf nodes of a B-tree, which would avoid one extra page of I/O. This condition might be ephemeral, given that newly created tables are often populated soon afterward. The hint is effective in avoiding such a scenario if you know that perhaps the table won't have enough rows to trigger a recompile or that the performance impact of this condition would be detrimental enough to the system to warrant the hint.

Earlier versions of this hint semantically meant "seek on the first column of the index." This precluded some scenarios in which seeking on multiple columns was advantageous. In SQL Server 2012, you also can specify more than one column to direct the Query Optimizer to try to generate a plan that forces seek operations that include multiple columns. The details of this are explained at *http://msdn.microsoft.com/en-us/library/ms187373(v=SQL.110).aspx*.

The primary scenario where this hint is interesting is to avoid locks in OLTP applications. This hint precludes an index scan, so it can be effective if you have a high-scale OLTP application where locking is a concern in scaling and concurrency. The hint avoids the possibility of the plan taking more locks than desired. The Query Optimizer doesn't explicitly reason about locking in plan selection; it doesn't prefer a plan that has fewer locks, but it might prefer a plan that it thinks will perform more quickly that also happens to take fewer locks. Be sure to hint high-scale applications only when necessary, especially for this hint because a poor hint can cause the system to behave substantially worse than an unhinted plan.

FAST <number_rows>

The Query Optimizer assumes that the user will read every row produced by a query. Although this is often true, some user scenarios, such as manually paging through results, don't follow this pattern; in these cases, the client reads some small number of rows and then closes the query result. Often a similar query is submitted in the near future to retrieve another batch of rows from the server. In the costing component, this assumption affects the plan choice. For example, hash joins are more efficient for larger result sets but have a higher startup cost (to build a hash table for one side of a join). Nested loops joins have no startup cost but a somewhat higher per-row cost. So, when a client wants only a few rows but doesn't specify a query that returns only a few rows, the latency of the first row can be slower because of the startup costs for stop-and-go operators such as hash joins, spools, and sorts.

The *FAST <number_rows>* hint supplies the costing infrastructure with a hint from the user about how many rows the user will want to read from a query. Internally, this is called a *row goal*, which simply provides an input into the costing formulas to help specify what point on the costing function is appropriate for the user's query.

The *TOP()* syntax in SQL Server also introduces a row goal. If you supply *TOP(@param)*, the Query Optimizer might not have a good value to sniff from the T-SQL context. In this scenario, you would want to use the *OPTIMIZE FOR* hint (described later in this section).

MAXDOP <N>

MAXDOP stands for maximum degree of parallelism, which describes the preferred degree of fan-out to be used when this query is run (in SKUs that support parallel query plans). For expensive queries, the Query Optimizer attempts to use multiple threads to reduce a query's runtime. This means that within the costing functions, some portions of the costs of a query are divided over multiple processor cores, reducing the overall cost compared to an otherwise identical serial plan. Very complex queries can actually have multiple zones of parallelism, meaning that each zone can have up to *MAXDOP* threads assigned to it during execution.

Large queries can consume a nontrivial fraction of the resources available to the system. A parallel query can consume memory and threads, blocking other queries that want to begin execution. In some cases, reducing the degree of parallelism for one or more queries is beneficial to the overall health of the system to lower the resources required to run a long-running query. This helps workloads that don't use the resource governor to manage resources. Often, a server that services mixed workloads would be a good candidate for considering this hint, when needed.

OPTIMIZE FOR

The Query Optimizer uses scalar values within the query text to help estimate the cardinality for each query operator. This ultimately helps choose the lowest-cost plan because cardinality is a major input into the costing functions. Parameterized queries can make this process more difficult because parameters can change from one execution to the next. Considering that SQL Server also automatically parameterizes queries, this design choice affects more queries than you would expect. When estimating cardinality for parameterized queries, the Query Optimizer usually uses a less accurate estimate of the average number of distinct values in the column or sniffs the parameter value from the context—usually only on recompile, unfortunately.

This sniffed value is used for cardinality estimation and plan selection, but it's not used to simplify the query or otherwise depend on the specific parameter value. So parameter sniffing can help pick a plan that's good for a specific case. Because most data sets have nonuniform column distributions, the value sniffed can affect the runtime of the query plan. If a value representing the common distribution is picked, this might work very well in the average case and less optimally in the outlier case (a value with substantially more instances than the average case). If the outlier is used to sniff the value, the plan picked might perform noticeably worse than it would have if the average case value had been sniffed. This can be a problem because of the plan-caching policy in SQL Server; a parameterized query is kept in the cache, even though the values change from execution to execution. When a recompile happens, only the information from that specific context is used to recompile.

The *OPTIMIZE FOR* hint allows the query author to specify the actual values to use during compilation. This can be used to tell the Query Optimizer, "I expect to see this common value at runtime," which can provide more plan predictability on parameterized queries. This hint works for both the initial compilation and for recompiles. Although specifying a common value is usually the best approach, you should test out this hint to ensure that it gives the desired behavior.

Listing 11-13 shows the *OPTIMIZE FOR* hint used to force the query plan to account for an average value in the optimization of the query. Notice that when the value of 5000 is used to compile the query (as shown in Figure 11-88), a different index is picked than when it's not (as shown in Figure 11-89) because 5000 is a very common value and is not as selective as the predicate on *col2*. Parameter values can cause index changes, join order changes, and other more complex changes to your query plan: testing forced parameters is highly recommended.

LISTING 11-13 Parameter sniffing example

```
CREATE TABLE param1(col1 INT, col2 INT);
go
SET NOCOUNT ON;
BEGIN TRANSACTION;
DECLARE @a INT=0;
WHILE @a < 5000
BEGIN
INSERT INTO param1(col1, col2) VALUES (@a, @a);
SET @a+=1;
END;
WHILE @a < 10000
BEGIN
INSERT INTO param1(col1, col2) VALUES (5000, @a);
SET @a+=1;
END;
COMMIT TRANSACTION;
go
CREATE INDEX i1 ON param1(col1);
go
CREATE INDEX i2 ON param1(col2);
go
DECLARE @b INT;
DECLARE @c INT;
SELECT * FROM param1 WHERE col1=@b AND col2=@c;
```

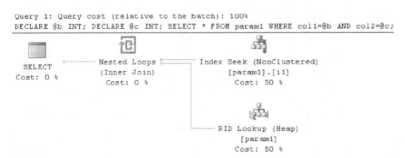

FIGURE 11-88 Sniffed parameters using *i2*.

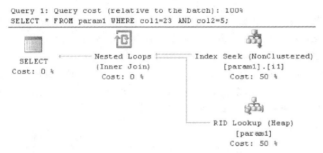

FIGURE 11-89 Non-sniffed parameters using index *i1*.

```
DECLARE @b INT;
DECLARE @c INT;
SELECT * FROM param1 WHERE col1=@b AND col2=@c option (optimize for (@b=5000))
```

Note These examples demonstrate only that the plans change, not that these two plans perform differently. This technique can be used on arbitrarily complex queries to hint plans.

Using the *OPTIMIZE FOR* hint instructs the Query Optimizer to use a known common value when generating the plan so that it works for a wide range of parameter values.

PARAMETERIZATION {SIMPLE | FORCED}

The *SIMPLE* parameterization model has existed in SQL Server for many releases. It corresponds to the concept of the trivial plan explained earlier in this chapter.

FORCED parameterization always replaces most literals in the query with parameters. Because the plan quality can suffer, you should use *FORCED* with care, and you should have an understanding of the global behavior of your application. Usually, *FORCED* mode should be used only in an OLTP system with many almost-equivalent queries that (almost) always yield the same query plan. Essentially, you are betting that the plans won't change between possible parameter values. If all the queries are very small, the risk of this bet is smaller. The reasoning for this hint is that some OLTP systems with ad hoc queries spent a large fraction of their time compiling the same (or similar) queries repeatedly. When possible, this is a good case to consider adding parameters into your application's queries.

NOEXPAND

By default, the query processor expands view definitions when parsing and binding the query tree. Although the Query Optimizer usually matches the indexed views during optimization, as well as portions of any query even when the indexed view wasn't specified, in some cases the internal queries are rewritten so that matching indexed views isn't possible anymore. The *NOEXPAND* hint causes the query processor to force the use of the indexed view in the final query plan. In many cases, this can speed up the execution of the query plan because the indexed view often precomputes an expensive portion of a query. However, this isn't always true—the Query Optimizer might be able to find a better plan by using the information from the fully expanded query tree.

USE PLAN

The *USE PLAN N'xml plan'* hint directs the Query Optimizer to try to generate a plan that looks like the plan in the supplied XML string. The Query Optimizer has been instrumented to use the shape of this plan as a series of hints to guide the optimization process to get the desired plan shape. Note that this doesn't guarantee that the exact same plan is selected, but it will usually be identical or very close.

The common user of this hint is a DBA or database developer who wants to fix a plan regression in the Query Optimizer. If a baseline of good/expected query plans is saved when the application is developed or first deployed, these can be used later to force a query plan to change back to what was expected if the Query Optimizer later determines to change to a different plan that's not performing well. This could be necessary to force a join order to avoid deadlocks or merely to get the right physical plan shape and algorithms to be chosen. In some scenarios, the Query Optimizer doesn't have enough information to make a good decision about a portion of the query plan (for example, the join order), which can lead to a suboptimal plan choice. DBAs should use this option with care; forcing the original query plan can actually degrade performance further because the plan was likely created for different data volumes and distributions. Try out a plan hint on a test database before deploying it, when possible.

Although SQL Server 2012 supports additional query types, some (including the following) aren't supported with this feature.

- Dynamic, Keyset, and Fast Forward cursors

- Queries containing remote tables

- Full-text queries

- DDL commands, including *CREATE INDEX* and *ALTER PARTITION FUNCTION*, which manipulate data

In the context of rules, properties, and the Memo, the *USE PLAN* hint is used by the Query Optimizer to control both the initial shape of the query tree (for example, the initial join order after the tree is normalized early in Optimization) as well as the rules that are enabled to run for each group in the Memo. With join orders, the Query Optimizer enables only join order transformations that led to the configuration specified in the plan hint. Physical implementation rules are also hinted, meaning that a hash aggregate in the XML plan hint requires that the implementation rule for hash aggregation be enabled and that the stream aggregation rule be disabled.

The following example demonstrates how to retrieve a plan hint from SQL Server and then apply it as a hint to a subsequent compilation to guarantee the query plan:

```
CREATE TABLE customers(id INT, name NVARCHAR(100));
CREATE TABLE orders(orderid INT, customerid INT, amount MONEY);
go
SET SHOWPLAN_XML ON;
go
SELECT * FROM customers c INNER JOIN orders o ON c.id = o.customerid;
```

The *SELECT* statement returns a single row and single column of text of XML that contains the XML plan for the query. It's too large to include in this book, but it starts with

```
<ShowPlanXML xmlns="http://schemas.microsoft.com/sqlserver/2004/07/showplan" Version="1.0" ...
```

After you copy the XML, you need to escape single quotes before you can use it in the *USE PLAN* hint. Usually, I copy the XML into an editor and then search for single quotes and replace them with double quotes. Then you can copy the XML into the query using the *OPTION (USE PLAN '<xml .../>')* hint. (The hint was again shortened for space.)

```
SET SHOWPLAN_XML OFF;
SELECT * FROM customers  c INNER JOIN orders o ON c.id = o.customerid
OPTION (USE PLAN '<ShowPlanXML xmlns="http://schemas.microsoft.com/sqlserver/2004/07/showplan"
Version="1.0" ...');
```

This technique enables you to force one query plan in scenarios when you can manipulate the query submitted to the server. The names used in the XML plan format are logical (table names instead of *object_id*), so taking a *USE PLAN* hint from one table and using it on another with the same physical schema (columns, indexes, and so on) should be possible with only minor modifications. A very straightforward way to copy a plan from one table to another table with the same structure, or from one database or SQL Server instance to another, is to create a *plan guide* incorporating the *USE PLAN* hint. Chapter 12 covers plan guides.

Hotfixes

The SQL Server engineering team is extremely careful about making changes to the Query Optimizer when those changes could lead to plan quality regressions. Unfortunately, changing the Optimizer's model can often cause unintentional side-effects because almost every customer uses this portion of the product. The SQL Server team has been working on delivering features that minimize the risk of regression for customers, especially in production environments. As part of this effort, the team has been formalizing the way it delivers hotfixes for releases of SQL Server after the initial release of each major version.

Starting several years ago, most optimizer hotfixes are controlled in a new way. You must turn on a special traceflag (4199) that enables all fixes that could possibly affect query plans. This benefits customers who have applications in production and should now have minimal fear of regressions when installing any service releases. The downside is that they might miss some hotfixes that would help their application. Customers are strongly encouraged to enable this traceflag only for a specific release in which they are seeing a problem for their specific application. Usually this flag is enabled as the result of a discussion with Microsoft Customer Support.

The 4199 traceflag is supposed to be scoped within a major release, although over the past few releases the SQL Server engineering team hasn't removed the 4199 traceflag requirement for some fixes from one major release to the next. Generally, you should expect to revalidate your query plans for major releases to ensure that they are acceptable.

Note The 4199 traceflag isn't used for security or wrong-results fixes. These are enabled by default, even if the changes are plan affecting (although this is almost never an issue in SQL Server when such a fix is necessary).

Conclusion

The Query Optimizer is a complex component with many internal features. Although it's not always possible to know exactly why the Query Optimizer would choose a specific plan, knowing a little about the Query Optimizer's design can help a DBA or database developer examine any query plan and diagnose any problems. Knowing how the Query Optimizer works can also help reinforce good database design methodologies that can improve the quality of your application and reduce problems in deployment.

This chapter explains the mechanisms used in query processing and optimization, including trees, rules, properties, and the Memo framework. These ideas are used through different stages of optimization to try to find a reasonable plan quickly. The examples throughout the chapter demonstrate many of the operators and how they are used to implement user-submitted SQL queries. Finally, the use of the statistics profile output can help identify poorly optimized queries, and it can use statistics and hints to get the Query Optimizer to select a better plan.

Plan caching and recompilation

Kalen Delaney

We've looked at the query optimization process and the details of query execution in Microsoft SQL Server. Because query optimization can be complex and time-consuming, SQL Server frequently and beneficially reuses plans that have already been generated and saved in the plan cache, rather than produce a completely new plan. However, in some cases, using a previously created plan might not be ideal for the current query execution, and creating a new plan might result in better performance.

This chapter looks at the SQL Server 2012 plan cache and how it's organized. Most discussion is relevant to SQL Server 2005 and later versions as well, and I will tell you when a behavior or feature was introduced in a version after SQL Server 2005. You will learn about what kinds of plans are saved and under what conditions SQL Server might decide to reuse them. This chapter looks at what might cause an existing plan to be re-created. It also looks at the metadata that describes the contents of plan cache. Finally, we'll see how to encourage SQL Server to use an existing plan when it might otherwise create a new one, and how to force SQL Server to create a new plan when you need to know that the most up-to-date plan is available.

The plan cache

Understanding that the plan cache in SQL Server isn't actually a separate area of memory is important. Releases prior to SQL Server 7 had two effective configuration values to control the size of the plan cache, which was then called the *procedure cache*. One value specified a fixed size for the total usable memory in SQL Server; the other specified a percentage of that memory (after fixed needs were satisfied) to be used exclusively for storing procedure plans. Also, in releases prior to SQL Server 7, query plans for ad hoc SQL statements were never stored in cache; only the plans for stored procedures are stored in the cache (the reason it was called procedure cache in older versions). As of SQL Server 7, the total size of memory is dynamic by default, and the space used for query plans is also very fluid.

Plan cache metadata

The first part of this chapter explores the different mechanisms by which a plan can be reused. To observe this plan reuse (or non-reuse), you need to look at only a couple of different metadata objects. About a dozen different metadata views and functions provide information about the contents of the plan cache, not including the metadata that gives you information about memory usage by the plan cache. Later, this chapter provides more details available in the plan cache metadata, but for now, you will use just one view and one function. The view is *sys.dm_exec_cached_plans*, which contains one row for each plan in cache, and we look at the columns *usecounts*, *cacheobjtype*, and *objtype*. (The value in *usecounts* allows you to see how many times a plan has been reused; the possible values for *cacheobjtype* and *objtype* are described in the next section.) Also, the value in the column *plan_handle* is used as the parameter when you use the *CROSS APPLY* operator to join the *sys.dm_exec_cached_plans* view with the table-valued function (TVF) *sys.dm_exec_sql_text*. Listing 12-1 shows this query, which this chapter refers to as the *usecount* query.

LISTING 12-1 The usecount query

```
SELECT usecounts, cacheobjtype, objtype, [text]
FROM sys.dm_exec_cached_plans P
    CROSS APPLY sys.dm_exec_sql_text(plan_handle)
WHERE cacheobjtype = 'Compiled Plan'
    AND [text] NOT LIKE '%dm_exec_cached_plans%';
```

Clearing plan cache

Because SQL Server has the potential to cache almost every query, the number of plans in cache can become quite large. (Later, this chapter describes a very efficient mechanism for finding a plan in cache.) Having many cached plans doesn't cause a direct performance penalty, aside from the memory usage. However, if you have many very similar queries, the lookup time for SQL Server to find the right plan can sometimes be excessive. Also, from a testing and troubleshooting standpoint, having many plans to look at can sometimes make finding just the plan you need difficult. SQL Server provides a mechanism for clearing out all the plans in cache, and you probably want to do that occasionally on your test servers to keep the cache size manageable and easy to examine. You can use any of the following commands.

- **DBCC FREEPROCCACHE**   This command removes all cached plans from memory. SQL Server 2008 added the capability to add parameters to this command to allow SQL Server to remove a specific plan from cache, all plans with the same *sql_handle* value, or all plans in a specific resource governor resource pool. Later, this chapter discusses how to use this procedure, when I discuss the contents of the plan cache.

- **DBCC FREESYSTEMCACHE**   This command clears out all SQL Server memory caches, in addition to the plan caches. Later, the section "Cache stores" discusses a bit more about the different memory caches.

- **DBCC FLUSHPROCINDB (<dbid>)**   This command allows you to specify a particular database ID, and then clears all plans from that particular database. Notice that the *usecount* query in Listing 12-1 doesn't return database ID information, but because the *sys.dm_exec_sql_text* function has that information available, you can add the *dbid* to the *usecount* query.

 Tip Don't use these commands on your production servers because they could affect the performance of your running applications. Usually, you want to keep plans in cache.

Caching mechanisms

SQL Server can avoid compilations of previously executed queries by using four mechanisms to make plan caching accessible in a wide set of situations.

- Ad hoc query caching
- Autoparameterization
- Prepared queries, using either *sp_executesql* or the prepare and execute method invoked through your API
- Stored procedures or other compiled objects (triggers, TVFs, etc.)

To determine which mechanism is being used for each plan in cache, you should look at the values in the *cacheobjtype* and *objtype* columns in the *sys.dm_exec_cached_plans* view. The *cacheobjtype* column can have one of six possible values.

- *Compiled Plan*
- *Compiled Plan Stub*
- *Parse Tree*
- *Extended Proc*
- *CLR Compiled Func*
- *CLR Compiled Proc*

This section looks at only *Compiled Plan* and *Compiled Plan Stub*. Notice that the *usecount* query limits the results to row having one of these two values.

The *objtype* column has 11 different possible values:

- *Proc* (stored procedure)
- *Prepared* (prepared statement)
- *Adhoc* (ad hoc query)
- *ReplProc* (replication filter procedure)
- *Trigger*

- *View*

- *Default* (default constraint or default object)

- *UsrTab* (user table)

- *SysTab* (system table)

- *Check* (CHECK constraint)

- *Rule* (rule object)

This chapter focuses mainly on the first three values—*Proc, Prepared,* and *Adhoc*—but many caching details that apply to stored procedures also apply to replication filter procedures and triggers.

Ad hoc query caching

If the caching metadata indicates a *cacheobjtype* value of *Compiled Plan* and an *objtype* value of *Adhoc*, the plan is considered to be an ad hoc plan. Prior to SQL Server 2005, ad hoc plans were cached occasionally, but it wasn't something on which you could depend. However, even when SQL Server caches your ad hoc query plans, you might not be able to depend on their reuse. When SQL Server caches the plan from an ad hoc query, the cached plan is reused only if a subsequent batch matches exactly. This feature requires no extra work to use but is limited to *exact* textual matches. For example, if the following three queries are each executed as a separate batch in the *AdventureWorks2012* sample database, the first and third queries use the same plan, but the second one needs to generate a new plan:

```
SELECT * FROM Person.Person WHERE LastName = 'Raheem';
SELECT * FROM Person.Person WHERE LastName = 'Garcia';
SELECT * FROM Person.Person WHERE LastName = 'Raheem';
```

You can verify this by first clearing out the plan cache and then running the three queries in separate batches. Then run the *usecount* query from Listing 12-1:

```
USE AdventureWorks2012;
DBCC FREEPROCCACHE;
GO
SELECT * FROM Person.Person WHERE LastName = 'Raheem';
GO
SELECT * FROM Person.Person WHERE LastName = 'Garcia';
GO
SELECT * FROM Person.Person WHERE LastName = 'Raheem';
GO
SELECT usecounts, cacheobjtype, objtype, [text]
FROM sys.dm_exec_cached_plans P
    CROSS APPLY sys.dm_exec_sql_text (plan_handle)
WHERE cacheobjtype = 'Compiled Plan'
    AND [text] NOT LIKE '%dm_exec_cached_plans%';
```

You should get two rows back because the *NOT LIKE* condition filters out the row for the *usecount* query itself. The two rows indicate that one plan was used only once, and the other was used twice:

usecounts	cacheobjtype	objtype	text
1	Compiled Plan	Adhoc	SELECT * FROM Person.Person WHERE LastName = 'Garcia'
2	Compiled Plan	Adhoc	SELECT * FROM Person.Person WHERE LastName = 'Raheem'

Note The results shown in this section are obtained with the Optimize for Ad Hoc Workloads configuration option set to 0, which is the default when you install SQL Server. This option is discussed later in this chapter.

The results show that with a change of the *LastName* value, the same plan can't be reused. However, to take advantage of reusing ad hoc query plans, you need to make sure that not only are the same *LastName* values used in the queries, but also that the queries are identical, character for character. If one query has a new line or an extra space that another one doesn't have, they aren't treated the same. If one query contains a comment that the other doesn't have, they aren't identical. Also, if one query uses a different case for either identifiers or keywords, even in a database with a case-insensitive collation, the queries aren't the same. If you run the following code, notice that none of the queries can reuse the same plan:

```
USE AdventureWorks2012;
DBCC FREEPROCCACHE;
GO
SELECT * FROM Person.Person WHERE LastName = 'Raheem';
GO
-- Try it again
SELECT * FROM Person.Person WHERE LastName = 'Raheem';
GO
SELECT * FROM Person.Person
WHERE LastName = 'Raheem';
GO
SELECT * FROM Person.Person WHERE lastname = 'Raheem';
GO
select * from Person.Person where LastName = 'Raheem';
GO
SELECT usecounts, cacheobjtype, objtype, [text]
FROM sys.dm_exec_cached_plans P
    CROSS APPLY sys.dm_exec_sql_text (plan_handle)
WHERE cacheobjtype = 'Compiled Plan'
    AND [text] NOT LIKE '%dm_exec_cached_plans%';
```

Your results should show five rows in *sys.dm_exec_cached_plans* for these five statements, each with a *usecounts* value of 1. You also might have other rows reflecting other batches being executed by other SQL Server processes or by SQL Server Agent.

Note The *SELECT* statements are all in their own batch, separated by *GO*. If no *GO*s were used, you would see only one batch. Each batch has its own plan containing the execution plan for each individual query within the batch. For the reuse of ad hoc query plans, the entire batch must be identical.

A few special kinds of statements are always considered to be ad hoc.

- A statement used with *EXEC*, as in

  ```
  EXEC('SELECT FirstName, LastName, Title FROM Employees WHERE EmployeeID = 6')
  ```

- A statement submitted using *sp_executesql*, if no parameters are supplied

Queries that you submit via your application with *sp_prepare* and *sp_prepexec* aren't considered to be ad hoc.

Optimizing for ad hoc workloads

If most of your queries are ad hoc and never reused, caching their execution plans might seem like a waste of memory. Later, this chapter talks about how the maximum size of plan cache is determined. Having tens of thousands of cached plans for ad hoc queries that have little likelihood of reuse probably isn't the best use of SQL Server's memory. For this reason, SQL Server 2008 added a configuration option, still available in SQL Server 2012, that you can enable in those cases where you expect most of your queries to be ad hoc. When this option is enabled, SQL Server caches only a stub of the query plan the first time any ad hoc query is compiled, and only after a second compilation is the stub replaced with the full plan.

Controlling the optimize for ad hoc workloads setting

Enabling the Optimize for Ad Hoc Workloads option is very straightforward, as shown in the following code:

```
EXEC sp_configure 'optimize for ad hoc workloads', 1;
RECONFIGURE;
```

You can also enable this option by using SQL Server Management Studio, on the Advanced page of the Server Properties sheet, as shown in Figure 12-1.

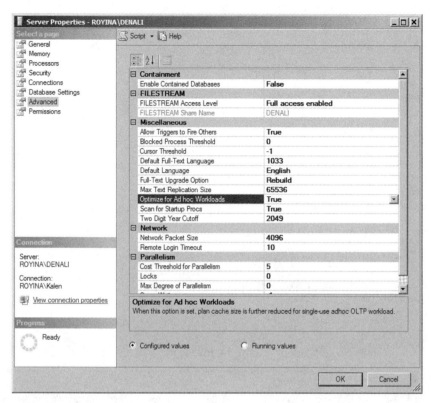

FIGURE 12-1 Using the Server Properties sheet in Management Studio to enable the Optimize for Ad Hoc Workloads option.

The compiled plan stub

The stub that SQL Server caches when Optimize for Ad Hoc Workloads is enabled is only about 300 bytes in size and doesn't contain any part of a query execution plan. It's mainly just a placeholder to keep track of whether a particular query was compiled previously. The stub contains the full cache key and a pointer to the actual query text, which is stored in the SQL Manager cache. Later, the section "Plan cache internals" discusses cache keys and the SQL Manager. The *usecounts* value in the cache metadata is always 1 for compiled plan stubs because they are never reused.

When a query or batch that generated a compiled plan stub is recompiled, the stub is replaced with the full compiled plan. Initially, the *usecounts* value is set to 1 because the previous query isn't guaranteed to have exactly the same execution plan. All that's known is that the query itself is the same. I will execute some of the same queries used in the previous section after enabling the Optimize for Ad Hoc Workloads option, so you can see what the *usecounts* query displays. I need to modify my *usecounts* query slightly, and rather than look for rows that have a *cacheobjtype* value of *Compiled Plan*, I look for *cacheobjtype* values that start with *Compiled Plan* (see Listing 12-2).

LISTING 12-2 Examining cached ad hoc plans with Optimize for Ad Hoc Workloads set to 1

```
EXEC sp_configure 'optimize for ad hoc workloads', 1;
RECONFIGURE;
GO
USE AdventureWorks2012;
DBCC FREEPROCCACHE;
GO
SELECT * FROM Person.Person WHERE LastName = 'Raheem';
GO
SELECT usecounts, cacheobjtype, objtype, size_in_bytes, [text]
FROM sys.dm_exec_cached_plans P
        CROSS APPLY sys.dm_exec_sql_text (plan_handle)
WHERE cacheobjtype LIKE 'Compiled Plan%'
        AND [text] NOT LIKE '%dm_exec_cached_plans%';
GO
SELECT * FROM Person.Person WHERE LastName = 'Raheem';
GO
SELECT usecounts, cacheobjtype, objtype, size_in_bytes, [text]
FROM sys.dm_exec_cached_plans P
        CROSS APPLY sys.dm_exec_sql_text (plan_handle)
WHERE cacheobjtype LIKE 'Compiled Plan%'
        AND [text] NOT LIKE '%dm_exec_cached_plans%';
GO
```

The first execution of the *usecounts* query returns the following:

usecounts	cacheobjtype	objtype	size_in_bytes	text
1	Compiled Plan Stub	Adhoc	272	SELECT * FROM Person.Person WHERE LastName = 'Raheem';

The second execution shows the replacement of the stub with the compiled plan:

usecounts	cacheobjtype	objtype	size_in_bytes	Text
1	Compiled Plan	Adhoc	16384	SELECT * FROM Person.Person WHERE LastName = 'Raheem';

The stub is generated when the plan is compiled, not when it's executed, so you would see this same behavior if you examined only the query plan twice with one of the *SHOWPLAN* options, without ever executing the query. Notice that the size of the stub in the output from the first execution is less than 300 bytes, and the size of the plan in the second execution is two pages.

If the Optimize for Ad Hoc Workloads option is set to 1 and then is set back to 0 after Compiled Plan Stubs are placed in the plan cache, the stubs aren't removed immediately from cache. Similar to when the option was set to 1, any resubmission of the same ad hoc T-SQL batch replaces the stub with the compiled plan, and then no further stubs are created.

Even with this special mechanism for improving the caching behavior when your workloads use primarily ad hoc queries, this doesn't mean that ad hoc workloads are a good idea. Sometimes you have no control over the kind of queries being submitted to your SQL Server; in that situation, you might find this option beneficial. In fact, having this option on really has no negative side, so you might consider always setting the value to 1 when a new instance is installed. However, if you and your developers can control how your queries are submitted, you should consider other options, such as Prepared Queries or stored procedures, as discussed later in this chapter.

If you are running the sample queries as you are reading, you might want to turn off the Optimize for Ad Hoc Workloads option at this point, so that the rest of the examples can give the same results that are discussed. However, in general, you have no reason not to keep this option set to 1.

```
EXEC sp_configure 'optimize for ad hoc workloads', 0;
RECONFIGURE;
GO
```

Simple parameterization

For certain queries, SQL Server can decide to treat one or more of the constants as parameters. When this happens, subsequent queries that follow the same basic template can use the same plan. For example, these two queries that run in the *AdventureWorks2012* database can use the same plan:

```
SELECT FirstName, LastName, Title FROM Person.Person
WHERE BusinessEntityID = 6;
SELECT FirstName, LastName, Title FROM Person.Person
WHERE BusinessEntityID = 2;
```

Internally, SQL Server parameterizes these queries as follows:

```
(@1 tinyint)SELECT [FirstName],
[LastName], [Title]
FROM [Person].[Person]
WHERE [BusinessEntityID] = @1
```

You can observe this behavior by running the following code and observing the output of the *usecount* query:

```
USE AdventureWorks2012
GO
DBCC FREEPROCCACHE;
GO
SELECT FirstName, LastName, Title FROM Person.Person WHERE BusinessEntityID = 6;
GO
SELECT FirstName, LastName, Title FROM Person.Person WHERE BusinessEntityID = 2;

GO
SELECT usecounts, cacheobjtype, objtype, size_in_bytes, [text]
FROM sys.dm_exec_cached_plans P
    CROSS APPLY sys.dm_exec_sql_text (plan_handle)
WHERE cacheobjtype = 'Compiled Plan'
    AND [text] NOT LIKE '%dm_exec_cached_plans%';
GO
```

You should get three rows returned, similar to the following:

usecounts	cacheobjtype	objtype	size_in_bytes	text
1	Compiled Plan	Adhoc	16384	SELECT FirstName, LastName, Title FROM Person.Person WHERE BusinessEntityID = 2;
1	Compiled Plan	Adhoc	16384	SELECT FirstName, LastName, Title FROM Person.Person WHERE BusinessEntityID = 6;
2	Compiled Plan	Prepared	32768	(@1 tinyint)SELECT [FirstName], [LastName], [Title] FROM [Person].[Person] WHERE [BusinessEntityID] = @1

Notice that the two individual queries with their distinct constants are cached as ad hoc queries. However, these are considered *shell* queries and are cached only to make it easier for SQL Server to find the parameterized version of the query if the exact same query with the same constant is reused later. These shell queries don't contain the full execution plan, but instead contain a pointer to the full plan in the corresponding prepared plan. Notice that their size is less than the size of the Prepared Plan, which contains the entire execution plan.

Note Don't confuse a shell query with a plan stub. A shell query contains the complete text of the query and uses about 16 KB of memory. Shell queries are created only for those plans that SQL Server thinks are parameterizable. A plan stub, as mentioned previously, uses about only 300 bytes of memory and is created only for unparameterizable, ad hoc queries, and only when the Optimize for Ad Hoc Workloads option is set to 1.

In the output shown in the preceding table, the third row returned from *sys.dm_exec_cached_plans* has an *objtype* value of *Prepared*. (The order of the returned rows isn't guaranteed. You should have two rows with a *cacheobjtype* value of *Adhoc* and one row with a *cacheobjtype* value of *Prepared*.) The query plan is associated with the prepared plan, and you can observe that the plan was used twice. Also, the text for that *Prepared* row shows a parameter in place of a constant.

By default, SQL Server is very conservative about deciding when to parameterize automatically. SQL Server automatically parameterizes queries only if the query template is considered to be safe. A template is safe if the plan selected doesn't change, even if the actual parameter values change. This ensures that the parameterization won't degrade a query's performance. The *Person.Person* table used in the preceding queries has a unique index on *BusinessEntityId*, so any query that has an equality comparison on *BusinessEntityId* is guaranteed never to find more than one row. A plan using a seek on that unique index can be useful, no matter what actual value is used.

However, consider a query that has either an inequality comparison or an equality comparison on a non-unique column. In those situations, some actual values might return many rows, and others return no rows or only one. A nonclustered index seek might be a good choice when only a few rows are returned, but it could be a terrible choice when many rows are returned. So a query for which more than one possible best plan is available, depending on the value used in the query, isn't considered safe, and it's not parameterized. By default, the only way for SQL Server to reuse a plan for such a query is to use the ad hoc plan caching described in the preceding section (which doesn't happen if the constant values in the query are different).

In addition to requiring only one possible plan for a query template, many query constructs normally disallow simple parameterization. Such constructs include any statements with any of the following elements:

- *JOIN*
- *BULK INSERT*
- *IN* lists
- *UNION*
- *INTO*
- *FOR BROWSE*
- *OPTION* query hints
- *DISTINCT*
- *TOP*
- *WAITFOR* statements
- *GROUP BY, HAVING, COMPUTE*
- Full-text predicates
- Subqueries
- *FROM* clause of a *SELECT* statement that has a table-valued method or full-text table or *OPENROWSET* or *OPENXML* or *OPENQUERY* or *OPENDATASOURCE*
- Comparison predicate of the form EXPR <> a non-null constant

Simple parameterization is also disallowed for data modification statements that use the following constructs:

- *DELETE/UPDATE* with a *FROM* clause
- *UPDATE* with a *SET* clause that has variables

Forced parameterization

If your application uses many similar queries that you know could benefit from the same plan but aren't autoparameterized, either because SQL Server doesn't consider the plans safe or because they use one of the disallowed constructs, SQL Server provides an alternative. A database option called *PARAMETERIZATION FORCED* can be enabled with the following command:

```
ALTER DATABASE <database_name> SET PARAMETERIZATION FORCED;
```

When this option is enabled, SQL Server treats constants like parameters, with only a very few exceptions. These exceptions, as listed in *SQL Server Books Online*, include the following.

- *INSERT...EXECUTE* statements.

- Statements inside the bodies of stored procedures, triggers, or user-defined functions. SQL Server already reuses query plans for these routines.

- Prepared statements that are already parameterized on the client-side application.

- Statements that contain XQuery method calls, in which the method appears in a context in which its arguments would typically be parameterized, such as a *WHERE* clause. If the method appears in a context in which its arguments wouldn't be parameterized, the rest of the statement is parameterized.

- Statements inside a T-SQL cursor. (*SELECT* statements inside API cursors are parameterized.)

- Deprecated query constructs.

- Any statement that's run in the context of *ANSI_PADDING* or *ANSI_NULLS* set to *OFF*.

- Statements that contain more than 2,097 literals.

- Statements that reference variables, such as *WHERE T.col2 >= @p*.

- Statements that contain the *RECOMPILE* query hint.

- Statements that contain a *COMPUTE* clause.

- Statements that contain a *WHERE CURRENT* OF clause.

Be careful when setting this option on for the entire database because assuming that all constants should be treated as parameters during optimization and then reusing existing plans frequently can lead to very poor performance. An alternative that allows only selected queries to be autoparameterized is to use plan guides, as discussed at the end of this chapter. Also, plan guides can also be used to override forced parameterization for selected queries, if the database has been set to *PARAMETERIZATION FORCED*.

Drawbacks of simple parameterization

A feature of autoparameterization that you might have noticed in the output from the *usecount* query shown previously is that SQL Server makes its own decision as to the data type of the parameter, which might not be the data type you think should be used. In the earlier example, looking at the *Person.Person* table, SQL Server chose to assume a parameter of type *tinyint*. If you rerun the batch and use a value that doesn't fit into the *tinyint* range (that is, a value less than 0 or larger than 255), SQL Server can't use the same autoparameterized query. The following batch autoparameterizes both *SELECT* statements, but it can't use the same plan for both queries:

```
USE AdventureWorks2012
GO
DBCC FREEPROCCACHE;
GO
SELECT FirstName, LastName, Title FROM Person.Person WHERE BusinessEntityID = 6;
GO
SELECT FirstName, LastName, Title FROM Person.Person WHERE BusinessEntityID = 622;
GO
SELECT usecounts, cacheobjtype, objtype, [text]
FROM sys.dm_exec_cached_plans P
    CROSS APPLY sys.dm_exec_sql_text (plan_handle)
WHERE cacheobjtype = 'Compiled Plan'
    AND [text] NOT LIKE '%dm_exec_cached_plans%';
GO
```

The output from the *usecount* query should show two ad hoc shell queries and two prepared queries. One prepared query has a parameter of type *tinyint*, and the other is *smallint*. As strange as it might seem, even if you switch the order of the queries and use the bigger value first, you get two prepared queries with two different parameter data types.

The only way to force SQL Server to use the same data type for both queries is to enable *PARAMETERIZATION FORCED* for the database.

As mentioned, simple parameterization isn't always appropriate, which is why SQL Server is so conservative in choosing to use it. Consider the following example. The *Person.Person* table in the *AdventureWorks2012* database has 19,972 rows and 3,814 pages, so you might expect that a table scan reading 3814 pages would be the worst possible performance for any query accessing the *Person.Person* table. Now create a nonclustered, non-unique index on the *PersonType* column:

```
USE AdventureWorks2012
GO
CREATE INDEX IX_Person_PersonType ON Person.Person (PersonType);
GO
```

If you enable forced parameterization for the *AdventureWorks2012* database, the plan used for the first *SELECT* is also used for the second *SELECT*, even though the constants are different. The first query returns 273 rows, and the second returns 18,484. Typically, a nonclustered index seek would be chosen for the first *SELECT* and a clustered index scan for the second because the number of qualifying rows exceeds the number of pages in the table. However, with *PARAMETERIZATION FORCED*, that's not what you get, as you can see when you run the following code:

```
USE AdventureWorks2012;
GO
ALTER DATABASE AdventureWorks2012 SET PARAMETERIZATION FORCED;
GO
SET STATISTICS IO ON;
GO
DBCC FREEPROCCACHE;
GO
SELECT * FROM Person.Person WHERE PersonType = 'EM';
GO
SELECT * FROM Person.Person WHERE PersonType = 'IN';
GO
SELECT usecounts, cacheobjtype, objtype, [text]
FROM sys.dm_exec_cached_plans P
    CROSS APPLY sys.dm_exec_sql_text (plan_handle)
WHERE cacheobjtype = 'Compiled Plan'
    AND [text] NOT LIKE '%dm_exec_cached_plans%';
GO
ALTER DATABASE AdventureWorks2012 SET PARAMETERIZATION SIMPLE;
GO
```

When you run this code, you see that the first *SELECT* required 847 logical reads and the second required 56,642—almost 14 times as many reads as would have been required if scanning the table. The output of the *usecount* query shows that forced parameterization was applied and the parameterized prepared plan was used twice:

usecounts	Cacheobjtype	objtype	Text
1	Compiled Plan	Adhoc	SELECT * FROM Person.Person WHERE PersonType = 'EM';
1	Compiled Plan	Adhoc	SELECT * FROM Person.Person WHERE PersonType = 'IN';
2	Compiled Plan	Prepared	(@0 varchar(8000))select * from Person.Person where PersonType = @0

In this example, forcing SQL Server to treat the constant as a parameter isn't a good thing, and the script sets the database back to *PARAMETERIZATION SIMPLE* (the default) as the last step. Notice also that while you're using *PARAMETERIZATION FORCED*, the data type chosen for the parameterized query is the largest possible regular character data type.

So what can you do if you have many queries that shouldn't be parameterized and many others that should be? As you've seen, the SQL Server query processor is much more conservative about deciding whether a template is safe than an application can be. SQL Server guesses which values are really parameters, whereas your application developers should actually know. Rather than rely on SQL Server to parameterize your queries automatically, you can use one of the prepared query mechanisms to mark values as parameters when they are known.

The SQL Server Performance Monitor includes an object called SQLServer:SQL Statistics that has several counters dealing with automatic parameterization. You can monitor these counters to determine whether many unsafe or failed automatic parameterization attempts have been made. If these numbers are high, you can inspect your applications for situations in which the application developers can take responsibility for explicitly marking the parameters.

Prepared queries

As you saw previously, a query that SQL Server parameterizes shows an *objtype* of *Prepared* in the cached plan metadata. Two other constructs have prepared plans, both which allow a programmer to control which values are parameters and which aren't. Also, unlike with simple parameterization, the programmer also determines the data type that should be used for the parameters. One construct is the SQL Server stored procedure *sp_executesql*, which is called from within a T-SQL batch; the other is to use the prepare-and-execute method from the client application.

The sp_executesql procedure

The stored procedure *sp_executesql* is halfway between ad hoc caching and stored procedures. Using *sp_executesql* requires that you identify the parameters and their data types, but it doesn't require all the persistent object management needed for stored procedures and other programmed objects.

Here's the general syntax for the procedure:

```
sp_executesql @batch_text, @batch_parameter_definitions,
    param1,...paramN
```

Repeated calls with the same values for *@batch_text* and *@batch_parameter_definitions* use the same cached plan, with the new parameter values specified. The plan is reused as long as the plan hasn't been removed from cache and is still valid. Later, the section "Causes of recompilation" discusses those situations in which SQL Server determines that a plan is no longer valid. The same cached plan can be used for all the following queries:

```
EXEC sp_executesql N'SELECT FirstName, LastName, Title
    FROM Person.Person
    WHERE BusinessEntityID = @p', N'@p int', 6;
EXEC sp_executesql N'SELECT FirstName, LastName, Title
    FROM Person.Person
    WHERE BusinessEntityID = @p', N'@p int', 2;
EXEC sp_executesql N'SELECT FirstName, LastName, Title
    FROM Person.Person
    WHERE BusinessEntityID = @p', N'@p int', 6;
```

Just like with forcing autoparameterization, using *sp_executesql* to force reuse of a plan isn't always appropriate. Looking at the same example used earlier when the database was set to *PARAMETERIZATION FORCED*, you can see that using *sp_executesql* is just as inappropriate:

```
USE AdventureWorks2012;
GO
SET STATISTICS IO ON;
```

```
GO
DBCC FREEPROCCACHE;
GO
EXEC sp_executesql N'SELECT * FROM Person.Person
    WHERE PersonType  = @p', N'@p nchar(2)', 'EM';
GO
EXEC sp_executesql N'SELECT * FROM Person.Person
    WHERE PersonType  = @p', N'@p nchar(2)', 'IN';
GO
SELECT usecounts, cacheobjtype, objtype, [text]
FROM sys.dm_exec_cached_plans P
    CROSS APPLY sys.dm_exec_sql_text (plan_handle)
WHERE cacheobjtype = 'Compiled Plan'
    AND [text] NOT LIKE '%dm_exec_cached_plans%';
GO
SET STATISTICS IO OFF;
GO
```

Again, you can see that the first *SELECT* required 847 logical reads and the second required 56,642. The following output of the *usecount* query shows the parameterized query being used twice. Note that with *sp_executesql*, you don't have any entries for the ad hoc (unparameterized) shell queries.

usecounts	cacheobjtype	objtype	text
2	Compiled Plan	Prepared	(@p nchar(2))SELECT * FROM Person.Person WHERE PersonType = @p

The prepare-and-execute method

This last mechanism is like *sp_executesql* in that parameters to the batch are identified by the application, but with some key differences. The prepare-and-execute method doesn't require the full text of the batch to be sent at each execution. Instead, the text is sent once at prepare time, and a handle that can be used to invoke the batch at execute time is returned.

ODBC and OLE DB expose this functionality via *SQLPrepare/SQLExecute* and *ICommandPrepare*. You can also use this mechanism via ODBC and OLE DB when cursors are involved. When you use these functions, SQL Server is informed that this batch is meant to be used repeatedly.

Caching prepared queries

If your queries have been parameterized at the client using the prepare-and-execute method, the metadata shows you prepared queries, just as for queries that are parameterized at the server, either automatically or by using *sp_executesql*. However, queries that aren't parameterized—either under simple or forced parameterization—don't have any corresponding ad hoc shell queries in cache containing the unparameterized actual values; they have only the prepared plans. You can't reliably detect whether a prepared plan was prepared by SQL Server using simple or forced parameterization or by the developer through client-side parameterization. If you see a corresponding shell query, you can know that the query was parameterized by SQL Server, but the opposite isn't always true. Because the shell queries have zero cost, they are among the first candidates to be removed when SQL Server is under memory pressure. So a lack of a shell query might just mean that ad hoc plan was already removed from cache, not that a shell query never existed.

Compiled objects

When looking at the metadata in *sys.dm_exec_cached_plans*, we've seen compiled plans with *objtype* values of *Adhoc* and *Prepared*. The third *objtype* value is *Proc*, which you will see used when executing stored procedures, user-defined scalar functions, and multistatement table-valued functions (TVFs). With these objects, you have full control over what values are parameters and what their data types are when executing these objects.

Stored procedures

Stored procedures and user-defined scalar functions are treated almost identically. The metadata indicates that a compiled plan with an *objtype* value of *Proc* is cached and can be reused repeatedly. By default, the cached plan is reused for all successive executions and, as you've seen with the *sp_executesql*, this isn't always desirable. However, unlike the plans cached and reused with *sp_executesql*, you have an option with stored procedures and user-defined scalar functions to force recompilation when the object is executed. Also, for stored procedures, you can create the object so that a new plan is created every single time it's executed.

To force recompilation for a single execution, you can use the *EXECUTE...WITH RECOMPILE* option. The following is an example in the *AdventureWorks2012* database of forcing recompilation for the execution of a stored procedure:

```
USE AdventureWorks2012;
GO
CREATE PROCEDURE P_Type_Customers
  @custtype nchar(2)
AS
  SELECT BusinessEntityID, Title, FirstName, Lastname
  FROM Person.Person
WHERE PersonType = @custtype;
GO

DBCC FREEPROCCACHE;
GO
SET STATISTICS IO ON;
GO
EXEC P_Type_Customers 'EM';
GO
EXEC P_Type_Customers 'IN';
GO
EXEC P_Type_Customers 'IN' WITH RECOMPILE;
```

If you look at the output from *STATISTICS IO*, notice that the second execution used a suboptimal plan that required more pages to be read than would be needed by a table scan. This is the kind of situation that you might have seen referred to as *parameter sniffing*. SQL Server is basing the plan for the procedure on the first actual parameter—in this case, *EM*—and then subsequent executions assume that the same or a similar parameter is used. The third execution uses the *WITH RECOMPILE* option to force SQL Server to come up with a new plan, and you should see that the number of logical page reads is about the same as the number of pages in the table.

If you look at the following results from running the *usecounts* query, you should see that the cached plan for the *P_Customers* procedure has a *usecounts* value of 2, instead of 3.

usecounts	cacheobjtype	objtype	text
2	Compiled Plan	Proc	CREATE PROCEDURE P_Type_Customers @cust nchar(2) AS SELECT BusinessEntityID, Title, FirstName, Lastname FROM Person.Person WHERE PersonType = @custtype;

The plan developed for a procedure executed with the *WITH RECOMPILE* option is considered valid only for the current execution; it's never kept in cache for reuse.

Functions

User-defined scalar functions can behave exactly the same way as procedures. If you execute them using the *EXECUTE* statement instead of as part of an expression, you can also force recompilation. Listing 12-3 shows an example of a function that masks part of a national ID number (a U.S. Social Security number). It was created in the *AdventureWorks2012* sample database because the *HumanResources.Employee* table contains a Social Security number in the *NationalIDNumber* column.

LISTING 12-3 Observing cached plan for a user-defined scalar function

```
USE AdventureWorks2012;
GO
CREATE FUNCTION dbo.fnMaskIDNum (@ID char(9))
RETURNS char(11)
AS
BEGIN
  SELECT @ID = 'xxx-xx-' + right (@ssn,4);
  RETURN @ID;
END;
GO

DBCC FREEPROCCACHE;
GO

DECLARE @mask char(11);
EXEC @mask = dbo. fnMaskIDNum '123456789';
SELECT @mask;
GO
DECLARE @mask char(11);
EXEC @mask = dbo. fnMaskIDNum '123661111';
SELECT @mask;
GO
DECLARE @mask char(11);
EXEC @mask = dbo. fnMaskIDNum '123661111' WITH RECOMPILE;
```

```
SELECT @mask;
GO
```

If you run the *usecounts* query, notice that the cached plan for the function has an *objtype* of *Proc* and has a *usecounts* value of 2. If a scalar function is used within an expression, as in Listing 12-3, you can't request recompilation:

```
SELECT dbo. fnMaskIDNum (NationalIDNumber), LoginID, JobTitle
FROM HumanResources.Employee;
```

User-defined TVFs might or might not be treated like procedures, depending on how you define them. You can define a TVF as an inline function or as a multistatement function. However, neither method allows you to force recompilation when the function is called. Here are two functions that do the same thing:

```
USE AdventureWorks2012;
GO
CREATE FUNCTION Fnc_Inline_Customers (@custID int)
RETURNS TABLE
AS
 RETURN
 (SELECT FirstName, LastName, Title
 FROM Person.Person
 WHERE BusinessEntityID = @custID);
GO

CREATE FUNCTION Fnc_Multi_Customers (@custID int)
RETURNS @T TABLE (FirstName nvarchar(100), LastName varchar(100), Title nvarchar(16))
AS
BEGIN
 INSERT INTO @T
  SELECT FirstName, LastName, Title
   FROM Person.Person
   WHERE BusinessEntityID = @custID;
  RETURN
END;
GO
```

Here are the calls to the functions:

```
DBCC FREEPROCCACHE
GO
SELECT * FROM Fnc_Multi_Customers(6);
GO
SELECT * FROM Fnc_Inline_Customers(6);
GO
SELECT * FROM Fnc_Multi_Customers(2);
GO
SELECT * FROM Fnc_Inline_Customers(2);
GO
```

If you run the *usecounts* query, notice that only the multistatement function has its plan reused. The inline function is actually treated like a view, and the only way the plan can be reused would be if the exact same query were reexecuted—that is, if the same *SELECT* statement called the function with the exact same parameter.

Causes of recompilation

Up to this point, this chapter has discussed the situations in which SQL Server automatically reuses a plan and the situations in which a plan might be reused inappropriately so that you need to force recompilation. However, in some situations an existing plan isn't reused because of changes to the underlying objects or the execution environment. The reasons for these unexpected recompilations fall into one of two different categories: correctness-based recompiles and optimality-based recompiles.

Correctness-based recompiles

SQL Server might choose to recompile a plan if it has reason to suspect that the existing plan might no longer be correct. This can happen when explicit changes are made to the underlying objects, such as changing a data type or dropping an index. Obviously, any existing plan that referenced the column by assuming its former data type or that accessed data by using the now nonexistent index wouldn't be correct. Correctness-based recompiles fall into two general categories: schema changes and environmental changes. The following changes mark an object's schema as changed:

- Adding or dropping columns to or from a table or view

- Adding or dropping constraints, defaults, or rules to or from a table

- Adding an index to a table or an indexed view

- Dropping an index defined on a table or an indexed view if the index is used by the plan

- Dropping a statistic defined on a table that causes a correctness-related recompilation of any query plans that use that table

- Adding or dropping a trigger from a table

Also, running the procedure *sp_recompile* on a table or view changes the modification date for the object, which you can observe in the *modify_date* column in *sys.objects*. This makes SQL Server behave as though a schema change has occurred so that recompilation takes place at the next execution of any stored procedure, function, or trigger that accesses the table or view. Running *sp_recompile* on a procedure, trigger, or function clears all the plans for the executable object out of cache to guarantee that the next time it's executed, it will be recompiled.

Other correctness-based recompiles are invoked when the environment changes by changing one of a list of *SET* options. Changes in certain *SET* options can cause a query to return different results, so when one of these values changes, SQL Server wants to make sure a plan is used that was created in a similar environment. SQL Server keeps track of which *SET* options are set when a plan is executed, and you have access to a bitmap of these *SET* options by using the DMF called *sys.dm_exec_plan_attributes*. This function is called by passing in a plan handle value that you can obtain from the *sys.dm_exec_cached_plans* view and returns one row for each of a list of plan attributes. You need to make sure that you include *plan_handle* in the list of columns to be retrieved, not just the few columns used earlier in the *usecounts* query. The following is an example of retrieving all the plan attributes when you supply a *plan_handle* value:

```
SELECT * FROM sys.dm_exec_plan_attributes (0x06001200CF0B831CB821AA05000000000000000000000000)
```

Table 12-1 shows some possible results for the plan attributes, depending on the actual *plan_handle* value supplied. You will probably get different values for *objectid*, *dbid*, and *sqlhandle*.

TABLE 12-1 Attributes corresponding to a particular planhandle value

Attribute	Value	is_cache_key
set_options	4347	1
objectid	478350287	1
Dbid	18	1
dbid_execute	0	1
user_id	1	1
language_id	0	1
date_format	1	1
date_first	7	1
compat_level	110	1
status	0	1
required_cursor_options	0	1
acceptable_cursor_options	0	1
merge_action_type	0	1
is_replication_specific	0	1
optional_spid	0	1
optional_clr_trigger_dbid	0	1
optional_clr_trigger_objid	0	1
inuse_exec_context	0	0
free_exec_context	1	0
hits_exec_context	0	0
misses_exec_context	0	0
removed_exec_context	0	0
inuse_cursors	0	0
free_cursors	0	0
hits_cursors	0	0
misses_cursors	0	0
removed_cursors	0	0
sql_handle	0x02000000CF0B-831CBBE70632EC8A-8F7828AD6E6	0

Later in this chapter when we explore cache management and caching internals, you learn about some of these values for which the meaning isn't obvious. The chapter also goes into more detail about the metadata that keeps track of your plans. To get the attributes to be returned in a row along with each *plan_handle*, you can use the *PIVOT* operator and list each attribute that you want to turn into a column. The next query retrieves the *set_options*, the *object_id*, and the *sql_handle* from the list of attributes:

```
SELECT plan_handle, pvt.set_options, pvt.object_id, pvt.sql_handle
FROM (SELECT plan_handle, epa.attribute, epa.value
    FROM sys.dm_exec_cached_plans
        OUTER APPLY sys.dm_exec_plan_attributes(plan_handle) AS epa
    WHERE cacheobjtype = 'Compiled Plan'
    ) AS ecpa
PIVOT (MAX(ecpa.value) FOR ecpa.attribute
  IN ("set_options", "object_id", "sql_handle")) AS pvt;
```

The result is a value of 4347 for *set_options*, which is equivalent to the bit string 1000011111011. To see which bit refers to which *SET* options, you could change one option and then see how the bits have changed. For example, if you clear the plan cache and change *ANSI_NULLS* to *OFF*, the *set_options* value changes to 4315, or binary 1000011011011. The difference is the sixth bit from the right, which has a value of 32 (the difference between 4347 and 4315). If you didn't clear the plan cache, you would end up with two plans for the same batch, one for each *set_options* value.

Not all changes to *SET* options cause a recompile, although many of them do. The following is a list of the *SET* options that cause a recompile when changed:

ANSI_NULL_DFLT_OFF	DATEFIRST
ANSI_NULL_DFLT_ON	DATEFORMAT
ANSI_NULLS	FORCEPLAN
ANSI_PADDING	LANGUAGE
ANSI_WARNINGS	NO_BROWSETABLE
ARITHABORT	NUMERIC_ROUNDABORT
CONCAT_NULL_YIELDS_NULL	QUOTED_IDENTIFIER

Two of the *SET* options in this list have a special behavior in relation to objects, including stored procedures, functions, views, and triggers. The *SET* option settings for *ANSI_NULLS* and *QUOTED_IDENTIFIER* are actually saved along with the object definition, and the procedure or function always executes with the *SET* values as they were when the object was first created. You can determine what values these two *SET* options had for your objects by selecting from the *OBJECTPROPERTY* function, as follows:

```
SELECT OBJECTPROPERTY(object_id('<object name>'), 'ExecIsQuotedIdentOn');
SELECT OBJECTPROPERTY(object_id('<object name>'), 'ExecIsAnsiNullsOn');
```

A returned value of 0 means that the *SET* option is *OFF*, a value of 1 means that the option is *ON*, and a value of NULL means that you typed something incorrectly or don't have appropriate permissions. However, even though changing the value of either of these options doesn't cause any difference in execution of the objects, SQL Server can still recompile the statement that accesses the object. The only objects for which recompilation is avoided is for cached plans with an *objtype* value of *Proc*—namely, stored procedures and multistatement TVFs. For these compiled objects, the *usecounts* query shows you the same plan being reused but doesn't show additional plans with different *set_options* values. Inline TVFs and views create new plans if these options are changed, and the *set_options* value indicates a different bitmap. However, the behavior of the underlying *SELECT* statement doesn't change.

Optimality-based recompiles

SQL Server might also recompile a plan if it has reason to suspect that the existing plan is no longer optimal. The primary reasons for suspecting a non-optimal plan deal with changes to the underlying data. If any of the statistics used to generate the query plan have been updated since the plan was created, or if any of the statistics are considered stale, SQL Server recompiles the query plan.

Updated statistics   Statistics can be updated either manually or automatically. Manual updates happen when someone runs *sp_updatestats* or the *UPDATE STATISTICS* command. Automatic updates happen when SQL Server determines that existing statistics are out-of-date (or stale), and these updates happen only when the database has the option *AUTO_UPDATE_STATISTICS* or *AUTO_UPDATE_STATISTICS_ASYNC* set to *ON*. This could happen if another batch had tried to use one of the same tables or indexes used in the current plan, detected the statistics were stale, and initiated an *UPDATE STATISTICS* operation.

Stale statistics   SQL Server detects out-of-date statistics when it first compiles a batch that has no plan in cache. It also detects stale statistics for existing plans. Figure 12-2 shows a flowchart of the steps involved in finding an existing plan and checking to see whether recompilation is required. You can see that SQL Server checks for stale statistics after checking to see whether updated statistics are already available. If stale statistics exist, the statistics are updated, and then a recompile begins on the batch. If *AUTO_UPDATE_STATISTICS_ASYNC* is *ON* for the database, SQL Server doesn't wait for the update of statistics to complete; it just recompiles based on the stale statistics.

> **Note** Make sure that you perform thorough performance tests if you are considering setting *AUTO_UIPDATE_STATISTICS* to *OFF*. Although your queries might benefit from avoiding the time to update the statistics, frequently the plan generated because of the stale statistics can be much worse.

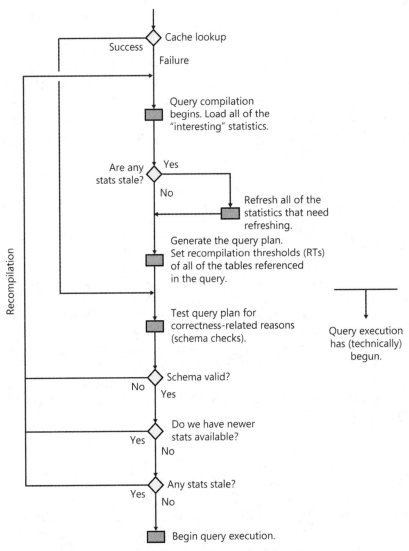

FIGURE 12-2 Checking an existing plan to see whether recompilation is necessary.

Statistics are considered to be stale if a sufficient number of modifications have occurred on the column supporting the statistics. Each table has a recompilation threshold (RT) that determines how many changes can take place before any statistics on that table are marked as stale. The RT values depend on the table type—that is, whether it's permanent or temporary—and on the current number of rows in the table at the time a plan is compiled. The exact algorithms for determining the RT values are subject to change with each service pack, so this book uses the algorithm for the RTM release of SQL Server 2012. The formulas used in the various service packs should be similar to this but aren't guaranteed to be exactly the same. N indicates the cardinality of the table.

- For both permanent and temporary tables, if N is less or equal to 500, the RT value is 500. This means that for a relatively small table, you must make at least 500 changes to trigger recompilation. For larger tables, at least 500 changes must be made, plus 20 percent of the number of rows.

- For temporary tables, the algorithm is the same, with one exception. If the table is very small or empty (*N* is less than 6 before any data modification operations), you need only six changes to trigger a recompile. A procedure that creates a temporary table (which is empty when created) and then inserts six or more rows into that table must be recompiled as soon as the temporary table is accessed.

  You can get around this frequent recompilation of batches that create temporary tables by using the *KEEP PLAN* query hint. Use of this hint changes the recompilation thresholds for temporary tables and makes them identical to those for permanent tables. So if changes to temporary tables are causing many recompilations, and you suspect that the recompilations are affecting overall system performance, you can use this hint to see whether performance has improved. The hint can be specified as shown in this query:

```
SELECT <column list>
FROM dbo.PermTable A INNER JOIN #TempTable B ON A.col1 = B.col2
WHERE <filter conditions>
OPTION (KEEP PLAN)
```

- Table variables have no RT value. This means that you won't get recompilations caused by changes in the number of rows in a table variable.

Modification counters The RT values, as you just learned, are the number of changes required for SQL Server to recognize that statistics are stale. In versions prior to SQL Server 2005, the *sysindexes* system table keeps track of the number of changes that had actually occurred in a table in a column called *rowmodctr*. These counters keep track of any changes in any row of the table or index, even if the change was to a column that wasn't involved in any index or useful statistics. SQL Server now uses a set of Column Modification Counters (*colmodctr*) values, with a separate count being maintained for each column in a table, except for computed nonpersisted columns. These counters aren't transactional, which means that if a transaction starts, inserts thousands of rows into a table, and then is rolled back, the changes to the modification counters are *not* rolled back. Unlike the *rowmodctr* values in *sysindexes*, the *colmodctr* values aren't visible to the user but are available internally to the Query Optimizer.

For very large tables, these RT values are also quite large—and in many cases, unacceptably large. For example, if your table has a million rows, you need to make 200,000 modifications to trigger a recompile. In many cases, a different query plan might be better well before 200,000 changes are made. You can set up your own jobs to update statistics more frequently on certain big tables, after running tests to verify that doing so will indeed improve query performance.

Another option is to use a traceflag added in SQL Server 2008R2 SP1, described in a blog post written by Microsoft engineer Juergen Thomas at *http://blogs.msdn.com/b/saponsqlserver/archive/2011/09/07/changes-to-automatic-update-statistics-in-sql-server-traceflag-2371.aspx*. Trace flag 2371 changes the RT for large tables and makes it a sliding scale. The Knowledge Base article doesn't publish the exact formula it uses (and it's subject to change, in any case). For a 25,000-row table, the

RT is still 20 percent, but for a table with 100,000 rows, the RT drops to 10 percent. A million-row table has an RT value of about 3 percent, and a 50 million–row table has an RT of about half a percent.

> **Note** As always, use this traceflag with care. It can enable your statistics to be kept much more up to date, but as you've seen, that can result in more frequent compilations, which might or might not end up giving you a better plan.

Tracking changes to tables and indexed views using colmodctr values   The *colmodctr* values that SQL Server keeps track of are continually modified as the table data changes. Table 12-2 describes when and how the *colmodctr* values are modified based on changes to your data, including *INSERT*, *UPDATE*, *DELETE*, *BULK INSERT*, and *TRUNCATE TABLE* operations. Although only table modifications are specifically mentioned, keep in mind that the same *colmodctr* values are kept track of for indexed views.

TABLE 12-2 Factors affecting changes to the internal values

Statement	Changes to colmodctr values
INSERT	All colmodctr values increased by 1 for each row inserted.
DELETE	All colmodctr values increased by 1 for each row deleted.
UPDATE	If the update is to nonkey columns, colmodctr values for modified columns are increased by 1 for each row updated. If the update is to key columns, colmodctr values are increased by 2 for all the columns in the table, for each row updated.
BULK INSERT	All colmodctr values increased by N where N is the number of rows bulk inserted.
TRUNCATE TABLE	All colmodctr values increased by N where N is the table's cardinality.

Skipping the recompilation step

In several situations, SQL Server bypasses recompiling a statement for plan optimality reasons, such as the following.

- **When the plan is a trivial plan**   A trivial plan is one for which no alternative plans are available, based on the tables referenced by the query and the indexes (or lack of indexes) on those tables. In these cases, where only one way exists to process a query, any recompilation would be a waste of resources, no matter how much the statistics had changed. Keep in mind that a query isn't guaranteed to continue to have a trivial plan just because it originally had a trivial plan. If new indexes have been added since the query was last compiled, multiple possible ways might be available to process the query.

- **If the query contains the *OPTION* hint *KEEPFIXED PLAN***   SQL Server doesn't recompile the plan for any optimality-related reasons.

- **If automatic updates of statistics for indexes and statistics defined on a table or indexed view are disabled**   All plan optimality-related recompilations caused by those indexes or statistics will stop.

> **Caution** Turning off the auto-statistics feature usually isn't a good idea because the Query Optimizer would no longer be sensitive to data changes in those objects, and suboptimal query plans could easily result. You can consider using this technique only as a last resort after exhausting all other alternative ways to avoid recompilation. Be sure to thoroughly test your applications after changing the auto-statistics options to verify that you're not hurting performance in other areas.

- **If all the tables referenced in the query are read-only** SQL Server doesn't recompile the plan if all tables that the query references are read-only.

Multiple recompilations

The earlier discussion on unplanned recompilation primarily described situations in which a cached plan would be recompiled before execution. However, even if SQL Server calculates that it can reuse an existing plan, in some cases stale statistics or schema changes might be discovered after the batch begins execution, and then a recompile would occur after execution starts.

Each batch or stored procedure can contain multiple query plans, one for each statement that can be optimized. Before SQL Server begins executing any of the individual query plans, it checks for correctness and optimality of that plan. If one of the checks fails, the corresponding statement is compiled *again*, and a possibly different query plan is produced. One reason this can happen is by mixing Data Definition Language (DDL) and Data Manipulation (DML) statements within your batch. Because the DDL can change the definition of a referenced object, plans for subsequent statements referencing that object are no longer correct and need to be recompiled.

In some cases, query plans can be recompiled even if the plan for the batch wasn't cached. For example, a batch that contains a literal larger than 8 KB is never cached. However, if this batch creates a temporary table and then inserts multiple rows into that table, the insertion of the seventh row causes a recompilation because the recompilation threshold has been passed for temporary tables. Because of the large literal, the batch wasn't cached, but the currently executing plan needs to be recompiled.

In SQL Server 2000, when a batch was recompiled, *all* statements in the batch were recompiled, not just the one that initiated the recompilation. SQL Server 2005 introduced statement-level recompilation, which means that only the statement that causes the recompilation has a new plan created, not the entire batch. This means that SQL Server consumes less CPU time and memory during recompilations.

Removing plans from cache

In addition to needing to recompile a plan based on schema or statistics changes, SQL Server needs to compile plans for batches if all previous plans have been removed from the plan cache. Plans are removed from cache based on memory pressure, as discussed later in the section "Cache size management." However, other operations can cause plans to be removed from cache. Some of these operations remove all the plans from a particular database, whereas others remove all the plans for the entire SQL Server instance.

The following operations flush the entire plan cache so that all batches submitted afterward will need a fresh plan. Note that although some of these operations affect only a single database, the entire plan cache is cleared.

- Upgrading any database to SQL Server 2012

- Running the *DBCC FREEPROCCACHE* or *DBCC FREESYSTEMCACHE* commands

- Changing any of the following configuration options:

  - *cross db ownership chaining*

  - *index create memory*

  - *cost threshold for parallelism*

  - *max degree of parallelism*

  - *max text repl size*

  - *min memory per query*

  - *min server memory*

  - *max server memory*

  - *query governor cost limit*

  - *query wait*

  - *remote query timeout*

  - *user options*

The following operations clear all plans associated with a particular database:

- Running the *DBCC FLUSHPROCINDB* command

- Detaching a database

- Closing or opening an auto-close database

- Modifying a collation for a database using the *ALTER DATABASE...COLLATE* command

- Altering a database with any of the following commands:

  - *ALTER DATABASE...MODIFY_NAME*

  - *ALTER DATABASE...MODIFY FILEGROUP*

  - *ALTER DATABASE...SET ONLINE*

  - *ALTER DATABASE...SET OFFLINE*

- *ALTER DATABASE...SET EMERGENCY*

- *ALTER DATABASE...SET READ_ONLY*

- *ALTER DATABASE...SET READ_WRITE*

- *ALTER DATABASE...COLLATE*

■ Dropping a database

You can clear a single plan from cache in a couple of different ways. First, you can create a plan guide that exactly matches the SQL text for the cached plan, and then all plans with that text are removed automatically. SQL Server 2008 provides an easy way of creating a plan guide from plan cache. (Plan guides are discussed in detail later in this chapter.) The second way to remove a single plan from cache involves *DBCC FREEPROCCACHE*, as shown with the following syntax:

```
DBCC FREEPROCCACHE [ ( { plan_handle | sql_handle | pool_name } ) ] [ WITH NO_INFOMSGS ]
```

This command now allows you to specify one of three parameters to indicate which plan or plans you want to remove from cache:

■ **plan_handle** By specifying a *plan_handle*, you can remove the plan with that handle from cache. The *plan_handle* is guaranteed to be unique for all currently existing plans.

■ **sql_handle** By specifying a *sql_handle*, you can remove the plans with that handle from cache. You can have multiple plans for the same SQL text if any of the cache key values are changed, such as SET options. The code in Listing 12-4 illustrates this.

LISTING 12-4 Removing a plan from cache based on its *sql_handle*

```
USE AdventureWorks2012;
GO
DBCC FREEPROCCACHE;
GO
SET ANSI_NULLS ON
GO
SELECT * FROM Person.Person WHERE PersonType = 'EM';
GO
SELECT * FROM Person.Person WHERE PersonType = 'SC';
GO
SET ANSI_NULLS OFF
GO
SELECT * FROM Person.Person WHERE PersonType = 'EM';
GO
SET ANSI_NULLS ON
GO

-- Now examine the sys.dm_exec_query_stats view and notice two different rows for the
-- query searching for 'EM'
SELECT execution_count, text, sql_handle, query_plan
FROM sys.dm_exec_query_stats
   CROSS APPLY sys.dm_exec_sql_text(sql_handle) AS TXT
      CROSS APPLY sys.dm_exec_query_plan(plan_handle)AS PLN;
GO
```

```
-- The two rows containing 'EM' should have the same value for sql_handle;
-- Copy that sql_handle value and paste into the command below:
DBCC FREEPROCCACHE(0x02000000CECDF507D9D4D70720F581172A42506136AA80BA);
GO
-- If you examine sys.dm_exec_query_stats again, you see the rows for this query
-- have been removed
SELECT execution_count, text, sql_handle, query_plan
FROM sys.dm_exec_query_stats
    CROSS APPLY sys.dm_exec_sql_text(sql_handle) AS TXT
        CROSS APPLY sys.dm_exec_query_plan(plan_handle)AS PLN;
GO
```

■ ***pool_name*** By specifying the name of a Resource Governor pool, you can clear all the cache plans associated with queries that were assigned to workload group via the specified resource pool. (Chapter 2, "The SQLOS," described the Resource Governor, workload groups, and resource pools.)

Plan cache internals

Knowing when and how plans are reused or recompiled can help you design high-performing applications. The more you understand about optimal query plans, and how different actual values and cardinalities require different plans, the more you can determine when recompilation is useful. When you are getting unnecessary recompiles, or when SQL Server isn't recompiling when you think it should, your troubleshooting efforts will be easier the more you know about how plans are managed internally.

This section explores the internal organization of the plan cache, the metadata available, how SQL Server finds a plan in cache, plan cache sizing, and the plan eviction policy.

Cache stores

The plan cache in SQL Server is made up of four separate memory areas, called *cache stores*. (Other stores in memory can be seen in the DMV called *sys.dm_os_memory_cache_counters*, but only four contain query plans.) The names in parentheses are the values shown in the *type* column of *sys.dm_os_memory_cache_counters*.

■ **Object Plans** *(CACHESTORE_OBJCP)* Object Plans include plans for stored procedures, functions, and triggers.

■ **SQL Plans** *(CACHESTORE_SQLCP)* SQL Plans include the plans for ad hoc cached plans, autoparameterized plans, and prepared plans. The memory clerk that manages the SQLCP cache store is also used for the SQL Manager, which manages all the T-SQL text used in your ad hoc queries.

■ **Bound Trees** *(CACHESTORE_PHDR)* Bound Trees are the structures produced by the algebrizer in SQL Server for views, constraints, and defaults.

- **Extended Stored Procedures** *(CACHESTORE_XPROC)*   Extended procs (Xprocs) are predefined system procedures, like *sp_executesql* and *sp_tracecreate*, that are defined by using a dynamic link library (DLL), not by using T-SQL statements. The cached structure contains only the function name and the DLL name in which the procedure is implemented.

Each plan cache store contains a hash table to keep track of all the plans in that particular store. Each bucket in the hash table contains zero, one, or more cached plans. When determining which bucket to use, SQL Server uses a very straightforward hash algorithm. The hash key is computed as *(object_id * database_id)* mod (hash table size). For plans associated with ad hoc or prepared plans, the *object_id* is an internal hash of the batch text. The DMV *sys.dm_os_memory_cache_hash_tables* contains information about each hash table, including its size. You can query this view to retrieve the number of buckets for each of the plan cache stores by using the following query:

```
SELECT type as 'plan cache store', buckets_count
FROM sys.dm_os_memory_cache_hash_tables
WHERE type IN ('CACHESTORE_OBJCP', 'CACHESTORE_SQLCP',
  'CACHESTORE_PHDR', 'CACHESTORE_XPROC');
```

Notice that the Bound Trees store has about 10 percent of the number of hash buckets of the stores for Object Plans and SQL Plans. (On a 64-bit system, the number of buckets for the Object Plan and SQL Plan stores is about 40,000; on a 32-bit system, the number is about 10,000.) The number of buckets for the Extended Stored Procedures store is always set to 127 entries.

To find the size of the stores themselves, you can use the view *sys.dm_os_memory_objects*. The following query returns the size of all the cache stores holding plans, plus the size of the SQL Manager, which stores the T-SQL text of all the ad hoc and prepared queries:

```
SELECT type AS Store, SUM(pages_in_bytes/1024.) AS KB_used
FROM sys.dm_os_memory_objects
WHERE type IN ('MEMOBJ_CACHESTOREOBJCP', 'MEMOBJ_CACHESTORESQLCP',
  'MEMOBJ_CACHESTOREXPROC', 'MEMOBJ_SQLMGR')
GROUP BY type;
```

Finding a plan in cache is a two-step process. The hash key described previously leads SQL Server to the bucket in which a plan might be found, but if the bucket has multiple entries, SQL Server needs more information to determine whether the exact plan it's looking for can be found. For this second step, it needs a cache key, which is a combination of several attributes of the plan. Earlier, you looked at the DMF *sys.dm_exec_plan_attributes*, to which you could pass a *plan_handle*. The results obtained were a list of attributes for a particular plan, and a Boolean value indicating whether that particular value was part of the cache key. Table 12-1 included 17 attributes that comprise the cache key, and SQL Server needs to make sure all 17 values match before determining that it has found a matching plan in cache. In addition to the 17 values found in *sys.dm_exec_plan_attributes*, the column *sys.dm_exec_cached_plans.pool_id* is also part of the cache key for any plan.

Compiled plans

The Object and SQL plan cache stores have two main types of plans: compiled plans and executable plans. Compiled plans are the type of object this chapter has looked at up to this point when examining the *sys.dm_exec_cached_plans* view. You've already seen the three main *objtype* values that can correspond to a compiled plan: *Adhoc*, *Prepared*, and *Proc*. Compiled plans can be stored in either the Object Store or the SQL Store, depending on which of those three *objtype* values they have. The compiled plans are considered valuable memory objects because they can be costly to re-create. SQL Server attempts to keep them in cache. When SQL Server experiences heavy memory pressure, the policies used to remove cache objects ensure that the compiled plans aren't the first objects to be removed.

A compiled plan is generated for an entire batch, not just for a single statement. For a multistatement batch, you can think of a compiled plan as an array of plans, with each element of the array containing a query plan for an individual statement. Compiled plans can be shared between multiple sessions or users. However, be aware that not every user executing the same plan will get the same results, even if the underlying data hasn't changed. Unless the compiled plan is an ad hoc plan, each user has her own parameters and local variables, and the batch can build temporary tables or worktables specific to that user. The information specific to one particular execution of a compiled plan is stored in another structure called the *executable plan*.

Execution contexts

Executable plans, or execution contexts, are considered to be dependent on compiled plans and don't show up in the *sys.dm_exec_cached_plans* view. Executable plans are runtime objects created when a compiled plan is executed. Just as for compiled plans, executable plans can be Object Plans, stored in the Object Store, or SQL Plans, stored in the SQL Store. Each executable plan exists in the same cache store as the compiled plan on which it depends. Executable plans contain the particular runtime information for one execution of a compiled plan and include the actual runtime parameters, any local variable information, object IDs for objects created at runtime, the user ID, and information about the currently executing statement in the batch.

When SQL Server starts executing a compiled plan, it generates an executable plan from that compiled plan. Each individual statement in a compiled plan gets its own executable plan, which you can think of as a runtime query plan. Unlike compiled plans, executable plans are for a single session. For example, if 100 users are executing the same batch simultaneously, 100 executable plans will be generated for the same compiled plan. Executable plans can be regenerated from their associated compiled plan, and they are relatively inexpensive to create. Later, this section looks at the *sys.dm_exec_cached_plan_dependent_objects* view, which contains information about your executable plans. Note that Compiled Plan Stubs, generated when the Optimize for Ad Hoc Workloads configuration option is set to 1, don't have associated execution contexts.

Plan cache metadata

You've already seen some of the information in the *sys.dm_exec_cached_plans* DMV when you looked at *usecount* information to determine whether your plans were being reused. This section looks at some of the other metadata objects and discusses the meaning of some of the data contained in the metadata.

Handles

The *sys.dm_exec_cached_plans* view contains a value called a *plan_handle* for every compiled plan. The *plan_handle* is a hash value that SQL Server derives from the compiled plan of the entire batch, and it's guaranteed to be unique for every currently existing compiled plan. (The *plan_handle* values can be reused over time.) The *plan_handle* can be used as an identifier for a compiled plan. The *plan_handle* remains the same even if individual statements in the batch are recompiled because of the correctness or optimality reasons discussed earlier.

As mentioned, the compiled plans are stored in the two cache stores, depending on whether the plan is an Object Plan or a SQL Plan. The actual SQL Text of the batch or object is stored in another cache called the SQL Manager Cache (SQLMGR). The T-SQL Text associated with each batch is stored in its entirety, including all comments. You can retrieve the T-SQL Text cached in the SQLMGR cache by using a data value called the *sql_handle*. The *sql_handle* contains a hash of the entire batch text, and because it's unique for every batch, the *sql_handle* can serve as an identifier for the batch text in the SQLMGR cache.

Any specific T-SQL batch always has the same *sql_handle*, but it might not always have the same *plan_handle*. If any of the values in the cache key change, you get a new *plan_handle* in plan cache. (Refer to Table 12-1 to see which plan attributes make up the cache keys.) The relationship between *sql_handle* and *plan_handle*, therefore, is 1:*N*.

You've seen that *plan_handle* values can be obtained easily from the *sys.dm_exec_cached_plans* view. You can get the *sql_handle* value that corresponds to a particular *plan_handle* from the *sys.dm_exec_plan_attributes* function discussed earlier. Here is the same query that was discussed earlier to return attribute information and pivot it so that three of the attributes are returned in the same row as the *plan_handle* value:

```
SELECT plan_handle, pvt.set_options, pvt.object_id, pvt.sql_handle
FROM (SELECT plan_handle, epa.attribute, epa.value
    FROM sys.dm_exec_cached_plans
        OUTER APPLY sys.dm_exec_plan_attributes(plan_handle) AS epa

    WHERE cacheobjtype = 'Compiled Plan'
    ) AS ecpa
PIVOT (MAX(ecpa.value) FOR ecpa.attribute
    IN ("set_options", "object_id", "sql_handle")) AS pvt;
```

The *sys.dm_exec_query_stats* view contains both *plan_handle* and *sql_handle* values, as well as information about how often each plan was executed and how much work was involved in the execution. The value for *sql_handle* is very cryptic, and determining which query each *sql_handle* corresponds to can be difficult. To get that information, you can use another function.

sys.dm_exec_sql_text

This function can take either a *sql_handle* or a *plan_handle* as a parameter, and it returns the SQL Text that corresponds to the handle. Any sensitive information that might be contained in the SQL Text (such as passwords) are blocked when the SQL is returned. The text column in the function's output contains the entire SQL batch text for ad hoc, prepared, and autoparameterized queries; for objects such as triggers, procedures, and functions, it gives the full object definition.

Viewing the SQL Text from *sys.dm_exec_sql_text* is useful in quickly identifying identical batches that can have different compiled plans because of several factors, such as *SET* option differences. For example, consider the following code, which executes two identical batches. This example is similar to the one shown as part of Listing 12-4 when I discussed using *DBCC FREEPROCCACHE* with a *sql_handle*, but this time, you see the *sql_handle* and *plan_handle* values. The only difference between the two consecutive executions is that the value of the *SET* option *QUOTED_IDENTIFIER* has changed. It's *OFF* in the first execution and *ON* in the second. After executing both batches, you can examine the *sys.dm_exec_query_stats* view:

```
USE AdventureWorks2012;
DBCC FREEPROCCACHE;
SET QUOTED_IDENTIFIER OFF;
GO
-- this is an example of the relationship between
-- sql_handle and plan_handle
SELECT LastName, FirstName, Title
FROM Person.Person
WHERE PersonType = 'EM';
GO
SET QUOTED_IDENTIFIER ON;
GO
-- this is an example of the relationship between
-- sql_handle and plan_handle
SELECT LastName, FirstName, Title
FROM Person.Person
WHERE PersonType = 'EM';
GO
SELECT st.text, qs. sql_handle, qs.plan_handle
FROM sys.dm_exec_query_stats qs
    CROSS APPLY sys.dm_exec_sql_text(sql_handle) st;
GO
```

You should see two rows with the same text string and *sql_handle*, but with different *plan_handle* values, as shown here. In the following output, the difference between the two *plan_handle* values is only a couple of digits, so it might be hard to see, but in other cases, the difference might be more obvious.

Text	sql_handle	plan_handle
-- this is an example of the -- relationship between -- sql_handle and plan_handle SELECT LastName, FirstName, Title FROM Person.Person WHERE PersonType = 'EM';	0x020000000F31773489883 22B57A36298C26C7C4A42BF E41E00000000000000000000 00000000000000000000	0x06000B000F317734B08FD AFF020000000010000000000 0000000000000000000000000 00000000000000000000
-- this is an example of the -- relationship between -- sql_handle and plan_handle SELECT LastName, FirstName, Title FROM Person.Person WHERE PersonType = 'EM';	0x020000000F31773489883 22B57A36298C26C7C4A42BF E41E00000000000000000000 00000000000000000000	0x06000B000F3177345082D AFF020000000010000000000 0000000000000000000000000 00000000000000000000

You can see that two plans correspond to the same batch text. This example should clarify the importance of making sure that all *SET* options that affect plan caching should be the same when the same queries are executed repeatedly. You should verify whatever changes your programming interface makes to your *SET* options to make sure that you don't end up with different plans unintentionally.

Not all interfaces use the same defaults for the *SET* option values. For example, the SQLCMD interface uses the ODBC driver, which sets *QUOTED_IDENTIFIER* to *OFF* for every connection, whereas Management Studio uses ADO.NET, which sets *QUOTED_IDENTIFIER* to *ON*. Executing the same batches from these two different clients results in multiple plans in cache.

sys.dm_exec_query_plan

This table-valued function takes a *plan_handle* as a parameter and returns the associated query plan in XML format. If the plan is for an object, the TVF includes the database ID, object ID, procedure number, and encryption state of the object. If the plan is for an ad hoc or prepared query, the *dbid* value will reflect the ID of the database where the statements were compiled, and the additional values are NULL. If the *plan_handle* corresponds to a *Compiled Plan Stub*, the query plan will also be NULL. Some of the preceding examples use this function.

sys.dm_exec_text_query_plan

This table-valued function takes a *plan_handle* as a parameter and returns the same basic information as *sys.dm_exec_query_plan*. The differences between the two functions are as follows.

- *sys.dm_exec_text_query_plan* can take optional input parameters to specify the start and end offset of statements with a batch.

- The output of *sys.dm_exec_text_query_plan* returns the plan as text data, instead of XML data.

- The text output for the query plan returned by sys.dm_exec_text_query_plan is unlimited in size. (The XML output for the query returned by sys.dm_exec_query_plan is limited to 128 levels of nested elements. If the plans exceeds that, NULL is returned.)

sys.dm_exec_cached_plans

This view is the one used most often for troubleshooting query plan recompilation issues. It's used in the "Plan cache metadata" section to illustrate the plan reuse behavior of ad hoc plans compared to autoparameterized and prepared plans. This view has one row per cached plan, and in addition to the *plan_handle* and *usecounts*, which you've looked at already, this DMV has other useful information about the cached plans.

- **size_in_bytes**   The number of bytes consumed by this cache object.

- **cacheobjtype**   The type of the cache object—that is, if it's a Compiled Plan, a Parse Tree, or an Extended Proc.

- **memory_object_address**   The memory address of the cache object, which can be used to get the memory breakdown of the cache object.

  Although this DMV doesn't have the SQL Text associated with each compiled plan, you can find it by passing the *plan_handle* to the *sys.dm_exec_sql_text* function. You can use the following query to retrieve the *text*, *usecounts*, and *size_in_bytes* of the compiled plan and *cacheobjtype* for all the plans in cache. The results are returned in order of frequency, with the batch having the most use showing up first.

```
SELECT st.text, cp.plan_handle, cp.usecounts, cp.size_in_bytes,
    cp.cacheobjtype, cp.objtype
FROM sys.dm_exec_cached_plans cp
    CROSS APPLY sys.dm_exec_sql_text(cp.plan_handle) st
ORDER BY cp.usecounts DESC;
```

- **pool_id**   The ID of the resource pool with which this plan is associated. As *DBCC FREEPROCCCACHE* allows specifying a particular resource pool's plans to be removed from cache, analyzing which pools are making the most use of plan cache can be useful for cache-tuning purposes.

sys.dm_exec_cached_plan_dependent_objects

This function returns one row for every dependent object of a compiled plan when you pass a valid *plan_handle* as a parameter. If the *plan_handle* isn't that of a compiled plan, the function returns NULL. Dependent objects include executable plans, as discussed earlier, as well as plans for cursors used by the compiled plan.

The following example uses *sys.dm_exec_cached_plan_dependent_objects*, as well as *sys.dm_exec_cached_plans*, to retrieve the dependent objects for all compiled plans, the *plan_handle*, and their *usecounts*. It also calls the *sys.dm_exec_sql_text* function to return the associated T-SQL batch.

```
SELECT text, plan_handle, d.usecounts, d.cacheobjtype
FROM sys.dm_exec_cached_plans
CROSS APPLY sys.dm_exec_sql_text(plan_handle)
CROSS APPLY
    sys.dm_exec_cached_plan_dependent_objects(plan_handle) d;
```

sys.dm_exec_requests

This view returns one row for every currently executing request within your SQL Server instance. It's useful for many purposes in addition to tracking down plan cache information. This DMV contains the *sql_handle* and the *plan_handle* for the current statement, as well as resource usage information for each request. For troubleshooting purposes, you can use this view to help identify long-running queries.

Keep in mind that the *sql_handle* points to the T-SQL for the entire batch. However, the *sys.dm_exec_requests* view contains the *statement_start_offset* and *statement_end_offset* columns, which indicate the position within the entire batch where the currently executing statement can be found. The offsets start at 0, and an offset of –1 indicates the end of the batch. The statement offsets can be used with the *sql_handle* passed to *sys.dm_exec_sql_text* to extract the query text from the entire batch text, as demonstrated in the following code. This query returns the 10 longest-running queries currently executing:

```
SELECT TOP 10 SUBSTRING(text, (statement_start_offset/2) + 1,
    ((CASE statement_end_offset
        WHEN -1
            THEN DATALENGTH(text)
        ELSE statement_end_offset
    END - statement_start_offset)/2) + 1) AS query_text, *
FROM sys.dm_exec_requests
    CROSS APPLY sys.dm_exec_sql_text(sql_handle)
ORDER BY total_elapsed_time DESC;
```

> **Note** Including the asterisk (*) in the *SELECT* list indicates that this query should return *all* the columns from the *sys.dm_exec_requests* view. You should replace the asterisk with the columns that you are particularly interested in, such as *start_time* or *blocking_session_id*.

sys.dm_exec_query_stats

Just as the text returned from the *sql_handle* is the text for the entire batch, the compiled plans that are returned are for the entire batch. For optimum troubleshooting, you can use *sys.dm_exec_query_stats* to return performance information for individual queries within a batch. This view returns performance statistics for queries, aggregated across all executions of the same query. This view also returns both a *sql_handle* and a *plan_handle*, as well as the start and end offsets like you saw in *sys.dm_exec_requests*. The following query returns the top 10 queries by total CPU time, to help you identify the most expensive queries on your SQL Server instance:

```
SELECT TOP 10 SUBSTRING(text, (statement_start_offset/2) + 1,
    ((CASE statement_end_offset
        WHEN -1
            THEN DATALENGTH(text)
        ELSE statement_end_offset
    END - statement_start_offset)/2) + 1) AS query_text, *

FROM sys.dm_exec_query_stats
```

```
        CROSS APPLY sys.dm_exec_sql_text(sql_handle)
        CROSS APPLY sys.dm_exec_query_plan(plan_handle)
ORDER BY total_elapsed_time/execution_count DESC;
```

This view has one row per query statement within a batch. When a plan is removed from cache, the corresponding rows and the accumulated statistics for that statement are removed from this view. In addition to the *plan_handle*, *sql_handle*, and performance information, this view contains two columns added in SQL Server 2008, which can help you identify similar queries with different plans.

- ■ *query_hash*   This value is a hash of the query text and can be used to identify similar queries with the plan cache. Queries that vary only in the values of constants have the same *query_hash* value.

- ■ *query_plan_hash*   This value is a hash of the query execution plan and can be used to identify similar plans based on logical and physical operators and a subset of the operator attributes. To look for cases where you might not want to implement forced parameterization, you can search for queries that have similar *query_hash* values but different *query_plan_hash* values. Both *query_hash* and *query_plan_hash* can also be captured with Extended Events in SQL Server 2012.

sys.dm_exec_cached_plans and *sys.dm_exec_query_stats* have two main differences. First, *sys.dm_exec_cached_plans* has one row for each batch that has been compiled and cached, whereas *sys.dm_exec_query_stats* has one row for each statement. Second, *sys.dm_exec_query_stats* contains summary information aggregating all the executions of a particular statement. It also returns a tremendous amount of performance information for each query, including the number of times it was executed, as well as the cumulative I/O, CPU, and duration information.

Keep in mind that *sys.dm_exec_query_stats* is updated only when a query is completed, so you might need to retrieve information multiple times if a large workload is currently running on your server.

sys.dm_exec_procedure_stats

This view returns one row for each cached stored procedure plan containing aggregate performance information for each procedure. When a stored procedure is removed from the cache, the corresponding row is eliminated from this view. The columns are similar to those in *sys.dm_exec_query_stats*. Another column indicates the type of stored procedure that has one of the following values: *SQL_STORED_PROCEDURE*, *CLR_STORED_PROCEDURE*, or *EXTENDED_STORED_PROCEDURE*.

Cache size management

This chapter has already discussed plan reuse and how SQL Server finds a plan in cache. This section looks at how SQL Server manages the size of plan cache and how it determines which plans to remove if no room is left in cache. Earlier, you saw a few situations in which plans would be removed from cache. These situations included global operations such as running *DBCC FREEPROCCACHE* to clear all plans from cache, as well as changes to a single procedure, such as *ALTER PROCEDURE*, which would drop all plans for that procedure from cache. In most other situations, plans are removed from cache only when memory pressure is detected. The algorithm that SQL Server uses to determine when and how plans should be removed from cache is called the *eviction policy*. Each cache store can have its own eviction policy, but this section covers only the policies for the Object Plan store and the SQL Plan store.

Determining which plans to evict is based on the plan's cost, as discussed in the next section. When eviction starts is based on memory pressure. When SQL Server detects memory pressure, zero-cost plans are removed from cache, and the cost of all other plans is reduced by half. As discussed in Chapter 2, two types of memory pressure lead to removal of plans from cache. These two types of memory pressure are referred to as *local* and *global* memory pressure.

With memory pressure comes the term *visible memory*. Visible memory is the directly address-able physical memory available to the SQL Server memory manager. On a 32-bit SQL Server instance, the maximum value for the visible memory is either 2 GB or 3 GB, depending on whether you have the */3 GB* flag set in your boot.ini file. In SQL Server versions prior to SQL Server 2012, memory with addresses greater than 2 GB or 3 GB was available indirectly, through *AWE-mapped-memory*, but this option was removed for the current version. On a 64-bit SQL Server instance, visible memory has no special meaning because all memory is directly addressable. When this chapter refers to visible target memory greater than 3 GB, keep in mind that that's only possible on a 64-bit SQL Server instance.

The term *target memory* refers to the maximum amount of memory that can be committed to the SQL Server process. Target memory is the lesser of the value you have configured for max server memory and the total amount of physical memory available to the operating system. So *visible target memory* is the visible portion of the target memory. You can see a value for visible memory, specified in kilobytes, in the *visible_target_kb* column in the *sys.dm_os_sys_info* DMV. This view also contains values for *committed_kb* and *committed_targe_kb*.

SQL Server defines a cache store pressure limit value, which varies depending on the version you're running and the amount of visible target memory. The formula for determining the plan cache pressure limit changed in SQL Server 2005 SP2. Table 12-3 shows how to determine the plan cache pressure limit in SQL Server 2000 and 2005, and indicates the change in SP2, which reduced the pressure limit with higher amounts of memory. SQL Server 2012 RTM uses the same formulas that were added in SQL Server 2005 SP2. Be aware that these formulas can be subject to change again in future service packs.

TABLE 12-3 Determining the plan cache pressure limit

SQL Server version	Cache pressure limit
SQL Server 2000	4 GB upper cap on the plan cache
SQL Server 2005 RTM & SP1	75 percent of visible target memory from 0 to 8 GB + 50 percent of visible target memory from 8 GB to 64 GB + 25 percent of visible target memory > 64 GB
SQL Server 2005 SP2 and SP3, SQL Server 2008, SQL Server 2008R2, SQL Server 2012	75 percent of visible target memory from 0 to 4 GB + 10 percent of visible target memory from 4 GB to 64 GB + 5 percent of visible target memory > 64 GB

Suppose that you are using SQL Server 2005 SP1 on a 64-bit SQL Server instance with 28 GB of target memory. The plan cache pressure limit would be 75 percent of 8 GB plus 50 percent of the target memory over 8 GB (or 50 percent of 20 GB), which is 6 GB + 10 GB, or 16 GB. On a 64-bit SQL Server 2012 RTM instance with 28 GB of target memory, the plan cache pressure limit would be 75 percent of 4 GB plus 10 percent of the target memory over 4 GB (or 10 percent of 24 GB), which is 3 GB + 2.4 GB, or 5.4 GB.

Local memory pressure

If any single cache store grows too big, it indicates local memory pressure, and SQL Server starts removing entries from only that store. This behavior prevents one store from using too much of the total system memory. If a cache store reaches 62.5 percent of the plan cache pressure limit, as described in Table 12-3, internal memory pressure is triggered and plans are removed from cache.

Prior to version 2012, single-page allocations and multipage allocations were treated separately, and the multipage allocations weren't included in the max server memory value; instead, they added to it. Also, single-page allocations and multipage allocations would trigger internal memory pressure separately. If a cache store reaches 75 percent of the plan cache pressure limit in single-page allocations or 50 percent of the plan cache pressure limit in multipage allocations, internal memory pressure was triggered, and plans were removed from cache. In SQL Server 2012, there is only one page allocator, called the *any-size page allocator*, can allocate either single-page units or multipage units. A straight 62.5 percent of the limit of allocations from the any-size page allocator triggers memory pressure.

For example, in the situation described just a few paragraphs earlier, the plan cache pressure limit was computed to be 5.4 GB. If any cache store exceeds 62.5 percent of that value, or 3.375 GB, internal memory pressure is triggered. If adding a particular plan to cache causes the cache store to exceed the limit, the removal of other plans from cache happens on the same thread as the one adding the new plan, which can cause the response time of the new query to be increased.

In addition to memory pressure occurring when the total amount of memory reaches a particular limit, SQL Server also indicates memory pressure when the number of plans in a store exceeds four times the hash table size for that store, regardless of the actual size of the plans. As mentioned previously when describing the cache stores, these hash tables have either about 10,000 or 40,000 buckets, for 32-bit and 64-bit systems, respectively. That means memory pressure can be triggered when either the SQL Store or the Object Store has more than 40,000 or 160,000 entries. The first query shown here is one you saw earlier, and it can be used to determine the number of buckets in the hash tables for the Object Store and the SQL Store, and the second query returns the number of entries in each of those stores:

```
SELECT type as 'plan cache store', buckets_count
FROM sys.dm_os_memory_cache_hash_tables
WHERE type IN ('CACHESTORE_OBJCP', 'CACHESTORE_SQLCP');
GO
SELECT type, count(*) total_entries
FROM sys.dm_os_memory_cache_entries
WHERE type IN ('CACHESTORE_SQLCP', 'CACHESTORE_OBJCP')
GROUP BY type;
GO
```

Prior to SQL Server 2008, internal memory pressure was rarely triggered (because of the number of entries in the hash tables) but was almost always initiated by the size of the plans in the cache store. However, in SQL Server 2008 or later, with Optimize for Ad Hoc Workloads enabled, the actual size of the SQL cache store can be quite small (each *Compiled Plan Stub* is about 300 bytes) so the number of entries can grow to exceed the limit before the size of the store gets too large. If Optimize for Ad Hoc Workloads isn't on, the size of the entries in cache is much larger, with a minimum size of 24 KB for each plan. To see the size of all the plans in a cache store, you need to examine *sys.dm_exec_cached_plans*:

```
SELECT objtype, count(*) AS 'number of plans',
     SUM(size_in_bytes)/(1024.0 * 1024.0 * 1024.0)
          AS size_in_gb_single_use_plans
FROM sys.dm_exec_cached_plans
GROUP BY objtype;
```

Remember that the ad hoc and prepared plans are both stored in the SQL cache store, so to monitor the size of that store, you have to add those two values together.

Global memory pressure

Global memory pressure applies to memory used by all the cache stores together and can be either external or internal. External global pressure occurs when the operating system determines that the SQL Server process needs to reduce its physical memory consumption because of competing needs from other server processes. All cache stores are reduced in size when this occurs.

Internal global memory pressure can occur when virtual address space is low. It can also occur when the memory broker predicts that all cache stores combined will use more than 80 percent of the plan cache pressure limit. Again, all cache stores will have entries removed when this occurs.

As mentioned, when SQL Server detects memory pressure, all zero-cost plans are removed from cache, and the cost of all other plans is reduced by half. Any particular cycle updates the cost of at most 16 entries for every cache store. When an updated entry has a zero-cost value, it can be removed. SQL Server can't free entries that are currently in use, but you can execute *DBCC FREESYS-TEMCACHE* with *MARK_IN_USE_FOR_REMOVAL* to cause a deferred removal of in-use cache entries so that they can be removed as soon as they are no longer used. SQL Server can remove unused dependent objects for an in-use compiled plan. Dependent objects include the executable plans and cursors, and up to half of the memory for these objects can be removed when memory pressure exists. Remember that dependent objects are inexpensive to re-create, especially compared to compiled plans.

Chapter 2 provides more information on memory management and memory pressure.

Costing of cache entries

The decision of what plans to evict from cache is based on their cost. For ad hoc plans, the cost is considered to be zero, but it's increased by 1 every time the plan is reused. For other types of plans, the cost is a measure of the resources required to produce the plan. When one of these plans is reused, the cost is reset to the original cost. For non–ad hoc queries, the cost is measured in units called *ticks*, with a maximum of 31. The cost is based on three factors: I/O, context switches, and memory. Each has its own maximum within the 31-tick total:

- **I/O** Each I/O costs 1 tick, with a maximum of 19.

- **Compilation-related context switches** Each switch costs 1 tick each, with a maximum of 8.

- **Compile memory** Compile memory costs 1 tick per 16 pages, with a maximum of 4.

When not under memory pressure, costs aren't decreased until the total size of all plans cached reaches 50 percent of the buffer pool size. At that point, the next plan access decrements the cost in ticks of all plans by 1. When memory pressure is encountered, SQL Server starts a dedicated resource monitor thread to decrement the cost of either plan objects in one particular cache (for local pressure) or all plan cache objects (for global pressure).

The *sys.dm_os_memory_cache_entries* DMV can show you the current and original cost of any cache entry, as well as the components that make up that cost:

```
SELECT text, objtype, refcounts, usecounts, size_in_bytes,
    disk_ios_count, context_switches_count,
    pages_kb as MemoryKB, original_cost, current_cost
FROM sys.dm_exec_cached_plans p
    CROSS APPLY sys.dm_exec_sql_text(plan_handle)
    JOIN sys.dm_os_memory_cache_entries e
    ON p.memory_object_address = e.memory_object_address
WHERE cacheobjtype = 'Compiled Plan'
    AND type in ('CACHESTORE_SQLCP', 'CACHESTORE_OBJCP')
ORDER BY objtype desc, usecounts DESC;
```

Note that you can find the specific entry in *sys.dm_os_memory_cache_entries* that corresponds to a particular plan in *sys.dm_exec_cached_plans* by joining on the *memory_object_address* column.

Objects in plan cache: the big picture

In addition to the DMVs discussed so far, another metadata object called *syscacheobjects* really is just a pseudotable. No DMVs existed prior to SQL Server 2005, but SQL Server did have about half a dozen pseudotables, including *sysprocesses* and *syslockinfo*, that took no space on disk and were materialized only when someone executed a query to access them, similarly to the way that DMVs work. These objects are still available in SQL Server 2012. In SQL Server 2000, the pseudotables were available only in the *master* database, or by using a full object qualification when referencing them. In SQL Server 2012, you can access *syscacheobjects* from any database using only the *sys* schema as a qualification. Table 12-4 lists some of the more useful columns in the *sys.syscacheobjects* object.

TABLE 12-4 Useful columns in sys.syscacheobjects

Column name	Description
bucketid	Internal hash table; helps SQL Server locate the plan more quickly. Two rows with the same bucket ID refer to the same object (for example, the same procedure or trigger).
cacheobjtype	Type of object in cache: Compiled Plan, Parse Tree, and so on.
objtype	Type of object: Adhoc, Prepared, Proc, and so on.
objid	One of the main keys used for looking up an object in cache. This is the object ID stored in sys-objects for database objects (procedures, views, triggers, and so on). For cache objects, such as Adhoc or Prepared, objid is an internally generated value.
dbid	Database ID in which the cache object was compiled.
Uid	The creator of the plan (for ad hoc query plans and prepared plans).
refcounts	Number of other cache objects that reference this cache object.
usecounts	Number of times this cache object has been used since its creation.
pagesused	Number of memory pages consumed by the cache object.
setopts	SET option settings that affect a compiled plan. Changes to values in this column indicate that users have modified SET options.
langid	Language ID of the connection that created the cache object.
dateformat	Date format of the connection that created the cache object.
Sql	Module definition or first 3,900 characters of the batch submitted.

In SQL Server 2000, the *syscacheobjects* pseudotable also includes entries for executable plans. That is, the *cacheobjtype* column could have a value of *Executable Plan*. As of SQL Server 2005, because executable plans are considered dependent objects and are stored completely separately from the compiled plans, they are no longer available through the *sys.syscacheobjects* view. To access the executable plans, you need to select directly from the *sys.dm_exec_cached_plan_dependent_objects* function and pass in a *plan_handle* as a parameter.

As an alternative to the *sys.syscacheobjects* view, which is a compatibility view and isn't guaranteed to exist in future versions, you can create your own view that retrieves the same information from the SQL Server Dynamic Management Objects. The script in Listing 12-5 creates a view called *sp_cacheobjects* in the *master* database. Remember that any objects with a name starting with *sp_*, created in the *master* database, can be accessed from any database without having to qualify the object name fully. Besides being able to access the *sp_cacheobjects* view from anywhere, another benefit of creating your own object is that you can customize it. For example, doing one more *OUTER APPLY*, to join this view with the *sys.dm_exec_query_plan* function, would be a relatively straightforward way to get the XML plan for each plan in cache.

```
USE master
GO
CREATE VIEW sp_cacheobjects

AS
    SELECT pvt.bucketid,
        CONVERT(nvarchar(18), pvt.cacheobjtype) AS cacheobjtype,
        pvt.objtype,
        CONVERT(int, pvt.objectid) AS objid,
        CONVERT(smallint, pvt.dbid) AS dbid,
        CONVERT(smallint, pvt.dbid_execute) AS dbidexec,
        CONVERT(smallint, pvt.user_id) AS uid,
        pvt.refcounts, pvt.usecounts,
        pvt.size_in_bytes / 8192 AS pagesused,
        CONVERT(int, pvt.set_options) AS setopts,
        CONVERT(smallint, pvt.language_id) AS langid,
        CONVERT(smallint, pvt.date_format) AS dateformat,
        CONVERT(int, pvt.status) AS status,
        CONVERT(bigint, 0) as lasttime,
        CONVERT(bigint, 0) as maxexectime,
        CONVERT(bigint, 0) as avgexectime,
        CONVERT(bigint, 0) as lastreads,
        CONVERT(bigint, 0) as lastwrites,
        CONVERT(int, LEN(CONVERT(nvarchar(max), fgs.text)) * 2) as sqlbytes,
        CONVERT(nvarchar(3900), fgs.text) as sql
FROM (SELECT ecp.*, epa.attribute, epa.value
  FROM sys.dm_exec_cached_plans ecp
    OUTER APPLY
      sys.dm_exec_plan_attributes(ecp.plan_handle) epa) AS ecpa
PIVOT (MAX(ecpa.value) for ecpa.attribute IN
    ("set_options", "objectid", "dbid",
    "dbid_execute", "user_id", "language_id",
    "date_format", "status")) AS pvt
OUTER APPLY sys.dm_exec_sql_text(pvt.plan_handle) fgs;
```

Notice that several of the output columns are hardcoded to a value of 0. For the most part, these columns are for data that hasn't been maintained since SQL Server 2000. In particular, these columns report on performance data for cached plans, which SQL Server 2000 maintained for each batch. Since then, it's maintained on a statement level and available through *sys.dm_exec_query_stats*. To be compatible with the *sys.syscacheobjects* view, the new view must return something in those column positions. If you choose to customize this view, you could choose to remove those columns.

Multiple plans in cache

SQL Server tries to limit the number of plans for a query or a procedure. Because plans are reentrant, this is easy to accomplish. You should be aware of some situations that cause multiple query plans for the same procedure to be saved in cache. The most likely situation is a difference in certain *SET* options, as discussed previously.

One other connection issue can affect whether a plan can be reused. If an owner name must be re-solved implicitly, a plan can't be reused. Suppose that user *sue* issues the following *SELECT* statement:

```
SELECT * FROM Sales;
```

SQL Server first tries to resolve the object by looking for an object called *Sales* in the default schema for the user *sue*. If no such object can be found, it looks for an object called *Sales* in the *dbo* schema. If user *dan* executes the exact same query, the object can be resolved in a completely differ-ent way (to an object in the default schema of the user *dan*), so *sue* and *dan* couldn't share the plan generated for this query. Because using the unqualified object name can lead to possible ambiguity, the query processor doesn't assume that an existing plan can be reused. However, the situation is dif-ferent if *sue* issues this command:

```
SELECT * FROM dbo.Sales;
```

Now you have no ambiguity. Anyone executing this exact query always references the same ob-ject. In the *sys.syscacheobjects* view, the column *uid* indicates the user ID for the connection in which the plan was generated. For ad hoc queries, only another connection with the same *user ID* value can use the same plan. The one exception is if the *user ID* value is recorded as –2 in *syscacheobjects*, which indicates that the query submitted doesn't depend on implicit name resolution and can be shared among different users. This is the preferred method.

 Tip Objects should always be qualified with their containing schema name, so that you never need to rely on implicit resolutions and the reuse of plan cache can be more effective.

When to use stored procedures and other caching mechanisms

Keep the following guidelines in mind when you are deciding whether to use stored procedures or one of the other query mechanisms.

- **Stored procedures**   These objects should be used when multiple connections are execut-ing batches in which the parameters are known. They are also useful when you need to have control over when a block of code is to be recompiled.

- **Ad hoc caching**   This option is beneficial only in limited scenarios. It's not dependable enough for you to design an application, expecting this behavior to control reuse of appropri-ate plans correctly.

- **Simple or forced parameterization**   This option can be useful for applications that can't be easily modified. However, when you initially design your applications, you should use methods that explicitly allow you to declare what your parameters and what their data types are, as described in the following two suggestions.

- **The _sp_executesql_ procedure**   This procedure can be useful when the same batch might be used multiple times and when the parameters are known.

- **The prepare and execute methods**   These methods are useful when multiple users are executing batches in which the parameters are known, or when a single user will definitely use the same batch multiple times.

Troubleshooting plan cache issues

To start addressing problems with plan cache usage and management, you must determine that existing problems are actually caused by plan-caching issues. Performance problems caused by misuse or mismanagement of plan cache, or inappropriate recompilation, can manifest themselves as simply a decrease in throughput or an increase in query response time. Problems with caching can also show up as out-of-memory errors or connection timeout errors, which can be caused by all sorts of different conditions.

Wait statistics indicating plan cache problems

To determine that plan-caching behavior is causing problems, one of the first things to look at is your wait statistics in SQL Server. This section will tell you about some of the primary wait types that can indicate problems with your plan cache.

Wait statistics are displayed when you query the _sys.dm_os_wait_stats_ view. The following query lists all the resources that your SQL Server service might have to wait for, and it displays the resources with the longest waiting list:

```
SELECT *
FROM sys.dm_os_wait_stats
ORDER BY waiting_tasks_count DESC;
```

Notice that not all wait types indicate a problem of some sort. Some waits are typical and expected. You can check out this blog post from Microsoft SQL Server support engineers for more details: _http://blogs.msdn.com/b/psssql/archive/2009/11/03/the-sql-server-wait-type-repository.aspx_.

Be aware that the values shown in this view are cumulative, so if you need to see the resources being waited on during a specific time period, you have to query the view at the beginning and end of the period. If you see relatively large wait times for any of the following resources, or if these resources are near the top of the list returned from the previous query, you should investigate your plan cache usage.

- **CMEMTHREAD waits**   This wait type indicates contention on the memory object from which cache descriptors are allocated. A very high rate of insertion of entries into the plan cache can cause contention problems. Similarly, contention can also occur when entries are removed from cache and the resource monitor thread is blocked. Descriptors are allocated from only one thread-safe memory object and, as you've seen, only a single cache store exists for ad hoc compiled plans.

Consider the same procedure being called dozens or hundreds of times. Remember that SQL Server caches the ad hoc shell query that includes the actual parameter for each individual call to the procedure, even though the procedure itself might have only one cached plan. As SQL Server starts experiencing memory pressure, the work to insert the entry for each individual call to the procedure can begin to cause excessive waits resulting in a drop in throughput or even out-of-memory errors.

SQL Server 2005 SP2 added some enhancements to caching behavior to alleviate some of the cache flooding that could occur when the same procedure or parameterized query was called repeatedly with different parameters. In all releases after SQL Server 2005 SP2, zero-cost batches that contain *SET* statements or transaction control aren't cached at all. The only exception is for those batches that contain only *SET* and transaction control statements. This isn't that much of a loss, as plans for batches containing *SET* statements can never be reused in any case. Also, as of SQL Server 2005 SP2, the memory object from which cache descriptors are allocated has been partitioned across all the CPUs to alleviate contention on the memory object, which should reduce *CMEMTHREAD* waits.

- **SOS_RESERVEDMEMBLOCKLIST waits**   This wait type can indicate the presence of cached plans for queries with a large number of parameters or with a large number of values specified in an *IN* clause. These types of queries require that SQL Server allocate in larger units, called *multipage allocations*. You can look at the *sys.dm_os_memory_cache_counters* view to see the amount of memory allocated in the multipage units:

```
SELECT name, type, single_pages_kb, multi_pages_kb,
    single_pages_in_use_kb, multi_pages_in_use_kb
FROM sys.dm_os_memory_cache_counters
WHERE type = 'CACHESTORE_SQLCP' OR type = 'CACHESTORE_OBJCP';
```

Clearing out plan cache with *DBCC FREEPROCCACHE* can alleviate problems caused by too many multipage allocations, at least until the queries are reexecuted and the plans are cached again. The cache management changes in SQL Server 2005 SP2 can also reduce the waits on *SOS_RESERVEDMEMBLOCKLIST*. Finally, you can consider rewriting the application to use alternatives to long parameters or long *IN* lists. In particular, queries that filter on long *IN* lists can almost always be improved by creating a table of the values in the list. Passing the table as a table-valued parameter (TVP) to a procedure that executes the query replaces the *IN* list filter by a *JOIN* with the TVP.

- **RESOURCE_SEMAPHORE_QUERY_COMPILE waits**   This wait type indicates a large number of concurrent compilations. To prevent inefficient use of query memory, SQL Server limits the number of concurrent compile operations that need extra memory. If you notice a high value for *RESOURCE_SEMAPHORE_QUERY_COMPILE* waits, you can examine the entries in the plan cache through the *sys.dm_exec_cached_plans* view:

```
SELECT usecounts, cacheobjtype, objtype, bucketid, text
FROM sys.dm_exec_cached_plans
    CROSS APPLY sys.dm_exec_sql_text(plan_handle)
WHERE cacheobjtype = 'Compiled Plan'
ORDER BY objtype;
```

If no results with the *objtype* value of *Prepared* exist, SQL Server isn't automatically parameter-izing your queries. You can try altering the database to *PARAMETERIZATION FORCED* in this case, but this option affects the entire database, including queries that might not benefit from parameterization. To force SQL Server to parameterize just certain queries, you can use plan guides, as discussed later in the section "Optimization hints and plan guides."

Keep in mind that caching is done batch by batch. If you try to force parameterization by using *sp_executesql* or prepare and execute, all statements in the batch must be parameterized for the plan to be reusable. If a batch has some parameterized statements and some using constants, each execution of the batch with different constants is considered distinct, and no value to the parameterization exists in only part of the batch.

Other caching issues

In addition to looking at the wait types that can indicate problems with caching, some other coding behaviors can negatively affect plan reuse.

- **Verify parameter types, both for prepared queries and autoparameterization**   With prepared queries, you actually specify the parameter data type, so making sure that you're al-ways using the same type is easier. When SQL Server parameterizes, it makes its own decisions as to data type. If you look at the parameterized form of your queries of type *Prepared*, you see the data type that SQL Server assumed. Earlier, this chapter showed that a value of 622 is assumed to be a different data type than 6, and two queries that are identical except for these specific values never can share the same autoparameterized plan.

  If the parameter passed is numeric, SQL Server determines the data type based on the preci-sion and scale. A value of 8.4 has a data type of *numeric* (2, 1), and 8.44 has a data type of *numeric* (3, 2). For *varchar* data type, server-side parameterization doesn't depend so much on the length of the actual value. Look at these two queries in the *AdventureWorks2012* database:

  ```
  SELECT * FROM Person.StateProvince
  WHERE Name = 'Victoria';
  GO
  SELECT * FROM Person.StateProvince
  WHERE Name = 'Vienne';
  GO
  ```

  Both queries can be autoparameterized to the following:

  ```
  (@0 varchar(8000))SELECT * FROM Person.StateProvine WHERE Name = @0
  ```

- **Monitor plan cache size and data cache size**   In general, as more queries are run, the amount of memory used for data-page caching should increase along with the amount of memory used for plan caching. One of the easiest places to get a comparison of the pages used for plan caching and the pages used for data caching is the performance counters. Look at the following counters: SQL Server: Plan Cache/Cache Pages(_Total) and SQLServer: BufferManager/Database pages.

Handling problems with compilation and recompilation

Tools are available for detecting excessive compiles and recompiles. You can use System Monitor, or one of the tracing or event-monitoring tools available with SQL Server or developed by third-party vendors, to detect compilations and recompilations. Keep in mind that compiling and recompiling aren't the same thing. Recompiling is performed when an existing module or statement is determined to be no longer valid or no longer optimal. All recompiles are considered compiles, but not vice versa. For example, when no plan is in cache, or when a plan is executing a procedure using the *WITH RECOMPILE* option or executing a procedure that was created with the *WITH RECOMPILE* option, SQL Server considers it a compile but not a recompile.

If these tools indicate that you have excessive compilation or recompilation, you can consider the following actions.

- If the recompile is caused by a change in a *SET* option, the SQL Trace text data for T-SQL statements immediately preceding the recompile event can indicate which *SET* option changed. It's best to change *SET* options when a connection is first made and avoid changing them after you have started submitting statements on that connection, or inside a store procedure.

- Recompilation thresholds for temporary tables are lower than for regular tables, as discussed earlier in this chapter. If the recompiles on a temporary table are caused by statistics changes, a trace has a data value in the *EventSubclass* column that indicates that statistics changed for an operation on a temporary table. Also, extended events in SQL Server 2012 can show this information in the *recompile_cause* column of the *sql_statement_recompile* event. You can consider changing the temporary tables to table variables, for which statistics aren't maintained. Because no statistics are maintained, changes in statistics can't induce recompilation. However, lack of statistics can result in suboptimal plans for these queries. Your own testing can determine whether the benefit of table variables is worth the cost. Another alternative is to use the *KEEP PLAN* query hint, which sets the recompile threshold for temporary tables to be the same as for permanent tables.

- To avoid all recompilations that are caused by changes in statistics, whether on a permanent or a temporary table, you can specify the *KEEPFIXED PLAN* query hint. With this hint, recompilations can happen only because of correctness-related reasons, as described earlier. An example might be when a recompilation occurs if the schema of a table that's referenced by a statement changes, or if a table is marked for recompile by using the *sp_recompile* stored procedure.

- Another way to prevent recompiles caused by statistics changes is by turning off the automatic updates of statistics for indexes and columns. Note, however, that turning off the Autostatistics feature usually isn't a good idea. If you do so, the Query Optimizer is no longer sensitive to data changes and will likely come up with a suboptimal plan. This method should be considered only as a last resort after exhausting all other options.

- All T-SQL code should use two-part object names (for example, *Inventory.ProductList*) to indicate exactly what object is being referenced, which can help avoid recompilation.

- Don't use DDL within conditional constructs such as *IF* statements.

- Check to see whether a stored procedure was created with the *WITH RECOMPILE* option. In many cases, only one or two statements within a stored procedure might benefit from recompilation on every execution, and you can use the *RECOMPILE* query hint for just those statements. Doing so is much better than using the *WITH RECOMPILE* option for the entire procedure, which means every statement in the procedure is recompiled every time the procedure is executed.

Optimization hints and plan guides

Chapter 11, "The Query Optimizer," looks at many different execution plans and discusses what it means for a query to be optimized. This chapter looks at situations in which SQL Server reuses a plan when it might have been best to come up with a new one, and you've seen situations in which SQL Server doesn't reuse a plan even if a perfectly good one is in cache already. One way to encourage plan reuse that has already been discussed in this chapter is to enable the *PARAMETERIZATION FORCED* database option. In other situations, where you just can't get the optimizer to reuse a plan, you can use optimization hints. Optimization hints can also be used to force SQL Server to come up with a new fplan in those cases in which it might be using an existing plan. Dozens of hints can be used in your T-SQL code to affect the plan that SQL Server comes up with, and some of them were discussed in Chapter 11. This section specifically describes only those hints that affect recompilation, as well as the mother of all hints, *USE PLAN*. Finally, this section covers a SQL Server feature called *plan guides*.

Optimization hints

All hints that you read about in this section are referred to in *SQL Server Books Online* as query hints, to distinguish them from table hints, which are specified in the *FROM* clause after a table name, and join hints, which are specified in the *JOIN* clause before the word *JOIN*. However, query hints are frequently referred to as *option hints* because they are specified in a special clause called the *OPTION* clause, which is used just for specifying this type of hint. An *OPTION* clause, if included in a query, is always the last clause of any T-SQL statement, as you can see in the code examples in the subsequent sections.

RECOMPILE

The *RECOMPILE* hint forces SQL Server to recompile a query. It's particularly useful when only a single statement within a batch needs to be recompiled. You know that SQL Server compiles your T-SQL batches as a unit, determining the execution plan for each statement in the batch, and it doesn't execute any statements until the entire batch is compiled. This means that if the batch contains a variable declaration and assignment, the assignment doesn't actually take place during the compilation phase. When the following batch is optimized, SQL Server doesn't have a specific value for the variable:

```
USE AdventureWorks2012;
DECLARE @PersonName nvarchar(100);
SET @PersonName = 'Abercrombie';
SELECT * FROM Person.Person WHERE LastName <= @PersonName;
```

The plan for the *SELECT* statement shows that SQL Server is scanning the entire clustered index because during optimization, SQL Server had no idea what value it would be searching for and couldn't use the histogram in the index statistics to get a good estimate of the number of rows. If you had replaced the variable with the constant 'Abercrombie', SQL Server could have determined that only a very few rows would qualify and would have chosen to use the nonclustered index that has *LastName* as the leading value. The *RECOMPILE* hint can be very useful here because it tells the optimizer to come up with a new plan for the single *SELECT* statement right before that statement is executed, which is after the *SET* statement is executed:

```
USE AdventureWorks2012;
DECLARE @PersonName nvarchar(100);
SET @PersonName = 'Abercrombie';
SELECT * FROM Person.Person WHERE LastName <= @PersonName
OPTION (RECOMPILE);
```

Note A variable isn't the same as a parameter, even though they are written the same way. Because a procedure is compiled only when it's being executed, SQL Server always uses a specific parameter value. Problems arise when the previously compiled plan is then used for different parameters. However, for a local variable, the value is never known when the statements using the variable are compiled, unless the *RECOMPILE* hint is used.

OPTIMIZE FOR

The *OPTIMIZE FOR* hint tells the optimizer to optimize the query as though a particular value has been used for a variable or parameter. Execution uses the real value. Keep in mind that the *OPTIMIZE FOR* hint doesn't force a query to be recompiled; it only instructs SQL Server to assume that a variable or parameter has a particular value in those cases in which SQL Server has already determined that the query needs optimization. Because Chapter 11 discusses the *OPTIMIZE FOR* hint, no further discussion about it is needed here.

KEEP PLAN

The *KEEP PLAN* hint relaxes the recompile threshold for a query, particularly for queries accessing temporary tables. As you saw earlier in this chapter, a query accessing a temporary table can be recompiled when as few as six changes have been made to the table. If the query uses the *KEEP PLAN* hint, the recompilation threshold for temporary tables is changed to be the same as for permanent tables.

KEEPFIXED PLAN

The *KEEPFIXED PLAN* hint inhibits all recompiles because of optimality issues. With this hint, queries are recompiled only when forced, or if the schema of the underlying tables is changed, as described earlier in the section "Correctness-based recompiles."

PARAMETERIZATION

The *PARAMETERIZATION* hint overrides the *PARAMETERIZATION* option for a database. If the database is set to *PARAMETERIZATION FORCED*, individual queries using the *PARAMETERIZATION* hint can avoid that and be parameterized only if they meet a strict list of conditions. Alternatively, if the database is set to *PARAMETERIZATION SIMPLE*, individual queries can be parameterized case by case. However, the *PARAMETERIZATION* hint can be used only with plan guides, which are discussed shortly.

USE PLAN

Chapter 11 describes the *USE PLAN* hint as a way to force SQL Server to use a plan that you might not be able to specify using the other hints. The plan specified must be in XML format and can be obtained from a query that uses the desired plan by using the option *SET SHOWPLAN_XML ON*. Because *USE PLAN* hints contain a complete XML document in the query hint, they are best used within plan guides, which are discussed in the next section.

Purpose of plan guides

Although in most cases that you are recommended to allow the Query Optimizer to determine the best plan for each of your queries, sometimes the Query Optimizer just can't come up with the best plan and you might find that the only way to get reasonable performance is to use a hint. This is usually a straightforward change to your applications, after you verify that the desired hint really will make a difference. However, in some environments, you have no control over the application code. In cases when the actual SQL queries are embedded in inaccessible vendor code or when modifying vendor code would break your licensing agreement or invalidate your support guarantees, you might not be able to simply add a hint onto the misbehaving query.

Plan guides, introduced in SQL Server 2005, provide a solution by giving you a mechanism to add hints to a query without changing the query itself. Basically, a plan guide tells the Optimizer that if it tries to optimize a query having a particular format, it should add a specified hint to the query. SQL Server supports three kinds of plan guides: SQL, Object, and Template, as explained shortly.

Plan guides are available in the Standard, Enterprise, Evaluation, and Developer editions of SQL Server. If you detach a database containing plan guides from a supported edition and attach the database to an unsupported edition, such as Workgroup or Express, SQL Server doesn't use any plan guides. However the metadata containing information about plan guides is still available.

Types of plan guides

The three types of plan types can be created using the *sp_create_plan_guide* procedure. The general form of the *sp_create_plan_guide* procedure is as follows:

```
sp_create_plan_guide 'plan_guide_name', 'statement_text',
    'type_of_plan_guide', 'object_name_or_batch_text',
    'parameter_list', 'hints'
```

This section discusses each type of plan guide, and then looks at the mechanisms for working with plan guides and the metadata that keeps track of information about them.

Object plan guides

A plan guide of type *object* indicates that you are interested in a T-SQL statement appearing in the context of a SQL Server object, which can be a stored procedure, a user-defined function, or a trigger in the database in which the plan guide is created. Suppose that you have a stored procedure called *Person.GetPersonByCountry* that takes a country as a parameter and, after some error checking and other validation, returns a set of rows for all customers in the specified country. Suppose further that your testing has determined that a parameter value of *US* gives you the best plan. Here is an example of a plan guide that tells SQL Server to use the *OPTIMIZE FOR* hint whenever the specified statement is found in the *Person.GetPersonByCountry* procedure:

```
EXEC sp_create_plan_guide
    @name = N'plan_US_PersonCountry',
    @stmt =
        N'SELECT Title, FirstName, LastName, City, StateProvinceCode, CountryRegionCode
            FROM Person.Person as p
            INNER JOIN Person.BusinessEntityAddress AS ea
                ON p.BusinessEntityID = ea.BusinessEntityID
            INNER JOIN Person.Address AS a
                ON ea.AddressID = a.AddressID
            INNER JOIN Person.StateProvince as sp
                ON a.StateProvinceID = sp.StateProvinceID
            WHERE sp.CountryRegionCode = @Country',
@type = N'OBJECT',
@module_or_batch = N'Person.GetPersonByCountry',
@params = NULL,
@hints = N'OPTION (OPTIMIZE FOR (@Country = N''US''))';
```

After this plan is created in the *AdventureWorks2012* database, every time the *Person.GetPerson-ByCountry* procedure is compiled, the statement indicated in the plan is optimized as if the actual parameter passed was the string 'US'. No other statements in the procedure are affected by this plan, and if the specified query occurs outside the *Person.GetPersonByCountry* procedure, the plan guide isn't invoked. (The companion website, which contains all the code used in all the book examples, also contains a script to build the *Person.GetPersonByCountry* procedure.)

SQL plan guides

A plan guide of type *SQL* indicates that you are interested in a particular SQL statement, either as a standalone statement or in a particular batch. T-SQL statements that are sent to SQL Server by CLR objects or extended stored procedures, or that are part of dynamic SQL invoked with the *EXEC (sql_string)* construct, are processed as batches on SQL Server. To use them in a plan guide, their type should be set to *SQL*. For a standalone statement, the *@module_or_batch* parameter to *sp_create_plan_guide* should be set to NULL so that SQL Server assumes that the batch and the statement have the same value. If the statement you are interested in is in a larger batch, the entire batch text needs to be specified in the *@module_or_batch* parameter. If a batch is specified for a SQL plan guide, the text of the batch needs to be exactly the same as it appears in the application. The rules aren't quite as strict as those for ad hoc query plan reuse, discussed earlier in this chapter, but they are close. Make sure that you use the same case, the same whitespace, and the other characteristics that your application does.

The following plan guide tells SQL Server to use only one CPU (no parallelization) when a particular query is executed as a standalone query:

```
EXEC sp_create_plan_guide
@name = N'plan_SalesOrderHeader_DOP1',
@stmt = N'SELECT TOP 10 *
          FROM Sales.SalesOrderHeader
          ORDER BY OrderDate DESC',
@type = N'SQL',
@module_or_batch = NULL,
@params = NULL,
@hints = N'OPTION (MAXDOP 1)';
```

After this plan is created in the *AdventureWorks2012* database, every time the specified statement is encountered in a batch by itself, it has a plan created that uses only a single CPU. If the specified query occurs as part of a larger batch, the plan guide isn't invoked.

Template plan guides

A plan guide of type *Template* can use only the *PARAMETERIZATION FORCED* or *PARAMETERIZATION SIMPLE* hints to override the *PARAMETERIZATION* database setting. Template guides are a bit trickier to work with because you have to have SQL Server construct a template of your query in the same format that it will be in after it's parameterized. This isn't hard because SQL Server provides a special procedure called *sp_get_query_template*, but to use template guides you need to perform several prerequisite steps. If you look at the two plan guide examples given previously, notice that the parameter called *@params* was NULL for both *OBJECT* and SQL plan guides. You only specify a value for *@params* with a *TEMPLATE* plan guide.

To see an example of using a template guide and forcing parameterization, first clear your procedure cache and then execute these two queries in the *AdventureWorks2012* database:

```
DBCC FREEPROCCACHE;
GO
SELECT * FROM Sales.SalesOrderHeader AS h
INNER JOIN Sales.SalesOrderDetail AS d
   ON h.SalesOrderID = d.SalesOrderID
WHERE h.SalesOrderID = 45639;
GO
SELECT * FROM Sales.SalesOrderHeader AS h
INNER JOIN Sales.SalesOrderDetail AS d
   ON h.SalesOrderID = d.SalesOrderID
WHERE h.SalesOrderID = 45640;
```

These queries are very similar, and the plans for both are identical, but because the query is considered too complex, SQL Server doesn't autoparameterize them. If, after executing both queries, you look at the plan cache, you should see only ad hoc queries. If you've created the *sp_cacheobjects* view described earlier in the chapter, you could use that; otherwise, replace *sp_cacheobjects* with *sys.syscacheobjects*:

```
SELECT objtype, dbid, usecounts, sql
FROM sp_cacheobjects
WHERE cacheobjtype = 'Compiled Plan';
```

To create a plan guide to force statements of this type to be parameterized, you first need to call the procedure *sp_get_query_template* and pass two variables as output parameters. One parameter holds the parameterized version of the query, and the other holds the parameter list and the parameter data types. The following code then *SELECT*s these two output parameters so you can see their contents. Of course, you can remove this *SELECT* from your own code. Finally, you call the *sp_create_plan_guide* procedure, which instructs the optimizer to use *PARAMETERIZATION FORCED* anytime it sees a query that matches this specific template. In other words, anytime a query that parameterizes to the same form as the query here, it uses the same plan already cached:

```
DECLARE @sample_statement nvarchar(max);
DECLARE @paramlist nvarchar(max);
EXEC sp_get_query_template
   N'SELECT * FROM Sales.SalesOrderHeader AS h
     INNER JOIN Sales.SalesOrderDetail AS d
        ON h.SalesOrderID = d.SalesOrderID
     WHERE h.SalesOrderID = 45639;',
   @sample_statement OUTPUT,
   @paramlist OUTPUT,
EXEC sp_create_plan_guide @name = N'Template_Plan',
   @stmt = @sample_statement,
   @type = N'TEMPLATE',
   @module_or_batch = NULL,
   @params = @paramlist,
   @hints = N'OPTION(PARAMETERIZATION FORCED)';
```

After creating the plan guide, run the same two statements as shown earlier, and then examine the plan cache:

```
DBCC FREEPROCCACHE;
GO
SELECT * FROM AdventureWorks2008.Sales.SalesOrderHeader AS h
INNER JOIN AdventureWorks2008.Sales.SalesOrderDetail AS d
   ON h.SalesOrderID = d.SalesOrderID
WHERE h.SalesOrderID = 45639;
GO
SELECT * FROM AdventureWorks2008.Sales.SalesOrderHeader AS h
INNER JOIN AdventureWorks2008.Sales.SalesOrderDetail AS d
   ON h.SalesOrderID = d.SalesOrderID
WHERE h.SalesOrderID = 45640;
GO
SELECT objtype, dbid, usecounts, sql
FROM sp_cacheobjects
WHERE cacheobjtype = 'Compiled Plan';
```

You should now see a prepared plan with the following parameterized form:

```
(@0 int)select * from Sales.SalesOrderHeader as h
   inner join Sales.SalesOrderDetail as d
   on h.SalesOrderID = d.SalesOrderID
   where h.SalesOrderID = @0
```

Managing plan guides

In addition to the *sp_create_plan_guide* and *sp_get_query_template* procedures, the other basic procedure for working with plan guides is *sp_control_plan_guide*. This procedure allows you to *DROP*, *DISABLE*, or *ENABLE* a plan guide by following this basic syntax:

```
sp_control_plan_guide '<control_option>' [, '<plan_guide_name>']
```

Six possible *control_option* values are available: *DISABLE*, *DISABLE ALL*, *ENABLE*, *ENABLE ALL*, *DROP*, and *DROP ALL*. The *plan_guide_name* parameter is optional because with any of the *ALL control_option* values, no *plan_guide_name* value is supplied. Plan guides are local to a particular database, so the *DISABLE ALL*, *ENABLE ALL*, and *DROP ALL* values apply to all plan guides for the current database. Also, plan guides behave like schema-bound views in a way; the stored procedures, triggers, and functions referred to in any object plan guide in a database can't be altered or dropped. So for the example object plan guide, as long as the plan guide exists, the *AdventureWorks2012.Person.GetPersonByCountry* procedure can't be altered or dropped. This is true whether the plan guide is disabled or enabled, and it remains true until all plan guides referencing those objects are dropped with *sp_control_plan_guide*.

The metadata view that contains information about plan guides in a particular database is *sys. plan_guides*. This view contains all the information supplied in the *sp_create_plan_guide* procedure plus additional information such as the creation date and last modification date of each plan guide. Using the information in this view, you can reconstruct the plan guide definition manually if necessary. Also, Management Studio allows you to script your plan guide definitions from the Object Explorer tree.

Plan guide considerations

For SQL Server to determine that an appropriate plan guide is available to use, the statement text in the plan guide must match the query being compiled. This must be an exact character-for-character match, including case, whitespace, and comments, just as when SQL Server is determining whether it can reuse ad hoc query plans, as discussed earlier in the chapter. Statement text that's close but not quite an exact match can lead to a difficult troubleshooting situation. When matching a SQL template, whether the definition also contains a batch that the statement must be part of, SQL Server does allow more leeway in the definition of the batch. In particular, keyword case, whitespace, and comments are ignored.

To make sure your plan guides use the exact text that is submitted by your applications, you can run a trace via SQL Server Profiler and capture the *SQL:BatchCompleted* and *RPC:Completed* events. After the relevant batch (the one you want to create a plan guide for) shows up in the top window of your Profiler output, you can right-click the event and select Extract Event Data to save the SQL Text of the batch to a text file. It's not enough to copy and paste from the lower window in the Profiler because the output there can introduce extra line breaks.

To verify that your plan guide was used, you can look at the XML plan for the query. If you can run the query directly, you can use the option *SET SHOWPLAN_XML ON* or you can capture the showplan XML through a trace. An XML plan has two specific items—*PlanGuideDB* and *PlanGuideName*—indicating that the query used a plan guide. If the plan guide was a template plan guide, the XML plan also has the items *TemplatePlanGuideDB* and *TemplatePlanGuideName*.

When a query is submitted for processing, if any plan guides are in the database at all, SQL Server first checks to see whether the statement matches a SQL plan guide or an object plan guide. The query string is hashed to make finding any matching strings in the database's existing plan guides faster. If no matching SQL or object plan guides are found, SQL Server then checks for a TEMPLATE plan guide. If it finds a TEMPLATE guide, it then tries to match the resulting parameterized query to a SQL plan guide. This gives you the possibility of applying additional hints to your queries by using forced parameterization. Figure 12-3, copied from *SQL Server Books Online*, shows the process that SQL Server uses to check for applicable plan guides.

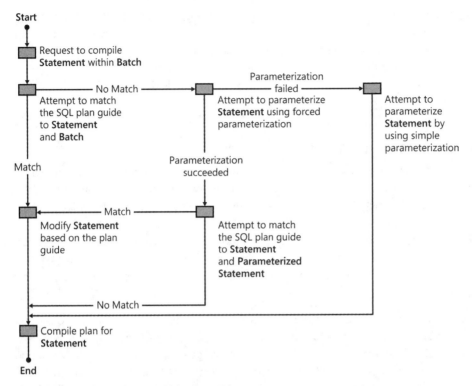

FIGURE 12-3 Checking for applicable plan guides.

The key steps are the following, which follow the flowchart from the top left: Take the top branch to the right, the middle branch down, and then right at the center, to the point where the statement is modified based on the plan guide and its hints.

1. For a specific statement within the batch, SQL Server tries to match the statement to a SQL-based plan guide, whose *@module_or_batch* argument matches that of the incoming batch text, including any constant literal values, and whose *@stmt* argument also matches the statement in the batch. If this kind of plan guide exists and the match succeeds, the statement text is modified to include the query hints specified in the plan guide. The statement is then compiled using the specified hints.

2. If a plan guide isn't matched to the statement in step 1, SQL Server tries to parameterize the statement by using forced parameterization. In this step, parameterization can fail for any one of the following reasons:

    - The statement is already parameterized or contains local variables.

    - The *PARAMETERIZATION SIMPLE database SET* option is applied (the default setting), and no plan guide of type *TEMPLATE* applies to the statement and specifies the *PARAMETERIZATION FORCED* query hint.

    - A plan guide of type *TEMPLATE* exists that applies to the statement and specifies the *PARAMETERIZATION SIMPLE* query hint.

Consider an example that involves the distribution of data in the *SpecialOfferID* column in the *Sales.SalesOrderDetail* table in the *AdventureWorks2012* database. Of the 12 different *SpecialOfferID* values, most of them occur only a few hundred times (out of the 121317 rows in the *Sales.SalesOrderDetail*) at most, as the following script and output illustrates:

```
USE AdventureWorks2012
GO
SELECT SpecialOfferID, COUNT(*) as Total
FROM Sales.SalesOrderDetail
GROUP BY SpecialOfferID
ORDER BY SpecialOfferID;

RESULTS:
SpecialOfferID  Total
--------------  -----------
1               115884
2               3428
3               606
4               80
5               2
7               137
8               98
9               61
11              84
13              524
14              244
16              169
```

Because the table has 1238 pages, for most of the values, a nonclustered index on *SpecialOfferID* could be useful, so here is the code to build one:

```
CREATE INDEX Detail_SpecialOfferIndex ON Sales.SalesOrderDetail(SpecialOfferID);
```

Assume that very few queries actually search for a *SpecialOfferID* value of 1 or 2, and 99 percent of the time the queries are looking for the less popular values. You want the Query Optimizer to auto-parameterize queries that access the *Sales.SalesOrderDetail* table, specifying one particular value for *SpecialOfferID*. So use the following template plan guide to autoparameterize queries of this form:

```
SELECT * FROM Sales.SalesOrderDetail WHERE SpecialOfferID = 4;
```

However, you want to make sure that the initial parameter that determines the plan isn't one of the values that might use a Clustered Index scan, namely the values 1 or 2. So you can take the autopa-rameterized query produced by the *sp_get_query_template* procedure, use it first to create a template plan guide, and then to create a SQL plan guide with the *OPTIMIZE FOR* hint. The hint forces SQL Server to assume a specific value of 4 every time the query needs to be reoptimized:

```
USE AdventureWorks2012;
-- Get plan template and create plan Guide
DECLARE @stmt nvarchar(max);
DECLARE @params nvarchar(max);
EXEC sp_get_query_template
    N'SELECT * FROM Sales.SalesOrderDetail WHERE SpecialOfferID = 4',
    @stmt OUTPUT,
```

```
    @params OUTPUT,
--SELECT @stmt as statement -- show the value when debugging
--SELECT @params as parameters -- show the value when debugging

EXEC sp_create_plan_guide N'Template_Plan_for SpecialOfferID',
    @stmt,
    N'TEMPLATE',
    NULL,
    @params,
    N'OPTION (PARAMETERIZATION FORCED)';

EXEC sp_create_plan_guide
    @name = N'Force_Value_for_Prepared_Plan',
    @stmt = @stmt,
    @type = N'SQL',
    @module_or_batch = NULL,
    @params = @params,
    @hints = N'OPTION (OPTIMIZE FOR (@0 = 4))';
GO
```

You can verify that the plan is being autoparameterized and optimized for a value that uses a non-clustered index on *SpecialOfferID* by running a few tests:

```
DBCC FREEPROCCACHE;
SET STATISTICS IO ON;
SELECT * FROM Sales.SalesOrderDetail
WHERE SpecialOfferID = 3;
GO
SELECT * FROM Sales.SalesOrderDetail
WHERE SpecialOfferID = 4;
GO
SELECT * FROM Sales.SalesOrderDetail
WHERE SpecialOfferID = 5;
GO
```

Notice in the *STATISTICS IO* output that each execution uses a different number of reads because it's finding a different number of rows through the nonclustered index. You can also verify that SQL Server is using the prepared plan by examining the *STATISTICS XML* output. If you set that option to ON and run the query looking for a value of 5, you should have a node in your XML document that looks very much like this:

```
<ParameterList>
<ColumnReference Column="@0" ParameterCompiledValue="(4)"
        ParameterRuntimeValue="(5)" />
</ParameterList>
```

Plan guides aren't intended to speed up query compilation time. Not only does SQL Server first have to determine whether a plan guide could be a potential match for the query being compiled, but the plan enforced by the plan guide also has to be one that the Query Optimizer would have come up with on its own. To know that the forced plan is valid, the Query Optimizer has to go through most of the process of optimization. The benefit of plan guides is to reduce execution time for those queries in which the Query Optimizer isn't coming up with the best plan on its own.

The main plan guide enhancements (after they were introduced in SQL Server 2005) have to do with making plan guides more usable. SQL Server 2008 added SMO and Management Studio support, including scripting of plan guides as part of scripting out a database. When a plan guide is scripted, it can be copied to other SQL Server databases or instances running the same queries.

Plan guide validation

One limitation of the original implementation of plan guides was that it was possible to change the physical design of a table (for example, dropping an index) in a way that could invalidate a plan guide and any queries using that plan guide would fail whenever they were executed. SQL Server 2008 and later versions can detect cases when changing the table design would break a plan guide. It can now recompile the query without the plan guide and to notify the administrator through trace events or Extended Events. Also, a new system function can be used to validate plan guides. This function can be used to detect physical database design changes that break existing plan guides and allow you to roll back the breaking transaction before it can break the system.

To validate all the existing plan guides in a system, you can use the *sys.fn_validate_plan_guide* function:

```
SELECT * FROM sys.plan_guides pg
CROSS APPLY
(SELECT * FROM sys.fn_validate_plan_guide(pg.plan_guide_id)) v;
```

The function returns nothing for valid plan guides. When the guide would generate an error, it returns a row. So you can incorporate this into any schema changes in the system:

```
BEGIN TRANSACTION;
DROP INDEX t2.myindex;
IF EXISTS(
SELECT * FROM sys.plan_guides pg
CROSS APPLY
  (SELECT * FROM sys.fn_validate_plan_guide(pg.plan_guide_id)) v
)
ROLLBACK TRANSACTION
ELSE
COMMIT TRANSACTION;
```

Freezing a plan from plan cache

SQL Server 2008 added a new stored procedure to allow you to create a plan guide automatically from a plan that has already been cached. The procedure *sp_create_plan_guide_from_handle* requires a *plan_handle* and a plan guide name as parameters and creates a plan guide using the execution plan stored in cache for that *plan_handle* value. The capability is called *plan freezing* because it allows you to ensure that a well-performing plan is reused every time the associated query is executed. Suppose that you've found that the plan just executed for the following query performs extremely well, and you want to make sure that plan is the one used on subsequent executions:

```
SELECT City, StateProvinceID, PostalCode FROM Person.Address ORDER BY PostalCode DESC;
```

To find the corresponding plan in cache, search for a text value that matches the query:

```
SELECT plan_handle
FROM sys.dm_exec_query_stats AS qs CROSS APPLY sys.dm_exec_sql_text(qs.sql_handle) AS st
WHERE st.text LIKE N'SELECT City,%';
```

As soon as you have that *plan_handle*, you can pass it as a parameter to the *sp_create_plan_guide_from_handle* procedure as follows:

```
EXEC sp_create_plan_guide_from_handle
    @name = N'Guide1_from_XML_showplan',
    @plan_handle = 0x06000600F19B1E1FC0A14C0A0000000000000000000000000
```

In several situations, plan guides and plan freezing can be particularly beneficial;

- You can use plan guides to provide a workaround for plan regressions after a server upgrade.

- You can disallow plan changes for critical plans in a well-performing system.

- You can troubleshoot a problematic query by freezing a good plan (assuming a good plan ever is used).

- Independent software vendors (ISVs) can create known good plans for shipping with their applications.

- You can optimize on a test system and then port the plan guide to your production system.

Conclusion

For all the caching mechanisms, reusing a cached plan avoids recompilation and optimization. This saves compilation time, but it means that the same plan is used regardless of the particular parameter values passed in. If the optimal plan for a specific parameter value isn't the same as the cached plan, the optimal execution time isn't achieved. For this reason, SQL Server is very conservative about auto-parameterization. When an application uses *sp_executesql*, prepare and execute, or stored procedures, the application developer is responsible for determining what should be parameterized. You should parameterize only constants whose range of values doesn't drastically affect the optimization choices.

This chapter looked at the caching and reuse of plans generated by the Query Optimizer. SQL Server can cache and reuse plans not only from stored procedures, but also from ad hoc and autoparameterized queries. Because generating query plans can be expensive, understanding how and why query plans are reused and when they must be regenerated is helpful. Understanding how caching and reusing plans work helps you determine when using the cached plan can be the right choice and when you might need to make sure SQL Server comes up with a new plan to give your queries and applications the best performance.

Transactions and concurrency

Kalen Delaney

oncurrency can be defined as the ability of multiple processes to access or change shared data at the same time. The greater the number of concurrent user processes that can be active without interfering with each other, the greater the concurrency of the database system.

Concurrency is reduced when a process that's changing data prevents other processes from reading that data or when a process that's reading data prevents other processes from changing that data. This chapter uses the terms *reading* and *accessing* to describe the impact of using a *SELECT* statement on your data. Concurrency is also affected when multiple processes attempt to change the same data simultaneously, but they can't all succeed without sacrificing data consistency. This chapter uses the terms *modifying*, *changing*, or *writing* to describe the impact of using the *INSERT*, *UPDATE*, *MERGE*, or *DELETE* statements on your data. (*MERGE* was introduced in SQL Server 2008. You can think of it as a combination of *INSERT*, *UPDATE*, and *DELETE*.)

In general, database systems can take two approaches to managing concurrent data access: optimistic or pessimistic. Microsoft SQL Server 2012 supports both approaches. Pessimistic concurrency was the only concurrency model available before SQL Server 2005. With SQL Server 2005, you specified which model to use by using two database options and a *SET* option called *TRANSACTION ISOLATION LEVEL*.

After I describe the basic differences between the two models, we look at the five possible isolation levels in SQL Server 2012, as well as the internals of how SQL Server controls concurrent access using each model. We look at how to control the isolation level, and we look at the metadata that shows you what SQL Server is doing.

Concurrency models

In either concurrency model, a conflict can occur if two processes try to modify the same data at the same time. The difference between the two models lies in whether conflicts can be avoided before they occur or can be dealt with in some manner after they occur.

Pessimistic concurrency

With pessimistic concurrency, the default behavior is for SQL Server to acquire locks to block access to data that another process is using. Pessimistic concurrency assumes that enough data modification operations are in the system that any specific read operation is likely affected by a data modification made by another user. In other words, the system behaves pessimistically and assumes that a conflict will occur. Pessimistic concurrency avoids conflicts by acquiring locks on data that's being read, so no other processes can modify that data. It also acquires locks on data being modified so that no other processes can access that data for either reading or modifying. In other words, readers block writers and writers block readers in a pessimistic concurrency environment.

Optimistic concurrency

Optimistic concurrency assumes that the system has few enough conflicting data modification operations that any single transaction is unlikely to modify data that another transaction is modifying. The default behavior of optimistic concurrency is to use row versioning to allow data readers to see the state of the data before the modification occurs. Older versions of data rows are saved, so a process reading data can see the data as it was when the process started reading and not be affected by any changes being made to that data. A process that modifies the data is unaffected by processes reading the data because the reader is accessing a saved version of the data rows. In other words, readers don't block writers, and writers don't block readers. Writers can and will block writers, however, which is what causes conflicts. SQL Server generates an error message when a conflict occurs, but it's up to the application to respond to that error.

Transaction processing

No matter what concurrency model you're working with, that you have an understanding of transactions is crucial. A transaction is the basic unit of work in SQL Server. Typically, it consists of several SQL commands that read and update the database, but the update isn't considered final until a *COMMIT* command is issued (at least for an explicit transaction). In general, when discussing a modification operation or a read operation, this chapter is talking about the transaction that performs the data modification or the read, which isn't necessarily a single SQL statement. The expression *writers will block readers* means that as long as the transaction that performed the write operation is active, no other process can read the modified data.

The concept of a transaction is fundamental to understanding concurrency control. The mechanics of transaction control from a programming perspective are beyond the scope of this book, but this chapter covers basic transaction properties. It also goes into detail about the transaction isolation levels because they directly affect how SQL Server manages the data being accessed in your transactions.

An implicit transaction is any individual *INSERT, UPDATE, DELETE,* or *MERGE* statement. (You can also consider *SELECT* statements to be implicit transactions, although SQL Server doesn't write to the log when *SELECT* statements are processed.) No matter how many rows are affected, the statement must exhibit all the ACID properties of a transaction, as explained in the next section. An explicit transaction is one whose beginning is marked with a *BEGIN TRAN* statement and whose end is marked by a *COMMIT TRAN* or *ROLLBACK TRAN* statement. Most examples in this chapter use explicit transactions because such transactions are the only way to show the state of SQL Server in the middle of a transaction. For example, many types of locks are held for only the duration of the transaction. You can begin a transaction, perform some operations, look around in the metadata to see what locks are being held, and then end the transaction. When the transaction ends, the locks are released; you can no longer look at them.

ACID properties

Transaction processing guarantees the consistency and recoverability of SQL Server databases. It ensures that all transactions are performed as a single unit of work, even in the presence of a hardware or general system failure. Such transactions are referred to as having the ACID properties, with ACID standing for *atomicity*, *consistency*, *isolation*, and *durability*. In addition to guaranteeing that explicit multistatement transactions maintain the ACID properties, SQL Server guarantees that an implicit transaction also maintains the ACID properties.

Here's a pseudocode example of an explicit ACID transaction:

```
BEGIN TRANSACTION DEBIT_CREDIT
Debit savings account $1000
Credit checking account $1000
COMMIT TRANSACTION DEBIT_CREDIT
```

Now take a closer look at each of the ACID properties.

Atomicity

SQL Server guarantees the atomicity of its transactions. *Atomicity* means that each transaction is treated as all or nothing: It either commits or aborts. If a transaction commits, all its effects remain. If it aborts, all its effects are undone. In the preceding DEBIT_CREDIT example, if the savings account debit is reflected in the database but the checking account credit isn't, funds essentially disappear from the database—that is, funds are subtracted from the savings account but never added to the checking account. If the reverse occurs (if the checking account is credited and the savings account isn't debited), the customer's checking account mysteriously increases in value without a corresponding customer cash deposit or account transfer. Because of the atomicity feature of SQL Server, both the debit and credit must be completed; otherwise, neither event is completed.

Consistency

The consistency property ensures that a transaction won't allow the system to arrive at an incorrect logical state; the data must always be logically correct. Constraints and rules are honored even in the event of a system failure. In the DEBIT_CREDIT example, the logical rule is that money can't be created or destroyed; a corresponding, counterbalancing entry must be made for each entry. (Consistency is implied by, and in most situations redundant with, atomicity, isolation, and durability.)

Isolation

Isolation separates concurrent transactions from the updates of other incomplete transactions. In the DEBIT_CREDIT example, another transaction can't see the work in progress while the transaction is being carried out. For example, if another transaction reads the balance of the savings account after the debit occurs, and then the DEBIT_CREDIT transaction is aborted, the other transaction is working from a balance that never logically existed.

SQL Server accomplishes isolation among transactions automatically. It locks data or creates row versions to allow multiple concurrent users to work with data while preventing side effects that can distort the results and make them different from what would be expected if users were to serialize their requests (that is, if requests were queued and serviced one at a time). This serializability feature is one of the isolation levels that SQL Server supports. SQL Server supports multiple isolation levels so that you can choose the appropriate tradeoff between how much data to lock, how long to hold locks, and whether to allow users access to prior versions of row data. This tradeoff is known as concurrency vs. consistency.

Durability

After a transaction commits, the durability property of SQL Server ensures that the effects of the transaction persist even if a system failure occurs. If a system failure occurs while a transaction is in progress, the transaction is completely undone, leaving no partial effects on the data. For example, if a power outage occurs in the middle of a transaction before the transaction is committed, the entire transaction is rolled back when the system is restarted. If the power fails immediately after the acknowledgment of the commit is sent to the calling application, the transaction is guaranteed to exist in the database. Write-ahead logging and automatic rollback and roll-forward of transactions during the recovery phase of SQL Server startup ensure durability.

Transaction dependencies

In addition to supporting all four ACID properties, a transaction might exhibit several other behaviors. Some people call these behaviors "dependency problems" or "consistency problems," but I don't necessarily consider them problems. They are merely possible behaviors, and except for lost updates, which are never considered desirable, you can determine which behavior to allow and which to avoid. Your choice of isolation level determines which of these behaviors is allowed.

Lost updates

Lost updates occur when two processes read the same data and both manipulate the data, changing its value, and then both try to update the original data to the new value. The second process might overwrite the first update completely. Suppose that two clerks in a receiving room are receiving parts and adding the new shipments to the inventory database. Clerk A and Clerk B both receive shipments of widgets. They both check the current inventory and see that 25 widgets are currently in stock. Clerk A's shipment has 50 widgets, so he adds 50 to 25 and updates the current value to 75. Clerk B's shipment has 20 widgets, so she adds 20 to the value of 25 that she originally read and updates the current value to 45, completely overriding the 50 new widgets that Clerk A processed. Clerk A's update is lost.

Lost updates are only one of the behaviors described here that you probably want to avoid in all cases. Keep in mind that in general, SQL Server won't allow lost updates at all, unless you write an application to specifically allow this behavior.

Dirty reads

Dirty reads occur when a process reads uncommitted data. If one process has changed data but not yet committed the change, another process reading the data will read it in an inconsistent state. For example, Clerk A has updated the old value of 25 widgets to 75, but before he commits, a salesperson looks at the current value of 75 and commits to sending 60 widgets to a customer the following day. If Clerk A then realizes that the widgets are defective and sends them back to the manufacturer, the salesperson has done a dirty read and taken action based on uncommitted data.

By default, dirty reads aren't allowed. Keep in mind that the process updating the data has no control over whether another process can read its data before the first process is committed. The process reading the data gets to decide whether it wants to read data that's not guaranteed to be committed.

Nonrepeatable reads

A read is nonrepeatable if a process might get different values when reading the same data in two separate reads within the same transaction. This can happen when another process changes the data in between the reads that the first process is doing. In the receiving room example, suppose that a manager comes in to do a quick check of the current inventory. She walks up to each clerk, asking the total number of widgets received today and adding the numbers on her calculator. When she's done, she wants to double-check the result, so she goes back to the first clerk. However, if Clerk A received more widgets between the manager's first and second inquiries, the total is different and the reads are nonrepeatable. Nonrepeatable reads are also called *inconsistent analysis*.

Phantoms

Phantoms occur when membership in a set changes. It can happen only when a query with a predicate—such as *WHERE count_of_widgets < 10*—is involved. A phantom occurs if two *SELECT* operations using the same predicate in the same transaction return a different number of rows. Suppose that the manager is still doing quick inventory checks. This time, she goes around the receiving room and notes which clerks have fewer than 10 widgets. After she completes the list, she goes back around to offer advice to everyone with a low total. However, if during her first walkthrough, a clerk with fewer than 10 widgets returned from a break but wasn't noticed by the manager, that clerk isn't on the manager's list even though he meets the criteria in the predicate. This additional clerk (or row) is considered to be a phantom.

Isolation levels

The behavior of your transactions depends on the isolation level. As mentioned earlier, you can decide which of the preceding behaviors to allow by setting an appropriate isolation level with the command *SET TRANSACTION ISOLATION LEVEL <isolation_level>*. Your concurrency model (optimistic or pessimistic) determines how the isolation level is implemented—or, more specifically, how SQL Server guarantees that the behaviors you don't want won't occur.

SQL Server 2012 supports five isolation levels that control the behavior of your read operations. Three of them are available only with pessimistic concurrency, one is available only with optimistic concurrency, and one is available with either. We look at these levels now, but a complete understanding of isolation levels also requires an understanding of locking and row versioning. In my descriptions of the isolation levels, I mention the locks or row versions that support that level, but locking and row versioning are discussed in detail later in the chapter.

Read Uncommitted

In Read Uncommitted isolation, all the behaviors described previously, except lost updates, are possible. Your queries can read uncommitted data, and both nonrepeatable reads and phantoms are possible. Read Uncommitted isolation is implemented by allowing your read operations to not take any locks, and because SQL Server isn't trying to acquire locks, it won't be blocked by conflicting locks acquired by other processes. Your process can read data that another process has modified but not yet committed.

In addition to reading uncommitted individual values, the Read Uncommitted isolation level introduces other undesirable behaviors. When using this isolation level and scanning an entire table, SQL Server can decide to do an allocation order scan (in page-number order), instead of a logical order scan (which would follow the page pointers). If concurrent operations by other processes change data and move rows to a new location in the table, your allocation order scan can end up reading the same row twice. This can happen when you've read a row before it's updated, and then the update moves the row to a higher page number than your scan encounters later. Also, performing an allocation order scan under Read Uncommitted can cause you to miss a row completely. This can happen when a row on a high page number that hasn't been read yet is updated and moved to a lower page number that has already been read.

Although this scenario isn't usually the ideal option, with Read Uncommitted you can't get stuck waiting for a lock, and your read operations don't acquire any locks that might affect other processes that are reading or writing data.

When using Read Uncommitted, you give up the assurance of strongly consistent data in favor of high concurrency in the system without users locking each other out. So when should you choose Read Uncommitted? Clearly, you don't want to use it for financial transactions in which every number must balance. However, it might be fine for certain decision-support analyses—for example, when you look at sales trends—for which complete precision isn't necessary and the tradeoff in higher concurrency makes it worthwhile. Read Uncommitted isolation is a pessimistic solution to the problem of too much blocking activity because it just ignores the locks and doesn't provide you with transactional consistency.

Read Committed

SQL Server 2012 supports two varieties of Read Committed isolation, which is the default isolation level. This isolation level can be either optimistic or pessimistic, depending on the *READ_COMMITTED_SNAPSHOT* database setting. Because the default for this database option is off, the default for this isolation level is to use pessimistic concurrency control.

> **Note** Unless indicated otherwise, when the text refers to the Read Committed isolation level, it's referring to both variations of this isolation level. Pessimistic implementation is referred to as Read Committed (locking), and optimistic implementation is referred to as Read Committed (snapshot).

Read Committed isolation ensures that an operation never reads data that another application has changed but not yet committed. (That is, it never reads data that logically never existed.) With Read Committed (locking), if another transaction is updating data and consequently has exclusive locks on data rows, your transaction must wait for those locks to be released before you can use that data (whether you're reading or modifying). Also, your transaction must put shared locks (at a minimum) on the visited data, which means that data might be unavailable to others to use. A shared lock doesn't prevent others from reading the data, but it makes them wait to update the data. By default, shared locks can be released after the data is processed; they don't have to be held for the duration of the transaction, or even for the duration of the statement. (That is, if shared row locks are acquired, each row lock can be released as soon as the row is processed, even though the statement might need to process many more rows.)

Read Committed (snapshot) also ensures that an operation never reads uncommitted data, but not by forcing other processes to wait. In Read Committed (snapshot), every time a row is updated, SQL Server generates a version of the changed row with its previous committed values. The data being changed is still locked, but other processes can see the previous versions of the data as it was before the data modification operation began.

Repeatable Read

Repeatable Read is a pessimistic isolation level. It adds to the properties of Committed Read by ensuring that if a transaction revisits data or a query is reissued, the data doesn't change. In other words, issuing the same query twice within a transaction can't pick up any changes to data values made by another user's transaction because no changes can be made by other transactions. However, the Repeatable Read isolation level does allow phantom rows to appear.

Preventing nonrepeatable reads is a desirable safeguard in some cases. The cost of this extra safeguard is that all the shared locks in a transaction must be held until the completion (*COMMIT* or *ROLLBACK*) of the transaction. (Exclusive locks must always be held until the end of a transaction, no matter what the isolation level or concurrency model, so that a transaction can be rolled back if necessary. If the locks were released sooner, it might be impossible to undo the work because other concurrent transactions might have used the same data and changed the value.) No other user can modify the data visited by your transaction as long as your transaction is open. Obviously, this can seriously reduce concurrency and degrade performance. If transactions aren't kept short or if applications aren't written to be aware of such potential lock contention issues, SQL Server can appear to stop responding when a process is waiting for locks to be released.

 Note You can control how long SQL Server waits for a lock to be released by using the session option *LOCK_TIMEOUT*. It's a *SET* option, so the behavior can be controlled only for an individual session. You can't set a *LOCK_TIMEOUT* value for SQL Server as a whole. You can read about *LOCK_TIMEOUT* in *SQL Server Books Online*.

Snapshot

Snapshot isolation—sometimes referred to as SI—is an optimistic isolation level. Like Read Committed (snapshot), it allows processes to read older versions of committed data if the current version is locked. The difference between Snapshot and Read Committed (snapshot) has to do with how old the older versions have to be. (You can find the details later in the section "Row versioning.") Although the behaviors prevented by Snapshot isolation are the same as those prevented by Serializable, Snapshot isn't truly a Serializable isolation level. With Snapshot isolation, you can possibly have two transactions executing simultaneously that give you a result that's not possible in any serial execution.

Table 13-1 shows an example of two simultaneous transactions. If they run in parallel, they end up switching the price of two books in the *titles* table in the *pubs* database. However, no serial execution occurs that would end up switching the values, whether we run Transaction 1 and then Transaction 2, or run Transaction 2 and then Transaction 1. Either serial order ends up with the two books having the same price.

TABLE 13-1 Two simultaneous transactions in snapshot isolation that cannot be run serially

Time	Transaction 1	Transaction 2
1	USE pubs; SET TRANSACTION ISOLATION LEVEL SNAPSHOT; DECLARE @price money; BEGIN TRAN	USE pubs; SET TRANSACTION ISOLATION LEVEL SNAPSHOT; DECLARE @price money; BEGIN TRAN
2	SELECT @price = price FROM titles WHERE title_id = 'BU1032';	SELECT @price = price FROM titles WHERE title_id = 'PS7777';
3	UPDATE titles SET price = @price WHERE title_id = 'PS7777';	UPDATE titles SET price = @price WHERE title_id = 'BU1032';
4	COMMIT TRAN	COMMIT TRAN

Serializable

Serializable is also a pessimistic isolation level. The Serializable isolation level adds to the properties of Repeatable Read by ensuring that if a query is reissued, rows aren't added in the interim. In other words, phantoms don't appear if the same query is issued twice within a transaction. Serializable is therefore the strongest of the pessimistic isolation levels because it prevents all the possible undesirable behaviors discussed earlier—that is, it doesn't allow uncommitted reads, nonrepeatable reads, or phantoms, and it also guarantees that your transactions can be run serially.

Preventing phantoms is another desirable safeguard. The cost of this extra safeguard is similar to that of Repeatable Read—all the shared locks in a transaction must be held until the transaction completes. Enforcing the Serializable isolation level also requires that you not only lock data that has been read, but also lock data that doesn't exist.

Suppose that within a transaction, we issue a *SELECT* statement to read all the customers whose postal code is between 98000 and 98100. On first execution, no rows satisfy that condition. To enforce the Serializable isolation level, we must lock that range of potential rows with postal codes between 98000 and 98100 so that if the same query is reissued, it continues to show that no rows still satisfy the condition. SQL Server handles this situation by using a special kind of lock called a *key-range lock*. Key-range locks require that the column have an index that defines the range of values. (In this example, that would be the column containing the postal codes.)

If that column has no index, Serializable isolation requires a table lock. (The following section discusses the different types of locks in detail.) The Serializable level gets its name from the fact that running multiple serializable transactions at the same time is the equivalent of running them one at a time—that is, serially.

For example, transactions A, B, and C run simultaneously at the Serializable level, and each tries to update the same range of data. If the order in which the transactions acquire locks on the range of data is B, C, and then A, the result obtained by running all three simultaneously is the same as though they were run sequentially in the order B, C, and then A. The term *serializable* doesn't imply that the order is known in advance. The order is considered a chance event. Even on a single-user system, the order of transactions hitting the queue would be essentially random. If the batch order is important to your application, you should implement it as a pure batch system. Serializable means only that you should have a way to run the transactions serially to get the same result you receive when you run them simultaneously. Table 13-1 illustrates a case where two transactions can't be run serially and get the same result.

Table 13-2 summarizes the behaviors possible in each isolation level and notes the concurrency control model used to implement each level. You can see that Read Committed and Read Committed (snapshot) are identical in the behaviors they allow, but the behaviors are implemented differently—one is pessimistic (locking), and one is optimistic (row versioning). Serializable and Snapshot also have the same No values for all the behaviors, but one is pessimistic and one is optimistic.

TABLE 13-2 Behaviors allowed in each isolation level

Isolation level	Dirty read	Nonrepeatable read	Phantom	Concurrency control
Read Uncommitted	Yes	Yes	Yes	Pessimistic
Read Committed (locking)	No	Yes	Yes	Pessimistic
Read Committed (snapshot)	No	Yes	Yes	Optimistic
Repeatable Read	No	No	Yes	Pessimistic
Snapshot	No	No	No	Optimistic
Serializable	No	No	No	Pessimistic

Locking

Locking is a crucial function of any multiuser database system, including SQL Server. Locks are applied in both the pessimistic and optimistic concurrency models, although the way other processes deal with locked data is different in each. The reason the pessimistic variation of Read Committed isolation is referred to as Read Committed (locking) is because locking allows concurrent transactions to maintain consistency. In the pessimistic model, writers always block readers and writers, and readers can block writers. In the optimistic model, the only blocking that occurs is that writers block other writers. But to really understand what these simplified behavior summaries mean, we need to look at the details of SQL Server locking.

Locking basics

SQL Server can lock data using several different modes. For example, read operations acquire shared locks, and write operations acquire exclusive locks. Update locks are acquired during the initial portion of an update operation, while SQL Server is searching for the data to update. SQL Server acquires and releases all these types of locks automatically. It also manages compatibility between lock modes, resolves deadlocks, and escalates locks if necessary. It controls locks on tables, on table pages, on index keys, and on individual rows of data. Locks can also be held on system data—data that's private to the database system, such as page headers and indexes.

SQL Server provides two separate locking systems. The first system affects all fully shared data and provides row locks, page locks, and table locks for tables, data pages, large object (LOB) pages, and leaf-level index pages. The second system is used internally for index concurrency control, controlling access to internal data structures and retrieving individual rows of data pages. This second system uses latches, which are less resource-intensive than locks and provide performance optimizations. The designers of SQL Server could have decided to use full-blown locks for all locking, but because of their complexity, they would slow down the system if they were used for all internal needs. If you examine locks using the *sys.dm_tran_locks* view, you can't see latches—you see only information about locks.

Another way to look at the difference between locks and latches is that locks ensure the logical consistency of the data and latches ensure the physical consistency. Latching happens when you place a row physically on a page or move data in other ways, such as compressing the space on a page. SQL Server must guarantee that this data movement can happen without interference.

Spinlocks

For shorter-term needs, SQL Server achieves mutual exclusion with a spinlock. Spinlocks are used purely for mutual exclusion and never to lock user data. They are even more lightweight than latches, which are lighter than the full locks used for data and index leaf pages. The requester of a spinlock repeats its request if the lock isn't immediately available—that is, the requester "spins" on the lock until it's free.

Spinlocks are often used as mutexes within SQL Server for resources that usually aren't busy. If a resource is busy, the duration of a spinlock is short enough that retrying is better than waiting and then being rescheduled by the operating system, which results in context switching between threads. The savings in context switches more than offsets the cost of spinning, as long as you don't have to spin too long. Spinlocks are used for situations in which the wait for a resource is expected to be brief (or if no wait is expected). The *sys.dm_os_tasks* dynamic management view (DMV) shows a status of *SPINLOOP* for any task that's currently using a spinlock.

Lock types for user data

This section examines four aspects of locking user data. First, look at the mode (type) of locking. Shared, exclusive, and update locks have already been mentioned, so this section goes into more detail about these modes as well as others. Next we look at the granularity of the lock, which specifies how much data is covered by a single lock. This can be a row, a page, an index key, a range of index keys, an extent, a partition, or an entire table. The third aspect of locking is the lock's duration. As mentioned earlier, some locks are released as soon as the data has been accessed, and some locks are held until the transaction commits or rolls back. The fourth aspect of locking concerns the ownership (scope) of the lock. Locks can be owned by a session, a transaction, or a cursor.

Lock modes

SQL Server uses several locking modes, including shared locks, exclusive locks, update locks, and intent locks, plus variations on these. The lock's mode determines whether a concurrently requested lock is compatible with locks that have already been granted. You can see the lock compatibility matrix at the end of this section, in Figure 13-2.

Shared locks   Shared locks are acquired automatically by SQL Server when data is read. Shared locks can be held on a table, a page, an index key, or an individual row. Many processes can hold shared locks on the same data, but no process can acquire an exclusive lock on data that has a shared lock on it (unless the process requesting the exclusive lock is the same process as the one holding the shared lock). Under the default isolation level, shared locks are released as soon as the data has been read, but you can change this by using query hints or a different transaction isolation level.

Exclusive locks   SQL Server automatically acquires exclusive locks on data when the data is modified by an *INSERT, UPDATE,* or *DELETE* operation. Only one process at a time can hold an exclusive lock on a particular data resource; in fact, as you see when lock compatibility is discussed later, no locks of any kind can be acquired by a process if another process has the requested data resource exclusively locked. Exclusive locks are held until the end of the transaction. This means the changed data usually isn't available to any other process until the current transaction commits or rolls back. Other processes can decide to read exclusively locked data by using query hints or changing the isolation level to Read Uncommitted.

Update locks   Update locks really aren't a separate kind of lock; they are a hybrid of shared and exclusive locks. They are acquired when SQL Server executes a data modification operation, but first SQL Server needs to search the table to find the resource that needs to be modified. By using query hints, a process can specifically request update locks and, in that case, the update locks prevent the conversion deadlock situation presented later in Figure 13-6.

Update locks provide compatibility with other current readers of data, allowing the process to later modify data with the assurance that the data hasn't been changed since it was last read. An update lock isn't sufficient to allow you to change the data; all modifications require that the data resource being modified have an exclusive lock.

An update lock acts as a serialization gate to queue future requests for the exclusive lock. (Many processes can hold shared locks for a resource, but only one process can hold an update lock.) As long as a process holds an update lock on a resource, no other process can acquire an update lock or an exclusive lock for that resource; instead, another process requesting an update or exclusive lock for the same resource must wait. The process holding the update lock can convert it into an exclusive lock on that resource because the update lock prevents lock incompatibility with any other processes. You can think of update locks as "intent-to-update" locks, which is essentially the role they perform. Used alone, update locks are insufficient for updating data—an exclusive lock is still required for actual data modification. Serializing access for the exclusive lock lets you avoid conversion deadlocks. Update locks are held until the end of the transaction or until they are converted to an exclusive lock.

Don't let the name fool you: Update locks aren't just for *UPDATE* operations. SQL Server uses update locks for any data modification operation that requires a search for the data before the actual modification. Such operations include qualified updates and deletes, as well as inserts into a table with a clustered index. In the latter case, SQL Server must first search the data (using the clustered index) to find the correct position at which to insert the new row. Although SQL Server is only searching, it uses update locks to protect the data; only after it finds the correct location and begins inserting does it convert the update lock to an exclusive lock.

Intent locks   Intent locks aren't really a separate mode of locking; they are a qualifier to the modes previously discussed. In other words, you can have intent shared locks, intent exclusive locks, and even intent update locks.

Because SQL Server can acquire locks at different levels of granularity, a mechanism is needed to indicate that a component of a resource is already locked. For example, if one process tries to lock a table, SQL Server needs a way to determine whether a row (or a page) of that table is already locked. Intent locks serve this purpose. They are discussed in more detail later in the section on lock granularity.

Special lock modes   SQL Server offers three additional lock modes: schema stability locks, schema modification locks, and bulk update locks.

- When queries are compiled, schema stability locks prevent other processes from acquiring schema modification locks, which are taken when a table's structure is being modified.

- A bulk update lock is acquired when the *BULK INSERT* command is executed or when the bcp utility is run to load data into a table. Also, the bulk import operation must request this special lock by using the *TABLOCK* hint. Alternatively, the table owner can set the table option called *table lock on bulk load* to True, and then any bulk copy *IN* or *BULK INSERT* operation automatically requests a bulk update lock.

  Requesting this special bulk update table lock doesn't necessarily mean it's granted. If other processes already hold locks on the table, or if the table has any indexes, a bulk update lock can't be granted. If multiple connections have requested and received a bulk update lock, they can perform parallel loads into the same table. Unlike exclusive locks, bulk update locks don't conflict with each other, so concurrent inserts by multiple connections is supported.

Conversion locks   Conversion locks are never requested directly by SQL Server, but are the result of a conversion from one mode to another. The three types of conversion locks supported by SQL Server 2012 are SIX, SIU, and UIX. The most common of these is the SIX, which occurs if a transaction is holding a shared (S) lock on a resource and an IX lock is needed later. The lock mode is indicated as SIX. Suppose that you issue the following batch:

```
SET TRANSACTION ISOLATION LEVEL REPEATABLE READ;
BEGIN TRAN
SELECT * FROM bigtable;
UPDATE bigtable
    SET col = 0
    WHERE keycolumn = 100;
```

If the table is large, the *SELECT* statement acquires a shared table lock. (If the table has only a few rows, SQL Server acquires individual row or key locks.) The *UPDATE* statement then acquires a single exclusive key lock to perform the update of a single row, and the X lock at the key level means an IX lock at the page and table level. The table then shows SIX when viewed through *sys.dm_tran_locks*. Similarly, SIU occurs when a process has a shared lock on a table and an update lock on a row of that table, and UIX occurs when a process has an update lock on the table and an exclusive lock on a row.

Table 13-3 shows most of the lock modes, as well as the abbreviations used in *sys.dm_tran_locks*.

TABLE 13-3 SQL Server lock modes

Abbreviation	Lock mode	Description
S	Shared	Allows other processes to read but not change the locked resource.
X	Exclusive	Prevents another process from modifying or reading data in the locked resource.
U	Update	Prevents other processes from acquiring an update or exclusive lock. This lock is used when searching for the data to modify.
IS	Intent shared	Indicates that a component of this resource is locked with a shared lock. This lock can be acquired only at the table or page level.
IU	Intent update	Indicates that a component of this resource is locked with an update lock. This lock can be acquired only at the table or page level.
IX	Intent exclusive	Indicates that a component of this resource is locked with an exclusive lock. This lock can be acquired only at the table or page level.
SIX	Shared with intent exclusive	Indicates that a resource holding a shared lock also has a component (a page or row) locked with an exclusive lock.
SIU	Shared with intent update	Indicates that a resource holding a shared lock also has a component (a page or row) locked with an update lock.
UIX	Update with intent exclusive	Indicates that a resource holding an update lock also has a component (a page or row) locked with an exclusive lock.
Sch-S	Schema stability	Indicates that a query using this table is being compiled.
Sch-M	Schema modification	Indicates that the structure of the table is being changed.
BU	Bulk update	Used when a bulk copy operation is copying data into a table and the *TABLOCK* hint is being applied (either manually or automatically).

Key-range locks   Additional lock modes—called *key-range locks*—are taken only in the Serializable isolation level for locking ranges of data. Most lock modes can apply to almost any lock resource. For example, shared and exclusive locks can be taken on a table, a page, a row, or a key. Because key-range locks can be taken only on keys, you can find details of key-range locks coming up in the "Key Locks" discussion.

Lock granularity

SQL Server can lock user data resources (but not system resources, which are protected with latches) at the table, page, or row level. (If locks are escalated, SQL Server can also lock a single partition of a table or index.) Also, SQL Server can lock index keys and ranges of index keys. Figure 13-1 shows the basic lock levels in a table that can be acquired when a resource is first accessed. Keep in mind that if the table has a clustered index, the data rows are at the leaf level of the clustered index and are locked with key locks instead of row locks.

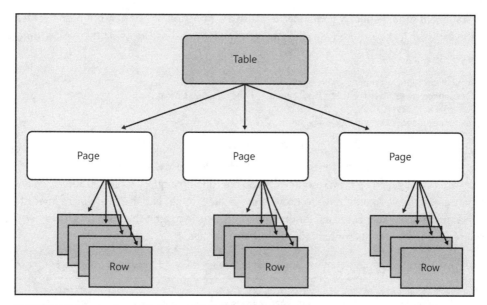

FIGURE 13-1 Levels of granularity for SQL Server locks on a table.

The *sys.dm_tran_locks* view keeps track of each lock and contains information about the resource, which item is locked (such as row, key, or page), the mode of the lock, and an identifier for the specific resource. Keep in mind that *sys.dm_tran_locks* is only a dynamic view used to display the information about the held locks. Like with all the DMVs, the actual information is stored in internal SQL Server structures that aren't visible to you at all. So when the text talks about information being in the *sys.dm_tran_locks* view, it's saying that the information can be seen through that view.

When a process requests a lock, SQL Server compares the lock requested to the resources already listed in *sys.dm_tran_locks* and looks for an exact match on the resource type and identifier. However, if one process has a row exclusively locked in the *Sales.SalesOrderHeader* table, for example, another process might try to get a lock on the entire *Sales.SalesOrderHeader* table. Because these are two different resources, SQL Server doesn't find an exact match unless additional information is already in *sys.dm_tran_locks*. This is what intent locks are for. The process that has the exclusive lock on a row of the *Sales.SalesOrderHeader* table also has an intent exclusive lock on the page containing the row and another intent exclusive lock on the table containing the row. We can see those locks by first running this code:

```
USE Adventureworks2012;
BEGIN TRAN
UPDATE Sales.SalesOrderHeader
SET ShipDate = ShipDate + 1
WHERE SalesOrderID = 43666;
```

This statement should affect a single row. Because a transaction has started but hasn't yet terminated, the exclusive locks acquired are still held. You can look at those locks via the *sys.dm_tran_locks*
view:

```
SELECT resource_type, resource_description,
       resource_associated_entity_id, request_mode, request_status
FROM sys.dm_tran_locks
WHERE resource_associated_entity_id > 0;
```

You can find more details about the data in the section "Viewing locks" later in this chapter, but
for now, just note that the reason for the filter in the *WHERE* clause is that you're interested only in
locks that are actually held on data resources. If you are running a query on a SQL Server instance
that others are using, you might have to provide more filters to get just the rows you're interested
in. For example, you could include a filter on *request_session_id* to limit the output to locks held by a
particular session. Your results should look something like this:

resource_type	resource_description	resource_associated_entity_id	request_mode	request_status
KEY	(92007ad11d1d)	72057594045857792	X	GRANT
PAGE	1:5280	72057594045857792	IX	GRANT
OBJECT		722101613	IX	GRANT

Notice three locks, even though the *UPDATE* statement affected only a single row. For the
KEY and *PAGE* locks, the *resource_associated_entity_id* is a *partition_id*. For the *OBJECT* locks, the
resource_associated_entity_id is a table. We can verify what table it is by using the following query:

```
SELECT object_name(722101613);
```

The results should tell you that the object is the *Sales.SalesOrderHeader* table. If a second process
tries to acquire an exclusive lock on that table, it finds a conflicting row already in *sys.dm_tran_locks*
on the same lock resource (the *Sales.SalesOrderHeader* table), and it's blocked. The *sys.dm_tran_locks*
view would show you the following row, indicating a request for an exclusive lock on an object that
can't be granted. The process requesting the lock is in a WAIT state:

resource_type	resource_description	resource_associated_entity_id	request_mode	request_status
OBJECT		722101613	X	WAIT

Not all requests for locks on resources that are already locked result in a conflict. A conflict occurs
when one process requests a lock on a resource that's already locked by another process in an incompatible lock mode. Two processes can each acquire shared locks on the same resource because shared
locks are compatible with each other. I discuss lock compatibility in detail later in this chapter.

Key locks   SQL Server 2012 supports two kinds of key locks, and which one it uses depends on the
isolation level of the current transaction. If the isolation level is Read Committed, Repeatable Read,
or Snapshot, SQL Server tries to lock the actual index keys accessed while processing the query. With
a table that has a clustered index, the data rows are the leaf level of the index, and you see key locks
acquired. If the table is a heap, you might see key locks for the nonclustered indexes and row locks for
the actual data.

If the isolation level is Serializable, the situation is different. We want to prevent phantoms, so if we have scanned a range of data within a transaction, we need to lock enough of the table to ensure that no one can insert a value into the range that was scanned. For example, we can issue the following query within an explicit transaction in the *AdventureWorks2012* database:

```
BEGIN TRAN
SELECT * FROM Sales.SalesOrderHeader
WHERE CustomerID BETWEEN 100 and 110;
```

When you use Serializable isolation, locks must be acquired to make sure no new rows with *CustomerID* values between 100 and 110 are inserted before the end of the transaction. Much older versions of SQL Server (prior to version 7.0) guaranteed this by locking whole pages or even the entire table. In many cases, however, this was too restrictive—more data was locked than the actual *WHERE* clause indicated, resulting in unnecessary contention. SQL Server now uses the key-range locks mode, which is associated with a particular key value in an index and indicates that all values between that key and the previous one in the index are locked.

The *AdventureWorks2012* database includes an index on the *Person* table with the *LastName* column as the leading column. Assume that we are in *TRANSACTION ISOLATION LEVEL SERIALIZABLE* and we issue this *SELECT* statement inside a user-defined transaction:

```
SELECT * FROM Person.Person
WHERE LastName BETWEEN 'Freller' AND 'Freund';
```

If *Fredericksen, French,* and *Friedland* are sequential leaf-level index keys in an index on the *Last-Name* column, the second two of these keys (*French* and *Friedland*) acquire key-range locks (although only one row, for *French*, is returned in the result set). The key-range locks prevent any inserts into the ranges ending with the two key-range locks. No values greater than *Fredericksen* and less than or equal to *French* can be inserted, and no values greater than *French* and less than or equal to *Friedland* can be inserted. That range includes all values that would exist between the two names 'Freller' and 'Freund' specified in the query.

Notice that the key-range locks imply an open interval starting at the previous sequential key and a closed interval ending at the key on which the lock is placed. These two key-range locks prevent anyone from inserting either *Fremlich* or *Frenkin,* which are in the range specified in the *WHERE* clause. The key-range locks would also prevent anyone from inserting *Freedman* (which is greater than *Fredericksen* and less than *French*), because *Freedman* isn't in the query's specified range. Key-range locks aren't perfect, but they do provide much greater concurrency than locking whole pages or tables while guaranteeing that phantoms are prevented.

SQL Server has nine types of key-range locks, and each has a two-part name: The first part indicates the type of lock on the range of data between adjacent index keys, and the second part indicates the type of lock on the key itself. Table 13-4 describes the key-range locks.

TABLE 13-4 Types of key-range locks

Abbreviation	Description
RangeS-S	Shared lock on the range between keys; shared lock on the key at the end of the range
RangeS-U	Shared lock on the range between keys; update lock on the key at the end of the range
RangeIn-Null	Exclusive lock to prevent inserts on the range between keys; no lock on the keys themselves
RangeX-X	Exclusive lock on the range between keys; exclusive lock on the key at the end of the range
RangeIn-S	Conversion lock created by S and RangeIn_Null lock
RangeIn-U	Conversion lock created by U and RangeIn_Null lock
RangeIn-X	Conversion of X and RangeIn_Null lock
RangeX-S	Conversion of RangeIn_Null and RangeS_S lock
RangeX-U	Conversion of RangeIn_Null and RangeS_U lock

Many of these lock modes are very rare or transient, so you don't see them very often in *sys. dm_tran_locks*. For example, the RangeIn-Null lock is acquired when SQL Server attempts to insert into the range between keys in a session using Serializable isolation. This type of lock isn't often seen because it's typically very transient. It's held only until the correct location for insertion is found, and then the lock is converted into an X lock. However, if one transaction scans a range of data using the Serializable isolation level and then another transaction tries to insert into that range, the second transaction has a lock request with a WAIT status with the RangeIn-Null mode. You can observe this by looking at the status column in *sys.dm_tran_locks*, which this chapter discusses in more detail later.

Additional lock resources   In addition to locks on objects, pages, keys, and rows, a few other resources can be locked by SQL Server. Generally, you don't need to be concerned with extent or database locks, but you see them if you are perusing *sys.dm_tran_locks*.

Extent locks   Locks can be taken on *extents*—units of disk space that are 64 KB in size (eight pages of 8 KB each). This kind of locking occurs automatically when a table or index needs to grow and a new extent must be allocated. You can think of an extent lock as another type of special-purpose latch, but it does show up in *sys.dm_tran_locks*. Extents can have both shared extent and exclusive extent locks.

Database locks   When you examine the contents of *sys.dm_tran_locks*, notice that most processes hold a lock on at least one database (*resource_type = DATABASE*). In fact, any process holding locks in any database other than *master* or *tempdb* has a lock for that database resource. These database locks are always shared locks if the process is just using the database. SQL Server checks for these database locks when determining whether a database is in use, and then it can determine whether the database can be dropped, restored, altered, or closed.

Because few changes can be made to *master* and *tempdb* and they can't be dropped or closed, database locks are unnecessary. Also, *tempdb* is never restored, and to restore the *master* database, the entire server must be started in single-user mode, so again, database locks are unnecessary. When attempting to perform one of these operations, SQL Server requests an exclusive database lock, and if any other processes have a shared lock on the database, the operation is blocked.

Allocation unit locks   You might occasionally see locks on allocation unit resources. Although all table and index structures contain one or more allocation units, when these locks occur, it means that SQL Server is dealing with one of these resources that's no longer tied to a particular object.

For example, when you drop or rebuild large tables or indexes, the actual page deallocation is deferred until after the transaction commits. Deferred drop operations don't release allocated space immediately, and they introduce additional overhead costs, so a deferred drop is done only on tables or indexes that use more than 128 extents. If the table or index uses 128 or fewer extents, dropping, truncating, and rebuilding aren't deferred operations.

During the first phase of a deferred operation, the existing allocation units used by the table or index are marked for deallocation and locked until the transaction commits. This is where you see allocation unit locks in *sys.dm_tran_locks*. You can also look in the *sys.allocation_units* view to find allocation units with a *type_desc* value of *DROPPED* to see how much space is being used by the allocation units that aren't available for reuse but also aren't currently part of any object. The actual physical dropping of the allocation unit's space occurs after the transaction commits.

Partition-level locks   You occasionally have locks on individual partitions, which are indicated in the lock metadata as HOBT locks. This can happen only when locks are escalated, and only if you have specified that escalation to the partition level is allowed (and, of course, only when the table or index has been partitioned). Later, the section "Lock escalation" looks at how you can specify that you want partition-level locking.

How to identify lock resources   When SQL Server tries to determine whether a requested lock can be granted, it checks the *sys.dm_tran_locks* view to determine whether a matching lock with a conflicting lock mode already exists. It compares locks by looking at the database ID (*resource_database_ID)*, the values in the *resource_description* and *resource_associated_entity_id* columns, and the type of resource locked.

SQL Server knows nothing about the meaning of the resource description. It simply compares the strings identifying the lock resources to look for a match. If it finds a match with a *request_status* value of *GRANT*, it knows the resource is already locked; it then uses the lock compatibility matrix to determine whether the current lock is compatible with the one being requested. Table 13-5 shows many of the possible lock resources that are displayed in the first column of the *sys.dm_tran_locks* view and the information in the *resource_description* column, which is used to define the actual resource locked.

TABLE 13-5 Lockable resources in SQL Server

resource_type	resource_description	Example
DATABASE	None; always indicated in the *resource_database_ID* column for every locked resource.	12
OBJECT	The object ID (which can be any database object, not necessarily a table). Reported in the *resource_associated_entity_id* column.	69575286
HOBT	Reported in the *resource_associated_entity_id* column as *hobt_id*. Used only when partition locking has been enabled for a table.	72057594038779904

resource_type	resource_description	Example
EXTENT	File number:page number of the first page of the extent.	1:96
PAGE	File number:page number of the actual table or index page.	1:104
KEY	A hashed value derived from all the key components and the locator. For a nonclustered index on a heap, where columns *c1* and *c2* are indexed, the hash contains contributions from *c1*, *c2*, and the *RID*.	ac0001a10a00
ROW	File number:page number:slot number of the actual row.	1:161:3

Note that key locks and key-range locks have identical resource descriptions because key range is considered a mode of locking, not a locking resource. When you look at output from the *sys.dm_tran_locks* view, you see that you can distinguish between these types of locks by the value in the lock mode column.

Another type of lockable resource is METADATA. More than any other resource, METADATA resources are divided into multiple subtypes, which are described in the *resource_subtype* column of *sys.dm_tran_locks*. You might see dozens of subtypes of METADATA resources, but most of them are beyond the scope of this book. For some, however, even though *SQL Server Books Online* describes them as "for internal use only," what they refer to is pretty obvious. For example, when you change properties of a database, you can see a *resource_type* of METADATA and a *resource_subtype* of DATABASE. The value in the *resource_description* column of that row is *database_id =<ID>*, indicating the ID of the database whose metadata is currently locked.

Associated entity ID   For locked resources that are part of a larger entity, the *resource_associated_entity_id* column in *sys.dm_tran_locks* displays the ID of that associated entity in the database. This can be an object ID, a partition ID, or an allocation unit ID, depending on the resource type. Of course, some resources, such as DATABASE and EXTENT, have no *resource_associated_entity_id*. An object ID value is given in this column for OBJECT resources, and an allocation unit ID is given for ALLOCATION_UNIT resources. A partition ID is provided for resource types PAGE, KEY, and RID.

No simple function exists to convert a partition ID value to an object name; you have to actually select from the *sys.partitions* view. The query in Listing 13-1 translates all the *resource_associated_entity_id* values for locks in the current database by joining *sys.dm_tran_locks* to *sys.partitions*.

LISTING 13-1 Creating a view to return all locks in the current database

```
CREATE VIEW DBlocks AS
SELECT request_session_id as spid,
    db_name(resource_database_id) as dbname,
    CASE
  WHEN resource_type = 'OBJECT' THEN
        object_name(resource_associated_entity_id)
     WHEN resource_associated_entity_id = 0 THEN 'n/a'
  ELSE object_name(p.object_id)
   END as entity_name, index_id,
     resource_type as resource,
     resource_description as description,
     request_mode as mode, request_status as status
```

```
FROM sys.dm_tran_locks t LEFT JOIN sys.partitions p
   ON p.partition_id = t.resource_associated_entity_id
WHERE resource_database_id = db_id();
```

For OBJECT resources, the *object_name* function is applied to the *resource_associated_entity_id* column. For PAGE, KEY, and RID resources, the *object_name* function is used with the *object_id* value from the *sys.partitions* view. For other resources for which no *resource_associated_entity_id* exists, the code just returns *n/a*.

Because the query references the *sys.partitions* view, which occurs in each database, this code is filtered to return only lock information for resources in the current database. The output is organized to reflect the information returned by the *sp_lock* procedure, but you can add any additional filters or columns that you need. Because the query in Listing 13-1 is used in many examples later in this chapter, it creates a *VIEW* based on the *SELECT* called *DBlocks*.

Lock duration

The length of time that a lock is held depends primarily on the lock's mode and the transaction isolation level in effect. The default isolation level for SQL Server is Read Committed. At this level, shared locks are released as soon as SQL Server has read and processed the locked data. In Snapshot isolation, the behavior is the same—shared locks are released as soon as SQL Server has read the data. If your transaction isolation level is Repeatable Read or Serializable, shared locks have the same duration as exclusive locks—that is, they're not released until the transaction is over. In any isolation level, an exclusive lock is held until the end of the transaction, whether the transaction is committed or rolled back. An update lock is also held until the end of the transaction, unless it has been promoted to an exclusive lock, in which case the exclusive lock (as is always the case with exclusive locks) remains for the duration of the transaction.

In addition to changing your transaction isolation level, you can control the lock duration by using query hints. Query hints for locking are briefly discussed later in this chapter.

Lock ownership

Lock duration is also directly affected by the lock ownership. Lock ownership has nothing to do with the process that requested the lock, but you can think of it as the "scope" of the lock. Lock owners, or lock scopes, come in four types: transactions, cursors, transaction_workspaces, and sessions. The lock owner can be viewed through the *request_owner_type* column in the *sys.dm_tran_locks* view.

Most of the locking discussion deals with locks with a lock owner of *TRANSACTION*. As you've seen, these locks can have two different durations, depending on the isolation level and lock mode. The duration of shared locks in Read Committed isolation is only as long as the locked data is being read. The duration of all other locks owned by a transaction is until the end of the transaction.

A lock with a *request_ownertype* value of *CURSOR* must be requested explicitly when the cursor is declared. If a cursor is opened using a locking mode of *SCROLL_LOCKS*, a cursor lock is held on every row fetched until the next row is fetched or the cursor is closed. Even if the transaction commits before the next fetch, the cursor lock isn't released.

In SQL Server 2012, locks owned by a session must also be requested explicitly and apply only to *APPLICATION* locks. A session lock is requested using the *sp_getapplock* procedure. Its duration is until the session disconnects or the lock is released explicitly.

Transaction_workspace locks are acquired every time a database is accessed, and the resource associated with these locks is always a database. A workspace holds database locks for sessions that are enlisted into a common environment. Usually, each session has just one workspace, so all DATABASE locks acquired in the session are kept in the same workspace object. In the case of distributed transactions, multiple sessions are enlisted into the same workspace, so they share the database locks.

Every process acquires a DATABASE lock with an owner of *SHARED_TRANSACTION_WORKSPACE* on any database when the process issues the *USE* command. The exception is any processes that use *master* or *tempdb*, in which case no DATABASE lock is taken. That lock isn't released until another *USE* command is issued or until the process is disconnected. If a process attempts to *ALTER*, *RESTORE*, or *DROP* the database, the DATABASE lock acquired has an owner of *EXCLUSIVE_TRANSACTION_WORKSPACE*. *SHARED_TRANSACTION_WORKSPACE* and *EXCLUSIVE_TRANSACTION_WORKSPACE* locks are maintained by the same workspace and are just two different lists in one workspace. The use of two different owner names is misleading in this case.

Viewing locks

To see the locks currently outstanding in the system, as well as those being waited for, the best source of information is the *sys.dm_tran_locks* view. You've seen some queries from this view in earlier sections; in this section you can look at a few more and find out what more of the output columns mean. This view replaces the *sp_lock* procedure.

Although calling a procedure might require less typing than querying the *sys.dm_tran_locks* view, the view is much more flexible. Not only do many more columns of information provide details about your locks, but as a view, *sys.dm_tran_locks* also can be queried to select just the columns you want, or only the rows that meet your criteria. It can be joined with other views and aggregated to get summary information about how many locks of each kind are being held.

All the columns (with the exception of the last column called *lock_owner_address*) in *sys.dm_tran_locks* start with one of two prefixes. The columns whose names begin with *resource_* describe the resource on which the lock request is being made. The columns whose names begin with *request_* describe the process requesting the lock. Two requests operate on the same resource only if all the *resource_* columns are the same.

resource_ columns

Most *resource_* columns have been discussed already, except the *resource_subtype* column was mentioned only briefly. Not all resources have subtypes, and some have many. The METADATA resource type, for example, has more than 40 subtypes.

Table 13-6 lists all the subtypes for resource types other than METADATA.

TABLE 13-6 Subtype resources

Resource type	Resource subtypes	Description
DATABASE	BULKOP_BACKUP_DB	Used for synchronization of database backups with bulk operations
	BULKOP_BACKUP_LOG	Used for synchronization of database log backups with bulk operations
	DDL	Used to synchronize Data Definition Language (DDL) operations with File Group operations (such as *DROP*)
	STARTUP	Used for database startup synchronization
TABLE	UPDSTATS	Used for synchronization of statistics updates on a table
	COMPILE	Used for synchronization of stored procedure compiles
	INDEX_OPERATION	Used for synchronization of index operations
HOBT	INDEX_REORGANIZE	Used for synchronization of heap or index reorganization operations
	BULK_OPERATION	Used for heap-optimized bulk load operations with concurrent scan, in the Snapshot, Read Uncommitted, and Read Committed SI levels
ALLOCATION_UNIT	PAGE_COUNT	Used for synchronization of allocation unit page count statistics during deferred drop operations

As mentioned earlier, most METADATA subtypes are documented as being for internal use only, but their meaning is often pretty obvious. Each type of metadata can be locked separately as changes are made. Here is a partial list of the METADATA subtypes:

- INDEXSTATS

- STATS

- SCHEMA

- DATABASE_PRINCIPAL

- DB_PRINCIPAL_SID

- USER_TYPE

- DATA_SPACE

- PARTITION_FUNCTION

- DATABASE

- SERVER_PRINCIPAL

- SERVER

Most other METADATA subtypes not listed here refer to SQL Server 2012 elements that aren't discussed in this book, including CLR routines, XML, certificates, full-text search, and notification services.

request_ columns

A couple of the most important *request_* columns in *sys.dm_tran_locks*—including *request_mode* (the type of lock requested), *request_owner_type* (the scope of the lock requested), and *request_session_id*—have been discussed already. Here are some of the others.

- **request_type**   In SQL Server 2012, the only type of resource request tracked in *sys.dm_tran_locks* is for a *LOCK*. Future versions might include other types of resources that can be requested.

- **request_status**   Status can be one of three values: *GRANT*, *CONVERT*, or *WAIT*. A status of *CONVERT* indicates that the requestor has already been granted a request for the same resource in a different mode and is currently waiting for an upgrade (convert) from the current lock mode to be granted. (For example, SQL Server can convert a U lock to X.) A status of *WAIT* indicates that the requestor doesn't currently hold a granted request on the resource.

- **request_reference_count**   This value is a rough count of number of times the same requestor has requested this resource and applies only to resources not automatically released at the end of a transaction. A granted resource is no longer considered to be held by a requestor if this field decreases to 0 and *request_lifetime* is also 0.

- **request_lifetime**   This value is a code that indicates when the lock on the resource is released.

- **request_session_id**   This value is the ID of the session that has requested the lock. The owning session ID can change for distributed and bound transactions. A value of –2 indicates that the request belongs to an orphaned DTC transaction. A value of –3 indicates that the request belongs to a deferred recovery transaction. (These are transactions whose rollback has been deferred at recovery because the rollback couldn't be completed successfully.)

- **request_exec_context_id**   This value is the execution context ID of the process that currently owns this request. A value greater than 0 indicates that this is a subthread used to execute a parallel query.

- **request_request_id**   This value is the request ID (batch ID) of the process that currently owns this request. This column is populated only for the requests coming in from a client application using Multiple Active Result Sets (MARS).

- **request_owner_id**   This value is currently used only for requests with an owner of *TRANSACTION*, and the owner ID is the transaction ID. This column can be joined with the *transaction_id* column in the *sys.dm_tran_active_transactions* view.

- **request_owner_guid**   This value is currently used only by DTC transactions when it corresponds to the DTC GUID for that transaction.

- **lock_owner_address**   This value is the memory address of the internal data structure used to track this request. This column can be joined with the *resource_address* column in *sys.dm_os_waiting_tasks* if this request is in the *WAIT* or *CONVERT* state.

Locking examples

Listings 13-2 through 13-9 show what many of the lock types and modes discussed earlier look like when reported using the *DBlocks* view described earlier in Listing 13-1.

In Listing 13-2, the data in the *Production.Product* table has no locks because the batch was performing only *SELECT* operations that acquired shared locks. By default, the shared locks are released as soon as the data has been read, so by the time the *SELECT* from the view is executed, the locks are no longer held, except for the ever-present DATABASE lock and an OBJECT lock on the view.

LISTING 13-2 *SELECT* with default isolation level

SQL BATCH

```
USE AdventureWorks2012;
SET TRANSACTION ISOLATION LEVEL READ COMMITTED;
BEGIN TRAN
SELECT * FROM Production.Product
WHERE Name = 'Reflector';
SELECT * FROM DBlocks WHERE spid = @@spid;
COMMIT TRAN
```

RESULTS FROM DBlocks

spid	dbname	entity_name	index_id	resource	description	mode	status
60	Adventureworks2012	n/a	NULL	DATABASE		S	GRANT
60	AdventureWorks2012	DBlocks	NULL	OBJECT		IS	GRANT

The code in Listing 13-3 filters out the database lock and the locks on the view and the rowset, just to keep the focus on the data locks. Because the *Production.Product* table has a clustered index, the rows of data are all index rows in the leaf level. The locks on the two individual data rows returned are listed as key locks. Also, two key locks at the leaf level of the nonclustered index on the table are used to find the relevant rows. In the *Production.Product* table, that nonclustered index is on the *Name* column. You can tell the clustered and nonclustered indexes apart by the value in the *index_id* column: the data rows (the leaf rows of the clustered index) have an *index_id* value of 1, and the nonclustered index rows have an *index_id* value of 3. (For nonclustered indexes, the *index_id* value can be anything between 2 and 250 or between 256 and 1005.) Because the transaction isolation level is Repeatable Read, the shared locks are held until the transaction is finished. Notice that the index rows have shared (S) locks, and that the data and index pages, as well as the table itself, have intent shared (IS) locks.

LISTING 13-3 *SELECT* with Repeatable Read isolation level

SQL BATCH

```
USE AdventureWorks2012;
SET TRANSACTION ISOLATION LEVEL REPEATABLE READ;
BEGIN TRAN
SELECT * FROM Production.Product
WHERE Name LIKE 'Racing Socks%';
SELECT * FROM DBlocks
WHERE spid = @@spid
```

```
AND entity_name = 'Product';
COMMIT TRAN
```

RESULTS FROM *DBlocks*

spid	dbname	entity_name	index_id	resource	description	mode	status
54	AdventureWorks2012	Product	NULL	OBJECT		IS	GRANT
54	AdventureWorks2012	Product	1	PAGE	1:16897	IS	GRANT
54	AdventureWorks2012	Product	1	KEY	(6b00b8eeda30)	S	GRANT
54	AdventureWorks2012	Product	1	KEY	(6a00dd896688)	S	GRANT
54	AdventureWorks2012	Product	3	KEY	(9502d56a217e)	S	GRANT
54	AdventureWorks2012	Product	3	PAGE	1:1767	IS	GRANT
54	AdventureWorks2012	Product	3	KEY	(9602945b3a67)	S	GRANT

In Listing 13-4, the locks held with the Serializable isolation level are almost identical to those held with the Repeatable Read isolation level. The main difference is in the mode of the lock. The two-part mode RangeS-S indicates a key-range lock in addition to the lock on the key itself. The first part (RangeS) is the lock on the range of keys between (and including) the key holding the lock and the previous key in the index. The key-range locks prevent other transactions from inserting new rows into the table that meet the condition of this query—that is, no new rows with a product name starting with *Racing Socks* can be inserted.

LISTING 13-4 *SELECT* with Serializable isolation level

SQL BATCH
```
USE AdventureWorks2012;
SET TRANSACTION ISOLATION LEVEL SERIALIZABLE;
BEGIN TRAN
SELECT * FROM Production.Product
WHERE Name LIKE 'Racing Socks%';
SELECT * FROM DBlocks
WHERE spid = @@spid
AND entity_name = 'Product';
COMMIT TRAN
```

RESULTS FROM *DBlocks*

spid	dbname	entity_name	index_id	resource	description	mode	status
54	AdventureWorks2012	Product	NULL	OBJECT		IS	GRANT
54	AdventureWorks2012	Product	1	PAGE	1:16897	IS	GRANT
54	AdventureWorks2012	Product	1	KEY	(6b00b8eeda30)	S	GRANT
54	AdventureWorks2012	Product	1	KEY	(6a00dd896688)	S	GRANT
54	AdventureWorks2012	Product	3	KEY	(9502d56a217e)	RangeS-S	GRANT
54	AdventureWorks2012	Product	3	PAGE	1:1767	IS	GRANT
54	AdventureWorks2012	Product	3	KEY	(23027a50f6db)	RangeS-S	GRANT
54	AdventureWorks2012	Product	3	KEY	(9602945b3a67)	RangeS-S	GRANT

The key-range locks are held on ranges in the nonclustered index on *Name* (*index_id* = 3) because that index is used to find the qualifying rows. The nonclustered index has three key locks because three different ranges need to be locked. The two *Racing Socks* rows are *Racing Socks, L* and *Racing Socks, M*. SQL Server must lock the range from the key preceding the first *Racing Socks* row in the index up to the first *Racing Socks*. It must lock the range between the two rows starting with *Racing Socks*, and it must lock the range from the second *Racing Socks* to the next key in the index. (So actually nothing could be inserted between *Racing Socks* and the previous key, *Pinch Bolt,* or between *Racing Socks* and the next key, *Rear Brakes*. For example, we couldn't insert a product with the name *Portkey* or *Racing Tights*.)

In Listing 13-5, the two rows in the leaf level of the clustered index are locked with X locks. The page and the table are then locked with IX locks. As mentioned earlier, SQL Server actually acquires update locks while it looks for the rows to update. However, these are converted to X locks when the actual update is performed, and by the time you look at the *DBLocks* view, the update locks are gone. Unless you actually force update locks with a query hint, you might never see them in the lock report from *DBLocks* or by direct inspection of *sys.dm_tran_locks*.

LISTING 13-5 Update operations

SQL BATCH

```
USE AdventureWorks2012;
SET TRANSACTION ISOLATION LEVEL READ COMMITTED;
BEGIN TRAN
UPDATE Production.Product
SET ListPrice = ListPrice * 0.6
WHERE Name LIKE 'Racing Socks%';
SELECT * FROM DBlocks
WHERE spid = @@spid
AND entity_name = 'Product';
COMMIT TRAN
```

RESULTS FROM *DBlocks*

spid	dbname	entity_name	index_id	resource	description	mode	status
54	AdventureWorks2012	Product	NULL	OBJECT		IX	GRANT
54	AdventureWorks2012	Product	1	PAGE	1:16897	IX	GRANT
54	AdventureWorks2012	Product	1	KEY	(6b00b8eeda30)	X	GRANT
54	AdventureWorks2012	Product	1	KEY	(6a00dd8966 88)	X	GRANT

In Listing 13-6, again notice that the key-range locks are on the nonclustered index used to find the relevant rows. The range interval itself needs only a shared lock to prevent insertions, but the searched keys have U locks so no other process can attempt to update them. The keys in the table itself (*index_id* = 1) obtain the exclusive lock when the actual modification is made.

LISTING 13-6 Update with Serializable isolation level using an index

SQL BATCH

```
USE AdventureWorks2012;
SET TRANSACTION ISOLATION LEVEL SERIALIZABLE;
BEGIN TRAN
UPDATE Production.Product
SET ListPrice = ListPrice * 0.6
WHERE Name LIKE 'Racing Socks%';
```

```
SELECT * FROM DBlocks
WHERE spid = @@spid
AND entity_name = 'Product';
COMMIT TRAN
```

RESULTS FROM *DBlocks*

spid	dbname	entity_name	index_id	resource	description	mode	status
54	AdventureWorks2012	Product	NULL	OBJECT		IX	GRANT
54	AdventureWorks2012	Product	1	PAGE	1:16897	IX	GRANT
54	AdventureWorks2012	Product	1	KEY	(6a00dd896688)	X	GRANT
54	AdventureWorks2012	Product	1	KEY	(6b00b8eeda30)	X	GRANT
54	AdventureWorks2012	Product	3	KEY	(9502d56a217e)	RangeS-U	GRANT
54	AdventureWorks2012	Product	3	PAGE	1:1767	IU	GRANT
54	AdventureWorks2012	Product	3	KEY	(23027a50f6db)	RangeS-U	GRANT
54	AdventureWorks2012	Product	3	KEY	(9602945b3a67)	RangeS-U	GRANT

Now look at an *UPDATE* operation with the same isolation level when no index can be used for the search. The locks in Listing 13-7 are similar to those in Listing 13-6, except that all the locks are on the table itself (*index_id* = 1). A clustered index scan (on the entire table) had to be done, so all keys initially received the RangeS-U lock, and when four rows were eventually modified, the locks on those keys were converted to RangeX-X locks. You can see all the RangeX-X locks, but not all the RangeS-U locks are shown for space reasons (the table has 504 rows).

LISTING 13-7 Update with Serializable isolation not using an index

SQL BATCH

```
USE AdventureWorks2012;
SET TRANSACTION ISOLATION LEVEL SERIALIZABLE;
BEGIN TRAN
UPDATE Production.Product
SET ListPrice = ListPrice * 0.6
WHERE Color = 'White';
SELECT * FROM DBlocks
WHERE spid = @@spid
AND entity_name = 'Product';
COMMIT TRAN
```

RESULTS FROM *DBlocks* (Abbreviated)

spid	dbname	entity_name	index_id	resource	description	mode	status
54	AdventureWorks2012	Product	NULL	OBJECT		IX	GRANT
54	AdventureWorks2012	Product	1	KEY	(7900ac71caca)	RangeS-U	GRANT
54	AdventureWorks2012	Product	1	KEY	(6100dc0e675f)	RangeS-U	GRANT
54	AdventureWorks2012	Product	1	KEY	(5700a1a9278a)	RangeS-U	GRANT
54	AdventureWorks2012	Product	1	PAGE	1:16898	IU	GRANT
54	AdventureWorks2012	Product	1	PAGE	1:16899	IU	GRANT
54	AdventureWorks2012	Product	1	PAGE	1:16896	IU	GRANT
54	AdventureWorks2012	Product	1	PAGE	1:16897	IX	GRANT
54	AdventureWorks2012	Product	1	PAGE	1:16900	IU	GRANT
54	AdventureWorks2012	Product	1	PAGE	1:16901	IU	GRANT

54	AdventureWorks2012	Product	1		KEY	(5600c4ce9b32)	RangeS-U	GRANT
54	AdventureWorks2012	Product	1		KEY	(7300c89177a5)	RangeS-U	GRANT
54	AdventureWorks2012	Product	1		KEY	(7f00702ea1ef)	RangeS-U	GRANT
54	AdventureWorks2012	Product	1		KEY	(6b00b8eeda30)	RangeX-X	GRANT
54	AdventureWorks2012	Product	1		KEY	(c500b9eaac9c)	RangeX-X	GRANT
54	AdventureWorks2012	Product	1		KEY	(c6005745198e)	RangeX-X	GRANT
54	AdventureWorks2012	Product	1		KEY	(6a00dd896688)	RangeX-X	GRANT

Very few of the locks in Listing 13-8 are actually acquired on elements of the *newProducts* table. In the *entity_name* column, you can see that most of the objects are undocumented—and usually invisible—system table names. As the new table is created, SQL Server acquires locks on nine different system tables to record information about this new table. Also, notice the schema modification (Sch-M) lock and other metadata locks on the new table.

LISTING 13-8 Creating a table

SQL BATCH

```
USE AdventureWorks2012;
SET TRANSACTION ISOLATION LEVEL READ COMMITTED;
BEGIN TRAN
SELECT *
INTO newProducts
FROM Production.Product
WHERE ListPrice between 1 and 10;
SELECT * FROM DBlocks
WHERE spid = @@spid;
COMMIT TRAN
```

RESULTS FROM *DBlocks* (Abbreviated)

spid	dbname	entity_name	index_id	resource	description	mode	status
54	AdventureWorks2012	n/a	NULL	DATABASE		NULL	GRANT
54	AdventureWorks2012	n/a	NULL	DATABASE		NULL	GRANT
54	AdventureWorks2012	n/a	NULL	DATABASE		S	GRANT
54	AdventureWorks2012	n/a	NULL	METADATA	user_type_id = 258	Sch-S	GRANT
54	AdventureWorks2012	n/a	NULL	METADATA	data_space_id = 1	Sch-S	GRANT
54	AdventureWorks2012	n/a	NULL	DATABASE		S	GRANT
54	AdventureWorks2012	n/a	NULL	METADATA	$seq_type = 0, objec	Sch-M	GRANT
54	AdventureWorks2012	n/a	NULL	METADATA	user_type_id = 260	Sch-S	GRANT
54	AdventureWorks2012	sysrowsetcol	NULL	OBJECT		IX	GRANT
54	AdventureWorks2012	sysrowsets	NULL	OBJECT		IX	GRANT
54	AdventureWorks2012	sysallocunit	NULL	OBJECT		IX	GRANT
54	AdventureWorks2012	syshobtcolum	NULL	OBJECT		IX	GRANT
54	AdventureWorks2012	syshobts	NULL	OBJECT		IX	GRANT
54	AdventureWorks2012	sysserefs	NULL	OBJECT		IX	GRANT
54	AdventureWorks2012	sysschobjs	NULL	OBJECT		IX	GRANT
54	AdventureWorks2012	syscolpars	NULL	OBJECT		IX	GRANT
54	AdventureWorks2012	sysidxstats	NULL	OBJECT		IX	GRANT
54	AdventureWorks2012	sysrowsetcol	1	KEY	(15004f6b3486)	X	GRANT
54	AdventureWorks2012	sysrowsetcol	1	KEY	(0a00862c4e8e)	X	GRANT
54	AdventureWorks2012	sysrowsets	1	KEY	(000000aaec7b)	X	GRANT
54	AdventureWorks2012	sysallocunit	1	KEY	(00001f2dcf47)	X	GRANT
54	AdventureWorks2012	syshobtcolum	1	KEY	(1900f7d4e2cc)	X	GRANT
54	AdventureWorks2012	syshobts	1	KEY	(000000aaec7b)	X	GRANT

54	AdventureWorks2012	NULL	NULL	RID	1:6707:1	X	GRANT
54	AdventureWorks2012	DBlocks	NULL	OBJECT		IS	GRANT
54	AdventureWorks2012	newProducts	NULL	OBJECT		Sch-M	GRANT
54	AdventureWorks2012	sysserefs	1	KEY	(010025fabf73)	X	GRANT
54	AdventureWorks2012	sysschobjs	1	KEY	(3b0042322c99)	X	GRANT
54	AdventureWorks2012	syscolpars	1	KEY	(4200c1eb801c)	X	GRANT
54	AdventureWorks2012	syscolpars	1	KEY	(4e00092bfbc3)	X	GRANT
54	AdventureWorks2012	sysidxstats	1	KEY	(3b0006e110a6)	X	GRANT
54	AdventureWorks2012	sysschobjs	2	KEY	(9202706f3e6c)	X	GRANT
54	AdventureWorks2012	syscolpars	2	KEY	(6c0151be80af)	X	GRANT
54	AdventureWorks2012	syscolpars	2	KEY	(2c03557a0b9d)	X	GRANT
54	AdventureWorks2012	sysidxstats	2	KEY	(3c00f3332a43)	X	GRANT
54	AdventureWorks2012	sysschobjs	3	KEY	(9202d42ddd4d)	X	GRANT
54	AdventureWorks2012	sysschobjs	4	KEY	(3c0040d00163)	X	GRANT
54	AdventureWorks2012	newProducts	0	PAGE	1:6707	X	GRANT
54	AdventureWorks2012	newProducts	0	HOBT		Sch-M	GRANT

The final example looks at the locks held when the table has no clustered index and the data rows are being updated. In Listing 13-9, the *newProducts* table has no indexes, so the lock on the actual row meeting the criteria is an exclusive (X) lock on the row (RID). For RID locks, the description actually reports the specific row in the form *File number:Page number:Slot number*. As expected, IX locks are taken on the page and the table.

LISTING 13-9 Row locks

SQL BATCH

```
USE AdventureWorks2012;
SET TRANSACTION ISOLATION LEVEL READ COMMITTED
BEGIN TRAN
UPDATE newProducts
SET ListPrice = 5.99
WHERE name = 'Road Bottle Cage';
SELECT * FROM DBlocks
WHERE spid = @@spid
AND entity_name = 'newProducts';
COMMIT TRAN
```

RESULTS FROM *DBlocks*

spid	dbname	entity_name	index_id	resource	description	mode	status
54	AdventureWorks2012	newProducts	NULL	OBJECT		IX	GRANT
54	AdventureWorks2012	newProducts	0	PAGE	1:6708	IX	GRANT
54	AdventureWorks2012	newProducts	0	RID	1:6708:5	X	GRANT

Lock compatibility

Two locks are compatible if one lock can be granted while another lock on the same resource is held by a different process. If a lock requested for a resource isn't compatible with a lock currently being held, the requesting connection must wait for the lock. For example, if a shared page lock exists on a page, another process requesting a shared page lock for the same page is granted the lock because the two lock types are compatible. But a process that requests an exclusive lock for the same page isn't granted the lock because an exclusive lock isn't compatible with the shared lock already held.

Figure 13-2 summarizes the compatibility of locks in SQL Server 2012. Along the top are all the lock modes that a process might already hold. Along the left edge are the lock modes that another process might request. (The locks modes were defined in Tables 13-3 and 13-4.) The chart is also available online in the SQL Server documentation at http://msdn.microsoft.com/en-us/library/ms186396(v=sql.105).aspx.

	NL	SCH-S	SCH-M	S	U	X	IS	IU	IX	SIU	SIX	UIX	BU	RS-S	RS-U	RI-N	RI-S	RI-U	RI-X	RX-S	RX-U	RX-X
NL	N	N	N	N	N	N	N	N	N	N	N	N	N	N	N	N	N	N	N	N	N	N
SCH-S	N	N	C	N	N	N	N	N	N	N	N	N	N	I	I	I	I	I	I	I	I	I
SCH-M	N	C	C	C	C	C	C	C	C	C	C	C	C	I	I	I	I	I	I	I	I	I
S	N	N	C	N	N	C	N	N	C	N	C	C	C	N	N	N	N	N	C	N	N	C
U	N	N	C	N	C	C	N	C	C	C	C	C	C	N	C	N	C	C	C	C	N	C
X	N	N	C	C	C	C	C	C	C	C	C	C	C	C	C	N	C	C	C	C	C	C
IS	N	N	C	N	N	C	N	N	N	N	N	N	C	I	I	I	I	I	I	I	I	I
IU	N	N	C	N	N	C	N	N	N	N	N	N	C	I	I	I	I	I	I	I	I	I
IX	N	N	C	C	C	C	N	N	N	C	C	C	C	I	I	I	I	I	I	I	I	I
SIU	N	N	C	N	C	C	N	N	C	N	C	C	C	I	I	I	I	I	I	I	I	I
SIX	N	N	C	C	C	C	N	N	C	C	C	C	C	I	I	I	I	I	I	I	I	I
UIX	N	N	C	C	C	C	N	C	C	C	C	C	C	I	I	I	I	I	I	I	I	I
BU	N	N	C	C	C	C	C	C	C	C	C	C	N	I	I	I	I	I	I	I	I	I
RS-S	N	I	I	N	N	N	I	I	I	I	I	I	I	N	N	C	C	C	C	C	C	C
RS-U	N	I	I	N	C	C	I	I	I	I	I	I	I	N	C	C	C	C	C	C	C	C
RI-N	N	I	I	N	N	N	I	I	I	I	I	I	I	C	C	N	N	N	N	C	C	C
RI-S	N	I	I	N	N	N	I	I	I	I	I	I	I	C	C	N	C	N	N	C	C	C
RI-U	N	I	I	N	C	C	I	I	I	I	I	I	I	C	C	N	C	N	N	C	C	C
RI-X	N	I	I	C	C	C	I	I	I	I	I	I	I	C	C	N	C	N	C	C	C	C
RX-S	N	I	I	N	N	C	I	I	I	I	I	I	I	C	C	C	C	C	C	C	C	C
RX-U	N	I	I	N	C	C	I	I	I	I	I	I	I	C	C	C	C	C	C	C	C	C
RX-X	N	I	I	C	C	C	I	I	I	I	I	I	I	C	C	C	C	C	C	C	C	C

FIGURE 13-2 SQL Server lock compatibility matrix.

Three possible values can be found at the point where the held lock and requested lock meet: *N* indicates no conflict, *C* indicates a conflict and the requesting process has to wait, and *I* indicates an invalid combination that could never occur. All the *I* values in the chart involve range locks, which can be applied only to KEY resources, so any type of lock that can never be applied to KEY resources indicates an invalid comparison.

Lock compatibility needs to be checked between locks on different resources, such as table locks and page locks. A table and a page obviously represent an implicit hierarchy because a table is made up of multiple pages. If an exclusive page lock is held on one page of a table, another process can't get even a shared table lock for that table. This hierarchy is protected using intent locks. A process acquiring an exclusive page lock, update page lock, or intent exclusive page lock first acquires an intent exclusive lock on the table. This intent exclusive table lock prevents another process from acquiring the shared table lock on that table. (Remember that intent exclusive locks and shared locks on the same resource aren't compatible.)

Similarly, a process acquiring a shared row lock must first acquire an intent shared lock for the table, which prevents another process from acquiring an exclusive table lock. Alternatively, if the exclusive table lock already exists, the intent shared lock isn't granted and the shared page lock must wait until the exclusive table lock is released. Without intent locks, process A can lock a page in a table with an exclusive page lock, and process B can place an exclusive table lock on the same table and think that it has a right to modify the entire table, including the page that process A has exclusively locked.

Note Obviously, lock compatibility is an issue only when the locks affect the same object. For example, two or more processes each can hold exclusive page locks simultaneously, as long as the locks are on different pages or different tables.

Even if two locks are compatible, the requester of the second lock might still have to wait if an incompatible lock is waiting. Suppose that process A holds a shared page lock. Process B requests an exclusive page lock and must wait because the shared page lock and the exclusive page lock aren't compatible. Process C requests a shared page lock that's compatible with the shared page already granted to process A. However, the shared page lock can't be granted immediately. Process C must wait for its shared page lock because process B is ahead of it in the lock queue with an incompatible request (exclusive page).

By examining the compatibility of locks, not only with processes granted locks but also with processes waiting, SQL Server prevents lock starvation, which can result when requests for shared locks keep overlapping so that the request for the exclusive lock can never be granted.

Internal locking architecture

Locks aren't on-disk structures. You won't find a lock field directly on a data page or a table header, and the metadata that keeps track of locks is never written to disk. Locks are internal memory structures: They consume part of the memory used for SQL Server. A lock is identified by *lock resource,* which is a description of the resource that's locked (a row, index key, page, or table). To keep track of the database, the type of lock, and the information describing the locked resource, each lock requires 64 bytes of memory on a 32-bit system and 128 bytes of memory on a 64-bit system. This 64-byte or 128-byte structure is called a *lock block.*

Each process holding a lock also must have a *lock owner,* which represents the relationship between a lock and the entity that's requesting or holding the lock. The lock owner requires 32 bytes of memory on a 32-bit system and 64 bytes of memory on a 64-bit system. This 32-byte or 64-byte structure is called a *lock owner block.* A single transaction can have multiple lock owner blocks; a scrollable cursor sometimes uses several. Also, one lock can have many lock owner blocks, as is the case with a shared lock. As mentioned, the lock owner represents a relationship between a lock and an entity, and the relationship can be granted, waiting, or in a state called *waiting-to-convert.*

The lock manager maintains a lock hash table. Lock resources, contained within a lock block, are hashed to determine a target hash slot in the hash table. All lock blocks that hash to the same slot are chained together from one entry in the hash table. Each lock block contains a 15-byte field that describes the locked resource. The lock block also contains pointers to lists of lock owner blocks. Each of the three states has a separate list for lock owners. Figure 13-3 shows the general lock architecture.

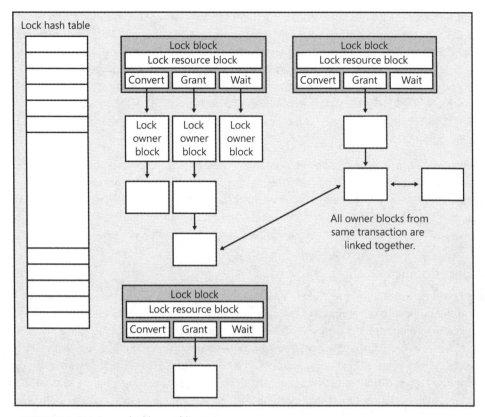

FIGURE 13-3 SQL Server locking architecture.

The number of slots in the hash table is based on the system's physical memory, as shown in Table 13-7. The upper limit is 231 slots. All instances of SQL Server on the same machine have a hash table with the same number of slots. Each entry in the lock hash table is 16 bytes in size and consists of a pointer to a list of lock blocks and a spinlock to guarantee serialized access to the same slot.

TABLE 13-7 Number of slots in the internal lock hash table

Physical memory (MB)	Number of slots	Memory used
< 32	$2^{14} = 16384$	128 KB
>= 32 and < 64	$2^{15} = 32768$	256 KB
>= 64 and < 128	$2^{16} = 65536$	512 KB
>= 128 and < 512	$2^{18} = 262144$	2048 KB
>= 512 and < 1024	$2^{19} = 524288$	4096 KB
>= 1024 and < 4096	$2^{21} = 2097152$	16384 KB
>= 4096 and < 8192	$2^{22} = 4194304$	32768 KB
>= 8192 and < 16384	$2^{23} = 8388608$	65536 KB
>= 16384	$2^{25} = 33554432$	262144 KB

The lock manager allocates in advance a number of lock blocks and lock owner blocks at server startup. On Non-Uniform Memory Access (NUMA) configurations, these lock and lock owner blocks are divided among all NUMA nodes. So when a lock request is made, local lock blocks are used. If the number of locks has been set by *sp_configure,* it allocates that configured number of lock blocks and the same number of lock owner blocks. If the number isn't fixed (0 means autotune), it allocates 2,500 lock blocks for your SQL Server instance. It allocates twice as many (2 * # lock blocks) of the lock owner blocks. At their maximum, the static allocations can't consume more than 25 percent of the committed buffer pool size.

When a request for a lock is made and no free lock blocks remain, the lock manager dynamically allocates new lock blocks rather than deny the lock request. The lock manager cooperates with the global memory manager to negotiate for server allocated memory. When necessary, the lock manager can free the dynamically allocated lock blocks. The lock manager is limited to 60 percent of the buffer manager's committed target size allocation to lock blocks and lock owner blocks.

Lock partitioning

For large systems, locks on frequently referenced objects can lead to performance bottlenecks. The process of acquiring and releasing locks can cause contention on the internal locking resources. Lock partitioning enhances locking performance by splitting a single lock resource into multiple lock resources. For systems with 16 or more CPUs, SQL Server automatically splits certain locks into multiple lock resources, one per CPU—a process called *lock partitioning.* Users can't control this process. (Don't confuse lock partitioning with partition locks, which are discussed later in the section "Lock escalation.") An informational message is sent to the error log whenever lock partitioning is active:

```
Lock partitioning is enabled. This is an informational message only. No user action is required.
```

Lock partitioning applies only to full object locks (such as tables and views) in the following lock modes: S, U, X, and SCH-M. All other modes—NL, SCH_S, IS, IU, and IX—are acquired on a single CPU. When each transaction starts, SQL Server assigns a default lock partition to it. During the life of a transaction, all lock requests that are spread over all the partitions use the partition assigned to that transaction. By this method, access to lock resources of the same object by different transactions is distributed across different partitions.

The *resource_lock_partition* column in *sys.dm_tran_locks* indicates which lock partition a particular lock is on, so you can see multiple locks for the exact same resource with different *resource_lock_partition* values. For systems with fewer than 16 CPUs, for which lock partitioning is never used, the *resource_lock_partition* value is always 0.

For example, consider a transaction acquiring an IS lock in REPEATABLE READ isolation, so that the IS lock is held for the duration of the transaction. The IS lock is acquired on the transaction's default partition—for example, partition 4. If another transaction tries to acquire an X lock on the same table, the X lock must be acquired on ALL partitions. SQL Server successfully acquires the X lock on partitions 0 to 3, but it blocks when attempting to acquire an X lock on partition 4. On partition IDs 5 to 15, which haven't yet acquired the X lock for this table, other transactions can continue to acquire any locks that don't cause blocking.

With lock partitioning, SQL Server distributes the load of checking for locks across multiple spin-locks, and most accesses to any specific spinlock are from the same CPU (and practically always from the same node), which means the spinlock shouldn't spin often.

Lock blocks

The lock block is the key structure in SQL Server's locking architecture, shown earlier in Figure 13-3. A lock block contains the following information.

- Lock resource information containing the lock resource name and details about the lock.

- Pointers to connect the lock blocks to the lock hash table.

- Pointers to lists of lock owner blocks for locks on this resource that have been granted. Four *grant lists* are maintained to minimize the amount of time required to find a granted lock.

- A pointer to a list of lock owner blocks for locks on this resource that are waiting to be converted to another lock mode. This is called the *convert list*.

- A pointer to a list of lock owner blocks for locks that have been requested on this resource but haven't yet been granted. This is called the *wait list*.

The lock resource uniquely identifies the data being locked. Figure 13-4 shows its structure. Each "row" in the figure represents 4 bytes, or 32 bits.

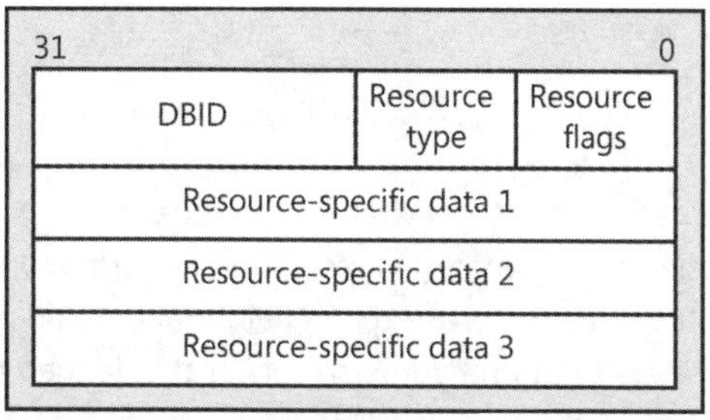

FIGURE 13-4 The structure of a lock resource.

Table 13-8 describes the meanings of the fields shown in Figure 13-4. The value in the *resource type* byte is one of the locking resources described earlier in Table 13-5. The number in parentheses after the resource type is the code number for the resource type (which we see in the section on the *syslockinfo* table a little later in the chapter). The meaning of the values in the three data fields varies depending on the type of resource being described. SR indicates a subresource (which is described shortly).

TABLE 13-8 Fields in the lock resource block

Resource type	Resource content		
	Data 1	Data 2	Data 3
Database (2)	SR	0	0
File (3)	File ID	0	0
Index (4)	Object ID	SR	Index ID
Table (5)	Object ID	SR	0
Page (6)	Page number		0
Key (7)	Partition ID	Hashed key	
Extent (8)	Extent ID		0
RID (9)	RID		0

The following are some of the possible SR (SubResource) values. If the lock is on a Database resource, SR indicates full database lock or bulk operation lock. If the lock is on a Table resource, SR indicates full table lock (the default), update statistics lock, or compile lock. If the lock is on an Index resource, SR indicates full index lock (the default), index ID lock, or index name lock.

Lock owner blocks

Each lock owned or waited for by a session is represented in a lock owner block. Lists of lock owner blocks form the grant, convert, and wait lists that hang off the lock blocks. Each lock owner block for a granted lock is linked with all other lock owner blocks for the same transaction or session so they can be freed as appropriate when the transaction or session ends.

syslockinfo table

Although the recommended way of retrieving information about locks is through the *sys.dm_tran_locks* view, another metadata object called *syslockinfo* provides internal information about locks. Before SQL Server 2005 introduced DMVs, *syslockinfo* was the only internal metadata available for examining locking information. In fact, the stored procedure *sp_lock* is still defined to retrieve information from *syslockinfo* instead of from *sys.dm_tran_locks*. This section won't go into full detail about *syslockinfo* because almost all the information from that table is available, in a much more readable form, in the *sys.dm_tran_locks* view. However, *syslockinfo* is available in the *master* database for you to take a look at. One column, however, is of particular interest—the *rsc_bin* column, which contains a 16-byte description of a locked resource.

You can analyze the *syslockinfo.rsc_bin* field as the resource block. For example, you can select a single row from the *Person* table in *AdventureWorks2012* using the Repeatable Read isolation level, so the shared locks continue to be held for the duration of the transaction. You can then look at the *rsc_bin* column in *syslockinfo* for key locks, page locks, and table locks:

```
USE AdventureWorks2012
GO
```

```
SET TRANSACTION ISOLATION LEVEL REPEATABLE READ
GO
BEGIN TRAN
SELECT * FROM Person.Person
WHERE BusinessEntityID = 249;
GO
SELECT rsc_bin, rsc_type
FROM master..syslockinfo
WHERE rsc_type IN (5,6,7);
GO
```

Here are the three rows in the result set:

```
rsc_bin                             rsc_type
----------------------------------- --------
0x805EFA5900000000000000000B000500  5
0x19050000010000000000000000B000600  6
0x710000000001F900CE79D5250B000700  7
```

The last 2 bytes in *rsc_bin* are the resource mode, so after byte-swapping, you can see the same value as in the *rsc_type* column. For example, you byte-swap 0500 to 0005 to resource mode 5 (a table lock). The next 2 bytes at the end indicate the database ID, and for all three rows, the value after byte-swapping is 000B, or decimal 11, which is the database ID of my *AdventureWorks2012* database.

The rest of the bytes vary depending on the type of resource. For a table, the first 4 bytes represent the object ID. The preceding row for the object lock (*rsc_type* = 5) after byte-swapping has a value of 59FA5E80, which is 1509580416 in decimal. You can translate this to an object name as follows:

```
SELECT object_name(1509580416)
```

This shows the *Person* table.

For a PAGE (*rsc_type* = 6), the first 6 bytes are the page number followed by the file number. After byte-swapping, the file number is 0001, or 1 decimal, and the page number is 00000519, or 9889 in decimal. So the lock is on file 1, page 1305.

Finally, for a KEY (*rsc_type* = 7), the first 6 bytes represent the partition ID but the translation is a bit trickier. We need to add another 2 bytes of zeros to the value after byte-swapping, so we end up with 0100000000710000, which translates to 72057594045333504 in decimal. To see which object this partition belongs to, I can query the *sys.partitions* view:

```
SELECT object_name(object_id)
FROM sys.partitions
WHERE partition_ID = 72057594045333504;
```

Again, the result is that this partition is part of the *Person* table. The next 6 bytes of *rsc_bin* for the KEY resource are F900CE79D525. This is a character field, so no byte-swapping is needed. However, the value can't be deciphered further. Key locks have a hash value generated for them, based on all the key columns of the index. Indexes can be quite long, so for almost any possible data type, SQL Server needs a consistent way to keep track of which keys are locked. The hashing function therefore generates a 6-byte hash string to represent the key. Although you can't reverse-engineer this value and determine exactly which index row is locked, you can use it to look for matching entries, just like SQL Server does. If two *rsc_bin* values have the same 6-byte hash string, they are referring to the same lock resource.

In addition to detecting references to the same lock resource, you can determine which specific keys are locked by using the undocumented value *%%lockres%%*, which can return the hash string for any key. Selecting this value, along with data from the table, returns the lock resource for every row in the result set, based on the index used to retrieve the data. The following example creates a clustered and nonclustered index on a tiny table and then selects the *%%lockres%%* value for each row, first using the clustered index and then using the nonclustered index:

```
CREATE TABLE lockres (c1 int, c2 int);
GO
INSERT INTO lockres VALUES (1,10);
INSERT INTO lockres VALUES (2,20);
INSERT INTO lockres VALUES (3,30);
GO
CREATE UNIQUE CLUSTERED INDEX lockres_ci ON lockres(c1);
CREATE UNIQUE NONCLUSTERED INDEX lockres_nci ON lockres(c2);
GO
SELECT %%lockres%% AS lock_resource, * FROM lockres WITH (INDEX = lockres_ci);
SELECT %%lockres%% AS lock_resource, * FROM lockres WITH (INDEX = lockres_nci);
GO
```

My results show that the first set of rows includes the lock resource for the clustered index keys, and the second set includes the lock resources for the nonclustered index:

lock_resource	c1	c2
(010086470766)	1	10
(020068e8b274)	2	20
(03000d8f0ecc)	3	30

lock_resource	c1	c2
(0a0087c006b1)	1	10
(14002be0c001)	2	20
(1e004f007d6e)	3	30

You can use this lock resource to find which row in a table matches a locked resource. For example, if *sys.dm_tran_locks* indicates that a row with the lock resource (010086470766) is holding a lock in the *lockres* table, you could find which row that resource corresponds to with the following query:

```
SELECT * FROM lockres
WHERE %%lockres%% = '(010086470766)'
```

Note that if the table is a heap and you look for the lock resource when scanning the table, the lock resource is the actual row ID (RID). The value returned looks just like the special value *%%physloc%%*, as discussed in Chapter 6, "Table storage":

```
CREATE TABLE lockres_on_heap (c1 int, c2 int);
GO
INSERT INTO lockres_on_heap VALUES (1,10);
INSERT INTO lockres_on_heap VALUES (2,20);
INSERT INTO lockres_on_heap VALUES (3,30);
GO
SELECT %%lockres%% AS lock_resource, * FROM lockres_on_heap;
```

Here are my results:

```
lock_resource                       c1           c2
--------------------------------    ----------   ----
1:169:0                             1            10
1:169:1                             2            20
1:169:2                             3            30
```

> **Caution** You need to be careful when trying to find the row in a table with a hash string that matches a particular lock resource. These queries have to perform a complete scan of the table to find the row you are interested in, and with a large table, that process can be very expensive.

Row-level locking vs. page-level locking

Although SQL Server fully supports row-level locking, in some situations, the lock manager decides not to lock individual rows and instead locks pages or the whole table. In other cases, many smaller locks are escalated to a table lock, as discussed in the next section, "Lock escalation."

Prior to SQL Server 7.0, the smallest unit of data that SQL Server could lock was a page. Although many people argued that this was unacceptable and that maintaining good concurrency was impossible while locking entire pages, many large and powerful applications were written and deployed using only page-level locking. If they were well designed and tuned, concurrency wasn't an issue, and some of these applications supported hundreds of active user connections with acceptable response times and throughput.

However, with the change in page size from 2 KB to 8 KB for SQL Server 7.0, the issue had become more critical. Locking an entire page means locking four times as much data as in previous versions. Beginning with version 7.0, SQL Server implements full row-level locking, so any potential problems because of lower concurrency with the larger page size shouldn't be an issue. However, locking isn't free. Resources are required to manage locks. Recall that a lock is an in-memory structure of 128 bytes with another 64 bytes for each process holding or requesting the lock. If you need a lock for every row and you scan a million rows, you need more than 64 MB of RAM just to hold locks for that one process.

Beyond memory consumption issues, locking is a fairly processing-intensive operation. Managing locks requires substantial bookkeeping. Recall that, internally, SQL Server uses a lightweight mutex called a *spinlock* to guard resources, and it uses latches—also lighter than full-blown locks—to protect non-leaf–level index pages. These performance optimizations avoid the overhead of full locking. If a page of data contains 50 rows of data, all of which are used, issuing and managing one lock on the page is apparently more efficient than managing 50. That's the obvious benefit of page locking—a reduction in the number of lock structures that must exist and be managed.

Suppose that two processes each need to update a few rows of data, and even though the rows aren't the same ones, some of them happen to exist on the same page. With page-level locking, one process would have to wait until the page locks of the other process were released. If you use row-level locking instead, the other process doesn't have to wait. The finer granularity of the locks means that no conflict occurs in the first place because each process is concerned with different rows. That's the obvious benefit of row-level locking.

Which of these obvious benefits wins? Well, the decision isn't clearly evident and depends on the application and the data. Each type of locking can be shown to be superior for different types of applications and usage.

The *ALTER INDEX* statement lets you manually control the unit of locking within an index with options to disallow page locks or row locks within an index. Because these options are available only for indexes, locking can't be controlled within the data pages of a heap. (Remember, however, that if a table has a clustered index, the data pages are part of the index and are affected by a value set with *ALTER INDEX*.) The index options are set for each table or index individually. Two options, *ALLOW_ROW_LOCKS* and *ALLOW_PAGE_LOCKS*, are both set to *ON* initially for every table and index. If both of these options are set to *OFF* for a table, only full table locks are allowed.

As mentioned earlier, during the optimization process, SQL Server determines whether to lock rows, pages, or the entire table initially. The locking of rows (or keys) is heavily favored. The type of locking chosen is based on the number of rows and pages to be scanned, the number of rows on a page, the isolation level in effect, the update activity going on, the number of users on the system needing memory for their own purposes, and so on.

Lock escalation

SQL Server automatically escalates row, key, or page locks to coarser table or partition locks as appropriate. This escalation protects system resources—it prevents the system from using too much memory for keeping track of locks—and increases efficiency. For example, after a query acquires many row locks, the lock level can be escalated because acquiring and holding a single lock probably makes more sense than holding many row locks. When lock escalation occurs, many locks on smaller units (rows or pages) are released and replaced by one lock on a larger unit. This escalation reduces locking overhead and keeps the system from running out of locks. Because a finite amount of memory is available for the lock structures, escalation is sometimes necessary to ensure that the memory for locks stays within reasonable limits.

The default in SQL Server is to escalate to table locks. However, SQL Server 2008 introduced the ability to escalate to a single partition using the *ALTER TABLE* statement. The *LOCK_ESCALATION* option of *ALTER TABLE* can specify that escalation is always to a table level, or that it can be to either a table or partition level. The *LOCK_ESCALATION* option can also be used to prevent escalation entirely. Here's an example of altering the *TransactionHistory* table (which you might have created if you ran the partitioning example in Chapter 8, "Special storage"), so that locks can be escalated to either the table or partition level:

```
ALTER TABLE TransactionHistory
SET (LOCK_ESCALATION = AUTO);
```

Lock escalation occurs in the following situations.

- The number of locks held by a single statement on one object, or on one partition of one object, exceeds a threshold. That threshold is currently 5,000 locks, but it might change in future service packs. The lock escalation doesn't occur if the locks are spread over multiple objects in the same statement—for example, 3,000 locks in one index and 3,000 in another.

- Memory taken by lock resources exceeds 24 percent of the memory used by the database engine.

When lock escalation is triggered, the attempt might fail if locks conflict. For example, if an X lock on a RID needs to be escalated and a different process holds concurrent X locks on the same table or partition, the lock escalation attempt fails. However, SQL Server continues to attempt to escalate the lock every time the transaction acquires another 1,250 locks on the same object. If the lock escalation succeeds, SQL Server releases all the row and page locks on the index or the heap.

> **Note** SQL Server never escalates to page locks. The result of a lock escalation is always a table or partition. Also, multiple partition locks are never escalated to a table lock.

Lock escalation can potentially lead to blocking of future concurrent access to the index or the heap by other transactions needing row or page locks on the object. Because SQL Server can't de-escalate the lock when new requests are made, lock escalation isn't always a good idea for all applications.

The *ALTER TABLE* statement also supports disabling lock escalation for a single table via the *DISABLE* option. Here is an example of disabling lock escalation on the *TransactionHistory* table:

```
ALTER TABLE TransactionHistory
SET (LOCK_ESCALATION = DISABLE);
```

SQL Server also supports disabling lock escalation using trace flags. Note that these trace flags affect lock escalation on all tables in all databases in a SQL Server instance:

- **Trace flag 1211** completely disables lock escalation. It instructs SQL Server to ignore the memory acquired by the lock manager up to the maximum statically allocated lock memory (specified using the locks configuration option) or 60 percent of the dynamically allocated memory. At that time, an out-of-lock memory error is generated. You should exercise extreme caution when using this trace flag because a poorly designed application can exhaust memory and seriously degrade the performance of your SQL Server instance.

■ **Trace flag 1224** also disables lock escalation based on the number of locks acquired, but it allows escalation based on memory consumption. It enables lock escalation when the lock manager acquires 40 percent of the statically allocated memory (as per the locks option) or 40 percent dynamically allocated memory. Note that if SQL Server can't allocate memory for locks because of memory use by other components, lock escalation can be triggered earlier. As with trace flag 1211, SQL Server generates an out-of-memory error when memory allocated to the lock manager exceeds the total statically allocated memory, or 60 percent of memory for dynamic allocation.

If both trace flags (1211 and 1224) are set at the same time, trace flag 1211 takes precedence. Remember that these trace flags affect the entire SQL Server instance. In many cases, controlling the escalation threshold at the object level is desirable, so you should consider using the *ALTER TABLE* command when possible.

Deadlocks

A deadlock occurs when two processes are waiting for a resource, but neither can advance because the other process prevents it from getting the resource. A true deadlock is a Catch-22 in which, without intervention, neither process can ever make progress. When a deadlock occurs, SQL Server intervenes automatically. This book refers mainly to deadlocks acquired due to conflicting locks, although deadlocks can also be detected on worker threads, memory, and parallel query resources.

> **Note** A simple wait for a lock isn't a deadlock. When the process that's holding the lock completes, the waiting process can acquire the lock. Lock waits are typical, expected, and necessary in multiuser systems.

In SQL Server, two main types of deadlocks can occur: a cycle deadlock and a conversion deadlock.

Cycle deadlocks

Figure 13-5 shows an example of a cycle deadlock. Process A starts a transaction, acquires an exclusive table lock on the *Product* table, and requests an exclusive table lock on the *PurchaseOrderDetail* table. Simultaneously, process B starts a transaction, acquires an exclusive lock on the *PurchaseOrderDetail* table, and requests an exclusive lock on the *Product* table. The two processes become deadlocked—caught in a "deadly embrace." Each process holds a resource needed by the other process. Neither can progress, and without intervention, both would be stuck in deadlock forever.

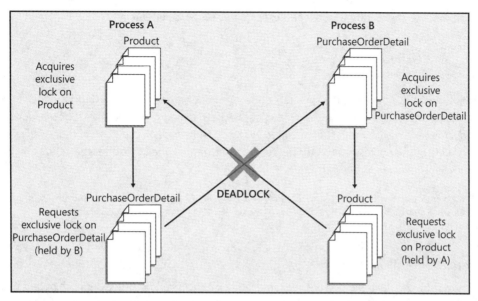

FIGURE 13-5 A cycle deadlock resulting from two processes, each holding a resource needed by the other.

You can actually generate the deadlock in SQL Server Management Studio, as follows:

1. Open a query window and change your database context to the *AdventureWorks2012* database. Execute the following batch for process A:

```
BEGIN TRAN
UPDATE Production.Product
    SET ListPrice = ListPrice * 0.9
    WHERE ProductID = 922;
```

2. Open a second window and execute this batch for process B:

```
BEGIN TRAN
UPDATE Purchasing.PurchaseOrderDetail
    SET ReceivedQty = ReceivedQty + 1
    WHERE ProductID  = 922
    AND PurchaseOrderID = 499;
```

3. Go back to the first window and execute this *UPDATE* statement:

```
UPDATE Purchasing.PurchaseOrderDetail
    SET ReceivedQty = ReceivedQty - 1
    WHERE ProductID  = 922
    AND PurchaseOrderID = 499;
```

At this point, the query should block. It's not deadlocked yet, however; it's waiting for a lock on the *PurchaseOrderDetail* table and has no reason to suspect that it won't eventually get that lock.

4. Go back to the second window and execute this *UPDATE* statement:

```
UPDATE Production.Product
    SET ListPrice = ListPrice * 1.1
    WHERE ProductID = 922;
```

At this point, a deadlock occurs. The first connection never gets its requested lock on the *PurchaseOrderDetail* table because the second connection doesn't give it up until it gets a lock on the *Product* table. Because the first connection already has the lock on the *Product* table, we have a deadlock. One of the processes receives the following error message (of course, the actual process ID reported will probably be different):

```
Msg 1205, Level 13, State 51, Line 1 Transaction (Process ID 57) was deadlocked on lock
resources with another process and has been chosen as the deadlock victim. Rerun the
transaction.
```

Conversion deadlocks

Figure 13-6 shows an example of a conversion deadlock. Process A and process B each hold a shared lock on the same page within a transaction. Each process wants to promote its shared lock to an exclusive lock, but can't do so because of the other process's lock. Again, intervention is required.

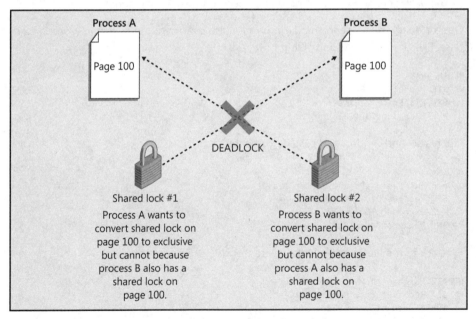

FIGURE 13-6 A conversion deadlock resulting from two processes wanting to promote their locks on the same resource within a transaction.

Deadlock detection, intervention, and avoidance

SQL Server automatically detects deadlocks and intervenes through the lock manager, which provides deadlock detection for regular locks. In SQL Server 2012, deadlocks can also involve resources other than locks. For example, if process A holds a lock on *Table1* and waits for memory to become available, but process B has some memory that it can't release until it acquires a lock on *Table1*, the processes deadlock. When SQL Server detects a deadlock, it terminates one process's batch, rolling back the active transaction and releasing all that process's locks to resolve the deadlock.

In addition to deadlocks on lock resources and memory resources, deadlocks can also occur with resources involving worker threads, parallel query execution–related resources, and MARS resources. Latches aren't involved in deadlock detection because SQL Server uses deadlock-proof algorithms when it acquires latches.

In SQL Server, a separate thread called LOCK_MONITOR checks the system for deadlocks every five seconds. As deadlocks occur, the deadlock detection interval is reduced and can go as low as 100 milliseconds. In fact, the first few lock requests that can't be satisfied after a deadlock has been detected immediately trigger a deadlock search rather than wait for the next deadlock detection interval. If the deadlock frequency declines, the interval can go back to every five seconds.

This LOCK_MONITOR thread checks for deadlocks by inspecting the list of waiting locks for any cycles, which indicate a circular relationship between processes holding locks and processes waiting for locks. SQL Server attempts to sacrifice the process that would be least expensive to roll back, considering the amount of work the process has already done. That process is killed and error message 1205 is sent to the corresponding client connection. The transaction is rolled back, meaning that all its locks are released, so other processes involved in the deadlock can proceed. However, certain operations are marked as golden, or unkillable, and can't be sacrificed. For example, a process involved in rolling back a transaction can't be sacrificed because the changes being rolled back could be left in an indeterminate state, causing data corruption.

Using the *SET DEADLOCK_PRIORITY* statement, a process can determine its priority for being sacrificed if it's involved in a deadlock. Priority levels range from –10 to 10, for 21 total. You can also specify the value *LOW*, which is equivalent to –5; *NORMAL*, which is equivalent to 0; and *HIGH*, which is equivalent to 5. Which session is sacrificed depends on each session's deadlock priority. If the sessions have different deadlock priorities, the session with the lowest deadlock priority is sacrificed. If both sessions have set the same deadlock priority, SQL Server sacrifices the session that's less expensive to roll back.

Note The lightweight latches and spinlocks used internally don't have deadlock detection services. Instead, deadlocks on latches and spinlocks are avoided rather than resolved. Avoidance is achieved via strict programming guidelines used by the SQL Server development team. These lightweight locks must be acquired in a hierarchy, and a process must not have to wait for a regular lock while holding a latch or spinlock. For example, one coding rule is that a process holding a spinlock must never directly wait for a lock or call another service that might have to wait for a lock, and a request can never be made for a spinlock that's higher in the acquisition hierarchy. By establishing similar guidelines for your development team for the order in which SQL Server objects are accessed, you can go a long way toward avoiding deadlocks in the first place.

In the example in Figure 13-5, the cycle deadlock could have been avoided if the processes had decided on a protocol beforehand—for example, if they had decided always to access the *Product* table first and the *PurchaseOrderDetail* table second. Then one of the processes gets the initial exclusive lock on the table being accessed first, and the other process waits for the lock to be released. One process waiting for a lock is typical and natural. Remember, waiting isn't the same as a deadlock.

You should always try to have a standard protocol for the order in which processes access tables. If you know that the processes might need to update the row after reading it, they should initially request an update lock, not a shared lock. If both processes request an update lock rather than a shared lock, the process that's granted an update lock is assured that the lock can later be promoted to an exclusive lock. The other process requesting an update lock has to wait. The use of an update lock serializes the requests for an exclusive lock. Other processes needing only to read the data can still get their shared locks and read. Because the holder of the update lock is guaranteed an exclusive lock, the deadlock is avoided.

In many systems, deadlocks can't be completely avoided, but if the application handles the deadlock appropriately, the impact on any users involved—and on the rest of the system—should be minimal. (*Appropriate handling* implies that when error 1205 occurs, the application resubmits the batch, which most likely succeeds on the second try. After one process is killed, its transaction aborted, and its locks released, the other process involved in the deadlock can finish its work and release its locks, so the environment isn't conducive to another deadlock.)

Although you might not be able to avoid deadlocks completely, you can minimize their occurrence. For example, you should write your applications so that your processes hold locks for a minimal amount of time; in that way, other processes won't have to wait too long for locks to be released. Even though you don't usually invoke locking directly, you can influence it by keeping transactions as short as possible. For example, don't ask for user input in the middle of a transaction; instead, get the input first and then quickly perform the transaction.

Row versioning

Early on, this chapter described two concurrency models that SQL Server can use. Pessimistic concurrency uses locking to guarantee the appropriate transactional behavior and avoid problems such as dirty reads, according to the isolation level you're using. Optimistic concurrency uses a technology called *row versioning* to guarantee your transactions. Starting with SQL Server 2005, optimistic concurrency is available after you enable one or both of the database properties *READ_COMMITTED_SNAPSHOT* and *ALLOW_SNAPSHOT_ISOLATION*. Exclusive locks can be acquired when you use optimistic concurrency, so you still need to be aware of all issues related to lock modes, lock resources, and lock duration, as well as the resources required to keep track of and manage locks.

The difference between optimistic and pessimistic concurrency is that with optimistic concurrency, writers and readers don't block each other. Or, by using locking terminology, a process requesting an exclusive lock doesn't block when the requested resource currently has a shared lock. Conversely, a process requesting a shared lock doesn't block when the requested resource currently has an exclusive lock.

You can avoid blocking because as soon as one of the new database options is enabled, SQL Server starts using *tempdb* to store copies (versions) of all changed rows, and it keeps those copies as long as any transactions exist that might need to access them. The space in *tempdb* used to store previous versions of changed rows is called the *version store*.

Prior to Server 2005, the tradeoff in concurrency solutions is that we can avoid having writers block readers if we are willing to risk inconsistent data—that is, if we use Read Uncommitted isolation. If our results must always be based on committed data, we need to be willing to wait for changes to be committed.

SQL Server 2005 introduced an isolation level called *Snapshot isolation* and a nonblocking flavor of Read Committed isolation called *Read Committed Snapshot Isolation (RCSI)*. These row versioning–based isolation levels allow a reader to get to a previously committed value of the row without blocking, so concurrency is increased in the system. For this to work, SQL Server must keep old versions of a row when it's updated or deleted. If multiple updates are made to the same row, multiple older versions of the row might need to be maintained. Because of this, row versioning is sometimes called *multiversion concurrency control*.

To support storing multiple older versions of rows, additional disk space is used from the *tempdb* database. The disk space for the version store must be monitored and managed appropriately, and some ways you can do that are pointed out later in this section. Versioning works by making any transaction that changes data keep the old versions of the data around so that a snapshot of the database (or a part of the database) can be constructed from these old versions.

Row versioning details

When a row in a table or index is updated, the new row is stamped with the transaction sequence number (XSN) of the transaction performing the update. The XSN is a monotonically increasing number that's unique within each SQL Server database. The concept of XSN isn't the same as log sequence numbers (LSNs), as discussed in Chapter 5, "Logging and recovery" (XSNs are discussed in more detail later). When updating a row, the previous version is stored in the version store, and the new row contains a pointer to the old row in the version store. Old rows in the version store might contain pointers to even older versions. All the old versions of a particular row are chained in a linked list, and SQL Server might need to follow several pointers in a list to reach the right version. Version rows must be kept in the version store only as long as operations might require them.

In Figure 13-7, the current version of the row is generated by transaction T3 and is stored in the regular data page. The previous versions of the row, generated by transaction T2 and transaction Tx, are stored in pages in the version store (in *tempdb*).

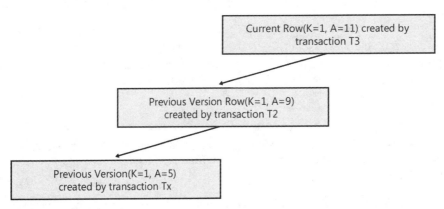

FIGURE 13-7 Versions of a row.

Row versioning gives SQL Server an optimistic concurrency model to work with when an application requires it or when the concurrency reduction of using the default pessimistic model is unacceptable. Before you switch to the row versioning–based isolation levels, you must carefully consider the tradeoffs of using this concurrency model. In addition to requiring extra management to monitor the increased use of *tempdb* for the version store, versioning slows the performance of update operations because of the extra work involved in maintaining old versions. Update operations bear this cost, even with no current readers of the data. Readers that use row versioning have the extra cost of traversing the link pointers to find the appropriate version of the requested row.

Also, because the optimistic concurrency model of Snapshot isolation assumes (optimistically) that not many update conflicts will occur, you shouldn't choose the Snapshot isolation level if you are expecting contention for updating the same data concurrently. Snapshot isolation works well to enable readers not to be blocked by writers, but simultaneous writers still aren't allowed. In the default pessimistic model, the first writer blocks all subsequent writers, but when using Snapshot isolation, subsequent writers can actually receive error messages, and the application needs to resubmit the original request. Note that these update conflicts occur only with the full Snapshot isolation, not with the enhanced RCSI.

Snapshot-based isolation levels

SQL Server provides two types of snapshot-based isolation, both of which use row versioning to maintain the snapshot. One type, RCSI, is enabled simply by setting a database option. When RCSI is enabled, no further changes need to be made. Any transaction that would have operated under the default Read Committed isolation will run under RCSI. The other type, snapshot isolation, must be enabled in two places. You must first enable the database with the *ALLOW_SNAPSHOT_ISOLATION* option, and then each connection that wants to use SI must set the isolation level using the *SET TRANSACTION ISOLATION LEVEL* command.

Read committed snapshot isolation

RCSI is a statement-level snapshot-based isolation, which means any queries see the most recent committed values as of the beginning of the statement. Look at the scenario in Table 13-9. Assume that two transactions are running in the *AdventureWorks2012* database, which has been enabled for RCSI, and that before either transaction starts running, the *ListPrice* value of product 922 is 8.89.

TABLE 13-9 A *SELECT* running in RCSI

Time	Transaction 1	Transaction 2
1	BEGIN TRAN UPDATE Production.Product SET ListPrice = 10.00 WHERE ProductID = 922;	BEGIN TRAN
2		SELECT ListPrice FROM Production.Product WHERE ProductID = 922; -- **SQL Server returns 8.89**
3	COMMIT TRAN	
4		SELECT ListPrice FROM Production.Product WHERE ProductID = 922; -- **SQL Server returns 10.00**
5		COMMIT TRAN

Notice where Time = 2, the change made by Transaction 1 is still uncommitted, so the lock is still held on the row for *ProductID* = 922. However, Transaction 2 doesn't block on that lock; it has access to an old version of the row with a last committed *ListPrice* value of 8.89. After Transaction 1 commits and releases its lock, Transaction 2 sees the new value of *ListPrice*. Because this is still Read Committed isolation (just a nonlocking variation), that read operations are repeatable isn't guaranteed.

You can consider RCSI to be just a variation of the default isolation level Read Committed. The same behaviors are allowed and disallowed, as indicated earlier in Table 13-2.

RCSI is enabled and disabled with the *ALTER DATABASE* command, as shown in this command to enable RCSI in the *AdventureWorks2012* database:

```
ALTER DATABASE AdventureWorks2012
  SET READ_COMMITTED_SNAPSHOT ON;
```

Ironically, although this isolation level is intended to help avoid blocking, if any users are in the database when the preceding command is executed, the *ALTER* statement blocks it. (The connection issuing the *ALTER* command can be in the database, but no other connections can be.) Until the change is successful, the database continues to operate as though it's not in RCSI mode. The blocking can be avoided by specifying a *TERMINATION* clause for the *ALTER* command, as discussed in Chapter 3, "Databases and database files":

```
ALTER DATABASE AdventureWorks2012
    SET READ_COMMITTED_SNAPSHOT ON WITH NO_WAIT;
```

If any users are in the database, the preceding *ALTER* fails with the following error:

```
Msg 5070, Level 16, State 2, Line 1
Database state cannot be changed while other users are using
the database 'AdventureWorks2008'
Msg 5069, Level 16, State 1, Line 1
ALTER DATABASE statement failed.
```

You can also specify one of the *ROLLBACK* termination options, mainly to break any current database connections.

The biggest benefit of RCSI is that you can introduce greater concurrency because readers don't block writers and writers don't block readers. However, writers do block writers because the usual locking behavior applies to all *UPDATE*, *DELETE*, and *INSERT* operations. No *SET* options are required for any session to take advantage of RCSI, so you can reduce the concurrency impact of blocking and deadlocking without any change in your applications.

Snapshot isolation

Snapshot isolation requires using a *SET* command in the session, just like for any other change of isolation level (for example, *SET TRANSACTION ISOLATION LEVEL SERIALIZABLE*). For a session-level option to take effect, you must also allow the database to use SI by altering the database:

```
ALTER DATABASE AdventureWorks2012
    SET ALLOW_SNAPSHOT_ISOLATION ON;
```

When altering the database to allow SI, a user in the database doesn't necessarily block the command from completing. However, if an active transaction is open in the database, *ALTER* is blocked. This doesn't mean that no effect occurs until the statement completes. Changing the database to allow full SI can be a deferred operation. The database can actually be in one of four states with regard to *ALLOW_SNAPSHOT_ISOLATION*: It can be *ON* or *OFF*, but it can also be *IN_TRANSITION_TO_ON* or *IN_TRANSITION_TO_OFF*.

Here is what happens when you *ALTER* a database to *ALLOW_SNAPSHOT_ISOLATION*.

- SQL Server waits for the completion of all active transactions, and the database status is set to *IN_TRANSITION_TO_ON*.

- Any new *UPDATE* or *DELETE* transactions start generating versions in the version store.

- New snapshot transactions can't start because transactions that are already in progress aren't storing row versions as the data is changed. New snapshot transactions would have to have committed versions of the data to read. No error occurs when you execute the *SET TRANSACTION ISOLATION LEVEL SNAPSHOT* command; the error occurs when you try to *SELECT* data, and you get this message:

```
Msg 3956, Level 16, State 1, Line 1
Snapshot isolation transaction failed to start in database 'AdventureWorks2012'
because the ALTER DATABASE command which enables snapshot isolation for this database has
not finished yet. The database is in transition to pending ON state. You must wait until
the ALTER DATABASE Command completes successfully.
```

- As soon as all transactions that were active when the *ALTER* command began have finished, *ALTER* can finish and the state change are complete. The database now is in the state *ALLOW_SNAPSHOT_ISOLATION*.

Taking the database out of *ALLOW_SNAPSHOT_ISOLATION* mode is similar, and again, a transition phase occurs.

- SQL Server waits for the completion of all active transactions, and the database status is set to IN_TRANSITION_TO_OFF.

- New snapshot transactions can't start.

- Existing snapshot transactions still execute snapshot scans, reading from the version store.

- New transactions continue generating versions.

Snapshot isolation scope

SI gives you a transactionally consistent view of the data. Any rows read are the most recent committed version of the rows as of the beginning of the transaction. (For RCSI, we get the most recent committed version as of the beginning of the statement.) Keep in mind that the transaction doesn't start at the *BEGIN TRAN* statement; for the purposes of Snapshot isolation, a transaction starts the first time the transactions accesses any data in the database.

For an example of SI, consider a scenario similar to the one in Table 13-9. Table 13-10 shows activities in a database with *ALLOW_SNAPSHOT_ISOLATION* set to *ON*. Assume that two transactions are running in the *AdventureWorks2012* database and that before either transaction starts, the *ListPrice* value of Product 922 is 10.00.

TABLE 13-10 A *SELECT* running in a *SNAPSHOT* transaction

Time	Transaction 1	Transaction 2
1	BEGIN TRAN	
2	UPDATE Production.Product SET ListPrice = 12.00 WHERE ProductID = 922;	SET TRANSACTION ISOLATION LEVEL SNAPSHOT
3		BEGIN TRAN
4		SELECT ListPrice FROM Production.Product WHERE ProductID = 922; -- **SQL Server returns 10.00** -- This is the beginning of -- the transaction
5	COMMIT TRAN	
6		SELECT ListPrice FROM Production.Product WHERE ProductID = 922; -- **SQL Server returns 10.00** -- Return the committed -- value as of the beginning -- of the transaction
7		COMMIT TRAN
		SELECT ListPrice FROM Production.Product WHERE ProductID = 922; -- **SQL Server returns 12.00**

Even though Transaction 1 has committed, Transaction 2 continues to return the initial value it read of 10.00 until Transaction 2 completes. Only after Transaction 2 is complete does the connection read a new value for *ListPrice*.

Viewing database state

The catalog view *sys.databases* contains several columns that report on the Snapshot isolation state of the database. A database can be enabled for SI and/or RCSI. However, enabling one doesn't automatically enable or disable the other. Each one has to be enabled or disabled individually using separate *ALTER DATABASE* commands.

The column *snapshot_isolation_state* has possible values of 0 to 4, indicating each of the four possible SI states, and the *snapshot_isolation_state_desc* column spells out the state. Table 13-11 summarizes what each state means.

TABLE 13-11 Possible values for the database option *ALLOW_SNAPSHOT_ISOLATION*

Snapshot isolation state	Description
OFF	Snapshot isolation state is disabled in the database. In other words, transactions with SI aren't allowed. Database versioning state is initially set to *OFF* during recovery. If versioning is enabled, versioning state is set to *ON* after recovery.
IN_TRANSITION_TO_ON	The database is in the process of enabling SI. It waits for the completion of all *UPDATE* transactions that were active when the *ALTER DATABASE* command was issued. New *UPDATE* transactions in this database start paying the cost of versioning by generating row versions. Transactions using Snapshot isolation can't start.
ON	SI is enabled. New snapshot transactions can start in this database. Existing snapshot transactions (in another snapshot-enabled session) that start before versioning state is turned *ON* can't do a snapshot scan in this database because the snapshot those transactions are interested in isn't properly generated by the *UPDATE* transactions.
IN_ TRANSITION_TO_OFF	The database is in the process of disabling the SI state and can't start new snapshot transactions. *UPDATE* transactions still pay the cost of versioning in this database. Existing snapshot transactions can still do snapshot scans. *IN_TRANSITION_TO_OFF* doesn't become *OFF* until all existing transactions finish.

The *is_read_committed_snapshot_on* column has a value of 0 or 1. Table 13-12 summarizes what each state means.

TABLE 13-12 Possible values for the database option *READ_COMMITTED_SNAPSHOT*

READ_COMMITTED_SNAPSHOT state	Description
0	READ_COMMITTED_SNAPSHOT is disabled.
1	READ_COMMITTED_SNAPSHOT is enabled. Any query with Read Committed isolation executes in the nonblocking mode.

You can see the values of each of these snapshot states for all your databases with the following query:

```
SELECT name, snapshot_isolation_state_desc,
       is_read_committed_snapshot_on , *
FROM sys.databases;
```

Update conflicts

One crucial difference between the two optimistic concurrency levels is that SI can potentially result in update conflicts when a process sees the same data for the duration of its transaction and isn't blocked simply because another process is changing the same data. Table 13-13 illustrates two processes attempting to update the *Quantity* value of the same row in the *ProductInventory* table in the *AdventureWorks2012*database. Two clerks have each received shipments of ProductID 872 and are trying to update the inventory. The *AdventureWorks2012* database has *ALLOW_SNAPSHOT_ISOLATION* set to *ON*, and before either transaction starts, the *Quantity* value of Product 872 is 324.

TABLE 13-13 An update conflict in *SNAPSHOT* isolation

Time	Transaction 1	Transaction 2
1		SET TRANSACTION ISOLATION LEVEL SNAPSHOT
2		BEGIN TRAN
3		SELECT Quantity FROM Production.ProductInventory WHERE ProductID = 872; -- **SQL Server returns 324** -- This is the beginning of -- the transaction
4	BEGIN TRAN UPDATE Production.ProductInventory SET Quantity=Quantity + 200 WHERE ProductID = 872; -- **Quantity is now 524**	
5		UPDATE Production.ProductInventory SET Quantity=Quantity + 300 WHERE ProductID = 872; -- **Process will block**
6	COMMIT TRAN	
7		-- Process receives error 3960

The conflict happens because Transaction 2 started when the *Quantity* value was 324. When that value was updated by Transaction 1, the row version with 324 was saved in the version store. Transaction 2 continues to read that row for the duration of the transaction. If both *UPDATE* operations were allowed to succeed, we would have a classic lost update situation. Transaction 1 added 200 to the quantity, and then Transaction 2 would add 300 to the original value and save that. The 200 added by Transaction 1 would be completely lost. SQL Server doesn't allow that.

When Transaction 2 first tries to perform the *UPDATE*, it doesn't get an error immediately—it's simply blocked. Transaction 1 has an exclusive lock on the row, so when Transaction 2 attempts to get an exclusive lock, it's blocked. If Transaction 1 had rolled back its transaction, Transaction 2 could have completed its *UPDATE*. But because Transaction 1 committed, SQL Server detected a conflict and generated the following error:

```
Msg 3960, Level 16, State 2, Line 1
Snapshot isolation transaction aborted due to update conflict. You cannot use snapshot
isolation to access table 'Production.ProductInventory' directly or indirectly in database'
AdventureWorks2012' to update, delete, or insert the row that has been modified or deleted
by another transaction. Retry the transaction or change the isolation level for the
update/delete statement.
```

Conflicts are possible only with SI because that isolation level is transaction-based, not statement-based. If the example in Table 13-13 were executed in a database using RCSI, the *UPDATE* statement executed by Transaction 2 wouldn't use the old value of the data. It would be blocked when trying to read the current *Quantity,* and then when Transaction 1 finished, it would read the new updated *Quantity* as the current value and add 300 to that. Neither update would be lost.

If you choose to work in SI, you need to be aware that conflicts can happen. They can be minimized, but as with deadlocks, you can't be sure that you will never have conflicts. Your application must be written to handle conflicts appropriately and not assume that the *UPDATE* has succeeded. If conflicts occur occasionally, you might consider it part of the price to be paid for using SI, but if they occur too often, you might need to take extra steps.

You might consider whether SI is really necessary and, if it is, you should determine whether the statement-based RCSI might give you the behavior you need without the cost of detecting and dealing with conflicts. Another solution is to use a query hint called *UPDLOCK* to make sure no other process updates data before you're ready to update it. In Table 13-13, Transaction 2 could use *UPDLOCK* on its initial *SELECT* as follows:

```
SELECT Quantity
FROM Production.ProductInventory WITH (UPDLOCK)
WHERE ProductID = 872;
```

The *UPDLOCK* hint forces SQL Server to acquire update locks for Transaction 2 on the selected row. When Transaction 1 then tries to update that row, it blocks. It's not using SI, so it doesn't see the previous value of *Quantity*. Transaction 2 can perform its update because Transaction 1 is blocked, and it commits. Transaction 1 can then perform its update on the new value of *Quantity,* and neither update is lost.

I will provide a few more details about locking hints at the end of this chapter.

DDL and snapshot isolation

When working with SI, you need to be aware that although SQL Server keeps versions of all the changed data, that metadata isn't versioned. Therefore, certain Data Definition Language (DDL) statements aren't allowed inside a snapshot transaction. The following DDL statements are disallowed in a snapshot transaction:

- *CREATE | ALTER | DROP INDEX*

- *DBCC DBREINDEX*

- *ALTER TABLE*

- *ALTER PARTITION FUNCTION | SCHEME*

On the other hand, the following DDL statements are allowed:

- *CREATE TABLE*

- *CREATE TYPE*

- *CREATE PROC*

Note that the allowable DDL statements create brand-new objects. In SI, simultaneous data modifications can't affect the creation of these objects in any way. Table 13-14 shows a pseudocode example of a snapshot transaction that includes both *CREATE TABLE* and *CREATE INDEX*.

TABLE 13-14 DDL inside a *SNAPSHOT* transaction

Time	Transaction 1	Transaction 2
1	SET TRANSACTION ISOLATION LEVEL SNAPSHOT;	
2	BEGIN TRAN	
3	SELECT count(*) FROM Production.Product; -- This is the beginning of -- the transaction	
4		BEGIN TRAN
5	CREATE TABLE NewProducts (<column definitions>) -- This DDL is legal	INSERT Production.Product VALUES (9999, ...) -- A new row is insert into -- the Product table
6		COMMIT TRAN

7	CREATE INDEX PriceIndex
	  ON Production.Product
	    (ListPrice)
	-- This DDL will generate an
	-- error	

The *CREATE TABLE* statement succeeds even though Transaction 1 is in SI because it's not affected by anything any other process can do. The *CREATE INDEX* statement is a different story. When Transaction 1 started, the new row with ProductID 9999 didn't exist. But when the *CREATE INDEX* statement is encountered, the *INSERT* from Transaction 2 has been committed. Should Transaction 1 include the new row in the index? You can't avoid including the new row, but that violates the snapshot that Transaction 1 is using, and SQL Server generates an error rather than creates the index.

Another aspect of concurrent DDL to consider is what happens when a statement outside the snapshot transaction changes an object referenced by a snapshot transaction. The DDL is allowed, but you can get an error in the snapshot transaction when this happens. Table 13-15 shows an example.

TABLE 13-15 Concurrent DDL outside the *SNAPSHOT* transaction

Time	Transaction 1	Transaction 2
1	SET TRANSACTION ISOLATION LEVEL SNAPSHOT;	
2	BEGIN TRAN	
3	SELECT TOP 10 * FROM Production.Product; -- This is the start of -- the transaction	

Time	Transaction 1	Transaction 2
4		BEGIN TRAN ALTER TABLE Purchasing.Vendor ADD notes varchar(1000); COMMIT TRAN
5	SELECT TOP 10 * FROM Production.Product; -- Succeeds -- The ALTER to a different -- table does not affect -- this transaction	
6		BEGIN TRAN ALTER TABLE Production.Product ADD LowestPrice money; COMMIT TRAN
7	SELECT TOP 10 * FROM Production.Product; -- ERROR	

For Transaction 1 in Table 13-15, the repeated *SELECT* statements should always return the same data from the *Product* table. An external *ALTER TABLE* on a completely different table has no effect on the snapshot transaction, but Transaction 2 then alters the *Product* table to add a new column. Because the metadata representing the former table structure isn't versioned, Transaction 1 can't produce the same results for the third *SELECT*. SQL Server generates this error:

```
Msg 3961, Level 16, State 1, Line 1
Snapshot isolation transaction failed in database 'AdventureWorks2012' because the object
accessed by the statement has been modified by a DDL statement in another concurrent transaction
since the start of this transaction. It is disallowed because the metadata is not versioned. A
concurrent update to metadata can lead to inconsistency if mixed with snapshot isolation.
```

In this version, any concurrent change to metadata on objects referenced by a snapshot transaction generates this error, even if no possibility of anomalies exists. For example, if Transaction 1 issues a *SELECT count(*)*, which isn't affected by the *ALTER TABLE* statement, SQL Server still generates error 3961.

Summary of snapshot-based isolation levels

SI and RCSI are similar in the sense that they are based on the versioning of rows in a database. However, how these options are enabled from an administration perspective and how they affect your applications have some key differences. This chapter has discussed many of these differences already, but for completeness, Table 13-16 lists both the similarities and the differences between the two types of snapshot-based isolation.

TABLE 13-16 Snapshot vs. read committed snapshot isolation

Snapshot isolation	Read committed snapshot isolation
The database must be configured to allow SI, and the session must issue the command *SET TRANSACTION ISOLATION LEVEL SNAPSHOT*.	The database must be configured to use RCSI, and sessions must use the default isolation level. No code changes are required.
Enabling SI for a database is an online operation. It allows a DBA to turn on versioning for one particular application, such as one that's creating large reports. The DBA can then turn off versioning after the reporting transaction is started to prevent new snapshot transactions from starting. Turning on SI in an existing database is synchronous. When the *ALTER DATABASE* command is given, control doesn't return to the DBA until all existing update transactions that need to create versions in the current database finish. At this time, ALLOW_SNAPSHOT_ISOLATION is changed to ON. Only then can users start a snapshot transaction in that database. Turning off SI is also synchronous.	Enabling RCSI for a database requires a *SHARED_TRANSACTION_WORKSPACE* lock on the database. All users must be kicked out of a database to enable this option.
Active sessions in the database have no restrictions when this database option is enabled.	No other sessions should be active in the database when you enable this option.
If an application runs a snapshot transaction that accesses tables from two databases, the DBA must turn on *ALLOW_SNAPSHOT_ISOLATION* in both databases before the application starts a snapshot transaction.	RCSI is really a table-level option, so tables from two different databases, referenced in the same query, can each have their own individual setting. One table might get its data from the version store, while the other table is reading only the current versions of the data. Both databases aren't required to have the RCSI option enabled.
The *IN_TRANSITION* versioning states don't persist. Only the *ON* and *OFF* states are remembered on disk.	No *IN_TRANSITION* states are used here. Only *ON* and *OFF* states persist.
When a database is recovered after a server crash, or after your SQL Server instance is shut down, restored, attached, or made *ONLINE*, all versioning history for that database is lost. If database versioning state is *ON*, SQL Server can allow new snapshot transactions to access the database, but must prevent previous snapshot transactions from accessing the database. Those previous transactions would need to access data from a point in time before the database recovers.	This object-level option isn't at the transaction level, so it's not applicable.
If the database is in the *IN_TRANSITION_TO_ON* state, *ALTER DATABASE SET ALLOW_SNAPSHOT_ ISOLATION OFF* waits for about 6 seconds and might fail if the database state is still in the *IN_TRANSITION_TO_ON* state. The DBA can retry the command after the database state changes to *ON*.	This option can be enabled only when no other active session is open in the database, so no transitional states are available.
For read-only databases, versioning is automatically enabled. You still can use *ALTER DATABASE SET ALLOW_SNAPSHOT_ISOLATION ON* for a read-only database. If the database is made read-write later, versioning for the database is still enabled.	Like for SI, versioning is enabled automatically for read-only databases.
Any long-running transactions might cause a DBA to wait a long time before the versioning state change can finish. A DBA can cancel the wait, and the versioning state is rolled back and set to the previous one.	This option can be enabled only when no other active session is open in the database, so no transitional states are available.
You can't use *ALTER DATABASE* to change the database versioning state inside a user transaction.	Like for SI, you can change the database versioning state inside a user transaction.
You can change the versioning state of *tempdb*. The versioning state of *tempdb* is preserved when SQL Server restarts, although the content of *tempdb* isn't preserved.	You can't turn this option *ON* for *tempdb*.

Snapshot isolation	Read committed snapshot isolation
You can change the versioning state of the *master* database.	You can't change this option for the *master* database.
You can change the versioning state of *model*. If versioning is enabled for *model*, every new database created will also have versioning enabled. However, the versioning state of *tempdb* isn't automatically enabled if you enable versioning for *model*.	This is similar to the behavior for SI, except it has no implications for *tempdb*.
You can turn this option *ON* for *msdb*.	You can't turn on this option *ON* for *msdb* because this can potentially break the applications built on *msdb* that rely on blocking behavior of Read Committed isolation.
A query in a SI transaction sees data that was committed before the transaction started, and each statement in the transaction sees the same set of committed changes.	A statement running in RCSI sees everything committed before the start of the statement. Each new statement in the transaction picks up the most recent committed changes.
SI can result in update conflicts that might cause a rollback or abort the transaction.	Update conflicts aren't possible.

The version store

As soon as a database is enabled for *ALLOW_SNAPSHOT_ISOLATION* or *READ_COMMITTED_SNAP-SHOT*, all *UPDATE* and *DELETE* operations start generating row versions of the previously committed rows, and they store those versions in the version store on data pages in *tempdb*. Version rows must be kept in the version store only as long as snapshot queries might need them.

SQL Server provides several DMVs that contain information about active snapshot transactions and the version store. This section won't examine all the details of all those DMVs, but we look at some of the crucial ones to help you determine how much use is being made of your version store and what snapshot transactions might be affecting your results. The first DMV we look at, *sys.dm_tran_version_store*, contains information about the actual rows in the version store. Run the following script to make a copy of the *Production.Product* table, and then turn on *ALLOW_SNAPSHOT_ISOLA-TION* in the *AdventureWorks2012* database. Finally, verify that the option is *ON* and that no rows are currently in the version store. You might need to close any active transactions currently using *AdventureWorks2012*:

```
USE AdventureWorks2012
SELECT * INTO NewProduct
FROM Production.Product;
GO
ALTER DATABASE ADVENTUREWORKS2012 SET ALLOW_SNAPSHOT_ISOLATION ON;
GO
SELECT name, snapshot_isolation_state_desc,
       is_read_committed_snapshot_on
FROM sys.databases
WHERE name= 'AdventureWorks2012';
GO
SELECT COUNT(*) FROM sys.dm_tran_version_store;
GO
```

As soon as you see that the database option is *ON* and no rows are in the version store, you can continue. As soon as *ALLOW_SNAPSHOT_ISOLATION* is enabled, SQL Server starts storing row versions, even if no snapshot transactions need to read those versions. So now run this *UPDATE* statement on the *NewProduct* table and look at the version store again:

```
UPDATE NewProduct
SET ListPrice = ListPrice * 1.1;
GO
SELECT COUNT(*) FROM sys.dm_tran_version_store;
GO
```

You should now see that 504 rows are in the version store because the *NewProduct* table has 504 rows. The previous version of each row, before the update, has been written to the version store in *tempdb*.

> **Note** SQL Server starts generating versions in *tempdb* as soon as a database is enabled for one of the snapshot–based isolation levels. In a heavily updated database, this can affect the behavior of other queries that use *tempdb*, as well as the server itself.

As shown earlier in Figure 13-7, the version store maintains link lists of rows. The current row points to the next older row, which can point to an older row, and so on. The end of the list is the oldest version of that particular row. To support row versioning, a row needs 14 additional bytes of information to keep track of the pointers. The actual pointer to the file, page, and row in *tempdb* needs 8 bytes, and 6 bytes are needed to store the XSN to help SQL Server determine which rows are current or which versioned row is the one that a particular transaction needs to access. You learn more about the XSN when we look at some of the other snapshot transaction metadata. Also, one of the bits in the first byte of each data row (the TagA byte) is turned on to indicate that this row has versioning information in it.

Any row inserted or updated when a database is using one of the snapshot–based isolation levels will contain these 14 extra bytes. The following code creates a small table and inserts two rows into it in the *AdventureWorks2012* database, which already has *ALLOW_SNAPSHOT_ISOLATION* enabled. You then find the page number using *sys,dn_db_database_page_allocations* (it's page 60763 in my output) and use *DBCC PAGE* to look at the rows on the page. The output shows only one of the rows inserted:

```
CREATE TABLE T1 (T1ID char(1), T1name char(10));
GO
INSERT T1 SELECT 'A', 'aaaaaaaaaa';
INSERT T1 SELECT 'B', 'bbbbbbbbbb';
GO
SELECT allocated_page_file_id, allocated_page_page_id, page_type_desc
    FROM sys.dm_db_database_page_allocations
        (db_id('AdventureWorks2012'), object_id('T1'), NULL, NULL, 'DETAILED');
DBCC TRACEON (3604);
DBCC PAGE('AdventureWorks2012', 1, 60763, 1);
```

```
OUTPUT ROW:
Slot 0, Offset 0x60, Length 32, DumpStyle BYTE
Record Type = PRIMARY_RECORD
Record Attributes =  NULL_BITMAP VERSIONING_INFO

Memory Dump @0x6207C060
00000000:    50000f00 41616161 61616161 61616102 00000000    P...Aaaaaaaaaaa.....
00000014:    00000000 000007c4 00000000                      ................
```

The new header information that indicates this row contains versioning information is in boldface, as are the 14 bytes of the versioning information. The XSN is all 0's in the row because it wasn't modified as part of a transaction that Snapshot isolation needs to keep track of. *INSERT* statements create new data that no snapshot transaction needs to see. If you update one of these rows, the previous row is written to the version store and the XSN is reflected in the row versioning information:

```
UPDATE T1 SET T1name = '2222222222' where T1ID = 'A';
GO
DBCC PAGE('AdventureWorks2012', 1, 60763, 1);
GO
OUTPUT ROW:
Slot 0, Offset 0x60, Length 32, DumpStyle BYTE
Record Type = PRIMARY_RECORD
Record Attributes =  NULL_BITMAP VERSIONING_INFO
Memory Dump @0x61C4C060
00000000:    50000f00 41323232 32323232 32323202 00001801    P...A2222222222.....
00000014:    00000100 00000cc4 00000000                      ..........Y.....
```

As mentioned, if your database is enabled for one of the snapshot–based isolation levels, every new row has an additional 14 bytes added to it whether or not that row is ever actually involved in versioning. Every row updated also has the 14 bytes added to it, if they aren't already part of the row, and the update is done as a *DELETE* followed by an *INSERT*. This means that for tables and indexes on full pages, a simple *UPDATE* could result in page splitting.

When a row is deleted in a database enabled for snapshots, a pointer is left on the page as a ghost record to point to the deleted row in the version store. These ghost records are very similar to the ones we saw in Chapter 7, "Indexes: internals and management," and they're cleaned up as part of the versioning cleanup process, as is discussed shortly. Here's an example of a ghost record under versioning:

```
DELETE T1 WHERE T1ID = 'B';
DBCC PAGE('AdventureWorks2012 ', 1, 60763, 1);
GO
--Partial Results:
Slot 1, Offset 0x80, Length 15, DumpStyle BYTE

Record Type = GHOST_VERSION_RECORD
Record Attributes =  VERSIONING_INFO
Memory Dump @0x5C0FC153

00000000:    4e280100 00010001 0017c400 000000    N........!.....
```

The record header indicates that this row is a *GHOST_VERSION_RECORD* and that it contains versioning information. The actual data, however, isn't on the row, but the XSN is, so snapshot transactions know when this row was deleted and whether they should access the older version of it in their snapshot. The *sys.dm_db_index_physical_stats* DMV discussed in Chapter 7 contains the count of ghost records due to versioning (*version_ghost_record_count*) and the count of all ghost records (*ghost_record_count*), which includes the versioning ghosts. If an update is performed as a *DELETE* followed by an *INSERT* (not in place), both the ghost for the old value and the new value must exist simultaneously, increasing the space requirements for the object.

If a database is in a snapshot–based isolation level, all changes to both data and index rows must be versioned. A snapshot query traversing an index still needs access to index rows pointing to the older (versioned) rows. So in the index levels, we might have old values, as ghosts, existing simultaneously with the new value, and the indexes can require more storage space.

The extra 14 bytes of versioning information can be removed if the database is changed to a non-snapshot isolation level. When the database option is changed, each time a row containing versioning information is updated, the versioning bytes are removed.

Management of the version store

The version store size is managed automatically, and SQL Server maintains a cleanup thread to ensure that versioned rows aren't kept around longer than needed. For queries running under SI, the row versions must be kept until the end of the transaction. For *SELECT* statements running under RCSI, a particular row version isn't needed after the *SELECT* statement is executed and can be removed.

The regular cleanup function is performed every minute as a background process to reclaim all reusable space from the version store. If *tempdb* actually runs out of free space, the cleanup function is called before SQL Server increases the size of the files. If the disk gets so full that the files can't grow, SQL Server stops generating versions. If that happens, a snapshot query fails if it needs to read a version that wasn't generated due to space constraints. Although a full discussion of troubleshooting and monitoring is beyond the scope of this book, note that SQL Server 2012 includes more than a dozen performance counters to monitor *tempdb* and the version store. These include counters to keep track of transactions that use row versioning. The following counters are contained in the SQLServer:Transactions performance object. Additional details and additional counters can be found in *SQL Server Books Online*.

- **Free space in tempdb** This counter monitors the amount of free space in the *tempdb* database. You can observe this value to detect when *tempdb* is running out of space, which might lead to problems keeping all the necessary version rows.

- **Version store size** This counter monitors the size in kilobytes of the version store. Monitoring this counter can help determine a useful estimate of the additional space you might need for *tempdb*.

- **Version generation rate and version cleanup rate** These counters monitor the rate at which space is acquired and released from the version store, in kilobytes per second.

- **Update conflict ratio**   This counter monitors the ratio of update snapshot transactions that have update conflicts. It's the ratio of the number of conflicts compared to the total number of update snapshot transactions.

- **Longest transaction running time**   This counter monitors the longest running time, in seconds, of any transaction using row versioning. It can be used to determine whether any transaction is running for an unreasonable amount of time, as well as help you determine the maximum size needed in *tempdb* for the version store.

- **Snapshot transactions**   This counter monitors the total number of active snapshot transactions.

Snapshot transaction metadata

The most important DMVs for observing snapshot transaction behavior are *sys.dm_tran_version_store* (which we briefly looked at earlier in this chapter), *sys.dm_tran_transactions_snapshot,* and *sys.dm_tran_active_snapshot_database_transactions.*

All these views contain the *transaction_sequence_num* column, which is the XSN mentioned earlier. Each transaction is assigned a monotonically increasing XSN value when it starts a snapshot read or when it writes data in a snapshot-enabled database. The XSN is reset to 0 when your SQL Server instance is restarted. Transactions that don't generate version rows and don't use snapshot scans don't receive an XSN.

Another column, *transaction_id,* is also used in some of the snapshot transaction metadata. A transaction ID is a unique identification number assigned to the transaction. It's used primarily to identify the transaction in locking operations. It can also help you identify which transactions are involved in snapshot operations. The transaction ID value is incremented for every transaction across the whole server, including internal system transactions, so whether or not that transaction is involved in any snapshot operations, the current transaction ID value is usually much larger than the current XSN.

You can check current transaction number information by using the view *sys.dm_tran_current_transaction,* which returns a single row containing the following columns:

- ***transaction_id***   This value displays the transaction ID of the current transaction. If you're selecting from the view inside a user-defined transaction, you should continue to see the same *transaction_id* every time you select from the view. If you are running a *SELECT* from *sys.dm_tran_current_transaction* outside a transaction, the *SELECT* itself generates a new *transaction_id* value and you see a different value every time you execute the same *SELECT,* even in the same connection.

- ***transaction_sequence_num***   This value is the XSN of the current transaction, if it has one. Otherwise, this column returns 0.

- ***transaction_is_snapshot***   This value is 1 if the current transaction was started under Snapshot isolation; otherwise, it's 0 (that is, this column is 1 if the current session has set *TRANSACTION ISOLATION LEVEL* to *SNAPSHOT* explicitly).

- **first_snapshot_sequence_num** When the current transaction started, it took a snapshot of all active transactions, and this value is the lowest XSN of the transactions in the snapshot.

- **last_transaction_sequence_num** This value is the most recent XSN generated by the system.

- **first_useful_sequence_num** This value is an XSN representing the upper bound of version store rows that can be cleaned up without affecting any transactions. Any rows with an XSN less than this value are no longer needed.

Now create a simple versioning scenario to see how the values in the snapshot metadata get updated. This isn't a complete overview, but it should get you started in exploring the versioning metadata for your own queries. Use the *AdventureWorks2008* database, which has *ALLOW_SNAPSHOT_ISOLATION* set to *ON*, and create a simple table:

```
CREATE TABLE t1
(col1 int primary key, col2 int);
GO
INSERT INTO t1 SELECT 1,10;
INSERT INTO t1 SELECT 2,20;
INSERT INTO t1 SELECT 3,30;
```

Call this session Connection 1. Change the session's isolation level, start a snapshot transaction, and examine some of the metadata:

```
SET TRANSACTION ISOLATION LEVEL SNAPSHOT
GO
BEGIN TRAN
SELECT * FROM t1;
GO
select * from sys.dm_tran_current_transaction;
select * from sys.dm_tran_version_store;
select * from sys.dm_tran_transactions_snapshot;
```

The *sys.dm_tran_current_transaction* view should show you something like this: The current transaction does have an XSN, and the transaction is a snapshot transaction. Also, note that the *first_useful_sequence_num* value is the same as this transaction's XSN because no other snapshot transactions are valid now. You can refer to this transaction's XSN as XSN1.

The version store should be empty (unless you've done other snapshot tests within the last minute). Also, *sys.dm_tran_transactions_snapshot* should be empty, indicating that no snapshot transactions were started when other transactions were in process.

In another connection (Connection 2), run an update and examine some of the metadata for the current transaction:

```
BEGIN TRAN
 UPDATE T1 SET col2 = 100
   WHERE col1 = 1;
SELECT * FROM sys.dm_tran_current_transaction;
```

Note that although this transaction has an XSN because it generates versions, it's not running in SI, so the *transaction_is_snapshot* value is 0. I refer to this transaction's XSN as XSN2.

Now start a third transaction in a Connection 3 to perform another *SELECT*. (Don't worry, this is the last one and we won't be keeping it around.) It is almost identical to the first, but with an important difference in the metadata results:

```
SET TRANSACTION ISOLATION LEVEL SNAPSHOT
GO
BEGIN TRAN
SELECT * FROM t1;
GO
select * from sys.dm_tran_current_transaction;
select * from sys.dm_tran_transactions_snapshot;
```

In the *sys.dm_tran_current_transaction* view, you see a new XSN for this transaction (XSN3), and you see that the values for *first_snapshot_sequence_num* and *first_useful_sequence_num* are both the same as XSN1. In the *sys.dm_tran_transactions_snapshot* view, you see that this transaction with XSN3 has two rows, indicating the two transactions that were active when this one started. Both XSN1 and XSN2 show up in the *snapshot_sequence_num* column. You can now either commit or roll back this transaction, and then close the connection.

Go back to Connection 2, where you started the *UPDATE*, and commit the transaction. Now go back to the first *SELECT* transaction in Connection 1 and rerun the *SELECT* statement, staying in the same transaction:

```
SELECT * FROM t1;
```

Even though the *UPDATE* in Connection 2 has committed, the original data values can still be seen because we are running a snapshot transaction. Examine the *sys.dm_tran_active_snapshot_database_transactions* view with this query:

```
SELECT transaction_sequence_num, commit_sequence_num,
   is_snapshot, session_id,first_snapshot_sequence_num,
   max_version_chain_traversed, elapsed_time_seconds
FROM  sys.dm_tran_active_snapshot_database_transactions;
```

The output isn't shown here because it's too wide for the page, but you should find many columns interesting. In particular, the *transaction_sequence_num* column contains XSN1, which is the XSN for the current connection. You could actually run the preceding query from any connection; it shows *all* active snapshot transactions in the SQL Server instance, and because it includes the *session_id*, you can join it to *sys.dm_exec_sessions* to get information about the connection that's running the transaction:

```
SELECT transaction_sequence_num, commit_sequence_num,
    is_snapshot, t.session_id,first_snapshot_sequence_num,
    max_version_chain_traversed, elapsed_time_seconds,
    host_name, login_name, transaction_isolation_level
FROM  sys.dm_tran_active_snapshot_database_transactions t
   JOIN sys.dm_exec_sessions s
     ON t.session_id = s.session_id;
```

Another value to note is in the *max_version_chain_traversed* column. Although now it should be 1, we can change that. Go back to Connection 2 and run another *UPDATE* statement. Although the *BEGIN TRAN* and *COMMIT TRAN* aren't necessary for a single statement transaction, they are included to clearly show that this transaction is complete:

```
BEGIN TRAN
 UPDATE T1 SET col2 = 300
   WHERE col1 = 1;
COMMIT TRAN;
```

Examine the version store, if desired, to see rows being added:

```
SELECT *
 FROM sys.dm_tran_version_store;
```

When you go back to Connection 1 and run the same *SELECT* inside the original transaction and then look again at the *max_version_chain_traversed* column in *sys.dm_tran_active_snapshot_database_transactions*, you should see that the number keeps growing. Repeated *UPDATE* operations, either in Connection 2 or a new connection, cause the *max_version_chain_traversed* value to just keep increasing, as long as Connection 1 stays in the same transaction. Keep this in mind as an added cost of using Snapshot isolation. As you perform more updates on data needed by snapshot transactions, your read operations take longer because SQL Server must traverse a longer version chain to get the data needed by your transactions.

This is just the beginning regarding how the snapshot and transaction metadata can be used to examine the behavior of your snapshot transactions.

Choosing a concurrency model

Pessimistic concurrency is the default in SQL Server 2012 and was the only choice in all versions of SQL Server prior to SQL Server 2005. Transactional behavior is guaranteed by locking, at the cost of greater blocking. When accessing the same data resources, readers can block writers and writers can block readers. Because SQL Server was initially designed and built to use pessimistic concurrency, you should consider using that model unless you can verify that optimistic concurrency really will work better for you and your applications. If you find that the cost of blocking is becoming excessive, consider using optimistic concurrency.

In most situations, RCSI is recommended over Snapshot isolation for several reasons.

- RCSI consumes less *tempdb* space than SI.

- RCSI works with distributed transactions; SI doesn't.

- RCSI doesn't produce update conflicts.

- RCSI doesn't require any change in your applications. One change to the database options is all that's needed. Any of your applications written using the default Read Committed isolation level automatically uses RCSI after making the change at the database level.

You can consider using SI in the following situations.

- The probability is low that any of your transactions have to be rolled back because of an update conflict.

- You have reports that need to be generated based on long-running, multistatement queries that must have point-in-time consistency. Snapshot isolation provides the benefit of repeatable reads without being blocked by concurrent modification operations.

Optimistic concurrency does have benefits, as follows, but you must also be aware of the costs:

- *SELECT* operations don't acquire shared locks, so readers and writers don't block each other.

- All *SELECT* operations retrieve a consistent snapshot of the data.

- The total number of locks needed is greatly reduced compared to pessimistic concurrency, so less system overhead is used.

- SQL Server needs to perform fewer lock escalations.

- Deadlocks are less likely to occur.

Now look at the other side. When weighing your concurrency options, you must consider the cost of the snapshot–based isolation levels.

- *SELECT* performance can be affected negatively when long-version chains must be scanned. The older the snapshot, the more time is needed to access the required row in an SI transaction.

- Row versioning requires additional resources in *tempdb*.

- Whenever either of the snapshot–based isolation levels are enabled for a database, *UPDATE* and *DELETE* operations must generate row versions. (Although *INSERT* operations usually don't generate row versions, as mentioned earlier, they might in some cases. In particular, if you insert a row into a table with a unique index, and if an older version of the row has the same key value as the new row and that old row still exists as a ghost, your new row generates a version.)

- Row versioning information increases the size of every affected row by 14 bytes.

- *UPDATE* performance might be slower because of the work involved in maintaining the row versions.

- *UPDATE* operations using SI might have to be rolled back because of conflict detection. Your applications must be programmed to deal with any conflicts that occur.

- The space in *tempdb* must be carefully managed. If very long-running transactions exist, all the versions generated by update transactions during the time must be kept in *tempdb*. If *tempdb* runs out of space, *UPDATE* operations won't fail, but *SELECT* operations that need to read versioned data might fail.

To maintain a production system using SI, you should allocate enough disk space for *tempdb* so that at least 10 percent free space is always available. If the free space falls below this threshold, system performance might suffer because SQL Server expends more resources trying to reclaim space in the version store. The following formula can give you a rough estimate of the size required by version store. For long-running transactions, using Performance Monitor to monitor the generation and cleanup rate using Performance Monitor can help estimate the maximum size needed:

```
[size of common version store] =
2 * [version store data generated per minute]
* [longest running time (minutes) of the transaction]
```

Controlling locking

SQL Server usually chooses the correct type of lock and the lock mode. You should override this behavior only if thorough testing has shown that a different approach is preferable. Keep in mind that setting an isolation level affects the locks that held, the conflicts that cause blocking, and the duration of your locks. Your isolation level is in effect for an entire session, and you should choose the one that provides the data consistency required by your application. Use table-level locking hints to change the default locking behavior only when necessary. Disallowing a locking level can adversely affect concurrency.

Lock hints

T-SQL syntax allows you to specify locking hints for individual tables when they are referenced in *SELECT, INSERT, UPDATE,* and *DELETE* statements. The hints tell SQL Server the type of locking or row versioning to use for a particular table in a particular query. Because these hints are specified in a FROM clause, they are called *table-level hints*.

SQL Server Books Online lists other table-level hints in addition to locking hints, but the vast majority of them affect locking behavior. They should be used only when you absolutely need finer control over locking at the object level than what's provided by your session's isolation level. SQL Server locking hints can override the current transaction isolation level for the session. This section mentions only some of the locking hints that you might need to obtain the desired concurrency behavior.

Many locking hints work only in the context of a transaction. However, every *INSERT, UPDATE,* and *DELETE* statement is automatically in a transaction, so the only concern is when you use a locking hint with a *SELECT* statement. To get the benefit of most of the following hints when used in a *SELECT* query, you must use an explicit transaction, starting with *BEGIN TRAN* and terminating with either *COMMIT TRAN* or *ROLLBACK TRAN*. The lock hint syntax is as follows:

```
SELECT select_list
FROM object [WITH (locking hint)]

DELETE [FROM] object [WITH (locking hint)]
[WHERE <search conditions>]
```

```
UDPATE object [WITH (locking hint)
SET <set_clause>
[WHERE <search conditions>]

INSERT [INTO] object [WITH (locking hint)
<insert specification>
```

 Tip Not all the locking hints require the keyword *WITH,* but the syntax that doesn't use *WITH* will go away in the next version of SQL Server. You are recommended to specify all table-level hints by using *WITH.*

You can specify one of the following keywords for the locking hint:

- **HOLDLOCK**   This hint is equivalent to the SERIALIZABLE hint. Using this hint is similar to specifying *SET TRANSACTION ISOLATION LEVEL SERIALIZABLE,* except that the *SET* option affects all tables, not just the one specified in this hint.

- **UPDLOCK**   This hint forces SQL Server to take update locks instead of shared locks while reading the table and holds them until the end of the transaction. Taking update locks can be an important technique for eliminating conversion deadlocks.

- **TABLOCK**   This hint forces SQL Server to take a shared lock on the table, even if page locks would be taken otherwise. This hint is useful when you know you escalated to a table lock or if you need to get a complete snapshot of a table. You can use this hint with HOLDLOCK if you want the table lock held until the end of the transaction block to operate in Repeatable Read isolation. Using this hint with a *DELETE* statement on a heap enables SQL Server to deallocate the pages as the rows are deleted. (If row or page locks are obtained when deleting from a heap, space won't be deallocated and can't be reused by other objects.)

- **PAGLOCK**   This hint forces SQL Server to take shared page locks when a single shared table lock might otherwise be taken. To request an exclusive page lock, you must use the XLOCK hint with the PAGLOCK hint.

- **TABLOCKX**   This hint forces SQL Server to take an exclusive lock on the table that's held until the end of the transaction block. All exclusive locks are held until the end of a transaction, regardless of the isolation level in effect. This hint has the same effect as specifying both the TABLOCK and the XLOCK hints together.

- **ROWLOCK**   This hint specifies that a shared row lock should be taken when a single shared page or table lock is usually taken.

- **READUNCOMMITTED | REPEATABLEREAD | SERIALIZABLE**   These hints specify that SQL Server should use the same locking mechanisms as when the transaction isolation level is set to the level of the same name. However, the hint controls locking for a single table in a single statement, as opposed to locking all tables in all statements in a transaction.

Note The READUNCOMMITTED hint is probably the least useful because of the availability of row versioning. In fact, anytime you find yourself needing to use this hint, or the equivalent NOLOCK, consider whether you can actually afford the cost of one of the snapshot-based isolation levels.

- **READCOMMITTED** This hint specifies that *SELECT* operations comply with the rules for the Read Committed isolation level by using either locking or row versioning. If the database option *READ_COMMITTED_SNAPSHOT* is *OFF*, SQL Server uses shared locks and releases them as soon as the read operation is completed. If *READ_COMMITTED_SNAPSHOT* is *ON*, SQL Server doesn't acquire locks and uses row versioning.

- **READCOMMITTEDLOCK** This hint specifies that *SELECT* statements use the locking version of Read Committed isolation (the SQL Server default). No matter what the setting is for the database option *READ_COMMITTED_SNAPSHOT*, SQL Server acquires shared locks when it reads the data and releases those locks when the read operation is completed.

- **NOLOCK** This hint allows uncommitted, or dirty, reads. Shared locks aren't requested so that the statement doesn't block when reading data that's holding exclusive locks. In other words, no locking conflict is detected. This hint is equivalent to READUNCOMMITTED.

- **READPAST** This hint specifies that locked rows are skipped (read past). READPAST applies only to transactions operating at the READ COMMITTED isolation level and reads past row-level locks only.

- **XLOCK** This hint specifies that SQL Server take an exclusive lock that's held until the end of the transaction on all data processed by the statement. This lock can be specified with either PAGLOCK or TABLOCK, in which case the exclusive lock applies to the specified resource.

Setting a lock timeout

Setting a *LOCK_TIMEOUT* also lets you control SQL Server locking behavior. By default, SQL Server doesn't time out when waiting for a lock; it assumes optimistically that the lock will be released eventually. Most client programming interfaces allow you to set a general timeout limit for the connection, so a query is canceled by the client automatically if no response comes back after a specified amount of time. However, the message that comes back when the time period is exceeded does not indicate the cause of the cancellation; it could be because of a lock not being released, because of a slow network, or because of a long-running query.

Like other *SET* options, *SET LOCK_TIMEOUT* is valid only for your current connection. Its value is expressed in milliseconds and can be accessed by using the system function *@@LOCK_TIMEOUT*. This example sets the *LOCK_TIMEOUT* value to five seconds and then retrieves that value for display:

```
SET LOCK_TIMEOUT 5000;
SELECT @@LOCK_TIMEOUT;
```

If your connection exceeds the lock timeout value, you receive the following error message:

```
Server: Msg 1222, Level 16, State 50, Line 1
Lock request time out period exceeded.
```

Setting the *LOCK_TIMEOUT* value to 0 means that SQL Server doesn't wait for locks. It cancels the entire statement and goes on to the next one in the batch. (This isn't the same as the READPAST hint, which skips individual rows.) To set *LOCK_TIMEOUT* back to the default, meaning that SQL Server will wait indefinitely, you need to change the value to -1.

The following example illustrates the differences between using READPAST, using READUNCOM-MITTED, and setting *LOCK_TIMEOUT* to 0. All these techniques let you avoid blocking problems, but the behavior is slightly different in each case.

1. In a new query window, execute the following batch to lock one row in the *HumanResources. Department* table:

```
USE AdventureWorks2012;
BEGIN TRAN;
UPDATE HumanResources.Department
SET ModifiedDate = getdate()
WHERE DepartmentID = 1;
```

2. Open a second connection and execute the following statements:

```
USE AdventureWorks2012;
SET LOCK_TIMEOUT 0;
SELECT * FROM HumanResources.Department;
SELECT * FROM Sales.SalesPerson;
```

Notice that after error 1222 is received, the second *SELECT* statement is executed, returning all 17 rows from the *SalesPerson* table. The batch isn't cancelled when error 1222 is encountered.

> **Warning** Not only is a batch not cancelled when a lock timeout error is encountered but any active transaction isn't be rolled back. If you have two *UPDATE* statements in a transaction and both must succeed if either succeeds, a lock timeout for one of the *UPDATE* statements still allows the other statement to be processed. You must include error handling in your batch to take appropriate action in the event of an error 1222.

3. Open a third connection and execute the following statements:

```
USE AdventureWorks2012;
SELECT * FROM HumanResources.Department (READPAST);
SELECT * FROM Sales.SalesPerson;
```

SQL Server skips (reads past) only one row, and the remaining 15 rows of *Department* are returned, followed by all the *SalesPerson* rows. The READPAST hint is frequently used with a *TOP* clause, particular *TOP 1*, where your table is serving as a work queue. Your *SELECT* must get a row containing an order to be processed, but it really doesn't matter which row. So *SELECT TOP 1 * FROM <OrderTable>* returns the first unlocked row, and you can use that as the row to start processing.

4. Open a fourth connection and execute the following statements:

```
USE AdventureWorks2012;
SELECT * FROM HumanResources.Department (READUNCOMMITTED);
SELECT * FROM Sales.SalesPerson;
```

In this case, SQL Server doesn't skip anything. It reads all 16 rows from *Department,* but the row for *Department 1* shows the dirty data that you changed in step 1. This data hasn't yet been committed and is subject to being rolled back.

Conclusion

SQL Server lets you manage multiple users simultaneously and ensure that transactions observe the properties of the chosen isolation level. Locking guards data and the internal resources that enable a multiuser system to operate like a single-user system. You can choose to have your databases and applications use either optimistic or pessimistic concurrency control. With pessimistic concurrency, the locks acquired by data modification operations block users trying to retrieve data. With optimistic concurrency, the locks are ignored, and older committed versions of the data are read instead. In this chapter, we looked at the locking mechanisms in SQL Server, including full locking for data and leaf-level index pages and lightweight locking mechanisms for internally used resources. We also looked at the details of how optimistic concurrency avoids blocking on locks and still has access to data.

Understanding the issues of lock compatibility and escalation is important if you want to design and implement high-concurrency applications. You also need to understand the costs and benefits of the two concurrency models.

CHAPTER 14

DBCC internals

Paul Randal

When anyone mentions consistency checking a Microsoft SQL Server database, the first thing that comes to mind is "DBCC." In SQL Server 7.0, DBCC stood for Database Consistency Checker, but Microsoft changed the acronym's meaning in SQL Server 2000 to Database Console Command. This change indicated that the DBCC family had grown to do much more than just check consistency and was intended to help dispel the perception that SQL Server databases required regular consistency checking because SQL Server itself caused corruption.

This chapter gives you a short explanation of the DBCC commands used for shrinking a file or database, which are some of the most misunderstood and misused of the non-consistency–checking DBCC commands. It will also provide a much more in-depth explanation of DBCC CHECKDB and its derivative commands. This division of information reflects the relative importance of these two command families.

Shrinking files and databases

I am often misquoted as saying, "You should never shrink a database," when in fact I say, "You should never regularly perform a shrink operation." Because of the detrimental effects of performing a shrink operation, shrinking should be performed only when absolutely necessary. For example, shrinking might be required when

- A large amount of data has been removed from a database, the database won't be populated with replacement data, and the disk space is required for other uses.

- A transaction log file has grown uncontrollably and needs to be resized.

- A transaction log file has an excessive number of virtual log files and needs to be resized.

Performing a database shrink operation (or individual data or log file shrinks) can incur a significant performance overhead and create performance problems later. For example,

- Shrinking a data file requires a lot of I/O, CPU, and buffer pool resources, generates a lot of transaction log records, and generally results in index fragmentation because of the way the algorithm works.

- Shrinking a log file doesn't consume any significant resources. However, if the log is shrunk too small, it must grow again, which requires the new portion of the log to undergo zero initialization, which stalls logging activity.

- Backups can't be taken while a shrink operation is in progress.

Shrinking a database shrinks each data file—one at a time—and shrinks the log file(s).

With *DBCC SHRINKDATABASE*, the size to which each file should be shrunk is determined by the target percentage of free space for the database to have after the shrink operation completes. If no target percentage is specified, all files are shrunk as far as possible, with zero free space remaining.

With *DBCC SHRINKFILE*, the size to which the file should be shrunk is the target size specified. If no target size is specified, the file is shrunk as far as possible, with zero free space remaining.

Data file shrinking

Data file shrinking works as follows:

1. Scan the file backward, using the Global Allocation Map (GAM) and Page Free Space (PFS) pages to find the highest page number allocated in the file.

2. Obtain an Exclusive Lock on the page.

3. Move all the records on the page to the lowest available empty page in the file, taking into account the allocation unit of which the page is part.

4. Repeat steps 1 through 3 until one of the following occurs.

   - The shrink operation has created the required amount of free space and/or reached the required target size.

   - A page is encountered that can't be moved, in which case shrinking stops and an explanatory message is displayed.

   - The shrink operation is cancelled, in which case all work performed so far is preserved.

Page linkages in indexes and Index Allocation Map (IAM) chains must be maintained when index or IAM pages move. This means updating the pages pointed to in the *m_prevPage* and *m_nextPage* fields of the page header of the page being moved, plus the page in the next higher level in the index.

To update the page in the next higher level in the index, a scan of that level must be performed to find which page points down to the page being moved. This is because a SQL Server index structure has no upward links, only downward links.

If the root page of an index or the first page in an IAM chain is moved, the metadata entry in the sys.sysallocunits system table must also be updated.

For data, index, and text pages, the records are moved between the source and destination pages individually, and any locks held on them are migrated too——that is, the lock resource is changed to be on the destination page. For IAM pages, the page is moved in one go.

When a record is moved between pages, any other records that point to the record being moved must be updated accordingly.

- For heap data records, any nonclustered indexes must be updated with the new physical location of the record being moved.

- For text records, the parent in the text tree (either another text record or a complex in-row root column in a data or index record) must be updated to the new physical location of the record being moved.

- Again for heap data records, any forwarding record must be updated with the new physical location of the record being moved.

The first two cases in this list can lead to shrink taking a very long time because of the algorithms used. Shrink can also take a long time because in most circumstances it waits indefinitely for the required exclusive page lock.

When a heap data record is moved, all nonclustered index records that point to it must be updated. In SQL Server 2000 this was done by the storage engine and was very fast, but since SQL Server 2005, the storage engine must ask the query processor to perform the update, in batches of 100 heap data records.

When a text record is moved, no back link identifies the text record or column that points to it, so a costly table/index or text tree scan must be performed to find the pointer to the record being moved so it can be updated. A similar problem occurs inside *DBCC CHECKDB* if a repair is removing a text record.

When text pages are moved, they can be compacted to reclaim empty space (from deleted/ truncated LOB values) in extents from *ROW_OVERFLOW_DATA* or *LOB_DATA* allocation units. This functionality is also present in the ALTER INDEX ... REORGANIZE code, where it's optional.

Also, any ghost records that aren't locked by active transactions are removed, as long as they aren't required to be kept around for versioning (in which case, the page they are on can't be moved at all).

If during the shrink operation SQL Server comes across a page that can't be moved, it stops and displays a message explaining what happened. Examples of such pages are those with ghost records involved in versioning, those that comprise columnstore indexes, and those involved in an online index operation where the index—not the index key—contains a LOB column.

The two options *NOTRUNCATE* and *TRUNCATEONLY* that can be used with *DBCC SHRINKDATABASE* and *DBCC SHRINKFILE* apply only to data file shrink operations. The *NOTRUNCATE* option specifies that the data movement portion of the shrink operation should be performed, but the file size shouldn't be reduced. The *TRUNCATEONLY* option specifies that the file size should be reduced to the size (of the highest allocated extent) immediately, but no data movement should be performed.

Log file shrinking

A log file shrink is a very simple operation. Any virtual log files at the end of the log file that aren't marked active can be removed from the log file. The shrink operation removes as many as it can to get the log file to the desired size (or as close to it as it can).

To shrink the log file smaller than the current highest virtual log file, the log must be cleared. This means you must truncate the log, either by performing a log backup (in the Full or Bulk-Logged recovery modes) or by executing a checkpoint in the Simple recovery mode. If the log can be cleared and the first virtual log file isn't marked active, the log wraps to the physical start of the log file, making the first physical VLF the active VLF, and a subsequent shrink enables the log to be shrunk further. (The log might not be cleared for other reasons. Query the *log_reuse_wait_desc* field of sys.databases to find out why.) This clear-then-shrink process might have to be executed several times to allow the log to shrink as far as possible, and might be very hard to achieve on a busy production system.

Contrary to some popular misconceptions, log records aren't moved by the shrink operation to allow log file shrinking. In fact, log records are never moved (or removed) by any operations on the log, because that would change their log sequence number, rendering crash recovery impossible.

DBCC SHRINKFILE

The *DBCC SHRINKFILE* command simply runs the appropriate shrink algorithm for the specified file, depending on whether the file is a log file or a data file. The only way to shrink a database to be smaller than the size it was created is to use *DBCC SHRINKFILE* on the individual files, because *DBCC SHRINKDATABASE* can't shrink a database below its initial size.

The *DBCC SHRINKFILE* command has two common uses.

- Shrinking the transaction log (as described earlier) after an uncontrolled growth
- Emptying a data file before removing it, using the *EMPTYFILE* option

When a data file is being emptied, its allocation threshold is set to zero (so no concurrent allocations can be made from the file while the shrink operation is progressing), and all data from the file is moved to other files in the filegroup. The pages being moved from the file being emptied are inserted into the other files in the filegroup, using the regular round-robin and proportional-fill algorithms in the allocation system—that is, the shrink mechanism doesn't control which pages are moved to which files.

AUTO_SHRINK

SQL Server provides a way to automatically shrink databases at set intervals using the database option *AUTO_SHRINK*. When this option is enabled, a background task wakes every 30 minutes and attempts to shrink the database to have 25 percent free space.

You shouldn't enable this setting: Even *Books Online* specifically states that the setting shouldn't be enabled. Automatically shrinking a database will likely lead to a shrink-grow-shrink-grow cycle, which wastes resources and results in massive index fragmentation. Similarly, you shouldn't have any scheduled task to perform any kind of shrink operation. I tried to remove this functionality when I was responsible for both DBCC and later the entire storage engine but was prevented because its removal would break backward compatibility.

The shrink functionality in SQL Server does have its uses, but it should be used very sparingly— never in an automated, regular way like auto-shrink—and with full knowledge of the resources it will use and very high potential for performance-degrading index fragmentation to result.

Consistency checking

Although SQL Server itself doesn't cause database corruptions, I/O subsystems—all the software and hardware between the SQL Server buffer pool and the metal oxide of the disk drives or memory chips of the solid-state drives—do cause the overwhelmingly vast majority of corruptions. For this reason, the common wisdom is that performing regular consistency checking is prudent because all database servers have an I/O subsystem of some sort. The definition of *regular*, in this sense, really depends on the situation and how confident you are with the integrity of your I/O subsystem. In general, perform- ing a consistency check once a week would be acceptable. If resource constraints are an issue in your environment, consider restoring a backup of the database to a secondary server and running your consistency checks there.

Consistency checking is the process of examining the physical and logical structure of the database to ensure that no corruptions can prevent the storage engine from being able to process part of the database or could lead to some incorrect behavior. Some simple examples of corruptions are as follows.

- A persisted computed column where the persisted value has been corrupted such that it no longer matches the result of the computation

- A data page where the page ID in the page header is incorrect

- An index where the key order of records is incorrect

Consistency checks in SQL Server have evolved significantly since SQL Server 7.0, when they used to run offline (that is, table locks were required). SQL Server 2000 saw the advent of consistency checks being online by default, with a new, highly efficient mechanism for scanning the database. With SQL Server 2005, the consistency checking and repair code inside the storage engine was sig- nificantly rewritten and enhanced. This was done to cope with the many new SQL Server features and rewritten subsystems and to increase the performance, reliability, and functionality of the consistency checks and repairs themselves. Both SQL Server 2008 and SQL Server 2012 added new functionality and further tweaks for performance and scalability.

The most comprehensive way to perform consistency checks on a database is to use the *DBCC CHECKDB* command. The major steps of *DBCC CHECKDB* are as follows:

1. Create a transactionally consistent, static view of the database.

2. Perform low-level consistency checks of the critical system catalogs.

3. Perform allocation consistency checks of the database.

4. Perform consistency checks of each table in the database.

    As long as no problems were found in the previous steps, the following cross-table consistency checks are performed.

    • Consistency checks of Service Broker metadata

    • Consistency checks between various system catalogs

    • Consistency checks of indexed views

    • Consistency checks of XML indexes

    • Consistency checks of spatial indexes

5. Output results.

Repairs are carried out at various steps, if necessary, but only if the user specified a repair option.

The "Shrinking files and databases" section of this chapter explains how the internals of *DBCC CHECKDB* work in SQL Server 2012, based on the steps listed here. For each option that can be specified, the following sections describe how it affects the behavior of *DBCC CHECKDB*. Finally, you see how repair works and learn about the other DBCC consistency-checking commands.

Getting a consistent view of the database

A consistent view of the database is necessary, because *DBCC CHECKDB* must analyze all allocated pages in the database and check the various links between structures on multiple pages. This means that the pages being analyzed—that is, the whole database—can't change while the consistency checks are running; otherwise *DBCC CHECKDB* reports all kinds of incorrect results. Because *DBCC CHECKDB* can't read all the allocated pages in the database instantaneously, the consistent view of the database must be maintained for the duration of the consistency checks. For the database to be simply unchanged over a long period isn't enough; the consistent view of the database must also be transactionally consistent so that no uncompleted changes appear in the view that *DBCC CHECKDB* sees.

Consider a transaction to insert a record into a table that has a nonclustered index, with a hypothetical consistency-checking process running concurrently that doesn't enforce a consistent view of the database. The way the query processor works is to insert the table record first and then insert the matching nonclustered index record. Because this hypothetical consistency-checking process doesn't have a consistent view, it might read the record in the table but not that in the nonclustered index, leading to a report that the nonclustered index is out of sync with the table.

How can this happen? As you see later in this chapter, *DBCC CHECKDB* reads the database pages in a special order to enhance performance. Using this mechanism, and continuing this example, it might read the nonclustered index page before the nonclustered index record is inserted but read the table page *after* the table record is inserted. It might then conclude that a corruption exists, but in reality the problem is that it saw the partial results of an in-flight transaction.

SQL Server 7.0 obtained a transactionally consistent view by taking locks at various levels in the database. This was too detrimental to workload performance, so SQL Server 2000 introduced online consistency checking and removed the need for blocking locks to be held. *DBCC CHECKDB* analyzed the transaction log after scanning the database and essentially ran recovery on its internal view of the database, thus producing a transactionally consistent view of the database.

The SQL Server 2000 solution was too unwieldy for many reasons, however, so it was replaced in SQL Server 2005 with a database snapshot, and the mechanism is the same in SQL Server 2012. This means that *DBCC CHECKDB* uses regular storage engine functionality with greatly reduced complexity.

As described in Chapter 4, "Special databases," a database snapshot is extremely space-efficient, containing only the database pages that have changed since the database snapshot was created. A combination of the database snapshot contents and the unchanged pages in the database provide an unchanging, transactionally consistent view of the database. This is exactly what *DBCC CHECKDB* needs to run online. Creating a database snapshot and then running the consistency-checking algorithms on the database snapshot is conceptually just the same as running the consistency-checking algorithms on a read-only copy of the database.

DBCC CHECKDB creates a database snapshot that can't be accessed by users—it's essentially hidden. This hidden database snapshot is created in a slightly different way from regular database snapshots. A regular database snapshot has one snapshot file corresponding to each data file in the source database, and each file must be explicitly named when the database snapshot is created. Because *DBCC CHECKDB* doesn't allow any user input to specify the filenames for the hidden database snapshot, it creates an NTFS alternate stream for each existing source database data file. You can think of an alternate stream as a hidden file that can be accessed through the file system path that points at the user-visible file. This mechanism works well and is transparent to users.

> **Tip** Because of isolated problems in the past, third-party NTFS filter drivers for antivirus or disk defragmentation products haven't coped correctly with NTFS alternate streams, leading to incorrect reports of database corruption. If all your databases suddenly start exhibiting massive corruption problems, try creating your own database snapshot and consistency checking it to see if the corruptions disappear. If they do, a filter driver is causing the problem.

Disk space issues

Sometimes an issue arises when the hidden database snapshot runs out of space. Because it's implemented using alternate streams of the existing data files, the database snapshot consumes space from the same location as the existing data files. If the database being checked has a heavy update workload, more and more pages are pushed into the database snapshot, causing it to grow. In a situation where the volumes hosting the database don't have much space, this can mean the hidden database snapshot runs out of space and *DBCC CHECKDB* stops with an error. An example of this is shown here (the errors can vary depending on the exact point at which the database snapshot runs out of space):

```
DBCC CHECKDB ('SalesDB2') WITH NO_INFOMSGS, ALL_ERRORMSGS;
GO
Msg 1823, Level 16, State 1, Line 5
A database snapshot cannot be created because it failed to start.
Msg 1823, Level 16, State 2, Line 1
A database snapshot cannot be created because it failed to start.
Msg 7928, Level 16, State 1, Line 1
The database snapshot for online checks could not be created. Either the reason is given in
a previous error or one of the underlying volumes does not support sparse files or alternate
streams. Attempting to get exclusive access to run checks offline.
Msg 5128, Level 17, State 2, Line 1
Write to sparse file 'C:\SQLskills\SalesDBData.mdf:MSSQL_DBCC20' failed due to lack of disk
space.
Msg 3313, Level 21, State 2, Line 1
During redoing of a logged operation in database 'SalesDB2', an error occurred at log record ID
(1628:252:1). Typically, the specific failure is previously logged as an error in the Windows
Event Log service. Restore the database from a full backup, or repair the database.
Msg 0, Level 20, State 0, Line 0
A severe error occurred on the current command. The results, if any, should be discarded.
```

In this case, the solution is to create your own database snapshot, placing the snapshot files on a volume with more disk space, and then to run *DBCC CHECKDB* on that. *DBCC CHECKDB* recognizes that it's already running on a database snapshot and doesn't attempt to create another one. If a database snapshot was created by *DBCC CHECKDB*, it's discarded automatically after the consistency-checking algorithms are complete.

While it runs, *DBCC CHECKDB* creates a database snapshot (if needed) and suspends the FILESTREAM garbage collection process. You might notice garbage collection run at the start of the consistency checking process; the creation of the hidden database snapshot starts with a checkpoint, which is what triggers FILESTREAM garbage collection. The suspension of garbage collection activity allows the consistency-checking algorithms to see a transactionally consistent view of the FILESTREAM data on any FILESTREAM data containers, as explained in more detail later in this chapter.

Alternatives to using a database snapshot

A database snapshot isn't required under the following conditions.

- The specified database is a database snapshot itself.

- The specified database is read-only, in single-user mode, or in emergency mode.

- The server was started in single-user mode with the *–m* command-line option.

In these cases, the database is already essentially consistent because no other active connections can be making changes that would break the consistency checks.

A database snapshot can't be created under the following conditions.

- The specified database is stored on a non–NTFS file system, in which case a database snapshot can't be created because it relies on NTFS sparse-file technology.

- The specified database is *tempdb*, because a database snapshot can't be created on *tempdb*.

- The *TABLOCK* option was specified.

If a database snapshot can't be created for any reason, *DBCC CHECKDB* attempts to use locks to obtain a transactionally consistent view of the database. First, it obtains a database-level exclusive lock so that it can perform the allocation consistency checks without any changes taking place. Offline consistency checks can't be run on *master or* on *tempdb* because these databases can't be exclusively locked. This means that allocation consistency checks are always skipped for *tempdb* (as was usually the case with SQL Server 2000, too). This also isn't possible if the database is an Availability Group replica, in which case error 7934 is reported if the database snapshot creation fails.

Rather than wait for the exclusive lock indefinitely (or whatever the server lock timeout period has been set to), *DBCC CHECKDB* waits for 20 seconds (or the configured lock timeout value for the session) and then exits with the following error:

```
DBCC CHECKDB ('msdb') WITH TABLOCK;
GO
Msg 5030, Level 16, State 12, Line 1
The database could not be exclusively locked to perform the operation.
Msg 7926, Level 16, State 1, Line 1
Check statement aborted. The database could not be checked as a database snapshot could not be
created and the database or table could not be locked. See Books Online for details of when this
behavior is expected and what workarounds exist. Also see previous errors for more details.
```

If the lock was acquired after the allocation checks are completed, the exclusive lock is dropped and table-level share locks are acquired while the table-level logical consistency checks are performed. The same time-out applies to these table-level locks.

One way or another, *DBCC CHECKDB* obtains a transactionally consistent view of the database that it's checking. After that, it can start processing the database.

Processing the database efficiently

A database can be thought of as one giant, interconnected structure with all tables linked back to system catalogs, and all system catalogs linked back to the lowest-level allocation metadata stored in *sys.sysallocunits*, which in turn has its first page fixed at page (1:20) in every database (with the possible exception of master). With the addition of the fixed-location allocation bitmaps, such as Page Free Space (PFS) and Global Allocation Map (GAM) pages, the entire database can be represented as a single entity-relationship diagram.

With this thought in mind, you can envision a consistency-checking algorithm for this meta-structure that starts with page (1:16) and the allocation bitmaps and progressively expands into the database-checking linkages between objects and structures as it goes. Whenever a page linkage is found, the link is followed to ensure that the correct page is linked. Whenever an allocation bitmap has a page marked as, for example, an IAM page, that page is checked to ensure that it really is an IAM page. This would be a *depth-first* algorithm.

Consider a data page with three data records, with each data record containing a link to two 8,000-byte large object (LOB) columns stored off row. Using the previous algorithm, the sequence of operations to consistency check the page includes the following:

1. Extract the page ID containing the first LOB column data from record 1.

2. Read that page to ensure that it has the correct LOB column data on it.

3. Extract the page ID containing the second LOB column data from record 1.

4. Read that page to ensure that it has the correct LOB column data on it.

5. Repeat steps 1 through 4 as necessary until the whole structure is processed.

As you can see, the algorithm described here is very inefficient. Pages are read as needed and in essentially random order. Pages can be processed multiple times, and the random nature of the page reads means that the I/O subsystem can't be used for read-ahead. In terms of algorithmic complexity, the algorithm would be described as having complexity O($n2$,or), or "order n-squared." This means that the algorithm takes exponentially longer to run as the number of elements on which it operates increases. In this case, n is the number of pages in the database.

This isn't how *DBCC CHECKDB* works in SQL Server 2012 (in fact, since SQL Server 2000). An O($n2$) algorithm is prohibitively expensive to run on large databases. Instead, *DBCC CHECKDB* uses an algorithm with complexity O($n*\log(n)$), which provides near-linear algorithmic scaling. In practice, the implementation of the algorithm doesn't scale completely linearly, but SQL Server 2012 contains an enhancement that solves a major bottleneck that was present in prior versions when running on very large databases. The rest of this section describes the algorithm used.

Performing fact generation

DBCC CHECKDB reads all the pages from the objects being consistency-checked in the most efficient way possible—in allocation order (that is, in the order they are stored in the data files) instead of by following page links and reading them in essentially random order. The mechanism for this is described later in this section.

Because the pages are read in strict allocation order as much as possible, validating all the relationships between pages immediately is impossible while they are being processed. Therefore, *DBCC CHECKDB* must remember what it knows about each page so that it can perform the relationship checking at a later stage. It does this by generating bits of information about a page called *facts*.

Continuing the previous example, as part of processing the data page, the following facts are generated. These facts are known as *parent text* facts.

- Two facts that the first record links to a LOB value (one fact for each LOB value). Each fact contains the following:

  - The page ID and slot ID—that is, the record number—of the data record

  - The page ID and slot ID where the LOB value should be stored, extracted from the text root stored in the data record

  - The text timestamp of the LOB value—that is, a unique ID that is assigned to that LOB value

  - The object ID, index ID, partition ID, and allocation unit ID of which the page is part

- Two facts that the second record links to a LOB value

- Two facts that the third record links to a LOB value

When each text page containing the actual LOB values is processed, part of the processing generates a fact that the LOB value was encountered. These facts are known as *actual text* facts. Each fact contains the following.

- The page ID and slot ID of the text record

- The text timestamp of the LOB value

- The object ID, index ID, partition ID, and allocation unit ID of which the page is part

At some later point in time, the facts are checked against each other (a process known as *aggregation*). As long as each LOB value has a matching parent text fact and actual text fact, *DBCC CHECKDB* recognizes that that particular LOB value linkage is free of corruption.

One more type of fact, apart from actual and parent facts, is known as a *sibling* fact. These are used when checking index B-tree linkages and describe the linked list that exists at each level of an index B-tree.

The consistency-checking algorithms for the different parts of the database structure use a variety of fact types and fact contents, but the basic algorithm is the same. The following fact types are used.

- Facts to gather allocation statistics about objects, indexes, partitions, and allocation units

- Facts to track FILESTREAM data

- Facts to track IAM chain linkages

- Facts to track IAM page bitmaps for a particular GAM interval

- Facts to track database files

- Facts to track extent allocations and ownership

- Facts to track page allocations and ownership

- Facts to track B-tree linkages

- Facts to track LOB value linkages

- Facts to track forwarding/forwarded records in heaps

Between generation and aggregation, the facts are stored in the query processor in memory used for a sort operation. Sometimes the size of the sort is larger than the memory available to the query processor; as a result, the sort "spills" to disk (into the *tempdb* database), thus generating (possibly significant) physical reads and writes in *tempdb*. Because each fact is essentially a table row, the fact must be split into table columns. Each fact is composed of five columns.

- ***ROWSET_COLUMN_FACT_KEY*** The page ID of a page that the fact describes, or the Log Sequence Number (LSN) of a FILESTREAM file

- ***ROWSET_COLUMN_FACT_TYPE*** The fact type

- ***ROWSET_COLUMN_SLOT_ID*** The slot ID of the record the fact describes, if any

- ***ROWSET_COLUMN_COMBINED_ID*** The object, index, partition, and allocation unit IDs of which the page is part

- ***ROWSET_COLUMN_FACT_BLOB*** A variable-length column to store any extra data required

If *tempdb* doesn't have enough space to store the DBCC sort, *DBCC CHECKDB* might fail. If this happens, error 8921 is reported, as shown here:

```
Msg 8921, Level 16, State 1, Line 1
Check terminated. A failure was detected while collecting facts. Possibly tempdb out of space or
a system table is inconsistent. Check previous errors.
```

Using the query processor

DBCC CHECKDB makes extensive use of the query processor to allow easy handling of the facts and to parallelize the consistency-checking process easily. The algorithm used to generate facts is as follows:

1. The DBCC code issues a query (using syntax available only within SQL Server) to the query processor, containing a pointer to a rowset and the name of a custom aggregation function.

2. The query processor queries the rowset for a row, essentially calling back into DBCC to get a fact to process.

3. DBCC sends back a single fact as a rowset row, using the column structure described earlier. If no facts are available, DBCC reads a page and processes it entirely, generating all necessary facts. The facts are stored in thread-local memory as a first-in-first-out (FIFO) queue, and a single fact is sent back to the query processor. One fact is returned from the head of the thread-local fact queue with each subsequent request from the query processor until no more facts are available. Only at that point is another page read and processed to generate facts, repopulating the fact queue.

4. The query processor stores the fact internally in sort memory and possibly also in the *tempdb* database.

After all the facts are generated for the objects being consistency-checked, the query processor completes the sort operation on them and then calls the custom aggregation function that DBCC supplied. The facts are sorted by the fact key and grouped by all columns except the type, so that the aggregation routine gets the facts in the correct order to allow successive facts to be matched easily.

Continuing the previous LOB linkage example, the facts are passed back to the aggregation routine in the following order. If the facts aren't in that order, matching facts without again remembering what had already been seen would be impossible.

- Actual text fact for a LOB value—really, LOB value 1 from record 1 on the data page

- Parent text fact for LOB value 1 in record 1 on the data page

- Actual text fact for a LOB value—really, LOB value 2 in record 1 on the data page

- Parent text fact for LOB value 2 in record 1 on the data page

The aggregation algorithm runs as follows:

1. The query processor calls the DBCC custom aggregation function with a single fact.

2. Facts are merged until a fact is passed from the query processor that doesn't match the facts being merged. For example, the actual and parent facts for LOB value 1 in the previous example are merged. The next fact is for LOB value 2, which is for a different part of the database structure.

3. When a mismatched fact is encountered, the merged set of facts is aggregated to determine whether any errors are present. Aggregation means that the facts are checked to see whether the right facts exist for the piece of database structure that they describe. For example, a LOB value must have an actual fact (that the value was actually encountered) and a parent fact (that some index or data record links to the LOB value).

4. If errors are present, an entry is made in the list of errors. The entry is generated using the information contained in the aggregated set of facts. Example errors are a LOB value that doesn't have a data or index record pointing to it.

5. The facts are discarded, and a new set of merged facts begins, starting with the mismatched fact that triggered aggregation.

6. The DBCC code signals to the query processor that it's ready to accept the next fact to merge and aggregate.

Figure 14-1 shows how the query processor and DBCC code interact while *DBCC CHECKDB* is executing.

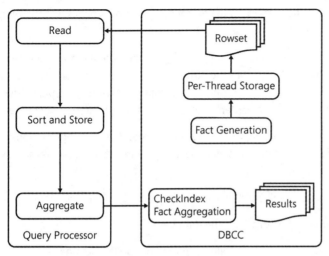

FIGURE 14-1 Interaction between the query processor and DBCC.

These algorithms are started by *DBCC CHECKDB* internally executing the following query:

```
DECLARE @BlobEater VARBINARY(8000);
SELECT @BlobEater = CheckIndex(ROWSET_COLUMN_FACT_BLOB)
FROM <memory address of fact rowset>
GROUP BY ROWSET_COLUMN_FACT_KEY
>> WITH ORDER BY
     ROWSET_COLUMN_FACT_KEY,
     ROWSET_COLUMN_SLOT_ID,
     ROWSET_COLUMN_COMBINED_ID,
     ROWSET_COLUMN_FACT_BLOB
OPTION(ORDER GROUP);
```

This query brings the query processor and the *DBCC CHECKDB* code together to perform the fact-generation, fact-sorting, fact-storing, and fact-aggregation algorithms. The parts of the query are as follows:

- **@BlobEater** This dummy variable serves no purpose other than to consume any output from the *CheckIndex* function (you should never have any, but the syntax requires it).

- **CheckIndex (ROWSET_COLUMN_FACT_BLOB)** The query processor calls this custom aggregation function inside *DBCC CHECKDB* with sorted and grouped facts as part of the overall fact aggregation algorithm.

- **<memory address of fact rowset>** *DBCC CHECKDB* provides this memory address of the OLEDB rowset to the query processor. The query processor queries this rowset for rows (containing the generated facts) as part of the overall fact generation algorithm.

- **GROUP BY ROWSET_COLUMN_FACT_KEY** This triggers the aggregation in the query processor.

- **>> WITH ORDER BY <column list>** This internal-only syntax provides ordered aggregation to the aggregation step. As explained earlier, the *DBCC CHECKDB* aggregation code is based on the assumption that the order of the aggregated stream of facts from the query processor is forced—that is, it requires that the sort order of the keys within each group is the order of the four keys in the query.

- **OPTION(ORDER GROUP)** This Query Optimizer hint forces stream aggregation. It forces the Query Optimizer to sort on the grouping columns and avoid hash aggregation.

This mechanism is used for the allocation consistency-checking and per-table consistency-checking phases of *DBCC CHECKDB*. By extension, this means that the same mechanism is also used by the *DBCC CHECKALLOC*, *DBCC CHECKTABLE*, and *DBCC CHECKFILEGROUP* commands.

If the internal query fails because of a memory shortage, error 8902 is reported. If the internal query fails for any other reason, generic error 8975 is reported. In either case, *DBCC CHECKDB* terminates.

> **Note** This mechanism uses the OLEDB protocol to communicate between the query processor and the *DBCC CHECKDB* part of the storage engine. This can lead to the OLEDB wait type appearing during wait statistics analysis. Another cause of this wait type can be third-party monitoring tools executing DMV queries, some of which also use the OLEDB protocol internally.

Processing batches

During the per-table logical checks phase, *DBCC CHECKDB* usually doesn't process all tables in the database together, nor does it usually process only a single table at a time. It groups tables into *batches* and runs the fact generation and aggregation algorithms on all tables in that batch. After all batches are processed, all tables in the database have been consistency checked.

DBCC CHECKDB breaks the database into a series of batches to limit the amount of space required in *tempdb* for fact storage. Each fact that's generated requires a certain amount of space, depending on the type of fact and its content. A more complex table schema requires more facts to be generated to allow all the aspects of the table's schema to be consistency-checked.

As you can imagine, for a very large database, the amount of space required to store all these facts very quickly exceeds the storage available in *tempdb* if all the tables in the database are consistency-checked in one batch.

The set of tables in a batch is determined while *DBCC CHECKDB* is scanning the metadata about tables at the start of the per-table logical checks phase. Batches always have at least one table, plus all its nonclustered indexes, and the size of each batch is limited by one of the following rules:

- If any repair option is specified, building the batch stops when it contains a single table. This is to guarantee that repairs are ordered correctly.

- When a table is added to a batch and the total number of indexes for all tables in the batch exceeds 512, building the batch stops.

- When a table is added to a batch and the total, worst-case estimation for how much *tempdb* space is required for all facts for all tables in the batch exceeds 32 MB, building the batch stops.

After a batch is built, the fact-generation and fact-aggregation algorithms are run on all the tables in the batch. This means that the internal query described earlier is issued once for each batch of tables.

Because of scalability enhancements in the *DBCC CHECKDB* code that were made during 2011, SQL Server 2012 contains a trace flag, 2562, that removes the batching mechanism and does the entire check in a single batch. This results in better performance on very large databases but has a side effect of increasing the tempdb usage from fact generation. This trace flag is described in the Knowledge Base article at *http://support.microsoft.com/kb/2634571*.

When a batch completes, various deep-dive algorithms can be triggered to find unmatched text timestamp values or unmatched nonclustered index records. At this point, unchecked assemblies can also be cleared.

If a table depends on a Common Language Runtime (CLR) assembly for the implementation of a CLR user-defined data type (UDT) or computed column and the assembly is subsequently changed using *ALTER ASSEMBLY* with the *WITH UNCHECKED DATA* option, all tables dependent on the assembly are marked as having unchecked assemblies in the system catalogs. The only mechanism to clear this setting is to run DBCC consistency checks against the affected tables. If no errors are found, the unchecked assembly setting is cleared.

Reading the pages to process

Part of the performance of the fact-generation and fact-aggregation algorithms comes from pages that comprise the tables and indexes in the batch being read very efficiently. As explained earlier, the pages don't have to be read in any specific order, because the facts are aggregated after all relevant pages are read (and all facts generated).

The fastest way to read a set of pages from a data file is to read them in *allocation order*, the physical order of the pages in the data files. This allows the disk heads to make one conceptual sweep across the disk rather than do all random I/Os and incurring excessive disk head seek time overhead.

The pages and extents that comprise each table and index in the batch are tracked by the IAM chains for the various allocation units in the table or index. When the batch is built, all these IAM chains are merged into a large bitmap that's managed by a scanning object inside *DBCC CHECKDB* known as the *MultiObjectScanner*. This bitmap then represents all the pages and extents in *sorted physical order* that comprise all the tables and indexes in the batch.

With this bitmap, all the necessary pages can be read (nearly) sequentially. The scanning object performs read-ahead on the pages to ensure that the CPU(s) never have to wait for the next page to process to be read into the buffer pool. The read-ahead mechanism is similar to that used in the rest of the storage engine, except that it's done round-robin among the physical volumes on which the logical data files are created. This is done to try to spread the I/O workload across the physical volumes because *DBCC CHECKDB* performs such a large amount of I/O.

Whenever the next page is required for processing, a call is made into the scanning object, which then returns multiple pages to the caller. The type of pages returned, or the object/index that the pages are part of, is completely irrelevant because of the nature of the fact generation and aggregation algorithms.

The scanning object was used to return a single page to the calling thread each time, but this was found to be inefficient during the 2011 scalability investigation mentioned earlier. The *DBCC_MULTIOBJECT_SCANNER* latch, which governs access to the scanning object, was found to be a contention point for parallel consistency checks, so the scanning object now returns multiple pages to each caller in SQL Server 2012.

This fix is also available in the latest updates to SQL Server 2008 and SQL Server 2008 R2 using trace flag 2562, as documented in the Knowledge Base article at *http://support.microsoft.com/kb/2634571*. That same article also describes trace flag 2549, which can produce some performance enhancements if each database data file is placed on a unique physical device.

 Note Sometimes random I/Os are necessary because some rows on the pages being read can have a portion of the row stored on a different (text) page because of the row-overflow feature. *DBCC CHECKDB* materializes an entire row in memory (except off-row LOB columns), which can involve a random I/O to read the row-overflow portion of the row.

Enablilng parallelism

DBCC CHECKDB can run using multiple processor cores in parallel to make more efficient use of system resources and process the database faster. It can run the current batch in parallel if all the following conditions are true.

- The SQL Server instance is Enterprise, Enterprise Eval, or Developer.

- More than 64 pages comprise all the tables and indexes in the current batch.

- The tables in the batch have no T-SQL-based or CLR-based computed columns.

- Parallelism hasn't been explicitly disabled with trace flag 2528.

If all these conditions are true, *DBCC CHECKDB* signals the query processor that it can be parallelized when it issues the internal query described earlier. The query processor then makes the final determination whether to use parallel threads. The query processor makes this determination based on the same factors that affect the parallelization of all other queries in SQL Server, such as the following.

- The instance's *MAXDOP* setting or the Resource Governor workload group *MAX_DOP* setting, if appropriate

- The projected query cost for parallelism

- The availability of resources on the server at the time the *DBCC CHECKDB* query for the batch is compiled for execution

The determination of whether to parallelize the internal query is performed each time the query is issued, which means that different batches in a single execution of *DBCC CHECKDB* might run with different degrees of parallelism.

Figure 14-2 shows the conceptual flow of data when the internal query runs in parallel. This diagram illustrates the data flow when the degree of parallelism is 3.

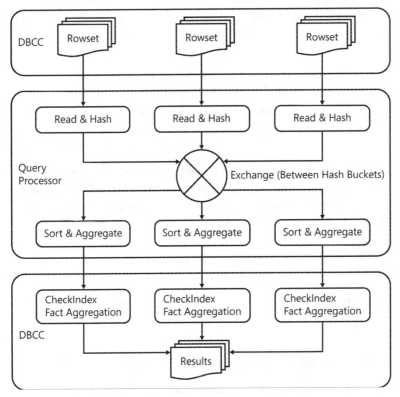

FIGURE 14-2 Conceptual data flow for the internal query with degree of parallelism = 3.

When the internal query runs in parallel, one thread is created for each degree of parallelism. During the fact-generation portion of the algorithm, each thread is responsible for requesting pages to process from the scanning object and completely processing each page. A page is processed only by a single thread. During the fact-aggregation portion of the algorithm, each thread is responsible for aggregating a separate, self-contained stream of facts, meaning that all pertinent facts for a particular part of an object's structure must be presented to that one thread. Cross-thread fact aggregation doesn't occur.

SQL Server has no control over which thread processes which page, so the pages comprising a single object might be processed by multiple threads. This could lead to problems during the fact-aggregation phase if facts that really should aggregate together are actually contained in the sorted and aggregated fact streams for a different thread. For this reason, when the internal query is parallelized, all facts are hashed by their *ROWSET_COLUMN_FACT_KEY* elements and then passed through an exchange operator into per-thread hash buckets before being sorted. This guarantees that all the facts for a particular part of an object's structure are presented to just one thread.

 Note The *DBCC CHECKTABLE* and *DBCC CHECKFILEGROUP* commands also can use parallelism in this way. *DBCC CHECKALLOC* can't run in parallel, however.

You can disable parallelism for all these DBCC commands by using trace flag 2528, if you determine that the parallelized command places too heavy a workload on the server. Note that disabling parallelism makes the DBCC command take more time to complete.

To allow efficient parallelism and scalability without artificial bottlenecks, all parts of the *DBCC CHECKDB* internals that are multithreading-aware—for example, the scanning object and the progress reporting object—are designed such that access to them from multiple threads don't cause scalability issues up to at least parallelizing across 32 processor cores.

Performing primitive system catalog consistency checks

The storage engine in SQL Server 2012 defines three of the system catalogs as being critical to its operations: *sys.sysallocunits*, *sys.sysrowsets*, and *sys.sysrscols*. SQL Server 2005 provided two more critical system tables—*sys.syshobts* and *sys.syshobtcolumns*—but these were folded into the *sys.sysrowsets* and *sys.sysrscols* tables, respectively, in SQL Server 2008. Collectively, these are the equivalent of the old *sysindexes, sysobjects,* and *syscolumns* tables. They hold all the base metadata that the storage engine needs to navigate around the table and index structures. *DBCC CHECKDB* also uses them for this purpose, although indirectly through the metadata subsystem in the Relational Engine.

These system catalogs each have a clustered index, and sys.sysallocunits also has a nonclustered index. *DBCC CHECKDB* needs to check that the clustered index leaf levels don't have obvious corruptions so that when it calls a metadata function to retrieve some information from one of them, the metadata function has a good chance of success.

The following checks are performed on the leaf level of these three clustered indexes.

- **Each page is read into the buffer pool.** This checks that the page has no I/O problems, such as a page checksum failure, invalid page ID, or plain failure of the I/O subsystem to read the page. Any pages that fail this operation report error 7985.

- **Each page is audited.** Page auditing (explained later in this chapter), generally makes sure that the page structure and page header look valid. The page must be a data page and must be allocated to the correct allocation unit. Any page that fails this check reports error 7984.

- **The leaf-level linked-list is checked.** All pages at a level in an index are in a double-linked-list. After all pages for the leaf level are read into the buffer pool and audited, the linkage of the pages are checked by following the next-page links through the leaf level and making sure that the previous-page link really does point to the previous page. Error 7986 or 7987 is reported if the linked-list is broken.

- **The leaf-level linked-list is checked for loops.** This is done while the linked-list linkages are checked by having two pointers into the page-linked list: one that advances at every step and one that advances at every second step. If they ever point to the same page before the faster-advancing pointer reaches the right-hand side of the leaf level, a loop results. Linkage loops can turn a range scan into an infinite loop (although I've never seen this occur on a customer system). Error 7988 is reported if a loop is detected.

If any of these checks fail, *DBCC CHECKDB* terminates with an appropriate message, such as the one here:

```
DBCC CHECKDB ('TestDB') WITH NO_INFOMSGS, ALL_ERRORMSGS;
GO
Msg 7985, Level 16, State 2, Line 1
System table pre-checks: Object ID 7. Could not read and latch page (1:20) with latch type SH.
Check statement terminated due to unrepairable error.
DBCC results for 'TestDB'.
Msg 5233, Level 16, State 98, Line 1
Table error: alloc unit ID458752, page (1:20). The test (IS_OFF (BUF_IOERR, pBUF->bstat))
failed. The values are 2057 and -4.
CHECKDB found 0 allocation errors and 1 consistency errors not associated with any single
object.
CHECKDB found 0 allocation errors and 1 consistency errors in database 'TestDB'.
```

It terminates because these critical system catalogs are necessary for *DBCC CHECKDB* to check the rest of the database. Note that the *DBCC CHECKDB* output lists no recommended repair level. These errors can't be repaired; the only option is to restore from your backups. If no problems are found, the next stage is to run database-level allocation consistency checks.

Performing allocation consistency checks

These checks verify the contents of and relationships between the various structures that track page and extent allocations in the database. The following structures are involved.

- PFS pages, which track the allocation status of individual pages within a 64 MB section of a data file (a PFS interval)

- GAM pages, which track the allocation status of all extents within a 4 GB section of a data file (a GAM interval)

- Shared Global Allocation Map (SGAM) pages, which track all mixed extents that have at least one page available for allocation with a GAM interval

- IAM pages, which track all pages and extents allocated to an allocation unit from a GAM interval

- IAM chains, which are a linked list of all IAM pages for an allocation unit (and hence track all pages and extents allocated to the allocation unit from all sections of all data files)

- The storage engine metadata in the three critical system tables, as described previously

The allocation consistency checks are very fast—in fact, magnitudes faster than the per-table and cross-table consistency checks. This is because the number of database pages that must be read to perform the allocation consistency checks is much smaller than the number that must be read to perform all the per-table and cross-table consistency checks.

Collecting allocation facts

Before any allocation consistency checks can be run, all the necessary information needs to be collected from the various allocation structures and stored as facts.

For each data file in each online filegroup in the database, the following actions are performed.

- The boot page—page (1:9) in file 1 of the database—and the file header page (page 0) in each data file are audited. Error 5250 is reported if this check fails and *DBCC CHECKDB* terminates. An 824 or 823 error also can possibly be thrown, which disconnects the connection to SQL Server.

- All PFS pages are read and processed. This provides a bitmap of all the IAM pages in the file, because the PFS page also tracks which pages are IAM pages. This also provides a bitmap of which pages in the file are from mixed extents. Each set of bitmaps collectively takes less space than all the PFS pages in the file because a PFS page stores 8 bits of information for each data file page.

- All GAM pages are read and processed. This provides a bitmap of all the allocated extents in the file.

- All SGAM pages are read and processed. This provides a bitmap of all mixed extents in the file that have at least one available page.

- The Differential Changed Map (DCM) pages and Minimally Logged Map (ML Map) pages are read while the GAM extent is being processed, just to ensure that they can be read correctly.

   At the start of every GAM interval is a special extent called the GAM extent, which contains the GAM and SGAM pages for that GAM interval. It also contains two other pages that track extents in that GAM interval—the DCM and the ML Map pages. The DCM pages track which extents were changed in the GAM interval since the last full database backup. The ML Map pages track which extents were changed in the GAM interval by minimally logged operations since the last transaction log backup.

- All IAM pages are read and processed to provide

   - A list of all the mixed pages in the file (pages allocated from mixed extents), and by derivation, a list of all mixed extents in the file. Remember that the first IAM page in an IAM chain contains an array—the single-page slot array—to hold up to eight mixed pages for the allocation unit it represents.

- A list of all the valid IAM pages in the file. This is necessary because a PFS page might be corrupt and mistakenly have a page marked as an IAM page, or a real IAM page might just be corrupt and unreadable.

- A list of all the allocated dedicated extents in the file.

- Linkage information for all IAM chains.

  All IAM pages in an IAM chain are linked in a doubly linked list. They also contain a sequence number, starting at 0 for the first IAM page in the chain and increasing by 1 for each IAM page added to the chain.

If any allocation page can't be read because its header is corrupt, error 8946 is reported (or error 7965 for a corrupt IAM page). This means that a large range of the database is excluded from the consistency checks. The excluded range is reported in error 8998.

After all the per-file information gathering, the storage engine metadata is processed as follows:

1. The page ID of the first IAM page of each IAM chain is stored in the system catalogs. If it wasn't stored somewhere, the storage engine wouldn't know where to find the list of pages and extents allocated to a table or index.

   These page IDs are used to generate the parent facts for the first IAM page in each IAM chain. This should match up with an actual fact generated during the per-file steps.

   During this phase, all system catalogs are checked to make sure that they are stored in the primary filegroup of the database. Error 8995 is reported if any are not.

2. Information about IAM chains currently waiting to be "deferred-dropped" is stored in an internal queue.

   Deferred-drop is an optimization introduced in SQL Server 2005 that prevents a transaction from running out of lock memory while dropping an IAM chain. It's the process by which an IAM chain with more than 128 extents is dropped, either by dropping and rebuilding an index or dropping and truncating a table. It doesn't have its actual pages and extents deallocated until after the transaction commits. The IAM chain is unhooked from *sys.sysallocunits*, though, and hooked into an internal queue.

   If *DBCC CHECKDB* didn't scan the internal queue as part of the allocation fact generation process, it might see all kinds of inconsistencies with the various allocation bitmaps.

The allocation facts are passed to the query processor, as described earlier, where they are sorted and grouped together. They are then passed back to *DBCC CHECKDB* so that they can be aggregated and any errors found.

Checking allocation facts

The allocation fact-aggregation algorithms perform the following consistency checks.

- Check that each extent in each GAM interval is allocated correctly. The possibilities here are that the extent should be

  - Marked in the GAM page as available for allocation.

  - Marked in the SGAM page as a non-full mixed extent.

  - Marked in exactly one of the IAM pages that cover the GAM interval.

  - Not marked in any of the allocation bitmaps, in which all pages in the extent must be mixed pages, referenced in various IAM pages' single-page slot arrays.

  Table 14-1 lists the possible combinations, with illegal states shown along with the resulting error number.

TABLE 14-1 Possible combinations of allocation bitmaps

GAM	SGAM	IAM	Legal	Meaning	Error
0	0	0	Y	Mixed extent with all pages allocated	N/A
0	0	1	Y	Dedicated extent allocated to an IAM	N/A
0	1	0	Y	Mixed extent with available pages	N/A
0	1	1	N	Illegal	8904
1	0	0	Y	Extent isn't allocated	N/A
1	0	1	N	Illegal	8904
1	1	0	N	Illegal	8903
1	1	1	N	Illegal	8904

  If two IAM pages have the same extent allocated, error 8904 is reported. Error 8904 is always accompanied by error 8913, which lists the second object (or allocation bitmap) that has the extent allocated. If an extent is a mixed extent but none of the mixed pages is seen, error 8905 is reported.

- Check that the PFS byte for each mixed and IAM page is correct. Error 8948 is reported for all pages that fail this check.

- Check that each page marked by a PFS page as being a mixed page appears somewhere in a single-page slot array on an IAM page. Error 8906 is reported for any pages that fail this check:

```
Msg 8906, Level 16, State 1, Line 1
Page (1:50139) in database ID 13 is allocated in the SGAM (1:3) and PFS (1:48528), but
was not allocated in any IAM. PFS flags 'MIXED_EXT ALLOCATED 0_PCT_FULL'.
```

- Check that each mixed page is allocated only in a single IAM page's single-page slot array. Error 8910 is reported for any doubly allocated pages.

- Check that the IAM pages in an IAM chain have monotonically increasing sequence numbers. Error 2577 is reported if this check fails.

- Check that no two IAM pages within the same IAM chain map the same GAM interval. Error 8947 is reported when this check fails.

- Check that all IAM pages within an IAM chain belong to the same allocation unit. Error 8959 is reported if this check fails.

- Check that IAM pages map valid portions of data files (for example, not in file ID 0 or 2). Error 8968 is reported if this check fails.

- Check that the linked list between IAM pages within an IAM chain is correct, including the pointer from the *sys.sysallocunits* catalog to the first IAM page in the IAM chain. Error 8969, 2575, or 2576 is reported if this check fails, depending on which linkage is broken:

```
Msg 2576, Level 16, State 1, Line 1
The Index Allocation Map (IAM) page (0:0) is pointed to by the previous pointer of IAM
page (1:79969) in object ID 0, index ID -1, partition ID 0, alloc unit ID 107504789946368
(type Unknown), but it was not detected in the scan.
```

- Check that an IAM page maps a GAM interval somewhere in the same filegroup as itself. Error 8996 is reported for any pages that fail this check.

- Check that all IAM, GAM, and SGAM pages that map the final GAM interval in a file don't have extents marked as allocated that are beyond the physical end of the file. Error 2579 is reported if this check fails.

When the allocation consistency checks are complete (and any repairs performed if a repair option was specified), the foundation has been laid for the logical consistency checks, discussed next.

Performing per-table logical consistency checks

These checks verify the consistency for all structures in a table and all its indexes. When this section uses the term "a table," it means "all partitions of the heap or clustered index, all partitions of all nonclustered and columnstore indexes, and any off-row LOB data." The table could be a regular table, an indexed view, an XML index, a system catalog, a spatial index, a Service Broker queue, or any other database object that's stored internally as a table.

All tables within a single batch are checked at the same time, using the fact-generation and fact-aggregation algorithms described earlier. The first batch contains the critical system tables, and subsequent batches are built and checked until all tables in the database are checked.

The consistency checks performed for each table follow this order:

1. Extract and check all metadata for the table.

2. For each page in the table, do the following:

    - Read and audit the page.

- Perform page-level consistency checks.

- Perform record-level consistency checks for all records on the page.

- For data and index records, perform column-level consistency checks on each column in each record.

3. Perform cross-page consistency checks as follows:

- Nonclustered index cross-checks

- B-tree consistency checks

- Off-row LOB data consistency checks

- FILESTREAM consistency checks

The remainder of this section explains each step in detail.

Metadata Consistency Checks

DBCC CHECKDB builds an internal cache of most of the metadata that describes each table. This metadata cache is used extensively during the various consistency checks, and for *DBCC CHECKDB* to access its own cache is much faster than to call continually into the metadata subsystem of the storage engine.

The metadata cache has the following hierarchy of information.

- **The Table metadata object**   holds the metadata describing a table and a linked list of index metadata objects.

- **The Index metadata object**   holds the metadata describing each index of a table, including the heap or clustered index, and a linked list of rowset metadata objects.

- **The Rowset metadata object**   holds the metadata describing each partition of each index.

Listing everything that the metadata cache tracks isn't necessary. Instead, you'll see some of the more interesting items that are tracked in each metadata object.

The table metadata cache object includes

- The page and record counts for use in the informational messages in the default output of *DBCC CHECKDB*.

- The count of errors found for the table.

- An expression evaluator that's used to calculate the expected values of persisted and indexed computed columns. This is obtained from the query processor and is necessary to be able to recalculate the value of computed columns to check their correctness.

- Status information, including whether the table has been found to contain an error.

If the CLR has been disabled, the expression evaluator can't be created and error 2518 is reported. If the CLR is enabled but a problem occurs while initializing the expression evaluator, error 2519 is reported. In either case, computed columns and UDTs aren't checked.

The index metadata cache object includes

- All metadata concerning any partitioning function that's used for the index, so each record can be checked to ensure that it's in the correct partition.

- Status information, including whether the index has been found to contain an error. For a nonclustered index, if an error has been found, the nonclustered index cross-checks aren't performed.

If the index being considered is on a filegroup other than that specified for *DBCC CHECKFILEGROUP*, it's not included in the checks and error 2594 is reported.

The rowset metadata cache object, the most extensive of the cache objects, includes various column and key counts as well as metadata to aid in FILESTREAM consistency checks.

If a table or index has a rowset (that is, a partition of an index or table) that resides on an offline or invalid filegroup, the table or index isn't included in the checks. For an offline filegroup, error 2527 is reported. For an invalid filegroup, error 2522 is reported.

As the rowset metadata cache objects are being constructed, the system catalog page counts for each allocation unit are tested to ensure that they aren't negative. This condition could occur in versions of SQL Server prior to SQL Server 2005. If a negative count is found, error 2508 is output:

```
Msg 2508, Level 16, State 3, Line 1
The In-row data RSVD page count for object "Receipts", index ID 0, partition ID 49648614572032,
alloc unit ID 49648614572032 (type In-row data) is incorrect. Run DBCC UPDATEUSAGE.
```

Also, a separate hash table includes every allocation unit ID present in the table with a link to the relevant rowset metadata cache object. This provides a very fast way to find the metadata describing a particular page (because each page has only an allocation unit ID in the page header), rather than have to do a costly search through the metadata cache.

If a specific index was requested to be consistency-checked but the index couldn't be found in the database metadata, error 2591 is reported.

As this cache is built, it's checked for consistency. If any errors are discovered (such as mismatches between the various columns counts and arrays), an 8901 or 8930 error is output, depending on the seriousness of the error. An 8901 error prevents a table being checked, but an 8930 error causes *DBCC CHECKDB* to terminate:

```
Msg 8930, Level 16, State 1, Line 1
Database error: Database 16 has inconsistent metadata. This error cannot be repaired and
prevents further DBCC processing. Please restore from a backup.
```

Page audit

All pages read by *DBCC CHECKDB*, no matter what type of page, go through an audit before being processed further. The audit process ensures that the page and its records are correct enough that deeper consistency-checking algorithms don't cause problems inside *DBCC CHECKDB*.

DBCC CHECKDB doesn't perform any physical I/Os itself—instead, it uses the buffer pool to read all pages that it processes. This allows *DBCC CHECKDB* to use the buffer pool's auditing, as well as re-duce complexity. Whenever the buffer pool reads a page into memory, the page is checked to ensure that no I/O errors occurred, and then any torn-page or page checksum protection is verified. If any problems are discovered, the usual 823 or 824 error is raised by the buffer pool but is suppressed by *DBCC CHECKDB* and translated into a DBCC-specific error message. These are usually errors 8928 and 8939:

```
Msg 8928, Level 16, State 1, Line 1
Object ID 1326627769, index ID 1, partition ID 72057594048872448, alloc unit ID
72057594055557120 (type LOB data): Page (1:69965) could not be processed. See other errors for
details.
Msg 8939, Level 16, State 98, Line 1
Table error: Object ID 1326627769, index ID 1, partition ID 72057594048872448, alloc unit ID
72057594055557120 (type LOB data), page (1:69965). Test (IS_OFF (BUF_IOERR, pBUF->bstat))
failed. Values are 12716041 and -4.
```

If the buffer pool audit fails, the page isn't processed any further. Otherwise, the DBCC page audit is performed as follows:

1. Check that the page ID in the page header is correct. This check is actually performed by the buffer pool when reading the page and *DBCC CHECKDB* is notified if the check fails. If this check fails while auditing a page from a critical system catalog during the primitive system catalog checks, error 5256 (which doesn't contain any metadata information) is raised:

   ```
   Msg 5256, Level 16, State 1, Line 1
   Table error: alloc unit ID 334184954400421, page (1:2243) contains an incorrect page ID
   in its page header. The PageId in the page header = (0:0).
   ```

   If this check fails in any other circumstance, an 8909 error is raised:

   ```
   Msg 8909, Level 16, State 1, Line 1
   Table error: Object ID 0, index ID -1, partition ID 0, alloc unit ID 844424953200640
   (type Unknown), page ID (1:26483) contains an incorrect page ID in its page header. The
   PageId in the page header = (0:0).
   ```

2. Check that the page type is valid for the allocation unit of which it is part. For instance, a data page shouldn't be present in the allocation unit for a nonclustered index. If this check fails, an 8938 error is raised:

   ```
   Msg 8938, Level 16, State 1, Line 1|
   Table error: Page (1:4667), Object ID 1877736499, index ID 1, partition ID
   72044394032172426, alloc unit ID 72044394045227020 (type LOB data). Unexpected page type
   1.
   ```

3. Check that each record on the page has the correct structure and doesn't have any bad pointers (such as one pointing into a different record or into free space). If any record structure
   audit checks fail, any of errors 8940 through 8944 can be raised:

```
Msg 8941, Level 16, State 1, Line 1
Table error: Object ID 0, index ID -1, partition ID 0, alloc unit ID 72057613244301312
(type Unknown), page (3:45522). Test (sorted [i].offset >= PAGEHEADSIZE) failed. Slot
114, offset 0x12 is invalid.
Msg 8942, Level 16, State 1, Line 1
Table error: Object ID 0, index ID -1, partition ID 0, alloc unit ID 72057613244301312
(type Unknown), page (3:45522). Test (sorted[i].offset >= max) failed. Slot 0, offset
0x72 overlaps with the prior row.
Msg 8944, Level 16, State 12, Line 1
Table error: Object ID 0, index ID -1, partition ID 0, alloc unit ID 72057613244301312
(type Unknown), page (3:45523), row 0. Test (ColumnOffsets <= (nextRec - pRec)) failed.
Values are 25 and 17.
```

As part of the page audit process, any page-compression information on the page is validated,
including the per-page compression information (CI) record that holds the prefixes (in an anchor record embedded within the CI record) and compression dictionary (an array of offsets plus values). Any
corruptions in this record are reported as 5274 errors.

When the page passes the audit process, the allocation unit ID in the page header is used to query
the metadata hash table described previously to find all the metadata that describes what's stored
within the page records. The page is then checked to determine whether it has been changed since
the previous full backup was performed. If so, and the relevant differential bitmap hasn't been set
correctly to indicate the change, error 2515 is reported:

```
Msg 2515, Level 16, State 1, Line 1
The page (1:24), object ID 60, index ID 1, partition ID 281474980642816, allocation unit ID
281474980642816 (type In-row data) has been modified, but is not marked as modified in the
differential backup bitmap.
```

After all these generic checks are performed, the page is processed further according to its type.

Data and index page processing

Data pages and index pages are processed using the same high-level algorithm, which does the following for each record.

- For records that have off-row LOB data, instantiate the record fully in memory (pulling in any
  row-overflow columns). For simple records without off-row LOB data, the record is processed
  directly from the page containing it.

- Check that the record length is correct, taking into account any versioning information appended to the end of the record.

- If the record contains data (that is, it isn't a ghost record), loop over all columns in the record
  and process them.

- Check that the record has no antimatter columns indicating a failed online index operation. Error 5228 or 5229 is output if this check fails:

```
Msg 5228, Level 16, State 3, Line 1
Table error: object ID 2073058421, index ID 0, partition ID 72057594038321152, alloc
unit ID 72057594042318848 (type "In-row data"), page (3:23345), row 12. DBCC detected
incomplete cleanup from an online index build operation. (The anti-matter column value is
14.)
```

- Check the versioning info for each record, if it exists. If a record has versioning info appended to it but the page header doesn't indicate that the page has versioned records on it, error 5260 is output. If a record has versioning info with a NULL version timestamp but a non-NULL version chain pointer, error 5262 is output.

 Note *DBCC CHECKDB* doesn't check the validity of the version store itself.

- Generate all necessary facts from the record and its contents—for example, B-tree linkage facts and LOB linkage facts.

For records that aren't stored on heap data pages, the records must be ordered by the defined clustered or nonclustered index keys. As the consistency checks progress through the page, the keys of the previous record are remembered so that they can be compared with the current record being processed. If the records aren't ordered correctly, error 2511 is output:

```
Msg 2511, Level 16, State 1, Line 1
Table error: Object ID 142675606, index ID 1, partition ID 72057594295025664, alloc unit ID
72057594301906944 (type In-row data). Keys out of order on page (1:1124457), slots 59 and 60.
```

For records that aren't stored in heap data pages, the records on a page must also have unique key values—that is, no two records can have the same keys. This applies even for indexes defined as non-unique, but only at the relational level. At the storage engine level, every record must be uniquely identifiable. If two records have the same keys, error 2512 is reported:

```
Msg 2512, Level 16, State 2, Line 1
Table error: Object ID 4, index ID 1, partition ID 262144, alloc unit ID 262144 (type In-row
data). Duplicate keys on page (1:4224) slot 9 and page (1:4224) slot 10.
```

The consistency checks of the various linkages between pages and records are discussed later in the section "Cross-page consistency checks."

After all records are processed, the following counters in the page header are checked.

- The count of records on the page (the slot count)
- The count of ghost records on the page

If the record count is incorrect, error 8919 is reported. If the ghost record count is incorrect, error 8927 is reported:

```
Msg 8927, Level 16, State 1, Line 1
Object ID 29, index ID 1, partition ID 281474978611200, alloc unit ID 281474978611200 (type
In-row data): The ghosted record count in the header (0) does not match the number of ghosted
records (1) found on page (1:309).
```

Non-leaf B-tree pages must have at least one record. If not, error 2574 is reported.

For data pages in a heap, the free space count is checked against the corresponding byte in the relevant PFS page. If the two don't match, error 8914 is reported:

```
Msg 8914, Level 16, State 1, Line 3
Incorrect PFS free space information for page (1:2511951) in object ID 357576312, index ID 0,
partition ID 72057594040156160, alloc unit ID 72057594044284928 (type In-row data). Expected
value 100_PCT_FULL, actual value 95_PCT_FULL.
```

Processing columns

For data and index records, each column is processed according to its type. Many checks described in this section result in a generic 2537 ("bad record") error message, with some specific text added into the error to identify the exact problem.

For *complex* columns, such as those that store LOB or FILESTREAM data or links, the column structure is checked as well as processed to extract the relevant linkage facts. If a corrupt complex column is found, error 8960 is output.

Columns are processed in many ways to support cross-page consistency checks, as discussed later in the section "Cross-page consistency checks."

Computed columns

As described earlier, an expression evaluator is compiled for each object that contains computed columns or CLR UDTs. If the expression evaluator can't be compiled, these columns can't be consistency checked.

The expression evaluator is called to evaluate persisted computed columns, or computed columns that exist in index records. It returns a value that's then compared against the persisted value in the data or index record. If the NULL status of the two values varies or a byte-comparison of the two values differs, error 2537 is returned.

For UDT columns, the comparison is done within the expression evaluator. It's passed the entire record that's being checked and returns a value of *True* or *False*, depending on the UDT comparison.

Note The expression evaluator object isn't thread-safe. This means that when *DBCC CHECKDB* is running in parallel across multiple processor cores, with one thread per processor core, only one processor core can access and use the expression evaluator at a time. Multiple processor cores can process pages from the same table with computed columns, so all the cores need access to the expression evaluator. Of course, internal synchronization occurs to prevent this and, inevitably, one or more processor cores might have to wait for access. As is the case with any mutual exclusion mechanism, this could affect the performance of heavily loaded systems with a large number of computed columns or CLR UDTs in the schema.

NULL and length checks   Three checks are performed here.

- Variable-length columns that are NULL must not have a nonzero data length. If this check fails, error 7961 is reported.

- A column that was created as NOT NULL can't have a NULL value. If this check fails, error 8970 is reported.

- A column can't be longer than the maximum in-row length as defined by its metadata. If this check fails, error 2537 is reported.

Data purity checks   Data purity checks verify whether the value of the column is within any bounds defined for the column's data type. An example is a corrupt *SMALLDATETIME* column value that had a "minutes past midnight" subvalue of 1440 or more into the next day.

As is documented in *SQL Server Books Online*, in versions prior to SQL Server 2005, importing "out-of-bounds" data values into a database was possible. From SQL Server 2005 onward, doing so is no longer possible. SQL Server 2005 introduced the concept of a database being "pure"—in other words, the database has no "out-of-bounds" data values. Pure databases have the data purity checks run by default, and they can't be disabled. Databases created on SQL Server 2005 onward are deemed pure from creation and remain so when upgraded to later versions.

Impure databases don't have the data purity checks run by default; they must be specifically requested with the *WITH DATA_PURITY* option. An impure database is one that was created before SQL Server 2005, has been upgraded to SQL Server 2012 in some way, and hasn't had the data purity checks run without errors. After data purity checks are run without errors, the database is irrevocably switched to being pure. A database's purity status is stored in the boot page.

Table 14-2 lists some of the SQL Server data types and the data purity validations performed for them.

TABLE 14-2 Data purity checks by data type

Data type	Data purity checks
TINYINT	None; all values are valid.
SMALLINT	None; all values are valid.
INT	None; all values are valid.
BIGINT	None; all values are valid.
MONEY	None; all values are valid.
SMALLMONEY	None; all values are valid.
UNIQUEIDENTIFIER	None; all values are valid.
TIMESTAMP	None; all values are valid.
IMAGE	None; all values are valid.
TEXT	Depending on the collation; validates any DBCS byte.
NTEXT	Validates that the length is a multiple of 2.
BIT	Ensures that the value is 0 or 1.
REAL or *FLOAT*	Validates that the floating-point value isn't outside the legal range.
DATETIME (and other date/time data types)	Validates the fields within the *DATETIME* (or other date/time data type) structure. For instance, the "days" field in a *DATETIME* value must be less than December 31, 9999, and greater than January 1, 1753.
DECIMAL or *NUMERIC*	Validates that the precision of the value is less than or equal to the defined precision. The scale of the value is equal to the defined scale, and the value is legal.
BINARY	Validates that the value has the correct length.
VARBINARY	Validates that the length is less than or equal to the maximum defined length.
VARBINARY(MAX)	None; all values are valid.
NCHAR	Validates that the length equals the defined length and that the length is a multiple of 2.
NVARCHAR	Validates that the length is less than or equal to the maximum defined length and that the length is a multiple of 2.
NVARCHAR(MAX)	Validates that the length is a multiple of 2.
CHAR	Validates that the length equals the defined length. Depending on the collation, validates any DBCS byte.
VARCHAR	Validates that the length is less than or equal to the maximum defined length. Depending on the collation, validates any DBCS byte.
VARCHAR(MAX)	Depending on the collation, validates any DBCS byte.
SQLVARIANT	Validates that the *SQLVARIANT* structure is valid and that the value contained within it is valid for its data type.
UDTs	Converts the value to the UDT and performs a byte comparison of the result with the original value.
XML	Performs structural validation of the XML value. This is performed by the XML subsystem.

Note Values compressed either through row compression, page compression, or *VARDECIMAL* must be uncompressed before being checked. This can add CPU overhead and extra runtime to *DBCC CHECKDB* if a large proportion of the table, filegroup, or database is compressed.

If any column value fails a data purity check, error 2570 is returned:

```
Msg 2570, Level 16, State 3, Line 1
Page (1:152), slot 0 in object ID 2073058421, index ID 0, partition ID 72057594038321152, alloc
unit ID 72057594042318848 (type "In-row data"). Column "c1" value is out of range for data type
"datetime". Update column to a legal value.
```

These errors can't be repaired and must be dealt with manually. The method for doing this is described in the Knowledge Base article at *http://support.microsoft.com/kb/923247.*

Partitioning checks   As described earlier, if the table or index being checked is partitioned, the index metadata cache object for it contains all information about the partitioning function used.

After all column value checks are completed, every record on the page is tested to ensure that it's in the correct partition. The column used for partitioning is extracted from each record and passed into a helper function within the query processor. The helper function evaluates the partition function and returns the partition ID that the record should be part of. If the partition ID returned doesn't match the partition ID that the page is part of, errors 8984 and 8988 are output:

```
Msg 8984, Level 16, State 1, Line 1
Table error: Object ID 2073058421, index ID 0, partition ID 72057594038452224. A row should be
on partition number 2 but was found in partition number 3. Possible extra or invalid keys for:
Msg 8988, Level 16, State 1, Line 1
Row (1:162:0) identified by (HEAP RID = (1:162:0)).
```

The 8984 error identifies the partition containing the error, whereas the 8988 error identifies the physical location of the incorrectly partitioned record, along with the index keys that can be used to access the record (or the heap physical RID if the incorrectly partitioned record is part of a partitioned heap).

Sparse column checks   The ability to define a column as *SPARSE* was a new feature in SQL Server 2008. Sparse columns that are NULL aren't stored in the record at all, not even in the NULL bitmap. This means that NULL values can truly take zero space in a record. When a sparse column is non-NULL, it's stored in a special sparse column array, which in turn is stored as a variable-length column in the record's variable-length column array. (Sparse column storage is described in detail in Chapter 8, "Special storage.") The consistency checking of the sparse column array is performed by the query processor and errors reported as for typical column corruptions.

Text page processing

Text pages are used to store LOB values—either actual LOB values that are stored off-row, or non-LOB variable-length columns that have been pushed off-row as row-overflow data. In all error messages involving text records or LOB linkages, the allocation unit type can be *LOB data* or *row-overflow data*.

Multiple types of text records are used in various ways to construct the loose text-trees that store LOB values. The text records are stored on two types of text pages: dedicated to a single LOB value or shared between multiple LOB values. Both types of text pages are processed using the same algorithm, which does the following for each text record.

- Instantiates the record and checks that it's a valid text record.

- Checks versioning info for each record, if it exists. If a record has versioning info appended but the page header doesn't indicate that the page has versioned records on it, error 5260 is output. If a record has versioning info with a NULL version timestamp but a non-NULL version chain pointer, error 5262 is output.

- Generates all necessary facts from the record and its contents (that is, LOB linkage facts).

When checking that a text record is valid, multiple types of text records with various structures must be part of that. Apart from regular record format structure checks, the following text-specific checks are performed:

- Deleted text records that have versioning info must have the correct row size. If this check fails, error 2537 is reported.

- The text record must be at least the minimum size required to hold a text-tree leaf-level node. If this check fails, error 2537 is reported.

- The text record must be on the correct text page type. If this check fails, error 8963 is reported:

```
Msg 8963, Level 16, State 1, Line 1
Table error: Object ID 1326627769, index ID 1, partition ID 72057594048872448, alloc unit
ID 72057594022622331 (type LOB data). The off-row data node at page (3:23345), slot 12,
text ID 89622642688 has type 3. It cannot be placed on a page of type 4.
```

- Non-leaf text records must not have more child nodes than are possible to store in their text record type, more child nodes than the size of their child links array, or more child nodes than the maximum permissible text-tree fan-out. If these checks fail, error 2537 is reported.

- The text record must have a valid type. If this check fails, error 8962 is reported.

Errors in text records are usually accompanied by an 8929 error, indicating the data or index record that links to the corrupt text record:

```
Msg 8929, Level 16, State 1, Line 1
Object ID 1326627769, index ID 1, partition ID 72057594048872448, alloc unit ID
72057594055622656 (type In-row data): Errors found in off-row data with ID 89622642688 owned by
data record identified by RID = (1:77754:1)
```

The next section discusses consistency checks of the various linkages between pages and records.

After all records are processed, the count of records on the page (the slot count) and the count of ghost records on the page are checked. If the record count is incorrect, error 8919 is reported; if the ghost record count is incorrect, error 8927 is reported.

The free space count is checked against the corresponding byte in the relevant PFS page. If the two don't match, error 8914 is reported:

```
Msg 8914, Level 16, State 1, Line 1
Incorrect PFS free space information for page (1:35244) in object ID 1683128146, index ID 1,
partition ID 223091033422352, alloc unit ID 81405523118118176 (type LOB data). Exected value
0_PCT_FULL, actual value 100_PCT_FULL
```

Cross-page consistency checks

As the various data, index, and text pages are being processed, facts are extracted from the records on the pages to support cross-page consistency checks. The various checks performed depend on the schemas present in the database and include

- The linkages between forwarding and forwarded records in heap data pages

- Intra B-tree page and record linkages

- The linkages between data/index records and text records

- Intra text-tree record linkages

- The linkages between data/index records and FILESTREAM files

- FILESTREAM container structure

- The linkages between base table records and nonclustered index records

Heap consistency checks   Cross-page consistency checks for a heap validate the linkages between forwarding and forwarded records. Forwarding/forwarded record pairs occur when a data record in a heap increases in size and the record's current page doesn't have the space to accommodate the size increase. The record is moved to a new location (becoming a forwarded record), and a small stub record (the forwarding record) is left in the original location to point to the record's real location.

The forwarded record points back to the forwarding record in case its location ever needs to change again, rather than create a chain of forwarding records. The original forwarding record is updated to point to the new location.

During regular processing of heap data pages, extra facts are generated from forwarding and forwarded records.

- Forwarding records generate a parent fact.

- Forwarded records generate an actual fact, with a note made of the link back to the forwarding record.

When the facts are aggregated, the following checks are made.

- The forwarded record linked to by a forwarding record must exist. If this check fails, error 8993 is reported:

```
Msg 8993, Level 16, State 1, Line 3
Object ID 357576312, forwarding row page (1:2386712), slot 8 points to page (1:2621015),
slot 18. Did not encounter forwarded row. Possible allocation error.
```

- The forwarding record linked back to by a forwarded record must exist. If this check fails, error 8994 is reported:

```
Msg 8994, Level 16, State 1, Line 1
Object ID 1967346073, forwarded row page (1:181506), slot 23 should be pointed to by
forwarding row page (1:83535), slot 66. Did not encounter forwarding row. Possible
allocation error.
```

- The forwarded record linked to by a forwarding record must link back to that forwarding record. If this check fails, error 8971 is reported:

```
Msg 8971, Level 16, State 1, Line 3
Forwarded row mismatch: Object ID 357576312, partition ID 72057594040156160, alloc unit
ID 72057594044284928 (type In-row data) page (1:3491303), slot 18 points to forwarded row
page (1:2506991), slot 22; the forwarded row points back to page (1:3423966), slot 1
```

- A forwarded record can't be linked to by multiple forwarding records. If this check fails, error 8972 is reported:

```
Msg 8972, Level 16, State 1, Line 3
Forwarded row referenced by more than one row. Object ID 357576312, partition ID
72057594040156160, alloc unit ID 72057594044284928 (type In-row data), page (1:2500650),
slot 2 incorrectly points to the forwarded row page (1:4361594), slot 4, which correctly
refers back to page (1:3472293), slot 20.
```

B-tree consistency checks   Cross-page consistency checks for a B-tree validate linkages within a B-tree level and between B-tree levels, as well as the consistency of key ranges across and between levels.

For pages at the leaf level of an index, page linkage facts are generated from the page headers, plus facts from the first and last records on the page (to give the key range contained on the page). For pages at the non-leaf levels of an index, all these facts are produced, as is a fact from every record on the page, containing a pointer to the page at the next level down in the B-tree that record references. When the facts are aggregated, the following checks are made.

- A page pointed to by the next-page linkage in a page's header must have the same B-tree level. If this check fails, error 2531 is reported.

- The child-page linkage from a non-leaf (parent) page can link only to a page that is one level below it in the B-tree. If this check fails, error 8931 is reported.

- The previous-page linkage must agree with the ordering of child-page links in the parent page. If a parent page has page B following page A, the previous-page linkage in page B's page header must link to page A. If this check fails, error 8935 is output:

```
Msg 8935, Level 16, State 1, Line 3
Table error: Object ID 1349579846, index ID 1, partition ID 72057594040811520, alloc unit
ID 72057594046382080 (type In-row data). The previous link (1:233719) on page (1:233832)
does not match the previous page (1:275049) that the parent (1:42062), slot 16 expects
for this page.
```

- If the next-page linkage in the page header of page A links to page B, the previous-page linkage in the page header of page B must link back to page A. if this check fails, error 8936 is reported:

```
Msg 8936, Level 16, State 1, Line 3
Table error: Object ID 1349579846, index ID 1, partition ID 72057594040811520, alloc unit
ID 72057594046382080 (type In-row data). B-tree chain linkage mismatch. (1:275049)->next
= (1:233832), but (1:233832)->Prev = (1:233719).
```

- A page can be linked to only by a single non-leaf page higher in the B-tree—that is, it can't have two child-page linkages from two "parent" pages. If this check fails, error 8937 is reported:

```
Msg 8937, Level 16, State 1, Line 3
Table error: Object ID 1349579846, index ID 1, partition ID 72057594040811520, alloc unit
ID 72057594046382080 (type In-row data). B-tree page (1:148135) has two parent nodes
(1:212962), slot 20 and (1:233839), slot 1.
```

- A page should be encountered only once by the *DBCC CHECKDB* scan. If this check fails, error 8973 is reported;

- A page must be encountered if a child-page linkage on a "parent" page links down to it and a page in the same level has a previous-page link to it. If this check fails, error 8976 is reported:

```
Msg 8976, Level 16, State 1, Line 1
Table error: Object ID 2073058421, index ID 1, partition ID 72057594038386688, alloc unit
ID 72057594042384384 (type In-row data). Page (1:158) was not seen in the scan although
its parent (1:154) and previous (1:157) refer to it. Check any previous errors.
```

- Every page in the B-tree must have a "parent page" with a child-page linkage that links to it. If this check fails, error 8977 is reported:

```
Msg 8977, Level 16, State 1, Line 3
Table error: Object ID 1349579846, index ID 1, partition ID 72057594040811520, alloc
unit ID 72057594046382080 (type In-row data). Parent node for page (1:163989) was not
encountered.
```

- Every page in the B-tree must have a previous page with a next-page linkage that links to it. This includes those on the left edge of the B-tree, where a fake linkage fact is created to make the aggregation work. If this check fails, error 8978 is reported:

```
Msg 8978, Level 16, State 1, Line 3
Table error: Object ID 1349579846, index ID 1, partition ID 72057594040811520, alloc unit
ID 72057594046382080 (type In-row data). Page (1:238482) is missing a reference from
previous page (1:233835). Possible chain linkage problem.
```

- Every B-tree page must have a "parent" page with a child-page linkage that links to it, and a previous page with a next-page linkage that links to it. This includes those pages on the left edge of the B-tree. When this isn't the case, the root page of the B-tree often has the problem, which is caused by a corrupt system catalog entry. This is why this error was created, which is really a combination of the two preceding errors. If this check fails, error 8979 is reported:

```
Msg 8979, Level 16, State 1, Line 1
Table error: Object ID 768057822, index ID 8. Page (1:92278) is missing references
from parent (unknown) and previous (page (3:10168)) nodes. Possible bad root entry in
sysindexes.
```

- The page linked to by a child-page linkage in a "parent" page must be encountered as a valid page in the B-tree by the *DBCC CHECKDB* scan. If this check fails, error 8980 is reported:

```
Msg 8980, Level 16, State 1, Line 1
Table error: Object ID 421576540, index ID 8. Index node page (1:90702), slot 17 refers
to child page (3:10183) and previous child (3:10182), but they were not encountered.
```

- The page linked to by the next-page linkage in a page's header must be encountered as a valid page in the B-tree by the *DBCC CHECKDB* scan. If this check fails, error 8981 is reported:

```
Msg 8981, Level 16, State 1, Line 3
Table error: Object ID 1349579846, index ID 1, partition ID 72057594040811520, alloc
unit ID 72057594046382080 (type In-row data). The next pointer of (1:233838) refers to
page (1:233904). Neither (1:233904) nor its parent were encountered. Possible bad chain
linkage.
```

- The next-page linkage in a page's header must link to a page within the same B-tree. If this check fails, error 8982 is reported.

- A page must be linked to by a "parent" page and previous page from within the same B-tree. If this check fails, error 8926 is reported:

```
Msg 8926, Level 16, State 3, Line 1
Table error: Cross object linkage: Parent page (0:1), slot 0 in object 2146106686, index
1, partition 72057594048806912, AU 72057594053394432 (In-row data), and page (1:16418)-
>next in object 366624349, index 1, partition 72057594049593344, AU 72057594054246400
(In-row data), refer to page [1:16768] but are not in the same object.
```

- The lowest key value on a page must be greater than or equal to the key value in the child-page linkage of the "parent" page in the next level up in the B-tree. If this check fails, error 8933 is reported:

```
Msg 8933, Level 16, State 1, Line 3
Table error: Object ID 1349579846, index ID 1, partition ID 72057594040811520, alloc unit
ID 72057594046382080 (type In-row data). The low key value on page (1:148134) (level 0)
is not >= the key value in the parent (1:233839) slot 0.
```

- The highest key value on a page must be less than the key value in the child-page linkage of the "parent" page for the next page at the same level of the B-tree. If this check fails, error 8934 is reported:

```
Msg 8934, Level 16, State 3, Line 3
Table error: Object ID 1349579846, index ID 1, partition ID 72057594040811520, alloc
unit ID 72057594046382080 (type In-row data). The high key value on page (1:275049)
(level 0) is not less than the low key value in the parent (0:1), slot 0 of the next page
(1:233832).
```

When a B-tree is corrupt, many of these errors commonly occur together for the same B-tree. Also, many of the errors where an expected page wasn't encountered are accompanied by a 2533 error:

```
Msg 2533, Level 16, State 1, Line 1
Table error: Page (3:9947) allocated to object ID 768057822, index ID 4 was not seen. Page may
be invalid or have incorrect object ID information in its header.
Msg 8976, Level 16, State 1, Line 1
Table error: Object ID 768057822, index ID 4. Page (3:9947) was not seen in the scan although
its parent (1:858889) and previous (1:84220) refer to it. Check any previous errors.
```

If you can determine that the missing page is allocated to another object, error 2534 is also reported, giving the actual object indicated in the page header.

LOB linkage consistency checks   As discussed earlier, LOB linkage facts are generated from text records and from complex columns in data or index records to allow consistency checking of text trees and of the linkages to off-row LOB columns or row-overflow data values. At aggregation time, the following checks are performed.

- The text timestamp in a text record must match the text timestamp in the data or index record complex column that links to it. If this check fails, error 8961 is reported:

```
Msg 8961, Level 16, State 1, Line 1
Table error: Object ID 434100587, index ID 1, partition ID 72057594146521088, alloc unit
ID 71804568277286912 (type LOB data). The off-row data node at page (1:2487), slot 0,
text ID 3788411843723132928 does not match its reference from page (1:34174), slot 0.
```

- Every text record must have a link to it from another text record or from a complex column in a data or index record. If this check fails, error 8964 is reported:

```
Msg 8964, Level 16, State 1, Line 1
Table error: Object ID 750625717, index ID 0, partition ID 49193006989312, alloc unit ID
71825312068206592 (type LOB data). The off-row data node at page (1:343), slot 0, text ID
53411840 is not referenced.
```

Multiple 8964 errors are commonly reported for text records on the same text page. This can happen if an entire data or index page can't be processed, and each record on the corrupt page has a complex column linking to a text record on the same text page.

- If a complex column in a data or index record links to a text record, the text record should be encountered by the *DBCC CHECKDB* scan. If this check fails, error 8965 is reported. This commonly happens when a text page can't be processed for some reason, in which case error 8928 is also reported:

```
Msg 8928, Level 16, State 1, Line 1
Object ID 1993058136, index ID 1, partition ID 412092034711552, alloc unit ID
71906736119218176 (type LOB data): Page (1:24301) could not be processed. See other
errors for details.
Msg 8965, Level 16, State 1, Line 1
Table error: Object ID 1993058136, index ID 1, partition ID 412092034711552, alloc unit
ID 71906736119218176 (type LOB data). The off-row data node at page (1:24301), slot 0,
text ID 1606680576 is referenced by page (1:24298), slot 0, but was not seen in the scan.
```

- A text record can have only one link to it. If this check fails, error 8974 is reported:

```
Msg 8974, Level 16, State 1, Line 1
Table error: Object ID 373576369, index ID 1, partition ID
72057594039238656, alloc unit ID 71800601762136064 (type LOB data). The
off-row data node at page (1:13577), slot 13, text ID 31002918912 is
pointed to by page (1:56), slot 3 and by page (1:11416), slot 37.
```

- The LOB linkage from a complex column in a data or index record must link to a text record contained within the same object and index. If this check fails, error 8925 is reported.

These errors commonly occur together and are usually accompanied by an 8929 error:

```
Msg 8961, Level 16, State 1, Line 1
Table error: Object ID 434100587, index ID 1, partition ID 72057594146521088, alloc unit ID
71804568277286912 (type LOB data). The off-row data node at page (1:2487), slot 2, text ID
341442560 does not match its reference from page (1:2487), slot 0.
Msg 8929, Level 16, State 1, Line 1
Object ID 434100587, index ID 1, partition ID 72057594146521088, alloc unit ID 72057594151239680
(type In-row data): Errors found in off-row data with ID 341442560 owned by data record
identified by RID = (1:34174:0)
```

The 8929 error contains the actual data or index record that links to the corrupt text record. This information can be found only by rescanning all data and index records at the end of the batch looking for complex columns that contain a text timestamp matching one in a text record that has been found to be corrupt. That this rescanning process (known as a *deep dive*) is performed is critical so that database repairs can remove both records: the corrupt text record and the record that contains a link to it.

FILESTREAM consistency checks   SQL Server 2008 introduced FILESTREAM storage—the ability to store LOB values *outside* the database in the NTFS file system. This permits very fast streaming access to the LOB values while maintaining transactional integrity with the relational data stored in the database. Chapter 8 describes FILESTREAM storage, but some of it is reviewed here so that you can understand how *DBCC CHECKDB* works with FILESTREAM data.

As with any multi-location storage system, link integrity is paramount so that *DBCC CHECKDB* in SQL Server 2012 performs rigorous consistency checking of the FILESTREAM storage attached to a database. In SQL Server 2012, the FILESTREAM feature was enhanced so that a FILESTREAM filegroup can contain multiple data containers, and FILESTREAM files are created in a round-robin fashion within them. The general FILESTREAM storage structure is as follows.

- The top level of a FILESTREAM data container is an NTFS directory.

- Each rowset (that is, a partition of a table or index) that contains FILESTREAM data has a rowset directory in the top level.

- Each column in the partition has a column directory in the rowset directory.

- The FILESTREAM data values for that column in each record in the partition are stored inside the column directory.

- A FILESTREAM log directory stored in the top level of each FILESTREAM data container can be thought of as a transaction log for the FILESTREAM storage.

These structures are present in each data container in a FILESTREAM filegroup. A table that has a FILESTREAM column will have corresponding rowset and column directories in all data containers for the FILESTREAM filegroup.

If the FILESTREAM log directory has been tampered with, the FILESTREAM scan fails and causes *DBCC CHECKDB* to terminate in various ways, depending on the corruption. For instance, if a file is created in the FILESTREAM log directory, *DBCC CHECKDB* fails, as shown here:

```
Msg 8921, Level 16, State 1, Line 1
Check terminated. A failure was detected while collecting facts. Possibly tempdb out of space or
a system table is inconsistent. Check previous errors.
Msg 5511, Level 23, State 10, Line 1
FILESTREAM's file system log record 'badlog.txt' under log folder '\\?\F:\Production\
FileStreamStorage\Documents\$FSLOG' is corrupted.
```

When *DBCC CHECKDB* starts, FILESTREAM garbage collection (GC) is prevented for the duration of the *DBCC CHECKDB* scan. FILESTREAM linkage facts are generated from the following.

- Table and index records that contain FILESTREAM columns

- The internal GC table, which contains information about which FILESTREAM files have been deleted logically (and hence don't have a linkage from a data/index record) but haven't yet been deleted physically

- The per-rowset and per-column directories in the FILESTREAM container(s)

- The actual FILESTREAM data files

At fact-aggregation time, the following consistency checks are performed.

- A FILESTREAM file must have a parent link from either a data/index record or the GC table. If this check fails, error 7903 is reported.

- The FILESTREAM link from a data/index record, or the GC table, must point to a valid FILESTREAM file. If this check fails, error 7904 is reported. For these two errors to be reported together, as shown here, isn't uncommon if a manual change has been made to a FILESTREAM data file:

```
Msg 7903, Level 16, State 2, Line 1
Table error: The orphaned file "0000001f-00000110-0001" was found in the FILESTREAM
directory ID 64a2a70b-f36b-4597-9d21-f751eae25003 container ID 65537 for object ID
245575913, index ID 0, partition ID 72057594039042048, column ID 3.
Msg 7904, Level 16, State 2, Line 1
Table error: Cannot find the FILESTREAM file "0000001e-0000013b-0002" for column ID 3
(column directory ID 64a2a70b-f36b-4597-9d21-f751eae25003 container ID 65537) in object
ID 245575913, index ID 0, partition ID 72057594039042048, page ID (1:275), slot ID 0.
```

- Each directory in the FILESTREAM data container directory structure must be part of the FILESTREAM storage structure. If the corrupt directory is in the top level of the FILESTREAM data container, error 7905 is reported; otherwise, error 7907 is reported:

```
Msg 7907, Level 16, State 1, Line 1
Table error: The directory "\64a2a70b-f36b-4597-9d21-f751eae25003\BadDirectory" under
the rowset directory ID e8b2f562-327f-4ee5-8489-ce6d9b4286ea is not a valid FILESTREAM
directory in container ID 65537.
```

- Each file in the FILESTREAM data container directory structure must be a valid FILESTREAM data file. If the corrupt file is in the top level of the FILESTREAM data container, error 7906 is reported; otherwise, error 7908 is reported:

```
Msg 7908, Level 16, State 1, Line 1
Table error: The file "\64a2a70b-f36b-4597-9d21-f751eae25003\corruptfile.txt" in the
rowset directory ID e8b2f562-327f-4ee5-8489-ce6d9b4286ea is not a valid FILESTREAM file
in container ID 65537.
```

- Each FILESTREAM rowset or column directory shouldn't be encountered more than once per data container by the *DBCC CHECKDB* scan. If this check fails, error 7931 is reported.

- Each FILESTREAM rowset directory should be in the correct FILESTREAM container(s) for a database. If this check fails, error 7932 is reported.

- Each FILESTREAM rowset directory must map to a valid partition in the database. If this check fails, error 7933 is reported.

- Each FILESTREAM column directory must match a column in a partition. If this check fails, error 7935 is reported.

- Each FILESTREAM column directory must match a FILESTREAM column in the partition. If this check fails, error 7936 is reported.

- Each FILESTREAM data file should be encountered only once by the *DBCC CHECKDB* scan in a FILESTREAM column directory. If this check fails, it indicates file-system corruption and error 7938 is reported.

- Each FILESTREAM data file must be linked to by only a single record in the table or index partition. If this check fails, error 7941 is reported.

- Each FILESTREAM file should be in the correct directory. If this check fails, error 7956 is reported.

- The FILESTREAM log file shouldn't be corrupt. If this check fails, error 7963 is reported.

Nonclustered index cross-checks The last of the cross-page consistency checks concerns nonclustered indexes. This has always been one of my favorite parts of the *DBCC CHECKDB* code base because of the intricacies of performing the checks efficiently. The nonclustered index cross-checks verify that

- Every record in a nonclustered index, whether filtered or nonfiltered, must map to a valid record in the base table—that is, the heap or clustered index.

- Every record in the base table must map to exactly one record in each nonfiltered, nonclustered index, and map to one record in each filtered index, where the filter allows.

If a nonclustered index record is missing, errors 8951 and 8955 are reported. Error 8951 reports the table name and the name of the index that's missing a record. Error 8955 identifies the data record that's missing a matching index record, plus the index keys of the missing index record.

If an extra nonclustered index record is present, errors 8952 and 8956 are reported. Error 8952 reports the table name and index name of the index with the extra record. Error 8956 identifies the index keys of the extra index record and the data record to which the index record links.

Commonly, a nonclustered index record is corrupt, so all four errors are reported as shown here:

```
Msg 8951, Level 16, State 1, Line 1
Table error: table 'FileStreamTest1' (ID 2105058535). Data row does not have a matching index
row in the index 'UQ__FileStre__3EF188AC7F60ED59' (ID 2). Possible missing or invalid keys for
the index row matching:
Msg 8955, Level 16, State 1, Line 1
Data row (1:169:0) identified by (HEAP RID = (1:169:0)) with index values 'DocId = '7E8193B4-
9C86-47C0-2207-BF1293BA8292' and HEAP RID = (1:169:0)'.
Msg 8952, Level 16, State 1, Line 1
Table error: table 'FileStreamTest1' (ID 2105058535). Index row in index 'UQ__
FileStre__3EF188AC7F60ED59' (ID 2) does not match any data row. Possible extra or invalid keys
for:
Msg 8956, Level 16, State 1, Line 1
Index row (1:171:1) with values (DocId = '7E8193B4-9C86-47C0-B407-BF2293BA8292' and HEAP RID =
(1:169:0)) pointing to the data row identified by (HEAP RID = (1:169:0)).
```

The mechanism to carry out these checks efficiently has changed in every release since SQL Server 7.0, becoming progressively more and more efficient. In SQL Server 2012, two hash tables are created for each partition of each nonclustered index: one for the actual records in that partition of the nonclustered index, and the other for the records that *should* exist in that partition of the nonclustered index (as calculated from the existing data records in the table).

When a nonclustered index record is processed, all columns in the record are hashed together into a *BIGINT* value. This includes

- The physical or logical link back to the base table (known as the base table RID)

- All included columns, even LOB and FILESTREAM values

The resulting value is added to the master hash value for actual records for the nonclustered index partition that the record is part of.

DBCC CHECKDB knows which nonclustered indexes exist for the table and what the complete nonclustered index record composition should be for each. When a data record is processed, the following algorithm is run for each matching nonclustered index record that should exist for the data record, taking into account any filter predicates for filtered nonclustered indexes:

1. Create the nonclustered index record in memory—again, including the base table RID, plus included columns.

2. Hash all columns in the index record together into a *BIGINT* value.

3. Add the resulting value to the "should exist" master hash value for the relevant nonclustered index partition that the index record is part of.

The premise that this algorithm works on is that if no corruption exists, the master hash values for the actual records and "should exist" records for each nonclustered index partition should match exactly at the end of the *DBCC CHECKDB* batch. No match, however, indicates a problem. The algorithm described here isn't without loss. Determining exactly which record is corrupt in a nonclustered index partition is impossible if the two master hash values don't match (this has always been the case since SQL Server 2000). In that case, a deep-dive check must be performed in which the table and its indexes are compared to find the exact corrupt record(s).

The deep-dive check can take a long time to run if it's triggered, which can significantly increase the runtime of *DBCC CHECKDB*. If a deep-dive check is triggered, error 5268 is output to the SQL Server error log, along with an error 5275 for each table that was searched. An example is shown here:

```
2012-04-30 16:34:09.750 spid52      DBCC CHECKDB is performing an exhaustive search of 1
indexes for possible inconsistencies.  This is an informational message only. No user action is
required.
2012-04-30 16:34:09.751 spid52      Exhaustive search of 'dbo.FileStreamTest1, UQ__
FileStre__3EF188AC7F60ED59' (database ID 17) for inconsistencies completed.  Processed 1 of 1
total searches.  Elapsed time: 5 milliseconds.  This is an informational message only. No user
action is required.
```

The deep-dive check uses the query processor to perform matches between the table and the index of concern, basically doing two left-anti-semi-joins using internal-only syntax. The query involved takes the form shown in Listing 14-1.

LISTING 14-1 Pseudo code for nonclustered index deep dive checks

```
SELECT <all information needed for errors 8951 and 8955 for an unmatched data record>
FROM <tablename> tOuter WITH (INDEX = <base table>)
WHERE NOT EXISTS
(
        SELECT 1
        FROM    <tablename> tInner WITH (INDEX = <nonclustered index>)
        WHERE
        (
                (([tInner].<index columns> = [tOuter].<index columns>)
                OR ([tInner].<index columns> IS NULL AND [tOuter].<index columns> IS NULL))
        AND
                (([tInner].<base table RID> = [tOuter].<base table RID>)
                OR ([tInner].<base table RID> IS NULL AND [tOuter].<base table RID> IS NULL))
        )
)
UNION ALL
SELECT <all information needed for errors 8952 and 8956 for an unmatched index record>
FROM <tablename> tOuter WITH (INDEX = <nonclustered index>)
WHERE NOT EXISTS
(
        SELECT 1
        FROM    <tablename> tInner WITH (INDEX = <base table>)
        WHERE
        (
                (([tInner].<index columns> = [tOuter].<index columns>)
                OR ([tInner].<index columns> IS NULL AND [tOuter].<index columns> IS NULL))
        AND
                (([tInner].<base table RID> = [tOuter].<base table RID>)
                OR ([tInner].<base table RID> IS NULL AND [tOuter].<base table RID> IS NULL))
        )
)
```

After the query is executed for each nonclustered index partition where the two master hash values didn't match, the batch is truly completed.

Performing cross-table consistency checks

Cross-table consistency checks involve validating nonphysical relationships between various tables in the database, such as the following.

- The metadata for a table must have matching metadata describing its columns. The two sets of data are stored in different system catalogs.

- A primary XML index must be an accurate representation of the XML column that it indexes. A primary XML index is stored as an internal table, separate from the table containing the XML column it indexes.

- An indexed view must be an accurate representation of the view definition. An indexed view is stored as an internal table, separate from the tables referenced in the view definition.

These cross-table consistency checks can't be run unless the tables involved have already been checked and have no consistency problems (or have had their consistency problems repaired).

Consider a case in which an XML index is based on an XML column in table *T1*. Table *T1* has a page that's damaged in such a way that it seems to be empty (because some records are inaccessible). If the XML index is checked before table *T1*, the XML index might seem to have extra information in it and be corrupt. In reality, however, the *T1* table is corrupt; the XML index needs to be rebuilt after any repair of table *T1*.

This might seem like a subtle difference, but *DBCC CHECKDB* needs to report the first-order consistency errors. The same logic holds for performing the other cross-table consistency checks, so depending on what consistency errors are found in earlier steps, some of the cross-table consistency checks might be skipped.

Service broker consistency checks

The Service Broker feature uses two types of tables in the database.

- System catalogs that store metadata about Service Broker usage in the database (for example, conversations, endpoints, and queues)

- Internal tables that are used to store the Service Broker queues

Both table types have the same physical structure as user tables but have different attributes governing their behavior and accessibility by users. Their physical structures are checked as part of the logical consistency checks described earlier.

Another level of checking is performed for the data contained with the Service Broker system catalogs and queues, similar to the system catalog consistency checks described earlier in the chapter. These checks validate such things as the following:

- A conversation must have two endpoints.

- A service must be related to a valid contract.

- A service must be related to a valid queue.

- A message must have a valid message type.

These checks aren't performed by *DBCC CHECKDB*; instead, they are performed by the Service Broker subsystem itself, on the behalf of *DBCC CHECKDB*. Any consistency errors are reported back to *DBCC CHECKDB* for inclusion in the final set of user results as an 8997 error, with the same format as the 8992 cross-catalog consistency-check error.

Cross-catalog consistency checks

SQL Server versions prior to SQL Server 2005 exhibited confusion about when *DBCC CHECKCATALOG* should be run to validate the relationships between the various system catalogs. To remove this confusion, SQL Server 2005 first included the *DBCC CHECKCATALOG* functionality inside *DBCC CHECKDB*.

The entire metadata subsystem in the Relational Engine was rewritten for SQL Server 2005 and as part of that effort, a new set of system catalog consistency checks was written, with some additions in SQL Server 2008, but nothing extra for SQL Server 2012. The checks are more comprehensive and efficient than the corresponding checks in SQL Server 2000 and earlier and are performed by the metadata subsystem on behalf of *DBCC CHECKDB* (they can also be performed by using the *DBCC CHECKCATALOG* command).

These checks operate only on the system catalogs dealing with Relational Engine metadata. The storage engine metadata system catalogs are checked during the per-table consistency checks described earlier. Some examples of the checks include the following.

- For all column metadata, the matching table metadata must exist.

- All columns referenced in a computed column definition must exist.

- All columns included in an index definition must exist.

Any consistency errors reported back to *DBCC CHECKDB* for inclusion in the final set of user results as 8992 errors in the following format:

```
Msg 8992, Level 16, State 1, Line 1
Check Catalog Msg 3853, State 1: Attribute (object_id=1977058079) of row
(object_id=1977058079,column_id=1) in sys.columns does not have a matching row
(object_id=1977058079) in sys.objects.
Msg 8992, Level 16, State 1, Line 1
Check Catalog Msg 3853, State 1: Attribute (object_id=1977058079) of row
(object_id=1977058079,column_id=2) in sys.columns does not have a matching row
(object_id=1977058079) in sys.objects.
```

 Note These checks aren't run on the *tempdb* database.

Indexed-view consistency checks

Although an indexed view is a first-class object in the database, it's stored as though it were an internal table with a clustered index, so its physical structure is checked for corruptions as part of the per-table consistency checks. Those consistency checks don't check that the *contents* of the indexed view match the view definition (that is, that the internal table doesn't have any extra or missing rows).

The simple way to describe the indexed view consistency check is that it uses the *indexed view* definition (which is stored in the system catalogs) to generate a temporary copy of the indexed view. It then uses the query processor to run two left-anti-semi-joins between the actual indexed view and the temporary indexed view. This query reports any missing or extra rows in the actual indexed view.

In reality, the temporary copy of the indexed view might not actually be created in its entirety, depending on which query plan the query processor uses when running the query. Listing 14-2 shows the query that *DBCC CHECKDB* uses, which similar to the one used for the nonclustered index deep dive cross-checking in Listing 14-1.

LISTING 14-2 Pseudo code for indexed view checks

```
SELECT <identifying columns of missing rows>
FROM <materialize the view temporarily> tOuter WITH (NOEXPAND)
WHERE NOT EXISTS
(
        SELECT 1
        FROM <actual view> tInner WITH (INDEX = 1)
        WHERE
        (
                ([tInner].<view columns> = [tOuter].<view columns>) OR
                ([tInner].<view columns> IS NULL AND [tOuter].<view columns> IS NULL)
        )
)
UNION ALL
SELECT <identifying columns of extra rows>
FROM <actual view> tOuter WITH (INDEX = 2)
WHERE NOT EXISTS
(
        SELECT 1
        FROM <materialize the view temporarily> tInner WITH (NOEXPAND)
        WHERE
        (
                ([tInner].<view columns> = [tOuter].<view columns>) OR
                ([tInner].<view columns> IS NULL AND [tOuter].<view columns> IS NULL)
        )
)
```

The *NOEXPAND* hint instructs the query processor to perform an index scan of the indexed view rather than expand it into its component parts. Any extra rows in the indexed view are reported as 8907 errors, and any missing rows are reported as 8908 errors.

This check can be very time-consuming and space-consuming. The more complex the *indexed view* definition and the larger the table(s) over which it is defined, the longer it takes to material-ize a temporary copy of the indexed view and the more likely it is to take up space in *tempdb*. This check hasn't been performed by default since SQL Server 2008 and must be enabled by using the *EXTENDED_LOGICAL_CHECKS* option.

XML-index consistency checks A primary XML index is stored as an internal table with a clustered index. A secondary XML index is stored as a nonclustered index on the primary XML index internal table. The consistency checks must validate that the XML indexes contain an accurate shredded repre-sentation of the XML values in the user table.

The mechanism for doing this is similar to that for the indexed-view consistency checks and can be visualized by using the same style of query, although a T-SQL query isn't used. In this case, the two left-anti-semi-joins can be thought of as between the actual XML index and a temporary copy of the XML index generated by the XML subsystem. Any extra rows in the XML index are reported as 8907 errors, and any missing rows are reported as 8908 errors.

This check can be very costly to run. The more complex the XML schema and the larger the XML column values, the more time is required to generate the temporary copy of the XML index, and the more likely it takes up space in *tempdb*. This check also hasn't been performed by default since SQL Server 2008 and must be enabled by using the *EXTENDED_LOGICAL_CHECKS* option.

Spatial-index consistency checks   A spatial index is stored as an internal table with a clustered index. The consistency checks must validate that the spatial index contains an accurate decomposed representation of the spatial values in the user table.

The mechanism for doing this is similar to that for the indexed-view consistency checks and can be visualized using the same style of query, although a T-SQL query isn't used. In this case, the two left-anti-semi-joins can be thought of as between the actual spatial index and a temporary copy of the spatial index generated by the spatial subsystem. Any extra rows in the spatial index are reported as 8907 errors, and any missing rows are reported as 8908 errors.

This check can be very time-consuming and space-consuming, depending on how the spatial index was defined. The higher the number of cells at each grid level of decomposition inside the index bounding box and the higher the number of stored matching grid cells per spatial value, the more time is required to generate the temporary copy of the spatial index and the more likely that copy will take up space in *tempdb*. Like with the other index consistency checks, this check hasn't been performed by default since SQL Server 2008 and must be enabled by using the *EXTENDED_LOGICAL_CHECKS* option.

Understanding DBCC CHECKDB output

DBCC CHECKDB outputs information in four ways.

- Regular output, consisting of a list of errors and informational messages to the connection issuing the *DBCC CHECKDB* command

- A message in the SQL Server error log

- An entry in the Microsoft Windows application event log

- Progress reporting information in the *sys.dm_exec_requests* catalog view

Regular output

By default, *DBCC CHECKDB* reports the following.

- A summary of the Service Broker consistency checks

- A list of allocation errors, plus a count of these errors

- A list of errors in which the affected table can't be determined, plus a count of these errors

- For each table in the database (including system catalogs),

  - The number of rows and pages

  - The list of errors, along with a count of these errors

- A summary count of allocation and consistency errors

- The minimum repair level that must be specified to fix the reported errors

Listing 14-3 shows an example of *DBCC CHECKDB* output for a database containing some corruption.

LISTING 14-3 Example DBCC CHECKDB output where corruption is present

```
DBCC results for 'CorruptDB'.
Service Broker Msg 9675, State 1: Message Types analyzed: 14.
Service Broker Msg 9676, State 1: Service Contracts analyzed: 6.
Service Broker Msg 9667, State 1: Services analyzed: 3.
Service Broker Msg 9668, State 1: Service Queues analyzed: 3.
Service Broker Msg 9669, State 1: Conversation Endpoints analyzed: 0.
Service Broker Msg 9674, State 1: Conversation Groups analyzed: 0.
Service Broker Msg 9670, State 1: Remote Service Bindings analyzed: 0.
Service Broker Msg 9605, State 1: Conversation Priorities analyzed: 0.
Msg 8909, Level 16, State 1, Line 1
Table error: Object ID 0, index ID -1, partition ID 0, alloc unit ID 0 (type Unknown), page ID
(1:158) contains an incorrect page ID in its page header. The PageId in the page header = (0:0).
CHECKDB found 0 allocation errors and 1 consistency errors not associated with any single
object.
DBCC results for 'sys.sysrscols'.
There are 637 rows in 8 pages for object "sys.sysrscols".
DBCC results for 'sys.sysrowsets'.
There are 92 rows in 1 pages for object "sys.sysrowsets".
DBCC results for 'sys.sysallocunits'.
There are 104 rows in 2 pages for object "sys.sysallocunits".
DBCC results for 'sys.sysfiles1'.
There are 2 rows in 1 pages for object "sys.sysfiles1".

----some results removed for brevity

DBCC results for 'sys.queue_messages_1977058079'.
There are 0 rows in 0 pages for object "sys.queue_messages_1977058079".
DBCC results for 'sys.queue_messages_2009058193'.
There are 0 rows in 0 pages for object "sys.queue_messages_2009058193".
DBCC results for 'sys.queue_messages_2041058307'.
There are 0 rows in 0 pages for object "sys.queue_messages_2041058307".
DBCC results for 'sales'.
Msg 8928, Level 16, State 1, Line 1
Object ID 2073058421, index ID 1, partition ID 72057594038386688, alloc unit ID
72057594042384384 (type In-row data): Page (1:158) could not be processed.  See other errors for
details.
There are 4755 rows in 20 pages for object "sales".
CHECKDB found 0 allocation errors and 1 consistency errors in table 'sales' (object ID
2073058421).
DBCC results for 'sys.filestream_tombstone_2121058592'.
There are 0 rows in 0 pages for object "sys.filestream_tombstone_2121058592".
DBCC results for 'sys.syscommittab'.
There are 0 rows in 0 pages for object "sys.syscommittab".
CHECKDB found 0 allocation errors and 2 consistency errors in database 'CorruptDB'.
repair_allow_data_loss is the minimum repair level for the errors found by DBCC CHECKDB
(CorruptDB).
DBCC execution completed. If DBCC printed error messages, contact your system administrator.
```

Although this output is comprehensive, the informational messages are redundant. In regular operation, the important information concerns the corruptions that might be present in the database. Using the *NO_INFOMSGS* option is recommended to reduce the output only to the essential information. Here is the output from *DBCC CHECKDB* of the same corrupt database, but with the *NO_INFOMSGS* option specified:

```
Msg 8909, Level 16, State 1, Line 1
Table error: Object ID 0, index ID -1, partition ID 0, alloc unit ID 0 (type Unknown), page ID
(1:158) contains an incorrect page ID in its page header. The PageId in the page header = (0:0).
CHECKDB found 0 allocation errors and 1 consistency errors not associated with any single
object.
Msg 8928, Level 16, State 1, Line 1
Object ID 2073058421, index ID 1, partition ID 72057594038386688, alloc unit ID
72057594042384384 (type In-row data): Page (1:158) could not be processed.  See other errors for
details.
CHECKDB found 0 allocation errors and 1 consistency errors in table 'sales' (object ID
2073058421).
CHECKDB found 0 allocation errors and 2 consistency errors in database 'CorruptDB'.
repair_allow_data_loss is the minimum repair level for the errors found by DBCC CHECKDB
(CorruptDB).
```

As you can see, this version of the output is easier to read.

When *DBCC CHECKDB* is executed on the *master* database, it's also run on the hidden resource database, *mssqlsystemresource,* so the output contains the results for both databases.

If *DBCC CHECKDB* must terminate prematurely for any reason, and the failure can be controlled by *DBCC CHECKDB*, error 5235 is output, containing one of the error states shown in Table 14-3.

TABLE 14-3 Error state descriptions for error 5235

Error state	Description
0	A fatal metadata corruption was detected. One or more 8930 errors (described earlier) accompanies the 5235 error.
1	An invalid internal state was detected inside *DBCC CHECKDB*. One or more 8967 errors (described earlier) accompanies the 5235 error.
2	The primitive checks of the critical system tables failed. One or more of errors 7984 through 7988 (described earlier) accompanies the 5235 error.
3	The emergency mode repair failed because the database couldn't be restarted after rebuilding the transaction log. Error 7909 accompanies the 5235 error, as described in more detail later in this chapter.
4	An access violation or assert occurred, even though *DBCC CHECKDB* was re-engineered in SQL Server 2005 to avoid these occurrences.
5	An unknown failure caused *DBCC CHECKDB* to terminate, although a graceful termination was possible.

Error reporting to Microsoft

From SQL Server 2008 onward, whenever an error is found by *DBCC CHECKDB*, a dump file is created in the instance log directory, along with a textual summary of the errors in XML form and a copy of the current SQL Server error log file. If the instance has been configured to provide feedback to Microsoft, these files are uploaded automatically. The SQL Server team uses the information contained within them to determine how common various corruptions are. This helps decide where engineering effort should be invested in future consistency-checking and repair functionality.

SQL Server error log output

Each time *DBCC CHECKDB* completes successfully, an entry is added to the SQL Server error log for the consistency-checked database. An example follows:

```
2012-05-02 16:36:12.270 spid56      DBCC CHECKDB (master) executed by APPLECROSS\paul found 0
errors and repaired 0 errors. Elapsed time: 0 hours 0 minutes 0 seconds.  Internal database
snapshot has split point LSN = 000000cf:00000171:0001 and first LSN = 000000cf:0000016f:0001.
This is an informational message only. No user action is required.
```

Notice that the entry lists the elapsed time that *DBCC CHECKDB* took to complete. This is included so that database administrators can gain an understanding of the average run time of *DBCC CHECK-DB* for a particular database without having to resort to manual timing. The entry also lists which options were specified. This can be useful to determine whether a database was previously repaired.

The entry also lists some metadata information about the database snapshot that *DBCC CHECKDB* created. This can be useful to Product Support when debugging corruption issues.

If *DBCC CHECKDB* terminates prematurely, an abbreviated entry is entered in the error log. If a high-severity error in the storage engine causes *DBCC CHECKDB* to terminate uncontrollably, no entry is made in the error log. The error-log-entry generation is one of the last things that *DBCC CHECKDB* does when it completes. This means that if an error occurs that, for instance, terminates the connection running the command, *DBCC CHECKDB* can't generate the error log entry.

Application event log output

DBCC CHECKDB generates a matching application event log entry each time it writes output to the SQL Server error log. Each time *DBCC CHECKDB* completes successfully, an entry is added to the Application event log detailing the number of errors found and fixed (see Figure 14-3).

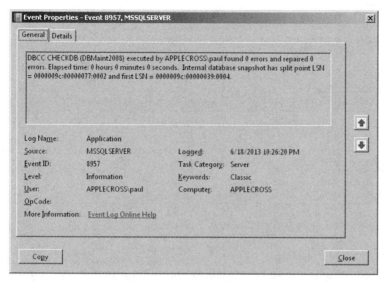

FIGURE 14-3 Application event log entry when *DBCC CHECKDB* completes as usual.

If *DBCC CHECKDB* finds errors, three entries are added to the event log, containing metadata for the error-reporting dump file described earlier.

If *DBCC CHECKDB* decides to terminate prematurely, an abbreviated entry is entered into the event log. If the SQL Server error log entry isn't generated because *DBCC CHECKDB* terminated uncontrollably, the application event log entry also isn't generated.

Progress reporting output

DBCC CHECKDB, *DBCC CHECKTABLE*, and *DBCC CHECKFILEGROUP* all report their progress in the *sys.dm_exec_requests* catalog view. The two columns of particular interest are *percent_complete*, which is self-explanatory, and *command*, which gives the current phase of execution of the DBCC command being executed. Table 14-4 lists the various phases of *DBCC CHECKDB* in order of execution. The *SQL Server Books Online* topic "DBCC" provides a similar list, but it includes several errors and omissions.

TABLE 14-4 Progress reporting phases of execution

Phase	Description	Granularity of reporting
DBCC ALLOC CHECK	Allocation consistency checks	This step is considered a single unit of work—that is, progress starts at 0 percent and jumps to 100 percent when the step completes.
DBCC ALLOC REPAIR	Allocation repairs, if specified	One unit of work per allocation error is found in the previous step, and progress is updated when each repair operation completes. For example, with eight errors found, each repair increments the progress by 12.5 percent.
DBCC SYS CHECK	Per-table consistency checks of critical system tables	Progress is calculated as a fraction of the total number of database pages that must be read and processed. Progress is updated after every 1,000 processed pages.

Phase	Description	Granularity of reporting
DBCC SYS REPAIR	Critical system table repairs, if specified and possible	See the description for *DBCC ALLOC REPAIR*.
DBCC TABLE CHECK	Per-table consistency checks of all tables	See the description for *DBCC SYS CHECK*.
DBCC TABLE REPAIR	User table repairs, if specified	See the description for *DBCC ALLOC REPAIR*.
DBCC SSB CHECK	Service Broker consistency checks (and repairs if specified)	This step is considered a single unit of work.
DBCC CHECKCATALOG	Cross-catalog consistency checks	This step is considered a single unit of work.
DBCC IVIEW CHECK	Indexed-view, XML-index, and spatial-index consistency checks, if specified	One unit of work for each indexed view, XML index, and spatial index is checked.
DBCC IVIEW REPAIR	Indexed-view, XML-index, and spatial-index repairs, if specified	See the description for *DBCC ALLOC REPAIR*.

 Note No phase is reported for primitive system table checks. This phase runs so quickly that when progress reporting was added into the *DBCC CHECKDB* code for SQL Server 2005, the development team didn't think that including a separate progress reporting phase was worthwhile.

DBCC CHECKTABLE reports the following phases.

- *DBCC TABLE CHECK*

- *DBCC IVIEW CHECK*, if no errors were found by the previous step

- *DBCC TABLE REPAIR*, if errors were found and a repair option was specified

DBCC CHECKFILEGROUP reports the following phases: *DBCC ALLOC CHECK, DBCC SYS CHECK*, and *DBCC TABLE CHECK. DBCC CHECKFILEGROUP* doesn't support repair operations.

Reviewing DBCC CHECKDB options

SQL Server Books Online shows the following syntax diagram for *DBCC CHECKDB*. The rest of this section explains the options in this syntax, with additional information to that in *SQL Server Books Online*.

```
DBCC CHECKDB
[
    [ ( database_name | database_id | 0
        [ , NOINDEX
        | , { REPAIR_ALLOW_DATA_LOSS | REPAIR_FAST | REPAIR_REBUILD } ]
        ) ]
    [ WITH
        {
            [ ALL_ERRORMSGS ]
            [ , EXTENDED_LOGICAL_CHECKS ]
            [ , NO_INFOMSGS ]
            [ , TABLOCK ]
```

```
        [ , ESTIMATEONLY ]
        [ , { PHYSICAL_ONLY | DATA_PURITY } ]
    }
  ]
]
```

NOINDEX

The *NOINDEX* option makes *DBCC CHECKDB* skip the nonclustered index cross-checks on user tables—that is, nonclustered index cross-checks are always performed on system tables when this option is specified. These checks are very CPU-intensive, so turning them off can make *DBCC CHECKDB* run faster. This option is rarely used because the *PHYSICAL_ONLY* option does a much better job of disabling CPU-intensive checks and making *DBCC CHECKDB* run faster.

Repair options

You can specify three repair options, although the *REPAIR_FAST* option has been changed in such a way that it does nothing from SQL Server 2005 onward and exists only for backward compatibility. The *REPAIR_REBUILD* option attempts to repair errors only when losing data isn't possible. The *REPAIR_ALLOW_DATA_LOSS* option attempts to repair all errors, including those in which data will likely be lost (the option name was carefully chosen). The repair process and specific repairs are discussed in much more detail later in this chapter.

> **Note** These options require that the database be in single-user mode. Running repair is usually used only as a last resort when restoring from a backup isn't possible.

ALL_ERRORMSGS

The *ALL_ERRORMSGS* option exists only for backward compatibility with earlier versions in which *DBCC CHECKDB* would report only the first 200 error messages. In SQL Server 2012, *DBCC CHECKDB* always lists all errors found.

> **Important** Running *DBCC CHECKDB* using the *ALL_ERRORMSGS* option from within SQL Server Management Studio limits the number of errors to 1,000. To work around this, you must use *sqlcmd*.

EXTENDED_LOGICAL_CHECKS

The *EXTENDED_LOGICAL_CHECKS* option enables the cross-table consistency checks for indexed views, XML indexes, and spatial indexes. Because these checks are so expensive to run, they are switched off by default from SQL Server 2008 onward.

In SQL Server 2005, when the indexed view and XML index checks were introduced, these checks were on by default. As such, when the database is set to the 90 compatibility level, the

EXTENDED_LOGICAL_CHECKS option is ignored and these cross-table consistency checks are always performed.

NO_INFOMSGS

When the *NO_INFOMSGS* option is specified, the output doesn't include any informational messages. This can make the output easier to read when errors are present. Although this isn't the default, I recommend that this option always be specified.

TABLOCK

The *TABLOCK* option forces *DBCC CHECKDB* to take database and table locks to obtain its transactionally consistent view of the database—that is, the consistency checks are performed offline and concurrent activity might be blocked. The locking behavior when this option is specified was described earlier in the section "Alternatives to using a database snapshot."

ESTIMATEONLY

The *ESTIMATEONLY* option calculates how much space might be required in *tempdb* for the sort that holds the facts generated by the consistency-checking algorithms, taking into account all other specified options.

DBCC CHECKDB goes through the motions of building all the batches of objects to check (as described earlier), but it doesn't actually check them. Instead, it uses the metadata that it has gathered about each table and index to produce an estimate of the number of each type of fact that it generates. The various numbers are multiplied by the size of each fact type and added together to form a total size for that batch. The batch with the highest total size is the one that's reported.

The estimation algorithms are very conservative in their calculations to ensure that an accurate maximum size is returned. The actual amount of *tempdb* space taken up might be considerably lower. For example, the estimation algorithm estimates the number of facts required to track forwarding and forwarded records by simply counting all the records in a heap and multiplying by two. This is almost never the case, but it is a sufficient estimation.

When *ESTIMATEONLY* is specified, the output doesn't contain any error or informational messages. Instead, the output has the following format:

```
Estimated TEMPDB space needed for CHECKALLOC (KB)
-------------------------------------------------
32

(1 row(s) affected)

Estimated TEMPDB space needed for CHECKTABLES (KB)
--------------------------------------------------
750

(1 row(s) affected)

DBCC execution completed. If DBCC printed error messages, contact your system administrator.
```

PHYSICAL_ONLY

The *PHYSICAL_ONLY* option makes *DBCC CHECKDB* skip the CPU-intensive per-table and cross-table consistency checks. When this option is specified, *DBCC CHECKDB* does the following.

- Create a transactionally consistent, static view of the database.

- Perform low-level consistency checks of the critical system catalogs.

- Perform allocation consistency checks of the database.

- Read and audit all allocated pages from each table in the database.

With the *PHYSICAL_ONLY* option, *DBCC CHECKDB* skips checking all B-tree linkages and all checks of FILESTREAM data. By skipping all the CPU-intensive consistency checks, the *PHYSICAL_ONLY* option turns *DBCC CHECKDB* from a CPU-bound process into an I/O-bound process. This usually results in *DBCC CHECKDB* running significantly faster.

Because this option forces all allocated pages in the database to be read into the buffer pool, using it is an excellent way to test all existing page checksums.

The *PHYSICAL_ONLY* option has these restrictions.

- It's mutually exclusive with the *DATA_PURITY* option.

- It's mutually exclusive with any repair option.

- It switches on the *NO_INFOMSGS* option.

DATA_PURITY

The *DATA_PURITY* option forces the per-column data purity checks to be run, as described earlier in this chapter. By default, these checks are run on databases that are marked as being pure. A pure database is one that was created on SQL Server 2005 onward, or an upgraded database that has had *DBCC CHECKDB* with the *DATA_PURITY* option run without finding any corruptions (which irrevocably marks the database as pure).

For all other databases, the data purity checks are run only when this option is specified. The *DATA_PURITY* and *PHYSICAL_ONLY* options are mutually exclusive.

Performing database repairs

Apart from performing consistency checks on a database, *DBCC CHECKDB* can repair most corruption that it finds. I say "most" and not "all" because *DBCC CHECKDB* can't repair some corruption, including the following.

- Corruption in the leaf level of a critical system catalog clustered index

- Corruption in a PFS page header

- Data purity errors (error 2570)

- Errors from system catalog cross-checks (error 8992)

If any such corruption is present, *DBCC CHECKDB* repairs as much as it can and indicates which corruptions can't be repaired with a 2540 error:

```
The system cannot self repair this error.
```

This book isn't the place to discuss when repair should be used, but restoring from valid backups always allows data loss to be minimized and is usually the preferred course of action. Database repair functionality really exists as a last resort when backups aren't available.

Usually, you should view repair as a last resort for two reasons.

- Most repairs that *REPAIR_ALLOW_DATA_LOSS* enables are to delete whatever is corrupt and fix up all linkages to and from the corrupt object. This is always the fastest, easiest to engineer, most easily proved, correct, and infallible way to remove a corruption.

- Not all corruptions can be repaired, as explained earlier.

However, if no backups are available, repair might be necessary. The necessary repair level to use is reported at the end of the *DBCC CHECKDB* output in an 8958 error:

```
repair_rebuild is the minimum repair level for the errors found by DBCC CHECKDB (ProductionDB).
```

The repairable corruptions fall into two groups: those that can be repaired without losing data (for example, corruptions in nonclustered indexes, indexed views, XML or spatial indexes, or in a forwarding <-> forwarded record linkage), and those that require data loss (that is, most corruptions involving heaps and clustered indexes).

For those corruptions in the first group, the *REPAIR_REBUILD* option is sufficient. For those in the second group, the *REPAIR_ALLOW_DATA_LOSS* option is required. If *REPAIR_ALLOW_DATA_LOSS* isn't specified, some corruptions might not be repaired, and *DBCC CHECKDB* uses an 8923 error to explain that the reason is because a lower repair level was specified:

```
The repair level on the DBCC statement caused this repair to be bypassed.
```

Repair mechanisms

If a repair option was specified, after *DBCC CHECKDB* completes each phase of the consistency checks, repairs are carried out then. This ensures that subsequent consistency checks and repairs are performed on a database without lower-level corruptions present.

When repair is required to run, the repair subsystem inside *DBCC CHECKDB* is passed the list of corruptions that the consistency checks found. The corruptions aren't repaired in the order that they are found—instead, they are sorted according to how intrusive the repair is. Consider a nonclustered index that has a corrupt IAM page and a missing record. The repair for the corrupt IAM page is to rebuild the nonclustered index, and the repair for the missing record is simply to insert a new nonclustered index record. If the missing record was fixed before the corrupt IAM page was fixed, the insertion of the new record is wasted because the nonclustered index is then completely rebuilt to repair the corrupt IAM page.

Therefore, ranking all corruptions by how intrusive their repairs are and performing the most intrusive repairs first makes sense. This usually allows less intrusive repairs to be skipped because they can be repaired as a side effect of performing a more intrusive repair. Continuing the example, the nonclustered index IAM page corruption is ranked higher than the missing nonclustered index record. When the index is rebuilt to repair the corrupt IAM page, the new index includes the missing record, thus fixing the missing-nonclustered-index-record corruption as a side effect.

Repair ranking also prevents the repair system from inadvertently causing more corruption. Consider a table that has a corrupt nonclustered index and a corrupt page at the leaf level of the clustered index. The more intrusive repair (deallocating the clustered index leaf-level page) must be performed first. This guarantees that when the nonclustered index is rebuilt, the rebuild uses an error-free clustered index as its base. If the nonclustered index was rebuilt first, and *then* the clustered index leaf-level page was deallocated, the nonclustered index is corrupt.

Each repair is performed within a separate transaction to allow *DBCC CHECKDB* to cope with a repair failing but then continue repairing other corruptions.

The output from *DBCC CHECKDB* contains details of the repair that was performed. The complete list of all corruptions with their repairs is well beyond the scope of this book, but example repairs include the following.

- Fixing incorrect record counts on a data or index page

- Fixing incorrect PFS page bytes

- Removing an extra record from a nonclustered index

- Inserting a single record into a nonclustered index (a much more efficient alternative than rebuilding a large nonclustered index to repair a single record)

- Moving a wrongly partitioned record to the correct partition

- Rebuilding a nonclustered index

- Rebuilding an indexed view, XML index, or spatial index

- Deleting orphaned off-row LOB values or FILESTREAM files

- Rebuilding a clustered index

- Deallocating a data record, with a consequent cascading delete of all nonclustered index records and off-row LOB or FILESTREAM values referenced by the record

- Deallocating an entire data page, with the consequent cascading deleted

- Setting or unsetting bits in the various GAM, SGAM, and IAM allocation bitmaps

- Fixing previous-page and next-page linkages in an IAM chain

- Truncating an IAM chain at a corrupt IAM page, stitching together the IAM chain remnants, and performing the consequent rebuilds and cascading deletes

- Resolving pages or extents that are allocated to multiple objects

Repairs that involve data loss have other possible consequences. If a table affected by repair is involved in a foreign-key relationship, that relationship can be broken after running repair, so *DBCC CHECKCONSTRAINTS* should be performed. If a table affected by repair is part of a replication publication, the repairs aren't replicated, so the subscription(s) should be reinitialized after running repair.

Also, an undocumented repair option, *REPAIR_ALL*, allows GAM and SGAM pages to be repaired. It's undocumented because these two repairs can't be undone if you decide to roll back the repair operation as described next.

Emergency mode repair

One additional piece of repair functionality is triggered only when the database is in EMERGENCY mode. EMERGENCY mode is used when the transaction log for the database has been damaged and no backups are available to restore from. In this case, regular repairs don't work; repairs are fully logged and this can't occur if the transaction log is damaged.

In SQL Server 2000 and earlier, EMERGENCY mode was undocumented and was used to allow the transaction log to be rebuilt by using the undocumented *DBCC REBUILD_LOG* command. Unfortunately, this procedure became publicized on the Internet but usually without all necessary steps. For this reason, I decided to add a documented and supported method of rebuilding a transaction log and recovering the database in SQL Server 2005. The feature is called *emergency mode repair* and its mechanism is unchanged for SQL Server 2012.

When the database is in EMERGENCY mode and SINGLE_USER mode, and *DBCC CHECKDB* is run with the *REPAIR_ALLOW_DATA_LOSS* option, the following steps are taken:

1. Force recovery to run on the transaction log (if it exists).

   This is essentially recovery with *CONTINUE_AFTER_ERROR*, in a similar vein to using *CONTINUE_AFTER_ERROR* with either *BACKUP* or *RESTORE*. The idea behind this is that the database is already inconsistent because either the transaction log is corrupt or something in the database is corrupt in such a way that recovery can't complete.

   Presuming that the database is inconsistent and the transaction log is about to be rebuilt, salvaging as much transactional information as possible from the log, before it's discarded and a new one is created, makes sense.

   This recovery with *CONTINUE_AFTER_ERROR* functionality is possible only from within *DBCC CHECKDB*.

2. Rebuild the transaction log if it's corrupt.

3. Run the full set of consistency checks on the database with the *REPAIR_ALLOW_DATA_LOSS* option.

4. Bring the database online.

> **Tip** The vast majority of the time, this operation completes successfully, although with data loss. However, I have seen it fail in production, especially on corrupt file systems, so again, backups are the recommended way to avoid data loss.

What data was deleted by repair?

In the unfortunate case where you have no choice but to use the *REPAIR_ALLOW_DATA_LOSS* option, some data is inevitably lost, as explained earlier. Your task becomes figuring out what data is lost so that it can be re-created or what other parts of the database are fixed up to reflect the loss.

Before running repair, you could try examining some of the pages that *DBCC CHECKDB* reports as corrupt to see if you can tell what data is on them. Consider the following error:

```
Server: Msg 8928, Level 16, State 1, Line 2
Object ID 645577338, index ID 0: Page (1:168582) could not be processed. See other errors for
details.
```

You can try using *DBCC PAGE* to examine page (1:168582). Depending on how badly the page is corrupt, you might see some of the records on the page and figure out what data is lost when the page is deallocated by the repair operations.

After running repair, you might be able to tell what data has been deleted. Unless you are intimately familiar with the data in the database, you have two options:

- Create a copy of the corrupt database before running repair so you can compare the pre-repair and post-repair data and see what's missing. This can be tricky to do if the database is badly corrupt; you might need to use the *WITH CONTINUE_AFTER_ERROR* options of *BACKUP* and *RESTORE* to do this.

- Start an explicit transaction before running repair. Not very well known is that you can run repair inside a transaction, as long as you're not performing an emergency-mode repair. After repair completes, you can examine the database to see what repair did, and if you want to undo the repairs, you can simply roll back the explicit transaction.

After the repair is completed, you might be able to query the repaired database to find out what data has been repaired. Consider the case where a repair deleted a leaf-level page from a clustered index with an identity column. Constructing queries that find the range of records deleted, such as the following, might be possible:

```
-- Start of the missing range is when a value does not have a plus-1 neighbor.
SELECT MIN(salesID + 1) FROM DemoRestoreOrRepair.dbo.sales as A
WHERE NOT EXISTS (
        SELECT salesID FROM DemoRestoreOrRepair.dbo.sales as B
```

```
        WHERE B.salesID = A.salesID + 1);
GO
-- End of the missing range is when a value does not have a minus-1 neighbor
SELECT MAX(salesID - 1) FROM DemoRestoreOrRepair.dbo.sales as A
WHERE NOT EXISTS (
        SELECT salesID FROM DemoRestoreOrRepair.dbo.sales as B
        WHERE B.salesID = A.salesID - 1);
GO
```

At the very least, after running a repair, you should perform a full backup and root-cause analysis of the corruption to find out what caused the problem.

Using consistency-checking commands other than DBCC CHECKDB

This section explains what each *DBCC CHECK...* command does. Historically, much confusion has resulted over what all the different consistency-checking DBCC commands do, which ones should be performed, and in what order. *DBCC CHECKDB* includes the functionality of all *DBCC CHECK...* commands except *DBCC CHECKIDENT* and *DBCC CHECKCONSTRAINTS*.

DBCC CHECKALLOC

DBCC CHECKALLOC performs primitive system-catalog consistency checks and allocation consistency checks on the database. It uses a database snapshot by default and has the same options as for *DBCC CHECKDB*, except for *PHYSICAL_ONLY*, *REPAIR_REBUILD*, and *DATA_PURITY*. None of these options make sense for allocation consistency checks.

If informational messages are allowed, it outputs comprehensive information about the number of pages and extents allocated to each allocation unit in the database, along with the first IAM page in the IAM chain and the root page. This information isn't returned when the allocation consistency checks are performed as part of *DBCC CHECKDB*. Listing 14-4 shows some example output.

Listing 14-4 Output of the DBCC CHECKALLOC Command

```
DBCC results for 'CorruptDB'.
***********************************************************************
Table sys.sysrscols              Object ID 3.
Index ID 1, partition ID 196608, alloc unit ID 196608 (type In-row data). FirstIAM (1:188). Root
(1:189). Dpages 8.
Index ID 1, partition ID 196608, alloc unit ID 196608 (type In-row data). 10 pages used in 1
dedicated extents.
Total number of extents is 1.
***********************************************************************
<some results removed for brevity>
***********************************************************************
Table sys.syscommittab           Object ID 2137058649.
Index ID 1, partition ID 72057594038583296, alloc unit ID 72057594042580992 (type In-row data).
FirstIAM (0:0). Root (0:0). Dpages 0.
Index ID 1, partition ID 72057594038583296, alloc unit ID 72057594042580992 (type In-row data).
0 pages used in 0 dedicated extents.
Index ID 2, partition ID 72057594038648832, alloc unit ID 72057594042646528 (type In-row data).
```

```
FirstIAM (0:0). Root (0:0). Dpages 0.
Index ID 2, partition ID 72057594038648832, alloc unit ID 72057594042646528 (type In-row data).
0 pages used in 0 dedicated extents.
Total number of extents is 0.
File 1. The number of extents = 25, used pages = 174, and reserved pages = 195.
        File 1 (number of mixed extents = 18, mixed pages = 139).
    Object ID 3, index ID 1, partition ID 196608, alloc unit ID 196608 (type In-row data), data
extents 1, pages 10, mixed extent pages 9.
    Object ID 5, index ID 1, partition ID 327680, alloc unit ID 327680 (type In-row data), data
extents 0, pages 2, mixed extent pages 2.
    Object ID 7, index ID 1, partition ID 458752, alloc unit ID 458752 (type In-row data), data
extents 0, pages 4, mixed extent pages 4.
    Object ID 7, index ID 2, partition ID 562949953880064, alloc unit ID 562949953880064 (type
In-row data), index extents 0, pages 2, mixed extent pages 2.
<some results removed for brevity>

    Object ID 2073058421, index ID 1, partition ID 72057594038386688, alloc unit ID
72057594042384384 (type In-row data), data extents 2, pages 23, mixed extent pages 9.
The total number of extents = 25, used pages = 174, and reserved pages = 195 in this database.
        (number of mixed extents = 18, mixed pages = 139) in this database.
CHECKALLOC found 0 allocation errors and 0 consistency errors in database 'CorruptDB'.
DBCC execution completed. If DBCC printed error messages, contact your system administrator.
```

DBCC CHECKTABLE

DBCC CHECKTABLE performs primitive system-catalog consistency checks, per-table consistency checks on the single table specified, and cross-table consistency checks on indexed views that reference the specified table. Cross-table consistency checks aren't performed if any corruptions were found in the table specified, even if the corruptions were repaired. This is slightly more restrictive behavior than for *DBCC CHECKDB*.

Also, a nonclustered index ID can be specified that limits the nonclustered index cross-checks to only that nonclustered index. This can't be specified if any repair options are used.

DBCC CHECKTABLE uses a database snapshot by default and has the same set of options as *DBCC CHECKDB*, including repairs. The command's output is limited to the table being checked.

DBCC CHECKFILEGROUP

DBCC CHECKFILEGROUP performs the following checks.

- Primitive system-catalog consistency checks

- Allocation consistency checks on the filegroup

- Per-table consistency checks on all tables stored in the filegroup

- Cross-table consistency checks, as long as the indexed views, XML indexes, and spatial indexes are stored within the filegroup and the tables on which they are based are also stored within the filegroup

It uses a database snapshot by default and has the same set of options as *DBCC CHECKDB*, except for *PHYSICAL_ONLY*, *DATA_PURITY*, and any repair options. The following subtleties are involved in the per-table consistency checks when a table and all its nonclustered indexes are *not* stored within the same filegroup.

- If a table is stored within the filegroup specified but one or more nonclustered indexes are stored in other filegroups, they aren't checked for consistency.

- If a nonclustered index is stored within the filegroup specified, but the table (heap or clustered index) is stored in another filegroup, the nonclustered index isn't checked for consistency.

As a basic principle, *DBCC CHECKFILEGROUP* doesn't perform cross-filegroup consistency checks.

The output of this command is the same as for *DBCC CHECKDB* except that it doesn't report any Service Broker details, and only tables within the specified filegroup are checked.

DBCC CHECKCATALOG

DBCC CHECKCATALOG performs primitive system catalog consistency checks and cross-catalog consistency checks. It uses a database snapshot by default and has only the *NO_INFOMSGS* option. If a database snapshot can't be created, it requires an exclusive database lock to run. Assuming that neither a database snapshot nor an exclusive lock can be acquired on *tempdb*, *DBCC CHECKCATALOG* can't be run on the *tempdb* database (either as part of *DBCC CHECKDB* or as the standalone command).

The output of this command is empty unless any corruption is found.

DBCC CHECKIDENT

DBCC CHECKIDENT checks that the identity value for the specified table is valid—that is, larger than the highest identity value contained in the table—and resets it automatically if necessary. It works by scanning the rows in the specified table to find the highest identity value and then comparing it with the next identity value stored in the table metadata.

This command can also be used to reset the identity value manually, if required. Be careful when doing this, however, so as not to produce duplicate values accidentally in the identity column.

If the command is just checking the identity value, the table is locked with an intent-share lock, with minimal impact on concurrent operations. If a new value has been specified, the table is locked with a schema-modification lock for the short time required to modify the table metadata.

 Note The *SQL Server Books Online* topic for this command, "DBCC CHECKIDENT (Transact-SQL)," at *http://msdn.microsoft.com/en-us/library/ms176057.aspx* describes the various options and their effects.

DBCC CHECKCONSTRAINTS

DBCC CHECKCONSTRAINTS checks the enabled *FOREIGN KEY* and *CHECK* constraints defined within the database. It can check a single constraint, all the constraints on a table, or all constraints in the database. If the *ALL_CONSTRAINTS* option is specified, it also checks any disabled *FOREIGN KEY* and *CHECK* constraints.

This command works by creating a query to find all rows that violate the constraint being checked. The query uses an internal query hint to tell the query processor that *DBCC CHECKCONSTRAINTS* is running and that it shouldn't short-circuit the query because of its knowledge of existing constraints.

DBCC CHECKCONSTRAINTS doesn't use a database snapshot and runs under whatever the session isolation level is set to. You must have the session option *CONCAT_NULL_YIELDS_NULL* set to *ON*; otherwise, the command fails with error 2507. If any rows violate a constraint, the row's keys are output along with the table name containing the row and the name of the violated constraint.

> **Tip** You should run *DBCC CHECKCONSTRAINTS* after performing any kind of DBCC repair because the repairs don't take any constraints into account.

Conclusion

As you can see from the descriptions in this chapter, the consistency checks that SQL Server 2012 can perform on a database are extremely comprehensive and have evolved significantly from earlier releases in terms of breadth, depth, and efficiency.

Also, you can see why *DBCC CHECKDB* can take such a long time to complete on a large, complex database. I've tried to include information on most corruption errors that *DBCC CHECKDB* can report, as well as background on the consistency-checking mechanisms that it used to arrive at its conclusions.

This information should help you if and when you encounter corruption in your own databases.

Index

Symbols

3-byte positive number, storing dates, 212
16-byte pointer, 386
$FSLOG folder, 401

A

accent sensitivity/insensitivity (AI/AS) tokens, 218
access
    datbase, 130–131
    FILESTREAM data, storage, 395–396
access methods
    storage engine, 14–15
ACID properties, 15
ACID properties, transaction processing, 767–768
actions
    Extended Events, 77
    package0.attach_activity_id, 97
    package0.attach_activity_id_xfer, 97
active state (VLFs), 178
active_workers_count (sys.dm_os_schedulers), 43
actual execution plans, 519
actual text facts, 847
Actual XML Showplan, 663
adding
    columns to tables, 281
    constraints (tables), 281–282
ad hoc query caching, 706–711, 747
Adhoc value (objtype columns), 705
admin events, 76
advanced index operations, 560–567
    dynamic index seeks, 560–563
    index intersections, 565–567
    index unions, 562–564
AdventureWorks, 100

AdventureWorks2012
    security, 132
AdventureWorks2012 database
    creating snapshot, 156
affinity
    ALTER SERVER CONFIGURATION setting, 38
    dynamic, 41
    process
        binding schedulers to CPUs, 41–42
    schedulers, 38
    workers, 39
Affinity64 I/O Mask option, 29
Affinity I/O Mask option, 29
Affinity Mask configuration option, 40
affinity (sys.dm_os_threads), 44
AFFINITY value, 63
Aggregate operator, 504
aggregating data
    Extended Events UI, 93–95
aggregation, 847
aggregation algorithm, 849
Aggregation dialog box, 94
aggregations, 545–556
    hash, 552–556
    scalar, 545–548
    stream, 548–552
AI/AS (accent sensitivity/insensitivity) tokens, 218
algorithms
    aggregation, 849
    Backup Compression, 30
    depth-first, 846
    fact-aggregation, 850
    fact-generation, 848
    fact-sorting, 850
    fact-storing, 850
    LRU-K, 49
    O(n2), 846
    O(n*log(n)), 846

ALL_ERRORMSGS option (DBCC CHECKDB), 891
allocation
    pages, 149
    regions, 160
    tempdb database optimizations, 146–147
allocation bitmaps, 859
allocation consistency checks, 856–860
    checking allocation facts, 859–860
    collecting allocation facts, 857–858
allocation strategies, LOB data, 393
allocation structures, heap data modifications,
    286–288
allocation unit locks, 783
allocation units, 245
ALLOW_PAGE_LOCKS (XML index option), 460
ALLOW_ROW_LOCKS (XML index option), 460
ALLOW_SNAPSHOT_ISOLATION option, 815–817
ALTER ANY USER database permission, 166
ALTER COULMN clause (ALTER TABLE
    command), 280–281
ALTER DATABASE command, 107, 109, 115, 140, 813
    changing compatibility levels, 137
    MODIFY FILE option, 142
    switching recovery models, 193
ALTER DATABASE statement, 114–119
    FILEGROUP keyword, 110
ALTER EVENT SESSION statement, 83
ALTER FULLTEXT INDEX DDL statement, 499
ALTER INDEX command, 361–364
    REORGANIZE option, 365–366
ALTER INDEX REBUILD operation, 190
ALTER INDEX statement
    manually controlling unit of locking, 804
altering
    databases, 114–119
        space allocation, 116–119
        user-defined space, 116
altering tables, 279–286
    adding columns, 281
    changing data types, 280–281
    constraints, 281–282
    dropping columns, 283
    internals, 283–286
    sparse columns (storage format), 413–414
alternatives to database snapshots, 844–845
ALTER RESOURCE GOVERNOR DISABLE
    command, 71
ALTER SEQUENCE command, 242
ALTER SERVER CONFIGURATION SET PROCESS
    AFFINITY CPU, 42–43

ALTER SERVER CONFIGURATION setting, 38
ALTER statement
    CONTAINMENT option, 163
ALTER TABLE command, 279–280
    ALTER COULMN clause, 280–281
    dropping columns, 283–284
    manipulating constraints, 281–283
    SQL Server execution, 283–286
    WITH VALUES clause, 281
ALTER TABLE statement
    escalating table locks, 805
AlwaysOn Availability Groups, 156
    contained users, 163
analysis
    indexes, 302–307
        dm_db_database_page_allocations
            function, 306–307
        dm_db_index_physical_stats DMV, 302–305
    page compression, 440–441
analysis phase of recovery, 174
analytic events, 76
analyzing query plans, 525–600
    advanced index operations, 560–567
        dynamic index seeks, 560–563
        index intersections, 565–567
        index unions, 562–564
    aggregations, 545–556
        hash aggregations, 552–556
        scalar aggregations, 545–548
        stream aggregations, 548–552
    bookmark lookup, 531–533
    data modification statements, 598–599
    joins, 533–544
        hash joins, 542–544
        merge joins, 539–542
        nested loops joins, 534–539
        properties, 544
    parallelism, 580–598
        bitmap filtering, 597–598
        broadcast partitioning, 596–597
        DOP (degree of parallelism), 582–583
        exchange operator, 583–586
        hash joins, 595
        hash partitioning, 595–596
        inner-side parallel execution, 593–594
        load balancing, 589–590
        merge joins, 594–595
        nested loops joins, 590–591, 592–593
        round-robin exchange, 592
        scan operators, 586–588

scans and seeks, 526–528
seekable predicates and covered columns, 528–531
subqueries, 566–580
CASE expressions, 578–580
correlated scalar subqueries, 570–577
noncorrelated scalar subqueries, 567–569
removing correlations, 576–577
unions, 555–559
anchor record (CI records), 438
ANSI_DEFAULTS database option, 234
ANSI_null_default database option, 234
ANSI_NULL_DEFAULT option, 126
ANSI_NULLS database option, 234
ANSI_NULLS option, 126
ANSI_NULLS (Set option), 724
ANSI_PADDING option, 127
ANSI properties information, 206–207
ANSI_WARNINGS option, 127
anti-semi-join, 537
ANY aggregate, 568
appending LOB data into columns, 393
application event log, DBCC CHECKDB output, 888–889
Apply operators (Query Optimizer), 621–622
approximate numeric data types, 208
architecture
Extended Events, 73
Query Optimizer, 624–630
auto-parameterization, 625–626
before optimization, 625
Memo, 627–630
parameterization limitations, 627–628
Simplification phase, 625
trivial plan, 625–626
ARITHABORT option, 127
assert operator, 568
associated entity ID, lock resources, 784–785
asynchronous statistics update feature, 631
atomicity property (transactions), 767
attributes
plan handle values, 722–723
ROWGUIDCOL, 397
authentication, 130–131
databases, 164–165
AUTO_CLOSE option, 125
AutoCreatedLocal route, 169
auto-create statistics, 630
AUTO_CREATE_STATISTICS option, 126
AUTO_GRID spatial index, 476

auto-grid specification, 473
autogrowing files
tempdb database, 147
automatic file expansion, 106–107
automatic shrinkage, 108
automatic truncation, virtual log files, 184–185
AUTO option (CHANGE_TRACKING specification), 499
auto options, 125–126
auto-parameterization, Query Optimizer, 625–626
AUTO_SHRINK database option, 841–842
autoshrinking log files, 187–188
autoshrink option
tempdb database and, 147
AUTO_SHRINK option, 126
autotruncate mode, 51
auto-update statistics, 630
AUTO_UPDATE_STATISTICS option, 126
avg_fragmentation_in_percent value, 364
avoidance, deadlocks, 809–811
awe_allocated_kb column (sys.dm_os_memory_clerks), 58

B

back pointer, 430
Backup Compression DEFAULT, 29
backup page compression, 443
backups
Backup Compression DEFAULT, 29
databases, 136, 188–201
choosing backup type, 194–195
partial backups, 198
partial restore, 200
recovery models, 190–194
restoring files and filegroups, 197–198
restoring pages, 198–200
restoring with standby, 200–201
types of backups, 189–190
balanced tree indexes. See B-tree indexes
batch-based operator model, 618
batches, 67
batches, processing databases, 851–852
batch hash table build operator, 607
batch mode parallelism, 667–669
batch processing, 603–608
Query Optimizer, 662–666
column orientation within batches, 664–665

grouping rows for repeated operations, 662–663

logical database design best practices, 666

bcp utility, bulk-loading data, 238

best practices

tempdb database, 147–148

BIGINT data type, 496

BIGINT value, 880

BIN2 binary collation, 218

binary collations

Windows collations, character data types (tables), 223–224

binary data types, 230

binary large object. *See* BLOB

BIN binary collation, 218

binding

components, 12

schedulers to CPUs, 41–42

bit data types, 230

bitmap filtering, 597–598, 601–602

bitmap operators, 660

@BlobEater variable, 850

BLOB (binary large object)

Filestream Access Level option, 30

blocked_event_fire_time column (sys.dm_xe_ sessions), 97

Blocked Process Threshold option, 31

blocking_exec_context_id (sys.dm_os_waiting_ tasks), 45

blocking iterators, 516

blocking_session_id (sys.dm_os_waiting_tasks), 45

blocking_task_address (sys.dm_os_waiting_tasks), 45

bookmark lookups, 531–533

bottom-up type queries, 470

bounding box, GEOMETRY data type, 472

Bound Trees cache store, 732

bracketed identifiers, 206

broadcast partitioning, parallelism, 596–597

B-tree consistency checks, 872–875

B-tree indexes, 297, 299–302, 457

creating, 313–315

IGNORE_DUP_KEY option, 313–314

MAXDOP option, 314

STATISTICS_NORECOMPUTE, 314

large key column example, 300–301

management, 360–370

ALTER INDEX command, 361–364

detecting fragmentation, 363

dropping indexes, 360

online index building, 367–370

rebuilding indexes, 366–367

removing fragmentation, 364–366

narrow key column example, 301–302

structure, 308–312, 315–332

clustered indexes, 316–322

clustering key dependency, 308–311

constraints, 312

index row formats, 315–316

nonclustered B-tree indexes, 311–312

nonclustered indexes, 322–332

B+ trees, 299

buckets_avg_length column (sys.dm_os_memory_ cache_hash_tables), 58

buckets_avg_scan_hit_length column (sys.dm_os_ memory_cache_hash_tables), 58

buckets_count column (sys.dm_os_memory_cache_ hash_tables), 58

buckets_in_use_count column (sys.dm_os_memory_ cache_hash_tables), 58

buckets_max_length column (sys.dm_os_memory_ cache_hash_tables), 58

buckets_min_length column (sys.dm_os_memory_ cache_hash_tables), 58

Buffer Manager, 172

buffer pool, 47

buffer pools

sizing, 55–57

buffers

dirty, 52

free buffer list, 49–50

page management in data cache, 49

BUFFER section (DBCC PAGE command output), 256

bulk import operations, 190

BULK INSERT command, 190

bulk-loading data, 238

BULK_LOGGED recovery model (databases), 192–193

bulk update locks, 777

bushy hash join tree, 543–544

Business Intelligence edition, 2

C

cacheobjtype column, values, 705

cache optimizations

tempdb database, 146–147

caches

memory management, 52–53

metadata, 53

plan, 53

CACHESTORE_COLUMNSTOREOBJECTPOOL, 48

cache stores, 53, 732–733
Cache value property, SEQUENCE objects, 241
caching plan. *See* plan cache
candidate cells, 480
CAP_CPU_PERCENT value, 63
cardinality estimation, Query Optimizer, 638–643
Cartesian products, 600
CASE expressions, subqueries, 578–580
case sensitivity/insensitivity (CS/CI) tokens, 218
catalog metadata
    sessions, 96
catalog views, 4–5
catalog view (tables)
    constraints, 277–278
    queries, 246–248
CD (column descriptor) row format, 426–432
CDocidRankWtToDocidRankAdaptor iterator, 504
CD Region (CD format), 427
Cell_Attributes, spatial indexes, 458, 476
CellID, spatial indexes, 458, 476
cells-per-object optimization rule, 474
CELLS_PER_OBJECT value, 473
cell tessellation levels, 472
changes in log file size (logging and recovery),
        178–188
    autoshrinking, 187–188
    maintaining recoverable logs, 185–187
    viewing log file size, 188
    virtual log files, 178–185
        automatic truncation, 184–185
        observing, 179–181
        using multiple files, 181–183
CHANGE_TRACKING parameter, full-text
        indexes, 493, 499
changing
    table data types, 280–281
character data types (tables), 213–230
    collation
        selection, 217–218
        SQL Server collations, 224–230
        viewing options, 218
        Windows collations, 218–224
CHECK constraint, 276
CheckIndex function, 850
checking consistency, 841–901
    allocation consistency checks, 856–860
        checking allocation facts, 859–860
        collecting allocation facts, 857–858
    alternatives to DBCC CHECKDB, 898–901
    consistent view of database, 842–845

cross-table consistency checks, 881–885
    cross-catalog consistency checks, 882–883
    indexed view consistency checks, 883–885
    Service Broker feature, 882
DBCC CHECKDB options, 890–893
DBCC CHECKDB output, 885–890
    application event log, 888–889
    error reporting to Microsoft, 888–889
    progress reporting output, 889–890
    regular output, 885–887
    SQL Server error log, 888
performing database repairs, 893–897
per-table logical consistency checks, 860–866
    data and index page processing, 864–866
    metadata consistency checks, 861–862
    page audits, 863–864
primitive system catalog consistency
        checks, 855–856
processing columns, 866–881
    computed columns, 866–869
    cross-page consistency checks, 871–881
    text page processing, 870–871
processing databases efficiently, 845–855
    batches, 851–852
    parallelism, 853–855
    performing fact generation, 846–848
    query processor, 848–851
    reading pages to process, 852–853
CHECKPOINT, 403
CHECKPOINT command, 51
checkpoint operations, 173
checkpoints, 50–52
    indirect, 29
CHECKSUM option, 128
Check UDX operator, 471
Check value (objtype columns), 706
CI (compression information) records, 437
    rebuilding, page compression, 440–441
CI/CS (case sensitivity/insensitivity) tokens, 218
classifier function, 62–63
cleanup function, 826
clearing plan cache, 704–705
clock_hand column (sys.dm_os_memory_cache_
        clock_hands), 59
clock_status column (sys.dm_os_memory_cache_
        clock_hands), 59
Close method, 514
CLR Compiled Func value (cacheobjtype
        columns), 705

CLR Compiled Proc value (cacheobjtype columns), 705

clustered indexes, 298, 457, 855
    B-tree index structure, 316–322
    clustering key dependency, 308–311
    rebuilding, 369

clustering key
    spatial indexes, 458

clustering key dependency, B-tree indexes, 308–311

CMEMTHREAD waits, 748

code
    locking, 16
    Resource Governor, 68–70
    versioning, 16

cold-cache assumption, costing model, 644–645

Collapse operator, 676

collation
    character data types (tables)
        selection, 217–218
        SQL Server collations, 224–230
        viewing options, 218
        Windows collations, 218–224

collation behavior
    contained databases, 166–168

collecting allocation facts, allocation consistency checks, 857–858

colmodctr (Column Modification Counters) values, 727–728

column-based DDL keywords, 493

column descriptor (CD) row format, 426–432

Column Modification Counters (colmodctr) values, 727–728

column prefix page compression, 435–436

column processing, 866–881
    computed columns, 866–869
    cross-page consistency checks, 871–881
        B-tree consistency checks, 872–875
        FILESTREAM consistency checks, 876–881
        heap consistency checks, 871–872
        LOB linkage consistency checks, 875–877
    text pages, 870–871

COLUMNPROPERTYEX function, 501

COLUMNPROPERTY function, 336

columns
    cacheobjtype, values, 705
    catalog views, 4, 5
    DMVs (Dynamic Management Objects), 42–45
    events, 76
    facts, 848
    first_snapshot_sequence_num, 828

first_useful_sequence_num, 828

friendly name, 9

is_read_committed_snapshot_on, 817

last_transaction_sequence_num, 828

max_version_chain_traversed, 830

node tables, 461

objtype, values, 705–706

recovery_model, 9

resource_lock_partition, 798

spatial indexes, 458, 476

syscacheobjects object, 745–746

sys.database_files, 102–103

sys.databases view, 120

sys.dm_db_database_page_allocations function, 306–307

sys.dm_os_memory_cache_clock_hands, 59

sys.dm_os_memory_cache_counters, 58

sys.dm_os_memory_cache_hash_tables, 58

sys.dm_os_memory_clerks, 57–58

sys.dm_os_process_memory, 56

sys.dm_os_schedulers, 43

sys.dm_os_sys_info, 56

sys.dm_os_tasks, 44–45

sys.dm_os_threads, 44

sys.dm_os_waiting_tasks, 45

sys.dm_os_workers, 44

sys.dm_xe_sessions, 96–97

transaction_id, 827

transaction_is_snapshot, 827

transaction_sequence_num, 827

Columns dialog box, 92

COLUMN_SET constructs, sparse columns, 414–417

columns (tables)
    adding to tables, 281
    defined, 203
    dropping from tables, 283
    minlen, 263
    xmaxlen, 263

columnstore indexes, 297, 370–380, 603–608
    creating, 370–372
    metadata, 376–380
    partitioning, 452–454
    storage, 371–375

columnstore indexes, Query Optimizer, 660–661, 670–671

columnstore index scan operator, 607

column store object pool, 48

columnstore plan shape, 669

column (sys.database_files), 102

combinations of allocation bitmaps, 859

commands. *See also* operations
ALTER DATABASE, 107, 109, 115, 140, 813
    changing compatibility levels, 137
    MODIFY FILE option, 142
    switching recovery models, 193
ALTER INDEX, 361–364
    REORGANIZE option, 365–366
ALTER RESOURCE GOVERNOR DISABLE, 71
ALTER SEQUENCE, 242
ALTER TABLE, 279–280
    ALTER COULMN clause, 280–281
    dropping columns, 283–284
    manipulating constraints, 281–283
    SQL Server execution, 283–286
    WITH VALUES clause, 281
BULK INSERT, 190
CHECKCONSTRAINTS, 901
CHECKFILEGROUP, 899–900
CHECKPOINT, 51
CREATE DATABASE, 104, 105, 106, 156
CREATE FUNCTION, 260–261
CREATE INDEX, 313–314
    DROP_EXISTING option, 360–361, 362–363
    FILLFACTOR option, 362
    INCLUDE syntax, 312–313, 313–314, 314–315,
        332–333, 360–361, 361–362, 362–363,
        363–364
    SORT_IN_TEMPDB option, 363
CREATE PARTITION SCHEME, 445
DBCC
    consistency checking, 841–901
    shrinking files and databases, 837–841
DBCC CHECKALLOC, 898–899
DBCC CHECKCATALOG, 883
DBCC CHECKIDENT, 900
DBCC CHECKTABLE, 890
DBCC FREESYSTEMCACHE, 743
DBCC LOG, 177
DBCC LOGINFO, 179
DBCC PAGE, 250, 824
DBCC SHOW_STATISTICS, 632–633
DBCC SHRINKDATABASE, 108, 109, 178, 187, 838
DBCC SHRINKFILE, 107, 108, 109, 840
DBCC SQLPERF('logspace'), 188
DBCC TRACEOFF, 23
DBCC TRACEON, 23
DDL
    code, 68–70
DELETE, 672–673
DROP DATABASE, 135

DROP INDEX, 360
FREEPROCCACHE, 731
INSERT, 671–672
INSERT INTO . . . SELECT, 190
RECONFIGURE, 25
RESTORE, 161
    WITH RECOVERY option, 196
RESTORE DATABASE, 198
ROLLBACK TRAN, 171
SELECT INTO, 190, 277
SET, displaying query plans, 519
SET TRANSACTION ISOLATION LEVEL, 813
T-SQL BULK INSERT, 238
UPDATE, 671
UPDATE STATISTICS, 725
commited_kb column (sys.dm_os_sys_info), 56
commit record, 172
commit_target_kb column (sys.dm_os_sys_info), 56
common subexpression spools, 623
compatability, locks, 794–795
compatibility levels, 137–138
compatibility views, 3–4
compensation log records, 172
compilation
    troubleshooting, 751–752
compilation-related context switches, costs, 744
compiled objects, 719–721
    functions, 720–721
    stored procedures, 719–720
compiled plan cache stores, 734–735
Compiled Plan Stub value (cacheobjtype
        columns), 705
Compiled Plan value (cacheobjtype columns), 705
compile memory costs, 744
components
    binding, 12
    Database Engine, 10–17
        protocols, 11–12
        query processor, 12–14
        storage engine, 14–17
    parsing, 12
composite indexes, seekable predicates, 529
composition of spatial indexes, 475–477
compression
    spatial indexes, 474
compression information (CI) records, 437
    rebuilding, 440–441
compression of data, 423–443
    pages, 433–442
        analysis, 440–441

backup compression, 443
CI record building, 440–441
column prefix compression, 435–436
dictionary compression, 436–437
metadata, 441
performance issues, 442–443
physical storage, 437–439
rows, 424–432
CD (column descriptor) format, 426–432
enabling, 425–426
vardecimal, 423
compressions
Backup Compression DEFAULT, 29
computed columns, indexes, 333–338
creating, 335–336
implementation, 336
permissible functions, 334–335
persisted columns, 337–338
schema binding, 335
SET options, 333–334
computed columns, processing, 866–869
Compute Scalar operator (Query Optimizer), 618, 659, 683–684
Compute Sequence operator (Query Optimizer), 619
concatenation operator, 556
CONCAT_NULL_YIELDS_NULL database option, 234
CONCAT_NULL_YIELDS_NULL option, 127
concurrency
locking, 774–811, 832–836
basics, 774–775
compatability, 794–795
deadlocks, 806–811
escalation, 804–805
examples, 789–795
hints, 832–836
internal architecture, 796–803
lock types for user data, 775–786
row-locking versus page-locking, 803–805
spinlocks, 775
viewing locks, 786–789
models, 765–766
row versioning, 811–832
choosing concurrency model, 830–832
details, 811–812
snapshot-based isolation levels, 813–830
transaction processing, 766–774
ACID properties, 767–768
dependencies, 768–769
isolation levels, 770–775
concurrency management, 17

concurrency models, 16
Configuration Manager
moving the master database, 143
configuring
full-text indexes, 500–501
network protocols, 18
operating system
connectivity, 23
firewall settings, 23
nonessential services, 23
paging file location, 22
task management, 21–22
partially contained databases, 162–163
SQL Server 2012, 17–20
default network configuration, 18–19
network protocols, 18
system configuration, 21–33
connections
DAC (Dedicated Administrator Connection), 45
connectivity
disabling protocols, 23
consistency checking, 841–901
allocation consistency checks, 856–860
checking allocation facts, 859–860
collecting allocation facts, 857–858
alternatives to DBCC CHECKDB, 898–901
consistent view of database, 842–845
cross-table consistency checks, 881–885
cross-catalog consistency checks, 882–883
indexed view consistency checks, 883–885
Service Broker feature, 882
DBCC CHECKDB options, 890–893
DBCC CHECKDB output, 885–890
application event log, 888–889
error reporting to Microsoft, 888–889
progress reporting output, 889–890
regular output, 885–887
DBCC CKECKDB output
SQL Server error log, 888
performing database repairs, 893–897
per-table logical consistency checks, 860–866
data and index page processing, 864–866
metadata consistency checks, 861–862
page audits, 863–864
primitive system catalog consistency checks, 855–856
processing columns, 866–881
computed columns, 866–869
cross-page consistency checks, 871–881
text page processing, 870–871

processing databases efficiently, 845–855
batches, 851–852
parallelism, 853–855
performing fact generation, 846–848
query processor, 848–851
reading pages to process, 852–853
consistency property (transactions), 767
Constant Scan operator, 616, 683
constraints
B-tree indexes, 312
constraints (tables), 276–279
failures in transactions, 278–279
modifying, 281–282
names and catalog view information, 277–278
contained database authentication option, 162
contained databases, 162–169
collation changes, 166–168
configuring, 162–163
creating contained users, 163–166
detecting uncontained features, 168–169
contained users, creating, 162–165
Containment assumption, Query Optimizer, 637
CONTAINMENT option (ALTER and CREATE
DATABASE statements), 163
CONTAINS operator, 501
CONTAINSTABLE function, 502
ContainsTableSSERankForNear iterator, 504
ContainsTableSSERank iterator, 504
Contains UDX operator, 471
contention
tempdb database, 148–152
DDL contention, 153
DML contention, 148–152
context_switches_count (sys.dm_os_tasks), 44
controlling locking, 832–836
control_option values (sp_control_plan_guide
procedure), 758–759
controls
Resource Governor, 70–71
conventions
naming tables, 207–208
conversion deadlocks, 808–809
conversion locks, 777–778
copying
databases, 134–136
copy-on-write operations, 157
core-based licensing
schedulers, 38
correctness-based recompiles, 722–725
correlated parameters, 535

correlated scalar subqueries, 566, 570–577
correlations, subqueries, 576–577
cosine similarity, 508
costing
joins, 538
costing, cache entries, 743–744
costing, Query Optimizer, 643–645
Cost Threshold For Parallelism option, 32, 33
counters, performance, 826–827
COUNT(*) iterator, 514–515
covered columns, 528–531
covering optimization rule, 473
cpu_id (sys.dm_os_schedulers), 43
CPUs
binding schedulers to, 41–42
NUMA nodes, 36, 37
schedulers, 38
crash recovery, 172
crawl, 498
CREATE DATABASE command, 104, 105, 106, 156
CREATE DATABASE...FOR ATTACH DDL
statement, 505
CREATE DATABASE FOR ATTACH syntax, 141
CREATE DATABASE statement
CONTAINMENT option, 163
FILEGROUP keyword, 110
CREATE EVENT SESSION statement, 83
CREATE FULLTEXT CATALOG DDL statement,
492–493
CREATE FUNCTION command, 260–261
CREATE INDEX command, 313–314
DROP_EXISTING option, 360–361, 362–363
FILLFACTOR option, 362
INCLUDE syntax, 332–333
SORT_IN_TEMPDB option, 363
CREATE INDEX operation, 190
CREATE INDEX statement
monitoring space usage in tempdb, 154
CreateLSN column (VLFs), 180
CREATE PARTITION SCHEME command, 445
CREATE PRIMARY XML INDEX statement, 459
CREATE SCHEMA statement, 133
CREATE SEQUENCE permission, 243
CREATE SPATIAL INDEX DDL statement, 472
CREATE TABLE syntax, 203–204
CREATE VIEW statement
WITH SCHEMABINDING option, 335
creating
columnstore indexes, 370–372
contained users, 163–166

databases, 104–105
  multiple files, 111
database snapshots, 156–159
filegroups, 110, 112
FILESTREAM data storage database, 397–398
FILESTREAM data tables, 397–398
full-text indexes, 498–499
indexed views, 339–340
indexes, 313–315
  IGNORE_DUP_KEY option, 313–314
  index placement, 314
  MAXDOP option, 314
  STATISTICS_NORECOMPUTE, 314
indexes on computed columns, 335–336
objects
  in schemas, 134
tables, 203–204
  data types, 208–233
  delimited identifiers, 206–207
  naming, 204–205
  naming conventions, 207–208
  NULL values, 233–235
  reserved keywords, 205–206
  sparse columns (storage format), 412–413
  user-defined data types, 235–236
XML indexes, 459–463
  primary XML indexes, 460–463
  secondary XML indexes, 463
creation_time (sys.dm_os_threads), 44
cross-catalog consistency checks, 882–883
cross joins, 535
cross-page consistency checks, 871–881
  B-tree consistency checks, 872–875
  FILESTREAM consistency checks, 876–881
  heap consistency checks, 871–872
  LOB linkage consistency checks, 875–877
cross products, 600
cross-table consistency checks, 881–885
  cross-catalog consistency checks, 882–883
  indexed view consistency checks, 883–885
  Service Broker feature, 882
current_tasks_count (sys.dm_os_schedulers), 43
CURRENT_TIMESTAMP function, 211
current_workers_count (sys.dm_os_schedulers), 43
CURSOR_CLOSE_ON_COMMIT {ON | OFF}
    option, 125
CURSOR_DEFAULT {LOCAL | GLOBAL} option, 125
cursor options, 125
cycle deadlocks, 806–807
Cycle property, SEQUENCE objects, 241

D

DAC (dedicated administrator connection). *See* DAC
DAC (Dedicated Administrator Connection), 45–47,
    458
  connecting to, 45
  scheduler, 46
  SQL statements, 46
data
  integrity, constraints, 276–279
  internal storage, tables, 270–273
  modification
    indexes, 341–359
  row-level versioning
    tempdb database, 146
  storage
    data compression, 423–443
    FILESTREAM data, 394–405
    FileTable data, 404–410
    LOB (large object) data, 381–393
    metadata, 245–246
    partitioning, 444–455
    sparse columns, 411–423
    tables, 203–296
database collation, 217
Database Console Commands. *See* DBCCs
Database Engine
  components, 10–17
    protocols, 11–12
    query processor, 12–14
    storage engine, 14–17
database_id parameter (dm_db_database_page_
    allocations function), 306
database_id parameter (dm_db_index_physical_stats
    DMV), 302
database_id parameter (sys.dm_io_virtual_file_stats
    function), 159
database-level authentication, 165
database locks, 782–783
DATABASEPROPERTYEX function, 8, 501
databases, 139–144
  AdventureWorks, 100
  AdventureWorks2012
    creating snapshot, 156
    security, 132
  altering, 114–119
    space allocation, 116–119
    user-defined space, 116
  authentication, 164–165
  backing up, 136

backup and restore processes, 188–201
  choosing backup type, 194–195
  files and filegroups, 197–198
  partial backups, 198
  partial restore, 200
  recovery models, 190–194
  restoring pages, 198–200
  restoring with standby, 200–201
  types of backups, 189–190
copying, 134–136
creating, 104–105
  FILESTREAM data storage, 397–398
  multiple files, 111
definition, 99
detaching, 135–136
expanding, 106–109
  automatic file expansion, 106–107
  fast file initialization, 107–108
  manual file expansion, 107
features, 99
filegroups, 109–113
  default, 110–111
  primary, 110
files, 101–106
  log, 102
  primary data, 101–102
  properties, 102
  secondary data, 102
  sys.database_files, 102–103
instances, 99
master, 139–140
model, 140
moving, 134–136, 142–144
msdb, 141–142
newdb, 185
Northwind, 101
objects, 99
partially contained, 162–169
  collation changes, 166–168
  configuring, 162–163
  creating contained users, 163–166
  detecting uncontained features, 168–169
properties, 99
pubs, 101
reattaching, 135–136
recovery
  models, 190–194
resource, 140–141
restoring, 136
security, 129–134

  default schemas, 134
SemanticsDB, 505
setting options, 119–129
  auto options, 125–126
  cursor options, 125
  database recovery options, 128–129
  SQL options, 126–127
  state options, 122–125
shrinking, 106–109, 837–841
  automatic shrinkage, 108
  AUTO_SHRINK option, 841–842
  data file shrinking, 838–839
  DBCC SHRINKFILE command, 840
  log file shrinking, 840
  manual shrinkage, 108–109
snapshots, 155–161
  alternatives to, 844–845
  consistency checks, 843
  creating, 156–159
  management, 161
  space monitoring, 159–161
system base tables, 3
tempdb, 140, 144–156
  best practices, 147–148
  contention, 148–152
  objects, 144–145
  optimizations, 146–147
  space monitoring, 153–155
truncating, 185
versus schemas, 133
database state
  viewing, row versioning, 816–817
Database Tuning Advisor program, 484
database_uncontained_usage extended event
  detecting uncontained features in databases, 168
data cache, 47
  access to pages in, 48–49
  page management, 48–49
data compression, 423–443
  pages, 433–442
    analysis, 440–441
    backup compression, 443
    CI record building, 440–441
    column prefix compression, 435–436
    dictionary compression, 436–437
    metadata, 441
    performance issues, 442–443
    physical storage, 437–439
  rows, 424–432
    CD (column descriptor) format, 426–432

enabling, 425–426
vardecimal, 423
Data Definition Language (DDL) statements
ALTER FULLTEXT INDEX, 499
CREATE DATABASE...FOR ATTACH, 505
CREATE FULLTEXT CATALOG, 492–493
CREATE PRIMARY XML INDEX, 459
CREATE SPATIAL INDEX, 472
mixing with DML statements, 729
snapshot isolation, 819–822
data file shrinking, 838–839
Data Manipulation (DML) statements
mixing with DDL statements, 729
Data Manipulation Language (DML) statements,
13–14
data modification statements, 598–599
data page processing, per-table logical consistency
checks, 864–866
data pages, tables, 248–257
data rows, 249
deallocation, 291
examination of, 250–257
in-row, 245
LOB, 245
page header, 249
row offset array, 249–250
row-overflow, 245
data purity checks, processing columns, 867–869
DATA_PURITY option (DBCC CHECKDB), 893
data rows
unrestricted-length LOB data, storage, 389–392
data rows, tables, 249, 257–259
DATA section (DBCC PAGE command output), 256
data_space_id column (sys.database_files), 102
Data Storage page (Extended Exvents UI), 89
Datatype property, SEQUENCE objects, 240
data types
BIGINT, 496
spatial
GEOGRAPHY, 471
GEOMETRY, 471
tables, 208–233
changing, 280–281
character, 213–230
date and time, 210–213
numeric, 208–210
special data types, 230–233
user-defined, 235–236
UNIQUEIDENTIFIER, 507

XML
built-in SQL methods, 463
Data UDX operator, 471
data warehouses
query execution, 599–603
data warehousing
Query Optimizer, 659–669
batch processing, 662–666
columnstore indexes, 660–661, 670–671
plan shape, 667–670
datbases
security
access, 130–131
date data types, 210–213
datetime2 data type, 210
datetime data type, 210
datetimeoffset data type, 210
DBCC CHECKALLOC command, 898–899
DBCC CHECKCATALOG command, 882, 883
DBCC CHECKCONSTRAINTS command, 901
DBCC CHECKDB
tempdb database, 144
DBCC CHECKDB command
consistency checking
allocation consistency checks, 856–860
alternatives to DBCC CHECKDB, 898–901
cross-table consistency checks, 881–885
getting consistent views of databases,
842–845
options, 890–893
output, 885–890
performing database repairs, 893–897
per-table logical consistency checks, 860–866
primitive system catalog consistency
checks, 855–856
processing columns, 866–881
processing databases efficiently, 845–855
DBCC CHECKFILEGROUP command, 899–900
DBCC CHECKIDENT command, 900
DBCC CHECKIDENT(tablename) statement, 240
DBCC CHECKTABLE command, 889, 890
DBCC commands
consistency checking, 841–901
allocation consistency checks, 856–860
alternatives to DBCC CHECKDB, 898–901
consistent view of database, 842–845
cross-table consistency checks, 881–885
DBCC CHECKDB options, 890–893
DBCC CHECKDB output, 885–890
performing database repairs, 893–897

per-table logical consistency checks, 860–866

primitive system catalog consistency checks, 855–856

processing columns, 866–881

processing the database efficiently, 845–855

shrinking files and databases, 837–841

AUTO_SHRINK option, 841–842

data file shrinking, 838–839

DBCC SHRINKFILE command, 840

log file shrinking, 840

DBCC DBREINDEX operation, 190

DBCC FREESYSTEMCACHE command, 743

DBCC LOG command, 177

DBCC LOGINFO command, 179

DBCC MEMORYSTATUS tool, 691

DBCC_MULTIOBJECT_SCANNER latch, 853

DBCC OPTIMIZER_WHATIF statement, 602

DBCC PAGE command, 250, 824

DBCCs (Database Console Commands), 108

DBCC SHOW_STATISTICS command, 632–633

DBCC SHRINKDATABASE, 108

DBCC SHRINKDATABASE command, 109, 178, 187, 838

DBCC SHRINKFILE command, 107, 108, 109, 840

DBCC SQLPERF('logspace') command, 188

DBCC TRACEOFF command, 23

DBCC TRACEON command, 23

dbid-fileno-pageno identifier

hashing, 48

dbo schema, 205

DCM (Differential Changed Map) pages, 857

DDL commands

code, 68–70

DDL contention

tempdb database, 153

DDL (Data Definition Language) statements

ALTER FULLTEXT INDEX, 499

CREATE DATABASE...FOR ATTACH, 505

CREATE FULLTEXT CATALOG, 492–493

CREATE SPATIAL INDEX, 472

mixing with DML statements, 729

snapshot isolation, 819–822

deadlocks, 806–811

conversion deadlocks, 808–809

cycle deadlocks, 806–807

detection, intervention, and avoidance, 809–811

parallel, 586

deallocation

pages, 149

deallocation, data pages, 291

debug events, 76

debugging planning issues, Query Optimizer, 691–692

decimals, exact numeric data types, 209

declarative data integrity, 276–279

decorrelation, subqueries, 576–577

dedicated administrator connection. See DAC

Dedicated Administrator Connection (DAC), 458

deepest cell optimization rule, 473

DEFAULT constraint, 276

default filegroup, 110–111

Default group, 66

Default pool, 64

default schema, 205

default schemas, 134

Default value (objtype columns), 706

deferred drop, 858

deferred drop operations

tempdb database, 147

degree of normalization, data warehouses, 599

degree of parallelism (DOP), 582–583

DELETE command, 672–673

DELETE statement, 598–599

deleting

FILESTREAM data, 400

rows

heap data modifications, 288–292

modifying indexes, 346–353

delimited identifiers

naming tables, 206–207

denormalized dimensional model, data warehouses, 599

density

spatial indexes, 472

density information, Query Optimizer statistics, 634–636

multicolumn statistics, 641

dependencies, transactions, 768–769

depth-first algorithm, 846

design

Query Optimizer statistics, 631–634

detaching

databases, 135–136

DETAILED mode (mode parameter), 304

detecting fragmentation, B-tree indexes, 363

detecting uncontained features (partially contained databases), 168–169

detection, deadlocks, 809–811

deterministic functions, 334

Developer edition, 1–2

diagnostic stored procedures
    full-text indexes, 500–501
    spatial indexes, 484–491
dialog boxes
    Aggregation, 94
    Columns, 92
    Grouping, 93
    Performance Options, 21–22
dictionary area (CI records), 438
dictionary compression, pages, 436–437
DIFF (Differential Changed Map), 119
DIFF (Differential Changed Map) pages, 189
differential backups, 189, 195
Differential Changed Map (DCM) pages, 857
Differential Changed Map (DIFF), 119
Differential Changed Map (DIFF) pages, 189
dimensional data modeling, data warehouses, 600
dimension tables, 600, 659
dirty buffers, 52
dirty page tables (DPTs), 174
dirty reads, 769
disabling
    constraints (tables), 281–282
    protocols, 23
    Resource Governor, 71
disabling indexes, 361–362
Disk I/O settings, 28–30
disk pages, 15
disk space issues, consistent database view, 844–845
display options, query plans, 520–526
distinct aggregates
    hash aggreagation, 554–555
    scalar aggregation, 550–551
DISTINCT keyword
    scalar aggregate, 547
Distributed Query feature (Query Optimizer), 687–689
distribute streams exchange, 585
dm_db_*, 7
dm_db_database_page_allocations function, 306–307, 319, 329
dm_db_index_operational_stats function, 441
dm_db_index_physical_stats DMV, 302–305, 318, 328
dm_db_index_physical_stats function, 353
dm_exec_*, 6
dm_exec_requests DMV, 366
dm_exec_sessions DMV, 334–335
dm_io_*, 7

DML contention
    tempdb database, 148–152
DML (Data Manipulation Language) statements, 13–14
DML (Data Manipulation) statements
    mixing with DDL statements, 729
dm_logpool*, 7
dm_os_*, 6
dm_tran_*, 7
dm_tran_locks DMV, 325
DMVs (Dynamic Management Objects), 6–7
    dm_db_*, 7
    dm_exec_*, 6
    dm_io_*, 7
    dm_logpool*, 7
    dm_os_*, 6
    dm_tran_*, 7
    log pool, 177
    memory internals, 57–59
    monitoring space usage in tempdb, 153
    schedulers, 42–45
    sys.dm_db_uncontained_entities
        detecting uncontained features in databases, 168
    sys.dm_exec_cached_plans, 72
    sys.dm_exec_connections, 6
    sys.dm_exec_query_memory_grants, 72
    sys.dm_exec_query_resource_semaphores, 72
    sys.dm_exec_requests, 6, 72
    sys.dm_exec_sessions, 6, 72
    sys.dm_os_memory_brokers, 72
    sys.dm_resource_governor_configuration, 72
    sys.dm_resource_governor_resource_pools, 72
    sys.dm_xe_packages, 75
    sys.dm_xe_sessions, 96–97
DMVs (dynamic management views)
    full-text indexes, 500
docid map table, 494
DOCUMENT qualifier, 470
Document Similarity Index (DSI) semantic index, 506
domain integrity, 276
DONE value (task_state), 44
DOP (degree of parallelism), 582–583
DPTs (dirty page tables), 174
drawbacks
    parameterization, 715–717
DROP DATABASE command, 135
DROP DATABASE operation, 161
DROP_EXISTING option (CREATE INDEX command), 360–363

DROP INDEX command, 360
DROP INDEX operation, 191
dropped_event_count and dropped_buffer_count
        column (sys.dm_xe_sessions), 97
dropping
    columns from tables, 283
    constraints (tables), 281–282
DSI (Document Similarity Index) semantic index, 506
durability property (transactions), 768
duration, locks, 785
dynamic affinity, 41
dynamic cursor support, iterators, 516–517
dynamic index seeks, 560–563
Dynamic Management Objects (DMVs), 6–7
    dm_db_*, 7
    dm_exec_*, 6
    dm_io_*, 7
    dm_logpool*, 7
    dm_os_*, 6
    dm_tran_*, 7
    log pool, 177
    monitoring space usage in tempdb, 153
    schedulers, 42–45
    sys.dm_db_uncontianed_entities
        detecting incontained features in
            databases, 168
    sys.dm_exec_cached_plans, 72
    sys.dm_exec_connections, 6
    sys.dm_exec_query_memory_grants, 72
    sys.dm_exec_query_resource_semaphores, 72
    sys.dm_exec_requests, 6, 72
    sys.dm_exec_sessions, 6, 72
    sys.dm_os_memory_brokers, 72
    sys.dm_resource_governor_configuration, 72
    sys.dm_resource_governor_resource_pools, 72
    sys.dm_resource_governor_workload_groups, 72
    sys.dm_xe_packages, 75
    sys.dm_xe_sessions, 96–97
dynamic management views (DMVs)
    full-text indexes, 500

E

EditionID property, 2
editions
    memory configurations, 56
    SQL Server, 1–2
efficiently processing databases, 845–855
    parallelism, 853–855
    performing fact generation, 846–848

processing batches, 851–852
    query processor, 848–851
    reading pages to process, 852–853
ellipsoidal (round-earth) data, 231
EMERGENCY mode, 122, 123
EMERGENCY mode repair, DBCC CHECKDB, 896–897
enabling
    constraints (tables), 281–282
    FILESTREAM data storage access, 395–396
    Optimize for Ad Hoc Workloads option, 708–709
    Resource Governor, 62
    row compression, 425–426
endpoints
    TDS (tabular data stream), 12
EngineEdition property, 1–2
Enterprise edition, 1–2
Enterprise Evaluation edition, 1–2
entity integrity, 276
entries_count column (sys.dm_os_memory_cache_
        counters), 58
entries_in_use_count column (sys.dm_os_memory_
        cache_counters), 58
environmental changes, correctness-based
        recompilation, 722
equality (equijoin) predicates, 536
equijoin (equality) predicates, 536
error reporting to Microsoft, DBCC CHECKDB
        output, 888–889
escalation, locking, 804–805
estimated execution query plans, 518–519
ESTIMATEONLY option (DBCC CHECKDB), 892
etw_classic_sync_target target, 80, 90
ETW (Event Tracing for Windows), 76
Euclidean (flat-earth) data, 231
event_counter target, 81
event data
    querying, 84–85
Event Fields tab, 88–89
event_file target, 80
events, 76–77
    admin, 76
    analytic, 76
    columns, 76
    database_uncontained_usage extended
        detecting uncontained features in
            databases, 168
    debug, 76
    extended, full-text indexes, 501–502, 503–505
    operational, 76
    sqlserver.latch_suspend_end, 151

event sessions, 75
  catalog metadata, 96
  creating, 86–90
  Extended Events, 82–83
    creating, 83–84
  managing, 86–90
  removing, 86
  session-scoped options, 96–97
  stop, 86
Events page (Extended Events UI), 87–88
event_stream target, 81
Event Tracing for Windows (ETW), 76
event_type column (suspect_pages table), 198
exact numeric data types, 208
exchange operator (parallelism), 583–586
Exchange operator (Query Optimizer), 624
exclusive locks, 358, 776
exec_context_id (sys.dm_os_waiting_tasks), 45
execute method, 747, 748
EXECUTE...WITH RECOMPILE option, 719
execution cache plans, 734
execution contexts, 734
execution, queries
  analyzing plans, 525–600
    advanced index operations, 560–567
    aggregations, 545–556
    bookmark lookup, 531–533
    data modification statements, 598–599
    joins, 533–544
    parallelism, 580–598
    scans and seeks, 526–528
    seekable predicates and covered
      columns, 528–531
    subqueries, 566–580
    unions, 555–559
  batch processing, 603–608
  columnstore indexes, 603–608
  data warehouses, 599–603
  hints, 609
  query processing, 513–517
  reading query plans, 517–526
    display options, 520–526
    estimated vs. actual query plans, 518–519
    graphical plans, 517
    text plans, 518
    XML plans, 518
exist method, 464
EXISTS subqueries, 579
expanding
  databases, 106–109

automatic file expansion, 106–107
  fast file initialization, 107–108
  manual file expansion, 107
Express edition, 2
expression evaluator objects, 867
extended events
  full-text indexes, 501–502, 503–505
Extended Events, 73
  actions, 77
    package0.attach_activity_id, 97
    package0.attach_activity_id_xfer, 97
  architecture, 73
  ETW (Event Tracing for Windows), 76
  events, 76–77
  event sessions, 75, 82–83
    creating, 83–84, 86–90
    managing, 86–90
    removing, 86
    stopping, 86
  life cycle, 73–74
  maps, 79
  object names, 75
  packages, 75
  predicates, 78–79
  querying event data, 84–85
  targets, 80–82
    viewing content, 90–95
  types, 79
  User Interface, 86–97
    aggregating data, 93–95
    Data Storage page, 89
    Events page, 87–88
    General page, 86–87
    grouping data, 93–95
    viewing target data, 90–95
extended indexes, Query Optimizer, 689
EXTENDED_LOGICAL_CHECKS option, 884, 885
EXTENDED_LOGICAL_CHECKS option (DBCC
    CHECKDB), 891
Extended Proc value (cacheobjtype columns), 705
Extended Stored Procedures cache store, 733
extent fragmentation, 359
extent locks, 782
external fragmentation, 359

F

fact-aggregation algorithm, 850
fact-generation algorithm, 848
fact generation, DBCC CHECKDB, 846–848

facts
  actual text, 847
  consistency checking, 847
  parent text, 846
  sibling, 847
fact-sorting algorithm, 850
fact-storing algorthm, 850
fact tables, 600, 659
fast file initialization, 107–108
FAST N hint, 644–645
FAST <number_rows> hint, Query Optimizer, 695
fast recovery, 174
FDHOST.exe executable, 498
fibers
  compared to threads, 40
FILEGROUP keyword
  creating filegroups, 110
filegroups, 109–113
  backing up and restoring, 189, 197–198
  creating, 110, 112
  default, 110–111
  filestream, 113
  indexes, 111
  primary, 110
  tables, 111
FILEGROUP specification
  full-text indexes, 493
FILEGROWTH property, 105
file_guid column (sys.database_files), 102
Fileid column (sys.database_files), 102
FileId column (VLFs), 179
file_id parameter (sys.dm_io_virtual_file_stats
        function), 159
files
  backing up and restoring, 189, 197–198
  databases, 101–106
    log, 102
    primary data, 101–102
    properties, 102
    secondary data, 102
    sys.database_files, 102–103
  log
    shrinking, 109
  primary, 110
  shrinking, 837–841
    AUTO_SHRINK option, 841–842
    data file shrinking, 838–839
    DBCC SHRINKFILE command, 840
    log file shrinking, 840
  sparse, 156

FileSize column (VLFs), 179
Filestream Access Level option, 30
FILESTREAM consistency checks, 876–881
FILESTREAM data, storage, 394–405
  creating database, 397–398
  creating tables, 397–398
  enabling access, 395–396
  manipulating data, 399–404
    deleting, 400
    garbage collection, 402–404
    inserting data, 399
    logging changes, 401
    transactions, 401–402
    updates, 400
  metadata, 404–406
  performance, 409–410
filestream filegroups, 113
FILESTREAM garbage collection process, 844
FileTable storage, 404–410
FILLFACTOR option (CREATE INDEX command), 362
FILLFACTOR (XML index option), 460
filtered indexes, 332, 342
filtered indexes, Query Optimizer, 648–650
Filtered Statistics feature, Query Optimizer, 636–637
Filter-For-Pid-Level1 iterator, 504
Filtering (Predicate) tab, 88–89
Filter iterator, 480
Filter() method, 488
Filter operator, 504
firewall settings, 23
first_snapshot_sequence_num column, 828
first_useful_sequence_num column, 828
fixed-length columns, tables, 214–215
fixed-length rows, tables, 262–265
FixedVar format, 257
FOR ATTACH_REBUILD_LOG option, 136
forced parameterization, 627, 714, 747
FORCED parameterization model, 698
FORCESEEK hint, Query Optimizer, 695
FOREIGN KEY constraint, 276
formats
  index rows, B-tree indexes, 315–316
forwarded records, 363–364
forwarding pointer, 430
forward pointers, 293–294, 356–357
fragmentation
  B-tree indexes
    detecting, 363
    removing, 364–366
  index data modification, 359–360

free buffer list, 49–50

FREEPROCCACHE command, 731

Free Space in tempdb counter, 826

FREETEXT operator, 501

FreeTextSSETermRank iterator, 504

FREETEXTTABLE function, 502

freezing, plan cache, 763

frequency information, Query Optimizer statistics, 634–636

friendly name columns, 9

FSeqNo column (VLFs), 179

Fsize row header, 315

full backups, 189

full outer joins, 538

FULL recovery model (databases), 191

fulltext_avdl_[t_objectid] internal table (full-text indexes), 496

FULLTEXTCATALOGPROPERTY function, 501

full-text catalogs, 492–493

fulltext_docidfilter_[t_objectid] internal table (full-text indexes), 496–497

full_text_exec_query_stats event, 503–504

fulltext_index_docidmap_[t_objectid] internal table (full-text indexes), 496

fulltext_index_docidstatus_[t_objectid] internal table (full-text indexes), 495

fulltext_indexeddocid_[t_objectid] internal table (full-text indexes), 496

full-text indexes, 492–505

    configuring, 500–501

    creating, 498–499

    diagnostic information, 500–501

    extended event information, 503–505

    internal tables, 494–497

    maintenance, 499–500

    metadata views, 497

    query plans, 502–503

    status metadata, 500–501

    use in a query, 501–502

FulltextMatch function, 502

full_text_query_recompile event, 503–504

full-text search daemon launcher service (MSSQLFDLauncher), 492

fulltext_semantic_document_language extended event, 506

FULLTEXTSERVICEPROPERTY function, 501

fulltext_thesaurus_metadata_table internal table, 497

fulltext_thesaurus_phrase_table internal table, 497

fulltext_thesaurus_state_table internal table, 497

functions

    CheckIndex, 850

    classifier, 62–63

    cleanup, 826

    COLUMNPROPERTY, 336

    COLUMNPROPERTYEX, 501

    compiled objects, 720–721

    computed columns, indexes, 334–335

    CONTAINSTABLE, 502

    CURRENT_TIMESTAMP, 211

    DATABASEPROPERTYEX, 8, 501

    deterministic, 334

    dm_db_database_page_allocations, 306–307, 319, 329

    dm_db_index_operational_stats, 441

    dm_db_index_physical_stats ghost records, 353

    FREETEXTTABLE, 502

    FULLTEXTCATALOGPROPERTY, 501

    FulltextMatch, 502

    FULLTEXTSERVICEPROPERTY, 501

    GETANSINULL, 234

    IDENT_CURRENT. SCOPE_IDENTITY, 239

    IDENT_INCR(tablename), 237–238

    IDENT_SEED(tablename), 237–238

    indexed views, 334–335

    INDEXPROPERTYEX, 501

    NEWID, 232

    NEWSEQUENTIALID, 232

    nondeterministic, 334

    object_definition, 5

    OBJECTPROPERTY, 335

    OBJECTPROPERTYEX, 501

    partitioning, 444–446

    PathName, 404

    property, 8–9

    RangePartitionNew, 682

    REPLICATE, 266

    SCOPE_IDENTITY, 239

    SEMANTICKEYPHRASETABLE, 507

    SEMANTICSIMILARITYDETAILSTABLE, 509

    SEMANTICSIMILARITYTABLE, 508

    SERVERPROPERTYEX, 501

    SESSIONPROPERTY, 334

    STATMAN, 633

    sys.dm_exec_cached_plan_dependent_objects, 738

    sys.dm_exec_query_stats, 739–740

    sys.dm_exec_sql_text, 736–738

    sys.dm_exec_text_query_plan, 737

sys.dm_fts_index_keywords, 497
sys.dm_fts_index_keywords_by_document, 497
sys.dm_fts_index_keywords_by_property, 497
sys.dm_io_virtual_file_stats, 159
sys.fn_PhysLocFormatter
    locating physical pages, tables, 261–262
sys.fn_validate_plan_guide, 763
system, 8–9
TERTIARY_WEIGHTS ', 225

Grouping dialog box, 93
GROUP_MAX_REQUESTS property, 68
groups
    Default, 66
    Internal, 66
    workload
        properties, 67–68
growth column (sys.database_files), 103
GUID (globally unique identifier) data type, 231

G

GAM (Global Allocation Map) pages, 116, 838, 856
garbage collection
    FILESTREAM data, 402–404
gather streams exchange, 585
General page (Extended Events UI), 86–87
geography data type, 231
GEOGRAPHY data type, 471
GEOGRAPHY_GRID spatial index, 476
geometry data type, 231
GEOMETRY data type, 471
GEOMETRY_GRID spatial index, 476
GETANSINULL function, 234
GetRow method, 514
ghost-cleanup thread, 350
ghost records, 350–351, 364, 825–826
global aggregates, 589
Global Allocation Map (GAM) pages, 116, 838, 856
Global Fields (Actions) tab, 88–89
globally unique identifier (GUID) data type, 231
global memory pressure, plan cache, 743
GRANT CREATE TABLE TO statement, 133
granularity, locks, 778–784
    additional lock resources, 782
    allocation unit locks, 783
    associated entity ID, 784–785
    database locks, 782–783
    extent locks, 782
    identifying lock resources, 783–784
    key locks, 780–782
    partition-level locks, 783
graphical plans (queries), 517
gridding specifications, 473
GROUP BY clause
    stream aggregation, 548–552
GROUP BY operator, Query Optimizer, 692–693
    cardinality estimation, 640–641
grouping data
    Extended Events UI, 93–95

H

Halloween Protection feature, Query Optimizer
                updates, 674–675
handles, plan cache, 735–736
hash aggregations, 552–556
hashing, 48
hash joins, 542–544
    parallelism, 595
hash partitioning, parallelism, 595–596
hash tables, 48
hash union operators, 558
header, CI records, 438
heap consistency checks, 871–872
heap data modifications, 286–295
    allocation structures, 286–288
    deleting rows, 288–292
    inserting rows, 288
    updating rows, 292–295
Heap or B-Tree (hobt), 245
heaps
    deleting rows, 347–350
    inserting rows, 342
    nonclustered index rows, 322–327
heuristics, detecting star schemas, 600
HighMemoryResourceNotification flag, 50
hints, 609
    locking, 832–836
    plan cache optimization, 752–754
    Query Optimizer, 689–699
        debugging planning issues, 691–692
        FAST <number_rows> hint, 695
        FORCESEEK hint, 695
        GROUP BY operation, 692–693
        JOIN operations, 693–694
        MAXDOP<N> hint, 696
        NDEX=<indexname> | <indexid> hint, 694
        NOEXPAND hint, 699
        OPTIMIZE FOR hint, 696–698

PARAMETERIZATION hint, 698
UNION operations, 693–694
USE PLAN hint, 699–700
histograms, cardinality estimation, 639
hobt (Heap or B-Tree), 245
HOLDLOCK hint, 833
hotfixes, Query Optimizer, 700–701
Hungarian-style notation, 208

I

IAM (Index Allocation Map) chains, 838, 857
IAM (Index Allocation Map) page, 148
IAM (Index Allocation Map) pages, 118
IDENT_CURRENT. SCOPE_IDENTITY function, 239
identification
    index keys, 529–531
identifying lock resources, 783–784
IDENT_INCR(tablename) function, 237–238
IDENTITYCOL keyword, 238
IDENTITY property (tables), 237–240
IDENT_SEED(tablename) function, 237–238
ifts_comp_fragment [t_objectid]_[ordinal] internal
    table (full-text indexes), 495
IGNORE_DUP_KEY=ON option, 475
IGNORE_DUP_KEY option, creating indexes, 313–314
IGNORE_NONCLUSTERED_COLUMNSTORE_INDEX
    hint, 609
implementation
    computed columns, indexes, 336
IMPORTANCE property, 67
INCLUDE syntax (CREATE INDEX command), 332–
    333
Increment property, SEQUENCE objects, 240
Independence assumption, Query Optimizer, 637
Index Allocation Map (IAM) chains, 838
Index Allocation Map (IAM) page, 148
Index Allocation Map (IAM) pages, 118
index-at-a-time modifications, 358
Index Create Memory option, 32
indexed-view consistency checks, 883–886
indexed views, 333–335, 338–341, 881
    creating, 339–340
    permissible functions, 334–335
    requirements, 338–339
    schema binding, 335
    SET options, 333–334
    uses, 340–341
Indexed Views feature, Query Optimization,
    649–653

indexes
    advanced index operations, 560–567
        dynamic index seeks, 560–563
        index intersections, 565–567
        index unions, 562–564
    analysis, 302–307
        dm_db_database_page_allocations
            function, 306–307
        dm_db_index_physical_stats DMV, 302–305
    B-tree, 297, 299–302
        large key column example, 300–301
        management, 360–370
        narrow key column example, 301–302
        physical index structure, 315–332
        structure, 308–312
    clustered, 457. See clustered indexes
    columnstore, 297, 370–380, 603–608
        creating, 370–372
        metadata, 376–380
        storage, 371–375
    composite, 529
    computed columns, 333–338
        creating, 335–336
        implementation, 336
        permissible functions, 334–335
        persisted columns, 337–338
        schema binding, 335
        SET options, 333–334
    creating, 313–315
        IGNORE_DUP_KEY option, 313–314
        index placement, 314
        MAXDOP option, 314
        STATISTICS_NORECOMPUTE, 314
    data modification, 341–359
        deleting rows, 346–353
        fragmentation, 359–360
        inserting rows, 342
        locking, 358
        logging, 358
        splitting pages, 342–346
        table-level vs index-level, 357
        updating rows, 354–358
    filegroups, 111
    full-text indexes, 492–505
        configuring, 500–501
        creating, 498–499
        diagnostic information, 500–501
        extended event information, 503–505
        internal tables, 494–497
        maintenance, 499–500

metadata views, 497
query plans, 502–503
status metadata, 500–501
use in a query, 501–502
indexed views, 333–335, 338–341
creating, 339–340
permissible functions, 334–335
requirements, 338–339
schema binding, 335
SET options, 333–334
uses, 340–341
nonclustered. *See* nonclustered indexes
overview, 298–299
partitioning, 444–455
columnstore indexes, 452–454
functions and schemes, 444–446
metadata, 446–449
sliding window benefits, 450–453
semantic indexes, 505–510
single-column, 528
spatial indexes, 471–491
columns, 458
composition of, 475–477
diagnostic stored procedures, 484–491
ensuring use, 478–479
nearest neighbor queries, 481–484
purpose of, 472–476
query plans, 479–480
spatial queries, 477
special indexes versus ordinary indexes, 457–458
XML
creating and maintaining, 459–463
query plans, 465–467, 470–471
schema-validated columns, 469–470
secondary XML indexes, 468–469
XQuery, 463–465
INDEX hint, 609
index_id parameter (dm_db_database_page_
allocations function), 306
index_id parameter (dm_db_index_physical_stats
DMV), 303
index keys
identification, 529–531
index-level data modification, indexes, 357
index merge joins, 540–542
Index metadata objects, 861
index operations, 14, 190
index page processing, per-table logical consistency
checks, 864–866
index population, 498

INDEXPROPERTYEX function, 501
index ranges
read-ahead, 60
index rows, B-tree indexes, 315–316
index seek, 527
index selection, Query Optimization, 645–654
filtered indexes, 648–650
indexed views, 649–653
indirect checkpoints, 29
inequality predicates, 536
INFORMATION_SCHEMA, 7
information schema views, 7
inner-side parallel execution, 593–594
input fraction, 525
in-row data pages, 245
INSERT command, 671–672
inserting
FILESTREAM data, 399
rows
heap data modifications, 288
modifying indexes, 342
INSERT INTO . . . SELECT command, 190
INSERT statement, 598–599
Installation Wizard
SQL Server collations, character data types
(tables), 228
installing
SQL Server 2012, 2
instance-level logins permissions, 163
instance-level objects, 162
instances, 57
databases, 99
multiple, 57
integers, exact numeric data types, 208
integrity (data), constraints, 276–279
intent locks, 776
intermediate index pages
splitting, 344
Internal_Filter_Efficiency property, 487
internal fragmentation, 359
Internal group, 66
internal locking architecture, 796–803
internal objects
tempdb database, 145
internal organization, plan cache, 732–744
cache stores, 732–733
compiled plans, 734–735
costing entries, 743–744
execution contexts, 734
metadata, 735

handles, 735–736

sys.dm_exec_cached_plan_dependent_objects
function, 738

sys.dm_exec_cached_plans view, 738–739

sys.dm_exec_procedure_stats view, 740–743

sys.dm_exec_query_stats function, 739–740

sys.dm_exec_requests view, 739–740

sys.dm_exec_sql_text function, 736–738

sys.dm_exec_text_query_plan function, 737

Internal pool, 64

internal queries, parallelism and, 854

internal query optimizations
spatial indexes, 477

internal storage, tables, 243–276
catalog view queries, 246–248
data and time data, 270–273
data pages, 248–257
data rows, 249
examination of, 250–257
page header, 249
row offset array, 249–250
data rows, 257–259
data storage metadata, 245–246
fixed-length rows, 262–265
locating a physical page, 259–262
creating a function to perform
conversion, 260–261
sys.dm_db_database_page_allocations
DMV, 261
sys.fn_PhysLocFormatter function, 261–262
NULL values, 267–270
sql_variant data, 273–276
sys.indexes Catalog view, 244–245
variable-length columns, 267–270
variable-length rows, 265–267
internal tables, full-text indexes, 494–497
intersections, indexes, 565–567
intervention, deadlocks, 809–811
inverted index, full-text, 495–496
I/O costs, 744
ISABOUT clause, full-text index queries, 501
IsAboutSSESum iterator, 504
is_fiber (sys.dm_os_workers), 44
is_media_read_only column (sys.database_files), 103
is_name_reserved column (sys.database_files), 103
isolation levels
FILESTREAM data, 401
snapshot-based, row versioning, 813–830
DDL statements, 819–822

RCSI (read committed snapshot
isolation), 813–814
snapshot isolation, 814–815
snapshot isolation scope, 815–816
summary, 821–822
transaction metadata, 827–830
update conflicts, 817–818
version store, 823–827
viewing database state, 816–817
isolation (transactions), 768, 770–775
Read Committed isolation, 771
Read Uncommitted isolation, 770
Repeatable Read isolation, 771–772
Serializable isolation, 773–774
Snapshot isolation, 772
is_online (sys.dm_os_schedulers), 43
is_percent_growth column (sys.database_files), 103
is_preemptive (sys.dm_os_workers), 44
is_read_committed_snapshot_on column, 817
is_read_only column (sys.database_files), 103
is_sparse column (sys.database_files), 103
iterators, 513–517. *See also* operators
CDocidRankWtToDocidRankAdaptor, 504
ContainsTableSSERank, 504
ContainsTableSSERankForNear, 504
COUNT(*), 514–515
exchange operator (parallelism), 583–586
Filter, 480
Filter-For-Pid-Level1, 504
FreeTextSSETermRank, 504
IsAboutSSESum, 504
MergeUnion Merger Type HeapMerger, 504
properties
dynamic cursor support, 516
memory consumption, 515–516
non-blocking vs blocking, 516
SingleFragmentDocidFilter, 504
SingleFragmentSeekFilter, 504
Table-Valued Function [XML Reader], 471
Table-Valued Function [XML Reader with XPath
Filter], 470
TopNByRank, 504
TOP N Sort, 482
UDX, 471

J

join associativity, 628–629
join collocation, 656
JOIN operations, Query Optimizer, 693–694

joins, 533–544
  hash, 542–544
    parallelism, 595
  merge, 539–542
    parallelism, 594–595
  nested loops, 534–539
    parallelism, 590–591, 592–593
  properties, 544

K

kanatype sensitivity (KS) tokens, 218
KEEPFIXED PLAN hint, 754
KEEPIDENTITY option (T-SQL BULK INSERT
    command), 238
KEEP PLAN hint, 727, 753
key columns, 457
KeyHashValue, 325
key index specification
  full-text indexes, 493
key locks, 780–782
key range information, 457
key-range locks, 778, 781–782
keywords
  column-based DDL, 493
  DISTINCT
    scalar aggregate, 547
  FILEGROUP
    creating filegroups, 110
  IDENTITYCOL, 238
  LANGUAGE, 493
  locking hints, 833–834
  LOOKUP, 532
  naming tables, 205
  SELECT DISTINCT
    stream aggregation, 550–551
  STATISTICAL_SEMANTICS, 493, 505
-k option, 52
KS (kanatype sensitivity) tokens, 218

L

LANGUAGE keyword, 493
large_page_allocations_kb column (sys.dm_os_
    process_memory), 56
last_log_backup_lsn column (sys.database_recovery_
    status catalog view), 185
last_transaction_sequence_num column, 828
latches, 152

latches, deadlocks and, 810
Latin1_General_CI_AI collation, 217
lazy spools, 535
lazywriter, 49–50
leaf-level linked-list, 855
leaf-level pages, splitting, 344–347
leaf levels (indexes), 299–300
  nonclustered indexes, 322
leaf node level (B-tree indexes), 457
left deep hash join tree, 543–544
LEFT JOIN operator, 448
length check, processing computed columns, 867
life cycles
  Extended Events, 73–74
Lightweight Pooling option, 27, 40
limitations
  cardinality estimations, 642–643
  columnstore indexes, 607
  columnstores, 670–671
  Query Optimizer parameterization, 627–628
LIMITED mode (mode parameter), 303
load balancing, 589–590
load_factor (sys.dm_os_schedulers), 43
LOB data pages, 245
LOB data types, 230
LOB (large object) data
  storage, 381–393
    restricted-length/row-overflow, 382–386
    unrestricted-length, 386–393
LOB linkage consistency checks, 875–877
local aggregates, 589
locale (sys.dm_os_threads), 44
local memory pressure, plan cache, 742–743
lock blocks, 799–800
lock duration, 785
locked_page_allocations_kb column (sys.dm_os_
    process_memory), 56
lock granularity, 778–784
  additional lock resources, 782
  allocation unit locks, 783
  associated entity ID, 784–785
  database locks, 782–783
  extent locks, 782
  identifying lock resources, 783–784
  key locks, 780–782
  partition-level locks, 783
locking, 774–811
  basics, 774–775
  compatability, 794–795
  control, 832–836

deadlocks, 806–811
    conversion deadlocks, 808–809
    cycle deadlocks, 806–807
    detection, intervention, and avoidance,
        809–811
escalation, 804–805
examples, 789–795
hints, 832–836
index data modifications, 358
internal architecture, 796–803
lock types for user data, 775–786
    lock duration, 785
    lock granularity, 778–784
    lock modes, 775–778
    lock ownership, 785–786
Query Optimizer updates, 685–686
row-locking versus page-locking, 803–805
spinlocks, 775
viewing locks, 786–789
locking code, 16
locking operations, 17
lock modes, 775–778
    bulk update locks, 777
    conversion locks, 777–778
    exclusive locks, 776
    intent locks, 776
    key-range locks, 778
    schema modification locks, 777
    schema stability locks, 777
    shared locks, 775–776
    update locks, 776
LOCK_MONITOR thread, checking for
    deadlocks, 809
lock_owner_address (request_Columns), 788
lock owner blocks, 800
lock ownership, 785–786
Lock Pages in Memory, 55
lock partitioning, 798–799
locks
    Shared Table
        running DBCC CHECKDB in tempdb
            database, 144
    viewing
        request_Columns, 788–789
        resource_Columns, 786–787
Locks option, 27
LOCK_TIMEOUT, setting, 834–836
log backups, 189, 195
log cache
    transaction logs and recovery, 177

log files, 102
    LSNs (Log Sequence Numbers), 171–172
    shrinking, 109
    transaction logs, 171–177
        changes in log size, 178–188
        log cache, 177
        page LSNs, 175–176
        readable records, 176–177
        recovery phases, 174–175
log file shrinking, 840
logging
    FILESTREAM data changes, 401
    index data modifications, 358
logging optimizations
    tempdb database, 146
logical fragmentation, 359
logical operators, spools, 571
logical properties, 616
log marks, 191
log pool, 177
Log Sequence Number (LSN), 158
Log Sequence Numbers (LSNs), 171–172
    recovery and, 175–176
long data region (CD format), 429
Longest Transaction Running Time counter, 827
LOOKUP keyword, 532
lost updates, transactioin dependencies, 768–769
LowMemoryResourceNotification flag, 50
LRU-K algorithm, 49
LSN (Log Sequence Number), 158
LSNs (Log Sequence Numbers), 171–172
    recovery and, 175–176

M

maintaining recoverable logs, 185–187
maintenance
    full-text indexes, 499–500
    XML indexes, 459–463
        primary XML indexes, 460–463
        secondary XML indexes, 463
management
    B-tree indexes, 360–370
        ALTER INDEX command, 361–364
        detecting fragmentation, 363
        dropping indexes, 360
        online index building, 367–370
        rebuilding indexes, 366–367
        removing fragmentation, 364–366
    plan guides, 758

sparse columns (storage format), 411–414
  altering tables, 413–414
  creating tables, 412–413
version store, 826–827
Management Studio, 184
Management Studio Properties sheet, 517
managing
  database snapshots, 161
  memory
    in other caches, 52–53
  services
    SQL Server Configuration Manager, 19
  tasks, 21–22
manipulating
  FILESTREAM data, 399–404
    deleting, 400
    garbage collection, 402–404
    inserting data, 399
    logging changes, 401
    transactions, 401–402
    updates, 400
manual file expansion, 107
MANUAL option (CHANGE_TRACKING
      specification), 499
manual shrinkage, 108–109
many-to-many merge joins, 539–540
maps
  Extended Events, 79
master database, 139–140
  moving, 143
master merge, 500
MAX_CELLS parameter, 479
MAX_CPU_PERCENT value, 63
Max Degree Of Parallelism option, 32, 33
MAXDOP<N> hint, Query Optimizer, 696
MAXDOP N query hint, 582
MAXDOP option, creating indexes, 314
MAX_DOP property, 68
Maximum value property, SEQUENCE objects, 241
max-length data, LOB storage, 392–393
MAX_MEMORY_PERCENT value, 64
Max Server Memory option
  multiple instances, 57
Max Server Memory setting, 26
max_size column (sys.database_files), 103
MAXSIZE property, 105
MAX values, 63–64
max_version_chain_traversed column, 830
Max Worker Threads option, 27, 28
mechanisms for repairs, DBCC CHECKDB, 894–895

mechanisms, plan cache, 705–732
  ad hoc query caching, 706–711
  compiled objects, 719–721
    functions, 720–721
    stored procedures, 719–720
  parameterization, 711–717
    drawbacks, 715–717
    forced, 714
  prepared queries, 717–719
    caching, 718–719
    prepare-and-execute method, 718
    sp_executesql procedure, 717–718
  recompilation, 722–732
    correctness-based recompiles, 722–725
    multiple recompilations, 729
    optimality-based recompiles, 725–728
    removing plans from cache, 729–732
    skipping recompile step, 728–729
media recovery, 173, 197
Memo (Query Optimizer), 617, 627–630
memory, 47–61
  access to pages in data cache, 48–49
  buffer pool, 47
  buffer pool sizing, 55–57
  checkpoints, 50–52
  column store object pool, 48
  data cache, 47
  DMVs (Dynamic Management Objects), 57–59
  free buffer list, 49–50
  hash aggregates, 552
  hash joins, 543
  lazywriter, 49–50
  management in other caches, 52–53
  Memory Broker, 54
  monitoring with
        QueryMemoryResourceNotification
        API, 50
  NUMA (Non-Uniform Memory Access), 59–60
  page management in data cache, 48–49
  queries, 31
  read-ahead, 60
  sizing, 54–55
  SQL Server 2012 editions, 56
  system configuration settings, 26–27
  Target Memory, 56
  workers, 39
Memory Broker, 54
memory-consuming iterators, 515–516
memory nodes, 37

memory pressure, plan cache
  global, 743
  local, 742–743
merge join operator
  Properties sheet, 521
  ToolTip, 520
merge joins, 539–542
  parallelism, 594–595
MERGE operation (Query Optimizer), 676–678
MergeUnion Merger Type HeapMerger iterator, 504
MergeUnion operator, 504
merging exchanges, 585
metadata, 3–10
  columnstore indexes, 376–380
  data storage, 245–246
  FILESTREAM data, 404–406
  full-text indexes, 497, 500–501
  information schema views, 7
  layers, 9–10
  page compression, 441
  partitions, 446–449
  plan cache, 704, 735
    handles, 735–736
    sys.dm_exec_cached_plan_dependent_objects
      function, 738
    sys.dm_exec_cached_plans view, 738–739
    sys.dm_exec_procedure_stats view, 740–743
    sys.dm_exec_query_stats function, 739–740
    sys.dm_exec_requests view, 739–740
    sys.dm_exec_sql_text function, 736–738
    sys.dm_exec_text_query_plan function, 737
  Resource Governor, 71–72
  security policies, 9
  sessions, 96
  sparse columns (storage format), 419
  system functions, 8–9
  system metadata objects
    catalog views, 4–5
    compatibility views, 3–4
    Dynamic Management Objects, 6–7
  system stored procedures, 9
  transactions
    snapshot-based isolation levels, 827–830
metadata cache, 53
metadata consistency checks, 861–862
METADATA subtypes, 787
methods
  built-in SQL methods, XML data types, 463
  Close, 514
  execute, 747, 748

exist, 464
Filter(), 488
GetRow, 514
modify, 464
nodes, 464
Open, 514
prepare, 718, 748
query, 464
STDistance(), 472–473
value, 464
Microsoft Distributed Transaction Coordinator (MS
      DTC) service, 16
Microsoft SQL Server. See SQL Server
MIN_CPU_PERCENT value, 63
Minimal Logging Changed Map (ML), 119
minimally logged map (ML map) pages, 192
Minimally Logged Map (ML Map) pages, 857
minimally logged operations, database recovery
      models, 190–191
Minimum value property, SEQUENCE objects, 241
minlen columns, 263
MIN_MEMORY_PERCENT value, 64
Min Memory Per Query option, 31, 32
Min Server Memory option
  multiple instances, 57
Min Server Memory setting, 26
MIN values, 63–64
ML map (minimally logged map) pages, 192
ML Map (Minimally Logged Map) pages, 857
ML (Minimal Logging Changed Map), 119
m_nextPage field, 345
model database, 140
models
  database recovery, 190–194
    BULK_LOGGED recovery model, 192–193
    FULL recovery model, 191
    minimally logged operations, 190–191
    SIMPLE recovery model, 193
    switching models, 193–194
models, concurrency, 765–766
mode parameter (dm_db_database_page_allocations
      function), 306
mode parameter (dm_db_index_physical_stats
      DMV), 303
modes, lock. See lock modes
modification counters, optimality-based
      recompiles, 727–728
MODIFY FILE option (ALTER DATABASE
      command), 142

modifying
    constraints (tables), 281–282
    data
        indexes, 341–359
modify method, 464
moving
    databases, 134–136
    rows, 292–293
moving databases, 142–144
moving rows, 354–356
msdb database, 141–142
MS DTC (Microsoft Distributed Transaction
        Coordinator) service, 16
MSSQLFDLauncher (full-text search daemon
        launcher service), 492
mssqlsystemresource database, 140–141
multicolumn indexes, 529
MultiObjectScanner, 852
multi_pages_kb column (sys.dm_os_memory_
        clerks), 54
multiple files
    creating databases, 111
multiple instances, 57
multiple log files (virtual logs), 181–183
multiple recompilations, 729
multiple-row data (tables), constraints, 278–279
multirow subqueries, 566
MULTI_USER mode, 122

N

name column (sys.database_files), 102
Named Pipes, 11
names
    catalog views, 4
    compatibility views, 3
    objects
        Extended Events, 75
namespaces, 133
naming
    constraints (tables), 277–278
    tables, 204–208
        conventions, 207–208
        delimited identifiers, 206–207
        reserved keywords, 205
    Windows collations, character data types
        (tables), 218–219
Ncol field, 315
NDEX=<indexname> | <indexid> hint, Query
        Optimizer, 694

nearest neighbor queries
    spatial indexes, 481–484
nested loops joins, 534–539
    parallelism, 590–591, 592–593
network protocols
    configuring, 18
New Database window, 104
newdb database, 185
NEWID function, 232
NEWSEQUENTIALID function, 232
New Session window (Extended Events UI), 86–87
NEXT VALUE FOR (sequence objects), 240
nodes method, 464
node tables, 460
    columns, 461
NOEXPAND hint, Query Optimizer, 699
NOEXPAND hint, query processor, 884
NOINDEX option (DBCC CHECKDB), 891
NO_INFOMSGS option (DBCC CHECKDB), 887, 892
NOLOCK hint, 834
nonblocking iterators, 516
nonclustered indexes, 298, 855
    B-tree index structure, 311–312, 322–332
    cross-page consistency checks, 879–881
    rebuilding, 368–369
noncorrelated scalar subqueries, 566, 567–569
nondeterministic functions, 334
NONE (No Page Verify Option), 128
nonessential services
    configuring, 23
non-key columns, 457
non-leaf levels (indexes), 299–300
    clustered indexes, 317
    deleting rows, 353
nonmerging exchanges, 585
non-order-preserving exchanges, 585
non-pushable, non-sargable predicates, 647
nonrepeatable reads, transaction dependencies, 769
NON_TRANSACTED_ACCESS option, 406
Non-Uniform Memory Access. See NUMA
Non-Uniform Memory Access (NUMA)
        configurations, 798
nonunique nonclustered index rows, 330–331
Non-Updating Updates feature, Query
        Optimizer, 681–682
normalized data, data warehouses, 599
normalizing
    queries, 13
Northwind, 101

NOTRUNCATE option, shrinking files and
　　databases, 839
NO_WAIT option, 125
NTFS volumes
　　creating snapshots, 159
null bitmap, 315
null checks, processing computed columns, 867
NULL values
　　tables, 233–235, 267–270
NUMA nodes, 36
　　CPUs, 37
NUMA (Non-Uniform Memory Access)
　　memory, 59–60
　　schedulers, 40–41
　　SQLOS (SQL Server Operating System), 36–37
NUMA (Non-Uniform Memory Access)
　　configurations, 798
numeric data types, 208–210
NUMERIC_ROUNDABORT option, 127
nvarchar data, 382

O

object_definition function, 5
Object Explorer in Management Studio
　　creating databases, 104–105
Object Explorer pane, 2
object_id parameter (dm_db_database_page_
　　allocations function), 306
object_id parameter (dm_db_index_physical_stats
　　DMV), 303
Object Linking and Embedding. *See* OLE
object plan guides, 755–756
Object Plans cache store, 732
OBJECTPROPERTYEX function, 501
OBJECTPROPERTY function, 335
objects
　　compiled, 719–721
　　　　functions, 720–721
　　　　stored procedures, 719–720
　　creating
　　　　in schemas, 134
　　instance-level, 162
　　limit in databases, 99
　　names
　　　　Extended Events, 75
　　plan cache, 744–752
　　　　multiple plans, 746–747
　　　　stored procedures, 747
　　　　troubleshooting issues, 748–752

space usage
　　tempdb database, 153–155
SQLServer:Transactions performance, 826–827
syscacheobjects, 744–746
system metadata
　　catalog views, 4–5
　　compatibility views, 3–4
　　Data Management Objects, 6–7
　　tempdb database, 144–145
object stores, 53
objtype column, values, 705–706
observing virtual log files, 179–181
OFFLINE mode, 122, 123
OFFLINE setting
　　schedulers, 38
offset array (long data region), 429
offsets (CI records), 438
OFFSET TABLE section (DBCC PAGE command
　　output), 257
OLEDB protocol, 851
OLE DB rowsets, 12
OLE (Object Linking and Embedding), 12
OLTP databases vs data warehouses, 599–600
OLTP (Online Transaction Processing), 100
O(n2) algorithm, 846
one-to-many merge joins, 539–540
online index building, 367–370
Online Index rebuild, 475
ONLINE mode, 122, 123
ONLINE setting
　　schedulers, 38
Online Transaction Processing. *See* OLTP
O(n*log(n)) algorithm, 846
Open method, 514
operating system
　　configuring, 21–23
　　　　connectivity, 23
　　　　firewall settings, 23
　　　　nonessential services, 23
　　　　paging file location, 22
　　　　task management, 21–22
operational events, 76
operations. *See also* commands
　　ALTER INDEX REBUILD, 190
　　bulk import, 190
　　copy-on-write, 157
　　CREATE INDEX, 190
　　DBCC DBREINDEX, 190
　　DROP DATABASE, 161
　　DROP INDEX, 191

index, 190
minimally logged, 190–191
operations that clear cache plans of specific
databases, 730–731
operations that remove the entire plan
cache, 730
read, 157–158
revert
managing snapshots, 161
SELECT INTO, 182
operators. *See also* iterators
Aggregate, 504
assert, 568
batch hash table build, 607
bitmap, 660
Check UDX, 471
Collapse, 676
columnstore index scan, 607
Compute Scalar, 659, 683–684
concatenation, 556
Constant Scan, 616, 683
CONTAINS, 501
Contains UDX, 471
Data UDX, 471
Filter, 504
FREETEXT, 501
hash union, 558
logical, spools, 571
merge join
Proeprties sheet, 521
ToolTip, 520
MergeUnion, 504
PIVOT, 724
Query Optimizer, 617–624
Apply, 621–622
Compute Scalar, 618
Compute Sequence, 619
Exchange, 624
Se44mi-Join, 619–621
spools, 623
Scalar, 504
scan, 526–528
seek, 526–528
Segment, 659
Serializer UDX, 471
Sort, 675
Split, 675–676
STIntersects() spatial, 480
SWITCH PARTITION, 670
TextAdd UDX, 471

Window Spool, 658
optimality-based recompiles, 725–728
modification counters, 727–728
stale statistics, 725–727
updated statistics, 725
optimistic concurrency, 766, 811, 830–832
optimistic currency, 16
optimization
Query Optimizer, 613
optimization hints
plan cache, 752–754
optimizations
tempdb database, 146–147
optimized bitmap filtering, 601
Optimize for Ad Hoc Workloads option, 708–709
OPTIMIZE FOR hint, 753
OPTIMIZE FOR hint, Query Optimizer, 696–698
Optimizer (Query Optimizer). *See* Query Optimizer
OPTION (MAXDOP 1) query hint, 559
options, DBCC CHECKDB, 890–893
order, integrity checks, 279
orderly shutdowns, 51
order preserving exchanges, 585
ORDPATH numbering system, 463
output, DBCC CHECKDB, 885–890
application event log, 888–889
error reporting to Microsoft, 888–889
progress reporting output, 889–890
regular output, 885–887
SQL Server error log, 888
output fraction, 525
overview
indexes, 298–299
Query Optimizer, 611–613
tree format, 612–613
ownership, locks, 785–786
owners (tables), 204

P

-P SQL Server startup parameter, 603
package0.attach_activity_id action, 97
package0.attach_activity_id_xfer action, 97
packages
Extended Events, 75
PAD_INDEX (XML index option), 460
page allocation operations, 15
page audits, per-table logical consistency
checks, 863–864

PAGE clause, RESTORE DATABASE statement, 199
page_compression_attempt_count columns, 441
page-compression information, 864
page_compression_success_count columns, 441
Page Free Space (PFS) pages, 119, 286–288, 838
Page Free Space (PFS) page, tempdb database, 148
PAGE HEADER section (DBCC PAGE command
           output), 256
page headers, table data pages, 249
page ID, 847
PAGEIOLATCH waits, 152
PAGELATCH waits
    tempdb database, 151
page-locking, 803–805
page LSNs (Log Sequence Numbers)
    recovery and, 175–176
page management
    in data cache, 48–49
PageModCount value (CI records), 438
pages
    data compression, 433–442
        analysis, 440–441
        backup compression, 443
        CI record building, 440–441
        column prefix compression, 435–436
        dictionary compression, 436–437
        metadata, 441
        performance issues, 442–443
        physical storage, 437–439
    DCM (Differential Changed Map), 857
    DIFF (Differential Changed Map), 119, 189
    GAM, 856
    GAM (Global Allocation Map), 116, 838
    IAM (Index Allocation Map), 118
    ML map (minimally logged map), 192
    ML Map (Minimally Logged Map), 857
    ML (Minimal Logging), 119
    PFS, 856
    PFS (Page Free Space), 119, 838
    reading, database processing, 852–853
    restoring, 198–200
    SGAM (Shared Global Allocation Map), 117, 856
    splitting, indexes, 342–346
pages_in_use_kb column (sys.dm_os_memory_
           cache_counters), 58
pages_kb column (sys.dm_os_memory_cache_
           counters), 58
pages_kb column (sys.dm_os_memory_clerks), 58
PageType values, 383
PAGE_VERIFY option, 128

PAGE_VERIFY options, 128
paging file
    location, 22
PAGLOCK hint, 833
pair_matching target, 81
parallel deadlocks, 586
parallelism, 580–598
    bitmap filtering, 597–598
    broadcast partitioning, 596–597
    DOP (degree of parallelism), 582–583
    exchange operator, 583–586
    hash joins, 595
    hash partitioning, 595–596
    inner-side parallel execution, 593–594
    load balancing, 589–590
    merge joins, 594–595
    nested loops joins, 590–591, 592–593
    round-robin exchange, 592
    scan operators, 586–588
parallelism, efficiently processing databases,
           853–855
parallel query execution plans, 32
parameterization, 711–717
    drawbacks, 715–717
    forced, 627, 714
    Query Optimizer
        auto-parameterization, 625–626
        limitations, 627–628
    simple, 713
PARAMETERIZATION hint, 754
PARAMETERIZATION hint, Query Optimizer, 698
parameters
    CHANGE_TRACKING, full-text indexes, 493
    correlated, 535
    DBCC PAGE command, 250
    index-specific, 474
    MAX_CELLS, 479
    -P SQL Server startup, 603
    plan_handle, 731
    pool_name, 732
    sql_handle, 731
parameter sniffing, 719
parent_node_id (sys.dm_os_schedulers), 43
parent text facts, 846
Parse Tree value (cacheobjtype columns), 705
parsing
    components, 12
partial aggregates, 589
partial backups, databases, 198
partially contained databases, 162–169

collation changes, 166–168

configuring, 162–163

creating contained users, 163–166

detecting uncontained features, 168–169

partial restore, databases, 200

partition-aligned index views, Query Optimizer, 658

partitioned parallel scans, 655–656

partitioned tables, Query Optimizer, 654–657

updates, 682–685

Partition_Info view, 454

partitioning checks, processing columns, 869

partitioning, locks, 798–799

partitioning tables/indexes, 444–455

columnstore indexes, 452–454

functions and schemes, 444–446

metadata, 446–449

sliding window benefits, 450–453

partitioning types, parallel queries, 585

partition-level lock escalation, Query Optimizer, 686

partition-level locks, 783

partition_number parameter (dm_db_database_page_allocations function), 306

partition_number parameter (dm_db_index_physical_stats DMV), 303

partition switching, 608

PASSTHRU predicates, 579–580

PathName function, 404

PATH secondary XML index, 463, 468–469

PAUSE full-text operation, 500

pending_disk_io_count (sys.dm_os_schedulers), 43

pending_io_byte_average (sys.dm_os_tasks), 45

pending_io_byte_count (sys.dm_os_tasks), 44

pending_io_count (sys.dm_os_tasks), 44

PENDING value (task_state), 44

performance

FILESTREAM data, 409–410

page compression, 442–443

performance considerations

SQL Server collations, character data types (tables), 229

performance counters, 826–827

Performance Options dialog box, 21–22

performing database repairs, 893–897

performing fact generation, DBCC CHECKDB, 846–848

permissible functions

computed columns, indexes, 334–335

indexed views, 334–335

permissions

ALTER ANY USER, 166

CREATE SEQUENCE, 243

instance-level logins, 163

View Server State, 42

per-partitioned joins, 657–658

persisted columns

computed columns, indexes, 337–338

persisted computed columns, 457

per-table logical consistency checks, 860–866

data and index page processing, 864–866

metadata consistency checks, 861–862

page audits, 863–864

per-thread hash tables, parallel queries, 667

pessimistic concurrency, 16, 766, 811, 830–832

PFS (Page Free Space) pages, 119, 286–288, 838

PFS (Page Free Space) page, tempdb database, 148

PFS pages, 856

phantoms, transaction dependencies, 769

phases of execution, progress reporting, 889–890

phases of recovery

transaction logs, 174–175

physical index structure, B-tree indexes, 315–332

clustered indexes, 316–322

index row formats, 315–316

nonclustered indexes, 322–332

physical_memory_in_use_kb column (sys.dm_os_process_memory), 56

physical_memory_kb column (sys.dm_os_sys_info), 56

physical_name column (sys.database_files), 102

PHYSICAL_ONLY option (DBCC CHECKDB), 893

physical pages, tables, 259–262

creating a function to perform conversion, 260–261

sys.dm_db_database_page_allocations DMV, 261

sys.fn_PhysLocFormatter function, 261–262

physical properties, 616

physical storage

page compression, 437–439

sparse columns, 416–419

pipeline, Query Optimizer, 611

PIVOT operator, 724

planar data, 231

plan cache, 53

clearing, 704–705

global memory pressure, 743

internal organization, 732–744

cache stores, 732–733

compiled plans, 734–735

costing entries, 743–744

execution contexts, 734

metadata, 735

local memory pressure, 742–743

mechanisms, 705–732

    ad hoc query caching, 706–711

    compiled objects, 719–721

    parameterization, 711–717

    prepared queries, 717–719

    recompilation, 722–732

metadata, 704

objects, 744–752

    multiple plans, 746–747

    stored procedures, 747

    troubleshooting issues, 748–752

optimization hints, 752–754

plan guides, 754–764

    considerations, 759–764

    management, 758

    object plan guides, 755–756

    SQL plan guides, 756–757

    template plan guides, 756–757

previous versions, 703

size management, 740–741

plan freezing, 763

plan guides, 754–764

    considerations, 759–764

        freezing a plan, 763

        validation, 763–764

    management, 758

    object plan guides, 755–756

    SQL plan guides, 756–757

plan_handle parameter, 731

plan_handle value, 735–736

plan shape

    Query Optimizer, 667–670

pminlen value, 315

pool_name parameter, 732

pool sizing

    Resource Governor, 65–66

populating full-text indexes, 494

precision (numeric data types), 209

predefined columns, FileTable, 408–409

predicates

    equijoin (equality), 536

    Extended Events, 78–79

    inequality, 536

    non-pushable, non-sargable, 647

    PASSTHRU, 579

    pushing non-sargable predicates, 647

    sargable, 646

    seekable, 528–531

    spatial queries, 477

Prepared (prepared statement) value (objtype
    columns), 705

prepared queries, 717–719

    caching, 718–719

    prepare-and-execute method, 718

    sp_executesql procedure, 717–718

prepare method, 718, 748

primary data files, 101–102

primary file, 110

primary filegroup, 110

Primary_Filter_Efficiency property, 487

primary filter step, 480

PRIMARY KEY constraint, 276–278

PRIMARY KEY constraints, 312

primary principals

    schemas, 133

primary XML indexes, 460–463

primitive system catalog consistency checks,
    855–856

principals, 130

    primary

        schemas, 133

    schemas, 133

    secondary

        schemas, 133

PROBE column, semi-joins, 579

procedures

    sp_helpdb, 9

    system stored, 9

process affinity

    binding schedulers to CPUs, 41–42

    dynamic, 41

processing columns, 866–881

    computed columns, 866–869

    cross-page consistency checks, 871–881

        B-tree consistency checks, 872–875

        FILESTREAM consistency checks, 876–881

        heap consistency checks, 871–872

        LOB linkage consistency checks, 875–877

    text page processing, 870–871

processing databases efficiently, 845–855

    parallelism, 853–855

    performing fact generation, 846–848

    processing batches, 851–852

    query processor, 848–851

    reading pages to process, 852–853

processing pipeline, Query Optimizer, 611

Proc (stored procedure) value (objtype
    columns), 705

Profiler, 176

programmatic data integrity, 276

progress reporting output, DBCC CHECKDB, 889–890

Project operator (Query Optimizer), 618

properties

  ACID, 15

  database, 99

  database files, 102

  EditionID, 2

  EngineEdition, 1–2

  FILEGROWTH, 105

  Internal_Filter_Efficiency, 487

  iterators, 515–517

    dynamic cursor support, 516

    memory consumption, 515–516

    non-blocking vs blocking, 516

  joins, 544

  logical, 616

  MAXSIZE, 105

  physical, 616

  Primary_Filter_Efficiency, 487

  READONLY, 114

  READWRITE, 114

  Recovery (DATABASEPROPERTYEX function), 8

  ROWGUIDCOL, 232

  search framework, Query Optimizer, 614–616

  SEQUENCE objects

    Cache value, 241

    Cycle, 241

    Datatype, 240

    Increment, 240

    Maximum value, 241

    Minimum value, 241

    Starting value, 240

  SIZE, 105

  tables

    IDENTITY, 237–240

  workload groups, 67–68

Properties sheet

  merge join operator, 521

property functions, 8–9

PROPERTY secondary XML index, 463, 468

protocols

  disabling, 23

  Named Pipes, 11

  Shared Memory, 11

  SQL Server Database Engine, 11–12

  SSRP (SQL Server Resolution Protocol), 20

  TCP/IP, 11

pseudotables

  compatibility views, 4

pubs, 101

pull-based data flow, 584

purity checks, processing columns, 867–869

purpose, spatial indexes, 472–476

push-based data flow, 584

Q

queries

  execution

    analyzing plans, 525–600

    batch processing, 603–608

    columnstore indexes, 603–608

    data warehouses, 599–603

    hints, 609

    query processing, 513–517

    reading query plans, 517–526

  full-text indexes, 501–502

  memory resources, 31

  normalizing, 13

  prepared, 717–719

    caching, 718–719

    prepare-and-execute method, 718

    sp_executesql procedure, 717–718

  shell, 712

  star join, 600

  Star Join, 660

Query Execution, 12–14

query execution engine, 513

query executor, 14

Query Governor Cost Limit option, 32

querying

  even data, 84–85

QueryMemoryResourceNotification API, 50

query method, 464

Query Optimization, 12–14

query optimizer, 513

Query Optimizer, 851

  architecture, 624–630

    auto-parameterization, 625–626

    before optimization, 625

    Memo, 627–630

    parameterization limitations, 627–628

    Simplification phase, 625

    trivial plan, 625–626

  cardinality estimation, 638–643

  costing, 643–645

data warehousing, 659–669
  batch processing, 662–666
  columnstore indexes, 660–661, 670–671
  plan shape, 667–670
Distributed Query feature, 687–689
extended indexes, 689
hints, 689–699
  debugging planning issues, 691–692
  FAST <number_rows> hint, 695
  FORCESEEK hint, 695
  GROUP BY operation, 692–693
  JOIN operations, 693–694
  MAXDOP<N> hint, 696
  NDEX=<indexname> | <indexid> hint, 694
  NOEXPAND hint, 699
  OPTIMIZE FOR hint, 696–698
  PARAMETERIZATION hint, 698
  UNION operations, 693–694
  USE PLAN hint, 699–700
hotfixes, 700–701
indexed views, 340
index selection, 645–654
  filtered indexes, 648–650
  indexed views, 649–653
optimization, 613
overview, 611–613
  tree format, 612–613
partitioned tables, 654–657
search framework, 614–624
  Memo, 617
  operators, 617–624
  properties, 614–616
  rules, 614
statistics, 630–638
  density/frequency information, 634–636
  design, 631–634
  filtered, 636–637
  string, 637–638
updates, 670–686
  Halloween Protection feature, 674–675
  locking, 685–686
  MERGE operation, 676–678
  non-updating updates, 681–682
  partitioned table updates, 682–685
  partition-level lock escalation, 686
  sparse column updates, 681
  Split/Sort/Collapse optimization, 674–676
  wide update plans, 679–681
windowing functions, 658–660
<QueryPlan> element, displaying query plans, 524

query plans
  analysis, 525–600
    advanced index operations, 560–567
    aggregations, 545–556
    bookmark lookup, 531–533
    data modification statements, 598–599
    joins, 533–544
    parallelism, 580–598
    scans and seeks, 526–528
    seekable predicates and covered
      columns, 528–531
    subqueries, 566–580
    unions, 555–559
  full-text indexes, 502–503
  reading, 517–526
    display options, 520–526
    estimated vs. actual query plans, 518–519
    graphical plans, 517
    text plans, 518
    XML plans, 518
  SET commands, 519
  spatial indexes, 479–480
  XML indexes, 465–467, 470–471
query processing options, 31–33
query processor, 12–14, 848–851
  NOEXPAND hint, 884
Query Wait option, 31
QUOTED_IDENTIFIER option, 127, 206
quoted identifiers, 206
QUOTED_IDENTIFIER (Set option), 724

R

Random I/Os, 644
RangePartitionNew function, 682
ranges
  Windows collations, character data types
    (tables), 222–223
RCSI (read committed snapshot isolation), 813–814
  vs snapshot isolation, 821–822
readable records, transaction logs and
    recovery, 176–177
read-ahead
  index ranges, 60
  table scans, 60
READCOMMITTED hint, 834
Read Committed isolation (transactions), 771
READCOMMITTEDLOCK hint, 834
read committed snapshot isolation (RCSI), 813–814
  vs snapshot isolation, 821–822

reading pages, database processing, 852–853

reading query plans, 517–526

    display options, 520–526

    estimated vs. actual query plans, 518–519

    graphical plans, 517

    text plans, 518

    XML plans, 518

READ_ONLY mode, 123–124

READONLY property, 114

read operations, 157–158

READPAST hint, 834

READUNCOMMITTED hint, 833

Read Uncommitted isolation (transactions), 770

READ_WRITE mode, 123–124

READWRITE property, 114

reattaching

    databases, 135–136

rebinds, spools, 572

rebuilding CI records, 440–441

rebuilding indexes, 366–367

reclaiming pages, ghost cleanup background
        thread, 354

recompilation, 722–732

    correctness-based recompiles, 722–725

    multiple recompilations, 729

    optimality-based recompiles, 725–728

        modification counters, 727–728

        stale statistics, 725–727

        updated statistics, 725

    removing plans from cache, 729–732

    skipping recompile step, 728–729

    troubleshooting, 751–752

recompilation threshold (RT), 726–727

RECOMPILE hint, 752–753

RECONFIGURE command, 25

recoverable state (VLFs), 178

recovery

    databases

        models, 190–194

    transaction logs, 171–177

        changes in log size, 178–188

        log cache, 177

        page LSNs, 175–176

        readable records, 176–177

        recovery phases, 174–175

recovery interval, 184

Recovery Interval option, 28

Recovery Interval server configuration option, 51

recovery_model column, 9

RECOVERY_PENDING mode, 123

Recovery property (DATABASEPROPERTYEX
        function), 8

RECURSIVE_TRIGGERS option, 127

redo phase of recovery, 174

redo_target_lsn column (sys.master_files), 200

referential integrity, 277

regions

    allocation, 160

regular_buffer_size and total_regular_buffers column
        (sys.dm_xe_sessions), 96

regular output, DBCC CHECKDB, 885–887

relational operator elements, 518

<RelOp> element, displaying query plans, 525

removed_all_rounds_count column (sys.dm_os_
        memory_cache_clock_hands), 59

removing

    event sessions, 86

removing correlations, subqueries, 576–577

removing fragmentation, B-tree indexes, 364–366

REORGANIZE option (ALTER INDEX command),
        365–366

reorganizing indexes, 363

REPAIR_ALLOW_DATA_LOSS option (DBCC
        CHECKDB), 891, 894, 897

Repair options (DBCC CHECKDB), 891

REPAIR_REBUILD option (DBCC CHECKDB), 891

repairs, DBCC CHECKDB, 893–897

repartition exchange, 583–584

REPEATABLEREAD hint, 833

Repeatable Read isolation (transactions), 771–772

REPLICATE function, 266

ReplProc value (objtype columns), 705

request_Columns

    viewing locks, 788–789

request_exec_context_id (request_Columns), 788

request_lifetime (request_Columns), 788

REQUEST_MAX_CPU_TIME_SEC property, 68

REQUEST_MAX_MEMORY_GRANT_PERCENT
        property, 68

REQUEST_MEMORY_GRANT_TIMEOUT_SEC
        property, 68

request_owner_guid (request_Columns), 788

request_owner_id (request_Columns), 788

request_reference_count (request_Columns), 788

request_request_id (request_Columns), 788

request_session_id (request_Columns), 788

request_status (request_Columns), 788

request_type (request_Columns), 788

reserved keywords

    naming tables, 205

resource_address (sys.dm_os_waiting_tasks), 45
resource_Columns
    viewing locks, 786–787
resource database, 140–141
resource_description (sys.dm_os_waiting_tasks), 45
Resource Governor, 61–71
    classifier function, 62–63
    code example, 68–70
    controls, 70–71
    disabling, 71
    enabling, 62
    metadata, 71–72
    overview, 61–62
    pool sizing, 65–66
    resource pools, 63–64
    workload groups, 66–68
resource_lock_partition column, 798
Resource Monitor
    memory pressure, 53
    QueryMemoryResourceNotification API, 50
resource pools, 63–64
    Default pool, 64
    Internal pool, 64
    pool sizing, 65–66
RESOURCE_SEMAPHORE_QUERY_COMPILE
    waits, 749
restart recovery, 172
RESTORE command, 161
    WITH RECOVERY option, 196
RESTORE DATABASE command, 198
RESTORE DATABASE statement
    PAGE clause, 199
restore processes
    databases, 188–201
        choosing backup type, 194–195
        files and filegroups, 197–198
        partial backups, 198
        partial restore, 200
        recovery models, 190–194
        restoring pages, 198–200
        restoring with standby, 200–201
        types of backups, 189–190
restore recovery, 173, 197
restoring
    databases, 136
restricted-length LOB data, storage, 382–386
RESTRICTED_USER mode, 122
restrictions, DBCC CHECKDB PHYSICAL_ONLY
    option, 893
RESUME full-text operation, 500

reusable state (VLFs), 179
revert operation
    managing snapshots, 161
rewinds, spools, 572
right deep hash join tree, 543–544
ring buffer, allocation, 149
RING_BUFFER_ALLOC_TRACE ring buffer, 150
ring_buffer target, 80, 90
ROLLBACK AFTER integer [SECONDS] option, 124
ROLLBACK IMMEDIATE option, 124
ROLLBACK termination options, 814
ROLLBACK TRAN command, 171
root pages
    splitting, 343
round-robin exchange, parallelism, 592
rounds_count column (sys.dm_os_memory_cache_
        clock_hands), 59
routes
    AutoCreatedLocal, 169
    defined, 169
row-at-a-time model, 514
row-at-a-time modifications, 358
row-based operator model, 618
row-based processing, 514
ROWGUIDCOL attribute, 397
ROWGUIDCOL property, 232
row-level versioning of data
    tempdb database, 146
ROWLOCK hint, 833
row-locking, 803–805
row offset array, table data pages, 249–250
row operations, 14
row-overflow data pages, 245
row-overflow LOB data, storage, 382–386
rows
    data compression, 424–432
        CD (column descriptor) format, 426–432
        enabling, 425–426
ROWSET_COLUMN_COMBINED_ID coulmn
        (facts), 848
ROWSET_COLUMN_FACT_BLOB coulmn (facts), 848
ROWSET_COLUMN_FACT_KEY column (facts), 848
ROWSET_COLUMN_FACT_TYPE coulmn (facts), 848
ROWSET_COLUMN_SLOT_ID coulmn (facts), 848
Rowset metadata objects, 861
rowsets, 12
rows (tables)
    defined, 203
    deleting
        heap data modifications, 288–292

modifying indexes, 346–353
inserting
  heap data modifications, 288
  modifying indexes, 342
moving, 292–293
updating
  heap data modifications, 292–295
  modifying indexes, 354–358
rowversion data types, 231
row versioning, 811–832
choosing concurrency model, 830–832
details, 811–812
snapshot-based isolation levels, 813–830
  DDL statements, 819–822
  RCSI (read committed snapshot isolation), 813–814
  snapshot isolation, 814–815
  snapshot isolation scope, 815–816
  summary, 821–822
  transaction metadata, 827–830
  update conflicts, 817–818
  version store, 823–827
  viewing database state, 816–817
RT (recompilation threshold), 726–727
rules
  search framework, Query Optimizer, 614
Rule value (objtype columns), 706
runnable_tasks_count (sys.dm_os_schedulers), 43
RUNNABLE value (task_state), 44
RUNNING value (task_state), 44

S

sample databases
AdventureWorks, 100
AdventureWorks2012
  security, 132
Northwind, 101
pubs, 101
SAMPLED mode (mode parameter), 303
sargable predicates, 646
savings (storage), sparse columns, 420–423
scalar aggregations, 545–548
scalar functions, forcing recompilation, 720–721
Scalar operator, 504
scalar subqueries, 566
scale (numeric data types), 209, 212–213
scan operators, 526–528
  parallelism, 586–588
scans on clustered indexes, 527

scans on heaps, 527
scans on nonclustered indexes, 527
scheduler_id (sys.dm_os_schedulers), 43
scheduler_id (sys.dm_os_tasks), 45
Scheduler Monitor, 40
schedulers
affinity, 38
binding to CPUs, 41–42
core-based licensing, 38
CPUs, 38
DAC (Dedicated Administrator Connection), 46
DMVs (Dynamic Management Objects), 42–45
SOS, 38
SQL Server, 37–47
  dynamic affinity, 41
  fibers, 40
  NUMA (Non-Uniform Memory Access), 40–41
  tasks, 39–40
  threads, 40
  workers, 39
Windows, 37, 38
scheduling options, 27–28
schema
creating tables, 204–205
schema binding
computed columns, indexes, 335
indexed views, 335
schema changes, correctness-based recompilation, 722
schema modification locks, 777
schemas
creating objects in
  , 134
default, 134
INFORMATION_SCHEMA, 7
primary principals, 133
principals, 133
secondary principals, 133
versus databases, 133
schema stability locks, 777
schema-validated columns, XML indexes, 469–470
schemes, partitions, 444–446
SCOPE_IDENTITY function, 239
SC (supports supplementary characters) tokens, 218
Se44mi-Join operators (Query Optimizer), 619–621
search-ARGument-able predicates, 646
search framework, Query Optimizer, 614–624
Memo, 617
operators, 617–624
  Apply, 621–622

Compute Scalar, 618
Compute Sequence, 619
Exchange, 624
Se44mi-Join, 619–621
spools, 623
properties, 614–616
rules, 614
SEARCHPROPERTY LIST specification
full-text indexes, 493
secondary data files, 102
secondary principals
schemas, 133
secondary XML indexes, 463, 468–469
securables, 130
security
authentication
contained databases, 166
databases, 129–134
default schemas, 134
datbases
access, 130–131
security policies
metadata, 9
seekable predicates, 528–531
seek operators, 526–528
dynamic index seeks, 560–563
Segment operator, 659
SELECT *, 414
SELECT DISTINCT keyword
stream aggregation, 550–551
SELECT INTO command, 190, 277
SELECT INTO operation, 182
SE_MANAGE_VOLUME_NAME setting, 107
semantic indexes, 505–510
SEMANTICKEYPHRASETABLE function, 507
SemanticsDB database, 505
Semantic Search, 505–510
SEMANTICSIMILARITYDETAILSTABLE function, 509
SEMANTICSIMILARITYTABLE function, 508
semi-joins, 537
PROBE column, 579
reduction, 598
sequence objects (tables), 240–243
Sequence Project operator (Query Optimizer), 619
serial execution plans, 32
SERIALIZABLE hint, 833
Serializable isolation (transactions), 773–774
Serializer UDX operator, 471
server collation, 217

Server Core
install SQL Server 2012, 2–3
Server Name Indication (SNI), 37
SERVERPROPERTYEX function, 501
server property pages
SQL Server Management Studio, 25
Service Broker
msdb database, 141
Service Broker feature, consistency checks, 882
services
managing
SQL Server Configuration Manager, 19
SQL Server Browser, 20
session IDs (SPID)
compared to tasks, 39
session_id (sys.dm_os_tasks), 45
session_id (sys.dm_os_waiting_tasks), 45
SESSIONPROPERTY function, 334
session-scoped options, 96–97
sessions (event), 67, 82–83
catalog metadata, 96
creating, 83–84, 86–90
managing, 86–90
removing, 86
session-scoped options, 96–97
stopping, 86
SET commands, displaying query plans, 519
SET DEADLOCK_PRIORITY statement, 809
SET IDENTITY_INSERT tablename option, 238
SET options
computed columns, indexes, 333–334
indexed views, 333–334
recompilation, 724
SET option settings, creating an XML index, 459
SET QUOTED_IDENTIFIER ON option, 206
SET ROWCOUNT N operation, 671
SET SHOWPLAN_ALL ON text plans, 518
SET SHOWPLAN_TEXT ON text plans, 518
SET STATISTICS TIME ON tool, 691
SET STATISTICS XML ON output, 523
setting
database options, 119–129
auto options, 125–126
cursor options, 125
database recovery options, 128–129
SQL options, 126–127
state options, 122–125
setting LOCK_TIMEOUT, 834–836
settings
system configuration, 24–33

Disk I/O, 28–30
memory options, 26–27
query processing options, 31–33
scheduling options, 27–28
SET TRANSACTION ISOLATION LEVEL
command, 813
Set Working Set Size option, 26
SGAM (Shared Global Allocation Map) pages, 117,
856
SGAM (Shared Global Allocation Map) page, tempdb
database, 148
Shared Global Allocation Map (SGAM) pages, 117,
856
Shared Global Allocation Map (SGAM) page, tempdb
database, 148
shared locks, 775–776
Shared Memory, 11
Shared Table lock
running DBCC CHECKDB in tempdb
database, 144
shell queries, 712
short data cluster, 428
short data region (CD format), 428–429
SHOWPLAN_ALL output, 571
showplan options
graphical plans, 517
text plans, 518
XML plans, 518
shrinking
databases, 106–109
automatic shrinkage, 108
manual shrinkage, 108–109
log files, 109
shrinking databases
tempdb, 147
shrinking files and databases, 837–841
AUTO_SHRINK option, 841–842
data file shrinking, 838–839
DBCC SHRINKFILE command, 840
log file shrinking, 840
shutdowns
orderly shutdowns, 51
sibling facts, 847
side-tables, 458
simple parameterization, 713, 747
SIMPLE parameterization model, 698
SIMPLE recovery model (databases), 193
Simplification phase (Query Optimizer), 625
simultaneous transactions, 772
single-byte character strings, 214

single-byte character types
Windows collations, 219–220
single-column indexes, seekable predicates, 528
SingleFragmentDocidFilter iterator, 504
SingleFragmentSeekFilter iterator, 504
SINGLE_USER mode, 122
size column (sys.database_files), 103
size management
plan cache, 740–741
SIZE property, 105
sizing
buffer pools, 55–57
memory, 54–55
pools
Resource Governor, 65–66
skipping recompile steps, 728–729
sliding window benefits, partitions, 450–453
slot ID, 847
smalldatetime data type, 210
SMP (symmetric multiprocessing)
NUMA, 36
snapshot-based isolation levels, row
versioning, 813–830
DDL statements, 819–822
RCSI (read committed snapshot isolation),
813–814, 821–822
snapshot isolation, 814–815
snapshot isolation scope, 815–816
summary, 821–822
transaction metadata, 827–830
update conflicts, 817–818
version store, 823–827
viewing database state, 816–817
Snapshot isolation (transactions), 772
row versioning, 814–815
scope, row versioning, 815–816
snapshots (databases), 155–161
alternatives to, 844–845
consistency checks, 843
creating, 156–159
management, 161
space monitoring, 159–161
Snapshot Transactions counter, 827
SNI (Server Name Indication), 37
SNI (SQL Server Network Interface) protocol
layer, 11
snowflake schemas, 659
snowflake schemas, data warehouses, 600
SORT_IN_TEMPDB option, 154

SORT_IN_TEMPDB option (CREATE INDEX command), 363
SORT_IN_TEMPDB (XML index option), 460
sort merge joins, 540–542
Sort operator, 675
sort order
    SQL Server collations, character data types (tables), 225
    Windows collations, character data types (tables), 220–222
sort units
    tempdb database, 145
SOS_RESERVEDMEMBLOCKLIST waits, 749
SOS Scheduler, 38
space allocation
    altering databases, 116–119
space monitoring
    database snapshots, 159–161
    tempdb database, 153–155
sparse column checks, processing columns, 869
sparse columns (storage format), 411–423
    COLUMN_SET construct, 414–417
    management, 411–414
        altering tables, 413–414
        creating tables, 412–413
    metadata, 419
    physical storage, 416–419
    storage savings, 420–423
sparse column updates, Query Optimizer, 681
sparse files, 156
sparse vector, 417–418
spatial data types, 231
    GEOGRAPHY, 471
    GEOMETRY, 471
spatial-index consistency checks, 885
spatial indexes, 471–491
    columns, 458, 476
    composition of, 475–477
    diagnostic stored procedures, 484–491
    ensuring use, 478–479
    nearest neighbor queries, 481–484
    purpose of, 472–476
    query plans, 479–480
    spatial queries, 477
SpatialIntersectFilterOverGridIndex optimization, 477
SpatialJoinToApply optimization, 477
spatial queries, 477
SPATIAL_WINDOW_MAX_CELLS query hint, 479
SPATIAL_WINDOW_MAX_CELLS value, 491

sp_cacheobjects view, 745
sp_configure Recovery Interval option, 51
sp_configure stored procedure, 184
sp_control_plan_guide procedure, 758
sp_create_plan_guide_from_handle procedure, 763–764
sp_create_plan_guide procedure, 755
special data types (tables), 230–233
    binary data types, 230
    bit data types, 230
    LOB data types, 230
    rowversion data types, 231
    spatial data types, 231
    sql_variant data types, 231
    table data types, 231
    uniqueidentifier data types, 231
    xml data types, 231
special indexes
    full-text indexes, 492–505
        configuring, 500–501
        creating, 498–499
        diagnostic information, 500–501
        extended event information, 503–505
        internal tables, 494–497
        maintenance, 499–500
        metadata views, 497
        query plans, 502–503
        status metadata, 500–501
        use in a query, 501–502
    semantic indexes, 505–510
    spatial
        columns, 458
    spatial indexes, 471–491
        composition of, 475–477
        diagnostic stored procedures, 484–491
        ensuring use, 478–479
        nearest neighbor queries, 481–484
        purpose of, 472–476
        query plans, 479–480
        spatial queries, 477
    versus ordinary indexes, 457–458
    XML, 458–471
        creating and maintaining, 459–463
        query plans, 465–467, 470–471
        schema-validated columns, 469–470
        secondary XML indexes, 468–469
        XQuery, 463–465
sp_estimate_data_compression_savings stored procedure, 442
sp_executesql procedure, 717–718, 748

sp_filestream_force_garbage_collection procedure, 404

sp_fulltext_keymappings system stored procedure, 496

sp_fulltext_pendingchanges system procedure, 495

sp_fulltext_semantic_register_language_statistics_db system stored procedure, 505

sp_fulltext_semantic_unregister_language_statistics_db system stored procedure, 505

sp_get_query_template procedure, 757, 761

sp_helpdb procedure, 9

sp_help_spatial_geography_histogram system stored procedure, 491

sp_help_spatial_geography_index diagnostic procedure, 484

sp_help_spatial_geography_index_xml system stored procedure, 484

sp_help_spatial_geometry_histogram system stored procedure, 491

sp_help_spatial_geometry_index diagnostic procedure, 484

sp_help_spatial_geometry_index_xml system stored procedure, 484

SPIDs (session IDs)
  compared to tasks, 39

spilling
  hash aggregates, 552–553
  hash joins, 543

spinlocks, 775, 810

SPINLOOP value (task_state), 44

Split operator, 675–676

Split/Sort/Collapse optimization (Query Optimizer), 674–676

splitting pages, indexes, 342–346
  intermediate index pages, 344
  leaf-level pages, 344–347
  root pages, 343

sp_migrate_user_to_contained stored procedure, 164

spool operators (Query Optimizer), 623

spools
  lazy, 535

sp_sequence_get_range stored procedure, 242

SQL-92 standard, 7, 205

SQL Azure, 2

SQLCMD tool, 2

sql_handle parameter, 731

sql_handle value, 735

SQL_Latin1_General_CP1_CI_AS collation, 218, 227

SQLMail
  fiber mode, 40

SQL Manager Cache (SQLMGR), 735

SQL methods
  XML data types, 463–465

SQLMGR (SQL Manager Cache), 735

SQL options, 126–127

SQLOS (SQl Server Operating System)
  memory
    DMVs (Dynamic Management Objects), 57–59

SQLOS (SQL Server Operating System). *See* SQLOS
  memor
    column store object pool, 48
  memory, 47–61
    buffer pool, 47
    buffer pool sizing, 55–57
    checkpoints, 50–52
    column store object pool, 48
    data cache, 47, 47–50
    free buffer list, 49–50
    lazywriter, 49–50
    management in other caches, 52–53
    Memory Broker, 54
    NUMA (Non-Uniform Memory Access), 59–60
    page management in data cache, 48–49
    read-ahead, 60
    sizing, 54–55
  NUMA (Non-Uniform Memory Access)
    architecture, 36–37

SQLOS (SQL Server Operating Sytem)
  memory
    access to pages in data cache, 48

SQL plan guides, 756–757

SQL Plans cache store, 732

SQL PowerShell, 2

SQL Server, 1
  editions, 1–2

SQL Server 2012, 1
  configuring, 17–20
    default network configuration, 18–19
    network protocols, 18
    system configuration, 21–33
  editions
    memory configurations, 56
  installing, 2

SQL Server Agent service
  msdb database, 141

SQL Server Analysis Services
  schemas, 133

SQL Server Books Online
  editions, 1
SQL Server Browser service, 20
SQL Server collations, character data types
        (tables), 224–230
    defined collations during setup, 227–228
    Installation Wizard, 228
    performance considerations, 229
    sort orders, 225
    tertiary collations, 225–227
    traps, 229–230
SQL Server Configuration Manager
    configuring network protocols, 18
    configuring SQL Server 2012, 18–19
    implementing default network configuration,
        18–19
    managing services, 19
    moving the master database, 143
    SQL Server Browser service, 20
SQL Server Database Engine, 1
    components, 10–17
        protocols, 11–12
        query processor, 12–14
        storage engine, 14–17
SQL Server error log, DBCC CKECKDB output, 888
SQL Server Express, 2
SQL Server Express with Advanced Services, 2
SQL Server Express with Tools, 2
sqlserver.latch_suspend_end event, 151
SQL Server Management Studio, 2, 184
    Object Explorer pane, 2
    server property pages, 25
SQL Server Network Interface (SNI) protocol
        layer, 11
SQL Server Operating System. *See* SQLOS
SQL Server Profiler, 176
SQL Server Resolution Protocol (SSRP), 20
SQL Server Resource Governor. *See* Resource
        Governor
SQL Server schedulers, 37–47
    dynamic affinity, 41
    fibers, 40
    NUMA (Non-Uniform Memory Access), 40–41
    tasks, 39–40
    threads, 40
    workers, 39
SQLServer:Transactions performance object,
        826–827
SQL statements
    DAC (Dedicated Administrator Connection), 46

sqlvariant columns, 382
sql_variant data, tables, 273–276
sql_variant data types, 231
SQLXML
    fiber mode, 40
SRID, spatial index columns, 458
SSRP (SQL Server Resolution Protocol), 20
stack_bytes_used (sys.dm_os_threads), 44
stale statistics, optimality-based recompiles,
        725–727
Standard edition, 2
standards
    SQL-92, 7
standby, restoring with, 200–201
star join queries, 600
Star Join queries, 660
star schema, data warehouses, 600
star schemas, 659
started_by_sqlserver (sys.dm_os_threads), 44
START FULL POPULATION option (ALTER FULLTEXT
        INDEX statement), 499
START INCREMENTAL POPULATION s option (ALTER
        FULLTEXT INDEX statement), 499
Starting value property, SEQUENCE objects, 240
start parallelism exchange, 585
START UPDATE POPULATION option (ALTER
        FULLTEXT INDEX statement), 499
State column (sys.database_files), 102
state_desc column (sys.database_files), 103
statements, 67
    ALTER
        CONTAINMENT option, 163
    ALTER DATABASE, 114–119
        FILEGROUP keyword, 110
    ALTER EVENT SESSION, 83
    ALTER INDEX
        manually controlling unit of locking, 804
    ALTER TABLE
        escalating table locks, 805
    CREATE DATABASE
        CONTAINMENT option, 163
        FILEGROUP keyword, 110
    CREATE EVENT SESSION, 83
    CREATE INDEX
        monitoring space usage in tempdb, 154
    CREATE SCHEMA, 133
    CREATE VIEW
        WITH SCHEMABINDING option, 335
    DBCC CHECKIDENT(tablename), 240
    DBCC OPTIMIZER_WHATIF, 602

DDL (Data Definition Language)
  ALTER FULLTEXT INDEX, 499
  CREATE DATABASE...FOR ATTACH, 505
  CREATE FULLTEXT CATALOG, 492–493
  CREATE PRIMARY XML INDEX, 459
  CREATE SPATIAL INDEX, 472
  snapshot isolation, 819–822
  DELETE, 598–599
  GRANT CREATE TABLE TO, 133
  INSERT, 598–599
  RESTORE DATABASE
    PAGE clause, 199
  SET DEADLOCK_PRIORITY, 809
  UPDATE, 598–599
    WRITE clause, 190
  UPDATE STATISTICS, 606
  UPDATETEXT, 190
  WRITETEXT, 190
<StatementSetOptions> element, displaying query
  plans, 524
state options, 122–125
states, virtual log files, 178
STATISTICAL_SEMANTICS keyword, 493, 505
statistics
  optimality-based recompiles
    stale, 725–727
    updated, 725
  Query Optimizer, 630–638
    density/frequency information, 634–636
    design, 631–634
    filtered, 636–637
    string, 637–638
  wait, 748–749
STATISTICS_NORECOMPUTE option, creating
  indexes, 314
STATISTICS PROFILE output, 635
STATMAN aggregate function, 633
Status column (VLFs), 180
STDistance() method, 472–473
STIntersects operation, 488
STIntersects() spatial operator, 480
<StmtSimple> element, displaying query plans, 524
STOPLIST specification
  full-text indexes, 493
stop parallelism exchange, 585
stopping
  event sessions, 86
storage
  columnstore indexes, 371–375

data
  data compression, 423–443
  FILESTREAM data, 394–405
  FileTable data, 404–410
  LOB (large object) data, 381–393
  metadata, 245–246
  partitioning, 444–455
  sparse columns, 411–423
  tables, 203–296
storage engine, 14–17
  access methods, 14–15
  transaction services, 15–17
stored procedures, 719–720, 747
  sp_sequence_get_range, 242
stream aggregations, 548–552
String Statistics feature, Query Optimizer, 637–638
structure
  B-tree indexes, 308–312, 315–332
    clustered indexes, 316–322
    clustering key dependency, 308–311
    constraints, 312
    index row formats, 315–316
    nonclustered B-tree indexes, 311–312
    nonclustered indexes, 322–332
stub, Optimize for Ad Hoc Workloads option,
  709–711
subqueries, 566–580
  CASE expressions, 578–580
  correlated, 566
  correlated scalar subqueries, 570–577
  multirow, 566
  noncorrelated, 566
  noncorrelated scalar subqueries, 567–569
  removing correlations, 576–577
  scalar, 566
subtype resources, 786–787
supplementary characters (SC) tokens, 218
suspect_pages table, 198–199
SUSPECT state, 123
SUSPENDED value (task_state), 44
switching recovery models, 193–194
SWITCH operations, 658
SWITCH option, partitions, 450
SWITCH PARTITION operator, 670
symmetric multiprocessing. See SMP
syscacheobjects, 4
syscacheobjects object, 744–746
sys.column_store_segments catalog view, 376–380
sys.column_store_segments view, 454

sys.database_files
  columns, 102–103
sys.database_recovery_status catalog view, 185
sys.databases, 4, 5
sysdatabases, 3
sys.databases catalog view, 119–129
sys.databases view, 8, 120–129
  columns, 120
  state options, 122–125
sys.data_spaces columns, 446
sys.destination_data_spaces columns, 447
sys.dm_db_database_page_allocations DMV
  locating physical pages, tables, 261
sys.dm_db_file_space_usage DMV
  monitoring space usage in tempdb, 153
sys.dm_db_fts_index_physical_stats DMV, 506
sys.dm_db_session_space_usage DMV
  monitoring space usage in tempdb, 153
sys.dm_db_task_space_usage DMV
  monitoring space usage in tempdb, 153
sys.dm_db_uncontained_entities DMV
  detecting uncontained features in databases, 168
sys.dm_exec_cached_plan_dependent_objects
    function, 738
sys.dm_exec_cached_plans, 6, 72
sys.dm_exec_cached_plans view, 738–739
sys.dm_exec_connections, 6
sys.dm_exec_procedure_stats view, 740–743
sys.dm_exec_query_memory_grants, 72
sys.dm_exec_query_resource_semaphores, 72
sys.dm_exec_query_stats function, 739–740
sys.dm_exec_requests, 6, 72
sys.dm_exec_requests catalog view, 889
sys.dm_exec_requests view, 739–740
sys.dm_exec_sessions, 6, 72
sys.dm_exec_sql_text function, 736–738
sys.dm_exec_text_query_plan function, 737
sys.dm_fts_index_keywords_by_document
    function, 497
sys.dm_fts_index_keywords_by_property
    function, 497
sys.dm_fts_index_keywords function, 497
sys.dm_fts_index_population DMV, 500, 506
sys.dm_fts_memory_buffers DMV, 500
sys.dm_fts_memory_pools DMV, 500
sys.dm_fts_outstanding_batches DMV, 500
sys.dm_fts_population_ranges DMV, 500
sys.dm_fts_semantic_similarity_population DMV, 506
sys.dm_io_virtual_file_stats function, 159
sys.dm_os_memory_brokers, 72

sys.dm_os_memory_cache_clock_hands, 53
  columns, 59
sys.dm_os_memory_cache_counters
  columns, 58
sys.dm_os_memory_cache_hash_tables
  columns, 58
sys.dm_os_memory_clerks, 54
  columns, 57–58
sys.dm_os_performance_counters view, 188
sys.dm_os_process_memory, 56
  columns, 56
sys.dm_os_schedulers
  columns, 43
sys.dm_os_sys_info
  columns, 56
sys.dm_os_tasks, 44–45
sys.dm_os_threads, 44
sys.dm_os_waiting_tasks, 45
sys.dm_os_wait_stats view
  wait statistics, 748–749
sys.dm_os_workers, 44
sys.dm_resource_governor_configuration, 72
sys.dm_resource_governor_resource_pools, 72
sys.dm_resource_governor_workload_groups, 72
sys.dm_tran_current_transaction view, 827–828
sys.dm_tran_locks view
  viewing locks, 786–789
sys.dm_xe_packages, 75
sys.dm_xe_sessions
  columns, 96–97
sys,dn_db_database_page_allocations, 824
sys.fn_PhysLocFormatter function
  locating physical pages, tables, 261–262
sys.fn_validate_plan_guide function, 763
sys.fulltext_index_catalog_usages metadata
    table, 497
sys.fulltext_semantic_languages metadata view, 505
sys.fulltext_semantic_language_statistics_database
    metadata view, 505
sys.indexes, 4
sysindexes, 3
sys.indexes Catalog view, tables, 244–245
sys.language_model_mapping_table internal
    table, 505
syslockinfo tables, 800–802
sysmembers, 3
sysmessages, 3
sys.objects, 5
sysobjects, 3
sys.partition_functions columns, 447

sys.partition_range_values columns, 447
sys.partition_schemes columns, 447
sys.partitions view, 245
sys.plan_guides view, 759
sysprocesses, 4
sys.resource_governor_configuration, 71
sys.resource_governor_resource_pools, 72
sys.resource_governor_workload_groups, 72
sys schema, 205
sys.sysallocunits system catalog, 855
sys.syshobtcolumns table, 855
sys.syshobts table, 855
sys.sysrowsets system catalog, 855
sys.sysrscols system catalog, 855
sys.system_internals_partition_columns view, 264
sys.tables, 5
SysTab value (objtype columns), 706
system base tables, 3
system catalog consistency checks, 855–856
system configuration
    configuring, 21–33
    operating system, 21–23
    settings, 24–33
        Disk I/O, 28–30
        memory options, 26–27
        query processing options, 31–33
        scheduling options, 27–28
system databases
    master, 139–140
    model, 140
    moving, 142–144
    msdb, 141–142
    partially contained, 162–169
        collation changes, 166–168
        configuring, 162–163
        creating, 163–166
        detecting uncontained features, 168–169
    resource, 140–141
    snapshots, 155–161
        creating, 156–159
        management, 161
        space monitoring, 159–161
    tempdb, 140, 144–156
        best practices, 147–148
        contention, 148–152
        objects, 144–145
        optimizations, 146–147
        space monitoring, 153–155
system functions, 8–9
system_internals_allocation_units view, 446

system metadata objects
    catalog views, 4–5
    compatibility views, 3–4
    Dynamic Management Objects, 6–7
system stored procedures, 9
system tables
    Compatibility Views, 3–4
sysusers, 3

T

table data types, 231
table-level data modification, indexes, 357
Table metadata objects, 861
tables, 203–296
    altering, 279–286
        adding columns, 281
        changing data types, 280–281
        constraints, 281–282
        dropping columns, 283
        internals, 283–286
        sparse columns (storage format), 413–414
    constraints, 276–279
        failures in transactions, 278–279
        names and catalog view information, 277–278
    creating, 203–204
        data types, 208–233
        delimited identifiers, 206–207
        FILESTREAM data, 397–398
        naming, 204–205
        naming conventions, 207–208
        NULL values, 233–235
        reserved keywords, 205–206
        sparse columns (storage format), 412–413
        user-defined data types, 235–236
    data types, 208–233
        character, 213–230
        date and time, 210–213
        numeric, 208–210
        special data types, 230–233
        user-defined, 235–236
    dimension, 600
    fact, 600
    filegroups, 111
    hash, 48
    heap modification internals, 286–295
        allocation structures, 286–288
        deleting rows, 288–292
        inserting rows, 288
        updating rows, 292–295

IDENTITY property, 237–240
internal storage, 243–276
    catalog view queries, 246–248
    data and time data, 270–273
    data pages, 248–257
    data rows, 257–259
    data storage metadata, 245–246
    fixed-length rows, 262–265
    locating a physical page, 259–262
    NULL values, 267–270
    sql_variant data, 273–276
    sys.indexes Catalog view, 244–245
    variable-length columns, 267–270
    variable-length rows, 265–267
naming, 204–208
    conventions, 207–208
    delimited identifiers, 206–207
    reserved keywords, 205
NULL issues, 233–235
partitioning, 444–455
    columnstore indexes, 452–454
    functions and schemes, 444–446
    metadata, 446–449
    sliding window benefits, 450–453
per-table logical consistency checks, 860–866
    data and index page processing, 864–865
    metadata consistency checks, 861–862
    page audits, 863–865
sequence objects, 240–243
system
    Compatibility Views, 3–4
system base, 3
table scans
    read-ahead, 60
table-valued functions
    tempdb database, 145
Table-Valued Function [XML Reader] iterator, 471
Table-Valued Function [XML Reader with XPath
        Filter] iterator, 470
table variables
    tempdb database, 145
TABLOCK hint, 833
TABLOCK option (DBCC CHECKDB), 892
TABLOCKX hint, 833
tabular data stream (TDS)
    endpoints, 12
    packets, 11–12
TagB row header, 315
Tag Index (TI) semantic index, 506
Target Memory, 56

Target Recovery Time database configuration
        option, 51
TARGET_RECOVERY_TIME option, 29
targets
    Extended Events, 80–82
        viewing data, 90–95
tasks, 39–40
    Blocked Process Threshold option, 31
    compared to SPIDs (session IDs), 39
    managing, 21–22
task_state (sys.dm_os_tasks), 44
TCP/IP, 11
TDS (tabular data stream)
    endpoints, 12
    packets, 11–12
tempdb database, 140, 144–156
    best practices, 147–148
    contention, 148–152
        DDL contention, 153
        DML contention, 148–152
    objects, 144–145
    optimizations, 146–147
    space monitoring, 153–155
temporary tables, 166
Temp Tables Creation Rate performance
        counter, 153
Temp Tables for Destruction performance
        counter, 153
termination options, 124–125
tertiary collations
    SQL Server collations, character data types
        (tables), 225–227
TERTIARY_WEIGHTS function, 225
tessellation levels, cells, 472
TextAdd UDX operator, 471
TEXT_DATA pages, 388
text_in_row_limit value, 389
TEXT_MIXED pages, 388
text pages, processing columns, 870–871
text plans, queries, 518
threads
    compared to fibers, 40
    parallel query execution plans, 32
    serial execution plans, 32
three-part name specification, tables, 204
ticks, 744
time data
    internal storage, tables, 270–273
time data types, 210–213
TI (Tag Index) semantic index, 506

toggling on/off
    trace flags, 23
tokens, collations, 218
tools
    analyzing indexes, 302–307
        dm_db_database_page_allocations
            function, 306–307
        dm_db_index_physical_stats DMV, 302–305
    DBCC MEMORYSTATUS, 691
    SET STATISTICS TIME ON, 691
    SQLCMD, 2
ToolTip
    merge join operator, 520
    rewind and rebind information, 572
TopNByRank iterator, 504
TOP N Sort iterator, 482
Top operations, 671
TORN_PAGE_DETECTION option, 128
total_virtual_address_space_kb column (sys.dm_os_
        process_memory), 56
traceflag 1106, 149
trace flag 2549, 853
trace flag 2562, 853
trace flags, 23–24
    1211, 805
    1224, 806
    2371, 727
    toggling on/off, 23
tracking type, changing in full-text indexes, 493
transaction_id column, 827
transaction_is_snapshot column, 827
transaction logs, 171–177
    changes in log size, 178–188
        autoshrinking, 187–188
        maintaining recoverable logs, 185–187
        viewing log file size, 188
        virtual log files, 178–185
    LSN (Log Sequence Number), 158
    recovery
        log cache, 177
        page LSNs, 175–176
        phases, 174–175
        readable records, 176–177
    truncating, 176
transactions, 766–774
    ACID properties, 15, 767–768
    dependencies, 768–769
    isolation levels, 770–775
        Read Committed isolation, 771
        Read Uncommitted isolation, 770

        Repeatable Read isolation, 771–772
        Serializable isolation, 773–774
        Snapshot isolation, 772
    manipulating FILESTREAM data, 401–402
    metadata
        snapshot-based isolation levels, 827–830
    Recovery Interval option, 29
transaction sequence number (XSN), 811
transaction_sequence_num column, 827
transaction services, 15–17
Transact-SQL (T-SQL)
    catalog views, 5
tree format, Query Optimizer, 612–613
trie trees, 637–638
Trigger value (objtype columns), 705
trivial plans (Query Optimizer), 616, 625–626
troubleshooting
    plan cache issues, 748–752
TRUNCATEONLY option, shrinking files and
        databses, 839
truncating
    databases, 185
    transaction logs, 176
T-SQL BULK INSERT command, 238
T-SQL query constructs, 458
T-SQL Reference, 298
T-SQL syntax, 156
T-SQL (Transact-SQL)
    catalog views, 5
TYPE COLUMN specification
    full-text indexes, 493
type_desc column (sys.database_files), 102
types
    Extended Events, 79

U

UDTs (user-defined data types), 631
UDT (user-defined data type), 852
UDX iterator, 471
UMS (User Mode Scheduler), 38
uncontained features (partially contained databases),
        detecting, 168–169
undo phase of recovery, 173–174
Unicode character strings, 213
Uniformity assumption, Query Optimizer, 637
UNION ALL queries, 555–559
UNION operations, Query Optimizer, 693–694
UNION queries, 555–559
    indexes, 562–564

UNIQUE constraint, 276
UNIQUEIDENTIFIER data type, 507
uniqueidentifier data types, 231
UNIQUE KEY constraints, 312
universal unique identifier (UUID) data type, 231
unrestricted-length LOB data, storage, 386–393
    appending data into columns, 393
    data rows, 389–392
    max-length data, 392–393
Unused state (VLFs), 179
UPDATE command, 671
Update Conflict Ratio counter, 827
update conflicts
    snapshot-based isolation levels, row
        versioning, 817–818
updated statistics, optimality-based recompiles, 725
update locks, 776
updates
    FILESTREAM data, 400
    Query Optimizer, 670–686
        Halloween Protection feature, 674–675
        locking, 685–686
        MERGE operation, 676–678
        non-updating updates, 681–682
        partitioned table updates, 682–685
        partition-level lock escalation, 686
        sparse column updates, 681
        Split/Sort/Collapse optimization, 674–676
        wide update plans, 679–681
UPDATE statement, 598–599
    WRITE clause, 190
UPDATE STATISTICS command, 725
UPDATE STATISTICS statement, 606
UPDATETEXT statement, 190
updating
    rows
        heap data modifications, 292–295
        modifying indexes, 354–358
UPDLOCK hint, 819, 833
USE PLAN hint, 754
USE PLAN hint, Query Optimizer, 699–700
User Connections option, 26
user data
    lock types for, 775–786
        lock duration, 785
        lock granularity, 778–784
        lock modes, 775–778
        lock ownership, 785–786
user-defined data types (tables), 235–236
user-defined data types (UDTs), 631

user-defined data type (UDT), 852
user-defined scalar functions, forcing
        recompilation, 720–721
User Interfaces
    Extended Events, 86–97
        aggregating data, 93–95
        Data Storage page, 89
        Events page, 87–88
        General page, 86–87
        grouping data, 93–95
        viewing target data, 90–95
User Mode Scheduler (UMS), 38
user objects
    tempdb database, 145
user stores, 53
UsrTab value (objtype columns), 706
UUID (universal unique identifier) data type, 231

V

validation
    plan guides, 763–764
value-based encoding, 372
value method, 464
VALUE secondary XML index, 463, 468
varbinary data, 382
varchar(MAX) data type, 389
vardecimal (data compression), 423
vardecimal storage format property, 209
variable-length columns, tables, 214, 267–270
variable-length rows, tables, 265–267
variables
    @BlobEater, 850
VAS (virtual address space), 55–57
Version Cleanup Rate counter, 826
Version Generation Rate counter, 826
versioning
    tempdb database, 146
versioning code, 16
versioning info, 430
versioning operations, 15
versions
    Windows collations, character data types
        (tables), 219
version store
    snapshot-based isolation levels, row
        versioning, 823–827
    tempdb database, 146
Version Store Size counter, 826
very large databases (VLDBs), partial backups, 198

view
sys.databases, 120–129
viewa
sys.resource_governor_workload_groups, 72
view expansion preoptimization activity, 625
viewing
collation options, character data types
(tables), 218
database state, row versioning, 816–817
locks, 786–789
request_Columns, 788–789
resource_Columns, 786–787
log file size, 188
query plans, 520–526
resource database contents, 141
target data (Extended Events UI), 90–95
views
sys.databases
columns, 120
state options, 122–125
sys.databases catalog, 119
sys.dm_exec_cached_plans, 72
sys.dm_exec_query_memory_grants, 72
sys.dm_exec_query_resource_semaphores, 72
sys.dm_exec_requests, 72
sys.dm_exec_sessions, 72
sys.dm_os_memory_brokers, 72
sys.dm_os_schedulers, 43
sys.dm_os_tasks, 44–45
sys.dm_os_threads, 44
sys.dm_os_waiting_tasks, 45
sys.dm_os_workers, 44
sys.dm_resource_governor_configuration, 72
sys.dm_resource_governor_resource_pools, 72
sys.dm_resource_governor_workload_groups, 72
sys.dm_tran_current_transaction, 827–828
sys.dm_tran_locks
viewing locks, 786–789
sys.plan_guides, 759
sys.resource_governor_configuration, 71
sys.resource_governor_resource_pools, 72
View Server State permission, 42
View value (objtype columns), 706
virtual_address_space_available_kb column (sys.
dm_os_process_memory), 57
virtual_address_space_committed_kb column (sys.
dm_os_process_memory), 57
virtual_address_space_reserved_kb column (sys.
dm_os_process_memory), 56
virtual address space (VAS), 55–57

virtual log files. *See* VLFs
virtual_memory_committed_kb column (sys.dm_os_
memory_clerks), 58
virtual_memory_kb column (sys.dm_os_sys_info), 56
virtual_memory_reserved_kb column (sys.dm_os_
memory_clerks), 58
VLDBs (very large databases), partial backups, 198
VLFs (virtual log files), 178–185
automatic truncation, 184–185
observing, 179–181
states, 178
using multiple files, 181–183
volumes
NTFS, creating snapshots, 159

W

wait_duration_ms (sys.dm_os_waiting_tasks), 45
wait statistics, 748–749
wait_type (sys.dm_os_waiting_tasks), 45
warehouses, data, 599–603
Web edition, 2
WHERE clause
full-text index queries, 501
wide update plans, Query Optimizer, 679–681
width sensitivity (WS) tokens, 218
windowing functions, Query Optimizer, 658–660
windows
New Database, 104
Windows collations, character data types
(tables), 218–224
binary collations, 223–224
character ranges, 222–223
naming, 218–219
single-byte character types, 219–220
sort order, 220–222
versions, 219
Window Spool operator, 658
Windows principal contained users, 163
Windows scheduler, 37, 38
Windows Server 2008 R2 Server Core SP1
installing SQL Server 2012, 2
WITH (NOEXPAND) hint, 650
WITH RECOMPILE option, 720
WITH RECOVERY option, RESTORE command, 196
WITH SCHEMABINDING option (CREATE VIEW
statement), 335
WITH VALUES clause (ALTER TABLE command), 281
word breaker, 498

workers, 39
    affinity, 39
work files, tempdb database, 145
workload groups, 66–68
    Default group, 66
    Internal groups, 66
    properties, 67–68
work_queue_count (sys.dm_os_schedulers), 43
work tables, tempdb database, 145
write-ahead logging, 15, 172
WRITE clause, 190
WRITETEXT statement, 190
WS (width sensitivity) tokens, 218

X

XACT_ABORT SET option, 279
XLOCK hint, 834
xmaxlen columns, 263
xml data types, 231
XML data types, built-in SQL methods, 463–465
XML-Index consistency checks, 884–885
XML indexes, 458–471, 881
    creating and maintaining, 459–463
       primary XML indexes, 460–463
       secondary XML indexes, 463
    query plans, 465–467, 470–471
    schema-validated columns, 469–470
    secondary XML indexes, 468–469
    XQuery, 463–465
XML query plans, 518
XQuery, XML indexes, 463–465
XSN (transaction sequence number), 811

About the authors

 **KALEN DELANEY** (primary author) has been working with Microsoft SQL Server for over 26 years, and she provides advanced SQL Server training to clients around the world. She has been a SQL Server MVP (Most Valuable Professional) since 1992 and has been writing about SQL Server almost as long. Kalen has spoken at dozens of technical conferences, including almost every PASS Community Summit held in the United States since the organization's founding in 1999.

Kalen is a contributing editor and columnist for *SQL Server Magazine* and the author or co-author of many Microsoft Press books on SQL Server, including *Inside Microsoft SQL Server 7*, *Inside Microsoft SQL Server 2000*, *Inside Microsoft SQL Server 2005: The Storage Engine*, *Inside Microsoft SQL Server 2005: Query Tuning and Optimization* and *SQL Server 2008 Internals*. Kalen blogs at *www.sqlblog.com*, and her personal website can be found at *www.SQLServerInternals.com*.

 **BOB BEAUCHEMIN** (author) is a database-centric instructor, course author, writer, conference speaker, application practitioner and architect, and a Developer Skills Partner for SQLskills. Bob has been a Microsoft MVP since 2002. He's written and taught courses on SQL Server and data access worldwide since the mid-1990s, and currently writes and teaches SQLskills' developer and DBA-centric immersion course offerings. He is lead author of the books *A Developer's Guide to SQL Server 2005* and *A First Look at SQL Server 2005 For Developers*, and sole author of *Essential ADO.NET*. He's written numerous Microsoft whitepapers, as well as articles on SQL Server and other databases, database security, ADO.NET, and OLE DB for a number of magazines.

 **CONOR CUNNINGHAM** (author) is principal architect of the SQL Server Core Engine Team, with over 15 years experience building database engines for Microsoft. He specializes in query processing and query optimization, and he designed and/or implemented a number of the query processing features available in SQL Server. Conor holds a number of patents in the field of query optimization, and he has written numerous academic papers on query processing. Conor blogs at "Conor vs. SQL" at *http://blogs.msdn.com/b/conor_cunningham_msft*.

JONATHAN KEHAYIAS (author and technical reviewer) is a Principal Consultant and Trainer for SQLskills, one of the most well-known and respected SQL Server training and consulting companies in the world. Jonathan is a SQL Server MVP and was the youngest person ever to obtain the Microsoft Certified Masters for SQL Server 2008. Jonathan is a performance tuning expert, for both SQL Server and hardware, and has architected complex systems as a developer, business analyst, and DBA. Jonathan also has extensive development (T-SQL, C#, and ASP.Net), hardware and virtualization design expertise, Windows expertise, Active Directory experience, and IIS administration experience.

Jonathan frequently blogs about SQL Server at *http://www.SQLskills.com/blogs/Jonathan*, and can be reached by email at *Jonathan@SQLskills.com*, or on Twitter as *@SQLPoolBoy*. He regularly presents at PASS Summit, SQLBits, SQL Intersections, SQL Saturday events, and local user groups and has remained a top answerer of questions on the MSDN SQL Server Database Engine forum since 2007.

BENJAMIN NEVAREZ (author and technical reviewer) is a database professional based in Los Angeles, California, and author of *Inside the SQL Server Query Optimizer*, published by Red Gate books. He has 20 years of experience with relational databases, and has been working with SQL Server since version 6.5. Benjamin holds a Master's degree in computer science and has been a speaker at many technology conferences, including the PASS Summit and SQL Server Connections. His blog is at *http://benjaminnevarez.com* and can be reached by email at *admin@benjaminnevarez.com* and on twitter at *@BenjaminNevarez*.

PAUL S. RANDAL (author) is the CEO of SQLskills.com, the world-renowned training and consulting company that he runs with his wife Kimberly L. Tripp. He is also a SQL Server MVP and a Microsoft Regional Director. Paul worked at Microsoft for almost nine years, after spending five years at DEC working on the OpenVMS file system. He wrote various DBCC commands for SQL Server 2000 and then rewrote all of DBCC CHECKDB and repair for SQL Server 2005 before moving into management in the SQL team. During SQL Server 2008 development, he was responsible for the entire Storage Engine.

Paul regularly consults and teaches at locations around the world, including the SQLskills Immersion Events on internals, administration, high-availability, disaster recovery, and performance tuning. He also wrote and taught the SQL Server Microsoft Certified Master certification for Microsoft. He is a top-rated presenter at conferences such as the PASS Summit, and owns and manages the SQLintersections conferences. Paul's popular blog is at *www.SQLskills.com/blogs/paul* and he can be reached at *Paul@SQLskills.com* and on Twitter as *@paulrandal*.

Now that you've read the book...

Tell us what you think!

Was it useful?
Did it teach you what you wanted to learn?
Was there room for improvement?

Let us know at http://aka.ms/tellpress

Your feedback goes directly to the staff at Microsoft Press,
and we read every one of your responses. Thanks in advance!

 Microsoft